D0141071

HOMERIC DICTIONARY

GEORG AUTENRIETH

HOMERIC DICTIONARY

GEORG AUTENRIETH

Focus Classical Reprints
Focus Publishing
R. Pullins Company
Newburyport MA 01950

Published by Focus Publishing/R. Pullins Company
ISBN 1-58510-028-5

Focus Publishing/R. Pullins Co., Inc.
PO Box 369
Newburyport, MA 01950

All rights are reserved. No part of this publication may be produced on stage or otherwise performed, reproduced, stored in a retrieval system, transmitted by any means, electronic, mechanical, by photocopying, recording, or by any other media or means without prior written permission of the publisher.

PREFACE.

Dr. Georg Autenrieth, the compiler of the "Wörterbuch zu den Homerischen Gedichten," of which the present volume is a translation, is the Director of the Gymnasium at Zweibrücken, in the Bavarian Palatinate. A favorite scholar and intimate personal friend of that admirable man, Von Nägelsbach, of Erlangen, there devolved upon him, on the death of the latter, the editorial charge of his works, and Autenrieth's editions of the "Gymnasial Pädagogik," the "Homerische Theologie," and the "Commentary on the First Three Books of Homer's Iliad" gained him the repute of a thorough and judicious scholar, and led to his appointment, at an unusually early age, to the important position which he now holds.

In 1868, at the request of the publishing house of Teubner & Co., of Leipzig, he undertook the preparation of a school dictionary of the Iliad and Odyssey, which appeared in 1873. This work met with favorable criticism in Germany, was translated, within a year from its publication, into Dutch, and has passed to its second German edition. Of Autenrieth's special fitness for the task of compiling such a dictionary, his experience as a practical educator, his devotion for many years to the study of Homer, his numerous contributions to the admirable Commentary of Ameis, and the frequent citation of his name in Crusius's Homeric Lexicon (the last edition, that of Seiler and Capelle) furnish sufficient proof. Autenrieth's aim has been not only to convey, in the compactest form consistent with clearness, the results of Homeric study and criticism up to the present time, but also to communicate such collateral information as may serve to render the study of Homer interesting and attractive. Passages of doubtful or difficult interpretation are translated, and the derivations of words receive from the author, who has made the science of comparative philology a special study, particular attention. A novel feature of the work is the introduction into the text of nearly one hundred and fifty small wood-cuts—mainly representations of veritable antiques—which are designed to give to the student a vivid conception of the things mentioned by Homer, by placing before his eyes the warfare, navigation, costume, and sacrificial rites of the Homeric age.

It was the test of actual use which suggested to the editor the idea of translating this book. With it in his hand he read, first the Odyssey, then the Iliad. Tried by this test, it seemed to combine so many excellences that the wish arose in his mind that the work might be made generally accessible to students in America and in England. From the time when he decided to undertake the translation to the present date he has been in frequent correspondence with the author, calling his attention to articles which seemed obscure, and receiving from him the corrections and changes which have been incorporated into the second German edition. The number of additions made by the editor himself is considerable, and many articles have been entirely rewritten, as a comparison of the present with the German edition will show.

Autenrieth's dictionary rests especially upon the labors of three distinguished Homeric scholars—Von Nägelsbach, Döderlein, and Ameis. The frequent references which, in the original edition, are made to these commentators, have been omitted in the translation.

Autenrieth frequently employs a Latin to define a Greek word. The practice commends itself from its conciseness and its precision, and the translator has accordingly in most cases continued it; yet he has not felt that he could presuppose, in the case of American students, such an acquaintance with a large Latin vocabulary as would justify him in omitting to add (in most cases) an English translation.

The present dictionary was intended to be primarily one of Homeric forms. Hence the plan of the work requires that, in the definitions of words which are inflected, the first inflexional form actually occurring in Homer should begin the article, and not, in all cases, the first person singular present indicative active or the nominative singular. Whenever, in rare cases, a non-Homeric form occupies the first place, this is printed in thin-faced type. Occasionally, moreover, a verb which occurs only in a historical tense, and is therefore augmented, will be found in that place which the first person singular of its present indicative active would properly occupy: e. g., *ἐξ-έφθιτο*, a *ἅπαξ λεγόμενον*, will be printed but once (to save space), and will be found where (if it occurred in Homer) the present, *ἐκ-φθίνω*, would stand; so, likewise, *ἐξ-ήρπαξε* will occupy the place properly belonging to *ἐξ-αρπάζω*.

The necessity for extreme conciseness and the restriction of the work to Homeric usage cause some articles to lack that full account of the various meanings of a word, as developed one from the other, which is to be found in a general lexicon like that of Liddell & Scott. A certain baldness and inadequateness in the treatment of many words must, indeed, be a characteristic of such a dictionary. The test of the book, however, is its practical adaptation to the ends it is intended to serve. The writer's own experience has led him to believe that it is well adapted to meet the wants of the young student, as well as to be a companion in the reading of those professional men who have unwillingly let their acquaintance with Homer drop because of the inconvenience of carrying with them on a journey or to the seashore a cumbrous lexicon. It is his earnest hope that this book —so attractive in form, and procurable at so low a price—will render possible, alike in our secondary schools and in our colleges, the reading of a considerably larger portion of Homer than has heretofore been attempted.

The following suggestions as to the use of the book may be found serviceable:

Let the beginning be made by grounding the student carefully and thoroughly upon the forms and peculiarities of the Homeric dialect, with the necessary constant comparison of Homeric and Attic forms. During this stage, the use of the larger lexicon in connection with the present volume will be necessary. Two Books read in this way would suffice. This done, the second step would be to proceed much more rapidly, requiring of the students in recitation only an accurate and intelligent translation of the text and such knowledge as to the meaning and history of the words as this dictionary furnishes.

The editor's own experience leads him to believe that a pupil with this dictionary in his hands will easily read two pages of Homer in the time which, with the large lexicon, would be required for one page. The dictionary also supplies, in a good degree, the place of a commentary, and will be found equally full upon all parts of the two poems. The translator even ventures to hope that the present volume, while offering only legitimate help to the student, may operate to remove the temptation to resort to translations. He is aware of the feeling of dislike with which many teachers regard all special lexicons. That there are grave objections to their use when they cover only a part of the works of an author seems perfectly clear; for then the vocabulary becomes so brief and the range of meaning of the definitions so narrow that translation is rendered for the scholar a merely mechanical exercise. These objections, however, have little force as respects a special lexicon for the Homeric Poems. These poems represent to us every thing, in a connected form, which survives of Epic Greek literature. Not only do their forms differ so widely from those of Attic usage as to constitute a separate dialect, but their vocabulary is an extremely copious one,* and contains a great multitude of words which are used only once, or but a very few times. This latter class of words, it is evident, if occurring in Homer alone, can receive no better elucidation from a large dictionary than from a small one, while the outlay of time required in seeking them in a volume of 1600 pages is very great. The requirements of a scheme of liberal study in our times are so extensive that the necessity of economizing labor, whenever it can be done without detriment to mental discipline, is self-evident. It may be, indeed, that Greek and Latin will only be able to hold their place in our courses of higher education by welcoming and encouraging every legitimate help

* The Iliad and the Odyssey contain about 9000 different words.

by which the labor necessary for acquiring a knowledge of the two chief ancient languages, and gaining an acquaintance with their literatures, may be abridged.

There remains for the translator the pleasant duty of mentioning that the proofs of the dictionary have passed under the eye of Dr. Autenrieth, of Zweibrücken, and Prof. John H. Wright, late of Columbus, Ohio. The references have all been twice verified by himself. It will thus be seen that great pains have been taken to secure that accuracy which is at once so indispensable and, in a work like the present, so difficult to attain.

ROBERT PORTER KEEP.

WILLISTON SEMINARY, EASTHAMPTON, MASS., *Sept.* 1, 1876.

The editor avails himself of the opportunity afforded by a new issue of the Dictionary to incorporate the corrections which have accumulated since its first publication. He wishes to express his thanks to Dr. Drisler, Professors F. D. Allen and T. D. Seymour, and to Mr. Irving G. Stanton, an undergraduate student in Harvard College, for the valuable corrections which they have furnished, and to request similar favors in the future from all who may use the book.

R. P. K.

Sept. 1, 1878.

The issue of a new edition of the Dictionary again gives opportunity for the insertion of corrections, and for some additions which suggest a word of introduction.

On pp. xv., xvi. will be found a new Index, in which the attempt is made to enumerate, in connection with each cut, all the important objects which it illustrates. This Index, which forms an almost necessary supplement to that upon pp. xiii., xiv., was prepared and furnished to the editor by Professor John Williams White, of Harvard College.

Pp. xvii.–xxi. are occupied by an outline of the Peculiarities of the Homeric Dialect, based, in contents and arrangement, upon the excellent sketch which forms the first appendix to Koch's *Griechische Schulgrammatik*, 2d ed., Leipzig: B. G. Teubner, 1871. Such an outline seemed likely to be of especial service to those friends of the Dictionary—men in professional life—who wish to read Homer cursorily and from a text-edition, and who look to the Dictionary to furnish all the aid they require.

The editor would renew his suggestion that the Dictionary yields its best results if scholars are not encouraged to use it much until they have mastered, by the aid of Liddell and Scott, at least one book of Homer. Now that the amount of Xenophon required for admission to college is generally read by the aid of special vocabularies, the student comes to Homer, in most cases, without having used a general dictionary. This is the point at which the purchase of a Liddell and Scott should be insisted upon. The thorough study of the Homeric forms involves at every step their comparison with the corresponding Attic forms, and cannot be satisfactorily prosecuted by the aid of the Autenrieth alone.

When three books of the Iliad have been mastered, the scholar will be well prepared for the rapid reading of the Odyssey.

Passages especially suited for such reading are Bk. V. (Odysseus's departure from Calypso's island); Bks. VI. and VII. (his meeting with Nausicaa and his reception by Alcinous); Bks. IX. and X. (his account of his adventures with Cyclops, and on Circe's island). Any of these passages can be read by ordinary pupils, with the use of the Dictionary alone, at the rate of fifty to seventy-five lines per hour. And the result of a few weeks of such reading will be to develop the confidence of the student in his own power to translate (a prerequisite to reading at sight with any success) and to greatly increase his interest in Homer.

In addition to the obligations already acknowledged, the editor has to thank for corrections the following friends: Professor J. W. White, Professor O. M. Fernald, and Professor J. H. Wright.

R. P. K.

EASTHAMPTON, MASS., *July* 1, 1879.

In sending out the Fourth Edition of the Dictionary, the editor desires to express his thanks for the continuance of the favor with which, from the first, the book has been received. Acknowledgments of corrections and suggestions are due to Messrs. F. D. Allen, H. Drisler, A. C. Merriam, L. R. Packard, A. S. Pattengill, E. D. Perry, T. D. Seymour, J. H. Wright, E. G. Coy, T. D. Goodell. The editor has also had before him, in this revision, the third edition of the original work (Leipzig, 1881), containing much new matter. Perhaps the most noticeable changes will be found in the etymologies: these have been carefully revised, and some have been dropped as not supported by sufficient authority.

It is possible that not all teachers and scholars realize what can be done in the way of rapid reading by the use of the Dictionary, and attention is therefore called to the following extract from a letter from one of the professors in Greek in an important Western college:

"In view of your aim in making the book an aid to rapid translation, I think perhaps you will be interested in learning that my class of seventy-five freshmen have read ten books of the Odyssey, and one half of the class have read eleven books. As we do not require any Homer in preparation for college, they had to learn the Epic dialect to begin with. They have almost universally used your book."

With reference to this same matter, the account given by Professor A. C. Merriam, of Columbia College, of the results of his experiments in rapid reading (*Transactions of the American Philological Association*, Vol. XI., 1880), will be found suggestive.

For changes and corrections in this issue of the Homeric Dictionary, the editor acknowledges obligation to Messrs. B. Perrin, G. F. Nicolassen, and W. B. Richards.

R. P. K.

FREE ACADEMY, Norwich, Conn., *July*, 1886.

EXPLANATION OF REFERENCES.

References are made to the several books of the Iliad and the Odyssey respectively, according to the usage of the ancient commentators, by the large and small letters of the Greek alphabet. Thus A 10 signifies Iliad, Bk. I., line 10; and ω 8 signifies Odyssey, Bk. XXIV., line 8; or, in detail:

Α	Iliad	I.	Odyssey	α	Ν	Iliad	XIII.	Odyssey	ν
Β	"	II.	"	β	Ξ	"	XIV.	"	ξ
Γ	"	III.	"	γ	Ο	"	XV.	"	ο
Δ	"	IV.	"	δ	Π	"	XVI.	"	π
Ε	"	V.	"	ε	Ρ	"	XVII.	"	ρ
Ζ	"	VI.	"	ζ	Σ	"	XVIII.	"	σ
Η	"	VII.	"	η	Τ	"	XIX.	"	τ
Θ	"	VIII.	"	ϑ	Υ	"	XX.	"	υ
Ι	"	IX.	"	ι	Φ	"	XXI.	"	φ
Κ	"	X.	"	κ	Χ	"	XXII.	"	χ
Λ	"	XI.	"	λ	Ψ	"	XXIII.	"	ψ
Μ	"	XII.	"	μ	Ω	"	XXIV.	"	ω

The character † designates Homeric *ἅπαξ λεγόμενα.*

Two references connected by the word *and* designate *δὶς λεγόμενα.*

Il. or Od. affixed to a definition denotes that the word defined occurs only in the Iliad or only in the Odyssey.

The references in general are to be understood as explanatory, and not as exhaustive: they are uniformly made to the small Teubner edition of the Iliad and Odyssey, edited by Dindorf.

To aid the eye, the first word of each article, or, if that chance not to occur in Homer, the first Homeric form, is printed in full-faced type.

LIST OF ABBREVIATIONS.

acc.	signifies	accusative.
act.	"	active.
adj.	"	adjective.
adv.	"	adverb.
aor.	"	aorist.
cf.	"	confer, compare.
cogn.	"	cognate.
coll.	"	collective.
coll. forms	"	collateral forms.
comm.	"	commonly; common gender.
comp.	"	comparative.
compd.	"	compound.
conj.	"	conjunction.
constr.	"	construction.
dat.	"	dative.
dep.	"	deponent.
d., du.	"	dual.
epith.	"	epithet.
esp.	"	especially.
euphem.	"	euphemistically.
exc.	"	except.
fem.	"	feminine.
follg.	"	following.
foreg.	"	foregoing.
freq.	"	frequent.
fut.	"	future.
gen.	"	genitive.
imp.	"	imperative.
indic.	"	indicative.
inf.	"	infinitive.
instr.	"	instrumental.
intrans.	"	intransitive.
ipf.	"	imperfect.
irreg.	"	irregular.
iter.	"	iterative.
κ. τ. λ.	"	καὶ τὰ λοιπά, etc.
lit.	"	literally.
masc., msc.	"	masculine.
met.	"	metaphorical.
mid.	signifies	middle.
nom.	"	nominative.
neut., ntr.	"	neuter.
opp.	"	opposed to.
opt.	"	optative.
orig.	"	originally.
part.	"	participle.
pass.	"	passive.
pf., perf.	"	perfect.
pers.	"	person, personal.
plupf.	"	pluperfect.
pl.	"	plural.
pr., pres.	"	present.
prob.	"	probably.
q. v.	"	quod vide, see.
red.	"	reduplicated.
reg.	"	regular.
sc.	"	scilicet, supply.
signif.	"	signification.
sing., s., sg.	"	singular.
sq., sqq.	"	sequens, sequentia.
subj.	"	subject, subjunctive.
subst.	"	substantive.
sup.	"	superlative.
sync.	"	syncopated.
trans.	"	transitive.
verb.	"	verbal adjective.
v.	"	vide, see.
v. l.	"	varia lectio, different reading.
w.	"	with.
in tmesi, tm., tmesis	"	separation of preposition from verb in a compound.
in arsi	"	in the arsis (the accented syllable of the foot).
1, 2, 3	"	adjectives of one, two, or three terminations.

INDEX OF ILLUSTRATIONS.

PLATES, AT END OF THE VOLUME.

* Plates II., IV., and V. have been added by the translator.

INDEX OF OBJECTS ILLUSTRATED BY EACH CUT.

(The number of the cut comes first, then the page, then the words that the cut illustrates.)

THE CHIEF PECULIARITIES

OF THE

HOMERIC DIALECT.

IN GENERAL.

A. VOWELS.

1. **η** is regularly found when, in Attic, **ᾱ** only would be admissible, e. g. *ἀγορή*, *ὁμοίη*, *πειρήσομαι*.
2. Similarly, **ει** is sometimes found for **ε**, **ου** for **υ**, e. g. *ξεῖνος*, *χρύσειος*, *πουλύς*, *μοῦνος*.
3. More rarely **οι** is found for **ο**, **αι** for **α**, **η** for **ε**, e. g. *πνοιή*, *αἰετός*, *τιθήμενος*.
4. By what is called metathesis quantitatis, **αο** becomes **εω** (for ᾰω). Similarly, we have *ἕως* and *εἷος*, *ἀπερείσιος* and *ἀπειρέσιος* κ. τ. λ.

B. CONTRACTION OF VOWELS.

1. Contraction, when it occurs, follows the ordinary rules, except that **εο** and **εου** form **ευ**, e. g. *θάρσευς*, *βάλλευ*.
2. But the contraction often does not take place, e. g. *ἀέκων*; and a few unusual contractions occur, e. g. *ἱρός* (*ἱερός*), *βώσας* (*βοήσας*), *ἐυρρεῖος* instead of *ἐυρρέους* from *ἐυρρέ-εος*.
3. Two vowels which do not form a diphthong are often blended in pronunciation (synizesis), e. g. *Ἀτρειδέω*, *δὴ αὖ*, *ἐπεὶ οὐ*, *ἢ οὐ*.

C. HIATUS.

Hiatus is allowed:

1. After the vowels **ι** and **υ**.
2. When the two words are separated by cæsura or a mark of punctuation.
3. When the final (preceding) vowel is long and in arsis.
4. When the final (preceding) vowel, though naturally long, stands in thesis and has been shortened before the following short vowel.
5. When the final vowel of the preceding word has been lost by elision, e. g.:

   1. *παιδὶ ὄπασσεν*, – ⏑ ⏑ | – ⏑.
   2. *Ὀλύμπιε, οὔ νύ τ' Ὀδυσσεύς*, ⏑ | – ⏑ ⏑ | – ⏑ ⏑ | – –.
   3. *ἀντιθέῳ Ὀδυσῆϊ*, – ⏑ ⏑ | – ⏑ ⏑ | – ⏑.
   4. *πλάγχθη ἐπεί*, – ⏑ ⏑ | –.
   5. *ἄλγε' ἔδωκεν*, – ⏑ ⏑ | – ⏑.

Remark.—Many apparent cases of hiatus result from the loss of a digamma or other consonant, e. g. *τὸν δ' ἠμείβετ' ἔπειτα Ϝάναξ ἀνδρῶν Ἀγαμέμνων*.

D. ELISION.

Elision is much more frequent than in prose. **α, ε, ι, ο** are elided in declension and conjugation; **αι** in the endings *μαι, σαι, ται, σθαι*; **οι** in *μοι*; **ι** in *ὅτι*.

E. APOCOPE.

Before a consonant, the final short vowel of ἄρα, and of the preps. ἀνά, παρά, κατά, may be cut off (apocope).

Remark.—The accent in this case recedes to the first syllable, and the consonant (now final) is assimilated to the following consonant, e. g. κὰδ δύναμιν, κάλλιπε, ἂμ πεδίον.

F. CONSONANT-CHANGES.

1. Single consonants, esp. **λ, μ, ν, ρ,** and **σ,** at the beginning of a word, after a vowel, are frequently doubled, e. g. ἔλλαβον, τόσσος. So also a short final vowel before a follg. liquid is often lengthened by doubling (in pronunciation, though not in writing) the liquid, e. g. ἐνὶ μεγάροισι.
2. Metathesis of vowel and liquid is common, e. g. κραδίη and καρδίη, θάρσος and θράσος.

DECLENSION.

G. SPECIAL CASE-ENDINGS.

1. The termination **φι(ν)** serves for the ending of the gen. and dat. sing. and pl., e. g. ἐξ εὐνῆ-φι, βίη-φι, ὀστεόφι θίς, σὺν ἵπποισιν καὶ ὄχεσφι.
2. The three local suffixes θι, θεν, δε answer the questions where? whence? whither? e. g. οἴκοθι, οὐρανόθεν, ὅνδε δόμονδε.

H. FIRST DECLENSION.

1. For **ᾱ** we find always **η,** e. g. θύρη, νεηνίης, except θεά.
2. The nom. sing. of some masculines in **-ης** is shortened to **-ᾰ,** e. g. ἱππότα, νεφεληγερέτα.
3. The gen. sing. of masculines ends in **-αο** or **-εω,** e. g. Ἀτρείδαο and Ἀτρείδεω.
4. The gen. pl. of masculines ends in **-άων** or **-έων** (rarely contracted, as in Attic, into **-ῶν**), e. g. θεάων, ναυτέων, παρειῶν.
5. The dat. pl. ends in **-ησι** or **-ης,** rarely in **-αις,** e. g. πύλῃσι, σχίζῃς, but θεαῖς.

I. SECOND DECLENSION.

1. The gen. sing. has retained the old ending in **-ιο,** which, added to the stem, gives the termination **-οιο.** Rarely occurs the termination **-οο**—more commonly the Attic ending **-ου.** Cf. H. 39 Rem. a, 32 d. Cf. also G. 9, 2.
2. The gen. and dat. dual end in **-οιιν.**
3. The dat. pl. ends in **-οισι** or **-οις.**

K. THIRD DECLENSION.

1. The gen. and dat. dual end in **-οιιν,** e. g. ποδοῖιν.
2. Dat. pl. **-σι, -σσι,** usually joined to a consonant stem by a connecting vowel **ε,** e. g. πόδ-ε-σσιν and ποσσί, βελέεσσι, βέλεσσι, βέλεσι.
3. Stems ending in **-σ** are generally uncontracted in declension, but **-εος** often contracts into **-ευς.**
4. Words in **-ις** generally retain the **ι** in all their cases, e. g. μάντις, μάντιος.
   Remark.—For the various forms of πόλις, vid. sub voc. in Lex.
5. Stems in **-ευ** generally lengthen **ε** to **η** in compensation for the omitted **υ** (ϝ), e. g. βασιλῆος, βασιλῆι. But proper names may retain the **ε,** e. g. Τυδέα.

L. ADJECTIVES.

1. The feminine of adjs. of the 1st and 2d declensions is always formed in **η**, e. g. *ὁμοίη, αἰσχρή*, exc. *δῖα*.
2. The Attic rule, that compd. adjs. have only two terminations, is not strictly observed, and, vice versâ, some adjs. which in Attic have three terminations have only two in Homer.
3. Adjs. in **-υς** are often of only two terminations, and often change the fem. **-εια** to **-εα** or **-εη**. For the various declensional forms of *πολύς*, vid. sub voc. in Lex.
4. The comp. and superl. endings **-ίων** and **-ιστος** are much more extensively used in the Homeric than in the Attic dialect.

M. PRONOUNS.

1. For special forms of pers. prons., vid. sub vocc. *ἐγώ, νῶι, ἡμεῖς. σύ, σφῶι, ὑμεῖς. οὗ, σφωέ, σφέων*.
2. **ὁ, ἡ, τό**, in Homer, is dem. pron. In nom. pl. the forms **τοί** and **ταί** occur by the side of **οἱ** and **αἱ**. The forms beginning with **τ** have often relative signif., vid. sub voc. in Lex. *τοίσδεσσι* and *τοίσδεσι* are forms of *ὅδε*. *κεῖνος* is another form for *ἐκεῖνος*.
3. For peculiar forms of rel. pron., as well as for demonstr. meaning of some of these forms, vid. sub voc. *ὅς*.
4. For peculiar forms of interrog., indef., and indef. rel. prons., vid. sub vocc. *τίς, τις*, and *ὅστις*.

CONJUGATION.

N. AUGMENT AND REDUPLICATION.

1. The augment may be omitted; in this case the accent is thrown back as far as possible toward the beginning of the word. Monosyllabic forms with a long vowel take the circumflex, e. g. *λῦσε* (*ἔλυσε*), *βῆ* (*ἔβη*).
2. The 2d aor. act. and midd. is often formed in Homer by a reduplication. The only examples of a similar formation in Attic are *ἤγαγον, ἤνεγκον* (*ην-ενεκ-ο-ν*), and *εἶπον* (*εϝεϝεπον*). Among the examples of reduplicated aorists may be mentioned: *ἐπέφραδον* (*φράζω*), *ἐκέκλετο* and *κέκλετο* (*κέλομαι*), *πεφιδέσθαι* (*φείδομαι*), *πεπίθομεν* (*πείθω*), *πεπύθοιτο* (*πυνθάνομαι*), *ἀμπεπαλών* (*ἀναπάλλω*). Examples of a very peculiar reduplication are *ἐνίπ-απ-ον* (*ἐνίπτω*) and *ἐρύκ-ακ-ον* (*ἐρύκω*). Here the last consonant of the stem is repeated after a connecting **α**.
3. There are a few examples of a reduplicated fut. of similar formation with the reduplicated aor., e. g. *πεφιδήσομαι, πεπιθήσω*.

O. ENDINGS.

1. The older endings of the sing. number *μι, σθα, σι*, are common in Homer: *ἐθέλωμι* (subj.), *ἐθέλησι* (also written *ἐθέλῃσι*).
2. The ending of the 3d pers. dual in the historical tenses is **-τον** as well as **-την** in the act., **-σθον** as well as **-σθην** in the midd., voice. In 1st pers. pl., **μεσθα** is used for **μεθα**, and **μεσθον** for 1st pers. dual.
3. The 2d sing. midd. and pass. often loses **σ** and remains uncontracted, e. g. *ἔχηαι, βάλλεο, ἔπλεο* (also *ἔπλευ*), *ὠδύσαο*. In perf. midd., *βέβληαι* occurs for *βέβλησαι*.

4. For the 3d pl. endings **-νται** and **-ντο, -αται** and **-ατο** are often substituted, e. g. *δεδαίαται, γενοίατο*. Before these endings (*-αται* and *-ατο*) smooth or middle labial or palatal mutes are changed to rough, e. g. *τετράφαται* (*τρέπω*).
5. The inf. act. frequently ends in **-μεναι,** also shortened to **-μεν**, e. g. *ἀκουέμεναι, τεθνάμεν(αι)*. The 2d aor. inf. appears also in the form **-έειν**, e. g. *θανέειν*. There are one or two examples of a pres. inf. in *-ήμεναι* and *-ῆναι* from verbs in **-άω** and **-εω**, e. g. *φορῆναι* (= *φορεῖν*).
6. The endings **-σκον** and **-σκόμην** express repetition of the action, and are called iterative endings. They have the inflection of the ipf. of verbs in **-ω,** and are rarely augmented. They are attached to the ipf. and 2d aor. of verbs in **-ω** by the connecting vowel **ε**, rarely **α**, e. g. *ἔχ-ε-σκον, ῥίπτ-α-σκον, φύγ-ε-σκε*. When joined to the 1st aor., these endings follow directly after the connecting vowel of the aor., e. g. *ἐλάσα-σκε, μνησά-σκετο*. Verbs in **-μι** append the iterative endings directly to the stem: *ἔφα-σκον, στά-σκον, κέ-σκετο* (*κεῖ-μαι*), *ἔσ-κον* (= *εσ-σκον* from *εἰμί*).

P. MOOD-VOWELS OF SUBJUNCTIVE.

The long mood-vowels of the subj. are frequently shortened to **ε** and **ο**, e. g. *ἴομεν* for *ἴωμεν, θωρήξομεν* for *θωρήξωμεν, εὔξεαι* for *εὔξηαι* (= *εὔξῃ*). This shortening is especially common in 1st aor. subj., which might, in that case, easily be confounded with fut. indic.

Q. CONTRACT-VERBS.

1. Verbs in **-αω** appear in open, contracted, and expanded (assimilated) forms. The expansion consists in prefixing to the long contracted vowel a like-sounding, short, accented vowel, e. g. *ὁρόω, ὁράᾳ, ἐλόωσι, ἐλάαν*. Cf. G. 120, b.

   Remark.—Sometimes, for the sake of the requirements of metre, a long vowel is prefixed; or the short vowel is affixed, instead of prefixed, to the long, contracted vowel, e. g. *ἡβώωσα, ἡβώοντες*.
2. Verbs in **-εω** are generally uncontracted, but sometimes form **ει** from *εε* and *εει*, **η** from *εε*, **ευ** from *εο* or *εου*. In uncontracted forms the stem-vowel **ε** is sometimes lengthened to **ει.**
3. Verbs in **-όω** are generally contracted; in open forms the stem-vowel **ο** is generally lengthened into **ω.** Resolved forms are: *ἀρόωσι* for *ἀροῦσι, δηιόῳεν* for *δηιοῖεν*.

R. PECULIAR FORMATION OF PRESENT (EXPANDED) STEM.

1. Many presents in **-ζω** are formed from stems ending in **γ**, e. g. *πολεμίζω* (fut. *πολεμίξομεν*), *μαστίζω* (aor. *μάστιξεν*). The stem of *πλάζω* ends in **-γγ,** e. g. aor. pass. *πλάγχθην*.
2. Several presents in **-σσω** are formed from lingual stems, e. g. *κορύσσω* (perf. pass. ptc. *κεκορυθμένος*), *λίσσομαι* (aor. *ἐλλισάμην*).
3. *νίζω* shows a stem **νιβ,** e. g. *νίψασθαι*.
4. Several other vowel stems, additional to *καίω* and *κλαίω*, form the present stem by the addition of **ι,** e. g. *μαίομαι* (perf. *μέμαμεν*).

S. FORMATION OF FUTURE AND FIRST AND SECOND AORIST ACTIVE AND MIDDLE.

1. Such pure verbs as do not lengthen the final stem-vowel, in the formation of their tenses, before a single consonant, often double **σ** in the fut. and 1st aor. act. and midd., e. g. *αἰδέσσομαι, νείκεσσε, ἐτάνυσσε*. Sometimes the stems in **-δ** show a similar doubling of **σ**, e. g. *κομίσσατο*.

2. The fut. of liquid verbs is generally uncontracted, e. g. *μενέω, ἀγγελέω.* A few liquid stems take the tense-sign **σ**, e. g. *ἐκέλσαμεν* (*κέλλω*), *κένσαι* (*κεντέω*), *ὦρσε* (*ὄρ-νυμι*).
3. A few verbs form the 1st aor. act. and midd. without **σ**, e. g. *ἔχευα* and *χεῦα* (*χέω*=*χεύω*), *ἔσσευα* (*σεύω*), *ἠλεύατο, ἀλέασθαι* (*ἀλεύομαι*), *ἔκηα*, subj. *κήομεν*, inf. *κῆαι* (*καίω*).
4. **ο** and **ε** sometimes take the place of **α** as connecting vowels of the 1st aor., e. g. *ἷξον, ἷξες* (*ἱκνέομαι*), *δύσετο* (*δύω*). Similarly, the imvs. *βήσεο* (*βαίνω*), *ὄρσεο* and *ὄρσευ* (*ὄρ-νυμι*), *ἄξετε* (*ἄγω*), *οἶσε* (*φέρω*), and the infins. *ἀξέμεναι, σαώσεμεν, κελευσέμεναι*, occur; and a single example of an aor. ptc. with connecting vowel **ο** is seen in *δυσόμενος* (*α* 24).
5. A 2d aor. act. and midd. is often formed, similarly to the aor. of verbs in **-μι**, without a connecting vowel. Of this formation there are many instances, e. g. *ἔκτα, ἔκτᾰν, ἔκτᾰτο* (stem *κτᾰ*=*κτεν*), *σύτο* (*σεύω*), *ἔχυτο* (*χέω*), *λῦτο* (*λύω*), opts. *φθίμην, φθῖτο*—inf. *φθίσθαι*—ptc. *φθίμενος* (*φθί-ν-ω*), *ἔβλητο, βλῆσθαι* (*βάλλω*), *ἆλτο* (*ἅλλομαι*), *δέκτο* (*δέχομαι*), *ἔμικτο* and *μίκτο* (*μίγνυμι*). The imvs. *κέκλυθι* and *κέκλυτε* are similarly formed from a reduplicated stem.

T. FORMATION OF PERFECT AND PLUPERFECT.

1. In the forms *ἔμμορα* (*μείρομαι*) and *ἔσσυμαι* (*σεύω*) we see the same doubling of the initial consonant of the stem after the augment (reduplication), as if the stem began with **ρ**. The reduplication has been lost in *δέχαται* (=*δεδεγμένοι εἰσί*), and is irregular in *δείδεγμαι* (*δέχομαι*) and *δείδοικα* or *δείδια*.
2. The 1st perf. is formed from vowel-stems alone. The 2d perf. is very common, but always without aspiration, e. g. *κέκοπα* (*κόπτω*). There occur frequently forms from vowel-stems which have lost the tense-sign **κ**, esp. perf. ptcs., e. g. *πεφύασι* (=*πεφύκασι*), *βεβαρηότες* (*βαρέω*), *κεκμηῶτα* (*κάμνω*), *τεθνηῶτος* and *τεθνηότος* (*θνήσκω*).
3. In the plupf. the older endings **-εᾰ, -εᾰς, -εε(ν)** contracted **ει(ν)** or **η** appear, e. g. *ἐτεθήπεα, ᾔδεα κ. τ. λ.* (cf. *ᾔδεα*=*ηδεσαμ*, with Lat. videram; *ᾔδεας*=*ηδεσας*, with Lat. videras; *ᾔδεσαν*=*ηδεσαντ*, with Lat. viderant).

U. AORIST PASSIVE.

1. The 3d pl. indic. often ends in **-εν** instead of **-ησαν**, e. g. *ἔμιχθεν, φόβηθεν, τράφεν.*
2. The subj. remains uncontracted, the **ε** of the pass. sign is often lengthened to **ει** or **η**, and the follg. mood sign shortened to **ε** or **ο**, e. g. *δαείω* (stem *δα*), *δαμείῃς* or *δαμήῃς* (*δάμνημι*).

   Remark.—A very peculiar form is *τραπείομεν*, by metathesis, for *ταρπείομεν* (=*ταρπῶμεν*, 2d aor. pass. from *τέρπω*) (Ξ 314).

V. VERBS IN -μι.

1. Forms of the pres. indic. of verbs in **-μι** occur as if from verbs in **-εω** and **-οω**.
2. As the ending of the 3d pl. of the ipf. and 2d aor. act., **ν** often takes the place of **σαν**, e. g. *ἴεν* (*ἵεσαν*), *ἔσταν* and *στάν* (*ἔστησαν*), *ἔβαν* and *βάν* (*ἔβησαν*), *ἔφαν* and *φάν* (*ἔφασαν*), *ἔφυν* (*ἔφυσαν*).
3. In the 2d aor. subj. act., to meet the requirements of the verse, the mood sign is sometimes shortened and the stem-vowel lengthened. Thus arise such forms as *θείω, θείῃς*, and *θήῃς*; *στήῃς, γνώω, δώησι*, and *δώῃ*. Sometimes the **α** of the stem is weakened to **ε**, and this again protracted to **ει**. Thus arise the forms *στέωμεν* and *στείομεν* (=*στῶμεν*), *βείομεν* (=*βῶμεν*).
4. For peculiar Homeric forms from the verbs *ἵστημι, τίθημι, ἵημι, δίδωμι, εἶμι, εἰμί, οἶδα, ἧμαι*, and *κεῖμαι*, vid. sub vocc. in Lex.

A.

A- in composition—(1) so-called *α* privativum, see *ἀν-*.—(2) *α* copulativum, orig. **σα* (cf. *ἅ-μα*, English same), then *ἀ-*, *ἁ-*, *ὀ-* contains the idea of union or likeness, Lat. idem or unâ, e. g. *ἅπας*, *ἀολλής*, *ἄξυλος*, *ἀθρόος*, *ἀτάλαντος*, *ὄτριχες* (in words like *ἀθρόος* cf. *ἁμαρτῇ*, the existence of an *α* intensivum was formerly, but incorrectly, assumed).—(3) *α* protheticum, simple euphonic prefix (like *i* and *e* in Low Latin istatus, ispero; Italian esperanza; French espérance, état), e. g. *ἀλείφω*, *ἀμάω*, *ἀείρω*, *ἀμέλγω*, *ἀμύνω*, *ἀνεψιός*, *ἄποινα*, *ἀσπαίρω*, *ἄσταχυς*, *ἀστεμφής*, *ἀστήρ*.

ἆ, interjection expressive of pity or horror, freq. with *δειλέ*, *δειλοί*, *δειλώ*, ξ 361, Λ 816, Ρ 443.

ἀ-άατον [⏑ – ⏓ ⏑] acc. masc. and ntr. (*ἀ-*, *ἀϝάτη*), *involving harm, ruinous, destructive*; *Στυγὸς ὕδωρ*, Ξ 271, as banishing faithless mortals and perjured deities to the lower world; *ἄεθλον*, φ 91.

ἀ-αγές (*ἀϝαγές*, *ἄγνυμι*), *not to be broken, stout*, λ 575†. [⏑ – ⏑]

ἄ-απτοι, *ους*, (ΣΑΠ, *ἕπω*), intractabiles, *unapproachable*; *χεῖρες*, *χεῖρας*; esp. freq. in Il., e. g. Α 567, λ 502, χ 70, 248.

ἀάσχετος, lengthened from *ἄσχετος*.

ἀάω, (1) *injure*; (a) *τῇδ' ἄτῃ ἄασας* 2 sing. aor. Θ 237; κ 68, *ἄασαν* (– – –); (b) esp. of injury to understanding, *mislead, delude*; *ἄασε* (– ⏑ ⏑), φ 296; *ἆσε*, λ 61; with *φρένας*, φ 297, pass. Τ 136; *μέγ' ἀάσθη*, Π 685; *πολλὸν ἀάσθη*, Τ 113; cf. φ 301.—(2) mid. (a) *commit a folly*, *ἀασάμην* (– ⏑ ⏑ –); *ἀάσατο* (⏑ – ⏑ ⏑) *δὲ μέγα θυμῷ*, deceived himself greatly in his thought; Τ 95, *Ζεὺς ἄσατο* (– ⏑ ⏑) (v. l. *Ζῆν' ἄσατο*, see no. 1); (b) trans. *dupe, beguile*, *Ἄτη ἣ πάντας ἀᾶται*, Τ 91, 129. [aor. 1, act. and mid. ⏓ ⏓ ⏑ and ⏒ ⏒ ⏑ –; pass. ⏑ – –.]

ἀβάκησαν, δ 249† [⏑ ⏑ – ⏑], of doubtful deriv. (*βάζω*? *ἀϝαω*?), and meaning, *were befooled, suspected nothing*.

Ἄβαντες, inhabitants of Euboia, Β 536. [⏑ – ⏑]

Ἀβαρβαρέη, Trojan fountain-nymph, Ζ 22. (⏑ – ⏑ ⏑ –]

Ἄβας, *αντα*, son of dream-reader Eurydamas; slain by Diomedes, Ε 148. [⏑ – ⏑].

Ἄβιοι, *δικαιότατοι ἀνθρώπων*, Ν 6, fabulous tribe of the North. [⏑ ⏑ –]

Ἄβληρος, a Trojan, Ζ 32. [– – ⏑]

ἀ-βλῆτα (from *ἀβλής*, *βάλλω*), *ἰὸν*, non missum, *not discharged, new*, Δ 117†. [– – ⏑]

ἄ-βλητος, *not hit*, Δ 540†. [– – ⏑]

ἀ-βληχρός, 3, v. l. *ἀμβληχρός*, (*ἀ* prothetic, *μαλακὸς*), only at beginning of verse.—(1) *weak, feeble*, Ε 337, Θ 178.—(2) *θάνατος*, *gentle*, λ 135, ψ 282. [– – ⏑]

ἄ-βρομοι (*ἀ* prothetic, *βρέμω*), *loud-roaring, clamorous*, Ν 41. [– ⏑ ⏑]

ἀβροτάξομεν, from *ἀβροτεῖν*, i. e. *ἀμβροτεῖν*, *ἁμαρτεῖν*, aor. subj. *fail of, miss*; *τινός*, Κ 65†. [⏑ ⏑ – ⏑ ⏑]

ἀ-βρότη *νύξ*, *divine* night, Ξ 78†, δ 429. [⏑ ⏑ –]

Ἄβυδος [⏑ – ⏑], town on S. shore of Hellespont, Β 836. Hence *Ἀβυδόθεν*, Δ 500; *Ἀβυδόθι*, Ρ 584.

ἀγα-, prefix, *exceedingly*, mirum in modum, mirum quantum.

ἀγάασθαι, *ἀγάασθε*, see *ἄγαμαι*, miror.

ἀγαγεῖν-ἄγαγον, etc., see ἄγω.

ἀγάζομαι, see *ἄγαμαι*, miror.

ἀγαθός, 3, (*ἄγαμαι*), strictly = admirabilis, *good, capable*, in widest signif.—(1) of persons, *valiant, brave*, Δ 181, I 341; *efficient*, B 732, Γ 179; freq. with acc. of specification, πύξ, βοήν; common in signif. *noble* (cf. optimates), Ξ 113, Φ 109, (opp. χέρηες, ο 324); *bold, daring*, N 238, 284, 314, Φ 280 (opp. κακός, N 279, P 632).—(2) of things and circumstances, *excellent*, Z 478, ι 27, ν 246; *advantageous*, B 204, Λ 793, ρ 347; *noble*, Ω 632, δ 611; ἀγαθόν τε κακόν τε, blessing and curse, δ 237, 392, θ 63; ἀγαθοῖσι γεραίρειν, do honor, ξ 441; ἀγαθὰ φρονεῖν, bene velle, wish one well, α 43; sana mente uti, think rightly, Z 162; εἰς ἀγαθόν or ἀγαθὰ εἰπεῖν, advise with friendly intent; εἰς ἀγ. πείθεσθαι, follow good counsel. [⏑⏑⏑]

Ἀγάθων, son of Priamos, Ω 249. [⏑⏑–]

ἀγαιομένου, parallel form to *ἀγαμένου*, *viewing with indignation*, υ 16, κακὰ ἔργα, indignantis scelera; cf. β 67. [⏑–⏑⏑–]

ἀγα-κλεής, ές, (from κλέος), only gen. and voc., *greatly renowned*. [⏑–⏑–]

Ἀγακλέης, -κλῆος, Π 571, a Myrmidon.

ἀγα-κλειτός, 3, praeclarus, *illustrious, glorious*, epith. of men, of a Nereid, Σ 45, and of hecatombs. [⏑––⏑]

ἀγα-κλυτός, 3, praeclarus, *illustrious*. of men; δώματα. [⏑–⏑⏑]

ἀγάλλομαι, only pres., *have joy in* (τινί), *plume one's self upon*, P 473, Σ 132, Υ 222; *exult, make display*, B 462; νῆες, ε 176, *speeding gladly forward* under Zeus's fair wind.

ἄγαλμα (ἀγάλλομαι), *any thing splendid, beautiful, or precious*, Δ 144; votive offerings, γ 274, θ 509, μ 347; applied to sacrificial victim, γ 438; to horses, δ 602; personal adornments, σ 300, τ 257. [⏑––]

ἄγαμαι (ἄγη), aor. ἠγασάμην, ἠγασσάμην (also unaugmented); and from parallel form, **ἀγάομαι**; ἀγάασθε, ἀγάασθαι, ipf. ἠγάασθε; the form ἄγαμαι, only in signif. 1.—(1) admirari, *admire*, H 41, 404, Θ 29, and mirari, demirari, *gaze at with amazement*, σ 71; in π 203, θαυμάζειν, *behold with wonder*, joined with ἀγάασθαι, *be astonished*.—(2) in bad sense, (a) indignari, *be indignant, outraged at*, with acc., β 67; with dat., θ 565; *be vexed, annoyed*, Ψ 639; with κότῳ, Ξ 111; (b) invidere, *envy, grudge*, δ 181, with inf., ε 129; esp. freq. of envy of the gods, δ 181, ψ 211, θ 565, H 442. [⏑⏑–]

Ἀγαμεμνονίδης, *son of Agamemnon*, Orestes, α 30.

Ἀγαμέμνων, ονος. His grandfather was Tantalos, whose sons were Atreus and Thyestes (father of Aigisthos); Atreus's sons, Agamemnon and Menelaos; Agamemnon's children, Orestes, Chrysothemis, Laodike, Iphianassa; cf. B 104, I 287; his wife, Klytaimnestra. King in Mykenai, but at the same time πολλῇσιν νήσοισι καὶ Ἄργεϊ παντὶ ἄνασσεν, B 108; his wealth in ships, B 576, 610–14; commander-in-chief of Grecian host before Troy; εὐρυκρείων and ἄναξ ἀνδρῶν, A 172; κρείων, ποιμὴν λαῶν, δῖος; his bodily size, Γ 166, 178; B 477–83; ἀριστεία, exploits, Λ 91–661; honor accorded him, Ψ 887; sceptre, B 104; return from Troia, γ 143 sqq., 156, 193 sqq., 234 sq.; is murdered, γ 248 sqq., δ 91, 512–37, 584, λ 387–463, ω 20–97 [⏑⏑––]. Hence fem. adj. Ἀγαμεμνονέη.

Ἀγαμήδη (cf. Μήδεια), daughter of Augeias, granddaughter of Sun-god, Λ 740. [⏑⏑––]

ἄ-γαμος, 2, (from γάμος), *unmarried*, Γ 40†. [⏑⏑⏑]

ἀγά-ννιφον Ὄλυμπον (ἀγα-σνιφ., see νίφω), A 420, Σ 186; nivosum, *covered with deep snow, snow-capped*. [⏑–⏑⏑]

ἀγανός, 3, (from γάνυμαι), lenis, *pleasant, gentle*, ἔπεα, δῶρα; *kind, friendly*, εὐχωλαί, βασιλεύς (opp. χαλεπός), β 230; common phrase, οἷς ἀγανοῖς βελέεσσι, with his (or her) gentle missiles, describing a (*natural*) sudden, painless death dealt by Apollo upon men, by Artemis upon women, γ 280.

ἀγανο-φροσύνη, ἡ, comitas, *gentleness, friendliness*, λ 203, cf. β 230. [⏑⏑–⏑⏑⏑–]

ἀγανό-φρων, comis, *gentle, friendly*, Υ 467†. [⏑–––]

ἀγάομαι, see ἄγαμαι, miror.

ἀγαπάζω (parallel form of ἀγαπάω) and -ομαι, only prs., τινά, *receive kindly*, π 17, η 33; *espouse the cause of*, Ω 464. [⏑⏑– –]

ἀγαπάω, ἀγάπησα, ψ 214, *I lovingly received;* and φ 289, art thou not therewith content? [⏑⏑–]

ἀγαπ-ήνωρ, ος, *loving-manliness, manly*, O 392. [⏑⏑– –]

Ἀγαπήνωρ, Ἀγκαίοιο παῖς, B 609, king of Arkadians, vassal of Agamemnon, to whom he brought the equipment of sixty ships.

ἀγαπητός (ἀγαπάω), *beloved, dear*, always with παῖς, son, which is to be supplied in β 365. [⏑⏑–⏑]

ἀγά-ρροος (ἀγα-σρόϝος, ῥέω), *strong-flowing;* Ἑλλήσποντος, B 845, acc. M 30.

Ἀγασθένης (σθένος), son of Augeias, king in Elis, B 624.

ἀγά-στονος (στένω), fremens, *boisterous*, epith. of Ἀμφιτρίτη, μ 97†. [⏑–⏑⏑]

Ἀγάστροφος, a Trojan, Λ 338. [⏑–⏑⏑]

Ἀγαυή, a Nereid, Σ 42. [⏑– –]

ἀγαυός, 3, (from ἄγαμαι), admirabilis; *illustrious* (cf. clarissimus), an epithet applied, honoris causâ, to rulers, nations (Phaiakians, Trojans, ν 272 to Phoinikes, N 5 to Hippemolgoi); also freq. to suitors; ν 71 to the noble πομπῆες; ε 1 to Tithonos; and thrice to Persephoneia. [⏑–⏑]

ἀγγελίη, ἡ, (ἄγγελος), *tidings, message, report*, H 416, I 422, Ξ 355, O 174; ἀλεγεινή, λυγρή; πατρός, de patre, α 408, cf. β 30; *command*, ε 150, η 263; as causal gen., Γ 206, he came (because of) on a mission respecting thee; ἀγγελίην ἐλθόντα, Λ 140; cf. also ἀγγελίης in N 252, O 640, Γ 206; see also ἀγγελίης. ὁ. [–⏑⏑–]

ἀγγελίης, ὁ, (ἄγγελος), nuntius, *messenger*, handed down by old grammarians as nom. masc., like ταμίης and νεηνίης; thus we may explain Γ 206, N 252, O 640, Δ 384, Λ 140; also such passages as α 414, β 92, ν 381. [–⏑⏑–]

ἀγγέλλων (ἄγγελος), fut. ἀγγελέω, aor. ἤγγειλα, inf. O 159; nuntiare, *report, announce;* τί, also τινά, ξ 120, 123; with inf., *bid*, π 350, Θ 517.

ἄγγελος, ὁ and ἡ, (cf. German gellen, English yell, nightin-gale), nuntius, nuntia, *messenger;* common phrase, ἦλθέ τινι, Λ 715; Ὄσσα Διὸς ἀγγ., B 94; also of birds, ο 526.

ἄγγος, εος, τό, vas, *vase, bowl;* for victuals, β 289, and drink.

ἄγε, ἄγετε, (ἄγω), particle like age, agedum; *quick! come!* after ἀλλά, or before δή; with subj. or imp., cf. French allons! ἄγε often occurs with pl., e. g. γ 475; see also εἰ δ' ἄγε.

ἀγείρω (cf. gerere?), aor. ἤγειρα; pass. pf. ἀγήγερμαι, aor. ἠγέρθην, 3 pl ἄγερθεν; mid. aor. ἀγερόμην, inf. ἀγερέσθαι (written by ancient grammarians as pres. ἀγέρεσθαι), part. ἀγρόμενος. —(1) act. colligere, congregare, *collect, call together, assemble*, τ 197, ἀγορήν, concionem advocare; pass. and aor. mid. *gather together;* ἐς φρένα θυμὸς ἠγέρθη, consciousness (Δ 152, courage, presence of mind), *came back again*.

ἀγελαίη (ἀγέλη), βοῦς, βόες, βόας, gregaria, *belonging to a herd, feeding at large.* [⏑⏑– –]

Ἀγέλαος (ἄγω, λαός), (1) son of Damastor, suitor, χ 131, 247, Ἀγέλεως.—(2) son of Phradmon, a Trojan, Θ 257. —(3) Greek, Λ 302. [⏑⏑–⏑]

ἀγελείη (ἄγουσα λείαν), praedatrix, *bestower of spoil;* cf. ληῖτις, epith. of Athene, only at end of verse, ν 359. [⏑⏑– –]

ἀγέλη, ης, (ἄγω), grex, *herd* of cattle, exc. T 281, where it is a *drove* of horses; ἀγέληφι, Π 487, with the herd. [⏑⏑–]

ἀγεληδόν, gregatim, *in herds*, Π 160. [⏑⏑–⏑]

ἀγέμεν = ἄγειν.

ἄγεν = ἐάγησαν, from ἄγνυμι.

ἀ-γέραστος (γέρας), inhonoratus, *without a gift of honor*, A 119†. [⏑⏑–⏑]

ἄγερθεν, see ἀγείρω, congregati sunt.

ἀγέρωχοι, ων, (ἄγα, ἐρωή), *impetuous, brave in combat;* epith. of Trojans, Mysians, Rhodians, and of Periklymenos, λ 286; formerly explained, *very honorable*, as if from α copul. and γερα-οχος. [⏑⏑–⏑]

ἄγη μ' ἔχει (de)miror, *I am astonished*, Φ 221. [⏑–]

ἀγηγέραθ' (*ατο*), see *ἀγείρω*, congregati erant.

ἀγ-ηνορίη, *ης, ἡ*, (*ἀγήνωρ*), virtus, *manliness, courage*, M 46; X 457, of the courage which will not let Hektor rest; I 700, *pride*.

ἀγ-ήνωρ (*ἄγα, ἀνήρ*), ferox, *very manly*.—(1) *brave, bold*, σ 43, α 106; *high-hearted*, *θυμός*, δ 658; high-beating life, Υ 406; also, μ 414, of helmsman; elsewh. with *θυμός*, freq. = *noble, generous* mind.—(2) *haughty*, I 699, Φ 443. [⏑ – –]

'Αγήνωρ, *ορος*, son of Trojan Antenor and Theano, Λ 59, Φ 579, Υ 474, O 340.

ἀ-γήραος, ἀγήρως, 2, (*γῆρας*), aeternus, *ageless, of undecaying vigor*, always with *ἀθάνατος*, Θ 539; *αἰγίς*, B 447. [⏑ – ⏑ ⏑]

ἀγητός (*ἄγαμαι*), admirabilis (with *εἶδος*, acc. of respect); *surpassingly beautiful*, X 370, ξ 177. [⏑ – ⏑]

ἀγινέω (*ἄγω*), inf. *-έμεναι*, ipf. **ἠγίνεον** and *ἠγίνευν*, Σ 493; iter. *ἀγίνεσκον*, agere, *lead, bring*, sc. animals more comm.; also, *conduct*, sc. a bride, Σ 492; *haul* wood, Ω 784. [⏑ – ⏑ –]

ἀγκάζομαι, ipf. **ἀγκάζοντο** (*ἀγκάς*), *were raising in their arms* the body from the earth, P 722†.

'Αγκαῖος, (1) son of Lykurgos, chief of Arkadians, B 609.—(2) wrestler from Pleuron, vanquished by Nestor, Ψ 635.

(*ἀγκαλίς*, from *ἀγκάλη*) *ἐν* **ἀγκαλίδεσσι,** in complexu, *in the arms*, only X 503, Σ 555.

ἀγκάς, adv., brachiis, complexu, *into* or *in the arms*, with *ἔχε, ἑλών, λαβέτην, ἐλάζετο, ἔμαρπτε*, η 252. [– ⏑]

ἀγκίστροισι, ntr., (*ἄγκος*, uncus), hamis, *with fish-hooks*, μ 332. (Od.)

ἀγ-κλίνας = *ἀνακλίνας*, aor. part.

ἀγκοίνῃσι (*ἀγκών*), *Διὸς ἐν*, Jovis in complexu, in Zeus's embrace, λ 261.

ἄγκεα, *τὰ*, (cf. ad-uncus), *crooked winding valley, gorge*.

ἀγ-κρεμάσασα, aor. part. from *ἀνακρεμάννυμι*.

ἀγκυλο-μήτης, *εω*, (*μῆτις*), versutus, *crooked in counsel*, epith. of Kronos, occurs in nom. only, Δ 59. [– ⏑ ⏑ – –]

ἄγκυλον, *α*, (*ἄγκος*), only ntr., curvus, *bent, curved*, epith. of bow and of chariot, φ 264. [– ⏑ ⏑]

ἀγκυλό-τοξοι, *ους*, (*τόξον*), *bearing the bent bow*, B 848; epith. of Paionians. [– ⏑ ⏑ – ⏑]

ἀγκυλο-χείλης, *ου*, (*χεῖλος*), adunco rostro praeditus, *with hooked beak*, nom. sing. only τ 538, elsewh. pl., epith. of birds of prey. [– ⏑ ⏑ – –]

ἀγκών, *ῶνος, ὁ*, (*ἄγκος*), cubitus, *elbow*, ξ 494, K 80; Λ 252, in the middle of the arm, below the elbow; Π 702, *τείχεος, corner* of the wall.

ἀγλαϊεῖσθαι (*ἀγλαΐζω*), fut. splendere, *take delight in*, K 331†. [– ⏑ ⏑]

ἀγλαΐη, *ης, ἡ*, (*ἀγλαός*), *splendor, beauty*, ο 78; *dazzling beauty*, of Penelope, σ 180; of dogs; *display*, ρ 310; scatter the fine things which you now have, ρ 244; Epiodat. *ἀγλαΐηφι*, Z 510.

'Αγλαΐη, wife of *Χάροψ*, mother of *Νιρεύς, ὃς κάλλιστος ἀνὴρ ὑπὸ Ἴλιον ἦλθεν*, B 672.

ἀγλαό-καρποι, *μηλέαι*, apple-trees *with shining fruit*, η 115, λ 589. [– ⏑ ⏑ – ⏑]

ἀγλαός, *όν*, (*ἀ-γαλ-Fός*), only masc. and ntr., splendidus, *shining, bright, brilliant*.—(1) epith. of clear water; of polished gifts, esp. of gold or other metal; of ransom; of fame, H 203; so also in reproach, *κέραι ἀγλαέ*, famous with thy bow (and little else), = *ἀγλαϊζόμενος*, Λ 385.—(2) in wider signif.: *illustrious*, *υἱός, υἱόν*, δ 188 (always at end of verse), *τέκνα*; *stately*, T 385; *ἄλσος, sunny* grove, ζ 291, B 506. [– ⏑ ⏑]

(*ἀ-γνοέω*), sync. aor. iter. **ἀγνώσασκε,** for *ἀγνοήσασκε*, ψ 95; from *ἀγνοιέω*, only aor. ind. *ἠγνοίησεν*, subj. *ἀγνοιῇσι*, ω 218, part. *ἀγνοιήσασα*, υ 15; (*ἀγνώς*), ignorare, *fail to recognize*, A 537, neque cum conspicata Juno ignoravit, knew right well; so also N 28, ε 78.

ἁγνή (*ἅζομαι*), only fem., intaminata, *holy*; Artemis, Persephone; *ἑορτή*, φ 259. [– –]

ἄγνυμι (*Fάγνυμι*). **ἀγνυμενάων,** fut. *ἄξω*, aor. *ἔαξα, ἦξα*, inf. *ἆξαι*, pass. aor. *ἐάγην* (*ἄ*, exc. Λ 559), *Fάγη, Fάγεν* (= *ἐάγησαν*), frango, *break, shiver, shatter*.—(1) act., spears, yoke, chariot (at end of pole), Z 40, II 371; shoots of trees, M 148, Π 769; ships, mast.—(2) pass., spear, sword, Γ 367; cudgel, Λ 559; barbs of arrow, Δ 214; neck of Elpenor, κ 560; *suffer shipwreck*, κ 123.

ἀ-γνῶτες (γιγνώσκω, ἀγνώς), ignoti, *unknown*, ε 79†.

ἀγνώσασκε, see ἀγνοέω, ignorabat.

ἄ-γνωστον (γνωστός), ignotum, *unrecognized* (with τεύξω, reddam); *unrecognizable*, ν 191. (Od.)

ἄ-γονος (γόνος), *unborn*, Γ 40†. [⏑⏑⏑]

ἀγοράομαι (ἀγορή), pres. **ἀγοράασθε**, Β 337; ipf. *ἠγοράασθε, ἠγορόωντο*, aor. only 3 sing. *ἀγορήσατο*, usually at end of verse with *καὶ μετέειπεν*, and following oratio directa, β 160, σ 412; concionari, *speak publicly, harangue in the assembly;* Δ 1, **ἠγορόωντο**, *held assembly*. [⏑⏑–]

ἀγορεύω (*ἀγορή*), fut. *ἀγορεύσω*, aor. ind. only *ἀγόρευσεν*, Θ 29, inf. and imp. more common; concionari, loqui, dicere, *speak, say;* freq. *ἔπεα πτερόεντα, ἐνί* or *μετά τισι; μή μοι ἀγόρευε*, with acc., *speak* to me not of, Φ 99, Χ 261; *ἣν ἀγ.*, quam dico, which I *mean*, β 318; freq. *declare, θεοπροπίας*, and with part. *θεοπροπέων, prophesy; διηνεκέως τι*, relate at length, η 241, μ 56; *speak* (joined with idea of action of contrary import, ρ 66, σ 15), *παραβλήδην*, speaking maliciously, Δ 6; peculiar phrase, Β 788, *ἀγορὰς ἀγόρευον*, were discussing in the assembly, cf. Β 796, σ 380; *ὀνειδίζων ἀγορεύοις*, thou shouldst not insultingly *mention* my hungry belly (cf. also *πρόφερε*, Γ 64). [⏑⏑––]

ἀγορή, *ῆς*, *ἡ*, (*ἀγείρω*), concio.—(1) *convoked assembly of people* or *army* (cf. *ἄγυρις, βουλή*), *ἀγορήνδε καλεῖν* (through the heralds), *καθίζειν, ποιεῖσθαι, τίθεσθαι; ἐς δ' ἀγορὴν ἀγέροντο, εἰς ἀγορὴν κίον ἀθρόοι*, π 361; *εἰν ἀγορῇ ἴσαν ἀθρόοι*, Σ 497.—(2) *public speech*, Β 275; *discussion* in assembly, Β 788, Ο 283, δ 818, Ι 441, Β 370, Δ 400, Σ 106; *debate before tribunal*, Π 387.—(3) *place of meeting, market*, β 150, ζ 266, η 44, θ 503, π 377, υ 362; *ἀγοραί, meeting-places*, θ 16; *place of assembly*, Η 382; *time* (afternoon), μ 439 [⏑⏑–]; hence

ἀγορῆθεν, e concione, *from the assembly*, Β 264.

ἀγορήνδε, ad concionem, *to the assembly*, *καλέσσαι, κιόντες*, Α 54.

ἀγορητής (*ἀγορή*), concionator, *haranguer, speaker* (opp. *βουληφόρος*, Η 126); *λιγύς*, loud speaking, powerful; *ἐσθλός*.

ἀγορητύν, *τήν*, (*ἀγορητής*), facundia, *gift of speaking, eloquence*, θ 168†. [⏑⏑––]

ἀγός, *οἱ*, (*ἄγω*), dux, *chief*, Δ 519, Γ 231. [⏑⏑]

ἀγοστῷ, *ἕλε γαῖαν* —, palmâ, *with flat, outstretched hand*, Λ 425, Ν 508, 520, Ξ 452, Ρ 315, of mortally wounded. [⏑––]

ἄγραυλος, only **ἀγραύλοιο** *βοός*, **ἄγραυλοι** *ποιμένες*, Σ 162; *πόριες*, κ 410 (*ἀγρός, αὐλή*), *belonging to the farm enclosure*, epith. of domestic cow, as distinguished from the cows driven to or roaming in remote pasture; epith. also of herd of cattle, of calves.

ἄγρει and υ 149 *ἀγρεῖτε*, imp. from *ἀγρέω* (*ἄγρη, ἄγω*), *quick! forwards!* used alone or with *μάν, δή, νῦν*, followed by imp., or inf. used as imp. (literally *seize! lay hand upon!*).

ἄγρη, *ἡ*, (*ἄγω*), venatio, *hunt*, *ἐφέπεσκον*, were following the *chase*, μ 330. (Od.)

ἄγριος, 2, yet shows fem. termination in ι 119 (*ἀγρός*), agrestis, *wild*.—(1) of beasts, *fierce*, *τὰ ἄγρια*, ferae.—(2) of men, *ferocious;* of combatants, *savage*, α 199, ζ 120, θ 575, ι 215; of Polyphemos, Skylla, μ 119; Gigantes, η 206.—(3) *horrible, dreadful*, of tumult of conflict, *ἄτη, χόλος, θυμός*; Ω 41, rages grimly like a lion. [–⏑⏑]

Ἄγριος, son of Portheus in Kalydon, Ξ 117.

ἀγριο-φώνους *μετὰ Σίντιας*, θ 294†, to the *harsh-voiced* Sintians.

ἀγρόθεν (*ἀγρός*), rure, *from the field*, *κατιέναι, ἔρχεσθαι*, go home, ν 268. (Od.)

ἀγροιῶται, *οἱ*, ruricolae, *peasants;* also adj. *rustic*, Ο 272.

ἀγρόμενος, part. aor. mid. from *ἀγείρω*.

ἀγρόνδε, rus, *to the country, country-house*, ο 379.

ἀγρο-νόμοι (*νέμω*) *νύμφαι*, ζ 106†, ruricolae, *rural*. [⏑⏑⏑–]

ἀγρός, οῦ, ὁ, ager, rus, *field, land;* ἀγροῦ ἐπ' ἐσχατιῆς, *far out in the country;* κατ' ἀγρούς, ruri, *in the country* (for term opp. to ἀγρός, cf. π 383, ρ 182); villa, *country-seat,* λ 188, ο 428, π 330, ψ 139. [–⏑]

ἀγρότερος, 3, ferus, *wild,* σῦς κάπριος, αἶγες, ἔλαφοι, Φ 471; Ἄρτεμις, *ranging through the fields, the huntress.* [–⏑⏑⏑]

ἀγρόται, οἱ, ruricolae, *peasants,* π 218†.

ἀγρώσσων (ἄγρα), ἰχθῦς, ε 53†, piscans, *ever catching* fish; of sea-gull.

ἄγρωστιν (ἀγρός), μελιηδέα, ζ 90†, honey-sweet *field grass,* on which mules feed; identified by some with *dog's tooth,* by others with *panic.*

ἄγυια, ἡ, (ἄγω), does not occur in nom. sing., via publica, *wagon road;* σκιόωντο δὲ πᾶσαι ἀγυιαί, and darkness overshadowed all ways, i. e. every thing; also of the *streets* and *public squares* in cities, plateae, Ε 642, Ζ 391; μέσην εἰς ἄγυιαν [⏑–⏑] ἰοῦσαι, in publicum progressae, on the open street, Υ 254. [⏑––]

ἀγύρει, ιν, fem. (ἀγορά), coetus, *chance gathering* (cf. ἀγορή), *company, host;* νεκύων, νηῶν (fleet, laid up on the shore), Πυλίων. [⏑⏑–]

ἀγυρτάζειν (ἀγύρτης, ἀγείρω), τ 284, colligere, *collect by begging.*

ἀγχέ-μαχοι (ἄγχι, μάχη), cominus proeliantes, *fighting hand to hand* (opp. τοξόται); otherwise explained as *fighting in close array,* Ρ 165. [–⏑⏑–]

ἄγχι (cogn. with ἄγχω), prope, iuxta, *near, close to, hard by,* τινός; freq. with παρίστασθαι, στῆναι, ἐλθεῖν; ἄγχι μάλα, sc. ἐστί, τ 301; Υ 283, οἱ, is dat. of disadvantage, ἄγχι being used absolutely, because the missile had struck and remained fixed so near him. [–⏑]

ἀγχί-αλον (ἅλς), acc., maritimam, *near the sea;* epith. of Χαλκίς and Ἀντρών. [–⏑⏑⏑]

ἀγχι-βαθής (βάθος) θάλασσα, ε 413†, *deep near* the shore. [–⏑⏑–]

ἀγχί-θεοι (θεός), diis propinqui, *related to the gods;* of Phaiakians. [–⏑⏑–]

ἀγχι-μαχηταί (μαχητής), cominus proeliantes, *fighting hand to hand*= ἀγχέμαχοι, Β 604, ἀνέρες; also of whole tribes. [–⏑⏑––]

ἀγχί-μολον (μολεῖν), ntr. acc. with adverbial force, prope, *near;* usually with dat. with ἐλθεῖν, ἔρχεσθαι, ρ 260; ἐπὶ ἦλθεν, χ 205, ω 502; only in Ω 352, ἐξ ἀγχιμόλοιο ἰδών, e propinquo conspicatus; ρ 336, *close after him* Odysseus entered the house.

ἀγχί-νοος (νόος), *quick of apprehension,* ν 332†; *self-possessed.* [–⏑⏑⏑]

Ἀγχίσης, (1) son of Κάπυς, father of Αἰνείας, ἄναξ ἀνδρῶν, Ε 268.—(2) father of Ἐχέπωλος, from Σικυών, Ψ 296. [–––]

Ἀγχισιάδης, (1) Αἰνείας, Ρ 754.—(2) Ἐχέπωλος. [––⏑⏑–]

ἄγχιστα, see ἄγχιστος, proximum.

ἀγχιστῖνοι, αι, (ἄγχιστος), conferti, *close together, one after another,* Ρ 361, χ 118.

ἄγχιστον (ἄγχι), proximum, *very near, close by;* proxime aberat, *least distant,* ε 280; pl. *nearest,* with gen.; ἄγχιστα ἐοικώς and ἐίσκω, nearest resembling, I compare (him) first with.

ἀγχόθι (ἀγχοῦ), with gen., prope a, *hard by,* ν 103. [–⏑⏑]

ἀγχοῦ (ἄγχι), prope, *near,* with ἵστασθαι, ναίειν, ξυμβαλέσθαι, ζ 5.

ἄγχε (from ἄγχω, ipf.), *was choking,* Γ 371†.

ἄγω (ago), ἄξω, aor. ἦξα (imp. ἄξετε, inf. ἀξέμεν, ἀξέμεναι), mid. ἠξάμην (ἄξεσθε, ἄξοντο); comm. form ἤγαγον, subj. ἀγάγωμι, mid. ἠγαγόμην (also unaugmented); agere, *lead, bring, drive;* I. act. (1) *lead, conduct, bring,* Λ 842, Ω 564 (in ρ 218 ὡς is prep., *brings* like *to* like), ρ 243, η 248, δ 312; βοῦν, ἵππους, *put to;* ἑκατόμβην, Α 431; of lioness's cubs, Ρ 134; bones of the fallen, Η 335; (a) *bring* or *carry with one,* Γ 401, Ι 664, Λ 650, Α 390, 184, δ 601; of persons and things; (b) *plunder, carry off, make away with;* prisoners and booty, beside Ω 764, cf. Ι 594, Υ 194, Ε 484, Ψ 512; Λ 332, the goddesses of dark death were carrying away, cf. Ε 614 and Ν 602.—(2) *transport, remove,* vehere, persons and things as subj. ναῦται, α 172; also freq. νῆες, even ἄξων, Ε 839; (a) *carry away,* νεκρόν, κόπρον, cf. Λ 598, Α 338, κ 551; *recover,* κ 268;

(b) *fetch*, things living or without life, Α 184, Γ 105, Θ 368, Ψ 613, 50, Ω 778, β 326, γ 424, ξ 27, φ 266.—(3) *bring to pass, occasion*, Ω 547; sport, σ 37, tempest.—(4) κλέος, *spread abroad* renown, ε 311; cf. παιήονα ἄγ., Χ 392, *raise* a song of exultation.—(5) *guide, control*, combat, Λ 721; water, Φ 262; esp. the army, *steer* ships, Β 580, 631, 557; λόχον, ξ 469, insidias struere. The part. ἄγων is often added to verbs of motion, where it is not necessary to the sense, for the sake of greater vividness, α 130, δ 525, ο 47, cf. γ 118.—II. mid. (1) *take with one* one's effects, or what one regards as one's own, clothes, ζ 58, cf. Γ 72, Δ 19, Χ 116; booty, κ 35, 40, cf. Η 363; prizes, Ψ 263; captives, Ζ 455.—(2) γυναῖκα, *bring home* as wife; of bridegroom, *take to wife*, Ι 146, Π 190, Χ 471; of father, who brings to his son in marriage, κούρην δ 10; of brother, to brother, ο 238; of master, to his slave, φ 214; of those who accompany the bride, ζ 28.

ἀγών, ῶνος, ὁ, (ἄγω), comitium, *place of meeting*.—(1) *assembly*, ἵζανεν, Ψ 258; λῦτο, Ω 1.—(2) *place where assembly meets:* (a) θεῖος, Η 298, *area before the temple, temple enclosure;* Σ 376, *hall of the gods*, yet cf. θ 264; νεῶν, *space behind the ships*, i.e. between the ships and the shore, *the encampment at the ships; νεῶν ἐν ἀγῶνι*, Π 500, differs in meaning from Ο 428; (b) *place* or *scene of combat, arena*, including the space reserved for spectators, Ψ 531. [⏑ –]

ἀ-δαημονίη (ἀδαήμων), inscitia, *inexperience*, ω 244†. [⏑ ⏑ – ⏑ ⏑ –]

ἀ-δαήμων, ον, gen. ονος, (δαήμων), imperitus, *unacquainted with*, τινός, ρ 283. [⏑ ⏑ – –]

ἀ-δάκρυτος (δακρύω), lacrimis carens, *tearless, dry*, δ 186. [⏑ – – ⏑]

Ἄδαμας, αντος, son of Ἄσιος from Troja, Ν 771, 759.

ἀ-δάμαστος (δαμάζω), inflexibilis, *inflexible*, Ἀίδης, Ι 158†. [⏑ ⏑ – ⏑]

ἀδδεές, see ἀδειής, impudens, *shameless*.

ἀδδηκώς, ἀδδήσειε, see ἀδέω, pertaesus.

ἄδδην, see ἄδην, *to satiety*.

ἀ-δειής (δέος), intrepidus, *undismayed*, Η 117, but κύον ἀδδεές, impudens, *shameless* hound, as abusive epithet; later form ἀδεές. [– ⏑ ⏑; Η 117, ⏑ – –.]

ἀ-δελφειοῦ, ἀδελφεός, οἱ, όν, (ἀ copul. and δελφύς, uterus), frater, *own-brother*.

ἀ-δευκέϊ, έα, (δεῦκος, decus), indignus, *disgraceful;* φῆμις, ζ 273, *slanderous* gossip.

ἀ-δεψήτῳ, ον, (δέψω), crudus, *untanned*, υ 2 and 142.

(ἀδέω) only opt. aor. **ἀδδήσειε**, perf. part. ἀδδηκότες, also written ἀδήσειε, ἀδηκότες, and ἀδηκότες, (sat-ur) satiatum fastidire, *be satiated, loathe from excess*, τινί, δείπνῳ; καμάτῳ, ὕπνῳ, *be overwhelmed with*.

ἄδην, ἄδην, (ἀδέω, orig. ἄδδην = σάδ-ϳην). *to satiety*, ἔδμεναι, and *to excess;* esp. ἐλάαν τινὰ κακότητος, πολέμοιο, etc., drive one into misery (war), *until he has had enough of it.* [⏑ –; Ε 203, – –.]

ἀ-δήριτος (δῆρις), non depugnatus, *uncontested*, Ρ 42†. [⏑ – – ⏑]

ἀδινάων Σειρήνων, ψ 326, seems to mean *sweet-singing, seducing* Sirens (Ϝαδινάων, from ἡδύς, ἕαδα). [⏑ ⏑ – – –]

ἀ-δινοῦ, ά, όν, (δίω), commotus, Π 481, *moved, agitated*.—I. epith. (1) of κῆρ, *throbbing with anxiety*, τ 516.—(2) μέλισσαι, Β 87, μυῖαι, Β 469, *buzzing;* μῆλα, oves trepidantes, *restless, flurried*, α 92, δ 320.—(3) γόος, sobbing, *whimpering* lament, Σ 316, Ψ 17, etc. (Σειρῆνες, see foreg.)—II. adverbial, ἀδινόν, ἀδινά, *vehemently, with utterance broken by sobs*, with στενάχω, στοναχέω, στεναχίζω, κλαίω (ἀδινώτερον, *more dolefully*, π 216), γοάω, μυκᾶσθαι, κ 413.—III. adv. **ἀδινῶς** ἀνενείκατο, flebiliter suspiravit, Τ 314, cf. 338. [⏑ ⏑ –]

ἀ-δμής, ῆτες, (δάμνημι), indomitus.—(1) *untamed;* of mules, δ 637, cf. ἀδμήτην.—(2) *unmarried;* of a virgin. (Od.)

ἀ-δμήτην (δάμνημι), indomitam, *unbroken*, not yet brought under the yoke; of beasts of draught, Κ 293, Ψ 266, 655.

Ἄδμητος, father of Εὔμηλος, Β 713, Ψ 289, 391, 532; husband of Ἄλκηστις, Β 714.

ἄδον, aor. 2 from ἁνδάνω, placui.

ἄδος (see ἀδέω), μιν ἵκετο θυμόν,

disgust (with toil) entered his soul, Λ 88†. [- ⏑]

'Αδρήστεια, town on the Propontis, in what was afterward Mysia, B 828.

'Αδρήστη, handmaid of 'Ελένη, *δ* 123.

'Αδρηστίνη, daughter of *"Αδρηστος*, *Αἰγιάλεια*, E 412†.

"Αδρηστος, (1) from *"Αργος*, fugitive to *Σικυών*, succeeds *Πόλυβος* there as king; becomes also king in Argos, harbors *Τυδεύς*, and gives him his daughter in marriage, cf. Ξ 121; his swift steed *'Αρείων*, Ψ 347.—(2) son of *Μέροψ*, from *Περκώτη*, founder of *'Αδρήστεια*, leader of Trojan allies from thence, B 830, Λ 328.—(3) Trojan slain by Menelaos, Z 37, 51 et sq.—(4) Trojan slain by Patroklos, Π 694.

ἀδροτῆτα (*ἀδρός*), acc. from *ἀδροτής*, coupled with *ἥβην* and *μένος*, *full bodily maturity*, Il. (Cf. *ἀνδροτῆτα*.)

ᾰ-δυτον (*δύω*, *not to be entered*), fanum, *shrine*, only E 448, 512.

ἀ-εθλεύειν (*ᾰεθλον*), certare, *institute, or contend in, a gymnastic contest; ἐπί τινι*, in honor of some one, Ψ 274; Ω 734, *toiling* for a merciless master. [⏑ – – –]

ἀέθλιον, τὸ, (*ᾰεθλον*).—(1) certamen, *contest for a prize*, *θ* 108, Π 590.—(2) *implements of combat, weapons*, *φ* 4, 117.—(3) *prizes in contest*, *ἀρέσθαι*, carry off; *ἀνελεῖν*, *ἀνελέσθαι*, win; *φέρεσθαι*, bring in, I 127. [⏑ – ⏑ ⏑]

ᾰ-εθλον, *τό*, (*ᾰϜεθλον*, vadari; German wetten, English bet).—(1) pl. certamina, *prize contests*, *θ* 160, *ω* 89.—(2) sing. and pl. *prize;* for such a prize, λ 548; having come, entered, for the prize, Λ 700. [⏑ – ⏑]

ᾰ-εθλος (*ᾰθλων*, *θ* 160), *ὁ*, (*ᾰεθλον*), (1) certamen, *prize contest*, distinguished from *πόλεμος*, Π 590; varieties, *θ* 103, Ψ 646, 753; *καταθήσω*, *τ* 572; *ἐκτελέειν*, *φ* 135, *χ* 5.—(2) *combat* (in war), Γ 126; *τελεῖν*, *γ* 262; *μογεῖν*, *δ* 241; *hardships* of every sort, *ψ* 248, 350, esp. *Εὐρυσθῆος*, those imposed by Eurystheus upon Herakles.

ἀεθλο-φόρος (*ἀθλοφόρος*), praemium certaminis ferens, *bearing away the prize, victorious;* only of horses, X 22.

ἀεί, αἰεί (at close of verse), **αἰέν** (cogn. with *αἰϜών*, aevum), semper, *always;* often strengthened by *ἀσκελέως*, *ἀσφαλές*, *διαμπερές*, *ἐμμενές*, *μάλα*, *νωλεμές*, *συνεχές*; also *αἰεὶ ἤματα πάντα*.

ἀείδω (*ἀϜείδω*), fut. *ἀείσομαι*, aor. ind. *ᾰεισε*, imp. *ᾰεισον*, inf. *ἀεῖσαι*, cantare, *sing*.—(1) trans. *sing*, *παιήονα*, *κλέα ἀνδρῶν*, minstrels' lays, heroic songs; of something, *μῆνιν* (cf. "sing and say," Nibelungen Lied), *relate in song*, *'Αχαιῶν νόστον*, *α* 326, *Δαναῶν κακὸν οἶτον*, *α* 350, *'Αχαιῶν*, *θ* 489 (*λίην κατὰ κόσμον*, very becomingly, altogether in order); *ἵππου κόσμον*, 492, with *ὡς*, 514, and with acc. and inf. 516.—(2) intrans. *sing; μάλ' ἀεῖσαι*, sing merrily; with adj. used adverbially, *καλόν*, *α* 155 and often, so probably A 473, Σ 570; *λίγ'*, loud, *κ* 254; also of nightingale (*ἀϜηδών*); of bow string, it *sang*, i. e. *twanged* under the touch, *φ* 411. [⏑ – –, exc. *ρ* 519.]

ἀ-εικείην, *ας*, fem. (*ἀϳεικείη*, *ϳέϳοικεν*), strictly dedecus.—(1) deformitas, *disfigurement*, Ω 19.—(2) *ἀεικείας φαίνειν*, *υ* 308; behave *unseemly*, proterve agere. [⏑ – – – –]

ἀ-εικέλιος, 2 and 3, (*ἀϳεικέλιος*, from *ϳείκελος*), indecorus, turpis, *unseemly, shameful*, *ἀλαωτύς*, *πληγαί*; *wretched*, Ξ 84, *τ* 341; *ill-favored, filthy*, *ζ* 242, *ν* 402, *υ* 259, *ρ* 357, *ω* 228 [⏑ – ⏑ ⏑ ⏑]; adv. *ἀεικελίως*, *ignominiously*, *π* 109, *υ* 319; *wretchedly*, *θ* 231.

ἀ-εικής, *ές*, (*ϳέϳοικε*), indignus, *unbecoming, unseemly*.—(1) *νόος οὐδὲν ἀ.*, mind altogether faultless; *οὔ τοι ἀεικές*, nec vero dedecet.—(2) *disgraceful, ignominious; ἔργον*, indignum facinus; *λοιγός*, *πότμος*, *στόνος*, K 483, *λώβη*.—(3) turpis, *mean, poor; ἀεικέα ἕσσαι*, thou art vilely clad, *πήρη*.—(4) vilis, *small, mean*, *μισθός*, M 435, *ᾰποινα*. [⏑ – – –]

ἀ-εικίζει (*ἀεικής*), ipf. *ἀείκιζεν*, fut. *ἀεικιῶ*, aor. subj. *ἀεικίσσωσι*, mid. *ἀεικισσαίμεθα*, *ἀεικίσσασθαι*, pass. *ἀεικισθήμεναι*, foedare, *maltreat, insult*, Π 545, *σ* 222, Ω 54; *disfigure*, T 26; for yea (*δή*), he even insults in his wrath the lifeless clay (*κωφήν*), Ω 54. [⏑ – – – –]

ἀείρων (*ἀϜείρω*), pl. *αἴροντας*, aor. *ἤειρα* and *ᾰειρα*, mid. I. *ἀειράμην*, pass. *ἀέρθην* (*ἀερθείς*, *ἀρθείς*), plupf. *ᾰωρτο*, tollere, *raise up*, (1) in strict sense (from ground and otherwise), I 465; stones, Ξ 411, H 268; corpses, Π 678, P 724; the wounded, Ξ 429; *swing on high* the lash, Ψ 362; *brandish* a spear, Υ 373, Θ 424; freq. with ὑψόσε, e. g. Υ 325; hence also ὑψόσ' ἀειρόμενος, *raising one's self* on high, *rising*, Φ 307. Also pass. ι 393, μ 249, 255, and ὑψόσ' ἀερθείς, μ 432, θ 375; of horses, ὑψόσ' ἀειρέσθην, Ψ 501; of birds, ἀρθείς, N 63, τ 540, ἀέρθη; the fortunes of the Trojans rose aloft, Θ 74. Part. ἀείρας, for greater vividness, with verbs of bearing, placing, e. g. Τ 380, α 141, β 425, ρ 335. Of ships (γ 312, ἄειραν), *carry*, ἄχθος.—(2) promere, *bring forth, produce*; οἶνον, Z 264, esp. mid. (out of one's store), Z 293, ο 106, ρ 335.

ἀ-εκαζόμενος, η, (ἀέκων), invitus, *unwillingly*, σ 135, τ 133; also with πολλά, quite against one's will. [⏑⏑–⏑⏑⏑]

ἀ-εκήλια (ἔκηλος), ἔργα παθέειν, Σ 77†, literally *unwished-for things*, suffer doleful woes, cf. sq.

ἀ-έκητι (ἕκητι), contra voluntatem, *against the will of*, with gen., ζ 287; esp. freq. with θεῶν, M 8, γ 28. [⏑⏑⏑–⏑]

ἀ-έκων, ουσ(α), (ἀϝέκων, from ἑκών), invitus, *unwilling*.—(1) *without design*, Π 264.—(2) *reluctant, against one's will; οὐκ ἄκοντε*, gladly; ἀέκοντος ἐμεῖο, me invito, *in spite of* me; against their wish, to their annoyance, Θ 487, cf. Π 369; vi me invitum retinebit, O 186; notice also σὲ βίῃ ἀέκοντος ἀπηύρα, with acc., vi nolentem privavit, robbed thee by force, against thy will; A 430, cf. δ 646. [⏑⏑–]

ἄελλα, ἡ, (ἄημι), procella, *gust of wind, stormy wind*, χειμέριαι, B 293; παντοίων ἀνέμων; also in simile, to describe onset of heroes, Λ 297, M 40, N 795. [⏑–⏑]

ἀ-ελλής κονίσαλος ὤρνυτο, turbidus pulvis surrexit, *a thick cloud of* dust rose, Γ 13†. [⏑––]

ἀελλό-πος Ἶρις, *storm-footed*, i. e. *swift-footed* Iris (Il.); cf. ποδήνεμος. [⏑––⏑]

ἀ-ελπέα, insperatam, Zeus has given me to see land which I *never expected to behold*, ε 408†.

ἀ-ελπτέοντες (ἔλπω), desperantes eum salvum esse, *despairing* of his safety, H 310†. [⏑–⏓–]

ἀε-νάοντα (from αἰὲν νάοντα) ὕδατα, juges aquae, *never-failing* springs, ν 109† (v. l. αἰενάοντα). [–⏑⏑–⏑]

ἀ-έξω (ἀϝέξω, cogn. with augeo, German wachsen, English wax), only pres. and ipf., *increase*, Z 261, ι 111; *nourish, let grow up*, υἱόν, ν 360; μέγα πένθος, cherish great grief; ἀέξεσθαι, *come to manhood*, of Telemachos, χ 426; *prosper*, ἔργον, ξ 66; ἀέξετο ἱερὸν ἦμαρ, the sacred day *advanced*, Θ 66, ι 56.

ἀ-εργίης (ϝέργον) ἕνεκα, pigritiae causa, *out of sloth*, ω 251†. [⏑–––]

ἀ-εργός, όν, (ϝέργον), piger, *idle, lazy*. [⏑–⏑]

ἀερθείς, ἄερθεν, part. and 3 pl. aor. pass. from ἀείρω, sublatus.

ἀερσί-ποδες, ων, (ἀείρω), ἵπποι, tolutarii equi, *quick-trotting, high-stepping* horses, cf. Ψ 501 (Il.). [⏑–⏑⏑⏑]

ἄεσα, ἀέσαμεν, aor. from ἰαύω, dormivi.

ἀεσι-φροσύνῃσιν (ἀεσίφρων), dat. pl. temere, *thoughtlessly*, ο 470.

ἀεσί-φρων, ονος, (ἀάω, φρένες), amens, *thoughtless, light-headed*, φ 302, Ψ 603, Υ 183. [⏑⏑––]

ἀζαλέοιο, ης, ην, ας, (ἄζομαι), aridus, *dry, parched, withered*; of trees; ox-hide shield, H 239; ὄρος, Υ 491. [–⏑⏑]

Ἀζεΐδαο, Ἄκτορος, *the son of Azeus*, B 513. [–⏑⏑–⏑]

ἄζη, τῇ, (ἄζω), situ inquinatum, covered with *dust, dirt*, χ 184†. [––]

ἀ-ζηχής, ές, (διέχω), penetrans, continuus, *unceasing*, of pain; *penetrating*, of sound of combat; adverbial, ἀζηχές, perpetuo, *incessantly*, Δ 435, O 658, σ 3. [––⏑]

ἄζομαι (ἅγιος), only pres. and ipf., vereri, *dread, shrink from*; esp. before the gods, τινά; religioni habere, with inf., Z 267, ι 478; with μή, Ξ 261. [–⏑⏑]

ἀζομένη (ἄζω), arescens, *becoming dry*, Δ 487†. [–⏑⏑–]

ἀηδών (ἀϝείδω) χλωρηίς, luscinia, the *songstress* in green foliage, τ 518; Ἀηδών, the daughter of Pandareos, is meant, the wife of Ζῆθος of Thebai, mother of Itylos, whom she slew by mistake while intending, out of jealousy, to kill the son of Niobe, her sister-in-law; after this deed, transformed into a nightingale, she ever sadly repeated the name of her murdered son, Ἴτυ, Ἴτυ.

ἀ-ήθεσσον (ἀ-ηθεσ-jω, ἦθος) αὐτῶν, insueti erant, (the horses) *were as yet unaccustomed* to the sight of corpses, K 493†. [⏑ — — ⏑]

ἄημι (ἄϝημι, cf. ventus, English wind), 3 du. **ἄητον**, inf. ἀῆναι, ἀήμεναι, part. ἀέντες, ipf. ἄη, ἄει, pass. ἀήμενος. (1) *blow*, of wind, always act.; ἀήμενος, ventis exagitatus.—(2) Φ 386, δίχα δέ σφιν ἐνὶ φρεσὶ θυμὸς ἄητο, their minds *wavered* to and fro. [⏑ — ⏑]

ἀήρ, fem., *gloom*, E 864, ι 144; *fog*, η 143; see also ἠήρ.

ἀήσυλα (=ἀ-ΐσυλα) ἔργα, facinora violenta, *deeds of violence*, E 876†. [⏑ — ⏑ ⏑]

ἀήτης, ου, ὁ, (ἄϝημι), ventus, *wind*, only Ξ 254; elsewh. with ἀνέμοιο, ζεφύροιο, ἀνέμων, flatus, *blast, gusts*.

ἄητο, see ἄημι.

ἄητον θάρσος ἔχουσα, with *stormy* courage, impetuoso animo, Φ 395†. (Of uncertain derivation; cf. θυμὸς ἄητο and ἀήσυλα, E 876; scarcely related to αἴητος.)

ἀθάνατος, 3, (θάνατος), *immortal;* also subst., e.g. A 503, Ω 61, A 265; freq. with θεοί; in phrase ἀθάνατος καὶ ἀγήραος; also predicated of bodily members, A 530, N 19, and of *imperishable* possessions (δ 79, B 447) of the gods; opp. βροτοί, Λ 2, ε 2; θνητοί, Ξ 199; ἄνδρες, π 265; ἀθ. κακόν, Charybdis, μ 118. [— ⏑ ⏑ ⏑]

ἄθαπτος, only masc. (θάπτω), inhumatus, *unburied.* [⏑ — —]

ἀθεεί, οὐκ ἀθ., (θεός), non sine numine, *not without divine guidance*=it is really a *special providence* that—, σ 353†. [⏑ ⏑ —]

ἀθεμίστιος, οι, α, (θέμις), nefarius, *criminal;* ἀθεμίστια εἰδέναι, live *impiously, godlessly.* [⏑ ⏑ — ⏑ ⏑]

ἀθέμιστος, ων, (θέμις), ferus, *lawless*, ι 106; nefarius, *wicked;* opp. ἐναίσιμοι, ρ 363. [⏑ ⏑ — ⏑]

ἀθερίζω, ipf. ἀθέριζον, (ἀθερές), contemno, *despise*, always with negation, A 261, θ 212, ψ 174. [⏑ ⏑ — —]

ἀθέσφατος, 2, (ἀ, θεός, φημί), immensus, *immeasurable, boundless;* γαῖα, θάλασσα, ὄμβρος, νύξ; also joined hyperbolically with οἶνος and σῖτος. [⏑ — ⏑ ⏑]

Ἀθῆναι, *Athens*, capital of Attika, B 546, 549, γ 278, 307; also sing. εὐρυάγυιαν Ἀθήνην, η 80.

Ἀθηναίη, ης, the goddess *Athene*, Διὸς ἐκγεγαυῖα, ἀγελείη, γλαυκῶπις, ἠύκομος, κούρη Διός (αἰγιόχοιο), λαοσσόος, ληῖτις, ἐρυσίπτολις, cf. Ἀτρυτώνη, Τριτογένεια, esp. Παλλάς; fosters the arts, ζ 232, ψ 160, esp. domestic and feminine accomplishments, I 390, β 116; as goddess of war, Ἀλαλκομενηίς, she protects cities, and is the especial patron of wary warriors like Odysseus; see Ἀθήνη.

Ἀθηναῖοι, *Athenians*, B 551, 558, Δ 328, N 196, 689, O 337.

Ἀθήνη, parallel form of Ἀθηναίη; Ἀλαλκομενηίς, γλαυκῶπις, ἐυπλόκαμος, πολύβουλος, etc.; η 80, the city *Athens.*

ἀθηρ-ηλοιγός (ἀθήρ, λοιγός), lit. *chaff-destroyer*, designation of winnowing-shovel in Teiresias's prophecy to Odysseus, λ 128†.

ἀθλήσαντε and **ἀθλήσαντα** (part. aor. from ἀθλέω), laboribus exerceri, *toil, drudge*, H 453, O 30.

ἀθλητῆρι, οὐδ' — ἔοικας, neque enim certatoris similis es, nor dost thou resemble *one who takes his part in manly contests*, θ 164†.

ἆθλος, see ἄεθλος.

ἀθλοφόροι, see ἀεθλοφόρος.

Ἀθόω, ἐξ —, *from Athos* (nom. sing. Ἀθόως), Ξ 229†, the well-known rocky promontory of Akte in Chalkidike, now Monte Santo.

ἀθρέω, only aor. **ἀθρήσειε**, ἀθρῆσαι, intueri, cernere, *gaze*, εἰς; *perceive*, τινά; *comprehend*, τ 478. [— — — ⏑]

ἀ-θρόος, 3, only pl., cuncti, *(all) together, in crowds*, Ξ 38, Σ 497; ἠγερέθοντο, β 392; freq. ἀθρόα πάντα; also written ἀθρόοι. [— ⏑ ⏑]

ἄ-θυμοι (θυμός), animo destituti, *faint-hearted, despondent*, κ 463†. [⏑ — —]

ἀθύρματα, τά, (ἀθύρω), ludicra, *playthings*, O 363; elegantiae minutulae, *child's toys*, σ 323; *ornaments, trinkets*, ο 416. [⏑ — ⏑ ⏑]

ἀθύρων, part. from ἀθύρω, O 364†, per lusum, *in sport.* [⏑ — —]

αἰ (perh. old case-form of relative; cf.

παραί, *ὑπαί*, as also *εἰ*; this relative force may be traced in λ 348, *αἴ κεν ἔγωγε ἀνάσσω*, *as true as that* I reign; *so sure as* I reign) never stands alone, but I. expressing a wish, optative use.—(1) *αἶ γάρ*, utinam, *would that*, always with opt., (a) where fulfillment of wish is regarded as possible, Θ 538, N 825, Π 97, Σ 464, X 454, γ 205, ζ 244, θ 339, ι 523, ο 156, 536, ρ 163, 251, σ 235, τ 309, υ 236, φ 200, 372 (*αἶ γὰρ δή*, Δ 189, K 536, Σ 272, X 346, δ 697, τ 22, υ 169, ρ 513); (b) where fulfillment of wish is regarded as impossible, π 99: the formula, *αἶ γάρ, Ζεῦ τε πάτερ καὶ Ἀθηναίη καὶ Ἄπολλον*, is followed by opt. in sense of (a) above, B 371, Δ 288, Π 97, σ 235; in sense of (b) above, H 132, δ 341 = ρ 132; by inf. in sense of (a), η 311; in sense of (b), ω 376.—(2) **αἴθε** (cf. *εἴθε*), utinam, *oh that! would that!* (a) where fulfillment of wish is conceived as possible, with opt. Δ 178, X 41, η 331, ξ 440, ρ 494, σ 202, υ 61; (b) where fulfillment is conceived as impossible, with opt. Π 722; with ipf. *ὤφελλε*, Ξ 84, σ 401; with aor. *ὄφελον*, A 415, Γ 40, Σ 86, Ω 253, ν 204.—II. interrogative use, **αἴ κε** (never separated by intervening word), si, *whether*, with subj. ξ 118, *εἰπέ μοι, αἴ κέ ποθι γνώω τοιοῦτον ἐόντα, Ζεὺς γάρ που τόγε οἶδε, εἴ κέ μιν ἀγγείλαιμι ἰδών*; so also after *ὄφρ' ἴδητε*, Δ 249; *πειρήσομαι*, E 279, ω 217; and freq. without a preceding verbum tentandi, A 66, Z 94, H 243, K 55, Λ 797, 799, Ω 301, α 379, β 144, γ 92, ν 182, δ 34, *αἴ κέ* **ποθι Ζεὺς**; so also α 379, β 144, μ 215, χ 252, ρ 51, 60, *αἴ κέ ποθι*, strictly = si qua, *if, if in any case;* the opt. occurs only in oratio obliqua, *αἴ κε γένοιτο*, H 387, yet see A 207.—III. conditional use, *αἴ κε* (never separated by intervening word), si, *if, perhaps*, (1) with subj., (a) where fut. follows in principal sentence, θ 496, ρ 230; (b) where opt. follows in principal sentence, Ω 688; (c) where inf. follows in principal sentence, E 260.—(2) with opt. (where a wish is involved) where opt. follows in principal sentence, ν 389.—(3) in a period, where there is an ellipsis of one of its members, *αἴ κ' ἐθέλῃσθα*, Σ 457, δ 322, μ 49, υ 233; after *ὄψεαι*, Θ 471, N 260, T 147, δ 391, ω 511 (to be distinguished from *εἰ ἐθέλεις*, π 82, ρ 277), Δ 353 *ἢν ἐθέλῃσθα καὶ αἴ κέν τοι τὰ μεμήλῃ*.

ἀι- has been sometimes regarded by some as a strengthening prefix = *very, exceedingly*, cf. *ἀίζηλος*.

αἶα, *αἴης*, *αἶαν*, (probably from *γαια*), terra, *earth, land*, *φυσίζοος*; *πατρίδος αἴης*; *Ἀχαιΐδος αἴης*; *πᾶσαν ἐπ' αἶαν*, over the whole earth; *Θρῃκῶν αἶαν*.

Αἰαίη, (1) *νῆσος*, island *Aeaea*, home of Kirke, κ 135, λ 70, *ὅθι τ' Ἠοῦς ἠριγενείης οἰκία καὶ χοροί εἰσι καὶ ἀντολαὶ Ἠελίοιο*, μ 3 sq., a fabulous region far in N. W. (the Romans located it at Circeii); hence (2) *δολόεσσα*, the goddess Kirke herself, ι 32; μ 268, 273, sister of Aietes.

Αἰακίδης, *descendant of Aiakos*, (1) son, Peleus, Π 15, Σ 433, Φ 189.—(2) grandson, Achilleus.

Αἰακός, son of Zeus, father of Peleus, grandfather of Achilleus, Φ 189.

Αἴας, *αντος*, (*ΑἴϝFας*), (1) *Τελαμώνιος*, *Τελαμωνιάδης*, *μέγας*, son of Telamon from Salamis, half-brother of Teukros, *ἕρκος Ἀχαιῶν*, bulwark of the Achaians ("a tower in battle"), *φέρων σάκος ἠύτε πύργον*, Λ 485; *πελώριος*, Γ 229; λ 550, *ὃς πέρι μὲν εἶδος πέρι δ' ἔργα τέτυκτο τῶν ἄλλων Δαναῶν μετ' ἀμύνονα Πηλείωνα*; *ὅπλων κρίσις*, λ 543 sqq.—(2) *Ὀιλῆος ταχὺς* (cf. Ψ 793) *Αἴας*, *μείων*, *Ὀιλιάδης*, Oileus's son, leader of Lokrians; for his presumption swallowed up in the sea near the *Γυραὶ πέτραι*, δ 499.—(3) the two heroes often coupled in dual or pl., e. g. *Αἰάντε δύω, θεράποντες Ἄρηος, θοῦριν ἐπιειμένοι ἀλκήν, πολέμου ἀκορέστω*; H 175, *Αἴαντε* = Aias and Teukros.

Αἰγαί, lit. "wave city," in *Αἰγιάλεια*, *Ἀχαϊκαί*; a town in Achaia, seat of worship, Θ 203, and favorite haunt, of Poseidon, N 21, ε 381.

Αἰγαίων', acc. lit. "wave-demon," popul. epith. of sea-giant *Βριάρεως* (the "mighty," the "crusher"), only A 404.

αἰγανέης, gen. *έῃσιν*, *έας*, (*αἴξ*), venabulum, *hunting-spear*, ι 156, also thrown for amusement. [– ⏑ ⏑ –]

Αἰγείδην, *Θησέα τ'*, in interpolated verse, A 265, *Aigeus's son.*

αἴγειος, 3, (*αἴξ*), caprinus, *of or belonging to a goat.*—(1) *τυρός*, cheese of goat's milk, Λ 639.—(2) ἀσκός, goatskin bottle, see ἀσκός; κυνέη, goatskin cap, ω 231.

αἴγειρος, ἡ, populus nigra, *black poplar;* as tree in lower world, κ 510.

αἴγεον (= αἴγειον) ἀσκόν, *goatskin bottle*, ι 196†.

Αἰγιάλεια, daughter of Adrestos, wife of Diomedes, Ε 412†. [–⏑⏑–⏑]

αἰγιαλός, ῷ, όν, litus, *shore, beach*, μεγάλῳ, πολυηχέι, κοῖλον. [–⏑⏑⏑–]

Αἰγιαλός (ora maritima, coast-line), (1) division in N. Peloponnesos, afterward Achaia, Β 575†.—(2) town in Paphlagonia, Β 855†.

αἰγίβοτος (βόσκω), capras alens, *abounding in goats*, δ 606; *goat pasture*, ν 246. [–⏑⏑⏑–]

αἰγίλιπος, κατ' — πέτρης, Ι 15, Π 4, of doubtful deriv. and signif.; the second part is perhaps from λίπτομαι, *loved and haunted by goats* alone, for men too steep. [–⏑⏑⏑–]

Αἰγίλιπα τρηχεῖαν, name of village in, or island near, Ithaka, Β 633†.

Αἴγιναν, acc., island in Saronic gulf, opposite Peiraieus, still bearing its ancient name, Β 562†. [–––]

Αἴγιον (cf. Αἰγιαλός), afterward chief city of the Achaian league, Β 574†. [–⏑–]

αἰγί-οχος (αἰγίς), *Aigis-holding*, epith. only of Zeus, though it might also be with propriety applied to Athene and Apollon, ω 164. [–⏑⏑⏑–]

αἰγίς, ίδος, ἡ, (strictly *storm-cloud*, cf. ἐπαιγίζω), *Aigis*, represented as *a ponderous shield* with a hundred golden tassels, Β 448; hence ἐρίτιμος; the handiwork of Hephaistos, Ο 309; the means in Zeus's hands, Ρ 593, Δ 166; or at his command, in the hands of Apollon, of exciting tempests and of spreading dismay among men, Ο 229; described, Ε 738, Β 448; serves esp. in battle, seconded by ἔρις, ἀλκή, ἰωκή, as means of spreading terror and flight; above all when borne by Athene, Β 448, χ 297; in Ε 738 and Σ 204, it would at first sight appear as if the later conception, which regards the Aigis as the movable breast armor of the goddess, and with which she is uniformly represented in sculpture (cf. cut No. 17), might be traced, but ἀμφιβάλετο refers as often rather to the τελαμών by which the shield was suspended over the shoulder; cf. also θυσανόεσσαν.

Αἴγισθος, son of Thyestes, seducer of Klytaimnestra; despite the warning of Zeus, α 35, he murdered her returning husband, ὥς τίς τε κατέκτανε βοῦν ἐπὶ φάτνῃ, γ 196, λ 409, δ 512 sqq.; wherefore eight years later Orestes slew him and his own mother Klytaimnestra, λ 410, α 30, γ 196.

αἴγλη, ἡ, (cogn. with γαλήνη), splendor, *radiance;* λευκή, *gleaming brightness* of sky, of daylight, ζ 45; also of sun and moon; of weapons, Β 458, Τ 362, οὐρανὸν ἷκε.

αἰγλήεντος (αἴγλη), ἀπ'—Ὀλύμπου, de splendido Olympo, from *resplendent* Olympos, Α 532.

αἰ-γυπιός, ὁ, (ἀίσσω, γύψ), *vulture, lammergeyer*, Π 428, χ 302, ἀγκυλοχεῖλαι, γαμψώνυχες; with ὄρνις, Η 59. [–⏑⏑–]

Αἰγύπτιος (when ultima is long, Αἰγυπτίης to be read with synizesis), Aegyptius.—(1) an *Egyptian*, δ 83. —(2) *Egyptian*, ξ 263, ρ 432.

Αἰγύπτιος, name of an aged Ithakan, β 15.

Αἴγυπτος, ἡ, Aegyptus.—(1) river Nile, ἐυρρείτην, ξ 257.—(2) Aegypt, the land of (magic) herbs, δ 355; Αἴγυπτόνδε, in Aegyptum.

αἰδεῖο = αἰδέεο, imp. from αἰδέομαι, verere, *respect, reverence*, ι 269.

αἰδέομαι (αἰδώς), pr. imp. αἴδεο, ipf. αἴδετο, fut. αἰδέσ(σ)ομαι, aor. mid. ᾐδεσάμην and αἰδεσσάμην, pass. ᾐδέσθην, αἰδέσθην, 3 pl. αἴδεσθεν, vereri, *feel shame*.—(1) τινά, *reverence* or *stand in awe of*, Α 23, Ζ 442, Χ 124, γ 96, φ 28, Ι 640; also joined with δείδια; was ashamed of his tears in the presence of the Phaiakians, θ 86.—(2) with inf., vereri, *shrink from*, by reason of religious or other scruples, ξ 146, π 75, υ 343, χ 312, Χ 82, out of regard to propriety, ζ 221, σ 184, where εἰσιέναι is to be supplied.

ἀΐδηλος, ον, (of doubtful derivation; ἀι-, δαίω, cf. δαΐς, δαυλός, or δήϊος, δηλεῖσθαι).—(1) perniciosus, *destroying*, πῦρ.—(2) protervus, *violent, insolent*, of Ares, Ε 897, θ 309; Athene, Ε 880; suitors, π 29, ψ 303; Melanthios, χ 165. **ἀιδήλως**, *with reckless violence*, Φ 220. [⏑ ⏑ – –]

'Αΐδης, 'Αιδωνεύς, gen. 'Αΐδαο [⏑ ⏑ – –], 'Αΐδεω [⏑ ⏑ – –], and "Αιδος [⏓ ⏑ ⏑], dat. 'Αϊδι [⏑ ⏑ ⏓], 'Αιδωνῆι, acc. 'Αΐδην, *Aides*, *Hades*, god of lower world, ἐνέροισιν ἀνάσσων, ἄναξ ἐνέρων, Ζεὺς καταχθόνιος, Ι 457, cf. Ο 188, πελώριος, κλυτόπωλος, ἴφθιμος, κρατερός, πυλάρτης, also στυγερός: freq. "Αιδος δόμον εἴσω, or εἰς δόμον, ἐν δόμοις, etc.; often also only "Αιδόσδε (sc. δόμονδε), or simply prep. ἐν, εἰς, followed by gen. "Αιδος, without proper case of δόμος.

αἰδοίων τε μεσηγὺ καὶ ὀμφαλοῦ, between *privy parts* and navel, Ν 568†.

αἰδοῖος, 3, (αἰδώς).—(1) verecundus, ἀλήτης, *shamefaced, bashful*, ρ 578. —(2) venerandus, *revered, venerated, august*, applied to all persons connected with one by ties of relationship or obligation: of the ταμίη, α 139; of kings, gods; of friends, guests, suppliants; often joined with φίλος or δεινός; ο 373, αἰδοιοῖσιν ἔδωκα = have given to the *needy*; in λ 360, αἰδοιότερος καὶ φίλτερος, more *respected* and beloved. **αἰδοίως** τ' ἀπέπεμπον, τ 243, *with due regard to the claims of a guest, with fit escort.*

αἴδομαι, see αἰδέομαι.

"Αιδος, "Αιδόσδε, see 'Αΐδης.

ἀιδρείη, ησι, (ἄιδρις), inscitia, *folly*, Η 198, μ 41; ἀιδρείῃσι νόοιο, κ 231, 257, λ 272. [⏑ – – – –]

ἄιδρις, ι, (ἄϝιδρις, from ϝίδμεναι), ignarus, *unacquainted with*, χώρου; *stupid*, Γ 219. [⏑ – ⏑]

αἰδώς, οῦς, ἡ, pudor.—(1) subj. *sense of shame*; υ 171, οὐδ' αἰδοῦς μοῖραν ἔχουσιν, not a spark of shame; *scruple*, ἐν φρεσὶ θέσθε αἰδῶ καὶ νέμεσιν, Ν 122, cf. Ο 561, with δέος, Ο 657; reverentia, *regard*, with φιλότης, Ω 111, ξ 505; with τιμή, θ 480; *diffidence*, γ 14.—(2) obj. *disgrace, dishonor*, used elliptically sc. ἔστω, Π 22, or ἐστίν, γ 24; with acc. and inf., Ε 787; *privy parts* = αἰδοῖον, Χ 75; Β 262, hide thy nakedness.

αἰεί, αἰέν, see ἀεί.

αἰει-γενετάων, θεῶν, and θεοῖς αἰειγενέτῃσιν (regular formula for closing the verse), *born to unending life, eternal, immortal*, ω 373.

αἰει-νάοντα, see ἀενάοντα, *ever flowing, never failing.*

αἰετός (cogn. with οἰωνός, avis), aquila, *eagle*, τελειότατος πετεηνῶν, favorite of Zeus, Jovis ales, Ω 311; bird of omen; μορφνὸς θηρητήρ, dusky bird of prey; high-soaring, Μ 201, Χ 308; hook-beaked, τ 538. [– ⏑ ⏑]

ἀίζηλον (ἀι, ζῆλος = δῆλος), τὸν μὲν ἀίζηλον θῆκεν θεός, Β 318, cum deus perillustre fecit exemplar, the god made it a *conspicuous* omen.

αἰζήιος ἀνήρ (= αἰζηός), vegetus homo, *vigorous* man, only Ρ 520, μ 83.

αἰζηός (ἀι, cf. ἥβη?), vegetus, robustus, *vigorous, robust*, with ἀνήρ, and as subst. with θαλεροί, ἀρηίθοοι, κρατερός; used as equivalent to man, μ 440.

Αἰήτης, son of "Ηλιος and Πέρση, brother of Κίρκη; robbed by Jason of the golden fleece, μ 70; ὀλοόφρων, κ 137. [– – –]

αἴητον, πέλωρ, Σ 410, epith. of "Ηφαιστος, of doubtful origin and meaning, perhaps best explained as from ἄημι, with intensive prefix ἀι, *breathing strongly, hard-puffing.* [– – ⏑]

αἰθαλόεις, εσσα, εν, (αἴθω), fumosus, fuliginosus, *smoky, black with smoke or soot*, μέλαθρον, μέγαρον, Β 414, χ 239; κόνις, of ashes that have burnt out and lost their glow, pulvis niger.

αἴθε, utinam, see αἰ, I. 2.

Αἴθη, name of mare, lit. *fiery, Sorrel*, Ψ 295.

αἰθήρ, έρος, ἡ, (αἴθω), aether, *space filled by light of day* (αἴθρη), situated under the heaven, οὐρανός, to which it is considered to belong, and separated by the clouds from the ἀήρ, which belongs to the earth; αἰθέρι ναίων, as dat. of place (locative), dwelling in aether. In Ο 20, Here hangs from a cord made fast in οὐρανός, and swings ἐν αἰθέρι καὶ νεφέλῃσιν; Π 365, as when a cloud rises from Olympos, out of the gleaming *light of day*, and mounts into heaven, i. e. the cloud seems to be generated out of the transparent aether, and then rising perpendicularly, subsequently spreads over the sky. See "Ολυμπος.

Αἰθίκεσσι, dat. pl., to the *Aithikes*, a tribe west of Mount Pindos, Β 744†. [– – ⏑ ⏑]

Αἰθίοπες, ων, εσσιν, ας and ῆας,

τηλόθ' ἐόντας and ἐσχάτους ἀνδρῶν, ἀμύμονας, *Aethiopians*, "burnt faces," dwelling on Okeanos' stream, in two divisions, east and west, a pious folk whom the gods loved and often visited. It is nowise unreasonable to suppose that some tidings of the existence of a black race may have found its way to the Greeks of the Homeric age.

αἰθόμενος (αἴθω), flagrans, ardens, *burning*, πῦρ, etc., ἄστυ, Φ 523.

αἴθουσα, ης, porticus, *hall, porch;* epithets; polished (smoothly planked), resounding. We distinguish two αἴθουσαι, see Table II. at end of volume. —(1) on either side of vestibule, after passing the entrance door; αἴθ. αὐλῆς, φ 390, ν 176, χ 449.—(2) after traversing the αὐλή, just before entering into the banqueting-hall, μέγαρον; this latter, αἴθουσα δώματος, served as sleeping-room for guests, γ 399, δ 297, and was roofed.

αἴθοπα, ι, (αἴθω), acc. and dat. fulgidus, coruscus, radians, *sparkling*, χαλκός, οἶνος; *red*, of smoke mixed with flame, κ 152. [– ◡ ◡]

αἴθρη, ην, (αἴθω), aether, *light of day, clear sky*, ἀνέφελος, ζ 44, P 646, μ 75. [– –]

Αἴθρη, mother of Theseus, follows Helene as captive to Troja, Γ 144.

αἰθρη-γενέτης, Βορέης, *sprung from aether*, ε 296†.

αἰθρη-γενέος, ὑπὸ ῥιπῆς — Βορέαο, under the blast of *aether-born* Boreas, O 171.

αἴθρῳ δεδμημένος, frigore confectus, overcome *by cold*, ξ 318†.

αἰθυίῃ, fem., *water-hen*, ε 337 and 353.

αἴθων, ωνος, fulgens, fulvus, *shining, tawny;* of horses, see Αἴθων; also of cattle, eagle, lion, and metal implements, σ 372, B 839.

Αἴθων, ωνος, name (1) assumed by Odysseus, τ 183.—(2) of horse, Θ 185, which we should best describe as *Sorrel*.

αἴκ', see αἴ(κε).

ἀικάς, τὰς, (ἀίσσω), τόξων, telorum impetus, *storm* or *hail* of arrows, O 709†. [– – –]

ἀικῶς (ἀ̓ϝικῶς. ϝέϝοικε) = ἀεικῶς, turpiter, *ignominiously*, X 336†. [◡ – –]

αἷμα, ατος, τό, sanguis, *blood*, (1) in the veins, Ψ 717, also of gods, E 339, 870.—(2) cruor, *carnage*, K 298; in sausage, σ 119.—(3) of descent, *blood relationship, kin*, joined with γενεή.

αἱμασιάς λέγειν, septa colligere, plant out a *thorn-hedge*. [– ◡ ◡ –]

αἱματόεις, εσσα, εν, *bloody*.—(1) sanguineus, σμῶδιξ *bloody* wales, ψιάδες drops *of blood*.—(2) cruentatus, *blood-besprinkled*.—(3) sanguinarius, *murderous*, ἤματα. [– ◡ ◡ –]

Αἱμονίδης, Λαέρκης, P 467†.

Αἱμονίδης, Μαίων, from Thebes, Δ 394†.

αἱμο-φόρυκτα (φορύσσω), δὲ δὴ κρέα ἤσθιον, and were eating pieces of flesh *all bloody* (crudas), υ 348†.

αἵμονα, θήρης (cogn. with amans?), *skilled in* the chase, E 49†.

αἱμυλίοισι λόγοισι θέλγει, *persuasive, persistent*, α 56†.

Αἵμων, ονος, κρείων; ἕταρος Νέστορος, Δ 296†.

αἰν-αρέτη (αἰνός), voc. *terribly-brave* (contains at once recognition of bravery and censure for the faults which attend it), Π 31†.

Αἰνείας, gen. Αἰνείαο, Αἰνείω, ἐὺς πάις Ἀγχίσαο and of Aphrodite; ascending pedigree as follows: Anchises, Kapys, Assarakos, Tros, Erichthonios, Dardanos, Zeus; represented as in feud with Priamos the great-grandson of Tros, N 460, Υ 180, 307; favorite of the gods, E 344, Υ 291.

αἰνέω (αἶνος), prs., -ήσω, -ησα, comprobare, *approve, praise;* opp. νείκει, K 249; esp. of oracle, αἰνεῖ, π 403.

αἰνίζομ(αι), with περί and ἔξοχα Βροτῶν ἁπάντων, prae omnibus te mortalibus praedīco, *praise* thee above all other mortals, N 374 and θ 487.

Αἴνιον, a Paionian, slain by Achilleus, Φ 210†.

αἰνόθεν αἰνῶς = αἰνοῦ αἰνότερον, non ferendum in modum, *horribly*, H 97†.

Αἰνόθεν, *from Ainos* (in Thrake), Δ 520†.

αἰνό-μορος (μόρος), infortunatus, *child of misfortune*.

αἰνο-παθέα (πάθος), acc. with μάλα, me perquam infortunatam, ah me, *poor sufferer!* σ 201†.

αἶνος, laudatio, laus, *praise*, Ψ 795.

αἰνός, *ή, όν*, terribilis, formidolosus, *frightful, dreadful, horrible*, in different grades of intensity; *αἰνότατε Κρονίδη*, dread son of Kronos; as we sometimes use *dreadfully* = *extremely, exceedingly, very; αἰνότατον περιδείδια*, N 52, *α* 208; freq. *αἰνὸν ἄχος*, *dire* woe; often with *δηϊοτῆτι, φύλοπις, κάματος, κότος*, etc.; **αἰνά,** adverbial, *τεκοῦσα* = wretched mother that I am, A 414; with *ὀλοφύρομαι παθοῦσα*, having encountered such sorrow, X 431; **αἰνῶς,** adv. esp. with *δείδια, ἐοικέναι*; intensively with *κακά*, *ρ* 24, cf. *τ* 324.

αἴνυμαι, **αἴνυται,** *αἴνυτο*, and part. prs. comprehendere, *take*, Λ 374, 580, N 550, O 459, Φ 490, *ι* 225, 232, 429, *φ* 53; *seize*, *ξ* 144, *χ* 500.

αἴξ, **αἰγός,** *ή, ὁ*, dat. pl. *αἴγεσιν*, capra, caper, *goat*.

ἀίξασκον, iter. aor., from *ἀίσσω*.

Αἰολίδης, *son of Aiolos*, see *Κρηθεύς, Σίσυφος*.

Αἰολίην, *νῆσον*, island *of Aiolos*, with surrounding wall of bronze, *κ* 1 sqq.; identified by the ancients with Strongyle or Lipara.

αἰόλλῃ (*ἀι-, Ϝολ-*, volvo), *ὅτε γαστέρα ἔνθα καὶ ἔνθα*—, as when one *turns this way and that* a paunch full of fat and blood, *υ* 27†.

αἰολο-θώρηξ, splendida lorica armatus, *with glancing mail*, Γ 83.

αἰολο-μίτρης (*μίτρη*), *with glancing* (because plated with metal) *girdle*, E 707†.

αἰολό-πωλος, *with glancing* (with metal trappings) *steeds*, Γ 185†.

αἰόλος, *ον, οι*, (*ἀι-Ϝολ-*, volvo), micans.—(1) of movement; *quick-moving, swift-footed*, T 404; *wriggling*, X 509; *buzzing*, *χ* 300; *μέσον αἰόλοι*, of wasps, pliant in the middle, because their body in the middle is so slender. —(2) of the impression which rays of light falling upon smooth, moving surfaces make; *shimmering, glancing, gleaming;* of weapons, of snakes, M 208.

Αἴολος, (1) *Ἱπποτάδης*, son of Hippotes, lord of winds, *κ* 2 (36, 60, ‒ ‒ ‒, for *Αἰόλοο*).—(2) father of Sisyphos, Z 154.

Αἴπειαν, *καλήν*, town on Messenian gulf, I 152, 294.

αἰπεινός (*αἰπύς*), arduus, *precipitous, steep*, of localities; cf. *ζ* 123.

αἰπήεσσαν, montuosam, *high-lying, mountainous*, Φ 87†.

αἰπήν and *ά*, (*αἰπύς*), only with *πόλιν*, and in Il. with *ῥέεθρα*, *high-lying, plunging sheer down.*

αἰπόλιον, properly, *belonging to the αἰπόλος*; caprarum grex, *herd of goats; αἰπόλια πλατέ' αἰγῶν*, wide-grazing (dispersed widely) herds of goats, *ξ* 101.

αἰ-πόλος (for *αἰγπ.*, *πέλομαι*, versari), *goatherd*, also with *ἀνήρ* and with *αἰγῶν*.

Αἰπύ, town subject to Nestor, B 592†.

αἰπύς, *εῖα, ύ*, praeceps, arduus, *precipitous, sheer.*—(1) of localities: Olympos, mountains, towns, islands, *lofty;* of noose, *hung high aloft*, λ 278. —(2) *bursting headlong in, sudden, utter*, *ὄλεθρος, φόνος, χόλος*.—(3) arduus, *hard*, *πόνος*, toil of combat; N 317, he shall find it hard.

Αἰπύτιον *παρὰ τύμβον*, at funeral mound *of Aipytos* (progenitor of royal line) in Arkadia, B 604†.

αἱρεῖ, *είτω, -ήσω*, aor. *εἷλον, ἕλον* (*Ϝέλον*), iter. *ἕλεσκον*; mid. *αἱρεύμενοι, αἱρήσομαι, εἱλόμην, ἑλόμην*, prehendere, *take.*—I. act. (1) *seize, lay hold of*, *χεῖρά τινος*, *σ* 258, Ω 361; *τινὰ χειρός*, by the hand; by the hair, Φ 242; also with acc., Θ 319, K 335, M 397, Σ 416, Φ 242; *δουρός*, grasp the spear, Π 406; *ὀδὰξ οὖδας*, mordicus humum (of mortally wounded); *ἐπὶ μάστακά τινα χερσί*, lay one's hands upon some one's mouth, hold the mouth shut with the hands; *τινὰ προτὶ οἷ* = (*ἀγκὰς*) *ἑλεῖν*, *embrace*, *η* 252, λ 210; *overtake* in running, *θ* 330; *win* prizes, Ψ 779, *κῦδος*; *χροῒ εἵματα*, *put on* garments (also *ἑλέσθαι*, *ψ* 132).—(2) metaphorically, *take possession of*, *ἄλγος, ἄτη*, Π 805; so of various emotions, joy, grief, courage, astonishment, longing, fear; *ἔνθεν ἑλών*, *taking up the story* where, *θ* 500.—(3) tollere, *take away from*, Ω 579; *rob*, A 356; *capture*, B 37, N 42; *take captive*, Φ 102; *slay*, Π 306, Δ 457, and freq.—II. mid. (1), *take one's own*, or *for one's self;* also with *ἀπό*, E 210; *τεύχεα ἀπ' ὤμων*, *lay off*, H 122; cf. O 125, Z 472, also spoliare, *strip off*, P 206.—(2) *take to one's self*, as food, *δόρπον, δεῖπνον, πιέειν*, *take with one*, φ 40, K 501; *receive*, ξ 297, ο 367, Σ 500; *enjoy*, H 482; *attain, reach a decision*, Σ 501; *take an oath of*, ὅρκον τινί and τινός.—(3) *choose, select*, K 235, B 127, ε 121.—(4) *rob*, μ 246, Σ 445.

῎Α-ιρος, *No Iros, unhappy Iros*, σ 73†.

αἴρω, see ἀείρω.

῎Αις, see Ἀίδης.

αἶσα, ἡ, (ἴσος), portio, *allotted share*.—(1) pars, *part*, τ 84, Σ 327; τίω δέ μιν ἐν καρὸς αἴσῃ (cf. Attic phrase, ἐν οὐδενὸς μέρει τίθεσθαι).—(2) *propriety*, κατ' αἶσαν, suitably; opp. ὑπὲρ αἶσαν, Z 333.—(3) *length of life*, vitae portio, A 416.—(4) *destiny*, sors; ἰῇ αἴσῃ, to one destiny; κακῇ α., to misfortune; θανάτοιο α., to death; αἰσά μοι ἐστι, I am destined, ε 206, ψ 315.—(5) *destiny*, as controlling power, Υ 127, η 197; ὑπὲρ αἶσαν, Z 487, contrary to fate's decree; Διός, δαίμονος α., decree pronounced by Zeus, by divinity; ὑπὲρ Διὸς αἶσαν, in disregard of Zeus's fateful decree, P 321; κακὴ Διὸς α. παρέστη ἡμῖν, the ill destiny sent by Zeus reached us; πεπρωμένος αἴσῃ, handed over to fate.

Αἴσηπον, acc., son of Abarbaree and Bukolion, Z 21†.

Αἴσηπος, river on Mount Ida.

ἄισθε, ἀίσθων, ipf. and part. (ἄϝω), always with θυμόν, animam efflans, exspirans, *breathing out* one's life, Π 468. [⏑ – –]

αἴσιμον, η, α, (αἶσα).—(1) fatalis, *decreed by fate*.—(2) decorus, *becoming*, idoneus, *suitable;* aequus, *just;* αἴσιμα εἰδέναι, think justly, be right-minded.

αἴσιος (αἶσα), *auspicious*, propitius, *opportune*, Ω 376†.

ἀίσσουσι, -ων, aor. ἦιξα, (ἀίξω, ἀῖξαι, ἀίξας), ἀίξασκον; mid. ἀίξασθαι; aor. ἠίχθην, (ἀιχθήτην), impetu ferri, *move with eager haste*.—I. act. (1) *hasten*, Ω 711, ο 183, ω 488; ἦιξε πέτεσθαι, flew rapidly; ἀίξας, in haste; πρόσσω, φόβονδε, ἀπό τινος, *fly*, of birds; of arrows (*speed*); of chariot (*sped over the ground*), Ψ 369; of thoughts (*rove*, O 80); τοὶ δὲ σκιαὶ ἀίσσουσι, but they *flit about* like shadows, trepidant, κ 495.—(2) *charge, come rushing on*, ἀντίοι, δοχμώ, λικριφίς, esp. in hostile signif., φασγάνῳ, ἔγχεϊ, *charge upon* (*strike, thrust*, etc.); Σ 506, with these they rose quickly up, —II. dep. = act. signif., X 195, Ψ 773, Z 510; Π 404, the reins *slipped from* his hands.

ἄ-ιστος (ϝίδμεναι, ἰδεῖν), ignotus, *of which nothing is known or seen; disappeared without leaving a trace, vanished, lost;* Ξ 258, and he would have cast me out of the upper air, and submerged me *out of sight* in the sea. [⏑ – –]

ἀιστώσειαν, from ἀιστόω, (ἄιστος), *cause to disappear*, υ 79, *annihilate;* ἀιστώθησαν, *vanished*, κ 259.

αἰσυητῆρι, v. l. for αἰσυμνητῆρι, Ω 347†, *princely*.

Αἰσυήταο, (1) γέροντος τύμβος, Trojan, father of Antenor, B 793†.—(2) διοτρεφέος υἱόν, Alkathoos, N 427†.

αἰσυλό-εργος (ϝέργον), v. l. for αἴσυλα ῥέζων, or ὀβριμόεργος, E 403†, nefarius, *high-handed, wicked*.

ἀίσυλα (ἄ-ισος), only with ῥέζειν and μυθήσασθαι; nefaria, turpia, do or speak *evil*. [– ⏑ ⏑]

Αἰσύμηθεν, Θ 304†, *from Aisyme*, in Thrake. [– – – ⏑]

αἰσυμνητῆρι κούρῳ, *princely* youth, Ω 347†.

αἰσυ-μνήτης, msc. (αἶσα, μνῆμα), cf. ἱερομνήμων), *umpire, unprejudiced referee*, θ 258†.

Αἴσυμνον, acc., Grecian chief, slain by Hektor, Λ 303†.

αἶσχος, ntr. (αἰδέομαι), ignominia, dedecus, *disgrace*, λ 433, σ 225; pl. *spoken insults*, Z 351, 524, if I must listen to *words of contumely* for thy sake; α 229, *outrageous acts*.

αἰσχρός, turpis, *disgraceful*, (1) B 216, *ugly*.—(2) *injurious, insulting*, ἔπεα; adv., αἰσχρῶς ἐνένιπεν, *ignominiously* reproved.

αἰσχύνω (αἶσχος), aor. ᾔσχυνε, foedare.—(1) *disfigure*, Σ 24, 180, Ω 418. —(2) *insult*, Z 209, β 86; Ψ 571, *tarnish* my fame.—(3) mid. verecundari, *have scruple, hesitation*.

Αἴσονα, acc., *Aison*, son of Kreteus and Tyro, father of Jason, king in Iaolkos, λ 259.

αἴτει, imp. prs., fut. -ήσω, rogare; *ask*, τινά τι, some one for something; *beg, sue for*, Ω 292, τινί τι; seek as wife, N 365.

αἰτιάασθαι, see *αἰτιάομαι*.

αἰτιάασθαι (*αἰτία*), only pres. and ipf., usually resolved, incusare, *accuse of*; α 32, what charges the mortals bring against the gods!

αἰτίζειν (*αἰτέω*), only pres., only Od., rogare.—(1) *ask*, δ 650.—(2) *beg, importune*.

αἴτιος, οι, (*αἰτία*), culpandus, reus, *guilty of* something (in bad sense), Τ 86, 'tis no fault of mine; *σοὶ δ' οὔτι μνηστῆρες αἴτιοι εἰσίν*, the suitors are nowise responsible for that, β 87.

αἰτιόωνται, 3 pl. pres., *αἰτιόῳο*, *-ῳτο*, 2 and 3 sing. opt. from *αἰτιάομαι*.

Αἰτώλιος, *Aitolian*.

Αἰτωλός, Ψ 471, ξ 379; *-οί*, *the Aitolians* in Hellas, Ι 531, 549, 597.

αἰχμάσσουσι, fut. from *αἰχμάζω*, *αἰχμάς*, youths *should hurl the spears*, Δ 324†.

αἰχμή, ή, (*ἀκίς*, acutus), cuspis, *point*, *ἔγχεος*, *δουρός*; then *the whole spear*, Ο 542.

αἰχμητά and **αἰχμητής**, ὁ, *spearman, warrior*, Γ 179; also adj., *fighting with spear, warlike*, Β 543.

αἶψα (=*αἰπέσα*, from *αἰπύς*), extemplo, *forthwith; αἶψα δ' ἔπειτα*, immediately after; *μάλ' αἶψα, αἶψα μάλα*, very quickly; *αἶψα καὶ ὀτραλέως*, at once and quickly.

αἰψηρός, ή, (*αἶψα*), citus, Τ 276, he dissolved the *quickly dispersing* (prolepsis) assembly, β 257, δ 103, *soon comes* a surfeit of the chilling lament for the dead.

ἄιον (*ἄηναι*), *ἐπεὶ φίλον*— *ἦτορ*, when I *was breathing out* my life, Ο 252†.

ἀΐων (*ἀϝίω*), only pres. and ipf. *ἄιον*, sentio, *perceive*.—(1) by senses, *πληγῆς*.—(2) by mind, σ 11.—(3) *learn of*, by hearsay: *οὐκ ἀΐεις*, knowest thou not? by sense of hearing, *κτύπον*, *ὄπα*, voice, usually with gen. *φθογγῆς*, exc. ω 48; *regard*, Ο 378, Ψ 199.

αἰών, *ῶνος*, ὁ, (ή, Χ 58), (*αἰϝών*, aevum), *lifetime*, Δ 478, Ι 415; *life*, anima, Τ 27, Χ 58; with *ψυχή*, Π 453, ι 523.

ἀ-κάκητα, masc. (*ἀ* priv., *κακός*), *deliverer*, applied to Hermes, ω 10.

ἀκαλα-ρρείταο (*ἧκα*, *ῥέω*), *ἐξ* — *βαθυρρόου Ὠκεανοῖο*, from the *smoothly flowing*, deep-streaming Okeanos, Η 422, τ 434.

ἀ-κάμαντι, α, (*κάμνω*), indefessus, *untiring*, Π 823.

Ἀκάμας, *αντος*, (1) son of Antenor and Theano, leader of Dardanians, Ξ 478.—(2) son of Eussoros, leader of Thrakians, Ζ 8.

ἀ-κάματον (*κάματος*), indefessus, *πῦρ*, *untiring, smouldering* fire. [⏑ ⏑ ⏑ ⏑]

ἀκάνθας (*ἀκή*), acc. pl. from *ἄκανθα*, carduos, *thistles*, ε 328†. [⏑ – –]

Ἄκαστος, king of Dulichion, ξ 336†.

ἀκαχείατο, 3 pl. plupf., **ἀκαχεῖν**; **ἀκαχήσω, ἀκαχημένος**, see **ἀκαχίζω**.

ἀκ-αχίζω, aor. *ἤκαχε*, *ἀκαχεῖν*, and *ἀκάχησε*; mid. *ἀκαχίζομαι*, pf. *ἀκάχημαι*, 3 pl. *ἀκηχέδαται*, part. also *ἀκηχεμένη*, *αι*, inf. *ἀκαχῆσθαι*, plupf. 3 pl. *ἀκαχείατο*, aor. *ἀκάχοντο*, *-οιτο* (*ἄχος*); *distress, afflict*, π 432, Ψ 223; mid. *distress one's self*, pf. *grieve*, *θυμῷ*, *-όν*, *ἦτορ*, in heart; because of something, *τινός τινί*; with part., λ 486; *πυκινῶς*, υ 84; *λίην*, Ζ 486; *μάλα*, Π 16 (cf. *ἄχνυμαι*).

ἀκαχμένος, 3, (*ἀκή*), acutus, *sharpened, pointed; ἔγχος ἀκ.* (*ὀξέι χαλκῷ*), lance *tipped* (with sharp bronze point); *πελεκὺς ἀμφοτέρωθεν ἀκ.*, double-edged axe, ε 235.

ἀκάχοιτο, see *ἄχνυμαι*.

ἀκέομαι, **ἀκειόμενον**, οι, aor. *ἠκεσάμην* (imp. *ἄκεσσαι*), sedare, *assuage*.—(1) *heal, repair*, ξ 383; *make good*, κ 69, Ν 115.—(2) *slake* thirst.

ἀ-κερσε-κόμης (*κείρω*), *with unshorn, flowing hair*, Phoibos, Υ 39†.

ἀκέσματα (*ἀκέομαι*), pl., *as means of alleviating pain*, Ο 394†.

Ἀκεσσαμενοῖο, gen., a king of Thrake, father of Periboia, Φ 142†.

ἀκεσταί (*ἀκέομαι*) *φρένες*, *tractable*, Ν 115†.

ἀκέων, *ουσα*, *ουσα*, (*ἀκαλός*), sedatus, tacitus, *silent*, Α 34; *ἀκέων* is generally used adverbially; a neuter form, *ἄκεων* (cf. *ἀκήν*), may have once existed, which was afterward confounded in common use with the part. *ἀκέων*.

ἀ-κήδεστοι, *unburied*, Ζ 60; *ἀκηδέστως*, *pitilessly*, Χ 465.

ἀ-κήδεις and **ἀκήδεσεν**, from *ἀκηδέω* (*κηδέω*), negligere, *disregard, slight*, esp. the dead, wounded; always with negative, Ψ 70.

ἀ-κηδής, ές, (κῆδος), incuriosus.—(1) act. *unfeeling*, Φ 123, ρ 319; *without sorrow*, Ω 526.—(2) pass. *neglected*, ζ 2(τ 18; *unburied*, ω 187, Ω 554.

ἀ-κήλητος (κηλέω), νόος, *inflexible* purpose, κ 329†.

ἀκήν, ancient acc., cf. ἄκεων, placide, tacite, *silent*, with ἴσαν, ἔσαν; also common phrase, ἀκὴν ἐγένοντο σιωπῇ, became hushed in silence, π 393. [⏑ –]

ἀ-κηράσιον (κήρ), intactum, *not meddled with, pure*, οἶνον, ι 205†. [⏑ – ⏑ ⏑ ⏑]

ἀ-κήρατος, ον, (κήρ), integer, *untouched, pure*, Ω 303.

1. **ἀ-κήριοι** (κήρ), incolumes, *uninjured*, ψ 328.

2. **ἀ-κήριον** and οι, (κῆρ).—(1) inanimus, *dead*.—(2) ignavus, *spiritless, cowardly*, δέος, Ε 812.

ἀκηχέδαται, ἀκηχέαται, ἀκηχεμένη, see ἀκαχίζω.

ἀκιδνότερος, 3, (κεδνός?), neglectus, miser, *more insignificant*, in figure; *more wretched*, σ 130.

ἄ-κικυς (κικύς), imbecillus, *feeble*; only in Od. [⏑ – ⏑]

ἀ-κίχητα (κιχάνω), διώκων, negata persequens, pursuing *the unattainable*, Ρ 75†. [⏑ ⏑ – ⏑]

ἄ-κλαυτος (κλαίω), illacrimabilis, (1) *unwept*.—(2) δ 494, *tearless*.

ἀ-κλεής (κλέος), acc. sing. ἀκλέα, better ἀκλεᾶ, pl. ἀκληεῖς, *inglorious*; adv. ἀκλειῶς.

ἀ-κλήρῳ (κλῆρος), sine patrimonio, *portionless, needy*, λ 490†.

ἀκμῆς (ἄκρος), ἐπὶ ξυροῦ ἵσταται, in discrimine res est, stands on the razor's *edge*, Κ 173†.

ἀκμηνός (ἀκμή), θάμνος ἐλαίης, *full-grown* olive-tree, ψ 191†.

ἄκμηνος (ἄκμη, ieiunia), famelicus, *unsatisfied, hungry*, with gen. (only Τ).

ἀ-κμῆτες, pl. (κάμνω), indefatigati, *fresh, unwearied* (only Il.).

ἀκμό-θετον (ἄκμων), *anvil-block*.

ἄκμονα, -ας, incudem, es, *anvil* (ἄκμων).

ἄκνηστιν, κατ', in spina dorsi, in the *backbone*, κ 161†.

ἀκοίτης, ὁ, **ἄκοιτις,** ἡ, coniux, *husband, wife*, ε 120, Ι 397, and freq.

ἀκόλους, frusta, *morsels*, ρ 222†. [⏑ ⏑ –]

ἀ-κομιστίη, *lack of care, neglect*, φ 284.

ἀκοντίζω (ἀκόντιον), aor. ἀκόντι(σ)σα, iaculari, *hurl javelin*, τινός, ἐπί τινι, εἴς τινα; αἰχμάς, δοῦρα, ἔγχεϊ, δουρί.

ἀκοντισταί, άς, iaculatores, *spearmen, lancers*, σ 262.

ἀκοντιστύν, acc. fem., *game of the dart, spear contest*, Ψ 622†. [ῠ]

ἀ-κόρητος (κορέννυμι), insatiabilis, *insatiate*, with gen., Υ 2.

ἄκος, τό, (ἀκέομαι), remedium, *cure, remedy*, χ 481.

ἄ-κοσμα (κόσμος), ἔπεα, indecentia, *unbecoming*, Β 213†.

ἀκοστήσας (ἀκοστή), ἐπὶ φάτνῃ, *having fed abundantly* (on barley) at the manger (Il.).

ἀκουάζεσθε, ονται, ωνται, (ἀκούω), ausculto, *listen, hearken*; τινός, Δ 343, ye are they who *are first invited* to the feast.

ἀκουή, ἡ, (ἀκούω), auditus.—(1) *sound*, Π 634, one hears it from far away.—(2) fama, *tidings, report* (hearsay).

ἄ-κουρον (κοῦρος), filio carentem, *without male heir*, η 64†.

ἀκούω, -σομαι, ἤκουσα, audio, *hear*, (1) Μ 442, Ο 129, β 423; *listen*, Τ 79, α 370, ἀοιδοῦ; *hear*, with acc., κ 221; ὄπα, φθόγγον, στόνον, ὑλαγμόν, or with gen. μυκηθμοῦ, μ 265, αὐτῆς (mid., Δ 331), φθογγῆς, κωκύτου οἰμωγῆς, στοναχῆς κτύπου (φ 291, μύθων καὶ ῥήσιος); τινός τι; or with gen. of participle στενάχοντος, θ 95, ι 497.—(2) comperire, *learn of by hearsay*, κλέος, Ω 543; with inf., Ζ 386; with gen. of partic. in Il., only Ω 490; λ 458, ρ 115, α 289; with gen. alone, δ 114; περί τινος; ὑπέρ σέθεν, Ζ 524; ex aliquo audire, τινός, μ 389, ἔκ τινός τι, ο 374.—(3) exaudire, *give ear to*, with gen. and dat., also with part.; audientem esse, *obey*, Τ 256, η 11, ὁμοκλητῆρος; pres. used with signif. of perf., δ 688.

ἀ-κράαντος (κραιαίνω), irritus, *unaccomplished, vain*. [– – – –]

ἀκραεῖ and αέα, (ἄκρος, ἄημι), impetuosus, *blowing strongly, fresh*, β 421. [– – ⏓ ⏓]

ἄκρη (ἄκρος), summa pars, *summit*, *promontory*; κατ' ἄκρης, a vertice, from the summit; then, from top to bottom, i. e. utterly, N 772.

ἄκρηθεν, in κατάκρηθεν, see κάρ.

ἄ-κρητος, 2, (κεράννυμι), merus, *unmixed*, *pure*, ω 73.

ἀκρίδες, αἱ, *locusts*, Φ 12†.

ἄκριας (ἄκρις, from ἄκρη), δι', amid the windy *mountain-tops*, ι 400. (Od.)

Ἀκρισιώνη, *daughter of Akrisios*, Δανάη, Ξ 319†.

ἀ-κρῐτό-μῦθος (ἄκριτα, μῦθος), *senseless babbler*, B 246; useless are the *confused* dreams, τ 560.

ἄ-κρῐτος, 2, (κρίνω).—(1) *undistinguished*, *common*, τύμβος.—(2) *endless*, *beyond measure*, also with πολλά; adverbially ἄκριτον, *unceasingly*.

ἀ-κρῐτό-φυλλον ὄρος, *thickly overgrown* (with foliage), B 868†.

ἀκρο-κελαινιόων, *growing black on surface*, *with troubled surface*, Φ 249†.

ἀκρό-κομοι (κόμη), with *hair* tied up on the *crown of head*, Δ 533†.

ἄκρον (ἄκρος), summum, *point*, *summit*, *promontory*.

Ἀκρόνεως, name of a Phaiakian, θ 111.

ἀκρό-πολις, citadel of Troja, only θ 494, 504.

ἀκρο-πόλοισιν (πέλομαι), ἐν—ὄρεσσιν, on *lofty* mountains, E 523.

ἀκρο-πόρους (πείρω), acumine transfigentes, ὀβελούς, *with penetrating points*, *sharp-pointed*, γ 463†.

ἄκρος, 3, (ἀκή, acies), extremus, summus, *at the point or end or top*, *outermost*, *topmost*, *highest*, *the extremity of*; tail, Ψ 519; hand, foot, Π 640, shoulder, rudder; πόλις ἄκρη, ἄκρη πόλις, upper city; *edge*, *surface*, etc.; κατ' ἄκρης, see ἄκρη; adverbially ἄκρον, Υ 229, *along the top*.

Ἀκταίη, a Nereid, Σ 41†.

1. **ἀκτή** (ἄγνυμι), mola, always with ἀλφίτου (or Δημήτερος), *barley meal*; in opposition to the whole kernels, οὐλαί, ξ 429.

2. **ἀκτή**, litus, *coast*, often προβλῆτες ἀκταί, tongues of land, promontories, κ 89.

ἀ-κτήμων (κτῆμα), carens, *not possessing*, with gen., I 126.

ἀκτίνεσσι, ἀκτῖσιν, fem., (ἀκτίς), Ἠελίοιο, radiis, *beams* of Helios.

Ἀκτορίδαο, gen., *descendant of Aktor*, Echekles, Π 189†.

Ἀκτορίς, attendant of Penelope, ψ 228†.

Ἀκτορίων, name for either of the *sons of Aktor*; the two were called Ἀκτορίωνε, and also Μολίονε, after their mother Molione, Λ 750.

Ἄκτωρ, (1) Ἀζείδης, son of Azeus, B 513.—(2) father of Μενοίτιος, Λ 785, Π 14.—(3) father of the Ἀκτορίωνε, son of Φόρβας, brother of Αὐγείας.—(4) father of Ἐχεκλῆς.

ἄκυλος, ἡ, *edible acorn*, κ 242†. [⏑ ⏑ ⏑]

ἀκωκή (ἀκή), cuspis, *point*, of missiles, χ 16.

ἄκων, οντος, ὁ, (ἀκή), iaculum, *dart*, K 335, Δ 137, ξ 531.

ἄκων = ἀέκων, invitus, *unwillingly*.

ἅλαδ(ε) (ἅλς), in mare versus, *seaward*, A 308, also with εἰς. [⏑ ⏑ ⏑]

ἀλάλημαι, see ἀλάομαι, vagari.

ἀλαλητός, ῷ, masc. (ἀλαλά), clamor, *shout*, *war-cry*; also *cry of fear*, and, ω 463, *of joy*. [⏑ ⏑ – ⏑]

ἄλαλκε, -εῖν, -ών, see ἀλέξω.

Ἀλαλκομενηΐς, epithet of Ἀθήνη, from the Boiotian city Ἀλαλκομεναί, near the lake Triton (see Τριτογένεια), Δ 8, E 908. [⏑ – ⏑ ⏑ – ⏑]

ἀλάομαι, **ἀλᾶσθε**, imp. ἀλόω, ipf. ἠλώμην, aor. ἀλήθην, pf. ἀλάλημαι, -ησθε, ἀλάλησθαι, ἀλαλήμενος, vagari, *wander*, *rove*, δ 368, ο 276, 492, γ 302, ε 377; ἀλώμενος, vagatus, errans.

ἀλαός, οῦ, caecus, *blind* [⏑ ⏑ ⏑; κ 493. μάντιος ἀλαοῦ, or v. l. μάντηος ἀλᾰοῦ].

ἀλαο-σκοπιήν (σκοπιή), οὐδ'—εἶχε, nor did he keep a *blind*, i. e. a *careless watch*. [⏑ ⏑ – ⏑ ⏑ ⏑ –]

ἀλάωσεν (ἀλαόω, from ἀλαός), ὀφθαλμοῦ, caecavit, *blinded*, (Od.). [⏑ ⏑ – ⏑]

ἀλαπαδνός, 3, infirmatus, *feeble*, σθένος, στίχες, etc.

ἀλαπάζω, ει, ipf. ἀλάπαζε, fut. -ξω, aor. ἀλάπαξα (ἀλαπαδνός), infirmare, esp. with πόλιν, *sack*; φάλαγγας, *rout*, also *slay*.

ἀλαστέω (ἄλαστος), only ipf. **ἠλάστεον**, aor. part. ἀλαστήσας, aegre fero, *be indignant*.

Ἀλαστορίδην, Tros. Υ 463.

ἄλαστος, *ον*, (*λαθέσθαι*), horrendus, *never to be forgotten, dreadful*, *ἄχος, πένθος, ἄλαστον ὀδύρομαι.*

Ἀλάστωρ, *ορος*.—(1) a Lykian, E 677.—(2) leader of the Pylians, Δ 295.—(3) father of Tros.

ἀλᾰωτύν, *τήν*, (*ἀλαός*), *ὀφθαλμοῦ*, excaecationem, *blinding*, ι 503†.

ἀλγέω, aor. subj. *ἀλγήσετε*, part. *ἀλγήσας*, (*ἄλγος*), dolere, *feel pain;* in Il. of bodily pain; Od., *μ* 27, in more general sense.

ἄλγιον (comp. from *ἄλγ-ος*), peius, *worse;* in exclamations: cf. French, tant pis, so much the worse; with dat. in threats, that shall be the worse for him; also *ἀλγίστη δαμάσασθαι*, difficillima domitu, *very hard* to tame, break.

ἄλγος, dolor, *pain, grief, distress*, only of mind, esp. *πάθεν ἄλγεα θυμῷ, κρατέρ' ἄλγεα πάσχων, ἄ. θεῖναι, δοῦναι, τεύχειν, κάλλιπ' ὀπίσσω*, etc.

ἀλδαίνω (*ἀλ-δ-*, alo), only aor. *μέλε' ἤλδανε ποιμένι λαῶν* (Od.), aluit, she *filled out* his limbs.

ἀλδήσκοντος (*ἀλ-*, alo), *λήϊου*, crescentis, *growing*, Ψ 599†.

ἀλέασθαι, see *ἀλέομαι*.

ἀλεγεινός, 3 (*ἄλγος*), dolore afficiens, *painful.*—(1) of bodily pain, *αἰχμή, ἐδύνη.*—(2) in wider signif., molestus, aerumnosus, *grievous, mournful, ἀγγελίη, Ἄρης, ἀγηνορίη.*—(3) difficilis, *hard, πυγμαχίη, μάχη, πνοιή, κύματα, hard to struggle with; ἵπποι ἀ. δαμήμεναι*, hard to break, cf. Ψ 655; hard to endure, *σ* 224. [⏑ ⏑ – ⏑]

Ἀλεγηνορίδαο, *Προμάχοιο*, *son of Alegenor*, Ξ 503†.

ἀλεγίζω (*ἄλγος*), always with *οὐ*, contemno, *not to concern one's self about*, *τινός*.

ἀλεγύνειν (*ἄλγος*), only with *δαῖτα, δαῖτας*, parare cenam, *give* (strictly, *prepare*), a banquet, *entertain* (Od.).

ἀλέγω (*ἄλγος*), *trouble one's self, heed;* I 504, who follow, *troubled*, behind Ate; usually with negation: contemno, *despise*, *τινός*; hence *οὐκ ἀλέγουσαι, shameless, insolent; ζ* 268 = *ἀλεγύνουσι*, they attend to the rigging.

ἀλεείνω (*ἀλέη*), only pr. and ipf., *avoid, shun, τινά, τι*; also with inf. [⏑ ⏑ – –]

1. **ἀλέη** (*ἀλέϝ-ομαι*), *escape*, X 301†.

2. **ἀλέη** (sol ?), *warmth of sun*, *ρ* 23†.

ἀλείατα (*ἄλειαρ, ἀλέω*), farina triticea, *wheaten flour*, *υ* 108†.

ἀλείς, *εἶσα, έν*, aor. pass. part., from *εἴλω*.

Ἀλείσιον, town in Elis, B 617, Λ 757.

ἄλεισον, *τό*, *drinking goblet*, usually costly, cf. *ο* 469; with handles, *χ* 9. [⏑ – ⏑]

ἀλείτης, *ου*, (*ἀλιταίνω*), sceleratus homo, *reckless offender*, Γ 28, *υ* 121. [⏑ – –]

ἄλειφαρ, *ατος*, (*ἀλείφω*), only gen. and dat., unguentum, *ointment; fat*, for anointing corpses; *γ* 408, shining with fat. [⏑ – ⏑]

ἀλείφω (*λίπα*), **ἤλειψαν,** *-άμην*, only aor., and usually with *λίπ' ἐλαίῳ*, ungere, *anoint;* oblinere, *smear* with wax, *μ* 200. [⏑ – ⏑]

Ἀλεκτρυόνος, *υἱός*, i. e. *Λήϊτος*, an Argonaut, P 602†.

ἄλεν, ἀλέν, see aor. from *εἴλω*.

ἀλεξάμενος, ἀλέξασθαι, aor. mid. from *ἀλέξω*.

Ἀλέξ-ανδρος, name given by Greeks to *Πάρις*; epithets, *δῖος . . . Ἑλένης πόσις ἠυκόμοιο, θεοειδής, βασιλεύς*, Δ 96; not characterized by Homer as so effeminate and feeble as in later representations (Γ 16, 39, 59), yet usually represented with the bow (Λ 369, 507, 581), and as betraying a sensual character; cf. also Γ 442, Z 290, Γ 39, Ω 28, 763, Δ 94.

ἀλεξ-άνεμον (*ἄνεμος*), *χλαῖναν*, ventum arcentem, *protecting against the wind*, *ξ* 529. [⏑ – ⏑ ⏑ ⏑]

ἀλεξητῆρα *μάχης*, defensor pugnae, *stemmer of battle*, one who bears the brunt in the fight, Υ 396†.

ἀλεξί-κακος (*κακόν*), mala arcens, *warding off ill or evil, protecting*, K 20†.

ἀλέξω (*ἀλκή*), inf. *ἀλεξέμεν(αι)*, fut. *ἀλεξήσω*, red. aor. *ἄλαλκε*, subj. *ἀλάλκῃσι*, inf. *ἀλαλκεῖν, -έμεναι, -έμεν*, aor. opt. *ἀλεξήσειε*, and subj. mid. *ἀλεξώμεσθα*, arceo, *ward off, τί, τινί*, dat. commodi, *τινί τι*; mid. *keep off from one's self* (*τινά*), se defendere (ab aliquo).

ἀλεώμεθα and **-εύεται,** *-όμενος*, aor. *ἠλεύατο, ἀλεύατο, -ντο*, opt. *ἀλέαιτο*, imp. *ἄλευαι, ἀλέασθε*, inf. *ἀλέασθαι*, part. ἀλευάμενος (subj. ἀλέϝηται, ἀλεϝώμεθα, aor. or pres.), evitare, *avoid, escape*, τί, esp. the weapons, the wrath of any one, esp. of the gods, Ε 444, Π 711, ι 277; hence, secondly, (vereri), *stand in dread of, be on one's guard before*, ι 274, with inf.

ἄλεται (aor. subj. from ἄλλομαι), insilierit.

ἀλετρεύουσι (ἀλετρίς), *grind*, η 104†.

ἀλετρίς (ἀλέω), γυνή, *female slave who grinds corn*, υ 105†.

ἀλεύεται = ἀλέϝεται, see ἀλεώμεθα.

ἀλέω, see καταλέω.

ἀλεωρή (ἀλεϝωρή, ἀλέομαι), munimentum, *defense*, τινός, against some one; but Ω 216, *flight*. [⏑ ⏑ – – –]

ἄλη, ἡ, (ἀλάομαι), oberrationes, roaming without knowledge whither, nor hope of rest, ceaseless *wandering* of Odysseus and his companions, ο 345. (Od.) [⏑ –]

ἀληθείη, ἡ, (ληθω), veritas, *truth*, ἀποείποι, παιδὸς (de filio) πᾶσαν μυθήσομαι, καταλέξω. [⏑ – – – –]

ἀληθείς (aor. part. from ἀλάομαι), vagatus.

ἀληθής, ές, (λήθω), verus, ἀληθὲς ἔνισπε, γ 247; elsewh. ἀληθέα μυθήσασθαι, εἶπε, πάντ' ἀγορεύσω, verum loqui, *speak the truth, tell truly;* only Μ 433 ἀληθής, proba, *honest*. [⏑ – –]

Ἀλήιον, πεδίον τὸ, *Aleïan* plain in Asia Minor (v. sq. = plain where no harvest grows—barren waste), Ζ 201†.

ἀ-λήιος (λήιον), sine arvis, *without corn land, poor*, cf. ἄκληρος. [⏑ – ⏑ ⏑]

ἄ-ληκτος (λήγω), *unceasing;* adverbially ἄλληκτον, *unceasingly*.

ἀλήμεναι, ἀλῆναι (inf. 2 aor. pass. from εἴλω), congregari.

ἀλήμονες (ἀλήμων, ἄλη), errabundi, *roving*, ρ 376.

ἄληται (aor. subj. from ἄλλομαι), saliat.

ἀλητεύειν (ἀλήτης), vagari, *roam about*, σ 114, (Od.)

ἀλήτης, ῃ, ην, masc. (ἀλάομαι) erro, *tramp, beggar*, ρ 576. (Od.)

Ἀλθαίη, wife of Οἰνεύς in Καλυδών, mother of Μελέαγρος, Ι 555†.

ἄλθετο (from ἄλθομαι), χείρ, *was healing*, Ε 417†.

ἀλι-αέες (ἅλς, ἄϝημι) οὖροι, venti maritimi, *blowing on the sea*, good sea-winds, δ 361†. [⏑ ⏑ – ⏑ ⏑]

Ἁλίαρτον, ποιήεντα, *Haliartos*, in Boiotia, with its rich meadows, Β 503†.

ἀ-λίαστος (λιάζομαι), obstinatus, *stubborn, unceasing* (only Il.). [⏑ ⏑ – –]

ἀλίγκιος, *like*, with which it seems to be etymologically connected.

ἁλιεύς, ῆος, (ἅλς), maritimus, π 349; elsewh. piscator, *fisher*. [⏑ ⏑ –]

Ἀλιζῶνες, tribe of Trojan allies from Pontos led by Ὀδίος.

Ἁλίη βοῶπις, a Nereid, Σ 40†. [⏑ ⏑ –]

Ἁλι-θέρσης, son of Mestor, friend of Odysseus, Ithakan, β 157, ρ 78. (Od.)

ἁλι-μυρήεντα, των, (μύρω), maris aestu oppletus, *reached by salt water, briny*, ε 460, Φ 190.

1. **ἅλιος**, ίοιο, 3, (ἅλς), maritimus, *belonging to the sea;* of old man of the sea, δ 365, etc.; ἅλιαι = Nereids, ω 47.

2. **ἅλιος** — (ἄημι? vâ-nus?), *fruitless;* of missiles, words, speeches, e. g. Ε 715, Ω 92. [⏑ ⏑ ⏑]

Ἅλιος, (1) a Lykian, Ε 678.—(2) son of Alkinoos, θ 119, 370. [⏑ ⏑ ⏑]

ἁλιο-τρεφέων (ἅλς), φωκάων, in mari nutritarum, the seals which *find their food in the sea*, δ 442†. [⏑ ⏑ – ⏑ ⏑ –]

ἀλίωσε, -ῶσαι (aor. from ἀλιόω, ἅλιος), *render fruitless, baffle*, ε 104; *hurl in vain*, Π 737. [⏑ ⏑ – ⏓]

ἁλι-πόρφυρα (σαλι-πορφύρα), ntr. pl. purpurata, *sea-purple* (Od.).

ἅλις (ϝάλις; ἐϝάλην), confertim, *in heaps*, in swarms, in crowds, in quantities, Β 90, Γ 384, Ξ 122, Φ 236; abunde, *abundantly*, Ι 137, Ρ 54, Φ 352; ἅλις δέ οἱ, Ι 376, he has done it *enough* (already); *enough and more than enough*, ἦ οὐχ ἅλις ὅτι (ὡς), is it not enough (that)? [⏑ ⏑]

ἁλίσκομαι (ἐϝάλην), aor. ἥλω, subj. ἁλώω, opt. ἁλῴην, ἁλοίην, inf. ἁλῶναι, part. ἁλούς, capi, *be taken captive, be seized*, of men, towns; θανάτῳ, *overtaken by death; be slain, fall in battle*, Χ 253, ο 300; Ε 487, lest ye, as if caught in the meshes of a net, become a prey.

ἀλιταίνω (ἀλάομαι?), aor. ἀλιτόμην (Ι 375, ἤλιτον); part. pf. ἀλιτήμενος, violare, *sin against*, τινά, τί, Ω 586; with part., Τ 265; θεοῖς ἀλιτήμενος, *transgressor* in the sight of the gods, δ 807.

ἀλιτήμων, ονος, (ἀλιταίνω), violentus, *transgressor*, Ω 157.

ἀλιτρός (ἀλιταίνω), nefarius, *offender, sinner; δαίμοσιν*, against the gods; also in milder signif., *rogue, rascal*, ε 182. [⏑ – ⏑]

'Αλκά-θοος, Αἰσυήταο υἱός, son-in-law of 'Αγχίσης, Ν 428. [– ⏑ ⏑ ⏑]

'Αλκ-άνδρη, Πολύβοιο δάμαρ, in Thebes, δ 126†.

"Αλκ-ανδρος (='Αλέξανδρος), a Lykian, Ε 678.

ἄλκαρ (ἀλκή), only nom. and acc., *protection, defense, safety*, τινί, τινός, Ε 644 and Λ 823.

ἀλκή, ῆς, ἀλκί, (ἀλκῇ, ω 509), (arceo, ἀλέξω), fortis defensio, *defense, power of defense, prowess;* common phrase, θούριδος ἀλκῆς, δ 527, *impetuous defense*, i. e. *self-defense*, cf. Ν 330; with μένος, fury; with σθένος, steadfastness, χ 237; with ἠνορέη, manly endurance, ω 509; freq. ἀλκὶ πεποιθώς, ζ 130; ἐπιειμένος ἀλκήν. As divinity, Ε 740.

"Αλκηστις, Πελίαο θυγατρῶν εἶδος ἀρίστη, wife of "Αδμητος of Pherai in Thessaly, mother of Εὔμηλος, Β 715† sq. [– – ⏑]

ἀλκὶ πεποιθώς, see ἀλκή.

'Αλκι-μέδων, Λαέρκεος υἱός, chief of Myrmidons, Ρ 481, Π 197. [– ⏑ ⏑ –]

'Αλκιμίδης ('Αλκίμου υἱός), i. e., Μέντης, χ 235†. [– ⏑ ⏑ –]

ἄλκιμος, ον, (ἀλκή), defendens, *capable of self-defense, brave, bold*, opp. δειλός, Ν 278; applied also as epithet to ἔγχος, υ 127, also to δοῦρε.

"Αλκιμος, (1) father of Mentor.—(2) charioteer of Achilleus.

'Αλκί-νοος, son of Ναυσίθοος, king of Φαίηκες in Σχερίη, husband of 'Αρήτη; his daughter Ναυσικάα, and his sons Λαοδάμας, "Αλιος, Κλυτόνηος; 'Αλκινόου ἀπόλογοι, tale of Odysseus at the court of Alkinoos, ι—μ. [– ⏑ ⏑ ⏑]

'Αλκ-ίππη, slave of 'Ελένη, δ 124†.

'Αλκ-μαίων, son of 'Αμφιάραος and 'Εριφύλη, brother of 'Αμφίλοχος, ο 248†.

'Αλκμάων, Θεστορίδης, Greek, Μ 394†.

'Αλκμήνη, wife of 'Αμφιτρύων in Thebes, mother of 'Ηρακλέης by Zeus, and of 'Ιφικλέης by Amphitryon.

ἀλκτῆρα, ες, masc., (ἀλκή), *defender*, ξ 531, *safeguard*. [– – ⏑]

'Αλκυόνη, name given to Κλεοπάτρη, wife of Μελέαγρος, daughter of Μάρπησσα, Ι 562.

ἀλκυόνος, πολυπενθέος οἶτος, alcedinis, *kingfisher*, Ι 563†.

ἀλλ'=(1) ἄλλο.—(2) ἀλλά.

ἀλλά, ἀλλ', (from ἄλλα), orig. adv., then adversative conj., in contrasted clauses, (1) *but, on the contrary*, Α 25, α 190; freq. after negation, μ 404, Φ 276, θ 312.—(2) subjoining additional circumstance, immo, *nay, but, rather*, Α 94, 165; after question expecting a negative answer, α 68.—(3) corresponding to a concession, expressed or understood, *but, yet*, Α 24, β 107; in apodosis, after a condition expressed or implied, Α 281, Θ 154; μέν or εἰ may be omitted, Α 287, α 42; also εἴπερ τε —ἀλλά τε; ἀλλὰ καὶ ὥς, but even thus; ἀλλ' οὐδ' ὥς, but not even thus.—(4) beginning anew, changing subject, *but, yet, then*, Α 135, 233, 281, Γ 433, α 6, 16, 22, 195.—(5) breaking off, *but, yet*, α 169, 267; ἀλλ' ἤτοι, sed vero, *but yet*, Α 140.—(6) repelling an ungrounded assumption (καί νύ κε), ι 79.—(7) after ἄλλος, ἕτερος, with negative, *than*, Φ 275, θ 311, μ 403, φ 70, γ 377.—(8) in appeal, Α 32, 259, 274, ι 269, κ 69; freq. phrases, ἀλλ' ἄγε, ἀλλ' ἄγετε, with subj., β 404; ἀλλὰ μάλα, ε 342.—(9) with other particles, ἀλλ' ἄρα, see ἄρα, ἀλλὰ γάρ, ξ 355; ἀλλά τε, *but still*, Α 81; ἀλλ' ἤτοι, see no. 5.

ἄλ-λεγον, ἀλ-λέξαι, ipf. and aor., from ἀναλέγω, colligere, *gather*.

ἄλλη (ἄλλος), (1) aliâ, alibi, *elsewhere; ἄλλον ἄλλῃ*, alium alibi, *one in one direction, another in another*.—(2) aliorsum, ἄλλυδις ἄλλῃ, alias alio, *every one in a different direction;* Α 120, (distinction) the honor (due to me) comes to naught; Ο 51, mean very differently.

ἄ-λληκτος=ἄληκτος, *unceasing, unwearied*.

ἀλλ-ήλοιιν, gen. du., pl. -ων, -οις, -ῃσι, -ους, -ας, inter se, *of one another, to one another, one another, mutually;* also with prepositions (avoided by a periphrasis, ι 47); μ 101, near *to each other* are they (the rocks).

ἀλλο-γνώτῳ (γνῶναι), ἐνὶ δήμῳ,

apud exteros, in a *foreign* land, β 366†.

ἀλλοδαπός, 3, (ἄλλος), exterus, extraneus, *strange*, *foreign;* also subst., *stranger*. [– ⏑ ⏑ ⏑]

ἀλλοειδέα [– ⏑ ⏔ ⏔], see ἀλλοίδεα.

ἄλλοθεν (ἄλλος), aliunde, *from elsewhere*, B 75; γ 318, *from abroad;* ἄ. ἄλλος, alius aliunde, *one from one side, another from another*=undique. [– ⏑ ⏑]

ἄλλοθι (ἄλλος), alibi, *elsewhere*, *abroad;* γαίης, β 131, but in ρ 318= procul a patria. (Od.) [– ⏑ ⏑]

ἀλλο-θρόων, -ους, gen. acc. pl. (θρόος), always with ἀνδρῶν or ἀνθρώπους (Od.), aliter sonantium, *talking otherwise* from one's own people, *speaking a strange tongue*.

ἀλλο-ϊδέα (i. e. ἀλλοϝιδέα, _ ⏑ ⏑ ⏔), transformia, *looking differently*, ν 194† (cf. π 181).

ἀλλοῖος, -ῳ, -ον, (ἄλλος), alius speciei, of *another sort;* π 181, *different looking;* τ 265, *inferior*, *commonplace*.

ἅλλομαι (salio), aor. 2 and 3 pers. sing. ἆλσο, ἆλτο, subj. ἅληται, ἅλεται, part. ἅλμενος, salio, *leap*, *spring;* ἐξ ἵππων χαμᾶζε; *hasten*, θύραζε; *start up*, Υ 62; *fly*, Δ 125; *hasten to*, ἐπί τινα; *charge upon*, ἐπί τινι.

ἀλλο-πρόσ-αλλον, -ε, acc. voc., applied to Ares, E 831 and 889; desultorius, *inconstant*, *changeable* (cf. ἑτεραλκής. [– ⏑ ⏑ – ⏑]

ἄλλος, η, ο, (alius), (1) *another*, adj. and subst., with gen., with τίς, οὔ τις ἄλλος εἰ μή (ἀλλά, Σ 403, Φ 275), non alius nisi; ἄλλον instead of ἐμέ, etc., B 360, 200; and freq. in antithetical clauses, ἄλλος (or ὁ, cf. I 594, or ἕτερος) μέν—ἄλλοι δέ, without μέν—δέ, M 267, Σ 536; μέν τ' ἄλλ'—αὐτὰρ ἐπ' ἄλλα, N 799; ἄλλο δέ τοι ἐρέω, κ. τ. λ., verse marking, in Homer, a transition, π 299; (a) *other*, *additional*, reliquus, Γ 223; ἄλλο, *besides*, Ξ 249; ἄλλο τόσον, as much *more;* (οἱ) ἄλλοι, *the rest;* ἔξοχον (ὑπείροχον) ἄλλων, ε 105; (b) used when it can with difficulty be translated into English=*besides*, *moreover*, *as for the rest* (cf. nous autres Français), Θ 211, B 191, α 132, β 412, ο 407, N 622, α 157, B 665, etc.; (c) for emphasis, in apposition with compar., O 569, X 106; and πλησίος, Δ 81 and often; (d) with other forms or cases of ἄλλος, cf. alius alium, B 75, see ἄλλυδις, ἄλλοθεν, δ 236.—(2) alieni, *strangers*, *intruders*, υ 213.—(3) *untrue*, δ 348.

ἄλλοσε (ἄλλος), *to* or *in another place*, ψ 184 and 204. [– ⏑ ⏑]

ἄλλοτε (ἄλλος), alias, *at another time*, *formerly;* often doubled with or without μέν—δέ; in first member, ὅτε μέν often substituted for ἄλλοτε μέν; in second member, often ἄλλοτε δ' αὖτε, *now—then*, *now—now*, Φ 464, Λ 65, Σ 159; ἄλλοτε ἄλλῳ, modo huic, modo illi; ἄλλοτ' ἐπ' ἄλλον, modo in hunc, modo in illum. [– ⏑ ⏑]

ἀλλότριος, 3, (ἄλλος), *strange*, *belonging to another*.—(1) alienus, ἀλλότρια, *others' goods*, cf. α 160; υ 347 (cf. ἀλλοιδέα and π 181), with *distorted* cheeks they were laughing, laughed with strange grimaces.—(2) exterus, φώς, *stranger*, hence *enemy*, π 102; γαίη, *foreign* land.

ἄ-λλοφος (λόφος), non cristatus, *without crest;* κυνέη, K 258†. (See cut, under κυνέη.)

ἀλλο-φρονέων, -ντος, see φρονέω.

ἄλλυδις (ἄλλος), alio, *to another place*, always with ἄλλος, alius alio, or with ἄλλῃ, *now in one way*, *now in another;* N 279, the coward changes, *from moment to moment*, i. e. *every moment*, his color. [– ⏑ ⏑]

ἀλ-λύεσκον, εν, iter. ipf. from ἀναλύω, retexebat, *unravel*, β 105, τ 150. (Od.).

ἄλλως (ἄλλος), aliter, *otherwise*, (1) in strict signification, ε 286, φ 429; *besides*, ε 267; *for some other reason*, ρ 577; *already*, *without this*, φ 87.—(2) melius, *better*, θ 176, υ 211, ω 107, E 218, Ξ 53, T 401.—(3) incassum, *in vain*, ξ 124, Ψ 144.—(4) alioquin, *in other circumstances*, ο 513.

ἅλμα, ατι, ασι, (ἅλλομαι), saltus, *leaping*, as a game, θ 103 and 128.

ἅλμη, ἡ, (ἅλς), aqua marina, *seawater*, *brine*, ε 53. (Od.)

ἁλμυρὸν (ἅλμη) ὕδωρ, aqua marina, *salt water*, δ 511. (Od.)

ἀ-λογήσει (λεγ-, cf. ἀλέγω), contemnere, *disregard*, *despise*, O 162, 178.

ἁλόθεν (ἅλς), ἐξ—, e mari, *from the sea*, Φ 335†. [⏑ ⏑ ⏑]

ἀλοία (ἀλωή), ipf. from ἀλοιάω, contudit, she *smote;* γαῖαν χερσίν, I 568†. [⏑ – –]

ἀλοιφή, ἡ, (ἀλείφω), adeps, *fat*, I 208, P 390, Ψ 32; for rubbing in, to render pliant, φ 179; unguentum, *ointment*, ζ 220, σ 179.

Ἄλον, acc., **Ἀλόπην**, acc., towns in domain of Achilleus, B 682†.

ἀλο-σύδνης (ἅλς, Gothic sunus, son), gen. mari natae, *daughter of the sea*, Υ 207, δ 404.

ἄ-λοφος, see ἄλλοφος.

ἄ-λοχος (λέχος), uxor, *she who shares the bed, wife*, Z 299, γ 264; also the *concubine* is called ἄλοχος; adjectives, μνηστή, αἰδοίη, κυδρή, καλλικρήδεμνοι, κεδνή, πολύδωρος.

ἀλόω, ἀλόωνται, see ἀλάομαι, vagari.

ἅλς, ἁλός, ὁ, sal, *grain of salt*, ρ 455 = ne hilum quidem; — ἡ, *the briny deep, sea* (near the shore), A 308. [⏑ ⏑]

ἆλσο, 2 sing. aor. from ἅλλομαι, saliisti.

ἄλσος, ει, εα, έων, ntr. (alere), lucus, *grove*, usually with altar, and sacred to a divinity, B 506, ζ 321.

Ἄλτης, king of the Λέλεγες, father of Λαοθόη, Φ 85.

ἆλτο, 3 sing. aor. from ἅλλομαι, saluit.

Ἀλύβαντος, ἐξ —, out of *Wandering*, ω 304†, word formed by a pun out of ἀλάομαι.

Ἀλύβης, τηλόθεν ἐξ —, *from Alybe*, whence silver comes, B 857†.

ἀλυσκάζω (ἀλύσκω), only pres. and ipf., evitare, *avoid*, τι, Z 443, ρ 581.

ἀλύσκανε (ἀλύσκω), effugiebat, *was seeking how to escape*, χ 330†. [⏑ – ⏑ ⏑]

ἀλύσκων (ἀλεύομαι), ἀλύξω, ἤλυξα, effugio, *avoid, escape*, κῆρας, ὄλεθρον; μ 335, clam me subduxi sociis, χ 363, 382.

ἀλύσσοντες (from ἀλύσσω, see ἀλύων), *confused*, X 70, *maddened in spirit;* ἀλαλύκτημαι, K 94, *I am beside myself.* [⏑ ⏑ – – –]

ἄ-λυτον, 2, (λύω), insolubilis, *not to be loosed*, N 360. [⏑ ⏑ ⏑]

ἀλύων, ουσ(α), ἀλάομαι, perturbata mente esse, furere, *be beside one's self*—(1) with joy, σ 333, 393.—(2) with pain; ι 398, he dashed it with his hands wildly from him. [⏑ ⏓ –]

Ἀλφειός, river in Ἦλις; then the river-god, γ 489.

ἀλφεσί-βοιος (ἀλφεῖν, βοῦς), boves comparans, *bringing in cattle*, i. e. *making wealthy*, see ἕδνα, Σ 593†.

ἀλφηστάων, -ῇσιν, -άς, (ἀλφεῖν), victum quaerentes, ζ 8, ν 261, *hard-working*, contrasted with ῥεῖα ζώοντες; others translate *flour-eating, fruit-eating.* (Od.)

ἀλφίτου (albus), ἀκτή, β 355, *barley-meal;* elsewh. **ἄλφιτα**, *barley-groats* or *meal* (the porridge made of them), β 290, etc.; μυελὸς ἀνδρῶν, λευκά, ἐπιπαλύνειν. [– ⏑ ⏑]

(ἀλφεῖν), aor. ἦλφον, opt. **ἄλφοι**, 3 pl. ἄλφοιν, υ 383, so Ameis, (German arbeit), parere, *bring in, yield*, ὦνον, βίοτον, ο 452, ρ 250. (Od.)

Ἀλωῆος, *of Aloeus*, the father of Ὦτος and Ἐφιάλτης, husband of Ἰφιμέδεια. [⏑ – – ⏑]

ἀλωή (ἀλοιάω), area, *threshing-floor*, Υ 496; also *orchard* and *vineyard;* Σ 561, *corn-field;* see γουνός.

ἁλώῃ, ἁλῴη, ἁλώμενος, from ἁλίσκομαι, capi.

ἀλώμενος, from ἀλάομαι, errans.

ἁλώω, from ἁλίσκομαι, aor. subj. captus sim.

ἄμ, ἀμ, instead of ἀνά before labials.

ἅμα (from σάμα, cf. Σαμοκλῆς, ὁμός), una, simul, *at once, at the same time.* —(1) adv., A 343; ἅμ' ἄμφω, H 255; often with τὲ—καί, B 281; with following δέ, T 242.—(2) prep. with dat., simul, *at same time with*, ἅμ' ἠελίῳ ἀνιόντι, καταδύντι; una, *beside, with*, A 348, α 428; ἕπεσθαι, go with, attend. so, τροχόωντα, θέουσα, run after; α 98, Π 149, *swift as* the wind. [⏑ ⏑]

Ἀμαζόνες ἀντιάνειραι, Γ 189, dwelt on the river Thermodon in Pontos; made a plundering foray into Phrygia, B 814, Z 186. [ᾰ]

Ἀμάθεια, a Nereid, Σ 48†. [⏑ ⏑ – ⏑]

ἀμάθοιο (ψάμαθος) βαθείης, E 587†, he fell into deep *sand.* [⏑ ⏑ – ⏑]

ἀμᾰθύνει, πῦρ, solo aequat, *destroys*, I 593†. [⏑ ⏑ – –]

ἀ-μαιμάκετος, 3, (μαιμάσσω), saeviens, *furious*, Z 179, Π 329; ξ 311, the mast *tossed to and fro* by the waves, like a man reeling in drunkenness.

ἀμαλδύνω (σμερδ-, mordeo?), only aor. **ἀμαλδῦναι**, -ύνας, and pass. ἀμαλδύνηται, conterere, *destroy;* only with τεῖχος. (Il.)

ἀμαλλο-δετήρ, ὁ, (ἄμαλλα, δέω), *binder of sheaves.* (Il., Σ.)

ἀμαλήν, -ῇσι, (mollis), teneram, *tender;* of lamb, dog.

ἄμ-αξα, ἡ, (ἅμα, ἄξων), parallel form ἅμαξα, plaustrum, *four-wheeled freight wagon,* ι 241; also the constellation of the Great Bear, Σ 487, ε 273; cf. ἅρμα, ἀπήνη. [ᾰ]

ἀμαξ-ιτόν (ἅμαξα, εἶμι), κατ' —, viâ publicâ, *wagon-road,* X 146.

ἀμάρης (μύρω? mare?), ἐξ —, *canal for irrigation,* Φ 259†. [⏑⏑–]

ἁμαρτάνω (ἀ-, μέρος), ἁμαρτήσομαι, aor. ἥμαρτον and ἤμβροτον—(1) impertem fieri esse, *lose,* φ 155, ι 512; then (2) in general, *fail of; miss,* τινός; λ 511, *mistook* not the word, spoke the right word; Ω 68, *failed not to bring* gifts; η 292, *let not* presence of mind *fail* her.—(3) peccare, *fail, err;* with ὑπερβήη, I 501; χ 154, I myself have *overlooked* this.

ἁμαρτῇ (ἅμα, ἄραρον), simul, *simultaneously,* χ 81. [ᾰ]

ἁμαρτο-επές (ἔπος), temere locutus, speaking *thoughtlessly,* N 824†. [ᾰ]

Ἀμᾰρυγκεΐδης Διώρης, B 622, Δ 517. [ᾰ]

Ἀμᾰρυγκέα θάπτον Ἐπειοὶ Βουπρασίῳ, his burial in Messene, with funeral games, described, Ψ 630†.

ἀμα-τροχόωντα, see τροχόωντα, *running about after me.*

ἀμα-τροχιάς (τροχός), acc. pl., concursus impactarum rotarum, *running together, clash of chariots,* Ψ 422†. [⏑–⏑⏑–]

ἀ-μαυρὸν (ἀ-, μάρμαρος) εἴδωλον, *pale, dim, lurid,* δ 824 and 835. (Od.) [ᾰ]

ἀ-μᾰχητί (μάχη), sine pugna, *without contest,* Φ 437†. [ῑ]

ἀμάω (Ger. mähen, Eng. mow), ipf. **ἤμων,** aor. ἀμήσαντες, -σάμενος, manu colligere, *gather together, collect,* ι 247; *mow.* [⏓––]

ἀμβ-, see **ἀναβ-.**

ἀμ-βᾰτός (ἀνα-βαίνω), aditum praebens, *that may be scaled,* Z 434.

ἀμ-βλήδην (ἀναβάλλομαι), adv. exorsa, *as prelude, at first,* X 476†.

ἀμ-βολάδην (ἀναβάλλω), adv., *bubbling up,* Φ 364†.

ἀμ-βροσίη (ἀμβρόσιος), *ambrosia,* adj. used as subs., strictly signifies *immortal* and *conferring immortality;* used by the gods as food; as ointment, for embalming, for perfume; also as food for horses of the gods.

ἀμ-βρόσιος (ἄμβροτος), divinus, *immortal, divine,* E 369.—(1) that which the gods send, νύξ, ὕπνος, or (2) belongs to them; πλοκάμους, χαῖται, κάλλεϊ, ἑανόν, πέπλον, even of their horses, εἶδαρ and κάπῃσιν. [–⏑⏑⏑]

ἄμ-βροτος, ο , (βροτός), *immortal,* Υ 358, θ 365, θεός; then like ἀμβρόσιος, *divine.*—(1) νύξ.—(2) αἷμα, εἵματα, τεύχεα, ἐλαίῳ, ἱστόν, ἵπποι.

ἀ-μέγαρτος (μεγαίρω), only sing., invisus, *unenviable, doleful, dreadful* (proleptically of battle, B 420); *mighty* blast, λ 400; *miserable,* ρ 219. [ᾰ]

ἀμείβω (moveo), fut. ἀμείψω, -ομαι, aor. ἠμείψατο, alternare, *alternate, change.*—I. act., *exchange,* τί, τινός, for something, πρός τινα, with some one; ὀλίγον γόνυ γουνὸς ἀμ., pedetentim cedendo; οἱ ἀμείβοντες, *rafters.*—II. mid., (1) *change with each other,* ἀμειβόμενος, alternans, A 604, *relieving one another;* θ 379, *in quick alternation* (of dance); α 375, *passing from one house to another;* θρώσκων ἀμείβεται, O 684, leaps in turn.—(2) *answer,* δ 382; μύθῳ, κ 71; (μυθῳ, -οισι, ἐπέεσσι) τινά, some one; εὖ δώροις τινά, *make* beautiful gifts *in return.*—(3) *pass over,* I 409, κ 328.

ἀ-μείλικτον (μειλίσσω), ὄπα, implacabilem, *harsh, inexorable* words. (Il.) [ᾰ]

ἀ-μείλιχος, 2, (μειλίσσω), inexorabilis, *implacable, relentless.* [ᾰ]

ἀ-μείνων, ον (Old Lat. mānus= bonus), melior, *better, more excellent, superior, more favorable, more advantageous* (opposed in signif. to χέρηα, Δ 400); μέγ' ἀμείνων, multo praestantior; α 376, more profitable and *better.*

ἀ-μέλγω, only pr. and ipf., mulgeo, *milk;* pass., Δ 434, *yielding* white milk. [ᾰ]

ἀ-μέλησε (μέλω), aor., always with negation; οὐκ ἀμ. τινός, curabat, *he bethought himself of.* [ᾰ]

ἄμεναι, inf. from ἄω, satiare.

ἀ-μενηνός, 2, (μένος), debilis, *feeble*, E 887; νεκύων ἀμ. κάρηνα, *feeble heads* of the dead (periphrasis) = the *feeble* dead; ὀνείρων, *unsubstantial.* [ᾰ]

ἀ-μενήνωσεν (ἀμενηνός), debilitavit, *made ineffective*, N 562†. [ᾰ]

1. **ἀ-μέρδω** (μέρος), aor. ἄμερσε, -σαι; pass. pres. ἀμέρδεαι, aor. subj. ἀμερθῇς, privare, *deprive*, θ 64; pass., *lose, be deprived of*, X 58.

2. **ἀ-μέρδω** (μάρμαρος), only pres. and pf., *make lustreless, blind*, τ 18; *dazzle, blind* by excess of light, N 340.

ἀ-μέτρητος, 2, (μετρέω), immensus, *immeasurable*, τ 512 and ψ 249. [⏑ – – ⏑]

ἀ-μετρο-επής (μέτρον, Ϝέπος), immoderate loquax, *immoderate talker*, B 212†.

ἀμητῆρες (ἀμάω), messores, *reapers*, Λ 67†. [≃ – – ⏑]

ἄμητος (ἀμάω), messis, *reaping, harvest;* metaph. for *slaughter*, T 223†. [≃ – ⏑]

ἀ-μηχανίη (ἀμήχανος), desperatio, *helplessness, despair*, ι 295†. [ᾰ]

ἀ-μήχανος, 2, (μῆχος), *helpless.*—(1) act., miser, *wretched*, τ 363.—(2) pass., difficilis, *impossible*, Ξ 262; Θ 130, *irremediable mischief;* τ 560, *useless* dreams; *unyielding*, O 14, T 273; *stubborn, hard-hearted*, Π 29; N 726, *thou canst not* (for thou art too obstinate) yield to, etc.

Ἀμισωδάρου υἷες (Ἀτύμνιος, Μάρις), in Karia, Π 328†. [ᾰ]

ἀ-μιτρο-χίτωνες (μίτρη, χιτών), *wearing coat of mail without girdle*, or the word may mean *wearing both coat of mail and girdle*, χιτών in this cmpd. = θώρηξ, Π 419†. [⏑ – ⏑ ⏑ – ⏑]

ἀμιχθαλόεσσαν (ὀμίχλη), Λῆμνον, vapore obductam, *foggy, misty, smoky*, since Lemnos is a volcanic island, Ω 753†. [ᾰ]

ἄμμε, ἄμμες, ἄμμι, see ἡμεῖς.

ἀμ-μίξας, aor. part. from ἀναμίγνυμι, admiscens.

ἀμ-μορίην (μόρος), *misfortune*, υ 76†.

ἄμ-μορος, 2, (μέρος), expers, ε 275, Σ 489, *deprived of* the bath of the ocean, of the Great Bear, which never sinks below the horizon in Greece; elsewh. *unfortunate.*

ἀμνίον, ntr., *basin in which the blood of victims was caught*, γ 444‡. (See cut.)

Ἀμνίσῳ, ἐπ', *at Amnisos*, harbor of Knosos, τ 188†. [ῐ]

ἀ-μογητί (μογέω), sine labore, *without trouble*, Λ 637†. [ῐ]

ἀμόθεν (ἀμός), τῶν, alicunde (orsa), *from any point soever; beginning with any point whatever*, relate to us, α 10†. [ᾰ]

ἀμοιβάς (ἀμείβω), χλαίνη, mutatoria, *for a change*, ξ 521†. [ᾰ]

ἀμοιβή, ἡ, (ἀμείβομαι), retributio, *recompense, gift in return, restitution.* (Od.) [ᾰ]

ἀμοιβηδίς, *in turn*, Σ 506 and σ 310.

ἀμοιβοί (ἀμείβω), succedanei, *as substitutes* (in exchange for former aid furnished by Priam), N 793†. [ᾰ]

ἀμολγῷ (ἐν), νυκτὸς, *in darkness*, of night. [ᾰ]

Ἀμοπάονα, Πολυαιμονίδην, slain by Τεῦκρος, Θ 276†. [⏑ ⏑ – ⏑ ⏑]

ἀμός, 3, (also ἁμός) = ἡμέτερος. [ᾰ]

ἄ-μοτον (μέμαα, moveo), vehementer, *insatiably, unceasingly, eagerly;* esp. with μέμαα, κλαίω, κεχολωμένος, τανύοντο. [ᾰ]

ἀμπ-, see ἀναπ-.

ἀμπελόεντ(α), -εσσαν, (ἀμπελό-εις), B 561, Γ 184, vitibus abundans, *full of vines, abounding in vines;* of districts and towns. (Il.)

ἄμπελος, ἡ, *grape-vine, vine.* (Od.)

ἀμ-πεπαλών, aor. part. from ἀναπάλλω, vibrans.

ἀμ-περές (ἀνά, περάω), always διὰ δ' ἀμπερές, penitus, *through and through.*

ἄμπ-εχεν, ἅλμη ὤμους, circumdabat, *covered, lay thick upon*, ζ 225†.

ἀμ-πήδησε, aor. from ἀναπηδάω, exsiluit.

ἀμ-πνεῦσαι, ἄμ-πνυε, ἀμ-πνύνθη, ἄμ-πνυτο, see ἀνα-πνέω.

ἄμπ-ῡκα (ἀμπέχω), *head-band, fillet,* ornament of woman's head, χ 469. (See cut.)

ἀμῡδίς (Aeolic instrumental case, from ἀμός; parallel form, ἄμυδις), una, simul, *at once,* (1) *together,* καθίζειν, κικλήσκειν, etc., πάντ' ἄμυδις, *all together,* μ 413, M 385.—(2) *at once, immediately,* I 6, N 336, Ψ 217, ξ 305. [ᾰ]

'Αμῠδῶνος, ἐξ —, *Amydon,* city of Παίονες, on the river 'Αξιός, in Makedonia, B 849 and Π 288. [ᾰ]

'Αμῡθάονα, acc., son of Κρηθεύς and Τυρώ, father of Βίας and Μελάμπους, λ 259†. [⏑⏑–⏑⏑]

'Αμύκλαι, ας, city in Lakonia, near the Eurotas, twenty stadia S.E. of Sparta, residence of Tyndareos, B 584†. [ᾰ].

ἀ-μύμων, ονος, [μῶμος], irreprehensus, *faultless,* used esp. of external appearance, but also in a more general sense, *excellent, glorious* (fortunate, α 232, μ 261). [⏑––]

ἀμύντωρ, -ορα, -ας, (ἀμύνω), acc., defensor, *defender, protector.* [ᾰ]

'Αμύντορος, 'Ορμενίδαο, gen., father of Φοῖνιξ, I 448. [ᾰ]

ἀμύνω (μύνη, munio), arcere, propulsare, *ward off,* (1) act., N 814, τινί τι, I 674, Π 835; τινός, from some one, τι, M 402, O 731; ἀπὸ, ρ 538; *help, defend,* τινί, E 486, Λ 674, λ 500; τινός, N 109; περί τινος, P 182; ἀπό τινος, Π 75, 80.—(2) mid., *defend one's self,* β 62, χ 106, 116; *ward off,* τί, N 514, P 510; *protect,* τινός, M 155, I 531; ναῦφι, N 700; περί τινος, M 170, 243. [⏑––]

ἄμυσσεν, ἀμύξεις, (ἀμύσσω, mucro), ipf., fut. lacerare, *scratch, tear,* T 284, out of grief; A 243, θυμόν, thou shalt *gnaw* thy soul with vexation. [ᾰ]

ἀμφ-ἄγάπαζον, -όμενος, (ἀγαπάζω), ipf. act. and pres. mid., amplecti, *receive hospitably,* Π 192, ξ 381.

ἀμφ-ἄγέροντο (ἀγείρω), ipf., μιν —, circa eam conveniebant, *were grouping themselves* about her, Σ 37†.

ἀμ-φάδιον, adj. (φάος), γάμον, *open, publicly declared,* ζ 288; esp. **ἀμφαδίην,** adv. palam, *openly,* H 196. [ᾰ]

ἀμ-φᾰδὰ γένοιτο, detegeretur, that the thing should *come to light;* ἀμφαδόν, palam, *openly, undisguisedly* (opp. κρυφηδόν, ξ 330; δόλῳ, α 296), *publicly.*

ἀμφὶ δ' ἀίσσονται (ἀίσσω), undique concitantur, *spring upon it from all sides,* Λ 417; ὤμοις, *float round his shoulders,* Z 510, O 267. [ᾰ]

ἀμφί τ' ἀλεῖψαι (ἀλείφω), aor. inf., perungere, *anoint thoroughly,* Ω 582†.

ἀμφ-ἄράβησε (ἀραβέω), aor., his armor *crashed around him,* Φ 408†.

ἀμ-φᾰσίη (φάναι), μιν—ἐπέων λάβε, *speechlessness* took possession of him, P 695, δ 704.

ἀμφ' αὖον **ἀύτευν** (ἀυτέω), ipf. aridum circa sonabant, *gave a dull sound,* M 160†. [ῡ]

ἀμφ-ἄφάω (ἅπτω), part. **ἀμφ-αφόων,** -όωσα, mid. inf. -άασθαι, ipf. -όωντο, contrectare manibus, *feel of all around, touch, grasp;* also with χερσί, *handle,* θ 215.

ἀμφ-εποτᾶτο, ipf. from ἀμφιποτάομαι, circumvolitabat, B 315†.

ἀμφ-έπω, see ἀμφιέπω.

(ἀμφέρχομαι), only aor. **ἀμφ-ήλυθε,** versabatur circa, *sounds about me,* ζ 122; *rose about me,* μ 369. (Od.)

ἀμφ-έχανε, devoravit, see ἀμφιχαίνω.

ἀμφ-έχυτ', circumfundebatur, see ἀμφιχέω.

ἄμφ-ηκες (ἀκή), utrimque acutus, *two-edged,* of sword, π 80.

ἀμφ-ήλυθε, circumiit, from *ἀμφέρχομαι.*

ἄμφ-ημαι, only **ἀμφὶ δ' εἵατο,** circumversabantur, O 9†.

ἀμφ-ηρεφέᾱ (*ἐρέφω*), utrimque contectam, *close-covered,* A 45†.

ἀμφ-ήριστον (*ἐρίζω*), ambiguum (victorem), *doubtful* (his victory doubtful), Ψ 382†.

ἀμφί (see *ἀμφίς*), utrimque, *on both sides,* often synonymous with *περί.* —I. adv., utrimque, β 153, 427, σ 173; *round about,* γ 32, 429, φ 122; exchanged with *περί,* Σ 564, O 647; *ἀμφὶ περί* (sometimes wrongly written as one word), Φ 10, Ψ 191, λ 609; *περί τ' ἀμφί τε,* with acc., P 760; so *περί,* κ 262.—II. prep., (1) with gen., de, *about, concerning,* Π 825, θ 267.—(2) with dat., (a) local, circa, *around, among,* B 388, Γ 328, Σ 231, M 396, Δ 493; *ὀβελοῖσιν ἔπειραν,* proleptically, pierced the meat so that it was *around* the spit, A 465, cf. Ψ 30; *ἀμφὶ πυρί,* on the fire, θ 426; *with,* λ 423, I 470; (b) causal, *because of = for,* Γ 70, 157, α 48, δ 153, λ 546, Λ 672; de, *with respect to,* ρ 555, δ 151, H 408.—(3) with acc., local; circa, *about,* Ω 588, B 461, A 409; *within,* Λ 706; *ἀμφί τινα,* any one in company with those about him, χ 281, Γ 146.

Ἀμφί-ἄλος, a Phaiakian, θ 114. [ῐ]

ἀμφῐ-άλῳ, *ἐν Ἰθάκῃ,* mari cincta, *sea-girt.* (Od.)

Ἀμφῐ-άρᾱος, son of *Οἰκλῆς,* great-grandson of *Μελάμπους,* pious and brave; seer, and king of Argos; he participated in the Argonautic expedition and in the Kalydonian boar-hunt, and finally, through the treachery of Eriphyle, in the expedition of the Seven against Thebes, o 244. [ᾰ]

ἀμφῐ-ἀχυῖαν (*ἄχος*), as she flew *shrieking about,* B 316†.

ἀμφι-βαίνω, ipf., pf., plupf.; only ipf. (aor. P 359) in tmesi; *surround,* cingere, *τι,* μ 74; *τινί,* Π 66; Z 355, θ 541, *occupies* the thought, heart; *μέσον οὐρανόν,* stand at zenith; *τί,* tenere, *possess, protect,* esp. of perf. and plupf. with dat.

ἀμφι-βάλλει, fut. *-βαλεῦμαι, cast about,* (1) amicire, induere, *put on,* of garments, weapons, etc., always in tmesi *τινά τι,* also without acc. of the person (also mid., *clad one's self*), *τί, τινί* (dat. of pers., ξ 342; of thing, E 722, N 36) *τι*; *ἀμφιβαλόντες,* P 742, *putting on* strength; fut. only mid., *I will equip myself.*—(2) circum ponere, ψ 192, *building upon this* (as foundation); *χεῖρας, χεῖρε—δειρῇ Ὀδυσῆι,* ψ 208, or *τινί, τινά, embrace; γούνασί τινος,* amplecti genua; δ 454, *seize;* ρ 344, as much as his hands could hold *in their clasp;* K 535, *encompass, resound about.*

ἀμφί-βᾰσῐν, *resistance,* E 623†.

ἀμφι-βρότης, *-ην,* (*βροτός*), hominem undique tegentis, *covering the entire man, ἀσπίδος,* B 389, Λ 32. (Il.)

Ἀμφι-γένεια, town subject to Nestor, B 593†.

ἀμφῐ-γυήεις (*γυῖα*), ambidexter, *strong-armed,* only at close of verse, usually subst. *work-master,* with *περικλυτός,* of *Ἥφαιστος,* θ 300.

ἀμφῐ-γύοισιν (*γυῖον*), *ἔγχεσιν,* almost always at close of verse, utrimque acutis, *sharp at both ends,* π 474; see *οὐρίαχος.* (See annexed cuts.) [ῠ]

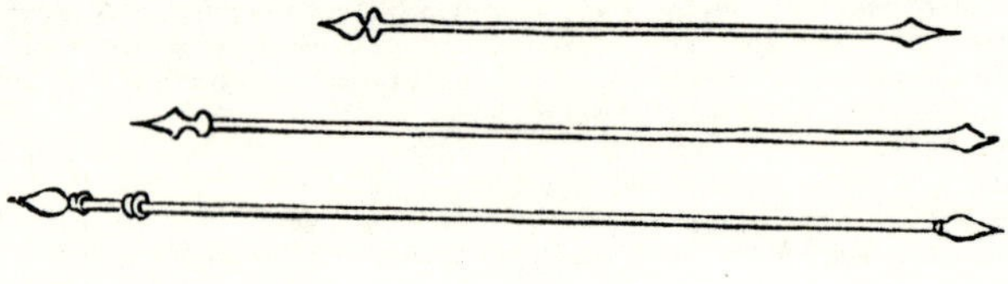

ἀμφι-δαίω, only **-δέδηε, -δεδήει**, (*δαίω*), perf. plupf., circa exarsit, *rages round about*, *τι*, Z 329. (Il.)

Ἀμφι-δάμας, *-αντος*, (1) from *Κύθηρα*, K 268.—(2) from *Ὀπόεις*, Ψ 87.

ἀμφῐ-δάσειαν (*δασύς*), *αἰγίδα*, circa villosam, *shaggy all around, with shaggy border*, O 309†.

ἀμφῐ-δῑνέω, **-δεδίνηται**, pf. pass., Ψ 562, *round whose edge goes a border* (casting) of tin; θ 405, *encloses* it.

ἀμφι-δρῠφής (*δρύπτω*), quae genas lacerat, *with both cheeks torn from grief*, B 700†.

ἀμφί-δρῠφοι (*παρειαί*), circa laceratae, (both) *torn from grief*, Λ 393†.

ἀμφί-δῠμοι, duplices, *double* (outer and inner harbor), δ 847†.

ἀμφῐ-ελίσσης, *-αι*, *-ας*, (*ἑλίσσω*), gen. sing., nom. and acc. pl., utrimque curvatae, *curved at both ends*, only of ships at rest, γ 162. [–⏑⏑––] (The cut represents a Phoenician ship, as represented on an Egyptian monument.)

ἀμφι-έννυμι (*ἕννυμι*), fut. **ἀμφῐ-έσω**, aor. *-εσ(σ)α*, and mid. *-άμην*, (no pres. or ipf.), amicire, *put on, don*, *τινά τι*, T 393, ξ 23; mid., induere sibi, *dress one's self in*, ψ 131, K 23.

ἀμφι-έπων, only pr. (imp. and part.) and ipf., *ἄμφεπε*, also in tmesi, circa versari, *to be busy about*; *τινά*, Λ 473, *surround* (mid.); *πῦρ*, *envelop in flame*; apparare, *dress*, θ 61; *arrange*, B 525; *ἀμφιέποντες*, seduli, *busily*, γ 118.

ἀμφι-εῦσε (*εὕω*), ambussit, *singed round about*, ι 389†.

ἀμφ-ίζανε (*ἱζάνω*), circa adhaerebat, *hung upon*, Σ 25†.

ἀμφῐ-θᾰλής (*θάλος*), undique affluens, *rich*; others interpret, *having father and mother still alive*, X 496†.

Ἀμφῐ-θέη, wife of *Αὐτόλυκος*, grandmother of *Ὀδυσσεύς*, τ 416†.

ἀμφί-θετος *φιάλη*, *reversible* cup, i. e. with double bowl and base, which may stand upon or be drunk from either end, the base serving also as bowl (cf. *ἀμφῐ-κύπελλον δέπας*), Ψ 270. (Ψ.)

ἀμφῐ-θέουσιν (*θέω*), circumsiliunt, *run about*, κ 413†.

Ἀμφιθόη, a Nereid, Σ 42†.

ἀμφῐ-κᾰλύπτει (also in tmesi), with fut. and aor. (calim, occulo, Ger. hüllen, Eng. hull, of grain), obvolvo, *wrap around, veil*, B 262; *shelter, enclose*, Ψ 91, δ 618, θ 511; *becloud*, of swoon, Υ 417; of sleep, υ 86; *θανάτου μέλαν νέφος*, Π 350, cf. M 116, E 68, δ 180; *ἔρως με φρένας*, love *engrossed* my heart; *τινί τι*, *surround*, Ξ 343, N 420, P 132, θ 569, E 507.

ἀμφι-καρῆ, *double-headed*, v. l., ρ 231.

ἀμφῐ-κεάσσας (*κεάζω*), *having hewed off all around* (the bark), ξ 12†.

Ἄμφι-κλος, a Trojan, Π 313†.

ἀμφι-κόμῳ (*κόμη*), frondoso, *shady*, P 677†.

ἀμφῐ-κύπελλον, *δέπας*, *double-cupped* goblet, whose base is bowl-shaped, and may be drunk from, γ 63. [ῠ]

ἀμφῐ-λάχαινεν, sarriebat, *was digging about*, ω 242†.

Ἀμφί-λοχος, son of *Ἀμφιάραος*, from *Ἄργος*, a seer, ο 248†.

ἀμφῐ-λύκη (lucere), *νύξ*, diluculum, *gray of early dawn*, H 433†. [ῡ]

ἀμφῐ-μάσασθε, 1 aor. imp. mid., *σπόγγοισι*, *wipe off all over*, υ 152†.

ἀμφῐ-μάχονται, *fight around*, (1) *τί*, *besiege*, Z 461.—(2) *τινός*, *fight for* (as a prize), of defenders and assailants, Π 496; cf. *ἀμφὶ νέκυι*, Π 526. (Il.)

Ἀμφί-μᾰχος, (1) son of *Κτέατος*, leader of *Ἐπειοί*, N 203.—(2) son of *Νομίων*, leader of *Κᾶρες*, B 870.

Ἀμφῐ-μέδων, son of *Μελανεύς*, a suitor, χ 242.

ἀμφῐ-μέλαιναι, *-ας*, *φρένες*, *dark on both sides, darkened* (lit. diaphragm, *dark on both sides*), metaph. of soul, *darkened by rage or grief*, of instantaneous effect of strong feeling. (Il.)

ἀμφῐ-μέμῡκεν (*μυκάομαι*), circumsonavit, *re-echoed*, κ 227; in tmesi, aor. *-μῦκε*, *-ον*, *resounded*, Υ 260, M 460.

Ἀμφι-νόμη, a Nereid, Σ 44.

Ἀμφί-νομος, son of *Νῖσος*, from *Δουλίχιον*, a suitor, χ 89.

ἀμφι-ξέω, only **ἀμφέξεσα,** dolavi, *I hewed round about,* ψ 196†.

Ἄμφῖος, (1) son of Σέλαγος, from Παισός, ally of the Trojans, E 612.—(2) son of Μέροψ, a Trojan chief, B 830.

ἀμφῐ-πέληται, circumsonet, *resounds,* α 352†.

ἀμφῐ-πένονται, and ἀμφεπένοντο, ipf., curant, *attended,* ο 467; *take up, tend* (the wounded); *assail,* Φ 203, Ψ 184.

ἀμφι-περί, see ἀμφί.

ἀμφι-περι-στρέφεται, see περιστρέφ.

ἀμφι-περι-στρώφα, see περιστρώφα.

ἀμφῐ-πεσοῦσα (πίπτω), amplexata, *embracing, clinging to* (her lifeless husband), θ 523†.

ἀμφι-πολεύειν (ἀμφίπολος), only pr., curare, *till,* ὄρχατον; βίον, *watch over;* υ 78, *attend, serve* (ironical). (Od.)

ἀμφί-πολος, ἡ, (πέλομαι), comes, *female attendant* (not a slave), without whom the noble dame of the heroic age never appears in public, α 331.

ἀμφι-πονέομαι, only ipf. **-επονεῖτο** and fut. -πονησόμεθα, curare, *attend* (so also ἀμφιπένονται), Ψ 681; *superintend,* Ψ 159, υ 307.

ἀμφι-ποτάομαι, only **ἀμφ-εποτᾶτο,** circumvolitabat, *was fluttering about,* B 315†.

ἀμφῐ-ρύτῃ (ῥέω), νήσῳ ἐν —, circumflua, *sea-girt,* α 50. (Od.) [ῠ]

ἀμφίς (from ἄμφω, old instr. case, Φ 162; weakened to ἀμφί, which orig. stood before σέκαστον [ἕκαστον], Λ 634, 748, τ 46; and in composition, ἀμφισέχω, α 54, γ 486, θ 340; replaced at close of verse by ἀμφίς, η 4, ζ 266, E 723, Φ 442), utrimque, *on both sides.* —I. adv., (1) Σ 519; Φ 162, hurl the spears *from both hands at once;* ἔχειν, have on both sides, carry; α 54, hold asunder; *round about,* H 342, Γ 115.—(2) *apart,* N 706; *singly,* χ 57, cf. X 117; εἶναι, π 267, with gen., *be far from,* τ 221, O 709.—(3) *differently,* φράζεσθαι, φρονεῖν, B 13, N 345.—II. prep. (always following the word it governs, except ἀμφὶ *before* (σ)έκαστος), (1) with gen., *far away from,* ξ 352, π 267, Θ 444; *on one side of,* Ψ 393; *in all its parts, narrowly,* B 384.—(2) with dat., *on either end,* E 723.—(3) with acc., *about, around,* Ξ 274, ζ 266, Λ 635, 748, τ 46.

ἀμφίσταμαι, only ipf. and aor. **ἀμφέσταν,** ἀμφ-έστησαν, circumstare, obsidere, Σ 233; in tmesi, η 4, ι 380, ω 58.

ἀμφὶ- (νέφος) **ἔστεφε,** cinxit, *crowned with,* Σ 205†.

ἀμφ-εστρᾰτόωντο, τήν, obsidebant, *were besieging,* Λ 713†.

ἀμφι-στρεφέες (στρέφω), flexiles, *turning all ways,* Λ 40†.

ἀμφι-τίθημι, induere, *put on,* τινί τί; in tmesi, yet **ἀμφιτεθεῖσα,** *placed upon,* K 271; mid. ἀμφέθετο, *girded on,* φ 431; in tmesi, θ 416, K 149.

ἀμφὶ- (ἑανὸς) **τρέμε,** circa tremebat, *trembled round about,* Φ 507†.

Ἀμφι-τρίτη, sea-goddess (not represented in Homer as wife of Poseidon), ε 422, μ 97, 60.

ἀμφι-τρομέω, τοῦ δ' — καὶ δείδια, *tremble for,* and fear lest, δ 820†.

Ἀμφι-τρύων, ωνος, only with παῖς, υἱός (Ἡρακλέης), and ἄκοιτιν (Ἀλκμήνην), king of Τίρυνς, E 392, γ 266.

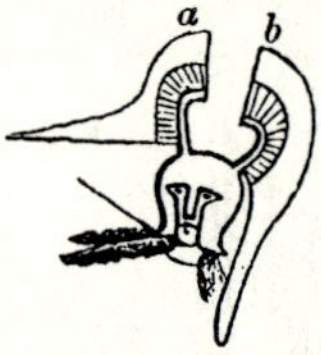

ἀμφί-φᾰλον (φάλος) κυνέην, *double-plumed,* strictly, *double-ridged;* helmet *with double* or *divided crest.* (See cut, *a* and *b.*)

ἀμφι-φοβέω, only **-εφόβηθεν,** aor. pass. μιν, *were put to flight around* him, Π 290†.

ἀμφῐ φορεύς, ὁ, (ἀμφίς, φέρω), *two-handled vase* or *jar* for wine; also, ω 74, for ashes of the dead. (See the following cuts, the first two from Egyptian, the others from Greek, originals.)

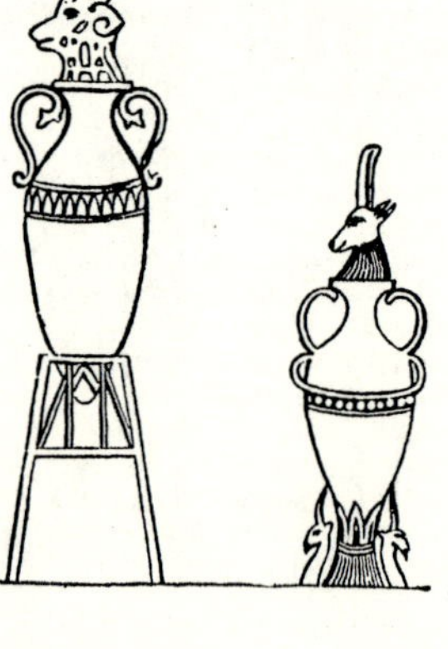

ἀμφὶ (*μάλα*) **φράζεσθε**, *weigh carefully*, Σ 254†.

ἀμφ-έχᾰνε, aor. (*χαίνω*), devoravit, *yawns on every side*, Ψ 79†.

ἀμφι-χέω, aor. *χεῦε*, *χέε*, circumfundo.—(1) in tmesi, *τί τινι*, circumdare, *shed about*, Ρ 270, θ 278.—(2) aor. mid. *ἔχυντο*, *thronged about*, χ 498; *were laid round them*, θ 297 (tmesis); *τινά*, *sound in one's hearing*, Β 41; *encompass* (tmesis), *τινί*, Ν 544, Π 414; also aor. pass. -*εχύθη*, δ 716, Ξ 253, Ψ 63; *embrace*, π 214; Ψ 764, before the dust-cloud rose.

ἀμφι-χυθείς, -*ῆναι*, see *ἀμφι-χέω*, amplexus.

ἀμφί-χῠτον (*χέω*), circumfusum, *encompassing* (earthen wall), Υ 145†.

Ἀμφίων, *ονος*, (1) son of *Ἴασιος* and *Χλῶρις*, king of *Ὀρχομενός*, λ 283.—(2) son of Zeus and *Ἀντιόπη*, brother of *Ζῆθος*, founder of *Θῆβαι*, λ 262.—(3) leader of the *Ἐπειοί*, Ν 692. [ῑ]

ἀμφότερος, *η*, *ον*, ambo, *both*; *ἀμφότερον—τε—τε* (*καί*), utrumque et—et; *ἀμφοτέρῃσι* (*χερσί*), κ 264 (Ε 416), ambabus (manibus); *χεῖρε ἀμφοτέρας*, ω 398.

Ἀμφοτερός, a Lykian, Π 415†.

ἀμφοτέρωθεν, utrimque, *from* or *on both sides*, *at both ends*, κ 167.

ἀμφοτέρωσε, in utramque partem, *in both directions*, Θ 223. (Il.)

ἀμφ-ουδίς (*οὖδας*), humi, *on the ground*, *at his feet*, ρ 237†.

ἀμ-φράσσαιτο, aor. from *ἀναφράζομαι*, agnosceret.

ἄμφω (ambo), ambo, utrique, *both* (sides), Α 363 (Β 124); *the two pieces*, μ 424.

ἄμφ-ωτον (*οὖς*), *two-handled*, χ 10†.

ἀμῷεν, opt. pres. from *ἀμάω*, meterent.

ἀ-μωμήτοιο (*μῶμος*), irreprehensus, *irreproachable*, Μ 109†.

1. **ἄν** (possibly from *ἀμός*, strictly, aliquâ), *somehow*, similar in its use to *κέ*; hence, I., with opt., mere (subjective) supposition, sumtio ficti; Ρ 711, *οὐ γάρ πως ἂν Τρώεσσι μάχοιτο*, non enim Troes impugnaverit, he *would* (could) not, unarmed, *attack* the Trojans; in hypothetical periods, sumtio ficti, conclusion of expressed or implied supposition made without regard to fact, *ἢ τ' ἂν ἀμυναίμην* (*εἴ μοι δύναμίς γε παρείη*), ego vero me defenderim, I *would defend* myself, β 62; in relative periods, *ὅς νῦν γε καὶ ἂν Διὶ πατρὶ μάχοιτο*, who now at least *would fight* even with father Zeus, Ε 362; also with assumption contrary to fact, sumtio falsi, Α 232.—(2) in interrogations, α 65, *πῶς ἂν ἔπειτ' Ὀδυσῆος ἐγὼ θείοιο λαθοίμην*; how *should* (*could*) *I forget?* in requests, ζ 57, *οὐκ ἂν δή μοι ἐφοπλίσσειας ἀπήνην*, *couldst* (wouldst) *thou not?*—(3) in dependent relation after past tenses, *προΐεις* (*με*) *ὄφρ' ἂν ἑλοίμην*, ut acciperem, didst send me that *I might receive*, ω 334; hypothetically, in oratione obliqua, *στεῦτο νικησέμεν εἴπερ ἂν—ἀείδοιεν* (oratio recta would be *ἐάνπερ ἀείδωσι*), he stood and boasted that he would *conquer* even though (as he said) the Muses *should sing*, Β 597.—II. with indic., (1) past tense (supposition contrary to fact), sumtio falsi, *οὐκ ἂν τόσσα θεοπροπέων ἀγόρευες*, non tam multa vaticinatus loquereris, *wouldst* not *be talking* so much, disclosing (forsooth) the will of the gods, β 184; hypothetically, ε 39, quae—ne ex Troia quidem abstulisset, si incolumis rediisset, as he *would* not *have brought* away from Troy, had he returned home without mishap.—(2) with future, seldom, Χ 66, *αὐτὸν δ' ἂν πύματόν με—ἐρύουσι*, me ipsum postremo dilaceraverint, me last of all *shall* the dogs *rend*.—III. with subj., denoting that which is soon to take place, scarcely different from simple future.—(1) in principal sentences, *τάχ' ἄν ποτε θυμὸν ὀλέσσῃ*, soon *shall* he *lose* his life; thus esp. freq. with aor. subj., also (2) in dependent sen-

tence, ὃν δ' ἂν ἐγὼν—νοήσω, quem conspicatus ero, whomsoever I *shall have perceived*, Θ 10 (yet subj. pres., ἴῃ, τ 332); ὡς ἂν ἐγὼ εἴπω, quomodo ego locutus ero? how *shall I speak?* Α 510, ὄφρ' ἂν—τίσωσι, quoad honorabunt, until *they shall honor*.—"Αν and κέ in one sentence, ζ 259, ε 361. [⏑; but – by position before Ϝερύσαιτ', Θ 21; σϜῷ, Θ 406, where orig. initial consonants have disappeared.]

2. ἄν by apocope for ἀνά, before ν, Κ 298; before τ, Ε 167; before στόμα, ε 456; and in ἂν δέ, sc. ὤρνυτο, Γ 268, Ψ 755 (cf. 812, 709, and θ 110–118).

3. ἀν-, negative prefix, cf. Lat. in-, Eng. in-, un- (cogn. with ἄνευ, possibly with ἀνά), shortened before consonants to so-called ἀ privativum, which also (as ἀνα-) appears before vowels when in the ancient form a spirant, σ, Ϝ, or j, was heard: ἀνάϜεδνος, ἀϜαγής.

ἀνά, ἄν, before labials ἄμ (opp. κατά), *up, aloft*.—I. adv., ἀλλ' ἄνα, but *up! quick!* Σ 178, σ 13; *thereon*, Σ 562; *upon*, β 416; mixed, pouring *in* (upon the water) the wine, γ 390; often separated by tmesis from the verb to which it belongs.—II. prep., (1) with gen., ἀνὰ νηὸς (νεῶν) βαίνειν, *embark*, α 210.—(2) with dat., *aloft on, upon*, Α 15, Ο 152, ψ 275, Σ 177; ω 8, *to* each other.—(3) with acc., strictly per, *along* a line (contrast successively with κατά, *on different points of a surface*, passim per—; ἐν, with dat., *at one point within a given boundary*; εἰς, with acc., *to such a point*.—(1) of space, *aloft to*, or *in*, ἀναβαίνειν, χ 132; τιθέναι, Κ 466; *in* my breast, and rose *to* my mouth, ἀνὰ στόμα, Χ 452; ῥῖνας, ω 318; *along*, Κ 339; ἀν' ἰθύν, *straight forward*; (a) *throughout, along*, with verbs of motion, Ε 74, Κ 362, 298, Ο 657, 101, Ν 270, Ρ 257, Σ 546, Υ 319, Ψ 321, Ω 166, ψ 136, also figuratively, Ψ 716; (b) with other verbs, *throughout the confines of, over, amid*, ἀν' Ἑλλάδα, Ν 117, Β 575, β 291, ξ 286; ἀνὰ στόμ' ἔχειν, having (their names) *in* thy mouth, Β 250: ἀνὰ θυμὸν φρονεῖν, judge *in* one's soul; also, ὁρμαίνειν, θαμβεῖν, ὀίεσθαι; follg. the governed word, νεῶν ἀνά, ν 32.—(2) temporal, ἀνὰ νύκτα, per noctem, all night *through*, Ξ 80. [⏑ ⏑]

1. **ἄνα**, see ἀνά, I.

2. **ἄνα**, voc. from ἄναξ.

ἀνα-βαινέμεν, ἀμ-βαίνειν, -βήσομαι, -έβη, often in tmesi, *go up*, μ 77; with acc., *ascend* (*to*), οὐρανόν, ὑπερώια, ἅρματα; ζ 29, permeat homines, *goes abroad among* men; ἀνά τι, χ 132, 143; εἴς τι, Ξ 287, Π 184, χ 143, ε 470; with dat., Κ 493, per corpora ingredientes; ἐν δίφροισι, Ψ 132; ἐς δίφρον, Π 657, Χ 399; with gen., νηός (νεῶν), *embark upon*; also absolute (before taking ship for Troy), α 210, cf. Α 611; also trans. in tmesis, Α 143, τινά, *put on board*; cf. ο 475, ἀναβησάμενοι, *having taken us into their ship*.

ἀνά-βαλλε, **ἀμ-βαλλώμεθα**, (1) procrastinare, *postpone*, τ 584; tmesis, ρ 262; mid., Β 436.—(2) mid., ordiri, *make a prelude*, ἀείδειν, α 155, ρ 262.

ἀνα-βέβρῦχεν (βρέχω) ὕδωρ, scaturivit, *bubbled up*, Ρ 54† (v. l. ἀναβέβροχεν).

'Ανα-βησί-νεως, a Phaiakian, θ 113†.

ἀνά-βλησις (ἀναβάλλω), dilatio, *postponement*, Β 380. (Il.)

(ἀνα-βραχεῖν), aor. **ἀν-έβρᾰχε**, *rattled aloud*, Τ 13; *creaked aloud*, φ 48.

(ἀνα-βρόχω), only **ἀνα-βρόξειε**, μ 240, as often as *she gulped down*; and ἀναβροχέν, λ 586, vanished as if *sucked up*.

ἀνα-βρύζω, -βρύχω, see ἀναβέβρυχε, scaturivit.

(ἀνα-γιγνώσκω), only aor. ἔγνων, etc., agnoscere, *know again*, δ 250, τ 250; Ν 734, maxime vero ipse sentit, the fortunate possessor *knows* it best of all; λ 144, quomodo talem me agnoscat, *recognize* me for such as I am.

ἀναγκαίη (=ἀνάγκη), necessitas, *necessity, want*, Ζ 85; dat., *perforce*, Δ 300; αναγκαίηφι δαμέντες, Υ 143.

ἀναγκαῖος, η, ον, (ἀνάγκη), (1) violentus, *constraining*; ἦμαρ, day *of constraint*, servitus; μύθῳ, word *of force*, χρειοῖ, dira necessitate.—(2) coactus, *perforce*, δμῶες (captivi), πολεμισταί, inviti.

ἀνάγκη, necessitas, *constraint, necessity*, κρατερή; τινί ἐστι (with inf.), necesse est, Κ 418, Ω 667 (Ε 633, Υ 251); ἀνάγκῃ, vi, *of necessity*, κ 434, vel coacti; ὑπ' ἀνάγκης, out of *compulsion*. [⏑ – –]

ἀνα-γνάμπτω, only **ἀν-έγναμψαν**, retro curvabant, *unloosed*, and ἀνεγνάμφθη, *was bent back*, P 44.

ἀν-άγουσι, -άξω, aor. -ήγαγον, *bring up, conduct, carry to* a place.—(1) on land, δ 534, ξ 272, ρ 441 (to the interior), cf. Θ 203; producere, *bring forth*, σ 89.—(2) by water, on shipboard, τινά, τί, *carry away* (home, γ 272), N 627, Γ 48, Z 292; *despatch*, σ 115; *bring back*, O 29; *guide hither*, I 338; ἀνάγοντο (opp. κατάγοντο), *put to sea*, τ 202.

ἀνα-δέδρομε, imminebat, see ἀνατρέχω.

(ἀνα-δέρκω), **ἀν-έδρακεν** ὀφθαλμοῖσιν, aperuit oculos, *opened again* his eyes, Ξ 436†.

ἀνα-δέσμην (δέω) πλεκτήν, (twisted or plaited) *head-band*, X 469†. (See cut.)

(ἀνα-δέχομαι), only **ἀνεδέξατο**, excepit, *received*, E 619; and ipf. ἀνεδέγμεθα, suscepimus, *have undergone*, ρ 563.

(ἀνα-δύομαι), only in the forms **ἀνδύεται**, -εδύσετο, and 2 aor. -έδυ, -δύῃ, -δῦναι, emergere, *emerge*, ε 322; with gen., A 359, ε 337; with acc., *arose* to the wave (surface) of the sea, A 496; recedere, *draw back*, ι 377; εἰς, H 217; and acc. without prep., N 225, cf. 214, out of the combat.

ἀν-ά-εδνον (ἀ-ἔεδνα), *without bridal gifts*, I 146. (Il.) [⏑ ⏑ – ⏑]

ἀν-αείρω, imp. -**άειρε**, aor. ind. -άειρε, opt. -αείραι, inf. -αεῖραι, part. -αείρας—tollere, *lift up* (tmesis, H 130, X 399, χεῖρας, τεύχεα); limbs, θ 298; the opponent in wrestling, *carry off* a prize. (Il. Ψ.)

ἀνα-θηλήσει (θηλέω), revirescet, *shall bloom again*, A 236†.

ἀνα-θήματα (τίθημι), δαιτός, additamenta cenae, *ornaments, delights* of the banquet, α 152, φ 430. (Od.)

ἀνα-θρώσκων, exsultans, *bounding*, N 140†.

ἀν-αιδείης (ἀναιδής), gen. ἐπέβησαν, trod the path of *insolence*, χ 424; -είην ἐπιειμένος, I 372, clad in *impudence*.

ἀν-αιδής, ές, (αἰδώς), impudens, *insolent, shameless*, ρ 449, of the suitors; applied to inanimate objects, κυδοιμός, πέτρη, N 139, and λᾶας, λ 598.

ἀν-αίμονες (αἷμα), sanguine carentes, *bloodless*, i. e. without mortal blood, E 342†. [⏑ – ⏑ ⏑]

ἀν-αιμωτί (αἷμα), sine caede, *without bloodshed*, σ 149. [ῑ]

ἀναίνομαι, ipf. ἀναίνετο, aor. ἀνήνατο, ἠνήνατο, etc. (αἴνυμαι)—negare, *deny*, Σ 500, ξ 149, I 116; recusare, *refuse*, Σ 450, Ψ 204, I 585; spernere, *repel, reject* (opp. ὑποδέχεσθαι), H 93, σ 287, I 510, 679; γ 265, *spurn*.

ἀν-αιρέω, -ήσεσθαι, aor. -εῖλον, -ειλόμην, tollere, *take up*.—(1) *lift from the ground*, γ 453; mid., *take up for one's self*, οὐλοχύτας; *take up in one's arms*, Π 8; *lift up* and *sweep away*, υ 66.—(2) comprehendere, *lay hold of*, A 301, σ 16; mid., capere, *take*, arms, N 296; cloak, ξ 530; goblet, χ 9; *come to reason*, τ 22.—(3) accipere, *bear off*, prizes, Ψ 736; mid., 823, φ 117 (or in signification 2).—(4) conducere, *to take into one's service*, σ 357.

ἀν-αΐσσουσι, aor. ἀν-ήιξα, *spring up, rise suddenly* from a sitting posture, A 584, σ 40, for combat, etc., H 106, Ψ 203; *gush forth* (pr. only in this sense), X 148; with acc., *leap upon*, Ω 440.

ἀν-αίτιος (αἰτία), insons, *innocent*, Υ 297, υ 135.

ἀνα-καίω, always with πῦρ, only **ἀνέκαιε** (and -ον), accendit, *kindled*, ι 251 (υ 123). (Od.)

ἀνα-κεράννυμι, only **ἀνὰ-κέρασσεν**, aor., *filled and mixed*, γ 390†.

ἀνα-κηκίει, ipf. -κήκιε, *gush forth*. (Il.)

ἀνα-κλίνω, only 1 aor. act. (part. **ἀγκλίνας**) and pass. part., ἀνα-κλινθείς, reclino, *make to lean upon*.—(1) τινὰ πρός τι, σ 103; τόξον ποτὶ γαίῃ, *bracing* against the ground, Δ 113, cf. τ 577; *open*, doors (opp. ἐπιθεῖναι), λ 525, χ 156, Θ 395; ἀνακλινθείς, supinus, *leaning back*, ν 78, ι 371, δ 794.

ἀν-ακοντίζω, only ipf. **ἀνηκόντιζε**, *shot forth*, αἷμα, E 113†.

ἀνα-κόπτω, ipf. **ἀν-έκοπτε**, *shoved back*, φ 47†; see ὀχεύς.

ἀνα-κράζω, aor. **ἀν-έκρᾰγον**, since *I have once for all broken silence*, ξ 467†.

ἀνα-κρεμάννυμι, aor. part. **ἀγ-κρεμάσασα**, *after she had hung it up*, α 440†.

ἀνακτορίῃσι (ἄναξ) ὕεσσιν, *belonging to the master*, ο 397†.

ἀνα-κυμβαλιάζω, **ἀν-εκυμβᾰλίαζον,** *fell rattling over*, Π 379†. [ῐ]

ἀνα-λέγω, ipf. **ἄλ-λεγον,** aor. inf. ἀλλέξαι, colligere, *gather*, Φ 321. (Il.)

ἀν-αλκείῃσι δαμέντες, overmastered *by fear*, Ζ 74. (Il.)

ἄν-αλκις, ιδος, acc. -ιδα (-ιν, γ 375), ignavus, *defenseless, cowardly*, Ο 62.

ἄν-αλτον (alere), insatiabilem, *insatiable*, σ 114. (Od.)

ἀνα-λύω, ipf. iter. **-ἀλ-λύεσκεν,** part. ἀλ-λύουσαν, aor. ἀν-έλυσαν, solvere, *untie*, ι 178 (in tmesi); retexere, *unravel*, β 105. (Od.)

ἀνᾰ-μαιμάει πῦρ ἄγκεα, grassatur per, *rages through*, Υ 490†.

ἀνᾰ-μάξεις, fut. (μάσσω) σῇ κεφαλῇ, *shalt wipe off* on thy own head, *expiate with* thy life, τ 92†.

ἀνα-μένω, aor. **ἀν-έμεινα,** exspectavi, *was awaiting*, τ 342†.

ἀνα-μετρήσαιμι (μετρέω), aor., emetirer, *remeasure the road to*, μ 428†.

ἀνα-μίγνυμι, see ἀναμίσγω.

ἀνα-μιμνήσκω, **ἀν-έμνησας,** aor., commonuisti, *hast reminded*, ταῦτα, γ 211†.

ἀνα-μίμνω, only ipf., manere, *await*, Λ 171; *stand fast*, Π 363. (Il.)

ἀνα-μίσγω, ipf. and aor. (tmesis), ἀμμίξας, admiscere, *to mix with, mix together*, κ 235, δ 41, Ω 529.

ἀνα-μορμύρω, ipf. iter. **ἀν-εμορμύρεσκε,** efferbuit, *seethed up*, μ 238†.

ἀνα-νέομαι, **ἀν-νεῖται,** oritur, *rises*, κ 192†.

ἀνα-νεύω, only ipf. and aor., abnuere, *deny, refuse*, Ζ 311; with inf., Π 252; ὀφρύσι, vetare, *forbid*, ι 468; without inf., φ 129; καρήατι, Χ 205.

ἄν-αντα, sursum, *up-hill*, Ψ 116†.

ἄναξ, κτος, (Ϝάναξ), voc. ὦ ἄνα, of gods; dat. pl. ἀνάκτεσι, ο 557, tutor, dominus, *master, ruler*.—(1) as *possessor*, δ 87.—(2) as *ruler*, (a) of gods, Ζεῦ ἄνα, Διὶ Κρονίωνι ἄνακτι, etc.; Apollo, Η 23; κλῦθι ἄναξ, Π 514; Poseidon, Hephaistos, ἀν. ἐνέρων Ἀιδωνεύς; (b) of men, e.g., Ι 164; common phrase, ἄναξ ἀνδρῶν, Α 172, Α 7.

ἀνα-ξηραίνω, **ἀγ-ξηράνῃ,** aor. subj., exsiccat, *dry up*, Φ 347†.

ἀν-οίγεσκον, see ἀνοίγνυμι, aperiebant.

ἀνα-πάλλω, only (1) aor. part. **ἀμπεπᾰλών,** vibratam, *having poised and drawn back*, Γ 355.—(2) mid. ἀναπάλλεται, Ψ 692, aor. ἀν-έπαλτο, exsiluit, *sprang up*, Θ 85.

ἀνα-παύω, aor. **ἀν-έπαυσε,** τινά τινος, arcuit, *hinders from*, Ρ 550†.

ἀνα-πείρω, aor. part. **ἀμ-πείραντες,** transfixa, *having spitted*, Β 426†.

ἀνα-πεπταμένας, see ἀναπετάννυμι, apertas.

ἀνα-πετάννυμι, expando, *spread out*; only (1) ἀνὰ δ' ἱστία—**πέτασσαν,** *unfurled, shook out* the sails, Α 480, etc.—(2) ἀνα-πεπταμένας, apertas, *open* (opp. ἐπικεκλιμένας, Μ 121), θύρας.

ἀνα-πηδάω, aor. ἀμ-πήδησε, exsiluit, *sprang up out of*, Λ 379†.

ἀνα-πίμπλημι, only fut. **-πλήσειν** and 1 aor., explere, *fill up, accomplish* (one's fate), Θ 34, Λ 263, Δ 170; *endure* woes, ε 207, 302, Ο 132.

ἀνα-πλέω, fut. **-πλεύσεσθαι** and ipf., *sail up*, στεινωπόν, ad fretum, μ 234; ἐς Τροίην.

ἀνά-πνευσις (πνέω) πολέμοιο *recovering of breath, respite* from battle, Λ 801. (Il.)

ἀνα-πνέω, ipf. and aor. **-έπνευσα** and ἄμ-πνυε, pass. ἀμ-πνύνθη, and plupf. mid. ἄμ-πνυτο, respirare, *respire, take breath, come to one's senses*, Π 42; τινός, *receive from* (only 1 aor. act.).

ἀν-άποινον (ἄποινα), non redemptam, *without ransom*, Α 99†. [ᾰ]

ἀνα-πρήσας (πρήθω) δάκρυ, lacrimas exprimens, *letting tears flow*, β 81.

ἀν-άπτω, religare, *attach*, of cables, μ 162; **ἀν-ῆφθω** imp. aor. pass., religantor ad mâlum, μ 51; suspendere, *hang up*, γ 274; μῶμον, *impute fault*, β 86.

ἀνά-πυστα (πεύθομαι), nota, *notorious*, λ 274†. [ᾰ]

ἀνα-ροιβδέω, see ἀναρροιβδέω.

ἀν-αρπάζω, only aor. **-ήρπασε,** -αρπάξας, eripere, *snatch out*, Χ 276; *carry off*, Ι 564; *snatch away*, Π 437, esp. of sudden gusts of wind, δ 515.

ἀνα-ρ-ρήξας, and -ρήξειε (ῥήγνυμι), lacerare, *tear open*; evertere, *destroy*, Η 461. (Il.)

ἀνα-ρ-ριπτέω, only pres. and ipf. (ἀν-ερρίπτουν, ν 78), aor. -έρριψαν—ἅλα (πηδῷ, κ 130, is to be supplied), *turn up* with oar-blades; cf. torquent spumas et caerula verrunt. (Od.)

ἀνα-(ρ)-ροιβδέω, -εροίβδησε, devorare, *swallows up*, μ 104. (Od.)

ἀν-άρσιοι (ἄρω), alienati, *not fitting, incongruous*, hence *hostile* (opp. θυμήρης), (Od., Ω 365).

ἄν-αρχοι (ἀρχός), sine duce, *without leader*, B 703, 726.

ἀνα-σεύω, **ἀνέσσυτο,** 2 aor. mid., exsiluit, *sprang forth*, Λ 458†.

ἀνα-σπάω, **ἀν-εσπάσατο,** ἔγχος, *drew* his spear *forth*, N 574†.

ἄνασσα, ης, (ἄναξ), domina, *mistress, queen* (only ζ 149 of a mortal).

ἀνάσσω (ἄναξ), fut. -άξω, aor. mid. -άξασθαι (ipf. ἄνασσε), tueri, A 7, dominari, *be sovereign, rule, reign over*.—(1) persons ; comm. with dat., A 180, also with μετά, Δ 61, ἐν, η 62; with gen., K 33; with acc. (duration of time), ἀνάξασθαι γένεα, *ruled* through three generations of men, γ 245.—(2) country and city; with gen., A 452, ρ 443; with dat., B 108; with ἐν, Π 572, λ 276.—(3) κτήμασιν, α 117, cf. δ 93; τιμῆς, Υ 181; *be master of* Priam's sovereignty over the Trojans, ω 30; pass., *be ruled*, τινί, δ 177.

ἀνα-σταδόν, adv. (cf. σταδίῃ), assurgendo, *standing upright*, Ψ 469. (Il.)

ἀνα-στεναχίζω, **ἀν-εστενάχιζε,** ipf., ingemuit, *wailed aloud*, K 9†.

ἀνα-στενάχουσι, and ipf. ἐστενάχοντο, lamentari, *bemoan, bewail aloud; τινά*, Ψ 211. (Il.)

ἀνα-στοναχίζω, v. l. for ἀναστεναχίζω.

ἀνα-στρέφω, only aor. opt. **ἀν-στρέψειαν,** everterent, *overturn*, Ψ 436; and -στρέφομαι, γαῖαν, peragro, *wander through*, ν 326.

ἀνα-στρωφῶν (-στρωφάω), versans, *turning it over and over*, φ 394†.

ἀνα-σχέμεν, ἀνά-σχεο, see ἀνέχω, perferre.

ἀνασχόμενος, -σχέσθαι, -σχών, tollens, see ἀνέχω.

ἀνα-τέλλω, aor. **ἀνέτειλε,** emisit, *caused to spring up* (as food), E 777†.

ἀνα-τίθημι, fut. **ἀναθήσει,** ἐλεγχείην, ignominia afficiet, *will heap* insult upon me, X 100†.

ἀνα-τλάς, part. of aor. **ἀνέτλην,** *endure, withstand* (poison), κ 327. (Od.)

ἀνα-τρέπομαι, aor. **ἀνετράπετο,** eversus est, *fell backward*, Z 64. (Il.)

ἀνα-τρέχω, only pf. **-δέδρομε,** and aor. **-έδραμεν, -ον.**—(1) *run up, spout up*, P 297; wales *started up* under the blows, Ψ 717; Σ 437, *shot up*; ε 412, *up rises* the sheer rock.—(2) *run back;* Λ 354, cito immensum.

ἄν-αυδος (αὐδή), mutus, *speechless*, ε 456. (Od.)

ἀνα-φαίνω, only pres. act. and mid., and aor. act. -φῆναι, monstrare.—(1) *were feeding* by turns *the flame* (to give light), σ 310.—(2) *disclose*, A 87; *displaying*, Υ 411; *show* loquacity, δ 159; *betray*, δ 254.—(3) mid., *appear*.

ἀνᾰ-φανδόν (-φαίνω), Π 178†, and **-φανδά** (Od.), *openly, before the eyes of all*.

ἀνα-φέρω, only aor. 1 **ἀν-ένεικα,** *brought up*, λ 625, and -ενείκατο, *drew a long-drawn sigh*, T 314.

ἀνα-φλύω, ipf. **ἀνὰ δ' ἔφλῠε,** ebulliebat, waves *were boiling up*, Φ 361†.

ἀνα-φράζομαι, aor. opt. **ἀμφράσσαιτο,** agnosceret, *should recognize*, τ 391†.

ἀνα-χάζομαι, pres., ipf., part. aor. -χασσάμενος, recedo, *was retiring*, E 600; also with ἄψ, ὀπίσω, τυτθόν, πολλόν.

ἀνα-χέω, **ἀνὰ-χεῦε,** aor., infudit, *poured therein*, ι 209†.

ἀνα-χωρείτω, pres., fut. aor. 1, recedo, *withdraw*, χ 270; also with ἄψ, ρ 461, K 210.

ἀνα-ψύχειν (ψῦχος), pres. ipf., and K 575 -έψυχθεν, 3 sing. aor. pass., refrigerare, *cool*, δ 568; E 795, *assuage, alleviate*. [⏑– ––]

ἀνδάνει (Ϝανδάνω, (σϜ)ἀδύς, suavis), ipf. ἑήνδανε (ἐϜήνδανε), ἥνδανε, pf. ἑαδότα (ϜεϜαδότα), aor. εὔαδε (for ἔϜαδε) and ἅδε, placere, *please, delight, gratify*; esp. with θυμῷ, κ 373; with two datives, A 24, O 674 (π 398, by speech); σ 422, gratum, *acceptable*.

ἄν-διχα, *asunder*, Π 412; *in twain*. (Il.)

ἀνδρ-άγρια (ἄγρη), spolia, *spoils of arms*, Ξ 509†.

'Ανδρ-αιμονίδης, i. e. Θόας, H 168†.

'Ανδρ-αίμων, ονος, king of Αἰτωλοί in Καλυδών, B 638, ξ 499.

ἀνδρακάς, viritim, *man by man, each*, ν 14†. (v. l. ἄνδρα καθ'.)

ἀνδρα-πόδεσσι, mancipiis, *slaves*, Η 475†.

ἀνδρ-αχθέσι (ἄχθος), ingentibus, *with man-burdening* stones, κ 121†.

ἀνδρεϊ-φόντῃ (φένω), homicidae, *man-slaying*, Ἐνυαλίῳ, Β 651. (Il.)

ἄνδρεσσι, dat. pl. from ἀνήρ.

ἀνδρο-κμήτῳ (κάμνω), manibus facto, *wrought by men's hands*, Λ 371†.

ἀνδρο-κτἄσίη (κτείνω), only gen. sing. pl., nom. pl., caedes, *slaughter of men* (in battle). (λ 612, Il.)

Ἀνδρο-μάχη, daughter of Ἠετίων in Θήβῃ ὑποπλακίῃ; wife of Hektor, ἄλοχος πολύδωρος, λευκώλενος, Ζ 371, 395, Χ 460, etc. (Il.)

ἀνδρόμεος, ον, (ἀνήρ), humanus, *human* flesh, ι 297; pieces of human flesh, ι 374; blood, χ 19; body, Ρ 571; ὅμιλος, tumult *of men*, tumultuous crowd, Λ 538.

ἀνδροτῆτα (ἀνδροτής), *valor* (better reading, as regards sense, than ἀδροτῆτα, *vigor*, but unmetrical).

ἀνδρο-φάγοιο (φαγεῖν), Κύκλωπος, homines devorans, *eating man's flesh*, κ 200. [ᾰ]

ἀνδρο-φόνος, ον, (φένω), viros occidens, *man-slaying*, Ἄρης, Ἕκτωρ, χεῖρες, Achilleus, Ω 479, vegetable poison, α 261.

ἀν-δύεται, see ἀναδύω, *shun*.

ἀν-εγείρεις, pres., and 1 aor. ἀνέγειρα, excitare, *wake up*, ἐξ ὕπνου, ἐκ λεχέων, δ 730; κ 172, *encouraged*.

ἀν-έγνω, aor. from ἀναγιγνώσκω, agnovi.

ἀν-εδέγμεθα, ipf. from ἀναδέχομαι, suscepimus, *we have sustained*.

ἀν-έδραμον, aor. from ἀνατρέχω, exortae sunt, *started up*.

ἀν-έεδνος, see ἀνάεδνος, sine dote.

ἀν-είργω, ipf. **ἀνέεργον** (for ἀνέϝεργον), cohibebat, *was holding back*, Γ 77; also ὀπίσσω, Ρ 752. (Il.)

ἀν-έζω, only 1 aor. part. **ἀν-έσαντες,** *having placed him upon*, Ν 657; opt. ἀνέσαιμι, should *bring upon the nuptial bed*, Ξ 209. (Il.)

ἄν-ειμι, -εισι, (ἰέναι), subire, (1) *go up*, κ 146, 274; ἅμ' ἠελίῳ ἀνιόντι, oriente, *with the dawn*, ψ 362.—(2) redire, *return*, Χ 499, Ζ 480; σὺν νηΐ, κ 332; ἄψ, Τ 290.—(3) adire ad, Χ 492.

ἀν-είμονος (εἷμα), gen., veste carentis, *destitute of bedclothing*, γ 348†.

ἀν-είρεαι (ἔρομαι), ipf. ἀνείρετο, interrogo, *inquire*, δ 420, τινά τι; with μεταλλᾶν, α 231; τί, ask respecting, ν 238.

ἀν-εκτός, -όν, (ἔχω), tolerabilis, *endurable*, υ 83; usually with οὐκέτ', also ἀνεκτῶς, ι 350, in a fashion no longer to be endured.

ἀν-ελθών, aor. part. from ἀνέρχομαι, reversus.

ἀν-έλκων, ipf. ἄν-ελκε, attrahere, *draw up, draw*, Μ 434, φ 128, 150; *draw back*, Λ 375; mid., *draw out and recover* (one's spear), χ 97; *tear out* (one's hair), Χ 77.

ἀν-ελών, see ἀναιρέω.

ἄνεμος, ου, ventus, *wind*; ζαής, λιγέων, δυσαής; ἀνέμου ἴς, hurricane, τ 186, θύελλα, ἄελλα, πνοιαί, ἀήτης, ἰωή, βία, ἀυτμένα; as symbol of swiftness, Μ 207, Ω 342, Κ 437; ταμίης, Aiolos, κ 21. Chief winds, νότος, εὖρος; see also Ψ 195, ε 383.

ἀνεμο-σκεπέων (σκέπας, ε 443), *sheltering against the wind*, Π 224†.

ἀνεμο-τρεφές (τρέφω), ventis auctus, *swollen by the wind*, Ο 625, Λ 256; made from a tree *toughened by exposure to wind*.

ἀνεμώλιος, ον, (for ἀνεμώνιος), futilis, *useless*, Υ 123; vanus, *vain*, Ε 216; **-ια** βάζειν, Δ 355; adv. -ιον, Φ 474.

Ἀνεμώρεια, ἡ, town in **Φωκίς,** Β 521†.

ἀνενείκατο, see ἀναφέρω, respiravit.

ἀν-έπαλτο, see ἀναπάλλω, vibravit.

ἀν-ερείπομαι, only aor. **ἀν-ηρείψαντο,** abripuerunt, *snatched away*, α 241.

ἀν-ερύω, aor. **ἀνά** θ' ἱστία λεῦκ' **ἐρύσαντες,** *hoist*, μ 402. (Od.)

ἀν-ερχόμενον, aor. -ελθών, (1) *go up*, cf. ἄνειμι, κ 97; *shoot up*, ζ 163.—(2) *return*, ἄψ, Δ 392, Ζ 187.

ἀν-ερωτάω, ipf. **ἀνειρώτων,** *questioned repeatedly*, δ 251†.

ἀν-έσαιμι, ἀνέσαντες, imponerem, see ἀνέζω.

ἄν-εσαν, aor., **ἀν-έσει** fut., from ἀνίημι.

ἀν-έσσυτο, aor. from ἀνασεύω, exsiluit.

ἀν-έστιος (ἑστία), *hearthless, homeless*, I 63†.

ἄνευ (ἀν- privative, in-, un-), with gen., sine, *without*; θεοῦ, invito deo, β 372, cf. O 213; δηΐων, procul ab hostibus, N 556.

ἄνευθεν, -θε,—(1) procul, *far away*, B 27, Δ 277, X 300 (opp. ἔγγυθι), Ψ 241; κιών, A 35; ἰόντος, Ψ 452.—(2) sine, with gen., *without*, X 39, π 239; θεοῦ, invito deo, E 185, cf. Π 89; procul a, *far from*, κ 554; μέγα ἄν. νῶιν, remotissimum a nobis, X 88.

ἀ-νέφελος αἴθρη, innubilus aether, *cloudless* blue sky, ζ 45†. [ᾱ-σνεφ.]

ἀν-έχω, aor. ἀνέσχον (inf. ἀνασχέμεν) and ἀνέσχεθον (inf. ἀνσχεθέειν), mid. fut. ἀνέξομαι (inf. ἀνσχήσεσθαι), aor. ἀνεσχόμην (imp. ἀνάσχεο, ἄνσχεο), sustinere, *hold up*. I. act. τί, Ξ 499, X 80, χ 297, ρ 291; χεῖρας, in combat (boxing), σ 89; in prayer, θεοῖς, A 450; σκῆπτρον, in making oath, H 412; *maintain*, τ 111; *hold back*, Ψ 426; *jut forth, emerge*, ε 320, P 310.—II. mid. (1) *hold one's self up, bear up, endure*, E 285, π 277 with part.; A 586, Ψ 587, *forbear*; λ 375, *stay awake*.—(2) *hold up before one*, σκῆπτρον, K 321; χεῖρας, σ 100; δούρατα; often ἀνασχόμενος, exsurgens, *lifting up* arm for striking, Γ 362.—(3) perferre, *endure, tolerate*, τί, χ 423, η 32; *entertain*, ρ 13; τινὰ ἄλγε' ἔχοντα, E 895; with part., *would gladly* sit, δ 595.

ἀ-νεψιός, ὁ, (nepos), *sister's son, nephew*, O 422.

ἄν-εω (ἄϝημι), mutus, *speechless*.—(1) pl. from ἄνεως; muti, ἐγένεσθε, etc., B 323, I 30, β 240.—(2) adv., ψ 93, ἧστο.

ἀν-ήγαγον, aor. from ἀνάγω.

ἀν-ήῃ, 3 sing. aor. subj. from ἀνίημι.

ἀν-ήϊον, see ἄνειμι.

ἀν-ήκεστος, ον, (ἀκέομαι), insanabilis, *inappeasable*, E 394. (Il.)

ἀν-ηκούστησε (ἀκούω), οὐδ' — πατρός, obsequium detrectavit, *was rebellious*, O 236. (Il.)

ἀν-ήμελκτοι (ἀμέλγω), *unmilked*, ι 439†.

ἀν-ήνοθεν (ἄνθος), perf., ebullivit, *gushed forth*, Λ 26†. See ἐνήνοθε.

ἀν-ηνύστῳ (ἀνύω) ἐπὶ ἔργῳ, *endless, aimless*, π 111†.

ἀν-ήνορα (ἀνήρ), acc., non virilem, *unmanly*, κ 301. (Od.)

ἀνήρ, -έρος, ἀνδρός, dat. pl. ἀνδράσι, ἄνδρεσσι (perhaps ϝανήρ, P 65, Λ 371; cognate with Sabine word nero).—(1) vir, *man*; (a) as distinguished from γυνή, ο 163; (b) in age, λ 449; (c) emphatically, *man indeed, hero*, E 529, I 189; cf. in combat, Δ 472; (d) of occupation and nationality; with ἰητρός, Λ 514, ἐλαφηβόλος, Σ 319; νομῆες, αἰπόλοι, χαλκῆες, ἐπακτῆρες; Σίντιες; δήμου, unus e plebe, B 198.—(2) maritus, *husband*, λ 327, ω 196, α 292, ζ 181.—(3) homo, *human being*, often with βροτοί, θνητοί, *among mortals*, ρ 354; πατὴρ ἀνδρῶν τε θεῶν τε, A 544; opp. gods, ε 119; opp. giants, φ 303, κ 120. [ᾱ in arsi, and in trisyllabic forms.]

ἀν-ήροτος (ἀρόω), non culta, *unploughed*, ι 109. (Od.)

ἀν-ήφθω, perf. pass. imp. from ἀνάπτω, alligantor.

Ἄνθεια, town in Μεσσήνη, I 151. (Il.)

Ἀνθεμίδης, Σιμοείσιος, son of Ἀνθεμίων, Δ 488†. [– ⏑ ⏑ –]

Ἀνθεμίων, ωνος, father of Σιμοείσιος in Troia, Δ 473†.

ἀνθεμόεντος, ι, (ἄνθος), floridus, *flowery*, B 467; *adorned with flowers*, λέβης, γ 440; κρητῆρα, ω 275; cf. cut No. 98.

ἀνθερεῶνος, ῶνα, masc. (ἄνθος), mentum, *chin*; to take by the chin in token of supplication, A 501.

ἀνθερίκων, gen. pl. (ὁ ἀνθέριξ), ἐπ'—, per aristas, *over the ears of grain*, Υ 227†.

ἀνθέω, **ἀνθῆσαι**, aor., *bloom*, λ 320†.

Ἀνθηδών, όνος, town in Βοιωτία, B 508†.

ἄνθινον (ἄνθος) εἶδαρ, floridum cibum, *food of flowers, flowers as food*, ι 84†. [– ⏑ ⏑]

ἀνθ-ίσταντο, ipf., aor. ἀντ-έστη, resistere, *resist*, Π 305, Υ 70. (Il.)

ἄνθος, εος, (ad-or), flos, *blossom, flower*, I 542; fig., N 484; *young shoots, youthful herbage*, ι 449.

ἀνθρακιήν, τήν, (ἀνθρακιή), prunae, *heap of glowing coals*, I 213†. [– ⏑ ⏑ –]

ἄνθρωπος, ου, (ϝαν. ἀνήρ, β 65, λ 365, Σ 288), homo, *man*, (opp. to gods, Σ 107, γ 48; to animals, ζ 125, Π 315);

homines, *mankind, the world*, ρ 354, I 340, Ξ 361, Ω 535, ψ 125, α 95, cf. ν 123 and θ 29; quisquam, *any one*, ν 400.

ἀνιάζω (ἀνίη), ipf. ἀνίαζον, pertaesum esse, *be disgusted with, weary of*, δ 460, 598, Σ 300: θυμῷ, indignari, *indignant, grieved in heart*, Φ 270, χ 87; trans. *annoy, distress*, Ψ 721, τ 323. [ῐ]

ἀνιάω (ἀνίη), ἀνιήσω, pass. ἀνιᾶται, ἀνιηθείς, act., taedio afficere, *incommode*, υ 178, τ 66; pass., *be annoyed, wearied*, γ 117; τινί, α 133, ο 335; B 291, 'tis indeed hard to *return out of weariness*. [⏑ – – –]

ἀν-ιδρωτί, sine sudore, *without sweat*, O 228†. [⏑ – – –]

ἀνίη, ης, molestia, *burden, weariness*, ο 394, υ 52; μ 223, unendurable *bane; trouble, plague*, η 192, ρ 446. (Od.) [ῑ]

ἀνιηθείς, aor. pass. from ἀνιάω, pertaesus.

ἀν-ίημι, 2 sing. **-ἱεῖς**, 2 sing. opt. -ιείης, fut. -ήσω, aor. 1. -ῆκα, -έηκεν, 2 -εσαν, subj. 3 sing. -ίῃ (conjectural false reading, ἐσεῖ, σ 265), -ήῃ, mittere. —(1) *send forth*, δ 568; μ 105, *vomit forth*.—(2) *loose*, δεσμόν; *open*, πύλας (mid. κόλπον, *laying bare* her bosom, X 80; αἶγας, *skin*, β 300); *let go*, σ 265, ὕπνος, B 34; ω 440, *forsake; give reins to*, E 880.—(3) *loose upon, urge on*, incitare, Υ 118, β 185; ἐπί τινι, against, E 405, 882; with inf., Ξ 362; excitare, *stir up against, impel*, P 705, esp. θυμός τινα, also with inf., X 252, ξ 465. [ἀνῖει, ἀνῑέμενος; elsewh. ῐ.]

ἀνῑηρός (ἀνίη), molestus, *troublesome*, ρ 220, 377; ἀνιηρέστερον, *the more troublous for him*, β 190. (Od.)

ἀ-νιπτό-ποδες, Σελλοί, illotis pedibus, *with unwashed feet*, Π 235†.

ἀ-νίπτοισι (νίπτω), illotis, *unwashed*, Z 266†.

ἀν-ίστημι, I. ipf. **-ίστη**, fut. ἀν(α)-στήσω, aor. 1. -έστησε, imp. ἄνστησον, part. ἀνστήσασα, excicre, *bid or make stand up*, η 163; χειρός, *supporting with his hand*, ξ 319; *disperse*, A 191; *wake up*, K 32; *call to life* the dead, Ω 756; *deport, transfer*, ζ 7; excitare, *stir up to battle*, O 64, Σ 358.—II. **ἀνίσταμαι**, fut. -στήσεσθαι, aor. -έστην (du. ἀνστήτην, 3 pl. -έσταν, part. -στάς ἀν-στᾶσα, inf. ἀνστήμεναι, for imp. see ἄνα under ἀνά-, I.), surgere, *rise up*.—(1) from seat (of whatever sort), I 195, ε 195, Σ 410, or from bed, Ξ 336, υ 124. —(2) for *action* (of whatever sort), θ 258, μ 439, with inf., incipere, υ 380; *to speak*, τοῖσι δ' ἀνέστη, *rose up* (before or among them), cf. τοῖσι δ' ἀνιστάμενος μετέφη, A 58; for combat, battle, δ 343, B 694; τινί, σ 334; ἄν repeated, Ψ 709; freq. in tmesi, e. g. θ 118.—(3) from sick-bed, O 287; from grave, Φ 56.

ἀν-ίσχων, ἴσχοντες, part., tollens, *raising*, E 798, O 369; ἀνὰ δ' ἴσχεο = ἀνάσχεο, *hold thyself erect*, i. e. *be of good courage*.

ἀν-ιχνεύων (ἴχνος), investigans, *tracking back*, X 192.

ἀν-νεῖται, see ἀνανέομαι, oritur.

ἀ-νοήμων, imprudens, *unreflecting*, β 270. (Od.)

ἀν-οίγω, **ἀνέῳγε**, ἀνῷγε, ipf., and iter. ἀναοίγεσκον, aperio, *open*, κ 389, Ξ 168, Ω 228.

ἀν-ολέθρους (ὄλεθρος), incolumes, *untouched by destruction*, N 761†.

ἄνομαι, see ἄνω.

ἄ-νοον, κραδίην, quam excors fuisti, *silly, foolish* heart, Φ 441†.

ἀνόπαια, see ὀπαῖα.

ἀν-όρνυμι, see ἀνῶρτο.

ἀν-ορούω, only aor. **-όρουσεν**, **-σαν**, **-σας**, exsilio, *spring up*, ἐκ θρόνων, ὕπνου, ἐς δίφρον, P 130; Ἠέλιος, climbed swiftly up the sky, γ 1.

ἀ-νόστιμον (νόστος), reditu interclusum, ἔθηκαν, reddiderunt, *cut off his return*, δ 182†.

ἀ-νόστους (νόστος), reditu carentes, ἔθηκαν, *made void their return*, ω 528†.

ἄ-νουσοι (νοῦσος), sine morbo, *without disease*, ξ 255†.

ἀν-ούτατος (οὐτάω), non cominus vulneratus, *unwounded*, Δ 540†.

ἀν-ουτητί, nor did any one draw near *without inflicting a wound*, X 371†. [ῑ]

ἀν-στάς, -στᾶσα, -στησον, -στήτην, στήσεσθαι, etc., see ἀνίστημι.

ἀν-στρέψειαν, see ἀναστρέφω.

ἀν-σχεθέειν, -σχεο, -σχήσεσθαι, etc., see ἀνέχω.

ἀν-σχετά (ἀνέχω), οὐκ, intolerabilia, *unendurable*, β 63†.

ἄντ' = **ἄντα** (old instr. case, *ἀντί*, German prefix ant, ent), adversum, *opposite;* adv., and prep. with gen., (1) e regione, *in the vicinity of*, Β 626; coram, *in presence of, before*, ζ 141, she remained standing *before* him, χ 232; α 334, holding the veil *before* her cheeks; *straight forward*, *ἰδεῖν*, *τιτύσκεσθαι*; *ἄντα ἐῴκει*, properly ore (instr.) similis fuit, was like him *in countenance.*—(2) in hostile sense, adversus, contra, *against*, *ἰέναι*, Υ 75, 355; *ἐλθεῖν*, *πολεμίζειν*, *στήμς*, *ἔγχος ἀεῖραι*; *ἀνασχομένω*, having drawn back their hands (to strike); δ 159, *before thee, to thy face.*

ἀντ-άξιος, *ον*, aequi pretii, *equivalent to*, with gen., Ι 401, Λ 514. (Il.)

ἀντάω (*ἄντα*), ipf. *ἤντεον*, fut. *ἀντήσω*, aor. *ἤντησα*, occurrere, *meet*, Δ 375, δ 201; *τινί*, Η 423, Ζ 399; *τινός*, *encounter*, *ὀπωπῆς*, δ 327; Η 158, then might he soon *take part in battle*, i. e. *find an opponent; meet in hostile encounter*, π 254.

Ἄντεια, *δῖα*, wife of *Προῖτος*, Ζ 160†.

ἄντην (*ἄντα*), strictly, *the face*, *εἰσιδέειν*, Τ 15, Ω 223, cf. ε 77; acc. of specification, *in respect to countenance*, with *ἐναλίγκιος*, *εἰκέλη*; acc. of direction, *face to face, openly*, co-oram, palam, Α 187, Κ 158, Ο 247, Ω 464, γ 120, ζ 221, θ 213, 158; *in battle*, Λ 590, Σ 307, Χ 109; *forward*, Θ 399; *in front*, Μ 152.

Ἀντηνορίδης, son of *Ἀντήνωρ*, *Ἑλικάων*, Γ 123; pl. Λ 59, sons of Antenor.

Ἀντήνωρ, *ορος*, son of *Αἰσυήτης*, husband of *Θεανώ*, Γ 262, Λ 59, 262.

ἄντηστιν (*ἀντάω*), *κατ'* —, *at the junction* of the men's and women's apartments, *opposite the entrance of the house* (see table III. at end of volume), ex adverso, υ 387†.

ἀντί (locative from *ἄντα*), prep. with gen., strictly (1) *in the face of*, adversum, Ο 415, Φ 481; δ 115, *before the eyes.* — (2) placed over against as equivalent, loco, *instead of*, Ι 116, θ 546, υ 307, χ 290.

ἀντί', ἀντία, see *ἀντίος*.

ἀντι-άνειραι, *-ανείρας*, *matching-men*, of Amazons, Γ 189. (Il.)

ἀντιάω, **ἀντιόω** (*ἀντί*), fut. *ἀντιάσω*, *ἀντιόω*; aor. *ἀντιάσαιμεν*, etc., occurrere, *meet*, η 293, μ 88, ν 312, Κ 551, *encounter*, Ο 297 (with dat., Ζ 127, Φ 431, σ 147), with gen., Η 231; Ν 290, *strike; have or take part, share*, with acc., only Α 31; elsewh. with gen., Α 67, Μ 356, Ν 215, Υ 125, Ψ 643 (mid. Ω 62), α 25; φ 402, would that he might *enjoy* just as much good luck as —, χ 28; ω 56, *participate in* the funeral ceremonies of her son.

ἀντι-βίοις, dat. pl. (*βία*), adversis, *hostile*, *ἐπέεσσι*, Α 304, σ 415; **ἀντίβιον,** adv., with verbs of combating, Γ 20, 435, Λ 386; so also **ἀντιβίην,** Α 278, Ε 220, Φ 226. (Both advs. only Il.)

ἀντι-βολέω (*ἀντί*, *βάλλω*), *-ήσω*, aor. **ἀντι-βόλησε,** *come in the way of*, cf. *ἀντιάω*, occurrere.—(1) *meet accidentally, encounter*, Π 790, Ω 375, ζ 275, η 16; with gen., only δ 547, σ 272 *shall be my lot*, φ 306; elsewh. with dat., e. g. Η 114.—(2) *meet intentionally* (a) as friend, Κ 546, η 19, κ 277; (b) as foe, Λ 365, Μ 465; *τινί*, Π 847, ν 229.—(3) interesse, *have part in*, *μάχης*, Δ 342; *φόνῳ*, *τάφῳ*.

ἀντί-θεος, 3, *godlike*, distinguished in rank, might, size, beauty; common epithet of kings, Ε 663; heroes, Ι 623, Ω 257, α 21, ο 90; Odysseus's companions, δ 571; nations, ζ 241, Μ 408; suitors, ξ 18; Penelope, λ 117; Polyphemos, α 70. [ῐ]

ἀντί-θυρον (*θύρη*), *κατ'* —, *opposite the entrance* (out of doors), π 159†. [ῐ]

Ἀντί-κλεια, daughter of *Αὐτόλυκος*, wife of *Λαέρτης*, λ 85, ο 358.

Ἄντι-κλος, name of a Greek warrior in the wooden horse, δ 286.

ἀντι-κρύς, ἀντικρύ, ex adverso, *opposite.* — (1) coram, *face to face with*, Ε 130, 819, Η 362; *Ἕκτορος*, Θ 310. — (2) *straightforward*, Ν 137; *outright, utterly*, Π 116, 380, Ψ 673, 867, κ 162; often joined with foll. prep., e. g. *παραί*, *διά*, *κατά*, *ἀνά*; also in compounds, e. g. *διέσχε*, Ε 100; *διῆλθε*, Ψ 876, cf. Δ 481. [– – ⏑, Ε 130, 819.] [ῠ]

Ἀντί-λοχος, son of *Νέστωρ*, Δ 457, Ν 554, Π 320, Ν 93, Ο 569, Ε 565, γ 452, δ 187.

Ἀντί-μαχος, a Trojan, Λ 123, 132, 138, Μ 188.

'Αντί-νοος, Εὐπείθεος υἱός, α 383; the most insolent of the suitors, β 84, π 418, χ 22, ω 424.

ἀντίον, see ἀντίος.

'Αντι-όπη, daughter of 'Ασωπός, mother of 'Αμφίων and Ζῆθος, λ 260.

ἀντίος, 3, (ἀντί), adversus, *against, towards*.—(1) ἦλυθε, Υ 463; τινός, Χ 113; π 160, ἰδεῖν, look *up*.—(2) with friendly intent, obviam (ire), (*go*) *to meet*, Ζ 54, Ρ 257; τινί, Η 20; τινός, Β 185, Λ 594, Φ 539, π 14; **ἔσταν,** Λ 535.—(3) with hostile intent, contra, ἵστασθαι, ἐλθεῖν, ἔγχε' ἄειραν, ἐείσατο, ἀίξας, τ 445, Λ 94, 216, (ἀίσσουσι, Λ 553, Ρ 662); τινί, Ο 584, Υ 422; elsewh. τινός, e. g. Η 98, Ο 694, Ρ 8, 31, χ 90.

ἀντίον, adv., *in opposition, against*.—(1) in friendly signif., coram, *before, in presence of*, ρ 529; answer, ηὔδα τινά, Γ 203, β 208, α 213; ἵζεν, etc., ε 198, ψ 165, τινός, Ι 218; π 160, look *up*; κατέθηκε, ρ 334; ἀίξασθαι πυλάων, Χ 195.—(2) in unfriendly signif., contra, τινός, εἴπῃ, Α 230; ἰέναι, Ε 256; ἐλθεῖν, Η 160. Similar significations has **ἀντία,** (1) coram, τινός, Γ 425, ο 377.—(2) contra, *against*, with verbs of combating, Υ 88, 80, 113, 333, Χ 253, α 78. [ῐ]

ἀντιόω, see ἀντιάω.

ἀντι-πέραια (πέραν), adversa, *the lands lying over against*, Β 635†.

ἀντ-ίσχω, **ἀντ-ίσχεσθε,** contra opponite, *oppose, interpose* (tables against arrows), gen., χ 74†.

ἀντι-τορέω, aor. **τορήσας,** perforare, only δόμον, *break into*—, Κ 267; *pierce*, χροός, Ε 337.

ἄν-τιτα (τίω), ἔργα, talio, *requital, vengeance*, ρ 51; cf. β 76.

'Αντι-φάτης, ᾱο, (1) a Trojan, Μ 191.—(2) son of Μελάμπους, ο 242.—(3) king of the Λαιστρυγόνες, acc. -ῆα, κ 114. [ᾰ]

ἀντι-φερίζεις, ειν; τινί, (τι), *match one's self against*, Φ 411. (Φ)

ἀντι-φέρεσθαι, *measure one's self with*, μάχῃ, Ε 701; with acc. of respect, Φ 482.

'Αντί-φονος, son of Priam, Ω 250†.

"Αντι-φος, (1) a son of Priam, Δ 489, Λ 109.—(2) son of Αἰγύπτιος, β 19.—(3) 'Ιθακήσιος, ρ 68.—(4) son of Ταλαιμένης, Β 864; leader of Μῄονες.—(5) son of Θεσσαλός, leader of Greek islanders, Β 678, 'Ηρακλείδης.

ἄντλος, ου, ὁ, sentina, *bilge-water, hold*, μ 411. (Od.)

ἀν-τολαί (τέλλω), ortus, 'Ηελίοιο, *rising-places* of the sun, μ 4†.

ἄντεσθαι, ομένη, αι, (ἄντα), only pres., ipf., occurro, *encounter*, Β 595, Θ 412; τινί, Χ 203; *join*, τινί, Δ 133; *come together* with hostile purpose, Ο 698, Π 788.

ἄντρον, antrum, *cave*, ι 216, ω 6. (Od.)

'Αντρών, ῶνος, town in Thessaly, Β 697†.

ἄν-τυξ, γος, ἡ, (τέγος).—(1) *metal rim of shield*, Ζ 118; serving to bind together the layers of metal or leather, of which the shield was composed (see the cut).—(2) *rim of chariot*; rim surrounding (περίδρομος) the body (δί-

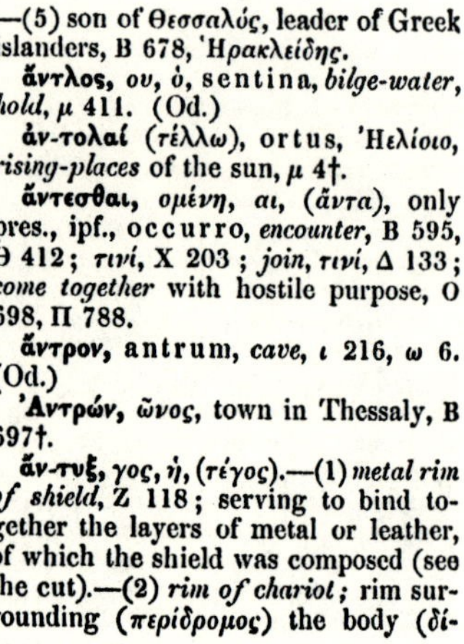

chariot, sometimes double, E 728; it served also as place of attachment for the reins. (See the cut.)

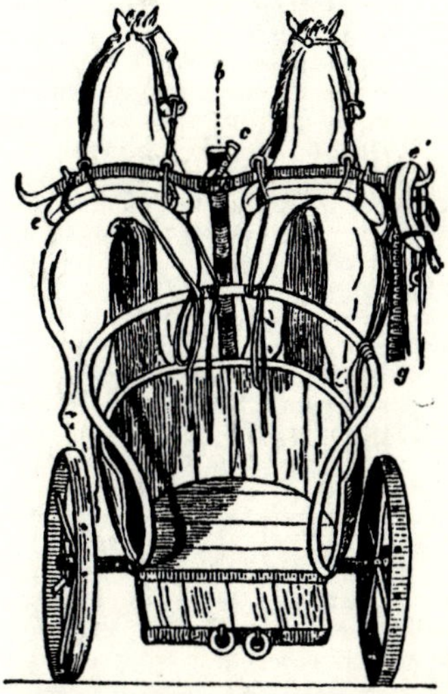

ἄνυμι (ἀνύω), **ἤνῦτο**, ipf., cito ei successit opus, *was progressing*, ε 243†.

ἄνῦσις, -ιν, ἡ, (ἀνύω), *accomplishment*, successus; B 347, they will accomplish nothing; δ 544.

ἀνύω (ἄνω), fut. -ύσω, -ύσ(σ)εσθαι, conficere.—(1) τινά, *consume*, ω 71. —(2) δ 357, ο 294, *traverse;* proficere, *effect* (nothing), Δ 56; mid., π 373. [⏑ ⏑ –]

1. **ἄνω**, ipf. ἦνον, conficere.—(1) *were completing*, γ 496.—(2) pass. ἄνεται, ἄνοιτο, *draw to a close*, K 251, Σ 473. [⏑ –; K 251, – ⏑ ⏑]

2. **ἄνω** (ἀνά), sursum, *upwards*, λ 596; porro, from down south *upwards*, i. e. *to the northward*, Ω 544. [⏑ –]

ἄνωγα (ἄγχω?), pf. (imp. ἄνωχθι, -ώχθω and -ωγέτω, -ωχθε and -ώχετε, inf. -ωγέμεν); plupf. ἠνώγεα (3 sing. ἠνώγει and -ειν, ἀνώγει), also forms like pres. ipf. ἀνώγει, -ετον; ἤνωγον, ἄνωγον; fut. ἀνώξω, aor. ἤνωξα, iubere, *command*, constr. like κελεύω, β 113, ρ 508 (τινί, only υ 139); θυμός (ἐποτρύνει καὶ) ἀνώγει, Z 439, T 102, Θ 322, σ 409, etc.

ἀνῷγεν, ipf. from ἀνοίγω, aperiebat.

ἀνώγω, see ἄνωγα, iussi.

ἀν-ωθέω only **ἀν-ώσαντες**, ο 553†, *having shoved off* from land.

ἀν-ωιστί (ὀίω), necopinato, *unexpectedly*, δ 92†. [ῑ]

ἀν-ώιστον (ὀίω), inopinatum, *unimagined*, Φ 39†.

ἀν-ώνῠμος (ὄνομα), sine nomine, *nameless*, θ 552†.

ἀν' ὦρτο (ὄρνυμι), aor. in tmesi, surrexit, *arose*, Ψ 812, θ 3.

ἄνωχθε, -θι, -θω, imp. from ἄνωγα, iubete, etc.

ἄξαντος, -ασθε, -έμεν, -έμεναι, -ετε, from ἄγω.

ἀξίνη, *ησι*, ἡ, bipennis, *double battle-axe* of Trojans, O 711. (See cut.)

ἄξιος, 3, (ἄγω), *counterbalancing, equivalent*, τινός, O 719, Ψ 562; *worth a gift in return*, τινός, α 318; *equal in strength*, Θ 234; *corresponding to* one's station or requirements, *suitable*, I 261, Z 46, N 446, υ 383; *worth*, Ψ 885; βοός, θ 405, πολέος.

Ἀξιός, river in Paionia, Φ 141, B 849.

ἀ-ξύλῳ (σα-, ξύλον), lignis abundante, *dense forest*, Λ 155†. [– ⏑ –]

Ἄξυλος, son of Τεύθρας in Ἀρίσβη, Z 12†.

ἄξων, ονος, (axis), *axle*, E 838, Λ 534. (Il.)

ἀοιδή, ῆς (ἀϝοιδή, from ἀείδω).—(1) cantus, *singing, the power to sing*, B 595, N 731, θ 44, 253; *song*, α 328, 159, 421; ἀοιδῆς ὕμνον, θ 429, *strains of the bard*.—(2) carmen, *song, ballad, story; that song* men hear most willingly, α 351; mournful song, α 340; funeral lament, elegy, Ω 721; with pregnant signif. *song, subject for song*, ω 197, 200, γ 204, (v. l. πυθέσθαι), θ 580.

ἀοιδιάει, -ουσα, (ἀοιδή), καλόν, ὀπὶ καλῇ, sweetly *sings*, only κ 227, ε 61. [ᾰ]

ἀοίδιμοι, cantabiles, *subject for song, notorious,* (infames), Ζ 358†. [ᾰ]

ἀ-οιδός, οῦ, (ἀϝείδω), cantor, *singer* (of funeral ode), Ω 720; elsewh. *singer* and *poet*, regarded with special favor by the gods (θ 43, 479, 487, ρ 518, αὐτοδίδακτος, χ 347; e. g. Φήμιος, Δημόδοκος), hence θεῖος, ρ 385, θ 479, sqq., and highly honored.

ἀ-ολλέες, έα, (σα-, ϝολλ, εἰλέω), conferti, *crowded together*, in throngs, Ε 498, Ο 306; cuncti, Ν 39, γ 165, 412; ἅπασαι, *all together*, χ 446.

ἀολλίζω, only aor. **ἀόλλισαν, -σσασα,** and pass. **ἀολλίσθησαν, -θήμεναι** (ἀολλέες), congregare, *collect*, Ζ 270, Ο 588. (Il.)

ἄορ, ορος, τὸ, (ἀείρω, ἄσϝορ, English sword), gladius, *sword*, in form =ξίφος, θ 403, 406, κ 294, 321; acc. pl., ἄορας, ρ 222. [⏑⏑; ⏑⏑⏑, in arsi –⏑⏑.] (See cut.)

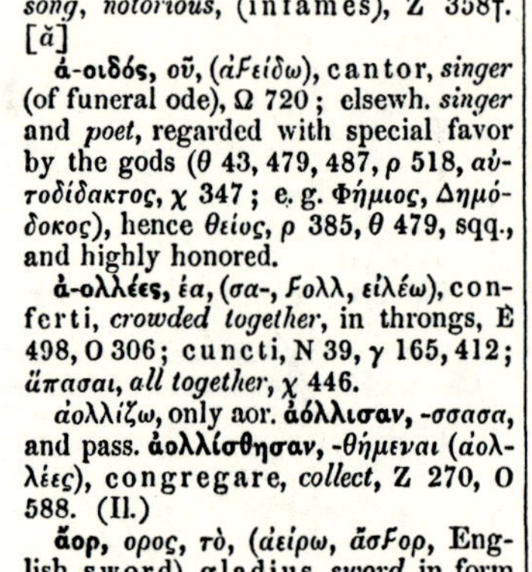

ἀορτήρ, ῆρα, etc., masc. (ἀείρω, ἀσϝορτ.), balteus, *sword-belt* =τελαμών (see cut), λ 609; Λ 31, ἀορτήρεσσιν, *with hooks* or *handles*; of *strap* on wallet, ν 438.

ἀ-οσσητήρ, ῆρα, ες, ας, masc. (socius, ἀ-σοκjητήρ), defensor, *companion in battle*, Ο 254; *helper*, δ 165, ψ 119.

ἄ-ουτον (οὐτάω), non percussum, *unwounded*, Σ 536†.

ἀπ-αγγέλλω, only ipf. **ἀπαγγέλλεσκε,** and 1 aor., renuntio, *report*, τί, Ι 626; *bring tidings*, τινί, Ρ 640, ο 210.

ἀπ-άγχων, strangulans, *throttling*, τ 230†.

ἀπ-άγουσιν, fut. -άξω, aor. -ήγαγον, abducere, *lead away;* always with pers. obj., exc. σ 278, *bring with them from their own estates;* always with pers. subj., exc. Ο 706.

ἀπ-αειρόμενον, πόλιος πεδίονδε, campum petentem, withdrawing from the city, and *seeking* the plain, Φ 563†.

ἀπ-αίνυτο, ipf., also (ἀποϝαίνυται, -το, cf. μ 419) only pres. and ipf., adimere, *take away, rob*, Λ 582, Ο 595, μ 419; τί τινος, ρ 322 (v. l. ἀπαμείρεται), Ν 262.

Ἀπαισός, Trojan town, Β 828†; see Παισός.

ἀπ-αΐξας (ἀΐσσω), κρημνοῦ, desiliens, *springing down from* a crag, Φ 234†.

ἀπ-αιτίζοντες, res repetentes, *reclaiming*, β 78†.

ἀπ-άλαλκε, -οι, (ἀλκή), imp. and opt. 2 aor., arcere, *ward off*, δ 766, Χ 348, τί τινος. [ᾰ]

ἀ-πάλαμνος (παλάμη), sine palmis, *not knowing how to swim, helpless*, Ε 597†. [ᾰ]

ἀπ-ἄλεξήσειν, -ήσαιμι, fut. and aor. opt., arcere, *keep off*, τινά τινος, Ω 371; ρ 364, but not even thus could she *keep some one from* maliciously insulting him, cf. ρ 462.

ἀπ-αλθήσεσθον, 3 du. fut., ἕλκεα, *shall they be healed* of their wounds, Θ 405, 419.

ἀπ-αλοιάω, **ἀπ-ηλοίησεν,** ἄχρις, contudit penitus, *crushed* utterly, Δ 522†.

ἀπᾰλός, 3, tener, *tender*, δειρή, αὐχένος, ἦτορ, παρειάων (πόδες, Τ 92, of Ἄτη, as ἠεροφοῖτις, like the Ἐρινύς), χεῖρας, φ 151; ἁπαλὸν γελάσαι, *heartily*, ξ 465.

ἀπᾰλο-τρεφέος, σιάλοιο, bene saginatae, *well-fed*, Φ 363†.

ἀπ' ἀμήσαντες (ἀμάω), *after having cut* (hacked) *off*, φ 301†.

ἀπ-αμβροτεῖν, see ἀφαμαρτάνω.

ἀπ-αμειβόμενος, and ipf. -ετο (former with προσέφη, latter with φώνησέν τε), respondens, *answering*, Α 84, δ 824, θ 400, λ 347.

ἀπ-αμείρεται, v. l. for ἀποαίνυται, ρ 322†.

ἀπ-αμύνω, only aor. (in tmesi ἀμῦναι, Α 67, β 59), act. and mid.; and ipf.

ἀπήμυνεν, arcere, *ward off*, mid. *defend one's self*, λ 579, O 738; *τινά*, *defend one's self against*, Ω 369, π 72.

ἀπ-αναίνομαι, only aor. *-ηνήναντο*, *-ανήνασθαι*, recusare, *decline*, *refuse*, only H 185, κ 297.

ἀπ-άνευθε(ν), (1) procul, *far away*, K 434; *κιών*, A 35; *out from it*, T 374.—(2) separatim, *apart*, κ 524, K 425.—(3) with gen., sine, *without the knowledge*, A 549; *far from*, A 48, ι 36; follg. its gen., *μάχης*, Λ 283.

ἀπάντῃ (*ἅπας*), quoquoversus, *on every side*, Il. and θ 278.

ἀπ-ήνυσαν (*ἀνύω*), pervenerunt, *accomplished* the journey home again, η 326†.

ἅ-παξ (*σα-*, *παγῆναι*), semel, *once*, μ 22; *once for all*, 350. (Od.)

ἀπ-αράσσω, only aor. **ἀπήραξεν,** and in tmesi **ἄραξεν,** detruncare, *smote to the earth*, Ξ 497. (Il.)

ἀπ-αρέσσασθαι (*ἀρέσκω*), reconciliare sibi, that a king should *conciliate* a man, T 183†.

ἀπ-άρχομαι, *-αρξάμενος*, sacra ordiri, *to begin the sacred rites* by cutting off hair from the forehead of the victim, γ 446.

ἅ-πᾱς, -πᾱσα, -πᾰν, universus, *entire*, *all*; pl., cuncti, *all together*; ο 158, *nothing but kindness*; δ 616, argento solidum, *of massive silver*; ξ 196, *in a year and a day*. (The trisyllabic forms scarcely found, exc. at end of line.)

ἄ-παστος (*πασσάμενος*), non pastus, *not having eaten*, *fasting*, with *ἐδητύος*, carens, *without* food, cf. δ 788.

ἀπ-ᾰτάω, fut. **-ατήσω,** aor. **ἀπάτησε(ν)** (*ἠπ-*), fallo, *deceive*, δ 348. [ᾰ]

ἀπ-άτερθε, seorsim, *apart*, B 587; *far from*, E 445. [ᾰ]

ἀπάτη, *ης*, dolus, *deceit*, Δ 168; pl. fallaciae, *tricks*, O 31. [ᾰ]

ἀπατήλια, ntr. fallacia, only ξ 127, *βάζει*, speaks *falsely* to her, and 288, skilled in *deceit*.

ἀπᾰτηλόν, fallax, *deceitful*, A 526†. [ᾰ]

ἀπ-ητίμησε (*ἀτῑμάω*), prorsus contempsit, *greatly insulted*, N 113†.

ἀπ-αυράω (cogn. with *Ϝερύω* ?), only ipf. **ἀπηύρων, ας, α,** fut. *-ουρήσουσι*, q. v., aor. part. **ἀπούρας,** eripere, *wrest away*, A 356; *τί*, I 107; *τινί τι*, ν 132, γ 192, (*θυμόν*, P 236, Φ 296); *τινά τι*, P 125, Ψ 291, 560, (*θυμόν*, Υ 290); not *τινός τι*, A 430 (but gen. absol.), T 88, σ 273, I 107; see also *ἀέκων*.

ἀπᾰφίσκει, and 2 aor. *ἤπαφε*, mid. **ἀπάφοιτο,** ludificari, *delude*, *beguile*, only λ 217, ψ 216. [ᾰπ]

ἀπ-έειπε, see *ἀπ-εῖπον*.

ἀπ-έεργε, see *ἀπο-έργω*.

ἀπειλεῖς, *εῖτε*, fut. *-ήσω*, ipf. *ἀπειλήτην*. — (1) minari, *threaten*, *τινί*, *ἀπειλάς*, N 220, Π 201; *μῦθον*, A 388; with inf., A 161, Θ 415, O 179.—(2) gloriari, *boast*, Θ 150; with inf., θ 383.—(3) vovere, *utter a vow*, *τινί*, Ψ 863, 872. [⏑ –]

ἀπειλαί, *άων*, *άς*, minae, *threats*, I 244, N 219; then iactantia, *boasting*, Ξ 479, Π 200.

ἀπειλητῆρες, iactatores, *boasters*, H 96†.

1. **ἄπ-ειμι,** subj. *-ἔῃσι*, ipf. *-έην*, *-εσαν*, fut. *-έσσεται*, *-εσσεῖται*; often in tmesi, abesse, *be far from*, *τινός*, τ 169; *τόσσον*, as far away, ε 400; *δουρηνεκές*, as far as a spear is cast; *be absent*, *wanting*, Υ 7, σ 146.

2. **ἄπ-ειμι,** imp. *-ιθι*, part. *-ιών*, ipf. *ᾔε*, abire, *go away*, ρ 478; *ἄψ*, K 289.

ἀπ-εῖπον (*Ϝέπω*, voco), ind. also *ἀπέϜειπε*, *-Ϝείπω* (subj.), *-Ϝείποιμι* (opt.), *-Ϝειπ(ε)* (imp.), *-Ϝειπεῖν* (inf.), *-Ϝειπών* (part.), and without *Ϝ*; **ἀπ-** *ειπών*, etc. —(1) *speak out* (fully), *deliver*, an errand, π 340; a mission, H 416; the truth, Ψ 361; *μῦθον ἀπηλεγέως*, *speak out* regardless of feelings, α 373.—(2) negare, *say no*, A 515, I 431, 510, 675.—(3) renuntiare, *give solemn warning*, *τινί*, α 91; *μῆνιν*, T 35, 75, *renounce*.

Ἀπειραίη, *she who springs from Apeira*, **Ἀπείρηθεν** (*Ἤπειρος* ?), η 8, 9†.

ἀ-πειρεσίην, *οι*, *αι*, and **ἀ-περείσια,** ntr. pl. (*πέρας*, *πείρατα*), infinitus, *boundless*, *infinite*, *vast*, *πολλοί*, τ 174; *γαῖαν*, *ὀϊζύν*, *ἄποινα*, *ἔεδνα*.

ἀ-πείρητος (*πειράομαι*), imperitus, *unskillful*, opp. *ἐὺ εἰδώς*, β 170; non tentatus, *untried*, P 41.

ἀ-πείρῐτος (*πείρατα*), infinitus, *boundless*, κ 195†.

ἀ-πείρων, *-ονος*, (*πείρατα*), infinitus, *immeasurable*, Ω 545; *endless*, η

286; δεσμοί, *in which the end can not be found, indissoluble*, θ 340.

ἀπ-εκ-λελάθεσθε (λήθω), imp., obliti sitis, *forget altogether*, ω 394†.

ἀ-πέλεθρον (πλῆθος ?), immensam, *immeasurable*, ἶν', vim, E 245; and immensum quantum, sprang back *enormously far*, Λ 354.

ἀπ-έμεσσεν (ἐμέω), aor., evomuit, *spat out*, Ξ 437†.

ἀπ-εμνήσαντο, see ἀπο-μιμνήσκομαι, meminerunt.

ἐνάριζον (ἔναρα), **ἀπ' ἔντεα**, ipf., spoliabant, *were despoiling*, τινά, only M 195, O 343.

ἀπ-ένεικας, αν, aor. from ἀποφέρω, abstulisti.

ἀπ-έπλω, ipf. from ἀποπλώω, naves solvit.

ἀπερείσιος, see **ἀπειρεσίην**, infinitus.

ἀπ-ερύκω, -ξω, arcere, *ward off, scare away*, τινά; also in tmesi, Ω 156.

ἀπ' ἐρύσαι (ἐρύω), tmesis; detrahere, *tear off*, ξ 134†. [ῠ]

ἀπ-έρχομαι, -ῆλθε, -ελήλυθα, abire, *go away*, τινός, β 136, Ω 766; *leave*, Ω 514 (tmesis).

ἀπ-ερωεύς (ἐρωή), exstinctor, *thwarter, annihilator*, ἐμῶν μενέων, Θ 361†.

ἀπ-ερωήσειας (ἐρωέω), opt. aor. πολέμου, decederes, wouldst thou miserably *withdraw from* battle, Π 723†.

ἄπ-εσαν, see ἄπειμι, aberant.

ἀ-πευθής (πεύθομαι), (1) ignarus, *ignorant*, only γ 184.—(2) ignotus, *unknown*, only γ 88.

ἀπ-εχθαίρει, only δ 105, μοι ὕπνον, *makes hateful*; and aor. subj. ἀπεχθήρω, oderim, *hate*, Γ 415.

ἀπ-εχθάνεαι, 2 sing., aor. -ήχθετο, inf. -έχθεσθαι (ἔχθος), odisse, *hate*, π 114, cf. 96; elsewh. odio esse, *be hated*, τινί, Δ 53, Z 140, I 614, Φ 83. [⏑ – ⏑ ⏑]

ἀπ-έχω, -ομαι, fut. ἀφέξω, -ομαι, ἀποσχήσει, aor. -σχῃ, -σχωνται, ipf. ἔχοντο, prohibere, *keep away, hold off*, τί, τινά τινος (τινί, Ω 19), τ 572; an enemy, Z 96; X 324 (tmesi); χεῖρας (so also mid. tmesi, χ 316), A 97, υ 263; ἑκὰς νηῶν, ο 33; mid., *hold one's self aloof from*, τινός, M 248, Θ 35, Ξ 78, 206; abstinere, *abstain*, ι 211; parcere, *spare*, μ 321, τ 489.

ἀπ-ηλεγέως (ἀλέγω), ἀποειπεῖν μῦθον, speak out *without scruple*, only α 373, I 309.

ἀ-πήμαντον (πημαίνω), incolumem, *uninjured*, τ 282†.

ἀπ-ήμβροτον, aor. from ἀφαμαρτάνω, decrravi.

ἀ-πήμων, ονος, (πῆμα), sine damno.—(1) fortunatus, *safe, unharmed*, A 415, ε 40, δ 519, ν 39, N 744.—(2) prosper, *favoring, kindly*, οὖρος, η 266; speech, escort, *healthful*, Ξ 164.

ἀπήνη, ης, plaustrum, *freight wagon*, four wheeled, Ω 324; with tent-like cover, ζ 70; not unlike the Roman rheda. (See cut.)

ἀπ-ηνήναντο, aor. from ἀπαναίνομαι, recusabant, *refused*.

ἀπ-ηνής, έος, *unfriendly, harsh*, A 340; θυμός, O 94; νόος, Π 35; μῦθος, O 202.

ἀπ-ήραξεν, aor. from ἀπαράσσω, detruncavit, *struck off*.

ἀπ-ηύρων, aor. from ἀπαυράω, eripui.

ἀπ-ήωροι (ἀείρω), procul pendentes, *high-hanging* (Odysseus hangs upon one of the roots which project from the land), μ 435†.

ἀ-πιθέω, only fut., and aor. 1 **ἀπίθησε, σαν** (πείθω), adversari, *disobey*, only with οὐκ and οὐδ', χ 492.

ἀ-πινύσσειν, and -ων, (πινυτός), amentem esse, *lack understanding*, ε 342; κῆρ (acc.), *be unconscious*, O 10.

ἀπίης, ἐξ — γαίης, from a *remote* land, Α 270, π 18. [⏑ ⏑ –]

Ἀπισάων, ονος.—(1) Ἱππασίδης, a Greek, Ρ 348.—(2) Φαυσιάδης, a Trojan, Λ 582.

ἀ-πίστεον, ipf. (ἄπιστος), οὔ ποτ'—, desperavi, *was doubting*, ν 339†.

ἄ-πιστος (πιστός), sine fide, (1) *faithless*, Γ 106.—(2) *incredulous*, ξ 150.

ἄπ-ισχε = ἄπεχε, *hold away*, λ 95†.

ἁπλοΐδας, acc. pl. (ἁπλόος), χλαίνας, *single* cloak or mantle, i. e. to be wrapped only once around the body, only Ω 230, ω 276.

ἄ-πνευστος (πνέω), sine spiritu, *breathless*, ε 456†.

ἀπό, ab, prep. with gen., after its case ἄπο, ξ 525; freq. with words to which the (orig. instr.) suffix -φι is appended, Λ 374, 351, 44, Θ 300, Ο 313, Κ 347, Π 246, Ω 268; also with words having suffix -θεν; very freq. in tmesi, in which case the compound word must be sought (e. g. Π 82 under ἀφαιρεῖν).—(1) *from* starting-point, *out*, *away*, Ο 610, 714, Ζ 472, Ε 13, Λ 645; ἀπ' οὔδεος, Μ 448, cf. Ψ 730; fight, etc., *from*, i. e. *on*, ἀφ' ἵππων, ἀπὸ νεῶν, Ο 386, ι 49; fasten to (cf. pendere a), λ 278; ἀπ' αἰῶνος νέος ὤλεο, depart *from* life (cf. recens a), Ω 725; ἀπὸ δ' αὐτοῦ, *from* the meal to something else, *immediately after*, Θ 54 (no other examples of temporal use).—(2) separation, *away from*, *from*, Ω 514, Ι 437, Δ 535, Υ 278, Κ 465, 575, Ν 640, Π 436, 733; οἶον ἀπ', φ 364; after ἐκτός, Κ 151, *outside of*; νόσφιν, Ε 322; τῆλε, ε 315.—(3) remoteness; *far from*, ξ 525; ἀπ' Ἄργεος, Ν 227; ἀπ' οὔατος, Χ 454; *out of* my hearing, ἀπ' ὀφθαλμῶν, e conspectu, Ψ 53; ἀπὸ σκοποῦ οὐδ' ἀ. δόξης, *contrary to* our intention and meaning, λ 344; ἀ. θυμοῦ εἶναι, odio esse; θυμὸς ᾤχετ' ἀπὸ μελέων, Ν 672, cf. Η 131, Π 861, Ρ 17, ο 354.—(4) origin: *out of*, *from*, Μ 97; τ 163, for thou didst not spring from an ancient oak nor from a rock, so also converse speaking from a tree or a rock (as shepherd with shepherdess), Χ 126; κάλλος ἀπὸ χαρίτων, *from* the Graces (as source); μ 187, ἀπὸ στομάτων ὄπα, *out of* our mouth; Μ 306, *from* his swift hand; Θ 279, sending destruction *from* his strong bow; ἀπὸ σπουδῆς, *in* earnest, Η 359. [⏑ ⏑; ⏑ – before σνευρῆς, Ϝρίου.]

ἀπο-αίνυμαι = ἀπαίνυμαι, adimere.

ἀπο-αιρέομαι (Ϝαιρέω?) = ἀφαιρέομαι, adimere.

ἀπο-βαίνω, fut. -βήσομαι, aor. -έβην, 3 sing. -εβήσατο and -σετο, abire, *go away*, πρὸς μακρὸν Ὄλυμπον, Ω 468, etc.; *dismount*, ἐξ ἵππων ἐπὶ χθόνα, Γ 265, cf. Λ 619; ἐπὶ χθονί, Ω 459; ἵππων, Ρ 480; *disembark*, νηός, ν 281; *forsake*, σχεδίης, ε 357.

ἀπο-βάλλω, aor. inf. -βαλέειν, only in tmesi, abicere, *throw off*, τί, Β 183, ζ 100; χαμαί, Φ 51; χαμάδις, τ 63; Π 793, *cast down from* his (τοῦ) head (κρατός) the helmet; δάκρυ παρειῶν, *let* tears *fall from* his cheeks, δ 198; νῆας ἐς πόντον, *push off* to sea, δ 359.

ἀπό-βλητον, -α, (βάλλω), contemnendus, only found with οὔτοι, *not to be despised*, Β 361 and Γ 65.

ἀπο-βλύζων, ebulliens, *letting spirt out of the mouth*, οἶνου, Ι 491†.

ἀπο-βρίξαντες (βρίζω, βαρύς), conniventes, *having fallen asleep*, ι 151 and μ 7.

ἀπο-γυιώσῃς, aor. subj., (γυῖα), debilites, *shouldst unnerve*, Ζ 265†.

ἀπο-γυμνωθέντα (γυμνόω), nudatum armis, *disarmed*, κ 301†.

ἀπο-δαίω, only fut. **ἀποδάσσομαι**, and aor. inf. -δάσσασθαι—τινί τινος, only Χ 118, Ω 595, and Ρ 231, ἥμισυ τῷ ἐνάρων, partiri, *share*.

ἀπὸ δειδίσσετο, deterruit, *frightened back*, Μ 52†.

ἀπο-δειρο-τομήσω, fut., aor. -εδειροτόμησα (τέμνω), iugulare, *slaughter*, men, Σ 336, Ψ 22; *sheep*, λ 35.

ἀπ-εδέξατο, aor. from -δέχομαι, recepit, *accept*, Α 95†.

ἀπο-διδράσκω, **ἀπο-δράς**, aor. part. (διδράσκω), qui aufugit, *escape by stealth*, (ἐκ) νηός, only (π 65) ρ 516.

ἀπο-δίδωμι, fut. -δώσομεν, aor. -έδωχ' (= κε), 3 sing. subj. -δῷσι, opt. -δοῖτε, inf. -δοῦναι (tmesis -δόμεναι), opt. aor. pass., -δοθείη, reddere, *deliver up*, Γ 285, Ε 651, Η 84, χ 58, 61; *restore*, Λ 98, Σ 499, β 78, θ 318; τοκεῦσι θρέπτρα, requite parents for one's nurture.

ἀπο-δίωμαι (δίω), subj., exturbem, *drive out of*, E 763†. [ῐ]

ἀπο-δοχμώσας (δοχμόω), aor. part., inflexam ponere, αὐχένα, *bend to one side*, ι 372†.

ἀπο-δράς, see ἀποδιδράσκω, qui aufugit.

ἀπο-δρύφοι, opt., aor. 3 sing. -δρυψε, subj. δρύψωσι, aor. pass. -δρύφθη, 3 pl. -έδρυφθεν, cutem lacerare, *stripped* the muscles *from* the shoulder, Π 324; τινά, ρ 480; ε 426, then would his skin (acc. of respect) *have been stripped off*, cf. 435. [ῠ]

ἀπο-δύνω, ipf. **-έδυνε**, exuit, *threw off*, χ 364; so also 2 aor. part. ἀποδύς; but fut. -δύσω and aor. -έδυσα, τινά, nudare, *strip off*, B 261; spoliare, *despoil of*, Δ 532, Σ 83; also in tmesi.

ἀπο-δυσάμενος, ε 349, better reading -λυσάμενος.

ἀπο-δῷσι, aor. subj. from ἀποδίδωμι, reddat.

ἀπό-εικε (ϝείκω), imp., recede, *retire from*, κελεύθου, Γ 406†.

ἀπο-εῖπον, see ἀπ-εῖπον.

ἀπο-έργαθε, and -εέργαθε ipf., (ϝέργω), separavit, *held aloof from*, τινός, Φ 599; *removed from*, φ 221; also in tmesi.

ἀπο-έργω, ipf. -εεργε, (ϝέργω), also in tmesi, separare, *keep away from*; τινός, Θ 325, λ 503; *drive away*, Ω 238.

ἀπό-ερσε, aor., subj. -έρσῃ, opt. -έρσειε, (ϝέρσε, ϝέρρω), abripuit, had *washed one away*, Z 348. (Il.)

ἀπ-εθαύμασε, aor., (θαυμάζω), demirata est, *wondered at*, with acc., ζ 49†.

ἀπό-θεστος (θέσσασθαι), spretus, *despised*, ρ 296†.

ἀπο-θνήσκων, part., pf. -τεθνηῶτος, moribundus, *expiring*, λ 424; X 432, defuncti.

ἀπο-θρώσκων, part., in tmesi, 3 pl. ipf. θρῶσκον, part. aor. θορόντες, θοροῦσα, exsilio, *spring up*, ψ 32; *spring down from*, νηός, B 702; νευρῆφι, *fly from the string*, O 314; *rise*, α 58.

ἀπο-θύμῐα (θυμός), ntr., ingrata, *things displeasing*, *offense*, Ξ 261†. [ῡ]

ἀπ-οικίζω, only aor. **ἀπῴκισε**, deduxit, *transferred*, μ 135†.

ἄ-ποινα, ων, (ποινή), poenae, mulcta, *fine*, *recompense*, *satisfaction*, T 138; esp. *ransom*, A 13; τινός, for any one, A 111, Ω 137. (Il.)

ἀπ-οίσω, see ἀποφέρω, auferam.

ἀπ-οίχομαι, only prs., *go away*; τινός, deserere, *abandon*, Λ 408, T 342; -οιχόμενος, digressus, absens, ξ 8, φ 70.

ἀπ-εκαίνυτο, ipf., superavit, *excelled*, only θ 127, 219.

ἀπο-καίω, only 3 sing. opt. aor. **κῆαι** (in tmesi), comburat, *consume*, Φ 336†.

ἀπὸ ἐκάπυσσεν, aor. from καπύω, efflavit, *gasped forth* her life (swooned), X 467†. [ᾰ]

ἀπο-κείρω, only aor. (ἔ)**κέρσε** (in tmesi), and -εκείρατο, dissecuit, *cut through*, N 546; totondit, *sheared his* hair, Ψ 141. (Il.)

ἀπο-κηδήσαντε, du. part. aor., (κηδέω), negligentes, *through your negligence*, Ψ 413†.

ἀπο-κῑνέω, only aor. iter. **-κινήσασκε**, subj. -κινήσωσι, amovebat, *moved away*, Λ 636 and χ 107, *dislodge*, τινά τινος.

ἀπο-κλίναντα, aor. part., (κλίνω), ἄλλῃ, deflectentem, *turn off*, interpreting differently, τ 556†. [ῑ]

ἀπο-κόψειν, fut., and aor. -έκοψα, (κόπτω), also in tmesi, abscindo, *cut off*, Λ 146, Φ 455, ι 325; Π 474, *cut loose* the out-running horse, i. e. the reins by which he drew.

ἀπ-εκόσμεον, ipf., auferebant, *clear off*, η 232†.

ἀπ-εκρέμᾰσε, aor., (κρεμάννυμι), inflexuit, *let droop*, Ψ 879†.

ἀπο-κρινθέντε, du. part. aor. pass., (κρίνω), separati, i. e. *parted from the throng*, E 12†.

ἀπ-έκρυψεν, aor., inf. -κρύψαι, occultare, *hide*, Λ 718; *deny*, *conceal*, ρ 286; *shelter*, *save*, Σ 465.

ἀπο-κτάμεν(αι), aor. inf., see following word.

ἀπο-κτείνω, 1 aor. -έκτεινε, usually 2 aor. -έκτανε, -έκταμεν, -έκτανον, subj. -κτάνῃ, inf. -κτάμεν(αι), interimo, *kill*, ξ 271; *slaughter*, μ 301; with pass. signif. 2 aor. mid. -έκτατο, -κτάμενος, interemtus, P 472, Δ 494, Ψ 775.

ἀπ-έλαμπε, -ετο, ipf., resplendebat, *shone forth resplendent*, Z 295, σ 298, T 381; X 319, *flashed back* (the splendor from the spear-point).

ἀπο-λείβεται (λείβω), destillat,

trickles off (from the closely woven linen), η 107†.

ἀπο-λείπουσιν, ipf. -έλειπεν, relinquere (with οὐδέ), *quit*, M 169; *leave over*, ι 292, (I 437, tmesis, *remain behind*).

ἀπο-λεψέμεν, fut. inf., (λέπω), detruncare, lit. *peel off, cut off*, v. l. ἀποκοψέμεν, Φ 455†.

ἀπ-ολέσκετο, aor. iter., from ἀπόλλυμι, peribat.

ἀπο-λήγω, ipf. -έληγε, fut. -(λ)λήξεις, aor. subj. -(λ)λήξῃς, -ωσι, opt. -(λ)λήξειαν (λήγω), desistere, *abandon, cease*, τινός, H 263, ν 151, μ 224; with part., τ 166; *vanishes*, Z 149.

ἀπο-λιχμήσονται, fut. mid., (λιχμάω, lig-urio), delambent, *lick off* (blood from wound), Φ 123†.

ἀπο-λλήξεις, see ἀπολήγω, desistes.

ἀπ-όλλυμι, fut. -ολέσσω, aor. -ώλεσα, I. perdere.—(1) *lose*, πατέρα, πόσιν, θυμόν, βίοτον, β 46, δ 814, K 452, β 49. —(2) *annihilate, kill, destroy*, E 758, 648. II. -όλλυμαι, aor. -ωλόμην (-όλοντο), iter. -ολέσκετο, pf. -όλωλεν, perire. —(1) *be lost, disappear*, δ 62, λ 586, 556, ρ 253.—(2) *perish* (opp. σαωθῆναι, O 502), I 230, Ψ 81; ὀλέθρῳ, ὄλεθρον, μόρον, γ 87, ι 303.

Ἀπόλλων, ωνος, son of Ζεύς and Λητώ, brother of Ἄρτεμις, like her, bringing death, see ἀγανός; god of the sun and of light, Φοῖβος, Λυκηγενής; of prophecy (his oracle in Πυθώ, θ 79), A 72, θ 488; of music, A 603 (yet not known to Homer as μουσαγέτης, leader of the Muses); of poesy; of youth, τ 86; guardian of flocks and herds; epithets, ἀκερσεκόμης, ἀφήτορος, διίφιλος, ἑκατηβόλος, ἕκατος, ἑκηβόλος, ἑκάεργος, ἰήιος, λαοσσόος, παιήων, χρυσαόρου, Σμινθεύς, Φοῖβος.

ἀπο-λούσῃ, aor. subj., opt. -λούσειαν, (λούω), abluere, *wash off*, Ξ 7; τινά τι, Σ 345; mid. fut. -λούσομαι, aor. -σασθαι, τι, *wash from off one's self*, ὤμοιϊν, ζ 219.

ἀπο-λυμαίνεσθαι, ipf. -ελυμαίνοντο, (λυμαίνω), sordes abluere, *cleanse one's self by bathing*, A 313 sq. (Il.)

ἀπο-λῡμαντῆρα, acc., -ες nom. pl., (λυμαίνω), δαιτῶν, purgator, *one who clears off* the tables by devouring the fragments, *plate-licker*, ρ 220 and 377.

ἀπο-λύσομεν, fut., aor. -έλυσε (λῦσε), mid. fut. -λυσόμεθα, aor. -λυσάμενος (λύω), solvere.—(1) *undo*, γ 392; τινός, *loose from*, φ 46, μ 421.—(2) *release*, A 95, for ransom (Il.).—(3) mid. τινὰ χρυσοῦ, *ransom* with gold, X 50; *loosen from one's self, untie*, ε 349. [ῡ]

ἀπο-μηνίσει, fut., aor. part. -μηνίσας, (μηνίω), succensere, *be angry*, π 378; τινί, B 772. [ῐ]

ἀπ-εμνήσαντο, aor., (μιμνήσκω), therefore *they have remembered* (repaid) him, Ω 428†.

ἀπ-ώμνυ and -υε, -υον, ipf., aor. ὤμοσα, (ὄμνυμι), iureiurando renuntiare, *swear not* to do; ὅρκον, κ 381. (Od.)

ἀπ' ὀμόργνυ, ipf., and -ομόρξατο, -ξαμένω, aor. mid., (ὀμόργνυμι), abstergere, *wipe off*, E 798; τινός, E 416; *wipe clean*, Σ 414; mid. *wipe any thing off from one's self*, B 269, Ψ 739; *wipe one's self clean of* any thing, σ 200.

ἀπ-εμῡθεόμην, ipf., (μυθέομαι), dissuasi, (earnestly) *dissuaded*, I 109†.

ἀπ-όναιο, -οναίατο, see ἀπονίνημι.

ἀπο-ναίω, only aor. subj. **-νάσσωσι,** and aor. mid. **-ενάσσατο;** Π 86, remittant domum, *send away;* mid. demigraverat, *withdraw to*, ο 254.

ἀπο-νέωνται, pres. subj., inf. -νέεσθαι [– ⏑ ⏑ –], ipf. -νέοντο, redire, *return, go home*, π 467; with **προτί, ἐπί** (ἐς) with acc., **-δε, παλιμπετές, ἄψορροι** (-ον).

ἀπ-όνηθ' (-όνητο), **-ονήμενος,** see ἀπονίνημι, frui.

ἀπο-νίζοντες, -ουσα, part. pres., ipf. -ενίζοντο, and aor. imp. -νίψατε, part. -νίψαντες, -νιψαμένη, -οι, from pres. **-νίπτεσθαι,** abluere, *wash off*, τινά, τ 317; τί, H 425, ω 189; *wash clean*, ψ 75; mid. *wash off from one's self*, K 572; *wash one's self clean*, σ 172, 179, χ 478.

ἀπ-ονίνημι, only fut. mid., **-ονήσεται,** aor. **-όνητο** (opt. **-όναιο,** part. -ονήμενος), perfrui, *have enjoyment, profit, advantage*, π 120; τινός, ω 30, Ω 556; οὐδ', nihil profecit.

ἀπο-νίπτεσθαι, -νίψατε, etc., see ἀπο-νίζοντες, abluere.

ἀπο-νοστήσειν, fut., (νοστέω), always after ἄψ, rediturum esse, *return*, A 60, ω 471.

ἀπὸ or **ἄπο νόσφι(ν)** (should always be written separately), (1) separatim, *apart*, B 233; procul, *away*, A 555, O 548, σ 268, ε 350.—(2) after its object, τινός, procul, A 541, ε 113, μ 33 (ο 529); cf. νόσφιν ἀπό, K 416, O 244.

ἀπὸ ἔξεσε (ξέω), aor., abscīdit, *cut* (lit. *shaved*) *off*, E 81†.

ἀπ-οξύνουσι, and aor. inf. -οξῦναι, praeacuere, *bring to a point, make taper*, ζ 269, ι 326 (v. l. ἀπο-ξῦσαι, *smooth off*).

ἀπο-ξύσας (ξύω), aor. part., expoliens, *smoothing off* (wrinkles), I 446†. (inf. -ξῦσαι v. l., ι 326.) [ῡ]

ἀπο-παπτᾰνέουσι, fut., (παπταίνω), terga dabunt, *will turn in flight*, Ξ 101†.

ἀπό-παυε, imp., fut. -παύσει, aor. -έπαυσας, -ε, -αν, reprimo, *keep off*, τινά, Σ 267; τί, *check, hinder*, T 119; τινός, *repress*, A 323; from any thing, Φ 340; with acc. and inf., μ 126, σ 114; mid. **-παύεαι,** imp. -εο, fut. -σομαι, desisto, *desist*, Φ 372, E 288; τινός, from something, α 340, A 422, Π 721, Θ 473.

ἀπο-πέμπω, inf. -πεμπέμεν, ipf., fut. ἀπ- and ἀπο-πέμψει, etc., 1 aor. -έπεμψα, dimittere, *send away*, ξ 108, ρ 76; *send off*, Φ 452, ο 83, ψ 23, β 113; *dismiss*, ε 146, 161; *strangers with escort*, κ 65, 73, ω 285.

ἀπο-πέσῃσι, aor. subj., from -πίπτω, deciderit.

ἀπο-πέτομαι, only follg. forms from 2 aor. -επτάμην: **ἀπὸ ἔπτατο,** -πτάμενος, η, avolavit, *flew away*, arrow, dream; life, θυμός, (of animals), Π 469, κ 163, τ 454; ψυχή, (of men), λ 222.

ἀπ-έπιπτον, ipf., -πέσῃσι, subj. 2 aor., (πίπτω), decĭdo, *fall down*, only Ξ 351, ξ 129.

ἀπὸ πλάζει, in tmesi, pres. only α 75, πατρίδος, *keeps him away from*; elsewh. only aor. pass. -επλάγχθης, etc., *be driven from one's course*, θ 573; with gen. ο 382, ι 259 (-θεν), μ 285; *rebound*, X 291, N 578, 592.

ἀπο-πλείειν, inf., ipf. -έπλειον, (πλέϝω), navibus proficisci, *sail away*, I 418, θ 501.

ἀπο-πλήξας, aor. part., (πλήσσω), detruncare, *strike off*, κ 440†.

ἀπο-πλύνεσκε, ipf. iter., (πλύνω), diluebat, was *washing clean*, ζ 95†. [ῡ]

ἀπ-έπλω (πλώω, πλέϝω), ipf., avecta est, *had sailed away from*, γαίης, ξ 339†.

ἀπο-πνείων, ουσα(αι), part., (πνέϝω), exhalans, *breathing forth*, life, fire, smell, δ 406.

ἀπο-πρό, πολλόν, Π 660, *far away*; τυτθὸν ἀ. νεῶν, H 334, *not far from*.

ἀπο-προ-αιρέω, only **-ελών,** *take away from what lies before*, ρ 457†.

ἀπο-προ-έηκε, aor. from ἀπο-προΐημι, delegavit.

ἀπό-προθεν, procul, (from) *far away*, στῆτε, ζ 218; ρ 408, the house would hold him *aloof*.

ἀπό-προθι, procul, *far away*, Ψ 832.

ἀπο-προ-ίημι, part. **-ιείς** and aor. -έηκε, delegavit, *sent away*, ξ 26; *shot forth*, χ 82; *let fall*, χ 327. [⏑ – – ⏑ –]

ἀπο-προ-τέμνω, only aor. part. **-ταμών,** desecans, *cut off from*, with gen., θ 475†.

ἀπο-πτάμενος, aor. part. from πέτομαι, avolans.

ἀπο-πτύει, 3 sing. and part. pres., (πτύω), exspuitare, *spit forth*, Ψ 781; *dash forth*, Δ 426. [ῡ]

ἀ-πόρθητος (πορθέω), non excisa, *not destroyed*, M 11†.

ἀπ-ορνύμενον, part., profectum, *having set out from*, Λυκίηθεν, E 105†. [ῡ]

ἀπ' ὄρουσε, -σαν, aor., (ὀρούω), also in tmesi, desiliit, *sprang away*, E 297, P 483; *rebounded*, Φ 593; *sprang down*, E 20.

ἀπο-ρραίσει and -ρραῖσαι, fut. and inf. aor., (ῥαίω), eripere, *wrest away from*, α 404.

ἀπὸ ῥῆξε, -ρρήξας, aor. ind. and part., (ϝρήγνυμι), abrupit, *break off, shatter*, Z 507, Π 587; hinges, M 459.

ἀπ-ερρίγασι, for ϝεϝρίγασι, pf., (ϝριγέω), perhorrent, *shrink from*, β 52†.

ἀπὸ ἔρριψε, ἀπο-ρρῖψαι, -ρρίψαντα 1 aor., (ϝρίπτω), excutere, *put off, lay aside* (anger), I 517; veil, X 406.

ἀπο-ρρώξ (ϝέϝρωγα, ϝρήγνυμι), *branch* (of the Styx), κ 514; *morsel* (of Nectar), ι 359; as adj. **-ρρῶγες,** *steep*, ν 98†.

ἀπ-έσσυτο, -εσσύμεθα, aor. mid., (σεύω), se proripuit, *hurried away*, ι 396; δώματος, Z 390.

ἀπ-εσκέδασεν, -σκέδασον, tmesis,

indic. and imp. aor., (σκεδάννυμι), propulit, *scattered*, λ 385; *dismissed*, Τ 309. [⏑ – ⏑ ⏑ ⏑ ⏑]

ἀπο-σκίδνασθαι (σκίδνημι), digredi, *disperse*, Ψ 4†.

ἀπο-σκύδμαινε, imp., (σκυδμαίνω), *be indignant at*, τινί, Ω 65†.

ἀπο-σπένδων, part., (σπένδω), libans, *pouring out a libation*, γ 394. (Od.)

ἀπο-στᾰδόν and **-ά**, adv., (σταδίη), only Ο 556, ζ 143, *standing far away*.

ἀπο-στείχων, part. pres., and aor. -έστιχε, imp. ἀπόστιχε, abscedere, *go away*, λ 132, Α 522.

ἀπο-στίλβοντες, pres. part., nitentes, *gleaming* with oil, with gen., γ 408†.

ἀπο-στρέψοντας, fut. part., **-στρέψασκε**, aor. iter., -ψῃσι, -ψαντε(ς), (στρέφω), averto, *twist back*, hands and feet, χ 173; *turning about*, γ 162; *turn back in flight*, Ο 62; *roll back*, λ 597; *recall*, Κ 355.

ἀπ-εστῠφέλιξεν, -ξαν, aor., (στυφελίζω), retudit, *forced back*, Π 703; Σ 158, τινός.

ἀπο-σφήλωσι, aor. subj., -σφήλειε, opt., (σφάλλω), aberrare faciat, *cause to drift away*, γ 320; lead them astray from object of their labor, cause them to fail of the result of their toil (through the death of Menelaos), Ε 567.

ἀπο-σχέσθαι, aor. inf., see ἀπέχω, abstinere.

ἀπὸ ἔσχισεν (σχίζω), discidit, *split off, split in sunder*, δ 507†.

ἀπο-τάμνω, ipf. **-έταμνε** (in tmesi: τάμνε, 1 aor. τάμε, subj. τάμῃσι, opt. τάμοι), pres. mid. -ταμνόμενον, decidere, *cut off, cut open;* throats, Γ 292, Χ 328; thread, Ψ 867; reins, halter, Ο 87; *cut off for one's self*, Χ 347.

ἀπο-τηλοῦ, procul, *far away*, ι 117†.

ἀπο-τίθημι, only aor. **-έθηκα** (also in tmesis), and aor. mid. **θέτο** (tmesis), and inf. -θέσθαι, deponere, *put away, lay off*, garments and weapons, esp. freq. in mid., habit of fault-finding, Ε 492.

ἀπο-τῖνύμενοι, part. pres., ipf. -ετίνυτο, (τίνω), τινά τινος, ulcisci pro, *take vengeance for*, β 73, Π 398. [ῠ]

ἀπο-τίνειν, -έμεν; -ετον, imp., -τίνων; fut. -τίσεις, aor. -έτισε, etc., inf. -τῖσαι, solvere, *pay back*, τιμήν, mulctam, a fine, Γ 286; *pay*, Ψ 487; *atone for*, Χ 271, Φ 399, γ 195, σὺν μεγάλῳ Δ 161, Ι 512, χ 168, ν 193; Σ 93, *atone for* slaying and despoiling Patroklos; *make good*, Α 128, Ι 634, β 132; *recompense*, Θ 186, χ 235; mid. **-τίσομαι**, etc. fut., aor. -ετίσατο, *avenge one's self upon, punish*, ulcisci, τί, λ 118, ν 386; ποινὴν ἑτάρων, exact satisfaction for his companions, ψ 312. [ῑ]

ἀπο-τμήγουσι, aor. opt. -τμήξειε, part. -τμήξας, abscindere, *cut off, sever*, Σ 34, Λ 146, κ 440; fig. *cut off, intercept*, Κ 364, Λ 468; *plough, tear* (hill-sides), Π 390.

ἄ-ποτμος, infortunatus, *ill-starred*, Ω 388; sup. -ότατος, α 219.

ἀπο-τρεπέτω, imp. prs., fut. -τρέψεις, aor. -έτραπε, avertere, *turn away from*, τινά τινος, Μ 249, Υ 256, 109; reducere, *turn back*, Λ 758; *scare back*, Ο 276; mid. aor. **-ετράπετο**, etc., *turn one's self away*, Μ 329; ἀπὸ νόσφι, *turn away the face*, ε 350; *turn about*, Κ 200.

ἀπο-τρίψουσι, fut., (τρίβω), deterentur, many footstools, thrown from both sides about his head, as he is made a target of throughout the house (gen. absol. of part.), (as they slip down) *shall rub off* his ribs; coarse jest of goatherd Melantheus, ρ 232†.

ἀπό-τροπος (τρέπω), remotus, (live) *retired*, ξ 372†.

ἀπο-τρωπῶσι, subj. -ῶμεν (-τρωπάω), avertere, *drive back*, Υ 119; *forbid*, π 405; mid. -τρωπᾶσθε, imp., -ετρωπῶντο, ipf., τινός, tergiversamini, *turn the back upon, delay about;* with inf., *shrink from*, Σ 585.

ἀπ-ούρας, aor. part. from ἀπαυράω, eripere.

ἀπ-ουρήσουσι, fut., eripient (-αυράω), or **ἀπ-ουρίσσουσι**, amovebunt terminos (οὖρος), *remove the boundary stones*=intrude upon his fields, Χ 489†

ἀπο-φέρω, only fut. **-οίσετον**, -οίσειν, aor. -ένεικας, -αν, aufero, *carry home*, π 360; *bear back*, Ε 257; *drive away* (at sea), Ξ 255; *bring back*, Κ 337.

ἀπό-φημι, and aor. mid. imp. -φασθε, pronuntio, ἀντικρύ, *I say it to thy face*, Η 362; *deliver* this message, Ι 422.

ἀπ-έφθιθεν, 3 pl. aor. pass., (φθίω), perierunt, only in interpolated verses of Od., ε 110.

ἀπο-φθῐνύθουσι (φθίω), pereunt, Ε

643; θυμόν, Π 540, perdunt, *lose life.* [ῠ]

ἀπο-φθίω, perdo, prs. pass. opt. -φθίμην, imp. -φθίσθω, part. -φθιμένου, -οιο, -ον, -η; mid. aor. with pass. signif. -έφθιτο, aor. pass. 3 pl. -(έ)φθιθεν, ψ 331 (and interpolation, ε 110); perire, *perish,* ὀλέθρῳ, in destruction, ο 268, Τ 322, ω 88; mortua, ο 357; occisi, Σ 499.

ἀπο-φώλιος, -οι, -α, (φύω, φώς), sine fetu, *not unblessed with offspring* is intercourse with the gods, λ 249; =ἀφυής (non-Homeric), *unfruitful,* i. e. *aimless, foolish,* ε 182; *unseemly,* ξ 212; *vile,* θ 177.

ἀπο-χάζεο, imp. prs., (χάζομαι), recede a, *go away from,* τινός, λ 95.

ἀπὸ χεῦεν, for ἔχεϝεν, aor., (from χέω), excussit, *threw down from* the table, only χ 20, 85.

ἀπο-ψύχοντα (ψύχω), part., exspirantem, *fainting,* ω 348; elsewh. ἱδρῶ, with ipf. mid. **-εψύχοντο,** *were letting the sweat dry off from* their garments, and pass. -ψυχθείς, *having cooled off.* [ῡ]

ἀπ-πέμψει, fut. from ἀποπέμπω, dimittet.

ἄ-πρηκτον, -ους, acc., (πρήσσω), irritum, *endless,* Β 121, 376; *with or against which nothing can be done, hopeless, incurable,* μ 223, β 79; active, *unsuccessful,* Ξ 221.

ἀ-πριάτην (πρίαμαι), adv., gratis, *without money, for nothing,* ξ 317; *without ransom,* Α 99. [ᾰ]

ἀ-προτί-μαστος (-μαίομαι), intacta, *undefiled,* Τ 263†.

ἄ-πτερος (πέτομαι), ἔπλετο μῦθος, τινί, non excidit, nor did the word *escape her, she perceived its sense,* ρ 57. (Od.)

ἀ-πτῆσι, dat. pl., (-πτήν), implumibus, *unfledged,* Ι 323†.

ἀ-πτο-επές (ἐπτοίηθεν, ἔπος), audacter loquens, *rash-speaking,* Θ 209†.

ἀ-πτόλεμος, -ον, -ους, imbellis, *unwarlike,* Β 201. (Il.)

ἅπτω, only aor. part. **ἅψας,** aptans, *making fast,* φ 408; ἀψαμένη ἀπό, *suspending a noose on high upon,* λ 278; elsewh. only mid. prs. **ἅπτεσθαι,** ipf. ἥπτετο, fut. ἅψεσθαι, aor. ἥψατο, ἀψάσθην, etc., *cling to,* τινός, Π 9; *hit, strike,* Θ 67, Ρ 631; *touch, clasp,* τινός, τ 344 (also with double gen., τ 348); esp. with γούνων, γενείου (supplicare), Α 512, 500, Ω 357; *lay hold of,* Θ 339, Β 152; *clasp,* δ 522; *lay hands on,* τινός, β 423; *lay hold of* in eating, δ 60, κ 379; τ 28=sits at my table; sc. πυρός, take fire, ι 379; aor. pass. ἐάφθη, ἐπὶ, *fell after, sank upon* him, Ν 543.

ἀ-πυργωτόν (πύργος), immunitam, *unfortified,* λ 264†.

ἄ-πῡρον, -ους, (πῦρ), kettle or tripod, *not yet placed over the fire,* Ψ 267, Ι 122. (Il.)

ἀ-πύρωτον (πῦρ), ignis expertem, *untouched by fire*=ἄπυρον, Ψ 270†. [ῡ]

ἄ-πυστος (πυθόμενος), (1) ignotus, *unknown,* α 242.—(2) ignarus, *uninformed of,* τινός, δ 675. (Od.)

ἀπ-ωθέω, only fut. **-ώσω** (inf. -σέμεν), aor. -ῶσε, etc., mid. fut. -ώσεαι, etc., aor. -ώσατο, repellere, *push back,* Ω 446, χ 76; *cast off,* ο 280, β 130, Υ 489; *drive from one's course* (at sea), ι 81, cf. ν 276; *tear away,* Ε 308; τινός, *drive away from,* Θ 96; mid. *drive away from one's self* (enemies), Θ 206, Ο 503; *dislodge, push aside,* α 270, Θ 533, Ω 508.

ἄρα, before consonants ἄρ, enclitic ῥα, always postpositive, (ἀραρεῖν), orig. adv. containing the idea of being firmly fixed, denotes, as conjunction, a natural inference from what precedes, *now, now then, no doubt, exactly, therefore, then.*—(1) of what is fixed by decree of fate, esp. in phrase οὐδ' ἄρ' ἔμελλεν, δ 107, λ 553, ν 293, ι 475, Κ 336, Μ 3; Β 419, λ 139; Ψ 670, δ 605.—(2) of what experience has taught to regard as fixed, ν 209, π 420, Ε 532.—(3) often joined with causal conjs., γάρ ῥα, Α 113, 236; ἐπεί ῥα, ο 390, α 263; ὅτι ῥα, because *you know,* Α 56.—(4) εἴτ' ἄρα, if *namely,* Α 65; εἰ μὴ ἄρα, unless *indeed,* Ζ 75, ψ 242.—(5) recapitulating, with demonstratives, *precisely, to wit,* Β 482, Γ 153, Α 405; ὥς ἄρα, φ 163, Α 428, 584, Γ 13, Η 7; with τοὔνεκα, ἔνθεν, τότε, τῆμος, etc.; with relatives, Η 182 *just the* one which, ξ 449, υ 106, Ζ 131; ὅς ῥα, who, *you see* = since he.—(6) with weakened force, *without doubt, naturally, of course, surely,* Α 46, 56; εἴτ' ἄρα, Α 65, cf. 93; in questions, τίς τ' ἄρ, α 346, Α 8; κατ' ἄρ' ἕζετο, Α 68;

in first member of antithetical period, followed by δέ: μέν ῥα, B 1; δ' ἄρα, *then in due course*, A 471; οὐδ' ἄρα, A 330; αὐτὰρ ἄρα, B 103.—(7) denoting a subtle, inherent sequence of thought, often untranslatable, H 360, B 433.—(8) ἄρα, ῥα, following participles, θ 458, ν 380; sometimes doubled, π 213. [⏑ ⏑]

ἀράβησε (ἀραβέω), aor., δὲ τεύχε' ἐπ' αὐτῷ, his armor *rang* around him, ω 525. [ᾰ]

ἄρᾰβος ὀδόντων, *chattering* of teeth, K 375†.

Ἀραιθυρέη, town in Argos, B 571†.

ἀραιή, etc., adj. fem., tenuis, *thin, slender*, κ 90, Π 161; legs of Hephaistos, Σ 411; *delicate*, E 425. [ᾰ]

ἀρᾶται, etc., prs. (-άομαι), inf. ἀρήμεναι, χ 322; ipf. ἠρώμην, ἆτο, fut. -ήσεται, aor. ἠρήσατο, -αντο, etc., precari.—(1) *pray*, η 1; πολλά, fervently, δαίμοσιν, ἀθανάτοισι, πάντεσσι θεοῖσι (see cut, for attitude); εὐχομένη, *imploring, supplicating*, Z 304, I 567; grieving sore, with inf., Ψ 209; with acc. and inf., δ 827.—(2) *wish, long for*, with inf., N 286, Δ 143, α 366; *call down upon*, Ἐρινῦς, *curse*, β 135; with acc. and inf., τ 533.

ἀράρισκε, I. ipf., 1 aor. ἄρσε (with imp., inf., part.), 2 aor. ἤραρε, ἄραρον, (artare), coniungo, *fit together*, rafters, Ψ 712; *fit upon*, τί τινι, ξ 23; *close*, β 353; β 289, *seal up* in jars; M 105, *formed themselves in close array* with their shields; *build* (put together) a wall with stones, Π 212; parare (ἀρτύω) γέρας, A 136; θάνατον καὶ κῆρα, π 169; θυμὸν ἐδωδῇ, *satisfy*.—II. pf. ἄρηρε, (part. ἀρηρώς, ἀρᾰρυῖα, etc.), plupf. ἀρήρει, (2 aor. ἤραρεν, ἄραρον, but only Π 214, δ 777), and 3 pl. aor. pass. ἄρθεν, and part. aor. mid. ἄρμενος, artari, *be closely joined together*, of ranks, O 618, Π 211; of jars *standing close together* against wall, β 342; *close tightly*, I 475, ψ 42, Σ 275; with dat.: *joined together* with or of (metal plates, O 530; palisades, M 56; *paved* with flags, ζ 267); *lie close upon, fit*, Γ 338, Σ 600, ε 234 (also with prep., σ 378); *please*, δ 777; *hold fast to*, ε 361; *fitted to*, ε 254; K 265, with ἐν; *be provided with*, Λ 31, E 744, Ξ 181, ζ 70, κ 553.

ἄραρον, aor., ἀραρυῖα, pf. part., see ἀράρισκε.

ἄρασσεν, ipf., compegit, *drove home and made fast*, ε 248†.

ἀράχνιᾰ, τά, aranea, *spider's web*, only θ 280, π 35.

ἀργαλέος, η, ον, (ῥίγιον?), arduus, *impossible, difficult*, A 589, M 63, β 244; also in pers. constr., A 589, δ 397; difficilis, *difficult to manage, shocking, violent*, K 107, P 385, O 10, Λ 812, λ 400.

Ἀργεάδης, Πολύμηλος, Π 417†.

Ἀργεῖος, η, ον, inhabitant of Ἄργος; freq. in pl. as collective designation of Greeks, B 159, A 79, Γ 286, 99.

Ἀργεϊ-φόντης (ἄργει instr., φαν, *clear-shining*), epith. of Ἑρμῆς, *swift messenger*, a popular (mistaken) etymology seems to have been the origin of the myth of the Argos-slayer, B 103.

ἀργεννάων, -ῶν, -ῇσι, -ῇς, (from ἀργεσινάων), candidus, *white*, Γ 198, 141.

ἀργεστᾶο Νότοιο, only Λ 306, Φ 334, rapidi, *rapid*.

ἀργής, ῆτος, (also -έτι, έτα, dat. acc.), *dazzling white, bright*; of linen, fat, lightning, Γ 419.

ἀργι-κέραυνε, voc., (κεραυνός), fulmen coruscum gerens, *wielder of the dazzling thunderbolt*, T 121; fulminator, *thunderer*, Υ 16. (Il.)

ἀργῖνόεντα, acc., candidum, *gleaming*; epith. of town in Kreta, because of chalk cliffs near it, only B 647, 656.

ἀργῐ-όδοντος, etc., (-όδους), *white-toothed*, epith. of dogs and swine.

ἀργί-ποδᾶς (πούς), acc., *swift-footed*, Ω 211†. [ῐ]

Ἄργισσα, town in Θεσσαλία, B 738‡.

ἄργμᾰτᾰ, τά, (ἄρχεσθαι), *consecrated pieces of flesh* burned at *beginning* of sacrifice, ξ 446†.

Ἄργος, ὁ, name of the faithful hound of Odysseus, ρ 292†.

Ἄργος, εος, ntr.—(1) town on river Inachos in Argolis, domain of Diomedes, ο 224, φ 108, Z 224, Ξ 119, γ 180, B 559; ἱππόβοτον, ο 239, 274.—(2) in wider sense, realm of Agamemnon, who dwelt in Mykene, B 108, 115, A 30, I 22, O 30, N 379, γ 263, Δ 171.—(3) probably, the entire Peloponnesos, δ 174; Ἀχαιικοῦ, γ 251; ἱπποβότοιο, Z 152; so often joined with Ἑλλάδα, which latter word then designates Northern Greece; cf. Ἴασον, σ 246.—(4) Πελασγικόν, domain of Achilleus, B 681, Ω 437, ω 37, Z 456, valley and plain of river Peneios.—(5) in widest sense, the whole of Greece, M 70, N 227, Ξ 70; also Ἀχαιικόν, ἱπποβότοιο, B 287, I 246, δ 99; πολυπύρῳ, O 372. Not all passages admit of satisfactory explanation, e. g. H 363, δ 562.

ἀργήν, *οί, ούς, white,* ο 161, Ψ 30; *swift* (with and without πόδας), κύνες, β 11.

Ἄργοσδε = εἰς Ἄργος.

ἀργύρεος, *έη, εον,* (ἄργυρος), argenteus, *of silver,* δ 615; *inlaid* or *adorned with silver,* E 727, A 219. [ῠ]

ἀργῠρο-δίνης, (δίνη), *silver-eddying,* of rivers, B 753. (Il.) [ῑ]

ἀργῠρό-ηλος, *ηλον, ον,* (ἧλος), *adorned with silver studs* or *knobs, silver-studded;* ξίφος, θρόνος, φάσγανον, B 45, η 162, Ξ 405.

ἀργῠρό-πεζα (-πεδja), *silver-* (in whiteness) *footed,* Θέτις, A 538. (Il.)

ἄργῠρος, *ου,* ὁ, (ἀργός), argentum, *silver,* B 857, ψ 200.

ἀργῠρό-τοξος, *bearing the silver bow,* Ἀπόλλων; also subst., A 37.

ἀργύ-φεον (ἀργός, φα-), ntr., *dazzling-white,* ε 230. [ῠ]

ἄργῠ-φον, α = ἀργύφεον, ntr. Σ 50, κ 85.

Ἀργώ (lit. *swift*), ship of Argonauts, μ 70.

ἀρδμός, *-οί,* aquatio, *watering-place,* ν 247.

ἀρειῇ (ἀρά), minis, *by threats,* P 431. (Il.)

Ἀρεθούσῃ, κρήνῃ in Ithaka, ν 408†.

ἄρειον, τεῖχος, see follg. word.

ἀρείων, acc. sing. *-είω* and *-είονα,* nom. pl. *-είους, -είονες,* ntr. **ἄρειον,** (ἀραρεῖν), *compact,* τεῖχος, Δ 407, T 33; fortis, ι 48; then, *surpassing,* praestans, Ψ 588, β 277; β 277, opp. κακίους, ν 133, opp. χείρονα. [ᾰ]

Ἀρείων, name of horse of Ἄδρηστος at siege of Θήβη, Ψ 346.

ἄ-ρεκτον (ῥέζω), infectum, *unaccomplished,* T 150†.

ἀρές, voc., (from ἀρής, ἀρε-ίων), *Oh brave one,* restore in E 31, 455.

ἀρέσαι, -έσασθαι, see ἀρέσκω.

ἀρέσθαι, inf. aor. from ἄρνυμαι, comparare.

ἀρέσκω, only **ἀρέσαι,** inf. 1 aor., *make amends;* also fut. mid. **ἀρεσσόμεθα,** and aor. ἀρεσσάσθω, *-σσασθαι, appease,* τινά; reconciliare, δώροις, etc.

ἀρετᾷ, *-ῶσι, thrive,* only θ 329, τ 114.

Ἀρετάων, a Trojan, Z 31†.

ἀρετή, *ῆς,* (ἀρείων), praestantia, *excellence,* of whatever sort, Υ 411, Ψ 276; *superiority, accomplishment,* δ 725, σ 251, O 642, Υ 242; *capacity, prowess,* ξ 212, Ψ 571; virtus, Θ 535, N 237, θ 239; *skill,* ρ 322; *success,* ν 45, σ 133; *prosperity,* ξ 402.

ἀρετῆτα, conjecture for ἀδροτῆτα.

ἀρή, *ῆς,* preces, (1) *prayer,* δ 767. —(2) imprecatio, *curse* (ἀρέων, I 566), ρ 496; *destruction,* M 334; with λοιγόν, Ω 489; *calamity,* χ 208. [⏑ –; in arsi – –]

ἄρηαι, aor. subj. from ἄρνυμαι, compares.

ἀρήγω, fut. *-ξω,* (ἄρκιον, ἀλκή), opitulari, τινί, *aid,* A 77. (Il.) [ᾰ]

ἀρηγών, *-όνες,* fem., (ἀρήγω), *helper,* E 511 and Δ 7. [ᾰ]

ἀρηΐ-θόων (ἄρης, θοός), *swift in battle, valiant,* Θ 298. (Il.)

Ἀρηΐ-θοος, (1) κορυνήτης, son of Μενέσθιος from Βοιωτία, H 10, 137.—(2) θεράπων of Ῥίγμος, Υ 487.

ἀρηι-κτᾰμένῳ, in pugna caeso, *slain in battle,* X 72.

Ἀρηΐ-λυκος, (1) father of Προθοήνωρ, Ξ 451.—(2) a Trojan, Π 308.

ἀρήϊος (ἄρης), *warlike, martial,* B 698, ψ 220; τεύχεα, ἔντεα, of weapons, armor, Z 340, K 407.

ἀρηΐ-φᾰτοι, *ους,* (φένω), in pugna caesi, *slain,* λ 41, T 31. [ῐ]

ἀρηΐ-φῐλος, *-ον, -οι,* Marti gratus, *loved by Ares, valiant,* ο 169. (Il.) [ῐ]

ἀρήμεναι, inf. from ἀράομαι, precatus esse.

ἀρημένος, *-ον, overcome, burdened,* Σ 435, σ 53.

ἀρήν, see ἀρνός.

ἀρηρομένος, pf. pass. from ἀρόω, aratus.

Ἀρήνη, town subject to Νέστωρ, B 591, Λ 723.

Ἄρης, -ηος, -ηϊ, -ηα, -ην (also -εος, -εϊ, and -ει), voc. Ἄρες (see ἀρές), god of war and of the tumult of conflict, E 890 sqq.; son of Ζεύς and Ἥρη, brother of Ἔρις, father of Δεῖμος and Φόβος; common epithets, ἀλλοπρόσαλλος, ἆτος πολέμοιο, βροτολοιγός, δεινὸς ἐνυάλιος, θοῷ, θοῦρος, μιαιφόνος, ὄβριμος, ταλαυρινὸν πολεμιστήν, χάλκεος, etc.; his favorite abode, N 301 sqq., θ 361; his size, E 860; cf. E 385, θ 267 sqq.; brave heroes are called ὄζος or θεράποντες Ἄρηος; cf. follg.

ἄρης (ἔρις?), orig. *the god* Ἄρης (cf. Ἥφαιστος), then his element, *the tumult of battle*, ὀξὺν ἄρηα ἐγείρειν, B 440; ξυνάγειν, B 381; φέρειν πολύδακρυν, Γ 132; ἔριδα, etc.

ἄρησθε, subj. aor. from ἄρνυμαι, comparetis.

Ἀρήτη, daughter of Ῥηξήνωρ, wife of Ἀλκίνοος, η 54, ν 66. (Od.) [ᾱ]

ἀρητήρ, ῆρος, ὁ, (ἀράομαι), *one who prays, a priest*, A 11. [ᾱ]

Ἀρητιάδης, Νῖσος, π 395. [ᾱ]

ἄ-ρητον (perh. from ἄϝρητον = ἄρρητον, cf. εἴρηκα, from ἔ-ϝρηκα), infandum, *unspeakable*, P 37, Ω 741; others interpret, *accursed, shocking*, from ἀράομαι.

Ἄρητος, (1) son of Νέστωρ, γ 414. —(2) son of Πρίαμος, P 535.

ἄρθεν, conferti sunt, 3 pl. aor. pass. from ἀραρίσκε.

ἀρθμήσαντε, part. aor. (ἀρθμέω), ἐν φιλότητι, *having been brought together* (in combat), separated in friendship, H 302†.

ἄρθμιοι (ἀραρίσκω), coniuncti, *allied*, π 427†.

ἀρῐ- (ἀρείων), intensive, inseparable prefix, *exceedingly, very*. [ᾰ]

Ἀρι-άδνη, κούρη Μίνωος, λ 321, Σ 592.

ἀρί-γνωτος, η, ον, *recognizable*, N 72, δ 207; famose, = *infamous*, ρ 375 (where — — — ⏑).

ἀρι-δείκετος, *illustrious*, λ 540; usually with gen. part. ἀνδρῶν, λαῶν, θ 382.

ἀρί-ζηλος, η, (δῆλος), valde clarus, *conspicuous*, Σ 519; *clear, shrill*, Σ 219 (B 318, ἀίζηλον). ⏑ — — ⏑ adv. **-ζήλως**, *clearly*, μ 453†.

ἀριθμήσω, fut. (ἀριθμέω), aor. -ήσας, pass. -ηθήμεναι, numerare, *count, reckon up*; δίχα, *divide into two companies*, κ 204.

ἀριθμῷ, -όν, numero, *number*, λ 449. [ᾰ]

Ἄριμοις, εἰν—, name of a region in Κιλικία, B 783†. [ᾰ ῐ]

ἀρι-πρεπής, -ές, *conspicuous, distinguished*; Z 477, Τρώεσσιν, among the Trojans.

Ἀρίσβας, αντος, father of Λειώκριτος, P 345†. [ᾰ]

Ἀρίσβη, town in Troia; Ἀρίσβηθεν, *from Arisbe*, B 838. [ᾰ]

ἀριστερός, όν, sinister, *left*, ἐπ' ἀριστερά (-όφιν, N 309), sinistrorsum, ε 277; *foreboding ill*, υ 242. [ᾰ]

ἀριστῆος, gen., pl. -ῆες, nobilis, optimates, *chiefs*, O 489, H 73, ο 28.

ἀριστεύειν, ipf. iter. ἀριστεύεσκε, excellere, *be the best or bravest*, usually with inf. μάχεσθαι, Λ 746; with gen. τ.νός, (μεθ' ἡμέας, δ 652); with both gen. and inf., Z 460.

ἄριστον (ἦρι), *breakfast*, π 2, Ω 124. [ᾰ]

ἄριστος, η, ον, (ἀρείων, ἀρι-), and **ὥριστος** = ὁ ἄρ., optimus, *the best, most excellent, most capable, bravest, first*; of things animate and inanimate; among, with gen. part., A 69; with ἐν (with verbs), Z 7, O 296; with dat. of manner (or respect), I 54, θ 247, π 419, ν 297; with acc. of respect, Γ 39, Ψ 483, λ 469, γ 370, also followed by inf., θ 123; often intensified by advs., μέγ', ὄχ', ἔξοχ', διακριδόν (M 103, O 108), decidedly; Ζεύς, Ξ 213, T 95, τ 303, N 154; princeps, e.g. Γ 274, K 214, Z 209, I 3, (by birth, rank, or other title to honor); *advantageous*, I 103, Γ 110, ν 154; Z 56, σοὶ—πεποίηται, *honorably* (indeed) has been their conduct toward thee! [ᾰ]

ἀρι-σφαλέα, acc., (σφάλλομαι), lubricum, *slippery*, the ground, ρ 196†.

ἀρι-φραδής and -έα, ntr., (φράζομαι), *very plain, easy to recognize*, σῆμα, ὀστέα, Ψ 240; adv., **φραδέως** = ἀριζήλως, v. l. ψ 225†.

Ἀρκάδες, inhabitants of **Ἀρκᾰδίη**, B 611, 603, in the Peloponnesos. (Il.) [ᾰ]

Ἀρκείσιος, son of Ζεύς, father of **Ἀρκεισιάδης**, i.e. Λαέρτης, π 118, ω 270. (Od.)

Ἀρκεσί-λαος, leader of the Βοιωτοί, B 495, O 329. [ῐ]

ἀρκέω, only ipf. **ἤρκει**, fut. **ἀρκέσει**, aor. ἤρκεσε (ἀλκή), arcere, *keep off*, τινί τι, Z 16; ἀπό τινός τι, N 440; patrocinari, *protect*, τινί, π 261, Φ 131.

ἄρκιος, -ον, (ἀρκέω), *sufficient*, K 304; B 393, ei non erit opportunitas, shall have no further *opportunity* to; certum, O 502.

ἄρκτος, ὁ and ἡ, ursus, *bear*, λ 611; ἡ, constellation of the *Great Bear*, or *Wain*, Σ 487, ε 273; septem triones.

ἅρμα, ατος, τό, (ἀραρίσκω), *chariot*, ἀγκύλον, ἐύξοον, ἐύτροχον, θοόν, καμπύλον; usually in pl., δαιδαλέοισιν, ποικίλα χαλκῷ (adorned with gold and silver, K 438), κολλητοῖσιν; esp. *war chariot*, drawn by horses, hence these often named with it, E 199, 237, Δ 366; the Homeric chariot differed in no essential respect from that in use centuries earlier by the Egyptians and by the Asiatics; for description of separate parts, cf. ἄντυξ, ἄξων, ῥυμός, ἕστωρ, ἴτυς, ἐπίσσωτρα, πλῆμναι, κνήμη, δίφρος, ζυγόν (see cut No. 10, and tables I. and II.).

Ἅρμα, village in Βοιωτία, B 499†.

ἁρμᾰτο-πηγός (πήγνυμι), ἀνήρ, *chariot-builder*, Δ 485†.

ἁρμα-τροχιή (τρόχος), *wheel-rut*, Ψ 505†.

ἄρμενος, *fitting*, part. aor. mid. (ἀράρισκε).

ἁρμόζεο, imp. pres. mid., aor. act. ἥρμοσε, from ἁρμόζω, strictly, *fit together*, Γ 333, the cuirass *fitted him; fit together*, beams, ε 247; 162, unite them together into a raft.

Ἁρμονίδης, ship-builder in Troy, (ἁρμόζω), E 60†. [ῐ]

ἁρμονίάων, ῃσι, gen. dat. pl., (ἁρμόζω), *bands, slabs*, one side flat, the other curved; serving to bind together the raft: see *d*, in cut; also *k*, in cut No. 35. Also fig., *bond, compact*, χ 225.

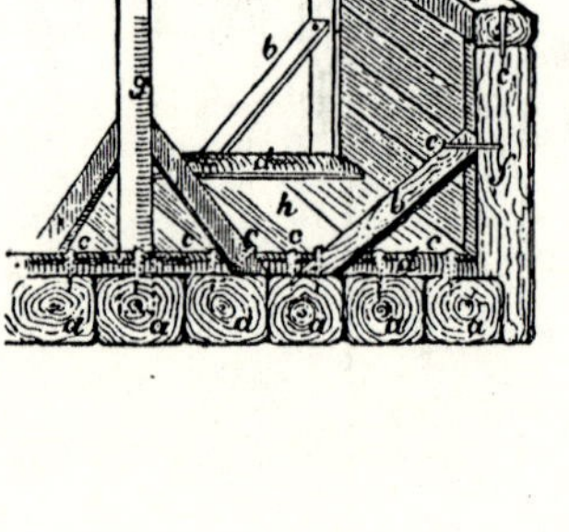

ἀρνειός, ὁ, aries, *ram*, Γ 197, ι 444; with ὄιν, κ 527, 572.

ἀρνεῖται, etc., ipf. ἠρνεῖτο, aor. ἀρνήσασθαι, (ἀρνέομαι), negare, recusare, στερεῶς, Ψ 42; *withhold*, φ 345.

ἀρνευτῆρι, dat., (ἐρευνᾶν), *diver*, μ 413; cf. Π 747 sq.

Ἄρνη, town in Βοιωτία, H 9, B 507. With initial ϝ, B 507?

ἄρνα, acc. sing., du. -ε, pl. regular, dat. only -εσσιν, gender comm. (ϝαρν-, Γ 310), *sheep, lamb*, δ 85, Δ 102.

ἄρνυμαι, pres. ipf., aor. ἤρατο, -άμεθα and ἀρόμην, etc., comparare, *procure for one's self*, μισθόν; *gain*, κλέος, κῦδος, εὖχος, νίκην, ἀέθλια (also gain for another, τινί, A 159, I 303, Δ 95, Π 84); also *carry off as share of booty*, Ψ 592, I 188; ἀνδράγρια, Ξ 510; *receive*, Ξ 130; experiri, *take upon one's self*, δ 107, α 390; *carry*, as burden, νηῦς, Υ 247; *seeking to gain*, α 5, X 160. [– ⏑ ⏑; ⏑ – –.]

ἀροίμην, etc., aor. opt. from ἄρνυμαι.

ἄροσις, ἡ, (ἀρόω), arva, *arable land*, ι 134; ψιλήν, unwooded. [ᾰ]

ἀροτήρ, ῆρες, arator, *plough-man*, Σ 542. [ᾰ]

ἀρότοισιν, arationibus, *by cultivation*, ι 122†. [ᾰ]

ἄροτρον, τό, (ἀρόω), aratrum, *plough*, πηκτόν, firmly put together, N 703.

ἄρουρα, ης, (earth), *plough-land*, Z 195, M 422, N 707; *field*, K 7, Ψ 599; *ground*, Γ 115; ζείδωρος, corn-bearing earth, δ 229 (used in altogether general sense, cf. also τ 593 = upon the earth). As goddess = Γαῖα, B 548. [ᾰ]

ἀρόωσι (ἀρόω, cf. obsolete Eng. ear, to plough), arant, *plough*, ι 108; **ἀρηρομένῃ**, perf. pass., aratae, Σ 548. [ᾰ]

ἁρπάζω, fut. -ξω, aor. ἥρπαξα, ἥρπασε, etc., rapio, *rob, carry off*, Σ 319, N 528; *draw out*, Π 814; *carry off*, ο 250; *sweep away*, ε 416.

ἁρπακτῆρες (ἁρπάζω), *robbers*, Ω 262†.

ἁρπᾰλέων, *eagerly sought* (gains), θ 164; **ἁρπαλέως**, *greedily*, ξ 110. (Od.)

Ἁρπᾰλίων, son of Πυλαιμένης, N 644.

ἅρπη, unknown bird of prey, perh. *falcon*, T 350†.

ἅρπυιαι, rapaces, *snatchers*, personified *storm-winds*, by whom those who have mysteriously disappeared are conceived of as *borne away* (not the Harpies, Monsters, of later myths), *α* 241.

ἄ-ρρηκτος (*-ϝρηκτος*, *ϝρήγνυμι*), *indissoluble, firm*, with ἄλυτος, Ν 360; *θ* 275, *indestructible.*

ἄ-ρρητος (*ϝρητός*, ver-bum, Eng. word), *unspoken*, *ξ* 466; *unspeakable*, see *ἄρητον*.

ἄρσην, *ενος*, masculus, *masculine, male*, Θ 7, *ι* 425.

᾿Αρσί-νοος, father of ῾Εκαμήδη, of island Τένεδος, Λ 626†. [ι]

᾿Αρτᾰκίη, name of fountain in country of Λαιστρυγόνες, *κ* 108†. [ῐ]

ἀρτεμέα, *-έεσσι*, acc. sing., dat. pl., incolumis, *safe and sound*, Ε 515, *ν* 43.

῎Αρτεμις, *ἀγνή*, *ἰοχέαιρα*, *χρυσηλάκατος*, *χρυσήνιος*, *χρυσόθρονος*, *ἀγροτέρη*, *κελαδεινή*, daughter of Ζεύς and Λητώ, sister of ᾿Απόλλων, death-goddess (cf. *ἀγανός*), intaminata venatrix, *ε* 123, *ρ* 37; as huntress, haunting the mountains of Peloponnesos, *ζ* 102.

ἀρτῐ, prefix, *suitable, excellent.*

ἀρτῐ-επής (*ϝέπος*), *speaking excellently; μύθων, glib-tongued*, Χ 281†.

ἄρτῐα (*ἀράρισκε*), *suitable things*, *θ* 240; *friendly*, *τ* 248.

ἄρτῐ-πος (*πούς*), pedibus valens, *strong* or *swift of foot*, Ι 505, *θ* 310.

ἀρτί-φρων, mente valens, *intelligent* (*friendly*), *ω* 261†.

ἄρτον, *ους*, acc., *wheaten bread*, *ρ* 343, *σ* 120. (Od.)

ἀρτύνω (*ἄρτιος*), fut. *-υνέουσι*, aor. part. *-ύνας*, mid. ipf. aor. *ἠρτύνατο*, pass. aor. *ἀρτύνθη*, compono, paro, *put in order, form in close array*, Μ 43, 86, Ο 303; *prepare*, *α* 277, *ξ* 469, *ω* 153; *devise*, *λ* 366; pass., Λ 216, *the battle began*; mid., *put in order for one's self, arrange*, *δ* 782; *place*, Β 55.

ἀρτύει, prs., ipf. *ἤρτῦε*, (cf. *ἀρτύνω*), parare, *δ* 771, *υ* 242; *make ready*, Σ 379. [ῠ]

᾿Αρύβας, a native of Sidon, *ο* 426†. [ῠ]

ἀρχε-κάκους, *beginning mischief*, Ε 63†.

᾿Αρχέ-λοχος, son of ᾿Αντήνωρ, Ξ 464.

᾿Αρχε-πτόλεμος, ᾿Ιφιτίδης, charioteer of ῞Εκτωρ, Θ 128.

ἄρχευε, *-ειν*, pres., (*ἀρχός*), *τινί*, ducere, *command*. (Il.)

ἀρχή (*ἄρχω*), initium, *beginning*, *ἐξ ἀρχῆς*, *of old*, *α* 188; *τινός*, *φ* 4, Γ 100, Λ 604; *occasion*, Χ 116.

ἀρχός, dux, *leader*, Β 493, Ε 39, *θ* 162, *δ* 653, *χ* 48.

ἄρχω (and mid., but without pf., plupf., and pass.), I. active: praeire, (1) *precede*, Α 495, Γ 420; *lead the way*, *ε* 237; *τινί*, *ω* 9.—(2) ducere, *lead*, Ρ 262; *τινί*, Β 805, Ε 592, *ξ* 230; *τινός*, Β 494, Μ 93, *κ* 205; *νηῶν*, Β 576; *τινὶ μάχεσθαι*, Π 65.—(3) regnare, *rule*, only *ζ* 12.—II. act. (and mid.*), incipere, inire, *commence, begin*.—(1) with inf., Β 84, *θ* 90*, Η 324, Φ 437, Ν 329; with dat. of interest, *τινί*, Η 324*, Ι 93*; esp. *τοῖσι δὲ . . . ἦρχ' ἀγορεύειν*, Α 571, *β* 15 (also Β 378 sc. *μαχήσασθαι*; *ξ* 428* sc. *ὠμοθετεῖν*).—(2) with gen., *make a beginning with, begin*, Ι 97, Δ 335, *φ* 142* (*ἔκ τινος*, *ψ* 199*).—(3) *τινί τινος*, Ο 95, *ζ* 101*; common phrase, *τοῖς ἄρα μύθων ἦρχε*, Β 433, *α* 28, and *τοῖσιν δ' . . . ἤρχετο μύθων*. (Od.)

ἀρωγή, *ἡ*, (*ἀρήγω*), auxilium, *help, aid*, in battle or combat; Φ 360, why should I concern myself with *giving succor?* (Il.) [ᾰ]

ἀρωγός, *-οί*, *-ούς*, opitulator, *helper, advocate*, in battle and before tribunal, *σ* 232. [ᾰ]

ἆσαι, (1) aor. from *ἄω*, satiare. —(2) aor. from *ἀάω*, obcaecare.

ἄσαιμι, opt. aor. from *ἄω*, satiarem.

᾿Ασαῖος, a Greek, Λ 301†.

ἄσαμεν, aor. from *ἰαύω*, dormivimus.

ἀσάμινθος, *ἡ*, labrum, *bathing-tub*, *δ* 48. [ᾰ]

ἄσασθαι, aor. inf. from *ἄω*, satiare.

ἄσατο, aor. of *ἀάω*, obcaecare, *blind.*

ἄ-σβεστος, 3, (*σβέννυμι*), *unextinguishable*, fire, laughter; *unceasing*, *βοή*, *κλέος*, *η* 333.

ἄσεσθαι, fut. mid. from *ἄω*, satiare.

ἀ-σημάντοισιν (*σημαίνω*), sine ductore, *without a shepherd or leader*, Κ 485†. [ᾰ]

* Denotes that the form referred to is in mid. voice.

ἆσθμα, -ατι, (ἄισθω), *short-drawn breath, panting*, O 10. (Il.)

ἀσθμαίνων (ἆσθμα), anhelans, *panting, gasping*, Φ 182. (Il.)

Ἀσιάδης, son of Ἄσιος, Ἀδάμας, Φαῖνοψ.

Ἀσίνη, in Ἀργολίς, B 560†. [ᾰ ῑ]

ἀ-σινέας, acc. pl. from -ής, (σίνομαι), illaesas, *unmolested*, λ 110. (Od.) [⏑ ⏑ ⏓]

Ἄσιος, ου, (1) son of Δύμας, a Phrygian; brother of Ἑκάβη, Π 717.—(2) son of Ὕρτακος from Ἀρίσβη, ally of Trojans, M 95.

ἄσῑν, τόσσην, situm, *slime*, Φ 321†. [ᾰ]

ἄ-σῖτος, sine cibo, *without food*, δ 788†. [ᾰ]

Ἀσίῳ ἐν λειμῶνι, *in the Asian* meadow; from Asia, a district in Lydia, from which the name was gradually extended to the whole continent, B 461. [ᾱ ῐ]

Ἀσκάλαφος, son of Ἄρης, leader of Βοιωτοί, B 512.

Ἀσκᾰνίη, a town in Bithynia, on lake of same name, B 863, N 793. [ῑ]

Ἀσκάνῖος, (1) son of Ἱπποτίων, N 792.—(2) leader of the Φρύγες, B 862. [ῑ]

ἀ-σκελέες, -ές, (σκέλλω), tabe confecti, *wasted*, κ 463; ntr. and adv. **ἀσκελέως** with *αἰεί*, *unceasingly*, T 68.

ἀσκέω, 3 sing. ipf. **ἤσκειν**, aor. *ἤσκησε*, etc., pf. pass. *ἤσκηται*, *work out with skill and care*, K 438; *smooth out*, α 439.

ἀ-σκηθής, -έες, (σκάζω), incolumis, *uninjured, unscathed*, ξ 255.

ἀσκητόν, ntr., (ἀσκέω), *curiously wrought*, δ 134. (Od.)

Ἀσκληπιάδης = Μαχάων, Δ 204. (Il.) [ᾰ]

Ἀσκληπιός, Thessalian prince, a famous physician, father of Ποδαλείριος and Μαχάων, Δ 194. (Il.) [– – ⏓ ⏑]

ἄ-σκοπος, temerarius, *thoughtless*, Ω 157.

ἀσκός, ὁ, uter, *leather bottle*, usually a goat skin (see cut, after a Pompeian painting), Γ 247; elsewh., corium, *hide*, κ 19.

ἄσμενος, ῳ, οι, (ἕαδα, σϝαδ-), lubens, *glad*, ι 63; Ξ 108, it would please me.

ἀ-σπάζομαι, only ipf. **ἠσπάζοντο**, (σπάω), amplectebantur, *were making welcome* (by reaching out hands to draw toward one), χερσί; cf. K 542.

ἀ-σπαίρων, part. ipf., *move convulsively, quiver*, K 521; πόδεσσι, χ 473, τ 231.

ἄ-σπαρτα (σπείρω), non sata, *unsown*, ι 109†.

ἀ-σπάσιος, 3 and 2, (ἀσπάζομαι).—(1) acceptus, *welcome*, Θ 488.—(2)

lubens, *joyful*, ε 397, *to his joy* the gods have delivered him; so also **ἀσπασίως**, adv. [ᾰ]

ἀσπαστός, όν, acceptus, *welcome*, ψ 239; ε 398, *a grateful thing*.

ἄ-σπερμος (σπέρμα), sine prole, *without offspring*, Υ 303†.

ἀ-σπερχές (σπέρχομαι), ntr., studiose, *eagerly*, Σ 556; μενεαίνω, be *vehemently* enraged with.

ἄ-σπετος, 2, (ἔ-σπετε), infandus, *unutterable*, Ρ 332; with πολλά, Λ 704, δ 75; *enormously great*, Τ 61, Π 157; *countless, unlimited*, χ 407, Λ 245; *endless supplies* for his needs, ν 424.

ἀσπῐδῐώτας (ἀσπιδιώτης), scutatos, *shield-bearing*, Β 554 and Π 167.

ἀσπίς, ἴδος, ἡ, *shield*, (1) *the great oval shield* (see cut); epithets, ἀμφιβρότη, ποδηνεκής; more than 2 ft. broad, 4½ ft. high, and weighing about 40 lbs.; Agamemnon's shield described, Λ 32–40; it was carried over the left shoulder, sustained by the τελαμών and by the πόρπαξ, or ring within the shield.—(2) *smaller circular shield*, *πάντοσ' ἐίση* (see cut), with only two handles; or with one central handle for the arm and several for the hand (see cut No. 12): it was of about half the size and weight of the larger ἀσπίς; cf. description of Sarpedon's shield, Μ 294 sqq. The shield consisted generally of 4 to 7 layers of ox-hide (ῥινοί, Ν 804); these were covered by a metal plate, and the whole was firmly united by rivets, which projected on the outer convex side of the shield; the head of the central rivet, larger than the rest, was the ὀμφαλός, and was usually fashioned into the form of a head; instead of the plate above mentioned, concentric metal rings (δινωτήν, εὔκυκλος) were sometimes substituted. The rim of the shield was called ἄντυξ, and the convex surface bore some device analogous to our coat of arms, Ε 182, Λ 36, cf. Ε 739. The shield of Achilleus, Σ 478–608, which was large and round, does not exactly correspond to either of the two ἀσπίδες above described.

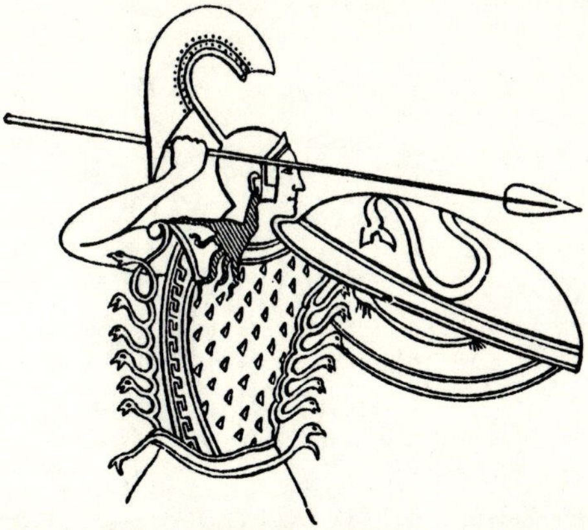

ἀσπιστάων, gen. pl., (-τής), scutatorum, *shield-bearing*, Δ 90. (Il.) [ᾱ]

Ἀσπληδών, όνος, a town in Βοιωτία, Β 511†.

ἀ-σπουδί (σπουδή), μὴ μὰν — γε, may I at least not perish *without combat*, Χ 304. (Il.) [ῑ]

ἄσσα = ἅ τινα.

ἄσσα, ὁπποῖ', *what sort of*, τ 218†.

Ἀσσάρᾰκος, son of Τρώς, Υ 232, 239 (supreme deity of Assyrians). [ᾰ]

ἆσσον, comp. from ἄγχι, propius, *nearer*, τινός, ρ 303; with twofold comparative termination, **ἀσσοτέρω**, ρ 572; τινός, τ 506.

ἀ-στᾰχύεσσιν (from ἄσταχυς), aristis, *with its ears of grain*, Β 148†. [ῠ]

ἀ-στεμφέα, ές, acc., *firm, persistent, unyielding*, Γ 219; adv. **-έως**, δ 419, 459.

Ἀστέριον, τό, a town in Θεσσαλία, Β 735†.

Ἀστερίς, an imaginary island S. of Ithaka, δ 846†.

ἀστερόεντος, ι, α, (nom. -όεις; ἀστήρ), stellatus, *starry*, ι 527; *spangled* (for ornament), Π 134 and Σ 370. (See cut on follg. page, also No. 22.)

Ἀστεροπαῖος, son of Πελάγων, leader of Λύκιοι, Μ 102, Φ 179.

ἀστεροπή, ἡ, *lightning*. (Il.)

ἀστεροπητής, Ὀλύμπιος, fulminator, *sender of lightning*, Α 580. (Il.)

ἀστήρ, -έρος, ἀστράσι, dat. pl., stella, *star*, e. g. Sirius, E 5, X 26; ἕσπερος, X 317, ν 93; stella cadens, *falling star*, Δ 75.

ἀστοί (ἄστυ), *citizens*, Λ 242 and ν 192.

ἀστράγἄλον, acc., -ων, -οισι, (strangulare?), *neck-vertebra*, κ 560; pl., *game of dice*, cf. our jack-stones, Ψ 88. (See cut, after an ancient painting in Resina.) [ᾰ]

ἀστράπτει, aor. part. -άψας, (ἀστεροπή), fulgurat, *gleams*, *lightens*, B 353. (Il.)

ἄστρα, τά, astra, *constellations*, μ 312; sank toward the horizon, K 252.

ἄστυ, εος, (Ϝάστυ), *habitations*, α 3; *city*, e. g. Ἴμβρου; ἄστυδε, in urbem, κ 104; P 144, civitatem et urbem.

Ἀστύἄλος, a Trojan, Z 29†. [ῠ]

Ἀστυ-άναξ, epithet conferred by Trojans, in honor of Hektor, upon Σκαμάνδριος, his son, Z 403.

ἀστῠ-βοώτην, acc., (βοάω), *calling throughout the city*, Ω 701†.

Ἀστύ-νοος, (1) son of Προτιάων, a Trojan, O 455†.—(2) a Trojan leader, E 144†. [ῠ]

Ἀστῠ-όχεια, mother of Τληπόλεμος, B 658†.

Ἀστῠ-όχη, mother of Ἀσκάλαφος and Ἰάλμενος, B 513†.

Ἀστύ-πῠλος, a Paionian, Φ 209†. [ῠ]

ἀ-σύφηλον, ntr., *insulting*, I 647 and Ω 767. [ῠ]

ἀ-σφᾰλὲς (σφάλλω) αἰεί, *immutable*, ζ 42, = **ἀσφαλέως**, P 436; θ 171, *steadily*, *without faltering*.

Ἀσφᾰλίων, servant of Μενέλαος, δ 216†. [ῐ]

ἀ-σφάρᾰγον, τόν, (φάρυγξ ?), *windpipe*, X 328†. [ᾰ]

ἀ-σφοδελὸν λειμῶνα, acc., *asphodel-meadow*, λ 539. (The asphodel is a plant of the lily kind.) (Od.)

ἀ-σχᾰλάᾳ, -όωσι, 3 sing. pl., -άαν inf., -όων prs. part., (σχολή), *be impatient*, B 297; τινός, at —, τ 159, 534; *to be beside one's self* (with grief), X 412. [ᾰ]

ᾰ-σχετος, ον, (and ἀάσχετον), *irresistible*, E 892; μένος, in courage, β 85; *overpowering* grief, Π 549, Ω 708.

Ἀσωπός, a river in Βοιωτία, Δ 383.

ἀ-τάλαντος (σα-, τάλαντα), *balancing*, *equal*, τινί (θεόφιν, γ 110, 409); μῆτιν, in counsel. (Il.) [ᾰ]

ἀ-τᾰλά-φρονα, acc., *harmless*, *tender*, Z 400†.

ἄταλλε, ipf., *skip*, *gambol* (cf. Psalm 104, 26), N 27†. [ᾰ]

ἀτᾰλαί, -ῇσι, and -ὰ φρονέοντες, *frisking*; λ 39, Σ 567, *light hearted*. [⏑⏑–]

ἀτάρ (from αὖ, τε, ἄρ? ἀτᾶρ, ε 108, τ 273), sed, *but*, *however*, at, *but*, *yet*.—(1) after μέν, A 166, Z 86, 125; also ἀτὰρ αὖτε, K 420; attamen, and *yet*, after ἦ μήν, vero, *verily*, I 58.—(2) without μέν, introducing a new thought. δ 236, A 506, B 313; after μάψ, B 214; after voc. not easily translatable, *for indeed*, Z 429 (in contrast with 413–28), X 331.—(3) after ἐπεί, in apodosis, M 144; following a wish, φ 404. [⏑⏑]

ἀ-ταρβής (τάρβος), impavidus, *fearless*, N 299†. [ᾰ]

ἀ-τάρβητος (ταρβέω), impavidus, *fearless, intrepid*, Γ 63†. [ᾰ]

ἀ-ταρπῖτός, ἡ, (ἀταρπός), *path*, Σ 565 and ρ 234. [ᾰ]

ἀ-ταρπόν, τήν, (τραπῆναι?), semita, *path, footway*, Ρ 743 and ξ 1. [ᾰ]

ἀ-ταρτηρέ, -οῖς, (τάρταρος?), *infernal, horrible*, Α 223. [ᾰ]

ἀτασθᾰλίαι, αἱ, (ἀτάσθαλα), scelus, *wantonness* (sin), μ 300. [ᾰ ῐ]

ἀτασθάλλων, -ουσα, prs. part., (ἀτάσθαλα), *acting wantonly*, σ 57 and τ 88. [ᾰ]

ἀτάσθᾰλος, ον, (ἄτη), scelestus, *wanton, presumptuous, wicked*, ῥέζειν, ἐώργει; esp. μηχανάασθαι ἀτάσθαλα, practice wickedness, Χ 418, π 86. [ᾰ]

ἅ τε, never as in Attic=tanquam, see ὅς τε.

ἀ-τειρής, -έα, -έας, (τείρω), *not to be worn out*, (1) *hard*, χαλκός.—(2) *unyielding, enduring*, Γ 60, Ο 697. [ᾰ]

ἀ-τέλεστος, -ον, -α, (τέλος), *without purpose, without result, unaccomplished*; π 111, *without ceasing*. [ᾰ]

ἀ-τελεύτητον, -ῳ, (τελευτάω), *unfulfilled*, Δ 175 (cf. π 111), *unfinished*.

ἀ-τελής (τέλος), *unaccomplished*, ρ 546†.

ἀτέμβω (ἀτέων), only pres., act. and pass., *vex, deceive*, pass. carere, *be deprived of, be without*, τινός, ι 42, Ψ 445, 834.

ἄτερ, with gen., sine, *without*, Ε 473; Ζηνός (cf. β 372), invito Jove; procul, *apart from*, Α 498.

ἀ-τέραμνον (τείρω), *hard*, ψ 167†. [ᾰ]

ἀ-τερπής, -έα, (τέρπω), *joyless* region, η 279; Τ 354, *tormenting*. [ᾰ]

ἀ-τέρπου, gen., (τέρπω), *doleful*, Ζ 285†. [ᾰ]

ἀτέοντα, acc. part. from ἀτέω (ἄτη), temerarium, *foolhardy*, Υ 332†. [– ⏑⏑ ⏑]

ἄτη, ης, (ἀάω), noxa, *bane, hurt*, μ 372; *folly, infatuation*, Β 111, Θ 237; euphemistically for *sin, crime*, Ζ 356, δ 261, Τ 270. [ᾰ]

ἀ-τίζων, part. from ἀτίζω (τίω), contemnens, *unheeding*, Υ 166†. [ᾰ]

ἀ-τῑμάζω, ipf. iter. ἀτιμάζεσκε, aor. ἠτίμασε, (ἀτιμάω), despicere, *treat with disrespect, dishonor*, φ 332, σ 144, Α 11. [ᾰ]

ἀ-τῑμάω, ipf. ἀτίμα, fut. and aor. ἠτίμησα (τιμάω), despicere, *treat with contempt*, Ξ 127; *maltreat*, Α 356, ξ 57. [ᾰ]

ἀ-τίμητον (τιμή), contemtum, *despised*, μετανάστην, Ι 648 and Π 59. [ᾰ]

ἀ-τῑμίησιν (ἄτιμος), assail *with insults*, ν 142†. [ᾰ]

ἄ-τῑμος (τιμή), inhonoratus, *despised*; comp. -ότερον, sup. -οτάτη; π 431, *without making return*. [ᾰ]

ἀ-τῐτάλλω, inf. ἀτιταλλέμεναι, ipf. ἀτίταλλεν, aor. ἀτίτηλα; pass. part. prs. ἀτιταλλομένην, *rear*, of gods, Ω 60; of men, λ 250; of animals, ο 174. [ᾰ]

ἄ-τῐτος (τίω), *unpaid* (penalty for), Ξ 484; *unavenged*, Ν 414.

Ἄτλας, αντος, father of Καλυψώ, η 245, α 52.

ἄ-τλητον, -ῳ, (τλῆναι), *unendurable*, Ι 3 and Τ 367.

ἆτος (ἄ-ατος, ἄμεναι), insatiabilis, *insatiable*, τινός, ν 293. (Il.)

ἀ-τρᾰπῖτοί = ἀταρπιτοί, *paths*, ν 195†.

Ἀτρεΐδης, ου, *son of Atreus*, title of Ἀγαμέμνων and of Μενέλαος; also in pl. and du., ω 24, λ 397, Α 16, 17, Γ 182.

Ἀτρεΐων, ωνος, *son of* Ἀτρεύς, Ἀγαμέμνων, Α 387, Β 192. (Il.)

ἀ-τρεκές (ἄτρακτος), ntr. as adv., *undistorted, real, true*, Ε 208; adv. **-έως**, *truly*, ρ 154.

ἀ-τρέμᾰ and before vowels (exc. Ο 318) **ἀτρέμας** (τρέμω), *motionless*, τ 212; *calm*, Β 200.

Ἀτρεύς, father of Ἀγαμέμνων and of Μενέλαος; his sceptre, Β 105.

ἀ-τρίπτους (τρίβω), *not hardened, tender*, φ 151†.

ἄ-τρομος, ον, (τρόμος), intrepidus, *fearless*, Ε 126. (Il.)

ἀ-τρῠγέτοιο, ον, gen. acc., (τρύω), *unwasting, restless, unresting*, epith. of the sea, and Ρ 425, of αἰθήρ, *glimmering*; the ancients derived the word from τρυγᾶν, *unfruitful*; opp. γαίην πολυφόρβην, Α 316.

Ἀτρῡτώνη, Διὸς τέκος—, (ὀτρύνω), Ἀθηναίη, δ 762.

ἄττᾰ (cf. in Swiss dialect Aetti), term of endearment used in addressing elders=*father*, π 31.

ἀτυζομένω, οι, part. pres., and aor.

ἀτυχθείς, from ἀτύζω (ἄτη ?), strictly, *blinded, dazed, frightened; fleeing bewildered* over the plain, Z 38; *terrified at*, Z 468; *amazed*, ψ 42. [ᾰ]

Ἀτυμνϊάδης, son of Ἀτύμνιος, Μύδων, E 581†. [ᾰ]

Ἀτύμνιος, son of Ἀμισώδαρος, Π 317, 328.

αὖ, rursus, *again, on the contrary*, adversative conjunction, (1) nearly equals δέ, B 493; after μέν, Λ 109; νῦν αὖ, *but* now, ν 149; εἰ δ' αὖ, σ 371; but if *on the contrary; again, moreover*, B 671, 678, 681, Γ 200.—(2) *on the other hand*, Γ 323, Δ 240; δ' αὖ, but *again*, Δ 17, Z 229; esp. freq., τὸν δ' αὖ ἀντίον ηὖδα, α 213, 230.—(3) denuo, *also, again*, A 540, υ 88; αὖ νῦν, ε 129, δεύτερον αὖ.

αὐαίνω, **αὐανθέν,** aor. pass. part., (αὔω), siccatum, *when it was dry*, ι 321†.

αὐγάζομαι (αὐγή), *discern*, Ψ 458†.

Αὐγειαί, town, (1) of Λάκωνες, B 583†.—(2) of Λοκροί, B 532†.

Αὐγείας, *αο*, father of Ἀγαμήδη, Λ 701, 739.

αὐγή, ῆς, *bright light, radiance*, N 341, ζ 305; pl., *beams*, of sun, of light of day, Διός, N 837.

Αὐγηιάδης, *son of* Αὐγείας, Ἀγασθένης, B 624†.

αὐδάω, imp. **αὔδα,** ipf. ηὔδα, aor. (iter. αὐδήσασκε), part. αὐδήσας, *speak*, ἔπος, Z 54, ν 199; ἀντίον—τινά, alloqui, *address*, Γ 203; ἔπος, E 170; μεγάλα, *boast* loudly, δ 505.

αὐδή, ῆς, *voice*, A 249, Σ 419, T 418; φ 411 (of the swallow).

αὐδήεις, εσσα, *speaking with human voice*, T 407, ε 334; v. l. οὐδήεσσα, *earthly*.

αὐ-έρυον, ipf., aor. αὐ-έρυσαν (ἀν-Fερύω), *draw out*, M 261; *bend back* (head of victim), A 459.

αὔη, αὔη, see αὔοι, accenderet.

αὖθ', (1)=αὖτε.—(2) Λ 48, M 85, β 369, σ 48=αὖθι.

αὖθι, (1) eodem loco, *on the spot, here, there*, A 492; with following determination of place by prep., ι 29.—(2) illico, *at once*, σ 339.

αὐίαχοι, pl., (ἀ-Fίαχοι), *speechless*, N 41†. (Others interpret, *shouting loudly*.)

αὐλείου, *ησι*, (αὔλειος, αὐλή), *belonging to the αὐλή, of the court*, α 104. (Od.)

αὐλή, ῆς, (FAΣ), *court enclosure*, (1) before the house; with gate, gate-way, portico, stables, slave-quarters, altar, and θόλος; see table III.—(2) before the cave of Πολύφημος, ι 239; before the tent of Ἀχιλλεύς, Ω 452; round the palace of Αἴολος, κ 10.

αὔλῃ, v. l. instead of αὐλῇ, κ 10.

αὐλιζομενάων, pres. part. from αὐλίζομαι (αὐλή), *penned in*, μ 265. (Od.)

αὖλιν, acc., (ἰαύω), *place of repose*, χ 470.

Αὐλίς, ἴδος, rendezvous of Greeks before sailing for Troja, town in Βοιωτία, B 303.

αὐλός, οῦ, (ἀFῆναι), (1) *wind instrument, flute*, Σ 495, K 13.—(2) *socket* in which point of lance was fitted, P 297; *holes* or *eyes*, receiving the tongue of a buckle, τ 227.—(3) *stream of blood*, χ 18.

αὐλῶπις, ιδι, (αὐλός), *with upright socket* to receive the plume, E 182. (Il.) (See *b* in cut; see also cuts 17, 18, 122.)

αὖος, 3, (εὔω), siccus, *dry*, P 493; αὖον, of sound, *dull, hollow, grating*, M 160, N 441.

ἄ-υπνος, -ους, (ὕπνος), *sleepless*, (1) of persons, ι 404, κ 84.—(2) νύκτας, I 325. [ᾰ]

αὔρη (ἄFημι), aura, *breeze*, ε 469†.

αὔριον (ἦρι), *to-morrow morning*, Θ 535, η 318.

ἀυσταλέος (αὖος), squalidus, *unanointed, unkempt*, τ 327†. [ᾰ]

αὐτ-άγρετα, ntr. pl., (ἀγρεῖν), *self-chosen, attainable*, π 148†.

αὐτάρ (αὖτε, ἄρα), *but, however*, adversative conj., differing from δέ chiefly in marking a contrast more strongly, (1) after *μέν*, A 127, B 103, *α* 215; also *αὐτὰρ ὁ αὖτε*, B 107, and *αὐτὰρ ἄρα*, B 103; after *εἰ*—, Γ 290; after a wish, *φ* 404.—(2) at beginning of sentence, *but, yet, now*, A 118, 348; *αὐτὰρ ὁ*, Γ 18; in transitions esp. with *ἐπεί, ἐπήν*, A 458, 464, 467, *ω* 467. [– ⏑, the first syllable always in arsi.]

αὖτε (*αὖ, -τε*), lit. *on that occasion; then, further, moreover, but*, (1) adversative, with *νῦν*, A 237; *τότε*, B 221; *ἔνθα*, Z 234; Γ 180, *also; further*, B 407, and *δεύτερον αὖτε*; *on the other hand*, H 345; with *δέ*, Γ 76, 121, *β* 203, 331; like *δέ* in apodosis, A 137, Δ 321. —(2) *hereafter*, A 340, B 225, 370; *again* (in disapproval), A 202; cf. also Z 73, 81, H 335.

ἀϋτέω (2 *αὔω*), only ipf. 3 sing. and pl. **ἀΰτει, ἀΰτευν**, *call aloud*, Υ 50, Φ 582; *call upon*, Λ 258; of things, *ring, resound*, M 160. [ᾰ]

ἀϋτή, *ῆς*, (2 *αὔω*), *cry*, *ζ* 122, B 153; esp. *battle-cry*, Δ 331, Ξ 96; *battle*, O 718.

αὐτ-ῆμαρ (*ἦμαρ*), *on the same day*, *γ* 311; A 81, *to-day*.

αὐτίκα (cf. *ἡνίκα, πόκα*), *forthwith, straightway*, *ξ* 403, Δ 160, A 199; often with *νῦν*, Z 308; *ἐπεί*, M 393; *ἔπειτα*, T 242; *μάλα*, *κ* 111.

αὖτις (*αὖ, τέ*), *again*, rursus, *back again*, A 425, B 208; with *ἄψ*, *φ* 139; *πάλιν*, E 257; *once more, again*, A 513, 522, H 462, Δ 15, *κ* 461, see *ἐξαῦτις*; *on the other hand, in turn*, H 170, *ο* 439; *another time, in future*, Γ 440, *α* 317.

ἀϋτμή, *-ήν*, (German Athem; *ἀϜῆναι*?), *breath*, I 609, Ξ 174; *μ* 369, *scent; scorching heat*, *ι* 389; *blast*, *λ* 400, Σ 471. [ᾰ]

ἀϋτμένα, acc. from *ἀϋτμήν*, masc., (*ἀϋτμή*), *breath*, Ψ 765; *blast*, *γ* 289.

αὐτο-δίδακτος (*διδάσκω*), *self-taught*, *χ* 347†.

αὐτόδιον (*αὐτοῦ*), e vestigio, *straightway*, *θ* 449†.

αὐτό-ετες (*ἔτος*), *in the same year*, *γ* 322†.

αὐτόθ' = *αὐτόθι*.

αὐτόθεν (*αὐτ-οῦ*), *from the very spot*, Υ 120; elsewh. with *ἐξ*—, *from one's seat, chair*, T 77, *ν* 56, *φ* 420.

αὐτόθι (= *αὐτοῦ*), *on the spot*, K 443; often with more definite limitation following: e. g. *ἀγρῷ*, ruri, *λ* 187; or *ἐν*, with dat., *ι* 29; *κατ'*, K 273.

αὐτο-κᾰσιγνήτη, soror germana, *own sister*, *κ* 137†.

αὐτο-κᾰσίγνητος, *ου*, frater germanus, Γ 238; see *κασίγνητος*. (Il.)

Αὐτό-λῠκος, *ου*, father of *Ἀντίκλεια*, mother of *Ὀδυσσεύς*, *τ* 394 to 466, K 267.

αὐτό-μᾰτος, 3, (*μέμαα*), spontaneus, *of one's own accord*, B 408. (Il.)

Αὐτο-μέδων, *οντος*, son of *Διώρης*, charioteer of *Ἀχιλλεύς*, P 536, Π 145.

Αὐτο-νόη, handmaid of *Πηνελόπεια*, *σ* 182†.

Αὐτό-νοος, (1) a Greek, Λ 301†.—(2) a Trojan, Π 694†.

αὐτο-νυχί (*νύξ*), *this very night*, Θ 197†.

αὐ-τός, *ή, ό*, lit. *again he*, (1) idem, *same*, pron. of identity, preceding subst., *θ* 107, M 225; with demonstr. (*τόν*), Z 391, *δ* 654, A 338, *η* 55.—(2) ipse, pron. of emphasis, opposition, A 47, 51, 112, 161, Γ 301, A 4, *λ* 602; immediately under, N 615; middle of the road, *κ* 158; dat. (with and without *σύν*), together with, I 194, *θ* 186, *ν* 118; of one's own free will, *β* 168, Θ 218; *alone*, Θ 99, N 729; often with preceding pers. pron., *τ* 93, *γ* 49, *ξ* 331, Ψ 312, *α* 279, K 389, Ω 292; pers. pron. must sometimes be supplied, *χ* 38, Ω 430, B 263; with enclitic pron. forms preceding, *ε* 179, 190, K 242, *β* 33, *λ* 134, *δ* 66; following, E 459, *χ* 345, X 346, *δ* 244; in reflexive sense, *φ* 249, *ξ* 51, *θ* 68, *κ* 416, *β* 125, *δ* 247, H 338; with possessive prons., *α* 409, *χ* 218, *π* 197, K 204, *ο* 262, *δ* 643, O 39, *β* 138. —(3) as pron. 3 pers. (only in oblique cases), Λ 633, *κ* 302, *β* 154, P 546, B 347.

αὐτο-στᾰδίῃ, *ἐν*—, (*ἵστασθαι*), *hand-to-hand fight*, N 325†.

αὐτο-σχεδίῃ, *-ην*, (*σχεδόν*), *close combat*, O 510; acc. cominus.

αὐτο-σχεδόν, *-ά*, (*σχεδόν*), cominus, *hand to hand*, O 386, Π 319.

αὐτοῦ (*αὐτός*), eodem loco, *on the spot*, usually more closely defined by following preposition, *θ* 68; illico, *β* 250, Φ 114; hic, ibi.

αὐτόφι(ν) = *αὐτῷ*, T 255; = *αὐτῶν*, Λ 44; = *αὐτοῖς*, N 42; always with prep.

Αὐτό-φονος, father of *Πολυφόντης* of *Θήβη*, Δ 395†.

αὐτο-χόωνον, acc., (*χόανος*) *σόλον*,

of mass of stone in its natural rough shape, *massive* quoit, Ψ 826†.

αὔ-τως (*αὐτός*), (1) eodem modo, *just so*, Χ 125 ; esp. *ὡς δ' αὔτως, so in this very way*, ζ 166.—(2) sponte, *even without this*, Α 520 ; *utterly, simply*, Β 138, υ 379, Γ 220, Ζ 400, Ψ 268 ; just as you are, Σ 198. —(3) sic (temere), *thus*, with ellipsis, as you propose, as he was, Α 133, υ 130 ; in vain, Β 342. (Reading often doubtful between *αὔτως* and *οὕτως*.)

αὐχενίους, acc. pl., (*αὐχήν*), *τένοντας, neck* sinews, γ 450†.

αὐχήν, *ένος, ὁ*, cervices, *neck*, of men and animals, Ζ 117, κ 559.

αὐχμεῖς, 2 sing. prs. from *αὐχμέω* (*αὐχμός*), *be dry*, i. e. *unanointed, squalid*, ω 250†.

1. **αὔοι** (*αὔω, εὔω*), accenderet, where *he could not obtain fire* from other source, v. l. *αὔῃ*, that *he may not be forced to seek fire* from elsewhere, ε 490†.

2. *αὔω*, only ipf. **αὖε**, and 1 aor. **ἤϋσε** and *ἄυσε* (*ἀῦσαι, ἀύσας*, etc.), *call aloud*, (1) vocare, *call upon, τινά*, Λ 461, Ν 477, ι 65.—(2) clamare, *call aloud*, of things, *ring*, with *μέγα, δεινόν, καρφαλέον*; *αὖον*, of harsh, dry sound (cf. aridum); *διαπρύσιον*, piercingly ; (*ἐπὶ*) *μακρόν*, so as to be heard a great distance, aloud (Ε 347, Θ 160), Γ 81, ζ 117.

ἀφ-αιρέω, fut. mid. **-αιρήσεσθαι**; aor. **-εῖλον**, etc., also *ἀπο-αίρεο*, prs. imp., (*Ϝαίρεο* ?), *-εῖσθαι, ἀπο-Ϝεῖλε(το)*, often in tmesi, adimere, (1) act., *take away*, ι 313 ; *τί τινος*, Ε 127, ι 416 ; *τί τινι*, ξ 455.—(2) *take away to hold for one's self*, Γ 294, Π 54, Ι 336 ; *τινά τι*, Θ 108, Χ 18, Α 182 ; *remove from one's self*, μ 199 ; *take away*, Α 299, ζ 91 ; *θυμόν* (life) *τινος*, and *τινά*; *frustrate, νόστον, νόστιμον ἦμάρ τινι, βίας τινός*; *take off* armor, *ὤμων*, Η 122; *ὤμοιϊν*, Π 560.

ἄ-φᾰλον (*φάλος*), *without crest, ταυρείην—τε καὶ ἄλλοφον*, Κ 258†. [ᾰ]

ἀφ-ᾰ́μαρτεν, *-ών, -ούσῃ*, and **ἀπήμβροτεν**, aor. from *ἁμαρτάνω—τινός*, (1) *miss*, deerrare a, Θ 302.—(2) *lose*, orbari, Ζ 411. (Il.)

ἀφ-ᾰμαρτο-επής, *missing the point, rambling speaker*, Γ 215†.

ἀφ-ανδάνει (*ἀνδάνω*), *displeases*, π 387†.

ἄ-φαντος, *-οι*, (*φαίνω*), *unseen, leaving no trace behind*, Ζ 60†. (Il.)

ἄφαρ, statim, *at once, instantly*, Φ 528. When joined with *δέ* (exc. Ψ 593, θ 409) it begins the sentence ; when used alone, it follows one or more words. [⏑⏑]

Ἀφᾰρεύς, *ῆος, Καλητορίδης*, name of a Greek leader, Ν 541.

ἀφ-αρπάξαι, aor. inf., (*ἁρπάζω*), deripere, *τι τινός, wrench away from*, Ν 189†.

ἀφάρ-τεροι, celeriores, *swifter*, Ψ 311†.

ἀφαυροῦ, *-ότερος, -ον, -ότατος, -η*, (*φάϜος*), *insignificant*, debilis, *weakly*, Η 235, υ 110.

ἀφάω, **ἀφόωντα**, (*ἅπτω*), tractantem, *busy with handling, τι*, Ζ 322†. [ᾰ]

Ἀφείδας, *αντος, Πολυπημονίδης*, fictitious, assumed name, ω 305†.

ἀφείη, aor. opt. from *ἀφίημι*, iacularetur.

ἄφενος (opes), *possessions*, esp. in cattle, ξ 99, Α 171. [ᾰ]

ἀφ-έξω, *-ξομαι*, fut. from *ἀπέχω*, prohibebo.

ἀφ-ήμενος (*ἧμαι*), seorsum sedens, *sitting apart*, Ο 106†. [ᾰ]

ἀφ-ήτορος, gen. (*ἀφίημι*), sagittarii, *of the archer=ἑκηβόλου*, Ι 404†. [ᾰ]

ἄ-φθῖτος, 2, (*φθίω*), aeternus, *unwasting, imperishable*, only of possessions, exc. Ι 413, Ω 88.

ἀφ-ίημι, reg., collat. forms of ipf. *ἀφίει, ἠφίει*, aor. *ἀφέηκε*, subj. *-ἑῃ, -ήῃ*, opt. *-είη* (*ἵημι*), dimittere, (1) *send away*, Α 25 ; *drive away*, Β 263, Λ 642 ; *shed* blossom, η 126 ; *let fall*, Μ 221 ; *μένος, slackened* its force, Ν 444 ; *release*, Υ 464 ; mid. ψ 240 ; pass., *are emitted from*, Δ 77.—iaculari, *hurl*, weapons, lightning, etc., Κ 372, Ψ 432, Ρ 631, χ 251, ω 539, Θ 133. [⏑⏑–⏑; χ 251 ⏑–⏑⏑.]

ἀφ-ῑκάνω (*ἱκάνω*), pervenio, *come to, reach, πρός τι*, Ζ 388 ; *δεῦρο*, huc, Ξ 43 (Od. only with acc.).

ἀφ-ίκομαι, only fut. **-ῖξεαι**, perf. inf. *-ῖχθαι*, aor. *-ικόμην*, etc. (tmesis, μ 2), pervenio, with acc., *come to* (a person), *arrive at* (a place), φ 25, α 332, φ 42, ο 489, also with *εἰς, ἐπί, ποτί*, κατά, ὑπό; *reach*, Ω 329, θ 202; Σ 395, trouble *came upon* me.

ἀφ-ίστημι, I. trans., only mid. *ἀποστήσωνται*, *demand pay for themselves for*, N 745.—II. intr., *-ἵσταμαι*, pf. *-ἕστατε*, *-ἑστᾶσιν*, *-ἑσταίη*, *-ἑσταότες*, plupf. *-ἕστασαν*, aor. *-ἔστη*, *stand away*, *stand off*, Ψ 517, N 738; *νόσφιν*, λ 544; *τινός*, from a person, ψ 101; from a thing, Δ 340.

ἄ-φλαστον, aplustre, *ornamental knob on stern of ship, figure-head*, O 717†. [⏑ – ⏑] (See cut, also No. 41.)

ἀ-φλοισμός (*φλοῖσβος*), spuma, *foam*, O 607†.

ἀφνειός, 2, *-ότεροι*, *-ότατος*, (*ἄφενος*), opulentus, *wealthy*, *rich in*, *τινός* (means of subsistence, gold, etc.); *flourishing* house, α 232; coupled with *μέγα δυναμένοιο*, λ 414.

ἀφ-ωπλίζοντο (*ὁπλίζω*), ipf., *ἔντεα*, *laid off their armor*, Ψ 26†.

ἀφ-ορμηθεῖεν, opt., and *-θέντες*, aor. pass. part., (*ὁρμάω*), proficisci, *ναῦφιν*, *set out from* the ships; *depart*, β 375.

ἀφόωντα, see *ἀφάω*, tractantem.

ἀ-φρᾰδέουσι, pres. indic., *-έοντι*, part. (*ἀ-φραδής*), amentem esse, *be foolish*, η 294, I 32.

ἀ-φρᾰδέες, *έων*, (*φράζομαι*), *senseless*, λ 476; *foolish*, β 282; adv. *-έως*, *foolishly*, Γ 436.

ἀ-φρᾰδίῃ, dat. sing., (*φράζομαι*), *ignorance*, B 368; elsewh. dat. pl. *-ίῃσι*, *folly*, Π 354, ξ 481; *νόοιο*, K 122.

ἀ-φραίνω (*φρήν*), *be mad*, H 109, υ 360.

ἄφρεον, ipf. (*ἀφρός*), spumabant, breasts *were covered with foam*, Λ 282†. [– ⏑⏑ = *ἄφρευν*.]

ἀ-φρήτωρ (*φρήτρη*), *no respecter of race*, I 63†.

'Αφροδίτη, *ης*, daughter of Ζεύς, Γ 374, Υ 105; and of Διώνη, E 370; also Κυθέρεια, Κύπρις, from her seats of worship; *δῖα*, *ἐυστεφάνου*, *φιλομμειδής*, *χρυσέη*; wife of Ἥφαιστος, θ 267 sq.; goddess of love, E 429, δ 261, Γ 54; and of beauty, T 282; of love's charms, Ξ 214 (see *κεστός*); attended by Χάριτες, σ 192; mother of Αἰνείας. As common noun = *hot passion*, χ 444.

ἀ-φρονέοντες, pres. part., (*ἄφρων*), *foolish*, O 104†.

ἀφρός, *οῦ*, spuma, *foam* of waves, of lion, Υ 168. (Il.)

ἀφροσῠ́νης, *-άων*, gen., (*ἄφρων*), *folly*, H 110; pl., *foolish behavior*, π 278, ω 457.

ἄ-φρων, *-ονι*, *-ονα*, (*φρήν*), *thoughtless*, Δ 104, E 875, Λ 389; Ω 157, *foolish*.

ἀ-φύλλοισιν, dat. pl., (*φύλλον*), *leafless*, *stripped of leaves*, B 425†. [ᾰ]

ἀφύξειν, fut. from *ἀφύσσω*.

ἀ-φυσγετόν, acc., *slime*, Λ 495†. [ᾱ]

ἀφύσσων, ipf. *ἄφυσσεν*, *-ον*, fut. *ἀφύξειν*, aor. *ἠφύσαμεν*, part. *ἀφύσσας*, mid. ipf. *ἠφύσσετο*, aor. *ἠφυσάμην*, *ἀφυσσάμεθα*, *ἀφυσσάμενος*, fundere, *draw*, *pour into* (mid. for one's self), wine or water, ι 9, 85; with *ἀπὸ*, *ἐκ*, *ἐν*, or with simple gen., ψ 305; η 286, *I was scattering* the leaves over myself; A 171, do I intend to *acquire for* thee, *σοί*.

'Αχαιαί, *Achaian women* (with beautifully braided hair). (Od.) [ᾰ]

'Αχαιιάδες, *ων*, E 422, *Achaian women*, E 424 (with beautiful mantles). [ᾰ]

'Αχαιϊκόν, acc. msc. and ntr. nom., *Achaian*, I 521, 141, γ 251. [ᾰ]

'Αχαιίς, *ίδος*, land of 'Αχαιοί, *Achaia*, Northern Greece, Γ 75, λ 166, ν 249, A 254, φ 107; pl. as subst., *Achaian women*, I 395; contemptuously, B 235. [ᾰ]

'Αχαιοί, *ῶν*, chief tribe of Greeks in Θεσσαλία, Μεσσήνη, Ἄργος, 'Ιθάκη;

collective appellation of the Greeks, A 2, α 90; epithets, ἀρηιφίλων, δῖοι, ἑλίκωπες, ἐυκνήμιδες, κάρη κομόωντες (κοῦροι), μεγάθυμοι, μένεα πνείοντες, χαλκοχιτώνων. [ᾰ]

ἀ-χἄρίστερον (ἄχαρι), ingratius, *more unwelcome*, υ 392†. [ᾰ]

ἀ-χάριστα, ntr. pl., (χάρις), ingrata, *unpleasing*, θ 236†. [ᾰ]

Ἀχελώιος, river-god, (1) in Greece (Αἰτωλία), Φ 194†.—(2) in Φρυγία, Ω 616†.

ἀχέρδῳ (ἡ ἄχερδος), *wild pear-tree*, ξ 10†. [ᾰ]

ἀχερωΐς, *white poplar*, N 389. (Il.) [ᾰ]

Ἀχέροντα, acc., (Ἀχέρων, ἀ-χέρων, cuncta abripiens), *the chasm, abyss* (not river), of lower world, κ 513†. [ᾰ]

ἀχεύων, prs. part., (ἄχος), *troubled for*, τινός, ξ 40; εἵνεκα, φ 318; θυμόν, *grieved* at heart. [ᾰ]

ἀχέων, ουσα, part. prs. (ἄχος), *grieving*, τινός, B 694; κῆρ, at heart. [ᾰ]

ἄχθομαι, ipf. ἤχθετο (ἄχθος), (1) *be laden*, ο 457.—(2) moleste fero, *take ill, be pained or afflicted with*, τί, N 352, E 361; ὀδύνῃσι, *tormented* with pains; κῆρ, *vexed* at heart.

ἄχθος, τό, (ἄχος), onus, *burden*, Υ 247; ἀρούρης, *dead weight* upon the earth, of idle, useless man, υ 379.

Ἀχιλεύς, Ἀχιλλεύς, ῆος, (Πηλείδης), son of Πηλεύς and Θέτις, Αἰακίδης, king of Μυρμιδόνες, foster-child of Φοῖνιξ, pupil of Χείρων, hero of the Iliad: his destiny, I 410 sq.; expedition against Troy, B 681; forays, I 328, A 392, B 690, see Βρισηίς; μῆνις, A; πρεσβεία, I; death of his friend Πάτροκλος, Π 827; μηνίδος ἀπόρρησις, T 56; Ἕκτορος ἀναίρεσις, X; Ἕκτορος λύτρα, Ω; his death, ε 310, ω 37 sq.; epithets, δαΐφρων, δῖος, διίφιλος, θεοῖς ἐπιείκελ(ε), θεοείκελ(ε), πελώριον, ποδάρκης δῖος, ποδώκης, πτολιπόρθῳ, ῥηξήνορος, πόδας ταχύν, (πόδας) ὠκύς. (See cut, in next column, from Panathenaic Amphora.)

ἀχλύς, ύος, ἡ, caligo, *mist*, E 127, Υ 321; of death, Π 344; *swoon*, E 696; *grief*, Υ 421. [– ⏑ ⏑, nom. and acc. – –.]

ἤχλῦσε, aor. from ἀχλύω, *grew dark*, μ 406. (Od.)

ἄχνη, ῃ, ην, *foam of water*, Λ 307; *chaff*, E 499, pl.

ἄχνῠμαι, pres., ἄχνυτο, ipf., (ἀκαχίζω, ἄχος), dolere, *grieve, mourn*, θυμός (ἐνὶ στήθεσσι, Ξ 38), κῆρ ἄχνυται (ἐν θυμῷ, Z 524), ἀχνυμένῃ κραδίῃ, Ω 584; ἄχνυσθαι κῆρ, in heart, ω 420; τινός, λ 558, for some one; with part., Σ 320.

ἄ-χολον, *dissipating-wrath*, others translate *mild, soothing*, δ 221†. [ᾰ]

ἄχομαι (ἄχος), only σ 256, τ 129, *I mourn*. [ᾰ]

ἄχος, εος, τό, also pl., (ἄγχω), *grief, pain*, τινός, over some one, for something, Θ 124, N 417, ο 358; περί, φ 249; sorrow seizes, θυμὸν ἵκανεν, ἀμφεχύθη τινά, γένετό τινι (κατὰ θυμόν); ἀπὸ πραπίδων ἔλθοι, roll a stone from one's heart; cf. Υ 282, K 145; εἷλε, ἔλλαβε, τύψε τινά (θυμόν), N 581, Ξ 475, T 125; τινί ἐστι, I 249; ἄχεος νεφέλη, P 591. [ᾰ]

ἀ-χρεῖον, ntr. = adv., (χρεῖος), B 269, looked *foolishly* about, as one who has *no* χρεῖος, i. e. knows not what he shall do; σ 163, *constrainedly* (a forced laugh without cause) (164, οὔτι πάρος γε).

ἀ-χρημοσύνη (χρήματα), inopia, *want*, ρ 502†.

ἄχρῐ(ς) (κατ' ἄκρης), prorsus, *altogether*; σ 370, perhaps *until*.

ἀχῡρμιαί (ἄχυρον), *heaps of chaff*, Ε 502†. [ᾰ]

ἄψ (ἀπό), *back, back again*, ἀπονοστήσειν, Θ 499; ἀπιών, Κ 289; with gen. *back from*, Μ 420; ἀπό, Μ 390; ἀποφέρω, Κ 337; and freq. with cmpds. of ἀπό-; with πάλιν, *back again*, Σ 280; αὖτις, Θ 335.

'Α-ψευδής, a Nereid, Σ 46†.

ἀψῖδες, αἱ, (ἅψος), maculae, *meshes*, Ε 487†.

ἀψο-ρρόου (ῥέω) Ὠκεανοῖο, of the Okeanos stream which *flows back into itself*, i. e. *encircling*, Σ 399.

ἄψο-ρροι, -ον, (ῥέω, -σροος), reduces, *back*, with verbs of motion; usually ntr., retro, κ 558.

ἅψεα (ἅπτω), artus, *joints, limbs*, δ 794 and σ 189.

ἄω, inf. **ἄμεναι**, fut. ἄσειν, aor. subj. ἄσῃ, opt. ἄσαιμι, inf. ἆσαι, mid. fut. or aor. imp. ἄσεσθε, aor. inf. **ἄσασθαι** (aveo), (1) satiari, Φ 70, eager to *sate itself* with human flesh; γόοιο ἆσαι, Ψ 157, cf. κλαυθμοῖο ἄσεσθε.—(2) satiare, τινά τινος, Ε 289; τινί, Λ 817.

ἄωροι (ἀείρω) = μετ-έωροι, penduli, *dangling*, i. e. *formless, useless, misshapen*, μ 89†. [ᾰ]

ἄωρτο, plupf. pass. from ἀείρω, pendêbat.

ἀωτεῖς, εἶτε, (from ἀωτέω, ἄημι), dormire, with acc. ὕπνον, Κ 159 and κ 548. [ᾰ]

ἀώτου, ῳ, ον, (ἄημι, αϝωϝτος), floccus, *lock of wool*, οἰός, α 443; *nap of linen*, Ι 661; *fleece, sheep's wool*, ι 434; on sheep's back; spun, Ν 599. [ᾰ]

B.

βάδην (βαίνω), pedetentim, *step by step, slowly*, Ν 516†.

βάζω, pres., ipf., and perf. pass. βέβακται, loqui, *speak*, esp. with ntr. adjs., e. g. ἄρτια, fit things, Ξ 92; cf. Ι 58, Δ 355, σ 392, δ 32, ξ 127; ἔπος, θ 408.

βᾰθῠ-δινήεις, **δῑνήεντος**, -α, *full of deep eddies*, Φ 15.

βᾰθῠ-δῑνης (δῖναι), *deep-eddying*, Υ 73; always of rivers, exc. κ 511.

βᾰθυ-ζώνους, acc., (ζώνη), *deep-girdled*, i. e. with girdle low down over the hips, Ι 594. (See cut.)

Βᾰθῠ-κλῆς, ῆα, son of Χάλκων, a Μυρμιδών, Π 594†.

βᾰθύ-κολποι, ων, (κόλπος), *with deep folds* or *bellies in garment*, i. e. with garment falling low or in deep folds over and below the girdle, which its folds hid from sight; the word may be translated *deep-girdled*; epithet of Trojan women, Σ 122. (Il.) (See cut.)

βᾰθῠ-λειμον, acc. comm., (λειμών), *with rich meadows*, i. e. *with deep soil*, Ἄνθειαν, Ι 151. (Il.)

βᾰθῠ-λήϊον, *with deep-*, i. e. *high-waving grain, fruitful*, Σ 550†.

βαθύνω, only ipf. **βάθῡνε**, *deepen, hollow out*, Ψ 421†.

βᾰθῡ-ρρείταο (-σρειταο, ῥέω), *deep-flowing* Okeanos, Φ 195†.

βᾰθῡ-ρρόου, όου, (-ρροος), *with deep current, deep-streaming* Okeanos, and Φ 8, river.

βᾰθύς, εῖα, (-έης, -έην), ύ, sup. -ιστον, (1) vertically: altus, *high, deep,* Τάρταρος; *low lying,* of court, chasm, plowed land, sandy shore, forest, storm, and fog, T 125, *deep* in the heart.—(2) horizontally: *deep, stretching far into* the land; of bay, B 560; of shore pierced by numerous inlets, B 92; to the limits of the *broad* plough-land, Σ 547.

βᾰθύ-σχοινον (σχοῖνος), *deeply overgrown with rushes,* Δ 383†.

βαίνω, ipf., fut., 1 aor. ἔβησα, trans.; 2 aor. ἔβην (βᾰ́την, ἔβαν, subj. βείω, -ῃ or βήῃ, βείομεν, βήμεναι), pf. βέβηκα, *stand, tread* (βεβάασιν, inf. βεβάμεν, part. βεβαώς), fut. mid. βήσομαι, also aor. (ἐ)βήσετο, -σατο, *go,* πάλιν, redire; νόσφι, secedere; B 134, βεβάασι, praeterierunt; *set out,* θ 49; hence often with inf., βῆ (βάν, βεβήκει) δ' ἰέναι, ῥ' ἴμεν, etc., σ 428; with pres. part., B 302, 665, ξ 207; fut., Λ 101; cf. α 424; aor., ω 488, N 582.—(1) *go* (whither?), πῇ, Z 377 (B 339, Θ 229, what *is become of?*); χαμᾶζε, with -δε Οὔλυμπόνδε, οἴκαδε, Ἀιδόσδε, cf. also λ 277, 627; (a) with acc., *go and take one's place by the side of,* Γ 262; with ἀνά, Δ 209; διά, Θ 343; εἰς, ἐς (Οδυσῆα, χ 202); κατά, *stalks* over the heads of men, T 93; throughout, B 47; go for, δ 701, A 424; μετά, sequi, β 406; adire, Δ 292, λ 563; aggredi, Π 864; παρά, T 40; πρός, Z 313; ὑπέρ, χ 182.—(b) with gen. διά, ρ 26; διέκ, σ 185; ἐπί, I 589 (χέρσου, ἠπείρου, ἵππων, I 589); ὑπέρ, ρ 575; ἰθύς, E 849.—(c) with dat. ἀμφί, tueri, *guard,* A 37; ἐν, N 618; ἐπί, accedere, *draw near,* P 574; aggredi, Λ 460, Π 751.—(2) (where?), ἐπὶ χθονί, incedere, *walk,* Δ 443; ἐν νηυσί, avehi, *sail away,* α 210.—(3) (whence?), ἀπὸ πύργου, κατ' Ἰδαίων ὀρέων; 1 aor. ἀφ' (ἐξ) ἵππων, *cause to dismount, dash down, shoot down;* ἐπὶ Βουπρασίου ἵππους, *bring* horses to Bouprasion.

βᾰ́λᾰνον, τήν, glandem, *acorn,* ν 409, and ἄκυλον, edible acorn, κ 242.

Βᾰλῐ́ος, one of the horses of Ἀχιλλεύς. T 400. (Il.)

βάλλω, reg. as in Attic, exc. fut. βαλέω, aor. subj. βάλῃσθα, opt. βάλοισθα, plupf. 3 sing. βεβλήκειν, pf. pass., 3 pl. βεβλήαται, plupf. -ήατο (the forms βεβολημένος, and plupf. βεβόλητο and 3 pl. -ήατο only of inward [mental] feelings); aor. mid. with pass. signif., βλῆτο, subj. βλήεται, opt. βλεῖο, part. βλήμενος, mitto, iacio.—(1) *throw,* I 588, *was struck;* esp. tela mittere, *discharge missiles* (opp. ἐλαύνω, ρ 279; τύπτειν, Y 378, O 495; οὐτάσαι, Ξ 424); *shoot,* Θ 282, Γ 82; also lapides coicere, *hurl stones.*—(2) *strike, hit,* Φ 591, Λ 380 (and *wound*); τόν ῥ' ἔβαλεν κεφαλήν, in the head, etc., O 433, N 411; also κατὰ (ἀσπίδα δουρί, E 537), Λ 108, M 189, and πρὸς στῆθος, Λ 144; βλῆσθαι, pass., χ 253; ἕλκος, vulnus infligere, *inflict wound;* ἐν κονίῃσι, deicere, *lay low in,* cf. προτὶ γαίῃ, *sank* to the earth, λ 423; χαμαί, χ 188; fig., *wounded* (ἦτορ or κῆρ), ἄχεϊ, πένθεϊ; *reach,* οὔατα, ἀκτῖσιν, ε 479; conspergere, *bespatter,* ἄντυγα, ἡνίοχον.—(3) in wider signif., mittere, fundere, *send, pour,* ὕπνον ἐπὶ βλεφάροισι, δάκρυ (χαμάδις, δ 114), *let fall,* λ 424, sc. χεῖρας; *shake off,* P 457 (βάλλεσθαι, *discharge,* εἰς ἅλα); εἰς κακόν τινα, *plunge,* μετὰ νείκεα, *involve in,* φιλότητα μετά τισιν, *conclude* friendship; ὄμματα ἑτέρωσε, *turn* (περὶ τέρμα, mid. of horses, drive round the turning-post), ἵππους πρόσθε, *drive by;* Ψ 639, πρόσθε, superare, *be superior;* ponere, *place,* esp. *throw* the arms *about* some one, *embrace* (ἀμφί, περί, πρός τινι) (mid. ἐν θυμῷ, φρεσί, animo volvo, *turn over* in mind, I 435, μ 218, A 297; *take* to heart, O 566).—(4) amicire, *put on* garments or weapons, also mid., Γ 334 and freq.; *put* wheels *on* axle, ἀμφ' ὀχέεσσιν; *make fast,* ἐφ' ἱστῷ, μ 423; pass., *were spread,* λ 194.

βαμβαίνων (βαίνω, cf. παμφαίνων), trepidans, *quivering* (with terror), K 375†.

βάν = ἔβαν (ἔβησαν).

βάπτῃ, subj. from βάπτω, *dips,* ι 392†.

βαρβᾰ́ρο-φώνων, gen. pl., *harsh-speaking,* B 867†.

βάρδιστοι = βράδιστοι, from βραδύς, tardissimi, *slowest.*

βαρέω, only **βεβᾰρηότα,** ότες, (βαρύς), gravati, *weighed down with,* οἴνῳ (φρένας, τ 122); γ 139, *drunken.*

βαρύθει (βαρύθω, βαρύς), gravescit, *pains* (me), Π 519†. [⏑⏑–]

βαρύνω, only ipf. (ἐ)**βάρῡνε**, pres. pass. βᾰρῡ́νεται and aor. part. βᾰρυνθείς, -θέν (βαρύς), gravare, *disable*, χεῖρα; *oppress by weight*, Θ 308.

βᾰρύς, ὺν, ι 257, εῖα, ύ, gravis, *heavy woe*, Κ 71; *grievous* pains, Ε 417; *strong* delusion, Β 111; *harsh* voice, ι 257; χεῖρες, *mighty* arms; κῆρες, *dread*, *inexorable*; βαρὺ and βαρέα στενάχειν, moaning *loudly*, sobbing *heavily*, ε 420; esp. βαρὺ στενάχων, θ 95.

βᾰρυ-στενάχων, better βαρὺ στενάχων, see βαρύς.

βασίλεια, ης, αν, fem. of follg., regina, *queen*; γυναικῶν, *queenly* dame, λ 258; *princess*, ζ 115.

βᾰσῐ-λεύς, ῆος, ὁ, (βάσις, λαός), *leader of people*, princeps, (1) subst., *prince*, *king*, exercising functions of commander-in-chief, priest, and judge; *nobles*, α 394; Σ 556, *master*, *lord*.—(2) used adjectively with ἄναξ, υ 194; ἀνήρ, Γ 170; comp. βασιλεύτερος, ον, *more kingly*; super. -τατος, Ι 69, *most princely*.

βᾰσῐλευέμεν, prs., ipf., fut., regnare, *be king* (Z 425, *queen*), τισί, Β 206; ἔν τισι, β 47; κατὰ δῆμον, χ 52; Πύλον, ἐν Ἰθάκῃ.

βᾰσῐληΐδος τιμῆς, regiae dignitatis, *royal* honor, Ζ 193†.

βᾰσῐλήϊον γένος, regium genus, scion of the *royal* stock, π 401†.

βάσκ' ἴθι, imp. from βάσκω (βαίνω), *haste* and go, Β 8. (Il.)

βαστάζοντα, pres. part., and aor. ἐβάστᾰσε, *grasp*, *raise*, λ 594. (Od.)

βάτην = ἐβήτην, 3 du. aor. from βαίνω.

Βατίεια, height on the plain of Troy before the city, Β 813†.

βάτων, gen. pl. from ἡ βάτος, sentis, *thorn-bushes*, *thorns*, ω 230†.

βεβάασι, βεβάμεν inf., βέβασαν plupf., βεβαώς perf. part. from βαίνω.

βεβαρηότα, see βαρέω, gravatum.

βεβίηκε, pf. from βιάω, coegit.

βεβλήαται, -το, pf. and plupf. pass. from βάλλω, ictus est, erat.

βεβολήατο, plupf. pass., -ημένος, pf. pass. part. from βάλλω, ictus.

βεβρώθοις, intensive form of pf. opt., (βιβρώσκω), devorares, Δ 35†.

βεβρωκώς, βεβρώσεται, pf. part., 3 fut. with pass. signif., from βιβρώσκω.

βέῃ, βείομαι, see βέομαι.

βείω, aor. subj. = βῶ, see βαίνω.

βέλεμνα, τά, acc., (βάλλω), tela *missiles*, flying wide, Ο 484; Χ 206, sharp.

Βελλερο-φόντης, ῃ, ην, son of Γλαῦκος, Ζ 155, 220. His true name, according to the Scholiast, was Ἱππόνοος. (Ζ.)

βέλος, εος, τό, (βάλλω), telum, *missile*, in widest sense, spear, arrow, stone, even the foot-stool, ρ 464; and the rocky mountain-summit, ι 495; Apollo's missiles, see ἀγανός; missiles of the Εἰλείθυιαι, Λ 269; ἐκ (ὑπὲκ, Σ 232) βελέων, out of shot, outside of battle; joined with verbs, Μ 159, Δ 498, Ε 174, Ε 106, 278, ρ 464, Θ 67, Λ 576.

βέλτερον (Ϝελέσθαι), *preferable*, *better*, *more advantageous*, with inf., Ο 511; praestat aut—aut—, quam (cf. Hor. Sat. 1, 1, 8), Ο 197; with εἰ, ζ 282, if she herself had gone abroad and found.

βένθος, εος, τό, also pl., (βάθος), profundum, *depth*, esp. of the sea, βένθεα, α 53 (βένθοσδε, δ 780); of the forest, ρ 316.

βέομαι, βείομαι, (βήομαι), 2 sing. βέῃ, fut., (βίος), vivam, Ο 194, *will not live*, i. e. *order my life* according to the will of Zeus. (Il.)

βέρεθρον, ου, τό, (βιβρώσκω), vorago *abyss*, *chasm*, μ 94.

βῆ = ἔβη.

βηλοῦ, ῷ, masc., (βαίνω), liminis, *threshold*, Α 591, Ψ 202. (Il.)

βῆμεν = ἔβημεν, **βήμεναι** = βῆναι (**βήσαμεν**, βῆσε, βήσατο, βήσετο unaugmented forms), see βαίνω.

Βῆσσα, town in Lokris, Β 532†.

βήσσης, gen., ῃ, αν, etc., (βαθύς), *glade*, *glen*, *valley*, *ravine*, Γ 34, Χ 190, κ 210.

βητ-άρμονες (βῆναι, ἁρμονία), *dancers*, θ 250 and 383.

βιάζετε, 2 pl.; elsewh. only prs. ipf. mid., (βιάζω), domo, vim affero, *constrain*, μ 297; mid. also with pass. signif., Ο 727, Λ 576.

βίαια ἔργα (βία), deeds *of violence*, β 236†; adv. **-αίως**, per vim. (Od.)

Βίας, αντος, (1) father of Λαόγονος and of Δάρδανος, Υ 460†.—(2) leader of Ἀθηναῖοι, N 691†.—(3) from Πύλος, Δ 296†.

βιάω=βιάζω, pf. **βεβίηκε,** mid. prs., 3 pl. ind. βιόωνται, opt. -ῴατο, ipf. βιόωντο, fut. -βιήσεται, aor. -ατο, *beset*, Π 22; *maltreat*, ψ 9; *overreach*, Ψ 576; *withhold*, τινά τι, Φ 451; Λ 558, *overmasters.*

βίβημι, βιβάσθω, βιβάω, assumed pres. of **βιβάς,**-άντα, **βιβάσθων** (Il.), and of **βιβῶντα** acc. masc., **βιβῶσα** fem., *stride along*, usually with μακρά (βιβάσθων so always), H 213, N 809, Γ 22; ι 450, with mighty strides. [⏑–]

βιβρώσκω, only **βεβρωκώς,** χ 403, βοός, *having eaten of; τι*, X 94; and **βεβρώσεται,** β 203, comedetur, *shall be devoured.*

βίη, ης, dat. with instr. suffix βίηφιν, vis, robur, *force, strength*, Λ 561, H 288, φ 185, O 165, P 569; in periphrasis, e. g. Πριάμοιο, Ἡρακληείη = the mighty Priamos, Herakles, Γ 105, B 658; βίηφιν, βίῃ, ο 231, per vim; οὐκ ἐθέλοντα, N 572; ἀέκοντα, O 186, α 403; with κάρτος, σ 139, δ 415, ζ 197; pl. *violence*, Ψ 713, γ 216; sing., ψ 31; βίῃ ἀέκοντος (gen. absol.), δ 646, A 430.

Βι-ήνωρ, ορος, a Trojan, Λ 92†.

βῖον, τόν, vitam, *life*, ο 491. (Od.)

βιός, οῖο, ὁ, arcus, *bow*, A 49, Δ 125.

βίοτος, οιο, ὁ, sing., vita, H 104, α 287; victus, *provisions*, bona, *substance*, Ξ 122, γ 301, λ 116, 490, ο 446.

βιόω, only aor. imp. **βιώτω,** vivat, *let him live*, Θ 429; inf. βιῶναι, ξ 359; mid. **ἐβιώσαο,** servavisti, *hast saved me*, θ 468.

βιῴατο, -όωνται, -όωντο, see βιάω.

βλάβω (μαλακός), only pass. **βλάβεται,** pf. βεβλαμμένον, aor. ἔβλαβεν, βλάβεν = ἐβλάβησαν and βλαφθείς, etc., act. (ἔ)βλαψας, etc. (see βλάπτω), debilitare, *weaken, injure*, physically, T 166, H 271, Ψ 774; mentally, X 15; φρένας, ξ 178; I 512, *baffle;* impedire, pass., *is confused*, T 82; *impede*, Π 331; 660, *wounded* in the heart (see also βλάπτω).

βλάπτω, only prs. ipf., (see βλάβω), impedio, *incommode, hinder*, ν 22; τινός, α 195; *delude, infatuate* (φρένας, O 724), I 507, φ 294; τῇ ἐνὶ, *entangled* in which, O 647; cf. Z 39, ὄζῳ ἔνι.

βλεῖο, opt. aor. mid. from βάλλω, ferireris.

βλεμεαίνει, -ων, prs., (βάλλω ?), se iactare, *exult in*, always with σθένεϊ, only θυμὸς . . . περὶ σθένεϊ βλεμεαίνει, heart *beats high* in its strength, P 22†.

βλεφᾰροιϊν, and pl., (τὸ βλέφαρον, βλέπω), palpebra, *eyelid* (conceived of as the seat of sleep), K 26, Ξ 165, α 364, μ 366, ι 389.

βλήεται, βλήμενος, aor. mid. from βάλλω, feriatur.

βλήτροισι, ntr., (βάλλω ?), *rivets*, or perh. better, *rings, bands*, O 678†.

βληχήν, τήν, (blacterare), *bleating*, οἰῶν, μ 266†.

βλοσῠροῖσι, -ῦσι, (voltuosus), horridis, *horrible, dreadful*, H 212, O 608. (Il.)

βλοσῠρ-ῶπις, ἡ, horrido voltu, *with awful countenance*, Λ 36†.

βλωθρή, ήν, procera, *tall*, N 390, ω 234.

βλώσκω, only pf. **μέμβλωκε,** ρ 190, and 2 aor. subj. **μόλῃ** and part., *come*, also of time, Ω 781, ρ 190.

βο-άγρια, τά, *shields of ox-hide*, M 22 and π 296.

Βο-άγριος, ου, river of Λοκροί, B 533.

βοάᾳ, pl. **βοόωσι,** part. acc. **βοόωντα,** pl. **-όωντες,** aor. ἐβόησα, etc., clamare, *shout*, B 198; *resound*, P 265; *call aloud*, I 12, ε 400; with acc. of kindred meaning, μέγα, μακρά, σμερδνόν, ὀξύ.

βόειος, **βοείην, -ον,** etc., (masc. wanting), and **βοέου,** έῃ (ntr. wanting), *of an ox* or *oxen*, bubulus, *ox-* (dung, Ψ 777), esp. *of ox-leather*, E 452, Δ 122 (P 492, shields); freq. as subst. (sc. δορή), *ox-hide*, P 389, υ 142 (χ 364 and Σ 582, with βοός).

βοεύς, dat. pl. **βοεῦσι,** *thongs of ox-hide*, on sails, β 426, ο 291.

βοή, ῆς, ἡ, clamor, *cry*, esp. *cry of alarm*, χ 77, κ 118, ξ 266; and *battle-cry*, Λ 50, 500, 530; βοὴν ἀγαθός, good at the battle-cry, i. e. brave in battle, hero, γ 311 and freq.; also *cry of pain, of distress*, Z 465, ω 48, ι 401; βοὴν ἔχον, sonabant, resounded, Σ 495.

Βοηθοΐδης, Ἐτεωνεύς, ο 95. (Od.)

βοη-θόον (βοῇ θοϝόν), *swift in battle, warlike*, bellicum, P 481; bellicosum, N 477.

βο-ηλᾰσίη (ἐλαύνω), *cattle-lifting*, Λ 672.

βοητύς, ἡ, (βοᾶν), vociferatio, *clamor*, α 369†.

βόθρον, gen. etc., masc., scrobs, *hole in the ground*, for planting trees, for sacrificial blood, P 58; *natural trough* for washing clothes, λ 25.

Βοίβη, name of town in Θεσσαλίη. Hence **Βοιβηὶς λίμνη,** B 712, 711†.

Βοιώτιος, subst., **Βοιωτοί,** *Boiotians*, B 494 and freq. (Il.)

βολαί, άων, ῇσι, fem., (βάλλω), iactus, ictus; ὀφθαλμῶν, *glance*, δ 150. (Od.)

βόλεται, etc., see βούλομαι.

βομβέω, only aor. **βόμβησε,** σαν, *rang*; θ 190, *hummed, whizzed*; μ 204, *rushed roaring* through the water.

βοόων, -όωντα, -όωντες, see βοάω, clamans.

βορέης, έαο, ὁ, (ὄρος), aquilo, *north wind*. Personified, *Boreas*, Ψ 195.

βόσιν, acc. fem., pastum, *food*, T 268†.

βόσκει, prs., ipf. act. and pass. (iter. βοσκέσκοντο), fut. act., pasco, βοῦς, αἶγας, αἰπόλια, κήτεα, μ 97; ξ 325, *give subsistence; feed, nourish*, σ 364; mid., pasci, *feed, graze*, δ 338, φ 49.

βοτάνης, τῆς, (βόσκω), herba, *fodder, grass*, N 493 and κ 411. [⏑ ⏑ –]

βοτῆρας, τούς, (βόσκω), pastores, *shepherds*, ο 504†.

βοτοῖσι, τοῖς, ntr., (βόσκω), pecoribus, *flocks*, Σ 521†.

βοτρῦδόν, adv., (βότρυς), *like a bunch of grapes, in a swarm*, B 89†.

βότρυες, οἱ, uvae, *grape-clusters*, Σ 562†.

βού-βοτος, ἡ, (βοτός), *cattle-pasture*, ν 246†.

βού-βρωστις, ἡ, *ravenous hunger*, Ω 532†.

βουβῶνα, τόν, inguen, *groin*, Δ 492†.

βου-γάϊος, ε, *braggart*, usually derived from βοῦς and γαίω, perh. better, βοῦς, γέγαα, *big and awkward as an ox*, abusive epithet, applied to a big but cowardly fellow, N 824, σ 79.

Βούδειον, town in Φθίη, Π 572†.

βου-κολέων, part. prs., ipf. iter. -κολέεσκες (βου-κόλος), pascere (boves), *pasture*, E 313; but Υ 221, ἵπποι βουκολέοντο, equae pascebantur, *graze*.

Βου-κολίδης, αο, Σφῆλος, O 338†.

Βου-κολίων, ωνι, son of Λαομέδων, Z 22†.

βου-κόλος, ῳ, ον, οι, ὁ, (-πόλος), *cattle-herd*, ἄνδρες, N 571; ἀγροιῶται, λ 293.

βουλευτῇσι (βουλευτής, from βουλεύω), γέρουσι, old men *of the council*, Z 114†.

βουλεύουσιν, inf. -ευέμεν, fut. (inf. βουλευσέμεν), 1 aor.; mid. prs., I 99, 1 aor., (βουλή), *take counsel, deliberate*, B 347; with βουλήν, -άς, I 75, K 147; *discuss, discourse with one another*, A 531, ν 439; ἐς μίαν (βουλήν), B 379, harmoniously; meditari, *meditate*, τί, K 311; *devise*, ε 179 (mid., B 114); *suggested* this plan, ε 23; *bethink one's self*, ὅπως, ι 420; *think of*, with inf., ι 299.

βουλή, ῆς, ἡ, consilium, (βούλομαι), (1) *will*, Διός, A 5, M 241; and *decree*, Ζηνός, (θεῶν), H 45, P 469; *plan*, β 372; *designs, counsels*, Διός, N 524, θ 82; θεῶν, λ 276; cf. 437.—(2) *proposal, counsel*, κ 46, ξ 337, μ 339, K 43; ἀρίστη φαίνετο, freq. πυκινὴν ἠρτύνετο, callidum struebat consilium, B 55; pl. *plans*, μητιόωντες, Υ 154, B 340.—(3) *discernment, shrewdness*, A 627, N 728, I 54, λ 177, μ 211.—(4) *council of nobles*, cf. senatus; opp. ἀγορά, concio, γ 127, B 53, 194, 202.

βουλη-φόρος, οι, (φέρω), *giving counsel, advising*, ἀγοραί, ι 112; ἀνήρ, A 144; ἄναξ, M 414; also subst. *counselor*, E 180, H 126.

βούλομαι, (also βόλεται, -εσθε, ἐβόλοντο, α 234), only prs. and ipf., (βουλή), velle, (1) decernere, τινί τι, *grant, accord*, H 21, Θ 204, P 331.—(2) *wish*, with inf. (and acc.), τό, λ 358; βούλεται, A 67, is subjunctive; μέγα, *desire* greatly.—(3) malle, *prefer*, ρ 187 (ι 96); with and without following ἤ, ρ 228; with πολύ, A 112.

βου-λυτόν-δε (λύω), the sun began to decline toward *eventide*, lit. *toward the time of unyoking plough-cattle*, ι 58.

βου-πλῆγι, from -πλήξ, (πλήσσω), *with the ox-goad*, Z 135†.

Βου-πράσιον, οιο (περᾶν, cf. Oxford), A 756, 760. (Il.)

βοῦς, ἡ, ὁ, dat. pl. βόεσσι, acc. βόας, βοῦς, bos, usually fem., *cow, the cows* of Helios, μ 379; yet also masc., *bullock, ox*, in which case another word is often added to make the gender more clear, ἄρσενα(ς), ταύροιο; pl. *cattle, kine*, βοῶν ἔργα = ἄροσις, ploughed lands; slaughter cattle, ἱερεύειν (cf. O 633, γ 450); adjectives ἀγελαίη, ἀγραύλοιο, εἰλίποδες, ἕλικες, ἐριμύκων, ὀρθοκραιράων; as symbol of flight, pecorum ritu, Λ 172. Βοῶν ἀγέλαι, herds of cattle, constitute the chief wealth, cf. ἀλφεσίβοια; hence βοῶν ἴφθιμα, perh. costly (usually explained as mighty), κάρηνα, Ψ 260; as means of exchange and measure of value, Ψ 885, see ἐννεαβοίων; bestowed as prizes in athletic contests; κέρας, μ 253, horn guard just above hook, to prevent fish from biting off the line; ῥινὸς βοός (cf. βοὸς βοείην, Σ 582), oxhide, Υ 276; shield of ox-hide, K 155. Also as fem. subst., (acc. βῶν), *ox-hide*, H 474, untanned; the *shield* made from the same, ἀζαλέην, H 238; αὔας, M 137; ἐυποιητάων, τυκτῇσι.

βου-φόνεον, 3 pl. ipf., (φονή), *were slaughtering cattle*, H 466†.

βο-ῶπις, usually πότνια Ἥρη, voc. ῐ, Α 551, *ox-eyed, with large, calm eyes;* otherwise applied, H 10, Σ 40.

Βοώτης, ὁ, lit. *Herdsman*, the constellation Arcturus, α 272†.

βρᾰδύς, έες, comp. **βράσσων**, sup. **βάρδιστοι**, tardus, *slow;* with inf. θείειν, Ψ 310; νόος, K 226; in proverb, θ 329.

βρᾰδῦτῆτι, τῇ, (βραδύς), tarditate, *slowness*, T 411†.

βρᾰχίονος, α, ες, (ὁ βραχίων), brachium, *arm*, πρυμνοῖο, *shoulder*, στιβαροί, firm. [⏑ – ⏑ ⏑]

βράχε, ἔβρᾰχε, ipf., *creak*, μέγα, loud, E 838; *rattled*, δεινόν, *roared*, Φ 9; *shrieked aloud*, of Ares, E 859; of wounded horse, Π 468.

βρέμει, -εται, (fremo), *roar*, B 210, Ξ 399. (Il.)

βρέφος, τό, acc. ἡμίονον, mule *foal*, yet in the womb, Ψ 266†.

βρεχμόν, τόν, *forehead*, E 586†.

Βριάρεως = Αἰγαίων, name of hundred-armed water-giant, A 403†.

βριαρῇ, ήν, (βριαρός, βρί-θω), gravis, *heavy*, only of helmet, Λ 375, T 381. (Il.)

βρίζοντα (βαρύς), *drowsy*, Δ 223†.

βρῑ-ήπυος, *loud shouting, roaring* (cf. Ξ 398 sqq.), N 521†.

βρῑθοσύνῃ (βρίθω), *with the weight*, E 839 and M 460.

βρῑθύ, adj. ntr., *ponderous*, only with ἔγχος—μέγα στιβαρόν, α 100.

βρίθῃ, prs., ipf. βρῖθον, aor. ἔβρισα, pass. only pres. part., Θ 307; also perf. act. βέβρῑθε, and plupf. βεβρίθει (βαρύς), gravare, *weigh down*, Θ 307; turgere, *be full of*, Σ 561; τινί, π 474, τ 112; τινός, ι 219; *be drenched with* water, Π 384; urgere, *charge*, M 346; *be superior* through gifts, ζ 159; βεβρῑθυῖα, *heavy*, only Φ 385.

Βρῑσεύς, ῆος, king and priest in Λυρνησσός, A 392, I 132, 274; father of follg.

Βρῑσηΐς, ΐδος, daughter of Βρισεύς, the occasion of the μῆνις Πηληιάδεω, A 184. (Il.) (See cut, after a Panathenaic Amphora.)

βρομέωσι, subj., (βρόμος), *buzz*, Π 642†.

βρόμος (βρέμω), *roar, crackling*, Ξ 396†.

βροντάω, only aor. (ἐ)**βρόντησε**, only of Ζεύς, *thunder; μεγάλ', δεινόν*, loud, terribly; ἄμυδις, peal on peal.

βροντῆς, ῇ, ήν, fem., (βροντή, βρόμος), tonitru, δεινήν, dread *thunder*, Φ 199.

βροτέη (βροτός) φωνῇ, humana voce, τ 545†.

βροτόεντα, ntr. pl., (βρότος), cruentata, *bloody*, ἔναρα, Ξ 509. (Il.)

βροτο-λοιγός, only sing. masc., of Ἄρης and of heroes, *man-destroying*, E 31. (Il. and θ 115.)

βροτός, οῦ, (orig. μροτός from μόρος, mors), mortalis, *mortal*, adj. ἀνήρ, E 361, and subst. T 2, θνητοῖσι, γ 3; δειλοῖσι, ὀϊζυροῖσι, μερόπεσσι, ἐπιχθόνιος; Ψ 331, κατατεθνηῶτος, hominis mortui; Υ 248.

βρότον, τόν, μέλανα, ω 189, elsewh. (Il.) αἱματόεντα, *blood from a wound, gore.*

βροτόω, only **βεβροτωμένα**, cruentata, *gory*, τεύχεα, λ 41†.

βρόχον, τόν, and pl. -οι, laqueum, *noose*, λ 278 and χ 472.

Βρυσειαί, town in Λακονική, B 583†.

βρυχάομαι, only pf. **βέβρῡχε**, ὡς, ἐβεβρύχειν, 3 sing., *roar; shriek*, falling with death wound, N 393, Π 486.

βρύει (βλύω), efflorescit, ἄνθεϊ λευκῷ, *swells with* white bloom, P 56†.

βρώμης, τῆς and -ην, (βιβρώσκω), cibi, *food*, κ 379. (Od.)

βρῶσις, -ιν, ἡ, (βιβρώσκω), cibus, *food*, always with πόσις, potus, *drink*. (Od., and T 210.)

βρωτύν, τήν, (βιβρώσκω), cibum, *food*, T 205 and σ 407.

βύβλῐνον, τό, ὅπλον, lit. *made of papyrus = braided, twisted*, φ 391†.

βυκτάων, τῶν, *whistling, howling*, κ 20†.

βυσσο-δομεύων, pres. part., and pl. ipf. βυσσοδόμευον (βυσσός, δέμω), always with κακά (φρεσί), ρ 66, *secretly devise.* (Od.)

βυσσόν, τόν (βύθος), profundum, *deep, depths*, Ω 80†.

βύω, only **βεβυσμένον**, τόν, confertum, *stuffed full of*, δ 134†.

βῶλος, ὁ, gleba, *clod*, σ 374†.

βωμός, ὁ, (βαίνω), gradus, *step*, η 100; *stand, rack*, Θ 441; esp. *altar*, θυήεις, smoking, fragrant with incense, Θ 48; ἐύδμητον, A 448. (See cut.)

Βῶρος, (1) Maionian, father of Φαῖστος, E 44†.—(2) son of Περιήρης, husband of Πολυδώρη, daughter of Πηλεύς, Π 177†.

βῶν, acc. from βοῦς, scutum, *shield.*

βώσαντι, aor. part. from βοάω.

βωστρεῖν, inf. = imp., *call loudly upon* μ 124†.

βωτῐ-άνειρη, *man-nourishing, fruitful*, A 155†.

βώτορες, ας, (βόσκω), ἄνδρες, pastores, *shepherds*, M 302†.

Γ.

γαῖα, ης, ἡ, terra, *earth*, (1) as division of universe, ρ 386; opp. heaven, Ξ 174, Θ 16, Υ 58, ε 184, α 54; opp. sea, ε 408, μ 242, 282, 315; *world*, Γ 447, Ω 351, σ 130.—(2) *country*, *land*, O 81, θ 284, 555, ζ 119; *particular land*, A 254, H 124, ε 280; *native country*, Γ 244, α 21, ν 188.—(3) *surface of earth*, *ground*, N 508, A 245, Θ 65, Φ 168; ὑπὸ γαῖαν, Τ 259; fruitful, τ 111; *place of burial=grave*, γ 16, λ 549, ν 427; pulvis, H 99.

Γαῖα, as deity, Tellus, *Earth*, O 36.

Γαιήϊον υἱόν, son of Γαῖα, *earth-born*, Τιτυός, η 324†; cf. λ 576.

γαιή-οχος (ἔχω), *earth-possessing*, *earth-surrounding*, epithet of Ποσειδάων, I 183, α 68.

γαίων, pres. part., (γαίω, gaudeo), κύδεϊ, *exulting in* his glory, A 405.

γάλα, ακτος, τό, lac, *milk*, E 902.

γαλα-θηνούς, τούς, (θῆσθαι), *sucking*, *tender*, δ 336 and ρ 127.

Γαλάτεια, name of a Nereid, Σ 45†. [⏑⏑–⏑]

γαλήνη, ην, ἡ, (γάλα, γελᾶν), *smooth surface of water*, *calm of the sea*, μ 168. (Od.)

γαλόῳ, ων, dat. sing., nom. gen. pl., glos, *husband's sister*, Γ 122. (Il.)

γαμβρός, ὁ, (1) gener, *son-in-law*, Z 249.—(2) *brother-in-law*, N 464 and E 474.

γαμέω, aor. ἔγημε, γῆμε, uxorem ducere, *marry*=θέσθαι γυναῖκα, φ 72; mid. γαμέεσθαι, aor. γήμασθαι, *to give one's self in marriage*, of the woman, τινί, nubere; but in I 394, fut. γαμέσσεται, of the parents, *to get a wife for* their son; α 36, *took as his wife*.

γάμος, ὁ, *marriage*, ρ 476; *marriage-feast*, T 299, α 226.

γαμφηλῇσι, dat. pl., (γόμφος), maxillae, *jaws*, N 200. (Il.)

γαμψ-ώνυχες (γναμπτός? ὄνυξ), αἰγυπιοί, *with crooked claws*, π 217.

γανόωντες, όωσαι, (γαίω), *gleaming*, *bright*, *luxuriant*.

γάνυται, -νται, fut. -νύσσεται, (γάνος), gaudere; φρένα, *glad* at heart, N 493.

Γανυμήδης, son of Τρώς, cup-bearer of Zeus, E 266 and Υ 232.

γάρ (γέ, ἄρα, γᾶρ, B 39, λ 580), always second word in its clause, apparent exc., like ρ 317, explained by considering that the two preceding words make but one idea; particle denoting immediate, indisputable certainty, *yes*, *yes doubtless*, *namely*, *for*.—I. independently, without relation to another clause, (1) in declaration, A 408, ρ 78; ἦ γάρ, A 293, 342, 355; ἀλλὰ γάρ, but yet, H 242, κ 202.—(2) after relatives, K 127 (τ' ἄρ?); and in a question, after the interrogative word, e. g. πῶς γάρ, etc., e. g. κ 337, 383, 501; emphasizing (cf. δή), K 424, Σ 182.—(3) in wishes, with opt., εἰ γάρ, N 825, ρ 513; αἲ γὰρ (δή), B 371, ζ 244 (Δ 189, ι 523).—II. with relation to another sentence, (1) which may be co-ordinate, and connected by a pron. (τῷ, then, therefore, τῶν), or by a conj., P 227, H 73, ξ 496, υ 273.—(2) which may inclose, as a parenthesis, the clause with γάρ, M 326, α 301; thus esp. freq. after vocs., Ψ 156, κ 174; and after ἀλλά, ξ 355, cf. H 328 sq.—(3) which has its truth confirmed, *for*, A 9, 55, 78, 120, 177; γὰρ may even be transferred to the preceding, instead of remaining in the following sentence, e. g. A 81, B 123.—(4) which thus receives explanation of its meaning, *to wit*, *namely*, A 195, δ 86. Joined with other particles: ἀλλὰ γάρ, but *really*; γὰρ δή, *for* of a truth; γάρ οὖν, *for* indeed; γάρ ῥα, *for* certainly; γάρ τε, namque; γάρ τοι, *for* surely. [⏑; in arsi ᾱ.]

Γάργᾰρον, τό, south peak of Ἴδη in Τροίη, Ξ 292. (Il.)

γαστήρ, έρος, ἡ, (and sync. forms, -τρός, -τρί), venter, (1) *pit of belly*, Δ 531, E 539; *womb*, Z 58.—(2) *belly*, *paunch*, Π 163; *hunger*, ζ 133; *fasting*, T 225.—(3) *paunch* stuffed with minced meat, *blood sausage*, σ 44.

γάστρην, τήν, *belly*, of a caldron, θ 437.

γαυλοί, οἱ, *milk-pails*, ι 223†.

γδουπέω, see δουπέω.

γέ, enclitic particle, Lat. quidem, used with great variety of meaning, often untranslatable, (1) restrictive; *at all events, at least*, A 60, 81, β 62, α 229; γέ μέν, *but yet*, B 703; often to emphasize a relation subsisting between two parties, also doubled, e. g. σέ γε, θ 488, Γ 143; cf. πρίν γε, A 97.—(2) causal, A 352.—(3) emphatic with voc., τ 215; esp. with pron., A 173, 216, 261, 525, α 46, 47, 163, 226, 403; with pron. in second member of the period, Γ 409. —(4) γέ often seems to be used only to give greater force of sound to a word, e. g. ὅ γε, cf. hi-ce, hic, in Latin, α 222, β 132.

γεγάᾶσι, -ἄῶτα(ς), pf. indic. and part., from γίγνομαι, nati sunt, B 866, ζ 62, ω 84; usually=εἰσίν, ἐόντες, ε 35.

γέγηθε, ει, pf. and plupf., from γηθέω, gavisus est.

γέγωνε, pf. with pres. signif., inf. -εῖν and -έμεν, part. -ώς, plupf. 1 sing. ἐγεγώνευν, 3 sing. -ει, also 1 sing. and 3 pl. γεγώνευν, *make one's self heard* (by a call, as is often specified, M 337, Θ 227; ε 400, ὅσσον τε γέγωνε βοήσας, as far as one shouting *can be heard*), τινί, *cry out to*, Ξ 469, ρ 161; in distress, μ 370; Ω 703, shouted throughout the whole city.

γεγωνέω, see γέγωνε.

γείνεαι, ομένῳ, ipf. -όμεθα, aor. ἐγείναο, ατο, γείνατο, -ασθαι, (γένος), prs. ipf., nasci, *to be born*, X 477, to a like fate; aor., gigno and pario, *beget, bring forth*; λ 299, brought forth to Tyndareos.

γείτονες (nom. γείτων), vicini, *neighbors*, δ 16. (Od.)

γελαστά, ntr. pl., (γελάω), ridicula, θ 307†.

(γελάω), prs. **γελόω**, part. γελόωντες and -ώοντες (false reading -οίωντες, υ 390), ipf. 3 pl. γελώων, aor. (ἐ)γέλασσε(ν), 3 pl. γέλασσαν, part. γελάσσας, also forms with one σ, (γέλος), ridere, *laugh*, ἡδύ, ἀχρεῖον; ἐπί(τι), laugh at, laugh over, ἐπ' αὐτῷ, at him, B 270; my heart laughed within me, ι 413; χείλεσι, of feigned, forced laughter, O 101; γναθμοῖς ἀλλοτρίοισιν, υ 347, with distorted grin; χθών, T 362, *was smiling.*

γελοίων, incorrect reading for γελώων, see γελάω, ridebant, υ 347.

γελοίιον, ntr., (γέλως), ridiculum, B 215†.

γελοίωντες, false reading for γελώοντες, see γελάω, ridentes, υ 390.

γελόω, -όωντες, -ώοντες, see γελάω.

γέλως (dat. -ῳ), acc. -ω; and **γέλος**, dat. -ῳ, acc. -ον, risus, ἄσβεστος, unextinguishable=uncontrollable *laugh;* ἔχει τινά, indulge in, be overcome by laughter; σ 100, laughed themselves almost to death.

γενεή, ῆς, ἡ, (γένος), genus, (1) *descent, origin, race*, Φ 157; of animals, E 265; *home*, α 407; *family*, Z 145; joined with τόκος, ο 175, *birthplace* and its young; gens, *house*, α 222, Υ 306; *descendants*, Φ 191, δ 27; *rank*, Λ 786.—(2) *generation*, Z 149; plur. only A 250; aetas, *age*, γενεῆφι ὁπλότερος, etc., B 707, O 166.

γενέθλη, ης, ἡ, only sing., (γένος), origo, *race, stock*, εἶναι (ἐκ) γενέθλης τινός, aliquo oriundum esse; τῶν γενέθλης ἐγένοντο, there were born to him six of their stock, E 270; cf. T 111; B 857, *home* of silver.

γενειάδες, αἱ, *beard*, π 176†.

γενειάω, aor. part. **γενειήσαντα**, *beginning to grow a beard*, σ 176 and 269.

γένειον, ου, ῳ, mentum, *chin*, ἁψαμένη Ὀδυσῆα γενείου, τ 473, as sign of homage, elsewh. as supplicantium gestus, attitude of suppliants, A 501. (See cut under γουνοῦμαι.)

γένεσις, ἡ, (γένος), origo, *source*, θεῶν, πάντεσσι, Ὠκεανός. (Ξ.)

γενετῆς, τῆς, (γενέσθαι), only ἐκ, inde e natu, *from the hour of birth*, σ 6.

γενναῖον, ntr., (γέννα), οὔ μοι, non ex indole mea est, *suitable to one's birth*, or *descent*, E 253†.

γένος, ευς, τό, (γίγνομαι), genus, cf. γενεή; (1) *family*, ζ 35; *race*, as a whole, ἀνδρῶν, ἡμιθέων ἀνδρῶν, βοῶν.—(2) *generation*, γ 245; aetas, *age*, Γ 215. —(3) *scion*, Z 180.—(4) *extraction*, γένος εἰμί (ἐκ) τινος, aliquo ortus sum; also of the *home*, ο 267, B 852.

γέντο, 3 sing. aor., prehendit=λάζετο, with acc. Σ 476, N 241. (Il.)

γένυς, ἡ, pl. -ύων, acc. ῦς, maxilla, *under jaw;* also of jaw of boar, Λ 416.

γεραιός, έ; αί, άς, senex, *old, aged*, with ἄττα and παλαιγενές, P 561;

freq. ὁ γ., A 35; fem., Z 87; comp. -αίτερος, ον, senior(em).

γεραίρεις, -ειν, prs., ipf. γέραιρεν (γέρας), honorare, *show honor*, H 321, ξ 437.

Γεραιστός, οῦ, promontory of Εὔβοια; now Geresto, γ 177†.

γεράνων, gen. pl., gruum, from ἡ γέρανος, *crane*, Γ 3. (Il.)

γερᾰρόν, acc. masc., comp. **-ώτερος,** Γ 170 and 211, *stately*.

γέρας, τό, pl. **γέρα,** *honor*, Δ 323; *precedence, prerogative*, λ 175; *gift of honor*, A 118; *rendered to the gods*, Δ 49; *gift*, υ 297; θανόντων, *last honors* of the dead, viz., burial, the thrice-repeated call, the funeral mound, and a column, Ψ 9, ω 190.

Γερήνιος (ἱππότα), Νέστωρ, from Γερηνός in Ἦλις, B 336.

γερούσιον, acc. masc., (γέρων), senatorium, *belonging to the old men of the council*, of wine, ν 8; of oath, X 119.

γέρων, οντος, (1) senex, adj., *aged*, A 358, Θ 100, Φ 85; σάκος γέρον, vetustum, *old*, χ 184; subst., *old man*, opp. νέοι, I 36, παῖδας, Θ 518; ἁλίοιο =Νηρέως, Πρωτέως, Φόρκυνος, *old man* of the sea; honorable title of Λαέρτης, β 227.—(2) *elder, member of the council* or βουλή, cf. Lat., senator.

γεύσεται, -σόμεθα, -σεσθαί, fut., aor. inf. γεύσασθαι, (γεύω), gustare, *taste*, ρ 413, προικός; elsewh. fig. ironical, φ 98, Υ 258; temptemus inter nos, *try*.

γεφύρη, αι, ας, agger, *dam, dike*, E 88; πτολέμοιο, ordines, *rows* of combat, i. e. of combating hosts, Δ 371, Θ 378, 553. (Il.) [⏑‒‒]

γεφύρωσε, aor. from γεφυρόω, exaggeravit, *dammed* it up, Φ 245; *made a causeway*, O 357. [ῡ]

γῆ, ἡ, terra, *earth*, ν 233, ψ 233, Φ 63.

Γῆ, Γῇ, dat., Tellus, *Earth*, as goddess, T 259, Γ 104.

γηθεῖ, prs., ipf. ἐγήθεεν, etc., also fut., aor. γήθησε, etc., pf. γέγηθε, plupf. -θει (γηθέω), gaudeo, *rejoice*, θυμῷ, H 189; κατὰ θυμόν, N 416; φρένα, Θ 559, in his heart; so also with ἦτορ, κῆρ, θυμός τινι (τινος), N 494; at any thing, τι, or with ὅτι, οὕνεκα, and follg. clause.

γηθοσύνῃ, τῇ, (γηθέω), *for joy*, N 29 and Φ 390. [ῡ]

γηθόσῡνος, η, -οι, laetus, κῆρ, *glad at heart*; because of something, τινί, N 82, ε 269.

γηράς, see γηράσκω.

γῆρας, αος, αϊ and αι, τό, (γέρων), senectus, Ξ 86; λυγρῷ, in a wretched *old age* (opp. τ 368), χαλεπόν, στυγερῷ; ἐς γῆρ., up to old age; ἔχειν γῆρ., ω 249; ἔχει τινά, Σ 515; ἱκάνει, ἔπεισι; ἐπὶ γήραος οὐδῷ, on the threshold of hoary old age, ο 348.

γηράσκει, prs., ipf. γήρασκε, aor. ἔγηρα (ἐγήρα), part. γηράς, (γῆρας), senesco, *grow old*, P 197; of hale old age, δ 210; maturescit, *ripen*, η 120.

γῆρυς, ἡ, *speech*, Δ 437†.

Γίγαντες, dat. εσσι, *Giant-race* in Θρινακίη, η 59, 206, and κ 120.

γίγνομαι, fut. etc. reg. as in Attic, aor. iter. γενέσκετο, pf. γέγονε, see also γεγάασι, plupf. γεγόνει, (γένος), (1) nasci, *be born*, δ 418, ζ 201, κ 350, μ 130; crescere, *grow*, ν 245, υ 211; *arise*, Π 634, Σ 212, Ξ 415, O 607, μ 326; fieri, *arise, begin*, A 49, K 375, N 283, Ψ 505, δ 417; obtingere, *fall to one's lot, happen*, [N 659], γ 228, A 188, Ω 45; ε 299, what now last of all shall *come upon* me?—(2)=εἶναι, β 320, μ 87, ξ 157, O 490, T 386; exstare, Δ 245; *come to be*, Z 82, H 99; ἐπὶ πῆμα, come to ruin; Δ 382, ὁδοῦ, and ὁδοῖο πρὸ γένοντο, profecerunt, *progressed* on the way.

γιγνώσκω (not γινώσκω), reg., but aor. subj. γνώω, ομεν, ωσι, inf. γνώμεναι, fut. mid. γνώσεαι, (-gnosco), (1) sentio, intelligo, *perceive, understand*, τ 160, π 136, N 223, Π 658; with ὅτι, Θ 175, E 331; ὅτ', P 623, γ 166; ὡς, X 10; with εἰ, si, Φ 266; with obj. attracted from follg. clause, E 85; with part., *recognize*, ο 532; nosse, *know*, X 356; τινός, *know*, φ 36; *learn to know*, Σ 270.—(2) agnosco (of senses), *recognize*, Λ 651, O 241, υ 94; by his shield, E 182.—(3) callere, *understand*, β 159.

γίνομαι, un-Homeric, see γίγνομαι.

γινώσκω, un-Homeric, see γιγνώσκω.

γλάγος, τό, (γάλα), lac, *milk*, B 471 and Π 643.

γλακτο-φάγων, gen. pl., (γάλα, φαγεῖν), lacte vescentium, *living on milk*, N 6†.

Γλαύκη, Νηρηΐς, Σ 39†

γλαυκιόων, pres. part. from γλαυκιάω, *with glaring eyes*, Υ 172†.

γλαυκή, θάλασσα, *gleaming*, Π 34†.

Γλαῦκος, (1) Ἱππολόχοιο πάϊς, Λυκίων ἀγός, Η 13; Ζ 119, guest-friend *of* Διομήδης.—(2) son of Σίσυφος, father of Βελλεροφόντης, Ζ 154 sqq.

γλαυκ-ῶπις, ιδος, (acc. also -ιν, α 156), voc. ῖ, only of Ἀθήνη, *with gleaming eyes, bright-, glaring-eyed*, α 44, Α 206. The type of expression recognizable in Attic tetradrachm. (See cut No. 43.)

Γλᾰφῦραι, town in Θεσσαλίη, Β 712†.

γλαφυρός, ή, όν, (nom. masc. wanting), cavus, *hollow*, esp. of ships, Β 454; of grotto, Σ 402, β 20, α 15; rock, Β 88; φόρμιγξ, θ 257; *deep, spacious*, μ 305.

γλήνη, ης, ην, (γαλήνη), pupilla, *pupil of eye*, ι 390; Θ 164, then, perh. because figures are reflected in miniature in the eye, contemptuous epithet, *timid coward!*

γλήνεα, τά, (radical syllable ΓΑΛ), (gleaming) *jewelry*, Ω 192†.

Γλίσας, αντος, town of Βοιωτοί, Β 504†.

γλουτόν, ούς, acc., clunem, *rump, buttocks*, Ε 66, Θ 340. (Il.)

γλῠκερός, ή, όν, comp. -ώτερον, (γλυκύς), dulcis, gratus, *sweet, dear*, Λ 89, ξ 194; φάος, dear to me as the light, π 23.

γλῠκῠ-θῡμος, mitis animi, *of mild temper*, Υ 467†.

γλῠκύς, ύ; fem. γλυκερή, comp. -ίων, -ιον, dulcis, *sweet*, Α 598, 249; gratus, *grateful*, ὕπνος, ἵμερος; acceptus, *dear*, ε 152, Β 453.

γλῠφῖδας, τάς, (γλύφω), *notches on the arrow*, φ 419. (See cuts Nos. 96, 97.)

γλῶσσα, ης, ή, lingua, (1) *tongue*, Ε 292, Ρ 618, Β 489, Π 161; τάμνειν, cut out the *tongues of victims*, γ 332.—(2) *language*, Β 804, Δ 438.

γλωχῖνα, τήν, (γλῶσσα), *end of the strap* or *thong* of the yoke, Ω 274†. (See cut under ζυγόν, letter *b*, No. 49.)

γναθμοῖο, όν, and pl. masc., (γένυς, gena), maxilla, Ν 671, π 175; σ 29, I would beat all the teeth out of his *jaws* upon the ground; υ 347, with distorted jaws, disfigured countenance.

γναμπτόν, ntr., and masc. fem. and ntr. pl., (γνάμπτω), (1) curvus, *curved*, δ 369.—(2) *flexible, pliant*, of limbs of living beings, ν 398; metaph. *placable*, νόημα, Ω 41.

γνάμψε, aor., (γνάμπτω), ἐν—, supplantavit, *bent* in his knee, tripped up, Ψ 731; ὑπὸ—, bent under, passed under, Ω 274. (See cut under ζυγόν.)

γνήσιον, acc. masc., -ιοι, (γενέσθαι), legitimum, *genuine*, υἱόν; opp. νόθον, ξ 202.

γνύξ (γόνυ) ἔριπε, -ών, fell *upon the knee*, Ε 309. (Il.)

γνῷ, γνώμεναι, γνώομεν, aor. from γιγνώσκω.

γνώρῖμος, notus, *acquaintance*, π 9†.

γνωτός, όν, fem. -αί, (1) notus, *evident*, Η 401, ω 182.—(2) cognatus, *relative*, Ο 350, Γ 174; *brother*, Ρ 35.

(γοάω) **γοόων, -ντες,** (γοῶντες), **-ντας, -όωσα,** part. pres., opt. γοάοιμεν, **-άοιεν,** inf. γοήμεναι, 3 pl. ipf. γόον, γόων, iter. γοάασκεν, fut. γοήσεται, (γόος), lamentari, *sob*, θ 92; esp. in lamentation for dead, *wail*, τινά, Ξ 502, Ζ 500, Φ 124; πότμον, Π 857.

γόμφοισι, masc., *with nails, with pins*, ε 248†.

γονή, ήν, (γέγονα), proles, *offspring*, Ω 539 and δ 755.

γόνος, οιο, ον, masc., (γέγονα), origo, *origin*, α 216; proles, *offspring*, δ 12; commonly = filius, σ 218, Ζ 191, Ν 449, Ω 59; *young*, of cattle, μ 130.

Γονόεσσα, ή, town near Πελλήνη, Β 573†.

γόνυ, τό, all other forms with lengthening of first syllable, gen. γούνατος, γουνός, pl. γούνατα, γοῦνα, gen. γούνων, dat. -ασι, -εσσι, genu, *knee*, κάμπτειν, rest, ἐπὶ γοῦνα ἕζεσθαι, sit down; γοῦνα βλάβεται, tremble; πήγνυνται, are stiff; ἐπὶ and ποτὶ γούνασι, Χ 500; Ε 408, in gremio, cf. also ἐν γούνασι πῖπτε, Ε 370; θεῖναί τι ἐπὶ γούνασι θεοῦ, as gift, Ζ 92; θεῶν ἐν γούνασι κεῖται, *lies at the disposal of* the gods, α 267.—(2) genua, as seat of *pity*, in phrases like the follg., ἅψασθαι, ἑλεῖν, λαβεῖν, ἀντίον ἐλθεῖν, λίσσεσθαι γούνων, etc., Α 500; cf. Eurip. Iph. T. 361 sqq., 1069 sq.; Plin. Historia Naturalis, XI., 45, (103).—(3) as seat of *physical power, strength*, λύειν τινὸς γούνατα = slay any one, and λύεται γούνατά τινος, knees sink under him; γ. ὀρώρῃ, as long as I can move my limbs.

γόον, ipf. from γοάω.

γόος, ου, and οιο, ον, pl. ους, masc., (βοή?), lamentatio, δ 758; πατρός, *lament* for one's father, Ω 507; esp. of the sobbing (ἀδινοῦ) *lamentation* for the dead, Σ 316; κρυεροῖο, chilling weeping; δακρυόεντος, tearful lamentation; γόον δ' ὠίετο θυμός, his soul foreboded death.

Γοργείη, ην, with κεφαλή, head *of the* Γοργώ, Ε 741.

Γοργῦθίων, ωνα, son of Πρίαμος and of Καστιάνειρα, Θ 302†.

Γοργώ, οῦς, ἡ, a dread-inspiring monster, Λ 36.

Γόρτυν, ῦνος, city in Κρήτη, γ 294 and Β 646.

γοῦν, i. e. γ' οὖν, in εἴ γ' οὖν, *if however; ἐμέ γ' οὖν*, me quidem certe.

γουνάζομαι, prs., and fut. άσομαι, (γόνυ), supplico, *beseech, implore*, τινά, (ὑπέρ, πρός), τινος, for the sake of, by; γούνων, τοκήων, by my knees, by (my) parents, Χ 345.

γούνατα, ασι, εσσι, see γόνυ.

Γουνεύς, leader of two tribes of Πελασγοί, Β 748†.

γουνοῦμαι, only pres., and ipf. γουνούμην, λ 29, (γόνυ), supplico, τινά, with inf., supplicando vovere, *supplicate and vow to offer*, κ 521. (See the cut, from ancient gem, representing Dolon and Ulysses.)

γουνός, ῷ, όν, masc., (γόνυ), strictly *curve, winding* (applied by Herodotos to Attica, because of its irregular form), *corner*, α 193; ἀλωῆς, garden-plot, Σ 57.

γραίης, τῆς, (γρῆυς), vetulae, *old woman*, α 438†.

Γραῖα, town in Βοιωτία, Β 498†.

γραπτῦς, τάς, nom. ἡ γραπτύς, (γράφω), *scratches*, ω 229†.

γράφω, (en-grave), only aor. **γράψεν,** part. γράψας, *scratch, engrave*, Ζ 169; *penetrate to*, Ρ 599.

Γρήνῑκος, river *Granicus*, rising in Mount Ἴδη, Μ 21†.

γρῆυς and γρηῦς (τ 346), dat. γρηΐ, voc. γρῆυ and γρηῦ, (γεραιός), *old woman*, also with παλαιγενέϊ, παλαιή.

γῠᾶλον, οιο, οισι, ntr., only θώρηκος (q. v.), *convexity*, Ν 507; γυάλοισιν ἀρηρότα, fitted together of *convex* (*metal*) *plates*, Ο 530. (Il.)

Γῡγαίη, λίμνη, lake in Μῃονίη, Υ 391. Nymph of this lake, Β 865.

γυῖα, ων, τά, artus, *joints*, only of arms and feet, Ψ 627, Ε 811, κ 363; λύονται γυῖα (see γόνυ), are wearied, Ν 85; in death, Η 16.

γυιόω, only fut. **γυιώσω,** σειν, *lame*, Θ 402 and 416.

γυμνός, οῦ, όν, nudus, *naked*, ζ 136; *uncovered*, τόξον (i. e. taken out of the γωρυτός); usually *unarmed, defenseless*, Φ 50, Ρ 122, Χ 124.

γυμνόω, **γυμνοῦσθαι,** aor. (ἐ)γυμνώθη, -θείη, -θέντα (γυμνός), nudari, *lay off one's clothes*, ζ 222, κ 341; with gen., χ 1; *unprotected, unarmed*, Μ 389, 428; *unprotected* against attack, Μ 399.

γῠναικείας, διὰ βουλάς, muliebribus dolis, *woman's* designs, λ 437†.

γῠναι-μᾰνές, voc., (μαίνομαι), *mad after women*, Ἀλέξανδρος, Γ 39. (Il.)

γῠναίων, δώρων, *gifts to a woman*, λ 521 and ο 247.

γυνή, γυναικός, etc., (quean, queen), *woman*.—(1) as designating sex, *woman, female*, Ο 683, Ω 708, Τ 110, Λ 269; θηλύτεραι, Θ 520; as contemptuous epithet, Θ 163, Χ 125; often with distinguishing title, to mark occupation, χερνῆτις, ταμίη; in general signif., mulieres, Τ 301, Ω 722; δῖα γυναικῶν, Γ 171; γ. δμωαί, also without δμωαί=*maid-servants*, ρ 75, υ 6.—(2) uxor, *wife*, Ζ 160, Ι 394, Ζ 516, Κ 422, Δ 162, θ 523; χήρη, vidua, *widow*, Ζ 432; *concubine*, Ω 497.—(3)

hera, *mistress*, ξ 123, X 48; *queen*, π 334.—(4) opp. θεά, Π 176; θνητάων, Υ 305; Ω 58, has sucked the breast of a woman (mortal).

Γῦραὶ πέτραι, **Γῦραίην** πέτρην, and **Γῦρῆσι**, name of rocky cliffs near Νάξος, δ 500, 507.

γῦρὸς ἐν ὤμοισιν, *round*-shouldered, τ 246†.

Γυρτιάδης=Ὕρτιος, Ξ 512†.

Γυρτώνη, town in Πελασγιῶτις, on the river Πηνειός, Β 738†.

γύψ, only **γῦπε**, γῦπες, εσσι, vultures, λ 578, X 42, χ 30.

γωρῦτῷ, τῷ, *bow-case, quiver*, φ 54†.

(See cuts, from ancient Greek and Assyrian representations.)

Δ.

δ'=(1) δέ, (2) δή, in δ' αὖ, δ' αὖτε, also in δ' οὕτως and εἰ δ' ἄγε, see δή ad. fin.

ΔΑ; pres. δι-δά-σκω (q. v.), aor. **δέδαεν**, docuit; τινά τι, ζ 233, θ 448; with inf., υ 72. In pass. signif. pf. **δεδάηκας**, ε, -ότες, and **δεδαώς**, novisse, *have been taught*, i. e. *know*, β 61, ρ 519; aor. pass. **ἐδάην**, cognovi, Γ 208; subj. δαείω, ῶμεν, discam; inf. δαῆναι, cognoscere, δ 493, and δαήμεναι, nosse, Z 150; comperire, *learn*, ν 335; τινός, *understand* any thing, Φ 487; aor. mid. **δεδάασθαι**, experiri, *test*, *try*, π 316; fut. δαήσεαι, noveris, *thou shalt know*, γ 187; τινός, τ 325.

δαήμονος, ι, α; ε; ες (δαήμων, δέδαα), τινός, peritus, *skilled in*, θ 159; Ψ 671, πάντεσσ' ἔργοισι.

δαῆναι, δαήσεαι, δαῶμεν, see ΔΑ.

δαήρ, έρα, voc. δᾶερ, pl. -έρων [⏑⏑ –], (δαϝηρ, Lat. levir), frater mariti, *brother-in-law*, Z 344, Ω 762. (Il.)

δάηται, see δαίω.

δαί, after τίς: quis-nam, what *pray*, α 225; v. l. τίς δέ.

δαΐ, dat. from δαΐς.

δαιδάλεος, 3, (δαίδαλα), *skillfully wrought, delicate, graceful*, I 187, κ 315, α 131.

δαιδάλλων, pres. part., (dolare), *elaborate skillfully, decorate*, Σ 479 and ψ 200.

δαίδᾰλον, τό, only τ 227; elsewh. pl., (dolare), *piece of skillful workmanship* (in metal), *ornament*, Ξ 179, E 60.

Δαίδᾰλος, famous artist and artisan from Κνωσός, Σ 592†.

δαΐζω, fut. ξω, etc., pf. pass. δεδαϊγμένος, (δαίω), lacerare, *cleave, tear in sunder*, esp. *wound*, by a cut or thrust, *pierce, cut through*, with or without mention of the weapon; and so generally, *cut down, slay*, B 416, H 247, Φ 147; ξ 434, *divide;* δεδαϊγμ. ἦτορ, Ρ 535 and Σ 236, confossum, *wounded* in the heart, *transfixed* (ὀξέϊ χαλκῷ). Distinguish fig. heart *rent* (by grief), ν 320; mind *confused* or *divided* (in perplexity or in doubt), I 8, Ξ 20.

δᾰϊ-κτᾰμένων, gen. pl., (δαΐς), *fallen in battle*, Φ 146 and 301.

δαιμόνιος, *ίη*, of person *standing under influence of a god* (δαίμων), this influence may be friendly or unfriendly, hence the word has opposite significations; either *admirable*, or more commonly, *wretch, luckless wight*, '*strange being*' (Bryant), ξ 443.

δαίμων, ονος, ὁ, *divinity*, (1) =θεός, A 222, ο 261, φ 196, 201; of specified divinity, Γ 420.—(2) numen divinum, *divine power*, P 98; as unfriendly, with κακός, στυγερός, etc., ω 149; Θ 166, *death;* in general, *the divinity*, in its influence upon human life, hence *δαίμονος αἶσα*, etc.

δαίνυ(ο), aor. mid. from *δαίνυμι*, epulabaris, Ω 63.

δαίνυμι, **δαινύντα,** with pres. mid.; ipf. (*δαίνυ'=ἐδαίνυε*), aor. *ἔδαισα*, and mid. *δαίνυντο*, opt. *δαινῦτο*, pl. *-ύατο*, fut. *δαίσειν*, aor. mid. *δαισάμενοι*, (*δαίω*), dispertio, *divide, distribute*, a portion of food, *δαῖτα*; *give a marriage- or funeral-feast*, δ 3, Ψ 29; mid., epulari, *feast*, Ω 665, σ 408, τ 425; *consume, feed upon*, κρέα καὶ μέθυ, ι 162; *ἑκατόμβας*, *μῆρα*; *hold a banquet*, *εἰλαπίνην*, *δαῖτα*, *δαίτην*.

δαΐς, (1) **δαΐδες,** ων, ας, (*δαϝίδες*, *δέδηα*), faces, *pine splinters*, σ 310; *torches consisting of a number of such splinters bound together*, α 428, Σ 492. (See cut.)—(2) **ἐν δαΐ** (*δαϝί*, *δεδήϝεν*, Υ 18), *λυγρῇ*, *λευγαλέῃ*, *heat of combat*, Ν 286. (Il.)

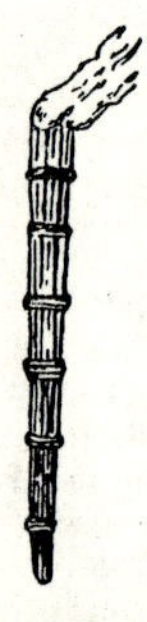

δαίς, τός, ἡ, also pl. *δαῖτες*, ας, (*δαίω*, *δαίνυμι*), *portion, share*; *ἐίση*, due share; then, convivium, *meal, banquet*, α 225, κ 124, Ι 487, Α 424; Ψ 48, let us now comply with the *invitation to the banquet*, odious though the feast be; =cibus, β 245; *ἔντεα δαιτός*, table utensils. (The root syllable always stands in arsi.)

δαίτη, **δαίτης,** ην, ῶν, ῃσι, (*δαίς*), convivium, *banquet*, ρ 220; **-ηθεν,** de convivio, κ 216.

δαιτρεύειν, inf., ipf. *δαίτρευον*, fut. *-εύσων*, aor. *-εῦσαι*, (*δαιτρός*), *distribute*, Λ 687; esp. food, ξ 433.

δαιτρόν, τό, (*δαίω*), *portion*, Δ 262†.

δαιτρός, ὁ, (*δαίω*), structor, *carver, distributor*, α 141. (See cut.)

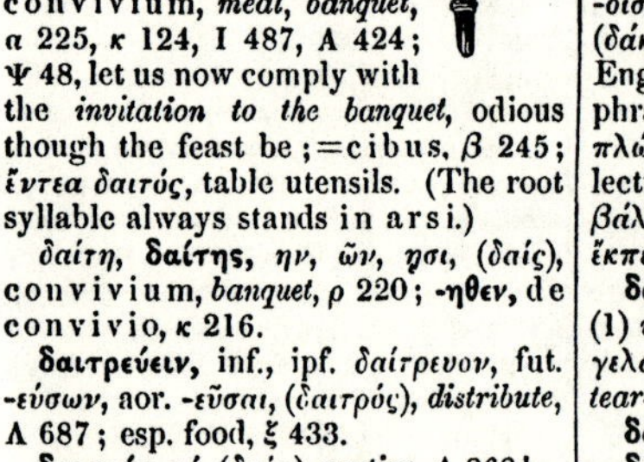

δαιτροσύνης, τῆς, (*δαιτρός*), *art of carving and distributing*, π 253†.

δαιτῡμόνες, οἱ, dat. *-εσσι*, (*δαιτύς*), convivae, *banqueters*, also with *ἀνδρῶν*, ο 467, χ 12. (Od.)

δαιτύος, τῆς, (*δαίω*), ἐκ, de cena, from the *feast*, Χ 496†. [– ⏑ ⏑]

Δαίτωρ, ορα, a Trojan, Θ 275†.

δαΐ-φρων, ονος, only sing., (*δαῆναι*), expertus, *skillful, tried*, of heroes, e. g., Β 23, Σ 18, Λ 791, Ζ 162; in works of art or skill, θ 373; in women's accomplishments, *ἔργα γυναικῶν*, ο 356.

δαίω, (1) prs. **δαίωσι,** ipf. *δαῖε*, pl. *δαῖον*, in pass. sense: pf. *δέδηεν*, plupf. *δεδήει*, pass. part. *δαιόμενον*, η, ων, ipf. *δαίετο*, and aor. subj. mid. *δάηται*, (*δαϝ-ίς*), incendere, *kindle, set in a blaze*, of fire, cities, etc., Σ 227; pass. ardere, *blaze*, *ἔρις*; *μάχη*, Υ 18; *ὄσσε*, *sparkle*, ζ 132 (*πυρί*, Μ 466).

—(2) **δαίεται, -όμενος,** ipf. *δαίετο*, and perf. 3 pl. *δεδαίαται*, (*δαίς*), dividitur, *is divided*, in mid. signif. *distribute* ο, 140 and ρ 332; *ἦτορ*, laceratur, α 48.

δάκνω, only aor. 3 sing. **δάκε,** inf. **δᾰκέειν,** mordeo, *bite*, Σ 585; *sting*, Ρ 572; stung Hektor's heart, Ε 493. (Il.)

δάκρυ, τό, pl. *υα*, *υσιν*, and **δάκρῠον,** *-οισι*, and gen. of separation, **-όφιν,** (*δάκ-νω*, Lat. dacruma, Goth. tagr, Eng. tear), lacrima, *tear*, esp. common phrases, *δάκρυ* (*χέων*, *-ουσα*, etc., β 24; *πλώειν*, *ἀναπρήσας*), where sing. is collective=*δάκρυα*, β 81; *εἴβειν*, (*κατα*) *βάλλειν*, *ἧκε* and *χύτο ἀπ' ὀφθαλμῶν*, *ἔκπεσε*, *ῥέε*; *ὀμόρξασθαι*, *τέρσοντο*.

δακρῠόεις, εσσα, εν, lacrimosus, (1) *weeping*, Φ 493; *tearful*, δ 801; *-όεν γελάσασα*, laughing *through tears*.—(2) *tear-bringing*, *μάχη*, *ἰῶκα*, Λ 601.

δάκρυον=*δάκρυ*.

δάκρυ πλώω, not one word, but two, swim in *tears* (*δάκρυ*), τ 122†.

δάκρυ χέων, *ουσα*, etc., see each word.

δακρύω, aor. **δάκρῡσα,** σ(ε), part. *δακρύσας*, pass. pf. *δεδάκρῡσαι*, *νται* (*δάκρυ*), lacrimare, *shed tears*, pf. pass., *be tearful*, Π 7.

δᾰλός, ῷ, όν, masc., (*δαϝίω*), *firebrand*, *αἰθόμενος*, blazing *torch*, Ν 320.

ΔΑΜ, to this root belong, (1) prs. **δαμάᾳ,** *όωσι*.—(2) **δαμνᾷ,** 3 sing. prs., ipf. (*ἐ*)*δάμνα*.—(3) **δάμνημι,** *ησι*, prs., mid. *δαμνᾷ* (*-ασαι*), *αται*, *ασθαι*, part. *δαμναμένους*, ipf. mid. *δάμνατο*, pf. pass. *δεδμημένος*, plupf. *δεδμήμην*, *ητο*,

-ήμεσθα, 3 pl. -ηντο, γ 305, -ήατο, fut. act. δαμάσσομεν (mid. -σσεται); aor. δάμασσεν (mid. -άσσατο, opt. -ασαίατο); pass. 1 aor. δαμάσθη, σθείς, and imp. δμηθήτω; 2 aor. ἐδάμην, δάμεν (=ἐδάμησαν), subj. δαμείω, ήῃς, ήῃ, ήετε, opt. -είη, inf. -ήμεναι, (domare, Eng. tame), (1) *tame*, Ρ 77, δ 637.—(2) *give as wife*, τινί, Σ 432, Γ 301.—(3) *overpower*, βίηφι, ἀνάγκῃ, ἶφι; *weaken, exhaust*, Θ 231; χεῖμα, ξ 488; στίβη, ρ 24; αἴθρῃ, καμάτῳ, ξ 318, Φ 52; ἁλί, ε 454; *reduce to subjection* (Ζ 159), pass., *be subject to*, Γ 183, Ε 878, γ 304, λ 622; *overcome*, δεσμός, μοῖρα, χ 413; (φρένας) οἴνῳ; τινὰ ἐπέεσσι, πληγῇσι (δ 244, foedare, *disfigure*) Διὸς μάστιγι; π 105; λοιμός, ἔρος θυμόν, Ξ 316; *succumb*, Ξ 353, γ 269; *give over into any one's power in battle*, τινά τινι, ὑπό τινι, ὑπό τινος, Π 434; χερσί τινος, ὑπὸ χερσί (δουρί) τινος, ὑπὸ σκήπτρῳ τινί, Ζ 159; deicere, *slay*, δουρί, βέλεϊ, δεδμημένος εὕδει ἔγχει ἐμῷ, Ξ 482; pass., *be slain, fall by hand of*, τινί, τινὸς δουρί (χερσι), ὑπὸ δουρί, ὑπό τινος, κηρί; *slay*, of arrows, Λ 478, Ε 278; θυμόν, Ξ 439, *held unconscious* (elsewh. with θυμόν, *overcome, control*, Σ 113, λ 562), conterere, *shatter*, Υ 266, Φ 401; mid., *subject one's self*, used like active, yet the following forms in pass. signif., δαμναμένους, and inf. δάμνασθαι, Θ 244, and ipf. δάμνατο, Λ 309.

δάμαρ, τι, τα, ἡ, (δμηθεῖσα, Σ 432), uxor, *wife*, τινός, υ 290. [⏑–, Ξ 503.]

Δάμασος, a Trojan, Μ 183. [⏑⏑⏑]

Δᾰμαστορίδης, (1) Τληπόλεμος, Π 416.—(2) Ἀγέλαος, *a suitor*, υ 321.

δαμάω, δαμείω, δάμεν, δαμήῃ, δαμήμεναι, δαμνάω, δάμνημι, δαμόωσι, see ΔΑΜ.

Δᾰνάη Ἀκρισιώνη, daughter of Ἀκρίσιος, mother of Περσεύς, Ξ 319†.

Δᾰνᾰοί, ῶν, collective designation of the Greeks who shared in the expedition against Troy.

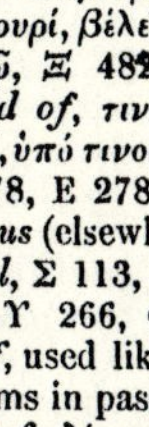

δᾱνά, ntr. pl., (δανός, δαϝίω), arida, *dry*, ο 322†.

δᾴος, τό, (δάϝος, δαϝίω), facem, *torch, firebrand*, μετὰ χερσὶν ἔχουσα(ι) (Od. and Ω 647). [⏑⏑] (See cut.)

δά-πεδον, -ῳ, τό, (πέδον), *ground*, λ 577; esp. pavimentum, *pavement*, floor beaten until it was hard, esp. in houses, δ 627; λ 420, *floor of men's apartment*.

δάπτει, ουσι, ἔμεν, fut. δάψει, aor. ἔδαψας, ε, (δαίω, dapes), lacerare, *rend*, Ν 831; *consume*, Ψ 183. (Il.)

Δαρδᾰνίδης, son of Δάρδανος; Πρίαμος, Ἶλος.

Δαρδᾰνίη, ἡ, city founded by Δάρδανος, Υ 216†.

Δαρδάνιαι πυλαί, of Troy, Ε 789, Χ 194, 413.

Δαρδάνιοι = Δάρδᾰνοι = Δαρδᾰνίωνες (fem. Δαρδανίδες, Σ 122, 339), inhabitants of Δαρδανίη, of same race as Ἴλιοι, called also Τρῶες, in connection with whom they are often named as representatives of the ἐπίκουροι, Β 819, 839, Γ 456.

Δάρδᾰνος, (1) son of Ζεύς, father of Ἶλος and Ἐριχθόνιος, progenitor of Τρῶες (Δαρδάνιοι), founder of Δαρδανίη, Υ 215, 219, 304.—(2) son of Βίας, Υ 460†.

δαρδάπτουσι (δάπτω), only 3 pl. prs., devorant, *devour*, Λ 479, ξ 92.

Δάρης, ητος, priest of Ἥφαιστος, Ε 9 and 27.

δαρθάνω, **ἔδρᾰθε**, aor., dormivit, *slept*, υ 143†.

δασάσκετο, δάσασθαι, see δατέομαι.

δά-σκῐος, ον, fem., (σκιά), umbrosa, *thick-shaded*, Ο 273 and ε 470.

δασμός, ὁ, (δατέομαι), distributio (praedae), *division* (of the booty), Α 166†.

δάσονται, δάσσατο, ασθαι, see δατέομαι.

δα-σ-πλῆτις, *hard-smiting, dread*, ο 234; derivation unknown.

δᾰσῠ-μαλλοι (μαλλός), *thick-fleeced*, ι 425†.

δᾰσείας, ύ, densas, *shaggy*, ξ 49 and 51.

δᾰτέομαι, prs. and ipf., (3 pl. δᾰτεῦντο, έοντο), fut. δάσονται, aor. δασσάμεθα, αντο, ασθαι and ἐδάσαντο, δάσασθαι and δατέασθαι, iter. δασάσκετο, perf. pass. 3 sing. δέδασται, (δαίω), dividere, *divide among themselves*, πατρώια, μοίρας, ληίδα, κρέα, κατὰ μοῖραν ἐφ' ἡμᾶς, ἄνδιχα, τριχθά, ξ 208, ζ 10, ρ 80, Σ 511; dissecabant, *cut in sunder*, Υ 394; conculcabant, *were treading* (to dust), and in this sense *dividing*, Ψ 121; Σ 264, *share with each other* the fury of combat, fight on both sides with equal fury.

Δαυλίς, *ίδος, ἡ,* town of *Φωκῆες*, Β 520†.

δάφνῃσι, dat. pl., (*δάφνη*), lauris arboribus, *with laurel* or *bay trees*, ι 183†.

δα-φοινός, *όν, οί,* and **δα-φοινεόν,** Σ 538†, *blood-red*, Β 308; *tawny*, Λ 474.

δέ, particle serving to continue the narrative, usually untranslatable, *and, farther, again, but, also*, (1) introducing additional or corresponding circumstances, Α 3, 5, 10, 16, α 3, 4, 28, 44; in contrast, Α 4, 20, 29, 57, α 19, 20, 26; after *μέν*, Α 126, 141, α 13, 24, 66, the two uses often hard to distinguish; after interrogatives, Α 540; second member of antithesis often precedes instead of following, Ζ 46, μ 220, π 130.—(2) introducing an apodosis (cf. *αὖ*), correlative, Ζ 146, λ 592; hypothetical, Α 137, Μ 246, μ 54; in period consisting of two members, Μ 10–17, γ 470–74; cf. Α 57, 137, 193, Η 148; *δ' ἄρα*, ζ 100, η 142.—(3) adversative, in sentence inserted between the two members of the period, υ 227; after negative sentence, ι 145; to mark a fact, in opposition to a mere assumption (esp. *νῦν δέ*), Α 354, 417, Β 82, α 166, β 79; the true in opposition to the false (*τὸ δέ, τὰ δέ*), χ 32, ψ 152.—(4) continuative, with causal force, apparently instead of *γάρ*, Α 259, Β 26; continuative, apparently supplying the place of a relative, Α 162, Β 209 sq., Δ 541, α 3, 52 sq.; instead of subordinative conjunction, Ζ 148, β 313, ι 292.—(5) recapitulating, after a parenthesis, μ 356; after vocative, γ 247; *δ' αὖτε*, but again, σ 48; *δέ τε*, Α 403, Β 90; *δέ* as third word instead of second in the clause, θ 540, φ 299.

-δε, remnant of ancient pron., (1) *τοίςδεσσι*, *to* those *there*, otherwise indecl., e. g. *ὅ-δε*, the one *there*, so with other pronouns.—(2) *towards, -ward*, *κλισίηνδε, οἰκόνδε, ὅνδε δόμονδε.*

δέατο, ipf., (*δίϝατο*), and **δοάσσατο** (*δϝ-ασσατο*), aor. subj. *δοάσσεται*, Ψ 339. (ΔΙϜ *δῆλος*), videbatur, *appeared*, ζ 242; *seemed*, ο 204.

δέγμενος, see *δέχομαι*, opperiens, *awaiting*.

δέδαα, *άασι, άηκα, αήμενος, αώς*, see ΔΑ.

δεδαίαται, δέδασται, see *δατέομαι*, divisa sunt.

δεδαϊγμένος, pf. pass., (*δαΐζω*), laceratus.

δέδηε, ήει, see *δαίω* 1, exarsit.

δεδίασι, see *δείδω*, veriti sunt, *feared*.

δεδισκόμενος, ο 150 = **δειδισκόμενος,** γ 41, ipf. *δειδίσκετο*, (*δείκνυμι*), salutare, *bid welcome* (by gesture), *δέπαϊ, δεξιτερῇ χειρί.* (Od.)

δεδμήατο, δεδμημένος, see ΔΑΜ.

δεδοκημένος, see *δοκάω.*

δέδορκε, *ώς*, see *δέρκομαι.*

δεδραγμένος, see *δράσσομαι.*

δέελον = *δῆλον*, conspicuum, Κ 466†.

δεῖ, opus est, *it behooves*, Ι 337†.

δείδεκτο, -δέχαται, -το, plupf. and pf. from *δείκνυμι.*

δειδήμονες (*δείδω*), timidi, Γ 56†.

δείδια, *ιθι, ιμεν, ίμεν*, see *δείδω.*

δειδισκόμενος, see *δεδισκόμενος.*

δειδίσσεο, *ίσθω*, imp., *εσθαι*, inf. prs., fut. *δειδίξεσθαι*, aor. *-ασθαι*, (*δείδω, δίω*), territare, *terrify*; only Β 190, pass., trepidare, *fear*. (Il.)

δείδοικα, see *δείδω.*

δείδω (always in first foot of verse), fut. *δείσεται, -εσθαι*, aor. *ἔδδεισας, ε*, and *δεῖσε, σαν*, etc., pf. *δείδοικα, ας, ε*, other form **δείδια,** *ιε, ιμεν, ίασι*, imp. *ἴθι, ἴτε*, inf. *-ίμεν*, part. *-ιότες*, plupf. *ἐδείδιμεν, ισαν*, (*δέος*), metuo, timeo, *fear*; revereri, *stand in awe of*, ξ 389, π 306; *μή*, with indic., ε 300; with prs. or aor. subj. (after principal tenses), with opt. (after hist. tenses); with inf. when subject remains the same; (*ἐνὶ*) *θυμῷ, κῆρι, κατὰ φρένα*, in one's heart, in one's thought; *περί τινος, τινῶν πέρι* (*ἀμφί*); (*μάλ'*) *αἰνῶς*; Ε 827, fear not so much Ares; revereri, ξ 389, *revering* Zeus Xenios, and taking pity on thee, π 306.

δειελιήσας, aor. part., (*δείελος*), qui coenavit, *having supped*, or toward evening, ρ 599†.

δείελον (*δείλη*), vespertinum, *ἦμαρ*, ρ 606, late in the afternoon; *δείελος*, vespera, *evening*, Φ 232.

δεικανόωντο, ipf., from *-νάομαι*, (*δεικνύμενος*, δ 59), consalutabant =*extend hospitable welcome*, by motion of cups, O 86; or with words, ω 410.

δείκνυμι, prs., only **δεικνύς** and *-νύμενος*, fut. *δείξω*, etc., aor. *δεῖξε*; mid. pf. 3 pl. *δειδέχαται*, plupf. 3 sing. *δείδεκτο*, 3 pl. *δειδέχατο*, (*δίκη*), monstrare, *show*, *point out*, act. and mid., Ψ 701; *σῆμα*, *τέρας*, *give a sign* or *portent*, *teach*; mid., consaluto, *make welcome* (by gesture, or with words), *κυπέλλοις*, *δεπάεσσι*, *μύθοις*, I 196, δ 59, I 224, 671, Δ 4, X 435, η 72.

δείλη, *afternoon*, Φ 111†.

δείλω, only **δείλετο**, *declined toward setting*; v. l. of Aristarchus for *δύσετο*, η 289†.

δειλός, *ή*, *όν*, (*δεῖσαι*), ignavus, *cowardly*, N 278, A 293; *wretched*, *miserable*, θ 351; miser, P 38, X 431, Ψ 223; esp. in phrase *δειλοῖσι βροτοῖσι*, λ 19, and *ἆ δειλ'* (*δειλέ*), *δειλώ*, *-οί*, heu te miserum, etc.

δεῖμα, *τό*, (*δεῖσαι*), terrorem, E 682†.

δείματο, ομεν, see *δέμω*.

Δεῖμος, *ον*, (*δείδω*), Terror, *terror of combat* personified, Δ 440. (Il.)

δεινός, *ή*, *όν*, (*δέος*), horrendus, *dread*, *terrible*, B 321, 755; *δεινὸν δέρκεσθαι*, Γ 342, and *δεινὰ ἰδών*, O 13, λ 608 and elsewh. = adv. Π 566, E 439, Δ 420, Θ 133; *vast*, *great*, H 346, O 309, Ξ 385; *mighty*, E 839; venerandus, *venerated*, θ 22. (Orig. form *δϝεινός*, cf. Γ 172.)

δείους, *τοῦ*, gen. from *δέος*, timoris, cf. the form *σπείους*.

δειπνέω, ipf. **ἐδείπνεε**, plupf. *δεδειπνήκει*, also aor., (*δεῖπνον*), coenare, *take a meal*, ξ 111.

δείπν-ηστος, *ὁ*, (*δειπνέω*), *meal-time* (afternoon), ρ 170†.

δειπνίσσας, aor. part. from *-ίζω*, (*δεῖπνον*), *after having entertained him at his table*, δ 535 and λ 411.

δεῖπνον, *ου*, *τό*, (*δάπτω*, dapes), cena, *chief meal* (in the afternoon, see *δόρπον*, υ 392), *repast*, B 381, K 578; *ἑλέσθαι*, ρ 176; *food*, ο 316; *fodder*, B 383.

δείρας, *αντος*, aor. part. from *δέρω*.

δειρῆς, *ῇ*, *ήν*, *αί*, *ῇσι*, collum, cervices, *neck*, *throat*, Γ 371, T 285, μ 90.

δειρο-τομήσεις, *ει*, fut., and *-ῆσαι*, *σας*, aor. from *δειροτομέω*, (*τέμνω*), iugulare, *cut the throat*, *behead*, Ψ 174, χ 349.

Δεισ-ήνωρ, *ορα*, a Lykian, P 217†.

δέκᾰ, decem, *ten*; as a round number, η 253, B 489; **δεκάκις**, decies; **δεκάς**, *άδος*, Eng. decade; **δέκατος**, decimus, as a round number, ξ 325; **δεκάχῑλοι**, centum milia.

δέκτῃ, *τῷ*, (*δέχομαι*), mendico, *beggar*.

δέκτο, aor. from *δέχομαι*, excepit.

δελφῖνος, *τοῦ*, and **-ῖνας**, *τούς*, delphini, *dolphin*, Φ 22 and μ 96.

δέμας, *τό*, (*δέμω*), *frame*, *build of body*, A 115; joined with *εἶδος*, *φυή*, *αὐδή*; freq. *δέμας*, as acc. of specification, *in figure*, also with gen., *like*, cf. instar, Λ 596.

δέμνια, *τά*, (*δέω*), *wooden bedstead* (with cords), τ 318, λ 189.

δέμω, ipf. 1 sing. **δέμον**, aor. *ἔδειμε*, (and mid. *-ατο*), subj. *δείμομεν*, pass. pf. *δεδμημένοι*, plupf. (*ἐ*)*δέδμητο*, (domus), *build*, I 349, H 337.

δενδίλλων, pres. part., of doubtful origin, *address one's self in turn to*, *ἐς*, I 180†.

δένδρεον, *έῳ*, *τό*, (*δένδρον*), arbor, *tree*. [Γ 152, τ 520; – ⏑͡ –.]

δενδρήεντι, dat. masc., nom. fem. *-εσσα*, (*δενδρήεις*), *woody*, ι 200, α 51.

Δεξᾰμένη, daughter of *Νηρεύς*, Σ 44†.

Δεξιάδης, i. e. *Ἰφίνοος*, H 15.

δεξῐός, *ῇ*, *όν*, (*δέχομαι*), (1) dexter, *on the right hand or side*, *ἐπὶ δεξιά* and *δεξιόφιν*, N 308; esp. *δεξιῇ* [K 542, – ⏑͡ –], *αί*, dextra (manus); also fides interposita, *pledges of faith*, B 341.—(2) faustus, *propitious*, ο 160.

δεξῐτεροῖο, *όν*, *ῆς*, *ῇ*, *ήν*, *ῆφι* = *δεξιοῖο*, etc., dextri, A 501, Λ 377.

δέξο, aor. imp. from *δέχομαι*.

δεόντων, imp. from *δέω*, false reading for *διδέντων*.

δέος, *τό*, *δείους*, gen., (*δείδω*), timor, *fear*, A 515; nihil tibi timendum; with inf., M 246.

δέπας, *τό*, *αϊ* and *αι*, pl. *α*, *άων*, *άεσσι* and *ασσι*, (*δάπτω?*), *vase* or *cup for drinking*; only Λ 632, as *mixing-bowl*. (See cut.)

δέρκεσθαι, prs., ipf. iter. *δερκέσκετο*, pf. *δέδορκεν*, *ώς*, aor.

ἔδρακον, tueri, *look*, δεινόν, σμερδαλέον, πῦρ, with fiery glance, ἐπὶ χθονί; joined with ζῆν, live and "see the light of the sun;" *behold*, N 86.

δέρμα, τό, ατι, ατα, ασι, (δέρω), *hide*, stripped off, pellis; *skin*, on human body, cutis; hide dressed for shield, Z 117; skin prepared for bottle, β 291.

δερμάτῐνοισιν (δέρμα), *leathern* (row-locks), δ 782 and θ 53.

δέρον, ipf. from δέρω.

δέρτρον, τό, *membrane which contains the bowels;* penetrating into the *intestines*, λ 579†.

δέρω, ipf. ἔδερον, δέρον, aor. ἔδειραν, δείραντας, *strip off the hide, flay*, A 459, τ 421.

δέσμᾰτα, τά, (δέω), vincula, X 468, *head-band.* (See cut No. 8.)

δεσμός, οῖο, ὁ, (δέω), vinculum, *band*, κρατερός, ἀργαλέος, θυμαλγέϊ, νηλέϊ, ὀλοῷ; χαλεπός, *fetter; halter*, Z 507; *rivets* for securing handles to tripod, Σ 379; *hawser*, ν 100; *knot*, ξ 348; *latch-string*, φ 241.

δέσποινα, ης, ἡ, (δεσπότης), *mistress*, also with ἄλοχος and γυνή, γ 403 (cf. πότνια).

δεταί (δέω) καιόμεναι, burning *fagots*, A 554 and P 663.

δευήσεσθαι, see δεύω.

Δευκᾰλίδης, Ἰδομενεύς, M 117. [ῐ]

Δευκᾰλίων, ωνος, (1) son of Μίνως, king of Κρήτη, N 451 sq., τ 180 sq.—(2) a Trojan, Y 478.

δεῦρο, δεῦτε (possibly δέ-ϝρω-θι, δέ-ϝρ-ιτε), huc i, *come here*, θ 292; allons! *hither*, δεῦρ' ἴθι, ἄγε δεῦρο, δεῦτ' ἄγετε; often with subj. of exhortation.

δεύτᾰτος, ον, (δεύτερος), ultimus, *last*, T 51.

δεῦτε, see δεῦρο.

δεύτερος, ῳ, ον, οι, (δύω), alter, secundus, Ψ 265; with gen. of compar., Ψ 248; **-ον,** iterum, with αὖ, αὖτις, αὖτε; τὰ δεύτερα, *second prize*, Ψ 538.

1. **δεύει,** prs. 3 sing., ipf. ἔδευε and δεῦε, iter. δεύεσκον, pass. -εται, -ετο, -οντο, *drench, moisten*, N 655, B 471.

2. δεύω, only prs. **δεύεαι,** -ῃ, opt. 3 pl. δευοίατο, etc., ipf. ἐδεύετο, fut. δευήσεαι, -ήσεσθαι, aor. ἐδεύησε, egere, *miss, want*, τινός; θυμοῦ, vita privatos, Γ 294; οὐ δεύεσθαι οὕτω, will not *be* so *wanting* (in battle) (πολέμου); P 142, *be deficient in*—, (τινός); *be inferior to*, (τινός); ἐδεύησε, with infin., ι 540, it just missed hitting the rudder.

δέχαται, δέχθαι, see δέχομαι.

δέχομαι, 3 pl. δέχαται, fut. and 1 aor. reg., 2 aor. **ἐδέγμην,** δέκτο, imp. δέξο, inf. δέχθαι, part. δέγμενος, pf. δέδεξο, imp. δεδεγμένος, 3 fut. δεδέξομαι, (δέκα), excipere, accipere, *receive*, παρά τινος (ἐμεῦ πάρα, Ω 429), τινός τι, τινί τι, *receive at hand of*, υ 271; *accept*, κῆρα, death; *await attack of*, Y 377; ἔγχεϊ, etc.; esp. 2 aor. *await*, with part., Δ 107; τινὰ ὁππότε λήξειε, I 191; εἰσόκεν ἔλθῃς, K 62 (δεδεγμένος, A 124, nactus, *having received at the hands of*), *stand one's ground against* in combat. Intrans. only T 290, sic mihi semper malum excipit malum, *succeeds.*

δεψήσας, aor. part. from δέψω, *knead*, μ 48†.

1. δέω, aor. **δῆσεν,** caruit, *stood in need of*, Σ 100† (δεῖ, see separately).

2. δέω, prs. imp. **δεόντων,** ipf. mid. δέοντο, aor. δῆσε, -σαν, imp. -σάντων, mid. aor. iter. δησάσκετο, plupf. pass. δέδετο, -ντο, ligare, vincire, *tie, bind*, men, Ξ 73, Φ 30; cattle, βίῃ, N 572; (ἐν) δεσμῷ; ἔκ τινος, to something, κ 96, X 398; Ψ 854 (ποδός, by the foot); ὅπλα ἀνὰ νῆα, *make fast* tackle throughout the ship, β 430; ἐρετμὰ ἐπὶ κληῖσιν, to the thole-pins; παρ' ἅρμασιν, to the chariot, Θ 544; τινὰ κελεύθου, *hinder* one's journey.

δή (cognate with jam, Eng. yea, yes?), particle marking a conclusion, cf. in meaning, jam, with various signif., according to the words with which it is connected.—(1) in general, *evidently*, and of time, *now, already*, τὰ δή, *just* that, νῦν δή, *at this very moment*, B 284; now *finally;* δὴ τότε, then *indeed*, ν 92; γὰρ δή, for *surely;* οὕτω δή, *just* so; it strengthens superlatives, *confessedly* the best, A 266; ἄλλοι δή, others, *be they who they may;* after interrogative words gives greater definiteness, τίς δή, quis tandem, who *pray;* πῇ δή, B 339; in commands, strengthens the command, *yet, only*, A 295, 514, 545; common phrases, ἄγε δή, agedum; ἴθι δή, μὴ δή, *only* do not, A 131; so also with expressions of wish, αἶ γὰρ δή, if *only.*—(2) in dependent clauses, ὡς δή, that *without doubt*, A 110; οὕνεκα δή, because *indeed; ἐπεὶ δή*, since *now;* in relative clauses, ἐξ οὗ δή, when *once for all*, A 6; in temporal clause, ὅτε δή, when *now*, as soon as; in conditional clause, εἰ δή (ἢν δή), if *now*, if *really*, if *at all events*, expressing a supposition which can not be contradicted; in interrogative clause, εἰ δή, whether *really*, α 207; in final clause, ἢ ἵνα δή, is it *perhaps* that thou mayest give *as is to be expected?* H 26; δὴ αὖτε, *actually* again; δ', better δὴ αὖ, αὖτε, οὕτως, pronounced with synizesis, A 131, 338, 540, δ 400; δή is often merged by synizesis with following word, Λ 138, 386, μ 330; yet never so, δὴ ἔπειτα. δή always follows the emphatic word, exc. in δὴ τότε, γάρ, πάμπαν.

δηθά, δήθ', diu, *long*, B 435, α 49. [– ⏑]

δηθύνειν, subj. δηθύνησθα, ipf. δήθῡνεν, (δηθά), cunctari, *linger*, A 27, Z 503.

Δηι-κόων, ωντος, (hostes speculans), a Trojan, E 533 sqq.

1\. **δηΐοιο**, ον, (δέδηε, δαίω, 1), *blazing*, πῦρ, B 415; πόλεμος, *hot* combat, Δ 281.

2\. **δήϊος**, ον, hostilis, ἄνδρα, Z 481, and hostis, B 544.

Δηϊοπίτης, ην, son of Πρίαμος, Λ 420†.

δηϊοτῆτος, ι, α, nom. δηιοτής, ἡ, (δήϊος), caedes, *slaughter*, usually with αἰνῆς, H 174.

Δηί-οχος, ον, a Greek, O 341†.

δηιόω, only prs. forms, e. g., Λ 153, Ψ 176, δ 226, and ipf. pass., N 675; all other forms, prs. ipf. fut. aor. also pass. from **δηόω**, prs. part. δηῶν, more commonly δηιόων, (δήϊος), caedere, concidere, *slay, cut in pieces*, χαλκῷ, Θ 534; lacerare, *rend*, P 65; Σ 195, *fighting* with the spear for—.

Δηί-πυλος, ῳ, companion at arms of Σθένελος, E 325†.

Δηί-πυρος, ον, a Greek, N 576.

Δηί-φοβος, οιο, son of Πρίαμος, M 94, δ 276.

δηλέομαι, only fut. and aor., (δαλός, deleo), laedere, *hurt*, χαλκῷ, χ 368; violare (ὑπὲρ, Δ 67), ὅρκια; nocere, *harm*, Ξ 102; by theft, θ 444, ν 124.

δηλήματα, τά, (δηλέομαι), *destroyers*, μ 286†.

δηλήμονα, ες, nom. δηλήμων, (δηλέομαι), infestus, *baneful*, Ω 33; βροτῶν, *destroyer*, σ 85.

Δῆλος, ῳ, ἡ, a famous island, sacred to Apollo and Artemis, ζ 162†.

δῆλον (δέελον), manifestum, ν 333†.

Δημήτηρ, τερος, τερα, (τρος, τρα), prob. = Γῆ μήτηρ, *Demeter; ἀνάσσης*, Ξ 326, ε 125, B 696; ἀκτή, barley meal.

δημιο-Fεργοί, *workers for the community, handicraftsmen*, e. g. seers, physicians, carpenters, bards, heralds, ρ 383.

δήμιος, ον, *belonging to the people;* publicus; δήμιον, *public affair; δήμια πίνειν*, publice, at public expense.

δημο-βόρος, *devourer of the people*, of grinding, avaricious βασιλεύς, A 231†.

δημο-γέροντος, ες, (γέρων), *elder of the people*, Γ 14. (Il.)

Δημό-δοκος, ου, name of blind bard in Σχερίη, θ 44. (Od.)

δημόθεν (δῆμος) ἀγείρας, publice collectum, having levied *from among the people*, τ 197†.

Δημο-κόων, ωντα, son of Πρίαμος, Δ 499†.

Δημο-λέων, οντα, son of Ἀντήνωρ, Υ 395†.

Δημο-πτόλεμος, ον, a suitor of Πηνελόπεια, χ 266. (Od.)

δῆμος, ου and οιο, ὁ, *commons, community*, (1) civitas, *body of citizens*, opp. βουλὴ γερόντων and βασιλεύς, θ 157; with πόλις, Γ 50, town and *people;* so often = *people, the public*, e. g. M 213 = δήμου ἀνήρ, unus ex plebe.—(2) *country-district* with its inhabitants, Z 158, I 634, Ω 481; Ὀνείρων δῆμος, land of Dreams.

δημῷ, όν, dat. acc., from δημός, *fat*, of man and beasts, ἀργέτι, Λ 818; πίονα, X 501, exuberant fat; Ψ 243.

Δημ-οῦχος, ον, Φιλητορίδην, Υ 457†.

δήν (orig. δFήν), diu, *long; οὔτι μάλα δήν*, N 573; οὐδ' ἄρ (οὔτοι) ἔτι δήν, β 36, ζ 33; οἰχομένοιο, β 215.

δηναιός (δήν) μάλ' οὐ, minime longaevus, by no means *long lived*, E 407†.

δήνεα, τά, (δαῆναι), consilia, *counsels, arts*, ψ 82, Δ 361.

δηῶν, δηόω, see δηιόω.

δηρῑάασθον, 3 du. indic., δηρῑάασθαι

inf., -άασθων imp. prs., ipf. δηρῑόωντο; also from δηρίομαι; aor. δηρίσαντο, also aor. pass. in act. signif. δηρινθήτην, (δῆρις), *contend*, P 734 (with words, only θ 76, 78, M 421).

δῆριν, τήν, *rivalry*, ω 515; *battle*, P 158.

δηρινθήτην (=δῆριν ἐθέσθην, P 158), see δηρῑάασθον.

δηρόν, acc. masc. and neut., (δήν), diuturnum, *long*, χρόνον, Ξ 206; elsewh.=diu, B 298.

δησάσκετο, aor. from δέω, vinciebat.

δῆσε, from δέω, (1) caruit.—(2) ligavit.

δήω, **δήεις,** ομεν, ετε, invenies, N 260; *find out, attain*, I 418.

Δία=Ζῆνα, see Ζεύς.

διά, prep., I. with gen., per, *through*, A 398, Γ 61, 357, λ 581; κυνέης διὰ χαλκοπαρῄου, M 183, P 294; στήθεσφιν, E 57; ὄρεσφι, K 185; ἔπρεπε δ. πάντων, was conspicuous even *among* all, M 104; *throughout, amid*, ι 298, Δ 495, Z 226, I 468, N 755.—II. with acc. (1) per, *through, throughout*, A 600, K 375, M 62, X 190, ι 447, ρ 72; διὰ στόμα ἄγειν, in ore habere, to have *in one's mouth, upon one's lips*; trans, *across*, H 247, Θ 343, K 298; of time, *during*, per, δ. νύκτα, B 57, Θ 510, ι 143; νύκτα δι' (ὀρφναίην), K 83, 142, 297, 386, Ω 363.—(2) propter, *because of*, A 72, ψ 67; ope, *by means of*, θ 520, O 41, 71, K 497, θ 82, λ 276; auxilio, 'Αθήνης, θ 520. [⏑⏑, –⏑ at beginning of verse.]

δια-βαινέμεν, inf. prs., -βήμεναι aor., traicere, *cross over*, εὖ διαβάς, *placing his legs far apart*, i. e. *planting himself firmly*, M 458.

δια-γιγνώσκω, inf. aor. -γνῶναι, agnoscere, *recognize*, H 424; dignoscere, *distinguish*. (Il.)

δια-γλάψᾱσα (γλάφω), excavans, *scoop out*, δ 438†.

δι-άγω, **δι-ήγᾰγον** aor., transportaverunt, *carry over*, υ 187†.

διὰ δᾶσάσκετο, διὰ δατέοντο, dispertiebat, *distributed*, see δατέομαι.

διὰ ἔδαψας, ε, see δάπτει, laceravisti.

δια-δέρκομαι, aor. opt. **δια-δρᾰ́κοι,** *look through at, pierce through*, Ξ 344†.

δι-εδηλήσαντο (δηλέομαι), laceravissent, ξ 37†.

δι-άει, see δι-άημι, perflat.

δια-είδεται (εἶδον), prs. pass., cernitur, *is discerned*, N 277; fut. mid. -είσεται, prae se feret, *display*, Θ 535.

δια-ειπέμεν, inf., imp. δίειπε (Ϝεῖπε), δ 215 and K 425, *talk over fully, relate precisely*.

δι-άημι, only 3 sing. ipf. **δι-άη,** better reading δι-άει, prs., perflare, *blow through*, ε 478. (Od.)

δι-εθείωσε, aor., (θειόω, θέειον), *fumigate* (with sulphur), χ 494†.

δια-θρύπτω, aor. pass. **δῐᾰ-τρῠφέν,** confractum, *shivered*, Γ 363†.

διαίνω, ipf. **δίαινε,** pass. διαίνετο, aor. ἐδίηνε, humectare, *moisten*, X 495. (Il.)

δι-αιρέω, aor. **διὰ ἕλε,** dissecuit, *cut through*, Υ 280†.

δια-κεάζω, aor. inf. **διὰ κεάσσαι,** discindere, *split*, ο 322†.

δια-κείρω, aor. inf. **διακέρσαι,** interrumpere, *frustrate*, Θ 8†.

δια-κλάσσας, aor. part., (κλάω), diffringens, *breaking in twain*, E 216†.

δια-κοσμέω, ipf. **-εκόσμεον,** aor. mid., -εκοσμήσαντο, aor. pass. opt. -κοσμηθεῖμεν, part. -θέντες, (κόσμος), dispertio, *dispose*; χ 457, *put in order*.

δια-κρῐδόν (κρίνω) ἄριστος, *decidedly* the best, M 103 and O 108.

δια-κρίνω, reg., fut. 3 sing. -κρῐνέει, mid. -κρῐνέεσθαι (also in pass. signif.); aor. pass. 3 pl. -έκρῐθεν, opt. -κρινθεῖτε, inf. -κρινθήμεναι, pf. part. -κεκρῐμέναι, (κρίνω), separare, *separate*, B 475; B 387, *shall part* the fury of the men, i. e. the furious combatants; cf. H 292; pass., *be parted, separate peacefully*, Γ 98, ω 532; dignoscere, *distinguish*, θ 195.

δῐ-άκτορος, ου, ὁ, (διάγω), *guide, conductor*, 'Αργεϊφόντης, α 84; epith. of Hermes as *messenger* of the gods, and *guide* of Priamos, Ω; of Odysseus, κ; of souls of departed, ω.

δια-λέγομαι, aor. **δι-ελέξατο,** ἀλλὰ τί ἤ μοι ταῦτα φίλος—θυμός, why does my heart thus *converse with* me? Λ 407, and freq.

δι-άμησε, aor. -αμάω, dissecuit, *cut through*, Γ 359 and H 253.

δια-μελεϊστί, see μελεϊστί.

διε-μέτρεον, ipf., (-μετρέω), metabantur, *were measuring off*, Γ 315†.

δια-μετρητῷ, metato, *laid off*, Γ 344†.

δῐ-εμοιρᾶτο, ipf., -άομαι, (μοῖρα), dispertiit, *portioned out*, ξ 434†.

δῐ-αμ-περές, also διὰ δ' ἀμπερές, (πείρω), *piercing through*, (1) *through and through*, penitus; *successively*, deinceps, Η 171, χ 190, ξ 11.—(2) perpetuo, *forever, constantly*, λ 558, ν 59; ἤματα πάντα, δ 209.

δῐ-άν-δῐχᾰ (δίχα), bifariam; μερμηρίζω, hesitated *between two resolves;* Ι 37, gave them *but one of two things*.

δῐ-ήνῠσεν, aor., (ἀνύω), οὔπω—ἀγορεύων, *finished* narrating, ρ 517†.

διὰ πεῖρεν, aor. from πείρω, transfixit, Π 405†.

δια-πέρθω, fut. 1 aor., and 2 aor. **-επράθομεν,** ον, ἔειν, evertere, *overthrow*, but διεπράθετο, ο 384, eversa est.

δια-πέτομαι, see δι-ίπταμαι.

δια-πλήσσοντες, part. from -πλήσσω, *splitting*, Ψ 120; aor. inf. πλῆξαι, θ 507.

δια-πορθήσας, aor. part. from -πορθέω, diripere, *sack*, Β 691†.

δια-πρᾰθέειν, aor. from δια-πέρθω, evertere.

δια-πρήσσω, prs. ipf., (πέρας), emetiri, *pass over, accomplish*, κέλευθον, πεδίοιο; *spend*, ἤματα, with part. Ι 326; λέγων, *finish* narrating, ξ 197, cf. ρ 517.

δῐα-πρό, penitus, *right through*, with gen. after verbs of motion, Ε 281; without gen., Ε 66, Μ 184, 404.

δῐα-πρῠσῐον (διαπρό), penetrans, reaching *far and wide*, Ρ 748; *piercingly*, ἤυσεν.

δῐ-επτοίησε, aor. from -πτοιέω, conterruit, *startle and scatter*, σ 340†.

δῐ-αρπάζουσι, auferunt, *carry off*, Π 355†.

δια-ρ-ραίουσι, and fut., aor. -ῥαῖσαι, fut. mid. -ῥαίσεσθαι, percellere, *shatter*, μ 290; evertere, *overthrow*, πόλιν; perdere, *destroy*, α 251; dilacerare, Ρ 727.

διὰ ῥήξασθαι, aor. from ῥήγνυμι, dirumpere, *break through*, Μ 308†.

δια-ρ-ρίπτασκεν (Fρίπτω), iter. aor., traiciebat, *shot through*, τ 575†.

δια-σεύομαι, only aor. **διέσσυτο,** pervolavit, *flew* (*charged, hastened*) *through*, with acc. and with gen., Ο 542, δ 37.

δια-σκεδάννυμι, aor. **-εσκέδᾰσε,** ειε, disiecit, *scatter*, ε 369; comminuit, *shatter*, η 275; ρ 244, would he *scatter* to the winds all thy fine things=insolence.

δια-σκιδνᾶσι, from -σκίδνημι, dispellunt, Ε 526†.

δια-σκοπῐᾶσθαι, from -σκοπιάομαι, speculari, *spy out*, Κ 388 and Ρ 252.

δια-σχίζω, aor. **-έσχισε,** pass. -εσχίσθη, discindere, *part, cleave asunder*, ι 71 and Π 316.

διὰ τάμε, 3 sing. 1 aor., subj. -τάμῃ, (τέμνω), dissecuit, Ρ 522 and 618.

διὰ τελευτᾷ, from τελευτάω, perficit, *bring fully to pass*, Τ 90†.

δια-τινάξῃ, aor. subj. from -τινάσσω, discusserit, *shatter*, ε 363†.

δια-τμήγω, aor. **-τμῆξαι,** ας, 2 aor. -έτμαγον, aor. pass. 3 pl. -έτμαγεν, (ἔταμον), *cleave*, ε 409, μ 174; traiciens, *crossing*, according to others, *parting*, Φ 3; pass., *have become dispersed*, Π 354; *part, separate;* Μ 461, *were shattered, flew asunder*.

δια-τρέχω, aor. **-έδραμον,** *run over* (the sea), γ 177 and ε 100.

δι-έτρεσαν, aor. from -τρέω (Ρ 729, tmesis), diffugerunt, *scattered*, Λ 481. (Il.)

δια-τρίβειν, only pres., and aor. -τρίψας, conterere, *rub*, Λ 846; tempus terere, Τ 150, morari, *delay; lose time* on the road, ὁδοῖο, β 404; τινὰ ὃν γάμον, *put off* one with her wedding, β 204.

δια-τρῠγῐος, *bearing in succession*, ω 342†.

δια-τρῠφέν, see διαθρύπτω, comminutum, *shivered*.

δι-εφαίνετο, ipf., *was visible through*, νεκύων, Θ 491; *glowed through*, ι 379.

δια-φθείρω, fut. **-φθέρσει,** pf. -έφθορας, evertet, *destroy*, Ν 625; Ο 128, periisti, *thou art doomed* (threat).

διὰ φορέουσι, from φορέω, divulgant, *spread abroad*, τ 333†.

δια-φράζω, only redup. aor. **-επέφρᾰδε,** *indicate*, Υ 340; *tell*, Σ 9; *admonish*, ζ 47.

δι-ἀφύσσω, ipf. **ἄφυσσε** (tmesis), aor. -ήφῠσε, pass. prs. -αφυσσόμενον, *draw off, consume*, π 110; *tear away*, τ 450; *cut through* and *let gush forth*, ἔντερα.

δια-χέω, only aor. **-ἔχευαν**, (ἔχεϝαν), disseeuerunt, *cut up*, γ 456.

διδάσκω, prs., inf. σκέμεναι, aor. 3 sing. δίδαξε, pass. pres., part., and δεδιδάχθαι, pf. inf., (ΔΑ), doceo, *teach*, τινά τι, θ 481, χ 422; pass., discere, *learn*, πρός τινος, of one, Λ 831; part. with gen., modo edoctus, one who has just begun to learn, *tyro*, Π 811.

δίδημι, only imp. **διδέντων**, and ipf. 3 sing. δίδη, (δέω), vincire, *bind*, Λ 105 and μ 54.

διδῠμάονε, du., -οσι, dat. pl., (δίδυμοι), gemini, *twins*, Π 672, also παῖδε.

δίδῠμοι, οισι, (δύω), gemini, *twins*, Ψ 641; duplicibus, *twofold*, τ 227.

δίδωμι, collat. form διδόω; irreg. forms, διδοῖς, διδοῖσθα, inf. διδόμεν, διδοῦναι, imp. δίδωθι, δίδου, ipf. (ἐ)δίδου, 3 pl. δίδοσαν, δίδον, fut. διδώσομεν, ώσειν, δωσέμεναι; aor. 3 pl. δόσαν, subj. δώῃ, δώομεν, δώωσιν, inf. δόμεν(αι), aor. iter. δόσκον, εν, ον, (dare), *give*, *present*, Χ 470, ι 197, freq. with inf., χ 253; with inf. of purpose, Λ 20; *bestow*, *accord*, of gods (opp. ἀνένευσε, Π 250; ἐάσει, ξ 444), Η 288, Ι 37, 255; with inf., Σ 293, Γ 322; ὁδόν, prosperous journey, οὖρον, Η 4; also of evils, *decree*, *inflict*, ἄτην, δ 262, etc.; tradere, τινὰ κυσί; ἀχέεσσι, *deliver over to*, Ψ 390, ω 219, Ψ 512, abducendam; collocare filiam, *give* daughter *in marriage*, δ 7; ἀνέρι μητέρα, β 223; *offer*, ν 378; *pay*, Φ 42, α 431.

δίε, see δίω, persecutus est, *pursue*.

δι-έδραμον, see διατρέχω.

δι-έεργον (ἐϝεργον), ipf., *separated*, *parted*, Μ 424†.

δια-ϝειπέμεν, inf., imp. δίειπε, (ϝεῖπον), δ 215 and Κ 425, *tell fully*, *converse of*.

δι-είρεαι, 2 sing. indic., -είρεο, imp., (εἴρομαι), perquirere, *question*, Α 550, δ 492.

δῐ-έκ, with gen., *out through*, προθύρου, μεγάροιο, σ 101, 185.

δι-ελαύνω, aor. **διὰ ἔλασσεν** (imp. -σσον), and **διήλασεν**, plupf. pass. ἐλήλατο, *drive through*, with gen., Κ 564; of spear, *thrust through* (with gen.), Ν 595; also διαπρὸ—ἐλάσσαι, Ν 647.

δι-ελθέμεν, see δι-έρχομαι.

δίενται, εσθαι, prs., (δίω), *speed* across the plain, Ψ 475; *be frightened off from*, with gen., Μ 304. [⏑ – –]

δῐ-εξ-ίμεναι, inf., (εἶμι), *go out through*, Ζ 393.

δι-εξ-ερέεσθε (ἐρέομαι), inquiritis, *question*, Κ 432†.

δι-επέφρᾰδε, see διαφράζω, explicuit.

δι-έπρᾰθον, see διαπέρθω, evertit.

δι-έπτᾰτο, see διίπταμαι, pervolavit.

δι-έπουσιν, ipf. δίεπε, διείπομεν, (ἕπω), exsequi, *perform*, Α 166, μ 16; persequi, *chase away*, Ω 247; *pass through*, Β 207.

δι-ήρεσα, aor. from -ερέσσω, *paddled hard*, μ 444 and ξ 351.

διερός, ῳ, *living*, ζ 201; *quick*, ι 43.

δι-έρχεται, etc., pres. fut. aor., transire per, *pass through*, with acc., Γ 198; with gen., Υ 100, ζ 304; διαπρὸ ἤλυθεν, Η 260.

δι-έσσυτο, aor. from -σεύομαι, pervolavit.

δι-έτμᾰγεν, aor. from -τμήγω, discesserunt, disiecti sunt.

δι-έχω, aor. **διέσχε** and **δι'—ἔσχεν**, prominebat, *project out*, Ε 100; with gen., Ν 519.

δί-ζηαι, pres. 2 sing., etc., (δι-ἴῃ-, ianus? strictly, *go*, *go to seek*, cf. Italian, cercare), quaerere, *seek*, Ἄσιον εἴ που (si qua) ἐφεύροι, Ν 760; *seek to win*, *woo*, τινί τι, π 391.

δί-ζῠγες (ζυγῆναι), biiugi, *yoked two abreast*, Ε 195 and Κ 473.

δίζε, ipf., (δίζω, from δϝίς, δύο), dubitabat, *debated*, Π 713†.

Δίη, ῃ, an island = Νάξος, λ 325.

διη-κόσιοι, ων, ducenti, Ι 383, Θ 233.

δι-ηνεκέα, acc. masc., έες, έεσσι, -έσσι, adv. **-έως**, (ἤνεγκον), continuus, *continuous*, *unbroken*, *long*; adv., *at length*, *minutely*, δ 836.

δι-ήρεσα, aor. from -ερέσσω.

δίηται, see δίω.

δι-ίημι, **διὰ δ' ἧκε**, with gen., *shot through*, φ 328, ω 177.

δι-ίκεο, aor., fut. -ίξομαι, (ἱκνέομαι), *go through*; recensere, *review*, Ι 61, Τ 186.

δῑι-πετέος, gen., (ΔιϝΙ, πετ-ής), *fallen from Zeus*, i. e. *from heaven*, of rivers, Π 174.

δι-ίπταμαι, aor. **δι-έπτάτο,** E 99, O 83, pervolavit, *flew through.*

δι-ίσταμαι, reg., (pf. -έσταμεν), *separate;* Π 470, *parted from each other;* A 6, *quarrel;* Φ 436, *stand aloof.*

δῐκαζέμεν, inf. prs., 3 pl. ipf. δίκαζον, 3 pl. aor. δίκασαν, imp. δικάσσατε; prs. mid., (δίκη), *pass sentence upon,* τισί; between two persons, ἐς μέσον τισί, Ψ 574; mid., *seek justice,* μ 440.

δῐκαιον, ῳ, οι, comp. -ότερος, sup. ότατος, ων, adv. αίως, (δίκη), iustus, aequus, *just, equitable,* γ 52; οὐδὲ δίκαιον, nor is it *right,* υ 294; *in due form,* ξ 90; σ 414, upon a thing *rightly* said, a just request.

δῐκασ-πόλον, -οι, (πέλω), *lawgiver,* A 238; ἄνδρα, λ 186.

δίκη, ης, ἡ, (δείκνυμι), *usage, custom;* τ 168, for such is *the way; right,* ius, Π 388, pervert *justice;* εἰπεῖν, give *judgment;* pl., *decisions;* δίκῃ, iure, *duly, rightly.*

δι-κλῖδες (κλίνω), *double-folding,* of door and gates, M 455. (See cut, representing ancient Egyptian doors.)

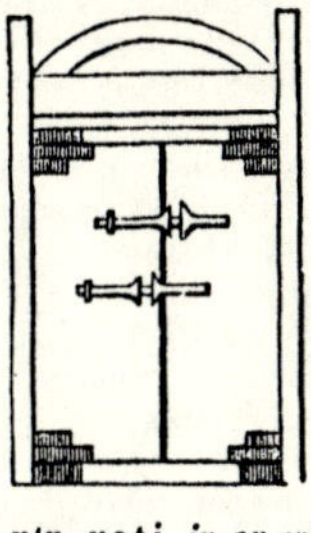

δικτύῳ, ntr., reti, *in* or *with the net,* χ 386†.

δῑνεύοι, etc., prs. ipf., (iter. δινεύεσκε), versari, *move about,* Δ 541; *turn about,* τί, Σ 543; *fly in circles,* Ψ 875; Σ 606, *turn somersaults;* oberrare, *wander about,* Ω 12.

δῑνέω, ipf. δινέομεν, (ἐ)δίνεον, also mid. 3 du. δινείσθην, (δίνη), *whirl,* Ψ 840; *turn around,* ι 384, 388; mid. (and act., Σ 494), *whirl about;* oberrare, *roam,* ι 153 (δινηθῆναι, π 63).

δίνη, ης, and pl., vortex, *eddy.* (Il. Φ.)

δῑνήεις, εντος, *eddying,* Φ 125.

δῑνωτοῖσι, τήν, (δινόω), *inlaid,* τ 56.

δῑο-γενής, voc. -ές, (Ζεύς, divo), *sprung from Zeus,* A 337.

Διόθεν, Jovis iussu, O 489, Ω 194, 561.

δῐ-οϊστεύω, aor. **-οϊστεύσῃ,** εύσειας, εῦσαι, (ὀιστός), *pierce with arrow,* with gen., τ 578. (Od.)

Δῐο-κλῆς, ῆος, son of Orsilochos of Pherai, γ 488.

δι-όλλυμι, pf. **δῐ-όλωλε,** *be plundered,* β 64†.

Δῐο-μήδη, daughter of Phorbas of Lesbos, slave of Achilleus, I 665†.

Δῐο-μήδης, εος, Τυδέος υἱός, Ψ 472 (H 163), husband of Aigialeia, E 412; king of Argos, B 567; his exploits, ἀριστεία, E; dealings with Glaukos, Z 232–236.

Δίον, ου, town in Euboia, B 538†.

Δῐονύσου, λ 325†, see Διώνυσος.

δι-οπτεύσων, fut., speculaturus, *to spy about,* K 451†.

δι-οπτῆρα, τόν, (διοπτεύω), speculatorem, *scout,* K 562†.

διὰ ὀρύξας, aor. part. from ὀρύσσω, *digging a long straight trench,* φ 120†.

δῖος, α, ον, (δῖϝος), illustris, *illustrious, divine, noble,* of gods, men, horses, elements; also of Λακεδαίμονα.

Δῖος, ον, son of Priamos, Ω 251†.

διο-τρεφέος, ές and pl., -ής, (Διός, τρέφω), *nourished, cherished by Zeus,* A 176.

δί-πλᾰκι, α, dat. acc., *double mantle,* Γ 126.

δι-πλόος, duplex, Δ 133; διπλῆν χλαῖναν, *double* mantle, see δίπλακι.

δί-πτῠχα, acc., from -πτύξ, (πτύσσω), *double, folded in two layers,* κνίσην, A 461, γ 458.

δί-πτῠχον, acc., from -πτῠχος, *thrown twice around* his shoulders, ν 224†.

δίς (δϝίς), bis, τόσσον, *twice* as far, ι 491†.

δισ-θᾰνέες, bis mortales, μ 22†.

δισκέω, ipf. **ἐδίσκεον,** *hurled the discus,* θ 188†.

δίσκον, ῳ, ον, οισι, from δίσκος, ὁ, (δικεῖν), *quoit, discus,* of metal, stone, wood; κατωμαδίοιο (cf. Statius, Thebais, VI., 646–721), attitude illustrated by the cut, see follg. page, after Myron's famous statue the discus-thrower (Discobolos); δίσκου οὖρα, τά = **δίσκουρα,** *a quoit's cast,* Ψ 431, 523.

δῑφῶν, part. from διφάω, *diving* (for oysters), Π 747†.

δίφρος, ου, οιο, ὁ, etc., (1) *seat* or *stool*, without back or arms, τ 97 (see cut No. 79).—(2) *seat* or *box* of chariot, E 728, esp. of war-chariot, Γ 262; word also designates the *chariot* itself, or in γ 324, a *traveling chariot*. (See cut No. 10.)

δῐχᾰ (δϝίς), bifariam, diverse, in two parts, *twofold*, *in doubt*, *at variance*, Σ 510, γ 127; ο 412, *in halves*.

διχθά (δίχα), *twofold*, α 23; my heart was divided, Π 435.

διχθάδῐας, α, acc. pl., (διχθά), duplices, *twofold*, I 411; Ξ 21=δίχα.

δίψα, ῃ, αν, sitis, *thirst*, Φ 541. (Il.)

διψάων, part. from διψάω, sitiens, *thirsting*, λ 584†.

δίω, only aor. **δῖον,** ε, mid., pres. subj. inf., *flee*, X 251; *be anxious for*, τινί; mid., aspellere, *drive away*, φ 370, υ 343; *repel from*, ἀπό τινος, Π 246.

δῐ-ῶσε, aor. from ὠθέω, dirupit, *tore away*, Φ 244†.

διώκω, prs., ipf. 3 du. διώκετον, K 364; act., ipf. mid., pres. pass., *drive*, of ship and horses; insequi, *pursue*, E 65 (also consequi, *overtake*, X 199); ποσὶν ταχέεσσι, X 173; *drive away*, σ 409; also *gallop*, *speed*, with like signif. in act. and mid., μ 182, ν 162; δόμοιο, domo pellere; πεδίοιο, per campum, through the plain.

Δῐώνη, ης, E 381; mother of Ἀφροδίτη, E 370.

Δῐώνῡσος, οιο, (and Διονύσου, λ 325), Z 132, 135, Ξ 325, ω 74.

Δῐώρης, εος, (1) Ἀμαρυγκείδης, chief of Ἐπειοί, Δ 517.—(2) father of Αὐτομέδων, P 429.

δμηθείς, -θήτω, see ΔΑΜ, domitus.

δμῆσιν, τήν, (δάμνημι), domationem, *taming*, P 476†.

δμήτειρα, victrix, Ξ 259†, = sq.

Δμήτωρ, ορι, victor, *Tamer*, ρ 443†.

δμωαί, άων, (ῶν), ῇσι, αἱ, (δμώς), *female slaves*, η 103; often captives in war, ζ 307; freq. with γυναῖκες, Z 323, χ 421.

δμώς, ωός, pl. δμῶες, ώων, (ΔΑΜ), *slaves*, often captives in war, δ 644, π 140; with ἄνδρες, μ 230. (Od. and T 333.)

δνοπαλίζω, ipf. **ἐδνοπάλιζεν,** fut. -ίξεις, (δινόω, πάλλω ?), *wrap around*, ξ 512; *grapple with*, *overthrow*, deicere, Δ 472.

δνοφερή, ήν, όν, (δνόφος), *dark*, *dusky*, Π 4, ν 269.

δοάσσατο, see δέατο, videbatur.

δοιῇ, ἐν, in dubio, *in perplexity*, I 230; also **δοιώ,** οἱ, αἱ, ά, duplices, *twofold*, β 46, Ω 527, τ 562; duo, M 455, X 148.

δοκάω, only mid. **δεδοκημένος;** also prs. 3 sing. **δοκεύει,** and aor. part. -εύσας, *observe sharply*, *watch*, τινά, O 730, Ψ 325, ε 274.

δοκέω, έεις, έει, (εῖ), aor. δόκησε, *intend*, with inf., H 192; videri, *seem*, pers., Z 90, Ψ 459, and impers., M 215, α 376; δόκησέ σφισι θυμὸς ὣς ἔμεν ὡς εἰ, their heart felt as if; ὡς ἐμῷ θυμῷ δοκεῖ εἶναι ἄριστα=ἐμοί, ν 154; δόκησέ οἱ κατὰ θυμόν, υ 93.

δοκόν, τήν, and pl. οἱ, οἴσιν, (δέκτο), *beam*, esp. in roof, χ 176.

δόλῐος, ίης, etc., (δόλος), fallax, *deceitful*, δ 455. (Od.)

Δολῖος, οιο, (ου), slave of Πηνελόπεια, ω 397. (Od.)

δολῐχ-αύλους (αὐλός) αἰγανέας, spears *with long socket*, ι 156†.

δολῐχ-εγχέας, adj. acc. pl. from -ής, (ἔγχος), *having long spears*, Φ 155†.

δολῐχ-ηρέτμοιο, οι, οισι, (ἐρετμός), *long-oared*, *using long oars*, of ships and Phaiakians, θ 191. (Od.)

δολῐχόν, ή, ήν, *long*, longus, O 474; diuturnus, ψ 243 (ntr., diu, K 52); *of distance*, ὁδόν, πλόον.

δολῐχό-σκῐον (σκιά), *casting long shadows*, Γ 346; or perh. -σκίον from κίων, *long-shafted*?

δολόεντα, όεσσα, (δόλος), dolosus, *artful*, η 245. (Od.)

δολόμητις, ιν, voc. -μῆτα, from -μήτης, (μῆτις), *wily;* Αἴγισθος, Κλυταιμνήστρη (Ζεῦ, A 540).

Δολοπίων, ονος, father of Ὑψήνωρ, E 77†.

δόλος, ου, ὁ, dolus, *trick;* δόλῳ, per dolum; λάθρη ἀνωϊστί, γ 235, δ 453, κ 232; opp. ἀμφαδόν, α 296; κράτεϊ, H 142; βίηφι, ι 406; *plot*, θ 276 (the wooden horse, θ 494; *bait*, μ 252); ὑφαίνειν, ε 356.

δολο-φρονέων, έουσα, (φρονέω), *wily-minded*, Γ 405, κ 339.

δολο-φροσύνην, τήν, pl. -νσι, *wile*, T 97 and 112.

Δόλοψ, οπος, (1) tribe on river Ἐνιπεύς in Thessaly, I 484, Λ 302.—(2) name of son of Λάμπος, O 525.

Δόλων, ωνος, Εὐμήδεος υἱός, K 314, spy, from whom Bk. 10, Il., receives its name. (See cut No. 26.)

δόμος, οιο, ου, ὁ, (δέμω), *building, house*, δ 618; pl., designating the *complex of rooms* which make up the house, ρ 85; also *rooms*, ζ 303, θ 57; *dwelling of gods*, η 81, λ 627, δ 834; of men, α 380, η 88; of animals, M 301, 169; in restricted signif., *hall*, α 126; in wider signif., *home, habitation* (ὅνδε) δόμονδε, ω 220.

δονᾰκῆα, τόν, acc., nom. -εύς, *thicket of reeds*, Σ 576†.

δόναξ, ἄκας, ὁ, (δονέω), arundo, *reed*, K 467 ; *shaft of arrow*, Λ 584.

δονέουσι, 3 pl. prs., aor. ἐδόνησε and part., agitare, *shake*, P 55; *drive*, M 157.

δόξης, gen., (δόξα), οὐδ' ἀπὸ—, nec praeter opinionem, not disappointing *expectation*, K 324 and λ 344.

δοροῖσι, nom. ὁ δορός, (δέρω), *leather bag*, β 354 and 380.

δορπέομεν, prs., ipf. (δορπείτην), also fut. aor, (δόρπον), cenare, *sup*, ο 302, Ψ 11.

δόρπον, cenam, *evening meal*, chief meal of day; ἑλέσθαι, Λ 86, prepare one's supper.

δόρυ, τό, -ατα, also (cf. γόνυ) parallel forms, δούρατος, ατι, ατα, ασι, and δουρός, ί; ε; α, ων, εσσι, (1) lignum, *wood*, ἐλάτης, Ω 450; τάμνετο, ε 243; trabs, *beam*, Γ 61; *ship-timber*, O 410, cf. μ 441; θ 507, hollow *belly* (of wooden horse).—(2) *shaft of spear*, Θ 494; μείλινον, E 666; *spear*, chief weapon of heroes, B 382, E 73; Γ 78, grasping the spear by the middle; χάλκεον, Π 608; χαλκοβαρές, λ 532; κεκορυθμένον χαλκῷ, χ 125.

Δόρυ-κλος, ον, Πριαμίδην, νόθον υἱόν, Λ 489†.

δόσις, ἡ, -σιν, (δίδωμι), *gift;* ζ 208, though small (to thee) dear (to me): ἀνήνασθαι, refuse a gift, σ 287.

δόσκον, aor. iter., see δίδωμι.

δοτῆρες, οἱ, (δίδωμι), *dispensers*, T 44 and θ 325.

δούλειον (δοῦλος) εἶδος, servilis habitus, ω 252†.

δούλη, ης, (δοῦλος), *female slave*, Γ 409, δ 12.

δούλιον ἦμαρ, servitutis dies, *bondage*, ξ 340.

Δουλῑχιον, island S. E. of Ithaka, inhabited by Epeioi, B 625, α 246; Δουλιχιόν-δε, *to D.*, B 629; Δουλιχιεύς, *inhabitant of D.*, σ 424.

δουλῐχο-δείρων, gen. pl., (δειρά), *long-necked*, B 460 and O 692.

δουλοσύνην, τήν, (δοῦλος), servitutem, χ 423†.

δουπέω, prop. γδουπέω (κτύπος), aor. ἐγδούπησαν, Λ 45; δούπησεν δὲ πεσών, *he fell with a crash; fall*, N 426; δεδουπότος ἐς τάφον, *sunk into his grave*, Ψ 679.

δοῦπος, ου, ὁ, (κτύπος), fremitus, strepitus (cf. French, le bruit), any dull, heavy sound, *din*, I 573; *noise, tread*, K 354, π 10; *clash* of spears, Λ 364; *roar*, Δ 455, ε 401; *hum* of javelins, Π 361.

δουρᾰτέου, ου, (δουράτεος, δόρυ), lignei, θ 493 and 512.

δουρ-ηνεκές (δόρυ, ἤνεγκον), *a spear's throw*, K 357†.

δουρὶ κλειτός = δουρι-κλυτός, όν, hasta inclutus, *renowned in the use of the spear*, E 55, ο 52, ρ 71.

δουρῑ-κτητήν, acc., (κτητός, κτάομαι), *captured in battle*, I 343†.

δοῦρα, δούρατος, see δόρυ.

δουρο-δόκης, της, (δέχομαι), *case* or *stand for spears*, perh. a ring on a column in the vestibule, α 128†.

δόχμια, obliqua, *obliquely*, Ψ 116; and **δοχμώ,** *sideways*, M 148.

δράγματα, τά, (δράσσομαι), manipuli, *handfuls of grain* gathered by the reaper, and cut by a single stroke of the sickle, Λ 69 and Σ 552.

δραγμεύοντες, *gatherers of the handfuls,* as they fall from the sickle, into bundles for the binders, Σ 555†.

δραίνεις, prs., (*δρᾶν*), moliris, *undertake,* K 96†.

Δρακίος, leader of Ἐπειοί, N 692†.

δράκων, *οντα, οντες,* ὁ, (*δρακεῖν*), anguis, *snake,* X 93; *dragon,* Z 181, M 202.

δράσσομαι, pf. part. **δεδραγμένος,** *grasping* (with hand), N 393 and Π 486.

δρᾰτά (*δαρτά, δέρω*), excoriata, *flayed,* Ψ 169†.

δράω, opt. **δρώοιμι,** exsequerer, *execute as servant,* (*δρηστήρ*), ο 317†.

δρεπάνας, *τάς,* (*δρεπάνη*), falces, *sickles,* Σ 551†.

δρέπᾰνον, *τό, sickle, reaping-hook,* σ 368†.

δρέπω, aor. **δρεψάμενοι,** *plucking, culling,* μ 357†.

Δρῆσος, *ον,* a Trojan, Z 20†.

δρηστῆρες, *οἱ,* (*δράω*), famuli, *slaves, workmen,* π 248; **δρήστειραι,** *αἱ,* famulae, *female slaves, work-women,* κ 349. (Od.)

δρηστοσύνῃ, *τῇ,* (*δρηστήρ*), *in service,* ο 321†.

δρῑμύς, *εῖα, ύ, piercing, sharp;* Λ 270, piercing missile overcomes; ω 319, *keen,* irresistible wish.

δρῖος, masc., (*δρῦς*), arbustum, *thicket,* ξ 353†.

δρόμος, *ὁ, -ου, -ον, -οι,* (*δραμεῖν*), cursus, *running,* θ 121; of horses, Ψ 300; *home-stretch,* Ψ 373; *race-courses* (*cattle-runs,* Gladstone), δ 605.

Δρύας, *αντος,* (1) king of *Λαπίθαι,* A 263†.—(2) father of *Λυκόοργος,* Z 130†.

δρύϊνον, acc. masc., (*δρῦς*), *oaken,* φ 43†.

δρῡμά, *τά,* (*δρῦς*), *oak-thicket, πυκνά,* κ 150.

δρῡ-όχους, *τούς,* (*δρῦς, ἔχω*), *ribs* of ship or boat, τ 574†. (See cut.) Later the same word designates the keelson, as holding fast the ribs, the lower ends of which are inserted into it. (See cut, where *fe* designates the *stem; b g, keelson; i h, mast; o, o, o, ribs.*)

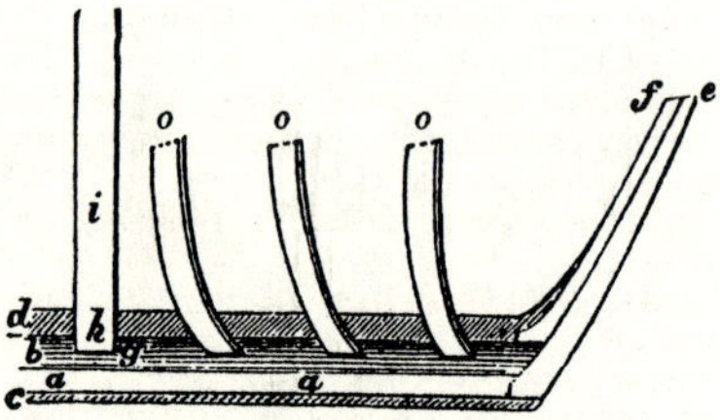

Δρύοψ, *οπος,* son of *Πρίαμος,* Υ 455.

δρῦς, *ὑός, ἡ,* (*δόρυ*), arbor, *tree,* Λ 494, N 389; quercus, *oak,* ξ 328; *οὐκ ἀπὸ δρυὸς οὐδ' ἀπὸ πέτρης,* X 126, 'tis no time now to talk, at ease, from *oak* or rock with this one; τ 163, thou art not, as the ancient proverb says, from *oak* or rock; cf. non es e saxo sculptus aut e robore dolatus (Cic. Acad. Posteriora, 31, 100), where the sense is slightly different.

δρῡ-τόμος, *ων, ὁ,* (*τέμνω*), lignator, *wood-chopper,* Ψ 315; with *ἀνήρ,* A 86.

δρύφθη, see *ἀπο-δρύφω.*

δρύφω, 3 sing. aor. **δρύψε,** mid. aor. **δρυψαμένω,** Π 324, *tear away; β* 153, *tearing each other's* cheeks and necks.

δρώοιμι, *ώωσι,* see *δράω.*

δῦ=*ἔδυ* (*δύομαι*).

δῡόωσι, 3 pl. prs. from *δύω,* (*δήιος*), *alter the appearance of for the worse, disfigure,* υ 195†.

δύη, *ης, η, ῃς,* fem., (*δυς-*), miseria, *misery, want,* ξ 338, σ 53. (Od.) [⏑ –]

Δύμας, *αντος,* (1) father of Ἑκάβη, Π 718†.—(2) one of the *Φαίηκες,* ζ 22†.

δύμεναι, inf. aor. from *δύω.*

δύναμαι, *ασαι,* etc., ipf., (also *δύνατο, ἀμεσθα*), fut. reg., 2 sing. also *δυνήσεαι,* aor. *δυνήσατο* and (*ἐ*)*δυνάσθη,* posse, *be able,* in every sense, physically, φ 247; valere, *avail, dare,* α 78; λ 414, *μέγα δυναμένοιο,* of a rich and potent man; is sum qui, δ 644; *δύναται γὰρ ἅπαντα,* ξ 445; *θεοὶ δέ τε πάντα δύνανται,* κ 306; often with negative (*οὔ τι,* α 78).

Δυναμένη, *ης,* a Nereid, Σ 43†.

δύναμις, *ει, ιν, ἡ,* (*δύναμαι*), *power,* κ 69; robur, *strength,* υ 237, N 786, 787; *πὰρ δύναμιν,* beyond one's strength; *δ. πάρεστιν,* as far as strength reaches.

δύνω, part. δύων, δύομαι, ipf. δῦνε, δύοντο, iter. δύσκε, fut. δύσομαι, εαι, aor. ἔδυν, 3 sing. δῦ, opt. δύη, part. δύντα, aor. mid. ἐδύσατο, δύσετο, opt. δυσαίατο, pf. δέδῦκε, intrare, *enter, make one's way into*, στρατόν, (καθ') ὅμιλον, πόλεμον (-οιο στόμα), οὐλαμόν; imbibitur, *sinks in*, P 392; induere, *put on*, χιτῶνα, (ἐς)τεύχεα, ἔντεα, θώρηκα; also with ἐν and dat.; intrare, πόλιν, πύλας, τεῖχος, δόμον, σπέος, (ὑπὸ, ἐς) πόντον, θαλάσσης κόλπον, *sink, go under* the earth, χθόνα, γαῖαν (of dead); of sun, *sink into the sea, set*, of evening, Φ 232, Θ 487; of stars, ε 272, Λ 63.—With prepositions, εἰς, Θ 271; εἴσω, Π 340 (οἱ—, Φ 118); δέρτρον ἔσω, λ 579, *burrowing into;* δόμον εἴσω, Λ 263; of passions and emotions, δύνει, δύεταί τινα, *enter, come upon, take possession of*, χόλος, Ἄρης; ἄχος ἦτορ, Τ 367; ὀδῦναι μένος, Λ 268; λύσσα ἑ, Ι 239; κάματος γυῖα, Ε 811. [ῠ in prs. ipf. act. and mid., elsewh. and in δύνω only ῡ, e. g. subj. aor. δύω.]

δύο, δύω, duo, *two*, with du. and pl., Γ 116; Κ 224, when two go in company, one thinks for the other.

δυοκαίδεκα, duodecim, *twelve.*

δυόωσι, see δυάω.

δυς-, insep. prefix, opp. εὖ, like our un-, miss- (cf. un-rest, mis-chance), conveys idea of *hard, bad, evil, untoward.* (See δύη.)

δυσ-āής, ᾱέος, ἄήων, (ἄημι), male flans, *ill-blowing, stormy*, μ 289.

δῦσ-άμ-μορος, ε, οι, (μόρος), perquam infortunatus, *most miserable*, Χ 428. (Il.)

δῦσ-ἄριστο-τόκεια (τόκος), *unhappy mother of a hero*, Σ 54†.

δύσεο, ετο, aor. mid. from δύνω.

δύσ-ζηλοι (ζῆλος), *exceeding jealous, suspicious*, η 307†.

δῦσ-ηλεγέος, έα, (ἀλέγω), *painful, doleful*, Υ 154 and χ 325.

δῦσ-ηχέος, gen. from -ηχής, (ἠχέω), *loud roaring*, πόλεμος, also θανάτοιο, *ill-boding* death, Π 442. (Il.)

δυσ-θαλπέος, gen. from -θαλπής, (θάλπος), *ill-warming, chilly*, P 549†.

δυσ-κελάδου, gen., (κέλαδος), *ill-sounding, shrieking* (fear), Π 357†.

δυσ-κηδέα, acc. from -κηδής, (κῆδος), *dreadful*, ε 466†.

δυσ-κλέᾶ, acc. from -κλεής, (κλέος), infamem, *inglorious*, Β 115 and Ι 22.

δύσκον, 3 sing. **δύσκε,** ipf. from δύνω.

δυσ-μενέων, έοντες, (μένος), malignus, *bearing ill-will*, β 72. (Od.)

δυσ-μενέες, έεσσι, (μένος), infesti, hostiles, *enemies*, Κ 100, π 121.

δύσ-μητερ, voc., my mother, yet *no mother*, ψ 97†.

δύσ-μορος, ῳ, ον, (μόρος), infortunatus, *ill-fated*, α 49.

Δύσ-πᾰρι, voc., *hateful Paris*, Γ 39 and Ν 769.

δυσ-πέμφελος, *stormy*, Π 748†.

δυσ-πονέος, gen. from -πονής, (πόνος), *toilsome*, ε 493†.

δύστηνος, οιο, etc., pl. ων, infelix, miser, *wretched, miserable*, λ 76, Χ 59.

δυσ-χειμέρου, ον, (χεῖμα), hiemalis, *wintry;* of Dodona, Β 750 and Π 234.

δῦσ-ώνῠμος, οι, (ὄνομα), infamis, *ill-omened, hateful*, Ζ 255, τ 571.

δῦσ-ωρήσωσι, aor. from -ωρέω, (ὥρα), *keep wearisome watch*, Κ 183†.

δύω=δύο.

δύων, see δύνω.

δῠώδεκ(α) = δυοκαίδεκα, Κ 488, Β 637; **δῠωδέκατος,** η = δωδέκατος, Α 493.

δῠωδεκά-βοιον, *worth twelve oxen*, Ψ 703†.

δῠω-και-εικοσί-μετρον, *holding twenty-two measures*, Ψ 264†.

δῠω-και-εικοσί-πηχυ, *twenty-two cubits long*, Ο 678†.

δῶ, τό (=δῶμα), Α 426.

δώδεκα, duodecim, Ζ 248; with πάντες, πᾶσαι, *twelve* in all; **δωδέκατος,** η, duodecimus, β 374.

Δωδωναῖος, *Dodonaian*, epithet of Zeus, see follg.

Δωδώνη, ης, in Ἤπειρος, oldest oracle of Zeus, ξ 327.

δώῃ and **δώῃσι,** 3 sing. subj. aor. from δίδωμι.

δῶμα, ατος, τό, (δέμω), *house;* also *palace*, κ 398; δώματα ναίειν, dwell, live, yet in ο 227 with adj.; δώματα, rooms=aedes, *house*, ο 109; *largest apartment of house, meeting-place of men*, χ 494; δῶμ' Ἀΐδαο=Ἀΐδαο δόμον, inferos, lower world.

δωρήσαιτο, opt. aor. from δωρέομαι,

(*δῶρον*), donaret, *would give*, K 557†.

δωρητοί (*δωρεῖσθαι*), *open to gifts, reconcilable*, I 526†.

Δωριέες, tribe in *Κρήτη*, τ 177†.

Δώριον, town, subject to *Νέστωρ*, B 594†.

Δωρίς, a Nereid, Σ 45†.

δῶρον, *ῳ, ων, οις, οισι*, (*δίδωμι*), donum, *gift; ὕπνου, Ἀφροδίτης, θεῶν*; *present, περίκλυτα, κάλλιμα, ἐρικύδεα*.

δωτῆρες, pl., (*δίδωμι*) *ἐάων*, *givers* of good, θ 325†.

δωτίνην, *τήν*, pl. *-ῃσι*, (*δίδωμι*), *gift, present*, λ 352. [ῑ]

Δωτώ, a Nereid, Σ 43†.

δῶτορ, voc. from *δώτωρ*, *ἐάων*, *giver* of good, θ 335†.

δώωσι, aor. subj. from *δίδωμι*.

E.

ἕ', ξ 222, false reading for *ἔα*=*ἦν*.

ἕ, enclitic, and *ἑέ*, see *οὗ*.

ἔα=(1) ipf. sing. *ἦν*, eram. [◡ ⏗] —(2) imp. prs. and 3 sing. ipf. from *ἐάω*. [◡ –]

ἐάγη, aor. pass. from *ἄγνυμι*, rupit.

ἑαδότα, perf. part. from *ἁνδάνω*, gratum.

ἐάλη, aor. pass. from *εἰλέω*.

ἑανοῦ, *ῷ, όν*, (*ϝεσθής*), *enveloping*, E 734; *pliant*, Σ 613.

ἑανός, *οῦ, ὁ*, (*ϝεσθής*), vestis, *garment*, Φ 507, Γ 419.

ἔαξε, *αν*, aor. from *ἄγνυμι*, discidit.

ἔαρος, *τοῦ*, (*ϝέαρος*), veris, *spring*, Z 148.

ἔασιν=*εἰσίν*.

ἕαται, το, see *ἧμαι*.

ἐάφθη, aor. pass. from *ἅπτω*, (*ἕπω*), *sank after* him.

ἐάω, **ἐῶ**, 3 sing. *ἐᾷ*, pl. *εἰῶσι*, subj. *εἰῶ, ἐᾷς, ἐᾷ, εἰῶμεν, εἰῶσι*, opt. 3 sing. *ἐῷ*, imp. *ἔα*, inf. *ἐάαν*, ipf. (3 sing. also *ἔα*, iter. *εἴασκον, ες, ε, εἴασχ'*, Λ 125, and *ἔασκες, εν*), fut. reg., so also aor. *εἴασα* (also *ἔασας, ε*, subj. *ἐάσω*), *let, permit*, (*οὐκ*—, impedire, *prevent*); with inf., e. g. *κεῖσθαι*, T 8; *κατακεῖσθαι*, Ω 523; *ζώειν*, χ 222; *κάρη ἕλκεσθαι*, X 398, K 344; T 65, *let us dismiss*= obliviscamur; *leave, say no more of*, ξ 171, 183 (*τινά, τί*); omittere, *let alone, let be*, Π 731, P 13, Υ 456, δ 212; *withhold*, i. e. *let alone giving*, ξ 444; relinquo, Δ 226, κ 166. [ᾰ in prs. and ipf.; *ἐᾷ, ἔα, ἐῶμεν, ἐάσουσιν*, often pronounced with synizesis.]

ἐάων (*ἐύς*), bonorum, Ω 528; with *θεοὶ δωτῆρες*, θ 325 (possibly from fem. *ἔη, good*).

ἑβδομάτῃ and **ἕβδομος**, septimae, -us.

ἔβλητο, aor. mid. from *βάλλω*, ictus est.

ἐγγεγάᾱσι, pf. from *ἐγγίγνομαι*.

ἐγ-γείνωνται, subj. prs., ingignant, *engender*, T 26†.

ἐγ-γίγνομαι, only pf. **ἐγ-γεγάασι** *Ἰλίῳ*, Troiae nati sunt, Z 493 and P 145.

ἐγ-γνάμπτω, see *γνάμπτω*.

ἐγ-γυαλίζει, fut. *ξω*, aor. *ἐγγυάλιξε*, (*γύαλον*), *put into the hand*, θ 319; *hand over*, π 66; *confer, κάρτος*, etc.

ἐγ-γύαι, ἐγ-γυάασθαι, from *ἐγγύη*, (*γυῖα*), *δειλαί τοι δειλῶν γε καὶ*, worthless *to receive* are the *pledges* of the worthless, θ 351†. (*ἐγγυάω, give pledge.*)

ἐγγύθεν, (*ἐγγύς*), ex propinquo= *near*, Λ 723; temporal, T 409; and *εἶναί τινι*, propinquum esse, *related*, η 205.

ἐγγύθι, prope, of space, H 341; with gen., *near to*, I 76, ν 156; of time, K 251; with dat., X 300.

ἐγγύς (*ἄγχι*), adv., prope, *near*, Γ 344; with *στῆναι, ἰέναι, εἶναι*; with gen., N 247, P 484; temporal, with dat., X 453.

ἐγδούπησε, see *δουπέω*.

ἐγείρω, aor. *ἤγειρα, ἔγειρε*, excitare, *wake up*, Ψ 234; ο 8, anxiety for his father *kept him awake*; *ἐξ ὕπνου*, ο 44;

arouse, to combat, P 544; *stir* the fight, Υ 31, Ε 496, Ν 357; Ἄρηα, Β 440; τινά, Ε 208; ἕκαστον, quemque ex urbibus excitavi, Ρ 222; μένος, *fire* courage.—Mid. prs. ἐγειρομένων, aor. ἔγρετο, οιτο, ἔγρεσθαι, όμενος, pf. ἐγρήγορθε, -όρθασι, inf. -όρθαι, whence part. pres. **ἐγρηγορόων**, *watch*; υ 100, as they wake; ἔγρεο, wake up, Κ 159.

ἔγκατα, *τά*, dat. ἄσι, viscera, *entrails*, Ρ 64.

ἐγ-κατ-έπηξα, ε, (in tmesi, Η 441), aor. from πήγνυμι, *thrust into*; κουλεῷ, the scabbard, λ 98.

ἐγ-κατα-τίθημι, mid. aor. 3 sing. **ἐγκάτθετο**, imp. -θεο, imposuit; λ 614, let not the craftsman who *conceived* this belt by (lit. in) his art, hereafter attempt any thing further, i. e. he would only injure his reputation; ψ 223.

ἔγ-κειμαι (ἐνὶ **κείμην**, ξ 501, δ 127), fut. **ἐγ-κείσεαι**, with dat., in iis iacebis, *shalt* not *sleep in* them, Χ 513.

ἐγ-κεράννυμι and -κεράω, ipf. **ἐν κερόωντο**, and aor. **ἐγκεράσασα**, with dat., *mix in* or *with*, κρητῆρσιν, υ 253 (Θ 189).

ἐγ-κέφᾰλος, οιο, ὁ, cerebrum, *brain*, Γ 300, ι 290.

ἐγ-κλάω, see ἐνι-κλᾶν.

ἐγ-κλίνω, pf. **ἐγκέκλιται**, *lies upon* you, Ζ 78.

ἐγ-κονέουσαι, prs. part., (διά-κονος ?), *in haste*, η 340 and ψ 291.

ἐγ-κοσμεῖτε, imp. prs., disponite, *put in order* (within), ο 218†.

ἐγ-κρύπτω, aor. **ἐν-έκρυψε**, with dat., *bury in* ashes, ε 488†.

ἐγ-κυκάω, see κυκάω.

ἐγ-κυρέω, aor. **ἐνέκυρσε**, with dat., incidit in, *met*, Ν 145†.

ἔγρεο, ετο, εσθαι, **ἐγρήγορθε**, θασι, θαι, όων, see ἐγείρω.

ἐγρηγορτί (ἐγρήγορα), adv., *awake*, Κ 182†.

ἐγρήσσεις, οντα, οντες, (ἐγείρω), indic. and part. pres., vigilare, *keep watch*, Λ 551, υ 33.

ἐγχείη, ης, ἡ = ἔγχος, *lance*, Ν 339.

ἐγ-χείῃ, subj. from ἐγχέω.

ἐγχέλυες, *αἱ*, anguillae, *eels*, Φ 203.

ἐγχεσί-μωροι, ων, ους, *mighty with the spear*, γ 188.

ἐγχέσ-πᾰλος, οι, (πάλλω), *spear-brandishing*, Β 131.

ἐγ-χέω, aor. **ἔχευε** = ἔχεϝε, ἔχεαν, subj. ἐγχείῃσι, also in tmesi, (χέω), infundere, *pour in*, with dat., γ 40, and with ἐν, ζ 77; mid. ἐνεχεύατο, *poured in for herself*, τ 387.

ἔγχος, εος, τό, *spear*, *lance*, for hurling and thrusting, the most honorable weapon: the shaft, δόρυ, was of ash, μείλινον, Χ 293, about 7 ft. long, δολιχόσκιον; the upper end, **καυλός**, was fitted with a bronze socket, **αὐλός**, into which the point, ἀκωκή, αἰχμή, was inserted, Π 802, being held fast by the πόρκης; the lower end, οὐρίαχος, was furnished with a ferule or spike, σαυρωτήρ, for sticking into the earth. The warrior carried two spears—for hurling (at distance of about 12 paces), and for thrusting from above. Hektor's spear was 16 ft. long, Ζ 319. (See also σῦριγξ, and cut No. 22.)

ἐγ-χρίμπτω, only aor. **ἐγχρίμψας**, *let graze*, Ψ 334; mid. ipf. -χρίμπτοντο, pass. aor. imp. and part. ἐγ-χριμφθείς, ἐνιχριμφθέντα, (χρίω), *almost touch* the stake, Ψ 338; Ρ 405, *press forward to* the gates; Η 272, ἀσπίδι, *dashed flat against* his shield; Ρ 413, *were crowding* constantly *forward;* Ν 146, *approach closely.*

ἐγών, ἐγώ, ego, forms as in Attic, but gen. ἐμεῖο, ἐμεῦ, ἐμέο, μευ, ἐμέθεν.

ἐδάην, cognovi, see ΔΑ.

ἐδᾰνῷ, dat., (ϝιδ-, σϝήδύς), *sweet*, Ξ 172†.

ἐδάσατο, -σσατο, see δατέομαι, dispertiit, *distributed.*

ἔδᾰφος, τό, (οὐδός), *floor of ship*, ε 249†. (See next page.) *a*, μεσόδμη, *mast-box; b*, *beams running parallel to*, *c*, ἐπηγκενίδες, *gunwale; d*, κληῖδες, *rowlock*, *thole-pin; e*, σκαλμοί, part of the gunwale on which the oar rests, *bed of the oar; f*, ζυγά, *cross-planks; g*, θρῆνυς, *braces* for the feet of the oarsmen; *h*, ἴκρια, *ribs; i*, τρόπις, *keel; k*, ἁρμονιαί, *slabs*, sustaining the floor; *l*, ἔδαφος, *floor; m*, *keelson*, was probably not distinguished from *i*, *keel.* (See also plate No. IV., at end of vol.)

ἔδδεισε, ἐδείδιμεν, etc., δείδω, timuit.

ἐδέδμητο, plupf. from δέμω, aedificatum erat.

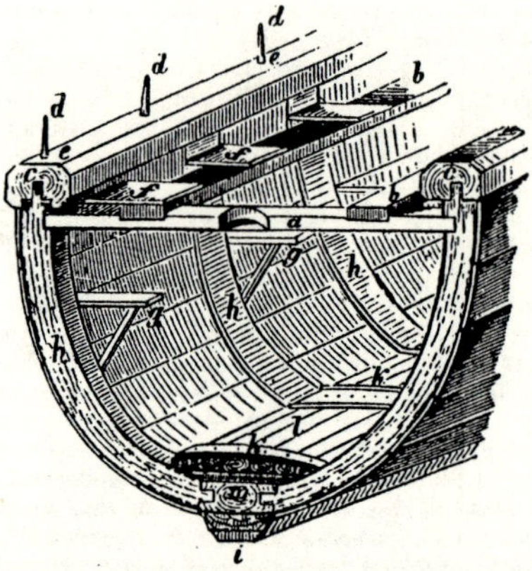

ἔδεκτο, aor. from δέχομαι, excepit, *received.*

ἐδητύος, τῆς, gen. from -τύς, (ἔδμεναι), cibi, *food*, Α 469, κ 384.

ἔδμεναι, inf. from ἔδω, edere.

ἕδνα, ἔεδνα, τά, (ἐϜεδνα, (σϜ)ηδύς), *bridal gifts*, chiefly cattle, (1) *suitor's presents to bride.*—(2) *to her father and relatives*, σ 276 sqq.—(3) *dowry of bride*, portion given her by her father, α 277.

ἔδομαι, fut. of ἐσθίω, comedam, ι 369.

ἕδος, τό, gen. pl. -έων, (ἕζομαι), sedes, (1) *act of sitting, time* or *reason* for it, οὐχ ἕ., non vacat (mihi) sedere, Λ 648.—(2) *sitting place, seat*, Α 534.—(3) *seat, abode*, Θ 456, ζ 42; *situation*, ν 344.

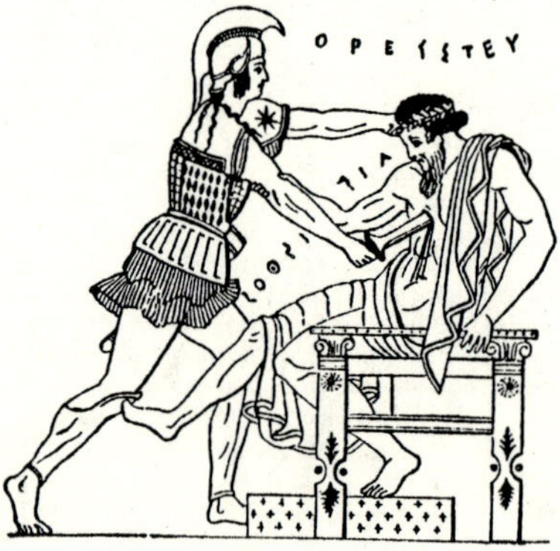

ἔδρᾰθον, aor. from δαρθάνω, dormivit.

ἕδρη, ης, ἡ, (ἕζομαι), (1) *seat, stool* (see cut; also No. 79), Τ 77.—(2) *rows of seats*, e. g. stone benches in the ἀγορά, θ 16; and elsewh., e. g. γ 7; τίειν ἕδρῃ, honor with a seat, i. e. show to a place of honor.

ἑδριάασθαι, inf., ipf. ἑδριόωντο, (ἕδρη), *sit down*, γ 35; *take seats in council*, Κ 198, η 98.

ἔδυν, aor. from δύνω, δύομαι.

ἔδω, inf. ἔδμεναι, ipf. ἔδον, iter. ἔδεσκεν, fut. ἔδομαι, εαι, ονται, pf. part. ἐδηδώς, pass. ἐδήδοται (ΕΔ, edo), *eat, devour*, of men and animals; σῖτον ἔδοντες = ἀλφησταί, bread-eating; θυμόν, κ 379, and κραδίην, Ω 129, metaph. *consume* one's soul with toil and pain; ι 75, *devour*, οἶκον (νήποινον, impune); ν 419, βίοτον; ξ 417, the fruit of the sweat of our brow.

ἐδωδή, ῆς, ἡ, only sing., (ἔδω), *food, meat, fodder*, Τ 167; ἤραρε θυμὸν ἐδωδῇ, strengthened his soul with meat, ξ 111.

ἑέ, see οὗ.

ἔεδνα = ἕδνα.

ἐεδνώσαιτο, aor. opt., (ἐδνόω, ἔεδνα 3), that he *may portion off* his daughter, β 53†.

ἐεδνωταί (ἔεδνα 3), κακοί, stingy *givers* (of dowry), Ν 382†.

ἐεικοσά-βοιον, α, (βοῦς), *worth twenty cattle*, α 431 and χ 57.

ἐείκοσιν = εἴκοσιν.

ἐεικοσ-όροιο (ἐρέσσω), *twenty-oared*, ι 322†.

ἐεικοστόν = εἰκοστόν, Ω 765 [and Od.

ἐείλεον, see εἰλέω.

ἐεισάμενος, etc., see εἴδω II. and εἶμι.

ἐεισάσθην, from εἶμι.

ἐέλδομαι, see ἔλδομαι.

ἐέλδωρ, τό, nom. and acc., (ἐϜέλδωρ, velle), desiderium, *wish, desire*, Α 41, ψ 54.

ἐέλμεθα, μενος, σαι, see εἰλέω.

ἐέλπομαι = ἔλπομαι.

ἐεργάθω = ἐργάθω.

ἔεργε, γμένος, from ἔργω.

ἐέργνυμι, see κατεέργνυμι.

ἐερμένον and -μέναι, σ 296, pf. pass., and **ἔερτο,** plupf. from stem ΣΕΡ, (σειρά, ὅρμος, series), necklace on which were *strung alternately* gold and amber beads, or a golden necklace *strung* (at intervals) with amber beads, ο 460; Ε 89, *firmly united.*

ἐέρση, -ήεις, see ἐρσ-.

ἔερτο, see ἐερμένον.

ἐέρχατο, see ἔργω.

ἐέσσατο, στο, see ἕννυμι.

ἐέσσατο, see following word.

ἕζω, aor. **εἷσα,** imp. εἷσον, part. ἕσας, ἕσασα, *set down, place,* ξ 280; λόχον, *lay* an ambush; ἐν κλισμοῖσι, κατὰ κλισμούς τε θρόνους τε; ἐπὶ θρόνου, *bid to be seated;* υ 210, ἐπὶ—, *set over; δῆμον* Σχερίῃ, *settled* in Scheria; here belongs also aor. mid. **ἐέσσατο,** imposuit, *take on board* (ship), ξ 295.—Mid. pres. **ἕζομαι, -εαι,** ipf., considere, *take a seat;* subsedit, *crouched down,* Χ 275, du. ἑζέσθην; with (inanimate) pl. subject, **κῆρες,** Θ 74, settled down upon, touched the surface of the earth; ἐπὶ δίφρῳ, ἐπὶ γοῦνα, ἐν λέκτρῳ, ἐν κλισμῷ, ἐπὶ δίφρου, ἀνὰ μέλαθρον, κατὰ κλισμούς τε θρόνους τε, ἐς θρόνους, ποτὶ βωμόν, ἐπ' ἐρετμά, took their places at the oars.

ἔῃ=ᾖ, subj. from εἰμί.

ἔηκε=ἧκε, aor. from ἵημι.

ἔην=ἦν.

ἑήνδανε=ἥνδανε from ἁνδάνω.

ἑῆος (ἐῆος), see ἐύς.

ἔης=ἧς, rel. pron. from ὅς.

ἑῆς, poss. pron. gen. from ἑός.

ἔησθα, 2 sing. ipf., **ἔῃσι,** 2 sing. prs. subj. from εἰμί.

ἔθ'=ἔτι.

ἔθειραι, αἱ, -ας, *horse-hair,* of mane, tail, plume of helmet, Θ 42, Π 795.

ἐθείρῃ, subj. prs., colat, *till,* Φ 347†.

ἐθελοντῆρας, τούς, (ἐθέλω), *volunteers,* β 292†.

ἐθέλω (θέλοιεν, only ο 317), subj. ἐθέλωμι, ipf. ἔθελον, ἠθέλετον, την, etc., iter. ἐθέλεσκες, ε, ον, fut. ἐθελήσεις, etc., aor. ἐθέλησα, *be resolved,* Β 391; *be ready,* Τ 187; οὐκ—, recuso, Α 112; I've no thought, θ 223; ἐθέλων, lubens; οὐκ ἐθέλων, invitus, ο 280; πολλὰ μάλ' οὐκ—, sorely against his will; μηδ' ἔθελε, *venture not, attempt not,* Β 247; *wish,* Δ 37, Ι 397, ι 262; μάλα, would gladly, Δ 318; θυμός, κῆρ (μοι) ἐθέλει; also ᾧ θυμῷ τις ἐθέλει, ἐκπάγλως, desire exceedingly; *be able,* γ 120; *desire,* ζ 64, ν 40, σ 113, Η 182. In Α 133, ὄφρα=in order that.

ἔθεν=οὗ, reflexive pron., see οὗ.

ἐθηεύμεθα, ipf. from θηέομαι.

ἔθνος, τό, -εα, (Ϝέθνος), *company, band, host,* ἑτάρων, λαῶν, νεκρῶν; *swarm, flock,* μελισσάων, ὀρνίθων, μυιάων; *herd,* χοίρων, ξ 73.

ἔθορε, aor. from θρώσκω, saluit, *sprang.*

ἔθρεψε, aor. from τρέφω, nutrivit.

ἔθων, part. prs., pf. **εἴωθε** (ἔωθε) -ώς, (σϜέθω, σϜέο, ἕο), suetus, consuevit, Θ 408; Ι 540, *laying waste continually;* Π 260, provoke *in their wanton way;* but in Ε 231, solitus.

εἰ (from pron. ὅς, as also αἰ), orig. *as;* this signif. recognizable in Δ 321.—I. optative use: cf. utinam, with opt., Κ 111, Ο 571, Π 559, Ω 74, δ 388; esp. with γάρ, α 255, Ρ 561; with κέν, ο 545.—II. interrogative use: si, *if, whether* (in MSS. often confounded with ἤ, ν 415), with indic., Β 300, Ε 183, τ 325; fut., Α 83, Ζ 367; subj., Ο 16, π 138; opt. and subj., Ξ 163; tentative use: freq. after such verbs as πειρήθη, Τ 385; γνώμεναι, Φ 266; μενοίνεον, Μ 59; also after other verbs when an ellipsis is to be supplied, e. g. *to see,* followed by opt. or indic., Κ 206, 19, Μ 122, Ψ 40, Ο 571.—III. conditional use: si, *if,* (εἴ ποτ' ἔην γε, see under I. ἦ), εἰ μή, nisi, *unless,* without verb, after negations, μ 326; other combinations, e. g. εἰ δέ, εἰ δ' ἄγε, etc., see under special heads.—(1) when the condition is formal rather than real, i. e. the sentence is not really hypothetical; indic. pres., Μ 233, Λ 178, 280; εἰ ἐθέλεις, with follg. inf., ο 80; ipf., Δ 321; aor., Α 290, Ε 104, Σ 305 (εἴ ποτε, Α 39, γ 98); pf., Α 173, Ζ 128, Ι 42, γ 93; the principal sentence is entirely uninfluenced in form by the condition, Μ 233, Π 452, 494, Ζ 142, Α 290, Σ 305, Ζ 128, Χ 390.—(2) with condition likely to be realized, seldom indic., Σ 427; more often fut., Α 135, 137, Ν 375, β 115, Ο 163, Α 294 (principal sentence is free to take any form, Α 135, Υ 26, 130); usually subj., Ε 258, Α 340, ε 221; often with κέν, Φ 553, α 288, Λ 324, Ι 135, Γ 281, 284, Ι 412, 414, Λ 315; rarely with ἄν, Φ 556, Γ 290; the principal sentence unaffected by the conditional clause, M 71, A 324, I 277, H 77, E 212, I 363, Δ 415.—(3) condition wholly uncertain, with no expectation of being realized; here the optative (never in iterative sense), Δ 34, P 102, I 379, Ξ 209, Π 73; also with *κέν*, I 141, 283, A 60; after negations *οὐδ' εἰ*, Θ 22, χ 61 (*κεν*, I 445, K 381); *ὡς εἴ τε*, *as if*, κ 420, ι 314; in the principal sentence, opt. with *κέν* (*ἄν*, Θ 22, I 445).—(4) condition contrary to reality; indic. ipf. for present time, the verb of the principal sentence, instead of following in indic. ipf, is often potential, Ω 220; indic. aor. for past time, (also Λ 310, ipf. joined with aor.), Λ 750, δ 363, O 460, Π 686, 700, Ψ 527; plupf., δ 363; in principal sentence we expect aor. indic. with *κέν*; yet we also find in principal sentence *κέν* with opt., E 311, 388, B 81, α 236, P 70; irreg., B 488, Γ 453. Irregularities in the hypoth. period are common, e. g. the conclusion (principal sentence) begins often with *τῷ*, *ἤτοι*, *ἤ τ'*.—IV. concessive use: *εἰ καί* (yet not in every case, e. g. B 367), *if also*, and *καὶ εἰ*, *even if*, with indic., O 51; with opt., χ 13, I 318; with subj., E 351; *εἴ περ*, see this word.

εἰᾰμενῇ, *τῇ*, (*ἧμαι*?), *depression*, Δ 483 and O 631.

εἰᾰνοῦ=*ἑ.ινοῦ*, Π 9†.

εἰᾰρινῇ, *ῇσι*, *οῖσι*, (*Fέαρ*), *ὥρῃ*, *springtime*; *ἄνθεσι*, spring blossoms, B 89.

εἴασε, aor. **εἴασκε**, ipf. iter. from *ἐάω*.

εἵαται, το, see *ἧμαι*, **εἵατο**=*ἧσαν*.

εἶβεις, etc., ipf. *εἶβον*, *ε*, (*λείβω*), *δάκρυον*, θ 531, *shed tears*; often with *κατά*, Π 11.

εἰ γάρ, see *εἰ* I.

εἴ γε, siquidem, *if at least*, *since*, usually separated as *εἰ ἐτεόν γε*, ι 529; except *εἴ γε μέν*, ε 206, and *εἴ γ' οὖν—γε*, E 258 (see *γοῦν*).

εἰδᾰλίμας, acc., (*εἶδος*), venustas, *comely*, ω 279†.

εἶδᾰρ, *τό*, *-ᾰτᾰ*, (*ἔδω*), cibus, λ 123, α 140; *ἄνθινον*, flowery *food*; *fodder*, E 369.

εἰ δέ, (1) *but if*, π 387 and freq.—(2) **εἰ δ' ἄγε** (*ἄγετε*), usually explained by ellipsis of *βούλει*; perh. better as an old imp. from *εἶμι*, instead of *ἴθι δή* (cf. *τί δέ*, *εἰ δέ*, I 262), vade age! *come go!* P 685, *Ἀντίλοχ'*, *εἰ δ' ἄγε δεῦρο*, *διοτρεφές*, *ὄφρα πύθηαι*; later, its signif. having been forgotten, it is joined with *ἄγετ'*, X 381; and with pl. verbs, Z 376, Θ 18; often with vocatives, the verb following in imp. (yet sometimes fut., φ 217, A 524, I 167, Ψ 579; or subj., ι 37, ω 336), A 302 (*μήν*, vero), Π 667, T 108; or subj. of exhortation, X 381.

εἰ δή, *if now*, *seeing that*, expressing conviction; also in indirect questions, *whether now*. (See *δή* 2.)

Εἰδοθέη, daughter of Proteus, a sea-goddess, δ 366.

ειδ-, I. prs., (*εἴδημι*), subj. *εἰδέω*, opt. *εἰδείην*, classed with *οἶδα*; mid. **εἴδεται** (stem FIΔ, video, Eng. wit), *-όμενος*, *-η*, videor, *seem*, A 228; with inf., Ω 197, ι 11; part., similis—, *δέμας*, *like* in bodily shape; lucere, Θ 559, N 98.—II. aor. **εἰσάμην**, *ἐείσατο*, (*ἐ*)*εισάμενος*, *η*, videbar, M 103; *appeared*, Ω 319; *ὡς ὅτε*, ε 281; *seemed*, with inf., θ 295, β 320, B 215; *was like*, *φθογγήν*, in voice, B 791; part., similis, *τινί*, N 45, 216, ζ 24.—III. fut. **εἴσομαι**, cognoscam, *recognize*, K 88; sciam, *know*, β 40, π 246; experiar, *find out*, Θ 532, χ 7; *αἴ κε*, with subj., Θ 111, Π 243, *ἤ*; also **εἰδήσεις**, *ειν*, *έμεν*, sciam, η 327, ζ 257, cogniturum esse.—IV. perf. **οἶδα**, novi, *I know*, with which are classed follg. forms, 2 sing. *οἶδας*, 3 pl. *ἴσασι*, ξ 89; *ἰδέω*, Ξ 235, and *εἰδέω*, *ομεν*, *ετε*, inf. *ἴδμεναι*, *ἴδμεν*, part. *ἰδυίῃσι*, plupf. *ᾔδεα*, 2 sing. *ἠείδης*, *ἠείδεις*, *ᾔδησθα*, 3 sing. *ἠείδη*, *ει*, *ᾔδεεν*, *η*, 3 pl. **ἴσαν**—*ἔκ τινος*, ex aliquo, from some one, X 280; (*μάλ'*) *εὖ*, ψ 175, (*οὐ*)*σάφα*, (not) accurately, certainly; *περὶ κείνου*, de illo, concerning him, ρ 563; *παλαιά τε πολλά τε*, have been through much, η 157; *πλείονα*, more experienced, T 219; with gen., peritum esse, M 229, O 412, P 5, nondum peperisse; with follg. *ὅ*, δ 771; *ὅττι*, Λ 408; *ὅτ' ἄν*, Θ 406; *ὡς*, ε 423; *εἰ*, δ 712; *εἴ κε*, β 332; with indirect question, Λ 653, ι 348, λ 463; with attraction, B 409, N 275, ρ 373; part., P 402; calleo, *know how*, with inf., H 238, 358; with acc., *understand*, *ἔργα*, H 236, B 832, θ 134; esp. with ntr. adj., *be versed in*, *practice*, *ἤπια*, τ 329, 332, B 213, ι 189, 428; *χάριν τινί*, gratiam habere, *thank*; *εὖ εἰδώς*, with gen., peritissimus; σάφα—, with inf., Ο 632; with acc., Ν 665, δ 534; fem., Α 365, and ἰδυίῃσι πραπίδεσσι, of Ἥφαιστος, with inventive mind, η 92.—V. aor. **εἶδον** (ἔϝιδον), also ἴδον, subj. ἴδω(μι), mid. **ἰδόμην**, subj. ἴδηαι, opt. ἰδοίατο, vidi, Δ 275, Χ 25, ξ 29; opp. πυθόμην, ψ 40; νοῆσαι, Ε 475; ὀφθαλμοῖσιν (without ἐν), very often; intelligo, *perceive*, Δ 249, with subj.; with acc. part., Τ 283, 292, γ 221, Δ 223, 232; spectare, *behold*, λ 94; visitare, α 3; *look*, εἴς τινα, τι (ὀφθαλμοῖσι, π 477), πρός, ἄντα, Ν 184; ἐσάντα, λ 143; ἀντίον, π 160; κατένωπα, Ο 320, straight forward, into one's countenance, ἀχρεῖον, ὑπόδρα; mid., videre, *see*, with part., Δ 374, 516, (ἐν) ὀφθαλμοῖσι (Σ 135), Ο 600; ἐνὶ φρεσί, in thought; cognoscere, Φ 61, φ 159; ἰδέσθαι, *to look upon*, Γ 194; θαῦμα, θ 366; εἰς ὦπα, τ 383.

εἶδος, dat. εἴ, ntr., (εἶδον), species, *outward form* or *appearance*, esp. of countenance; often joined as acc. of specification with adjs., *in form*, *beauty*, Γ 124; often coupled with μέγεθος, φυήν, always of human beings, exc. ρ 308, to judge from his (such an) appearance.

εἴδωλον, τό, ῳ, α, ων, (εἶδος), species, *illusive image*, Ε 449; *phantom*, δ 796; esp. (καμόντων), *shades* of the dead who flit about in the lower world, κ 476.

εἶθἄρ, statim, *immediately*, Α 579.

εἴθε (see αἴθε, εἰ, I.). utinam, *oh that!* with opt., β 33, ξ 468, Δ 313: εἴθ', γ 90=εἴτε, sive.

εἰ καί, si etiam, *even if*, Υ 371; etiamsi, *although*, Ψ 832. (Β 367, see ἤ καί.)

εἴ κεν, see εἰ, III., 2, 3.

εἶκε, ipf., (1) from εἴκω, *yield*.—(2) from εἴκω, *appear*.

εἴκελος (also ἴκελος), η, ον, (II. εἴκω), similis, *like*, τινί, λ 207; αὐδήν, in voice.

εἰκοσάκις, vicies, *twenty times*, I 379.

εἴκοσι, ἐείκοσι, viginti, *twenty*.

εἰκοσῖν-ήρῖτα (cf. ἐρήρης). *joined twenty times*, *twenty-fold*, Χ 349†.

(ἐ)εικοστόν, ῷ, vicesimum, o. (Ω 765.)

ἔικτο, τον, την, **ἐικυῖα**, see II. εἴκω.

I. εἴκω, **εἴκετε**, imp., εἴκων, ipf. εἶκε, 1 aor., iter. εἴξασκε, (ϝεικ-), *retire before any one*, τινί, Ρ 230 (χάρμης, *withdraw from* battle; τὸ ὃν μένος, *be inferior in* courage); θυμῷ εἴκων, from impulse, ν 143; θυμῷ εἴξας, in consequence of impulse; τινός, *retire from*, σ 10, χ 91; *be inferior in*, τινί (πόδεσσι, ξ 221); Χ 321, where he might most easily be wounded; Ψ 337, give him the reins with thy hands, i. e. give him free rein.

II. εἴκω (JIK ?) ipf. **εἶκε** (ἤικε), pf. **ἔοικα** (ϝέϝοικα), 3 du. ἔικτον, part. ἐοικώς and εἰκώς, ἐοικυῖα and ἐικυῖα, plupf. ἐῴκειν, εις, ει(ν), ἐίκτην, ἐοίκεσαν, mid. plupf. ἔικτο, ἤικτο, (1) similem esse, *resemble*, τινί τι, in any thing, Υ 371, Ψ 379, α 208, τ 380; ἄντα, Ω 630; εἰς ὦπα, in countenance, Γ 158; ἄγχιστα, maxime, πάντα, in all respects.—(2) decēre, *beseem*, ἔοικέ τοι οὔτοι ἀεικές, I 70; οὐδὲ μὲν οὐδὲ ἔοικε, nec vero decet (personal, χ 348, decet me); Κ 440, with acc. and inf., Β 190, 233, α 278 (χ 196, sc. καταλέχθαι, ω 273, sc. πορεῖν).—(3) convenit, *suit*, Σ 520, I 399. **ἐοικώς** (εἰκώς), (1) similis, τινί, Α 47, Ψ 430, γ 124 sq. —(2) meritus, *deserved*, α 46.—(3) *what is becoming*, *suitable*, δ 239.

εἰλἄπινάζων, ουσι, part. and 3 pl. prs., (εἰλαπίνη), epulans, *feasting*, β 57.

εἰλἄπῖναστής, ὁ, conviva, *guest*, Ρ 577†

εἰλἄπίνη, ἡ, compotatio, *drinking bout*, α 226.

εἶλἄρ, τό, (ϝεῖλαρ, εἰλέω), munimentum, *defense*, Η 338, ε 257.

εἰλάτῐνος, ον, οισι, αι, *of pine*, β 424, Ξ 289.

εἷλε, aor. from αἱρέω.

Εἰλείθυια, ἡ, *Eileithyia*, daughter of Hera, τ 188; usually pl. as *sister-goddesses who preside over childbirth*, Τ 119, Λ 270.

Εἰλέσιον, town in Βοιωτία, Β 499†.

εἰλέω, aor. ἔλσαν, 3 pl. inf. ἔλσαι and ἐέλσαι, part. -σας; pass. pf. ἐέλμεθα, μένος, aor. ἐάλη [ᾰ], 3 pl. ἄλεν, inf. ἀλήμεναι, ῆναι, part. ἀλείς, (FΕΛ), *crowd together*, *confine*, Ν 524; esp. *force back* enemy, Φ 295; game, λ 573; *shut in*, μ 210, Σ 447; *hold back*, Β 294; *smite with* lightning, shatter and sink in the sea, η 250; pass.. *in close array*, Ε 782; obsideri, *shut up in siege*, Ε 203; includi. *crowded together*, Μ 38, Σ 287; *collect themselves* *in one body*, E 823, Π 714, Φ 534, Ψ 420; contrahi, *cower*, *crouch* (gather strength for a bound, onset), Π 403, Υ 168, Φ 571, X 308.

εἰλήλουθα, *μεν*, *ει*, pf. and plupf. = ἐλήλυθα, ει, see ἔρχομαι.

εἰλι-πόδεσσιν, *ποδας*, (*πούς*), *bringing the feet close together*, of oxen or cows, which plait their hind-legs as they go, each describing, alternately, an arc of a circle about the other, and occasioning a rolling gait; others translate *trailing-footed*, and explain of the hind-feet, which approach successively the fore-feet on the opposite side, α 92 and freq.

εἶλον, *όμην*, aor. from *αἱρέω*.

εἰλῠάται, pf. pass. from *εἰλύω*.

εἴλῡμα, *τό*, (velamen, Ϝειλ., English, veil), *wrapper*, ζ 179†.

εἰλῡφάζει, 3 sing. and part. **εἰλῡφόων,** *whirl about*, Υ 492, Λ 156†.

εἰλύω, fut. **εἰλύσω,** pass. pf. *εἴλῡμαι*, 3 pl. *-ύαται*, part. *-μένος*, plupf. *εἴλῡτο*, obvolvere, *wrap*, *envelop*, E 186, υ 352; *cover*, ξ 479, Π 640.

εἶμα, *τό*, *-τι*, *-τα*, *-σι*, (*Ϝέσμα*, *ἕννυμι*), vestimentum, *garment*; ζ 214, *as clothing*.

εἶμαι = *Ϝέσμαι*, pf. pass. from *ἕννυμι*.

εἵμαρται, *το*. pf. and plupf. from *μέρω*.

εἱμένος = *Ϝεσμένος*, *ἕννυμι*, indutus.

εἰ μή, nisi, also after *ἄλλος*, μ 326.

εἰμί (*ἐσμί*, esse), 2 sing. *ἐσσί* (never *εἶ*), 1 pl. *εἰμέν*, 3 pl. *ἔασι*, subj. *ἔω*, *εἴω*, 3 *ἔῃσι*, *ᾖσι*, 3 pl. *ἔωσι*, *ὦσι*, opt. 2 *ἔοις*, 3 *ἔοι*, inf. *ἔ(μ)μεν(αι)*, part. *ἐών*, *ἐοῦσα*, *ἐόν*; ipf. 1 *ἔα*, *ἦα*, *ἔον* (*ἔην*, Λ 762 *ἤην*? Ο 82, τ 283), 2 *ἔησθα*, *ἦσθα*, 3 *ἔην*, *ἤην*, *ἦεν*, du. *ἤστην*, pl. *ἔσαν* (mid. *εἴατο*, correct to *ἕατο*, υ 106), iter. *ἔσκον*, ε; fut. *ἔσσομαι*, *-σεαι*, *-σεῖται*, *-σόμεθα*, *-σονται*, also *ἔσεαι*, *ἐσόμεσθα*.—Pres. indic. is enclitic; exes. 2 sing., epic 3 pl. *ἔασιν*, and forms in signif. *exist*; esse, suppetere, *be*, *be at hand*, ξ 496; *ἔνδον ἐόντων*, of her store; with inf. of purpose or obj., δ 215, Ω 610; *ἠώς*, ο 50; *μῦθοι*, δ 214, to-morrow also we shall be able to converse with each other; B 393, surely he shall find no means; cf. β 355, σ 371, Δ 271, Ψ 412; *ἔστι τί μοι*, habeo aliquid, have any —, ο 336, σ 3; *ὄνομ' ἐστί* (*τινι*, with nom. of name, σ 5); *ἔστι δέ τις*, *ἔσκε δέ*, introductory formula, γ 293, ο 417; *originate with*, α 33; *spring from*, *τινός*, α 215; cf. Υ 106 sq., β 274, γ 123, ξ 204, ν 130, Z 211, T 111, Ψ 347; *be in life*, *exist*, ω 263, β 119, ω 351, ζ 201; *οὐ δήν*, Z 131; *οὐκέτ' ἐόντος*, mortui, X 384, α 289; *take place*, *ὅπως ἔσται τάδε ἔργα*, what turn these things will take; *ὡς ἔσεταί περ*, as it will also come to pass; *εἴη κεν καὶ τοῦτο*, this might well come to pass, ο 435; *τίσις*, α 40; *ἐσσόμενοι*, posteri; *ἐόντα—ἐσσόμενα πρό τ' ἐόντα*, praesentia futura praeterita; *be*, as verb copula, *αἶσα*=*αἴσιμον*, is fated, with inf. (A 416); *ἢ ποτ' ἔην γε*, alas! it was he; *παρήιον ἔμμεναι*, to be an ornament, Δ 142; *ἀπὸ θυμοῦ μοι*, mihi odio eris; *οὐχ ἕδος ἐστί*, non vacat sedere; impersonal, *ὧδε*, Σ 266; *οὕτω*, λ 348, π 31; *ἐμοὶ ἀσμένῳ*, mihi gaudio, would be grateful to me, Ξ 108; *ἔστι*, it is possible, with inf., *οὐκ ἔστι*, M 327 = *οὔπως*, nullo modo, δ 193; with acc. and inf., ε 103, *οὐ — μῆχος* (expedient, remedy); *ἣ θέμις ἐστί*, sicut fas est; *οὐ θέμις*, Ξ 386, nefas est. (Ellipsis of *ἐστί* is frequent, in various forms, e. g. *ἔῃ*, Ξ 376; *ἔστω*, O 502.)

εἶμι, 2 sing. *εἶσθα*, subj. *ἴῃσθα*, *ἴῃς*, *ἴῃσι*, *ἴομεν*, *ἴωσι*, opt. *εἴην*, *εἴη*, T 209, *ἰείη*, inf. *ἴ(μ)μεν(αι)*, ipf. *ἤιον ἤια*, *ἤιες ἴες*, *ἤιεν ᾖε ἴε*, *ᾔομεν*, *ἤισαν ἴσαν ἤιον*, aor. mid. (*ἐ*)*είσατο*, ire, *go*, in widest range of meaning; usually with fut. signif., ξ 526 (yet not so in comparisons, e. g. δ 401); with fut. part., Γ 383, Ξ 200, O 136, P 147; *ὁδόν*, go by a road; *ἄγγελος*, as messenger for, *τινί*, Λ 652, K 286, examples of different constructions:—*δῶ*, *χορόν*, σ 194; *πεδίοιο*, through the plain, *ἄστυ-*, *Οὔλυμπόν-*, *Αἴγυπτόν-*, *πόλεμόν-*, *ἤπειρόνδε*, *πρὸς Ὄλυμπον*, *παρά τινα*; *μετά τινα*, *seek for*, *go to fetch*, N 247, ψ 83; *ἐς δαῖτα*, *ἐπὶ δόρπον*, *ἐπὶ δεξιά*, *ὑπὸ γαῖαν*=*εἰς Ἄιδος*, *ἄντα θεῶν*, *ἐπὶ νηός ἐν νηΐ*, *sail*,—*pass*, *ἔτος*, β 89; *return*, δ 670, γ 257, A 169, Γ 305; incedere, *walk* (majestic), ζ 102, H 213; *rise to go*, *go away*, then as exhortation (*βάσκ'*, *ἀλλ'*, *δεῦρ'*), *ἴθι*; *fly*, B 87, M 239, X 309; *plough the waves*, A 482; *penetrate*, Γ 61, Δ 138; of stars, *pursue their* *course*, X 27, Ψ 226; φάτις, *go abroad*, ψ 362; *advance* (of enemy), Γ 2, 8, M 88, P 759, χ 7; ἐπί τινι, ἀντί τινος, ἰθύς τινος, straight upon, ἀντίος, H 98, χ 89. [ῐ-, ῑομεν.]

εἰν=ἐν.

εἰνά-ετες (ἔτος), adv., *nine years*, γ 118.

εἰνάκῐς, novies, *nine times*, ξ 230†.

εἰν-ᾰλίη, αι, (ἅλς), adj., marina, *of the sea*, *sea-*, ο 479 and ε 67.

εἰνά-νῠχες (-νύχ-), adj. pl., *nine nights long*, I 470†.

εἰνάτερες, ων, αἱ, janitrîces, *brothers' wives*, Z 378.

εἴνᾰτος, nonus, *ninth*, B 295.

εἵνεκα=ἕνεκα.

εἰνί=ἐν.

εἰν-οδῖοις, adj., (ὁδός), *in the way*, Π 260†.

εἰν-οσῖ-γαιος=ἐννοσίγαιος.

εἰν-οσί-φυλλον, acc., (φύλλον), *leaf-shaking*, *with quivering foli·ge*, ι 22.

εἴξασκε, iter. aor. from εἴκω, cedebat.

εἷο=οὗ, χ 19, Δ 400, sibi inferiorem, inferior to *himself*.

εἰοικυῖαι, pf. part. from ἔοικα, II. εἴκω.

εἷος=ἕως.

εἶπα, -έμεν(αι), see εἶπον.

εἴπερ, *if only*, *if for once*, *as sure as*, contains often an emphatic assertion; the leading idea or important word often precedes, θ 408; with indic. preterit, ζ 282; fut., K 115, M 223, Π 263; subj. pres., M 245; aor., K 225, Φ 576, X 86, 191; opt., N 288 (apodosis, οὐκ ἂν πέσοι), Υ 100 (οὔ με νικήσει); additional examples with past tense of indic., Π 618 (τάχα κεν κατέπαυσε), Π 847 (πάντες κ' ὄλοντο).

εἶπον (ἔϝειπον, ϝέπος), aor., parallel form iter. εἴπεσκεν, subj. εἴπωμι, ησθα, indic. 1 sing. εἶπα, 2 pl. εἴπατε (ἔσπετε, see this word), *say*, *speak*, τινί or πρός τινα; τί τινι, *bid* one execute something γ 427; τινά, (1) *address*, B 59.—(2) *call*, *tell*, τ 334, Θ 373 (attraction, τ 219), ω 337.—(3) (εὖ) τινά, *speak* (well) of one, α 302; περί τινος, ἀμφί τινι, de aliquo; ἐν (μετά) τισι, before, in presence of; ἔπος, A 108, 543 (σ 166, say something); μῦθον, T 85; ἀγγελίην, θεοπρόπιον, θέσφατα; δίκην, give judgment; ὑπέροπλον, speak arrogantly; σάφα, clearly, accurately; καί ποτέ τις εἴπῃσι, olim dicturus sit aliquis.

εἴ ποτε, si quando, *if ever*; εἴ ποτ' ἔην γε, see I. ἤ.

εἴ που, sicubi, *if any where*, γ 93,

εἴ πως, si qua, *if in any way*, serve to state more mildly an assertion or suspicion, K 206, O 571, δ 388, π 148, Δ 17.

εἰράων, τῶν, *meeting-places*, Σ 531†.

εἴργω, un-Homeric, Ψ 72, see ἔργω.

εἴρερον, τόν, (σειρά, servus), servitutem, *slavery*, θ 529†.

εἰρεσίη, ης, ἡ, (ἐρέσσω), remigium, *rowing*, μ 225. (Od.)

Εἰρέτρια, αν, town in Εὔβοια, B 537†.

εἴρηαι, see ἔρω III.

εἴρημαι, see (1) εἴρω, *say*.—(2) ἔρω, *ask*.

εἰρήνη, ης, ἡ, (εἴρημαι), *peace*, ἐπ' εἰρήνης, in pace.

εἴρια, τά, (ἔριον, ἀρνός), vellera, *wool*; εἴ. ξαίνειν, card wool, χ 423.

εἰρο-κόμῳ, τῇ, (κομ-έω), lanas curanti, *dressing wool*, *spinning*, Γ 387†.

εἴρομαι, see ἔρω III.

εἰρο-πόκων, οις, gen. and dat. pl. from -πόκος, (πέκω), *wool-fleeced*, *woolly*, ι 443 and E 137.

εἶρος, τό, (εἴρια), vellus, *fleece*, δ 135 and ι 426.

εἰρύαται, το, see ἐρύομαι and ἐρύουσι.

εἴρω (FEP, ver-bum), fut. ἐρέω, έει, έουσι, έων, έουσα, pass. pf. εἴρηται, ημένα, plupf. εἴρητο (fut. εἰρήσεται), aor. ῥηθέντι,—*say*, A 297; *announce*, ἔπος, ἀγγελίην, φόως; παρέξ, falso, ψ 16.

εἴρω, see ἐερμένον.

εἰρωτᾷς, prs., ipf. εἰρώτα, ἠρώτα; (εἴρομαι), interrogare, *ask*, ο 423. (Od.)

εἰς, before vowels and βαίνω, **ἐς** (εἰν, ἐν, in), prep. with acc., (cf. in with acc. in Latin).—(1) of place, *into*, *to*, εἰς ἅλα (δῖαν, δ 577), ἅλαδε, κ 351; λαύρην, χ 128; with κατέθηκεν, υ 96; with designations of place, also names of cities, *to*, Θ 203; τρέπεσθαι, turning themselves *toward*, α 421; elsewh. of object or aim, e. g. ἐς θήρην, μάχην, πόλεμον; apparently with gen., sc. δόμον, κ 512, Z 378, Ω 160, 482, ν 23, esp. with 'Αίδαο; δ 581, sc. ῥοάς; yet cf. ξ 258; ἐς δίσκουρα, *at a discus-throw;* look *upon,* Ω 484, θ 170, π 477; εἰς ὦπα, α 411; εἰς ἄντα, ε 217, *in* the face; distributive, Β 126, in decurias distribueremur, *by* tens, ι 135;—of end or purpose: εἰπεῖν (μυθεῖσθαι, Ψ 305) εἰς ἀγαθόν, Ι 102, advise one *for* his good; εἰς ἄτην, *to* my ruin, μ 372; Ε 737, *for* the combat;—of result: Β 379, come *to* one conclusion.—(2) of time, *up to, for,* ἐνιαυτόν, δ 595, λ 356; ἐς τί, quousque, how long; εἰς ὅτε κεν, *until* when, with subj., β 99.

εἰσ-, in compounds, see ἐσ-.

εἶς (εἰς) = ἐσσί, (εἰμί), es, only before vowels, exc. ρ 388.

εἷς, μία, ἕν, unus, a, um; Δ 397, ἕνα οἶον, μία μούνη, μί' οἴη, β 412, *one single one;* so εἷς, *only one, a single one,* υ 313, χ 138; idem, *same,* Ν 487, Ο 511, *once for all;* ο 106 = nearly aliquem, *some one;* ἕνα αἰεί, i. e. one after another, χ 117.

εἶσα, see ἕζω.

ἐς ἀγείρομεν, ipf. ἐσαγείρετο, aor. -ατο, *collect into,* Α 142 (v. l. ἐν δ'—); ξ 248, collected itself into; Ο 240, was just coming back to life.

εἰσ-άγω, reg., aor. freq. in tmesi, ἐς δ' ἄγαγε, introducere, *lead in;* Ζ 252, ἐσάγουσα, *bringing with her* (by chance); elsewh. with design, e. g. Λ 778; Ω 447, *bid come forward, be seated;* προτέρω, δ 36; Κρήτην ἑταίρους, brought safely to Krete, γ 191; δόμον, into the house; *bring in,* ξ 419, τ 420.

εἰσάμενος, ατο, (1) from εἴδομαι, similis. — (2) from εἶμι = ἐείσατο, ivit.

εἰσ-ανα-βαίνοι, opt. prs., ipf. -έβαινον, aor. -έβην, *mount,* Θ 291; *go back to,* Ζ 74; *go up to,* Ω 700; Ω 97, Σ 68, *went up* the shore, π 449 (tmesis, τ 602).

εἰσ-αν-άγουσι, *carry off into* bondage, with acc., θ 529†.

εἰσ-αν-ιδών, intuitus, *looking up into,* with acc., Π 232 and Ω 307.

εἰσ-αν-ιών (εἶμι), with acc., *climbing* the sky, Η 423†.

εἰσ-άντα (εἰς ἄντα), *in the face, straightforward,* ο 532, also ἐσάντα.

εἴσατο, aor., see εἶμι and εἶδον.

εἰσ-αφ-ίκανεν, ipf., *came to,* χ 99.

εἰσ-αφ-ικόμην, only subordinate modes, pervenire ad, *arrive at,* with acc., μ 84, ψ 66, Υ 336.

εἰσ-βαίνω, ipf. and aor., *embark upon, enter,* τι, ι 103, δ 48, θ 314; Μ 59, *come in;* ἐς δ' βῆσε, *drove in,* Α 310.

εἰσ-εῖδον, ε, see εἰσοράω.

εἴσ-ειμι, ipf. ἐς δ' ᾔιεν, ἴτην, *go in; μετ' ἀνέρας,* among the men; *enter,* χ 470; Ω 463, in conspectum veniam.

εἰσ-ελάων, *drive in,* κ 83; εἰσ-έλασσαν, *ran in* the ship, ν 113; drive into battle, Ο 385.

εἰσ-ερύσαντες (ἐρύω), aor. part., *having dragged it into* the cave, μ 317†.

εἰσ-έρχεο, fut. ἐσελεύσομαι, aor. εἰσῆλθε, ἐς δ' ἦλθε, ἔσελθε, etc., also ἐσέρχεται, intrare, *enter,* τί, ρ 275; ἔς τι, δ 802; εὐνήν, δ 338; incessere, *enter into, come upon,* Ρ 157, ο 407; Β 798, very often have I been present in battles; ingredi, Φρυγίην.

ἐίση, ης, ῃ, ην, αι, (ἐϝισϝη, fem. from ἔϝισος = ἴσος), aequus, *like, proportionate,* epithet of (1) δαιτός (δαῖτας, λ 185), *fitting* share, Α 468; *equal,* i. e. *equally divided,* feast.—(2) νῆες, νῆας, νηός, *symmetrical, well-proportioned,* ε 175.—(3) ἀσπίδα παντόσ' ἐίσην, *uniform* on every side, circular.—(4) φρένας ἔνδον (nearly = ἐναίσιμοι, σ 220), *well-balanced, thoughtful, reasonable.*

εἶσθα = εἶς, from εἶμι.

εἰσ-ιέμεναι, prs. part. mid. from εἰσίημι, *seeking to enter,* χ 470.

εἰσ-ίθμη, ἡ, (εἶμι), *entrance,* ζ 264†.

ἐίσκω, prs. indic., ipf. ᾔισκε, ομεν, ἐίσκομεν (ἴκελος), *liken,* (1) with reflexive pron. and dat., *assume form* (appearance) of any one, ν 313.—(2) *discern resemblance,* τινά τινι, ἄγχιστα, πάντα altogether, ἐνωπαδίως, ψ 94; *compare,* Γ 197; ι 321, *judged it* as large as.—(3) censere, *hold,* with acc. and inf., Ν 446, *may we think* it an equivalent?

εἰσ-νοέω, only aor. **εἰσενόησα,** ε, *discern,* Ω 700†.

εἴσ-οδος, ἡ, *entrance,* κ 90†.

εἰσ-οιχνεῦσι, εῦσαν, 3 pl. indic. and part., (οἴχομαι), with acc., *enter,* ζ 157 the choral dance.

εἰσόκε(ν) = εἰς ὅ κε, dum, with subj., (1) *until,* Γ 409, θ 318.—(2) *as long as,* Ι 609.

εἴσεται, fut., (1) from εἶμι, ibit.—(2) from οἶδα, sciet, see ΕΙΔ, IV.

εἰσ-οράω, prs. **εἰσορόωσι,** opt. -ορόῳτε, part. -ορόων and -ῶν, mid. pres. imp. -οράασθε, inf. -άασθαι, ipf. -ορόωντο; aor. εἰσεῖδον εἴσιδον, iter. ἐσίδεσκεν (ψ 94), mid. -ίδοντο, ἰδέσθην, ἴδηται, (often in tmesi, σ 219, 320), intueri, *look upon*, ὀφθαλμοῖσιν, π 477; ἐνωπαδίως = ἄντην, *gazed* into his eyes; ψ 94, ἐσίδεσκεν, instead of usual reading ἤισκεν (ἤσκεν); *behold*, Η 214, with part. Σ 235, θ 526; π 277, endure *the sight; θεὸν ὥς*, dei instar suspicere, *gaze upon* one as a god; spectare, *behold* (mid.), Ψ 448; the infin. is often used after verbs of comparing where it seems superfluous, ι 324, γ 246, ζ 230; Ξ 345, whose rays are the most piercing to the sight.

ἔισος, see ἐίση.

εἰσ-πέτομαι, only aor. **εἰσέπτατο,** with acc., involavit, *fly into*, Φ 494†.

εἴσω, ἔσω, (εἰς), introrsum, *within*, freq. after acc., Π 364, ο 40, Ζ 284, sc. δόμον; with gen., η 135, θ 290; with pregnant signif., seeming to have partially the force of a prep., Ν 553, κ 91; η 13, and carried *in* to her the evening meal.

εἰσωποὶ ἐγένοντο νεῶν, they arrived *just opposite* (εἰς ὦπα) the ships, Ο 653†.

εἶται = Ϝέσται, vestitus est, ἕννυμι.

εἴ τε—εἴ τε, sive—sive, *either—or*, with indic., Α 65; and subj., Μ 239.

εἶτε = εἴητε, opt. from εἰμί.

εἰῶ = ἐάω.

εἴω = ὦ, subj. from εἰμί.

εἴωθα, pf. of ἔθω.

εἴων, ipf. from ἐάω.

εἵως = ἕως.

ἐκ, before vowels **ἐξ,** prep. with gen., ex, (1) local: *out of*, *forth from*, Ι 344, Κ 15, Λ 239, σ 29; ὕπνου, Ε 413; Κ 107, turn his heart *from* wrath; ζ 224, washed himself *in* the river; partitive, Δ 96, Ο 680, Ω 397; ἐκ πάντων, prae omnibus, β 433; *from*, ε 283, Ζ 257, Ν 493, Π 365, Υ 377; ἵππων, ἕδρης, θρόνου, θυμοῦ *from* the heart; *on the part of*, η 70, α 313; *from—to*, Π 640, Χ 397; ἄρχεσθαι, begin *with; away from*, Γ 273, Σ 107, ζ 226; Λ 163, βελέων, *out of* shot; = ἐκτὸς ἀπό, *away from*, i. e. *from elsewhere than*, λ 134; translated *by*, *to*, or *upon*, with many verbs, e. g. κρεμάσας, θ 67, Θ 19; ἧκα, Ο 18; τείνας, Ε 322; ἧν, Λ 38; ἀνήφθω, μ 51; δῆσε, Ψ 853; so also with προσφυέα, τ 58, and ω 8; cf. Σ 480.—(2) temporal: *from—to*, Τ 290, one misfortune *after* another, Ω 535, Ξ 86; ἐξ οὗ, ex quo, since, Α 6, Θ 295 sq.; ἐκ τοῦδε, λ 168; ἐκ τοῖο, henceforth, Α 493; ἐξ ἔτι πατρῶν, since the days of our ancestors.—(3) causal: *springing from*, (γένος, Ψ 347), εἶναι ἔκ τινος, Υ 106, α 207; γενέσθαι, Ε 897, 548, Ζ 206, κ 350; γενεή, Φ 157, cf. Α 63; γαίης, α 406, cf. ο 425; ἐκ νυκτῶν, μ 286, β 136; *in consequence of*, Ι 566, Λ 308, ψ 224; ἔριδος, Η 111; denoting the prime mover, α 33, π 447, Β 669, ἐκ Διός; κλύειν ἐκ, from one's mouth, τ 93; from some other country, Π 13. Examples of anastrophe, Ε 865, Ξ 472, Ω 743, ρ 518.

Ἑκάβη, ης, Δύμαντος θυγάτηρ, wife of Πρίαμος, Ζ 293, Π 718. (Il.)

ἑκά-εργος, ον, ε, (σε-κᾰ-Ϝεργ-ος, from ἐέργω, not from ἔργον), as god of death, *he who banishes, he who shuts up far away* (in the grave or in the lower world), Ι 564. (Il. and θ 323.)

ἐκάη, aor. pass. from καίω, combustus est.

ἕκᾰθεν (ἑκάς), e longinquo, *far, far away* (usually from stand-point of speaker), ρ 25; *far and wide*, Β 456.

Ἑκα-μήδη, ης, daughter of Ἀρσίνοος, maid-servant of Νέστωρ, Λ 624.

ἑκάς (σϜε=Lat. se+κάς), adj., *for one's self, alone*, Υ 422; usually adv., *remote*, ἀπό, Σ 256; freq. used as prep. with gen., *far from*, Ν 263, γ 354, ξ 496.

ἑκαστέρω, *farther than*, gen., η 321†; and ἑκαστάτω, *farthest off*, Κ 113†.

ἑκάστοθι, *in each division*, γ 8†.

ἕκαστος, η, ον, (σϜε—κα=unusque), unusquisque, *each one;* in apposition often in pl., where we should expect the sing., ν 76; sing. distributive apposition, κ 397; with demonstratives, τά, ταῦτα, μ 16; ξ 436, *one to each.*

ἑκάτερθε(ν), utrimque, *on both sides*, ὅμιλον, = the two armies, Γ 340, α 335, ζ 19.

ἑκᾰτη-βελέτāο, gen. from -έτης, *sender of missiles*, Α 75†.

ἑκᾰτη-βόλος, ον, (ϝέκατος, βέλη), *sender of missiles*, epith. of Ἀπόλλων, Α 370, θ 339, Ο 231.

ἑκατόγ-χειρον, acc., (χείρ), centimanum, *hundred-handed*, Α 402†.

ἑκατό(ν)-ζῦγος (ζυγόν), *with hundred rowers'-benches*, Υ 247† (hyperbolically).

ἑκατόμ-βης, της, -ῃ, -ας, (βόες), *hecatomb, great public sacrifice*, etymologically *of a hundred oxen*, but, in fact, of far less, Ζ 93, 115; often part or all of the victims are rams; pl. used of a single sacrifice, Β 321.

ἑκᾰτόμ-βοιος, ον, α, *worth a hundred oxen*, Β 449; *a hundred oxen*, Φ 79. (Il.)

ἑκᾰτόμ-πεδον, better **-ποδον,** *a hundred feet* (each way), Ψ 164†.

ἑκᾰτόμ-πολις, *hundred-citied*, of Κρήτη, Β 649†. (Yet see τ 174.)

ἑκᾰτόμ-πυλοι, *with hundred gates*, Θῆβαι Αἰγύπτιοι, Ι 383†.

ἑκᾰτόν, centum, *hundred*, Ι 85; freq. as large round number, Β 448, Ξ 181; so also in compounds, e. g. with -βης, -πολις, -πυλοι.

ἑκάτοιο (ϝέκατος, ἵημι), missor, *shooter*, Α 385. (Il.)

ἐκ-βαίνοντα, prs. part. ipf., aor. often in tmesi, ἐκ δ' ἔβαν, Γ 113, (βαίνω), exire, *go out*, Α 437, 439; descendo, *descend*, πέτρης; 1 aor., *set on land*, Α 438, ω 301.

ἐκ-βάλλων, prs. part., ipf. aor. usually in tmesi, ejicere, *cast forth*, Φ 237; dejicere, *hurl down from*, Ε 39; excutere e manibus alicuius, β 396; fundere, *let fall*, δάκρυα; emittere, *utter*, ἔπος; excîdere, *hew out*, ε 244.

ἔκ-βᾰσις, ἡ, *landing-place*, ε 410†.

ἐκ-βλώσκω, only aor. **ἔκμολεν,** processit ex, *went forth*, Λ 604†.

ἐκ-γεγάμεν, άτην, αώς, άονται, see ἐκγίγνομαι.

ἐκ-γελάσας, aor. part., (γελάω), *laugh out*; ἡδύ, heartily, π 354, σ 35; but Ζ 471, ἐκ δέ, thereat laughed.

ἐκ-γίγνομαι, aor. **ἐξεγένοντο,** pf. γεγάτην, άασι, inf. άμεν, part. -ἄῶτι, ἄυῖα, often in tmesi, *spring from*, τινός, Φ 185, Ο 641, ζ 229.

ἔκ-γονος, ον, ὁ and ἡ, filius, filia, *child, offspring*, Ε 813, λ 236.

ἐκ-δέρω, only aor. part. **ἐκδείρας,** detractam, *having flayed*, κ 19†.

ἐξ-εδέχοντο, (τινί τι), *received from* him, Ν 710†.

ἐκ-δέω, ipf. **ἐξέδεον,** aor. inf. ἐκδῆσαι, *bind upon*, with gen., Ψ 121 and χ 174.

ἔκ-δηλος, conspicuus, μετὰ πᾶσιν, Ε 2†.

ἐκ-δια-βάντες (βαίνω), τι, *having passed quite over*, Κ 198†.

ἔκ-δοτε, aor. imp., (δίδωμι), tradite, *deliver over*, Γ 459†.

ἔκ-δυνε, ipf., exuit, *put off*, α 437; **-ἐδύοντο,** exuerunt sua, Γ 114; aor. -δύς, ξ 460, but μεγάροιο, *escaping from*; so Π 99, opt. -δῦμεν, with acc., may we escape; ξ 341, ἔδυσαν, *stripped from* my body.

ἐκεῖθι, ibi, ρ 10†.

ἐκεῖνος and **κεῖνος,** η, ο, ille, μέν τοι ὅδ' αὐτὸς ἐγώ, in truth I who am here am *he*, ω 321, cf. Τ 344; κεῖνος ἀνήρ, δ 145, ρ 243; freq. with follg. rel. sentence, e. g., ξ 156; κἀκεῖνος = καὶ ἐκεῖνος, now usually replaced by the reading καὶ κεῖνος.—**κείνῃ,** illâ, *there*, ν 111†.

ἐκέκαστο, plupf. from καίνυμαι, superabat.

ἐκέκλετο, see κέλομαι; **ἐκέκλιτο,** plupf. from κλίνω; **ἔκηα,** see καίω.

ἐκη-βολίαι, *skill in shooting missiles*, Ε 54†.

ἐκη-βόλος, ον, (ϝέκη, jacula, βάλλω). *shooting*; also subst., Α 96. (Il.)

ἔκηλος, ον, οι, and **εὔκηλος,** οι, (Ϝέκηλος, ἐϜέκηλ. ἑκών), *of good cheer, at ease, unmolested*, Ε 805, Ζ 70, β 311, λ 184, φ 289, ξ 479.

ἕκητι (Ϝέκητι), favore, *by grace or aid* (of a god), with gen., τ 86. (Od.)

ἐκ-θνήσκω, only aor. 3 pl. **ἔκθᾰνον** γέλῳ, risu emoriebantur, (nearly) *died* of laughter, laughed themselves (almost) to death, σ 100†.

ἐκ-θρώσκει, aor. ἐξέθορε, ἔκθορε, freq. ἐκ θόρε, exsilire, *spring forth*, Η 182; with gen., desiluit, Θ 320; prosiluit, Ο 573; with gen., εὐνῆφι, Ο 580, Κ 95, *leaps from* my breast (from throbbing).

ἐξ-εκάθαιρον, ipf., purgabant, *cleanse*, Β 153†.

ἐκ-και-δεκά-δωρα, ntr. pl., *sixteen palms* (δῶρα) *long* (of horns of wild goat), Δ 109†.

ἐκ-καλέω, only aor. part. act. and aor. mid. **ἐξεκαλεῖτο,** καλεσσάμενος, *summon*, mid., *for one's self*, τ 15, ω 1.

ἐκ-καλυψάμενοι, mid., (καλύπτω),

(capita) revelantes, *unveiling their heads* (which they had previously covered in token of grief), κ 179†.

ἐκ-κατέ-παλτο, better οὐρανοῦ ἐκ κατ., (πάλλομαι), *sprang down from* heaven, T 351†.

ἐκ-κατ-ιδών, better Περγάμου ἐκ κατ., *looking down from* Pergamos, Δ 508 and H 21.

ἐκ-κίεν, ipf. from κίω, *came forth,* ω 492†.

ἐξ-έκλεψεν, aor., (κλέπτω), *stole away* (from his chains), E 390†.

ἐξ-εκῠλίσθη, aor. pass., (κυλίω), *rolled headlong down from,* Z 42 and Ψ 394.

ἐκ-λανθάνω, only **-λέλαθον,** *made quite forget,* κιθαριστύν, B 600; mid. aor. **-λελάθοιτο,** οιντο, έσθαι, with gen., -λάθετο, οντο, with gen., Π 602; with inf., κ 557, *forget utterly.*

ἔκλε', ipf. pass. = ἐκλέεο, from κλείω, *thou wast celebrating.*

ἐκ δέ με πάντων **ληθάνει,** *makes—forget* all my sufferings, η 221†.

ἔκ-λησιν, τήν, (λήθω), *forgetting and forgiving* (bring about), ω 485†.

ἐκ-λύσομαι, fut. from -λύω, exsolvam, *set free from,* with gen., κ 286; ἐξελύθη, better ἐξεσύθη, E 293.

ἔκ-μολεν, aor. from -βλώσκω, *went forth.*

ἐκ-μυζήσας, aor. part. from -μυζάω, (μύξα), exsugere, *suck out,* Δ 218†.

ἐκ-νοστήσαντι, see νοστῆσαι.

ἔκ-παγλος, ον, α, οις, sup. **-ότατ',** adv. -ως, (πάγος, cf. ῥιγεδανῆς and καταρριγηλά), strictly, *frosty,* ξ 522; horridus, *horrible, dreadful,* Φ 589, A 146, κ 448; ntr. sing. adverbially, N 413, X 256; so also ntr. pl. used like adv. ἐκπάγλως, only with verbs of hating and loving, and always in signif. *exceedingly, beyond measure* (exc. A 268, B 357).

ἐκ-παιφάσσειν, (φάος), emicare, *rush madly into the fray,* E 803†.

ἔκ-παλτο, aor. mid., (πάλλω), with gen., excussa est, *spirted out,* Υ 483†.

ἐκ-πεπᾰταγμένος (πατάσσω) φρένας, lit. with senses *beaten out of* one, *stricken* in mind, σ 327†.

ἐκ-πέμπεις, ipf. fut. 1 aor., (also mid.), freq. in tmesi, emittere, *send forth,* Ω 381, π 3; M 28, *wash away; conduct forth,* Ω 681; *cast out,* with gen.

ἐκ-πέποται, pf. from -πίνω, epotatum est, *has been drunk up.*

ἐκ-περάω, 3 sing. **-περᾷ,** pl. -όωσι, aor. -ησεν—ἀντικρύ, *pierced through* on the opposite side; μέγα λαῖτμα (ἁλός, θ 561), *traverse* the mighty deep.

ἐκ-πέρθω, only fut. and aor. 1 (and 2 ἐξεπράθομεν), evertere, *destroy,* only of cities; A 125, πολίων, *we have pillaged* from the cities. (Il.)

ἐκ-πεσέειν = -πεσεῖν, aor. from πίπτω, casurum esse ex—.

ἐκ-πεφυυῖαι, pf. from -φύω, enatae.

ἐκ-πίνω, aor. **ἔκπιε,** ebibit, *drank up;* perf. pass. **-πέποται,** quantum epotatum est, χ 56. (Od.)

ἔκ-πιπτον, 3 pl. ipf., fut. -πεσέειν, aor. ἔκπεσε, ον, also in tmesi, excĭdere, *fall out,* Φ 492, Ψ 467; with gen., Λ 179; τινί, *escaped from* her hand, X 448; δάκρυ, *streamed from* his eyes; χειρός, from the hand; η 283, having got clear of the water *I sank down* (on the shore).

ἐκ-πλήσσουσι, aor. pass. -πλήγη, 3 pl. ἔκπληγεν, perturbare, *confuse* (N 394. φρένας, in mind); Σ 225, *were terrified.*

ἐκ-ποτέονται, 3 pl. prs., (πίπτω), decĭdunt (ex aëre), *fall down from* Zeus = from the sky, T 357†.

ἐκ-πρεπέα, acc., nom. -ής, (πρέπω) ἐν πολλοῖσι, *conspicuous* among many, B 483†.

ἐκ-προ-καλεσσαμένη, aor. mid. from -καλέω, with gen., *having called him forth to herself,* β 400†.

ἐκ-προ-λιπόντες, aor. from λείπω, egressi ex, *having gone out of,* with acc., θ 515†.

ἐξ-έπτῠσεν, aor. from -πτύω, exspuit, *spat forth,* with gen., ε 322†.

ἐκ-πεύσεται, fut., aor. πῠθέσθαι, explorare, *search out,* K 308 and 320 (better θεῶν ἐκ, Υ 129).

ἐκρέμω, 2 sing. ipf. from κρέμαμαι, suspensa eras.

ἐκ δ' **ῥέε,** ipf. from ῥέω = ἔσρεϝε, effusum est, *flowed forth,* N 655.

ἐξ-έρρηξε, aor. from ϝρήγνυμι, scidit, *snapped,* O 469; ὁδοῖο, *carried away* a part of the road.

ἐξ-εσάωσε, aor. from -σαόω, servavit, δ 501, from the sea, with gen.

ἐκ δὲ ἐσσεύοντο, ipf., aor. ἐξέσσυτο (B 809, Θ 58, tmesis), pass. -εσύθη, *rush forth* (of enemy); πυλῶν, from the gates; *hurried forth*, ι 438; μ 366, fled away from my eyes; ι 373, streamed from his throat; E 293, burst out.

ἐκ δὲ σπάσεν = ἐξέσπασε, mid. -σπάσ(σ)ατο, -σσαμένω, aor. from σπάω, extrahere, evellere, *wrench forth*, always of spear, with gen. of part of body whence it is drawn out, στέρνοιο, etc., Δ 530. (Il.)

ἐξ-έστρεψε, aor. from -στρέφω, with gen., *root up out of*, P 58†.

ἔκτα, aor. act., **ἔκταθεν,** aor. pass. 3 pl. from κτείνω.

ἐκ-τăδίην, acc. fem., (τείνω), extensam, *broad, with ample folds*, K 134†.

ἐκ-τάμνησι, subj., -τάμνοντε part., aor. -έταμον (ἔκταμε, imp.), *cut out* the thigh-bones or thigh pieces of victims; arrows from wound, Λ 515; *hew out, hew off*, trees, ι 320; *breaking off* the low growth (of wild boars), M 149.

ἔκταν = ἔκτασαν, aor. from κτείνω.

ἐκ-τανύω, only aor. **ἐτάνυσσα,** -τανύσας part., pass. -ετανύσθη, *stretch out*, Ω 18; *fall one's length*, prone (pass.), H 271; *lay low*, P 58; stretched out within it, ψ 201.

ἐκ-τελέω, τελέει, ipf. -ετέλειον, fut. έσω, aor. -εσσε, subj. -έσωσι, pf. pass. τετέλεσται, fut. τελέεσθαι, perficere, *bring to fulfillment, finish, achieve*, B 286, δ 7; γόνον, present with offspring; bring to pass, Σ 79; χ 5, has come to a close.

ἐκ-τίθημι, only aor. **ἐκ θῆκε** and **ἐκθεῖσαι,** extra ponere, υ 97, ψ 179.

ἐκ δ' ἐτίνăχθεν = -ησαν, pass. aor. from τινάσσω, *were dashed out*, Π 348†.

ἔκτοθεν (ἐκτός, ἐκ), extra, with gen., *separate from*; ι 239, the MSS. have ἔκτοθεν, but Ameis reads ἔντοθεν. (Od.)

ἔκτοθι (ἐκτός), extra, *outside of, far from*, νηῶν, O 391; πυλάων, X 439.

Ἑκτόρεος, Hectoreus, *of Hektor*, B 416; **Ἑκτορίδης** = Ἀστυάναξ, Z 401.

ἐκτός (ἐκ), extra, *outside*, Δ 151; with gen., *outside of*, Ψ 424; and with ἀπό, K 151, *apart from*.

ἕκτος, ον, sextus, um, *sixth*.

ἔκτοσε (ἐκτός), *out of*, with gen., ξ 277†.

ἔκτοσθε(ν) (ἐκτός), *outside*, H 341; with gen., *outside of, before*, I 552, η 112.

ἔκτŭπε, aor. from κτυπέω, tonabat, *thundered*.

Ἕκτωρ, ος, son of Πρίαμος (Ω) and of Ἑκάβη, X 80, 405, 430, Ω 747; husband of Ἀνδρομάχη, Z 390, Ω 723; "fighting for his household gods, he fell as *preserver*," Schiller, Siegesfest; οἷος γὰρ ἐρύετο Ἴλιον Ἕκτωρ, Z 403; slain by Achilleus in revenge for slaughter of Patroklos, Σ 115, X 326, 331, 361.

ἑκῦρή, ῆς, socrus, *mother-in-law*, X 451; **ἑκυρός,** έ, socer, *father-in-law*, Γ 172 (σϝεκυρ, svocr, Ger. schwieger).

ἐκ-φαίνω, fut. **ἐκφανεῖ,** *shall bring to light*; aor. ἐξεφάνη, 3 pl. ἐκ ἔφανεν and ἐξεφάανθη, apparuit, *appeared*, Σ 248, Θ 557; emicuit, *is revealed*, N 278; -φάανθεν, *sparkled*, T 17.

ἔκ-φασθαι (ἔκφημι), *utter*, κ 246 and ν 308.

ἐκ-φέροι, -έμεν (inf.), ipf. also ἔκφερε, ον, efferre mortuum, *carry out* the dead, Ω 786; surripere, *abstract*, ο 19; reportare, *carry off*, Ψ 785; πολέμοιο, *carry off out of* the fight; Φ 450, *brought about* the end of our service; *spring to the front, take the lead* (of horses), Ψ 376 sq.

ἐκ-φεύγω, aor. also **ἔκφυγε,** ομεν and in tmesi, inf. -έειν, effugere, ἁλός, *escape from* the sea; βέλος (χειρός, *slip from* the hand); τί, *avoid*.

ἐκ-φθέγξατο, see φθέγγομαι.

ἐξ-έφθῖτο, aor. from -φθί-νω, νηός, *had been consumed out of* the ships, ι 163 and μ 329.

ἐκ-φόρεον, ipf. 3 pl., (φέρω), *were carrying forth from*, οἴκων; ἐκφορέοντο, *were moving forth from*, νηῶν.

ἔκ-φῦγε, aor. from ἐκφεύγω.

ἐκ-φύομαι, only pf. **ἐκπεφῦυῖαι;** Λ 40, *growing out of*, αὐχένος.

ἐκ-χέω, ipf. **ἔκχεον,** effundere, aor. mid. ἐκχεύατο, *poured forth his* arrows; pass. ipf. χέοντο, plupf. -ἐκέχυντο, aor. -εχύθη, and aor. mid. -έχυτο (ἔκχυτο, ύμενοι, μένοιο), *stream out*; θ 279, *hung from*.

ἑκών (old part. ϝεκών), volens, *willingly*, Γ 66; sponte, Δ 43, *of free will*, yet reluctantly; *intentionally*, Z 523, K 372.

ἐλάαν, inf. from ἐλάω.

ἐλαίη, ης, ἡ, olea, *olive-tree*, ν 102.

ἐλάϊνος, ῳ, ον, and **ἐλαϊνέῳ,** εον, *of olive-wood*, ι 320, ε 236, Ν 612.

ἔλαιον, ῳ, τό, oleum, *olive-oil*, Ψ 281; λίπ(α) ἐλαίῳ, fat, i. e. abundantly with olive-oil, γ 466; ἐν ληκύθῳ, ζ 79; η 107, from the firmly woven stuff, the oil trickles off.

ἔλασ(α), ἔλασσε, ἐλάσασκε, see ἐλάω.

Ἔλασος, ον, a Trojan, Π 696†.

ἔλασσον, minus, *less*, Κ 357†.

ἐλάστρεον, ipf. 3 pl., (ἐλάω), *were driving* (plough-cattle), Σ 543†.

ἐλάτης, ην, *pine*; pl., *oars*, Η 5, μ 172.

ἐλατῆρι, τῷ, -α, -ες, (ἐλάω), aurigae, *charioteer*, Δ 145. (Il.)

Ἔλατος, ον, (1) ally of the Trojans, Ζ 33.—(2) suitor of Πηνελόπεια, χ 267.

Ἐλατρεύς, one of the Φαίηκες, θ 111, 129.

ἐλαύνω, see ἐλάω.

ἐλαφη-βόλος (ἀνήρ), *deer-hunter*, Σ 319†.

ἔλαφος, ἡ, -οιο, -οισιν, -ους, cerva, *hind*, Γ 24; symbol of cowardice, Α 225.

ἐλαφρός, αί, όν, ά; -ότερος, οι; -ότατος, οι, ην; adv. -ῶς, ε 240; levis, agilis, *nimble*, πόδας, θείειν; *swift*, Τ 416.

ἔλαχε, -ον, aor. from λαγχάνω.

ἐλάχεια, fem. from ἐλαχύς, ι 116, κ 509. *small* (ἐλάσσων), v. l. λάχεια.

ἐλάω, ἐλάαν, inf., **ἐλαύνω,** prs., ipf. ἔλων, fut. ἐλόωσι, aor. ἤλασσε, ἔλασσε, ἔλασε, iter. ἐλάσασκε, plupf. pass. ἠλήλατο, ἐλήλατο, 3 pl. ἐληλέδατο, *drive*, Δ 279, 299, Τ 281; *beset, discipline, exercise*, Ν 315; ἄδην κακότητος, in satietatem mali adigere, persecute him until he has had enough, ε 290; *drive away*, Ζ 158, Ω 532; *drive off*, Α 154, ι 405, 465, ο 235; ῥύσι' ἐλαυνόμενος, driving away cattle for himself in reprisal, Λ 674; ἅρμα, ἵππους, Ψ 334, Ω 696; νῆα, *sail* a ship, Ν 27, μ 47, 109; *row, sail*, ν 22, Η 6, η 319; *draw, lay out* in a given direction, Ι 349, Σ 564, ζ 9, η 86; *strike, hew, thrust*, with weapons, sceptre, Ε 80, Υ 475; οὐλήν, so as to leave a scar, φ 219; with whip, Ρ 614, γ 484, swung the lash to drive them forward; drive in (stakes), ξ 11; χθόνα μετώπῳ, strike the earth with the forehead; πρὸς γῆν κάρη τινός, strike off some one's head and dash it against the earth; *forge*, Μ 296; κολῳόν, prolong the brawl; ὄγμον, make one's way down a swath, in reaping or mowing; Π 518, my arm is pierced with sharp pains.

ἔλδεαι, εται, όμεναι, also **ἐέλδομαι,** etc., prs. ipf., desidero, *long for*, τινός, Ξ 276; also τι, *desire*, α 409; the part. construed like ἀσμενος, φ 209, Η 4; pass., Π 494. (Ϝελέσθαι, velle.)

ἔλε=εἷλε, aor. from αἱρέω.

ἐλεαίρω, prs., ipf. ἐλέαιρεν, iter. ἐλεαίρεσκον, (ἔλεος), misereri, *pity*, τινά, with part., Η 27, Ι 302; οὐκ ἐλ., with inf., thou involvest without compassion, υ 202.

ἐλεγχέες, *despicable*; **ἐλέγχιστος,** οι, ε, *most infamous*, Β 285.

ἐλεγχείη, ην, (ἔλεγχος), *reproach, disgrace*; τινὶ ἀναθήσει, κατέχευας, inflict upon, cover with, Χ 100, ξ 38.

ἔλεγχος, τό, -εα, probrum, *disgrace*; φ 333, why do ye reckon this (what people will say of ye), as disgrace? pl., *miscreants, cowards*, Β 235, Ω 260.

ἐλέγχει, prs. 3 sing., aor. subj. ἐλέγξῃς, *dishonor*; φ 424, *bring disgrace upon*; Ι 522, despise neither their words nor their mission.

ἑλέειν=ἑλεῖν, aor. from αἱρέω.

ἐλεεινός, όν, ά, -ότερος, -οτάτῳ, (ἔλεος), miserandus, *pitiable*, Φ 273; ntr., flebiliter, *pitifully*, θ 531; esp. pl., Χ 37, Β 314.

ἐλεέω, only fut. **ἐλεήσει,** aor. ἐλέησε, αἴ κ' ἐλεήσῃ, and part., (ἔλεος), misereri, *have pity upon*, τινά, Π 431, and τι, Ζ 94; with part., Ο 44, Ρ 346, ε 336.

ἐλεήμων, misericors, *compassionate*, ε 191†.

ἐλεητύς, ύν, ἡ, (ἔλεος), misericordia, *compassion*, ξ 82 and ρ 451.

ἔλεκτο, aor., see stem ΛΕΧ.

ἐλελίζω, aor. **ἐλέλιξε,** aor. mid. ἐλελιξάμενος, plupf. ἐλέλικτο, aor. pass. ἐλελίχθη, 3 pl. ἐλέλιχθεν, *shake*, Α 530, Χ 448; *rally*, Ρ 278; mid., *twist one's self*, Λ 39; *brandish* quivering sword, Ν 558; *whirl round and round*, μ 416, Ζ 109.

Ἑλένη, ης, wife of Μενέλαος; daughter of Ζεύς, Γ 199, 426, and of Λήδα;

sister of Κάστωρ and of Πολυδεύκης, Γ 238; 'Αργείη, Β 161, δ 184; Γ 91, 121, Ω 761, δ 12, 219, 279.

"Ελενος, ου, (1) son of Πρίαμος; the best seer of the Trojans, Ζ 76, Ν 576, Ω 249.—(2) a Greek, Οἰνοπίδης, Ε 707†.

ἑλεό-θρεπτον, *growing in marshes*, Β 776†.

ἔλεον, τόν, misericordiam, *pity*, Ω 44†.

ἐλεοῖσι, τοῖς, *dressers*, Ι 215 and ξ 432.

ἕλεσκον, ε, aor. iter. from αἱρέω.

ἑλετή, capienda, *to be caught*, neither plunder nor *choice* can make the breath of man return when once it has passed the barrier of the teeth, Ι 409†.

ἑλεῦ, imp. aor. mid. = ἑλοῦ, *take thy* spear, Ν 294.

ἐλεύθερον κρητῆρα, mixing-bowl *of freedom*, i. e. celebrating its recovery, Ζ 528; ἦμαρ, day of freedom = freedom, Ζ 455.

ἐλεφαίρονται, 3 pl., part. aor. ἐλεφηράμενος, decipere, *delude, overreach*, τ 565 and Ψ 388.

ἐλέφαντος, τοῦ, -ι, -α, *ivory*, Δ 141, Ε 583, δ 73, θ 404; symbol of whiteness, σ 196, ψ 200.

'Ελεφ-ήνωρ, ορος, Χαλκωδοντιάδης, ἀρχὸς 'Αβάντων, Β 540, Δ 467.

'Ελεών, ῶνος, town in Βοιωτία, Β 500.

ἐληλάδατο, ἐλήλαται, ατο, ἐληλέδατο, etc., see ἐλάω.

ἐληλουθώς, ἐλθέμεν(αι), see ἔρχομαι.

'Ελικάων, ονος, son of 'Αντήνωρ, husband of Λαοδίκη, Γ 123.

'Ελίκη, a town in 'Αχαιΐα, Β 575, Θ 203, with shrine of Ποσειδάων.

'Ελικώνιον ἄνακτα = Ποσειδῶνα, Υ 404.

ἑλίκ-ωπες, ας, -ώπιδα, *shining-eyed*, Α 98.

ἕλικες, ας, (usually digammated, Ϝέλικες, Ϝελίσσω), (1) adj. camurae, *crooked-horned*, βόες, never ταῦροι (explained by Ameis as for σέλικες, cf. σέλας, *shining, sleek*).—(2) subst. **ἕλικες** γναμπταί, Σ 401, *arm-bands bent into a spiral.* (See cut No. 12.)

ἑλισσέμεν, inf., aor. part. ἑλίξας, also mid., pres. ipf. εἱλίσσετο, ἑλίσσετο, aor. ἑλιξάμενος, pass. aor. ἑλιχθέντων (Ϝελισσ.), *turn*, Ψ 466, 309; pass., *whirled around* in the eddies, Φ 11; turn one's self (from flight), *rally*, Μ 74; mid., *go eagerly about*, Μ 49, Σ 372; *turning at bay*, Ρ 283; *turn round* (the goal), Ψ 309, Μ 408; *turned himself this way and that*, υ 28; *coiling himself* within his hole, Χ 95; *roll*, Ν 204.

ἑλκεσί-πεπλους, Τρωάδας, *wearing long, trailing robes.* (Il.)

ἑλκε-χίτωνες, 'Ιάονες, *trailing the tunic, wearing long tunic*, Ν 685†.

ἕλκεον, ipf., fut. ἑλκήσουσι, aor. ἥλκησε, aor. pass. ἑλκηθείσας, (ἕλκω), *were dragging* this way and that, Ρ 395, Χ 336; *carried off*, as captives, Χ 62; *maltreat*, λ 580.

ἑλκηθμοῖο, τοῦ, *carrying into captivity*, Ζ 465†.

ἕλκος, τό, -εος, -εϊ, -αε, vulnus, *wound*, Τ 49; ὕδρου, from the Hydra, Β 723.

ἑλκυστάζων, part. pres., *dragging*, Ψ 187 and Ω 21.

ἕλκει, etc., ἑλκέμεν(αι), inf., only prs. ipf. (unaugmented), act. mid. and pass. (cf. ἕλκεον), *draw*, Β 165, Κ 353, Υ 405; *drag*, Ω 52; Χ 401, from him as he was dragged along; ποδός, *drag* by the foot, σ 10; Π 406, drew him over the chariot-rim; drew the bow-string, Δ 122, φ 419; Θ 486, drawing after it, Μ 398, *tugged at it; raise, hoist*, of balance, sails, Χ 212, ο 291; vehere, *draw along*, Ψ 518; pass., Ε 665, *trailing along;* Ψ 715, *wrenched;* mid., *drew his* sword; *tore his* hair, Κ 15; *draws down* the skin over *his* forehead, Ρ 136; *drew his* seat nearer, τ 506.

ἔλλαβε = ἔλαβε, aor. from λαμβάνω.

'Ελλάς, άδος, ἡ, *Hellas*, the ancients understood as a Thessalian city and district in Φθιῶτις, under the sway of 'Αχιλλεύς, Β 684; now more correctly described as the tract between the Asopos and Enipeus; coupled with Phthia, Ι 395; λ 496, the realm of Peleus; καὶ μέσον "Αργος = the whole of Greece, see "Αργος; epithets, εὐρυχόροιο, Ι 478; καλλιγύναικα, Β 683, Ι 447.

ἐλλεδανοῖσι, τοῖς, *straw bands* for bundles of grain, Σ 553†.

"Ελληνες, οἱ, *inhabitants of* 'Ελλάς, primarily in Φθιῶτις; Β 684, in Northern Greece (β 530, Πανέλληνας).

'Ελλήσ-ποντος, ῳ, ον, *Hellespont*, with adjacent bodies of water, ω 82.

ἐλλισάμην, *σσετο*, aor. from *λίσσομαι*.

ἐλλιτάνευε, ipf. from *λιτανεύω*.

ἐλλόν, *τόν*, *young deer*, τ 228†.

ἕλοιμι, *ἑλών*, etc., aor. from *αἱρέω*.

ἕλος, *εος, τό*, (*Fέλος*), *meadow-land, marsh*, Δ 483, ξ 474.

Ἕλος (*Fέλος*, Veliae), (1) in *Λακωνική*, B 584, maritime city, named from its *marshes*.—(2) town of the *Πύλιοι*, B 594.

ἐλόωσι, see *ἐλάω*.

Ἐλπ-ήνωρ, *ορος*, companion of *Ὀδυσσεύς*, κ 552, λ 51, 57.

ἐλπῖδος, *τῆς*, spei; τ 84, there is still a portion *of hope*, a gleam of hope.

ἔλπει, mid. *ἔλπομαι*, ipf. *ἔλπετο* (*ἐFέλπεται, το*), pf. *FέFολπα, ε=ἔολπα, ε*, plupf. *ἐώλπει*, (volupe), *give hopes*, β 91, ν 380; mid., *expect*, P 406, γ 228, η 293, ζ 297; *think*, I 40, N 309, T 328, ι 419, φ 314; *fear*, O 110; *hope*, *ἐνὶ φρεσί, κατὰ θυμόν, θυμῷ*, but also *Τρωσὶν Fέλπετο θυμὸς ἐνὶ στήθεσσιν ἑκάστου*, O 701, 288, P 395; parenthetically, Σ 194; with acc. and inf., γ 375; inf. fut. prs. aor. pf.

ἐλπωρή *τοι ἔπειτα*, tum tibi spes est, ψ 287. (Od.)

ἔλσαι, *σας*, aor. from *εἰλέω*.

ἐλύω, aor. pass. **ἐλύσθη,** *είς* (*Fελυ-*, volv-), *bent itself*, i. e. *sank upon the ground*, Ψ 393, Ω 510; ι 433, *drawing one's self together*.

ἕλχ' = *ἕλκε*, from *ἕλκω*.

ἔλων, ipf. from *ἐλάω*.

ἕλωρ, *α*, (*Fέλωρ, Fελεῖν*), praeda, *spoil, prey* (of enemies, wild-beasts, birds); Σ 93, pay the penalty for *slaying and stripping* Patroklos.

ἐλώρια, *τά=ἕλωρα*, A 4, gave them to dogs and birds *to prey upon*, lit. *as prey*.

ἐμβᾰδόν, *on foot* (over the sea), O 505†.

ἐμ-βαίνων, part. prs., ipf. *ἔμβαινον*, aor., (also in tmesi), *ἔμβη, ητον*, subj. *ἐμβήῃ*, pf. *ἐμβεβαῶτα, -υῖα*, plupf. *βέβασαν, ἐν νηΐ*, vehi navibus, *embark for*, α 210; *ἅρμασιν ἐμβεβαῶτα*, currui insistentem, vehentem, *step into, mount, step upon*, Z 65, κ 164; Ψ 403, allons! *hasten! forward!* but A 311 and freq. *ἐν δέ*=eorum in numero, e. g. δ 653; Π 94, *enter the combat*; λ 4, *μῆλα ἐβήσαμεν*, *got on board*.

ἐμβάλλω, prs., ipf., aor. act. mid. *τί τινι*, injicere, *cast in, lay in*, imponere, Ω 645, δ 298; *thrust*, E 317 *εὐνήν*, *prepare*; T 394, *put in*; *hand over to*, H 188 (also *οἱ—χειρί, ἐν χερσί*, *take in the hand, give over into the hand of*, Φ 47, 104); *infuse*, P 451, N 82, courage, strength, flight, fear, longing; *μοι — φρεσὶν ἄτην*, blind the mind; *βάλλεσθαι ἐνὶ φρ.*, lay to heart; *θυμῷ τι*, think upon something; *νηΐ ἐμβάλλειν τινά*, embark; *κεραυνόν*, hurl upon; *κώπῃς*, lay one's self to the oar; Σ 85, gave thee to share the bed of a mortal.

ἐμ-βᾰσίλευεν, ipf., with dat., *in them ruled*, ο 413.

ἐμ-βέβᾰσαν, βεβᾰώς, βήῃ, βη, see *ἐμβαίνων*.

ἐμ-βρέμεται, *ἱστίῳ*, *roars in* the sail, O 627†.

ἔμβρῡον, *τό*, *new-born lamb*, (ι).

ἐμέθεν, ἐμεῖο, ἐμέο, ἐμεῦ, = *ἐμοῦ*.

ἐμέμηκον, see *μηκάομαι*.

ἔμεν(αι)=*εἶναι*.

ἕμεν(αι)=*εἶναι*, aor. inf. from *ἵημι*.

ἐμέων (*Fεμ-*), vomens, *spitting out*, O 11†.

ἔμικτο, aor. from *μίγνυμι*.

ἔμμαθε, aor. from *μανθάνω*.

ἐμ-μᾰπέως (*μαπέειν, μάρπτω*), continuo, *instantly*, E 836 and ξ 485.

ἐμ-μεμᾰώς, -υῖα, part. from *μέμαα*, *eager, persistent*. (Il.)

ἔμμεν(αι)=*εἶναι*.

ἐμ-μενὲς *αἰεί* (*μένω*), only at close of verse, *persistently, always*, N 517.

ἔμμορε, pf. from *μέρω*.

ἔμ-μοροι (*μόρος*), participes, *sharers in*, *τιμῆς*, θ 480†.

ἐμός, *ή, όν*, meus, a, um, no voc., β 96, τ 406; usually without article (yet Ψ 585, σ 254, Λ 608, and elsewhere *οὑμός*, Θ 360=*ὁ ἐμός*), *ἐμός ἐσσι* =*my* son, π 300 (*τῷμῷ τῇμῇ*, by crasis with article; better *τῷ ἐμῷ τῇ ἐμῇ*, pronounced with synizesis).

ἐμ-πάζομαι, prs., and ipf. *ἐμπάζετο*, respicere, *care for*, *τινός* (acc., π 422), usually with negative, exc. imp., α 271, 305.

ἔμ-παιος, *ον*, particeps, peritus, *conversant with*, υ 378, φ 400. (Od.)

ἐν-έπασσε, ipf., (*πάσσω*), intexebat, *was weaving in*, Γ 126 and X 441.

ἔμ-πεδος, *ον* (*ἐν πέδῳ*), *firmly stand-*

ing, ψ 203, N 512; τ 113, produces *unfailing* sheep, i. e. never fails to produce; *enduring*, Δ 314; so also ἴς, μένος; *firm, immovable*, νόος; κ 493, *unimpaired*, φρένες; *thoughtful* mind, discretion, σ 215, Z 352; cf. ἔμπ. οὐδ' ἀεσίφρων, Υ 183; cf. illico, *speedy*, θ 30; certus, *sure*, τ 250; ntr. ἔμπεδον μένειν, await, remaining *in one's place* (αὖθι, αὐτόθι, *there*), ἑστάθη; *without wavering, constantly* (θέει); στηρίξαι, support myself firmly.

ἐμ-πεσεῖν, aor. from ἐμ-πίπτω.

ἐν πήξεις, fut., and aor., (πήγνυμι), τινί μεταφρένῳ (ἥπατι) δόρυ (βέλος), *fix* or *plant in* (the back liver), E 40. (χ 83.)

ἔμπης (ἔμπεδα? not from πᾶς), prorsus, *at any rate, by all means*, (1) affirmative: P 632, Zeus *doubtless* guides them all; οὔ τινα ἔμπ., *no one whatever; ἔμπης* δ' οὐκ, *not at all* (cf. οὐ πάνυ); τ 302, *yet* I must give thee oath; in doubt and surprise; *yet* (however it may seem to you), σ 354, τ 37. —(2) concessive: quidem, *yet, although*, Ξ 98, T 308; without περ, δ 100, cf. 104; *still*, cf. French, toutefois, γ 2. 9; tamen, *nevertheless*, Ξ 174, σ 12, A 562, B 297, Θ 33, P 229; ἀλλ' ἔμπ., ἀλλὰ καὶ ἔμπ., υ 311, T 422; Ω 214; ἔμπης—ἀχνύμενοί περ, Ω 522 sq.; freq. phrase περ ἔμπης, which always stands at end of the verse, I 518, Ξ 1, σ 165, τ 356.

ἐμ-πίπληθι, imp. prs., -πίμπλαντο, ipf. mid., other forms from -πλήθω; fut. inf. ἐμ-πλησέμεν, aor., (3 pl. also -πλῆσαν), *fill full*, of something, τινός, Σ 351, X 312, τ 117; aor. mid. ἐμπλήσατο, ἐνιπλήσασθαι, *fill one's self*, η 221; X 312, *one's* heart; *one's* belly, ι 296; X 504, having satisfied his heart with dainties; pass. aor. 3 pl. ἐν-έπλησθεν, ἐνιπλησθῆναι, and aor. mid. ἔμ-πλητο, -πλῆτο, *be full of*; λ 452, sate myself with looking at my son.

ἐμ-πίπτει, ων, prs., ipf. -πῖπτε, fut. -πεσέεσθαι, aor. -ἔπεσε, etc., usually in tmesi, with dat., incĭdere, *fall into*, ε 318, ο 375, τ 469; incessit, *come upon*, Φ 385, χόλος, δέος; impetu ferri in, *charge upon*, ω 526, Π 81; irrumpo, irruo, *burst into, rush upon*, O 624, Λ 297, 311, 325, Φ 9; *penetrate*, Δ 134, O 451, χ 259; *break in upon*, β 45; *cast themselves into*, B 175, Λ 824; μοι—θυμῷ, the words *came to* my mind, μ 266.

ἐμ-πλείην and **ἐνί-πλειος,** ον, impletus, *filled with*, with gen., σ 119, τ 580. (Od.)

ἐμ-πλήγδην (πλήσσω), temere, *at random*, υ 132†.

ἔμ-πλην (πέλας), iuxta, *hard by*, with gen., B 526†.

ἐμ-πλήσατο, -ηντο, -ητο, see ἐμπίπληθι.

ἐμ-πλήσσω, see ἐνι-πλήξωμεν.

ἐμ-πνείοντε, part. prs., aor. ἔμπνευσε, ἐνέπνευσε, also in tmesi, subj. -πνεύσῃσι, τινί, afflare, *breathe upon; τινί τι* (μένος, θάρσος), inspirare, *suggest* a thought, τ 138; pass. **ἐμ-πνύνθη,** *recovered his senses*, E 697.

ἐμ-ποιέω, only ipf. **ἐν-εποίεον,** *fitted into*, H 438; tmesis, ποίησε ἐνὶ φρεσί, *put into* his heart.

ἐμ-πολόωντο, ipf., (πολάω), *gained for themselves by trading*, ο 456†.

ἔμ-πορος, ὁ, *one who goes on shipboard* as passenger, β 319 and ω 300.

ἐμ-πρήθω, see ἐνι-πρήθω.

ἐμ-πῦρι-βήτην, τρίποδα, *standing over the fire*, Ψ 702†.

ἐμ-φορέοντο, ipf., κύμασιν, innatabant, *were borne about in* the waves, μ 419 and ξ 309.

ἔμ-φῦλον, τόν, *of the same tribe*, ο 273†.

ἐμ-φύομαι, ipf., **-φῦοντο** ἐν χείρεσσι, ω 410; so also ἔν τ' ἄρα οἱ φῦ (aor.) χειρί, *he grew to* his hand=*grasped heartily* his hand, β 302; cf. κ 397; ἔφυν, ὀδὰξ ἐν χείλεσι φύντες, *biting hard* the lips, α 381; ἐμπεφυυῖα, *clinging closely; ἐμπεφύᾱσι*, innati sunt, *grow upon; ἐνέφυσε*, insevit, *implant*.

ἐν (**εἰνί, ἐνί, εἰν**), I. as adv., in co numero, *among them*, δ 653; intus, *therein*, ρ 270, Ω 472; sc. ἔστι, εἰσί, ἦν, δ 358, η 95, E 740 sq.—II. preposition, with dat., freq. in anastrophe, or separated from verb by tmesis, e. g. ἐστί, Σ 419, ἔασι, υ 105=Lat. in, προθύροισι, νεῶν ἐν ἀγῶνι; *upon, on*, οὔρεσι, ἵπποισι, καὶ ἅρμασι, νηυσὶν ἔβη, went *on* shipboard; inter, *among*, Γ 31, K 127, N 689, 829, Π 166; ἀνθρώποισι, Τρώεσσι, τοῖσι, *among* these, E 395, Υ 55, Ω 62, (μῦθον) ἔειπεν, ἐρέω; *in the* *midst of*, N 555, δηίοισι; coram, *in presence of*, A 109, I 121, πᾶσιν; ὀφθαλμοῖσι, *before* her eyes, θ 459; οἴνῳ ἔν, sprinkling them *with* wine, ω 73; *in* the shaft, N 608; *of* my bow, O 463; *upon* his limbs, Ω 359, ν 398; *at* the mouth, προχοῇς, λ 242. Apparently =εἰς, with acc., with πεσεῖν, βαλεῖν, βῆναι, ἔδυνον, θῆκε (ἐν χερσί—, βαλεῖν, λαβεῖν, O 229), κάθιζον, εἷσε, δῆσαν. ἐν, with gen., sc. δόμοις, cf. in French, chez, Z 47, η 132, κ 282.—Of states and conditions, πολέμῳ, δηιοτῆτι, φιλότητι, amice, πένθεϊ, θαλίῃ, θυμῷ, ὀνείρῳ, δοιῇ, in dubio, μοίρῃ, iure, rightly; αἴσῃ, X 61, divâ fortunâ; ἐν καρὸς αἴσῃ, I 378, I regard him not a whit.—Temporal, ὥρῃ ἐν εἰαρινῇ, *in* spring-time; penes, *in possession of*, H 102, κ 69.

ἐν-αίρω, inf. -έμεν, mid. -αιρόμενος, aor. ἐνήρατο (Ἄρης), interimere, *kill in battle, slay, murder*, game, Φ 485; fig., τ 263, *disfigure.*

ἐν-αίσῐμος, ον, οι, α, (ἐν αἴσῃ), *fitting, proper, seemly, just*, Ω 40, 425, ε 190, κ 383, ρ 363; *ominous*, β 182, B 353; *the future*, β 159.

ἐνᾰ-λίγκῐος, ον, οι, α, *like*, τινί τι, to some one, in something, α 371; ἄντην, in countenance.

ἐνάλιος, see εἰν-αλίῳ.

ἐν-ᾰ́μελγεν, ipf., *milked therein*, ι 223†.

ἔν-αντᾰ (ἐν ἄντῃ) τινός, coram, ex adverso, *over against*, Υ 67†.

ἐν-αντῐ́-βῐον, (stand, advance), *with hostile front against*, ξ 270, ρ 439, Υ 130.

ἐν-αντίος, ον, ω, οι, η, (ἀντί), adversus, *opposite*, στῆναι, ἐλθεῖν; *visible*, ζ 329; *lying opposite*, κ 89; esp. ntr. ἐναντίον, *against*, A 129; *opposed to*, N 106; τινί, *against*, O 304; νεικεῖν, Υ 252; *straightway*, ρ 544; *face to face*, χ 65, ψ 107; τινός, *before*, A 534, Υ 97. [ῐ]

ἔναξε, aor. from νάσσω.

ἔν-ᾰρᾰ, τά, -ων, (ἀρηρώς), spolia, *armor of slain foe:* usually βροτόεντα, O 347; praeda, *booty*, I 188.

ἐν-αργής, ές, εῖς, (ἀργός, argutus), *clear, in real form*, δ 841, η 201; Υ 131, the gods are dangerous when they appear in their real forms.

ἐν-ᾰρηρός (AP), *well fitted in*, ε 236†.

ἐνᾰρίζων, opt. ἐναρίζοι, ipf. ἐνάριζε, ον, aor. ἐνάριξα, ε, (ἔναρα), spoliare, *strip off*, τινά τι, P 187; also *slay*, A 191.

ἐν-ᾰρίθμῐος, ον, (ἐν ἀριθμῷ), *of account*, B 202; *filling up the number*, μ 65.

ἔνασσαν, aor. from ναίω.

ἐνάτη, εἰνᾰτος, nona, us, *ninth*, B 313, 295.

ἔν-αυλος, οι, ους, ὁ, (αὐλός), torrens, perh. denotes the *ragged bed* of the (in summer dry) water-courses in the Trojan plain; Π 71, fossa, *ditch.*

ἐν-δείξομαι, fut., (δείκνυμι), indicabo, *I will declare it*, Τ 83†.

ἔν-δεκᾰ, undecim, *eleven*, ξ 103, Φ 45 (round number).

ἐνδεκᾰ́-πηχυ, *eleven cubits long*, Z 319 and Θ 494.

ἑνδεκᾰ́τῳ, η, ῃ, undecimus, a, ae, *eleventh*, δ 588 (round number).

ἐν-δέξια (ἐν δεξιᾷ), dextra, *favorable*, σήματα, I 236; also adv., *from left to right*, ρ 365, A 597.

ἐν-δεόντων, imp. prs., aor. ἐνέδησε (-δῆσε), pass. plupf. -δέδετο, *entangle*, with dat. (in bonds; B 111, I 18, in delusion); *fasten upon*, ἐν-, ε 260.

ἐν-δῑ́εσαν, aor., (δίημι), were only (αὔτως) *setting on* the dogs, Σ 584† (prob. for ἐδίεσαν, *sought to terrify*).

ἐνδῖνων, τῶν, (ἔνδον), intestinorum, *entrails*, Ψ 806†.

ἔν-δῖος, οι, meridianus, i, *at midday*, δ 450 and A 726.

ἔνδοθεν (ἔνδον), intus, *from within*, also *within*, δ 293, 283, 467; with gen., Z 247, intra.

ἔνδοθῐ (ἔνδον), intus, *within*, Z 498; with gen., intra, Σ 287; *within* = ἐν φρεσί, when joined with θυμός, μῆτις, νόος; opp. θύρηφιν, χ 220.

ἔνδον (ἐν), intus, *in the house, tent*, etc., Σ 394; ἔνδον ἐόντων, of household store; with gen. = French chez, Υ 13, Ψ 200; so freq. = chez moi, toi, etc., *at home*, π 355, 462, φ 207, ψ 2.

ἐν-δούπησα, ε, aor. from δουπέω, *dropped like a plummet* into the water, μ 443 and ο 479.

ἐν-δῠκέως (δεῦκος, decus), decenter, *duly*, Ω 158, κ 65; *suitably, gallantly*, κομίζειν, attend, wait upon, φιλεῖν; *busily*, i. e. *greedily*, ξ 109.

ἔν-δυνε (=δῦν'), ον, ipf., aor. -εδύτην,

imp. -*δύτω*, part. -*δῦσα*, and mid. -*εδύσατο*, induere, *put on*, arma, *τὶ περὶ στήθεσσι*, Κ 131; in tmesi with dat., *clothe* in armor, Κ 254, Ξ 377, Ψ 131; Τ 367, unendurable woe *entered* his soul.

ἐν ἕηκε, aor. from *ἐν-ίημι*; **ἐνεῖκαι,** aor. inf. from *φέρω*.

ἔν-εστι, -*ειμεν*, prs., opt. -*είη*, ipf. -*έην* = -*ῆεν*, 3 sing., -*εσαν*, 3 pl., inesse, *τινί*, *be within*, Α 593 (*ἔνδον ἐν φρεσί*); in tmesi, Σ 419 (not so however in follg. examples, but simple verb *εἶναι*, β 345, η 291, μ 320, ν 438, σ 293; nor do we have compound verb in follg. examples, *ἔνι* sc. *εἰσί*, Σ 53, Υ 248, ι 126, 132, φ 288; *ἐν* sc. *ἐστί*, Φ 569, ι 134).

ἕνεκᾰ, ἕνεκεν, εἵνεκᾰ, causâ, *on account of*, with gen., placed before and after its case; cf. *οὕνεκα*.

ἐν-έκυρσε, see *ἐγκυρέω*, incidit in, *met*.

ἐνενήκοντα, nonaginta, *ninety*, Β 602.

ἐνένῑπεν, aor. from *ἐνίπτω*.

ἐν-έπω (for *ἐν-σέπω*), **ἐν-έποιμι,** imp. *ἔννεπε* (insece), part. *ἐνέποντα, ες*, -*έπουσα*, fut. *ἐνίψω, ἐνισπήσω*; aor. *ἔνισπες, ε* = *ἔννεπε*, 3 sing., subj. *ἐνίσπω, ῃ*, opt. *ἐνίσποις, οι*, inf. *ἐνισπεῖν*, imp. *ἐνίσπες*, γ 101 = *ἔνισπε*, *report*, *inform*, *τινί τι*; Λ 643 = ψ 301, referentes, *relating*.

ἐν-έρεισαν, aor. 3 pl. from *ἐρείδω*, infixerunt, *thrust into*, *τινί τι*, ι 383†.

ἔνερθεν, ἔνερθε, νέρθεν, νέρθε, (*ἔνεροι*), *from below*, Υ 57; usually *below*, Ν 75, Ξ 274, ι 385, Η 212, Υ 500, υ 352; esp. in reference to the feet; with gen., infra, *below*, Ξ 204, λ 302, Θ 16, Λ 252.

ἔνεροι, *ων, οισι, οἱ*, (*ἐνί*), inferi, *those beneath the earth*, Ο 188; comp. **ἐνέρτερος** *Οὐρανιώνων*, *lower* than the gods = in the lower world, Ε 898; pl. *θεοί*, Ο 225, *Τιτῆνες*.

ἔν-εσαν = *ἐνῆσαν*, ipf. from *εἰμί*.

ἐν-εστήρικτο, plupf. from *ἐν-στηρίζω*, infixa erat.

ἐν-ετῇσι, *ταῖς*, (*ἐνίημι*), fibulis, *with clasps* = (a variety of *περόναι*, σ 293), Ξ 180†.

Ἐνετοί, *ῶν*, a tribe *τῶν Παφλαγόνων*, Β 852†.

ἐν-εύδειν, ipf. *ἔνευδεν*, *sleep in* or *on*, γ 350. (Od.)

ἐν-ευναίων, gen. pl., (*εὐνή*), incubantium, *people to sleep in it*, π 35; but *ἐνεύναιον*, *place to sleep in*, ξ 51.

ἐν-ηείης, gen. (see follg.), *gentleness*, *amiability*, Ρ 670†.

ἐν-ηής, *έος, έα*, (aveo?), comis, *gentle*, *amiable*, Ψ 252, θ 200.

ἔν-ημαι, -ήμεθα, insidebamus, *sit within*, δ 272†.

ἐνήρατο, aor. mid. from *ἐναίρω*.

ἐνήνοθε (*ἄνθος*), strictly, *has blossomed forth*, *streams forth*, ρ 270†.

ἔνθᾰ, *there*, γ 120.—(1) local: ζ 266; with following explanatory clause, γ 365; *ἄρα*, just *where*, χ 335; *ἢ ἔνθα*, *to* or *fro*, κ 574; *καὶ ἔνθα*, *this way* and *that*, *long* and *broad*; *περ*, exactly *where*, ν 284; *τε*, for *ἔνθα δὲ*, θ 363; *thither*, ο 415.—(2) temporal: *thereupon*, ξ 345, Β 308; as introduction of a tale, α 11; continuative, Δ 293, Ε 155; *αὖ*, Ε 1; introducing apodosis, Β 308; *ἔπειτα*, κ 297.

ἐνθάδε, (1) eo, huc, *thither*, Ζ 256.—(2) hic, *here*, Α 171, Β 203. [– ⏑ ⏑]

ἔνθεν, (1) inde, *thence*, Δ 58, κ 108; ab illa (altera) parte, μ 230 (59, 211); ex iis, ξ 74.—(2) unde, *whence*, Η 472, Ω 597, δ 220, τ 62.—(3) dein, *then*, Ν 741.

ἐνθένδε, inde, hinc, Θ 527.

ἐν-θρώσκω, only aor. **ἔνθορε** (tmesi, Ε 161, Υ 381), insiluit, *sprung upon*, usually with dat.; *λάξ*, *gave a thrust* with the heel.

ἐν-θύμιος (*θυμός*), *taken to heart*, *subject of anxiety*, ν 421†.

ἐνί, see *ἐν*; *ἔνι* = *ἔνεστι*.

ἐνιαύσιον (*ἐνιαυτός*) *σῦν*, *yearling*, π 454†.

ἐνιαυτός, etc., annus; *περιπλομένων -ῶν*, as the seasons rolled on, the *year* came, α 16.

ἐν-ίαυε, ipf., *therein slept*, ι 187. (Od.)

ἐν-*ίημι*, **ἵησι,** etc., prs., ipf., fut., aor. (freq. in tmesi), immitto, *send in* or *into*, Ξ 131; Ψ 177, *cast in* the fire's might; *τινί τι*, Π 729; Φ 338, *τινὰ πυρί*, *set on* fire; *put to* (in harness), Π 152; ο 198, *lead to* concord; *πόντῳ νῆα*, *launch*; injicere, *τινί τι*, κ 317, Μ 441; *πόνοις*, *plunge into* hardships; inserere, *insert*, key, ear-rings, Ξ 182; inspirare, courage, wrath.

'Ενιῆνες, B 749† (Αἰνιᾶνες), tribe dwelling about Dodona.

ἐνι-κλᾶν, *frustrate*, only Θ 408, 422.

'Ενῖπεύς, ῆος, a river-god, λ 238†.

ἐν-ῑπή, ῆς, ῇ, ήν, άς, (ἴπτομαι), *reprimand*, E 492.

ἐνί-πλειος, ον, see ἔμπλειος.

ἐνι-πλησθῆναι, πλῆσωσι, see ἐμ-πίπλημι.

ἐνι-πλήξωμεν, ωσι, αντες, aor., from -πλήσσω, *rush into*, τινί, into the noose, χ 469. (Il.)

ἐνι-πρήθω, ipf. **-έπρηθον,** fut. πρήσω, aor. -έπρησεν, etc., lit. *fly forth in sparks*, (1) *inflate*, β 427, ἔμπρησεν.—(2) *kindle*, I 589; usually with πυρί, Θ 182; πυρός, Π 82.

ἐν-ίπτοι (ἰάπτω), opt., increpet, *scold, upbraid*, μέ, Ω 768; μὲ θυμὸν ὀνείδεσι, Γ 438; τινὰ μύθῳ (κακῷ, etc.), B 245; aor. **ἐνένῑπε,** αἰσχρῶς, Ψ 473, and **ἠνίπαπε** μύθῳ, at close of verse, υ 17.

ἐνι-σκίμψαντε, aor. part., and -σκίμφθη, aor. pass. from σκίμπτω, (σκήπτω), always with οὔδει; *lean upon* the ground, *bury in* the ground, P 437, 528. (Il.)

'Ενίσπη, town in Arkadia, B 606.

ἐνι-σπήσω, ἐνί-σπον, ες, see ἐν-έπω.

ἐνισσέμεν, ων, όμενος, ipf. ἐνίσσομεν, (ἐνίπτω), exc. X 497, always with ἐπέεσσιν, or like word, *upbraid*.

ἐνι-χριμφθέντα, *pressing forward*, see ἐγ-χρίμπτω.

ἐν-ίψω, fut. from ἐν-έπω.

ἐννέα, novem, *nine*, Π 785.

ἐννεᾰ-βοίων, gen. pl. ntr., *worth nine cattle*, Z 236†.

ἐννεα-καί-δεκα, *nineteen*, Ω 496†.

ἐννεά-πηχυ and **-πηχέες,** *nine cubits long*, λ 311.

ἐννεά-χιλοι, *nine thousand*, E 860.

ἔννεον, ipf. from 1. νέω.

ἐννε-όργυιοι, pronounce ἐνϝόργυιοι, *nine fathoms long*, λ 312†.

ἐνν-εσίῃσιν, dat. pl., (ἐνίημι), *at the command*; κείνης ἐνν., E 894†.

ἐννέ-ωρος, οιο, οι, οισι, *nine years old*, κ 19. [Pronounce ἐνϝώρ.]

ἐννήκοντα, *ninety*, τ 174†.

ἐνν-ῆμᾰρ, *nine days long*, η 253.

῞Εννομος, (1) οἰωνιστής, chief of Mysians, slain by Achilleus, B 858, P 218.—(2) a Trojan slain by Odysseus, Λ 422.

ἐνν-οσί-γαιος, ῳ, ον, ε, (ὠθέω, γαῖα), *earth-shaker* (also joined with γαιήοχος, I 183), epithet of Poseidon as causer of earthquakes, ε 423. [ῐ]

ἕννυμι (ϝέσνυμι, ϝεσθής, vestis), fut. **ἕσσω,** aor. ἕσσε (imp. ἕσσον), mid. ἕσσατο, ἐέσσατο, pass. prs. ipf., pf. ἕσσαι, εἶται, εἱμένος, plupf. sing. ἕσσο, ἕστο, du. ἕσθην, pl. εἵατο, induere, *put on*, εἵματα, τινά τι, η 265, π 457; mid., *clothe one's self*; pass., *wear*, τί, K 334, Ξ 350; εἵματα, or simply adj., κακά, ἀεικέα, καλά, *be* well or ill *clad*; (περὶ) χροΐ, on the body; ἀμφ' ὤμοισι, and ὤμοιϊν νεφέλην, O 308; εἱμένα χαλκῷ, clad in brass; Γ 57, hadst been clad in coat of stone=stoned to death.

ἐν-νύχῐος, οι, αι, *in the night-time*, Φ 37=ἔν-νυχος (νύξ), Λ 715†.

ἐν-οινο-χοεῦντες = χοέοντες (οἰνοχόος), *pouring in*, γ 472†.

ἐν-οπή, only sing., (ὄψ), (1) voces, *voices*; κ 147, *shout*.—(2) *tumult*, Π 782; joined with μάχη.

'Ενόπην, acc., town in Messenia, subject to Agamemnon, I 150, 292.

ἐν-όρνυμι, only aor. **ἐν-ῶρσας,** ε, -όρσῃ, τινί (Αἴαντι, Λ 544) τι, *excite in one*, fear, flight, courage, longing; **ἐνῶρτο,** aor. mid. γέλως θεοῖσι, *began among* the gods, θ 343 (also in tmesi).

ἐν-ορούω, only aor. **-όρουσε,** σαν, σας, σῃ, irruit, *broke in upon* (of hostile charge), τινί, Λ 149; Φ 182, *stepping upon*.

ἔν-ορχα, *uncastrated*, Ψ 147†.

ἐν-οσί-χθων = ἐνν-οσί-γαιος, with (εὐρὺ)κρείων, Λ 751, N 10.

ἐν-σκίμπτω, see ἐνι-σκίμπτω.

ἐν-έστακται, pf. pass. from -στάζω, instillatum est, *has been infused* in thy veins, β 271†.

ἐν-εστήρικτο, plupf. pass. from -στηρίζω, *remained sticking fast*, Φ 168†.

ἐν-στρέφεται ἰσχίῳ, *plays in* the hip-joint, E 306†.

ἐν-τᾰνύουσιν, fut. -τανύειν, φ 97; aor. ἐντάνυσε, ἐτάνυσσε, *stretch out within*, ψ 201; elsewh. always with νευρήν, *stretch tight*=*string*, or with τόξον, βιόν, *bend, string the bow*, τ 577. (Cf. the cut on follg. page, from antique gem.)

ἐν-ταῦθα, huc, *hither*, I 601†.

ἐν-ταυθοῖ, huc, ἧσο; hic, *here*, κεῖσο, Φ 122.

ἔντεα, *εσι*, ntr., strictly *cattle-gear;* then *δαιτός*, *table-furniture;* usually *armor*, esp. *breast-plate*, Γ 339; *ἀρήια*, fighting-gear, ψ 368, K 407.

ἐν-τείνω, only pass. pf. plupf. **ἐντέτᾰται**, *το*, *was lined with tightly stretched* straps, K 263; the front of the chariot *is ornamented* (*plaited*) *with* gold and silver straps, E 728; cf. Ψ 335, 436.

ἔντερον, *α*, intestina, (1) *gut*, φ 408.—(2) *bowels.*

ἐντεσῐ-έργους (*ἔντεα*, *Fεργ.*), *working in harness*, Ω 277†.

ἐντεῦθεν, inde, *thence*, τ 568†.

ἐν-τίθημι, ipf. **ἐν-ετίθει**, also fut. and aor. 1, 2 (*-θέμεναι*), mid. only 2 aor. (freq. in tmesi), imponere, *put* or *place*, *in*, *into*, or *upon*, *τινά τινι*, on fire, bed, anvil-block; *thrust* sword *into* the sheath, κ 333; *ἐνὶ φρεσί*, *suggest*, *infuse into* the mind, courage, etc., γ 77; *put* strength *into* the shoulders, P 569; *χερσί*, *put into* the hand; ξ 312, *give into* the hand; ο 357, *plunge into* premature old age; Δ 410, *place in* like honor, mid. also *θυμῷ*, *store up* wrath, etc., *in one's* heart; *μῦθον θυμῷ*, *take to* heart; *ἐν στήθεσσι θυμόν.*

ἔντο, 2 aor. from *ἐξ-ίημι.*

ἐντός, intus, with gen., intra, M 374.

ἔντοσθε(ν) (*ἔντοθεν*, ι 239, 338, conjectural v. l.) = *ἐντός*, M 296, Z 364, κ 92.

ἐν-τρέπεται, pass., *is* not (thy heart) *moved*, O 554 and α 60.

ἐν-τρέχοι *γυῖα*, if his limbs *played freely in* the armor, T 385†.

ἐν-τροπᾰλιζόμενος, *η*, *ην*, *turning frequently about*, Z 496, Λ 547. (Il.)

ἔντῡνον, ipf., and 1 aor. imp., (see *ἐντύω*), with aor. part., mid. pr. ipf. aor. (subj. *ἐντύνεαι*, pronounce *ἐντῡνῃαι*), parare, *adorn one's self*, *ἑαυτήν*, and mid.; *get ready*, *δέπας*; *prepare one's meal*, ο 500, Ω 124; *raise the strain*, μ 183; *get ready*, ζ 33.

ἐν-τῠπάς (*τύπτω*), *prostrate*, or better *closely wrapped in* his mantle, Ω 163†.

ἐντύω, ipf. **ἔντῡεν**, **ον**, (*ἔντεα*), *harnessed*, E 720; *made ready*, ψ 289.

Ἐνῡάλιος, sing., (*Ἐνυώ*), Ares as raging god of battle, P 211; elsewh. subst. *Enyalios.* [By synizesis, *-ῡᾰλῐῳ ’νδρεϊφόντῃ.*] (Il.)

Ἐνῡεύς, *ῆος*, king of Skyros, slain by Achilleus, I 668†.

ἐν-ύπνιον (*ὕπνος*), ntr. as adv., *in sleep*, B 56.

Ἐνῡώ, *ἡ*, *Enyo*, tumult of battle, personified companion of Ares, E 333, 592.

ἐν-ωπᾰδίως (*ἐν-ῶπα*), *face to face*, *clearly*, ψ 94†.

ἐν-ωπῇ, dat., (*ὄψ*), *openly*, E 374. (Il.)

ἐν-ώπῐα (*ὄψ*, cf. façade), *παμφανόωντα*, the bright shining *side walls* of the vestibule, see plate III. A and B.

ἕξ, sex, *six*, μ 90.

ἐξ-αγγέλλω, only **-ήγγειλεν**, aor., detulisset ad, *report to*, E 390†.

ἐξ-άγνυμι, only **-έαξεν**, and *ἄξῃ*, confregit, *break*, Λ 175.

ἐξ-αγόρευεν, ipf., *related*, λ 234†.

ἐξ-άγε, pr., ipf., aor., often in tmesi: educere, *lead out*, A 337; *τινά* (also *τινός*, from a place, *Σκυρόθεν*), ξ 264, N 379; *drag out*, *θύραζε*; exstruere, *raise* a mound, *τύμβον*, H 336.

Ἐξάδιος, one of the Lapithai, A 264†. [– ⏑ ⏑ ⏑]

ἑξά-ετες (*ἔτος*), ntr., *six years*, γ 115†.

ἐξ-αίνῠτο, ipf., (*αἴνυμαι*), tmesis, Δ 531, *θυμόν*, *took away* his life; ο 206, *took out from* the chariot and placed in the vessel's stern.

ἐξαίρετοι (*αἱρεῖσθαι*), eximii, ae, *chosen*, *choice*, δ 643, B 227.

ἐξ-αιρεύμην, ipf. mid., see follg.

ἐξ-αιρέω, only ipf. and aor. act. and mid., also in tmesi. (1) act., eximere, *take out*, Ω 229; eligere, ι 160, *γέρας*.—(2) mid., *select for one's self* (one's own use), arrows, sheep, birds, *choose for one's self* from booty, I 130, Λ 696, μ 123; *took away his* sense, *τινός* or *τινί*, Z 234; take away fear, fatigue from the limbs, *γυίων*; take away life, *θυμόν*, Μ 150; λ 201, *μελέων*; *τινά*, Π 58; *τινί*, υ 61, Λ 381; *τινός*, Φ 112; *τινί τι*, π 218.

ἐξ-αίρω, only aor. **ἐξήρᾰτο**, *carry off as booty from*, Τροίης, ι 39.

ἐξ-αίσιον, acc., (*αἶσα*), *unbecoming, undue*, δ 690, ρ 577; *presumptuous*, Ο 598.

ἐξ-αίσσω, only **ἀίξαντε**, *rushing forth from*; *ἠίχθη*, *has flown from* my hands, Γ 368.

ἔξ-αιτον, *ους*, (*αἴνυμαι?*), *choice, chosen*, wine, Μ 320; of oarsmen, hecatombs.

ἐξ-αίφνης (*αἰπύς*), *on a sudden*. (Il.)

ἐξ-ᾰκέονται, placant, *soothe*, aor. *-ακέσαιο*, Δ 36.

ἐξ-ἄλάωσας, *σε*, aor., (*ἀλαόω*), *thou hast utterly blinded*, *τινά*, *ὀφθαλμόν*. (Od.)

ἐξ-ᾰλᾰπάξειν, fut. and aor. *-αλαπάξαι*, (*ἀλαπάζω*), evertere urbes, *sack, storm*; only Ν 813, delere naves.

ἐκ ἀλέοντο, vitabant, *were shrinking from*, Σ 586†. [⏑⏑⏑–⏑]

ἐξ-άλλεται, and aor. part. *-άλμενος*, (*ἅλλομαι*), prosiliens, ex aula, *leaps out from* the enclosure, Ε 142; *τινῶν*, prae—, *springing to the lead*, Ψ 399.

ἐξ-ᾰνᾰ-βᾶσαι, part. aor., (*βαίνω*), escendentes in, *climbing up upon*, Ω 97†.

ἐξ-ᾰνᾰ-δῦσαι, 1 aor. part., 2 aor. part. *-δύς*, (*δύνω*), *emerge from*, *τινός*, δ 405. (Od.)

ἐξ-ᾰνᾰ-λῦσαι, aor., (*λύω*), *release*, *θανάτοιο*, from death, Π 442. (Il.)

ἐξ-ᾰνᾰ φανδόν (*φαίνω*), *openly*, υ 48†.

ἐξ-ᾰν-ῐεῖσαι, part., (*ἵημι*), emittentes, *sending forth*, Σ 471†.

ἐξ-ᾰνύω, fut., aor. *-ήνυσε*, (*ἀνύω*), perfecit, Θ 370; conficere aliquem, *kill*, Λ 365. (Il.)

ἐξ-ᾰπᾰτήσειν, fut., and aor. *-ησε*, (*ἀπατάω*), decipere, *deceive utterly*, Χ 299.

ἐξ-ᾰπ-ᾰφίσκω, aor. **-ήπᾰφε**, subj. *-φω*, aor. mid. *-απάφοιτο*, decipere, Ι 376.

ἐξ-ᾰπῖνης (*αἰπύς*), *suddenly*, ξ 29, Ε 91.

ἐξ-ᾰπ-έβησαν (*βαίνω*), *stepped down out of* the ship, (*νηός*), μ 306†.

ἐξ-ᾱποδῖωμαι, subj., (*δίω*), after *μάχης*, *hunt out of* the combat, Ε 763†.

ἐξ-ᾰπ-έδῦνε, ipf., exuit, *put off*, ε 372†.

ἐξ-ᾰπ-όλλυμι, pf. **-όλωλε**, deperiit, *τινός*, *disappeared from*; aor. *-ολοίατο*, pereant, *may they perish*, Ζ 60.

ἐξ-ᾱπο-νέεσθαι *μάχης* (better ἐξ *ἀπο-*), *return out of*—, Π 252. (Il.)

ἐξ-ᾰπ-ένῑζε, ipf., with which she *usually washed*, τ 387†.

ἐξ-ᾱπο-τῑνοις, *satisfy in full*, Φ 412†.

ἐξ-άπτων, ipf. *-ῆπτε*, aor. part. *ἅψας*, (*ἅπτω*), *bind to*, *τινός*; mid., Θ 20, *hang ye* all to it.

ἐκ ἄραξε, aor., (*ἀράσσω*), *dashed* the mast *out of* the keel, μ 422†.

ἐξ-ήρπαξε, aor. *-ξασα*, (*ἁρπάζω*), *snatched away*, μ 100; in Il. in good sense, *save*; in which case the subject is always a goddess.

ἐξ-άρχους (*ἄρχω*), *leaders* of the dirges, Ω 721†.

ἐξ-άρχων, ipf. *-ῆρχε* and *-ήρχετο*, (*ἄρχω*), *βουλάς*, *be author of* counsel, Β 273; mid., μ 339, *τινός*, *begin* something; a game, a dirge. Χ 430.

ἐξ-αύδᾱ, imp., (*αὐδάω*), proloquere, *speak out*, Π 19. (Il.)

ἐξ-αῦτῐς, rursus, *again*, Ε 134, δ 213.

ἐξ-ἀφ-αιρέω, mid. subj. aor. **-έλησθε** *ψυχάς*, *have taken* the life *from* them all (*ἐκ μελέων*), χ 444†.

ἐξ-ᾰφύοντες, part., *drawing out*, ξ 95†.

ἔξ-ῐδεν, aor., *looked out* far, *saw clearly*, Υ 342†.

ἐξείης (*ἔχω*), adv., deinceps, *in order*, Ο 137; *one after another*, Χ 240.

ἔξ-ειμι, *-εισθα*, inf. also *-ίμεναι*, ipf. *ἤιον*, (*ἰέναι*), exire, *go out*, *θύραζε*; *τινός*, β 139.

ἐξ-είπω, *ῃς*, *ῃ*, subj. *-οι*, aor. opt., *ἐξ-ερέω*, fut., esp. *ὧδε γάρ*, φ 337, and **ἐκ** (*μέν*, δ 376; *γάρ*, ο 318, ω 265, 324) *τοι ἐρέω*, *speak out*, Α 204.

ἔξ-εισθα, 2 sing. *ἔξ-ειμι*.

ἐξ-εκῠλίσθη, aor. pass. from *ἐκκυλίω*.

ἐξ-ελαύνω, only ipf. **-ήλαυνε**, and aor. *-ήλᾰσε*, *-έλᾰσε*, etc., *drive out*; *τινός*, Λ 562; *drive away from*, π 381; drive out, λ 292; driving out (his flocks), κ 83; sc. *ἵππους*, *ἅρμα*, *drive out*, seemingly intrans., Ω 323; *dash out* (teeth), σ 29.

ἐξ-ελεῖν, aor. from *-αιρέω.*

ἐξ-έλκουσα, part., ipf. *-έλκεν,* pass. pr. *-ελκομένοιο,* extrahere, *draw out,* the thread of the woof through the warp, Ψ 762; a polypus from his hole, ε 432.

ἐξ-έμεν = ἐξ-έμεναι, inf. aor. from *-ίημι.*

ἐξέμεν, inf. fut. from ἔχω.

ἐξ-εμέσειε, opt. aor. from *-εμέω,* evomeret, *disgorge,* μ 437. (Od.)

ἐξ-έμμορε, better θεῶν ἒξ ἔμμορε, ε 335, from μέρω, particeps factus est, *has obtained* from the gods dominion amid the waves of the sea.

ἐξ-ενᾰρίζεις, ων, fut. *-ίξεις,* aor. *-ενάριξε,* etc., (ἔναρα), spoliare, *strip* or *spoil* a foe, τινά, E 151; τεύχεα, P 537. (Il. and λ 273, χ 264.)

ἐξ-ερεείνοι, prs., ipf. *-ερέεινε,* (ἐρέω), *make inquiry,* absolutely, K 543; τί, μ 34; τινά, ψ 86; mid., K 81.

ἐξ-ερέεσθαι, pres., ipf. *-είρετο, -ερέοντο,* (ἐρέω), sciscitari, *inquire into, of,* τί, Υ 15; τινά, γ 24.

ἐξ-ερείπω, only aor. subj. **-ερίπῃ,** part. *-ρῐποῦσα, fall down,* P 440. (Il.)

1. **ἐξ-ερέω,** fut. from *-εῖπον.*

2. **ἐξ-ερέω, -ερέουσι,** pr. subj. *-έρσι,* opt. *-έοις,* part. *έοντες, -έουσα,* mid. prs. ipf. ἐρέοντο, (ἐρέω), (1) *ask,* I 671, γ 116, η 17; *question,* τινά, γ 24; *explore,* κνημούς.—(2) mid., *interrogate,* α 416, E 756.

ἐξ-ερύοι, opt. prs., aor. *-έρυσε, είρυσε, είρυσσαν,* iter. *-ερύσασκεν,* (ἐρύω), evellere, *draw out* or *away,* σ 86, χ 476; τί τινος, spear out of shield, Υ 323; laying hold of *was dragging away* by the foot, K 490; by the pole, K 505.

ἐξ-έρχομαι, only aor. **-ῆλῠθε,** ἦλθε, etc., egredi ex, *go out of,* with gen., φ 190, X 237; *march forth,* I 576.

ἐξ-ερωέω, only aor. **-ηρώησαν,** (ruere), *have run away,* Ψ 468†.

ἐξ-εσίην, acc., (ἵημι), ἐλθεῖν, going on *an embassy,* Ω 235 and φ 20.

ἐξ-έτεα, acc., (-έτης, ἔτος), sexennem, *six years old,* Ψ 266. (Il.)

ἐξ-έτι, with gen., inde, ex, *ever since,* I 106; a patrum memoria, θ 245.

ἐξ-εύροι, aor. opt., (εὑρίσκω), if he may any where *light upon* them, Σ 322†.

ἐξ-ηγείσθω, imp. with gen., (ἡγέομαι), edūcat, *let him lead out,* B 806†.

ἑξήκοντα, sexaginta, *sixty,* ξ 20.

ἐξ-ήλασε, *ασσαν,* aor. *-ελαύνω.*

ἐξ-ήλατον, acc., (ἐλαύνω), *beaten out,* M 295†.

ἑξ-ῆμαρ, *for six days,* ξ 249. (Od.)

ἐξ-ημοιβά (ἀμείβω), ntr., *for change, changes of raiment,* θ 249†.

ἐξ-ήπαφε, aor.. (*-απαφίσκω*), *deceive.*

ἐξηράνθη, aor. pass. from ξηραίνω.

ἐξ-ήρατο, aor. from *-αίρω.*

ἐξ-ηρώησαν, aor. from *-ερωέω.*

ἑξῆς = ἑξείης, *one after another,* μ 147. (Od.)

ἐξ-ίημι, only aor., emittere, (1) act. inf. **-έμεν(αι),** τινά, *send forth, release; remove* the desire for any thing; τινὸς ἔρον (εἵην, εἶναι), satiate one's self with, N 638, Ω 227; freq. πόσιος καὶ ἐδητύος ἐξ ἔρον **ἕντο,** *got rid of their* desire for food and drink—driven away from themselves hunger and thirst, A 469, α 150.

ἐξ-ῑθύνει (ἰθύνω), *straightens,* O 410†.

ἐξ-ῑκόμην, -ίκετο, aor., (ἱκνέομαι), with acc., *reach,* a place, a person, ν 206; *gain,* μ 166.

ἐξ-ῑ́μεναι, λ 530, exire; better ἐξ-έμεναι, from ἐξ-ίημι.

ἐξ-ίσχει, *extends,* μ 94†.

ἐξ-οίσουσι, fut. from φέρω.

ἐξ-οιχνεῦσι (οἰχνέω), exeunt, I 384†.

ἐξ-οίχεται, exiit, Z 379; tmesi, δ 665.

ἐξ ὤλεσαν, ὀλέσειε, aor., (ὄλλυμι), τινά, pessumdare, *utterly destroy;* τινὶ φρένας, *rob of* reason, H 360.

ἔκ τ' ὀνόμαζεν (from ὄνομα, hence *pronounce a name,* the name usually follows), always after ἔπος τ' ἔφατ', spoke the word and *uttered it aloud, proclaimed,* A 361, β 302, and freq.

ἐξ-ονομήνῃς, subj. and *-ονομῆναι,* inf. aor. (ὀνομαίνω), *mention by name,* Γ 166; *speak out,* ζ 66.

ἐξ-ονομᾰκλήδην, adv., (ὄνομα, καλέω), *mentioning by name,* X 415; call upon, μ 250.

ἐξ-όπῐθε(ν), adv., (ὄπισθεν), a tergo, Δ 298; κεράων, *behind* the horns.

ἐξ-οπῑ́σω, adv., (1) *backwards,* P 108; νεκροῦ, *back* from the corpse. (Il.)—(2) *hereafter, in future.* (Od.)

ἐξ-ορμήσασα, part. aor., (ὁρμάω), λάθῃσι (νηῦς), without thy intention *swerve from its course*, μ 221†.

ἐκ ὄρουσε, σαν, aor., (ὀρούω), proruerunt, *rushed forth*; Γ 325, exsiliit, *sprang forth*.

ἐξ-οφέλλω, only ipf. **-ώφελλεν,** large auxit, *greatly augment*, ο 18†.

ἔξ-οχος, οι; ον, α, (ἔχω), eximius, excellens inter, *distinguished among*, with gen., Ξ 118; with dat., φ 266, Β 483; ntr., egregie, ι 551, *by way of preference*; ἄλλων, *above* the others; ἔξοχα ἄριστοι, longe optimi, *far* the best.

ἐξ-ῠπ-ᾰν-έστη, aor., (ἵσταμαι), μεταφρένου, *started up from under* the skin of the back, Β 267†.

ἔξω, adv., foras, *forth*, ξ 526; with gen., ex, *out of*, χ 378; foris, extra, *without*, Ρ 265.

ἕξω, fut. from ἔχω. **ἔο, ἑοῖ,** see οὗ. **ἔοι**=εἴη. **ἔοικα,** see II. εἴκω. **ἑοῖο**= ἑοῦ, see ἑός. **ἔοις** = εἴης. **ἔολπα,** see ἔλπω. **ἔον**=ἦν. **ἔοργας,** ε, ώς, from ἔργω.

ἑορτή, *festival*; ἁγνή, holy, φ 258. (Od.)

ἑός, οῦ, οῖο, ῷ, όν; ἑοί, ῶν, οῖσι, ούς. ἑή, ῆς, ῇ, ήν; ῇσι. ἑόν, ἑά, (=ὅς, σϝός), suus, *his*, *her*, *own*, *αὐτοῦ*, Κ 204, δ 643; with pron., τόν, Ψ 295; τό, Κ 256.

ἐπ-ᾰγαλλόμενος, *exulting in*, Π 91†.

ἐπ-αγγείλῃσι (ἀγγέλλω), aor., deferat, *announce*, δ 775†.

ἐπ-αγείρειν, *bring together*, Α 126; mid., λ 632, *crowded to the spot*.

ἐπᾰγη, aor. pass. from πήγνυμι.

ἐπ-αγλᾰϊεῖσθαι (ἀγλαΐζω), superbiturum esse, *will glory in*, Σ 133†.

ἐπ-άγω, pres., and aor. adducere, *bring upon*, Λ 480; *induce*, ξ 392; incitare, sc. κύνας, *setting on* the dogs, τ 445; τινί τι, Ψ 188, *spread out over*.

ἐπ-άειραν (ἀείρω), only aor., tollere; τί τινος, *lift and place upon*, Η 426. (Il.)

ἐπὶ ἀέξῃ (ἀέξω), subj., *prospers*, ξ 65†.

ἔπᾰθες, ον, aor. from πάσχω.

ἐπ-αιγίζων (αἰγίς), *rushing on*, Β 148, ο 293.

ἐπ-αινέομεν (αἰνέω), prs. ipf. fut. aor., *agree*, η 226, Δ 380; *approving*, Β 335; τινί, assentiri; often in tmesi, Γ 461.

ἐπ-αινή (αἰνός), only sing., always of Περσεφόνεια, saeva, *dread*, Ι 457, κ 491.

ἐπ-ᾱΐσσω, pr., ipf., fut., aor. -αῖξαι, adorior, *rush upon*, absol., χ 187, Β 146, Ν 687; τινός, νεῶν, ἵππων (Il.); τινί, κ 295, Ψ 64; with dat. of instr., δουρί, ἔγχει, μοι μελίῃσι, ξ 281 (Od.); τινά, τί, invadere, *attack*; also with κατά, Σ 159 (Il.); mid. χεῖρες ὤμων -αΐσσονται, move lightly in the shoulders; αἴξασθαί τι, *rush at*, *seize*.

ἐπ-αιτήσειας, opt. aor., (αἰτέω), insuper postulaveris, *ask besides*, Ψ 593†.

ἐπ-αίτιοι (αἰτία), *blameworthy*, Α 335†.

ἐπ-ακούει, prs., aor. *hearken to*, ἔπος, πάντα, βουλήν; with indirect question, Σ 63; βουλῆς, interfuerant, *participate in*, Β 143.

ἐπ-ακτῆρες (ἄγω), venatores, τ 435, Ρ 135.

ἐπὶ ἀλήθην (ἀλάομαι), only aor., (part. at end of verse), *wander about*, πολλά, long, δ 81; over, to, with acc., δ 83, in tmesi, ξ 120, 380. [ᾰ]

ἐπ-ᾰλαστήσᾱσα (ἀλαστέω), indignabunda, *indignant*, α 252†.

ἐπὶ ἄλειψα (ἀλείφω), only aor., oblinere, *besmear*, μ 47, 177. [ᾰ]

ἐπ-ᾰλεξήσων (ἀλέξω), only fut., adesse, *assist in battle*, τινί; *ward off*, τινί τι, Υ 315, tmesis. (Il.)

ἐπ-ᾰληθείς, see ἐπὶ ἀλήθην, vagatus.

ἐπ-αλλάξαντες (ἀλλάσσω), *entwining in each other*, *connecting* (the ends of the cord of war), i. e. prolonging the contest; others translate, drawing the cord of war now this way, now that, Ν 359†.

ἐπ-άλμενος, see ἐφάλλομαι.

ἔπ-αλξις, ἡ, **-άλξιος,** ιν, ιες, εσιν, ις, (ἀλέξω), *breastwork*, *battlement*, Μ 263. (Il.)

Ἐπάλτην, a Lykian, slain by Patroklos, Π 415†.

ἐπ-ᾶλτο, aor. from ἐφ-άλλομαι.

ἐπ-ᾰμήσᾰτο (ἀμάω), sibi corrasit, *heaped up for himself*, ε 482†.

ἐπ-ᾰμείψομεν, fut., (ἀμείβω), *exchange*, ἀλλήλοις; πρός τινα; mid., ἄνδρας, *come in turn to*, Ζ 339. (Il.)

ἐπ-ᾰμοιβᾱδίς (see preceding), invicem; ἀλλήλοισιν ἔφυν, had grown *each into the other*, i. e. had intertwined their branches, ε 481†.

ἐπ-ἀμύντορα, acc., (see follg.), *defender*, π 263†.

ἐπ-ἀμύνειν, only pres. and imp. aor. -ἄμῡνον, *aid in battle*, absol., E 685; τινί, Θ 414. (Il.)

ἐπ-αν-θέμεναι (τίθημι), better reading, ἐπ' ἂψ θ., rursus claudere, *shut again*, Φ 535†.

ἐπ-άν-ίσταμαι, -έστησαν, aor., simul assurrexerunt, *stood up also*, B 85†.

ἐπ-ἀοιδῇ, dat. fem., (ἀείδω), incantatione, *by a spell*, τ 457†.

ἐπ-ἀπειλέω, only aor. **-ηπείλησε,** and part., minari, τί, *menace*, ν 127, N 582.

ἐπ-αραρίσκω, aor. **-ῆρσε,** *fit to*, τινί; -αρήρει, plupf., *fitted exactly*=*made fast* the gates, M 456.

ἐπ-ἀράς, acc. pl. fem., (ἀρά), *curses*, I 456†.

ἐπ-ἀρήγειν, only pres., and (in tmesi) aor. inf., *succor*, A 408; τινί, Ψ 783.

ἐπ-ἀρήρει, -αρηρώς, see ἐπ-αραρίσκω.

ἐπ-αρκέω, only **-ήρκεσε,** aor., *ward off*, τινί τι, ρ 568.

ἐπ-ἄρουρος (ἄρουρα), *serf*, λ 489†.

ἐπ-αρτέες, έας, (-αρτύω), instructi, parati, *equipped, ready*, τ 289. (Od.)

ἐπ-αρτύω, only ipf. **-ήρτυε,** *fitted on*, θ 447; *added*, γ 152. (Od.)

ἐπ-αρξάμενος, οι, ἄσθω, part. and imp. aor., (ἄρχω), δεπάεσσι, *having performed the dedicatory rites* with the cups, i. e. having filled the cups for the libation, A 471, γ 340.

ἐπ-ἀρωγός (ἀρήγειν), *helper*, λ 498†.

ἐπ-ασκέω, only pf. pass. **-ήσκηται,** the walled and turreted court *is skillfully joined* to it, ρ 266†.

ἐπ-ασσύτεροι, ους, αι, ntr. ον, (ἆσσον), *closer and closer, close together*, Δ 423; *in quick succession*, A 383, π 366.

ἐπ-αύλους (αὐλή), *cattle-pens*, stabula, ψ 358†.

ἐπ-αυρίσκω, only aor. act., **-αύρῃ,** εἶν, ἔμεν, mid. -ηαι, ωνται, and mid. prs. -ίσκονται, fut. -ήσεσθαι, attingere, consequi, (1) *touch*, τινός, Λ 573; impingi, *strike*, Ψ 340; κακόν (σε), *befall*, σ 107.—(2) (usually mid.) *partake of, enjoy*, reap fruit of, τινός, ρ 81; ironically, O 17, Z 353.

ἐπὶ ἄυσε (αὔω), aor., *hailed*, E 101. (Il.)

ἐπ-ήφυσε (ἀφύσσω), aor., *poured upon*, τ 388†.

ἐπ-έγειρε, imp. pr., and (tmesis) ipf.; aor. mid. -έγρετο, *waken*, χ 431; excitare, *arouse*, O 567; mid., expergisci, *wake up*.

ἐπ-έδραμεν, aor. from ἐπι-τρέχω.

ἐπ-έην, ipf. from ἔπ-ειμι.

ἐπ-εί, conjunction, *after that, after, when*, (1) temporal: (a) with indic. pret., of facts, A 57, Γ 99, κ 414; πρῶτα, A 235, ρ 573; τὰ πρῶτα, Z 489, θ 553; τὸ πρῶτον, δ 13.—(b) with subj., of uncertainty, υ 86, O 363; with expectation of realization, with κέν, T 402, X 125; with ἄν, Z 412, N 285 (see also ἐπήν); iterative with κέν, B 475.—(c) with opt., iterative, ω 254, Ω 14, and freq.; with ἄν in simple assumption, I 304.—(2) causal: *since*, with indic., Z 333, A 352, B 171, N 1; with preterit indic. in conditional sentence, O 228; after suppressed principal sentence, A 231, γ 103, ι 352.—(3) joined with other particles, αὐτὰρ ἐπεί, but *when*; ἐπεὶ ἄρ, -ῥα, *since* then; -γε, *since* at least; ἐπεὶ δή, *since, now* that; ἐπεὶ ἦ, *since* in truth, ι 276 [⏑⏑– επεjη]; ἐπεὶ οὖν, *when* then, well then *when*; ἐπεί περ, *seeing* that; ἐπεί τοι, *since* of a truth; αὐτίκ'—τε, simul atque, as soon as. [At beginning of verse, pronounce –– επjει; ἐπεὶ οὐ, synizesis επjου, exc. ε 364, θ 585.]

Ἐπειγεύς, son of Agakles, a Myrmidon, slain by Hektor, Π 571.

ἐπείγει, only pres. and ipf. (no aug.) act. pass. mid., (1) premere, *oppress*, M 452; urgeo, *beset*, Z 85, Ψ 623, Λ 157, E 622; propellere, *drive forward*, O 382, μ 167; pass., ο 297; *pursue* (subj.), K 361; agitare, *ply*, μ 205; exigere, *hurry on* the sale, ο 445; mid., *urge on* in one's interest, γάμον.; pass., incitari, *hasten*; part. ἐπειγόμενος, citatus, *eager*, ε 399, Ξ 519, Ψ 119; desiderans, *desirous*, with inf., ν 30; τινός, appetens, T 142; ὁδοῖο, longing for the departure; περὶ νίκης.

ἐπειδάν (ἐπεὶ δὴ ἄν), doubtful reading, N 285†.

ἐπειδή, see ἐπεί 3.

ἐπειή, see ἐπεί 3.

ἐπ-είη, see 1. ἔπ-ειμι.

1. **ἔπ-ειμι** (cf. ἐπί I., ἔπι), εἴη, opt., ipf. 3 sing. -έην = -ῆεν, 3 pl. -εσαν, fut. -έσσεται, *be upon*, B 259; β 344, *be found, remain*.

2. **ἔπ-ειμι** (ἰέναι), prs. with part., ipf. ᾔειν, ᾔισαν, ᾖσαν, fut. ἐπιείσομαι, aor. mid. ἐπιεισαμένη, Φ 424, accedere ad, *come upon; τινά*, A 29; τί, *count over, visit*, ψ 359, δ 411; ὀρυμαγδός τινι, *drew near*, P 741; aggredi (usually in tmesi), τινά, *go against*, Υ 454; with dat., Γ 15, Υ 176.

Ἐπειοί, tribe in north Elis, Λ 732, N 686, Δ 537.

Ἐπειός, υἱὸς Πανοπῆος, Ψ 665, 838, builder of wooden horse, λ 523.

ἐπεί-περ, see ἐπεί 3.

ἔπειτα (ἐπί, εἶτα), postea, *then, afterward*, (1) in general, of mere sequence, A 35, 48, 121, 387, 440, α 80, 84, 106; *αὐτίκ' ἔπειτα*, immediately *after*; *καὶ ἔπ.*, θ 520; *αὐτὰρ ἔπ.*, often after *πρῶτον μέν*.—(2) in apodosis δὴ ἔπ., α 84 and freq.—(3) referring back to what has been already stated, *so then, for*, α 106, γ 62.—(4) of futurity, *hereafter*, β 60, Ψ 551.—(5) of sequence in thought, *then, therefore*, γ 62, O 49, Σ 357; in questions, α 65, I 437; and *yet*, α 65, φ 29.

ἐπ-εκέκλετο, aor. from -κέλομαι.

ἐπ-έκερσε, aor. from -κείρω.

ἐπ-ελαύνω, aor. **ἐπὶ ἤλασε**, *welded on* (as eighth layer); -ελήλατο, plupf. pass., N 804. (Il.)

ἐπ-έλησε, aor. from -λήθω.

ἐπ-εμ-βεβαώς, pf., (βαίνω) οὐδοῦ, *standing on* the threshold, I 582†.

ἐπ-ενεῖκαι, inf. aor. from -φέρω.

ἐπ-ένειμε, aor. from -νέμω.

ἐπ-ενήνεον, ipf. from -νηνέω.

ἐπ-ενήνοθε, pf., (ἄνθος), strictly *bloomed upon* = grew thereon, B 219, K 134: yet θ 365, θεοὺς ἐπενήνοθεν must be translated *surrounds*, i. e. such as bathes and exhales from the gods.

ἐπ-εν-τανύσας, part. aor. from τανύω, χ 467†; supra intendens, *stretching* the rope *high over* the θόλος (to hang each one in a noose upon it). [ῠ]

ἐπ-εντύνονται, subj., [ῡ], se accingant ad—, τι, ω 89; **ἐπ-έντυε**, ipf., (ἔντεα), *harnessed*, Θ 382. (Il.)

ἐπ-έοικεν, pf., and -εῴκει, plupf., (ϝεικω), decet, *it is seemly*, υ 293; usually with acc. with inf., λ 186, A 126; τινί τι, *befits*, Ω 595; libet, I 392.

ἐπέπιθμεν, 1 pl. plupf. from πείθω.

ἐπέπληγον, 3 pl. red. aor. from πλήσσω.

ἐπ-έπλως, 2 sing. aor. from -πλώω.

ἐπεποίθει, plupf. from πείθω.

ἐπεπόνθει, plupf. from πάσχω.

ἐπ-έπτἄρε, aor. from -πταίρω.

ἐπ-έπτἄτο, aor. from -πέτομαι.

ἐπέπυστο, plupf. from πυνθάνομαι.

ἐπ-έρεισε, aor., (ἐρείδω), *put to it* vast strength, ι 538; *drove against*, E 856; also in tmesi, Λ 235.

ἐπὶ ἔρεψα (ἐρέφω), *roof over* = *build*, A 39†.

ἐπ-ερρώσαντο, aor. -ρώω.

ἐπ-έρυσσε, aor. from -ερύω, *drew to*, α 441; tmes. ἐρύσαντες, *having dragged thither*, μ 14; ἠπείροιο, *draw toward* the mainland, A 485. [ῠ]

ἐπ-έρχεαι, 2 sing., (-έρχομαι), pres., fut. -ελεύσομαι, aor. -ήλυθε, -ῆλθε, with subj., part.; pf. -ελήλυθα, often in tmesi.—(1) adoriri, *attack*, O 406.—(2) ἐς τι, *come to*, η 280; τι, permeare, *traverse*, δ 268, Σ 321, Ψ 251; adire, *approach*, π 27; redire, ρ 170; advenire, ω 354, of seasons and hours of day, *arrive, come on*, νύξ, κνέφας; of advance of enemies, τμήδην, struck and grazed; come over, ὕπνος.—(3) τινί, *draw near*, Δ 251, Υ 91, O 84; adoriri, E 219, K 485; *surprise*, ὕπνος, νοῦσος, νύξ.

ἐπεσβολίας, acc. pl., (see follg.). *forward talk*, δ 159†.

ἐπεσ-βόλον, acc. masc., (βάλλω), *scurrilous, impudent*, B 275†.

ἔπεσον, aor. from πίπτω.

ἐπ-έσπον, aor. from ἐφ-έπω.

ἐπ-έσσεται, fut. from 1. ἔπειμι.

ἐπ-έσσυται, pf. pass. from -σεύω.

ἐπ-έστη, aor. from ἐφ-ίστημι.

ἐπ-έσχον, aor. from -έχω.

ἐπ-ετήσιος (ἔτος), *throughout all the year*, η 118†.

ἕπευ, imp. from ἕπομαι.

ἐπ-ευφήμησαν, 3 pl. aor., (-ευφημέω); *reverently approved*, A 22, 376.

ἐπ-εύχεται, pres., also fut. aor. (εὔχομαι), (1) precari, *pray*, τινί, κ 533; φ 203, with inf.; *adding a petition thereto*, ξ 436.—(2) gloriari, *exult*, absol., χ 286, Φ 427; τινί, Λ 431, Π 829, Ξ 478.

ἔπεφνον, aor. from Φεν-.

ἐπέφρᾰδον, aor. from φράζω.

ἐπ-έχεις (ἔχω), pres., ipf. -εῖχε, -εχε, aor. -έσχον, praebeo, *offer* (wine, the breast), Χ 83; τινί, impono, *place upon*, ρ 410; instare, *attack*, τ 71 (tmesis, χ 75); τι, occupare, *extend over*, Φ 407, Ψ 190, 238; *check*, Φ 244, υ 266; *restrain* the mind from; sc. ἑαυτόν, *kept aloof*, φ 186. (See ἐπώχατο.)

ἐπ-ήβολος, particeps, *possessing*, β 319†.

ἐπ-ηγκενίδεσσιν, dat. pl., *uppermost streaks*, or *planks of ship*, forming the *gunwale*, ε 253†. (See cut No. 35, letter *c*.)

ἐπ-ῆεν, see 1. ἔπ-ειμι.

ἐπ-ηετανός, οἱ, ούς, όν, (αἰεί), *lasting constantly*, neut. *always, abundantly*, κ 427. (Od.)

ἐπ-ήιεν, from 2. ἔπ-ειμι.

ἐπ-ήλῠθον, redierunt, aor. from -έρχομαι.

ἐπ-ημοιβοί (ἀμείβω), *serving for a change*, ξ 513; ὀχῆες, *cross*-bars, *shutting one over the other in opposite directions.* (See cut No. 32.)

ἐπί τ' ἠμύει, *nods to* (the wind) with its ears, i. e. dips its heads to the wind, Β 148†.

ἐπήν=ἐπεὶ ἄν, *when, after*, (1) with subj., (a) of fut. expectation, δ 414, Ο 147, α 293, Π 96, Μ 369, δ 412, χ 254; (b) general supposition, θ 553, ξ 130, Τ 223.—(2) with opt., (a) dependent upon clause containing a wish, and thus attracted into opt., Ω 227; (b) iter., δ 222. (ἐπεὶ ἄν=ἐπεj-ήν=ἐπήν.)

ἐπ-ήνεον, -ησαν, see ἐπ-αινέομεν.

ἔπηξεν, aor. from πήγνυμι.

ἐπ-ήπῡον, ipf., (ἠπύω), ἀμφοτέροισι, utrisque acclamabant, *applaud*, Σ 502†.

ἐπ-ήρᾰτος, ον, ον, α, (ἐρατός), *lovely, pleasing*, δ 606, Χ 121.

ἐπ-ήρετμοι (ἐρετμός), *fitted with oars*; but β 403, *at the oar.* (Od.)

ἐπ-ηρεφέες, έας, (ἐρέφω), *overhanging, steep*, Μ 54, μ 59.

Ἐπήριτος, name coined by Odysseus, ω 306†.

ἐπ-ῆρσε, aor. from -αραρίσκω.

ἐπ-ῆσαν, see 2. ἔπ-ειμι.

ἐπ-ητής, ῇ, *discreet*, ν 332, σ 128. (Od.)

ἐπ-ήτριμοι, α, crebri, a, *numerous*, Σ 211. (Il.)

ἐπ-ητύος, gen., (-ητύς, -ητής), benevolentiae, φ 306†. [⏑ – ⏑ ⏑]

ἐπί, I. adv., *thereto*, Ο 321, Ψ 840, Θ 507, Κ 466; *thereupon*, γ 9, Λ 630; *on the upper part of it*, Π 612; *moreover*, ε 443, Σ 529; *thereon*, Ι 187. So naturally **ἔπι**=ἔπεστι, adest, θ 563; est, λ 367, Γ 45, Ε 178, Ν 104; imminet, *hangs over*, Φ 110.—II. prep. A. with acc., (1) of the point or goal (a) aimed at: *toward, to*, Β 218, α 149, χεῖρας ἴαλλον, ἆλτο, ἰών, Γ 154, Μ 375; νῆας, θῖνα, Α 440; in hostile sense, *upon, against*, Ε 590, Λ 343, Μ 375, 443, Ν 101, Ρ 504, Κ 85, Φ 248, ρ 295; *over*, α 146; *upon*, ε 84, Ν 682; ψ 76, =stopped my mouth; *upon*, ἕζετο; *at*, μ 171; (b) attained: *to*, ἷξε, Κ 470, θ 226; *upon*, e. g. descend from chariot upon, fall upon, Κ 541, χθόνα, Ψ 393, λ 18; sit upon, Ξ 437; (c) esp. with neut. pl., ἡμέτερα, *to* our house, ο 88; ἀριστερά, sinistrorsum, a sinistra, δεξιά.—(2) of purpose, (a) with verbs of motion, θ 395; cenatum ire, ω 394; cubitum, ξ 455; ἔργα; ω 466, ad arma concurrere, hastened to arm themselves; στίχας, *to*, i. e. *in* or *by* ranks; (b) with verbs of seeking, go *for*, fetch, γ 421, cf. φ 17, Ν 459.—(3) of extension (a) *over* a space, λ 577; πόντον, γαῖαν, νῶτα θαλάσσης, σ 131; ἄρουραν, χθόνα, Ω 532; ἄστεα, νῶτα, Β 308; (πάντας) ἀνθρώπους, *throughout* the whole world; ὅσσον, how far; τόσσον, so far, so large; ἥμισυ, as far as the middle; πολλά, far and wide; (b) in time: δηρόν, *for* a long time, Ρ 41; χρόνον, *for* a time, until, η 288.—(4) secundum, *according to*; ἶσα, uniformly; στάθμην, *by* the rule, straight. —B. with dat., (1) local: *upon, at*, βωμοῖς, cf. δ 134; χθονί, humi, in terris, πύργῳ, ἐσχάρῃ and ἐσχαρόφιν, γούνασι; *amid*, α 218; κτεάτεσσι, νηυσί, σταθμοῖσι, φάτνῃ, αὐτόφι, υ 221; *on, at*, cf. French sur, on the river, Λ 712; ῥηγμῖνι, θῖνι, κρήνῃ, ὁδῷ, κόλπῳ, μαζῷ, *upon*; over the corpse of, Λ 261; *in the place of*, Π 649, Ρ 400; βαίνειν ἐπὶ νηυσί, go *to* the ships, freq. with verbs of motion, esp. πίπτω, χέω, τίθημι (ἐπὶ φρεσί, enjoin upon), ἕζομαι, also κ 375. —(2) temporal: ἤματι, cf. French un jour; *after*, Η 163 sqq., Ψ 401, 514. —(3) attending circumstance: *with* this intention, τῷδ' ἐπὶ θυμῷ, π 111, *with* work unaccomplished, Δ 235.—(4) approach: *upon, at* or *near*, α 103, Κ 568, Γ 23, Ο 743, Ρ 574, νηυσί; εἶναι, succor; πέλομαι, come upon, ν 60; *at* or *against*, δ 822, χ 8, Α 382, Γ 15, Θ 327.—(5) additional circumstance: *over and above, besides*, η 216, ρ 454, χ 264, Ι 639.—(6) causal: *for*, δόρπῳ; motive: *because of*, π 19, Υ 35; *in honor of*, ἀεθλεύειν; with hostile intent, *against*, Κ 185; *upon* clear right, σ 414; *for*, Α 162, Κ 304, Ψ 574; condition: *upon*, Φ 445.—C. with gen., (1) local: *upon, in, on*, νηός, ἠπείρου, ἀγροῦ, νευρῆφιν, ἰκριόφιν, ἵππων, πύργου, *over* the battle-field, Ρ 368; *against*, η 278; with verbs of motion, βαίνω, ἵζω, ἕζομαι, τίθημι, ἐρύω, νηός, *upon* the ship; ἰκριόφιν, γ 353; δεξιόφιν, ἀριστερόφιν; ε 238, *to* the verge of the island, Λ 546, Ψ 374.—(2) temporal: εἰρήνης, pace, *in time of* peace, Ψ 332.—(3) of goal: make *for* Psyria, γ 171.—(4) ἐπὶ παιδὸς ἕπεσθαι, accompany a daughter, α 278; ἐφ' ὑμείων, *by* yourselves, Η 195.

ἐπὶ ἰάλλοντα, ipf. ἴαλλε, aor. -ίηλε, -ιῆλαι, injicere, τινί τι, *lay upon* (hand-fetters); immittere, *send upon*, β 316, ο 475; χ 49, *brought to pass*. [ῐ, with augm. ῑ.]

ἐπι-άλμενος, aor. part. from ἐφάλλομαι.

ἐπι-ανδάνει, see ἐφανδάνω.

ἐπ-ίαχον, tmesi, ἴαχε, ipf., (ἰάχω), acclamabant, Η 403; conclamabant, Ρ 723.

ἐπί-βαθρον (ἐπι-βατήριον), *fare, passage-money*, ο 449†.

ἐπι-βαινέμεν, -ειν, pr. ipf., fut. -βήσομαι, aor. -έβην, subj. είομεν, βήμεναι, mid. -εβήσετο, imp. -βήσεο; freq. in tmesi, *get a footing, stand*, I. absol., μ 434, Ε 666; βέβηκε, Π 69, has advanced, *has marched forth*.—(1) with gen., *set foot on, tread*, of country, city, etc.—(2) fig. *tread* (the path of insolence, χ 424; of mirth, ψ 52).—(3) *mount, go on board*, chariot, bed, scaffold, ship, Δ 99; *climb*, πύργων, Μ 444.—(4) with acc. Πιερίην, *traverse*.—II. trans. fut. act. ἐπιβήσετε, and 1 aor. -έβησε, (1) *set upon*, η 223.—(2) *bring to* great glory, Θ 285; bring to reason, ψ 13.—(3) *cause to mount*, Θ 129, 197; *bring upon*, Ι 546.

ἐπὶ βάλλον, ipf., aor. act. mid., freq. in tmesi, *throw, cast upon*, act. τινί τι, ξ 520; ζ 320, *ply* the whip; (νηῦς) Φεάς, *steered for*, mid., se injicere in, ἐνάρων; *cast lots with each other for*, ξ 209; pass. ipf., *lay over it*, τ 58.

ἐπι-βασκέμεν (see ἐπιβαινέμεν, II., 2), τινὰ κακῶν, *bring into* misfortune, Β 234†.

ἐπι-βήμεναι, aor. from ἐπι-βαινέμεν.

ἐπι-βήτορα, ας, acc., (-βήτωρ), ἵππων, *mounted warrior*; συῶν, *boar*.

ἐπι-βλής, ὁ, (βάλλω), obex, *bar*, Ω 453†. (See cut No. 60, and the adjacent representation of Egyptian doors; see also No. 32.)

ἐπι-βοάω, only mid. fut. **-βώσομαι,** *call upon*, for help, as witnesses, θεούς, α 378, Κ 463 (v. l. δωσόμεθα).

ἐπι-βου-κόλος (κέλομαι), βοῶν—ἀνήρ, *cattle-herd, herdsman*, γ 422. (Od.)

ἐπι-βρέμει, *set roaring*, Ρ 739†.

ἐπι-βρίθω, only aor. -έβρῑσαν, with subj. and opt., *fall heavily upon, fall heavily*, Ε 91; *make* the vines *heavy* (with fruit), ω 344.

ἐπι-βωσόμεθα, fut. from -βοάω.

ἐπι-βώτορι, dat., (-βώτωρ), μήλων, *shepherd*, ν 222†.

ἐπὶ ἐγδούπησαν (γδουπέω), *thundered approval*, Λ 45†.

ἐπι-γίγνεται, appetit, *approaches*, Ζ 148†. (Ο 358, read ὅσον τ' ἐπί, as far as.)

ἐπι-γιγνώσκω, only aor. subj. **-γνώῃ,** ὦωσι, *recognizes*, ω 217; *look upon*, us fighting, σ 30.

ἐπι-γνάμπτει, aor. -έγναμψε, flectit, *changes*, τινά, νόον τινός; *bending*, Φ 178; κῆρ, *bowing* her will.

ἐπι-γνώῃ, see -γιγνώσκω.

ἐπι-γουνίδα, τήν, (γόνυ), femur,

θεῖτο, would grow a stout *thigh*, ρ 225. (Od.)

ἐπι-γράβδην, adv., (-γράφω), βάλε, struck *scratching*, i. e. grazed, Φ 166†.

ἐπι-γράφω, only aor. **-έγραψε,** *graze*, χρόα, Ν 553; κλῆρον, *scratch, mark*.

Ἐπίδαυρος, ἡ, town in Argolis, Β 561†.

ἐπι-δέδρομε, pf. from -τρέχω.

ἐπι-δέξια, ntr. pl., dextrorsum, *toward the right* (*auspicious*, Β 353).

ἐπι-δευής, pl. -έες, εῖς, (δέομαι), egemus, we are *in need of*; οὐκ ἐπιδευεῖς (ἐσμεν), with gen., non egemus; βίης—, robore inferior; ω 171, sc. βίης, far too *weak*; ἐπιδευὲς ἔχῃσθα, with gen., *mayst fail* in nothing *of* thy right.

ἐπι-δεύομαι, ipf. -εδεύετο (δεῖ), egeo, *lack*; with gen., inferior sum, Ε 636; esp. μάχης, pugnando, in battle; but Ω 385, non sibi defuit in pugna contra Ach.; desiderantes, Σ 77.

ἐπι-δημεύεις (δῆμος), *stayest at home* (ἐν δήμῳ), π 28†.

ἐπι-δήμιος, ον, ον, οι, (δῆμος), *at home*; Ω 262, *domestic*; Ι 64, civilis.

ἐπι-δίδωμι, only fut. aor. act., *give besides*, Ψ 559; *give with her*, Ι 147; mid. fut. -δωσόμεθα (better βωσόμεθα), *bestow gifts upon*; and aor. subj. -δώμεθα, testes nobis adhibeamus, *take as witness*, Χ 254.

ἐπι-δινέω (δίνη), aor. -δινήσας, *having whirled it*, mid. -δινεῖται, secum volvit, *weighs* (in thought), υ 218; pass. -δινηθέντε, *wheeling* (in the air), β 151.

ἐπι-διφριάδος, τῆς, (δίφρος), *rim of body* or *box of chariot*, Κ 475†. (See cut No. 10, under ἄντυξ.)

ἐπι-δίφρια, ntr., (δίφρος), θεῖναι= ἐπὶ δίφρῳ, place *in the chariot*, ο 51 and 75.

ἐπ-ιδόντα, aor. from ἐφ-οράω, Χ 61.

ἐπι-δραμέτην, εῖν, aor. see -τρέχω.

ἐπί-δρομον (δρόμος), ntr., *that may be scaled*, Ζ 434†.

ἐπὶ δῦναι, aor. inf. expressing a wish; may the sun *set*, utinamne occidat, Β 413†.

ἐπι-δωσόμεθα, see -βοάω.

ἐπι-δώμεθα, see -δίδωμι.

ἐπι-είκελος, ον, ε, (ἴκελος), consimilis, *like*, θεοῖς, ἀθανάτοισι, Α 265.

ἐπι-εικέα, acc. and -ές, ntr., (-εικής, ἔοικε), *becoming, suitable*; Ψ 246, thus *of suitable size*; with ntr. (freq. with ὡς, as), ἐστίν is always to be supplied =decet.

ἐπι-εικτόν, ά, ntr., (εἴκω), concedendus, always with οὐκ, *unendurable* (unheard of), θ 307; elsewh., *invincible, unceasing*. (Il.)

ἐπι-ειμένος, pf. pass. part. from ἐπιέννυμι.

ἐπι-είσομαι, fut. from 2. ἔπ-ειμι.

ἐπι-έλπεο, imp. pres., -εται (tmesis), -όμενος, *have hope of*, Α 545.

ἐπι-έννυμι, aor. act. **-έσσαμεν,** pf. pass. **-ειμένος,** οι, super induere, *put on over*, υ 143; pass., praeditus; with acc., Η 164, Α 149.

ἐπι-ζά-φελος (φαλ-, Eng. swell), *raging, furious*, χόλος; adv., *vehemently*, with χαλεπαίνοι, μενέαινε.

ἐπ-ίηλε, see ἐπ-ιάλλω.

ἐπι-ήνδανε, see ἐφ-ανδάνω.

ἐπί-ηρα, see ἦρα.

ἐπι-ήρανα, ntr. pl., (ἐπίηρα), θυμῷ, *corresponding to the wish, desired*, τ 343†.

ἐπι-θαρσύνων, part., (θάρσος), *encouraging*, Δ 183†. [ῡ]

ἐπι-θεῖτε, 2 aor. opt., -τίθημι.

ἐπι-θήματα, ntr. pl., (τίθημι), *lids*, Ω 228†.

ἐπι-θρέξαντος, aor. from -τρέχω.

ἐπι-θρώσκουσι, and part., aor. always in tmesi, -θόρον, (τόσσον ἔπι, so far, Ε 772), insilire, *spring on board*, νηός; insultare, *leap upon* (in contempt), τύμβῳ; aggredi, *attack*, τινί, Θ 252, χ 303.

ἐπ-ιθύουσι, pres., aor. -ῑθύσαντες, (ἰθύς), irruentes, *rush upon*, π 297; also Σ 175.

ἐπι-ίστορα, acc., (οἶδα), conscium, *privy to*, i. e. *accomplice in*, heinous deeds; others, *performer* of great labors, φ 26†.

ἐπι-καίω, only ipf. ἐπὶ μηρί' **ἔκαιον,** comburebant, *were burning*, γ 9, and aor. **ἔκηε,** αν.

ἐπί-καρ, see III. κάρ.

ἐπι-κάρσιαι, pl. adj., (ἐπὶ κάρ), *headforemost*, ι 70†.

Ἐπικάστη, mother of Oidipus, λ 271†.

ἐπ-έκειντο, ipf., fut. -κείσεται, (κεῖμαι), *lay thereon*, i. e. *were closed*, ζ 19; instabit, *beset*, Ζ 458.

ἐπὶ κείρει, ipf. -κεῖρεν, aor. -κερσε, accīdo, *maim, baffle,* μήδεα; *mow down,* Π 394.

ἐπὶ κελάδησαν, aor., (κελαδέω), *shouted applause,* Θ 542. (Il.)

ἐπι-κέλλω, only aor. **-έκελσεν,** etc., *beach, let take the land,* νῆας, ι 148. (Od.)

ἐπι-κέλομαι, only aor. **-εκέκλετο,** invocabat, *call upon,* Ι 454†.

ἐπι-κεράννυμι, inf. aor. **-κρῆσαι,** admiscere, *mix in addition,* η 164†.

ἐπι-κερτομέων, part., (κέρτομος), τινά, irridens, *mocking,* only Ω 649, iocatus, *laughingly.*

ἐπί-κευθε, imp. pres., fut. -κεύσω, aor. subj. -κεύσῃς, celare, *conceal,* always with negative; with dat. and after other verbs, Ε 816, ε 143, σ 171; δ 744, rem te non celabo.

ἐπι-κίδναται (σκεδάννυμι), dispergitur, *diffuses itself over,* Β 850, Η 451. (Il.)

ἐπι-κλείουσι (κλέος), collaudant, *praise* the more, α 351†.

Ἐπικλῆς, ῆα, companion at arms of Sarpedon, slain by Aias, Μ 379†.

ἐπί-κλησιν, acc., (-κλησις), cognomine, καλεῖν τινα; Π 177, *according to report.*

ἐπι-κεκλῐμένας, pf. pass. part., (κλίνω), *closed* (doors), Μ 121†.

ἐπί-κλοπος, ον, (κλέπτω), καὶ ἐ., and, no doubt, *a sly fox* (who will steal the bow if he can), φ 397.

ἐπ-έκλῠε, ipf., (κλύω), audiebat, τί, τινός, ε 150.

ἐπι-κλώθω, only aor. **-έκλωσε,** σαν, σαντο, σωνται, *spin to, allot;* subj. always some deity; obj. either ὀιζύν, ὄλβον, or inf. after ὥς. (Od. and Ω 525.)

ἐπι-κόψων (κόπτω), caesurus, *to strike, to fell,* γ 443†.

ἐπι-κουρήσοντα, fut., (ἐπίκουρος), auxiliaturum, *to aid,* Ε 614†.

ἐπί-κουρος, οι, ων, ους, adiutor, *aider in battle,* Ε 478; adiutrix, Φ 431; esp. pl., auxilia (Troianorum), *allies* of Trojans.

ἐπι-κραίνω, aor. **-κρήνειε,** and imp. -κρήηνον, ipf. -εκραίαινε, (κρανίον), *accomplish;* τινί τι, *fulfill,* ἐέλδωρ, Α 455. (Il.)

ἐπι-κρᾰτέουσι, indic. and part. only pres., (κράτος), *have the upper hand,* Ξ 98; elsewh. *hold power, rule over.*

ἐπι-κρᾰτέως (κράτος), *mightily, victoriously,* Π 67. (Il.)

ἐπι-κρήηνον, -κρήνειε, see -κραίνω.

ἐπι-κρῆσαι, aor. inf. from -κεράννυμι.

ἐπ-ίκριον, antenna, *yard,* only ε 254 and 318.

ἐπὶ κῦρε, aor. -κύρσας, (κυρέω), *encounter* (in hostile signif. *kept always aiming at,* Ψ 821).

ἐπ-έλαμψε, aor., (λάμπω), *shone in,* Ρ 650†.

ἐπι-λανθάνω, see -λήθω.

ἐπι-λέγεσθε (λέγω), *collect in addition,* Θ 507†.

ἐπὶ ἔλειβε, ον, and aor. λεῖψαι, (λείβω), *pour a libation over,* ἱεροῖσι, μ 362.

ἔπι λεύσσει, after τόσσον τίς τ', better separated; one *sees* as far as, Γ 12†.

ἐπί-ληθον, ntr., (-λήθω), κακῶν, *causing forgetfulness of* ills, δ 221†.

ἐπι-λήθω, only aor. **-έλησεν,** *made forget,* τινός, υ 85; fut. mid. -λήσομαι, aor. -ελήθετο, oblivisci, τινός (also tmesis, -λάθωνται).

ἐπ-ελήκεον, ipf., *beat time,* θ 379†.

ἐπῐ-λίγδην βλῆτο ὦμον, received a stroke *grazing* his shoulder, Ρ 599†.

ἐπ-ιλλίζουσί μοι, *wink to* me, σ 11†.

ἐπ-ελώβευον, ipf., (λώβη), *mock at,* β 323†.

ἐπι-μαίνομαι, aor. **-εμήνατο,** τῷ, *was madly in love with* him (or τῷ may be construed with μιγήμεναι), Ζ 160†.

1. **ἐπι-μαίεο,** imp. prs., ipf., (μέμαα), τινός, *seek to gain, make for,* Κ 401, μ 220.

2. **ἐπι-μαίομαι,** ipf. **-εμαίετο** and aor. -εμάσσᾰτο, (ΜΑ), *lay hold of, grasp;* τὶ χεῖρ' = χειρί, ι 302; contrectare, *touch,* λ 591; touch with sceptre, ν 429; Ε 748, strike with whip; was reaching after, λ 531.

ἐπι-μάρτῠρος, οι, testis (deus), Η 76.

ἐπι-μάσσεται, etc., see 2. ἐπι-μαίομαι.

ἐπί-μαστον (-μαίομαι), contrectatum, one who has been *passed through* many hands, *filthy,* υ 377†.

ἐπι-μειδήσας (μειδάω), *smiling at* or *upon,* Δ 356; *with scornful smile,* Κ 400.

ἐπι-μέμφεαι, εται, *find fault with,*

τινί, π 97; τινός, B 225, what *art thou coveting?* A 65, 93, *be dissatisfied with.*

ἐπι-μένω, only imp. aor. **-μεινον**, *stay*, α 309; *wait* (ὄφρα, δ 587), with subj., Z 340.

ἐπ-εμήδετο, ipf., *πατρί*, *she devised* a trick *against* her father, δ 437†.

ἐπι-μῆνις, reading of Aristarchus, E 178†, *wrath thereat.*

ἐπ-εμήνιε (μηνίω) τινί, succensebat, *was at feud with*, N 460†.

ἐπι-μιμνήσκομαι, only aor. mid. **-μνησαίμεθα**, and pass. -μνησθείς, recordari, *call to mind*, A 65, δ 191.

ἐπι-μίμνω, *wait upon, superintend*, ᾧ, ξ 66. (Od.)

ἐπι-μίξ, adv., promiscue, *indiscriminately*, Ψ 242.

ἐπι-μίσγομαι, only pres., *have to do with*, τινί, ζ 205; accedere, *draw nigh to*, ζ 241; manus conserere cum, *contend with.*

ἐπι-μνησαίμεθα, aor., see -μιμνήσκομαι.

ἐπι-μύζω, only aor. **-έμυξαν**, *murmured at*, Δ 20. (Il.)

ἐπι-νέμω, aor. **-ένειμε** τινί τι, dispertiit, *distributed to*, I 216.

ἐπι-νεύω, ipf. **ἔνευε**, aor. -ένευσα, ε, annuit, *he nodded* with his helmet, i. e. its plumes nodded, X 314; *nod assent*, κάρητι, ὀφρύσι (tmesis), A 528, φ 431, as promise, or as sign previously agreed upon.

ἐπι-νεφρίδιον, adj. acc., (νεφρός), *over the kidneys*, Φ 204†.

ἐπι-νέω, only aor. **-ένησε**, Destiny *spun to* him at his birth with her thread, Y 128, Ω 210.

ἐπ-ενήνεον, ipf., (νέω, νηέω), νεκροὺς πυρκαϊῆς, *were heaping up* the corpses upon the funeral pile, H 428.

ἐπι-ξύνῳ (ξῡνός), communi, *common*, where several have rights, M 422†.

ἐπι-ορκήσω, fut., (-ορκέω), peierabo, *swear falsely*; πρὸς δαίμονος, per deum, T 188†.

ἐπί-ορκον, neut., (ὅρκος), periurum, *false*, T 264; subst. periurium, *false oath*, Γ 279 (vainly, K 332).

ἐπὶ ὄρονται, το, pres. ipf., (οὖρος), *watch over* them, ξ 104; *were serving*, γ 471.

ἐπι-οσσομένω, part. du., tuentes, τι; *having before their eyes, avoiding*, P 381†.

ἐπί-ουρα, see -οὖρον.

ἐπί-ουρος, ον, (οὖρος), Κρήτῃ, *ruler* in Kreta (Il.); ὑῶν, *chief* swine-*herd.* (Od.)

ἐπι-όψομαι, see ἐφ-οράω.

ἐπι-πάσσειν, ων, and ipf. πάσσε (tmesis), φάρμακα, *sprinkle* healing drugs (powder made of roots) *upon*, Δ 219. (Il.)

ἐπι-πείθεται, εο, ipf. -ετο, fut. -σεται, *obey*, τινί (ἐπέεσσι, O 162), μύθῳ; subj. θυμός τινι. (Od.)

ἐπὶ πελεμίχθη, simul vibrabatur, *quivered* as it struck, Π 612. (Il.)

ἐπὶ πέλεται, ονται, aor. -πλόμενον, *coming*, η 261; τινὶ θάνατος, *comes upon*; so also γῆρας, νοῦσος. (Od.)

ἐπ-έπτᾰτο, -πτέσθαι, aor., (πέτομαι), advolavit, *fly toward*, N 821.

ἐπι-πίλνᾰται (πέλομαι), *is there there*, ζ 44†.

ἐπι-πλάζω, only aor. pass. **-πλαγχθεὶς** πόντον, *driven about over—*, θ 14†.

ἐπὶ πλέων=πλείων, πλεῖν, ipf. -έπλεον, *sail over*, the sea, the waves, A 312, δ 474 in tmesi.

ἐπι-πλήσσεις, ων, fut. πλήξειν, vituperare, *rebuke*, M 211, Ψ 580; *striking, lashing*, K 500.

ἐπι-πλώσας, aor. part., aor. sync. -έπλως, part. -πλώς, (from ἐπιπλέων), *sail upon*, πόντον, γ 15.

ἐπι-πνείησι, subj., πνείουσα part., aor. subj. πνεύσωσι, cf. adflare navi, νηΐ, *breathe* or *blow upon*, δ 357.

ἐπι-ποιμένες, *shepherdesses*, μ 131†.

ἐπι-πρέπει, τοι, *is manifest*, ω 252†.

ἐπι-προ-έμεν, inf. aor. -ίημι.

ἐπι-προ-ίηλε, aor., (ἰάλλω), *set before* them, (σφωΐν), Λ 628†. [ῐ]

ἐπι-προ-έηκα, εν, and inf. -έμεν, *send forth to* Troy, Σ 439; νηυσί, embark for; Δ 94, *shoot at* Menelaos; *made for*, ο 299. [ῐ]

ἐπ-έπτᾰρε, aor., (πταίρω), μοὶ πᾶσιν ἔπεσσιν, *has been sneezing* all the while I spoke, ρ 545†.

ἐπι-πτέσθαι, inf. aor., see -έπτατο.

ἐπι-πωλεῖται (πόλος), obit, *inspect*, Δ 231; -επωλεῖτο στίχας, was scouring to find a combatant, Λ 264. (Il.)

ἐπι-ρρέζεσκον (Ϝρέζω), *were accustomed to sacrifice*, ρ 211†.

ἐπι-ρρέπῃ, subj., (Ϝρεπ.), ἡμῖν, *settle down upon* us, Ξ 99†.

ἐπι-ρρέει (σρεει, ῥέω), *flow upon* (surface); -έρρεεν, *were streaming toward* us, Λ 724. (Il.)

ἐπι-ρρήσσεσκον, ipf. iter., (ῥήσσω), *drove to, pushed home,* Ω 454, 456.

ἐπι-έρριψαν (Ϝρίπτω) μοι, in me coniecerant, *cast upon* me, ε 310†.

ἐπί-ρροθος (ῥέθος?), adiutor, -trix, *helper,* Δ 390. (Il.)

ἐπι-ρώομαι (ruo), only ipf. **-ερρώοντο,** υ 107, τῇσιν, at which *were busy,* were toiling night and day, aor. -ερρώσαντο, *flowed waving down,* Α 529.

ἐπι-σσείων, -σσείῃ, (σϜεjω), *brandish over, against,* τινί, Δ 167. (Il.)

ἐπι-σεύῃ, ipf. -έσευε, (freq. σσ, from σϜ), *send upon, let loose upon,* (τινί), dogs, monsters; met. ill-luck, dreams; pass. prs. ipf., pf. -έσσυται, -εσσύμενος, plupf. -έσσυτο, *rush up, upon,* χ 310; τί, ζ 20; ἔς τινα, Ν 757; τινί, Ο 347; -δε, ν 19; freq. in tmesi, often in hostile signification, *charge upon,* τινί, τί, Π 511, with gen.; *raging through* the plain, πεδίοιο; *bursting forth,* Ρ 737; *was hastening* to follow, Φ 601; so also with subject, θυμός.

ἐπί-σκοπος, ον, οι, (σκέπτομαι), *lookout, watch* (Κ 38, 342?), for something, τινός, θ 163; *guardian,* Ω 729, Χ 255.

ἐπι-σκύζωνται, subj., aor. opt. -σκύσσαιτο, indignari, *be indignant at,* τινί, η 306.

ἐπι-σκύνιον (scu-tum, cu-tis), *skin over the brows,* knitted in frowning, Ρ 136†. [ῠ]

ἐπι-σμῦγερῶς, misere, *sadly,* γ 195. (Od.)

ἐπί-σπαστον (σπάω), *of his own seeking,* σ 73. (Od.)

ἐπι-σπεῖν, inf. aor. from ἐφ-έπω.

ἐπι-σπέρχουσι, 3 pl. and part. -ων, incitans; ε 304, *rush to the spot.*

ἐπι-σπέσθαι, -σπών, see ἐφ-έπω.

ἐπι-σσείῃς, etc., see ἐπι-σείων.

ἐπι-σσεύῃ, see -σεύῃ.

ἐπί-σσωτρα, ων, οις, sing., Ψ 519, (σϜω-, σεύω), *tire.* (Il.)

ἐπι-στᾰδόν, adv., (ἵσταμαι), *stepping up to* in turn; π 453, were making ready (standing) *on the spot.*

ἐπ-ίσταμαι, prs. ipf., and fut. -ιστήσονται, *know how, understand,* with inf., Β 611; ᾗσι φρεσί, of intellectual comprehension, in one's thought, ἔργα, η 111; *be skillful, an adept in,* etc. (in this sense, part. very common); φόρμιγγος, φ 406; with *skillful* feet, Σ 599; ἄκοντι, in throwing the spear, also of animals; though knowing well in your hearts, δ 730.

ἐπ-ιστᾰμένως (-ίσταμαι), *skillfully,* Η 317; εὖ καί—, ψ 197.

ἐπι-στάτῃ, dat., (ἵσταμαι), accedenti, *beggar,* ρ 455†. [ᾰ]

ἐπὶ δὲ στενάχοντο (στενάχω), *wailed in reply,* Τ 301. (Il.) [ᾰ]

ἐπὶ δ' ἔστενε (στένω), *groaned in answer,* Ω 776†.

ἐπι-στεφέας (στέφω) οἴνοιο, *filled to the brim* with wine, Θ 232.

ἐπι-στέφομαι, only aor. **-εστέψαντο** ποτοῖο, *filled to the brim* with drink, Α 470.

ἐπ-ιστήμων (ἐπίσταμαι), *discreet,* through thought and instinct, π 374†.

ἐπί-στιον (ἵσταμαι), place where the ships *stand* when drawn up, ζ 265†.

ἐπ-εστονάχησε, aor., billows *roared* as they closed *upon* her, Ω 79†. [ᾰ]

ἐπὶ ἐστόρεσεν, aor., (στορέννυμι), *spread over,* ξ 50†.

ἐπι-στρέψας, part. aor., (στρέφω), *having turned* him *toward* the Achaians, Γ 370†.

ἐπι-στροφάδην, adv., (στρέφω), *turning in every direction, on every side,* Κ 483. [ᾰ]

ἐπί-στροφος (στρέφω) ἀνθρώπων, *conversant with* (in his wanderings), α 177†.

Ἐπί-στροφος, (1) leader of the Halizonians, Β 856†.—(2) son of Euēnos, slain by Achilleus, Β 692†.—(3) son of Iphitos, chief of Phokians, Β 517†.

ἐπι-στρωφῶσι (=άουσι) πόληας, circumeunt urbes, *haunt,* ρ 486†.

Ἐπίστωρ, a Trojan, slain by Patroklos, Π 695†.

ἐπι-σφυρίοις, dat. pl., (σφυρόν), ἀραρυίας, furnished *with clasps around the ankles,* Γ 331. (Il.) (See cut on next page.)

ἐπι-σχερώ, adv., (σχερός), *in a row, close together,* Ψ 125. (Il.)

ἐπι-σχεσίην, acc., (ἐπέχω), μύθου, *pretext,* φ 71†.

ἐπί-σχεσις, ἡ, (ἐπέχω), *restraint,* with inf., δ 451.

ἐπ-ίσχειν (ἔχω), (1) *hold to* their course, Ρ 465.—(2) τινί, impono, Ξ 241; θυμόν τινος, *restrain* one's thoughts *from*—; mid. part. *aiming at,* χ 15.

ἐπὶ τάνῦσε, σαν, (also σσ), only aor., *extend, stretch out over, extend over,* Ν

359, Π 567; *laid* it down *upon*, ο 283; *drew forward by*, α 442.

ἐπι-τάρροθος, *ον, ω, οι*, (ῥέθος), *springing to aid*; adiutor, *helper*. (Il. and ω 182.)

ἐπι-τείνω, only pass. pf. **-τέτᾰται,** plupf. *-τέτᾰτο—τινί, is spread over*, λ 19.

ἐπι-τέλλω, pr. ipf. aor. act. and mid., *lay upon*, mandare, *τινὶ τάδε, μῦθον* (*κρατερόν*), *ἐφετμάς*, Ε 818, *συνθεσίας*; *ὧδε, ὥς, πολλά*, earnestly, *εὖ*, sharply; mid. also *μύθῳ—ἠδὲ κελεύεις*, Κ 61; *impose*, λ 622, α 327; give orders, ρ 21; pass. plupf. *ἐπέταλτο, commands had been given*. [*ἐπῖ*, ψ 361.]

ἐπι-τέρπεται *ἔργοις, takes pleasure in*, ξ 228†.

ἐπι-τέτραπται, *-τετράφαται*, see *-τρέπω*.

ἐπι-τηδές (*τείνω*), intente, *intently*, ο 28; *quickly*, Α 142.

ἐπι-τίθημι, prs. ipf. fut., aor. 3 pl. **-έθηκαν,** subj. *-θείω*, opt. *-θεῖτε*, inf. *-θεῖναι, -θέμεναι*, aor. mid. *-έθετο, -θέμενος* (freq. in tmesi), *put to, add, τινί τι*, Η 364; *confer*, Ψ 400; *φρεσί, put into* the mind; *devising* trouble, Ε 384; *place upon*, κ 355; *τινὶ γούνασι*, τ 401; *pile* Ossa *on* Olympos, λ 315; *lay upon* (wound, altar), Δ 190, φ 267; *λεχέων*, Ω 589; *put on*, Π 137; also of veil, arrow on string, *τινί τι*, Θ 324; *impose*, θ 245, also punishment, destiny; *ἄτην*, send delusion into the mind; *φρένα τινί*, animum advertere ad, *apply* the mind *to, place before, τινί*; *close* door, also of stone serving as door, χ 157, 201, Φ 535, [λ 525]; pass. *πᾶσι ὀνόματα*, names *are given*, θ 554; mid. aor. *χεῖράς τινι*, lay his hands upon.

ἐπι-τῑμήτωρ, ultor, *guardian*, ι 270†.

ἐπι-τλήτω, imp. aor., (*-τλῆναι*), *be patient*, Ψ 591; *μύθοισιν, hearken patiently to—*.

ἐπι-τολμάτω, imp. prs., aor. *-ετόλμησε*, (*τολμάω*), *endure* to listen, α 353; ρ 238, held out.

ἐπί-τονος [ῐ] (*τείνω*), *back-stay*, μ 423†. (See cut, representing an Assyrian war-ship.)

ἐπ-ετοξάζοντο, ipf., (*τοξάζω*), *were shooting arrows at—, τῷ*, Γ 79†.

ἐπι-τρᾰπέουσι, prs., (*ἐτράπην*), *Τρωσί, intrust* the watch *to* the Trojans, Κ 421†.

ἐπι-τρέπω, ipf. **-έτρεπε,** aor. 1 (*-έτρεψεν*), aor. 2 (*-ετράπομεν*), pass. pf. (*-τέτραπται, -τετράφᾰται*), cedere, *give over to, τί*; with inf., the victory, (Κ 79, *γήραϊ, yield to*); *leave behind* him, η 149; *intrust*, ο 24, Ε 750, Β 25; *νεκρόν* (defendendum); *charge with*, Κ 59; *θεοῖσι* (*μῦθον*), *commit in confidence*; *σοὶ θυμός*, with inf., ι 12, thy heart *is inclined*.

ἐπι-τρέχω, ipf., **-έτρεχον,** aor. 1 *-θρέξαντος*, aor. 2 *-έδραμον*, etc.; pf. *-δέδρομεν*, accurro, *run up*, Δ 524, ξ 3?; *strike upon, graze*, Ν 409; *roll after*, Ψ 504; *is spread over*, ζ 45, υ 357.

ἐπι-τροχάδην, adv., (*τροχός*), *glibly*, Γ 213, σ 26.

ἐπι-φέρειν, prs. act. and mid., fut. *-οίσει*, aor. *-ένεικα* (freq. in tmesi), inferre, *bring upon, τινὶ Ἄρηα*, bellum; *κῆρα*, perniciem; *χεῖρας, lay* hands *upon*, π 438; *=have intercourse with*, Τ 261.

ἐπι-φθονέοις, opt. prs., *τινί τι, refuse, deny*, λ 149†.

ἐπι-φλέγει, *y*, prs., (*φλέγω*), comburit, *consumes*, Β 455. (Il.)

ἐπι-φράζω, only aor. **-έφραδε**, etc., act. (1) *point out*, κ 111; (2) *declare*, Λ 795; (3) *show how*, θ 68; mid. aor. -ἐφράσατο, subj. ἐπῐφράσσεται, opt. φρασσαίᾰτο, and pass. aor. -εφράσθης; *perceive* (by mind), σ 94; sentire, by senses, θ 94, νόησεν, took note (of the sound), *think thereon*, E 665; *meditate*, βουλήν; *devise*, τινὶ ὄλεθρον; ε 183, that thou hast thought of speaking this.

ἐπι-φρονέουσα, part. prs., (-φρων), *justly*, τ 385†.

ἐπι-φροσύνην, ας, acc., (-φρων), *thoughtfulness* (presence of mind), τ 22, assume *discretion*. (Od.)

ἐπί-φρων, **φρονι**, α, (φρήν), *discreet*; βουλήν, in counsel, ψ 12. (Od.)

ἐπ-εχείρεον, ipf., fut. -ήσειν, (χειρέω), τινί, *lay hand upon, partake of*, ω 386, 395.

ἐπι-χεῦαι, inf. aor., v. sq.

ἐπι-χέω (freq. tmesis), aor. 1 -έχευα (χεϜ), -χεε, inf. -χεῦαι, mid. ipf. -χέοντο, aor. -εχεύατο, 2 aor. -έχυντο, pass. pf. κέχῠται, aor. opt. χῠθείη, *pour upon*, τινί τι, δ 214; *pour out*, M 284; met. (sleep) *over*, τινί, βλεφάροισιν; τινὶ βέλεα, *showering over* them missiles, Θ 159; *heap up*, earth, funeral mound, bed of boughs, material of whatever sort (mid., *raise for one's self*), ε 257.

ἐπι-χθόνιος, masc. plur., (χθών), *earthly* (opp. οὐρανίωνες), A 266; also as subst., Ω 220; =*men*, ρ 115.

ἐπι-χράω, aor. **-έχρᾰον**, *fall upon*, τινί, Π 352; *annoy, distress* (*by wooing*), β 50; *do harm to*, κ 64.

ἐπι-χρίοντες, aor. part. -χρίσᾱσα, mid. prs. *besmear* (mid., *one's self*), ἀλοιφῇ, σ 172. (Od.)

ἐπι-ψαύῃ, subj. prs., (ψαύω), ὀλίγον πραπίδεσσι, *touches* the matter only a little with his mind, uses only a little his reason, θ 547†.

ἐπ-ιωγαί, pl., *places of shelter against* wind and wave, *roadstead*, ε 404†.

ἐπ-ιών, see 2. ἔπ-ειμι. **ἔπλε**, aor. from πέλω. **ἔπλεο**, ευ, ετο, aor. from πέλομαι.

ἔπληντο, aor. from πελάζω. **ἐποίσει**, fut. from -φέρω.

ἐπ-οίχεσθαι, όμενος, ipf. -ῴχετο, tmesis, Ξ 381.—(1) obire, *go to and fro, back and forth*, παντόσε, ἀνά, A 383; ζ 282, if she herself should *go abroad* and look for a husband there.—(2) τινά, accedere ad, *approach*, ρ 346, α 324; invadere, *attack*, E 330, A 50.—(3) τί, permeare, O 676; obire, ἱστόν, *ply* the loom (*going up and down* before it); ν 34, *go to* evening meal; ρ 227, σ 363, *attend to* work in the field.—(4) τινί, accedere ad, α 143.

ἐπόμεσθα, see ἕπω.

ἐπ-όμνυμι, fut. **-ομοῦμαι**, aor. ὅμοσσεν (tmesis), *swear in addition*, I 274.

ἐπ-ομφάλιον, ntr., (ὀμφᾰλός), the shield, *on the boss*, H 267†.

ἐπ-οπίζεο, imp. pr., (ὄπις), revereri, *reverence, stand in awe of*, ε 146†.

ἐπ-οπτάω, only ipf. **-ώπτων**, *broiled over* (the blazing wood), μ 363†.

ἐπ-οπτεύεσκε, ipf. iter., (ὀπτεύω), *superintended*, π 140†.

ἐπ-ορέγω, aor. act. only in tmesi, **ὀρέξῃ**, *reach to, confer upon*, E 225; mid. aor. part. -ορεξάμενος, *stretching one's self out towards, lunging at*, E 335.

ἐπ-ορνύω, ipf. **-ώρνυε**, aor. -ῶρσε, imp. ἔπορσον; freq. in tmesi, incitare contra, *excite* (courage, Υ 93) *against*, τινά τινί, M 253, ε 366; (in hostile signif.) *send* (*against*, τινί) warrior, storm, wild beast, waves, sleep (day of death, O 613).—Mid. ipf. ὤρνυτο, aor. -ῶρτο, plupf. ὀρώρει, surgere, *rise*; Ψ 112, τινί, *rise up against* (for combat).

ἐπ-όρομαι, see ἐπὶ ὄρονται.

ἔπορον, aor. see πόρον.

ἐπ-ορούω, only aor. **-όρουσε**, *charge upon, rush to*, (a) with dat., usually in hostile signif., Γ 379; τινὶ δουρί, Π 320; in friendly signif., E 793.—(b) with acc., P 481, spring upon the chariot.

ἔπος, ntr. (gen. sing. wanting), ἔπεϊ, only E 879, (Ϝεπ, voc), vox, *that which is spoken, word*, A 108, Σ 384, α 64; *prophetic utterance*, μ 266; in general signif. cf. vox, *promise, decree*; διακέρσαι, battle, Θ 8; *threat*, τελεῖν, fulfill, Ξ 44; sententia, I 100; plur., recital, δ 597; *legend*, Υ 204; *desire*, Ξ 212; ἔπεσιν καὶ χερσίν, with *word* and deed; ἔργον τε ἔπος τε, β 272; ἔπος often is nearly equal to *fact, thing*, A 652, γ 243; λ 146, usually with verb of saying; it is to be distinguished from μῦθος, δ 597.

ἐπ-οτρύνω, prs. ipf., aor. -ώτρῡνας,

etc., impellere, (1) *drive on, excite, encourage*, Z 439, ι 488, 561; τινά, with inf. (τινί, only κ 531; Π 524, dat. depends on κεκλόμενος, in other parallel examples on κελεύω); πολλά, eagerly; *stir up* (*irritate*, τινά, θ 185), πόλεμόν τινι, against any one; ἀγγελίας, send quickly tidings, ω 355; make haste with, mid., furnish quickly, our customary escort (πομπήν), θ 31.

ἐπ-ουράνιος, also dat. pl., (οὐρανός), caelestis, *heavenly*, with θεός, Z 129; opp. ἐπιχθόνιοι ἄνθρωποι.

ἐπ-οχήσεται, fut., (ὀχέομαι), *be carried upon, ride upon*, ἵπποις, P 449. (Il.)

ἐπ-όψεαι, -όμενος, fut. from ἐφ-οράω.

ἔπραθον, aor. from πέρθω.

ἑπτά [ᾰ], septem. **ἑπτα-βόειον,** *of seven folds of hide*, septemplex, H 266. (Il.) **ἑπτά-ετες,** *seven years*, γ 305. (Od.) **ἑπτα-καί-δεκα,** septemdecim, ε 278. **ἑπτᾰ-πόδην,** *seven feet long*, O 729†. **Ἑπτά-πορος,** river in Mysia, flowing from Mount Ida, M 20. **ἑπτᾰ-πύλοιο,** *of seven gated* (Thebes, Δ 406).

ἔπταρεν, aor. from πταίρω. **ἔπτατο,** aor. from πέτομαι.

ἔπτᾰχᾰ (διεμοιρᾶτο, divided), *into seven parts*, ξ 434†.

ἕπω, I. act. pres. and ipf. **ἕπον,** *were making ready*, μ 209; *be busy* (about, περί, O 555); τί, Z 321, *occupied with; μετά τινα, going after*, K 516.—II. mid. prs. ipf. εἵπετο, usually without augm. ἑπόμην, etc., fut. ἕψομαι, aor. ἑσπετο, etc., (orig. redup. form σε-ΣΕΠ, sequi), προτέρω, accede, *draw near*, Σ 387; comitor, *attend*, A 424; τινί, ζ 276; ἅμα, Γ 447 (τινί, M 87, β 11). μετά τινι, Σ 234; σύν τινι, η 304; τινά, N 492; praesto esse, *be at hand*, Θ 140; τινί, B 675, O 204, δ 643; what my strength is, and *with* what sort of arms *I am furnished*, υ 237; πομπῆες, πομπόν, *conduct;* with ntr. subj., *go with, sail after, fall after*, γ 165, Γ 376, Π 504, M 398 (*belong to*, I 513, Δ 415; *accompany*, Γ 255, α 278); *correspond in strength*, Δ 314; *follow*, with hostile intent, τινά, Λ 154; ἀμφί τινα, Λ 474, 565. [μ 209, v. l. ἔπι instead of ἕπει.]

ἐπ-ώνῠμον (ὄνομα), *by name*, I 562; ὄνομα, was *given to him*. (Od.)

ἐπ-ῶρτο, aor. mid. from -ορνύω.

ἐπ-ώχᾰτο, 3 pl. plupf. pass., (ἔχω), clausae erant, *had been shut*, M 340†.

ἔρα-ζε (ἔρα), *on the ground*, P 619, χ 20.

ἔρᾰμαι, ται, ipf. ἐράασθε, aor. ἠρᾰσάμην, (σ)σατο, ἐράσσᾰτο, (ἔρω), τινός (πολέμου, I 64), amans sum, *be in love with.*

ἐραννῆς, ήν, fem., (ἐρατός), *charming*, I 531, η 18.

ἔρᾰνος, ῳ, masc., *picnic*, α 226. (Od.)

ἐρά(σ)σατο, aor. from ἔραμαι.

ἐρατεινός, ῆς, ήν, άς, ά, (ἐρατός), *lovely, charming*, Γ 239, T 347, Γ 175, δ 13; *pleasing* (prowess), Z 156; *welcome*, ι 230.

ἐρᾰτίζων, part., (ἐρατός), κρειῶν, *craving* (flesh), Λ 551. (Il.)

ἐρᾰτά, ntr. pl., (ἔραμαι), *charming*, Γ 64†.

ἐργάζεσθαι, only prs., and ipf. εἰργάζετο, ἐργάζοντο, (Ϝέργον), *work, labor*, τινί; *perform, bring to pass*, ἔργα; ρ 321, do what is proper; ω 210, did what it pleased him to command; *wrought*, γ 435.

ἔργαθεν and **ἐέργαθεν,** ipf., (Ϝέργω), τὶ ἀπό τινος, *cut off*, E 147. (Il.)

ἔργον, sing. and pl., (Ϝέργον, A 395, Eng. work), (1) facinus, *deed*, M 366, I 443, α 338; *shocking deed*, γ 265, 275, π 346, φ 26, ω 426; *work*, opera, M 412; *action*, B 436; *task*, Z 324, 492, α 356 (T 133, unseemly toil = bondage); *action*, opp. deliberation, I 374; opp. word, A 395, 504; opp. discussion, T 242; *state of the case*, τ 391.—(2) opus, *tasks*, ι 250, ξ 228; φιλοτήσια, love affairs; ἔργα τέτυκταί τινος, opus est re.—(3) *work in field, husbandry*, π 140, 144; ἀνδρῶν βοῶν, κ 98, i. e. neither plough-*land* nor vine*yard; ἀνθρώπων*, αἰζηῶν, = rura, *fields*, B 751; (paterna), β 127, cf. 22, paternal *estates;* bona, ἀέξεται, *property* increases which is in my charge, ξ 66.—(4) *severe combat*, Δ 470, M 271; μέγα ἄρηος, Λ 734; μάχης, Z 522.—(5) opera, *what is wrought* or *made, works of skill*, N 432, I 128, 390, ζ 234; women's *works*, Z 289; of Hephaistos, ο 117; *accomplishments*, θ 245.—(6) res, A 294, Σ 77, Φ 19, δ 663; *matter*, B 252, A 573, X 450, Γ 321; ἀμήχανα, *evil* without remedy.

ἔργω (Fέργω), act. prs. **εἴργουσι,** aor. ἔρξαν, pass. prs. ἐργομένη, aor. ἐρχθέντα, pf. ἔρχαται, plupf. ἔρχατο, also act. pres. **ἐέργει,** *ουσι, ων,* ipf. ἔεργε, *ον,* pass. pres. ἐεργόμενοι, part., plupf. ἐέρχατο, *press,* (1) *shut in,* ἐντός (with gen.), *τι,* ξ 411, Φ 282, κ 283; ἐκ, outside of, Θ 213; *were covered,* P 354.—(2) *hold off,* ἀμφίς, utroque; τῆλε, procul; τινός, ἀπό τινος, ἐκτός, *keep away from;* μ 219, *separate;* τινός, N 525; *cutting off, parting,* M 201; *force back,* Π 395. (E 89, better reading ἐερμένα.)

ἔρδω (Fέργjω), prs. ipf. **ἔρδομεν,** *ον,* iter. -δεσκες, ε, pf. ἐοργώς, plupf. ἐώργει, fut. ἔρξω, ἐμεν, aor. ἔρξαν, imp. ἔρξον, inf. ἔρξαι, *perform,* sacrifice, deeds, β 236; *treat* well, ο 360; joined with τελευτᾶν, λ 80, α 293; τί τινι, ο 360, υ 314; κακόν τινα, E 175.

ἐρεβεννή, ῇ, ῶν, (ἔρεβος), ater, *black,* I 474. (Il.)

ἐρέβινθοι, pl., *chickpeas,* N 589†.

ἔρεβος, gen. ἐρέβευς, ἐρέβεσφι, *realm of darkness* (of the lower world), ἔρεβόσδε, *to Erebos,* υ 356, Π 327.

ἐρεείνεις, ε, prs., and ipf. ἐρέεινεν, (ἔρω), *ask,* absol., Γ 191, η 31; (ἐπέεσσι) τινά, ε 85; τινά τι; ἀμφί τινι, asked after—, ω 262; ipf. mid. μύθῳ, ρ 305.

ἐρεθίζω, only prs., ipf. ἐρέθιζον, (ἔρις), *irritate,* A 32, Ω 560.

ἐρέθω (ἔρις), only pres., *excite;* δ 813, *disquiet.*

ἐρείδοντες, prs., ipf. ἔρειδε, aor. ἔρεισε, mid. -σατο, -σάμενος, and pass.—(1) *press against, support firmly, lean upon,* τὶ πρός (περί) τι, (ἐπί) τινι; pass. pf. **ἐρηρέδαται,** *have been rammed down upon;* Ψ 284, *rest upon* (the ground, οὔδει); plupf. ἐρηρέδατο, *were set* (firmly); **ἠρήρειστο,** *stuck fast.*—(2) *press upon,* N 131; τινά, *beset* (with missiles); *crowd thickly together,* ἀλλήλοισιν.—(3) mid., *support one's self* on one's spear, τινί; χειρὶ γαίῃ, *lean* with the hand on the earth; ἐρεισθείς, *supporting one's self; struggle against* each other, Ψ 735; ἐρεισάμενος, *having planted himself firmly.*

ἐρεικόμενος, prs. part. pass., and aor. ἤρῐκε, *rend* (frangi), περὶ δουρί, *pierced* by the spear, N 441. (Il.)

ἔρειο, ἐρείομεν, see ἔρω II.

ἐρείπω (ripa?), *fall, tumble,* (1) trans. prs. and ipf. **ἔρειπε,** *tear down,* O 361; pass. plupf. ἐρέριπτο; (2) intr. aor. **ἤριπε,** ἐρίπῃσι, ἐρῐποῦσα πρηνής, forwards, ἐξοπίσω, backwards, γνύξ, on the knee, Υ 417.

Ἐρεμβοί, a fabled folk, δ 84†.

ἐρεμνῇ, *ήν,* (ἔρεβος), atrae, *dark, black,* M 375, ω 106.

ἔρεξα, aor. from ῥέζω.

ἐρέοντο, see ἔρω II.

ἐρεπτόμενοι, *ους,* depascentes, *feeding upon;* of lotus-eaters, ι 97.

ἐρέριπτο, plupf. pass. from **ἐρείπω.**

ἐρέσθαι, see ἔρω I.

ἐρεσσέμεναι, inf. pr., and ipf. ἔρεσσον, (ἐρετμός), remigare, *row,* I 361.

ἐρέται, pl., ἐρέτης, nom. ὁ (ἐρετμός), remiges, *rowers,* A 142.

Ἐρετμεύς, a Phaiakian, θ 112.

ἐρετμόν, pl. *ά, οῖς,* (remus, Eng. rudder), *oar,* λ 77. (The cut, from drawing on antique vase, represents a

different way of working the oars from that of the Homeric age; see cut 126.)

ἐρεύγομαι, prs., ipf. **ἐρεύγετο,** aor. ἤρυγε, (ructare), evomere, Π 162; ι 374, *belched forth; roar* (of sea, cattle).

Ἐρευθαλίων, leader of the Arkadians, slain by Nestor, H 136.

ἐρεύθων, part., aor. ἐρεῦσαι, (ἐρυθρός, rutilus), *redden, dye,* with blood, Λ 394. (Il.)

ἐρευνῶν (-άων), prs., ipf. ἐρεύνα, *track,* Σ 321; *seek,* χ 180.

Ἐρεχθεύς, *Erechtheus,* a national hero of the Athenians, B 547, η 81.

ἐρέχθων, part., pass. ἐρεχθομένην, *rack, waste,* ε 83; *buffet about,* Ψ 317.

ἐρέω, see (1) εἴρω, say.—(2) ἔρω, *ask.*

ἔρημον, *ῃ, ην, α, abandoned;* E 140, *desolate.*

ἐρηρέδαται, *το,* pf. and plupf. from ἐρείδω.

ἐρητύειν, ipf. ἐρήτῡε, pass. ἐρητῠ́εται, το, [elsewh. ῡ], aor. ἐρητύσειε, iter. ἐρητύσασκε, pass. ἐρήτυθεν, 3 pl., *hold back*, *check*, Λ 567, Β 164 ; mid. and aor. pass. *restrain one's self*, Ν 280 ; *remain*, Β 99 ; *allow itself to be controlled*, Ι 462 ; trans. only Ο 723.

ἐρι-, like **ἀρι-,** and per-, strengthening prefix, *very*, *much*.

ἐρι-αύχενες, ας, *with high-arching necks*, Λ 159. (Il.)

ἐρι-βρεμέτεω, gen. from -έτης, (βρέμω), *loud thundering*, Ν 624†.

ἐρι-βώλᾰκος, ι, α = **ἐρι-βώλου,** ον, no nom., (βῶλος), *with large, thick clods*, epithet of *fertile*, *fruitful* regions, ν 235, ε 34. (Il.)

ἐρί-γδουπος, ου, οιο, οι = **ἐρι-δούπου,** ῳ, ων, (δοῦπος), *loud thundering*, *roaring*, of river, shore; resounding, of vaulted porch; *echoing*, of horses' tread, Λ 152.

ἐρῑδαινέμεν, only prs. and aor. ἐρῑδήσασθαι, Ψ 792, (ἔρις), certare, *quarrel*, *contend*, τινί, ἀντία πάντων, over, about something; ἕνεκά τινος, περὶ πτωχῶν, with words or by deeds, in rivalry, β 206, Π 765.

ἐριδμαίνωσι, subj., (ἔρις), *irritate*, Π 260†.

ἐρι-δούπου, etc., see ἐρί-γδουπος.

ἐριζέμεν, prs., ipf. ἔριζε, iter. ἐρίζεσκον, aor. ἐρίσωσιν, ἐρί(σ)σειε, ειαν, ἐρίσαντε, also mid. subj. aor. ἐρίσσεται, (ἔρις), certare, *contend with*, *vie with*, some one, τινί, in respect to something, τί, Ι 389, ι 213 ; τινί, δ 80, ο 321 ; περί τινος, e. g. concerning eloquence, with inf., σ 38 ; *wrangle*, contend for fair division of property, Μ 423 ; be wroth with, τινί, Ν 109.

ἐρί-ηρος, ον, pl. -ες, ας, (ἀρηρώς), *strongly attached*, *trusty*, ἑταῖρος, ἀοιδόν, α 346.

ἐρι-θηλές, έων, έας, (θάλλω), *luxuriant* (blooming, verdant), Ε 90. (Il.)

ἔρῑθοι, οισιν, *reapers*, Σ 550, 560.

ἐρι-κυδέος, έα, fem. acc., (κῦδος), *famous*, *glorious*, of gods ; then θεῶν δῶρα, ἥβης, δαῖτα, κ 182.

ἐρι-μῡ́κων, ους, gen. acc., (μυκάομαι), *loud bellowing*, βοῦς, Ψ 775.

ἐρινεός, όν, caprificus, *wild fig-tree*, μ 103 ; Il. the great wild fig-tree, near the sources of the Skamandros, Ζ 433.

ἐρῑνόν, τό = ἐρινεός, reading of Aristarchus in ε 281†.

Ἐρῑνύς, pl. ύες, ύσιν, ύας = ῦς, the *Erinyes*, subterranean powers or goddesses, who fulfill curses and punish crimes, Ι 571. (See cut.)

ἔριον, see εἴρια.

ἐρι-ούνης and -ούνιος, ον, (ὀνίνημι), *helpful*, epithet of Hermes ; also subst. *Helper*, Ω 440.

ἔρῐς, ἴδος, ἴδι, ἴδα, and ἔρῐν, pl. ἔρῐδας, —(1) *strife*, *quarrel*, certamen, iurgium, rixa, pugna, Ε 732 ; ἔριδος νεῖκος, Ρ 384 ; Α 8, ἔριδι ξυν. μάχ., bring together *in strife*, cf. Υ 134, Υ 251 ; Υ 55, let loose dire *strife* among them ; *enmity* (heart-consuming, Η 210).—(2) *rivalry*, προφέρουσαι, displaying *rivalry* = in emulation ; θ 210, reveals to his host *his longing for* contests ; ἐξ ἔριδος, *in combat*.—(3) *Eris* or *Discord* personified, Δ 440, Λ 73.

ἐρι-σθενέος, gen., (σθένος), *mighty*, *all-powerful*, Zeus, Τ 355.

ἔρισμα (ἐρίζω), *occasion of variance*, Δ 38†.

ἐρι-στάφῠλον, acc., (σταφυλή), *large-clustered*, epithet of wine, ι 111, 358.

ἐρι-τίμοιο, ον, (τῑμή), *highly prized*, *precious*, Β 447 (Il.)

ἐρίφων, gen. pl., οισι, ους, haedorum, *kids*, ι 220. [ῐ]

Ἐρι-φύλη, wife and betrayer of Amphiaraos, λ 326†. [ῠ]

Ἐρι-χθόνιος, son of Dardanos, father of Tros, Υ 219, 230.

Ἐριῶπις, wife of Oileus, step-mother of Medon, Ν 697.

ἐρκείου, gen., (ἕρκος), *protector of the enclosure* or *court*, (epithet of Zeus, whose altar stood in court ; see plate III., at end of volume), χ 335†.

ἑρκίον (ἕρκος) *αὐλῆς*, *wall* or *hedge* of court, I 476, σ 102. [ĭ]

ἕρκος, sing., and pl. ἕρκεα, εσι, (1) *enclosure, hedge, railing* or *wall*, around fields, gardens, or court-yard of house, π 341, υ 164; ὀδόντων, *barrier, line* of the teeth, Δ 350, κ 328; χαλκείῳ = armatorum, O 567.—(2) *safeguard, defense* (against, gen.), also as epithet of heroes, A 284, Δ 299.

I. **ἕρμα,** pl. ατα, (ὅρμος, σειρά, series), *pendants, ear-rings,* prob. strings of beads, pl. (see cut to the left, an Athenian tetradrachm; see cut to the right, Sicilian dekadrachm); ὀδυνάων, *chain = succession* of sharp pangs, Δ 117.

II. **ἕρμα,** pl. ατα, (of doubtful connection with preceding), columen, (1) *props,* set in a row, on which the ship was supported when drawn up on shore, A 486.—(2) πύληος, *pillar, prop* of the city, Π 549.

Ἕρμαιος λόφος, hill *of Hermes*, offshoot of Mount Neion in Ithaka, π 471†.

Ἑρμῆς, acc. ῆν, and **Ἑρμείας,** είαο = είω, εᾳ, είαν, εία, *Hermes*, the messenger of the gods, *διάκτορος*; (in Od.), son of Maia, ξ 435; guide of Priamos, Ω 457; also escort of the dead, ω 1; cf. ἐριούνιος, σῶκος, ἀκάκητα, χρυσόρραπις, ἐύσκοπον.

Ἑρμιόνη, (1) daughter of Menelaos and of Helene, δ 14.—(2) city in Argolis, B 560.

ἑρμῖνα, acc., pl. -ῖσιν, (II. ἕρμα), *bed-posts,* θ 278. (Od.)

Ἕρμος, river in Aiolis, Υ 392.

ἔρνος, dat. εϊ, ntr., (ὄρνυμι), *sprig, shoot,* germen, ἐριθηλές, blooming, P 53 (ξ 175, ζ 163, Σ 56, symbol of youthful grace and beauty).

ἔρξω, fut. from ἔρδω.

ἔρομαι, see ἔρω.

ἔρος, ῳ, ον, nom. also ἔρως, Γ 442, Ξ 294, *love, passion,* τινός; desiderium, appetitus, A 469; ἐξ ἔρον εἶναι, take away, the wish for—, satiate with—, τινός.

ἑρπετά (ἕρπω), *moving, living* beings, δ 418†.

ἑρπύζων, οντα, part., (ἕρπω), *creeping, crawling,* Ψ 225; from grief or age.

ἕρπω, only prs., and ipf. **εἷρπον,** (serpo), *walk, move,* ρ 158, P 447.

ἐρράδαται, pf. pass. from ῥαίνω.

ἔρριγα, ησε, see ῥιγέω.

ἔρρε, έτω, ετε, imp., and ἔρρων, οντι, (Fέρρω), *go,* δ 367; *hobble about,* Σ 421; *sail,* Θ 239; imp. *begone!* off with thee! abi in malam rem.

ἔρση, αι, and **ἐέρση,** αι, ας, ros, pl. *dew-drops,* stained with blood, Λ 53; ι 222, *new-born lambs.*

ἑρσήεις, εντα, (ἕρση), *dewy, fresh,* recens, of lotus, Ξ 348; of Hektor's corpse, Ω.

ἐρύγμηλον, acc., (ἐρεύγομαι), mugientem, *bellowing,* Σ 580†.

ἐρυγόντα, aor. from ἐρεύγομαι.

ἐρῡθαίνετο, ipf. pass., (ἐρυθρός), *was reddened,* K 484. (Il.)

Ἐρυθῖνοι, place in Paphlagonia, B 855.

Ἐρύθραι, town in Boiotia, B 499.

ἐρυθρός, όν, άς, (rutilus, Eng. ruddy), *red, ruddy,* I 365.

ἐρυκακέειν, -κακον, see ἐρύκω.

ἐρύκανε, κ 429, better ἐρύκακε.

ἐρῡκανόωσι, subj. prs. from ἐρυκανάω, (ἐρύκω), retinebunt, *detain,* α 199†.

ἐρύκω, pres., ipf. ἔρῡκε, fut. ἐρύξω, aor. ἔρυξε, and red. ἠρύκακε, ἐρύκακε, ετε, κάκοι, κακέειν, retinere, *restrain, detain,* Z 217, λ 105; *hold fast,* θ 317; *check,* Υ 268; *hold back,* ο 68, γ 144; *detain,* ἵππους, E 262, 321; Γ 113, *held,* i. e. *placed them* in ranks; arcere, *keep away,* τ 16, Θ 178, Π 369, H 342, τινὰ μάχης, from the battle; τινί τι, *keep off,* ε 166, O 450; separare, K 161; mid. pres. cessare, *tarry,* δ 466, Ψ 443; in M 285 = act. *restrains* = *melts.*

Ἐρύλαος, a Trojan, slain by Patroklos, Π 411†.

ἔρῡμα (ἐρύομαι) χροός, *protection* for his body, Δ 137†.

'Ερύμανθος, mountain in Arkadia, ζ 103†.

'Ερύμας, αντος, a Trojan, (1) slain by Idomeneus, Π 345; (2) by Patroklos, Π 415.

ἐρῦομαι (σρυ, σερϝ, servo, Ω 430, ξ 107, ο 35), **ἐρύεσθαι,** (sync. ἔρῦσθαι, εἴρῦσθαι, as also ipf. ἔρῦσο, το, and εἴρῦτο, ντο), pr. ipf., fut. and aor. (σ and σσ); equally common also, parallel forms **εἰρυ-**, servare, *preserve, shield,* (1) τινά, Ρ 327; *watch,* κ 444, ρ 429, ψ 229, 151, (against outbreak of indignation, Ω 584); *watch over,* γ 268; observare, *respect,* Α 216; *lie in wait for,* π 463.—(2) *ward off,* τι, Β 859, Ε 538, Ψ 819; *defend* one's self against, Θ 143; τινί, *protect* [ῡ in fut. and aor. (exc. ξ 279) on acc. of σσ; in sync. forms, by contraction].

ἐρῦσ-άρματες, τας, (ἐρύω, ἅρμα), *chariot-drawing,* Ο 354. (Il.)

ἐρυσί-πτολι, see ῥυσί-πτολι.

ἐρύω, **ἐρῦουσι,** (ϝερύω, verro, the ϝ often disregarded, augm. ει); act. prs. ipf., fut. (σσ, also without σ, Λ 454), aor., pass. pf. εἰρύαται, -ύμεναι, plupf. εἴρῦτο, υντο; mid. prs. fut. (also ἐρύεσθαι), aor., vellere, trahere, *draw;* ἔθεν ἆσσον, nearer to him; αὖ, *lift* up; πάλιν, *draw* back, Ε 836; *hoist* aloft, χ 176; *drag off,* νεκρόν; *drag* behind chariot, Ω 16; draw the bow string, Ο 464 (αὖ, Θ 325); evellere, Φ 175, Ε 110; convellere, Μ 258, 261; lacerare, Ο 351; τινὰ χλαίνης, by the mantle.—Mid. reflexive, Ξ 79, nostras; χ 90, suum; Ξ 422, to their side; φ 125, toward one's self (see cut No. 37); κ 165, to me; νεκρόν, μάχης, *drag* out of the combat after having slain, Ε 456, Ρ 161. [ῡ even in fut. and aor., exc. Θ 21, Π 863, Χ 351, β 389; only through σσ; also pf. plupf. pass. ῡ, exc. Δ 248.]

ἔρχαται, το, pf. plupf. pass. from ἔργω.

ἐρχατόωντο, ipf. pass., (ἐρχατάω, ἔρχαται), *were penned up,* ξ 15†.

ἐρχθέντα, see ἔργω.

ἔρχομαι, prs., imp. also ἔρχευ, fut. ἐλεύσομαι, aor. ἤλθον (indic. also ἤλυθον, inf. also ἐλθέμεν, μεναι), pf. εἰλήλουθα, θας, θεν, θώς (Ο 81, ἐληλουθώς), plupf. εἰληλούθει, Δ 520, (1) *go,* vado, ι 448, εἰς ἀγορήν, ἀγορήνδε; *march,* Β 457; ἐπὶ πολλὴν γαῖαν, *journey* far; incedere, *move,* Η 208; χαμαί, on the ground; *fly,* Ρ 755, Π 478; *sink,* Ω 82; πεδίοιο, through the plain; μετ' ἄεθλα, to the games; μετά (τι, for something; τινα, to some one, sectari) ἅμα τινί, comitari; πρός τι, ἐπί τινα, accedere; ὁδόν, Α 151; ἐξεσίην, go on an embassy, Ω 235; imp. ἔρχεο, also agedum, ψ 254, ρ 529, 544.—(2) *come,* Κ 540, α 408; παρά, ἀπό, ἔκ τινος, ὑπὸ Ἴλιον, ἄντην, forward; ἀγχίμολόν τινι), σχεδόν, ἐγγύθεν, σχεδόθεν, near; ἄντιον, ἄντα τινός, obviam, to meet; ἀντίος, adversus; ἄγγελος = ἀγγελίης, as messenger; ἀμοιβοί, in exchange; ἐπίρροθος, ἐπίκουρος, as helper; φάος, succor; πεζός, on foot; ἐναργής, visibly, in bodily form; μόρσιμος, destined for her; ὑποχείριος, in the power of; ἐς ὁρμὴν ἔγχεος, within spear-throw; ἐκ βελέων, out of reach of weapons; θέων, ουσα, quickly; φθάμενος, before. ἐλθών, often used pictorially to render the description more vivid, Β 147, Π 521.—Of inanimate objects, summer, λ 192; dawn, μ 142; night, Ξ 77; star, ν 94; death, λ 135; age, ν 60; marriage, ζ 288; dream, Β 56; storm, μ 288; stream of blood, χ 18, σ 97.—(3) *go forth,* Ρ 741, Φ 62, Ψ 737, ρ 599; ἄλλῃ(η), away = is lost, Α 120; proficisci, *set out,* Ε 150, 198; redire, *return* (ἄψ, Ο 550, Κ 211; πάλιν, Ι 408, τ 533), Γ 428, Θ 12, Μ 225, π 23, 131, 206, = referri, *be brought back,* Σ 180; ἄλγος, depart from, Χ 43.—Also with simple acc., Α 322, δ 82, ξ 167; or -δε, ξ 373, κ 320; λέχοσδε, to bed; χορόνδε = εἰς χορόν, to the dance; with part. fut. denoting intention or purpose, α 281, κ 284, cf. Ξ 304, Ω 240.

'ΕΡΩ, I. mid. aor. subj. **ἐρώμεθα,** opt. ἔροιτο, imp. ἔρειο; inf. ἐρέσθαι.—II. pres. **ἐρέων,** subj. ἐρείομεν, opt. ἐρέοιμι, μεν; mid. pres. subj. ἐρέωμαι, inf. ἐρέεσθαι, ipf. ἐρέοντο.—III. mid. prs. **εἴρομαι,** εαι, subj. εἴρωμαι, ηται, ώμεθα, imp. εἴρεο, έσθω, inf. εἴρεσθαι, part. εἰρόμενος, ῳ, ῃ, αι, ipf. εἴρετο, οντο, fut. εἰρήσομαι, εἴρηαι, α 188, quaerere, *seek,* φ 31; elsewh. *ask,* τινά, Α 553, α 284, τί, after something, Η 128; τινὰ ἔπος ἄλλο, something else of one, γ 243; τινὰ δίκας, *seek* justice at one's hands; *ask* one *after*, τινά τινα, K 416, Ω 390; περί τι, ρ 571; περί τινος, α 405; ἀμφὶ πόσει, τ 95; A 513, *pray, implore.*

ἔρῳ, see ἔρος.

ἐρωδῖόν, acc., ardeam, *heron*, K 274†.

1. **ἐρωέω** (1. ἐρωή), fut. ήσει, fluere, *flow*, A 303 and π 441.

2. ἐρωέω (2. ἐρωή), imp. **ἐρώει,** είτω, fut. ήσουσι, aor. inf. ἦσαι, *cease*, τινός, T 170; with ὀπίσσω, Ψ 433, fall back; but N 57, trans. *you would drive back.*

1. **ἐρωή,** ῇ, ήν, (ῥώομαι, ῥέω, ruo), impetus, *sweep*, N 590; *power*, Γ 62; shower of weapons, Δ 542 (as measure of distance, flight of a spear, Ψ 529).

2. **ἐρωή** (ἐρωϜή, Old Ger. ruowa), πολέμου, *cessation, pause*, Π 302, P 761.

ἔρως, see ἔρος.

ἐρωτάω, see εἰρωτᾷς.

ἐσ-, see also εἰσ-.

ἐσ-αθρέω, aor. **ἐσ-αθρήσειεν,** conspiceret, *descry*, Γ 450†.

ἐσ-ακούω, aor. **ἐσάκουσε,** *give ear*, Θ 97.

ἐσ-άλλομαι, aor. **-ήλατο,** Π 558, and 2 aor. -ᾶλτο, -αλλόμενοι, irrumpere, *burst into*, τεῖχος, πύλας.

ἔσβην, εσεν, see σβέννυμι.

ἐσ-δέρκομαι, only aor. **-έδρακον,** εν, conspexit, adspexit, Ω 223 and (Od.).

ἐσ-δύνω, only ipf. ἐς τεύχεα **ἔδυνον,** and aor. δύντε, induere, *put on*, also fut. **ἐσδύσεαι,** te immiscebis, *take a part in*, ἀκοντιστύν, Ψ 622.

ἐσ-έρχεο, see εἰσ-έρχεο.

ἐσ-ήλατο, aor. from ἐσ-άλλομαι.

ἔσθην, aor. pass. from ἕννυμι.

ἐσθής, ῆτος, ῆτι, ῆτα, (Ϝεσθ., vestis), *clothing, clothes*, α 165, ζ 74; *garments* given by the Nereids, ω 67; *bed-clothing*, ψ 290. (Od.)

ἔσθος, τό = foreg., *garment*, Ω 94†.

ἐσθίω, prs., ipf. **ἤσθιον,** ε, (fut. see ἔδω), aor. ἔφαγον (φάγον), inf. φαγέμεν, έειν, etc., pass. ἐσθίεται, edere, *eat*, τί; *eat of*, τινός, ι 102; *consume*, also of fire; *devour*, μ 310; *partake of food*, ω 254, ρ 478; δ 318, is being devoured.

ἐσθλός, ή, όν, etc., (ἐστί, εὖ), *excellent, glorious*, κλέος; *valiant*, Δ 458, Z 443, I 319, N 733; *brave*, Π 837, Ω 167; *noble, good*, I 514, O 203, ζ 182, η 73, A 108, Z 489, θ 553; ntr., *good, blessing*, Ω 530, ο 488; *costly*, K 213; κ 523, ἐσθλά, *valuables.*

ἔσ-θορε, aor., (θρώσκω), *sprang in*, M 462, Φ 18.

ἔσθω, inf. **ἐσθέμεναι,** ipf. ἦσθε = ἐσθίω, *eat, partake of food*, ε 94, Θ 231, Ω 476; *consume*, β 75; *devour*, ι 479.

ἐσ-ιδέσθην, ἴδεσκεν, ἴδηται, etc., see εἰσ-οράω.

ἐσ-ιέμεναι, prs. part. mid., (ἵημι), *hurrying into*, χ 470†.

ἐσ-ίζηται, subj., (ἵζομαι), *places himself in* the ambuscade, N 285†.

ἐς ἐκᾰλέσσατο, aor., (καλέω), *called in his* wife, Ω 193†.

ἐσ-κᾰτᾰ-βαίνων, permeans, *traverse*, ω 222†.

ἔσκον, εν, see εἰμί.

ἐσ-εμάσσατο, aor., (μαίομαι), θυμόν, *distressed* my heart, P 564, Υ 425.

ἐσ-όψομαι, εται, fut. from εἰσ-οράω.

ἑσπέρῖος, οι, ων, ους, (ἕσπερος), vespertinus, *in the evening*, Φ 560; *of the west*, θ 29. (Od.)

ἕσπερος, ον, (vesper), *evening; ἀστήρ*, evening star; ποτὶ ἕσπερα (ntr. pl.), sub vesperam, toward evening, ρ 191.

ἕσπετε, imp. red. aor., see **ἵσπω.**

ἑσπόμεθα, etc., red. aor., see **ἕπομαι.**

ἕσσα, αι, άμενος, etc., aor. from ἕννυμι.

ἕσσαι, aor. inf. from ἕζω. **ἔσσεαι,** εῖται, ἐσσί, ἔσσ' = ἔσσο, see εἰμί. **ἐσσεύοντο,** see σεύω. **ἕσσο,** aor. mid. from ἕννυμι. **ἔσσυται,** etc., pf. pass. from σεύω.

ἐσσυμένως (σεύω), raptim, *hastily*, Ψ 55, ξ 347.

ἔστᾰμεν, 1 pl., ἔστᾰν, 3 pl. aor., **ἕστᾰμεν,** 1 pl. ἑστάμεν, inf. pf., ἕστατον, du. pf. plupf., **ἕστασαν,** 3 pl. plupf. from ἵσταμαι. **ἕστο,** plupf. pass. from ἕννυμι. **ἔστρωμαι,** το, pf. plupf. pass. from στορέννυμι.

ἕστορι, dat., *bolt at end of pole of chariot, yoke-pin*, Ω 272†. (See cut on follg. page, at centre; cf. also No. 49.)

ἐσ-φέρεται, prs. mid., ipf. act. **ἔσφερον,** *were carrying in*, η 6; *draws into its current*, A 495.

ἐσ-φόρεον, ipf., (φορέω), inferebant, *were carrying in*, τ 32; ὕδωρ, in aquam, into the water. (Od.)

ἔσχ', β 346 = ἔσκε, see εἰμί; elsewh. (Il.) aor. from ἔχω.

ἐσχάρῃ, dat., αι, όφιν, *portable hearth*

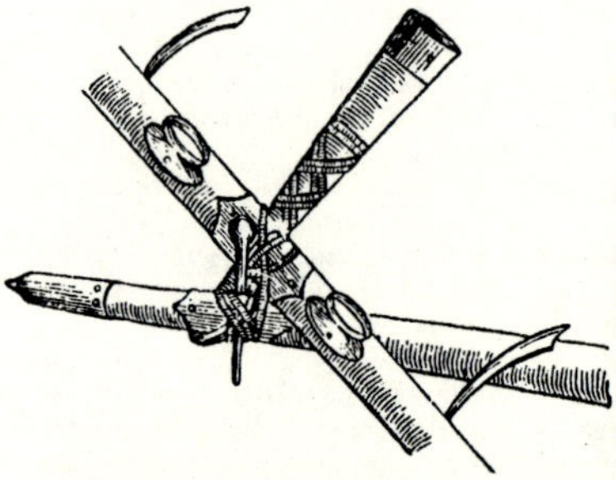

or *basin of coals*, ε 59, ζ 305, υ 123; in Odysseus's house *stationary fire-place*, yet portable fire-basins were doubtless common then as now in the East. (See cut No. 90; cf. also Pompeian warming-pan and water-warmer represented in the adjoining cut.) πυρὸς ἐσχάραι, watch-fires, K 418.

ἐσχατιῆς, ῇ, ήν, (ἔσχατος), ora e, *border, edge, remotest part;* subst. ξ 104, *remotest estate.*

ἔσχατον, acc., ἔσχατοι, (ἐξ), extremi; ἄλλων, ceteris exteriores, *outside of* the others, K 434; ἔσχατα, *at the outside.*

ἐσχατόωντα, όωσα, αν, (ἔσχατος), extrema, of cities, B 508, 616. *frontier town;* K 206, extra vagantem, *straggler.*

ἐσ-χέω, only aor. mid. **ἐσ-έχυντο,** *poured, rushed in at,* M 470. (Il.)

ἔσχον, εν, ετο, etc., see ἔχω.

ἔσω=εἴσω.

ἑταίρη, ην, and **ἑτάρη,** (ἕτᾰρος), socia, *companion, attendant,* I 2, Δ 441, ρ 271.

ἑταιρίσσαι, aor. act., -σσαιτο, mid., (ἑταιρίζω), τινί, comitari, *attend;* mid. τινά, *take as one's companion,* N 456. (Il.)

ἑταῖρος, no voc., and **ἕτᾰρος,** οιο, etc., du. ω, pl. adj., (ἔτης), sociatus, ἀνήρ, λαοί; Ἕκτορι; subst. socius, *companion; comrade,* Σ 80; in battle, danger, journey, esp. of followers of Odysseus in Od.

ἐτεθήπεα, plupf., see ταφών.

Ἐτεοκληείης, βίης=Eteoclis, Δ 386†; cf. 375 sqq., *Eteokles,* son of Oidipus and Epikaste.

Ἐτεό-κρητες, *genuine, primitive Kretans,* τ 176†.

ἐτεόν, ntr., (ἐστί), verum, *the truth,* B 300, O 53; ὡς ἐ. περ, these things ye must have heard, that they are in fact *true,* Ξ 125; ἐτεὰ νεικεῖν, utter many *just reproaches;* εἰ ἐτεόν (also with γέ, δή), if 'tis (really indeed) *true,* E 104 (M 217, γ 122, H 359); always at beginning or end of verse.

ἑτερ-αλκέα, acc., (ἕτερος, ἀλκή), νίκην, χ 236 (elsewh. Il.), *decisive;* δῆμον, *able to change the fortune of the fight,* O 738.

ἑτερ-ήμεροι (ἡμέρα), diebus alternantes, *on alternate days,* Λ 303†.

ἕτερος, η, ον, etc., (1) alter, plur. alteri, *other party,* Λ 71 (Υ 210, one set of parents); ἑτέρηφι=ἑτέρῃ, altera manu, γ 441, Π 734; doubled =unus—alter, *one—the other,* Γ 103; corresponds freq. to ἄλλος, N 731, I 313; joined with pron. ὁ, X 151, cf. υ 132; elliptically, Ω 528, H 420.—(2) secundus, M 93, κ 354, ν 69.—(3) alius, ι 302, I 302; ρ 266, one part is joined to another.

ἐτέρσετο, see τερσαίνω.

ἑτέρωθεν, ex altera parte, *from the other side; on the other side,* H 311, Γ 230.

ἑτέρωθι, *on the other side; elsewhere,* δ 531, O 348; corresponds to ἔνθεν, μ 235; =*from far away,* E 351.

ἑτέρως, aliter, *otherwise,* α 234†.

ἑτέρωσε, *in the other direction,* Δ 492, τ 470; *to one side,* Θ 306, 308; *in another direction*=*away,* Ψ 231; π 179, looked away.

ἐτέταλτο, see ἐπι-τέλλω. **ἐτετεύχατο,** plupf. pass., see τεύχω. **ἔτετμεν,** see τέτμον. **ἐτέτυκτο,** see τεύχω.

Ἐτεωνεύς Βοηθοΐδης, companion-at-arms of Menelaos, δ 22. (Od.)

Ἐτεωνός, town in Boiotia, B 497†.

ἔται, ῃσι, ας, pl., (Ϝέται = σϜέται, sui), *friends, retainers,* δ 3.

ἐτήτυμος, ον, (ἔτυμος), *truthful,* messenger, speech, words, ν 232; *real,* γ 241; ntr.=profecto, *actually, really,* A 558, Σ 128, εἰ δὴ καὶ πάμπαν ἐ., but if now even quite without doubt, N 111.

ἔτι (et, etiam), *still, yet,* (1) temporal continuance, B 344 sq., υ 12; ἔτι τυτθὸν ἐόντα; ἔτι καὶ νῦν, even now once more, A 455; *still,* B 344; οὐ—ἔτι, non iam, no longer, see οὐκέτι.—(2) strengthening, ἔτι καί, *even, still more,* B 229; πρὸς δ' ἔτι καὶ τόδε μεῖζον ἐνὶ φρεσί, π 291; with comparatives, μᾶλλον, ἄλλος, Z 411; ἕτερον, ξ 325. [⏑⏑; ⏑– before δήν, δηρόν; see these words.]

ἔτλην, ης, η, ητε, see τλῆναι.

ἑτοιμάζω, only aor. imp. **ἑτοιμάσατε,** άτω, and mid. 1 aor. -άσαντο, and opt. -άσαιντο = -ασαίατο, *make ready, prepare, provide,* A 118, ν 184.

ἑτοῖμος, η, α, adj., praesto, (1) *ready, at hand,* ὀνείατα; *feasible,* μῆτις. —(2) *evident, certain,* Ξ 53, Σ 96, θ 384.

ἔτορε, see τορέω.

ἔτος, εος, εϊ, ει; εα, έων, (Fέτος, vetus), annus, *year;* ἐπιπλόμενον, coming; περιτελλομένου, as the year came round; προτέρων, in by-gone years, Λ 691.

ἔτραπε, etc., see τρέπω.

ἔτραφεν, aor. pass. -έτην, aor act. from τρέφω.

ἔτῠμον, α, οισι, ntr., (ἐτεός), verum (dicere, K 534), pl., *truth,* τ 203; 567, bring *accomplishment;* ἔτυμον, *really,* ψ 26; οὐ ἔτ., falso, Ψ 440.

ἐτώσιον, α, (Fετώσ.), vanum, *fruitless,* ἔγχος, βέλεα.

εὖ, ἐύ, (for ἐσύ, ntr. from ἐύς), and **ἠύ,** *good* (in widest signif.), (1) adv., *well, skil'fully, carefully,* ν 20; joined with κατὰ κόσμον, fitly, in due form; καὶ ἐπισταμένως, εἰδέναι, γνῶναι, etc.; ἐϋφρονεῖν, well advising, intelligent, A 73.—(2) *morally well,* βάζουσι, φρονεῖν, bene velle, η 74; ἔρδειν τινά, bene facere.—(3) feliciter, *prosperously,* A 19, B 253.—(4) with ναιόμενος, *well* inhabited, habitable, so also ναιετάωσα; strengthening = *quite,* before πάντες, μάλα.—(5) in composition, before two consonants or a double consonant, usually ἐυ-, elsewh. εὐ-.

εὗ = οὗ, sui.

εὐ-αγγέλιον (ἄγγελος), *reward for good tidings,* ξ 152, 166.

εὔαδε = ἐFFαδε, aor. from ἁνδάνω, placuit, *pleased.*

Εὐ-αιμονίδης, *son of* **Εὐαίμων,** Eurypylos, grandson of Ormenos, E 76, H 167. (Il.)

εὐ-ανθέι, dat., nom. -ανθής, (ἄνθος), λάχνῃ, with *luxuriant, abundant* down, λ 320†.

Εὐ-άνθης, father of Maron, ι 197†.

Εὔ-βοια, island of the Abantes, B 536, γ 174, η 321.

εὔ-βοτος, *abounding in fine cattle,* ο 406†.

εὔγματα, pl., (εὔχομαι), κενά, empty *boastings,* χ 249.

ἐυ-γνάμπτοις, dat. pl., (γνάμπτω), *gracefully bent,* σ 294†.

εὐ-δείελος, ου, ον, (δέελος, δῆλος), *clearly-,* or *far-seen;* epithet of islands, esp. of Ithaka, β 167. (Od.)

εὐ-δῐκίας, acc., (δίκη), ἀνέχῃσι, maintains *justice,* τ 111†.

ἐυ-δμήτου, οιο, ῳ, ον, ων, ους, (δέμω), *well built, well fashioned;* wall, altar, A 448, η 100.

εὕδω, pres. subj. 2 sing. εὕδῃσθα, ipf. **εὗδον,** iter. εὕδεσκε, *sleep,* sweet sleep, sleep of death, Ξ 482; be still, E 524.

Εὔ-δωρος, son of Hermes and of Polymele; chief of Myrmidons, Π 186, 179.

εὐ-ειδέα, acc., (εἶδος), *well shaped beautiful,* Γ 48†.

εὐ-εργεσίη, ας, (ἔργον), *well-doing, kindness,* χ 235, 374†.

εὐ-εργής, έος, έα, έες, έων, (ἔργον), *well made, well* or *firmly wrought* (ship, chariot, seat); pl., bene factorum, χ 319.

εὐ-εργός, fem., (ἔργον), *excellent,* λ 434. (Od.)

εὐ-ερκέος, gen. from -ερκής, (ἕρκος), αὐλῆς, *well fenced, well enclosed;* ρ 267 (v. l. εὐεργέες), *with strong posts.*

ἐυ-ζύγου, gen., pl. -οι, (ζυγόν), *firmly built, well bound together* (with strong cross-beams), ν 116.

ἐύ-ζωνος, οιο, ους, (ζώνη), *beautifully girdled,* the girdle giving a graceful form to the garment, Z 467, A 429. (Il.) (See cut.)

εὐ-ηγενέος, έων, (γένος), *well* or *nobly born,* A 427. (Il.)

εὐ-ηγεσίης (ἡγεῖσθαι), ἐξ-, in consequence *of good government* (v. l. εὐεργεσίης), τ 114†.

εὐ-ηκέος, gen., -ής, (ἄκων), *well-pointed, sharp, piercing,* X 319†.

Εὐηνίνη, *daughter of Euenos,* Marpessa, I 557†.

Εὐηνορίδης, *son of Euenor,* Leiokritos, β 242. (Od.)

Εὐηνός, Evenus, (1) son of Selepios, B 693.—(2) father of Marpessa.

εὐ-ήνορα, acc. from -ωρ, (ἀνήρ), *manly, glorious, famous,* δ 622. (Od.)

Εὐήνωρ, ορος, father of Leiokritos.

εὐ-ῆρες, εα, ntr., (ἀρηρώς), *well poised, handy,* epithet of oars, λ 121. (Od.)

ἐύ-θριξ only **ἐύ-τριχας,** *with flowing mane,* Ψ 13. [ῐ]

ἐύ-θρονος, ον, (θρόνος) Ἠώς, *with beautiful throne, well throned,* Θ 565. (Od.)

εὐθύ, see εὐθύς.

εὔ-θυμος, *well disposed, kindly,* ξ 63†.

Εὔ-ιππος, a Trojan, slain by Patroklos, Π 417†.

εὐ-καμπέα, ές, (κάμπτω), *well bent, curved,* sickle, key, φ 6. (Od.)

εὐ-κεάτοιο, gen., (κείω), *easily cleft* or *split,* ε 60†. [ᾰ]

εὔκηλος, οι, (ἕκηλος, ε-Fεκ.), *quiet, unmolested,* A 554, γ 263.

ἐυ-κλεής, masc. pl. acc. **-κλεῖας,** ntr. sing. -κλεές, (κλέος), adv. **ἐυκλειῶς,** gloriosus, *famous,* K 281, φ 331.

ἐυ-κλείη, ης, *good reputation, fame,* Θ 285, ξ 402.

ἐυ-κλήϊς (κληΐς), *close shutting,* Ω 318†

ἐυ-κνήμῖδες, ας, (κνημίς), *well greaved* (Achaians, companions), A 17, β 402. (See cut under ἀμφι-βρότης.)

εὐ-κόσμως, *well disposed, well arranged,* φ 123†.

ἐυ-κτίμενον, η, ης, ην, (κτίω), bene cultus, *well tilled, laid out, appointed, built,* B 501, ι 130, Φ 77, ω 336. [ῐ]

ἐύ-κτῐτον (κτίω), *firmly built,* B 593†.

εὐκτά (εὔχομαι) γένηται, *occasion for triumph* (εὖχος, εὖγμα), Ξ 98†.

εὔ-κυκλον, ου, ους, (κύκλος), *well rounded, well rimmed* (Il.); *well wheeled,* ζ 58.

εὐ-λείμων (λειμών), *abounding in meadows, adapted for* (cattle) *pasturing,* δ 607†.

εὐλαί, άς, fem. pl., *maggots,* X 509. (Il.)

εὔληρα (ἐFλ. Fελίσσω ?), *reins,* Ψ 481†.

Εὔ-μαιος, son of Ktesios, Ormenides, ο 414; the illustrious swine-herd, π 461; faithful to his master Odysseus, cf. ξ 17–190, χ 267.

εὐ-μενέτησιν (μένος), *those who think rightly, the well disposed,* ζ 185.

Εὐ-μήδης, father of Dolon, Trojan herald, K 314, 412.

εὔ-μηλος (μῆλα), *abounding in sheep,* ο 406†.

Εὔ-μηλος, son of Admetos, Ψ 288. (Il.)

ἐϋ-μμελίης, ου, and ω, ην, αι, (also with single μ, σμελ.), *skillful with the spear,* γ 400. (Il.)

εὐνάζω, fut. εὐνάσω [ᾰ], mid. pr. εὐνάζεσθαι, ipf., (εὐνή), *put in ambush,* δ 408; mid., *lay one's self down, sleep,* υ 1. (Od.)

εὐ-ναιετάοντες, ας, (ναιετάω), *pleasant to dwell in, comfortable,* B 648, β 400. [ᾰ]

εὐ-ναιόμενον, ῳ, η, ην, (ναίω), *well inhabited, thickly peopled;* of cities, esp. Troia, A 164.

εὐνάω, aor. act. **εὔνησε,** pass. εὐνηθῆναι, (εὐνή), *place* (in ambush), δ 440; *still, quiet* (lament, wind); pass., *lay one's self to rest,* (ἐν)φιλότητι, of sexual intercourse, Γ 441.

εὐνή (no gen. dat. pl., but the form εὐνῆφι), *bed, couch,* of individual, I 618; of army, K 408; of wild animals, cattle; also *marriage bed, cohabitation; bedding,* τ 317, K 75, ψ 179; *bedstead,* α 427, β 2, θ 2. Plur., freq. *mooring stones*, which served as anchors, having cables (πρυμνήσια) attached to them, and being cast upon the land or on the bottom, A 436, 476.—**εὐνῆθεν** ἀνίστατο, arose *from his couch*, υ 124†.

Εὔ-νηος, son of Jason, king of Lemnos, H 468. (Il.)

εὔ-νητον, οι, ους, (ἐύ-ννητ., νέω), *well, firmly woven*, Σ 596.

εὐνῆφι, see εὐνή.

εὖνιν, acc., (Gothic, vans), *lacking*; ἔθηκεν, ποιήσας, orbavit, X 44, ι 524.

εὐ-νομίην (νόμος), *good order, obedience to laws*, ρ 487†.

ἐύ-ξεστον, ου, ῳ, οι, ῃ, ην, ας, (ξέω), *well scraped, smooth, polished*, Ω 275, 290, 271.

ἐύ-ξοον, ου, K 373, ἐύξου, (ξέω), *well planed, polished*; only ε 237, *polishing smoothly*.

εὔ-ορμος, ου, (ὅρμος), *affording good moorage* or *anchorage*, Φ 23. (Od.)

εὐ-πατερείη, ειαν, (πατήρ), *sprung from noble father, high-born*, epithet of Helene and of Tyro, Z 292, λ 235.

Εὐ-πείθης, εος, εα, father of Antinoos, slain by Telemachos, ω 523.

εὐ-πέπλῳ, ον, ων, fem., (πέπλος), *with beautiful mantle, beautifully robed*, E 424, ζ 49.

ἐυ-πηγής (πήγνυμι), *strongly built*, φ 334†.

ἐυ-πήκτου, ῳ, ων, (πήγνυμι), *firmly joined together, well built*, of ship, tent, apartment, B 661, ψ 41.

ἐυ-πλείην (πλεῖος), *well filled*, ρ 467†.

ἐυ-πλεκέες, έας, and **ἐυ-πλέκτῳ**, ους, *well plaited*, of body of chariot, tassels, cord, etc., Ψ 335, B 449, Ψ 115.

ἐυ-πλοίην, acc., (πλόος), *prosperous voyage*, I 362†.

ἐυ-πλοκᾰμῖδες and **ἐυ-πλόκᾰμος**, ῳ, ον, οι, οισι, (πλόκαμος), *adorned with beautiful tresses, fair-haired*, epithet of goddesses, ε 125, 390; of women, Z 380, β 119, X 442. (See cut No. 47.)

ἐυ-πλῠνές (πλύνω) φᾶρος, *well washed* (fair-shining), θ 392. (Od.)

εὐ-ποίητον, οιο, οισι, α, άων, ῃσι, (ποιέω), *well made, well wrought*, of works of skill, E 466, Π 106, 636.

εὔ-πρηστον (πρήθω) ἀυτμήν, *sparkling, fiery* breath, or *strong blowing*, Σ 471†.

ἐύ-πρυμνοι (πρυμνή), *with well-rounded sterns*, Δ 248†.

ἐύ-πυργον (πύργος), *well towered*, H 71†.

ἐύ-πωλον, acc., (πῶλος), *abounding in horses*, Ἴλιον, E 551, β 18.

εὐράξ, *on one side*, Λ 251, O 541.

εὐ-ρεής, see ἐυ-ρρεῖος.

εὑρίσκω, only aor. **εὗρον**, etc., mid. prs. imp. εὕρεο, opt.-οίμην, aor. εὕρετο, invenire, reperire. *find out, discover*; mid. τέκμωρ, goal, end, remedy; *invent* a name; *draw down upon one's self*, φ 304.

ἐύ-ρροος, ον, (σρο-, ῥέω), *beautifully flowing*, H 329, Φ 130.

Εὖρος, Eurus, *S.E. wind*, stormy, B 145; but warm, τ 206.

εὖρος, acc., τό, (εὐρύς), *in breadth*, λ 312†.

ἐυ-ρρεῖος, gen. and (Il.) **ἐυ-ρρείταο**, ην, (σρει-, ῥέω), *fair flowing*, Z 508, ξ 257.

ἐυ-ρραφέεσσι (ῥάπτω), *firmly sewed*, β 354, 380.

εὐρῠ-άγυια, αν, (ἀγυιά), *broad-streeted*, epithet of cities, Troia, δ 246, B 141.

Εὐρυ-άδης, suitor, slain by Telemachos, χ 267†.

Εὐρύ-ᾰλος, (1) son of Mekistos, companion of Diomedes, Z 20, Ψ 677.—(2) a Phaiakian, θ 115, 396.

Εὐρυ-βάτης, herald (1) of Agamemnon, A 320.—(2) of Odysseus, B 184, τ 247.

Εὐρυ-δᾰμας, (1) father of Abas and of Polyeidos, E 149.—(2) suitor, slain by Odysseus, χ 283.

Εὐρυ-δίκη, daughter of Klymenos, wife of Nestor, γ 452.

Εὐρύ-κλεια, daughter of Ops, α 429; nurse of Odysseus, and faithful housekeeper in his palace, τ 357, β 361.

εὐρυ-κρείων, *far-ruling*, Agamemnon, A 102; Poseidon, Λ 751.

Εὐρύ-λοχος, companion and cousin of Odysseus, κ 232, λ 23, μ 195, 339. (Od.)

Εὐρύ-μαχος, son of Polybos, α 399; suitor, slain by Odysseus, χ 82. (Od.)

Εὐρῠ-μέδουσα, attendant of Arete, η 8†.

Εὐρῠ-μέδων, (1) son of Ptolemaios, Agamemnon's charioteer, Δ 228.—(2) Nestor's servant, Θ 114, Λ 620.—(3)

king of the giants, father of Periboia, η 58.

εὐρυ-μέτωπον, οι, ων, ους, *broad-browed*, K 292, λ 289.

Εὐρυμίδης, *Eurymos's son*, Telemos, seer among the Kyklops, ι 509†.

Εὐρῦ-νόμη, (1) Okeanos's daughter, Σ 398.—(2) Penelope's stewardess, ρ 495, τ 97.

Εὐρῦ-νομος, son of Aigyptios in Ithaka, β 22. (Od.)

εὔρῡναν, aor. from εὐρύνω, *enlarged* (the arena of combat), θ 260†.

εὐρῦ-οδείης, gen., (ὁδός), *with broad ways* (ways open to all), Π 635, γ 453.

εὐρῦ-οπᾰ, voc., also old nom. for -όπης; acc. from -οψ, (ὄψ, vox), *far-thundering*, Ξ 203, Θ 206.

εὐρυ-πόροιο (πόρος) θαλάσσης, *traversable far and wide, with broad ways*, O 381. (Od.)

εὐρυ-πυλὲς (πύλη) Ἄιδος δῶ, *wide-gated*, Ψ 74, λ 571.

Εὐρῦ-πυλος, (1) son of Euaimon, from Thessaly, B 736, E 76, Z 36, Λ 580, 809.—(2) (son of Poseidon and of Astypalaia) from Kos, B 677.—(3) son of Telephos, slain by Neoptolemos, λ 520.

εὐρῦ-ρέεθρος, *broad-flowing*, Φ 141†.

εὐρὺ ῥέων, *broad-streaming*, B 849. (Il.)

εὐρύς, έος, έϊ, έα, ύν; fem. εὐρεῖα, ntr. εὐρύ, etc., *broad, wide*, applied to heavens, earth, sea, countries, (only B 575, to city and surroundings); elsewh. *broad;* comp. εὐρύτερος, *y*, Γ 194.

εὐρυ-σθενές, voc., *with far-reaching might*, epithet of Poseidon, ν 140. (Il.)

Εὐρυσθεύς, ῆος, son of Sthenelos, king of Mykenai, T 103 sqq.; imposes labors upon Herakles, O 639, Θ 363, λ 620.

Εὐρῦτίδης, *son of Eurytos*, Iphitos, Odysseus's guest-friend, φ 14, 37. (Od.)

Εὐρῦτίων, ωνα, Κένταυρον, φ 295†.

Εὔ-ρῦτος, (1) son of Aktor, Epeian, with his brother Kteatos, ally of Augeias, B 621; Μολίονε, Λ 709.—(2) son of Melaneus, king of Oichalia, B 730, φ 32; slain by Apollo, θ 224.

εὐρῦ-φυές (φύω), *wide growing*, i. e. with its two rows of kernels far apart, epithet of barley, δ 604†.

εὐρῦ-χόροιο, ῳ, ον, (χορός), *with broad dancing-places, with broad squares*, δ 635.

εὐρώεντα, acc., (εὐρώς), *mouldy, dank*, ψ 322.

Εὐρώπη, **Φοίνικος θυγάτηρ,** mother of Minos and Rhadamanthys, Ξ 321†.

ἐύς, ἐῆος, ἐύν, also **ἠύς,** ἠύν, ntr., ἠύ, (=ἐσύς, ἐσθλός), bonus, *good, excellent, brave*, B 653. (ἐύ and εὖ, also ἐάων, q. v.)

εὖσε, αν, aor. from εὕω, *singed*.

ἐύ-σκαρθμοι (σκαίρω), *lightly bounding*, N 31†.

ἐύ-σκοπος, ῳ, ον, (σκοπή), ἀργεϊφόντης, *far, sharply seeing* (Hermes); but λ 198, of Artemis.

ἐυ-σσέλμου, οιο, ῳ, and pl., (σϝέλμα, solum), *well decked*, of ships; *with good deck* (only at bow and stern), B 170, β 390. The Egyptian ships seem to have had a kind of caboose. (See cut.)

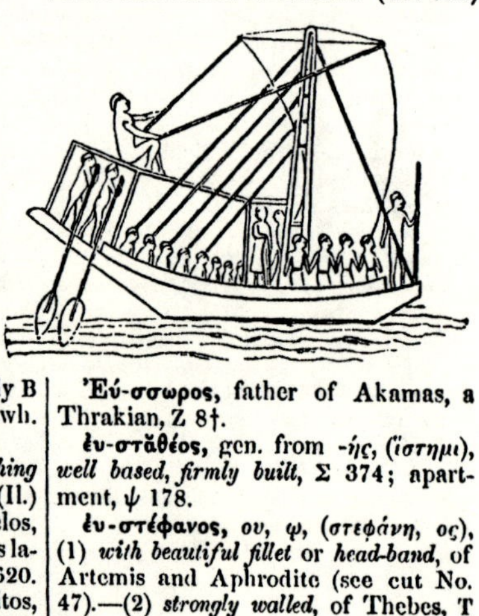

Ἐύ-σσωρος, father of Akamas, a Thrakian, Z 8†.

ἐυ-στᾰθέος, gen. from -ής, (ἵστημι), *well based, firmly built*, Σ 374; apartment, ψ 178.

ἐυ-στέφανος, ου, ῳ, (στεφάνη, ος), (1) *with beautiful fillet* or *head-band*, of Artemis and Aphrodite (see cut No. 47).—(2) *strongly walled*, of Thebes, T 99.

ἐυ-στρέπτοισι, dat. pl., (στρέφω), *tightly plaited* or *twisted*, β 426; so also **ἐυ-στρεφέι,** έα, ές, έεσσι, O 463; and **ἐυ-στρόφῳ,** N 599, of cords, ropes, string of bow and sling.

εὖτε (ὅτε), (1) quom, *when*, disjunctive: the sentence in which its clause stands connected with what precedes by another conjunction in the apodosis, γ 9; with subj. with (B 34), or without ἄν (η 202), to express general expectation, B 228.—(2) quasi, *as* = ἠΰτε, Γ 10.

εὐ-τείχεα, fem. acc., and **-τείχεον,** as fem., (τεῖχος), *strongly walled*, Π 57, A 129.

ἐυ-τμήτοισι, ους, (τέμνω), *well cut*, of straps, Ψ 684. (Il.)

ἐυ-τρεφέος, ές, έες, from -τρεφής, (τρέφω), *well nourished, fat*, ι 425. (Od.)

Εὔτρησις, village in Boiotia, B 502.

ἐυ-τρήτοισι (τιτράω), *well pierced*, Ξ 182†.

ἐύ-τριχας, nom. εὔθριξ, *with flowing mane*.

ἐύ-τροχον (τροχός), *well wheeled*, Θ 438.

εὔ-τυκτον (τεύχω), *well wrought*, Γ 336, δ 123.

εὐ-φημῆσαι, aor., -φημέω, (φήμη), bona verba loqui, favere linguis, *shun unlucky words, keep silence*, at sacrifice, I 171†.

Εὔ-φημος, son of Troizenos, chief of Kikones, B 846†.

Εὐ-φήτης, ruler over Ephyra in Elis, O 532†.

Εὔ-φορβος, Panthoos's son, Trojan, who having wounded Patroklos, Π 806, is slain by Menelaos, P 59.

ἐυ-φραδέως (φράζεσθαι), *thoughtfully, wisely*, τ 352†.

εὐ-φραίνοιμι, fut. -ανέω, ανέειν, aor. εὔφρηνε, ῆναι, (φρένες), exhilarare, *delight, gladden;* mid., β 311, *take one's pleasure*.

ἐὺ φρονέων, *well meaning and well judging, with kind and wise thought*, A 73, β 160.

ἐυ-φροσύνη, sing., and pl. -ῃσιν, laetitia, *mirth, gladness*, ζ 156.

ἐύ-φρων, ονα, (φρένες), laetus, Γ 246, *rejoicing the heart*.

εὐ-φυέα, acc. sing., pl. έες, *well grown, stately, shapely*, Δ 147. (Il.)

ἐυ-χάλκου, ον, ων, *wrought of fine brass, well mounted with brass*, Υ 322.

εὐχετάομαι, opt. **εὐχετοῴμην,** οῷτο, inf. -τάασθαι, ipf. εὐχετόωντο, (εὔχομαι), *wish*, (1) *pray to*, τινί, X 394.—(2) *boast*, M 391; μεγάλα, loudly; ἐπί τινι, χ 412.

Εὐχήνωρ, son of Polyeidos, N 663.

εὐχῇσι, nom. εὐχή, *by prayers*, κ 526†.

εὔχομαι, prs., ipf. εὔχοντο, fut., aor., (subj. εὔξεαι), *declare a wish*, ξ 463.—(1) precari, *pray*, θεῷ, Γ 296, Σ 75; μέγα, aloud; πολλά, devoutly; ὑπέρ τινος and τινί, in behalf of.—(2) vovere, *implore*, ο 353, τινί τι; inf.—(3) asseverare, *avow*, Σ 499; de se praedicare, *avouch myself*, esp. with εἶναι, α 180, usually of just pride.—(4) gloriari, *boast*, N 447.

εὖχος, τό, gloria, *fame*, E 654.

ἐυ-χροές, ntr., (χρώς), *bright-colored*, ξ 24†.

εὐχωλή, ῆς, ήν, αί, ῇσι, (εὔχομαι), preces, *prayer*, ν 357; votum, *vow*, A 65; gloriatio, *triumph*, Δ 450, Θ 229, B 160; my *pride*, X 433.

εὕω, prs. act. and pass. aor. **εὗσε,** σαν, *singe*, bristles of swine, I 468; eyelids of Kyklops, ι 379.

εὐ-ώδης, εϊ, ες, (ὄδωδα), *fragrant*, β 339.

εὐ-ώπιδα, acc. from -ῶπις, *fair-faced*, ζ 113. (Od.)

ἔφαγον, see **φαγεῖν**.

ἐφ-άλλομαι, aor. **ἐπᾶλτο,** ἐπ(ι)άλμενος, (ἅλλομαι, salio), insilio, *spring upon* (in hostile signif.), *charge upon*, τινί, N 643; ἵππων, *leap upon;* ω 320, *spring toward*.

ἔφ-αλον (ἐπί ἁλός), maritimus, B 538. (Il.)

ἔφαν, see *φημί*.

ἐφ-ανδάνω, **ἐπι-ανδάνει,** ipf. -ήνδανε (and ἐφήνδ., H 45), placere, *please*.

ἐφάνη, aor. pass. from *φαίνω*.

ἐφ-άπτω, pf. pass. **ἐφῆπται,** plupf. -ῆπτο, aor. mid. subj. ἐφάψεαι, (1) *hang over*, τινί, Φ 513.—(2) mid., attigeris, *touch*, ἠπείροιο, ε 348.

ἐφ-αρμόσσειε (ἁρμόζω) εἰ οἱ, whether they *fitted* him, T 385†.

ἐφ-εζόμενος, η, part., inf. prs., ipf. ἐφέζετο, pf. ἐφήμενος, aor. imp. ἔφεσσαι, inf. ἐφέσσαι, mid. -εσσάμενος (tmesis, ξ 295), insido, *sit upon*, τινί, δ 509; pf., ζ 309; aor. act., *take on board;* π 443, *set me on* his knee.

ἐφ-έηκα, ε, -είην, see ἐφ-ίημι.

ἐφ-έλκεται, with part., ipf. ἐφέλκετο, mid., *draw to one's self, attract;* pass., *trailing, dragging after*, Ψ 696.

ἐφ-έννυμι, see ἐπι-έννυμι.

ἐφ-έπων, I. act. prs., ipf. ἔφεπε, iter. -έπεσκον, fut. -έψεις, ειν, aor. -έσπον, ἐπι-σπεῖν, (ἕπω, sequor), (1) persequi, *pursue*, τινά, Λ 177.—(2) instigare contra, *turn against*, τινί, Π 732.—(3) percurrere, *rush through, over*, τί, τινάς, Υ 494, ι 121.—(4) *follow* *up* (occupation), τί, μ 330, ξ 195.—(5) fut. aor., assequi, *draw down upon one's self*, πότμον, etc., γ 134, Τ 294, Φ 100.—II. mid. fut. and aor., sequi, τινί, Δ 63, Ν 495; obsequi, *comply with*, γ 215, ξ 262.

ἐφ-έσσαι, ἐσσεσθαι, etc., see ἐφ-εζόμενος.

ἐφ-έστιος, ον, οι, (1) = ἐφ' ἑστίᾳ, *at one's own hearth*, γ 234; *native*, Β 125.—(2) = ἐφ' ἑστίαν, *to one's hearth*, ψ 55, η 248.

ἐφ-ετμή, ήν, έων, άς, (ἵημι), iussum, *command, behest*, Ξ 249.

ἐφ-εύρομεν, etc., aor., (εὑρίσκω), invenire, *come upon and find, surprise*, β 109, Δ 88.

ἐφ-εψῐόωνται, το, prs. ipf., (ἑψιάομαι), illudunt, *mock*, τινί, τ 331, 370.

ἐφ-ηγέομαι, see ἐπὶ στίχας.

ἐφ-ῆμαι, see ἐφ-έζω.

ἐφ-ημέριος, α, (ἡμέρα), *the day through*, δ 223; but φ 85, *every day, trivial* thoughts.

ἐφ-ημοσύνης, ην, gen. acc., (ἵημι), iussum, π 340.

ἔφησθα, aiebas, see φημί. **ἔφθης,** η, see φθάνω. **ἐφθίαθ'** (-ίατο), see φθίω.

Ἐφιάλτης, son of Aloeus (Poseidon), brother of Otos, giant, Ε 385, λ 308.

ἐφ-ίζᾰνε, etc., ipf., (ἵζω), insĭdebat, ὕπνος; assidebant, δείπνῳ, Κ 578.

ἔφ-ῑζε, ipf., iter. -ίζεσκε, insidebat, *sit upon*, τινί, γ 411, τ 55.

ἐφ-ίημι, ipf. **-ίει,** fut. -ήσω, aor. -ῆκε, ἐῆκε, subj. -είω, opt. -είην, imp. ἔφες, immitto, *send to*, τινά τινι, Ω 117; *launch at*, τί τινι, Α 382, Ο 444, τ 550; imponere, *place upon*, τινί τι; χεῖρας, lay hands upon; νόστον, *decree*; impellere, *constrain*, with inf., ξ 464, Σ 108; mandare, *propose*, τ 576; so also mid. -ιέμενος, and fut. -ήσομαι τινί τι, Ψ 82. [ῐ, but ῑέμενος, ῑεις, ῑει, exc. ω 180.]

ἐφ-ίκοντο, aor., (ἱκνέομαι), ἀλλήλων, *fell upon* one another, Ν 613†.

ἐφίληθεν, aor. pass. from φιλέω.

ἐφ-ίστατο, (1) ipf. and 2 aor. -έστη, *approached, drew near*, τινί, Κ 496, Ψ 201, Λ 644.—(2) pf. -εστᾶσι, inf. -εστάμεν(αι), part. -εστἄότες, plupf. -εστήκει, -έστᾰσαν, *stand by* (near), *upon, at*, τινί, Ν 133, Ζ 373, α 120, Σ 554, 515.

ἐφ-όλκαιον (ἕλκω), *rudder*, ξ 350†.

ἐφ-ομαρτεῖτον, ε, imp. prs., *follow close upon*, Θ 191. (Il.)

ἐφ-οπλίζοιμεν, prs., fut. -οπλίσσουσι, aor. with σσ (inf. ί(σ)σαι), *get ready*, repast, chariot, ship; mid. fut. -ισόμεσθα, *get ready our* supper, Ι 66.

ἐφ-ορᾷς, etc., prs., fut. ἐπιόψομαι, ἐπόψεαι, aor. ἐπιδόντα, ἰδεῖν, intueri, *behold, watch over;* visere, τινά, τί; *select*, Ι 167.

ἐφ-ορμάω, aor. **-ώρμησαν,** excitaverunt contra me, *stir up against*, Γ 165; elsewh. mid. -ορμᾶται, and aor. -ωρμήθην, irruere, adoriri, *attack*, τινά (τινί, tmesis, κ 214); cupere, *desire*, with inf., Ν 74; captabam, *strive*, λ 206.

ἐφ-ορμή, aditus, *entrance, approach*, χ 130† (only from the interior into the ὁδὸς ἐς λαύρην).

ἐφ-υβρίζων, insultans, Ι 368†.

ἔφ-υδρος (ὕδωρ), pluviosus, *wet*, ξ 458†.

ἐφ-ύπερθε(ν), desuper, supra, *above*, Ω 645, ι 383.

Ἐφύρη, (1) ancient name of Korinth, Ζ 152, 210.—(2) Pelasgic city in northern Elis, on the river Selleïs, residence of Augeias, Β 659, Ο 531, Λ 739.—(3) town in Thesprotia in Epeiros, α 259, β 328.—(4) town of the **Ἔφῡροι,** in Thessaly, afterward Krannon, Ν 301.

ἔχαδε, aor. from χανδάνω, *held*.

ἔχεε, αν, aor. from χέω, fudit, *pour*.

ἐχέ-θῡμος, cohibens cupiditatem; οὐκ ἐ., libidinosa, *lustful*, θ 320†.

Ἐχε-κλῆς, ῆος, son of Aktor, a Myrmidon, Π 189.

Ἔχε-κλος, (1) Agenor's son, slain by Achilleus, Υ 474†.—(2) a Trojan, slain by Patroklos, Π 694†.

Ἐχέμμων, ονα, Priamos's son, slain by Diomedes, Ε 160†.

Ἐχέ-νηος, an aged Phaiakian, λ 342. (Od.)

ἐχε-πευκές (πεῦκος), *pointed*, Α 51. (Il.)

Ἐχέ-πωλος, (1) descendant of Anchises, dwelling in Sikyon, Ψ 296.—(2) son of Thalysios, a Trojan, slain by Antilochos, Δ 458.

ἔχεσκον, ipf. iter. from ἔχω.

Ἔχετος, fabled king, βροτῶν δηλήμονα πάντων, φ 308. (Od.)

ἔχευα, ε, ατο, aor. from χέω, fudi.

ἐχέ-φρων, ονι, ονα, *thoughtful, prudent,* I 341. (Od.)

Ἐχέ-φρων, son of Nestor, γ 413.

ἔχησθα, subj. pres. from ἔχω.

ἐχθαίρουσι, pr. and ipf., aor. ἤχθηρε, (ἔχθος), oderunt, *hate,* γ 215.

ἔχθιστος (ἔχθος), *most hateful, most odious,* E 890. (Il.)

ἐχθοδοπῆσαι, aor., Ἥρῃ, *enter into hostilities against* Hera, A 518†.

ἔχθεσθαι, prs., ipf. ἤχθετο, (ἔχθος), odio esse, *be odious,* δ 756. (Od.)

ἔχθος, pl. εα, *hate, wrath,* ι 277.

ἐχθρός, fem. ῆς, αί, ntr. όν, *hateful,* ι 312.

Ἐχῖναι, a group of islands in the Ionian Sea, near Dulichion, B 625†.

Ἐχίος (ῐ), (1) father of Mekisteus, Θ 333.—(2) a Lykian, slain by Patroklos, Π 416.—(3) a Lykian, slain by Polites, O 339.

ἔχματα, pl., (ἔχω), *prop, support* (earth under mass of rock), Ξ 410, N 139; *bearers* of the towers, M 260; Φ 259, mud, rubbish from canal (as *holding back* the flow of water).

ἔχω, ipf. εἶχον and ἔχεν, iter. ἔχεσκον, ες, ε, fut. ἕξω, σχήσω, aor. ἔσχον, inf. σχέμεν, fut. mid. ἕξεται, σχήσεσθε, αι, aor. mid. ἐσχόμην, imp. σχέο, parallel forms, aor. ἔσχεθον, inf. σχεθέειν, Ψ 466. —**I. trans.** (1) tenere, *hold,* τί, ὑψοῦ, Z 509; (μετὰ) χερσί (Ω 724), Υ 420; πρόσθεν, Δ 113; ἀπὸ ἕο, out before him, N 163; ὄπιθεν, Ψ 136; τινά, ζ 281, τ 228, Σ 580; τινὰ ποδός, etc., Π 763, Δ 154, by the foot, hand, etc.; (ἐν) φρεσί (ο 445), B 33; πένθος, σ 324; *possess,* ρ 81; H 102, cords of victory *are held; hold together,* λ 219; *close,* M 456, χ 128; *enclose,* X 324; *shut out,* ι 301; *hold back,* τί τινι, Λ 96; τί τινος, δ 758; τινά, Λ 820, N 51, 687, Υ 27; τί τινι, *withhold,* ο 230; ἀμφίς, keep apart, α 54; *restrain,* T 119, X 412; tears, π 191; *choke,* T 418, τ 458; *let rest,* θ 537; sustineo, *hold ground, stand,* M 433, K 264; tenere, *guide, steer,* νῆα, ι 279; ἵππους, N 326; ἐπί τινι, χ 75, E 240; -δέ, Γ 263, Θ 139.—(2) habere, *have,* in widest signif., ἕλκος, πόνον, ποθήν, νόον; periphrasis with part., ξ 416, A 356; ἐπιδευὴς δίκης, have less, be lacking in what is right; *occupy,* ψ 46; *understand,* P 476; possideo, α 402, Γ 282; *inhabit, rest upon,* E 890, ζ 177, 183, μ 76, ν 245; *have as wife,* δ 569, pass., Z 398; *be lord over, care for, dispense,* α 53, δ 737, Λ 272; *manage,* T 43; *be heavy upon, compel,* κ 160, ξ 239; *abide with,* I 609; of mental states, etc., θάμβος ἔχει τινά, *seize,* cf. α 95, Φ 543; ὕπνος, ο 7; οἶνος, σ 391; ω 249, no kindly care awaits thee; pass., *be absorbed by,* X 409, ν 2; gestare, *wear, carry,* ρ 24, T 18, B 872; *indulge,* ὕβριν, δ 627; *practice,* χ 445; *make,* Π 105, Σ 495; keep, σκοπιήν, θ 302; *be able,* Π 110, μ 433. —**II. intr.** *persist,* Ω 27; ω 245, *goes on* well; *rise,* ὑψόσε, τ 38.—**III. mid.** *hold one's self fast, cling closely,* μ 433; to, τινός, ε 429; *hold ground, stand,* Π 501, I 235, P 639; *control one's self,* ρ 238; abstinere, *cease,* τινός, B 98, ν 151, N 630; στῆ σχομένη, stood still, ζ 141; haerere, *stick in the throat,* δ 705; ἄχεϊ, held fast by, not being able to get rid of, λ 279; πρὸς ἀλλήλῃσιν, sticking to one another, ε 329; pendere de, ἐκ, λ 346; *let be,* my friends, cessare, β 70; gestare, *wear.*

ἑψιαάσθων, imp., and -ασθαι, inf. prs., (ἑψία), *make merry,* ρ 530; with dat., φ 429.

ἐῶ, ἐῷ, indic. and subj. pres. from ἐάω.

ἔωθεν, pf. from ἔθων. **ἐῴκει,** see εἴκω II.

ἐώλπει, plupf. from ἔλπω.

ἔωμεν, neither in form nor meaning understood, T 402†; we should perh. read **χέωμεν** (from ΧΑσκω, χῆρος, cf. στέωμεν, φθέωμεν), aor. subj., when we *separate, withdraw ourselves* (with gen.) from battle.

ἐών, part. from εἰμί. **ἐῳνοχόει,** ipf. from οἰνοχοέω. **ἐώργει,** plupf. from ἔρδω.

ἕως [⏑ –, only β 78; elsewh. pronounced with synizesis, P 727, ε 123], **εἵως,** ν 315, and **εἷος** (should perh. be written ἧος), δ 90, ν 315, ο 153, etc.— I. quamdiu, *as long as,* ρ 358, followed in apodosis by τέως, τόφρα, δέ; quoad, *until,* with indic., ε 123; with subj. and κέ final, P 622, Ω 154; with opt. after past tenses, ε 386, with κέ, β 78; purely final=ut, δ 800, ι 376.—II. aliquamdiu (μέν), β 148.

ἕωσι, subj. pres. from εἰμί. **ἐῶσι,** from ἐάω.

Ἑωσ-φόρος, Lucifer, *morning star,* Ψ 226†.

Z.

ζα-, intensive prefix (from διά)= per-, *very*.

ζαής, acc. ζαῆν, (ἄημι), *strongly blowing, tempestuous*, μ 313.

ζα-θέοισι, ην, ας, *very divine, sacred*, of localities favored by the gods, O 432. (Il.)

ζά-κοτον, acc., (κότος), *surly, morose*, Γ 220†.

Ζάκυνθος, woody island in realm of Odysseus; now Zante, α 246, B 634. [ᾰ]

ζα-τρεφέων, έας, pl., (τρέφω), *sleek*, ξ 19.

ζα-φλεγέες, pl., (φλέγω), *full of fire*, Φ 465†.

ζα-χρηεῖς, ειῶν, (χράω), impetuosi, *raging, bold*, M 360. (Il.)

ζάω, see ζώω.

ζειαί, άς, *a coarse kind of barley, spelt*, δ 41, 604.

ζεί-δωρος, ον, (ζειή, δῶρον), *grain-giving* (plough-land, ἄρουρα), μ 386.

Ζέλεια, town at the base of Mount Ida in Troas, B 824. (Il.)

ζέσσεν, aor. from ζέω.

ζεύγλης, gen., (ζευγνύναι), *cushion between the neck and the yoke*, P 440. (Il.) (See cut No. 77, also 49, letter *d*.)

ζευγνύμεναι, ῦμεν, inf. prs., Π 145; aor. ἔζευξαν, ζεῦξε, iungo, *put to, yoke*, ὑπ' ὄχεσφιν, ὑφ' ἅρματα, ὑφ' ἅρμασιν; only Υ 495, *couple together;* also mid., *put to for one's self*. Pass. σανίδες ἐζευγμέναι, Σ 276, *joined*, i. e. *barred* gates. (See cut under δικλίδες.)

ζεύγεα, pl., from τὸ ζεῦγος, *a yoke, a pair* (of draught animals), Σ 543†.

Ζεύς, Διός, Διόθεν, Διί, Δία, and Ζήν, Ζηνός, Ζηνί, Ζῆνα, and Ζῆν' (not Ζῆν), *Zeus*, the father of gods and of men; also simply Ζεῦ πάτερ, (Diespiter), ὑψίζυγος; αἰθέρι ναίων, hence god of time; B 134, god of weather and of the clouds; Διὸς ὄμβρος, εὐρύοπα, ἐρίγδουπος πόσις Ἥρης, αἰγίοχος, ὑψιβρεμέτης, νεφεληγερέτα, κελαινεφέα, στεροπηγερέτα, τερπικέραυνος, ἀστεροπητῇ, ἀργικέραυνε, ἐριβρεμέτεω; hence sender of portents, τέραα, πανομφαίῳ; shaper of destiny, Διὸς τάλαντα, Π 658; βουλή, αἶσα, ὄσσα, α 282; θέμιστες, μητίετα, δοιοὶ πίθοι, Ω 527; protector of kings, διοτρεφέων, and διογενής; of beggars and suppliants, ξείνιος, ἱκετήσιος; of house and court, ἑρκείου; presides over fulfillment of oaths; ταμίης πολέμοιο.—Διὸς υἱός, esp. Herakles; κούρη, Athena; κοῦραι, the Λιταί and the Nymphs; Zeus himself is the son of Kronos, Κρονίδης, Κρονίων. His majestic person described, A 530; chief seat of his worship, Dodona, Π 233. The orig. meaning of the root of the word is the *brightness of the sky*, afterward personified; cf. δῖος, Lat. sub divo, *under the clear sky*.

Ζεφυρίη πνείουσα, *the western breeze*, η 119†, adj. from

ζέφυρος, only sing., (ζόφος), the rough *west wind*, the swiftest, bringing (to Asia Minor) rain and snow, only in fable land is it soft and balmy, η 119, δ 567; personified, Π 150, Ψ 200.

ζέω, **ζεῖ**, ipf. ζέεν, aor. ζέσσεν, fervet, *boil*, ὕδωρ; a caldron, Φ 362.

Ζῆθος, son of Zeus and of Antiope; with Amphion, founder of Thebes, λ 262; father of Itylos, τ 523.

ζηλήμονες, pl., *grudging, jealous*, ε 118†.

Ζήν, Ζῆν', see Ζεύς.

ζήτει, ipf. from ζητέω, requirebat, *seek*, Ξ 258†.

ζόφον, ον, (ζόφος, δνόφος), *darkness*, (1) *darkness of evening* into which the light of day (and fig. every thing living into death, υ 356, Ψ 51) subsides, γ 335; *evening* as region, *the setting sun, west*, ι 26, μ 81.—(2) *the realm of shadows*, O 191.

ζυγό-δεσμον, acc., *yoke-band*, cord or strap for fastening the yoke to the pole, Ω 270. (See cut under ζυγόν, *b*; and cut No. 45.)

ζυγόν, οῦ, όφιν, ῷ, ά, (jugum), (1) *yoke* or cross-bar by which beasts of draught were attached to whatever was to be drawn. (See adjacent cut, combined from several antique repre-

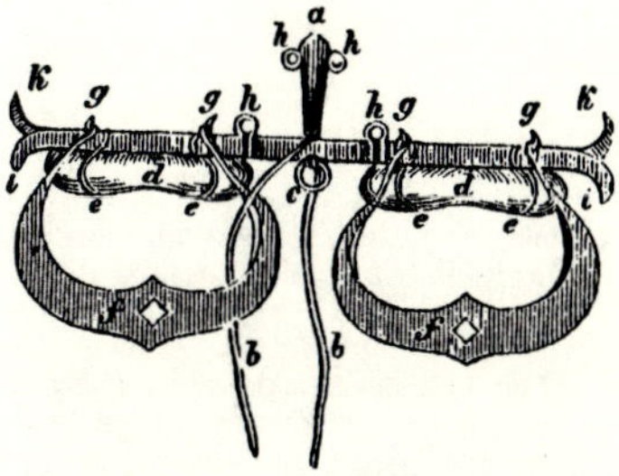

sentations.) *a*, ὀμφαλός; *b*, ζυγόδεσμος; *c*, κρίκος; *d*, ζεῦγλαι; *e*, straps to fasten in place the ζεῦγλαι; *f*, λέπαδνα; *g* and *h*, οἴηκες, points of attachment for the collars, and rings through which the reins pass; *i*, ζυγόν; *k*, projections to hold, e. g. the reins of the παρήορος. (Cf. also the Assyrian yoke on the chariot on board a ship, represented in adjoining cut.)—(2) *cross-*

bar of lyre (see φόρμιγξ), to which the strings were attached, I 187.—(3) pl., *cross-beams of ship* (see cut No. 35, under ἔδαφος).

ζω-άγρια, τά, (ζωός, ἄγρα), *reward for saving life*, Σ 407, θ 462.

ζώγρει, εἶτε, imp., (ζωός, ἀγρέω), *take alive*, i. e. *grant quarter*, τινά, K 378; only E 698, ipf. ζώγρει (ἐγείρω?), *revived, reanimated.*

ζωή, ήν, (ζάω), victus, *substance*, ξ 208. (Od.)

ζῶμα, ntr., (ζώννυμι), (1) *apron* of leather or of felt, extending from the flank to the upper part of the thigh, and serving to protect the part of the body left exposed between the cuirass and greaves (see cut under ἀστερόεντος; also cut No. 12, the figure of Aineias).—(2) *broad girdle* around the middle of boxers, like that of the tumbler in adjoining cut, Ψ 683.

ζώνην, acc., (ζώννυμι), (1) *woman's girdle* (see cut, also Nos. 47 and 65).—(2) *the waist*, B 479, Λ 234.

ζώννυσθαι, ipf. ζώννυτο and iter. ζωννύσκετο, aor. act. ζώσαντες, cingere, *put a girdle round the loins*, σ 76; elsewh. mid. se accingere, *gird one's self* (for combat), σ 30; *gird one's self with, gird on*, τί, Ψ 130; τινί, K 78; ζώννυνται, ω 89, is subjunctive.

ζωός, masc. (exc. λ 86, Σ 418), and **ζώς,** E 887; acc. ζών, Π 445, vivus, *living.*

ζωρότερον (ζωρός) κέραιε, make the mixture *stronger*, I 203†.

ζωστήρ, ῆρος, ὁ, (ζώννυμι), (1) *warrior's body-girdle*, of leather strengthened with metal plates, which covered the lower part of the θώρηξ, and the upper part of the μίτρη and of the ζῶμα (see cuts Nos. 78 [where the ζωστήρ is very broad], 3, and 85). (Il.)—(2) *girdle worn over the tunic*, ξ 72. (See cut No. 79.)

ζῶστρα, pl., (ζωστήρ), *girdles, belts* (that could be washed), ζ 38†.

ζώω, inf. ζωέμεν(αι) and -ειν, part. ζώοντος (and ζῶντος, A 88, from ζάω), ipf. ἔζωον, vivo, *live*, joined with ὁρᾶν φάος ἠελίοιο, δ 833 and freq.; with ἔστιν, ω 263; ῥεῖα ζώοντες, who live at ease.

H.

I. **ἦ**, particle of asseveration (*διαβεβαιωτικός*), always at beginning of sentence (*ἀρκτικός*), confirms an assertion (expressing subjective certainty); *in truth, certainly, to be sure* (usually with other particles), A 78, 229, 240, 254, 255; with particles expressing objective certainty: *γάρ*, yes to be sure, A 293; *δή*, evidently to be sure, A 518, *α* 384; with particles expressing subjective certainty: *μάν, μέν*, A 77, 140, 211; *μήν* (*καί*), nimirum (etiam), verily, B 291; *μάλα* (*δή*), most certainly indeed, Γ 204, *ι* 507, *σ* 201; *ἦ τοι*, q. v.; *που*, surely methinks; *ἄρα*, T 56, *μ* 280; *ἦ ῥά νυ*, M 164; *θήν, νυ, τε, κάρτα, μάλα*, *β* 325, *υ* 304.—Here belongs also **ἦ ποτ' ἔην γε** (acc. to G. Curtius instead of *εἰ*), yes (=alas!), it was he. —*ἦ* is also joined with other particles: **ἐπεὶ ἦ** (not so good *ἐπειή*) *πολὺ φέρτερος* (*μάλα*), *since in truth*, *ι* 276, A 156, 169, *κ* 465 [always ◡◡–]; and **τί ἦ**, why then, A 365, Z 55.

II. **ἦ** or **ἦε** (accent of ancient grammarians), interrogative particle, (1) [*ἐρωτηματικός*] (a) in simple direct question, *ἦ καί μοι νεμεσήσεαι*, *α* 158, A 133, 203; (b) in double direct question, utrum, *β* 30, 32.—(2) [*διαπορητικός, ἀπορηματικός*] in second member of a double question, cf. Lat. an (also *ἤ, ἠέ*); the double question may be: (a) direct, *β* 30, 32, *υ* 130; or (b) indirect, *α* 175, *λ* 493, 495; common phrase, *ἦε καὶ οὐκί*, or also not, *δ* 80.

ἤ or **ἠέ** (accent of ancient grammarians), A. simply interrogative, (1) =*εἰ*, *whether*, in indir. single question, *πευσόμενος ἤ που ἔτ' εἴης*, *ν* 415; (2) utrum, in indir. double question (*εἰ*, B 367), *οὐκ οἶδ' ἤ τις—ἠὲ καί*, *δ* 712, *α* 408.—B. [*διαζευκτικός*] (1) disjunctive, (a) aut, vel, sive, only in second or subsequent member of sentence, separating single ideas (vel, A 62) or clauses (aut, A 515); (b) *ἤ* may be several times repeated, cf. aut—aut, A 138; sive—sive, *β* 29, Σ 308, *ξ* 183, I 701, X 253, *ο* 300.—(2) in questions: (a) simple question marking opposition, *α* 391, or, dost thou hold? also *α* 298; (b) to continue an inquiry: or is it that? *β* 32; or indeed, *υ* 167 (in both these last cases it is better to read *ἦ*, an, and also in *ι* 253, *φ* 197). Many modern grammarians accent as oxytone (*ἤ*) the *ἦ*, an, of the previous article, II., *ἦ*, 2.—(3) *ἤ* comparative, quam, *than*; after comparatives, A 162; after *ἄλλος, ἕτερος, βούλεσθαι*, malle, A 112 (sc. *ἤ ἄποινα δέχεσθαι*); *ἔφθης*, *λ* 58. [*ἤ οὐκ* are usually pronounced as one syllable by synizesis.]

III. **ἦ**, aor. of defective verb (ait), always following a passage in oratio recta, and succeeded by (*ῥα*) *καί*, *he said*, and, *β* 321; *σ* 356, *ἦ ῥ' ἅμα τε*.

ᾗ, qua, corresponds to *τῇ*, ea, N 53.

ᾗ θέμις *ἐστίν*, sicut fas est, *as is right*, relative, B 73, *γ* 45, and freq.; demonstrative only *ω* 286.

ἦα=*ἔα*=*ἦν*, eram. **ᾖα**=*ᾔια* only *ε* 266, *ι* 212, at end of verse.

ἠβαιόν, αἰ, always at end of verse after *οὐδ'*, ne paululum (parvae) quidem, not even a (*very*) *little*; without neg. and in middle of verse, only *ι* 462, paulum, *a little way*.

ἡβάω, **ἡβῷμι**, *-ώοιμι* opt., *-ῶν, -ώοντες, -ώωσα* part. prs., *ἡβήσας*, *ψ* aor., *be in youth's prime*; *ε* 69, *luxuriant*.

ἥβη, only sing., pubertas, *youth*; *ἥβης μέτρον*, youthful prime; also vigor, *youthful strength*, Π 857.

Ἥβη, *Hebe*, daughter of Zeus and of Hera, wife of Herakles, *λ* 603; in Iliad she always appears as goddess performing some manual service for other divinities.

ἡβῷμι, *ἡβώοιμι*, see *ἡβάω*. **ἠγάασθε**, see *ἄγαμαι*. **ἤγαγον**, *-όμην*, see *ἄγω*.

ἠγά-θεον, *ἐῃ, έην*, (*ἄγαν, θεός*? or perh. from *θέα*=*beautiful*?), *sacred, very divine*, of localities, Z 133, *δ* 702.

ἤγειρα, aor. (1) from *ἀγείρω*, collegi.—(2) from *ἐγείρω*, excitavi.

ἠγάσσατο, aor. from *ἄγαμαι*, admiratus est.

ἡγεμονεύειν, prs., ipf., fut., (ἡγεμών), *lead the way for; τινί, conduct; πρόσθεν,* go in advance; ὁδόν, point out the way; τινί, ῥόον ὕδατι.—(2) (Il.) ducere exercitum, *lead* (the army), Π 92; τινῶν, B 527; τισίν, only B 816.

ἡγεμών, no dat. sing., dat. pl. -μόνεσσιν, (ἡγέομαι), *leader, guide* (Od.); *commander, chief,* opp. λαοί, B 365. (Il.)

ἡγέομαι, **ἡγείσθω,** imp., ipf. fut. 1 aor., in signif. and construction = ἡγεμονεύειν, (1) *guide, lead the way for,* opp. (ἅμ') ἕπεσθαι (M 251), θ 46, cf. β 405; πρόσθεν, Ω 96; craftily, X 247; in his folly, foolishly, ω 469.—(2) ducere, τισίν (τινῶν), aliquos, might *lead* them to their ranks, B 687; but E 211, Τρώεσσιν, dat. advantage.

ἠγερέθονται, εσθαι, ipf. -οντο, (ἀγείρω), *assemble themselves* (gradually one by one), Γ 231.

ἤγερθεν, aor. pass. from ἀγείρω = congregati sunt.

ἡγηλάζεις, ει, prs., (ἡγέομαι), *guide, lead,* ρ 217; λ 618, leadest some such wretched life as I.

ἡγήτορι, α, ι, ες, (ἡγήτωρ, ἡγεῖσθαι), duci, *leader,* λαῶν; freq. with μέδοντες, *chiefs in war* and leaders in council; principi, α 105.

ἠγοράασθε, ἠγορόωντο, ipf. from ἀγοράομαι, *sit in council, hold assembly.*

ἠδέ (orig. following ἠμέν), et, *and, also,* B 27, 79; with ἔτι, B 118; joined with καί, *and also,* A 334; O 663, ἠδὲ—καὶ—ἠδέ; with τέ, Z 446; ἠδὲ—καί, A 400; καί, Z 429 sq. See also ἰδέ.

ᾔδεα, ᾔδη, plupf. from οἶδα.

ἤδη (ἤ, δή), iam, *now,* in contrast (1) with what heretofore had no existence: *already,* A 250, β 89; καὶ ἄλλοτε, iam alias quoque; with part. B 663.—(2) contrasting the present moment with other time: *now,* A 456; *at once,* υ 315; with fut., α 303; with aor., Γ 98; freq. before or after νῦν: now at length, A 456; ξ 213, now already.

ἥδομαι, aor. **ἥσατο,** gavisus est, *rejoice,* ι 353†.

ἧδος, τό, (ἡδύς), commodum, *profit, advantage,* always in negative sense, μίνυνθα, οὐδέ τι, τί μοι (ἐστιν, ἔσσεταί τινος); paullum, neque quidquam, quid expediet? A 576, Λ 318, ω 95.

ἡδυ-επής, *sweet-speaking,* suaviloquens, A 248†.

ἡδύ-ποτοιο (ποτόν), *sweet to drink,* β 340. (Od.)

ἡδύς, εῖα, ύ, έος, ει, ύν, εῖαν, (σϜαδ-, εὔαδε, suavis, Eng. sweet), *sweet; ἡδὺ* γέλασσαν, dulce (heartily) riserunt; κνώσσουσα, softly slumbering, δ 809.

ἤε, ἠέ, see II. ἤ, ἤ. **ἦε,** erat, from εἰμί.

ᾐείδεις, ης, ει, εν, noverat, see ΕΙΔ IV.

ἠέλιος, only sing., [θ 271, Ἥλιος], (Lat. Ausēlius), sol, *sun;* sunrise, Λ 735, γ 1, τ 433; ἀντολαί, μ 4; midday, Θ 68; afternoon, Π 779, η 289; sunset, A 605, 475, Θ 485, β 388, κ 191; τροπαί, ο 404; πύλας, ω 12; his curved path in the heavens, (ὑπερίονος, α 8), λ 16, H 421, Θ 68; phrases signifying to shine, Λ 735, ἐπέλαμψε, ἀκτῖσιν ἔβαλλε, ἐπιδέρκεται ἀκτίνεσσιν, φάος (as figure of life, λ 93, Σ 11, 61, δ 540), αὐγή, ὑπ' αὐγάς, αἴγλη; μένος, vis, heat, Ψ 190, κ 160; epithets, ἀκάμαντα, (λαμπρός, τ 234; λευκός, Ξ 185), παμφανόωντα, φαεσίμβροτος; expressions for east, ν 240, M 239, (and west, κ 191).—*Sun* as god, cf. Lat. Sol, observing all things, Γ 277, Ξ 344, θ 271, (yet not so, μ 375); father of Kirke, κ 138; of Phaethusa and Lampetie, μ 133; propitiated by sacrifice, Γ 104, Τ 197; oath by the sun, Τ 259; his βόες καὶ μῆλα, μ 128, 322, τ 276, ψ 329.

ἦεν, erat. **ἠέπερ,** see ἤπερ.

ἠερέθονται, prs., ντο ipf., (ἀείρω), *float, flutter,* Φ 12; Γ 108, *be unsteady.*

Ἠερίβοια, μητρυιή of the Aloidae, second wife of Aloeus, E 389.

ἠέριοι, η, αι, (ἀήρ), matutini, *at early morn,* A 497, ι 52.

ἠερο-ειδέι, έα, ές, (-ειδής), *cloudy-gray,* πόντον, σπέος, πέτρην; but E 770, quantum acrium prospicit = as far as one sees *in the dim distance,* i. e. *through the haze.*

ἠερόεντος, τα, (ἀήρ), *cloudy, dark,* ζόφου; only Θ 13, Τάρταρον, and υ 64, κέλευθα.

ἠέρος, see ἀήρ.

ἠερο-φοῖτις (φοιτᾶν) Ἐρινύς, *walking in darkness,* I 571. (Il.)

ἠερο-φώνων (ἀείρω, φωνή), vocem tollentium, *loud-voiced,* Σ 505†.

Ἠετίων, ωνος, α, (1) father of Andromache, king of Thebe in Troas, Z 396, A 366.—(2) of Imbros, guest-friend of Priamos, Φ 43.—(3) a Trojan, P 590.

ἤην, erat, see *εἰμί.*

ἠήρ (see *ἀήρ*), **ἠέρος,** *ι, α,* fem., *fog, mist,* λ 15; esp. as means of rendering invisible, Γ 381; *darkness,* η 15 (41), 143; *πουλύν,* masc., from necessity of the verse, E 776.

ἠθεῖον, acc., *ἠθεῖε* voc., fem. *εἴη,* (*ἦθος,* suetus), carus, *beloved, dear,* ξ 147.

ἤθεα, pl. from *ἦθος,* (suetus), *accustomed places, haunts,* Z 511; ξ 411, *pens.*

ἤια, *τά,* (*ἰέναι*), pronounced with synizesis at end of verse, *ἤjα,* viaticum, *provisions, food,* N 103. (Od.)

ἠίων, *τῶν,* (*ἄημι?*), synizesis *ἠjων, chaff,* ε 368†.

ἤιε, ibat, from *εἶμι.*

ἠίθεος, *ον, οι,* (viduus), *unmarried youth,* Σ 567. [ῐ]

ἤικτο, *resembled,* see II. *εἴκω.*

ἤιξε, *sprang,* aor. from *ἀίσσω.*

ἠϊόεντι, dat., (*ἠιών*), *with changing banks,* E 36†; since rivers, like the Skamander, in warm countries, and with sources in near mountains, have in consequence of rains a broad, ragged bed out of all proportion to the ordinary size of the stream, and banks ragged and often high.

ἤιον, iverunt, from *εἶμι.*

Ἠϊόνες, sea-port in Argolis, B 561†.

Ἠιονεύς, (1) father of Thrakian king Rhesos, K 435.—(2) a Greek, slain by Hektor, H 11†.

ἤιε Φοῖβε, apostrophized, O 365, Υ 152, *gleaming* [?]. (*αὔως.*)

ἤισαν, iverunt, see *εἶμι.* **ἠίχθη,** aor. pass. from *ἀίσσω.*

ἠιών, **ἠϊόνος,** *α, ες, εσσι, ας,* fem., *shore, strand,* M 31, ζ 138.

ἦκα (*Ϝῆκα*), placide, *softly, gently, slightly,* Γ 155.

ἧκα, *ες, αν,* etc., misi, from *ἵημι.*

ἤκαχε, *troubled,* aor. from *ἀκαχίζω.*

ἠκέσατο, sanavit, *healed,* aor. from *ἀκέομαι.*

ἠ-κέστας, acc. pl., (*κεντέω*), *having never felt the lash, untamed,* Z 94. (Il.)

ἥκιστος (*Ϝῆκα*), *slowest, most sluggish,* Ψ 531†.

ἥκω, *ειν,* adveni, *come,* E 478, ν 325.

ἠλάκατα, *τά, wool,* or *woolen thread on distaff*; *στρωφῶσα, στροφαλίζετε,* ply the distaff, σ 315. (Od.) (See the first of the cuts below.) [ᾰ ᾰ]

ἠλᾰκάτη, *ην,* (*ἀράχνη*), *spindle,* Z 491. (Od.) (See the cuts, representing distaff and spindles.)

ἤλασα, *εν, αν, ἠμεσθα,* aor. act. and mid. from *ἐλάω.*

ἠλασκάζει, prs., *ων,* (*ἠλάσκω*), vagans, *wander;* ι 457, vagando effugiat.

ἠλάσκουσι, pres., and part. -*ουσαι,* (*ἀλάομαι*), *prowl about, swarm about,* B 470. (Il.)

ἠλᾶτο, vagabatur, from *ἀλάομαι.*

ἤλδανε, aluit, from *ἀλδαίνω.*

ἠλέ, see *ἠλεός.*

Ἠλεῖοι, *inhabitants of Elis,* Λ 671†.

ἠλέκτρου, *οισιν,* (*ἠλέκτωρ*), *amber,* δ 73. (Od.)

ἠλέκτωρ, splendens, *beaming* (sun), with and without *Ὑπερίων,* T 398, Z 513. (Il.)

ἠλεός, voc. *έ* and *ἠλέ, infatuated, crazed, φρένας,* in mind=*mad;* ξ 464, *confusing, maddening.*

ἠλήλατο, penetraverat, plupf. pass. from *ἐλάω.*

ἠλίβᾰτος, *ον, οι, steep, lofty,* ι 243, O 273.

ἠλῐθα *πολλή(ν),* satis multum, *very* much, Λ 677.

ἠλῐκίην (*ἧλιξ*), aetatem, *equals in age, fellows,* Π 808. (Il.)

ἥλῐκες, pl. from *ἧλιξ,* adultae, *full-grown,* σ 373†.

ἥλιος, see *ἠέλιος.*

Ἦλις, *ιδος, Elis,* division of Peloponnesos on west coast, inhabited in the north by Epeioi, in the south by Achaioi, B 615, δ 635.

ἤλιτε, aor. from ἀλιταίνω, peccavit.

ἠλῐτό-μηνον (ἀλιτεῖν, μήν), *untimely born*, T 118†.

ἤλκησε, aor., vim attulerat, from ἑλκέω.

ἧλοι, οισι, *nails, studs*, Λ 29. (Il.)

ἤλυθον, ες, aor. from ἔρχομαι.

Ἠλύσιον πεδίον, *Elysian fields*, abode of the blest, δ 563 sqq.† [ῡ]

ἤλφον, aor., (ἀλφεῖν), *have gained.*

ἥλω, capta est, aor. from ἁλίσκομαι.

ἠλώμην, vagabar, from ἀλάομαι.

Ἠλώνη, a city in Phthiotis, B 739†.

ἡμᾰσιν, dat. pl., (ἵημι), *at javelin throwing*, Ψ 891†.

Ἠμᾰθίη, ancient name of Makedonia, Ξ 226†.

ἠμαθόεντος, ι, α, comm., (ἄμαθος), arenosa, *sandy*, epithet of Pylos, α 93.

ἧμαι, σαι, σται, 3 pl. (ἧνται), ἕαται, εἵαται, imp. ἧσο, inf. ἧσθαι, part. ἥμενος, ipf. ἥμην, στο, σθην, 3 pl. ἧντο, ἕατο, εἵατο, sedeo, *sit*, ἥμενος ἢ ἕρπων, ρ 158; often with collateral meaning supplied by part. with which it is joined, A 134, B 137, Δ 412.

ἦμαρ, ατος, ατι, ατα, *day*, (a) as opposed to night, E 490; (b) *division of the year, season*, χειμέριον, etc.; (c) periphrastically with adj., e. g. ἐλεύθερον ἦμαρ, condition of freedom; δούλιον—, servitus; νόστιμον—, reditus, Z 455, σ 137; ἤματα πάντα, *always, forever; ἐπ' ἤματι, in one day*, but T 229, *one whole day;* ἤματι τῷ ὅτε, tum quum, B 351.

ἠμᾰτίη, αι, adj., (ἦμαρ), (1) diurna, die, *by day*, β 104.—(2) quotidianae, *daily*, I 72.

ἤμβροτον, ες = ἥμαρτον, ες, *missed.*

ἡμεῖς and ἄμμες, ἡμείων, -έων; ἄμμῐ(ν), ἡμῖν, encl. ἥμιν; ἄμμε, ἡμέᾶς (ἡμῆᾰς), ἧμας only π 372, *we.*

ἠμέν, usually corresponding to ἠδέ (καί), δέ, τέ, καί; *both, as well*, Π 664.

ἡμέρη, pl. αι, (other forms from ἦμαρ), dies, *day.*

ἡμερίς, ἡ, (ἥμερος), *cultivated vine*, ε 69†.

ἥμερον, acc., cicurem, *tame*, ο 162†.

ἡμέτερος, η, ον, etc., (ἡμεῖς), noster, *our;* ntr. subst. with εἰς-, -δε and ἐφ ἡμέτερα = *home*, β 55.

ἡμῐ- = semi-, *half-.*

ἡμῐ-δαής (δαίω), semiusta, *half-burnt*, Π 294†.

ἡμῐ-θέων, semi-deorum, *demigods*, M 23†.

ἡμῐ-όνειον, ην, adj., (ἡμί-ονος), *belonging to a mule, mule-*, of chariot, yoke, Ω 268.

ἡμῐ-ονον, acc., etc., (nom. and dat. sing. wanting), comm., mulus, *mule*, Ψ 266, 655.

ἡμῐ-πέλεκκα, *half axes, one-edged axes*, Ψ 851. (Il.)

ἡμῐσεες, εων, ntr., υ, semis, γ 155; ntr. usually subst., *half*, ρ 322.

ἡμῐ-τάλαντον, *half a pound* (gold), Ψ 751, 796.

ἡμῐ-τελής, *half complete, desolate*, B 701†.

ἦμος, quum (temporal), *when*, always at beginning of verse, exc. μ 439; followed in apodosis by τῆμος (ἄρα), δὴ τότε, δὴ or καὶ τότ' ἔπειτα, or (δὴ) ἄρα with indic. of histor. tenses; with subj. (= pres.), only δ 400.

ἠμύει, prs., aor. ἤμῡσε, σειε, (κάρη, καρήατι, with head), *nod;* B 148, it, the ploughed field, nods (to the breeze), with its heads of grain.

ἥμονες, pl., (ἵημι), ἄνδρες, *darters*, Ψ 886†.

ἤν (εἰ ἄν), si, *if, when*, (1) with subj. of pres. expectation, the verb of the principal clause standing in; (α) imp., φ 237, π 274; (β) fut., I 394, Δ 353; (γ) opt., μ 288; (δ) prs. subj., μ 121, Θ 482.—(2) with subj. of repeated action, verb of principal clause being pres., A 166, λ 159; often with πέρ, σ 318.—(3) = *whether*, with subj., α 282. (εἰ ἄν, ἐάν, ἤν.)

ἠναίνετο, negabat, from ἀναίνομαι.

ἤνεικε, καντο, tulit, aor. from φέρω.

ἠνεμόεντα, acc., -όεσσα, αν, ας, (ἄνεμος), *windy, breezy, airy*, (of towns, mountains, trees), πτύχας, τ 432.

ἡνία, τά, frena, *reins*, often adorned with gold or ivory, σιγαλόεντα, E 226. [ῐ]

ἠνίκα, *when*, with indic., χ 198†. [ῐ]

Ἡνιοπεύς, ῆα, son of Thebaios,

charioteer of Hektor, slain by Diomedes, Θ 120†.

ἡνῐ-οχεύς, **ἡνῐοχῆα**, ες, ας, (Il.), = ἡνίοχος.

ἡνιόχευεν, ipf., (ἡνίοχος), *held the reins, guided, drove*, Ψ 642.

ἡνίοχος, οιο, ῳ, ον, οι, οισι, ους, (ἡνία, ἔχω), *charioteer*, θεράπων, E 580, etc. The charioteer stood usually left of the πρόμαχος; among the Assyrians, the warrior (armed with bow) had also a second attendant, shield-bearer, with himself on the chariot (see cut); the Egyptian monuments represent only one warrior or triumphing king upon the war-chariot.

ἧντο, sedebant, from ἧμαι.

ἤνυτο, successit, from ἄνυμι.

ἠνώγεα, ει, iussit, from ἄνωγα.

ἦξε, fregit, from ἄγνυμι.

ἠοῖον, acc., οι, ων, fem. ῃ, ην, (ἠώς), matutinus; subst. *morning, dawn*, δ 447; elsewh. orientalis, *eastern*.

ἦος, see ἕως.

ἧπαρ, ατι, dat., jecur, *liver*, ι 301.

ἤπαφε, ludificatus est, see παραπαφίσκω.

ἠπεδανός, *feeble, weakly*, θ 311, Θ 104.

ἤπειρος, **ἠπείροιο**, ου, ῳ, ον, fem., (ἀ-πείρω?), *mainland, terra firma*, opp. sea and islands, cf. esp., B 635;

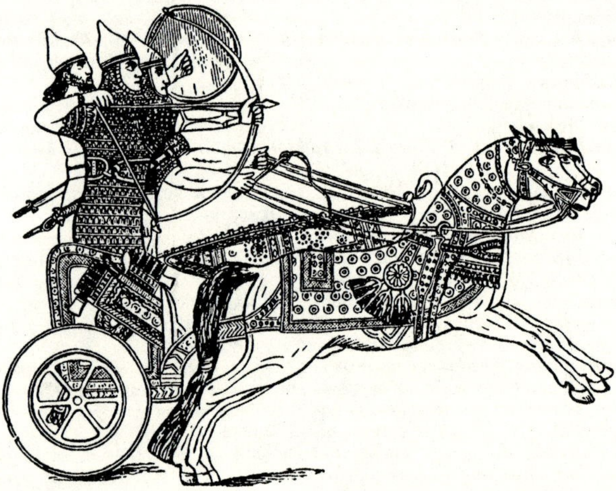

ἠνίπαπε, compellavit, *hail*, see ἐνίπτω.

ἦνῖν, acc. pl. ἦνῖς, (AN), *sleek, shining*, γ 382.

Ἠνοπίδης, Satnios, Ξ 444†. [ῐ]

ἠνορέη, ῃφι, ῃν, (ἀνήρ), *prowess, manhood*, Z 156.

ἤνοπι, dat., (ἦνοψ, AN), *gleaming, dazzling*, of naked metal, always with χαλκῷ, Π 408.

Ἤνοψ, (1) father of Satnios of Mysia, Ξ 445†.—(2) father of Klytomedes from Aitolia, Ψ 634.—(3) father of Thestor, of Troja, Π 401.

ἤντεον, obviam facti sunt, *meet*, from ἀντέω.

interior, opp. sea (coast), ι 49; yet used even of island, ε 56; ἤπειρόνδε, toward the land.

ἤπερ = ἠέπερ, quam, *than*, Ξ 468.

ᾗπερ (ὅσπερ), eadem qua, *just there* (thither), *where*, μ 81, Φ 4; *just as*, I 310.

ἠπεροπῆα, acc. from ἠπεροπεύς, λ 364†, and **ἠπεροπευτά**, voc. from -τής, *deceiver, seducer*, Γ 39 and N 769.

ἠπερ-οπεύεις, ει, ειν, prs., ipf. ἠπερόπευον, aor. -εύσῃς, (Ger. afterreden, ϝοπ), *deceive, cajole, seduce*, Γ 399.

ἠπῐό-δωρος (ἤπια), *kindly giving, bountiful*, Z 251†.

ἤπιος, ον, ον, η, α, *mild,* of persons, of remedies, Δ 218; of counsels, Δ 361.

ἠπύτα (ἠπύω), *loud voiced,* Η 384†.

Ἠπυτίδης, Periphas of Troja, P 324†.

ἠπύει, ipf. ἤπυε, *hail;* ρ 271, *sound shrill;* Ξ 399, *roar.*

ἦρα φέρειν τινί, also ἐπὶ . . . ἦρα, do a *favor,* gratify, humor, γ 164, Α 578 (Ϝῆρα, βούλομαι).

Ἡρακλείδης, (1) Tlepolemos, B 653. —(2) Thessalos, B 679.

Ἡρακλῆος, ηι, ῆα, often replaced in nom., as in other cases, by periphrasis, βίη Ἡρακληείη, voc. wanting, *Herakles,* son of Zeus and of Alkmene; his birth, T 98; ἄεθλοι, Θ 362, λ 623, φ 26; destroys Laomedon's Troja, Υ 145, E 642; makes conquest of Pylos, Λ 689 sqq., cf. also E 392, 397; death, Σ 117; his shade, λ 601; his wife (on earth) Megara (see Thessalos and Tlepolemos), in Olympos, Hebe. National hero. celebrated in popular songs before Homer's time, λ 602, 267. Epithets, θείοιο, θρασυμέμνονα, κρατερόφρονα; cf. φ 25.

Ἡρακληείη, ης, ῃ, ην, always with βίη, periphrasis for Herakles, Λ 690.

ἠράμεθα, see ἄρνυμι, *gain.*

ἤραρε, aor. from ἀραρίσκω.

ἤρατο, aor. mid. from αἴρω.

ἠρᾶτο, from ἀράομαι, precari.

Ἥρη, *Hera,* daughter of Kronos and of Rhea, sister and wife of Zeus; her education, Ξ 201 sqq.; relation to Zeus, Α 568, Ο 13, Ξ 153; hostile to Trojans; to Herakles; patron of Greeks; her children: Ares, Hephaistos, Hebe, Eileithyia; her favorite haunts, Argos, Mykenai, Sparta, Δ 51, 52. Epithets, Ἀργείη, βοῶπις πότνια, πρέσβα θεά, Διὸς κυδρὴ παράκοιτις; ἠυκόμοιο, λευκώλενος, χρυσόθρονος, χρυσοπεδίλου, Zeus gives her yet other (dishonorable) names, Ο 14; likewise Poseidon, Θ 209; δολοφρονέουσα.

ἠρήρει, plupf. from ἀραρίσκω.

ἠρήρειστο, plupf. pass. from ἐρείδω.

ἦρι, loc., (ἠέρι), mane, *at early morn,* I 360; with ἠῶθεν, τ 320.

ἠρι-γένεια, ης, αν, *early born,* epithet of ἠώς, δ 195. As substantive=Eos, *Child of dawn,* χ 197.

ἤριπε, fracta est, *break,* from ἐρείκω.

ἠρίον, τό, *sepulchral mound,* Ψ 126†.

ἤριπε, lapsus est, *slip,* from ἐρείπω.

ἤρυγε, vomuit, from ἐρεύγομαι. **ἠρῶ,** precabaris, from ἀράομαι. **ἠρώησαν,** cesserunt, *retire,* from ἐρωέω.

ἥρως, ωος, ωϊ (ῳ, Η 453, θ 483), ωα (ζ 303 [– ⏑ ⏑], ω' before vowels); pl. ωες, ώων, ώεσσι, ωας, *hero, warrior,* title of honor for the free and brave; standing alone as subst., Α 4, Κ 179; in address, Υ 104, Κ 416; with Δαναοί, Ἀχαιοί, likewise with single names, Δ 200, β 15, Φ 163; joined with θεράποντες Ἄρηος, B 110; γέρων, η 155. (Never=demigod.)

ἧσ' = (1) ἧσαι, Ο 245, sĕdes.—(2) ἧσο, π 44, conside.

ἧσαι, σται, sedes, sedet. **ἥσατο,** gavisus est, from ἥδομαι. **ἥσειν,** fut. from ἵημι. **ἦσθα,** eras.

ἤσκειν, *wrought,* ipf. from ἀσκέω.

ἧσο, conside, imp. from ἧμαι.

ἥσσων, pl. ονας, ntr. ον, deterior, ο 365; ὀλίγον ἧσσον, paullo minus, *little less.*

ἧσται, sedet. **ἥστην,** erant ambo.

ἡσυχίη, ἡ, quies, *peace, quiet,* σ 22†.

ἡσύχιον, acc. masc., tutum, *uninjured,* Φ 598†.

ᾐσχυμμένος, pf. pass. from αἰσχύνω.

ἤ τ' = ἤ τε, Γ 366.

ἤ τε—ἤ τε, sive—sive, *either—or.*

ᾐτιάασθε, όωντο, ipf. from αἰτιάομαι.

ἦ τοι (I. ἦ, and III. τοι), marks (1) calm assurance, *surely:* in address, Η 406, α 307, Η 191; in narration, Α 140, Ζ 201; after ἦ, ρ 372.—(2) marks antithesis=μέν, Α 68, ο 6, Η 188, Λ 487; quamquam, *and yet,* Χ 280; ἀλλ' ἦ τοι, but *by all means,* Α 211, Ω 48, ο 488, π 278; -μέν, sed vero, but *yet,* Α 140; with imp., *yet,* δ 238, κ 271; after ὡς, ε 24, and ὄφρα, γ 419; μέν before δέ, *by all means,* Γ 168; (ι 339 read ἤ τι; τοι, τ 599, is dat.).

ἦτορ, τό, *heart,* not as bodily organ, though used as synonymous with κραδίη, Κ 93; κῆρ, P 535; likewise with θυμός; also with ἐνὶ φρεσί, Π 242, Τ 169, Θ 413, ν 320, cf. B 490; ἐν κραδίῃ, Υ 169; synonymous with anima, Ν 84, Φ 201; *life,* E 250; *power of thought, mind,* Α 188; *heart, feelings,* I 497, 572; seat of astonishment, ρ 514; of joy, Ψ 647; of grief, E 364; of hope, π 92; of fear, Γ 31; of courage, Π 209; of desire, Ε 670; of wrath, Ξ 367; of appetite, Τ 307, Ι 705.

ἠυ-γένειος (*γένειον*), with *λίς* at end of verse (Il.), *δ* 456, with *λέων*, *strong-bearded*, from the long hairs ("feelers") around the lion's jaws.

ηὔδα, locutus est, ipf. from *αὐδάω*.

ἠΰ-κομος, οιο, (*κόμη*), *beautiful-, fair-haired*, Α 36.

ἠΰς, *ύν*, *ύ*, see *ἐΰς*.

ἤυσε, clamavit, from *ἀΰω*.

ἠΰτε (*ἠϝέ τε*), *as also*, (1) quam, *as*, *comparable to*, Δ 277.—(2) tanquam, quasi, *as it were*, Α 359.—(3) ceu cum, *as when*, *like*, Β 87.

Ἥφαιστος, no dat., (*σϝη-*, per se, *φαίνων*?), son of Zeus and of Hera, god of fire, and of arts which need the aid of fire; his wife, Charis, Σ 382 sqq.; but in Odyssey, the faithless Aphrodite; from childhood on, *ἀμφιγυήεις*, *κυλλοποδίων*, Σ 395 sqq.; his favorite abode, Α 593, *θ* 283; chief works: armor of Achilleus; net in which he entrapped Ares and Aphrodite, *θ* 274; brazen houses of gods on Olympos and their outfit; sceptre and aegis of Zeus; his titles, *χαλκεύς*, *κλυτοτέχνης*, *κλυτόεργον*, *κλυτόμητιν*, *πολύφρονος*, *περίκλυτος*, *πολυμήτιος*. Hephaistos is orig. nothing else than the element of fire, as may be recognized in Ι 468, and esp. in Β 426.

ἦφι (*σϝῆφι*, see *ὅς*) *βίηφι*, sua (vi), Χ 107†.

ἠχή, *ῇ*, (*ἠχώ*), *noise*, *roar*, *hum*, Β 209, Π 769.

ἠχήεντα, ntr., *ήεσσα*, fem., (*ἠχή*), *echoing*, *δ* 72; *roaring*, Α 157.

ἤχθετο, ipf. from *ἄχθομαι* and *ἔχθομαι*.

ἦχι, ubi, *where*, Α 607.

ἠῶθεν (*ἠώς*), mane, *early*; cras mane, *to-morrow at dawn*, Σ 136; with *μάλ' ἦρι*, cras multo mane.

ἠῶθι πρό, *before daybreak*, Λ 50.

ἠώς, *οῦς*, *οῖ*, *ῶ*, (aurora), *daybreak*, Φ 111, π 2; *dawn*, ε 390; cras mane, Θ 470, λ 375; *day*, Ω 31; *east*, ι 26. Personified, **Ἠώς,** Eos, *Aurora*; her son Memnon, *δ* 188; husband, Tithonos, Λ 1, but cf. ε 121, ο 250; abode, μ 3, Λ 1, Τ 1, χ 197; Ἑωσφόρος, Ψ 226, precedes her as she drives her chariot aloft, ψ 246; epithets, *ἠριγένεια*, *ῥοδοδάκτυλος*, *δῖα*, *ἐΰθρονος*, *κροκόπεπλος*, *χρυσόθρονος*.

Θ.

θαάσσεις, *έμεν*, ipf. *θάασσε*, sedere, *sit*, Ο 124.

θαιρούς, acc. pl., (*θύρα*), *hinges* of door or gate, Μ 459†. (See cuts from Egyptian originals; also under *ἐπιβλής*, No. 38.)

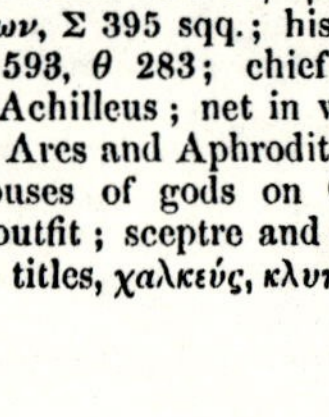

θάλάμης, gen., *bed*, *hole*, ε 432†.

θάλάμη-πόλος, *ἡ*, (*πέλεσθαι*, colere), *woman of the bedchamber*, *chambermaid*, η 8. (Od.)

θάλαμος, *ὁ*, no dat. pl., (*θέλυμνον*), *room* (opp. large hall, *μέγαρον δῶμα*), hence the rooms of the rear portion of the house [see table III., at end of volume], e. g. *women's chamber* (*δ* 121), *room for weapons* (τ 17), *store-room* (β 337), *bedchamber*, Γ 42[illegible].

θάλασσα, *ἡ*, (*ταράσσω*, orig. form *ταραχja*, Curtius), no pl., the *sea*, as element; when used of any particular sea it means the Mediterranean, Β 294.

θαλάσσια (*θάλασσα*) *ἔργα*, maritima (negotia), *belonging to the sea*, Β 614, ε 67.

θαλέθων, *οντες*, part., (*θάλλω*), *blooming*, ζ 63; *ἀλοιφῇ*, *teeming* with fat.

θάλεια, η, αν, (θάλος), always with δαίς, *abounding, goodly* feast, θ 76.

Θάλεια, name of a Nereid, Σ 39†.

θαλερός, οῖο, όν, ῷ, οἱ, ῶν, ούς, ή, ήν, (θάλλω), *blooming*, (1) *fresh, strong, thick*, μηρώ, χαίτη.—(2) *manly* voice was mute, φωνή; shedding *big* tears, δάκρυ; *rich, reeking*, ἀλοιφή; *thick and frequent* sob, γόος; entered into in the prime of youthful freshness, *blooming*, γάμος.

θᾰλέων, gen. pl. from τὸ θάλος, (θάλλω), *good cheer*, X 504†.

θαλίῃ, dat. pl. -ῃς, from ἡ θαλίη, (θάλλω), *abundance*, λ 603.

θαλλόν, acc. masc., (θάλλω), *foliage* (as fodder for goats), ρ 224†.

θάλλω, only pf. part. **τεθηλώς,** τεθαλυῖα, η, αν, plupf. τεθήλει, cf. θηλέω, *abound in, teem with*, dat.; part., *abundant, fresh*, ἐέρση, ν 245, cf. ε 467.

θάλος, acc., τό, (θάλλω), *shoot, scion*, X 87, ζ 157; see θαλέων.

θαλπιόων, part., (θάλπος), *warm*, τ 319†.

Θάλπιος, son of Eurytos, chief of the Epeians, B 620†.

θάλπων, οντες, part., (Od.), calefaciens, *warming*, φ 246.

θαλπωρή (θάλπω), *warming*, metaph. *comfort*, Z 412.

θᾰλύσια, τά, (θάλος), *offering of first-fruits, harvest offering*, I 534†. [ῡ]

Θᾰλῡσιάδης, Ἐχέπωλος, son of Thalysios, Δ 458†.

θᾰμά, frequenter, *often*, α 143, 209.

θαμβέω, only pl. ipf. **ἐθάμβεον,** aor. θάμβησεν, σαν, part. θαμβήσαντε, σασα, (θάμβος), *be struck with astonishment*, Γ 398, α 360; *gaze upon with wonder*, Ω 483.

θάμβος, ευς, ntr., *wonder, bewilderment*, ω 394.

θᾰμέες, έσι, έας, ειαί, ειάς, frequentes, *crowded, thick, frequent*, ε 252, Λ 552.

θαμίζεις, 2 sing. ind., and -ίζων part. prs., ipf. θάμιζε, frequentare, *come frequently, resort*; with part. = frequenter, θ 451.

θάμνος, ῳ, and pl., frondes, *bush, shrub, thicket*, ψ 190, Λ 156.

Θάμῠρις, Thrakian bard, vanquished and blinded by the Muses, B 595†. [ᾰ]

θάνᾰτος, sing., and οι μ 341, mors, nex, mortes; θανατόνδε, to *death*, Π 693. Personified, *Death*, twin-brother of Sleep, Ξ 231. [ᾰ ᾰ]

θάομαι, only 3 pl. 1 aor. **θησαίατο,** admirarentur, *admire*, σ 191†.

θάπτω, prs. ipf., 3 pl. aor. **θάψαν,** plupf. pass. ἐτέθαπτο, sepelire, *bury*, ὑπὸ χθονός, λ 52.

θαρσᾰλέος, ον, οι, η, ntr. comp. -εώτερον, adv. -έως, (θάρσος), ferox, *courageous, daring*; ρ 449, *impudent*.

θαρσέω, prs., pf. **τεθαρσήκασι,** also 1 aor., (θάρσος), *be bold*, also in bad signif. *be impudent*; part. *confident*; θ 197, with acc., *be of good courage* as regards the contest.

θάρσος, ους, ευς, (Eng. dare), audacia, *boldness*, also = *impudence*, P 570.

θάρσῡνος, adj., (θάρσος), *confident, relying upon*, οἰωνῷ, N 823.

θαρσύνω (subj.), prs., ipf. 1 sing. θάρσυνον, iter. θαρσύνεσκε, 2 sing. aor. θάρσυνας, (θάρσος), confirmare, *encourage*, Δ 233.

θάσσων, etc., comp. from ταχύς.

θαῦμα, τό, (θάομαι), miraculum, res mira, *wonder*, also with ἰδέσθαι, as exclamation, ρ 306; only κ 326, miratio, *surprise*.

θαυμάζω, prs., ipf. θαύμαζε, iter. -ξεσκον, mid. θαυμαζόμην, fut. θαυμάσσεται, aor. θαυμάσωσι, (θαῦμα), mirari, *wonder (at)*, B 320, γ 373; τινά, E 601, σ 411; τί, N 11, η 43; τό, on account of; with dependent sentence, B 320, Ω 629 sq.; with acc. and inf., E 601.

θαυμᾰνέοντες, fut. part. from θαυμαίνω, admiraturi, θ 108†.

Θαυμᾰκίη, town in Magnesia, under rule of Philoktetes, B 716†.

θάω, only mid. prs. inf. **θῆσθαι,** aor. θήσατο, *suck* (the breast of a mortal), Ω 58; *milk*, δ 89.

θεά, ᾶς, άν, αί, (**θέαιναι**), άων, ῇσι, ῇς, άς, dea, *goddess*, (opp. γυνή), Ξ 315, appos. with μήτηρ, νύμφαι.

Θεᾱνώ, Κισσηίς ἄλοχος Ἀντήνορος, Z 302, priestess of Athena in Ilios.

θέειον, only sing., sulfur, *sulphur*, as sacred instrument of purification; κακῶν ἄκος, χ 481; *with fumes of sulphur*, μ 417. (θέειον = θέϝειον, cf. θύω.)

θεειώσω, fut., and pres. mid. θεειοῦται, *fumigate and purify with brimstone* (one's house), ψ 50.

θεῖεν, opt. aor. from τίθημι.

θειλό-πεδον (θ' εἰλόπεδον?), *drying-*

place, a sunny spot in vineyard where grapes were dried, η 123†.

θεῖμεν, opt., θεῖναι inf. aor. from τίθημι.

θεινέμεν, inf., θείνῃ subj. prs., ipf. θεῖνε ἔθεινε, part. aor. θείνας and part. pres. pass., (fendo), *strike*, τινά τινι, with (the bow behind the ears), Φ 491.

θείομεν, subj. aor. from τίθημι.

θεῖος, ου, οιο, ον, ων, η, ης, ην, divinus, *divine*, B 41; also = *glorious*, β 341; sacer, H 298.

θείω, (1) = θέω, curro.—(2) = θέω, θῶ, aor. subj. from τίθημι.

θέλγω, prs., ipf. **θέλγε**, iter. θέλγεσκε, γ 264; fut. θέλξαι, aor. 1; pass. prs. opt. θέλγοιτο, aor. ἐθέλχθης, and 3 pl. ἔθελχθεν, *charm, cajole, bewitch*, Φ 276; *delude, deceive*, τινά, τινός, and τινὶ θυμόν, O 322, 594; *blind*, N 435.

θελκτήριον, α, τό, (θέλγω) = deliciae, *charm*; θ 509, *means of appeasing the gods.*

θέμεθλα and **θεμείλια**, τά, (θεῖναι), fundamenta, M 28; the first, fig. *bed* (roots) of the eye, Ξ 493; *lower part* of throat, near the jugulum, P 47.

θέμεν(αι) = θεῖναι, inf. aor. from τίθημι.

θέμις, ιστος, ιστι, ιστα, ι, ιστες, (θεῖναι), *custom, usage*, that which is laid down or established not by written law, but by old law, E 761, ι 112, 115; ἐστί, fas iusque est; with inf. ἣ θ. ἐ., sicut fas est, as is right, B 73; also with gen., ξείνων, with dat., Ξ 386; fatum, Διὸς θέμιστες; *decisions*, Π 387; *prerogatives*, joined with σκῆπτρον; τελεῖν, pay *dues, taxes*. Personified, *Themis*, β 68, Υ 4, O 87, 93.

θεμιστεύει, οντα, (θέμις), *give law*, τινί; τινός, *govern*, ι 114.

θέμωσε, aor. (θεμόω), coegit, *forced*, with inf., ι 486 and 542.

-θεν, suffix (cf. Lat. -tus). I. in general, (1) local, answering question whence, πεδόθεν, funditus; Τροίηθ-, οὐρανό-, οἰκό-; also with ἐξ, ἀπό; with verba movendi, φέρειν, ἄγειν; sentiendi, Ἴδηθεν μεδέων.—(2) denoting source, ε 477, Υ 305, cf. αἰνό-, οἰό-.—(3) specifying originator, O 489, π 447.—(4) temporal, ἠῶθεν, ὄπισθεν, postmodo. II. with designations of persons, θεό-, divinitus; πατρό-, Διό-, δημό-, ἐμέ- (with ἄνευ, O 213), σέ-, ἕ-; (1) with ablative force, audire ex, B 26, ζ 289; de, Ω 490; obedire, obey, O 199; after comparatives, A 114, ξ 56, Ψ 312; ὑπερέχω, I 419; also with ἐξ, ἀπό, πρό, E 96; πρόσθεν, E 56.—(2) with verba recordandi, θ 431, Δ 127; εἵνεκα, ἀέκητι, γ 213; ὑπέρ, Z 524; ἄνευ, P 407.—(3) joined with word in gen., υ 42, A 180, π 94, Σ 337; with ἄντα, ἀντίον, ἀντιᾶν, πειράζειν, ψ 114.—(4) instead of gen., δ 393, υ 232, π 439; but never instead of gen. partitive.

θένᾰρος, gen. from τὸ θέναρ, *flat of the hand*, E 339†.

θέο, imp. aor. act. from τίθημι.

θεο-δμήτων, gen. pl., (δέμω), a diis constructorum, *god-built*, Θ 519†.

θεο-ειδής, έα, acc., (εἶδος), *godlike, beautiful as the gods*, B 623, ο 271.

θεο-είκελος, ον, (ε), (ἴκελος), *like the gods*, in exterior, A 131.

θεόθεν, divinitus, *from the gods*, π 447†.

Θεο-κλῦμενος, seer in Ithaka, son of Polypheides, ο 256, υ 350.

θεο-προπέων, part., vaticinans, *prophesying*, A 109.

θεο-προπίης, gen., ην, ας, and **-πρόπιον**, gen. pl. ίων, (θεοπρόπος) = θεόφαντον, vaticinatio, vaticinium, *prophecy, oracle*, A 385.

θεο-πρόπος, acc. ον, (cf. ἀρι-πρεπής) = θεοφάντωρ, *one who discloses the will of gods*; vates, *seer* (N 70, οἰωνιστής), α 416.

θεός, οῦ, οῖς, ῷ, όφιν, όν, οί, ῶν, οῖσι, οῖς, ούς, comm., deus (dea), *god (goddess)*; of individual deities, Δ 514, Σ 394; then like numen, *the deity*, σὺν θεῷ, ἄνευ(θε) θεοῦ, ὑπὲρ θεὸν, ἐκ θεόφιν. [Often pronounced by synizesis, e. g. ξ 251, ℓj.]

θεουδής, έα, (θεο-Ϝαδής?), *pleasing the gods, pious*, τ 364. (Od.)

θεράπευον, 1 sing. ipf., (θεράπων), serviebam, *serve*, ν 265†. [ᾰ]

θεράπων, οντι, οντα, ε, ες, ας, *comrade, comrade at arms* (esquire, not servant), cf. λ 255, B 110, δ 23.

θερέω, see θέρομαι.

θερμαίνω, only subj. aor. **θερμήνῃ**, calefaceret, *warm, heat*, Ξ 7; opt. prs. pass. θερμαίνοιτο, calefieret.

θερμόν, ntr. ά, fervidum, a, *hot, warm*, ι 388.

θέρμετε, imp. prs., calefacite;

pass. ipf. 3 sing. *θέρμετο*, calefiebat, Ψ 381.

θέρος, *ευς, ει*, (fornax, fur-nus), aestas, *summer*, η 118.

Θερσί-λοχος, a Paionian, slain by Achilleus, Φ 209, Ρ 216.

Θερσίτης, slanderous demagogue in Greek camp, Β 212–69.

θέρεσθαι, prs., fut. mid. *θερσόμενος*, τ 507, pass. aor. subj. *θερέω*, fervescere, *be warm, warm one's self*, so also pass., ρ 23; *πυρός*, incendi, Ζ 331.

θές, imp. aor. from *τίθημι*.

θέσ-κελον, *α*, (*κέλω*), *wondrous*, *ἔργα*; ntr. adv., mirum in modum, Ψ 107.

θεσμόν, acc., (*θεῖναι*), *site*, ψ 296†.

Θέσπεια, town in Boiotia, Β 498†.

θεσπεσίοιο, gen., *ῳ, ον, η, ῃ, ην, άων*, adv. -*ως*, Ο 637 (*θεός* and *πέτομαι*?), *astonishing, tremendous*, in good and bad sense; *θεσπεσίῃ*, *by providential ordering*, Β 367.

θεσπι-δαές (*δαίω*), *πῦρ*, *fiercely blazing*, Μ 177.

θέσπιν, acc., (*σεπ-*, sequi?), *following, attending the deity; pious* or *divine, glorious*, *ἀοιδόν*, ρ 385; *ἀοιδήν*, α 328. (Od.)

Θεσπρωτοί, tribe dwelling about Dodona in Epeiros, π 427; their king Pheidon, ξ 316. (Od.)

Θεσσαλός, son of Herakles, father of Pheidippos and Antiphos, Β 679†.

Θεστορίδης, son of Thestor, (1) Kalchas, Α 69.—(2) Alkmaon, Μ 394.

Θέστωρ, (1) father of Kalchas.—(2) of Alkmaon.—(3) son of Enops, slain by Patroklos, Π 401†.

θέσ-φατος, *ον, α*, **θέσφαθ'** before rough breathing, (*θεός, φάναι, φαίνειν*), cf. fatum, ntr., *decrees of fate;* with *ἀήρ*, η 143 = *thick*.

Θέτις, *ιδος, ῑ, ῖν, ῑ*, a Nereid, mother of Achilleus by Peleus, Σ 431 sqq., Ω 62, cf. Α 502 sqq., 397 sqq.; epithets, *ἁλοσύδνη, ἀργυρόπεζα, ἠυκόμοιο, καλλιπλοκάμου, τανύπεπλε*.

θέω, **θέεις**, etc., prs., (inf. also **θείειν**), ipf. (iter. *θέεσκον*), fut. *θεύσεται, σθαι*, curro, *run;* of men and animals; part. joined with other verbs = ocius, *quickly, in haste*, Μ 343, Ζ 394, χ 106; also of ships, potter's wheel, vein, and in gen. of round or quick-moving things.

θεώτεραι, *θύραι*, divinae, ν 111†.

Θήβη and *Θήβῃσι, ας*, name of a city, (1) in Troas, at foot of Mount Plakos, residence of Eetion, Α 366, Ζ 397; destroyed by Achilleus. —(2) *ἑπταπύλοιο, ἐυστεφάνῳ, πολυηράτῳ, ἱερὰ τείχεα*, in Boiotia, orig. founded by Kadmos; **Θήβασδε,** *to Thebes*.

Θῆβαι, only pl., *ἑκατόμπυλοι*, city in Egypt on Nile (*Διὸς πόλις*), δ 126, Ι 381.

Θηβαῖος, (1) *a Theban;* but (2) as proper name, father of Eniopeus, Θ 120.

θήγει, *ων*, prs., *whet* (the teeth); imp. aor. mid. *θηξάσθω*, let each one *sharpen* well his spear, Β 382.

θηέομαι, only opt. **θηοῖο**, ipf. *θηεῖτο, ἐθηεύμεσθα, θηεῦντο*, aor. *θηήσατο, αντο, αιο*, and *θησαίατο*, 3 pl., (*θέα*), mirari, contemplari, *gaze at, admire*, Ω 418, η 133; *τινά*, σ 191; with part., ρ 64; *τί*, Κ 524, ο 132; *θυμῷ*, ε 76; joined with synonymous verb, Ψ 728, θ 265.

θήῃς, 2 sing. subj. aor. from *τίθημι*.

θηητήρ (*θηέομαι*), *beholder*, i. e. *fancier, connoisseur*, φ 397† (v. l. *θηρητήρ*).

θήιον, *θέειον*, sulfur, *brimstone*, χ 493†.

θήλεας, see *θῆλυς*.

θήλεον, ipf., (*θηλέω θάλλω*), (the meadows) *bloomed* (with violet blossoms, *ἴου*), ε 73†.

θῆλυς (also with fem. substs.), *υν*, fem. *εια, αι, ας*, and *θήλεας*, Ε 269, and **θηλύτεραι,** *άων, ῃσι*, λ 386, *gentler, feebler*, cf. gentle sex; femininus, muliebris, *female*.—(2) *fresh, refreshing* (dew, ε 467).

θημῶνα, *τόν*, (*θεῖναι*), congeriem, *heap*, ε 368†.

θήν, = in prose, *δήπου*, allied perh. to *δή*, *then, so then;* also *ἤ-, οὐ-* (*δή*).

θηοῖο, mirareris, opt. from *θηέομαι*.

θηρί, *θῆρε*, du., and *θῆρες, εσσιν, ας*, (Eng. deer), fera, *wild beast*, ε 473.

θηρευτῇσι, dat. pl., (*θήρη*), venatoribus, *hunters*, joined adjectively with *ἀνδράσιν* and *κύνεσσιν*, Μ 41. (Il.)

θηρεύοντα, part., (*θήρη*), venantem, *hunting*, τ 465†.

θήρη, *ης, ην*, (*θήρ*), venatio, *chase*, ι 158.

θηρητήρ, *α, ες, ας,* and **θηρήτορας,** I 544, (θήρη), venator, *hunter;* φ 397, better reading θηητήρ.

θηρίον, τό, (θήρ), *beast,* κ 171 and 180.

θῆτες, pl., (θεῖναι, conditio), *laborer on fixed terms, hired laborer, day laborer* (opp. δμῶες, vanquished serfs, slaves), δ 644†.

θησαίατο, 3 pl. opt. aor. from θηέομαι, mirarentur. **θήσατο,** *he sucked,* see θάω.

Θησεύς, acc. *έα,* λ 631, *Theseus;* national hero of Athens and Attika, A 265.

θῆσθαι, see *θάω.*

θητευέμεν, inf., -*εύσαμεν,* 1 pl. aor., (θητεύω, θῆτες), *work for hire, be a day laborer,* λ 489.

-θι (cf. Lat. -bi), suffix added to subst. and pron. stems to mark place *in which.*

θίς, *θινί, θῖνα,* masc., (θεῖναι ?), (1) acervus, *heap,* μ 45. — (2) elsewh. *strand.*

Θίσβη, town in Boiotia, *πολυτρήρωνα,* B 502†.

θλάω, only aor. **ἔθλᾶσε,** *θλάσσε, shattered,* E 307.

θλίβω, only fut. **θλίψεται** *ὤμους, will rub his* shoulders, ρ 221†.

θνήσκων, prs., aor. *ἔθανεν,* etc., inf. *θανέειν,* fut. *θανέεσθαι,* pf. *τέθνηκα,* part. *τεθνηώς, ῶτος* (and *ότος, ότα, ότας*), etc., *τεθνηκυῖαν;* pf. sync. *τεθνᾶσι, αίην, ης, η; τεθνάμεν(αι), τέθναθι, άτω,* mori, *die, ὑπὸ χερσίν τινος;* joined with *πότμον ἐπισπεῖν,* H 52; *οἰκτίστῳ θανάτῳ,* λ 412. *τεθνηῶτες* and *θανόντες,* mortui, *the dead.*

θνητός, *ή,* etc., (no ntr.), mortalis, Υ 41; *βροτόν,* π 212.

Θόας, *αντος,* (1) son of Andraimon, B 638; in Aitolia, Δ 527.—(2) *θεῖος,* son of Dionysos and of Ariadne, of Lemnos, Ξ 230.—(3) a Trojan, slain by Menelaos, Π 311.

Θόη, name of a Nereid, Σ 40†.

θοινηθῆναι, aor. pass., (θοινάω), *to be entertained,* δ 36†.

θόλον, *οιο,* only gen. sing., *building of circular form, with vaulted roof,* in court-yard of Odysseus. (See plate III., *k.*)

θοός (no gen. sing.), only gen. dat. and acc. pl. *θοῇ, άων, ῇσ(ιν),* adv. **θοῶς,** (θέω), citus, *quick,* with *δαῖτα,* θ 38, proleptically; *νύξ, swift-descending,* because night, in the countries on the Mediterranean, follows more speedily than with us the setting of the sun (cf. β 388); *νῆσοι, swiftly flitting by,* and sinking in the horizon, ο 299.

θοόω, only aor. **ἐθόωσα,** (*ἄκρον,* prae), acui, *brought to a point,* ι 327†.

θόρε, aor. from *θρώσκω.*

θοῦρος, *ον,* fem. *θούριδος, ῖν,* (θρώσκω), impetuosus, *rushing, raging, impetuous;* Ares, E 30; *ἀλκῆς, ἀσπίδα, αἰγίδα.*

θόωκος, *οι* = *θῶκος, οι.*

Θόων, *ωνος,* (1) a Phaiakian, θ 113. —(2) son of Phainops, slain by Diomedes, E 152.—(3) a Trojan, slain by Odysseus, Λ 422.—(4) a Trojan, comrade of Asios, slain by Antilochos, M 140, N 545.

Θόωσα, a nymph, daughter of Phorkys, mother of Polyphemos, α 71.

Θοώτης, herald of Menestheus, M 342.

Θράσιος, a Paionian, slain by Achilleus, Φ 210. [ᾰ]

θράσος, *τό,* Ξ 416 [ᾰ]=*θάρσος,* audacia, *boldness, courage.*

Θρᾰσύ-δημος, v. l. see **Θρασύμηλος.**

θρᾰσῠ-κάρδιος, *stout-hearted,* K 41. (Il.)

θρᾰσῠ-μέμνονα (*μίμνω*), *bravely steadfast;* Herakles, E 639.

Θρᾰσῠ-μήδης, son of Nestor, Π 321, K 255.

Θρᾰσῠ-μηλος, Sarpedon's charioteer, Π 463†.

θρασύς, *ύν, ειάων,* audax, *bold, daring, rash,* Λ 553.

θρέξασκον, aor. iter. from *τρέχω.*

θρέπτρα, *τά,* (=*θρεπτήρια* from *τρέφω*), praemia educationis, *return for bringing up, οὐδὲ τοκεῦσιν θρέπτρα φίλοις ἀπέδωκεν,* Δ 478 and P 302, nor did he recompense his parents for (their care in) bringing him up.

θρέψα, aor. from *τρέφω.*

Θρήκη, Θρήκηνδε, Θρήκηθεν, *Thrake,* a region in northern Greece beyond the Peneios, inhabited by Kikones and Paiones, B 845, Υ 485, Λ 222; traversed by river Axios; hence adj. **Θρηίκιον,** *ῳ, οι, ης, Thrakian;* sea, Ψ 230; *Σάμου* = island *Samothrake,* N 13; the inhabitants of Thrake are called **Θρῆκες**, *ὧν*, (sing. *Θρήικα*), also *Θρήικες ἀκρόκομοι*, Δ 533.

θρήνεον, *ἐθρήνεον*, ipf., (*θρηνέω*), *were raising the funeral song* (**θρῆνος**, Ω 721), Ω 722, ω 61.

θρῆνυς, *υϊ*, *υν*, *footstool*, (1) of the helmsman running athwart the ship, Ο 729.—(2) elsewh. *footstool*, either as in cut No. 113, from Assyrian original, attached to the chair, or usually standing free. (See cuts Nos. 73, 74, 113.)

Θρύξ, see *Θρύκη*.

θριγκός, *οῖσι*, *coping*, *cornice*, pl. *battlements*, ρ 267. (Od.)

θριγκόω, only aor. **ἐθρίγκωσεν**, *crowned the top* of the wall, to make it impassable, with bramble-bushes, ξ 10†.

Θρῑνᾰκίη, fable-island, pasture of the cattle of Helios, μ 135; the ancients identified it and located it in Sicily.

θρίξ, **τρίχα**, *ες*, *ας*, *θριξίν*, capillus, pilus, *hair*, also spoken of wool, and of bristles, Ψ 135.

θρόνα, *τά*, *flowers*, Χ 441†.

Θρόνῑον, town of the Lokrians, Β 533†.

θρόνος, *ου*, etc., *arm-chair*, with high back and footstool; cushions were laid upon the seat, and over both seat and back carpets were spread. (See cut, under *ἄμπυκα*; cf. also No. 113, where two chairs, from Assyrian and from Greek originals, are represented.)

θρόος, *ὁ*, *speech*, *tongue*, Δ 437†.

θρῡλίχθη, aor. pass., (*θρυλίσσω*), *was crushed*, Ψ 396†.

θρύον, *τό*, coll., *rushes*, Φ 351†. [ῠ]

Θρύον, *τό*, (lit. reedy), and **Θρυόεσσα** *πόλις* (lit. reed-town), a town on a ford of the Alpheios, Β 592, Λ 711.

θρώσκωσι, *ων*, prs., ipf., aor. *θόρε*, *θορών*, etc., salire, *leap*, *ἐπί* (*ἐν*) *τινι*, invadere, *attack*.

θρωσμῷ, dat., (*θρώσκω*), **πεδίοιο**, *rising* or *rise* of the plain (on Skamandros), Κ 160. (Il.)

θῠγάτηρ, *ἐρος*, *ός*, *ἐρι*, *ἐρα*, *ἐρες*, *ἐρεσσιν*; sync. *θυγατρός*, *ι*, *θύγατρα*, *τρες*, *τρῶν*, filia, *daughter*, Ο 197. [ῡ in forms of four and five syllables.]

θυέεσσιν, see *θύος*.

θύελλα, *ῃ*, *αν*, *αι*, *ας*, (*θύω*), *tempest* (of wind or of fire); also of *sudden gust* which, like the Harpies, snatches away those who suddenly and irrecoverably disappear, υ 63, δ 515. [ῠ]

Θυέστης, brother of Atreus, δ 517, Β 107; father of Aigisthos, who is hence called **Θυεστιάδης**, δ 518.

θυήεις (*θύος*), *smoking with incense*, *fragrant*, Θ 48.

θῡηλάς, *τάς*, (*θῡ́ω*), *part of the victim to be burned*, Ι 220†.

θῡμ-αλγέος, *ἐι*, *έα*, *ές*, (*ἄλγος*), *heart-paining*, *grieving*, π 69.

θῡμ-ᾱρέα, *ές*, *dear*, *welcome*, ρ 199, Ι 336.

Θυμβραῖος, a Trojan, slain by Diomedes, Λ 320†.

Θύμβρη, plain bordering on the Thymbrios, a branch of the Skamandros, Κ 430†.

θῡμ-ηγερέων (*ἀγείρω*), scarcely still *rallying the life* in one, *tired out*, η 283†.

θῡμ-ηδέα, ntr. pl., (*ἁδεῖν*), *delighting the heart*, *agreeable*, π 389†.

θῡμ-ῆρες (*ἐρί-ηρες*), *pleasantly*, κ 362†.

θῡμο-βόρου, *οιο*, *ῳ*, (*βορά*), *ἔριδος*, *heart-gnawing*, Η 301. (Il.)

θῡμο-δακής (*δακεῖν*), *stinging to the heart*, θ 185†.

Θῡμοίτης, a Trojan chief, Γ 146†.

θῡμο-λέοντα, acc., *lion-hearted*, Ε 639.

θῡμο-ραϊστής, *έων*, (*ῥαίω*), *life-destroying*, Ν 544. (Il.)

θῡμός, *οῦ*, *ῷ*, *όν*, (*θύω*), strictly, *that which is in constant motion* (blood as the vehicle of the anima), (1) *life*, *vital strength*, *ἑλέσθαι*, *ἀποπνείων*, etc.—(2) *heart*, as seat of emotions, courage; also *wrath*, *ἀπὸ θυμοῦ* = *ἀπο-θύμιος*; as feeling desire, *appetite* (even for food and drink).—(3) as seat of reason; *mind*, *thought*, *ἐν θυμῷ βαλέσθαι*, lay to *heart*.—(4) in general signif. *disposition*, *nature*, *heart*,—*ἐν στήθεσσι*, ψ 215; (*ἐν*) *θυμῷ*, locat., *in* (his) *heart*, *soul*, ν 145, υ 301, 304; *from the heart*, *seriously*, Ο 212, Ω 778; *κατὰ φρένα καὶ κατὰ θυμόν*, mente animoque, in mind and in soul, in the inmost heart; *θυμός*, used as equivalent to *one's own self*, ε 298, ο 202, Χ 122.

θῡμο-φθόρος, *ον*, *α*, (*φθείρω*), *destroying life*, *fraught with death*, *fatal*; Ζ 169, *inciting to murder*; *at risk of his life*, *wanton*, τ 323; δ 716, *consuming* (grief).

θόνων, part. prs., imp. θῦνε, besides these forms, ipf. θῦνε, ον, (θύω), *rush* or *dart along, charge*, Λ 342.

θυόεν, ntr., (θύος), *odorous*, Ο 153†.

θύον, gen., *arbor-vitae*, with fragrant wood, ε 60†.

θύεα, **θυέων**, ntr., *burnt-offerings*, Ζ 270.

θυο-σκόος, οι, (σκοϝεῖν), *one who, from the smoke rising from the burnt-offering, draws an omen*, Ω 221, φ 145.

θυόω, only pf. part. **τεθυωμένον**, (θύος), *fragrant*, Ξ 172†.

θύραζε, foras, *to the door, forth, out*, Ε 694, ε 410.

θυρα-ωρούς, acc. pl., (ὥρα), *guarding the doors*, Χ 69†.

θυρεόν, τόν, *door-stone*, placed by Polyphemos at mouth of his den, ι 240. (Od.)

θύρετρα, τά, (θύρη), *wings of a door, door*, Β 415; αὐλῆς, χ 137, near to the στόμα λαύρης (see plate III., o). [ῠ]

θύρη, no gen. and dat. sing., pl. gen. άων, dat. ῃσι, *door, folding doors, gate*, α 441, φ 47; *entrance*, ν 370; Β 788, ἐπὶ θύρῃσι,=*at the court* (cf. our phrase 'Sublime Porte,' as designation of Sultan, also [Xen.] βασιλέως θύραι). **θύρηθι**, ξ 352 = **θύρηφι**, foris, *forth*. θύραζε, foras. [ῠ]

θυσανόεσσαν (θύσανοι), *richly tasseled, many-tasseled*, Ε 738. (Il.)

θύσανοι, οις, (θύω), *tufts, tassels*, Β 448. (Il.) [ῠ]

θύσθλα, τά, (θύω), implements employed at orgies of Dionysos, *Thyrsi*, Ζ 134†. (See cuts.)

I. **θύων**, prs., ipf. θῦε, (θέω), (1) *heave, surge*; of water, Φ 234, rushing with swollen stream; αἵματι, *swam* in blood. —(2) saevire, Α 342, *raged*; περὶ πρὸ ἔγχεϊ, raged charging around and in front with his spear, Π 699.

II. **θύοντα**, part. prs., ipf. θῦε, aor. θῦσε, σαμεν, σαι, (θύος, tus), offer by throwing or pouring upon the fire to be *burnt* a part of, the first-fruits of, a meal, ξ 446, ο 260. (See adjoining cut.)

θυ-ώδεος, εα, (ὄδωδα), *fragrant*, δ 121. (Od.)

θωήν, τήν, multam, *penalty*, β 192, Ν 669.

(θῶκος) **θόωκος**, οι, **θῶκον**, ῳ, ους, (1) sedes, *seat*, β 14.—(2) consessus, *assembly*, β 26; θῶκόνδε, ε 3, to the assembly.

Θῶν, ῶνος, a noble Egyptian, δ 228†.

θωρηκτάων, οῖσι, from θωρηκτής, (θώρηξ), *cuirassed*, Φ 429. (Il.)

θώρηξ, no dat. pl., *breastplate, cuirass, corselet*, Λ 19 sqq.; usually of bronze, consisting of two plates (γύαλα). (See adjacent cut, also cuts Nos. 36 and 78.)

The cuirass fitted closely to the body, and was cut square off at the waist; the shoulder pieces (see cut) were drawn down by small chains and fastened to buttons (see cut No. 78); the metal plates were united by clasps (see cut No. 22); the upper part of the thighs was protected by the μίτρη, worn over the apron, ζῶμα, of leather or felt, by its metal flaps, πτέρυγες (Nos. 12, 36, 85), or plates (Nos. 3, 36, 78); over th θώρηξ, μίτρη, and ζῶμα was bound the ζωστήρ (Nos. 3, 78), below which projected the lower end of the χιτών (Nos. 3, 22, 36, 78; cf. λινοθώρηξ and χιτών).

θωρήσσω, pr., ipf. mid. 3 du. θωρήσσεσθον, N 301; fut. aor. act. and mid., (θώρηξ), *arm with breastplate*, or *cuirass*, mid. *arm one's self*, H 101; aor. pass. θωρήχθησαν, θῆναι, θέντες, Γ 340, Α 226, Θ 530, (σὺν) τεύχεσιν, Θ (530) 376.

θῶες, θώων, οἱ, *jackals*, Λ 474. (Il.)

I.

ἶα, ἰῆς, see ἴος. **ἰά**, see ἰός.

ἰαίνει, ομαι, εται, prs., ipf. ἰαίνετο, aor. ἴηνατε, ἰήνῃ, aor. pass. ἰάνθης, η, subj. ῇς, ῇ, calefacere, *warm*, pass., calefieri, κ 359; *cheer, lighten*, δ 549; pass. σφίν, iis gaudeo, *take delight in* them, freq. with θυμόν, φρένας. [ῐ]

Ἴαιρα, a Nereid, Σ 42†.

ἰάλλειν, prs., ipf. ἴαλλον, εν, aor. ἴηλα, ε, ον, ἰῆλαι, (ἐλθεῖν), mitto, *send forth*, usually with ἐπί, followed by dat. or acc.; ν 142, ἀτιμίῃσι, *assail* with insults. [ῐ]

Ἰάλμενος, son of Ares, chief of Boiotians, B 512. (Il.)

Ἰαμενός, Trojan chief, M 139†. [ῑ]

Ἰάνασσα, Ἰάνειρα, Nereids, Σ 47†. [ῑ]

ἰάνθη, aor. pass. from ἰαίνω.

ἰᾶτο, ipf., fut. ἰήσεται, aor. ἰήσασθαι, curare, *tend*, τινά, τί; *heal*, M 2, ι 525. [ῑ]

Ἰάονες, Ionians, N 685†. [⏑ – ⏑ ⏑]

Ἰᾰπετός, a Titan, Θ 479†.

Ἰάρδᾰνος, river (1) in Kreta, γ 292. —(2) in Elis, near Pheiai, H 135.

ἴασι (εἶμι), eunt.

Ἰᾰσίδης, son of Jasos, (1) Amphion, λ 283.—(2) Dmetor, ρ 443. [ῑ]

Ἰᾰσίων, ωνος, beloved by Demeter, slain by thunderbolt of Zeus, ε 125†. [ῑ]

Ἴᾰσον Ἄργος, σ 246† = the entire Peloponnesos. [ῑ]

Ἴᾰσος, (1) son of Sphalos, leader of Athenians, slain by Aineias, O 332. —(2) father of Amphion.—(3) father of Dmetor.

ἰαύειν, prs., ipf. ἴαυον, iter. ἰαύεσκον, -εν, aor. ἰαῦσαι, λ 261, and **ἄεσα**, σαμεν, σαν, ἀέσαι, ἄσαμεν, π 367, (FAΣ), pernoctare, *pass the night, sleep*, also with νύκτα, νύκτας, I 325, τ 340. [ῐ; ᾱ when augmented.]

ἰᾰχή, ῆς, ῇ, (Fιαχή), clamor, *cry, shout*; in field, hunt, or distress. [ῑ]

ἰάχων, ουσα, part. prs., ipf. ἴαχε, ον, (Fιάχω, Ger. wiehern?), *cry aloud*, of single person or of many, B 333; of things, strepere, *ring, roar, twang, hiss, resound, crackle*, Ψ 216. [ῐ; though orig. having F, it is often augmented, when ῐ becomes ῑ.]

Ἰᾰωλκός, town in Thessaly, εὐρυχόρῳ, λ 256, B 712.

ἰγνύην, τήν, (γόνυ), poplitem, *inner part of the knee, hollow of the knee*, N 212†. [ῠ]

Ἰδαῖος, (1) son of Dares, a Trojan, E 11.—(2) herald of Trojans, Γ 248; charioteer of Priamos, Ω 470. [ῑ]

Ἰδαῖος, *of Mount Ida, Idaean*, (1) Zeus, Π 605; Ω 291, Κρονίωνι.—(2) ὀρέων, Idaean mountains = Ida, Θ 170, Υ 189. [ῑ]

ἰδέ = ἠδέ, et, Γ 194, α 113.

ἴδε, ἰδέειν, ἴδεσκε, vidit, see ΕΙΔ V.

ἰδέω, sciam, see ΕΙΔ IV.

Ἴδη, ης, *Ida*, a mountain range, rich in springs, ravines, forests, and game, extending from Phrygia, through Mysia, toward the Hellespont, and subsiding into the plain near Troy, B 821, Λ 183; its summit, Γάργαρον; Zeus Ἴδηθεν, *from Ida* (as his seat), Θ 397, μεδέων, Γ 276.

ἴδηαι, cernas, see ΕΙΔ V.

Ἴδης, εω, father of Kleopatra, I 558†.

ἴδῐον, ntr., ίη, (viduus), privatum, *private*, δ 314. (Od.) [⏑ ⏑]

ἴδιον, ipf., (σFιδ-, Eng. sweat), *I was sweating*, υ 204†. [ῑ]

ἴδμεν(αι), scire, see ΕΙΔ IV.

ἰδνώθη, θείς, aor. pass. from ἰδνόω, (ὀπίσω), *bent* himself (backward), B 266.

ἰδοίατο, viderent, see ΕΙΔ V.

Ἰδομενεύς, ῆος and έος, son of Deukalion, grandson of Minos, chieftain in Kreta, Δ 265, M 117, B 645; σθένος Ἰδομενῆος, periphrasis=Idomeneus, N 248; his son Arsilochos, ν 259; comrade in arms Meriones, Ψ 113.

ἰδρείῃ, dat., (ἴδρις), *by skill* (in battle), Π 359. (Il.)

ἴδρις, ιες, (ἴδμεναι), peritus, *skilled, skillful,* with inf., η 108. (Od.)

ἱδρώοντα, ας, ουσα, ἱδρῶσαι, part. prs., fut. ἱδρώσει, aor. ἵδρωσα, (ἵδρως), sudare, *sweat,* ἱδρῶ, Δ 27; *be drenched with sweat,* B 388.

ἵδρυε, imp. prs., aor. ἵδρῡσε, σασα, *bid be seated,* B 191; aor. pass. **ἱδρύνθησαν,** *took their seats.* [ῠ]

ἱδρώς, dat. ῷ, acc. ῶ, (ἴδιον), sudor, *sweat,* with ἱδρόω, Δ 27.

ἰδυῖα, sciens, see ΕΙΔ IV. **ἴδω(μι),** see ΕΙΔ V. **ἴε, ἴεν,** ibat. **ἵει,** mittebat.

ἱείη=ἴοι, iret. **ἱέμενοι,** mid., **ἵεν,** ipf. 3 pl. aor. from ἵημι.

ἵενται, χ 304, and ἵεσθε, M 274, variae lectiones for ἵε- from ἵημι.

ἱέρειαν, τήν, (ἱερεύς), *priestess,* Z 300†. [ĭ]

ἱερεύς, ῆα, ῆες, and ἱρεύς, (ἱερός), *sacrificial priest* of a single god, also *soothsayer,* A 23. [ĭ]

ἱερεύετε, prs., ipf. ἱέρευον, iter. ἱρεύεσκον, υ 3; fut. ἱρευσέμεν, σειν, etc., aor. ἱέρευσεν, mid. ἱρεύσασθαι, τ 198; pass. plupf. ἱέρευτο, Ω 125, (ἱερεύς); *slaughter,* Z 174; *offer,* sacrifice, θεῷ; ξείνῳ, in the stranger's honor.

ἱερήιον, ήια, (ἱερεύς), victima, *victim, animal for sacrifice* or *slaughter,* ξ 94.

ἱερός, ή, όν, (ἴς?), *strong, mighty, fresh,* K 56, Δ 378, P 464, joined, in this signif., with ἴς, μένος, ἰχθύς; *holy,* of day, darkness, rivers, barley; sacer, *sacred,* of altar, grove, house, hecatombs, cities, localities, φ 108, α 2; *hallowed,* of threshing-floor, olive-tree.

ἱερόν, ά, and ἱρόν, ά, subst., sacrum, ῥέζειν, ἔρδειν=sacrificare, *sacrifice,* α 61; victimae, *victim,* A 147.

ἱζάνει, prs., ipf. ἵζανεν, ον, (ἵζω), consido, *sit; instituted* a contest, or *bade* the broad assembly *be seated,* Ψ 258.

ἵζει, prs. act. and mid., ipf. ἷζον and mid., iter. ἵζεσκε, (σιζjω, sîdo), *take one's seat,* with gen. of place, I 218, cf. π 53; *lie down, recline* (also mid.), Γ 326, χ 335; *bid be seated,* τινά, Ω 553; βουλήν, *hold a council.*

ἵηλε, αι, ον, aor. from ἰάλλω.

Ἰηλῡσός, town in Rhodos, B 656†.

ἵημι, peculiar forms: 3 pl. prs. ἱεῖσι, inf. ἱέμεναι, ipf. ἵει, ἵεν, aor. ἧκε, mitto, *send* (Π 152, *harness, put to*), *cast, let fall,* ἀπὸ ἕθεν, χαμᾶζε; φέρεσθαι, *hurled headlong,* esp. *shoot* (with and without obj.), τινός, ἐπί τινα; *let flow forth* (voice, a river its waters); *let loose* (hair), mid. cupio, *endeavor, strive after,* with gen., with inf. Ἔρεβόσδε, πρόσσω; *hasten,* ν 334; pres. part. mid. ἱέμενος, cupidus, *eager.* [ῐ in pres.; but freq., esp. in part. and ipf., ῑ.]

ἰήνατε, aor. from ἰαίνω, and **ἰήσασθε,** σθαι, from ἰάομαι. **ἴησι,** *eat.*

Ἰησονίδης, Euneos, son of **Ἰήσων,** leader of Argonauts, μ 72, H 469.

ἰητήρ, ῆρος, ῆρα, and **ἰητρός,** οί, οῖς, (ἰάομαι), medicus, *healer,* ρ 384, Π 28. [ῑ]

ἰθαι-γενέεσσι, dat. pl., (ἰθύς, -γενής), *born in lawful wedlock, legitimate,* ξ 203†. [ῐθ.]

Ἰθαι-μένης, father of Sthenelaos, Π 586†.

Ἰθάκη, native island of Odysseus; the ancients identified as Ithaka the present island Theaki, with mts. Νήριτος, Νήιος, Κόραξ; its harbor, Ῥεῖθρον; epithets, ἀμφιάλω, εὐδείελον, ἐυκτιμένης, κραναῆς, παιπαλόεσσαν, τρηχείης. Hence **Ἰθάκηνδε,** *to Ithaka;* the inhabitants, **Ἰθακήσιοι.** [ῐθᾰ.]

Ἴθακος, eponymous hero of island Ithaka, ρ 207†. [ῐθᾰ.]

ἴθι, imp. from εἶμι, often with ἄγε.

ἴθματα, τά, (ἰθύς), *straight flight,* E 778†.

ἰθύντατα, sup. from ἰθύς,

ἰθύνει, prs., ipf. ἴθῡνεν, ον; prs. ipf. mid., aor. pass. ἰθυνθήτην, (ἰθύς), *hew so as to be straight,* φ 121; *make straight,* ρ 341; *direct, guide* (missiles, ship), in a given direction, with acc., E 290, also ἐπί τινι; Π 475, pass., *placed themselves in line,* i. e. parallel to the pole; mid. reflexive, *was directing his* arrow, etc., χ 8.

ἰθυ-πτίωνα, acc., (πέτομαι, Υ 99), *straight-flying* (lance), Φ 169†. [– – – – ⏑]

I. **ἰθύς,** εῖα, ύ, *straightforward, straight, just,* Ψ 580; ἰθύντατα, *most fairly.*

II. **ἰθύς** and **ἰθύ,** adv., *straight at, straight for,* with gen., E 849; with verbs of motion, φέρειν, bring *against* (in hostile signif.).

III. **ἰθύν,** τήν, (ἴμεν), *undertaking, expedition,* δ 434, Z 79; *tendency, course,* π 304, upright or faithless *disposition;* ἀν' ἰθύν, straight upward. [ῑ]

ἰθύω, only aor. **ἴθῦσε,** σαν, (ἰθύς), *go straight forward, advance, attack* (of lion and warriors), M 48; with gen., O 693, νεός; with inf., *desire.*

Ἰθώμη, town in Thessaly, B 729†.

ἱκάνω, prs., ipf. aor. and prs. mid., (ἵκω), *arrive at, reach,* τινά, τι, with designations of place and names of persons; less freq. with prep.; γοῦνά τινος, supplicare alicui, come as suppliant; τόδ', come hither; noun denoting mental condition (e. g. grief, pain), is sometimes found as subj.; ἱκάνει τινὰ κραδίην (τινὶ ἦτορ), υ 228. [ῑ]

Ἰκάριος, father of Penelope, brother of Tyndareos, α 276, 329, δ 797. [ῑκᾰ.]

Ἰκάριος πόντος, S.W. of Asia Minor, B 145†. [ῑκᾰ.]

ἴκελος, ῳ, ον, οι, η, (ϝίκ, ἔοικα), similis, *like,* τινί, N 53. (See εἴκελος.)

Ἱκεταονίδης, *son of Hiketaon,* Melanippos, O 546†. [ῑ]

Ἱκετάων, (1) 'scion of Ares,' son of Laomedon, Priamos's brother, Γ 147, Υ 238.—(2) father of Melanippos, O 576. [ῑ]

ἱκέτευον, ipf., aor. ἱκέτευσα, etc., (ἱκέτης), supplicare, *approach as suppliant,* (εἰς) τινά (Π 574), η 292; with acc. and inf., λ 530. (Od.) [ῑ]

ἱκέτης, αο, εω, αι, άων, ῃσι, no dat. sing. or accus. pl., (ἵκω), supplex, *suppliant,* for protection, and esp. in search of purification from homicide (cf. Tlepolemos, Lykophron, Patroklos), ι 269, Φ 75. [ῑ]

ἱκετήσιος Ζεύς, *protector of suppliants,* ν 213†. [ῑ]

ἵκηαι, see ἱκνέομαι.

Ἰκμάλιος, τέκτων in Ithaka, τ 57†. [ᾰ]

ἰκμάς, ἡ, humor, *moisture,* Ρ 392†.

ἴκμενον (ϝίκω) οὖρον, *fair* following wind, A 479. (Od.)

ἱκνεύμεναι, prs. part., ἱκνεύμεσθα, ipf., (ἵκω), *arrive,* ι 128. (Od.)

ἴκρια, ἰκριόφιν, (ico), *deck,* which in the Homeric ship was partial, only fore and aft (see plate IV., at end of vol.); ε 252, *ribs of ship.* (See cuts Nos. 15 and 35.)

ἵκω, ipf. ἶκε, aor. ἶξον, ες, ε, mid. prs. ἵκομαι, subj. 2 sing. ἵκηαι, opt. 3 pl. ἱκοίατο, aor. ἱκόμην, fut. ἵξεται, σθαι, (ϝίκω), consequi, *reach,* τινά, τί; τέκμωρ, the goal; τέλος μύθων, substance of discourse, end proposed; ἥβης μέτρον, full strength of youth, *arrive at* dawn, old age; also with πρός, ἐπί, εἰς, μετά τι (τινα), οἴκαδε, δεῦρο (τόδ', ρ 524, 444, thither), so generally *come;* ὑπότροπον, reducem, come back, return; an abstract noun is freq. the subj., e. g. wrath, grief, longing, ἵκει τινά (φρένας); whom wandering (exile) and distress and grief *befall,* ο 345; *characterizes,* υ 228; δασμός, division (of spoils) arrives, A 166; χεῖρας, *fall into* hands of; also = supplicare, τινά, π 424, δ 516; cf. τὰ σὰ γοῦνα, ι 267. [ῑ, but ἵκετο.]

ἰλᾱδόν (ἴλη), adv., catervatim, *in troops,* B 93†.

ἵλᾱος, ον, (ἱλάω), placabilis, *propitious, gentle,* I 639. (Il.) [ῑ]

ἱλᾶονται, B 550. **ἱλάσκονται,** εσθαι, ipf. ἱλάσκοντο, fut. ἱλάσσομαι, σσεαι, ἱλασόμεσθα, and aor. ἱλασσάμενοι, (ἵλαος), placare, *reconcile one's self to, make propitious, appease;* θεὸν ταύροισι καὶ ἀρνειοῖς, μολπῇ, A 472. [ῑ]

Ἰλήιον πεδίον, plain *of Ilion,* Φ 558†. [ῑ]

ἱλήκῃσι, subj., opt. ἱλήκοι, imp. **ἵληθι,** (ἵλαος), *be gracious,* φ 365. (Od.)

Ἰλιόθεν, *from Ilios.* **Ἰλιόθι πρό,** *before Ilios.* **Ἰλιόφι** = Ἰλίου.

Ἴλιον, τό, O 71, elsewh. **Ἴλιος,** ἡ, (1) *Ilios* or *Ilion,* the residence of Priamos, and capital city of the Trojan plain (see plate V., at end of vol.); epithets, αἰπεινή, αἰπύ, ἐρατεινήν, εὐτείχεον, ἠνεμόεσσαν, ἱερήν, ὀφρυόεσσα, πύργον.—(2) in wider signif., *the region about*

Troy, Ἴλιον εἴσω, A 71, τ 182; Ἴλιον εἰσανέβαινον, β 172.

ἰλλάσι, ταῖς, (εἰλέω), *with twisted cords*, N 572†.

Ἶλος, (1) son of Tros, father of Laomedon, Υ 232; Ἴλου σῆμα, K 415; τύμβος, Λ 372; παλαιοῦ Δαρδανίδαο, Λ 166.—(2) son of Mermeros of Ephyra, α 259.

ἰλύος, τῆς, (lutum), *mud*, *slime*, Φ 318†. [ῑλῡ.]

ἱμάς, άντι, α, ων, εσσι, ας, masc., *leather strap* or *thong*, (1) in connection with the chariot, (a) *straps* in which chariot-box was hung, or, perh. more likely, the *network of plaited straps* enclosing the body of the chariot, E 727; (b) *the reins*, Ψ 324, 363; (c) *the halter*, Θ 544.—(2) *chin-strap of helmet*, Γ 371.—(3) *cestus* of boxers, see πυγμάχοι.—(4) *the leash* or *latch-string* by which doors were fastened and unfastened. See adjacent cut, in four divisions:

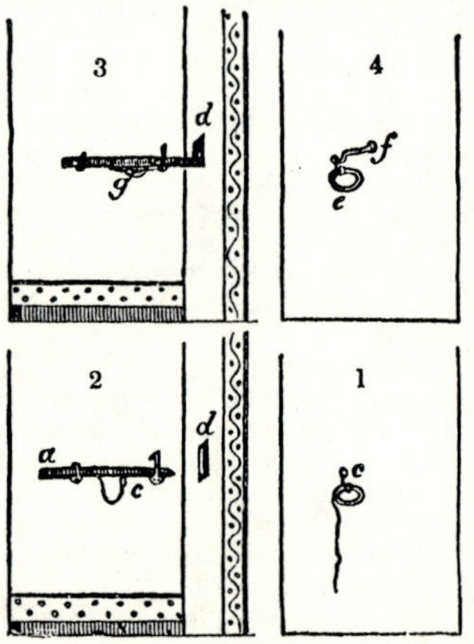

above, the closed, below the unfastened door; on the left, as seen from the inner side, on the right as seen from the outside. To close, now, the door from the outside, the string, hanging loosely in fig. 1, was pulled until it drew the bolt from the position of fig. 2 to that of fig. 3, when it was made fast by a knot difficult to untie to the ring, κορώνη, *e*, fig. 4. To open, from the outside, the string was first untied, and then the κληΐς, not unlike a hook (fig. 4, *f*), was introduced through the key-hole, *c*, and by means of a crook (*g*, fig. 3) at the end of it the bolt was pushed back from the position of fig. 3 to that of fig. 2 and the door opened, α 442.—(5) *bed-cord*.—(6) *magic girdle* of Aphrodite, Ξ 214, 219.—(7) *thong which makes the drill revolve*. (See cut No. 127.) [ῐ]

ἱμάσθλης, ην, gen. and acc. ῇ, (ἱμάς), *lash*, *whip*, Ψ 582.

ἱμάσσω, subj. ῃ, aor. ἵμασε, (ἱμάς), *lash*, E 589; *beat*, B 782, O 17.

Ἰμβρασίδης, son of Imbrasos, Peiroos, Δ 520†.

Ἴμβριος, *inhabitant of Imbros*, Φ 43; but proper name in N 171, 197; son of Mentor, son-in-law of Priamos, slain by Teukros.

Ἴμβρος, island on coast of Thrake, with capital city of same name, Ξ 281, N 33.

ἱμείρετε, ων, mid. -εαι, εται, όμενος, αιτο, (ἵμερος), desiderare, *yearn after*, with gen. or inf., ε 209, Ξ 163. [ῑ]

ἴμεν(αι)=ἰέναι, ire.

ἱμερόεις, όεντος, τα, όεσσαν, όεν, (ἵμερος), *charming*; γόος, *fond*, *passionate* lament; ntr. as adv., Σ 570.

ἵμερος, ον, (ἴσμαρος), desiderium, *longing*, τινός; *passionate longing*, *love*; πατρὸς γόοιο, yearning after tears = to weep for his father. [ῑ]

ἱμερτόν, masc., amoenum, *lovely*, B 751. **ἴμμεναι**=ἰέναι, ire.

ἵνα, pronominal adverb, quâ (viâ or ratione), *where*, *wherewith*, *therewith*, Γ 252; ἵνα περ, Ω 382, ν 364, ubi maneant; ζ 58, quo (plaustro) veheham.—(1) ubi, *where*, B 558, E 360, ι 136, δ 821, K 127 (τ' ἄρ?); *in circumstances in which* he would not be able to obtain fire from any other source, or ἵνα may be taken as final, *in order that* he may not need to kindle, ε 490.—(2) ut, *that*, *in order that*, never repeated (γ 78, not a genuine line), (a) with subj., after principal tenses, Ξ 484, Ψ 207, Γ 252, A 203, β 307, (joined with κε, μ 156), with imp., α 302, A 363, η 165 (also A 410); sometimes with subj. even after historical tenses, H 26, I 99, 495; (b) with opt. after historical tenses, γ 2, 77; after opt., ξ 408, even after principal tense, ρ 250; (c) subj. and opt. interchanged (text corrupt), O 598, cf. Ω 584 and 586. [⏑⏑, in arsi ⏑–.]

ἰνδάλλεται, το, (εἶδος), apparet, videtur, τίς τινι, with part., but τ 224, *it appears to me*, in my mind, *floats before me* in recollection.

ἴνεσι, dat. pl. from ἴς.

ἰνίον, ου, (Fῖν-), *bone of the back of the head, back of head*, E 73. (Il.)

Ἰνώ, see Λευκοθέα.

ἰξάλου αἰγὸς ἀγρίου, Δ 105†, apparently designates a species of wild goat=perh. *chamois*.

Ἰξιονίη = Ἰξίωνος, Ξ 317, mother of Peirithoos.

ἷξον, see ἵκω.

ἰξυῖ, τῇ, *waist*, ε 231. (Od.)

ἰο-δνεφές (ἴον, κνέφας), *violet, dark, violet blue*, of wool, δ 135. (Od.) [ῐ]

ἰο-δόκος, ον, (ἰός, δεκ, δέχομαι), *arrow-receiving*, φ 12, of quiver. [ῑ]

ἰο-ειδέος, gen., έα, (ἴον), *violet-colored, dark blue*, ε 56. [ῐ]

ἰόεντα (ἰός) σίδηρον, *rusty* iron; others interpret, *violet-colored, dark*, from ἴον, Ψ 850†. [ῐ]

ἰό-μωροι, adj. applied to Ἀργεῖοι, Δ 242, Ξ 479 (ἰό-της?), of doubtful deriv. and signif., *skilled in arrow-shooting*=*cowardly*; or *strong in wishing* and worthless in action.

ἴον, gen. from Fίον, (vio-lae), collective noun, *violets*, ε 72†.

ἰονθάδος, τῆς, barbatae, *shaggy*, ξ 50†. [ῐ]

ἰός, ῷ, όν, pl. ἰοί, (ἰά, Υ 68), ὧν, οἷσι, ούς, sagitta, *arrow*, Λ 515.

(ἴος) **ἰῷ, ἴᾰ,** ἰῆς, ἰῇ, unus, a, *one*, N 354, Δ 437. (Il. and ξ 435.) [ῐ]

ἰότητι, τα, (ἵμερος), τινός, *will, moving*, O 41.

ἰούλους, τούς, (οὖλος), *first growth of the beard, downy hair*, λ 319†. [ῐ]

ἰο-χέαιρα, αν, (ἰός, χέω), *arrow-shooting*, E 53.

ἱππάζεαι, 2 sing. prs., *thou art driving* (thy steeds), Ψ 426†.

Ἱππᾰσίδης, son of Hippasos, (1) Apisaon.—(2) Hypsenor.—(3) Charops, and his brother Sokos, Λ 431.

ἱππείου, ον, είων, ῃ, ῃσι, (ἵππος), *of* or *for horses, horse—*; λόφον, *horse-hair* plume, O 537.

ἱππεύς, ἱππῆες, ήων, εῦσι, ῆας, (ἵππος), *hero fighting from chariot, contestant for prize in chariot-race*, Δ 297, Ψ 262.

ἱππ-ηλᾰσίη (ἐλαύνω) ὁδός, road where *chariots may be driven*, H 340 and 439.

ἱππ-ηλάτᾰ, ὁ, (ἐλαύνω), *driver of horses, fighter from chariot, knight*, H 125, γ 436.

ἱππ-ήλᾰτος, *passable with chariots*; δ 607, *adapted to driving horses*.

Ἱππ-ημολγοί (ἀμέλγω), *mare-milkers, Hippemolgoi*, a Skythian tribe, N 5.

ἱππιο-χαίτην, acc., (χαίτη), *of horse-hair, of horse's mane*, Z 469.

ἱππιο-χάρμην, acc., (χάρμη), *fighter from a chariot*, Ω 257, λ 259.

ἱππο-βότοιο, ῳ, ον, (βόσκω), *horse-nourishing, horse-breeding*, epithet esp. of Argos, B 287.

Ἱππο-δάμας, αντα, Trojan warrior, slain by Achilleus, Υ 401.

Ἱππο-δάμεια, (1) daughter of Anchises, N 429.—(2) attendant of Penelope, σ 182.—(3) κλυτός, wife of Peirithoos, B 742.

ἱππό-δᾰμος, -δάμοιο, ου, ον, οι, ων, οισι, ους, (δαμᾶν), *horse taming*, epithet of heroes and of Trojans, γ 17, 181. (Il.)

Ἱππό-δᾰμος, slain by Odysseus, Λ 335†.

ἱππο-δάσεια, ης, ας, (δασύς), *with thick horse-hair plume, bushy with horse-hair*, N 714.

ἱππό-δρομος, *course for chariots*, Ψ 330†.

ἱππόθεν, *from the* (wooden) *horse*, θ 515, λ 531.

Ἱππό-θοος, (1) son of Priamos, Ω 251.—(2) Ληθοῖο Πελασγοῦ υἱός, P 289.

ἱππο-κέλευθε (κελεύω), *horse-urging, swift-driving*, Patroklos, Π 126. (Il.)

ἱππο-κόμου, ον, οι, ων, (κόμη), *decked with horse-hair*, Π 338.

ἱππο-κορυσταί, άς, (κορύσσω), *chariot-equipping, fighters from chariots*, epithet of heroes; also of Maionians and Paionians, B 1, Ω 677.

Ἱππο-κόων, cousin of Rhesos, K 518†.

Ἱππό-λοχος, (1) son of Antimachos, slain by Agamemnon, Λ 122.—(2) a Lykian, son of Bellerophontes, father of Glaukos, Z 206.

ἱππό-μᾰχος, *fighting on horse-back* (v. l. ἱππόδαμοι), K 431†.

Ἱππό-μᾰχος, son of Antimachos, slain by Leonteus, M 189†.

Ἱππό-νοος, a Greek warrior, slain by Hektor, Λ 303†.

ἱππο-πόλων (colere), *horse-rearing, horse-training*, Θρῃκῶν, N 4 and Ξ 227.

ἵππος, sing., du., (-οιϊν), and pl., comm., but usually fem., (no voc.), equus, equa, *horse, mare*, ἄρσενες, θήλεες, and θήλειαι. In battle and for common use, horses were not ridden but harnessed, hence du. and pl. =freq. *span*, i. e. *war-chariot with horses*, and this even when only the chariot is referred to, Γ 265, 113, Δ 142, E 163; opp. infantry, foot, Σ 153; opp. warriors, B 554; ἁλὸς ἵπποι, in simile, δ 708.

ἱπποσύνη, αων, ας, *art of fighting from chariot*, ω 40 and Il. [ῠ]

ἱππότᾰ, ὁ, *chariot fighter, knight*; esp. as epithet of Nestor, B 336, 628.

Ἱπποτάδης, *son of Hippotes*, Aiolos, κ 36†.

Ἱπποτίων, slain by Meriones, Ξ 514; father of Morys, N 792. [ῑ]

ἵππ-ουρις, ιν, (οὐρά), *with horse-tail plume*, T 382.

ἵπτομαι, only 3 sing. **ἴψεται,** aor. ἴψᾰο, (icere), castigare, *chastise*, spoken of gods and of kings, A 454, B 193.

ἱρεύς, see ἱερεύς. **ἱρεύσασθαι,** see ἱερεύω.

Ἱρή, town of Agamemnon, in Messene, I 150.

ἴρηξ, κος, ι, ες, ων = accipiter, *hawk*, O 237. [ῑ]

Ἶρις, ιν, ι, epithets: fleet as the wind, Θ 409; swift, B 786, E 353, 790, Θ 399, O 172; *Iris*, in the Iliad, messenger of the gods, with golden wings, Θ 398. She delivers on the battle-field messages to gods and men; to the latter, usually in assumed human form.

ἶριν, ἴρισσιν, (strictly acc. sing. and dat. pl. from preceding), *rainbow*, Λ 27, P 547.

ἱρόν, ά, see ἱερός.

Ἶρος, lit. *messenger*, nickname of Ἀρναῖος; impudent beggar and parasite of suitors, vanquished in boxing-match by Odysseus, σ 1 sqq., 73, 239.

ἴς, ἶνα, ἶνες, ἴνεσι, (Fίς), *sinews*, nervi, sing., *muscular strength*, vis; then, in general, *strength, force, power*, e. g. of wind and waves; freq. in periphrasis, with κρατερή or ἱρή, σ 3.

ἰσάζουσα, ipf. iter. mid. ἰσάσκετο, (ἴσος), aequans, *balancing*, M 435; *made herself equal*, Ω 607. [ῑ]

ἴσαν, (1) ibant.—(2) noverant, see ΕΙΔ IV.

Ἴσανδρος, son of Bellerophontes, slain by Ares, Z 197. (Il.)

ἴσασι, noverunt, see ΕΙΔ IV.

ἰσάσκετο, see ἰσάζουσα. **ἴσθι,** scito.

ἴσθμιον, τό, (ἰσθμός), *close-fitting necklace*, σ 300†. (See cuts, Nos. 2, 43, and 44, 65, 100.)

I. **ἴσκε,** ipf., (in-sece, *say*), *said; λέγων, spoke* relating, τ 203, χ 31.

II. **ἴσκοντες,** ουσα, (ἴσος), assimulare, *imitate, make like*, δ 279; ἐμὲ σοί, *taking* me *for* thee.

Ἴσμαρος, city of Kikones, ι 40.

ἰσό-θεος, *godlike* (in figure); epithet of heroes, Γ 310; in Odyssey, of Telemachos, α 324. [ῑ]

ἰσό-μορον, acc., *having an equal share, equally powerful, equal*, O 209†. [ῑ]

ἰσό-πεδον, acc., τό, *level ground*, N 142†.

ἴσος, ον, οι; η, ης, ῃ, ην, ας; ον, α, (Fῖσος, cf. ἐίση), *like*, par, in size, number, quantity, exterior, nature=idem or unus, N 704, also with φρονεῖν; aequus, *equal*, ἀτεμβόμενος ἴσης, cheated of his (of right belonging to him) just share; ἶσον ἐμοὶ φάσθαι, imagine himself my equal, A 187.—ἶσα (αἶσα ?), β 203, *reparation;* elsewh. e. g. ἶσον, adv., pariter, *on equal terms with*, ξ 203, with dat., I 616; κατὰ ἶσα =ἐπὶ ἶσα, *equally balanced, undecided;* of battle opp. ἑτεραλκέα.

Ἶσος, illegitimate son of Priamos, slain by Agamemnon, Λ 101†.

ἰσο-φαρίζει, οι, ειν, prs., (φᾶρος from φέρω), τινί, *make one's self equal, vie with, rival*, in any thing, τι, Z 101, I 390. (Il.)

ἰσο-φόροι, *drawing alike, equally strong*, σ 373†. [ῑ]

ἰσόω only **ἰσωσαίμην** (ἴσος) τοῖσιν ἐν, to them *would I compare* myself, η 212†.

ἴσπω only **ἔσπετε** = σέσπετε, imp. red. aor., (σεπ-, sec-), *declare*, B 484. (Il.)

ἵστημι, I. trans., collocare, prs.,

(imp. ἵστη, inf. ἱστάμεναι), ipf. also iter. ἵστασκε, fut. στήσειν, 1 aor. ἔστησε, στῆσα, ε, ἔστησαν (ἔστᾰσαν, Μ 56, γ 182; elsewh. read ἵστασαν), in general; *set, place*, of things; *cause to rise*, cloud, fog; excitare, pugnam, rixam, *rouse, begin*, battle, strife, π 292; *stop*, mill; νῆα, *bring to land*, τ 188; *weigh off*, τάλαντα, pounds; pass. aor. ἐστάθη *stood firm*, ρ 463. II. intr., *set one's self, stand*, mid. prs., ipf., fut., also act. 2 aor. **ἔστην**=στῆν, *I stood*, στῆμεν, ἔστητε, ἔστησαν, στῆσαν, ἵστᾰν, στάν, and iter. στάσκε, subj. στῶ, στήῃς, ῃ, ομεν, στέωμεν, dissyllable by synizesis, Α 348; inf. στήμεναι, pf. **ἕστηκα**, *I stand*, ας, ε, ασιν, (ἕστητε, Δ 243, 246?), and sync. pf. ἕστατον, μεν, τε, ἑστᾶσι, imp. ἕσταθι, τε, part. ἑστεῶτα, ες (in first foot of verse, θ 380, Β 170). ἑστᾰότος, α, ες, ων (in second foot); plupf. ἑστήκει, ἕστασαν, of things with and without life, *rise up, arise*, Α 535, cf. ὀρθός, dust, battle; μὴν ἱστάμενος, *coming, advancing* month; *stand firmly, still*. III. mid. **στήσασθαι**, *set up for one's self*, or something *of one's own*; μάχην, pugnam committere, join battle, Σ 533, ι 54.

Ἱστίαια (pronounce Ἱστjαίαν), city in Euboia, Β 537†.

ἱστίη, ἡ, (ἑστία), *hearth*, ξ 159. (Od.) [ῑ]

ἱστίον, ῳ, pl. α, (ἱστός), *sail, sails*, Α 481, 433, β 426. (See adjoining cut, from ancient coin bearing the inscription, ΝΙΚΟΜΗΔΙΩΝ . ΔΙΣ . ΝΕΩΚΟΡΩΝ.)

ἱστο-δόκη (δέχομαι), *mast-receiver, mast-crutch*, a saw-horse-shaped support on the after-deck to receive the mast when lowered, Α 434†. (Plate IV.)

ἱστο-πέδη (πέδη), *mast-stay*, a thwart or transverse beam with a depression into which the mast fitted, which was by this means, as well as by the ἐπίτονοι, prevented from falling forward, μ 51. (See cut, letter *b*.)

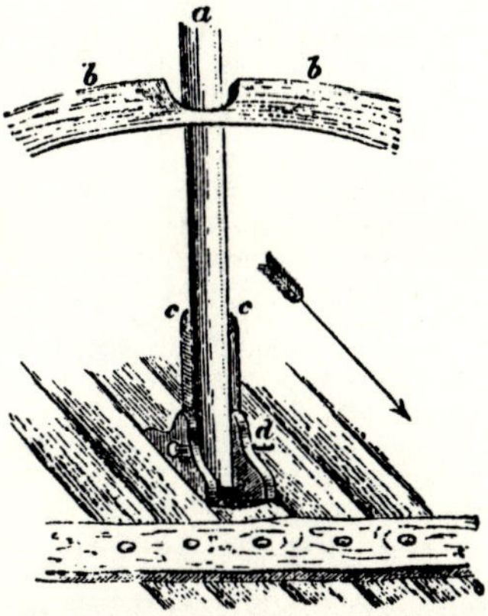

ἱστός, οῦ, ῷ, όν, οί, ούς, (ἵστημι, that which stands), (1) *mast* in middle of ship, held in place by μεσόδμη, ἱστοπέδη, πρότονοι, ἐπίτονοι; during stay in port the mast was unstepped and laid back upon the ἱστοδόκη (cf. preceding cut, and Nos. 64, 91, 109).—(2) *weaver's beam, loom*. The frame of the loom was not placed, as in modern hand-looms, in a horizontal position, but stood upright as appears in the cut, representing an ancient Egyptian

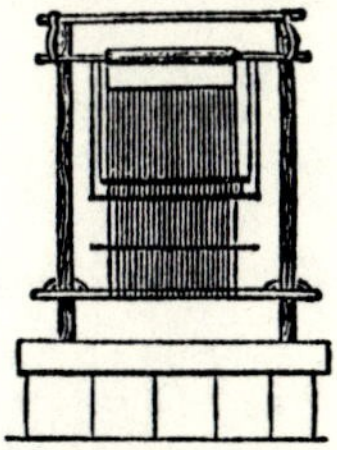

loom. The threads of the warp hung perpendicularly down, and were drawn tight by weights at their lower ends. To set up the beam and so begin the web is (ἱστόν) στήσασθαι. In weaving, the weaver passed from one side to the other before the loom (ἐποίχεσθαι) as he carried the shuttle (κανών), on which was wound the thread of the woof, through the warp, and then drew the woof home with a blow of the κερκίς.—(3) *warp*, and in general *web*, *woven stuff*.

ἴστω, scito, see ΕΙΔ IV.

ἴστορι, α, dat. acc., (οἶδα), *one who knows, judge*, Σ 501, Ψ 486.

ἰσχᾰλέοιο, gen. sing., (ἰσχνός), *dry, withered*, τ 233†.

ἰσχᾰνάας, α, mid. ἀσθω, ipf. iter. ἰσχανάασκον, also pres. **ἰσχάνει,** ipf. ἴσχανε, έτην, and **ἰσχανόωσι,** όων, όωσαν, mid. όωνται, όωντο, (ἴσχω), retinere, *detain*, ο 346; arcere, *keep off*, P 747; mid. *restrain one's self*, M 38; and *delay*, T 234; but with gen. or inf., *desire*, P 572, Ψ 300.

ἰσχίον, ῳ, α, (ἰξύς), *hip-joint*, E 306, κοτύλη; then coxa, *parts about the hips, flanks*, or *loins*, E 305. [ῐον.]

ἴσχωσι, prs., inf. ἰσχέμεν(αι), and ipf. act. and mid. (red. prs. from ἔχω), tenere, retinere, *hold, restrain*; τινός, arcere, *keep away from*, E 90; mid., *put restraint upon one's self, stay*, χ 367; *stop*, ω 54; τινάς, *desist from*.

ἰτέαι (Fιτ., vimen, withe), *willows*, Φ 350 and κ 510.

ἴτην, ibant ambo.

Ἴτῠλος, son of Aëdon, τ 522†. [ι]

Ἰτῠμονεύς, ῆα, son of Hypeirochos, slain by Nestor, Λ 672†. [ῐ]

ἴτυς, υν, (Fιτέη), *felloes of wheel*, Δ 486. (Il.) [ῐ]

ἴτω, ito, from εἶμι.

Ἴτων, ωνα, town in Thessaly, B 696†. [ῐ]

ἰῠγμῷ, dat., (ἰύζω), *cry of joy*, Σ 572†. [ῐ]

ἰύζουσιν, οντες, (ἰού), *scream* (with intent to scare away), ο 162 and P 66. [ῐ]

Ἰφεύς, έα, a Trojan slain by Patroklos, Π 417†.

Ἰφθίμη, daughter of Ikarios, wife of Eumelos, δ 797†.

ἴφθῑμος, η, α, etc., (τιμή ?), *strong, mighty*; deriv. and signif. still uncertain, A 3.

ἶφῐ (Fῖφι, really old case form from Fίς, ἴς), vi, *by violence*, κταμένοιο; *with might*, ρ 443.

Ἰφῐ-άνασσα, daughter of Agamemnon, I 145 and 287. [ῐφ.]

Ἰφι-δάμας, αντος, son of Antenor and of Theano, Λ 21 sqq. (Il.) [– ⏑ ⏑ –]

Ἰφι-κληείης, η, βίης, periphrasis for

Ἴφικλος, son of Phylakos, father of Podarkes and Protesilaos, B 705, N 698, Ψ 636, λ 289 sqq.

Ἰφι-μέδεια, wife of Aloeus and mother of Otos and Ephialtes, λ 305. [– ⏑ ⏑]

Ἰφί-νοος, son of Dexios, slain by Glaukos, H 14†. [– ⏑ ⏑]

ἴφια (Fίς) μῆλα, *fat* sheep, E 556, λ 108. [ῑφῐ.]

Ἶφῐς εὐζωνος, from Skyros, wife of Patroklos, I 667†.

Ἰφιτίδης, Archeptolemos, Θ 128†.

Ἰφῐτίων, ωνα, Ὀτρυντείδην, slain by Achilleus, Υ 382.

Ἴφῐτος (Fίφιτος), (1) Εὐρυτίδης, an Argonaut, guest-friend of Odysseus, slain by Herakles, φ 14–37.—(2) Ναυβολίδαο, an Argonaut, from Phokis, father of Schedios and Epistrophos, P 306, B 518.—(3) father of Archeptolemos.

ἰχθυάᾳ, pr. and ipf. iter. ἰχθυάασκον, (ἰχθύς), *fish*, μ 95 and δ 368.

ἰχθυόεντι, τα, (ἰχθύς), *abounding in fish, full of monsters of the deep*, ι 83, I 4, δ 381.

ἰχθύς and pl. ύες, ύσιν, ύας, ῦς, piscis, *fish*, only eaten in lack of other food, δ 368.

ἴχνια, pl. with the form **ἴχνεσι,** (Fίκω), vestigia, *steps*, β 406; ρ 317, odoratione, *scent*; but N 71 (see ἴκελος), *outlines, similar lines, resemblance*.

ἰχώρ, acc. ἰχῶ, (ἰκμάς), *fluid that flows in veins of the gods*, E 340 and 416. [ῑ]

ἴψ, pl. **ἶπες,** (Fισπ., vespa ?), *worm* that devours horn and wood, *borer*, φ 395†.

ἴψαο, ἴψεται, *chastise, strike*; see ἴπτομαι.

ἰωγῇ (Fάγνυμι) Βορέω ὑπ', under *shelter from* Boreas, ξ 533†. [ι]

ἰωή, ῆς, (αὐτή), *sound* (of voice), K 139; *tone, note*, ρ 261; *roaring, whistling* (of wind).

ἰωκή, pl. άς, also acc. sing. **ἰῶκα,** (διώκω), *attack*, E 521; personified, E 740. (Il.) [ῐ]

ἰωχμόν (ἰῶκα), ἀν', through *the battle-tumult*, Θ 89 and 158. [ῑ]

K.

κ' =(1) κέ, (2) καί.

κάββαλε, deiecit, from καταβάλλω.

κὰγ (κατά) γόνυ, *on the knee*, Υ 458†.

Κᾰβησόθεν, *from Kabesos*, Ν 363†.

κάγκᾰνᾰ, arida, *dry*, Φ 364.

καγχᾰλόωσι, όων, όωσα, (χάσκω), *laugh aloud, exult*, Γ 43.

καδ =κατά before δ, Φ 318. **καδδραθέτην,** aor. from καταδαρθάνω, ο 494.

καδδῦσαι, aor. part., penetrantes, from καταδύω.

Καδμεῖοι, *Kadmeioi, Thebans*, Δ 391; =**Καδμείωνες,** Δ 385.

Κάδμος, original founder of Thebes; his daughter Ino, ε 333†.

Κάειρα, fem. of Κάρ, *from Karia, Karian*, Δ 142†. [ᾰ]

καήμεναι, inf. aor. pass. from καίω, cremo.

καθ-αιρέω, fut. -**αιρήσουσι,** aor. -είλομεν, subj. -έλῃσι, part. -ελοῦσα; also in tmesi, ipf. ᾕρεε, εον, aor. ἕλον, ῃσιν, έειν, *take down*, Ω 268, ι 149; *close* the eyes of the dead, Λ 453; *overpower*.

κᾰθαίρειν (καθαρός), ipf. κάθαιρον, aor. ἐκάθηρε, κάθηραν, etc., *cleanse, clean*; σ 192, *adorn*; abluere, *wash off, away*, soil, blood, Ξ 171, ζ 93; τινά αἷμα, Π 667.

κᾰθ-αλλομένη, aor. **κατᾶλτο,** *rush down*, Λ 298†.

καθ-άπαξ, *once for all*, φ 349†. [⏑⏑–]

κᾰθ-άπτεσθαι, prs., ipf. καθάπτετο, (ἅπτω), compellare, *address*, ἐπέεσσι μαλακοῖσιν; also reprehendere, *upbraid*, Ο 127.

καθαρῷ, ά, purus, *clean*; ἐν κ., in a *clear, open space*, Θ 491; θάνατος, *honorable*.

κατ' ἕζεαι, subj. -εζώμεσθα, imp. -έζευ, ipf. καθέζετο, -εζέσθην, freq. in tmesi, consido, *sit down*; πρόχνυ, *placing herself* upon her knees, Ι 570.

καθέηκα = καθῆκα, from ἵημι. **καθείατο** = καθῆντο, from κάθημαι.

καθ-εῖσε, εἷσαν, aor., freq. in tmesi, (ἕζω), *bid be seated*, Η 57, Ψ 698; *set, place*, δ 524.

καθέξει, fut. from κατ-έχω.

κᾰθ-εύδετον, du., inf. prs., ipf. καθεῦδε, dormire, *sleep*, Α 611. (Od.)

κᾰθ-εψιόωνται (ἑψιάομαι) σέθεν, te irrident, *deride, insult*, τ 372†.

κᾰθ-ήμενος, etc., imp. κάθησο, pf., plupf. καθῆστο, pl. καθείατο, (ἧμαι), sedere, *sit*, Α 134 and Λ 76, Ω 403.

καθῆραι, αν, aor. from καθαίρω.

κᾰθ-ίδρυε, considere iussit, υ 257†.

κᾰθ-ίζᾰνον, 3 pl. ipf., considebant, *were gathering to the assembly and taking seats there*, ε 3†.

κᾰθ-ίζων, prs., ipf. καθῖζε, ον, often in tmesi, I. act. and mid., sedere, *sit*, ἐπὶ κλισμοῖς, etc.—II. act. prs. ipf. aor. κάθισαν, imp. ισον, part. ίσσας, *place*, Ι 488; considere iubeo, *bid be seated*, Τ 280, Ζ 360; *convoke*, β 69.

κᾰθ-ίημι, only -**ίετε,** aor. καθέηκα (elsewh. in tmesi), *let down, lower*; λαυκανίης, *pour down* through the throat, moisten the throat, Ω 642.

κᾰθ-ίκεο, ετο, (ἵκω), *touch, reach*, α 342.

κᾰθ-ίστα, imp. prs., aor. imp. στῆσον, inf. στῆσαι, *set down*; νῆα, *bring to land, anchor*; ν 274, *bring, carry*.

καθ-ορῶν, mid. -ορᾶται, ορώμενος, *look down upon*, τι, Ω 291.

κᾰθ-ύπερθεν, desuper, *from above*, Γ 337; supra, Μ 153, Σ 353; ultra, *besides*, Ω 545.

καί, (1) copulative: *as well as*, Ο 634, λ 417; et, *and*, Α 7, α 5; distributive=(et—et), *both—and*, λ 417, Α 395; uniting two imperatives (in transition of thought), σ 171; καὶ δέ, and besides, ξ 39; δή, and already, Α 161, μ 330; κ. μέν, and yet, Α 269; κ. τέ, and besides also, Α 521; κ. τόν, at beginning of verse, et hunc quidem, Ψ 748; *or even, or also*, β 374, instead of τέ, Β 49, Ζ 268, α 159.—(2) *also*, expressing a natural (logical or actual) harmony between two clauses: ὅς (τε), which *also*, Υ 165, Ε 62, λ 111; in protasis and apodosis, Ζ 476, Β 367; esp. freq. introducing apodosis, Α 478;

καὶ τότε δή—γάρ τε, Α 63, nam et, etenim; instead of rel. form, β 114; κ. λίην, yes to be sure, by all means, Α 553; ἔπειτα, and finally; ἠὲ καί (οὐκί), or also (not), δ 809; cf. French ou bien, Β 300; cf. Α 95; νῦν, and now also, joining to a general sentence a special illustration of truth previously announced, Α 109, Β 239, κ 43; καὶ ἄλλους, φ 293; κ. ἄλλοτε, previously also; κ. ἄλλως, already without this, φ 87; καὶ αὐτοί, α 33 (περ, Α 577), of themselves also, sponte.—(3) emphatic, *also, even:* e. g. καὶ δέ, besides, moreover, Ν 484; κ. βουλοίμην, Γ 41; δέ τε, Υ 28; μᾶλλον, etiam magis, even more, Θ 470.—(4) concessive, e. g. where force may be given by *although, though* thou shouldst destroy, Ρ 647; μάλα περ, with part., Α 217, Ρ 571.—(5) separated from ἄλλα, which it emphasizes, by δὲ or γὰρ intervening, ξ 39; κ., *also*, emphasizing the following word, Γ 184 (as well as to other places); καὶ εἰ=et si and etsi, even if; εἰ καί, etiamsi, if even, although; shortened in η 221; by elision, κ'; by crasis, χήμεῖς, καὐτός, κἀγώ, κἀκεῖνος.

καιετάεσσαν (κείω), *full of caverns*, δ 1† (v. l. κητώεσσαν, q. v.).

Καινεΐδης, Koronos, Β 746†.

Καινεύς, king of Lapithai, Α 264†.

καίνυμαι, ipf. **ἐκαίνυτο**, pf. κέκασται, σμένος, plupf. ἐκέκαστο, superiorem esse, excellere, *be superior, excel*, τισί, Δ 339, ι 509; ἐπί τινας, Ω 535, cf. ω 509; ἔν τισι, δ 725; μετά τισι, τ 82; τῶν, Ω 546; ἐπί τινι, excellere, Υ 35; superare, *surpass*, τινά τινι, Β 530, τ 395; with inf., β 158, γ 282.

καί—περ, always separated, *although*.

καιρίῳ, ιον, letalis, *fatal*, Θ 84; ἐν καιρ., in a vital part, Δ 185. (Il.)

καιροσέων, better καιροσσέων for καιρουσσῶν (καιροεσσέων, pronounced with synizesis), gen. pl. fem. from adj. καιρόεις, *with many* καῖροι, i. e. loops or thrums to which the threads of the warp were attached; κ. ὀθονέων, from the *fine-woven* linen, η 107†.

καίουσι, 3 pl. ind., subj. -ωμεν, inf. -έμεν, imp. part. prs., ipf. καῖε, aor. ἔκηε, κῆε, subj. κήομεν, opt. κήαι, αιεν, etc., mid. κήαντο, άμενος, οι, pass. prs., ipf. καίετο, ετο, etc., aor. ἐκάη, inf. καήμεναι, *kindle, burn;* mid. for one's self, Ι 88, 234; pass., ardere, cremari, *be lighted, blaze.*

κάκ=κατά by apocope and assimilation before κ.

κᾰκιζόμενον (κακός), *play the coward*, Ω 214†.

κακ-κεῖαι and **κακ-κῆαι,** see κατακαιέμεν.

κακ-κείοντες, see κατα-κείω.

κᾰκο-είμονας, acc. pl., (Fεῖμα), *ill-clad*, σ 41†.

κᾰκο-εργίης, gen. sing., (Fέργον), *ill-doing*, maleficentia, χ 374†.

κᾰκο-εργός, (Fέργον), maleficus, *villainous, importunate*, σ 54†.

Κᾰκο-ίλιον, acc., *evil Ilios*, τ 260, 597, ψ 19.

κᾰκο-μηχάνου, ε, (μηχᾰνή), *contriving evil, malicious*, π 418.

κᾰκο-ξεινώτερος, *having sorrier guests*, υ 376†.

κακο-ρραφίης, ῃ, ῃσι, (ῥάπτω), *maliciousness, evil device*, μ 26.

κακός, ή, όν, etc., malus, *bad, worthless, wicked*, in widest signif., in appearance, position, usefulness, courage, morals, way of thinking; hence *ugly, vile, useless, cowardly, low, injurious, fatal;* esp. as subst., **κακόν,** ά, = malum, a, *evil, pest;* of Skylla, μ 118; adv. **κακῶς,** male, Α 25, β 203; comp. **κακώτερος,** ον, *worse*, Τ 321; *feebler*, Χ 106; *malicious person*, ζ 275; **κακίων,** ιους, ιον, sup. κάκιστος, ον, *poorer*, ξ 56; *less honorable*, Ι 601; *worse*, σ 174; deteriores, β 277; *the worst*, δ 199.

κᾰκό-τεχνος (τέχνη), *devising evil, wily*, Ο 14†.

κᾰκότητος, gen., τι, τα, (κακότης), scelus, *wickedness, cowardice;* malum, *evil, misery, distress*, ρ 318; esp. in war, e. g. Λ 382.

κᾰκο-φρᾰδές, voc., (φράζω, φρήν), *bad in counsel, foolish*, malevole, Ψ 483†.

κᾰκόω, imp. **κάκου**, aor. κακῶσαι, etc., pf. pass. part. κεκακωμένος, οι, (κακός), vexare, τινά, *pain, injure, maltreat*, υ 99; ζ 137, *disfigured*, foedatus.

κάκτανε, see κατακτείνω. **κακώτερος,** see κακός.

κᾰλάμην, acc., (calamus, German halm), *reed*, Τ 222; looking upon the poor husk which remains, thou art yet able to recognize what I was, ξ 214.

κᾰλα-ύροπα, (from κάλως and ϝροπα), *shepherd's staff*, Ψ 845†.

κᾰλέω, prs. ipf. act. and pass. comm. uncontracted forms: καλέει, etc., yet not always, e. g. inf. καλήμεναι, part. καλεῦντες; ipf. κάλεον, pass. καλεῦντο, iter. καλέεσκον, καλέσκετο; fut. καλέει, έων, aor. ἐκάλεσσας, αν, also κάλεσας, κάλεσσαν, καλέσσας, etc. (with σ and σσ), mid. καλέσσατο, etc., perf. pass. κέκλημαι, plupf. κεκλήατο, 3 fut. κεκλήσῃ, (calare), (1) *call; ἄμυδις*, together; with εἰς-, -δε, ἐπὶ οἱ, βουλήν, to the council; θάνατόνδε, Π 693; invitare, *invite*, also mid.—(2) nominare, Α 403, pass. (esp. pf. and plupf. and 3 fut.); vocari, *be called, be, pass for*, κεκλημένος εἴη(ν), ζ 244 (Β 260); καλέσκετο, Ο 338, Ξ 210; also καλέω, ξ 147, *I call* him dearly loved, he *is* tenderly loved by me.

Κᾰλήσιος, companion of Axylos, slain by Diomedes, Ζ 18†.

Κᾰλητορίδης, Aphareus, Ν 541†.

κᾰλήτορα, acc., (καλέω), calator, *crier*, Ω 577†.

Κᾰλήτωρ, (1) son of Klytios, cousin of Hektor, slain by Aias, Ο 419.—(2) father of Aphareus.

καλλείπειν, καλλείψειν, see καταλείπω.

Καλλῐ-άνασσα and **Καλλῐάνειρα,** Nereids, Σ 46, 44†. [–⏑⏑–⏑]

Καλλίαρος, town in Lokris, Β 531†. [–⏑⏑⏑]

καλλῐ-γύναικα, *with beautiful women*, Hellas, Achaia, Sparta, ν 412.

καλλί-ζωνος, ων, (ζώνη), *with beautiful girdles* (see cut No. 47), Η 139.

Καλλῐ-κολώνη, lit. *Fair-mount*, near Ilios, Υ 151.

καλλι-κόμοιο (κόμη), cf. ἠΰκομος, *with beautiful hair*, Ι 449.

καλλι-κρήδεμνοι (κρή-δεμνον), *with beautiful fillets* or *head-bands*, δ 623†.

κάλλιμος, ον, α, *glorious*, λ 640. (Od.)

κάλλιον, see καλός.

καλλι-πάρηος, ῳ, ον, (παρειά), *beautiful-cheeked, fair-cheeked*, Α 143.

κάλλιπε, πέειν, see καταλείπω.

καλλι-πλοκάμου, οιο, ῳ, *with beautiful locks* or *braids*, cf. ἐυπλοκαμῖδες (πλόκαμος), Ξ 326. (See cut No. 47.)

καλλι-ρέεθρον, *beautifully flowing*, κ 107. (Od.)

καλλι-ρρόοιο, ῳ, ον, (-σροος, ῥόος), *beautifully flowing*, Β 752, ε 441.

κάλλιστος, see καλός.

καλλί-σφῠρος, ου, ον, *with beautiful ankles*, (σφυρά), *slender-footed*, ε 333.

καλλί-τρῐχος, α, ε, ες, ας, (θρίξ), *with soft fleece*, ι 336; *with beautiful manes*, Θ 348.

κάλλιφ'=κατέλιπε.

καλλι-χόρου (χορός), *with beautiful places, with large squares for the choral dance*, λ 581†.

κάλλος, εος, εϊ, *beauty*; σ 192, *means for enhancing beauty* [*unguent?*].

κᾱλός, ή, όν, adv. καλῶς, β 63; comp. **καλλίονες,** ιον, sup. κάλλιστος, ον, ους, αι, pulcher, δέμας, *beautiful*, of form, in build; *fitting, becoming*, τινί, for any one; εἰπεῖν, ἀγορεύειν, *well*. Adv. καλά, in the middle of verse, Θ 400, and καλόν with ἀείδειν, Α 473.

κάλους, acc. pl. from κάλως, *ropes, halyards*; which, passing through a hole at top of mast, and made fast at bottom of same, served to raise and lower the yard. (See cut.)

κάλπῐν, τήν, *water jar*, η 20†. (See cut, from picture on ancient vase, on next page.)

Κᾰλύδναι νῆσοι, near Kos, Β 677†.

Καλυδών, ῶνος, city on the river Euenos in Aitolia; ἐραννῇς, αἰπεινῇ, πετρήεσσαν, Ι 530, Ν 217, Β 640.

κάλυμμα, το, (κᾰλύπτω), *veil*, Ω 93†. (See cuts Nos. 2, 47, 66, 74.)

κάλῠκας, τάς, (κάλυξ), women's ornaments, Σ 401†; perhaps *cup-shaped ear-rings*. (See cut No. 8.)

κᾰλύπτρην, τήν, (καλύπτω), *woman's*

veil, ε 232. (Cf. adjoining cut, and Nos. 2, 47, 74.)

κἄλύπτων, part., prs., fut. *καλύψω*, aor. (ἐ)*κάλυψε*, also mid., pass. pf. *κεκαλυμμένος*, plupf. *κεκάλυφθ'* = *ἐκεκάλυπτο*, aor. *καλυφθείς*, (calim, occultus), *veil*, θ 85; *cover*, K 29, Ψ 693 (mid., *veil one's self*, Γ 141); *τινί*, *cover up with*, Σ 352; *πρόσθεν στέρνοιο* (*οἱ*), hold as protection before the breast (before one's self); *σάκος ἀμφί τινι*, protect one with the shield; pass., *wrapped up in*, α 443 (*ἐντυπάς*, closely); *hidden*, θ 503; fig. *τὸν δὲ σκότος ὄσσε*, Δ 461, so also *κατ' ὀφθαλμῶν νύξ*, N 580, darkness *overshadowed* his eyes; *τέλος θανάτοιο*, end of death, complete death, E 553; grief, a cloud of grief *enveloped* him, Λ 249, ω 315.

Κἄλυψώ, *οῦς*, daughter of Atlas, dwelling in Ogygia, where she rescues, and detains for seven years, the shipwrecked Odysseus, η 259; until compelled by command of Zeus to dismiss him, ε 28, η 265; epithets, *δολόεσσα*, *δεινὴ θεός*, *ἐυπλόκαμος*, *αὐδήεσσα*, *ἠυκόμοιο*, *νύμφη πότνια*.

Κάλχας, *αντος*, son of Thestor, Grecian seer before Troy, A 69, 86; *θεόπροπος οἰωνιστής*, N 70. (Il.)

κάμ = *κατά* by apoc. and assimil. before *μ*.

κάμαξι, dat. pl., (*ἡ κάμαξ*), *vine-poles*, *vine-props*, Σ 563†. [⏑ – ⏑]

κἄμἄτος, *οιο*, *ῳ*, *ον*, (*κάμνω*), labor, aerumna, fatigatio, *toil*, *distress*, *fatigue*; ξ 417, fruit of our toil.

κάμβαλε = *κατέβαλεν*, ζ 172.

κάμε, aor. from *κάμνω*, *wrought*.

Κάμειρος, town on west coast of Rhodos, B 656†. [ᾰ]

κἄμῖνοῖ, *τῷ*, nom. *καμινώ*, (*κάμινος*), *baker-woman*, σ 27†.

καμ-μίξας, aor. from *καταμίγνυμι*.

καμ-μονίην, *τήν*, (*κατα-μένω*), victory as reward of *endurance*, X 257†.

κάμ-μορον, *ε*, (*κατά-μορος*?), *ill-starred*, *hapless*, β 351; applied to Odysseus.

κάμνεις, *ει*, prs., ipf., aor. *ἔκαμον κάμε*, *ετον*, subj. *κάμω*, *ῃσι*, part. *καμόντα*, *ας*, *ων*; pf. *κέκμηκας*, *κεκμηώς*, *ῶτι*, *ῶτα*, *ότας*, mid. fut. *καμεῖται*, aor. *καμόμεσθα*, *ἐκάμοντο*, I. laborare, *weary one's self out*, *become tired*, Λ 802, κ 31, Z 261 sq., Θ 22, Δ 27; with acc. of part. *γυῖα*, *ὦμον*, *χεῖρα*, μ 280, Π 106; with part., φ 150, Φ 26, H 5; with neutr. subj., μ 232; *ὄσσε*, *πόδες*, Ψ 444; *καμόντες*, confecti, *those who have finished their toil*, the dead.—II. elaborare, *make ready with care and labor*, *work*, (aor. act.), Δ 187, ψ 189; with *τεύχων*, work skillfully; aor. mid., ι 130, would have transformed into a well-tilled, habitable island; acquire for one's self, Σ 341.

κάμπτω, only fut. **κάμψειν,** aor. *ἔκαμψε*, *κάμψῃ*, flecto, *bend*; Δ 486, *bend into* a tire; *γόνυ*, bend the knee = sit down to rest when weary with running, H 118; ε 453, let sink upon the ground.

καμπύλον, *α*, (*κάμπτω*), *bent*, *curved*, E 231. [ῠ]

κἄνάχησε, aor. from *-έω*, (*κάναχος*), *rang*, τ 469†. [⏑ ⏑]

κἄνἄχή, *ήν*, sonitus, strepitus, T 365, *gnashing*; ζ 82, *rattle* of harness of mule team in motion.

κἄνάχιζε, ipf., (*καναχή*), *creaked*, M 36; *re-echoed*, κ 399. [⏑ ⏑ – ⏑]

κάνεον, sing. and pl. *κάνεια*, *έοισι*, (*κάνη*), *basket* for wheaten bread; *dish* for meat and sacrificial barley, α 147, ρ 343. [ᾰ]

καν-νεύσας, aor. part. from *κατα-νεύω*.

κανών, *όνεσσι, όνας*, masc., (*κάνη*), (1) *shuttle* or *spool*, by which the thread of the woof was drawn through the thread of the warp, Ψ 761.—(2) *handle* on interior of shield, grasped by the left hand, Θ 193, N 407. (Il.) (See cuts Nos. 12, 17, 85; rudely represented in adjoining cut, after Assyrian relief.)

κάπ = *κατά*, before π and φ.

Κᾰπᾰνεύς, *ῆος*, one of the Seven against Thebes, father of Sthenelos, E 319; *ἀγακλειτοῦ, κυδαλιμοῖο*.

Κᾰπᾰνηιάδης and Κᾰπᾰνήιος *υἱός*, Sthenelos, E 109, 108.

κᾰπέτοιο, *ον*, from ἡ *κάπετος*, (*σκάπτω*), *ditch, grave*, Σ 564, Ω 797. (Il.)

κάπῃσι, dat. pl., praesepe, *manger*, δ 40, Θ 434. [ᾰ]

κάπνισσαν, 3 pl. aor. from *καπνίζω*, *lighted fires*, B 399†.

καπνός, *οῦ*, sing., (*καπύω*), fumus, *smoke*; μ 202, *cloud of spray* from violently agitated water.

κάπ-πεσον, *εν*, aor. from *καταπίπτω*.

κάπριος, *φ, ον*, (*κάπρος*), with and without *σῦς*, aper, *wild-boar*, M 42, P 282. (Il.)

κάπρου, *φ, ον, ω, οισι*, *wild-boar*, P 21; T 197, *boar*.

Κάπυς, *υος*, son of Assarakos, father of Anchises, Υ 239†.

καπύω, aor. in tmesi, *ἀπὸ* **ἐκάπυσσεν**, *breathed forth*, X 467†.

I. **κάρ** = *κατά*, before ρ.

II. **κᾰρός**, *ἐν—αἴσῃ*, (from *κείρω*?), = *a whittling*; cf. Lat. flocci; I care for him not *a whit*, I 378; the derivation of the word is uncertain.

III. **κάρ**, *ἐπὶ—*, *headlong*, Π 392†; here belong **κάρη**, *ητος, ητι*, and **καρήατος**, *-τι*, pl. *-τα*, also gen. **κρατός**, *τί*, pl. *κράτων, κρασίν*, K 152; *κράτεσφι*, K 156; also **κράατος**, *-τι*, acc. pl. *-τα*, and *κρᾶτα*, (*κορυφή, κόρυμβος*, Lat. cer-ebrum, cer-vices), caput, *head*, as part of body, also pl. θ 92, spoken of one head; of mountain summit, Υ 5; *λιμένος*, the end reaching farthest into the land, ι 140.—**κατὰ κρῆθεν**, *from head* (to foot), *utterly, entirely*, Π 548, λ 588.

Καρδᾰμύλη, town subject to Agamemnon, in Messene, I 150. [ῠ]

καρδίη, *ῃ*, see *κραδίη*, cor, *heart*.

Κᾶρες, Karians in S.W. of Asia Minor, *βαρβαροφώνων*, B 867. (Il.)

κάρη κομόωντες, *ας*, = capite comati, *long-haired*, B 11, α 90; of Achaians, who cut their hair only in mourning, or on taking a vow, Ψ 146, 151; while slaves and Asiatics habitually shaved their heads.

κάρηνα, *ων, τά*, (*κάρ* III.), capita, cacumina, *heads, summits*, also *battlements*, B 117. [ᾰ]

Κάρησος, river rising in Mount Ida, M 20†. [ᾰ]

κάρκαιρε, ipf., *quaked*, Υ 157†.

καρπᾰλίμοισι, dat. pl., adv. *-ίμως*, pernices, *swift, quick*, epithet of feet, Π 342, A 359, β 406.

καρπός, masc., only sing., fructus, fruges, *fruit*, *ἐπὶ καρπῷ* (σ 258), by the *ball, joint of the hand, wrist*.

καρρέζουσα, see *κατα-ρέζω*.

καρτερό-θῡμον, *ε, ων*, (*κρατερός*), *strong-hearted*, E 277, Ξ 512. (Il.)

καρτερός, see *κρατερός*.

κάρτιστος, *ον, ην, οι, οις*, (*κάρτος*), robustissimus, potentissimus; neutr., μ 120, *the greatest valor*.

κάρτος, see *κράτος*.

ἐκαρτύναντο, ipf. mid., (*καρτύνω*), *φάλαγγας*, *were strengthening* their ranks, Λ 215. (Il.) [ῡ]

Κάρυστος, fem., town at southern extremity of Euboia, B 539†. [ᾰ]

καρφᾰλέον, *έων*, ntr., (*κάρφω*), aridus, *dry*; of sound, *dull, hollow*, N 409. (Il.)

κάρφω, fut. **κάρψω**, aor. *κάρψε*, *shrivel up*, ν 398 and 430.

καρχᾰλέοι *δίψῃ*, *rough with thirst*, i. e. the throat rough and dry, Φ 541†.

καρχᾰρ-όδοντε, *ων*, *sharp-toothed*, *sharp-biting*, of dogs, Κ 360. (Il.)

κασί-γνητος, *οιο*, *ον*, etc., and **-γνήτη**, *ην*, *αι*, *ῃσι*, *own brother*, *sister* (of the same mother), Ζ 430, Δ 155, 441; also consobrinus, *cousin*, Ο 545.

Κάσος, island near Kos, Β 676†.

Κασσ-άνδρη, the most beautiful daughter of Priamos, prophetess, captive of Agamemnon, murdered by Klytaimnestra, Ν 366, Ω 699, λ 422.

κασσῐτέρου, *οιο*, *ῳ*, *ον*, *tin*, as ornament of weapons and chariots; *χεῦμα*, stream or border of tin, to give strength, Ψ 561.

Καστῐ-άνειρα, *καλή*, *Αἰσύμνηθεν*, mother of Gorgythion, Θ 305†.

καστορνῦσα, see *κατα-στορέννυμι*.

Κάστωρ, *ορος*, (1) son of Zeus and Leda, brother of Polydeukes and Helena, participated in Kalydonian boarhunt and in Argonautic expedition, Γ 237, λ 299 sqq.—(2) son of Hylakos, ξ 204.

κά-σχεθε instead of *κατ-έσχεθε*, Λ 702, retinuit.

κατά (and *καταί*, also *κάτα*, *κατ'*, in anastrophe and tmesi, also *κάτ'*, ρ 246; by assimilation also *καβ*, *καγ*, *καδ*, *κακ* [*καλ*?], *καμ*, *καπ* [before π and *φάλαρ'*], *καρ*, *κάτ-θανε*), I. with gen. of place: *from above down*, *down from*, *Οὐλύμποιο*, *οὐρανοῦ*, cf. κ 362; *down over*, *ὀφθαλμῶν*, *κρῆθεν*, desuper, *ἄκρης*, from crown (to sole), wholly; *ἵππων*, down from the chariot, Ε 111; *ῥινῶν*, *down into* the nostrils; ι 330, down into the depths of the cave, *χθονός*, *to* the ground (Γ 217), down under the ground, Ψ 100; *γαίης*, *upon* the ground.—II. with acc., (1) local: *down*, *ῥῖνας*, *through* the nostrils, cf. σ 97; *ὕδωρ*, *into* the water, cf. Ζ 136; *κέρας*, *on* the horn (horn sheath for the part of line next the hook); *in region of*, *upon*, *on*, *στῆθος*, *αὐχένα*, *στόμα*, *ἀσπίδα*, *ὁδόν*; *in neighborhood of*, *στρατόν*, usually per castra, passim in castris, *through* the camp, *everywhere throughout* the camp, Α 10, 409, 484; with verbs of motion, per, *through*, *νῆας*, *λαόν*, *ὦλκα*; then *within*, *in the midst of*, *Ἀχαιΐδα*, *Ἑλλάδα*, *μόθον*, *κλόνον*, *ὑσμίνην*, Φ 310; *ὕλην*, *ἄστυ*, *δῶμα*, *βωμόν*, *upon*; *θυμόν*, *in* heart, inwardly; *φρένα*, in mind; *φρ. καὶ κ. θυμόν*, in heart and mind.—(2) distributive: *στίχας*, *according to* ranks; *φῦλα*, Β 362; *σφέας*, *by* themselves; *ἕμ' αὐτόν*, ipse solus.—(3) *with*, *according to*: secundum, *κῦμα*, *ῥόον*, β 429; *θυμόν*, *according to* wish, Α 136, cf. Ι 108; *αἶσαν* (opp. *ὑπὲρ αἶσαν*) = *μοῖραν* (freq. *κατᾶ*, Π 367), *according to* propriety, fitly; *κόσμον*, in order; *οὐ κ. κ.*, shamefully, θ 489; *after the semblance of*, τ 233; *for the purpose of* trade, *πρῆξιν*, cf. *δαῖτα*, Α 424; *ληΐδα*, *χρέος τινός*, alicuius causa, *for the sake of* seeing Teiresias.

κατα-βαίνων, prs., ipf., aor. (3 pl. *ἔβησαν* and *ἔβαν*, subj. *βείομεν*, Κ 97; imp. *βῆθι*, inf. *βήμεναι*, *βῆναι*), mid. *-εβήσετο* (subj. *βήσεται*, imp. *βήσεο*), descendere, *step down*, *descend*, *τινός*, from, Ω 329; *οὐρανόθεν*, ζ 281; *εἴς τι*, *ἐπί τι*, *δόμον Ἀ. εἴσω*, ψ 252; also *θάλαμον*, β 337; but *κλίμακα*, descend the ladder; *ἐφόλκαιον*, climbing down along the rudder; only in σ 206, ψ 85, with pregnant signif., she descended (the ladder and left) the upper chamber.

κᾰτὰ βάλλων, prs., ipf., aor., (inf. *βαλέειν*); always in tmesi exc. ipf. *κατέβαλλεν*, Ο 357, and aor. *κάββαλε* (better so written than *κάμβαλε*); deiicere, *cast down*, Ψ 125, μ 252; destruere, *destroy*, Β 414; prosternere; deponere; effundere, *δάκρυ*; let *fall*.

κᾰτα-βείομεν, aor. subj. from *-βαίνω*.

κᾰτα-βλώσκοντα, part. prs., permeantem, *running about*, π 466†.

κᾰτα βρόξειε, opt. aor. from *-βρόχω*, devoraret, *swallow* (down), δ 222†.

κᾰτα-γηράσκουσι, prs., ipf. *-εγήρα*, senescunt, *grow old*, τ 360. (Od.)

κᾰτ-αγίνεον, ipf. from *ἀγινέω*, (*ἄγω*), devehebant, *carry down*, κ 104†.

κᾰτ-άγνυμι, fut. **ἄξω**, aor. *ἦξε*, *ἔαξε*, *αμεν*, subj. *ἄξῃς*, confringere; Ν 257, (pluralis maiestatis), *shatter*.

κᾰτ-άγων, part., *ειν*, inf. prs., fut. inf. *-αξέμεν*, aor. *-ήγαγε*, (also tmesis), mid. ipf. *-ήγετο*, *-άγοιντο*, aor. *-ηγαγόμεσθα*, deducere, *lead down*, λ 164; retulit, *bring back*, δ 258; *drive from one's course*, τ 186; mid., appellere, *land, bring to land* (νηί, κ 140), νηῦς, π 322.

κἄτὰ δάσονται, fut. from δαίω, inter se divident = lacerabunt, *tear*, X 354.

κἄτᾰ δάπτεται, pass. prs., aor. act. ἔδαψαν, δάψαι, lacerare, *wound*, π 92.

κἄτα-δαρθάνω, aor. 1 sing. 3 pl. **ἔδρᾰθον**, 3 du. καδδρᾰθέτην, subj. δρᾰθῶ, obdormivi, dormio, *sleep*; τοιόνδε, tam placide dormivi, ψ 18. (Od.)

κἄτᾰ-δέρκεται αὐτούς, *look down upon*, ἀκτίνεσσιν, λ 16†.

κἄτ-έδευσας, aor., (δεύω), conspersisti, *wet through*, I 490.

κατα-δέω, ipf. **ἔδει**, aor. (often tmesis) κατ-έδησεν, σαν, subj. δήσῃ, colligare, alligare, *bind fast*; ἐν δεσμῷ, vinculis; κελεύθους, νόστον, *stop*.

κἄτᾰ-δημο-βορῆσαι, inf. aor., (βιβρώσκω), communiter consumere, *consume in common*, Σ 301†.

κατα-δράθω, subj. aor. from -δαρθάνω, obdormiero, *fall asleep*.

κατα-δύεται, fut. δυσόμεθα, aor. -εδύσετο, (imp. δύσεο), and 2 aor. act. -έδυ (subj. δύω, inf. δῦναι, δύμεναι, part. δύς, δύντι, τα, τες, fem. δῦσα, pl. καδδῦσαι, T 25), freq. in tmesi, occidere, *set*, ἠέλιος, φάος ἠελίοιο; intrare, *enter*, δόμον, πόλιν, ὅμιλον, μάχην, μῶλον Ἄρηος; εἰς Ἀ. δόμους, κατά τι, T 25; induere, *put on*, τεύχεα.

κατα-ειμένος and **-είνυσαν**, see καταέννυμι.

κατα-είσατο, see κάτ-ειμι.

κἄτᾰ-έννυμι (Ϝέσνυμι, vestis), aor., contegebant, *cover*, Ψ 135, and pf. pass. -ειμένον, contectum, τ 431.

κἄτ-αζήνασκε (ἀζαλέος), exsiccabat, *parch, wither up*, λ 587†.

κἄτᾰ-θάπτειν and aor. inf. κατθάψαι, sepelire, *bury*, Ω 611. (Il.)

κατα-θείομαι, -θείομεν, see κατα-τίθημι.

κἄτ-έθελξε, aor. from θέλγω, *had charmed*, κ 213†.

κἄτα-θνήσκων, part. prs., aor. tmesis, 3 pl. θάνον and sync. κάτθᾰνε, pf. τεθνήκᾱσι, opt. τεθναίη, inf. τεθνᾰμεν, part. τεθνηῶτος, ῶτι, ῶτα, ώτων, ῶτας, τεθνηυίης, mori, defungi, *die*; part., mortuus, also joined with νέκυς, νεκροί, λ 37.

κἄτα-θνητός, ῶν, οῖσι, mortalis, *mortal*, ἄνδρεσσιν, ἀνθρώπων, K 440.

κατα-θρώσκω, only aor. κὰδ δ' ἔθορε, desiluit, *spring down*, Δ 79†.

κἄτᾰ-θύμιος, ον, *floating before the mind*; K 383, *think not of*—.

κἄτὰ χρόα καλὸν ἰάπτῃ, subj. prs., *harm her fair body, destroy her beauty*, β 376. (Od.)

κἄται-βᾰταί (βαίνω), *that may be descended, passable*, ν 110†.

κἄτ-ῄκισται, pf. pass., (αἰκίζω), foedata, *disfigured, soiled*, π 290 and τ 9.

κἄτ-ᾶΐξαντα, τε, ασα, see ἀΐσσω; ω 488, *springing down, in haste*.

κἄτ-αισχύνειν, subj. -ητε, part. οντα, (αἶσχος), foedare, *disgrace*, γένος; δαῖτα, *dishonor*.

κἄτᾰ-ίσχεται, see κατ-ίσχει.

κἄταῖ-τυξ (τεύχω), *low leather helmet* or *skull-cap*, K 258†. (See cut No. 121.)

κἄτᾰ-καίριον τέλος, *mortal spot*, Λ 439†.

κἄτᾰ-καιέμεν, inf., H 408, καίων, part. ipf. -έκαιον, aor. -έκηα, -έκηε, subj. κήομεν, inf. κῆαι (κακκῆαι), aor. pass. -εκάη, (also in tmesi), comburere, *burn*; pass., comburi; I 212, *burn out*, deflagraverat.

κατὰ καλύπτοι, opt. prs., aor. (ἐ)κάλυψεν, etc., (also in tmesi), aor. mid. κᾰλυψάμενος, occulere, *cover up* (by drawing *down* over the head the veil), κρᾶτα, having veiled his head, θ 92.

κατα-κεῖαι, better κῆαι, aor. from καίω.

κἄτᾰ-κείαται, 3 pl. ind. prs., κεῖσθαι, κείμενος, ipf. -έκειτο, iacent, cubare, *lie*; ἐπὶ πλευράς, on the side; fig. *rest*, Ω 523; Ω 527, positi sunt.

κἄτᾰ-κείρετε, ipf. -εκείρετε, aor. -έκειραν, *consume*, δ 686. (Od.)

κἄτᾰ-κείομεν, subj., imp. κείετε, (κεῖμαι), decumbere, *lie down*, in desiderative signif. only **κακκείοντες** ἔβαν, cubitum discesserunt, A 606, α 424.

κατα-κῆαι, κηέμεν, κήομεν, see κατακαίω.

κἄτα-κλάω, only ipf. 3 pl. **-έκλων**, and aor. pass. -εκλάσθη, conculcabant, *tread down*, Υ 227; τινὶ φίλον ἦτορ, δ 481, fig. my heart *broke*, gave way (from fear, grief); ι 256, δεισάντων, added as explanatory.

κἄτα-κλίνας, aor. part. from *κλίνω*, *having laid it down*, κ 165†.

Κἄτακλῶϑες, see Κλῶθες.

κἄτα-*κοιμάομαι*, only aor. **-εκοιμήϑημεν,** imp. *-ηθήτω*, inf. *-ηθῆναι*, *sleep*, Λ 731. (Il.)

κάτα κοιρανέουσι, see *κοιρανέω*.

κἄτ-εκόσμει, ipf., aor. mid. subj. *κοσμήσησθε*, (*κόσμος*), *put in order*, χ 440.

κὰδ κρέμᾰσεν (*κρεμάννυμι*), θ 67, 105, *ἐκ πασσαλόφιν*, *hung on* the nail.

κατάκρηθεν, see III. *κάρ*, funditus, *utterly*.

κατάκρης, see *ἄκρη*, funditus.

κἄτα-κρύπτουσι, *ων*, fut. *κρύψειν*, aor. part. *κρύψας*, *ασα*, occulere, *conceal*, *ὑπὸ κόπρῳ*, ι 329; *αὐτόν*, se, δ 247; also η 205, themselves.

κἄτα-κτείνει, *ειν*, subj. *ῃ*, *ωσι*, prs., fut. *κτενεῖ*, *κτᾰνέουσιν*, aor. opt. *κτείνειε*, inf. *κτεῖναι*, part. *κτείνας*, *αντα*, 2 aor. *ἔκτᾰνον*, *ες*, *εν* (also tmesis, Z 416), *ομεν*, subj. *κτάνῃ*, and aor. sync. 3 sing. *ἔκτα*, 1 sing. and 3 pl. *ἔκταν*, imp. **κάκτᾰνε,** inf. *-κτᾰμεν(αι)*, part. *κτάς*; aor. pass. 3 pl. **ἔκτᾰϑεν,** mid. with pass. signif. fut. *κτᾰνέεσθε*, and aor. *κτάμενος*, necare, *slay*, *kill*; α 75, E 558, π 106.

κἄτ-έκῡψε, aor. from *κύπτω*, *bowed himself*, Π 611. (Il.)

καταλαμβάνω (always in tmesi), see *λαμβάνω*.

κἄτα-λέγω (see also -λέχω), only fut. **-λέξω,** and aor. *-έλεξα*, *ας*, *εν* (also tmesis, λ 151), subj. *λέξῃς*, imp. *λεξον*, inf. *λέξαι*, enumerare, *recount*, τ 497; π 235, *narrate* to me, in detail, in order (*ἀριθμήσας*); *communicate*, *relate*, δ 256; *tell*, *disclose*, *πᾶσαν ἀλήθειαν*, *ταῦτα ἀλήθειαν*, as truth, in conformity with truth = *ἀτρεκέως* = *οὐ ψεῦδος*; *εὖ κατὰ μοῖραν* = *ἐν μοίρῃ*, fitly; *διίκεο καὶ κ.*, T 186.

κἄτᾰ-λειβομένοιο, pass., *trickling down*, Σ 109†.

κατα-λείπετε, *ειν*, ipf. *ἔλειπον*, *ε*, *ομεν*, fut. *λείψομεν*, *ουσι*, also (in tmesi): (*κὰδ*) *λείπεις*, ipf. *λεῖπεν*, aor. *λίπον*, *ε*; *λίπω*, *οιεν*; *λιπών*, *όντε*, *οὖσα*, *οὖσαν*, and by assimilation *καλ-λείπειν*, fut. *λείψω*, *ειν*, aor. *λιπον*, *ες*, *ε* (also *λιφ'*), inf. *έειν*, relinquere, *leave*, *τί*, Z 221; custodem, ο 89; *νέην*, as youthful mother, λ 447; *ἀγκλίνας*, left the door ajar, χ 156; deserere, Φ 414, *forsake*, *abandon*, *εὐχωλήν*; *give over*, as booty, *ἕλωρ*, with explanatory inf., γ 271, ε 344.

κἄτα-(*λέχω*), from stem ΛΕΧ, fut. **λέξεται,** 1 aor. *λέξατο*, imp. *λεξαι*, 2 aor. sync. *ἔλεκτο*, inf. *λέχθαι*, part. *λέγμενος*, (*λέχος*), *lay one's self down to rest*, ο 394.

κἄτὰ ἄλεσσαν, aor. from *ἀλέω*, since *they had ground out* (the wheat), υ 109†.

κατα-λήϑονται, obliviscuntur, *forget*, X 389†.

κἄτᾱ-λοφάδεια (*λόφος*) *φέρων*, carrying it *crosswise over his back* (the feet being tied together and held under the chin of the bearer), κ 169†.

κατα-λύσομεν, fut., aor. *ἔλῡσε*, (*λύω*), *loose from under* the yoke, *unharness*, δ 28; *destroy*, B 117.

κὰδ λωφήσειε, aor. from *λωφάω*, *κακῶν*, *recover itself from* the misery, ι 460†.

κατ-έμαρπτε, ipf., aor., (tmesi, *ἔμαρψε*), subj. *μάρψῃ*, consequi, *overtake*, Π 598, Z 364; corripere, *seize*, ω 390.

κἄτ-ᾰμήσατο, aor. mid., (*ἀμάω*), *had heaped upon himself*, Ω 165†.

κἄτ-ᾰμύξατο, aor. mid., (*ἀμύσσω*), *χεῖρα*, *has scratched* her hand, E 425†.

κἄτὰ ἀμφῐκᾰλύψας, aor. part., (*καλύπτω*), *κεφαλῇ ῥάκος*, *drawing down from around* my head my ragged garment, ξ 349†.

κἄτᾰ-νεύων, part., fut. *νεύσομαι*, aor. *ἔνευσα*, *σας*, *σε*, subj. *σω*, imp. *σον*, inf. *σαι*, part. *καννεύσας*, adnuere, *nod in assent* (opp. *ἀνα-*), *τινί τι*; also with inf. fut., δ 6; with *ὑπέσχεο*, *ὑπέστην*; also *κρατί*, *κεφαλῇ*. *permit*.

κἄτ-άνεται, pass., (*ἄνω*), consumitur, *use up*, *waste*, β 58. (Od.)

κατὰ νήσαντο (*νέω*), *ἅσσα οἱ . . . λίνῳ*, that which *they have spun to* him with the thread, η 197†.

κάτ-αντᾰ, deorsum, *downward*, Ψ 116†.

κατ-άντηστιν, see *ἄντηστιν*.

κατ-αντικρύ, see *ἀντικρύ*.

κατὰ πάτησαν, aor. from *πατέω*, conculcaverunt, *tread under foot*, *break*, Δ 157†.

κἄτά-παυμα (*παύω*), *alleviation*; *γόου*, *comfort* in their lamentation, P 38†.

κἄτᾰ-πανέμεν, inf. prs., fut. *παύσω*, *σέμεν*, inf. aor. *ἔπαυσα*, *ε*, *αν*, subj. *σῃ* and σομεν, finire, placare, *put end to, appease*, δ 583; comprimere (coërceri nos vis, β 244); τινά τινος, *hinder from;* ironically=slay, Π 618.

κατὰ ἐπέδησε, aor. from πεδάω, *has fettered*, of Ate or Moira, Τ 94, λ 292.

κατα-πέσσω, only aor. subj. **πέψῃ,** concoquat, *digest, repress*, Α 81†.

κατὰ πετάσσας, aor. part. from πετάννυμι, *spreading over it*, Θ 441†.

κατα - πέφνων, πέφνῃ, see κατα-φένω.

κᾰτᾰ-πήγνυμι, only aor. **ἔπηξεν,** αν, defixit, panxerunt, *stick fast, plant*, and sync. aor. mid. ἔπηκτο, fixus haesit, Λ 378.

κατα-πίπτω, only aor., in tmesi, Π 469; elsewh. **κάππεσον,** ε, έτην, ον, decidere, procidere, *fall down* (praeceps, πρηνής), ἐν κονίῃσιν, ἐπὶ γαίῃ, χαμᾶζε, ἁλί, *cast one's self into* the sea; θυμὸς παραὶ ποσί, courage utterly forsook them, Ο 280.

κατα -(φένω), only red. aor. subj. **πέφνῃ,** part. πέφνων, interimere, *slay*, Ρ 539.

κᾰτ-επλέομεν, ipf., appulimus, *put in*, ι 142†.

κατ-επλήγη, aor. pass. from πλήσσω, φίλον ἦτορ, *was struck* in his heart *with fear*, Γ 31†.

κᾰτᾱ - πρηνεῖ, έσσι, from πρηνής, *down turned;* with flat of the hand, χειρί, χερσί, Π 792.

κατὰ ἔπτηξαν, πτήξας, aor., and sync. 3 du. πτήτην, *crouch down; δείσαντε ὑπ' ὄχεσφιν*, under the chariot for fear, Θ 136.

κᾰτα-πτώσσουσι, inf. σσειν, part. σσοντ(α), τες, timidi sunt; extimescere, *yield to fear*, Ε 254. (Il.)

κᾰτα-πύθεται, putrescit, *become rotten*, ὄμβρῳ, Ψ 328†.

κᾰτ-αρῶνται, ipf. ηρᾶτο (ἀρά), imprecari, *call curses down upon*, τινὶ πολλά, Ι 454; ἄλγεα, τ 330.

κᾰτᾱ-ρῑγηλά, ntr. pl., (Ϝρῖγος), formidolosa, *horrible*, ξ 226†

κᾰτ-έρεξε, ipf., and καρρέζουσα, part. prs., (ὀρέγω ?), *stroke, caress*, χειρί τέ μιν κ., δ 610, Α 361.

κᾰτα-ρρέον, ntr. part., elsewh. tmesis, ῥέοντες, ipf. ἔρρεε, ῥέε, (σρεω), defluere, *flow down*, absol. and with τινός, ἐκ, Δ 149.

κᾰτ-άρχεσθαι, only ipf. **ἤρχετο** χέρνιβά τ' οὐλοχύτας τε, *began the sacred* hand-washing and the sprinkling of the barley meal, γ 445†.

κᾰτα-σβέννυμι, aor. **ἔσβεσε,** (tmesis, Π 293), σαν (tmesis, Ω 791), imp. σβέσατε, extinguere, rogum vino, *quench*, Ω 791. (Il.)

κατα-σεύομαι, only aor. **-έσσῠτο,** (ἐσϜυτο), ῥέεθρα, *streamed down into* the river-bed, Φ 382†.

κᾰτ-εσκίαον, ipf. from σκιάω, (σκιά), obumbrabant, *overshadow*, μ 436†.

κατὰ σμῦξαι, aor. inf., (σμύχω), *burn down*, Ι 653; pass. σμύχοιτο, Χ 411.

κατα-στορέννυμι, only aor. ἐστόρεσαν, στόρεσ(ε), and -εστόρεσαν, part. κᾶστορνῦσα, ρ 32, *spread out upon;* Ω 798, *cover over* (grave and contents), λάεσσι.

κᾰτ-έστῠγε and ἔστῠγον, 3 pl. aor., (στυγέω), horruit, *be horror-struck at*, τί, κ 113.

κατα-σχεθεῖν, see κατ-έχω.

κατὰ τεῖνε, aor., *drew in* (the reins), Γ 261. (Il.)

κᾰτᾰ-τήκω, only aor. **-έτηξεν,** liquefecit, *melt*, τ 206; and pass. τήκομαι φίλον ἦτορ, acc., my heart *is melting away;* τήκεται, liquefit, τ 205.

κατα-τίθημι, ipf. ἐτίθει, τίθεσαν, fut. -θήσω, ει, aor. ἔθηκα, εν, αν (also in tmesi), 2 aor. subj. θείομεν, inf. θεῖναι, and part. θέντε, mid. 2 aor. 3 pl. -έθεντο, subj. θείομαι, inf. θέσθαι; sync. 2 aor. act. 1 pl. **κάτθεμεν,** 3. θεσαν, imp. θετε, inf. θέμεν, mid. 2 aor. pl. θέμεθα, θέσθην, θέμενοι, deponere, collocare, *place, lay down*, τι ἐπὶ γαίῃ, χθονί, νηί, ἀπήνῃ, ῥυμῷ; ὑπ' αἰθούσῃ; ἐν λεχέεσσι, δήμῳ, ψαμάθῳ, οισιν; ἐπὶ χθονός, θρόνου; ἐς μυχόν, μέγαρον, θάλαμον, εἰς Ἰθάκην; but ἐκ καπνοῦ, put away out of the smoke; ἐπ' αὐτῷ, Ψ 381, holding their heads straight toward him; spread out a bed, τ 317; propose as prize in contest; ἄεθλον, (ἐπὶ σοί, in thine honor), institute a contest.—Mid., sibi or suum, am, etc., deponere.

κᾰτα-τρῦχω, indic. and subj. prs., exhaurio, *exhaust, consume*, ο 309.

καταῦθι, καταυτόθι, see αὖθι and αὐτόθι.

κατα-φαγέειν, ωσι, aor. from -εσθίω.

κἄτα-φέρω, only fut. **-οίσεται**, *με* Ἄϊδος *εἴσω*, *will bring* me to the grave, Χ 425†.

κἄτα-φθίσει, fut., (*φθίω*), perdet, *destroy*, ε 341; mid. aor. *-έφθῖτο*, exhausta erant; *φθίσθαι*, periisse; *φθιμένοιο*, *οι*, *οισιν*, defuncti.

κἄτα-φλέξω, fut. from *φλέγω*, cremabo, *consume*, *πυρί*, Χ 512†.

κἄτἄ-φῦλἄδόν (*φῦλον*), tributim, *in tribes*, *in clans*, Β 668†.

κατὰ (*δάκρυ*) **χέοντα**, *τες*, *τας*, *χέουσα*, *σαν*, *σαι*, (lacrimas), effundens; aor. *-έχευα* (for *ἔχεϝα*), *ας*, *εν*, *αν* (both forms freq. in tmesi), subj. *χεύῃ*, inf. *χεῦαι*, aor. mid. *κέχῦτο* and *ἔχυτο*, *-έχυντο*, infundere, offundere, *pour down upon*, *over*, *τινί τι*; effundere, *νιφάδας*, etc., *shower down*; *πέπλον*, *let fall*; proiicere, *cast down*, *θύσθλα*, *ἡνία*; superinfundere, *ἠέρα*, etc., *τινί*; *ἐλεγχείην*, etc., *τινί*, conspergere ignominia, *cover with* ignominy; *πλοῦτον*, Β 670. — Mid. *ὀφθαλμῶν* or (*οἱ*) *ὀφθαλμοῖσι*, oculis (eius) offusa est; *φλόξ*, diffusa est; *ὅπλα*, collapsa sunt.

κἄτα-χθόνιος (*χθών*), inferior, *subterranean*, *Ζεύς* = Aides, Ι 457†.

κἄτ-έαξε, *αμεν*, aor. from *-άγνυμι*.

κατ-έδει, ipf. from *-δέω*, colligavit, *bind*.

κἄτ-έδουσι, 3 pl., *ἔδων*, part. prs., pf. *ἐδηδώς*, devorare, comedere, *eat up*, *devour*, Τ 31; consumere, *οἶκον*, rem familiarem, τ 159; *ὃν θυμόν*, *consume*, *waste* one's heart.

κατὰ (*συφεοῖσιν*) **ἐέργνυ**, ipf., (*ϝέργνυμι*), *shut up* (in the hog-sties), κ 238†.

κατ-είβεις, *ετον*, mid. *-ειβόμενον*, ipf. *-είβετο*, elsewh. tmes. *κατὰ* (*δάκρυον*) *εἴβεις*, *ει*, *οι*, *ων*, ipf. *εἶβε*, effundere, *shed*; mid., defluere, *flow apace*, *trickle down*, and fig. effluxit vita, *ebb away*, ε 152.

κατ᾽ (*ὄσσε*) **ἰδών**, aor. part., *looking him straight in the eyes*, Ρ 167†.

κὰδ εἰλύσω, fut. from *εἰλύω* (*ϝελϝω*, volvo), involvam, *surround*, Φ 318†.

κἄτ-ειμι, *εισιν*, inf. *-ίμεν*, part. *-ιόντα*, *-ιοῦσα*, *αν*, ipf. *-ήϊεν*, aor. *καταείσατο*, delata est, *had flown*; *γαίης*, (*εἶμι*), *go*, or *come down*, *flow down*; appellentem, *enter harbor*, π 472.

κατ-έκταθεν, 3 pl. aor. pass. from *-κτείνω*.

κἄτ-εναίρω, only aor. mid. *-ενήρατο* *χαλκῷ*, ferro absumpsit, *slay*, λ 519†.

κἄτ-εναντίον (*ἀντίος*) *οἱ ἔλθω*, ei obviam fiam, *go to meet him*, Φ 567†.

κἄτ-ένωπα (*ἰδὼν Δαναῶν*), *in the face of*, *turned toward* the Danaoi, Ο 320†.

κατ-επ-άλμενος, *-ᾶλτο*, see *κατ-εφ-άλλομαι*.

κατὰ ἐπείγει, urget, *oppress*, Ψ 623†.

κατ-ερείπω, only pf. **-ερήρῐπεν**, collapsum est, and aor. *-ήριπεν ὑπ᾽ αὐτοῦ*, *are prostrated* under (by) it, Ε 92.

κατ-ερήτῦεν, *ον*, ipf., retinebat, *hold back*, τ 545, from tears.

κατ-ερύκω, *ει*, *ετε*, subj. *ῃ*, imp. *ε*, and **κατερύκᾰνε**, Ω 218; ipf. *-ερυκες*, *ε*, pass. prs. *ομαι*, *εται*, retinere, *hol l back*; cohibet, Φ 63; impedire; pass., *delays*.

κατ-ερύω, aor. *-είρῠσε*, pass. pf. *-είρυσται*, inf. *-ερύσθαι*, deducere (navem), *launch*, ξ 332. (Od.)

κἄτ-έρχεαι, *εται*, pass. *ομένης*, fut. *-ελεύσομαι*, aor. *-ήλῠθον*, *-ῆλθες*, *ε*, *ομεν*, *ον*, inf. *-ελθέμεν*, pass. *-ελθόντ(α)*, *go*, *come down*, *go*; *fly down*, *descend*, ι 484.

κατ-εσθίει, ipf. *-ήσθιε* (also in tmesi), aor. in tmesi, *φάγε*, *ωσι*, *έειν*, *devour*, spoken of animals and of Polyphemos, except α 8, π 429, γ 315, ο 12.

κατ-έσσυτο, aor. from *-σεύομαι*.

κατ-ευνάω, aor. opt. **-ευνήσαιμι**, pass. aor. part. *-ευνηθέντα*, parallel form indic. 3 pl. *-εύνασθεν*, Γ 448, sopire, *lull to sleep*; pass., decumbere, dormire, *lie down*, *sleep*.

κατ-εφ-άλλομαι, only aor. **-επᾶλτο**, part. *-επάλμενος*, desiluit, *shot d.wn*, Τ 351.

κατ-έχει (also in tmesi), *ουσι*, subj. *ἔχῃ κάτα*, pass. *-έχων*, *-εχούσας*, ipf. *ἔχεν κάτα*, *-έχεν*, fut. *καθέξει*, aor. *-έσχε*, subj. *σχῇ*; pass. *-έχονται*, ipf. *-είχετο*, *-έχοντο*, aor. mid. *-έσχετο*, part. *σχομένοις*, parallel forms: aor. act. **κατέσχεθον**, ipf. **κάσχεθε**, retinere, impedire; cohibere, *hold fast*, *hold b ck*, *restrain*; *τινά γαῖα*, *αἶα*, Β 699, *hold within its bosom*, cut off from light and life; Σ

332, moriar; τί, *prevail, bear sway*, ι 6; κεφαλήν, *bend over*; mid., se contegere, *cover one's self*; subsistere, *remain*, γ 284.

κᾰτ-ηπιόωντο, ipf. from ἠπιάω, leniebantur, *assuage*, E 417†.

κᾰτ-ηρεφές, acc. pl. masc. έας, (ἐρέφω), *covered over, vaulted, overhanging*, ε 367.

κατ-ήριπε, aor. from -ερείπω, corruit.

κατη-φείη, ην, (καταί, φάος, = with downcast eyes), *shame*, Π 498. (Il.)

κατ-ήφησαν, aor., part. σας, (-ηφέω), *were confounded*, ἐνὶ θυμῷ, π 342.

κατ-ηφέες, pl. from -ής, (-ηφών), *disgraced*, ω 432†.

κατ-ηφόνες, nom. pl. from ἡ κατηφών (cf. κατηφείη), abstract noun used as concrete, *disgraces=bringers of disgrace*, Ω 253†.

κάτ-θανε, aor. from -θνήσκω. **κατθάψαι,** aor. from -θάπτω. **κάτθεμεν,** 3 pl. ind., -θέμεν, inf. etc., see κατα-τίθημι. **κατ-ίμεν** = -ιέναι, see -ειμι.

κατ-ίσχει, 3 sing., inf. έμεν(αι), mid. pr. -ίσχεαι, εται, pass. κᾰτᾰίσχεται, retinere, *hold back*; tenere, *steer*; mid., sibi retinere, *keep for one's self*; pass., possidetur, *is occupied*, ι 122.

κατ-οίσεται, fut. from -φέρω.

κᾰτ-όπισθε(ν), pone, post, *in the rear, behind*, with gen.; adv., *behind, thereafter*, φ 116.

κάτω (κατά), deorsum, *down*, ψ 91.

κατ-ωθέω, aor. in tmesi, **κὰδ ἔωσε,** *threw down*, Π 410†.

κᾰτ-ωμᾰδίοιο, gen., (ὦμος), *hurled from* (above and behind) *the shoulder*, Ψ 431. (See cut No. 33.)

κᾰτ-ωμᾰδόν (ὦμος), *from over the shoulder* (of whip in lashing the horses), Ψ 500. (Il.)

κᾰτ-ωρῠχέεσσι (ὀρύσσω), *dug in, buried in the earth, firmly set*, ζ 267. (Od.)

Καύκωνες, tribe in Paphlagonia, K 429; in Elis, γ 366.

καυλῷ, όν, dat. acc. masc., (caulis), *spear-shaft* (part next the point), Π 115; *sword-hilt*, Π 338.

καύματος, gen. from τὸ καῦμα, (καίω), aestus, in consequence of the *burning heat*, E 865†.

καυστείρης, gen. from καύστειρα, (καίω), μάχης, *hot, raging* combat, Δ 342. (Il.)

Κᾰΰστριος, river in Ionia, B 461.

καὐτός, ἡ = καὶ αὐτός, ἡ, Z 260, ζ 282.

ΚΑΦ, only part. perf. **κεκαφηότα,** (καπύω), efflantem, exspirantem, with obj. θυμόν, *gasping out*, E 698.

κέ, κέν, (from pronominal stem ka), similar in use to ἄν, but: (1) enclitic. —(2) esp. common in relative clauses (149 κέν to 3 ἄν).—(3) often repeated in parallel clauses.—(4) used also with ἄν, N 127, see also below II. B, c, 3.—I. with indic.: (A) denoting simple subjective supposition, δ 546; also with fut., Δ 176; expectation with fut., A 175, π 297; repeated action, with aor., σ 263; esp. (B) in apodosis of conditional sentence, with past tense, when the protasis contains a false assumption, e. g., Λ 311, E 898; the protasis may be represented by a participle, λ 418; or may require to be supplied, ξ 62.—II. with subj.: (A) in principal sentence: subj. of expectation, A 184, Ξ 235; esp. with apodosis conceived of as likely to follow, A 324. —(B) in subordinate clause: (a) relative clause, subj. of wish, τ 403, ι 356; of expectation, κ 539, β 43, H 171.—(b) hypothetical relative clause (κεν often wanting) dependent upon: (1) principal sentence with verb in imper., θ 548, α 316, Ψ 855 (inf., Ψ 246).—(2) principal sentence with opt., A 294, τ 577.—(3) principal sentence with fut. indic., φ 280, I 397, P 229.—(4) principal sentence with pres. indic., Ξ 416, τ 565, Λ 409.—(5) principal sentence with past indic. in sense of the present (gnomic use), λ 432, A 218. —(6) subordinate clause with subj., Φ 103.—(c) in clause joined by conjunction to its principal sentence: (1) by final conjunction: ἵνα, only μ 156; ὄφρα, ut, 9 times, σ 183; ὡς, ut, 32 times, B 385; ὅπως, δ 545.—(2) temporal conjunction (subj. of expectation), ὄφρα, δ 588, K 444; ἕως, always with κεν, Γ 291; εἰς ὅ, always with κεν, β 98.—(3) temporal = conditional. ὅτε, ὁπότε, (α) a supposition having reference to future, A 567, X 366, K 130; (β) supposition without reference to time, Z 225, I 501, λ 218, (not εὖτε), ὄφρα, dum, while, τ 17, Ω 554; joined with ἄν, Λ 202, ζ 259, ε 361; εἰς ὅ κεν, Κ 90, Ι 610.—(4) εἰ, whether, χ 76, Α 407, δ 322, Υ 436, ξ 118, Π 861, Δ 249; εἰ, if, of future expectation, 111 times, Π 445, ρ 549, Ξ 369, Ε 763, φ 305, Α 137, Υ 302, φ 114, Ρ 40, Σ 92; of general expectation, Λ 391; ἐπεί, ξ 153, Χ 125, Λ 764, Α 173, Ρ 658.—III. with optative (A) in principal sentence. (I) concessive, Χ 253, Ν 486, Ω 619, φ 162. (II) optative denoting future time, (1) simple futurity, ο 506, σ 166, μ 387, κ 269, Ω 664, Φ 412, Β 160, Κ 57.—(2) conditioned probability, Ι 157, φ 77, Δ 171, Ρ 417.—(3) possible future, always κέν (or ἄν), Ρ 103, σ 223, 380.—(4) prevented realization, δ 595, α 236, Γ 410 (joined with sentence with εἰ, Β 81, Ε 311).—(5) assumed situation, κέν (or ἄν), λ 488, Ο 697, χ 138, ε 73, μ 83.—(6) mere possibility, Τ 218, Ι 57, μ 102, ι 131.—(B) in interrogative sentence: ἤ, ο 300; ἤ ῥα, ο 431, θ 337, σ 357; πῶς, ο 195, λ 144; τίς, Κ 303; ποῖοι ἤ, φ 197; in rhetorical direct question, Τ 90, Ρ 586, 149, Τ 82.—(C) in dependent sentence: (a) relative sentence, α 253, Γ 235; Ω 732, υ 368, ω 188, Ε 192, 483, Ο 735; with ἄν, Ν 127; (b) hypothetical relative, only δ 600; (c) in conjunctional sentence, (1) final, ὡς, ψ 135, ω 532, β 53; ὅπως, Α 344; ἕως, β 78.—(2) comparative, ὡς, ψ 60.—(3) temporal implying condition, ὅτε, ν 391, Ι 525.—(4) dubitative, expressing doubt, εἰ, whether, μ 112, ξ 120, Λ 792, Η 387.—(5) optative, expressing desire, εἰ γάρ, υ 236. —(6) conditional, protasis introduced by εἰ, if, preceding the principal sentence (this last with κέν), Ε 273, Ι 141, 363, τ 590, μ 345; principal sentence preceding, protasis (with κέν) following, Τ 322, η 314, Κ 380, Χ 220.

κεάζω, aor. **ἐκέασσε** κέασσε κέασε, opt. κεάσαιμι, pf. pass. κεκεασμένα, aor. pass. ἐκεάσθη, *split*, ξ 418, υ 161; *rend, shiver*, ι 132, η 250.

κέαται, το = κεῖνται, ἔκειντο, from κεῖμαι.

Κεβριόνης, son of Priamos, Θ 318; Hektor's charioteer, slain by Patroklos, Π 738.

κεδάννυμι, only aor. **ἐκέδασσε**, and pass. 3 pl. ἐκέδασθεν, part. θέντες, θείσης, parallel form to σκεδάννυμι, used for metrical convenience, dispergere, dissipare, *disperse, scatter*; γεφύρας, *bursts* the dikes, Ε 88.

κεδνοῖο, ή, ῇ, ήν, αί, άς, (ά), and sup. -ότατος, οι, (κεκαδμένος), insignis, *excellent*, ἄλοχος, μήτηρ, τοκῆες, ἀμφίπολος, ἄναξ, ἑταῖροι, κεδνὰ ϝιδυῖα, τ 346.

κέδρῖνον, acc., (κέδρος), *of cedar*, Ω 192†.

κέδρος, **κέδρον**, fem., *cedar*, of the tree and of the wood, ε 60†.

κειάμενος, κείαντες (κη-), see καίω.

κείαται, το = κεῖνται, ἔκειντο.

κεῖθεν, adv., (κεῖνος), illinc, dein, *thence, then*, Ο 234.

κεῖθι, illic, *there*, Γ 402.

κεῖμαι, κεῖσαι, κεῖαι, κεῖται, 3 pl. κεῖνται, κείαται, κέαται, κέονται, subj. κῆται, imp. κεῖσο, σθω, inf. κεῖσθαι, part. κείμενος, ipf. ἐκείμην, το, μεθα, and κείμην, μεθα, κεῖτο, iter. κέσκετο, 3 pl. κεῖντο, κέατο, κείατο, fut. κείσομαι, εαι, εται, ονται, cubare, jacere, positum, collocatum esse, of things having life, *lie*, with various modifications, e. g. sick, dead, β 102; feeble, wounded, despised, old, Σ 435; unburied, idle; μέγας μεγαλωστί, stretched out at his full vast length; πολλός τις, like a giant; of localities, ι 25; of things: *lie* (objects of value); *stand* (of articles of household furniture); propositum est, the prize is offered, Χ 163. With follg. constructions: **ἐπὶ** γαίης, χθονός, γαίῃ, χθονί, ἐννέα πέλεθρα, spread out over; **ἐν** ἄλγεσι, εἰν ἁλί, νεκύων ἀγύρει = ὁμοῦ νεκύεσσι, among the dead, θεῶν-γούνασι, rest in the power of the gods, α 267; λέκτρῳ, νήσῳ, νούσῳ, πεδίῳ, πυρί, ψαμάθοισι, χηλῷ, and with dat. without preposition, ὀλέθρῳ.

κειμήλιον, α, (κεῖμαι), *treasure, heirloom*; β 75, *landed property*.

κεῖνος, η, ο, older form of ἐκεῖνος, etc.

κεινῇ, ῇσι, κεῖν' = κεινά = **κενά**, χ 249, vacuus, inania, *empty*.

κείρει, 3 sing., imp. ετε, part. οντες, τας, ipf. ἐκείρετε, ον, fut. inf. κερέειν, 1 aor. (ἔ)κερσε, part. σαντες, (Ger. Scheere, Schaar, Eng. shear), *shear off*, κόμην; *cut off, lay waste, devour*;

mid. κειρόμενοι, ipf. κείροντο, aor. inf. κείρασθαι, κόμην, *cut one's hair* (in grief), Ψ 136.

κεῖσε, illo, *there;* Ψ 461, usque illuc, *thus far.*

1. **κείων,** part., *splitting,* ξ 425†.

2. **κείω,** inf. κειέμεν, part. κείων (and **κέων**), οντες, ουσα (fut. forms without tense-sign with desiderative force), *desiring to sleep,* freq. with verbs of motion, ξ 532.

κεκαδήσει, σόμεθα, see κήδω, *trouble.*

κεκαδών, οντο, see χάζομαι, cedo, *give way.*

κεκασμένος, σθαι, see καίνυμαι, excello, *surpass.* κεκαφηώς, see ΚΑΦ, exspirans.

κέκλετο, aor. from κέλομαι, vocabat.

κεκληγώς, see κλάζω.

κεκλήατο, ήσῃ, see καλέω.

κεκλόμενος, see κέλομαι. **κέκλυθι,** τε, see κλύω, ausculto. **κέκμηκας,** -ηώς, see κάμνω. **κεκοπώς,** see κόπτω. **κεκορήμεθα,** μένοι, ηότε, see κορέννυμι. κεκορυθμένα, see κορύσσω. **κεκοτηότι,** see κοτέω. **κεκράανται,** ντο, see κεράννυμι.

κεκρύφαλον, τόν, (κορυφή), *net to* confine the hair, Χ 469†. (See cut No. 44.)

κεκύθωσι, see κεύθω.

κελᾰδεινή, ῆς, όν, (κέλαδος), *sounding, rushing;* esp. freq. as epithet of Artemis, Π 183; as substantive, Φ 511.

κελάδησαν, aor. from κελαδέω, *shouted aloud* (in applause), Ψ 869†.

κέλᾰδον, τόν, (Ger. schellen?), *tumult* of combat, of hunt; in more general signif., *confusion,* σ 402.

κελάδων, οντα, part., *sounding,* Φ 16.

Κελάδων, stream in Elis, Η 133†.

κελαι-νεφέι, εῖ, έα, ές, (νέφος), *shrouded in dark clouds,* Zeus; as subst., ν 147; αἷμα, *dark.*

κελαινόν, ή, ῇ, *dark, black;* of blood, night, skin, wave, storm; of earth, Π 384.

κελᾰρύζει, prs., ipf. κελάρυζε, *run, trickle,* Φ 261.

κελεύθου, κέλευθον, οι, ους, fem. and pl. ntr. α, (callis), *path, way;* ntr. pl. in wider signif. ἀνέμων (λαιψηρά, airy), ἰχθυόεντα, ὑγρά, ἠερόεντα, gloomy ways (of death); masc. also = iter, *journey,* κ 539; πρήσσοντε, traversing; τιθέναι, θέσθαι, open a way; γεφυροῦν, make a way over a ditch; Γ 406, θεῶν; κ 86, *outgoings* of night and day; others, paths (of cattle), i. e. *pastures.*

κελευτιόων, όωντε, part. from -άω. (κελεύω), *animating,* Μ 265. (Il.)

κελεύω (no du. and 3 pl.), subj. ῃς, opt. οι, imp. ε, ετε, part. ων, οντος, ipf. ἐκέλευον, ες, ον, and κέλευον, ε, fut. -σω, inf. σέμεναι, aor. ἐκέλευσα, σε, σαν, and κέλευσα, σας, σε, σαν, imp. κέλευσον, part. σας, (κέλλω, pello), *drive on,* with the lash; iubere, *command,* τινά, Δ 286, δ 274; τά με θυμός, Η 68, η 187, as my heart *bids* me; τινί, Δ 428; τινί τι, mandare, Ζ 324, π 136; with inf., Β 74, δ 233; with acc. and inf., Β 11, β 263; with dat. and inf., Β 50, β 6; with dat. of indirect object, followed by acc. and inf., Ψ 129, ι 561, λ 44.

κέλητα, τόν, (from κέλλω, celer), κέληθ' ὥς, ἵππον, *courser, racer,* ε 371†.

κελητίζειν, inf., (κέλης), ἵπποισι, *ride a race-horse,* Ο 679†; where the feats of a skillful rider are described.

κέλλω, aor. **ἐκέλσαμεν,** inf. κέλσαι, part. κελσάσῃσι, (collis, pello), appellere, *bring to shore, beach,* νῆα (ἐν ψαμάθοισι); ι 149, *having run* the ships *to* land, we, etc.

κέλομαι (κέλλω), εαι (syniz.), εται, εσθε, ονται, opt. οίμην, imp. κελέσθω, εσθε, inf. σθαι, fut. κελήσεται, aor. ἐκέκλετο (after the trochaic cæsura), κέκλετο, part. κεκλόμενος, οι, *urge on,* τινὰ θυμός, ἴς, coegit; iubere, hortari, *command, exhort,* with inf., Α 386, γ 317; with acc. and infin., Α 74, γ 425; with dat., Ζ 286, Κ 419, η 335.

κέλσαι, aor. from κέλλω.

κεμάδα, τήν, *a two-year-old deer,* Κ 361†.

κέν, see κέ.

κενε-αυχέες, voc. pl. from -ής, (αὐχέω), *empty, idle boaster,* Θ 230†.

κενεάς, vacuas, κενεόν, ntr., νέεσθαι, ἰέναι, incassum, infecta re, *in vain, fruitlessly,* Β 298.

κενεῶνα, τόν, (κενεός), part of body between hips and ribs, *waist, small of back,* χ 295; acc. of part., Ε 284; elsewh. with ἐς.

κενά, inania, *empty,* see κεινός.

κένσαι, aor. from κεντέω.

Κένταυρος, *Centaur*, Eurytion, φ 295; pl., *Centaurs*, a wild Thessalian tribe, A 268.

κένσαι, inf. aor. from κεντέω, *goad on*, horses, Ψ 337†.

κεντρ-ηνεκέας, acc. pl., (κέντρον, ἔνεκα), stimulatos, *goaded on*, ἵππους, E 752. (Il.)

κέντροιο, ῳ, (κεντέω), stimuli (flagelli), *goad*, Ψ 387. (Il.)

κέντορες, οἱ, (κέντρον), ἵππων, stimulatores equorum, Kadmeians and Trojans, Δ 391, E 102.

κέονται, το, see κεῖμαι.

κεράασθε, see κεράννυμι.

κερᾰϊζέμεν, inf., part. ζων, ipf. κεράϊζε, ζετον, pass. prs. part. κεραϊζομένους, ην, (κείρω), destruere, populari, *destroy*, *lay waste*, Π 752, E 557; trucidare, *slay*, B 861.

κέραιε, see κεράννυμι.

κερᾰμεύς, ὁ, figulus, *potter*, Σ 601†.

κεράμῳ, ων, properly, *great earthen jar* buried in the earth (see cut), I 469; but in E 387, χαλκέῳ, serving as *dungeon* (cf. the pit into which Joseph was thrown by his brethren).

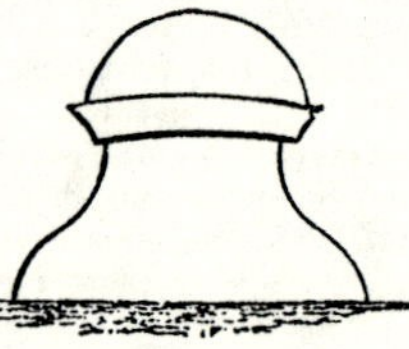

κεράννυμι; κεράω, κεραίω, give the forms prs. part. **κερῶντας,** imp. κέραιε, 1 aor. κέρασσε, part. κεράσασα, mid. prs. subj. κέρωνται, imp. κεράασθε, ipf. κερῶντο, ὁωντο, aor. κεράσσατο, σσάμενος, pass. pf. κεκράανται, plupf. κεκράαντο, temperare, *mix*, *prepare by mixing*, wine, bath; mid., *mix for one's self*, *have mixed*; alloy, mingle with gold, δ 132.

κερᾰο-ξόος (κέρας, ξέω) τέκτων, *worker in horn*, *horn polisher*, Δ 110†.

κεραόν, τόν, (κέρας), *horned*, Γ 24; κεραοί, are horned from their very birth, δ 85.

κέρας, αος, αι, ᾳ, pl. α, αων, ᾶσι, άεσσι, (κάρ, cere-brum, cornu), *horn*, of cattle, P 521; of wild-goat, Δ 109; as substance (where the resemblance in sound between κέρας and κραίνω is played upon), τ 566; as forming half of a bow, φ 395; hence = *bow*, κέραι ἀγλαέ, arcu superbiens; symbol of immobility, τ 211; *the sheath of horn* encasing the line just above the hook, and preventing it from being bitten off, Ω 81. [κέρᾱ, but shortened before a vowel, Δ 109, τ 211.]

κεραυνός, ῷ, όν, *thunderbolt*, *lightning*, O 117.

κεράω, see κεράννυμι.

κερδᾰλέος, ον, οισιν, ης, (κέρδος), comp. **κέρδιον,** sup. κέρδιστος, *advantageous*, Γ 41, β 74; *helpful*, K 44; *cunning*, ν 291, Z 153.

κερδᾰλεό-φρον, voc., *selfish*, A 149; *crafty*, Δ 339.

κέρδος, εα, έων, εσι, *gain*, π 311; good counsel, ψ 140; Ψ 709, κέρδεα ἐπίστασθαι, εἰδέναι, understand cunning arts; νωμᾶν, devise good counsel.

κερδοσύνῃ (κέρδος), per astutiam, *cunningly*, ξ 31.

κερκίς, ίδα, fem., *rod* (in later times comb), by a blow from which the threads of the woof were driven home into the warp, and the web made firm and close, ε 62. (See cut No. 63.)

κέρσε, αντες, see κείρω.

κερ-τομέωσι, subj., opt. έοι, part. έων, έοντες, έουσαν, ipf. ἐκερτόμεον, κερτόμεον, (-τομος), *taunt*, *tease*, Π 261.

κερτομίας, acc. pl., Υ 202; as subst. **κερτομίοισι,** οις, (κείρω, τέμνω, ω 240), *sharp-cutting*, sc. ἐπέεσσι, *taunting*, *derisive words*, yet the noun sometimes expressed, e. g. Δ 6.

κέρωνται, όωντο, see κεράννυμι.

κέσκετο, see κεῖμαι.

κεστὸν (κεντέω) ἱμάντα, *embroidered girdle*, Ξ 214.

ἐκεύθανον, ipf., occultabant, Γ 453†.

κευθμῶν, gen. pl. from ὁ κευθμός, latebra, *lairs*, N 28†.

κευθμῶνας, τούς, (κεύθω), latebras, *crannies*, ν 367; *hog-sties*, κ 283.

κεύθεσι, dat. pl. from τὸ κεῦθος, (κευθω), ὑπὸ—γαίης, *in the depths* of the earth, X 482, ω 204.

κεύθει, ετε, subj. ω, ῃ, imp. κεῦθε, ipf. ἔκευθε, κεῦθε, fut. κεύσω, aor. κύθε and subj. κεκύθωσι, pf. κέκευθε, plupf. ἐκεκεύθει, celare, occultare, *hide*, *cover*, *τινά, τί*, pass. 'Αιδι *κεύθωμαι*, s e p e l i a r ; also *νόος ἔνδοθι, θυμῶ, νόῳ, νοήμασι, ἐνὶ φρεσίν* ; *οὐδέ σε κεύσω*, n e c t e c e l a b o, nor will I *conceal* it from thee ; σ 406, no longer can ye *disguise* your eating and drinking; it is easy to see from your actions that, etc.

κεφαλή, *ῆς, ῇ, ήν, αί, έων, ῇσι, άς* ; *ῆφιν*, gen. du., (Ger. h a u p t, c a p - u t), c a p u t, *head*, *ἐκ κ.ῆς ἐς πόδας ἄκρους*, Π 640 ; *κὰκ*=*κατὰ κ.*; also of animals, I 548, Λ 39, Γ 273, Ψ 381 ; synonymous with *life*, Δ 162 ; in periphrasis, for a person, Λ 55, Σ 82, Ω 276 ; esp. in address, Ψ 94 ; common phrase, *κ.ὴν οὐδάσδε πελάσσαι* = lay at one's feet ; custom of kissing head and hands, φ 224, 225, χ 499 ; thence come speech and words, Λ 462, Π 77.

Κεφαλλῆνες, collective appellation of subjects of Odysseus on islands and mainland, B 631, ξ 100, υ 187, ω 355, 378, 429.

κεχάνδει, *ότα*, see *χανδάνω*. **κεχαρ**-*ησέμεν, ήσεται, ηώς, οίατο, οντο*, see *χαίρω*. **κεχαρισμ***ένος, ε, α, στο*, see *χαρίζεσθαι*. **κεχηότα,** see *χαίνω*. **κεχωλώ-,** see *χολόω*. **κεχρημένος,** see *χρα-*. **κέχυ(***ν***)***ται, το*, see *χέω*.

κέων, see *κείω* 2. **κῆ**-*αι, άμενος*, see *καίω*.

κήδεος, Ψ 160†, s e p e l i e n d u s.

κηδείους (*κήδω*,) c a r o s, *dear*, T 294†.

κηδεμόνες, *οἱ*, (*κήδω*), properly, s e p u l t o r e s, *mourners, nearer friends*, Ψ 163, 674.

κήδιστος, *οι*, (*κήδω*), c a r i s s i m u s, κ 225.

κῆδος, *εα, εσιν*, a e r u m n a, *trouble*, *τῶν ἄλλων οὐ-* ; *θυμοῖ*, grief ; l u c t u s, N 464, pl., *sorrows*.

κήδει, 3 sing., subj. *ῃ*, opt. *οι*, inf. *ειν*, pass. *ων*, ipf. *ἔκηδε*, and iter. *κήδεσκον*, fut. *-ήσοντες*, fut. red. *κεκαδήσει*, φ 153 ; mid. *κήδεαι, εται, ονται*, opt. *οιτο*, inf. *εσθαι*, pass. *όμενος, ῳ, ον, οι, η*, ipf. *κήδετο, οντο*, iter. *-έσκετο*, fut. *κεκᾰδησόμεθα*, *injure*, Φ 369, E 404 ; *θυμόν*, c r u c i a r e, *distress*, ι 402, Ω 240, 542 ; pass. part. prs. mid., *be concerned for*, person or thing, *τινός*, *care for*, H 204, A 196, ξ 146.

κῆεν, see *καίω*.

κήκιε, ipf., (*κίω*), *gush forth*, ε 455†.

κηλέῳ (*καίω*) *πυρί* (O 744, **κηλείῳ**), *in blazing* fire, Θ 217.

κηληθμῷ, dat., (*κηλέω*), *in rapture* (they listened), ν 2. (Od.)

κῆλα, t e l a, *weapons of the gods* ; even of snow, M 280. (Il.)

κήξ (*καϜαξ, κήυξ*) *εἰνᾰλίη*, *gull*, ο 479†.

κήομεν, subj. from *καίω*.

κῆπον, *ῳ, ους*, masc., (c a m p u s ?), *garden*, Φ 258, δ 737.

Κήρ, *ός, ί, α*, du. *ε*, pl. *ες, ας*, (*κείρω*, Ger. s c h e r e, s c h a r f, Eng. s h e a r), *mode of death*, (*μυρίαι*, M 326) *κῆρες θανάτοιο*, usher into Hades, ξ 207, B 302. Immediately upon the birth, the *Moira* or *Aisa* was determined for the life, and the *Ker* for the death (cf. I 411, where the choice of a twofold destiny is offered to Achilleus; the passage also shows that the Κήρ impels to destruction, cf. *κηρεσσιφορήτους*); when the time of death for the special favorites of Zeus approaches, he weighs the fortunes of combatants, e. g. Patroklos and Sarpedon, Achilleus and Hektor. (See cut, representing Hermes discharging this function.) Freq.

joined with *θάνατος*, β 283 ; *φόνον*, δ 273, β 165 ; hence with adj. *μελαίνῃ, αν*, Φ 66 ; like *θάνατος*, Π 687 ; often =death, Λ 360, 362, E 652, I 411 ; symbol of hate, A 228.

κῆρ, *ός, όθι, ί*, ntr., c o r, *heart*, Π 481 ; then, in wider signification, as the seat of understanding, will, and the varied emotions, and thus corresponding with varied range of meaning to our '*heart;*' hence (ἐν) φρεσίν, ἐνὶ στήθεσσιν, and ἐν θυμῷ, Z 523, which we may translate *within me;* (περὶ) κῆρι, exceedingly in heart, most heartily, ε 36; κηρόθι μᾶλλον (at close of verse), still more in heart, ρ 458; also used periphrastically like μένος, βίη, etc., B 851, cf. A 395.

κηρέσσι-φορήτους (φορέω), *urged on by their evil destinies*, i. e. to death, Θ 527†.

Κήρινθος, town on coast of Euboia, B 538†.

κηρόθι, see κῆρ.

κηρός, οἶο, όν = cera, *wax*, μ 175. (Od.)

κῆρυξ, ῡκος, ι, α; ε; ες, ων, εσσι, ας, *herald;* the heralds convoked the popular assembly, kept order at trials, bore as sign of their office a staff (see cut, from archaic relief, No. 120), which they handed over to him who had the right to speak; they served also as messengers of the chiefs and as their assistants in sacrifice; epithets, θεῖοι, Διὸς ἄγγελοι, Διὶ φίλοι. [P 324, pronounce κήρῡκj Ἠπυτίδῃ.]

κηρύσσειν, inf., part. -ων, οντος, ες, ipf. ἐκήρυσσον, (κῆρυξ), *proclaim as herald, summon, order*, πόλεμόνδε, ἀγορήνδε; P 325, in the office of herald.

κῆται, subj. from κεῖμαι.

Κήτειοι, Mysian tribe, followers of Eurypylos, λ 521†.

κῆτος, εος, εϊ, εα, εσι, *monster of the deep*, e. g. sharks and seals, Υ 147, δ 446.

κητώεσσαν (κῆτος) Λακεδαίμονα, *full of ravines*, B 581, δ 1.

Κηφισίς, ίδος, λίμνη, lake in Boiotia; later Κωπαΐς, E 709†, from

Κηφισός, river in Phokis, B 522†.

κηώδει, dat. from -ώδης, (καίω, κῆος?), *fragrant with sweet odors*, Z 483†.

κηώεντι, α, usually defined *fragrant;* and yet this signif. inconsistent with Γ 382; perh. better (κηϝ-, κύτος, căv-us) *vaulted*, epithet of treasure chambers, Ω 191.

κίδνᾶται, ipf. ἐκίδνατο, (σκιδ-, σκεδάννυμι), dispergitur, *is diffused*, ἠώς, Θ 1.

κῐθάριζε, ipf., φόρμιγγι, *was playing upon the lyre*, Σ 570†. (See cut, in next column, representing a Greek woman.)

κῐθᾰρις, ιν, fem., *cithara* (hence guitar), *lyre*, α 153; *skill in playing upon the cithara*, N 731.

κῐθᾰριστύν, τήν, (κιθαρίζω), *art of playing the cithara.* (See cut.)

κικλήσκεις, ει, ουσ(ι), inf. ειν, part. οντος, ουσα, ipf. κίκλησκε, ον, pass. pr. εται, mid. ipf. ετο, (καλέω), *call, summon*, κλήδην, nominatim, by name; invocans, I 569; nominant, ἐπίκλησιν, cognomine; mid., *call together to one's self*, ἄμυδις.

Κίκονες, Thrakian tribe, ι 47, B 846.

κῖκυς, ἡ, robur, *force*, λ 393†.

Κίλικες, tribe of Greater Phrygia, dwelling under two leaders in Θήβη ὑποπλακίῃ and in Lyrnessos, Z 397, 415.

Κίλλα ζαθέη, town in Troas, A 38, 452.

Κιμμέριοι, fabled people dwelling at entrance of Hades, λ 14†.

κινέω, aor. **κίνησε,** subj. σῃ (and σει? B 147, or perh. fut.?), inf. σαι, part. σας, pass. aor. κινήθη, 3 pl. ἐκίνηθεν, part. ηθέντος, commovere, *disturb, set in motion* (wasps, clouds), *push with the foot* (ποδί); Α 47, as he moved himself forward.

κῑνύμενος, οιο, ων, part., ipf. κίνυντο, (κινέω), proficiscor, *set out, march*, κ 556, Δ 281.

Κῑνύρης, ruler of Kypros, Λ 20†.

κῑνυρή, *wailing, whimpering*, Ρ 5†.

Κίρκη, daughter of Helios, sister of Aietes, inhabiting the island Aiaie, the enchantress, κ 230 sqq.

κίρκος, ον, *hawk* or *falcon* which flies in circles, ἴρηξ; Ἀπόλλωνος ἄγγελός, ο 526.

κιρνάς, part., κίρνη ipf. from κίρνημι; **ἐκίρνα,** ipf. from κιρνάω, (parallel form to κεράννυμι), miscere, *mix; οἶνον*, temperare, *mingle*, η 182.

Κισσηΐς, daughter of Kisses=Θεανώ, Ζ 299†.

Κισσῆς, ruler in Thrake; his grandson Iphidamas, Λ 223†.

κισσύβιον, ῳ, *bowl, basin*, ι 346. (Od.)

κίστῃ, *box, chest*, ζ 76†.

κιχάνω, ετε, opt. άνοι, ipf. (ἐ)κίχαν(ε), ἐκίχανον, and mid. **κιχάνομαι,** εται, όμενοι, fut. κιχήσομαι, σεαι, σεται, σόμεθα, inf. σεσθαι, aor. κιχήσατο, and parallel forms κίχημι, subj. κιχείω, ῃσι, είομεν, opt. είη, inf. ῆναι, ήμεναι, part. είς and ήμενον, ipf. κίχεις, εν, ήτην, (ἐ)κίχημεν, aor. ἔκιχε, ον, part. ών, [the unaugmented forms of two, four, and five syllables stand after caesura in third foot, the augmented forms of three and four syllables almost always at the end of the verse].—(1) reperire, consequi, *overtake, find*, τινά, τί, Γ 291, 383, Ζ 228, Π 342, Χ 303.—(2) invenire, *light upon*, Β 188, μ 122, ξ 139; with part., Α 26, Τ 289; with adj., δ 546.

κίχλαι, turdi, *thrushes*, χ 468†.

κῑ́ῃς, subj. prs., opt. κίοι, οίτην, οιτε, part. κιών, όντι, α, ε, ες, ας, οῦσα, ῃ, αι, ipf. ἔκιε, ον, or κί(εν), κίομεν, κίον, (cieo), *go, go away*, usually of persons; more rarely of things, animals, ships, etc., Ζ 422, ο 149, π 177.

κίων, ονος, ι, α, ες, ας, masc. and fem., columna, *pillar*, α 127, esp. *pillar* supporting the rafters. (See plate II. at end of volume, F and G.)

κλαγγή, ῆς, ῇ, (κλάζω), clamor, *any sharp sound, shout* of men, *cry* or *screech* of birds, cranes, *grunting* of swine, etc.; κλαγγῇ, Γ 5=**κλαγγηδόν,** Β 463, with a *din;* Α 49, *twang* of bow string.

κλάζοντε, part. du., aor. ἔκλαγξαν, part. κλάγξας, αντος, pf. part. κεκληγώς, ῶτες, ῶτας (MSS. οντες, ας), *make a loud, sharp sound, shriek;* Μ 125, *shouting loudly* (in battle); οὖλον, *screaming loudly* all at once; of birds, Π 429; *bellow, clash, rattle, roar.*

κλαίω, εις, ομεν, ετον, subj. ῃ(σι), ωμεν, opt. οισθα, οιμεν, inf. ειν, part. ων, οντα, ε, ες, εσσι, ας, ουσα, ούσης, ipf. ἔκλαιον, κλαῖον, εν, ον, and iter. εσκε, fut. κλαύσομαι, σονται, aor. κλαῦσε, σας, *weep, wail*, lament; esp. of lament for the dead (either of natural expression of grief, or of the more formal prescribed ceremony), τινά, Τ 300, π 450 (δ 169–185); τί, Ω 85, ψ 351; ἀμφί τινα, Σ 339.

κλαυθμοῦ, οῖο, όν, (κλαίω), fletus, *weeping*, esp. in lament for the dead, γόος, ρ 8.

κλαῦσε, aor. from κλαίω.

κλάσε, aor., (κλάω), fregit, ζ 128; aor. pass. ἐκλάσθη, fracta est, Λ 584.

κλεηδόνι, acc. κληηδόνα, (κλέος), fama, *tidings*, δ 317; elsewh. exclamation of favorable significance, *good omen*, cf. β 35.

κλειτῷ, όν, οί, ῶν, ούς, (κλέος, inclitus), *glorious, famous*, esp. of ἐπικούρων, Γ 451, and ἑκατόμβην, Α 447.

Κλεῖτος, (1) son of Mantios, ο 249. —(2) Πεισήνορος υἱόν, companion of Polydamas, slain by Teukros, Ο 445.

κλείω, (1) see **κλέω**.—(2) see **κληίω**.

Κλεόβουλος, a Trojan, slain by Aias, son of Oileus, Π 330†.

Κλεοπάτρη, wife of Meleagros= Ἀλκυόνη, Ι 556†.

κλέος, pl. α, (κλύω, clu-entes, Gothic, hliuma [sense of hearing], Ger. laut [sound]), quae fando audiuntur: (1) fama, *rumor, tidings* (σόν, ἐμόν, of thee, of me).—(2) gloria, κλέος (σοί) πρὸς Τρώων εἶναι, laudi tibi sunto inter Troianos, but they shall be an *honor* to thee before the Trojans, Χ 514; pl. ἀνδρῶν, laudes, *glorious deeds.*

κλέπτῃ, τῷ, (κλέπτω), *thief*, Γ 11†.

κλεπτοσύνῃ, τῇ, (κλέπτης), *knavery, trickery*, τ 396†.

κλέπτῃ, subj., κλέπτε, imp. prs., aor. ἔκλεψε, inf. κλέψαι, (καλύπτω, cal-im, oc-cul-o, clepo), furari, *steal;* νόον, fallere, deceive; νόῳ, cunningly get advantage of, A 132.

κλέομαι, ipf. ἔκλε(ο), pass. of **κλείουσιν,** subj. κλείω, (κλέϝ-ος), famâ celebrare, *make famous,* α 338, ν 299.

Κλεωναί, άς, town in Argolis, B 570†.

κλήδην (καλέω), nominatim, *by name,* I 11†.

κληηδόνα, see κλεηδόνι.

κλήθρη, alnus, *alder,* ε 64 and 239.

κληΐς, ῖδος, ι, α, ες, εσσιν, ῖσιν, (κλαϝ-, clav-is), (1) obex, repagula, *bolt, bar* (see cuts Nos. 32 and 38, both from Egyptian originals); cut No. 60, in four compartments, shows above the open, below the closed door: on the left as seen from within; on the right from without; *c, g, f,* mark the place of the key-hole, through which the thong, ἱμάς, α 442, ran, and the key was passed by which the bolt was first lifted (as is seen at *g*), ἀνέκοψεν, and then pushed back (ἀπῶσαν). The adjoining cut, from a Greek sepulchral

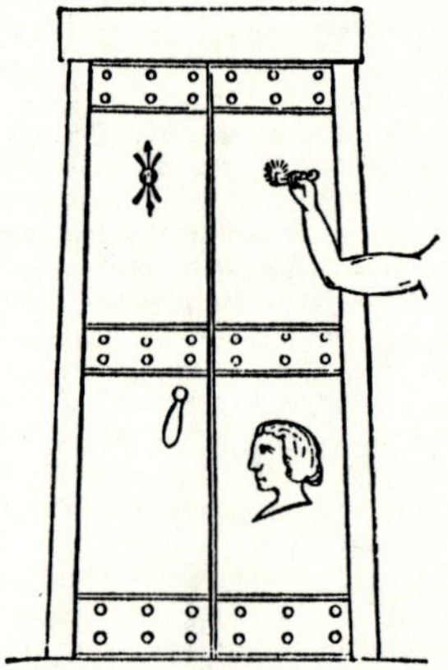

monument, as well as No. 32, presupposes double bolts, and above on the right we see the key as it is applied, and below on the other half of the door the loosened thong; these bolts of double doors are also called ἐπιβλῆς, ὀχῆες; κρυπτῇ, with hidden, concealed bolt.—(2) clavis, *key,* better described as *hook,* M 456. (See cut No. 60, *f, g.*)—(3) iugulum, *collar-bone.*—(4) curved *tongue* of buckle, σ 294. (See cut No. 104.)—(5) *thole-pins, rowlocks,* ἐπὶ κληῖσι, to which the oars were made fast by a thong, and round which they played, see cuts Nos. 126 and 35; for later, different arrangement, see cuts Nos. 41, 94, 64, and the Assyrian war-ship, cut No. 40. ἐπὶ κληῖσι, translate, *at the oars.*

κληϊσταί (κληΐω), *that may be closed,* β 344†.

κληΐω, aor. (ἐ)**κλήϊσε,** inf. ῖσαι, (κληϝίς), claudere, shut, ὀχῆας, *drew forward* the bolts closing the door, by means of the thong. (See cut No. 60.)

κλῆρος, ου, ῳ, ους, (κλάω ?), sors, (1) *lot,* a stone, or potsherd or broken (κλάω) twig, on which each man scratched his mark, H 175; the lots were then shaken in a helmet, and he whose lot first sprang forth was thereby selected for the matter in hand.—(2) *paternal estate,* patrimonium, ξ 64.

κλητοί, ούς, (καλέω), electos, I 165; invitati, ρ 386.

κλίμακα, τήν, (κλίνω), scalas, *stairs, ladder,* κ 558. (Od.)

κλιντῆρι, τῷ, (κλίνω), lectulo, *couch, sofa,* cf. adjacent cut, No. 73.

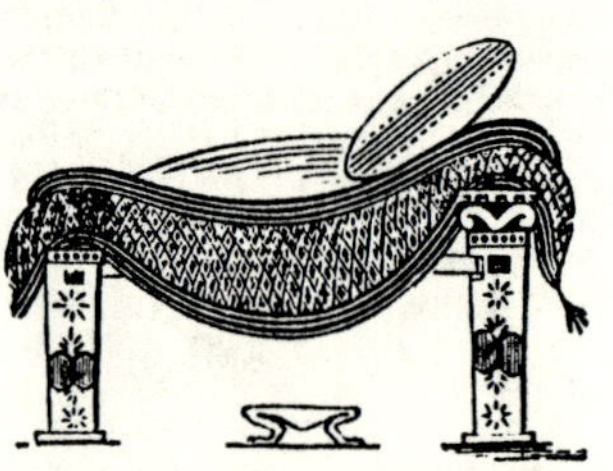

κλίνω, subj. **κλίνῃσι,** inf. κλῖνε, part. -ων, aor. ἔκλῖνε, αν, (κλῖναν), part. -ας, ασα, αντες, (clinare), *make to slope* or *incline,* one thing against another; τί τινι, πρὸς ἐνώπια, drew aside the chariots and *leaned them up* against the shining walls of the vestibule; ὄσσε πάλιν, oculos avertere, *turn away* the eyes; μάχην, inclinare pugnam, *turn the tide of* battle; τινάς, fugare, *put to flight;* pass. aor. (ἐ)κλίνθη, ἐκλίθη, -ῆναι, κλινθήτην, -ῆναι, *bend* *one's self, crouch down*, K 350; ἑτέρωσ', sank on one side; *lie down*; pf. κεκλίαται, κεκλιμένος, ον, οι, ων, η, plupf. κέκλῐτο, τινί, ad aliquid applicatus, innixus rei, *rest upon, lean upon*, Γ 135; iacēre, *lie*, χθονί, humi; situs, *situated*, ἁλί, ad mare, near the sea; λίμνῃ, accola lacus, *hard by*; mid., se applicare, *support one's self upon*, τινί.

κλῐσίης, ῃ, ην, αι, ῶν, ῃσι, ῃς, ας, (κλίνω), *earth hut* of shepherds, *shed* or *lodge, wigwam* of warriors, cf. Ω 450; *couch* or *easy chair*. (See cut No. 79.) **κλῐσίηθεν**, *from the hut*; κλῐσίηνδε, *to the hut*; κλῐσίηφι, *in the hut*.

κλῐσιον, τό, *buildings adjoining master's house*, (cf. in signif., Eng. Lean-to), for servants, strangers, etc., ω 208†.

κλισμῷ, όν, οῖσι, ούς, (κλίνω), *easy-chair, reclining chair*, α 145. (Cf. adjoining cut, or cut No. 113.)

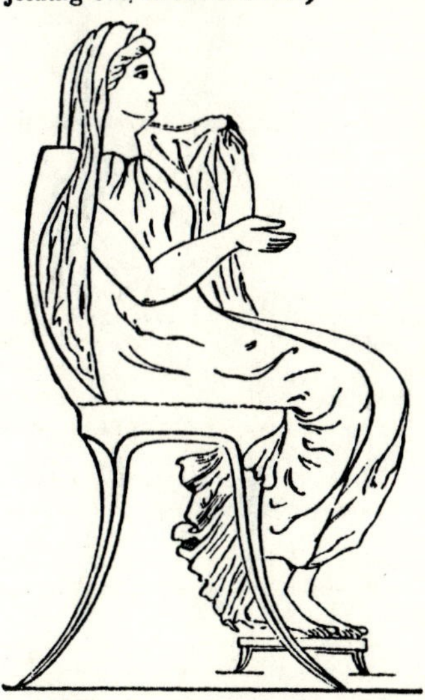

κλῖτῦν, acc. pl. ῦς, (κλίνω), clivus, *slope, hill-side*, ε 470.

κλονέει, ουσι, part. έων, έοντα, τε, τας, fugare, *put to flight* (τινά, Il.), absol., Λ 496; Ο 7, *drive before one*, proturbare; pass. κλονέονται, εσθαι, ipf. έοντο, conturbari, *rush wildly about, be driven in confusion*; ὁμίλῳ, in the fray; ὑπό τινι, Φ 527.

Κλονῖος, chief of the Boiotians, B 495; slain by Agenor, O 340.

κλόνον, τόν, turbam, *tumult*, Π 729; ἐγχειάων, press of spears.

κλοπῖων, gen. pl. from κλόπιος, (κλοπή), fallacium, *deceitful*, ν 295†.

κλοτοπεύειν, *make fine speeches?* T 149†. (Of doubtful deriv. and signif.)

κλῦδων, ὁ, (κλύζω), *billow, surge*, μ 421†.

κλύζεσκον, ipf. iter., (κλύζω), *were plashing*, Ψ 61; ἐκλύσθη δὲ θάλασσα, *was dashed high, rose aloft in foam*.

κλῦθι, imp. from κλύω, *hear*.

Κλυμένη, (1) a Nereid, Σ 47.—(2) an attendant of Helena, Γ 144; daughter of Minyas (Iphis), mother of Iphiklos, λ 326.

Κλύμενος, father of Eurydike, mortally wounded at Thebes, γ 452. [ῠ]

Κλῠται-μνήστρη, daughter of Tyndareos, sister of Helena, wife of Agamemnon; her paramour Aigisthos having slain at her desire her husband, she herself was slain with Aigisthos by her own son Orestes, A 113, γ 266, 310, λ 439. (See cut No. 36.)

Κλῠτίδης, son of Klytios.—(1) Δόλοψ.—(2) Πείραιος.

Κλῠτίος, (1) son of Laomedon, brother of Priamos, father of Kaletor, O 419, 427, Γ 147, Υ 238.—(2) father of Peiraios in Ithaka, π 327.—(3) father of Dolops.

κλῠτό-εργον (Ϝέργον), *maker of famous works, artist*, θ 345†.

Κλῠτο-μήδης, son of Enops, beaten in boxing-match by Nestor, Ψ 634†.

Κλυτό-νηος, son of Alkinoos, θ 119, 123.

κλῠτο-πώλῳ, *with noble steeds*, always epithet of Aides, E 654 sqq. (Il.) Probably in reference to rape of Persephoneie.

κλῠτός, οῦ, όν, οί; also comm. gender, (κλύω, in-clu-tus), *illustrious, glorious*; Ἐννοσίγαιος, ε 423; also of other gods and men, α 300; of places, Ω 437; of animals, ι 308; of things, ὄνομα, τ 183, ι 364.

κλῠτο-τέχνης, *famous for his art, renowned artist*, Α 571.

κλῠτό-τοξος, ῳ, ον, (τόξον), *with fa-*

mous bow, renowned archer, Δ 101, ρ 494.

κλύω, aor. **ἔκλυον,** ες, ε, ον, also κλῦον, imp. κλῦθι, κλῦτε, and aor. sync. κέκλυθι, τε, (cluere, in-clutus), (1) *hear*, ἔπος, ἀγγελίην, δοῦπον, αὐδήν, also with gen. ὀπός, vocem; with part., δ 505, τινὸς αὐδήσαντος; Γ 87, *hear from* me, the proposition of Alexander; also ἔκ τινος, ex aliquo.—(2) exaudire, *give ear to, hearken*, τινός, Α 43, 218, β 262, γ 385; also τινὸς αὐδῆς, μύθων, τινὶ ἀρῆς; less common with dat., τινί, Π 516.—(3) obedire, *hear and comply, obey*, τοῦ μάλα μὲν κλύον, ο 220.

Κλῶθες, lit. *the Spinsters;* as goddesses of fate, η 197†.

κλωμακόεσσαν (κλῶμαξ, grumus), *on rock terraces, rocky*, Β 729†.

κνέφας, ἄος, ας, (δνόφος), crepusculum, *twilight, dusk*, σ 370.

κνῆ, ipf. from κνάω; *she grated* (ἐπί, thereon), Λ 639†.

κνήμη, ην, αι, άων, ῃσιν, crus, part of leg between the knee and ankle, *shin*, Δ 519.

κνημίς, ῖδας, (κνήμη), ocrea, *greaves*, metal plates, lined with some soft material, bent around the shin-bone under the knee, and fastened by clasps at the ankle (see cut No. 39), only in Iliad; the word in the Odyssey, ω 229, signifies *leather leggins.*

κνημοῖσι, ούς, masc., saltus, *mountain valleys*, Β 821.

κνήστι, dat. from κνῆστις, (κνῆν), *knife for shaving* or *grating*, Λ 640†.

κνίση, only sing., (κνίδja, nidor ?), *fat*, esp. the *fat caul* or *diaphragm*, in which the thighs of the victim were wrapped, laid upon the fire and burned, together with the pieces of flesh piled upon them (Α 460); hence the word also signifies the *steam of the fat* or *sacrifice*, Α 66; **κνίσηεν,** *full of the steam of burnt sacrifice*, κ 10†. [v. l. κνίσση.]

κνυζηθμῷ (κνύζω), *with whimper, whimpering*, π 163†.

κνυζώσω, fut., and aor. κνύζωσεν, ν 401, 433, *make lustreless.*

κνώδἄλον, fera, *monster*, ρ 317†.

Κνωσός, μεγάλη πόλις, εὐρείῃ, in Kreta, Β 646, Σ 591, τ 178.

κνώσσουσα, part., *deeply slumbering*, consopita, δ 809†.

κόιλοιο, ον, η, ης, ῃ, ην, only χ 385, κοῖλον, (κόϝιλος, cav-us), *hollow;* λιμήν, *deep-embosomed, extending far into the land*, κ 92.

κοιμάω, aor. **(ἐ)κοίμησε,** σατε, imp. σον, part. σας, ασα, (κεῖμαι), *lull, hush to sleep*, τινά; *litter*, δ 336; consopire, *put to sleep*, also figuratively; mid. pr. κοιμᾶται, ipf. κοιμᾶτο, ῶντο, aor. (ἐ)κοιμήσατο, σαντα, subj. σωνται, imp. σασθε, and aor. pass. (ἐ)κοιμήθημεν, opt. θείη, inf. θῆναι, part. θέντι, ε, ες, *lay one's self down to sleep*, past tenses, *sleep; sleep the sleep of death*, Λ 241.

κοιρἄνέουσι, part. έων, έοντα, (κοίρανος), *be lord* or *master, rule*, ἀνά, κατά, διά τινας; dominari, *play the lord*, ν 377.

κοίρᾰνος, ε, οι, (κῦρος), *ruler;* also with λαῶν, ruler of the people, Η 234.

Κοίρᾰνος, (1) a Lykian slain by Odysseus, Ε 677.—(2) from Lyktos in Kreta, charioteer of Meriones, Ρ 611, 614, slain by Hektor.

κοίτῃ, τῇ, (κεῖμαι), *bed*, τ 341†.

κοῖτος, οιο, ου, ον, masc., *bed*, ξ 455; *night's rest, sleep*, η 138.

κολεόν, οῖο, ῷ, and κουλεόν, ῷ, ntr., (metal) *sword-sheath*, Α 194, 220.

κολλήεντα, ntr. pl., (κολλάω), ξυστὰ ναύμαχα, ship-spears, *united together with rings*, Ο 389†.

κολλητόν, οῖσι, ῇσι, άς, (κολλάω), *firmly bound together, compacted* or *shod with bands*, Ο 678, ψ 194.

κόλλοπι, dat. from κόλλοψ, *peg* on the lyre, round which the string was made fast, φ 407†.

κολοιῶν, ούς, graculorum, *jackdaws*, Π 583. (Il.)

κόλον, ntr., *docked, pointless*, Π 117†.

κολοσυρτόν, τόν, *noisy rabble*, Μ 147 and Ν 472.

κολούει, imp. ετε, (κόλος), mutilat, *leaves unfulfilled*, Υ 370; λ 340, *cut short, curtail.*

κόλπῳ, ον, οι, ους, (καλύπτω), *fold* or *belly* of garment round neck and breast, Ι 570; *bosom*, Ζ 136, 400; bosom of the sea, Σ 140.

ἐκολῴα, ipf. from κολῳάω, (κολῳός), *screamed, bawled*, Β 212†.

κολώνη (κέλλω), collis, *hill*, Β 811. (Il.)

κολῳὸν (φὸν ?) ἐλαύνετε, continue *noisy wrangling*, Α 575†.

κομόωντε, τες, part. from κομάω, (κόμη), ὄπιθεν, *with hair long* at back of head, shorn in front, B 542; κάρη, long-haired; ἐθείρῃσι, with long manes.

κομέω, **κομέουσι,** imp. είτων, inf. έειν, ipf. ἐκόμει (and iter. έεσκε), είτην, *take care of, tend* (by giving bath, food, bed, clothing), τινά, λ 250; also of animals, ρ 310, 319.

κόμη, ης, ην, αι, ας, (coma), *hair of head;* pl. ζ 231, thick flowing *locks;* also *foliage*, ψ 195.

κομῐδή, ῆς, ήν, cultus corporis, (see κομέω), *care, attendance,* bestowed on men, horses, also on garden, ω 245, 247.

κομίζω, ει, subj. ῃ, imp. κόμιζε, inf. ειν, έμεν, ipf. ἐκόμιζε, fut. κομιῶ, aor. ἐκόμισσα, (ἐ)κόμισε, αν, subj. ίσσῃ, imp. ισσον, (κομέω), (1) *wait upon, attend, care for,* Z 490, τινά, τί; esp. *receive as guest, entertain,* κ 73, ρ 113, cf. 111; τινά τινι, nutrire, υ 69; pass. όμενος, θ 451.—(2) *gather up,* ψ 355; *carry away,* Γ 378; *bear off,* Ξ 456, B 875; *bring,* Ψ 699; mid. aor. (ἐ)κομίσσατο, ίσαντο, opt. ίσαιο, *receive hospitably, entertain;* X 286, carry off in one's flesh.

κομπέω, ipf. **ἐκόμπει,** *clashed, rattled,* M 151†.

κόμπος, ὁ, (κόναβος), *stamping of feet,* θ 380; *grinding, gnashing* of tusks of boar.

κονάβησε, σαν, aor., ipf. **κονάβιζε,** (κόναβος), *resound* (of echo); *rattle, ring,* O 648, Φ 593, N 498. (Il. and ρ 542.)

κόνᾰβος, *din, crash,* κ 122†.

κονΐη, sing., and ῃσι, pulvis, *dust;* λ 600, rose from his head; with ὀμίχλῃ, N 336; στροφάλιγγι, Π 775, ω 39; *sand,* Ψ 502, 506; cineres, *ashes,* η 153. [ῑ when in final foot of verse.]

κόνις, ιος, ῐ, fem., pulvis, *dust,* N 335; *ashes,* Σ 23, λ 191.

κονί-σσαλος, ω, (σϝαλ), *dust-cloud, dust-whirl,* Γ 13. (Il.)

κονίοντες, part., fut. κονίσουσι, aor. ἐκόνῖσε, (κόνις), *make dust;* πεδίοιο, *raise a dust-cloud,* speeding over the plain, N 820; *making dusty,* Φ 407; pass. plupf. κεκόνῖτο, and pf. κεκονιμένοι, pulvere obducti, *covered with dust.*

κοντόν, τόν, (κεντέω), *pole,* ι 487†.

Κοπρεύς, father of Periphetes, O 639†.

κοπρήσοντες, fut. part., (κοπρέω), stercorandi causa, *for manure,* ρ 299†.

κόπρος, ὁ, only sing., fimus, stercus, lutum, *dung,* Ω 164; *farm-yard, cattle-stall,* Σ 575.

κόπτων, οντες, part, ipf. κόπτε, ον, aor. κόψε, ας; 2 pf. κεκοπώς, aor. mid. κόψατο, *beat, smite;* παρήιον, on the cheek; ποτὶ γαίῃ, strike to earth; *bite, sting,* M 204; decidere, detruncare, χ 477; *forge,* δεσμούς; mid., X 33, *smite one's own head.*

Κόρακος πέτρῃ, rocky mountain in Ithaka, ν 408†.

κορέννυμι, fut. **κορέεις,** έει, aor. opt. κορέσειε, satiare, *sate, satisfy,* τινά τινι, Θ 379; mid. (ἐ)κορέσσατο, σάμεθα, subj. σωνται, opt. σαίατο, inf. σασθαι, part. σάμενος, and pass. pf. κεκορήμεθα, ησθε, ημένοι, act. part. κεκορηότε, aor. also pass. ἐκορέσθην, satiari, *sate one's self* with, τινός; (κατὰ) θυμόν, in heart; also metaph. *be tired of,* τινός, or with part. τάμνων, κλαίουσα, υ 59.

κορέω, aor. imp. **κορήσατε,** *sweep out,* υ 149†.

κόρη, false reading, read κούρη.

κορθύεται (κόρυς, κάρ, III.), *raises itself aloft,* I 7†.

Κόρινθος, the city *Korinth,* the wealthy, on isthmus of same name, Isthmos, B 570; Κορινθόθι, *at Korinth,* N 664; ancient name, Ἐφύρη.

κορμόν, τόν, (κείρω), the *trunk of the tree* I hewed round about (beginning with the root and progressing toward the smaller end), ψ 196†.

κόρος, ὁ, satietas, taedium; τινός, *surfeit,* N 636, δ 103.

κόρσην, τήν, *temple,* Δ 502. (Il.)

κορῠθάϊκι, dat., (κόρυθα ἀίσσοντι), *helmet shaking, with waving plume,* X 132†.

κορῠθ-αίολος (κόρυθα αἰόλην ἔχων), *with glancing helm,* esp. epithet of Hektor and of Ares, B 816, Γ 83. (Il.)

κόρυμβα (κορυφή, κάρη) ἄκρα, the *heads* or *ends,* in which the stern of vessel terminated, cf. ἄφλαστα, I 241†. (See cut No. 21.)

κορῡνη, ῃ, (κόρυς), *battle mace* (of

iron). Hence comes **κορῡνήτης**, *ην*, *club-brandisher*, H 141, 9.

κόρυς, *υθος*, *θι*, *θα*, and *υν*; *θες*, *θων*, *θεσσι*, *ας*, fem., (*κάρη*, *κάρ*), *helmet*, with adjs. *βριαρήν*, *δαιδαλέην*, *ἱπποδασείης*, *ἱπποκόμου*, *λαμπομένης*, *λαμπρῆς*, *παναίθῃσι*, *τετραφάλῳ*, *φαεινῇ*, *χαλκήρεος*, *χαλκοπαρῄου*, N 131, 188. (See these adjs., and cuts under them.)

κορύσσων, part., ipf. *ἐκόρυσσε*, (*κόρυς*), *equip*, excitare, augere; pass. and mid. *κορύσσεαι*, *σσεται*, *σσόμενος*, *ον*, ipf. *κορύσσετο*, *σσέσθην*, aor. *κορυσσάμενος*, and pf. part. *κεκορυθμένος*, *ον*, *οι*, *α*, *equipped*; (*χαλκῷ*), *shod with*; *arm one's self*, *τεύχεσι*, *χαλκῷ*; *raise the head*, Δ 442, cf. 443, 424, cf. *κορθύεται*.

κορυστήν, du. *τά*, lit. *helmed*, hence *armed*, *ready for battle*, Δ 457, N 201. (Il.)

κορῡφῆς, *ῇ*, *ήν*, *αί*, *ῇσι*, *άς*, (*κόρυμβος*, *κόρυς*), vertex, *crest*; cacumen, *summit*, dat. without prep., E 554. (Il. and ι 121.)

κορῡφοῦται, from *-όω*, (*κορυφή*), *rises with arching crest*, Δ 426†.

Κορώνεια, city in Boiotia, south of lake Kopais, B 503†.

κορώνη, *ης*, *ῃ*, *αι*, *ῃσιν*, (corona, cornu, cur-vus), any thing *crooked* or *curved*, (1) the *ring* on the door, α 441. (See cut No. 72, and *κληΐς*.)—(2) the *curved end of the bow* over which the loop of the bow-string must be brought. (See cut No. 37, under *ἐντανύουσιν*.)—(3) *εἰνάλιαι*, *τανύγλωσσοι*, *sea-crows*, *cormorants*. ε 66.

κορωνίσι, dat. pl. fem., (*κορώνη*), *bent into shape of a horn*, *curved* (always in 4th foot of verse), of ships, τ 182. (See cuts Nos. 21, 41, 94, 95, 109.)

Κόρωνος, *Καινεΐδης*, father of Leonteus, king of the Lapithai, B 746†.

κοσμέω, ipf. **ἐκόσμει**, *εον*, aor. *ἐκόσμησε*, inf. *ῆσαι*, pass. aor. 3 pl. *κόσμηθεν*, part. *-θέντες*, (*κόσμος*), *arrange*, *order*, *equip* troops, *get ready* chariot; *δόρπον*, *prepare* evening meal, η 13; mid. *κοσμησάμενος πολιήτας*, *marshaling* his own countrymen, B 806.

κοσμηταί (*κοσμέω*), *well laid out*, η 127†.

κοσμήτορι, *ε*, usually *λαῶν*, *marshaler* of the people, usually of Atreidai and Dioskouroi; only in σ 152, Amphinomos. (Il.)

κόσμος, *ῳ*, *ον*, *arrangement*, *order*; constructio, *building*, *ἵππου*, θ 492; decus, ornamenta, *ornaments*, *trappings*, of women and horses; *κόσμῳ*, *in order*, *in rank and file*; *λίην*, *εὖ κατὰ κόσμον*, duly, becomingly, θ 489; *οὐ κ. κ.*, indecōre, shamefully, υ 181.

κοτέουσι, part. *έων*, *έοντος*, *τε*, *έουσ(α)*, pf. part. *κεκοτηότι*, τ 71; mid. ipf. *κοτέοντο*, aor. *κοτέσσατο*, subj. *ἐσσεται*, part. *εσσάμενος*, *η*, (*κότος*), succensere, *be angry with*, *τινί* (on account of something, *τινός*, Δ 168); also *οὕνεκα*, quod.

κοτήεις, *wrathful*, E 191†.

κότον, *τόν*, *grudge*, *rancor*, *wrath*, with dat. of person against whom feeling is felt, *τινί*; but Π 449, in whom thou wilt excite dire wrath.

κοτῡ́λην, *τήν*, properly *a little cup*; E 306, *hip-joint*.

κοτῡληδονόφιν, from *κοτυληδών*, (*κοτύλη*), *πρὸς*—, on the *suckers* at the end of the tentaculae of the polypus pebbles stick fast, ε 433†.

κοτῡλ-ήρῡτον (*ἀρύω*), *that may be caught in cups*, *streaming*, Ψ 34†.

κουλεόν, see *κολεόν*.

κούρη, sing. and pl., (gen. *άων*, dat. *ῃσι*), fem. from *κοῦρος*, *young girl* or *daughter*, cf. French fille; *τινός*, *Χρυσηΐδος*, A 111, for the daughter of Chryses; (*Διός*) *γλαυκῶπις*=Athene; also applied to youthful wives, A 98, Z 247.

κούρητες, *ων*, *εσσι*, (*κοῦρος*), *Ἀχαιῶν*, *Παναχαιῶν*, T 248, 193, *youthful chiefs*, *princes*, *princes' sons*.

Κουρῆτες, tribe in Aitolia, afterward expelled by Aitolians; their siege of Kalydon, I 529–599.

κουριδίου, *οιο*, *ῳ*, *ον*, *ης*, *ῃ*, *ην*, *ας*, (*κουρίξ* [Curtius], *κοῦρος*, *κούρη*?), *bridal*, *wedded*; nobilis, *noble*, A 243 (cf. 242, *μνηστῆς*), ο 22, in which latter case neither *κουριδίοιο* nor *φίλοιο* is subst. The signification of the word is not certainly known; others translate *youthful*, *princely*, A 114.

κουρίζων, part., (*κοῦρος*), *young*, *lusty*, χ 185†.

κουρίξ (*κουρά*), adv., *ἔρυσαν*, *by the hair*, χ 188†.

κοῦρος, *ῳ*, *ον*, *ω*, *οι*, *ων*, *οισιν*, *ους*, properly iuvenis, *youth*, *boy*, Ζ 59; *son*, τ 523 (yet N 95); cf. **κουροτέροισι**, Δ 316, φ 310, iunioribus, *fresh with youth*, *lusty*, θηρητῆρες; hence, *able to bear arms*, *valiant*, *noble*, β 96; used often (cf. Lat. equites) to denote persons of given rank, and may be translated *noble*, Α 473; κοῦροι Ἀχαιῶν, etc.

κουρο-τρόφος (*τρέφω*) ἀγαθή, bona nutrix iuvenum robustorum, ι 27†.

κοῦφα, ntr. pl., as adv., *quickly*, N 158†; **κουφότερον**, *with lighter heart*, θ 201†.

Κόων, son of Antenor, slain by Agamemnon, Λ 248–260, Τ 53.

Κόωνδ', see Κῶς.

κράατα, *τι*, *τος*, see III. *κάρ*.

κρᾰδαινόμενον, *η*, (*κραδαίνω*), vibratum, *quivering*, N 504. (Il.)

κραδάων, part. from *κραδάω*, vibrans, *brandishing*, H 213, τ 438.

κρᾰδίη, *ης*, *ῃ*, *ην*, and at beginning of verse *καρδίη*, (*κραδάω*), cor, *heart*; then as centre of circulation, anima, *life*; also animus, *courage*, Α 225, Μ 247; *heart* as *seat of emotion*, *desire*, Ι 646, with *θυμός*, Κ 220, Β 171, δ 548, etc., of *thought*, *reason*, Φ 441; thoughts were set, δ 260.

κραίνουσι, ipf. *ἐκραίαινε*, aor. imp. *κρῆνον*, *κρήηνον*, *ήνατ(ε)*, inf. *κρῆναι*, *κρηῆναι*, fut. mid. (as pass.) *κρανέεσθαι*, (creare), perficere, ε 170, *accomplish*, *fulfill*, *bring to pass*; Ι 626, the object of our mission does not appear to me likely to be brought to pass in this way; only θ 391, *bear sway*.

κραιπνόν, *οῖσι*, *αί*, *ά*, as adv. = *ὦς*, comp. -*ότερος*, rapidus, from wind and storm; elsewh. *quick*; Ψ 590, *hasty*, *hot*.

Κρᾰνάη, an island, Γ 445†.

κρᾰνᾰῆς, *ήν*, *rocky*, Ithaka, α 247. (Od.)

κρανέεσθαι, fut., see *κραίνουσι*.

κρᾰ́νειαν, acc., gen. *είης*, cornus, *cornel-tree*, its wood esp. hard, κ 242.

κρᾱνίῳ (*κρᾱ́νον*), cranio, *upper part of the skull*, Θ 84†.

Κρᾰ́πᾰθος, *ή*, Β 676, island near Rhodos; later Κάρπαθος.

κρᾶτα, *τί*, see III. *κάρ*.

κρᾰται-γῠ́ᾰλοι (*γύαλον*), *with strong breast-plates*, Τ 361†. (See cut No. 59.)

κρᾰταιΐς (*κράτος*), *with its weight*, *with overmastering force*, pondus, λ 597†.

Κρᾰταιΐν, *μητέρα τῆς Σκύλλης*, μ 124†.

κρᾰταιός, *οῦ*, *ώ*, *ή*, potens, *mighty*; *θηρός*=*λέοντος*, Λ 119.

κρᾰταί-πεδον (*κραταιός*) *οὖδας*, *hard-surfaced* earth, pavimentum, ψ 46†.

κρᾰτερός, *οῖο*, *οῦ*, *ῷ*, *όν*, *ώ*, *οῖσι*; *ή*, *ῆς*, *ῇ*, *ῆφι* (*βίηφιν*, thrice at end of verse), *ήν*, *αί*, *ῇσι*, *άς*; *όν*, (*κράτος*), and parallel form **καρτερός**, *όν*, *οί*, (*κάρτος*), *strong*, *mighty*, of persons, things, passions, etc.; adv. *κρατερῶς*, *strongly*, *mightily*, Θ 29; hold firm thy ground, Π 501.

κρᾰτερό-φρονος, gen., acc. *α*, (*ε*), (*φρήν*), *stout-hearted*, *dauntless*, animosus; of heroes and warriors, of lion, *θήρ*, Κ 184.

κρατερ-ώνυχες, *ας*, (*ὄνυξ*), *strong-hoofed*, *strong-clawed*, of horses, mules, and κ 218, of wolves and lions.

κρᾰ́τεσφι, see III. *κάρ*.

κρᾰτευτάων, gen. pl., (*κρατός*), explained by Aristarchus as *stones*, *head-stones*, on which the spits were rested in roasting meat; cf. our *fire-dogs*, *and-irons*, possibly in shape like the horns on the altar in cut No. 102, Ι 214†.

κρατέεις, *ει*, *ουσι*, inf. *έειν*, part. *έων*, (*κράτος*), *be mighty*, *rule over*, Α 288; *κρατέων*, with might; over any one, *τινῶν*; *τισίν*, *bear sway among*, λ 485.

κράτος, *εϊ*, and **κάρτος**, *εϊ*, robur, potentia, imperium, *might*, *power*, *mastery*, α 359; victoria, φ 280; *φέρεσθαι*, reportare, carry off victory.

κρατός, see III. *κάρ*.

κρᾰτῠ́ς = *κρατερὸς*, *ἀργειφόντης*, Π 181, ε 49, *mighty*.

κρέας, pl. *κρέ(α)'* (*κρέατ(α)'*, γ 33, ι 162), gen. *κρεῶν*, *κρειῶν*, dat. *κρέασιν*, (cruor), caro, *flesh*, pl. *pieces of flesh*, *dressed meat*. [*κρεα*, synizesis, ι 347.]

κρεῖον (*κρέας*), *meat-tray*, *dresser*, Ι 206†.

κρείσσων, *ονες*, *οσιν*, *ον*, (*κράτ-jων*), superior, *mightier*, *stronger*; ζ 182, nobler and better; *βίῃ*, superior in strength; with inf., φ 345.

Κρειοντιάδης, *son of* Κρείων, Lykomedes, Τ 240†.

κρείων, οντα, όντων, (ουσα, Χ 48), properly part., *ruling, ruler; εὐρὺ κρ.*, ruling far and wide, title esp. of Agamemnon, with reference to his position as generalissimo of Greek forces; also of Enosichthon, Zeus; also in one case of servant of Menelaos, δ 22.

Κρείων, (1) king of Thebes, father of Megara, λ 269.—(2) father of Lykomedes, Ι 84.

κρέμαμαι, see following.

κρέμαννυμι, fut. **κρεμόω**, aor. *κρέμᾰσε, ἄσαντες*, suspendere, *hang, hang up;* mid. ipf. *ἐκρέμω*, pendebas, thou didst hang, Ο 18.

κρέων, gen. pl. from *κρέας*.

κρήγῡον, *τὸ—εἶπας*, Α 106†, salutiferum, *good, useful, helpful.*

κρήδεμνον, ῳ, α, (*κάρη, δέω*), *headband;* in woman's attire, *a short veil*, as in adjacent cut, α 334; of cities, *battlements*, ν 388; of wine jar, *lid*, γ 392, (See cut No. 68.)

κρῆναι, aor. from *κραίνουσι*. **κρῆθεν,** see III. *κάρ*, funditus, *utterly.*

Κρηθεύς, *Αἰολίδης*, husband of *Τυρώ*, λ 237, 258.

Κρήθων, son of Diokles, slain by Aineias, Ε 542, 549.

κρημνοῦ, οῖο, όν, οί, ούς, (*κρέμαμαι*), *overhanging river bank*, esp. the *gullied banks* of the Skamandros, Φ 26, 175.

κρηναῖαι (*κρήνη*) *νύμφαι*, *fountain nymphs*, ρ 240†.

κρήνη, ης, ῃ, ην (δε), αι, έων, (*κάρηνα*, cf. caput), *fountain, spring, well*, Ι 14, ι 141. (Cf. cut No. 65.)

Κρῆτες, Β 645, Γ 230, *inhabitants of island* **Κρήτη**; described, τ 172, 175, *ἑκατόμπολιν, εὐρείης*; also pl. *Κρητάων*, as divided and speaking different languages, π 62; *Κρήτηνδε*, τ 186; *Κρήτηθεν*, Γ 233.

κρητῆρος, ι, α, ες, σι, ας, masc., (*κεράννυμι*), *mixing-vessel* in which wine and water, in ratio of $\frac{2}{5}$ and $\frac{3}{5}$, were mingled: *μίσγεσθαι; στήσασθαι*, place the mixing-bowl at hand, usually near the hearth, and often on a tripod (esp. when several *κρητῆρες* were used at the feast); the contents were afterward poured into the drinking-cups by means of the *πρόχοος*, γ 339; Ζ 527, set up in our palace a mixing-bowl in commemoration of freedom, in honor of the gods. Cut No. 7 shows (1) the *ἀμφιφορεύς*, from which the wine was poured into the upper smaller mixing bowl, on which the *πρόχοος* stands; the second mixing bowl served to contain the water, and then the contents of both bowls may be imagined as mixed in the largest mixing-bowl, which stands upon the tripod, and from which, by means of the *πρόχοος*, the diluted wine was distributed into the *δέπαα*. (Cf. cut No. 29.)

κρῖ, *τό*, nom. and acc., (*κριθή*), *λευκόν*, *barley*, Υ 496; also as food for horses, Ε 196, δ 41.

κριθαί, ῶν, έων, άς, (*κρῖ*, cer-es ?), *barley, barleycorn*, Λ 69.

κρίκε, aor. from *κρίζω*, *creaked*, of the yoke under a strain, Π 470†.

κρίκον, *τόν*, (*κίρκος*, circus), *yoke-ring*, Ω 272†. (See adjoining cut, from the antique; still clearer cuts Nos. 45, 49.)

κρίνῃ, ωσι, subj., οιμι opt., *κρῖνε* imp., ων, οντες part. prs., aor. *ἔκρινε*, ιναν, subj. *ίνωσι*, part. *ίνας*, cernere, *sieve, select;* eligere, *λοχόνδε*, for the ambuscade; pass. pf. part. *κεκριμένοι*, ους, η, electi, *chosen, selected* (Ξ 19, -ον, certum), and *κρινθέντε, ες*; decernere, *decide*, *νεῖκος*, the dispute; *σκολιὰς θέμιστας*, proleptically, *pervert* justice, mid. *κρίνονται*, subj. *ώμεθα*, aor. *ἐκρίνατο*, subj. *ηται, ωνται*, imp. *ασθων*, inf. *ασθαι*, part. *άμενος*, sibi eligere, *choose for one's self;* also, *measure one's self* in battle, *ἄρηι*, acie, Β 385; π 269, when our courage and that of the suitors is measured in my palace, cf. ω 507; ὀνείρους, *expound, interpret.*

κριόν, ἑ, masc., (κέρας), arietem, *ram,* ι 447, 461.

Κρῖσα, town in Phokis; ζαθέην, Β 520, near and southwest of Delphi.

κριτός, οἱ, (κρίνω), electus, *chosen,* Η 434 and θ 258.

κροαίνων, part., (κρούω), *galloping,* Ζ 507, Ο 264.

Κροῖσμος, a Trojan, slain by Meges, Ο 523†.

κροκό-πεπλος (πέπλος), *with saffron-colored mantle;* epithet of Eos, Θ 1. (Il.)

κρόκον, τόν, *crocus, saffron,* Ξ 348†.

Κροκύλεια, τά, island or village belonging to Ithaka, Β 633†.

κρόμυον, οιο, cepa, *onion,* Λ 630, τ 233.

Κρονίδης, ου, αο, ῃ, ην, η, *son of Kronos,* standing alone or with Zeus, Α 552, α 45, =**Κρονίων,** ίωνος (ίονος, Ξ 247, λ 620). (See following.)

Κρόνος, οιο, ου, ον, (κραίνω), father of Zeus, Poseidaon, Aides, of Hera, Demeter, and Hestia; overthrown with the Titans, Θ 415, 479, 383, Ε 721.

κροσσάων, ας, fem., (κόρση?), perh. *walls of the towers,* between foundations and battlements, Μ 258, 444.

κροτάλιζον, ipf., (κρόταλον), ὄχεα, *made rattle* (as they drew), *drew the rattling* chariots, Λ 160†.

κρόταφον, οιο, οισι, οις, masc., tempora, *temples;* sing., Δ 502, Υ 397.

κροτέοντες (κρότος) ὄχεα, *drawing the rattling* chariots, Ο 453†.

Κρουνοί, "Springs," name of locality in Elis, [ο 295]†.

κρουνώ, du., ῶν, ούς, pl., *sources,* Δ 454; of Skamandros, Χ 147, 208.

κρύβδα, Σ 168†, =**κρύβδην,** λ 455 (Od.), clam, *secretly.*

κρυεροῖο (κρύος, cru-or, Eng. gore), rigidus, *chilling, dread,* Ν 48, δ 103.

κρυόεντος, εσσα, (κρύος), horrendi, *chilling, horrible,* Ι 2. (Il.)

κρυπτάδίης, α, (κρύπτω), clandestina, *secret;* Α 542, clandestinis captis consiliis decernere.

κρυπτῇ κληΐδι, with a *secret* bolt, Ξ 168†.

κρύπτων, part., ipf. iter. κρύπτασκε, fut. κρύψω, aor. ἔκρυψαν, κρύψεν, subj. ψω, inf. ψαι, part. ψαντες, perf. pass. part. κεκρυμμένον, α, aor. κρύφθη, celare, *hide, conceal,* τί τινι (with desire for protection); pass. se celare, ὑπό τινι, sub re, *hide one's self* under any thing; τινά, aor., from some one; *keep secret,* ἔπος τινί, λ 443.

κρύσταλλος, ῳ, masc., (κρύος), glacies, *ice, clear ice,* ξ 477 and Χ 152.

κρυφηδόν (κρύφα), clam, *secretly,* ξ 330 and τ 299.

Κρῶμνα, locality in Paphlagonia, Β 855†.

κτάμεν(αι), ος, see κτείνω.

κτᾶσθαι, aor. ἐκτήσω, (ἐ)κτήσατο, pf. ἐκτῆσθαι, sibi comparare, *acquire for one's self,* property, servants, wife; τινί τι, alicui aliquid, υ 265; pf. possidere, *possess,* Ι 402.

κτεάτεσσιν (τὸ κτέαρ, κτάομαι), bonis, *property, possessions,* Ε 154, α 218.

κτεάτισσα, εν, part. ας, aor. from -ίζω, (κτέαρ), sibi comparare, *acquire for one's self; δουρί,* cf. δουρικτήτη, ferro = bello, Π 57. [ᾰ]

Κτέατος, son of Aktor and of Molione, Β 621.

κτείνεις, ει, ουσι, subj. ω, inf. ειν, part. ων, οντ(α), ες, ipf. ἔκτεινε, ον, κτεῖνε, ον, iter. κτείνεσκε, fut. κτενέω, έει (εῖ), έειν and κτανέω, έοντα, aor. (ἔ)κτεινε, opt. αιμι, inf. ναι, part. νας, αντες, ασα, 2 aor. ἔκτανον, ες, ε, κτάνον, ε, and 3 sing. ἔκτα, αμεν, αν, subj. κτέωμεν, χ 216, inf. κτάμεν(αι); pass. prs. κτεινώμεθα, εσθαι, όμενος, ῳ, ων, ους, ipf. κτείνοντο, 3 pl. aor. ἔκταθεν, and aor. 2 κτάσθαι, άμενος, οιο, ῳ, ον, ων, οισι, ης, with aoristic signif. only in Ν 262, Ο 554, Σ 337, interimere, *kill, slay;* pass., Ε 465, Ἀχαιοῖς = ὑπ' Ἀχαιῶν.

κτέρας (κτᾶσθαι), *possession,* Κ 216 and Ω 235; pl. **κτέρεα,** έων, always with κτερεΐζειν, bestow one's possessions upon one = justa facere, bury with due honors.

κτερίζω, fut. **κτεριῶ,** ιοῦσι, aor. opt. ίσειε, ειαν, and prs. imp. **κτερέιζε,** inf. έμεν, aor. -εΐξω, εΐξαι, (κτέρας), *bury,* efferre; ἀέθλοις, with funeral games; κτέρεα κτ., justa facere, bury with solemn pomp, α 291.

κτῆμαθ' = κτήματα, dat. ασιν, (κτᾶσθαι), *possession, property,* esp. the *treasures* carried off at the same time with Helen, Η 350, Ι 382.

Κτήσιος Ὀρμενίδης, father of Eumaios, ο 414†.

Κτήσιππος, from Same, son of Polytherses, a suitor, υ 288, χ 279; slain by Philoitios, χ 285.

κτήσιος, σιν, fem., (κτᾶσθαι), *property*, Ο 663.

κτητοί (κτᾶσθαι), *that may be acquired*, Ι 407†.

κτῐδέην (ἰκτίς), κυνέην, *helmet of weasel-skin*, Κ 335 and 458.

κτίζω, aor. **κτίσσε,** ἔκτῐσαν, incolere, *settle in a country*, with acc., Υ 216.

κτίλος, ον, aries, *ram*, Γ 196 and Ν 492. [ῐ]

Κτῐμένη, daughter of Laertes, sister of Odysseus, settled in marriage in Same, ο 363.

κτῠπέει, έων, έουσαι, aor. ἔκτῠπε, κτῠπε, *crash*, of falling trees, *thunder*, of Zeus; μέγα, loud; σμερδαλέα, terribly, Η 479, Θ 170.

κτῠπος, ου, ον, sonitus, *any loud noise, stamping* of feet, *blow* of horse's hoof, *foot-tread, tumult of battle, thunder*, Κ 532, φ 237.

κῠᾰμοι, *beans*, Ν 589†.

κῠᾰνεος, ον, οι, η, ην, αι, ῃσιν, (κύανος), *of steel*, only Σ 564; elsewh. always *steel-blue* or *dark-colored*, Ω 94.

κῠᾰνό-πεζαν, *with dark feet*, Λ 629†.

κῠᾰνο-πρωρείους (πρῷρα), νέας, γ 299; elsewh. **πρῳροιο;** always at end of verse, always with νεός, *dark-bowed, dark-prowed*, Ο 693, ι 482.

κῠᾰνοιο, gen., (blue) *steel*, Λ 24, 35, and η 87.

κῠᾰνο-χαῖτο = -χαίτης, dat. ῃ, (χαίτη), *dark-haired;* also subst., *the dark-haired one*, Ν 563; *dark-maned*, Υ 224.

κῠᾰν-ώπιδος (ὤψ), *dark-eyed*, μ 60†.

κῠβερνῆσαι, aor. inf., (κυβερνάω, guberno), *steer*, γ 283†.

κῠβερνήτης, εω, ην, voc. κυβερνῆτα, μ 217; αι = -ητῆρες, θ 557; gubernator, *pilot, helmsman*, Τ 43, Ψ 316. (Od.)

κῠβιστᾷ, 3 sing., ipf. 3 pl. κύβίστων, (κύβη), se praecipitat, *turn a somersault, tumble;* Φ 354, *were leaping about*.

κῠβιστητῆρε, ες, (κυβιστᾶν), *divers*, Π 750; elsewh. *tumblers*.

κῠδαίνων, ipf. κύδαινε, ον, aor. κύδηνε, inf. ῆναι, (κῦδος), *glorify, honor*, Ο 612; *ennoble*, π 212; θυμόν, *rejoice* the heart.

κῠδαλίμοιο, ον, ω, οισι, (κῦδος), *noble* in exterior, *glorious*, epithet of heroes; κῆρ, periphrastically, noble heart.

κῠδάνει, ipf. ἐκύδανον, (κῦδος), *exalt*, Ξ 73; superiores erant, Υ 42.

κῠδῐ-άνειρη, ᾶν, (κυδιᾶν), *man-ennobling, bringing renown*, ἀγορῇ, μάχῃ, Α 490, Ζ 124.

κῠδῐόων, τες, (κυδιάω, κῦδος), *triumphing, proud*, Φ 519. (Il.)

κύδιστε, ην, (κῦδος), *most glorious, exalted*, Α 122.

κῠδοίμεον, 3 pl. ipf., fut. ήσων, (κυδοιμός), saeviebant, grassabantur, *spread confusion*, Λ 324; Ο 136, ἡμᾶς, to *vent his rage against* us.

κῠδοιμός, οῦ, όν, *din* or *mêlée of battle; uproar*, also personified, Σ 535, Ε 593.

κῦδος, εϊ, ntr., *might, majesty, glory*, γ 57, 79, Ἀχαιῶν, pride of the Achaioi.

κῠδρή, ήν, (κῦδος), *glorious, illustrious*, λ 580.

Κύδωνες, tribe in northwest of Kreta, γ 292, τ 176.

κυέουσαν, part., ipf. ἐκύει, with acc., *bear in the womb*, Τ 117; Ψ 266, be with mule foal.

κῠθε, aor. from κεύθει, occuluit, *has hid*.

Κῠθέρεια, epithet of Aphrodite, θ 288; from island **Κύθηρα,** τά, southwest of promontory Malcia, where the worship of the goddess had been introduced by an early Phoinikian colony, ι 81, Ο 432; **Κυθηρόθεν,** *from Kythera;* adj. **Κυθηρίῳ,** ον, Κ 268, Ο 431.

κῠκόωντι, dat. part., ipf. ἐκύκα, aor. κύκησε, pass. prs. part. κυκώμενος, ον, η, aor. du. κυκηθήτην, ήθησαν, immiscere, *stir up and mix with*, pass., confundi, perturbari, *be struck with fear*, or *panic*, Υ 489; *be in commotion, foam up*, of the sea.

κῠκεῶ, = ειῶ, τόν, (from κυκεών, κυκᾶν), *mixed drink*, compounded of barley meal, grated goats' cheese, and (Pramnian) wine, Λ 624; Kirke adds also honey, κ 290, 234.

κυκλήσομεν, fut., (κυκλέω, κύκλος), *wheel away, carry forth*, of corpses, Η 332†.

κύκλου, ῳ, ον, οι, and α, *circle, ring;* δόλιον, circle with which hunters enclose game; ἱερῷ, sancto, solemn circle, as tribunal; κύκλῳ, round about; the rings on the outside of shield, or the layers which, lying one above another and gradually diminishing in size toward the ὀμφαλός, made up the shield, Λ 33, Υ 280; wheel, Ψ 340, pl. τὰ κύκλα.

κυκλόσε, in a circle, Δ 212 and Ρ 392.

κυκλο-τερές (τείρω), circular, ρ 209; Δ 124, stretch, draw into a circle.

Κύκλ-ωπες, wild race of giants, α 71, ζ 5. ι 166 sqq., related to Gigantes and Phaiakians, without towns, fear of gods, or social ties, ι 166; chief representative, ὁ **Κύκλωψ**, Polyphemos, the lawless monster, ι 428; one-eyed cannibal, κ 200; overreached by Odysseus, ι 366, 408.

κύκνων, τῶν, cygnorum, swans, Β 460 and Ο 692.

κυλίνδει, pass. ων, ον, pass. prs. εται, εσθαι, όμενος, η, ην, α, ipf. (ἐ)κυλίνδετο, volvere aliquid, roll, πῆμά τινι, moliri, metaph., roll calamity against; pass., volvi, be rolled, also throw one's self prostrate, wallow, in agony, Θ 86; in grief, κατὰ κόπρον, in the dirt (of the street, etc.); νῶιν πῆμα, evil is rolling upon us.

Κυλλήνη, mountain chain in northern Arkadia, Β 603; birthplace of Hermes, who is hence called, ω 1, **Κυλλήνιος**; yet the word in Ο 518 designates an inhabitant of the town Κυλλήνη, in Elis.

κυλλο-ποδίων, voc. -πόδῖον, (κυλλός, πούς), crook-footed, epithet of Hephaistos, Φ 331. (Il.)

κῦμα, τος, τι, τα, σι, ntr., (κύω), unda, also fluctus, wave, billow, Β 209, Κ 574; Β 396, ν 99, ventis agitata, keep off the waves raised by the wind; κατὰ κ., with the current.

κυμαίνοντα, part., (κῦμα), πόντον, fluctuantem, billowy, Ξ 229. (Od.)

κύμβᾰχος, ον, (κύβη), adj., on the head, Ε 586; subst., crown or top of helmet, in which the plume is fixed, Ο 536. (See cut No. 20, b.)

κύμινδιν, τήν, Ξ 291; ancient name of bird usually called χαλκίς, night-hawk.

Κῦμο-δόκη and **Κῦμο-θόη**, Nereids, Σ 39, 41†.

κυνᾰ-μυια, dog-fly, abusive epithet applied by Ares to Athena, Φ 394.

κυνέη, ης, ῃ, ην, (κύων), soldier's cap, of leather or weasel's skin, also of metal stiffened or adorned with metal, χαλκήρης (see cut, p. 58), also fitted with metal plates to protect the cheeks, χαλκοπάρῃος; with horse-hair plume, ἵππουρις, ἱπποδάσεια, cf. cuts Nos. 11, 85. Sometimes entirely of bronze = helmet. κυνέη αἰγείη is a goat-skin cap, like that of the oarsmen in cut No. 41. Ἄϊδος, cap of Hades, rendering invisible, Ε 845.

κύνεος (κύων), impudens, shameless, Ι 373†.

κῠνέω, ipf. **κύνει**, εον, aor. κύσα, (ἔ)κῦσε, (ἔ)κύσσε(ν), opt. κύσειε, inf. σσαι, osculari, kiss, υἱόν, πάντα, masc., π 21; γούνατα, χεῖρας, κεφαλήν τε καὶ ὤμους, μιν κεφαλήν τε καὶ ἄμφω φάεα καλά χεῖράς τ' ἀμφοτέρας, π 15, cf. ρ 39; κεφαλὰς καὶ χεῖρας, φ 225; ἄρουραν, one's native soil.

κυν-ηγέται (ἄγω), venatores, hunters, ι 120†.

κυνο-ραιστέων (synizesis), gen. pl. from -στής, (ῥαίω), fleas, ρ 300†.

Κῦνος, harbor-town of Lokris, Β 531†.

κύντερον, τατον, (κύων), impudentius, -issimum, shameless, horrible; Κ 503, what daring exploit he should perform.

κυν-ῶπα, voc. masc. from Α 159; **-ῶπις**, ιδος, fem., impudent; impudens, shameless, Γ 180.

Κῠπᾰρισσήεις, town in Elis, Β 593†.

κυπαρισσίνῳ (κυπάρισσος), of cypress wood, ρ 340†.

κυπᾰρισσος, ἡ, cypress, evergreen, ε 64†.

κύπειρον, τό, fragrant marsh-grass, food for horses, perh. galingal, δ 603.

κύπελλον, α, οις, (cupa, Eng. cup), goblet, usually of gold, general word for drinking-cup. Ω 305, cf. 285, Ι 670.

Κύπρις, ιν, and ιδα, Aphrodite, Ε 330; as goddess of island **Κύπρος**, whither her worship was brought by Phoinikians, δ 83; Κύπρονδε, Λ 21.

κύπτω, aor. opt. **κύψει'**, part. ψας, αντι, bow down, λ 585. (Il.)

κύρμα, τό, (κυρέω), what one lights upon, booty, prey, Ρ 272; usually with ἕλωρ, Ε 488.

κύρσας, aor. from *κύρω*.

κυρτόν, *ώ*, *ά*, (curvus), *rounded, arched, round*, B 218. (Il.)

κυρτωθέν, part. aor. pass. from *κυρτόω*, curvatum, *arched*, λ 244†.

κύρω, ipf. **κῦρε,** *collide with*, *ἅρματι*; aor. part. *κύρσας ἐπὶ σώματι*, *having lighted upon* a lifeless body; *αἰὲν ἐπ' αὐχένι κῦρε*, *was constantly aiming at* the neck, Ψ 821; mid., Ω 530, *κύρεται κακῷ*, *encounters, falls in with.*

κύστιν, *τήν*, *bladder*, E 67. (Il.)

Κύτωρος, town in Paphlagonia, B 853.

κυφός (*κύπτω*), *bowed, bent*, β 16†.

Κῦφος, town in Perrhæbia in Thessaly, B 748†.

κύω, see *κυέω* and *κυνέω*.

κύων, *κυνός*, *κύνα*, *κύον*, *κύνες*, *ῶν*, *σί(ν)* and *κύνεσσι(ν)*, *νας*, masc., six times fem., canis, *dog, bitch; θηρευταί, τραπεζῆες*; *'Αΐδαο* = Kerberos, Θ 368, λ 623; *sea-dog*, perhaps *seal*, μ 96; dog of Orion, X 29 = Seirios; as symbol of shamelessness, applied to women = feminae impudicae, then with general sense, impudens, impudent; dastardly dogs, N 623; with *λυσσητήρ*, rabida, raging hound, Θ 299.

κῶας, *εα*, *εσιν*. *fleece*, serving for seat or bedding, π 47, I 661, γ 38.

κώδειαν, *poppy-head*, Ξ 499†.

κωκυτός, *ὁ*, (*κωκύω*), (1) *howling, wailing*, X 409 and 447.—(2) as proper name, a river of the lower world, flowing out of the Styx, κ 514.

κωκύω, 3 sg. prs. **κωκύει,** ipf. *ἐκώκυε*, *ον*, aor. *ἐκώκυσεν*, *κώκυσ'*, part. *κωκύσασα*, *-άντων*, (1) *shriek, wail*, always of women, ε 37, β 361.—(2) trans., *lament*, *τινά*, ω 295.

κώληπα, *τήν*, (*κῶλον*?), poplitem, *bend* or *hollow of the knee*, Ψ 726†.

κῶμα, *τό*, (*κοιμάω*), sopor, *deep sleep*, σ 201.

Κῶπαι, town on lake Kopaïs in Boiotia, B 502†.

κώπη, *ῃ*, *ην*, *ῃσι(ν)*, *ῃς*, *ας*, (capio, Eng. haft), *sword-hilt*, A 219; *butt* or *handle of oar* (same word used to-day in Greece for oar), ι 489; incumbere remis, lay one's self to the oar, μ 214; *handle of key*, φ 7. (See cut No. 72.)

κωπήεντι, *τα*, (*κώπη*), *hilted*, Π 332, O 713.

κωρύκῳ, *τῷ*, perae, *leather sack* or *wallet*, ε 267. (Od.) [ῡ]

Κῶς, acc. *Κόωνδε*, *to Kos*. O 28, island in Ikarian sea, opposite the coast of Karia.

κωφῷ, *όν*, *ήν*, (*κόπτω*), (1) *blunted*, Λ 390.—(2) *noiseless, silent* (before it breaks), Ξ 16.—(3) *γαῖαν*, *dull, senseless, lifeless*, Ω 54.

Λ.

λᾶας, *ᾶος*, *ᾶι*, *ᾶαν*, du. *ᾶε*, pl. *άων*, *άεσσι*, saxum, *stone*, Γ 12, M 445, λ 594, ν 163, ξ 10; *hewn stone*, κ 211.

Λάας, *αν*, town in Lakonike, B 585†.

λαβρ-αγόρην, *τόν*, (*λάβρος*), *reckless talker*, Ψ 479†.

λαβρεύεαι, 2 sing. prs., (*λάβρος*), *talkest rashly*, Ψ 474 and 478.

λάβρος, *ον*, and sup. *-ότατον*, rapidus, *swift*, ο 293.

λαγχάνω, ipf. **ἐλάγχανον,** **λάγχανον,** aor. *ἔλαχον*, *λάχ(εν)*, *ομεν*, *ον*, subj. *λάχῃσιν*, *ῃ*, inf. *εῖν*, part. *ών*, *όντα*, sortiri, *obtain by lot*, *τί*, I 367, O 190; *ληΐδος αἶσαν*, praedae portionem, share of spoil; *Κὴρ λάχε γεινόμενον*, *had me allotted to her* at birth, i. e. *obtained power over me* from my birth; pf. *λελόγχᾱσι*, adepti sunt, *have obtained*, *τιμὴν δώρων*, *κτερέων*; red. aor. subj. *λελάχητε*, *ωσι*, *θανόντα πυρός*, mortuo ignem impertire, put in possession of fire = solemnly burn, H 80; *choose by lot*; ι 160. *fall by lot.*

λαγωόν, *ούς*, masc., lepŏrem, es, *hare*, K 361, ρ 295.

Λαέρκης, (1) son of Aimon, father

of Alkimedon, Myrmidon, Π 197.—(2) χρυσοχόος in Pylos, γ 425.

Λαέρτης, son of Akreisios, father of Odysseus, king in Ithaka, α 430, ω 206, 270, δ 111, χ 185, δ 555.

Λαερτιάδης, *son of Laertes*, Odysseus, Β 173, ε 203, ι 19, Γ 200.

λαζοίατο, 3 pl. opt. prs., ipf. λάζετο (ἐλάζετο, Ε 840), *take* into the hands (χερσί), μάστιγα; ἀγκάς, amplecti, embrace; γαῖαν ὀδάξ, bite the dust, fall in combat; μῦθον πάλιν, caught back again the words (of joy which were on his lips), ν 254.

λαθι-κηδέα, acc. masc., (λαθεῖν κῆδος), *banishing care*, Χ 83†.

λάθρῃ (λαθεῖν), clam, *secretly, unbeknown;* also with gen., τινός, aliquo; sensim, *imperceptibly*, Τ 165.

λάϊγγες, ας, (λᾶας), *pebbles*, ε 433 and ζ 95. [ᾱ]

λαῖλαψ, **λαίλαπι,** α, fem., *thunder-shower, hurricane;* also fig. with ἶσος, Μ 375, Υ 51.

λαιμόν, τόν, guttur, *throat, gullet*, Ν 388, Σ 34, χ 15. (Il.)

λάϊνεος and **λάινος,** ον, οι, (λᾶας), saxeus, *of stone, stony;* Μ 177, τεῖχος, yet the passage is of doubtful authenticity.

λαισήϊα, τά, (λάσιος ?), πτερόεντα, fluttering *shield* or *target*, Ε 453 and Μ 426, so called on account of the *fluttering apron* of untanned leather, λάσιος, hanging from the shield. (See adjoining cut, and esp. No. 85.)

Λαιστρυγών, όνος, όνες, fabled tribe of savage giants, κ 106, 119, 199. Hence adj., **Λαιστρυγονίη,** κ 82, ψ 318.

λαῖτμα, τό, (λαιμός ?), *depth* or *gulf* of the sea, used alone or with θαλάσσης, ἁλός, Τ 267. (Od.)

λαῖφος, ε(α), ntr., *shabby, tattered garment*, ν 399 and υ 206.

λαιψηρόν, οῖς, ά, (λαῖλαψ), rapidus, *nimble, swift*, λαιψηρὰ ἐνώμα, plied nimbly, Ο 269.

λάκε, aor. from λάσκω.

Λακεδαίμων, ονος, fem., district whose capital was Sparta, δῖαν, γ 326; ἐρατεινῆς, Γ 239; εὐρύχορον, ν 414; κοίλην κητώεσσαν, δ 1.

λακτίζων, part., (λάξ), *kicking with the heel, struggling convulsively*, of the mortally wounded, σ 99 and χ 88.

λαμβάνω, only 2 aor. **ἔλαβε,** also other augmented forms ἔλλαβ(ε), etc., (1) prehendere, *take hold of*, τι (ἐν) χείρεσσι; τινὰ ποδός, *grasp* by the foot, etc.; ἀγκάς, amplecti, *embrace;* τινός, also mid. ἐλλάβετ(ο), comprehendit, *seize*, and λελαβέσθαι, scil. αὐτοῦ, δ 388.—(2) of mental states, subjects such as χόλος, incessit, *take possession of, seize*, τινά (also with acc. of part., γυῖα).—(3) accipere, *receive.* —(4) capere, *take captive, carry off as booty;* η 255, domi recipiens.

Λάμος, king of Laistrygones, κ 81†.

λαμπετόωντι, part. pr., (-άω, λάμπω), *blazing*, Α 104.

Λαμπετίδης, *son of Lampos*, Dolops, Ο 526†.

Λαμπετίη, a nymph, daughter of Ἠέλιος, μ 132, 375.

Λάμπος, (1) son of Laomedon, father of Trojan Dolops, Γ 147, Ο 526. —(2) horse of Eos, ψ 246; of Hektor, Θ 185.

λαμπρός, όν, οῖσι, ῆσιν, sup. ότατος, *bright, shining*, τ 234. (Il.) λαμπρὸν παμφαίνῃσι, splendide luceat, Ε 6.

λαμπτήρων, gen. pl., ῆρσι, ῆρας, λάμπω), *fire pans* or *basins*, σ 307, τ 63; for holding blazing pine splinters, used to illuminate rooms. (See cuts on next page, after bronze originals from Pompeii.)

λάμπω, only prs. and ipf. (ἔ)**λάμπ(ε)** and λάμφ', act. and mid., splendere, *shine, gleam, be radiant;* subject a person, (χαλκῷ, πυρί, τεύχεσι), or thing,

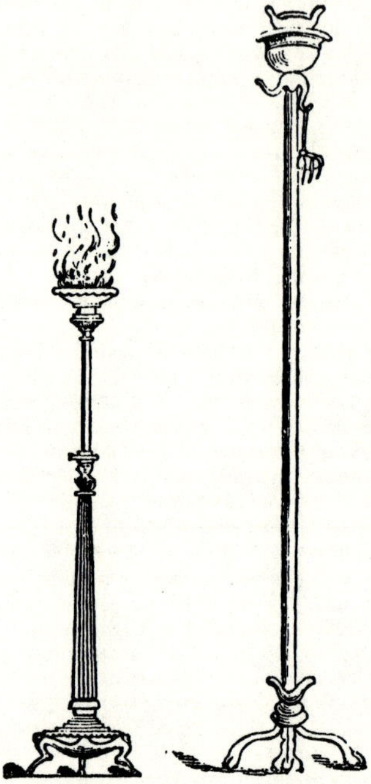

e. g. metal, torches, weapons, ὀφθαλμώ, ὄσσε, also πεδ. χαλκῷ, Υ 156.

λανθάνω, ipf. (ἐ)**λάνθανε,** ον, parallel form **λήθω,** chief forms: ipf. ἔληθον. λῆθ(ε), etc., iter. λήθεσκε, fut. λήσεις, aor. (ἔ)λαθ(ε), λάθον, 3 du. λαθέτην, mid. ipf. λανθᾰνόμην, prs. λήθεαι, ipf. λήθετο, aor. λάθετ(ο), opt. 3 pl. λαθοίατο, and aor. red. λελάθοντο, λελαθέσθω, pf. λέλασται, σμεθα, σμένος, ον, (1) latere, *escape notice of*, τινά, Α 561, Ν 272; with part., Ν 560, 721, π 156, θ 93, Ρ 89; also with ὅτι (ὅτε, Ρ 626), and ὅπως; λαθών (τινα), clam, *unperceived by*, Ι 477, Λ 251, ρ 305.—(2) λελάθῃ τινά τινος, Ο 60, *make forget*.—(3) mid. τινός, oblivisci, *forget*, Δ 127, γ 224.

λάξ, (calx), *with the heel*, joined with ποδί, Κ 158 and ο 45.

Λαό-γονος, (1) son of Trojan Onetor, slain by Meriones, Π 604.—(2) son of Trojan Bias, slain by Achilleus, Υ 460.

Λᾱο-δάμας, ντος, ντα, voc. δάμα, (1) son of Antenor, a Trojan, slain by Aias, Ο 516.—(2) son of Alkinoos, boxer, θ 119, 132, η 170, θ 117, 141.

Λᾱο-δάμεια, daughter of Bellerophontes, mother of Sarpedon, Ζ 198.

Λᾱο-δίκη, (1) daughter of Agamemnon, Ι 145, 287.—(2) daughter of Priamos, wife of Helikaon, Γ 124, Ζ 252.

Λᾱό-δοκος, (1) Antenor's son, Δ 87.—(2) comrade of Antilochos, Ρ 699.

Λᾱο-θόη, daughter of Altes, mother of Lykaon, Φ 85, Χ 48.

Λᾱο-μεδοντιάδης, (1) Priamos, Γ 250.—(2) Lampos, Ο 527.

Λᾱο-μέδων, son of Ilos, father of Priamos, Υ 237, Ζ 23, Ε 269, 640; his faithlessness, Φ 443; his daughter was wooed by Herakles, to whom she was promised by Laomedon on condition that Herakles freed her from the sea-monster which Poseidon had sent to ravage Troas. Herakles performed his part of the agreement, and when Laomedon refused Hesione, Herakles slew him, Ε 638 sqq.

λᾱός, etc. (no du.), masc., (κλαϝός? cluentes?), *people*, multitudo, Δ 199, Ε 573; usually pl., *soldiers, vassals*, γ 214, exercitus, *army*, opp. fleet or troops fighting from chariots.

λᾱο-σσόος, ον, (σεύω), *driving the people on* (to combat), *rousing the people*, epithet of Ares, Eris, Athene (Apollon, Amphiaraos), Ν 128, χ 210.

λᾱο-φόρον ὁδόν, *public way*, Ο 682†.

λᾰπάρης, gen., ην, fem., *the soft part of the body* between the hips and the ribs, *flank, loins*, Γ 359. (Il.)

Λᾰπίθαι, *Lapithai*, a tribe inhabiting Mount Olympos in Thessaly, Μ 128, 181, φ 297.

λάπτω, only fut. part. **λάψοντες,** *lap up* with the tongue, Π 161†.

Λάρῑσα, ης, town in Asia Minor near Kyme, Β 841, Ρ 301.

λάρνᾰκα, τήν, *chest*, Σ 413; *vase*, Ω 795.

λάρῳ, τῷ, laro, *cormorant*, ε 51†.

λᾱρόν, sup. -ώτατος, *dainty, choice*, Ρ 572, β 350.

λάσῐος, ον, οισι, ην, (δασύς?), villosus, *shaggy, woolly*, ι 433; epithet of στῆθος, also of κῆρ, as sign of strength and courage, Α 189.

λάσκω, only aor. **λάκε,** *crushed,*

cracked, bones, brass ; pf. λεληκώς, λελᾰκυῖα, *bellowing*, μ 85; *shrieking*, X 141.

λαυκᾰνίης, τῆς, gutturis, X 325, there appeared an unprotected spot *on the throat*. (Il.)

λαύρην, τήν, and (στόμα) λαύρης, *side passage*, pathway between the house of Odysseus and the outer wall (of the court), χ 128, 137. (See plate III., *i, n.*)

λᾰφύσσει, ετον, 3 du. Σ 583, glutire, *gulp down*, Λ 176. (Il.)

λάχε, aor. from λαγχάνω.

λᾰ́χεια, *with good soil for digging, fruitful*, ι 116 and κ 509.

λάχνη, η, *woolly hair, down*, K 134; *sparse hair*, B 219; λ 320, *sparse beard*.

λαχνήεντι, α, ας, (λάχνη), *hairy, shaggy*, I 548. (Il.)

λάχνῳ, τῷ, lana, *wool*, ι 445†.

λάω, pres. part. **λάων**, aor. λᾶε, *burying his teeth in*, τ 229.

λέβης, nom. sing., gen. pl. -ήτων, *caldron* for warming water, or for boiling food over fire, Φ 362; *wash-basin*, held under the hands or feet while water was poured from a pitcher over them (see cut), τ 386; ἀνθεμόεντα, adorned on the exterior with designs in imitation of palm leaves or flowers.

λέγωμεν, λέγε, ειν, ων, οντες, ipf. (ἔ)λέγ(ε), λέγομεν, aor. ἔλεξεν, mid. prs. λεγόμεθα, εσθε, εσθαι, ipf. λέγοντο, aor. λέξατο, αιτο, ασθαι, 2 aor. ἐλέγμην, λέκτο, pass. 1 aor. ἐλέχθην, legere, colligere, *pick up, gather*, ὀστέα, αἱμασιάς; numerare in, *count among*, ἐν, μετὰ τοῖσι; enumerare, *reckon up, narrate* (only Od. and B 222), τί, ξ 197, τ 203; τί τινι, ε 5, λ 374; mid., sibi colligere, sibi eligere, se adnumerare, *collect for one's self, select for one's self, add one's self to*; narrare, *relate*, N 292, γ 240; B 435, μηκέτι δὴ νῦν ταῦτα λεγώμεθα, let us now speak no longer of these things (but act); N 275, what need to relate these things? (See also ΛΕΧ.)

λειαίνω, fut. **λειανέω**, aor. 3 pl. λείηναν, part. ας, (λεῖος, lēvis), *smooth*, Δ 111; *level off*, θ 260.

λείβειν, ων, ipf. λεῖβε, ον, aor. λεῖψαι, part. ψαντε, (libare), effundere, *shed*, δάκρυα; libare, *pour a libation*, Ω 285; οἶνον, also with τινί, *perform a drink-offering*. (See adjoining cut; cf. also Nos. 24 and 102.)

λειμών, ῶνος, ι, α, ες, ας, (λείβω), *meadow*, ζ 292; λειμωνόθεν, *from the meadow*, Ω 451.

λεῖος, ῳ, η, ην, α, (lēvis), *smooth, even, level*; πετράων, ε 443, free from rocks; λεῖα δ' ἐποίησεν, made even.

λείπω, prs. ipf., also λεῖπ(ε), fut. λείψω, aor. ἔλιπον, also λίπον, ες, ε, έτην, ομεν, λίπ' = ἔλιπ', and λιπέ, imp., pf. λέλοιπεν; mid. prs., ipf. λείπετ(ο), aor. λιπόμην, relictus sum; pass. pf. λέλειπται, inf. -εῖφθαι, part. -μμένος, ον, οι, plupf. λελείμμην, -ειπτο, 2 fut. λελείψεται, aor. 3 pl. λίπεν, linquo, re-

linquere, *leave, forsake;* ξ 213, me deficiunt, *are wanting; fail,* ἰοὶ ἄνακτα.—Pass. and aor. mid., relinqui, remanere, *be left, remain;* ὄπισθεν, vivum, M 14, *survive;* τινός, *to be left behind one* (with acc. of distance? δουρὸς ἐρωήν); Π 507, postquam currus orbati sunt dominorum, after the chariots *had been forsaken* (λίπεν [v. l. λίπον]) by their masters.

λειριόεντα, όεσσαν, (λείριον), *lily-white; ὄπα, tender, delicate,* Γ 152. (Il.)

Λειώδης, son of Oinops, θυοσκόος of the suitors; he shares their fate, φ 144, χ 310.

Λειώκριτος, (1) son of Arisbas, slain by Aineias, Ρ 344.—(2) son of Euenor, suitor, β 242; slain by Telemachos, χ 294.

λείουσι, see λέων. **λέκτο,** see λέγω, and ΛΕΧ.

Λεκτόν, promontory on the Trojan coast, opposite Lesbos, Ξ 284.

λέκτρον, οιο, ῳ, οισι, (λέχω), lectus, *bed;* freq. pl., παλαιοῦ θεσμόν, to the site of the ancient bed; **λέκτρονδε** (with δεῦρο, hither), *to bed!* θ 292.

λελαβέσθαι, -βησι, see λαμβάνω.

λελάθῃ, οντο, see λανθάνω.

λελακυῖα, see λάσκω. **λελασμένος,** ον, see λανθάνω.

λελάχητε, ωσι, see λαγχάνω.

Λέλεγες, piratical tribe on south and west coast of Asia Minor, Κ 429, Φ 86.

λεληκώς, *shrieking,* see λάσκω.

λελιημένος, οι, pf., (λίην, λῆν), rapidus, *hastily,* with ὄφρα, Δ 465, Ε 690. (Il.)

λέλογχε, ασι, see λαγχάνω. **λέξεο,** λέξο, see ΛΕΧ.

Λεοντεύς, son of Koronos, one of the Lapithai, suitor of Helena, Β 745, Ψ 841.

λέπαδνα, τά, *breast collar,* strap passing around the breast of the horses and made fast to the yoke, Ε 730. (See above cut, *g;* also cut No. 49, *f.*)

λεπτάλέῃ (λεπτός), tenera, *delicate,* Σ 571†.

λεπτῷ, όν, οί, ῄ, ῇ, άς, ά, (λέπω), sup. -ότατος, η, *peeled, husked,* Υ 497; tenuis, tener; exiguus, *thin, fine, delicate, narrow.*

λέπω, aor. **ἔλεψεν;** ἕ = φύλλα, *has stripped off* from it the leaves, Α 236†.

Λέσβος, island on the coast of Asia Minor, opposite the gulf of Adramyttium, γ 169, Ω 544. Λεσβόθεν, *from L.,* Ι 664. **Λεσβίδας** γυναῖκας, Ι 129, 271.

λέσχην, τήν, (λέγω, *collect*), *place of meeting, country tavern,* σ 329†.

λευγάλέοιο, ῳ, οι, οισ(ι), η, ῃσι, (λοιγός, λυγρός, lugubris), miser, inhonestus, funestus, *wretched, shameful, ruinous,* πόλεμος, ἔπεα; Ι 119, ruinous obstinacy; adv., **λευγαλέως,** foede, *disgracefully,* Ν 723.

λεύκαινον, 3 pl. ipf., (λευκός), *made white with foam,* μ 172†.

Λευκάς, άδος, *Leukas,* lit. "White-rock" (cf. Ger. Weissenfels), at entrance of lower world, on border of Okeanos, ω 11†.

λευκ-άσπιδα, acc., and -ασπις, *with white shield, white-shielded,* Χ 294†.

Λευκοθέη = Ἰνώ, daughter of Kadmos; saves Odysseus from drowning by throwing him her veil, ε 334, 461.

λευκοῖο, ῷ, όν, οί, ούς, ῄ, ήν, έν, ά, comp. -ότερος, οτέρην, (lux, λεύσσω, γλαυκός), *bright, shining, gleaming,* lucens, splendens, nitens; candidus, *white,* Κ 437.

Λεῦκος, companion of Odysseus, Δ 491†.

λευκ-ώλενος, ῳ, ον, οι, (ὠλένη), *with white elbows, white armed,* epithet of

Hera, and of women in general, Α 55, 572.

λευρῷ (λεῖος), plano, *level*, η 123†.

λεύσσω, prs., ipf., λεῦσσ(ε), (λευκός), cernere, *see clearly; ἐπὶ τόσσον*, so far; *τινά*, conspicere, *behold*, Υ 346, θ 200.

λεχε-ποίην (λέχος, ποίη), *making his bed in the grass*, of river Asōpos, Δ 383; of towns, *meadowy, grassy*, Β 697.

λέχος, ει, ε(α), έων, έεσσ(ιν) έεσι, (λέχω), *bedstead*, ψ 189; *bed-clothing*, *στορέσαι*, make the bed, Ι 621, Ω 648, pl.; *πυκινόν*, firmly built, η 340, ψ 179; the entire bed, including couch and bedding, Α 609, Γ 447; *πορσύνειν*, prepare and share, γ 403, Γ 411; *τρητά*, smoothly polished; *δινωτά*, smoothly turned (posts and bars); pl., the whole bed, composed of all its parts, ε 1, δ 730, Ω 743; *bier, funeral couch*, ω 44, Ψ 165, Ω 720.

ΛΕΧ, (1) act.: aor. **ἔλεξα**, imp. λέξον, *put to rest*, Ω 635; fig., Ξ 252.—(2) mid.: fut. and 1 aor. and syncop. 2 aor. imp. λέξο, λέξεο, *lay one's self to rest*, θ 519, Ι 67, Ξ 350, δ 413, ρ 102; *lie at ease*, Β 435.

λέων, οντος, etc., (exc. οιν), dat. pl. λείουσι (λέουσι, Χ 262), leo, *lion*, bold in the midst of pursuit, Γ 23; attacks flocks or herds, Ε 140; λέοντα γυναιξίν (instead of λέαιναν), *destruction* to women, as goddess of sudden death.

λήγεις, imp. λῆγ', inf. -έμεναι, ipf. ἔληγε, λῆγ(ε), fut. λήξω, ειν, aor. 3 pl. λῆξαν, opt. αιμι, ειεν, *leave off, cease*, *τινός*, Ζ 107; or with part., Φ 224; *ἐν σοί* (with thee), Ι 97; *abate*, *μένος*, martial fury; *χεῖρας φόνοιο*, *stay* my hands *from* slaughter, χ 63.

Λήδη, wife of Tyndareos, mother of Kastor and Polydeukes, and of Klytaimnestra, λ 298, 300.

ληθάνει, ἐκ . . . *πάντων*, *does not allow me to think on* all, η 221†.

λήθη (λήθω), oblivio, *forgetfulness*, Β 33†.

Λῆθος, son of Teutamos, father of Hippothoos, Β 843, Ρ 288.

λήθω, see λανθάνω.

ληϊάδας (ληΐς) *γυναῖκας*, captivas feminas, *female captives*, Υ 193†.

ληϊ-βοτείρης (λήϊον, βόσκω) *συός*, *crop-destroying*, sow, σ 29†.

λ*ηΐζομαι*, fut. **ληΐσσομαι**, aor. λ*ηΐσσατο*, *carry off as booty*, *τινά*, α 398, Σ 28; *πολλά*, ψ 357.

λήϊον, ίου, *crop* (uncut), segetes, Β 147.

ληΐδος, τῆς, acc. ἴδα, (λάϝω), praeda, *prey, booty*, consisting of men, beasts, or treasure, Λ 677, κ 41. [ῐ]

ληϊστῆρες (ο 426, **ληΐστορες**), -σσι, (ληΐζομαι), praedatores, *pirates*, γ 73. (Od.)

ληϊστοί, ή, (ληΐζομαι), *may be plundered* (i. e. taken by plunder), Ι 406, 408.

ληϊτίδι, τῇ, (ληΐς), *the dispenser of booty* (Athena), Κ 460†.

Λήϊτος, son of Alektryon, chief of the Boiotians, Β 494, Ν 91, Ρ 601, Ζ 35.

ληκύθῳ, τῇ, *oil-flask, oil-bottle*, ζ 79 and 215.

Λῆμνος, *Lemnos*, an island west of Troas, with (probably in the time of Homer) a city of the same name, Ξ 230, 281; *ἠγαθέη*, sacred to Hephaistos (also to the Kabeiroi), on account of its volcano, Moschylos; now called Stalimene [(ἐ)ς τὴ(ν) Λῆμνον].

λήσω, σομαι, see λανθάνω.

Λητώ, οῦς, οῖ, voc. οἷ, *Leto, Latona*, mother of Apollon and of Artemis by Zeus, λ 580, Α 9, *ἐρικυδέος*, *ἠΰκομος*, *καλλιπαρῄῳ*.

λιαζόμενον, ipf. λιά ετο, aor. λιάσθης, η, εν, είς, effuger , *retire, withdraw* (from), *κῦμα*, *ὕπα ὶα*, *τινός*, or with prep.; *sink down*, Υ 418; *προτὶ γαίῃ*, *πρηνής*; *droop*, *πτερά*.

λιαρῷ, όν, tepidus, *warm, lukewarm*, Λ 477; *sweet, gentle*, Ξ 164.

Λιβύη, *Libya*, west of Aigyptos, δ 85, ξ 295.

λίγα, adv., (λιγύς), *shrilly, piercingly*, θ 527, κ 254.

λιγαίνω, ipf. 3 pl. **ἐλίγαινον**, (λιγύς), *cry with loud voice*, Λ 685†.

λίγδην (λακίς, lacero), *scraping, grazing*; *βάλλειν*, χ 278†.

λιγέως, adv. from λιγύς.

λίγξε, aor., (λίγγω? λίζω), *twanged*, Δ 125†.

λιγυ-πνείοντας (λιγύς), *whistling* (gusts), δ 567†.

λιγυρῇ, ήν, ῇσι, (λιγύς), *shrill-voiced*, Ξ 290; *ἀοιδή*, *loud-sounding, shrill* (the word orig. began with two consonants).

λιγύς, *ύν, ύ, έων; εῖα, είῃ, εῖαν,* adv. **λῐγέως** (orig. beginning with two consonants), *penetrating, clear, piercing, shrill, whistling, loud, φόρμιγγι, ἀγορητής.*

λῐγυ-φθόγγοισιν (φθόγγος), *loud-, clear-voiced,* B 50, β 6.

λῐγῠ-φώνῳ (φωνή), *harsh-screaming,* T 350†.

λίζω, see λίγξε.

λίην, (λῆν, desire), *gladly, fully, exceedingly;* with negative, *very much, altogether; καὶ λ.,* and *certainly,* and *by all means,* A 553. [ῑ, but ten times ῐ.]

λῐθάκι, dat. sing., (λίθος), *stony, hard,* ε 415†.

λῐθάδεσσι, *ταῖς,* (λίθος), *stone,* ξ 36. (Od.)

λιθέῳ, **εοι,** (λίθος), saxeus, *of stone,* ν 107.

λῐθος, *οιο, ον, ῳ, ον, οι, οισ(ι), ους,* masc. and fem. (twice), *rock,* γ 296; ν 156, *stone,* in field, or for building; *stone seats,* θ 6; symbol of firmness and harshness; λίθον ἔθηκεν=ποίησε.

λικμώντων, gen. pl. of part., (λικμάω, λικμός), *winnow,* E 500†.

λικμητῆρος, *τοῦ,* (λικμάω), *winnower,* who threw the grain with winnowing shovel against the wind, thus separating it from the chaff, N 590†.

λικριφίς, adv., (λέχριος, obliquus), *sideways, to one side,* Ξ 463.

Λῐκύμνιος, brother of Alkmene, slain by Tlepolemos, B 663†.

Λῐλαια, town in Phokis, at the source of the Kephisos, B 523†.

λιλαίομαι, prs., ipf. λιλαίετο, (λιλάσjομαι), cupere, gestire, desiderare, *desire,* with inf., or with gen. *τινός,* e. g. ὁδοῖο, ν 31; also of inanimate objects, missiles, χροὸς ἆσαι, etc., φόωσδε (sc. ἐλθεῖν), λ 223.

λῐμήν, *ένος, ένι, ένα, ες, έ(νεσ)σι, ας,* (λίμνη), portus, *harbor,* pl. also in signif. of *inlets, bays,* Ψ 745, ν 96, δ 846.

λίμνη, *ης, ῃ, ην,* (λείβω), lacus, stagnum, palus, *lake, swamp, marsh,* Φ 317; γ 1, *sea.*

Λιμν-ώρεια, lit. "she who guards a harbor," a Nereid, Σ 41†.

λῑμός, *ῷ, όν,* fames, *hunger, famine,* T 166, ε 166.

Λίνδος, town in Rhodos, B 656†.

λῑνο-θώρηξ (λίνον), *wearing a linen cuirass,* B 529. (As represented in adjoining cut; cf. also No. 12.)

λίνον, *οιο, ου, ῳ,* (λῖτα, linum), *flax, yarn, fishing-line, thread,* esp. the *thread of human destiny,* spun to each one at birth by Αἶσα and Κλῶθες, Υ 128, Ω 210, η 198 (see cut under ἠλᾰκάτη); *fisher's net,* E 487; *linen cloth, linen,* fleecy (as bed covering), I 661.

λίνον, *lay of Linos,* lament over the death of the youth Linos (perh. personification of spring), Σ 570†.

λῐπἄ (ἀλείφω, liquor), old oblique case of a subst., or acc. ntr. of adj., as adv.=*shining with fat, unctuously,* γ 466.

λῐπᾰρο-κρήδεμνος (κρήδεμνον), *with shining head-band,* Σ 382†.

λῐπᾰρο-πλοκᾰμοιο (πλόκαμος), *with shining braids,* T 126†.

λῐπᾰρῷ, *όν, οῖσι, ούς, ήν, άς, ά,* (λίπα, Ger. kleben), nitens, nitidus, *anointed, shining* (beautiful, white); *wealthy, comfortable,* λ 136; so also adv. **λιπαρῶς,** δ 210.

λῐπόω (λίπα), nitere, v. l., τ 72†.

I. **λίς,** *ῖν,* (λῖς, λέων), *lion,* Λ 239, 480.

II. **λῑς,** adj., (λισσός), *πέτρη, smooth* rock, μ 64, 79.

III. λίς, **λῖτί,** λῖτα, dat. acc., (λίνον), *linen;* cover of seat, κ 353; of chariot when not in use, Θ 441; of dead, Σ 352; of cinerary urn, Ψ 254.

λίσσομ(αι) from γλίτjομαι, pres.,

ipf. (ἐ)(λ)λίσσετο, etc., iter. λισσέσκετο, 1 aor. ἐλλισάμην, subj. λίσῃ, imp. λίσαι, 2 aor. ἐλιτόμην, opt. οίμην, inf. λιτέσθαι, precari, *beseech*, *pray*, τινὰ εὐχῇσι, εὐχωλῇσι λιτῇσί τε, Ζηνός, by Zeus, πρός, ὑπέρ τινος, for the sake of, by, γούνων (λαβών, ἀψάμενος), etc., β 68, I 451, κ 481; various constructions: with inf., with acc. and inf., with ὅπως, θάνατόν οἱ, sibi necem; ταῦτα ὑμέας, haec vos precor.

λισσὴ (λεῖος) πέτρη, lēve saxum, *smooth* rock, γ 293. (Od.)

λιστρεύοντα, part., *dig about*, ω 227†. (See follg.)

λίστροισι, dat. pl. ntr., *scraper* or *hoe* for cleaning the floor of large hall of house, χ 455†.

λῖτα, see III. λίς.

λῑτάνευε = ἐλλιτάνευε, ipf., fut. -εύσομεν, aor. ἐλλιτάνευσα, (λιταί), implorabat, *beseech*; πολλά, impense, earnestly, X 414; γούνων (ἀψάμενοι), by one's knees (grasping the knees), Ω 357.

λῖταί, ῇσι, (λίσσομαι), preces, *prayers*, with ἐλλισάμην, λ 34; personified, I 502–4, daughters of Zeus, *penitential prayers* following after their sister ἄτη (the blindness, the delusion which has caused the fault), moving limpingly and with eyes fixed on the ground.

λιτί, see III. λίς.

λό' = λόε, see λούω.

λοβοῖσιν, masc., auriculis, *lobes of the ears*, Ξ 182†.

λόγος, οισ(ιν), (λέγω), *story*, *tale*; *words*, *talk*, *language*, O 393.

λόε, εσσαι, etc., see λούω.

λοετρά, ῶν, τά, (λούω), lavacrum, *baths*, Ὠκεανοῖο, in Oceano, ε 275.

λοετρο-χόῳ, ον, (χέω), adj., *pouring* or *containing water for the bath*; τρίποδα, tripod with the water-kettle, Σ 346, θ 435; but υ 297, subst. *bath-maid*.

λοέω, see λούω.

λοιβῆς, ῇ, ήν, (λείβω), *libation*, Δ 49, Ω 70.

λοίγι(α) (λοιγός), perniciosa, *pestilent*, *deadly*, φ 533; *ending fatally* (ἔργα), A 518.

λοιγός, όν, masc., (lugēre), pernicies, interitus, *death*, *ruin*, by sickness or war; νεῶν, iacturam, *destruction*, Π 80.

λοιμός, οῖο, (λείβω?), lues, *pestilence*, A 61 and 97.

λοῖσθος (λοιπός), postremus, *last*, Ψ 536†. Hence **λοισθήϊον,** ultimum praemium, prize *for the hindmost*, Ψ 785 = λοισθήϊ(α), Ψ 751.

Λοκροί, *Lokroi*, a tribe occupying one of the divisions of Hellas, and dwelling on the Euripos, on both sides of Mount Knemis, B 527, 535, N 686.

λοπόν, τόν, (λέπω), τ 233†, *peel* (tunica), of an onion.

λούω, the forms may be classed under two stems, λοϝ- and λοε.—I. λοϝω (lavo), ipf. **λό-(ϝε)**, λοῦον, aor. λοῦσ(εν), αν, subj. λούσῃ, inf. λοέσαι (λοῦσαι), imp. λόεσον, λούσατε, part. λοέσασα, mid. prs. λούεσθαι λοῦσθαι, aor. λούσαντο, σαιτο, ασθε, ασθαι, pass. pf. λελουμένος. — II. ipf. λόεον, aor. λοέσσαι, σσας, mid. fut. λοέσσομαι, aor. λοέσσατο, σσάμενος, η, (parallel form λοϝέσω), lavare, *bathe*, *wash*, mid., *have one's self washed*, in waters of river, Z 508; Ὠκεανοῖο, washed by Okeanos.

λοφιήν, τήν, (λόφος), *comb*, or *bristly ridge* of boar's back, τ 446†.

λόφος, ον, ων, masc., (globus), (1) *crest* or *plume of helmet*, usually of horse-hair, E 743. (See adjoining cuts, and Nos. 3, 11, 12, 17, 18, 20, 36, 79, 122, 128.)—(2) cervices, *back of neck* of animals, Ψ 508; and of men, K 573. —(3) collis, *hill*, *ridge*, λ 596.

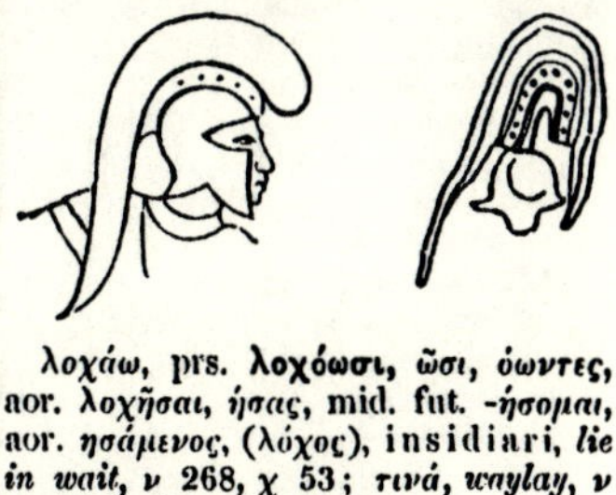

λοχάω, prs. **λοχόωσι,** ῶσι, όωντες, aor. λοχῆσαι, ήσας, mid. fut. -ήσομαι, aor. ησάμενος, (λόχος), insidiari, *lie in wait*, ν 268, χ 53; τινά, *waylay*, ν 425; so also mid., δ 670.

λόχμῃ, τῇ, (λόχος), *thicket*, *lair of wild beast*, τ 439†.

λόχος, ου, ῳ, ον, οι, (λέχω), *place for lying in wait*, (1) *the lying in wait*, *ambush*, A 379; λ 525, πυκινόν, crowded and κοῖλος, hollow, of wooden horse before Troy.—(2) *the men who lie in* *wait*, Θ 522; *πυκινόν*, numerous; *εἷσε*, Ζ 189, laid an ambush. **λοχόνδε,** *into the ambush*, Α 227; λόχῳ, *for the ambush*, Σ 513.—(3) δ 395, *way to capture.* —(4) *band, troop*, υ 49.

λύγοισι, *ους*, fem., (properly vitex agnus castus), *Abraham's balm, willow twig, osier*, ι 427; *μόσχοισι*, Λ 105, with tender willows.

λυγρός, *ῷ, όν, ὧν, οῖς*; *ῆς, ῇ, ήν*; *ά*, (lugeo, λευγαλέος), miserabilis, miserandus, funestus, *wretched, pitiable, ruinous*, Ω 531, Ρ 642, σ 134; perniciosus, δ 230, λ 432; ignavus, *worthless*, Ν 119, 237, σ 107; vilis, *contemptible*, π 457; adv. **λυγρῶς,** foede, Ε 763.

λύθεν = ἐλύθησαν, from λύω.

λύθρῳ, *τῷ*, (lues), cruore, *gore*, with and without *αἵματι*; *πεπαλαγμένος*, defiled, Ζ 268, cf. Λ 169, χ 402.

λῠκά-βαντος, *τοῦ*, (lux, *βαίνω*), *year*, ξ 161 and τ 306.

Λῠ́καστος, *ἡ*, a town in southern part of Kreta, Β 647†.

Λυκάων, (1) father of Pandaros, Ε 197, 95.—(2) son of Priamos and of Laothoe, Γ 333; slain by Achilleus, Φ 114 sqq.

λῠκέην, *τήν*, (λύκος), *wolf-skin*, Κ 459†.

λῠκη-γενεῖ (lux), *light-born*, epithet of Apollo as sun-god, Δ 101, 119.

Λῠκίη, (1) division of Asia Minor, Β 877; *Λυκίηνδε*, *to Lykia*, Ζ 168; *Λυκίηθεν*, *from Lykia*, Ε 105; the inhabitants, **Λύκιοι,** led by Glaukos, Η 13, and by Sarpedon, Ε 647, Ξ 426, Π 490.—(2) district on river Aisēpos; its chief town Ζέλεια, Β 824, Ε 173.

Λῠκο-μήδης, son of Kreon in Boiotia, Ρ 346, Τ 240.

Λῠκό-οργος, (1) son of Dryas, banishes from his land the worship of Dionȳsos (Bacchus), Ζ 134.—(2) an Arkadian, slays Areithoos, Η 142–148.

λύκοιο, *οι, ων, ους*, (ϝλύκος), lupus, *wolf*, Κ 334; symbol of blood-thirstiness, Δ 471, Λ 72.

Λῠκο-φόντης, a Trojan, slain by Teukros, Θ 275.

Λῠκό-φρων, son of Mastor, from Kythera, companion of Aias, Ο 430.

Λύκτος, city in Kreta, east of Knosos, Β 647, Ρ 611.

Λῡ́κων, a Trojan, slain by Peneleos, Π 335, 337.

λῦ́μᾰτ(α), *τά*, (lues, lu-strum), *filth, dirt*, Α 314, Ξ 171.

λυπρή (λύπη), tristis, *poor*, ν 243†.

Λυρνησ(σ)ός, town in Mysia, under sway of Thebe ὑποπλακίη, Β 690, Τ 60, Υ 92, 191.

Λῡ́σ-ανδρος, a Trojan, slain by Aias, Λ 491†.

λῡσι-μελής (*μέλος*, member; false derivation, υ 56 sq.), *relaxing the limbs*, ψ 343.

λύσιος, *ιν*, (λύω), *ransoming*, Ω 655; *θανάτου*, *rescue* from death, ι 421.

λύσσα, *αν*, fem., (λύκος), rabies, *martial rage*, Ι 239, Φ 542.

λυσσητῆρα, *τόν*, (λύσσα), *one who rages*, with *κύνα*, of Hektor, Θ 299†.

λυσσώδης (λύσσα), *raging*, of Hektor, Ν 53†.

λύχνον, *τόν*, (λευκός, lux), *light, lamp*, τ 34†.

λῡ́ων, prs., ipf. (also λύε, *ομεν, ον*), fut., aor. [also λῦσεν, *σαν, σασ(α)*], pass. pf. λέλυται, *υνται*, opt. *ῦτο*, plupf. *υντο*; aor. λῠ́θη, 3 pl. λῠ́θεν, also aor. mid. λύτο, λύντο, solvere, (1) *loose, open, release, let go; τινά τινι, set free* (*ἀποίνων*, for ransom).—(2) *dismiss*, assemblies; componere lites, *adjust* disagreements.—(3) *τινὸς* or *τινὶ γυῖα, μένος, ψυχήν*, interimere, *kill;* also of animals, with the weapon as subject, e. g. *πέλεκυς*, γ 450.—(4) *unnerve, weaken, γυῖα, γούνατα* (also as effect of amazement, σ 212), *βίην*; of sleep, *λύθεν δέ οἱ ἅψεα πάντα*, all her limbs *lost their strength.*—(5) delere, *break down, destroy, κάρηνα, κρήδεμνα*, towers, battlements; *μελεδήματα θυμοῦ*, *dissipate* cares, anxiety. — Mid. prs. *λυώμεθα ἵππους*, let us *put out our* horses; ipf. *λυόμην, οντο*, fut. *λύσομαι, μενος*, aor. *ἐλύσαο, ατο, σασθ(αι)*, 2 aor. *λύμην, λύτο, λύντο*, se, sibi, or sua solvere, *release, set free* (for one's self or one's own), freq., redimere, *ransom*, Α 13. [ῡ before σ, elsewh. in arsi; except thrice ῠ.]

λωβάομαι, aor. **λωβήσαιϝε,** opt. *λωβήσαιο*, *maltreat; τινά λώβην*, ignominia afficere, *do despite*, Ν 623.

λωβεύω, *εις*, (λώβη), *mock*, ψ 15 and 26.

λώβη, ης, ην, (labes), ignominia, *outrage, insult; τῖσαι, ἀποδοῦναι*, pay, atone for; *τίσασθαι*, exact retribution for; Σ 180, *shame* upon thee, if—; Γ 42, ignominiosus, *cowardly wretch.*

λωβητῆρα (λώβη) ἐπεσβόλον, *foul* slanderer, Β 275; λωβητῆρες ἐλεγχέες, vile *scoundrels.*

λωβητόν (λωβάομαι) τιθέναι τινά, make *contemptible*, Ω 531†.

λώϊον=λωΐτερον, melius, satius, *better, preferable;* ρ 417, largius, *more freely.*

λώπην (λέπω), *mantle*, ν 224†.

λωτοῦντα, part. from λωτόω, *Lotos-producing, clovery* fields, Μ 283†.

λωτός, οῖο, όν, masc., (1) *Lotos*, a kind of *clover*, food of horses (trifolium melilotus or lotus corniculatus, Linn.), δ 603, Ξ 348.—(2) *Lotus*—tree and fruit; the latter of the size of olives, and in taste resembling dates, still prized in Tunis and Tripoli, under the name of *Jujube*, ι 91 sqq.

Λωτο-φάγοι (see λωτός 2), *Lotos-eaters* on coast of Libya, ι 84 sqq.

λωφάω, fut. **λωφήσει,** *will retire*, Φ 292†.

M.

μ' usually = *με*; less often = *μοι*, Ζ 165, κ 19.

μά, from *μάν*, in oath; vero, with acc. of the divinity, or of the witness invoked (sc. ὄμνυμι): preceded by *ναί* =nae, it has an affirmative; by *οὐ*, a negative force.

Μάγνητες, a Thessalian tribe, sprung from Aiolos, Β 756.

μαζοῖο, ῷ, όν, masc., papilla, *nipple, teat*, then mamilla, mamma, esp. the *mother's breast; λαθικηδέα*, banishing cares; *ἐπέχειν*, offer; *ἀνέσχεν*, obsecrandi causa.

μαῖα, voc., *good mother, φίλη*, used esp. in addressing the nurse, υ 129, ψ 11.

Μαιάδος υἱός, Hermes; *Maia* is the daughter of Atlas, ξ 435†.

Μαίανδρος, the river with many windings which flows into the sea at Miletos, Β 869†.

Μαιμαλίδης, *son of Maimalos*, Peisandros, Π 194†.

μαιμάω, only prs. **μαιμώωσι,** ῶσι, ώων, ώωσα, etc., aor. *μαίμησε, eagerly desire*, Ν 75, 78, *itch* or *quiver with desire.*

μαινάδι, τῇ, (*μαίνομαι*), *mad woman*, Χ 460†.

μαίνεαι, etc., prs. and ipf. 3 sing. *μαίνετο*, (*μαν*, mens), furere, *rage, be furious*, of combatants, also of hand and weapons; with anger, of Polyphemos, ι 350; of fire on mountains; *madly raving* (under Bacchic frenzy), Ζ 132; of madness from wine, σ 406.

μαίεσθαι, fut. *μάσσεται*, (*μα-, μέμαα*), *seek*, ξ 356; perscrutari, *explore*, ν 367; find a wife for any one, Ι 394, [*μασσεται*, v. l. *γαμέσσεται*].

Μαῖρα (*μαρμαίρω*), lit. "shining" or "sparkling," (1) a Nereid, Σ 48†.—(2) attendant of Artemis, mother of Lokros, λ 326†.

Μαίων, son of Haimon in Thebai, Δ 394, 398.

μάκαρ, αρος, αρες, άρων, άρεσσι, sup. *μακάρτατος*, (macte), beatus, (1) *blessed*, of gods, opp. *δειλοὶ ὀϊζυροὶ βροτοί*.—(2) of men, *happy, fortunate*, λ 483.—(3) *wealthy*, α 217.

Μάκαρ, ος, son of Aiolos, ruling in Lesbos, Ω 544†.

μᾰκᾰρίζοι, opt. prs., (*μάκαρ*), *pronounce happy, τινά*, ο 538. (Od.)

μᾱκεδνής, gen. fem., (*μακρός*), *tall*, η 106†.

μᾰκελλαν, *τήν, broad, heavy hoe, mattock*, Φ 259†.

μακρός, ῷ, όν, οἱ, οἶσι; ή, ήν, αἱ, ῇσ(ι), άς; όν, ά, comp. *μακρότερον*, ην, also **μᾶσσον,** sup. *μακρότατ(α)*, τη, cf. *μήκιστον, long*, (1) of space, *κύματα; high and deep*, esp. *μακρόν, ά*; as adv., *far*, -ὸν ἀΰσας, always at close of verse (exc. Γ 81); ἀντεῖν, Θ 160, ζ 117; βιβάς.—(2) of time, diutinus, *long*.

μᾰκών, see μηκάομαι.

μάλᾰ, adv., (μαλερός?), sup. μάλιστα, (before or after the modified word), *eagerly*, ἐσθίειν; *gladly*, ἔκλυον; with adjs., *very*, *quite*; πάντες, *quite* all, all *together*; with demonstratives, *fully*, *utterly*, τοῖον; μάλα κνέφας, *utter* darkness; with advs., e. g. εὖ, πάγχυ, strengthens their meaning, *quite*, *utterly*, ρ 217; αὐτίκα, on the *very* moment; with verbs = valde; καί (or οὐδ') εἰ μάλα, quantumvis; μάλα περ with part. = quamvis; also with καί περ, Α 217.—(2) strengthening an assertion: *certainly*, *verily*, Γ 204; *no doubt*, ι 135; comp. **μᾶλλον**, *only the more*, *so much the more*, with κηρόθι, at heart, ε 284; with πολύ, ἔτι, καί, η 213; sup. **μάλιστα**, maxime, with gen. part., with ἐκ; *far*, *by far*, with other superlatives, Β 57, Ω 334. [μᾰ́λᾰ, by arsis often ⏑ –.]

μᾰλᾰκός, οῦ, ῷ, όν, οἱ, οῖσι; ῆς, ῇ, ήν, comp. -ώτερος (Ger. schmalz? mollis), *soft*, *mild*, *gentle*, *tender*, Β 42, γ 38; *spongy* meadow, Σ 541; mitis, dulcis, Κ 2, σ 201, Ζ 337; Χ 373, easier to handle; adv. **-ῶς**, placide, *softly*, γ 350.

Μάλεια, αν, ῶν, άων, southern promontory of the Peloponnesos, ι 80, τ 187, γ 287.

μᾰλεροῦ, ῷ, *devouring*; of fire, Ι 242. (Il.)

μαλθᾰκός (mollis), *effeminate*, *cowardly*, Ρ 588†.

μάλιστα, μᾶλλον, see μάλα.

μάν (= μήν), profecto, *verily*, *truly*, *in sooth*, Θ 373, Π 14; *come!* Ε 765; ἦ, Β 370; δή, Ρ 538; οὐ, Δ 512; αὖτε, by no means in his turn, Ν 414; μή, Θ 512; θην, but *yet* by no means, ε 211, v. l. μέν. [–]

μανθάνω, aor. **μάθον**, ἔμμαθες, εν, novi, *know*, ἔμμεναι ἐσθλός, Ζ 444.

μαντεύομαι, prs., ipf. μαντεύετο, fut. μαντεύσομαι, (μάντις), vaticinor, *divine*, *prophesy*, τινί τι, κακά, ἀτρεκέως, ρ 154.

μαντήϊα, τά, (μαντεύομαι), vaticinia, *predictions*, *oracles*, μ 272†.

Μαντῑνέη, a city in Arkadia, Β 607†.

Μάντιος, son of Melampus, brother of Antiphates, father of Polypheides and of Kleitos, ο 242, 249.

μάντις, ιος, (μάντηος in arsi, κ 493), ι, ιν, ιες, (μαίνομαι), *prophet*, *seer*, expounder of omens, which were drawn from flight of birds, from dreams, and from sacrifices, e. g. Teiresias, Kalchas, Melampus, Theoklymenos, Ω 221, Α 62.

μαντοσῡ́νη, ην, ας, (μάντις), *gift of divination*, Α 72; vaticinia.

μάομαι, see μαίομαι.

Μᾰρᾰθών (μάραθον, "fennel"), village in Attika, η 80†.

ἐμᾰραίνετο, ipf., aor. ἐμαράνθη, sensim extinguebatur, *died gradually away*, Ψ 228. (Il.)

μαργαίνειν (μάργος), furere, *rage*; *madly attack*, ἐπὶ θεοῖσιν, Ε 882†.

μάργε, voc., and ῃ, ην, vesanus, *furious*, *madman!* σ 2. (Od.)

Μᾱ́ρις, son of Amisodaros, slain by Thrasymedes, Π 319.

μαρμαίροντες, ας, α, (μαῖρα), *sparkling*, coruscantes, of weapons, eyes; of Trojans, χαλκῷ, *resplendent* with armor, Ν 801.

μαρμᾰρέην (μαῖρα), *flashing*, *sparkling*, of shield, shield-rim, sea, Ρ 594.

μαρμᾰ́ρῳ, ον, adj. and subst., [sc. πέτρος or πέτρη], (μαῖρα), stone of crystalline structure, which *sparkles* in the light, *block of stone*, Μ 380, ι 499.

μαρμᾰρῠγάς, τάς, (μαρμαρύσσω), ποδῶν, *quick twinkling* of dancers' feet, θ 265†.

μάρνᾰται, prs., (opt. -οίμεθα), ipf. (ἐ)μάρναο, ατο, άμεθα, elsewh. unaugmented, aor. ἐμαρνάσθην, pugnare, *fight*, (ἐπί) τινί, against some one, ἔγχει; περὶ ἔριδος, out of rivalry; as boxer, σ 31; with words, *wrangle*, Α 257.

Μάρπησσα, daughter of Euenos, wife of Idas, who recovered her after she had been carried off by Apollo, mother of Kleopatra, Ι 557 sqq.

μάρπτω, subj. **μάρπτῃσι**, ipf. ἔμαρπτε, μάρπτε, fut. μάρψει, aor. subj. μάρψῃ, inf. -αι, part. ας, comprehendo, *seize*, κ 116; ἀγκάς, complecti, embrace; consequi, *overtake*, Χ 201; attingere, *touch*, Ξ 228; Θ 405, inflixerit, *inflict upon*; ὕπνος, oppressit, *lay hold of*, υ 56.

μαρτῦρίῃσι, *ταῖς*, (*μάρτυρος*), testimonio, *on testimony of*, λ 325†.

μάρτῦρος, *οι*, testis, *witness*, π 423, A 338.

Μάρων, son of Euanthes, priest of Apollo in Ismaros, ι 197†.

Μάσης, *ητος*, town in Argolis, near Hermione, B 562†.

μάσσεται, fut. from *μαίομαι*, quaeret, *seek*.

μᾶσσον, see *μακρός*.

μάσταξ, **μάστᾰκ(α)**, *τήν*, (*μαστάζω*, mandere), *mouth*, δ 287, ψ 76; *mouthful, food*, I 324.

μαστίζω, aor. **μάστιξεν**, (*μάστιξ*), *was lashing*, *ἵππους*; *ἐλάαν*.

μάστιξ, **μάστῖγι**, *α*, *ας*, fem., flagellum, *whip*, *scourge*, ζ 316; *Διός*, M 37; N 812, *chastisement*.

μάστις, **μάστῖ**, *ιν*, fem., flagellum, *whip*, Ψ 500, ο 182.

μάστῑε, imp., *whip*, P 622; mid. prs. *μαστίεται πλευράς*, lashes his sides, Υ 171.

Μαστορίδης, *son of Mastor*, (1) Halitherses in Ithaka, β 158, ω 452. —(2) Lykophron, O 438, 430.

ματάω, *οὐκ* **ἐμάτησεν**, (*μάτην*), *be idle, delay, linger*, Π 474; nec cessavit, Ψ 510; *μὴ ματήσετον*, ne cessaveritis.

μᾰτεύσομεν, fut. quaeremus, *seek*, Ξ 110†.

μᾰτίῃ, *τῇ*, (*μάτην*), irrito labore, *useless labor*, κ 79†.

μαχαίρῃ, *αν*, *ας*, fem., *broad, short sacrificial knife*, Γ 271, Λ 844. (See following cut, and No. 115.)

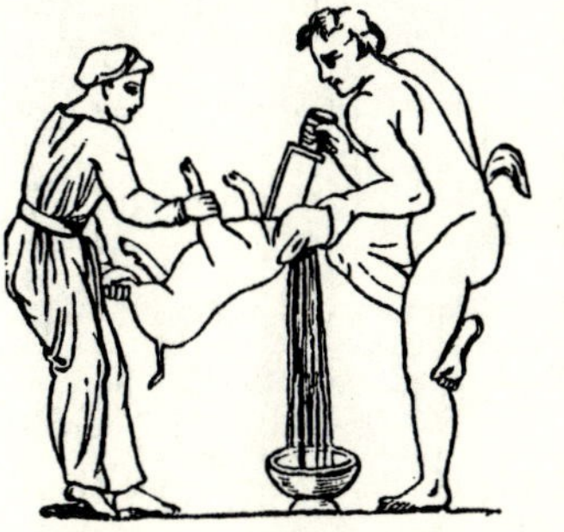

Μαχάων, voc. *ᾱον*, son of Asklepios, ruler in Trikka and Ithome in Thessaly, excelling in art of healing, Λ 512, 613, Δ 200, B 732; wounded by Hektor, Λ 506, 598, 651.

μαχειόμενος, *εούμενον*, see *μάχομαι*.

μάχη, *η*, *ῃ*, *ην*, *αι*, *ας*, pugna, *battle, combat, fight*; *μάχῃ* (*ἐνὶ*), in pugna, δ 497; *στήσασθαι*, set the battle in array, form one's line for battle, aciem instruere, ι 54; committere, join battle, fight a battle, *μάχεσθαι*, *τίθεσθαι*; *ἐγείρειν*, excitare, rouse the fight, N 778 = *ὀρνύμεν ὀτρύνειν*; also used of *single combat*, H 263 and Λ 255; *field of battle*, E 355.

μᾰχήμων (*μάχη*), *warlike*, M 247†.

μᾰχητής, *ήν*, *αί*, *άς*, (*μάχομαι*), pugnator, *warrior*, E 801.

μᾰχητόν (*μάχομαι*), *that may be vanquished*, μ 119†.

μαχλοσύνην (*μάχλος*), *lust*, Ω 30†.

μάχομαι, **μάχονται**, *όμεσθ(α)*, etc., ipf. *ἐμάχοντο*, *μαχόμην*, *οντο*, etc., parallel forms *μαχέομαι*, prs., opt. *μαχέοιτο*, *εοίατο*, A 344; *μαχειόμενος*, ρ 471; *εούμενον*, *οι*, ipf. iter. *μαχέσκετο*, H 140; fut. alternates between *μαχήσομαι* and *μαχέσσομαι*, etc., *μαχεῖται*, *ἔονται*; also aor. *μαχήσασθαι* and *έσασθαι*, *εσσάμεθ(α)*, *αίμην*, *άμενον*, pugnare, *fight*, of armies and of single persons, *ἀντία*, *ἐναντίον τινός*, (*ἐν*)*αντίβιον*, or (*ἐπί*) *τινί*; *μάχην*, Σ 533; for any thing, *περί τινος* (*τινί*, *ἀμφί τινι*), *εἵνεκα*; also of combat between beasts, and in general signif., e. g. of single combat and of quarrel with words, A 8, B 377; contradicere, I 32.

μάψ (*ἐμμαπέως*), raptim, temere, *hastily, rashly*, *ὀμόσαι*, *ἀτὰρ οὐ κατὰ κόσμον*; *recklessly, wantonly*, E 759, γ 138; cf. B 120, N 627, B 214; incassum, *in vain*, B 120; likewise **μαψιδίως**, E 374, β 58.

Μεγάδης, *son of Megas*, Perimos, Π 695†.

μεγᾰ-θῦμος, *ου*, *ον*, *ε*, *οι*, *ων*, (*θυμός*), *high-hearted*, animosus, B 53; usually of nations; of a bull, Π 488.

μεγαίρω, aor. *μέγηρε*, subj. *μεγήρῃς*, part. *-ας*, (*μέγας*), invidēre, *grudge*, *τινί τι*, Ψ 865; *βιότοιο*, *grudging* him the life of his enemy, N 563; *object*, with inf.; *οὔτι μεγ.*, nihil moror.

μεγᾰ-κήτεος, *εϊ*, *εα*, (*κῆτος*), *with great hollows*; *νηῦς*, *wide-bellied*; *πόντος*, *wide-yawning*, γ 158.

μεγαλ-ήτορος, ι, α, ες, ας, (ἦτορ), ferox, *great-hearted*, *haughty*, N 302, τ 176.

μεγαλίζομαι, imp. εο, (μέγας), superbio, *exalt one's self*, θυμῷ, K 69.

μεγάλως, adv. from μέγας.

μεγαλωστί, from μεγάλως, μέγας μ., *stretch'd over a vast space*, Σ 26, ω 40.

Μεγα-πένθης, son of Menelaos by a slave, ο 100, 103, δ 11.

Μεγάρη, daughter of Kreon in Thebai, wife of Herakles, λ 269†.

μέγᾰρον, οιο, ον, etc., *hall*, *large room*; μέγαρόνδε, *to the hall*, *into the hall*.—(1) *men's dining-hall*, *chief room of house*, the roof supported by columns, the light entering through the doors, the opening for the smoke overhead, and the loop-holes (ὀπαῖα) just under the roof. The cut, combined from different ancient representations, is de-

signed to show the back part of the μέγαρον in the house of Odysseus, cf. plate III. for ground-plan.—(2) *women's apartment*, behind the one just described, see plate III. G, also in pl., τ 16.—(3) *housekeeper's apartment in upper story* (ὑπερώιον), β 94.—(4) *sleeping-apartment*, λ 374.—(5) in wider signif. cf. aedes, in pl., *house*, A 396.

μέγας, αν, α (μέγ'), μεγάλου, ῳ, ω, οι, ων, οισι, ους; η, ης, ῃ, ην, ῃσι, ας; α; comp. μείζων, ονι, ονα, ονες; ον; sup. μέγιστος, ον, ε, ους, αι, ον, α, magnus, *great*, in various senses, e. g. also altus, longus, latus, amplus; ἔργον, facinus, *monstrous* deed; nimius, εἰπεῖν, speak *too big*, *too boldly*, provoking divine wrath; so also ntr. μέγα, with comp., multo, B 239; with super., longe, B 82; with positive, valde, B 480, Π 46; with verbs of mental condition or action, A 517, 256, B 27, Π 822, I 537, Π 237; also μεγάλ(α), *mightily*, *strongly*, *aloud*, A 450; with advs., valde; adv. **μεγάλως**, valde, *exceedingly*, π 432.

μέγεθος, τό, (μέγας), magnitudo (corporis), *bodily size*, B 58, ε 217.

Μέγης, ητος, acc. ην, son of Phyleus, Odysseus's sister's son, chief of the inhabitants of Dulichion and of the Echinades, E 69, N 692, O 520, 535, B 627, T 239.

μέγιστος, superl. from μέγας.

μεδέων, part., *bearing sway*; Ἴδηθεν, from Ida (as his seat), of Zeus, Γ 276.

Μεδεών, ῶνος, town in Boiotia, B 501†.

μέδομαι, **μέδεσθαι**, prs., ipf., fut. μεδήσομαι, (μεδέων), *be mindful of*, *pro-*

vide for, τινός, E 718, γ 334; κακά τινι, mala moliri, devise mischief.

μέδων, οντες, (μέδομαι), *lord*, ἁλός, α 72; pl., *counselors*, B 79.

Μέδων, οντος, (1) son of Oileus, step-brother of Aias, from Phylake, chief of warriors from Methone in Phthia, N 693, 695 sq., B 727; slain by Aineias, O 332.—(2) a Lykian, P 216.—(3) herald in Ithaka, δ 677, ρ 172, χ 357, 361, ω 439.

μεθ-αιρέω, only aor. iter. **μεθέλεσκε,** *reached after and caught*, excipiebat, θ 376†.

μεθ-άλλομαι, aor. part. **μετάλμενος,** *springing upon, after*, E 336, Ψ 345. (Il.)

μεθείω, subj. aor. from μεθ-ίημι.

μεθ-έλεσκε, aor. iter. from μεθ-αιρέω.

μεθέμεν, aor. inf. from μεθίημι.

μεθ-έπεις, ipf. μέθεπε, aor. part. μετασπών, (ἕπω), persequi, petere, *follow after, follow closely*, τινά, τί; pervenire, *arrive; ἵππους Τυδείδην, turned* the steeds *after* Tydeides; mid. aor. μετασπόμενος, consecutus; ipf. μετὰ-εἵπετο, subsequebatur, Σ 234.

μεθ-ήμενος, part., (ἧμαι), μνηστῆρσι, *sitting among* the suitors, α 118†.

μεθ-ημοσύνη, ῃσι, (μεθήμων), negligentia, *remissness*, N 108 and 121.

μεθ-ήμων, ονα, (ἵημι), negligens, *careless, remiss*, B 241, ζ 25.

μεθ-ίημι, ἱεῖς, ἱεῖ, δ 372, prs. and ipf. (others write ἱῃς, ἱῃ, and pres. ιεῖς, ιεῖ), prs. inf. ιέμεν(αι), subj. μεθιῇσι (sometimes written ἱῃσι), ipf. 3 pl. μεθίεν, fut. μεθήσω, etc., inf. ησέμεν(αι), aor. μεθέηκα, ε(ν), and μεθῆκεν, subj. μεθείω, ῃῃ (or εἱῃ, distinguish from opt. εἱη, ε 471), inf. ἕμεν, (ἵημι), (1) properly, *send after*, ἰόν; immittere, τὶ ἐς ποταμόν.—(2) dimittere, *let go*, τινά, also ῥῖγός με; *give up*, χόλον τινός, about any one, τινί, as a favor to some one, A 283; also νίκην, concedere, *give up to, surrender; τοῦτον ἐρύσαι*, hunc trahendum.—(3) with part., *cease*, Ω 48; τινός, χόλοιο Τηλεμάχῳ, *desist from, cease from* anger at wish of Telemachos; *neglect*, σεῖο τειρομένοιο, te saucium.—(4) cessare, *relax*, also with inf., N 234.

μεθ-ίστημι, fut. **μεταστήσω,** *substitute*, i. e. *exchange*, δ 612; mid. ipf. μεθίστατο ἑτάροισι, *retired among* his comrades, E 514.

μεθ-ομίλεον, ipf., (ὁμιλέω), τοῖσιν, *had dealings with them*, A 269†.

μεθ-ορμηθείς, aor. part., (ὁρμάομαι), persecutus, *make a dash after*, Y 192, ε 325.

μέθυ, τό, (Eng. mead), *wine*, ι 9, η 179.

μεθύοντι, ουσαν, (μέθυ), *drunken*, σ 240; ἀλοιφῇ, *soaked with* fat.

μειδάω, aor. **μείδησεν,** ῆσαι, ήσας, ασα, A 596, and μειδιάω, part. **μειδιόων,** όωσα, (σμειδ-, mirus, smile), subridere, *smile*, Ψ 786.

μείζων, ον, see μέγας.

μείλανι=μέλανι, nigro, Ω 79†.

μείλια, τά, (μέλι), *soothing gifts, gifts as means of reconciliation*, I 147 and 289.

μειλίγματα, τά, μειλίσσω, *that which appeases hunger*, sedamina appetitus, i. e. *dainty bits*, κ 217†.

μείλινον, see μέλινος.

μειλισσέμεν, prs. inf.; mid. prs. imp. -ίσσεο, (μείλιχος), placare (mortuos); πυρός, cf. construction with λαγχάνειν, *appease the dead* with fire, i. e. with funeral rites, H 410; mid., *extenuate*, γ 96.

μειλιχίη (μείλιχος), *softness*, i. e. *faintness* in fight, O 741†.

μειλίχιον, ιοισ(ιν), ίῃ, and **μείλιχος,** (μείλια), placidus, comis, mitis, *gentle, mild*; μῦθος, μειλιχίοις, sc. ἔπεσι; θ 172, *gentle, winning* modesty.

μείρεο, see μέρω.

μείς, ὁ, T 117; also **μηνός,** ί, μῆνα, ες, ας, ῶν, (metior) mensis, *month*, φθίνοντος, the waning month, i. e. as this month draws to a close, ξ 162.

μείων, see μικρός.

μελαγ-χροιής (χροιά, χρώς), *bronzed, swarthy*, π 175†.

μέλαθρον, ου, ῳ, όφιν, τό, (κμέλαθρον, camera), *vaulting of roof, rafters, roof*; τ 544, on the *ridge-pole* aloft (near the smoke-hole); χ 239, she, flying up to the roof of the sooty hall, sat there just like a swallow to look upon (i. e. on one of the cross-beams under the rafters; see cut under μέγαρον).

μελαίνετ(ο), ipf., (μέλας), *she colored herself dark* on her fair skin, her fair skin was stained by the dark blood; also of fresh upturned earth, E 354 and Σ 548.

Μελάμ-πους, ποδος, son of Amythaon, famous seer in Pylos. Wishing to fetch from Phylake in Thessaly the famous cattle of Iphiklos, and thus gain the beautiful Pero for his brother Bias, he was taken captive by herdsmen of Iphiklos, as he had predicted, and held prisoner for one year, when, in consequence of good counsel given by him, he was set free by Iphiklos, gained what he sought, and settled in Argos, λ 287 sqq., ο 225 sqq.

μελάν-δετα (*δέω*), *mounted in black*, i. e. *with dark hilt* or *scabbard*, Ο 713†.

Μελᾰνεύς, father of Amphimedon in Ithaka, ω 103.

Μελανθεύς = **Μελάνθιος**, son of Dolios, insolent goat-herd on estate of Odysseus, ρ 212, υ 173, φ 181, χ 135 sqq., 182; brother of the shameless maid-servant **Μελανθώ**, σ 321, τ 65.

Μελάνθιος, a Trojan, slain by Eurypylos, Ζ 36.

Μελᾰνιππος, (1) an Achaian chief, Τ 240.—(2) a Trojan, son of Hiketaon, slain by Antiochos, Ο 547–582.—(3) a Trojan, slain by Teukros, Θ 276.—(4) a Trojan, slain by Patroklos, Π 695.

μελᾰνό-χροος, 2 declension, τ 246, pl. -*χροες*, 3 declension, (*χρώς*), *black*, Ν 589.

μελᾰ́ν-ῡδρος (*ὕδωρ*), *with dark water*, Ι 14, υ 158, only at close of verse.

μελᾰ́νει, prs., *darkens*, (*μέλας*), spoken of the water of the sea, under its white surface-foam (v. l. *μελανεῖ*), Η 64†.

μέλας, αινα, αν, etc., pl. *μέλανες, αιναι, ανα*, dat. sing. *μείλανι*, Ω 79; dat. pl. masc. and ntr. wanting; comp. **μελάντερον**, *dark*, in different degrees up to *black* (opp. *λευκός*); of sea in commotion, when surface is ruffled by ripples, so that it does not reflect light, but appears *dark*, δ 359; *dark* (painted) ships, θ 34; land, spring (on account of depth); *pitch-dark*, Δ 277; *μέλαν*, as ntr. subst. the *dark*, i. e. *bark* of oak, *δρυός*. Metaph. *dark*, *gloomy*, of death, etc., *θανάτου νέφος, κήρ, ὀδύναι*.

Μέλας, son of Portheus, Ξ 117†.

μελδόμενος, part., (*σμέλδω*, Eng. melt), *filled with melting fat*, liquefaciens, Φ 363†.

Μελέ-αγρος, (*ᾧ μέλει ἄγρα*), son of Oineus and Althaia, husband of Kleopatra, slayer of Kalydonian boar. A quarrel arose between the Kuretes, of Pleuron, and the Aitolians, for the head and skin of the boar; the Aitolians had the upper hand until Meleager, on account of the curses of his mother, withdrew from the struggle; but he was afterward induced by his wife to enter the conflict again, and he drove the Kuretes vanquished into Akarnania, Ι 543 sqq., Β 642.

μελεδήματα, *τά*, (*μέλω*), *care, anxiety*, *θυμοῦ*, of the soul; *πατρός*, anxiety for his father kept him awake, ο 8.

μελεδών (*μέλω*), **μελεδῶνες** *ὀξεῖαι*, sharp *cares*, τ 517†.

μέλει, see *μέλω*.

μελεϊστί, adv., (*μέλος*), *limb from limb*, Ω 409, ι 291, σ 339.

μέλεος, *η, ον*, irritus; Ψ 795, *unrewarded*; ntr., incassum, *in vain*.

μέλι, *τος, τι, τό*, mel, *honey*, as food, υ 69; also as draught, mixed with wine; honey and fat were burned upon the funeral pyre, Ψ 170, ω 68; mixed with milk as libation to shades of dead, *μελίκρητον*. Metaph. of speech of well-disposed, Α 249, Σ 109. Cf. *μελίγηρυν*.

Μελί-βοια, town in Thessalian Magnesia, Β 717†.

μελῑ-γηρυν, *sweet-voiced*, μ 187†.

μελῐ́η, *ης, ῃ, ην, ῃσι*, fraxinus, *ash*, Ν 178, Π 767; *shaft of lance, lance*, freq. with *Πηλιάδα*, from mount *Πήλιον*; presented by the Centaur Cheiron to *Πηλεύς*, Π 143; *εὔχαλκον*, well shod with brass; *χαλκογλώχινος*, brazen-pointed.

μελῐ-ηδής, *έος, έα*, (*ἡδύς*), *honey sweet*, Σ 545, Κ 569, ι 94; fig. *ὕπνος*, *sweet*, *νόστον, θυμόν*, life.

μελι-κρήτῳ, *τῷ*, (*κεράννυμι*), *honey drink*, potion compounded of milk and honey as a libation to spirits of the lower world, κ 519, λ 27.

μέλινος, ρ 339, and **μείλινον**, *α*, (*μελίη*), fraxineus, beechen, *ashen*, Ε 655. (Il.)

μέλισσαι, *άων*, fem., (*μέλι*), *bees*, Μ 167.

Μελῐ́τη, a Nereid, Σ 42†.

μελί-φρων, *ονος, ονα*, (*φρήν*), *having mind, substance, essence like honey; honey sweet*=*μελιηδής*, dulcis.

μέλλω, *εις, ει, ετε, ουσι*, opt. *οι, οι-*

μεν, ipf. ἔμελλον, ες, (ε)ν, ετε, ον, and μέλλε, μέλλον, (1) is sum qui, *be able, can,* with inf. prs., Ξ 125, α 232, δ 200; with inf. aor., δ 377, χ 322; with πού, denoting probability or suspicion, *may well, must,* οὕτω που Διὶ μέλλει φίλον εἶναι, thus, methinks, must it please Zeus.—(2) like -urus sum, (a) *be on the point of,* α 232, ζ 135, with inf. fut. (prs. aor.); (b) *it is one's fate, destiny, I have to,* Λ 700, Π 46; often negatived, with inf. prs. aor.; *must,* Ω 46, ι 477.

μέλεα, έων, εσσι, ntr., membra, *limbs,* σ 70, Ρ 211; corpus, *body,* Η 131, Ν 672, ο 354.

μέλπηθρα, τά, (μέλπω), *sport,* κυνῶν, Ν 233; κυσίν, Ρ 255. (Il.)

μέλποντες, part., *extol in song,* Α 474; mid. ἐμέλπετο (φορμίζων), *was playing* (on the lyre), δ 17, ν 27; μελπομένῃσιν ἐν χορῷ, *celebrate a choral dance;* μέλπεσθαι Ἄρηϊ, fig., *dance a measure* in honor of Ares in close combat = fight on foot, Η 241.

μέλω, ι 20, elsewh. 3 prs. μέλει, ουσι; imp. έτω, όντων; inf. έμεν, ειν; part. ουσα, ipf. ἔμελε, μέλε, fut. -ήσει, ήσουσι, ησέμεν, pf. μέμηλε(ν), subj. ῃ, part. ώς, plupf. μεμήλει, curae esse, *it is a care,* to me, μοί τι; may often be translated personally, *care for, attend to, engage in,* ἔργα; Κ 92, angit, *distresses,* Ω 152, φρεσί, in thy soul; with inf., π 465; part., ε 6; ι 20, *be an object of interest;* μεμηλώς τινος, studiosus rei; mid. in similar signif. with act. prs. μελέσθω, angat; fut. μελήσεται, pf. μέμβλεται, plupf. μέμβλετο, χ 12.

μέμαα, du. **μέμᾰτον,** pl. ἄμεν, ἄτ(ε), άασι, imp. άτω, part. ἀώς, ῶτος, τι, τα, τε, τες, σιν, τας, (μεμᾱότες, ότε, Β 818), μεμᾰυῖα, αν, αι, plupf. μέμᾰσαν, (μαίομαι), *charge, press forward,* ἐπί τινι (yet not so, Φ 174), ἐγχείῃσι; gestire, moliri, *plan,* λ 315; with inf., appotens sum, *desirous,* τινός; part., cupidus, rapidus, *eager, quick.*

μεμακυῖαι, see μηκάομαι.

μέμβλωκε, see βλώσκω.

μέμβλεται, το, see μέλω.

μεμηκώς, see μηκάομαι.

μέμηλε, ει, ῃ, see μέλω.

μεμνώμεθα, ῴτο, see μιμνήσκω.

Μέμνων, ονος, son of Tithonos and of Eos, came to the aid of Priamos after the death of Hektor, and slew Antilochos, λ 522, cf. δ 188.

μέμονας, εν, pf., (mens), *have in mind, purpose,* with inf. prs. fut. or aor., ἶσα θεοῖσι (cf. φρονέειν ἶσα), thinks to make himself equal with the gods, Φ 315; διχθά, yearns with a twofold wish, hesitates.

μέμυκε, see μυκάομαι.

μέν (from μήν, μῖν, Η 77, 389, Λ 442, Χ 482), I. in affirmation: profecto, *in truth,* Α 216; μὲν δή, with imp., now then, Α 514; νῦν, now *certainly;* εἰ, if then *in fact;* ἦ, (1) in oath, *in very truth,* ξ 160; (2) in assertion: *truly, yet,* κ 65, λ 447; (3) in antithesis, Ω 416.—καὶ μέν, (a) and *yet,* Α 269; (b) but *even,* υ 45; (c) and *truly,* κ 13, τ 244; οὐ μέν, non profecto, not *indeed,* Β 203, Ρ 19, ρ 381 (see also II.); οὐ μὲν γάρ = ἐπεὶ οὐ μέν, α 78, 173; οὐ μέν τοι, ψ 266; οὐδὲ μέν, κ 447; οὐδὲ μὲν οὐδέ, Β 703; neque vero ne hi quidem, nor *by any means;* ἀτὰρ μέν, but *in truth,* β 122; μέν = δέ, Γ 308; after pronouns, in recapitulation, Α 234; in repetition, Α 267.—II. in first of two corresponding clauses, (1) without δέ, quidem, *indeed,* Α 211; also οὐ μὲν δή, but still not, ε 341; οὐ μέν τοι, yet by no means, σ 233; μὲν οὐδέ, (a) = ἀλλ' οὐ μὰν οὐδέ, nec vero ne—quidem, but not even, κ 551.—(b) but yet not, Τ 295; verily in no respect, δ 807; οὐδὲ μέν, but also not, Α 154; nor indeed, Ψ 311; after negative, οὐ, θ 553, γ 27.—(2) with following δέ, et—et, quidem—sed, cum—tum, *both—and, as well—as, although—yet,* Α 53 sq., α 22 sqq., Γ 51, α 24, γ 153.—(3) instead of δέ, ἀλλά may follow, Α 24; ἀτάρ, Α 166; αὖ, Λ 109; αὐτάρ, Α 127; αὖτε, Γ 240.—(4) other combinations: μὲν οὖν, so then, δ 780; μέν που, methinks indeed, Γ 308; μέν τοι (but β 294, δ 836, τοι = tibi): (a) in assertion, *yet really,* δ 157, π 267.—(b) introductory, before αὐτάρ, δ 411; before δέ, β 294.—(c) adversative, σ 233, Θ 294.

μενεαίνω, εις, ει, ομεν, ετε, ων, ipf. μενεαίνομεν, aor. μενεήναμεν, (μέμονα, mens, μῆνις), *eagerly desire,* with inf. aor. prs. (fut.), Ν 628, Δ 126; irasci, *be angry,* Τ 68, Ω 22, α 20, succensere alicui, τινί; but ἔριδι, *contend* in angry strife; Π 491, transfixus indignabatur.

μενε-δήιος, *withstanding the enemy, brave*, M 247 and N 228.

Μενέ-λᾱος, son of Atreus, brother of Agamemnon, his wife Helene seduced by Alexandros, Γ 27; slays Skamandrios, Pylaimenes, Peisandros, Dolops, Thoas, Euphorbus, Podes; ἀρήιος, ἀρηίφιλος, διοτρεφές, δουρικλειτός, κυδαλίμοιο, ξανθός; his return home, occupying eight years, δ 82 sqq.

μενε-πτόλεμος, οι, *persistent in battle, steadfast*, γ 442. (Il.)

Μενεσθεύς, son of Peteos, B 552, M 331; leader of the Athenians, N 195; πλήξιππον, Δ 327.

Μενέσθης, a Greek, slain by Hektor, E 609†.

Μενέσθιος, (1) son of Areithoos, slain by Paris, H 9.—(2) a Myrmidon, son of Spercheios, Π 173.

μενε-χάρμης, ην, αι, and **-χαρμος**, Ξ 376, (χάρμη), *stanch in battle, steadfast*.

μενο-εικέ(α), masc., ntr., ές, (εἴκω), *suiting the heart, satisfying*, largus, T 144, ζ 76.

μενοινώω (instead of άω), ᾷς, ᾷ=άᾳ, ῶν, prs., ipf. μενοίνα, εον, aor. -ησεν, subj. ήσῃ=ήσῃσι, O 82; ήσωσι, (μένος, μενεαίνω), cupio, peto, *desire, seek*, δ 480, ο 111, ρ 355; τινὶ κακά, moliri, *devise*, λ 532; *ponder*, M 59; πολλά, O 82.

Μενοιτιάδης, αο and εω, *son of Menoitios*, Patroklos, Π 554, Σ 93, I 211.

Μενοίτιος, son of Aktor, Λ 785; in Opus, Σ 326; father of Patroklos, Λ 605, T 24.

μένος, εος, εϊ, ος, εα, έων Θ 361, εα, ntr., (MEN, MA, mens, μῆνις), *vehement impulse*, ω 319, T 202, P 503; *force, might*, H 210; ἐν γούνεσσι, P 451; freq. with χεῖρες, Z 502, Υ 372, λ 502; κρατερόν, Π 38, K 479, N 60; coupled with ἀλκή (power of defense), I 706, Z 265, χ 226; πυρός, Z 182, λ 220; ἀνέμων, E 524; *vital force, life*, P 298, 29, Z 27; joined with ψυχή, E 296, Γ 294; θυμός, Θ 358; often in periphrasis, e. g. μ. Ἀτρείδαο = Ἀτρείδης, etc., Λ 268, Ψ 837, η 178, θ 423; ἱερόν, η 167, ν 20; μένε' ἀνδρῶν, Δ 447, Θ 61, δ 363; *resolve*, with θυμός, E 470, X 346; *courage, valor*, Φ 151, K 366, Π 529; πολύθαρσες, P 156; with θάρσος, E 2; B 536, Γ 8; *wrath*, Θ 361, A 207; *fury*, cf. ἔριδος, A 103; δάμασσε, λ 562; mens, *temper*, τ 493, E 892; in general signif. determined by context, ἐν φρεσί, Φ 145, A 103; ἐν θυμῷ, P 451, Ψ 468, X 312.

Μέντης, (1) chief of Kikones, P 73.—(2) son of Anchialos, α 180, chief of Taphians, α 105, guest friend of Odysseus, under whose form Athena visits Telemachos.

μέντοι, see μέν, ad fin., II., 4.

Μέντωρ, ορος, son of Alkimos, friend of Odysseus, in whose form Athena conducts Telemachos to Pylos, and seconds Odysseus against the suitors, β 225, 243, γ 22, 340, χ 206, 208, ω 446.

μένω, prs., ipf. ἔμεν(ε), ον, iter. μένεσκον, fut. μενέω, εις, ουσι, ειν, ων, aor. ἔμεινα, ας, ε, αμεν, αν, and μεῖν(ε), αμεν, ατ', αν; ῃ; ειας, (mens, maneo), (1) maneo, *remain, wait*, with inf., O 599; εἰσόκε, I 45; *hold one's ground in battle*, Π 659.—(2) τί, exspecto, *await*, O 709; τινά, ο 346; *withstand*, Z 126; *await*, A 535, Φ 609; *wait for*, τινά, Υ 480, Φ 571, ἠῶ, Λ 723; *sustain, resist*, O 406, X 93, M 169, I 355, there *he dared* once *to encounter* me alone.

Μένων, a Trojan, slain by Leonteus, M 193†.

Μερμερίδης, *son of Mermeros*, Ilos, α 259†.

μέρμερ(α), τά, (smar, maere, merke), *remarkable, signal* (ἔργα, πολέμοιο); in bad sense, *infamous, horrible*, K 48 (K 524, Θ 453). (Il.)

Μέρμερος, slain by Antilochos, Ξ 513†.

μερμηρίζω, εις, ει, ων, ipf. μερμήριζε, ον, aor. μερμήριξα, ε(ν), subj. ω, inf. -αι, (smar, schmerz ?), (1) deliberare, *ponder, reflect*, ἐνὶ (μετὰ) φρεσί, κατὰ φρένα (θυμόν), A 189; with ἤ—ἤ, utrum—an, ὡς, ὅπως, inf. ω 235.—(2) meditari, *imagine*, τινὰ ἀμύντορα, π 256, 261.

μέρμῑθι, τῇ, *cord*, κ 23†.

μέροπες, ων, εσσι, (mors), mortales, *mortal*, ἄνθρωποι, ων, also βροτοῖσιν, B 285.

Μέροψ, seer and ruler in Perkote on Hellespont, father of Adrastos and Amphios, B 831, Λ 329.

(μερω, μερομαι, μείρομαι), ipf. **μείρεο,** pf. 3 sing. *ἔμμορε*, plupf. pass. *εἵμαρτο* (for *σέσμαρτο*), *cause to be divided, receive as portion*, (a) with acc., I 616.—(b) with gen., *τιμῆς*, A 278, O 189, ε 335.—(c) plupf. pass., *it was decreed by fate*, with acc. and inf., Φ 281, ε 312, ω 34.

μεσαι-πόλῖος (*μέσαι*, locative from *μέσος*), *half-gray, grizzled*, N 361†.

Μεσαύλιος, servant of Eumaios, ξ 449, 455.

μεσηγύ(ς), see *μεσσηγύ*.

μεσήεις (*μέσος*), mediocris, *middling*, M 269†.

μεσό-δμης, *τῆς*, (*δέμω*), (1) prop. *what is constructed in the middle*, represented in the cut (see *a*) as a metal shoe

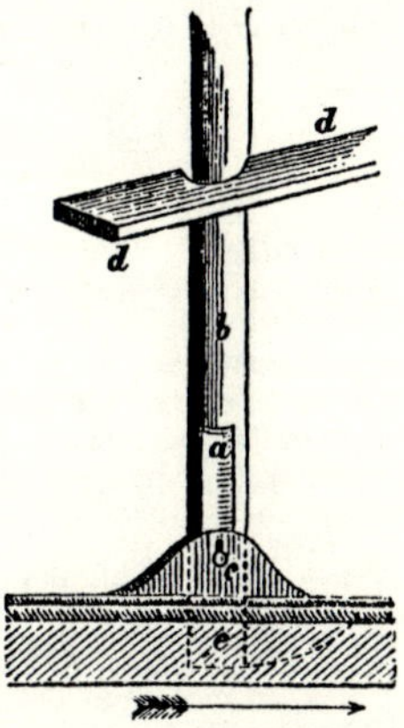

in which the foot of the mast was firmly fastened, so that it (the mast) could be turned backward on the pivot (*c*) to a horizontal position, until it rested upon the *ἱστοδόκη*, β 424. See also plate IV., where the *μεσόδμη* is somewhat differently represented as a three-sided trough, or mast-box.—(2) pl., *small spaces* or *niches* opening into the *μέγαρον*, and enclosed on three sides, behind by outside wall, on either side by the low walls which served as foundations of the columns, τ 37. (See table III., *r*, and cut No. 90.)

μέσον, etc., see *μέσσος*.

μεσσάτῳ, (*μέσσος*), *ἐν*, *in the middle*, Θ 223 and Λ 6.

μεσσ-αύλοιο, *ον*, (*αὐλή*), *court, farm-yard*, P 112; *cattle-yard*, Λ 548, *βοῶν*; of Polyphemos, κ 435.

Μέσση, harbor town near Tainaron in Lakonike, B 582†.

μεσσηγύ(ς) and *μεσηγύ(ς)*, *in the middle*, Λ 573, Ψ 521; *meantime*, η 195; elsewhere with gen., *between, betwixt*, χ 341. [ῡς, ῠ.]

Μεσσηίς, spring in Thessalian Hellas, Z 457†.

Μεσσήνη, district about Pherai, in what was afterward Messenia, φ 15; the inhabitants, **Μεσσήνιοι,** φ 18.

μεσσο-παγές (*πήγνυμι*), *fixed up to the middle; ἔθηκεν ἔγχος*, drove the spear *half its length firm* into the bank, Φ 172; v. l. *μεσσοπαλές*, *vibrating through half its length, quivering*.

μέσσος, nom. and gen. pl. wanting, dat. pl. *οισ(ιν)*; *η*, gen. sing., nom. and gen. pl. wanting, dat. pl. *ῃσ(ιν)*; *ον, α*, with parallel form **μέσῳ,** *ον, οισι*, (*μεδjος*, medius), medius, ntr., freq. as subst., *middle*; (*ἐν*)*μέσσῳ*, *ἐς* (*κατὰ*) *μέσον*, *δικάζειν*, judge impartially, Ψ 574; *ἐς μ. θεῖναι*, in medio proponere, offer as prize; *μέσον ὑπέρ*, half-way over; *μέσον αἰόλοι*, pliant in the middle.

μέσφ(α) (*μέσοφα*), *ἠοῦς*, *till* dawn, Θ 508†.

μετά, *amid, among*, B 446, Σ 515; *after*, Ψ 133; postea, *afterward*, ο 400.—Prep., (1) with dat., *amid*, also of things; *among*, *μ. νηυσίν*, N 668; also *between*, of two things, or such as exist in pairs, *γένυσσι*, *ποσσί* (*πέσῃ μ. π. γυναικός* = nascatur), *φρεσί*, in thought, properly intra praecordia, Δ 245; *πνοιῇς*, *στροφάλιγγι*, as it were with the breath of the wind, of the whirlwind; *πύματον μετὰ οἷς ἑτ.*, ultimum e sociis suis.—(2) with gen., *along with*, *μάχεσθαι μετά τινος*, *in league with* any one.—(3) with acc., inter, *amid*, infrequent, B 143; usually to denote direction *toward*, often with plural subst., Γ 264, H 35, K 205, P 458, 460, joined with *ἐς*, Δ 70, A 423, μ 247, cf. E 804; coupled with *ἐπί*, Π 534; also *after*, of individuals, K 73, ζ 115; in hostile sense, *ὁρμᾶσθαι*; of space, A 423; and of time, post; in order of worth, rank, secundum = *next after*; so also where a superlative is implied, e. g. ἀριστῆες, μετέπρεπε, Π 195; θ 583, the dearest *according to* blood and race; finally, with verbs of motion and of intention, *after*, *in pursuit of*, πλεῖν μετὰ χαλκόν, οἴχονται μετὰ δεῖπνον; denoting conformity with, secundum, μ. ὄγμον, *along* the furrow. In anastrophe μέτα = μέτεστι, so μέτα, φ 93, coupled with ἐν.

μετα-βαίνω, aor. imp. **-βηθι**, *pass over* (in narration, καὶ ἄεισον), θ 492; μετὰ δ' ἄστρα βεβήκει, μ 312, had passed over (the meridian) = were declining toward the horizon, μ 312.

μετὰ νῶτα **βαλών**, aor., terga vertens, *turn one's back*, Θ 94†.

μετ-εβούλευσαν, aor. from -βουλεύω, ἄλλως, *have changed their purpose*, ἀμφ' (de) Ὀδυσῆι, ε 286†.

μετ' ἄγγελος, Ο 144 and Ψ 199, is not a single word, but μετά belongs in one case to θεοῖσι, and in the other to ἀνέμοισι.

μετα-δαίνῦται, prs., fut. δαίσομαι, σεται (δαίνυμαι, δαίς), *have a share in the feast*, Ψ 207, with gen. partitive, elsewh. ἡμῖν, nobiscum.

μετα-δήμιοι, ον, (δῆμος), *among the people*, *in the community*, ν 46; *at home*, θ 293.

μετα-δόρπιος (δόρπος), adj., inter caenam, *during supper*, δ 194† (cf. 213, 218).

μετα-δρομάδην (δρόμος), *running after*, Ε 80†.

μετα-ίζειν (ἵζω), *sit among them*, π 362†.

μετ-αΐσσων, prs. part., -αΐξας, aor. part., *rushing after*, Φ 564.

μετ-εκίαθε, ον, ipf., (κιάθω), subsequi, *follow after*; τινά, persequi, Σ 581; transire, *pass over to*; πεδίον, permeare.

μετα-κλαύσεσθαι, fut., (κλαίω), postea fleturum esse, *shall hereafter lament*, Λ 764†.

μετα-κλινθέντος, aor. pass. part., (κλίνω), if the tide of battle *should shift about*, Λ 509†.

μετα-λλήξειε, αντι, aor. from λήγω (σλ- ?), χόλοιο, *cease from*, Ι 157. (Il.)

μετ-αλλῶ, ᾷς, ᾷ, ῶσιν, imp. ἄλλα, aor. ἄλλησαν, ῆσαι, (Ameis derives from μετά and λάω, *look after*), sciscitari, *search after*, Ε 516, ο 362; *inquire about*, τινά, Κ 125, Ν 780; τί, π 465, ξ 128; percontari, *question*, τινά, Α 553, τ 6; also τινά τι, or ἀμφί τινι, ρ 554; coupled with verbs of similar meaning, Α 550, γ 69, ψ 99, η 243.

μετάλμενος, aor. part. from μεθάλλομαι.

μετᾰ-μάζιον, ntr., (μαζός), στῆθος, on the breast, *between the nipples*, in the middle of the breast, Ε 19†.

μετ-έμισγον, ipf., fut. -μίξομεν, (μίσγω), *placed* (pine splinters) *in the midst*, σ 310; χ 221, *we will merge* thy possessions *with* those of Odysseus (for subsequent division among us).

μεταμώνια (for -ανεμώνια ?), ntr., vana, irrita, *vain*, *fruitless*; θεῖεν, reddant, Δ 363; v. l. μεταμώλια.

μετᾰ-νάστην, τόν, (ναίω), *new-comer*, *interloper*, inquilinum, Ι 648. (Il.)

μετ-ενίσσετο, ipf., (νίσσομαι), βουλυτόνδε, *passed over* (the meridian) *toward* (his place of unyoking) setting, Π 779.

μετ-αξύ, *between*, Α 156†.

μετᾰ-πανόμενοι (παύω), *resting between whiles*, Ρ 373†.

μετα-πανσωλή (παύω), intermissio, *rest*, *pause*, πολέμοιο, Τ 201†.

μετα-πρεπέ(α) τόν, (πρέπω), *conspicuous among*, ἀθανάτοισιν, eximiam inter immortalium (domos), Σ 370†.

μετα-πρέπω, ει, (tmesis, θ 172), ipf. -έπρεπον, ε(ν) (tmesis, σ 2), ον, (πρέπω), *be prominent among*, excellere, among, τισί, on account of, dat. Π 596, inf. Π 194.

μετα-σεύομαι, ipf. **-εσσεύοντο**, aor. ἔσσυτο, (σεύω, σϜυ-), *hurry after*, Φ 423; τινά, Ψ 389.

μετα-σπών, μετα-σπόμενος, see μεθέπω.

μέτασσαι, αἱ, (μετά), *yearlings*, properly those born in the *middle* one, of the three bearings in the year, *summer lambs*, ι 221†, see δ 86.

μετασσεύομαι, see μετα-σεύομαι.

μετ-έστενον, ipf., (στένω), postmodo deploravi, *lament afterward*, δ 261†.

μετα-στοιχί (στοῖχος), secundum lineam, *in a line*, *in a row*, side by side, Ψ 358 and 757.

μετα-στρέφω, fut. **-στρέψεις**, aor.

subj. στρέψῃ, ωσι, opt. ειε, convertere, K 107, *turn away* his heart *from* anger; O 52, *change* his purpose in conformity to thy and my will; *change* one's ways, O 203; β 67, *reverse* (your fortunes), sending misfortune instead of prosperity; pass. aor. μεταστρεφθείς, έντι, τα, τε, qui corpus convertit, *having turned themselves about*, P 732.

μετ-έθηκεν (τίθημι), κε—, *would not have caused* such a din *among* us, σ 402†.

μετα-τρέπομ(αι), ῃ, εται, τινός, properly, *turn one's self about at=regard, consider*, always with neg., A 160; exc. μετὰ δ' ἐτράπετο, aor., se convertit, *turned himself about*, A 199.

μετα-τροπαλίζεο, ipf., (τροπαλίζω), (non) revertebaris ad me, *turn about*, i. e. thou didst flee *without looking behind thee*, Y 190†.

μετ-αυδάω, only ipf. **ηὔδων**, α, (αὐδή), *spake among*, ἔπεα, Θ 496, α 31, B 109.

μετά-φημι, aor. **μετ-έφη** and **μετέειπον**, έειπ(εν) and έειφ', τοῖσι, *among* (them) he (she) *spoke*, B 411; B 795, allocuta est, not a genuine verse; tmesis, μετὰ ἔειπ., Γ 303, κ 561.

μετα-φραζόμεσθα, prs. 1 pl., (φράζομαι), postea considerabimus, *will afterward consider*, A 140†.

μετά-φρενον, ου, ῳ, and pl. α, of single person, M 428, (φρένες), properly, *behind the diaphragm, the back*.

μετα-φωνέω, ipf. -εφώνεον, ε(ν), (φωνή), τοῖσι, *made my voice heard among them*, κ 67, sc. τοῖσι.

μετ-έασι, from I. μέτ-ειμι.

μετ-έειπ., see μετά-φημι.

I. **μέτ-ειμι** (μέτα = μέτεστι, φ 93), 3 pl. **έασι**, ἔμμεναι = εἶναι, ἰών (tmesis, λ 78), subj. ἔω = εἴω, ἐῃ, fut. ἔσσομαι (tmesis, ἔσσεται, I 131), versari inter, *be among*, τισίν; only B 386, intercedet, *intervene*.

II. **μέτ-ειμι**, εισιν, ipf. tmesis, ᾔει, aor. mid. εισάμενος, (ἰέναι), *go after*, sequor; N 298, *march forth; go* or *ride among*, N 90, P 285.

μετ-εἶπον, etc., see μετά-φημι.

μετ-εισάμενος, see II. μέτ-ειμι.

μετ-είω, ἔμμεναι, see I. μέτ-ειμι.

μετ-έπειτα, *afterward*, Ξ 310, κ 519.

μετ-έρχομαι, εται, όμενος, fut. ελεύσομαι, aor. ἔλθοι, imp. ελθε, part. ελθών, *come upon*, α 229; τισίν, *come among*, α 134; ingruere, irruere, *attack*, λέων ἀγέληφι, μετ' ἐλάφους; στίχας, obire ordines, *pass through to marshal* the ranks, E 461; τινά, *seek for, pursue; πατρὸς κλέος, I go to seek* tidings of my father; ἔργα, *attend to* the farm; γάμοιο, curare.

μετ-έσσυτο, see μετα-σσεύομαι.

μετέω, see I. μέτ-ειμι.

μετ-ήορα, ntr., (ἀείρω), Θ 26, γένοιτο, would *be raised aloft*, would float in the air; into the air, Ψ 369.

μετ-οιχόμενος, η, ipf. ᾤχετο, ἀνὰ ἄστυ, permeare urbem; K 111, *go to seek;* persequi; comitari.

μετ-οκλάζει, *keeps changing his position* (from one knee to the other), N 281†.

μετ' ὄπασσα, (ὀπάζω), *gave* (to accompany them) *at the same time* a leader, κ 204†.

μετ-όπισθ(εν), *behind, in the rear* (toward the west), ν 241; λελειμμένοι, left behind; with gen., pone, *behind*, ι 539.

μετ-οχλίσσειε, aor. opt., (ὀχλίζω), *push back, away* (strictly with a lever), Ω 567.

μετρήσαντες, aor. part., (μετρέω), emensi, *having passed over*, γ 179†.

μέτρον, (α), ntr., *measure, measuring-rod*, M 422; *jar and its contents, measure*, H 471, of wine, of flour; measures of the way = length of the journey, δ 389; *full measure, prime*, ἥβης; ὅρμου, proper mooring-place.

μετ-ώπιον, adj., acc. sing. masc., (μέτ-ωπον), *on the forehead*, Λ 95 and Π 739.

μέτ-ωπον, ῳ, α, ntr., (ὤψ), frons, *forehead*, also *front of helmet*, Π 70.

μεῦ = (ἐ)μοῦ, see ἐγώ.

μέχρι(ς), with gen., tenus, *as far as*, θαλάσσης, N 143, and τέο μ., how long? Ω 128.

μή, negative prohibitory particle, ne: I. where the subject desires to avert something, (1) prohibition, with imp. pres., Π 22, Γ 414; aor., Δ 410, ω 248; subj. aor., E 684 (in threat, A 26; as mild assertion, ε 467); μή τι, do not in any way, true reading in α 315.—(2) exhortation, M 216, μὴ ἴομεν (subj.).—(3) wish, with opt., Γ

160; with ὄφελες, I 698; with inf., B 413; in imprecation, B 259.—(4) solemn promise, fut. indic., K 330; inf., ε 187; protest, indic., O 41; inf., T 261, Ψ 585.—(5) purpose, A 522, α 133.—(6) fear *lest*, ο 12, A 555; with indic. aor., ε 300; in independent clause, A 587; dependent upon other verbs, A 555, K 98, Π 446; in indirect question, K 101.—(7) threat, Ξ 46.—II. where the subject intends to deny the truth of its assertion: (1) in conditional clauses, nisi, *unless*, Γ 374 (invariable, except where an idea not the sentence is denied, cf. si non, Γ 289).—(2) in concessive sentence invariable, εἰ καί and καὶ εἰ, etc.—(3) in relative sentence implying a condition, δ 165; after indefinite general antecedent, B 302.—(4) in temporal clauses implying condition, π 197, N 319.—(5) always with infin.—(6) in interrogations expecting negative answer, num; always ἦ μή, *pray can it be? you don't mean?* ζ 200, ι 405, 406. With other particles: μὴ οὐ, ne non, *lest not*, A 28, 566; μὴ δή, *think not, I pray you*, A 131; μὴ μάν, Θ 512, see μάν. (For place in sentence, see οὐ.)

μηδέ, (1) *but not*, Γ 160.—(2) neque, *and not, nor*, ne—quidem, μηδέ τι, *nor by any means* (in first, second, and fifth foot), Δ 184, Y 121, γ 96. Also doubled, yet not correlative like μήτε—μήτε, but continuative, e. g. *nor—, also not*, Δ 303.

μηδέν, nihil, *nothing*, Σ 500†.

Μηδεσι-κάστη, illegitimate daughter of Priamos, wife of Imbrios, N 173†.

μήδεαι, εται, οίμην, εο, ipf. μήδετ(ο), δονθ' = δοντο, fut. μήσεαι, aor. (ἐ)μήσατ(ο), (μέδων, meditor), B 360, *take counsel for one's self; devise*, τινί τι, Ξ 253; κακά τινι, H 478; ὄλεθρόν τινι, ξ 300, κ 115; λυγρὸν νόστον, γ 132; τινά τι, *prepare for*, Ψ 24, X 395, ω 426; νόστον, parare, γ 160.

I. **μήδεα**, τά, (μέδων, meditor), *plans, counsels;* πυκνά, shrewd; εἰδώς, fertile in plans; πεπνυμένα, prudent; ἄφθιτα, enduring; φίλα, friendly; εὖ φρεσὶν οἶδεν, knows well in her thought, λ 445.

II. **μήδεα** (μαδᾶν, madere), *privy parts*, ζ 129, σ 87. (Od.)

Μηθώνη, home of Philoktetes, B 716.

μηκάομαι, only pf. **μεμηκώς**, μεμᾰκυῖαι, whence ipf. (ἐ)μέμηκον, ι 439; and aor. part. μᾰκών, *shrieking, screaming*, always of wounded animals, exc. σ 98; pf., of hard-pressed game, K 362; elsewh. balare, *bleat.*

μηκάδες, ας, fem., (μηκάομαι), *bleating* (she-goats), ι 124.

μη-κ-έτ(ι), non iam, *no longer*, B 259, 435, γ 240.

Μηκιστεύς, ῆος, έος, (1) son of Talaos, brother of Adrastos, father of Euryalos, B 566, Ψ 678.—(2) son of Echios, companion of Antilochos, slain by Polydamas, acc. -ῆ, O 339, Θ 333, N 422.

Μηκιστηϊάδης = Euryalos, Z 28.

μήκιστον, ους, longissimum, os, *tallest*, H 155; μήκιστα, *finally*, ε 299.

μῆκος, τό, (μᾱκρός), *lofty stature*, υ 71; elsewh. longitudine, *length.*

μήκων, ὁ, *poppy stalk*, Θ 306†.

μηλέαι, ας, pl. fem., (μῆλον), *apple-trees;* in synizesis, ω 340. (Od.)

μηλο-βοτῆρας, τούς, *shepherds*, Σ 529†.

I. **μῆλον**, ῳ, ων, τό, mâlum, *apple*, η 120, I 542.

II. **μῆλον**, ntr., μ 301, ξ 105, *small-cattle, domestic animals;* τί, *a single head;* esp. in pl., *herds of sheep and goats;* ἔνορχα, ἄρσενα, he-goats, rams.

μήλοπα, τόν, *shining white*, η 104†.

μήν (μάν), profecto, *verily, in truth* (never alone); ἦ—, B 291; οὐ—, Ω 52; ἄγε—, *on then*, A 302; καὶ μήν, *and verily*, Ψ 410, π 440; *also in truth*, T 45, λ 582.

μήν, νός, see μείς.

μήνη, ης, (μήν, mensis), *moon*, Ψ 455 and T 374.

μηνιθμόν, τόν, (μηνίω), *wrath*, Π 62 (only Π).

μήνῑμα, τό, (μηνίω), θεῶν, *cause of divine wrath, curse*, X 358.

μῆνις, ιος, ιν, fem., (μαίνομαι), ira, *wrath, rancor*, A 1.

μηνίει, prs., imp. μήνῑ(ε), ipf. (ἐ)μήνῑ(εν), aor. μηνίσας, (μῆνις), irasci, succensere, *be wroth with*, A 422, M 10, ρ 14.

Μήονες, *inhabitants of*, **Μηονίς**, *woman from*, **Μηονίη**, i. e. Lydia, Δ 142, Γ 401, B 864.

μή-ποτε, (1) nunquam, *never*, I 133.—(2) ne unquam, *lest ever*, X 106.

μή που, ne forte, *lest in any way*, Ξ 130, δ 775, τίς, with subj. in threat.

μή πω, with imp., ne (non) iam, *not yet, that not yet*, χ 431, ψ 59, P 422, Σ 134; with opt., ν 123.

μή πως, with subj. or opt.: *that in no way, lest somehow*, ι 102; expressing purpose or fear, with subj., P 95; in indirect question, *whether not*, K 101.

μῆρα, see μηρία.

μηρίνθοιο, ῳ, ον, fem., (μηρύω), *cord*, Ψ 854 (only Ψ).

μηρί(α) and **μῆρ(α)**, τά, (μηρός), *pieces of the flesh of the thighs*, which, together with other pieces, were wrapped in a double layer of fat (πίονα ὠμοθέτησαν), placed upon the altar (ἐπιθεῖναι), and burned, A 40, γ 456.

Μηριόνης, son of Molos, N 249; K 270, from Kreta; θεράπων, of Idomeneus, N 246; ἀτάλαντος Ἐνυαλίῳ, H 166; Ἄρηι, N 528; exploits, N 566, 650, Ξ 514, Π 342, 603.

μηρός, οῦ, όν, ῷ, οί, ούς, masc., femur, *ham, upper fleshy part of the thigh*; "to smite one's thighs" as sign of surprise or excitement, M 162; **ἐξέταμνον μηρία**, they cut out (from the thighs of the victims, sc. μηρῶν) the thigh-pieces, γ 456, q. v.

μηρύσαντο, aor. mid. from μηρύω, *drew up, furled by brailing up*, μ 170†. The process was what it is to-day. (See cut No. 5, Egyptian representation of a Phoenician ship.)

μήστωρα, ε, ες, ας, masc., (μήδομαι), properly, *deviser, preparer*; auctor, μ. φόβοιο, *author* of flight, but E 272, *well understanding* pursuit and flight; μ. ἀυτῆς, *raisers of* battle cry, cf. βοὴν ἀγαθός, elsewh. *counselor*.

Μήστωρ, son of Priamos, Ω 257†.

μήτε — μήτε, nec — nec, neve — neve, *neither—nor*; followed by simple τέ, N 230; μητέ τι, with imp., and do not, K 249, ξ 387.

μήτηρ, έρος, έρι, έρα, (ἐρ' ἐμὴν and ἐνί, ψ 113), voc. μῆτερ, acc. pl. έρας; also **μητρός**, ρί, mater, *mother*, of men, Δ 130, α 215; of animals, κ 414; freq. with epithets, πότνια, αἰδοίῃ, κεδνή; with μήλων = *producing, abounding in* sheep, Λ 222; — θηρῶν, in wild-beasts, Θ 47.

μήτῐ, see μήτις. **μήτῑ**, see μῆτις.

μητιάω, 3 pl. **μητιόωσι**, part. όωντι, ες, όωσι, όωσα, mid. prs. άασθε, ipf. μητιόωντο, (μῆτις), *deliberate*, H 45; *conclude*, βουλάς; *devise*, τί, κακά, νόστον τινί; Σ 312, κακά, male suadenti; mid., *debate with one's self, consider*.

μητίετα (μητίομαι), only of Ζεύς and Ζεῦ at close of verse, *all-wise, counselor*, A 175, 508.

μητιόεντα (μῆτις) φάρμακα, *helpful* herbs, δ 227†.

μητίομαι, fut. **ίσομαι**, aor. ισαίμην, ίσασθαι, (μητίομαι, μῆτις), *devise*, τινί τι, τινά τι; cf. μήδομαι, *perpetrate against* one.

μητιόωσα, όωσι, see μητιάω.

μῆτις, ῐς, ῑ, ῑν, fem., (metior), consilium, (1) *shrewdness, wisdom*, μῆτιν ἀτάλαντος, equal in *insight* to the gods. —(2) *proposal, plan*, P 634; ὑφαίνειν, think out, H 324, δ 678.

μήτῐς, **μήτῐ**, nullum, X 120, ν 46; usually separated, μή τι, e. g. with imp., *by no means*; also with subj. and inf. In most cases the force of the two words μή and τις, which are usually separated by a word, may be separately given, X 358, ν 229, Δ 234.

μητρο-πάτωρ, *one's mother's father*, Λ 224†.

μητρυιή, ῆς, noverca, *step-mother*, N 697. (Il.)

μητρώϊον δῶμα, materna domus, *maternal* home, τ 410†.

μήτρως, acc. ωα, avunculus, *maternal uncle*, Π 717. (Il.)

μηχανόωντας, part. pr. (for άοντας), mid. prs. -όωνται, opt. όῳτο, ipf. μηχανάασθε, όωντο, (μηχανή), *set at work, perpetrate*, σ 143; mid. in similar signif., also *devise*, π 134, τινὶ κακά.

μῆχος, τό, *help, remedy*, B 342.

Μῄων, see Μῄονες. **μία**, see εἷς.

μιαίνω, aor. subj. **μιήνῃ**, pass. pr. μιαίνεσθαι, ipf. μιαίνετο, aor. 3 pl. ἐμίανθεν and άνθησαν, *dye, stain*, Δ 141; pass., inquinari, *be soiled* (with blood and dust).

μῐαι-φόνος, ε, cruore inquinatus, *blood-stained*, Ares, E 31. (Il.)

μῐᾰρός (μιαίνω), cruore inquinatus, *stained*, Ω 420†.

μῑγαζομένους, part. prs., (*μίγνυμι*), *φιλότητι*, *united* in love, θ 271†.

μίγδᾰ, adv., (*μίγνυμι*), *promiscuously*, *θεοῖσι*, Θ 437; *together*, ω 77.

μίγνυμι, aor. inf. **μῖξαι,** pass. pf. *μεμιγμένον, οι, η, α*, plupf. *ἐμέμικτο*, aor. (*ἐ*)*μίχθη*, 3 pl. *ἔμιχθεν*, inf. *θήμεναι*, part. *θείς*, aor. 2 *ἐμίγην, ης, η, μίγη, ησαν*=*μίγεν*, subj. *ῇης, ἑωσι*, opt. *είην, ης, η, μιγεῖεν*, inf. *ήμεναι* and *ῆναι*, part. *έντα, εῖσα*, fut. *μιγήσεσθαι*, mid. fut. *μίξεσθαι*, aor. *ἔμικτο, μίκτο*; moreover, pass. **μίσγεαι,** *εται, ηται, έμεναι* and *εσθ(αι), εμένων*, ipf. *μίσγετο, όμεθ(α), οντο*, and iter. *μισγέσκετο, ἐμισγέσκοντο*, miscere, *mix*, *οἶνον καὶ ὕδωρ*; also wine with wine, Γ 270; *ἅλεσσι*, with salt; *γλῶσσα*, *mixed* language; pass., *come in contact*, with dat., *ἔγκασι*, *κονίῃ*; *have relations with*, *ξενίῃ*, *hold intercourse* in guest friendship, with dat., also *ἐν τισι, ἔς τινας*; also, *come into hostile relations with*, *τινί, παλάμῃσί τινος, ἐν δαΐ*; *be united in sexual intercourse*, esp. (*παρά*) *τινί*, with one; *φιλότητι καὶ εὐνῇ*, also *ἐν φιλότητι* or *εὐνῇ*, or *ἐν ἀγκοίνῃσί τινος*; Ο 33, *ἣν ἐμίγης*, whose embraces thou hast enjoyed.

Μίδεια, town in Boiotia on Lake Kopais, Β 507†.

μῑκρός, parvus, *small, little*; *δέμας*, in bodily stature, Ε 801; comp. **μείων,** minor; *κεφαλῇ*, *less* in stature, or *shorter* by a head, Γ 193.

μίκτο, *μῖκτο*, see *μίγνυμι*.

Μίλητος, (1) Ionian city in Karia, Β 868.—(2) city in Kreta, mother-city of foregoing, Β 647.

μιλτο-πάρῃοι (*μίλτος*, "vermilion," *παρειή*), *red-cheeked*, painted red on sides or bows, Β 637, ι 125.

Μῖμας, *ντος*, promontory in Asia Minor opposite Chios, γ 172†.

μιμνάζειν, inf. prs., (*μίμνω*), permanere, *remain*, Β 392 and Κ 549.

μίμνησκ(ε), imp. prs., fut. *μνήσει*, aor. *ἔμνησας, ήσῃ, ήσασα*, (*μένω*, mens), commonefacere, *remind*, *τινά τινος*; mid. prs., fut. *μνήσομαι*, etc., aor. *ἐμνήσατο, μνήσαντο*, opt. -*σαίατο*=*σαίαθ'*, imp. *μνῆσαι, ασθαι*, etc., iter. *μνησάσκετο*; moreover from *μνάομαι*, prs. **μνωομένω,** *ῳ*, ipf. *μνώοντ(ο)*, (1) *bethink one's self of, provide for*, with gen., *περί*, η 192; *φύγαδε*, think on flight.—(2) memorare, *mention*, *μνησθῆναί τινος*, δ 118.—(3) pf. *μέμνημαι*, (*σ*)*αι* and *ῃ, ητ(αι)*, etc., subj. *ὠμεθα*, opt. *ῇμην, ἐῳτο*, plupf. *μεμνήμην, ητο*, 3 fut. *μεμνήσομαι, ήσεσθαι*, meminisse, *remember*, *τινός* and *τινά, τί*; σ 267, curare, *care for*.

μίμνω, only prs. (part. *μιμνόντεσσι*, etc.) and ipf., also unaugmented *μίμνομεν, ον*, (*μι-μένω*), manere, permanere, *withstand*, enemy, rain, wind; exspectare, *await*, *ἠῶ*, π 367.

μῑν, Κ 347 *μῖν*, enclit., (for *ιμιμ*, old Lat. emem), eum, eam, id, ζ 48, Γ 232; never reflexive, δ 244; never for pl., ρ 268, κ 212.

Μῑνυείῳ (*ηιῳ*), *ειον*, *Minyeian*, from ancient stem of Minyai in Orchomenos, λ 284 and Β 511.

Μινυήιος, river in Elis, Λ 722.

μῑνύθει, *ουσι*, subj. *ῃ*, ipf. iter. *εσκον*, (*μίνυνθα*), minuo, *lessen, diminish*, Ο 492, ξ 17; minui, δ 467; μ 46, the skin round (the bones) *is wasting*.

μίνυνθα (minus), paullulum, *a little while*; *περ οὔτι μάλα δήν*, nor was it long=was quickly over, χ 473.

μῑνυνθάδιος, *ῳ, ον, οι*, comp. -*διώτερον*, Χ 54 (*μίνυνθα*), *brief* (of pain, life), Ο 612.

μῑνύριζε, imp. prs., ipf. 3 pl. *μινύριζον*, (*μινυρός*), *whimper, whine, moan*, Ε 889 and δ 719.

Μίνως, *ωος, ωα*, and *ω*, son of Zeus and of Europa; ruler in Knosos in Kreta, Ν 450; father of Deukalion and of Ariadne, λ 322; rules over his subjects in lower world, λ 568 sqq.

μισγ-άγκειαν, *τήν*, (*ἄγκος*), *meeting of mountain glens, basin*, Δ 453†.

μίσγω, see *μίγνυμι*.

μίσησε, aor. from *μισέω*, Ρ 272†, *suffered not* that he should—.

μισθός, *οῦ, οῖο, ῷ, όν, ούς*, (Ger. Miethe), *wages*, κ 84, σ 358.

μίστυλλε(ν), *ον*, ipf. from *μιστύλλω*, (mutilus), *cut up into bits*, preparatory to roasting flesh on the spit, Α 465.

μῑτον, *τόν*; *παρὲκ* —, forth from the *upright threads of the warp*, Ψ 762†. (See cuts Nos. 63, 129.)

μίτρη, *ης, ην*, fem., *band* or *girdle* round the waist and abdomen, below the *στατὸς θώρηξ*, the exterior of metal plates, the interior lined with wool (see cut No. 36), shorter than the *ζῶμα*, which it covered, while over both and the θώρηξ passed the ζωστήρ. (See cuts Nos. 3, 78.)

μιχθείς, see *μίγνυμι*.

μνάομαι, **μνᾷ**, *άασθαι* and *ᾶται*, *ῶνται*, *άσθω*, *ᾶσθαι*, *ώμενος*, ipf. *μνώμεθ(α)*, *ώοντο*, iter. *μνάσκετ(ο)*, (Ger. minne), *woo*, *γυναῖκα*, *ἄκοιτιν*, *δάμαρτα*, *ω* 125; used also absolutely: *μνωομένω*, etc.; see *μιμνήσκω*.

μνῆμ(α), *τό*, (*μέμνημαι*), *memorial*, *χειρῶν*, from Helen's hands (of her handiwork), *ο* 126.

μνημοσύνη (*μνήμων*) *πυρὸς γενέσθω*, let there be *remembrance* of, let us be mindful of fire, equivalent to a pass. of *μέμνημαι*, Θ 181†.

μνήμων (*μνῆμα*), memor, *φ* 95, and *φόρτου*, *bent on* freight.

μνῆσαι, *μνησάσκετο*, see *μιμνήσκω*.

Μνῆσος, a Paionian, slain by Achilleus, Φ 210†.

μνηστεύειν, prs., aor. part. *-εύσαντες*, (*μνηστή*), *woo*, *δ* 684 and *σ* 277.

μνηστῆρες, *ήρων*, *ῆρσι* and *ήρεσσι(ν)*, *ᾶς*, (*μνηστή*), *suitors*, proci, esp. of Penelope, in number 108, with ten servants, *π* 247.

μνῆστις, *ἡ*, (*μιμνήσκω*), *remembrance*, *δόρπου*, *ν* 280†.

μνηστός, only fem. **μνηστή**, *ῇ*, *ήν*, (*μνάομαι*), *wooed and won*, *wedded*, *ἄλοχος*; opp. *παλλακίς*, *δουρικτήτη*, etc., Ζ 246, *α* 36.

μνηστύος, *ύν*, gen. and acc. from *μνηστύς*, (*μνάομαι*), *wooing*, *courting*, *β* 199. (Od.)

μνωόμενος, *μνώμενος*, *ώοντο*, see *μνάομαι*.

μογέοντες, part., aor. (*ἐ*)*μόγησα*, *ας*, *αν*, *ἐμόγησε(ν)*, subj. *μογήσῃ*, part. *σας*, (*μόγις*), laborare, *toil*, *labor*; part. = aegre, *hardly*, Λ 636; fessum esse, *worn*, with dat. instrum., *ε* 224, also with gen.; and *ἐξ ἔργων*, *tired with* work in the fields; perpeti, *suffer*, *undergo*, *πολλά*, *εἵνεκά τινος* and *ἐπί τινι*, for the sake of.

μόγῐς, aegre, vix, *scarcely* [ῑ, Χ 412], Ι 355.

μόγῳ, *τῷ*, prae labore, *through my toil*, Δ 27†.

μογοσ-τόκος, *οι*, (*τίκτω*), *exciting pains* (of labor), Eilcithyia, Π 187. (Il.)

μόθον, *ον*, masc., (*σμυθ.*), *din of battle*, Η 117; *ἵππων*, of war-chariots.

μοῖρ(α), *ῃ*, *αν*, *αι*, *άων*, *ας*, (*μέρομαι*), pars, then portio, *part*, *portion*, in booty, the feast; *οὐδ᾽ αἰδοῦς μ. ἔχουσιν*, expertes sunt pudoris; then generally *share*, to every thing its share, *τ* 592; *proper share*, *κατὰ μοῖραν*, *suitably*; *ἐν μοίρῃ*, merito; opp. *παρὰ* (*ὑπέρ*, Υ 336) *μοῖραν*; finally, fatum, sors, the *lot in life* assigned to every one at birth, *θανάτου*; *μοῖρά ἐστιν* = *εἵμαρται*, *it is fated*, *ordered by destiny*, with inf.; opp. *ἀμμορίη*, in sense of *good fortune*; *doom*, Ζ 488; last of all, Fatum, *Destiny* as the blind controlling power, recognized even by the gods; plur. only Ω 49.

μοιρη-γενές, voc., *favored by* Μοῖρα at one's birth, *child of destiny*, Γ 182†.

μοιχ-άγρῐ(α), *τά*, (*μοιχός*, *ἄγρα*), *μ. ὀφέλλει*, owes the *fine imposed upon one taken in adultery*, *θ* 332†.

μολεῖν, see *βλώσκω*.

μόλῐβος, *ὁ*, plumbum, *lead*, Λ 237†.

Μολίων, *ονα*, (1) companion of Thymbraios, slain by Odysseus, Λ 322. —(2) **Μολίονε** = *᾽Ακτορίωνε*, Eurytos and Kteatos, Λ 709, 750.

μολοβρός, *όν*, ("filthy pig," so Curtius), *glutton*, as insulting epithet, *ρ* 219 and *σ* 26.

Μόλος, father of Meriones, Κ 269, Ν 249.

μολοῦσα, *μολών*, see *βλώσκω*.

μολπή, *ῆς*, *ῇ*, (*μέλπω*), lusus, *play*, *sport*, with music and dance, *ζ* 101, Α 472; *music* (vocal and instrumental); *dance*, Σ 572.

μολυβδαίνῃ, *τῇ*, (*μόλυβδος*), *piece of lead* attached to fishing-line as sinker, Ω 80†.

μονόω, only **μονωθείς**, *έντα*, part. aor. pass., and **μούνωσε**, aor. act., *propagate the race single*, so that there is in each case but a single heir, *π* 117; pass., *left alone*.

μόριμον (*μόρος*), *decreed by fate*, with inf., Υ 302†.

μορμύρων, *οντα*, part., (*μύρω*), *roaring by*, *ἀφρῷ*, with foam, Σ 403. (Il.)

μορόεντα (*μόρον*), *mulberry-colored* = *dark-colored*, so the old commentators; modern criticism has proposed other explanations, e. g. *shining*, from ΜΑΡ, yet nothing so far conclusive, *σ* 298.

μόρος, *ον*, masc., (1) from *μέρομαι*: *due* (cf. *μοῖρα*, *αἶσα*), *ὑπὲρ μόρον*, Φ

517, *α* 34; fatum, *destiny*, *doom* [λ 409], *π* 421, *υ* 241, Τ 421. —(2) abstract noun corresponding to *βροτός*, mors, *death*, Σ 465, Χ 280, Ω 85.

μόρσιμος, *ον*, ntr., (*μόρος*), *ἐστιν* (*ἦεν*), is (was) *ordered by fate*, with inf., Τ 417, Ε 674; also of persons, *destined to death*, Χ 13, to marriage, *π* 392; *ἦμαρ*, day of death, Ο 613.

Μόρυς, *υος*, son of Hippotion, Ν 792; a Mysian, slain by Meriones, Ξ 514.

μορύσσω. pf. pass. part. **μεμορυγμένα** or **-χμένα,** foedata, *stained*, *ν* 435†.

μορφή, *ήν*, venustas, *grace*, of speech; fills his words with grace, *θ* 170. (Od.)

μόρφνον, *swamp-eagle*, (*μορφνός*), or (cf. *ὄρφνη*) *dark-colored* (?), Ω 316†.

μόσχοισι, recentibus, *fresh*, *tender*, see *λύγοισι*, Λ 105†.

Μούλιος, (1) an Epeian, slain by Nestor, Λ 739.—(2) a Trojan, slain by Patroklos, Π 696.—(3) a Trojan, slain by Achilleus, Υ 472.—(4) a native of Dulichion, herald of Amphinomos, *σ* 423.

μουνάξ, adv., (*μοῦνος*), *singly*, *θ* 371.

μοῦνος, *ου*, *ῳ*, *ον*, *οι*, *η*, (*μόνος*), solus, *alone*, Α 467; unicus, *single*, *β* 365; *desolate*, *forsaken*, desertus, *κ* 157.

Μοῦσ(α), *αι*, *άων*, (mens, monere), *Muse*, *Muses*, daughters of Zeus, *θ* 488, Β 598, and of Mnemosyne, dwell in Olympos, Β 484, in number, nine, *ω* 60; sing before the gods, Α 604; *λίγεια*, *ω* 62; and inspire the bard, Α 1, *α* 1, Β 484.

μοχθήσειν, fut. from *μοχθέω*, (*μόχθος*), laboraturum, *will be worn*; *κήδεσι*, curis, Κ 106†.

μοχθίζοντα, part. from *μοχθίζω*, (*μόχθος*), *suffering*, c vulnere, Β 723†.

μοχλέω, ipf. **ἐμόχλεον,** (*μοχλός*), *heave up* (with levers), Μ 259†.

μοχλός, *ῷ*, *όν*, *οἶσι*, (moles), *lever*, *hand-spike*, not roller, *ε* 261; (in *ι*) *stake*.

Μύγδων, *ονος*, king of Phrygia, Γ 186†.

μῦδᾰλέας, acc. pl. fem., (madeo), madidas, *dripping* (with blood), Λ 54†.

Μύδων, *ωνος*, (1) son of Atymnios, charioteer of Pylaimenes, slain by Antilochos, Ε 580. —(2) a Paionian, slain by Achilleus, Φ 209.

μῦελόεντα, ntr., (*μυελός*), medullosa, *full of marrow*, *ι* 293†.

μῦελός, *όν*, masc., medulla, *marrow*, Υ 482; *ἀνδρῶν*, *β* 290, spoken of strengthening food.

μῦθέομαι, pr., and ipf. *ἐμῦθεόμην* (elsewh. unaugmented), iter. *μυθέσκοντο*, in ore habebant, *used to call*, Σ 289; fut. *ἤσομαι*, *σεαι*, aor. *ἤσατο*, etc., (*μῦθος*), *say*, *speak*, Η 76, Χ 184, *α* 124, λ 345; *κερτομίας*, utter taunts; with acc. with inf., Φ 462; *report*, Α 74, λ 328, *β* 202; with *οἷος*, *describe*, *τ* 245; *relate*, *μ* 155; also memorare, *speak of*, λ 517; interpretari, Α 74; *communicate*, *ν* 191.

μῦθο-λογεύειν, narrare, *relate*, *τινί τι*, *μ* 450.

μῦθος, *οιο*, *ου*, etc., dat. pl. *οισ(ιν)*, masc., *speech*, opp. *ἔργον*, Ι 443; oratio, narratio, *δ* 597; sermo, *conversation*, *δ* 214; iussum, *request*, *wish*, *ο* 196; consilium, *counsels*, Α 545; in general signif. = res, *matter*, its circumstances, its occasion; *φ* 71, *demeanor*, *conduct*.

μυίης, *μυῖαν*, *αι*, *άων*, *ας*, musca, *house-fly*, *carrion-fly*, *horse-fly*, the last as symbol of audacity, Ρ 570.

Μῠκᾰλη, promontory in Asia Minor, opp. Samos, Β 869†.

Μῠκᾰλησσός, town in Boiotia, Β 498†.

μῡκάομαι, part. **μυκώμεναι,** aor. 3 sing. *μῦκε*, 3 pl. *μῦκον*, pf. *μεμῡκώς*, plupf. *ἐμεμύκει*, (1) mugio, *bellow*, of cattle; of Skamandros in comparison, Φ 237.—(2) crepare, *creak*, *grate*, of city gates; *resound*, Υ 260.

μῡκηθμοῦ, *ῷ*, masc., mugitus, *lowing*, *bellowing*, Σ 575 and *μ* 265.

Μῠκήνη, daughter of Inachos, *β* 120; eponymous heroine of city **Μῠκήνη** (*-ηθεν*, *from M.*), and *ῆναι*, *Mykene* or *Mykenai*, residence of Agamemnon; the inhabitants **Μυκηναῖοι.**

μῦκον, aor. from *μυκάομαι*.

μῠλάκεσσι, *τοῖς*, *with millstones*, then generally, *mighty stones*, cf. saxis, Μ 161†.

μύλης, *ην*, *αι*, mola, (hand) *mill*, *υ* 106. (Od.) Without doubt, not very different, except that they were of ruder make, from the Roman handmills found in Switzerland, and represented in the cut on next page.

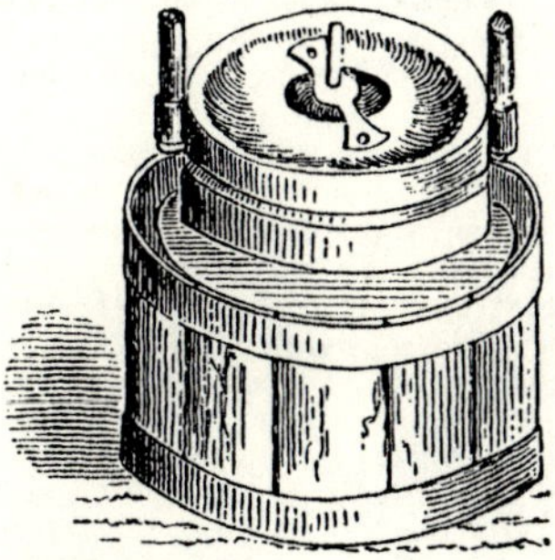

μῦλη-φάτου (*φένω*), *cracked* or *ground in a mill*, *β* 355†.

μῦλο-ειδέϊ (*μύλη*), *like a millstone*, Η 270†.

μύνῃσι, ταῖς, (munio), *through excuses*, *φ* 111†.

Μύνης, *ητος*, son of Euenos, slain by Achilleus, Β 692 and Τ 296.

μυρίκης, *ην*, *ῖκαι* Φ 350, *ησιν*, *tamarisk*, *marsh-shrub* (tamarix gallica Linn.), Κ 466. Hence **μυρίκινῳ** *ὄζῳ*, *tamarisk*-shoot, Ζ 39†.

Μυρίνη, an Amazon, whose funeral mound was called "Thorn-hill," *Βατίεια*, Β 814†.

μυρίον, *ίοι*, *ίαι*, *ίον*, *ί(α)*, innumerus, immensus, *countless*, θ 110, Β 468; *μυρίον*, with gen., immensum, *a vast quantity*, Φ 320.

Μυρμιδόνες, *εσσι*, a Thrakian tribe in Phthiotis, followers of Achilleus, Π 269, Β 684, Α 180, λ 495; their chief centres, Phthia and Hellas.

μύρονται, prs., part. and freq. ipf. 3 pl. *μύρονθ'*, (mare), *flow*, *dissolve in tears*, *lament*, Τ 340; *ἀμφί τινα*, Τ 6.

Μύρσινος, village in Elis, later *τὸ Μυρτούντιον*, Β 616†.

Μυσοί, (1) a tribe on the Danube, Ν 5.—(2) kindred with foregoing, *Mysians* in Asia Minor, occupying territory from River Aisepos to Mount Olympos, Β 858, Κ 430, Ξ 512, Ω 278.

μυχμῷ, *τῷ*, (*μύζω*), fremitus, *moaning*, *ω* 416†.

μυχοίτατος, *φ* 146, postremus, *farthest away from* (the rest); more common **μυχός**, *ῷ*, *όν*, (**ὅνδε**, *χ* 270), *ούς*, *rear portion*, *inner part*, of hall, house, cave, harbors, Φ 23; hence *μυχῷ*, *in the farthest*, *innermost corner of*, penitus, *κλισίης*, *Ἄργεος*, *σπείους*.

μύω, aor. 3 pl. **μῦσαν**, *have closed*, Ω 637†.

μυών, nom. sing., gen. pl. *ώνων*, masc., (*μῦς*, mus-culus), *mass of muscle*, *muscles*, Π 315, 324.

μῶλος, *ον*, masc., *tumult of battle*, Ρ 397; freq. with *Ἄρηος*, moil of war, Η 147.

μῶλυ, *τό*, *moly*, a magic herb, given by Hermes to Odysseus, to shield him against the spells of Circe, *κ* 305†. Identified by the ancients as a kind of *garlic* (allium nigrum Guan.).

μωμεύῃ, subj. prs. from *-εύω*, *ζ* 274†, and **μωμήσονται**, fut. from *-έομαι*, Γ 412†, vituperet, -abunt, *blame*, *reproach* (*μῶμος*).

μῶμον, *τόν*, *μ. ἀνάψαι*, set a *brand of shame* upon us, *β* 86†.

μώνυχες, *ας*, explained by ancient commentators as *μον-όνυχες*, *single-*, *uncloven-hoofed*, solidis ungulis, Ε 236, opp. cattle and sheep; a derivation from *μέμαα*, *eager-*, *quick-footed*, has been proposed by modern scholars.

N.

νῦ ἐφελκυστικόν, affixed to follg. forms: pl. *σι*; *εἴκοσι*; suff. *φι* and *νόσφι*; the particle *κε*; and to forms of the verb ending in *ε* and *ι* of 3d person.

ναί (*νή*, nae, ne), *verily*, Α 286; also with *μά*, q. v.

ναιετάω, part. *άων*, *όωσα*, (*α* 404, Β 648), *άοντα*, prs. and ipf., iter. *ναιετάασκον*, (*ναίω*), habitare, versari, *inhabit, exist,* Λακεδαίμονι, Γ 387; of localities, *are situated, inhabited,* sita est, *dwells,* where the island is conceived as a thing endowed with life = *exists,* α 404; also transitive, Β 539; part. εὖ ναιετάων, etc., *habitable.*

ναίω, prs., (inf. ναιέμεν), and ipf. (iter. ναίεσκε, ον), mid. εὖ ναιόμενον, η, etc., *inhabited, peopled,* of cities, (ναςjω), (1) *dwell,* κατά, περί, πρός τι; ἔν, παρά τινι; αἰθέρι, locat. *enthroned* in the aether; νῆσοι, *lie,* Β 626; trans., *inhabit,* οἰκία, Η 221, υ 288.—(2) 1 aor. νάσσα οἱ πόλιν, δ 174, would have *assigned him* a town *to dwell in;* also 1 aor. pass. 3 sing. νάσθη Ἄργεϊ, sedes posuit, *settled in—,* Ξ 119.

νάκην, τήν, αἰγός, *hairy skin,* ξ 530†.

νάπαι, αἱ, (γναμπτός), *forest glens* or *dells,* Θ 558 and Π 300.

νάρκησε, aor. from ναρκάω, *was palsied,* Θ 328†.

νάσθη, νάσσα, see ναίω.

νάσσω, aor. **ἔναξε,** *stamped down,* γαῖαν, φ 122†.

Νάστης, son of Nomion, leader of Karians, slain by Achilleus, Β 867 sqq.

Ναυβολίδης, *son of Naubolos,* (1) Iphitos, Β 518.—(2) a Phaiakian, θ 116.

ναύ-λοχον, οι, (λεχ, λέκτο), *ship-sheltering,* of harbors, δ 846 and κ 141.

ναύ-μαχα, pl. ntr., navalia, *for naval combat,* of ship-pikes, Ο 389†.

ναῦς, see νηῦς.

Ναυσί-θοος, son of Poseidon, father of Alkinoos, colonizes the Phaiakians in Scheria, η 56 sqq.

Ναυσι-κάα, daughter of Alkinoos, ζ 17 sqq., η 12, θ 457, 464.

ναυσι-κλειτοῖο, navibus clari, *renowned for ships,* intrepid seaman, ζ 22†, = **ναυσι-κλῦτοί,** epithet of Phaiakians and Phoenikians, ο 415.

ναῦται, άων, έων, ῃσι(ν), masc., nautae, *sailors,* Δ 76, θ 162.

Ναυτεύς, a Phaiakian, θ 112†.

ναυτιλίῃ, τῇ, navigatione, *seamanship,* θ 253†.

ναυτίλλεται, subj., εσθαι, inf., (ναυτιλίη), navigat, *sail,* δ 672 and ξ 246.

ναῦφι(ν), see νηῦς.

νάει, ουσι, ipf. (νᾶον, v. l. and better), **ναῖον,** *flow; ὀρῷ, ran over with* whey, ι 222.

Νέαιρα (possibly personification of new moon), name of nymph, mother by Helios of Lampetie and Phaethusa, μ 133†.

νεἄροί (νέος), teněri, *youthful,* Β 289†.

νεάτη, αι, elsewh. **νείατος,** ον, α, (νέος), properly novissimus, always local, extremus, *last,* Β 824; infimum, *lowest;* νείατος ἄλλων, imum e ceteris.

νεβρῷ, όν, οί, ούς, masc., (νέος), *fawn,* Θ 248; ἐλάφοιο, Χ 189; symbol of timorousness, Δ 243.

νέες, εσσι, see νηῦς.

νέηαι, see νέομαι.

νεη-γενέας, τούς, (-γενής), *new-born,* δ 336 and ρ 127.

νε-ήκεσι (ἀκή), *freshly whetted,* Ν 391 and Π 484.

νε-ήλῦδες (ἤλυθον), *newly come,* Κ 434 and 558.

νεηνίῃ, ίαι, adolescenti, *youth;* masc. ἀνδρί, ξ 524; fem. **νεήνιδι,** ισι, *maiden,* η 20, Σ 418.

νεῖαι, see νέομαι.

νειαίρῃ, αιραν, (see νεάτη, from νέος), inferior, *lower;* γαστήρ, lower part of belly, abdomen, Ε 539. (Il.)

νείατος, see νεάτη.

νεικείω, subj. είῃσι, είῃ, inf. ειν, part. ων, ipf. 3 pl. νείκειον, and iter. νεικείεσκε, ον, other forms from νεικέω, 3 pl. **νεικεῦσ(ιν),** imp. νείκεε, ει, inf. εῖν, ipf. νείκεε, (ἐ)νείκεον, iter. νεικε[illegible] fut. νεικέσω, aor. ἐνείκεσας, (ἐ)νείκε[illegible], (νεῖκος), (1) *quarrel,* τινὶ εἵνεκά τινος, ἔριδας καὶ νείκεα ἀλλήλοις, *contend* with railing and strife, Υ 252.—(2) *upbraid, reprove,* opp. αἰνεῖν, Κ 249, Ω 29; freq. with ἐπέεσσιν and with adj., Γ 38, ρ 374; μάλα, angrily; ἄντην, face to face, outright, ρ 239.

νεῖκος, εος, ει, εα, ntr., (νίκη ?), *heat of combat,* Μ 348; πολέμοιο, Ν 271; in general, *strife,* Γ 87; of Trojan war, ἔριδος νεῖκος, Ρ 384; φυλόπιδος, Υ 140; iurgia, *dissensions,* Ξ 205; with ἔρις, υ 267; *quarrel,* Ψ 483; *dispute,* θ 75, Δ 37; lites, *strife at law,* μ 440; *reproof,* Ι 448; *taunt,* Η 95.

νεῖμα = ἔνειμα, aor. from νέμω.

νειόθεν (νέος), *from below,* ἐκ κραδίης, *from the depths of* his heart, Κ 10†, and **νειόθι** λίμνης, *far below in the depths* of the sea, Φ 317†.

νειοῦ, *ῷ*, *όν*, fem., (*νέος*), *new land, fallow land*, land newly ploughed after having lain fallow; thrice ploughed, after such rest, in Σ 541, ε 127.

νεῖται, from *νέομαι*. *νειφέμεν*, v. l. for *νιφέμεν*.

νεκάδεσσιν, *ταῖς*, (*νεκρός*), *heaps of slain*, Ε 886†.

νεκρός, *οῖο*, *οῦ*, *οῖσ(ιν)*, etc., (necare), mortuus, *dead*, *τεθνηῶτα*, μ 10; *corpse*, Ψ 197, Δ 467; also with (*κατα*) *τεθνηῶτες*, Ζ 71, Σ 540.

νέκτᾰρ, *αρος*, (*νη-κτείνω*), *nectar*, reddish, fragrant drink of the gods, Δ 3; preserves from decay, Τ 38; *ἀπόρρωξ*, lit. "fragment," sample of nectar, i. e. wine of the choicest sort, ι 359.

νεκτᾰρέου, *ῳ*, (*νέκταρ*), Γ 385, Σ 25, *fragrant, perfumed with nectar.*

νέκῡς, *ῦος*, *υι*, *ῦν*, *ῦες*, *ύων*, *ύεσσι(ν)*, *ῦσιν*, *ῦας*, *ῦς*, (necare), = *νεκρός*, mortuus, *dead*, as subst., Ψ 160, 168, 190, Ν 509; *κατατεθνηῶτες*, Η 409, λ 37, κ 530; *corpse*, Ω 108.

νεμέθοντο, ipf., pascebantur, *were feeding*, Λ 635†.

νεμεσῶ, subj. *ῇσι*, imp. *α*, *ᾶτον*, aor. *νεμέσησαν*, subj. *σήσῃ*, fut. mid. *σήσεαι*, *σήσετ(αι)*, verbal adj. *σητός*, also **νεμεσσῶμαι**, *σσᾶται*, ipf. *ἐνεμέσσα*, aor. mid. *σσήσαιτο*, aor. pass. *νεμεσσήθη*, *θητε*, *θεν*, Β 223; *θωμεν*, *θείς*, *θεῖσα*, verbal adj. *σσητόν*, (*νέμεσις*), *take it ill, be vexed with*, *τινί* (*τι*), ζ 286, Ψ 494; indignari, *be angry with*, with part. φ 169, with *οὕνεκα*; mid., indignari (esp. aor. pass.), *become angry*, *τί*, *τινί*; with relative, α 158, or infin. clause, irasci; verbal adj., *causing indignation, reprehensible*, iniquum; only Λ 649, magni faciendus, reverendus, *to be dreaded.*

νεμεσίζομ(αι), only sing. prs. (imp. *-ζέσθω*), and ipf. *νεμεσίζετο*, (*νέμεσις*), magni facere, revereri, *dread, fear*, *θεούς*; *be wroth with for*, *τινί τι*, Ε 757; followed by acc. and inf., Β 296; *be ashamed*, Ρ 254, β 138.

νέμεσις, *έσσῑ* Ζ 335, *ιν*, fem., ignominia, *disgrace*, Ν 122, Ζ 351; (*ἐξ*) *ἀνθρώπων*, *censure* of men; *οὐ νέμεσις*, non vituperandum, 'tis no cause for anger.

νεμεσσάω, *σσητόν*, see *νεμεσῶ*, **νεμέσσ(ε)ι**, see *νέμεσις*.

νέμεϊ, *τῷ*, ntr., (*νέμεσθαι*), *wood-pasture, glade*, Λ 480.

νέμει, prs., ipf. *νέμε*, *ἔνεμον*, aor. *ἔνειμε*, *νεῖμεν*, *αν*, imp. *νεῖμον*, (1) distribuere, *dispense*, *τινί τι*, ζ 188.—(2) pascere, *drive to pasture*, ι 233; pass. *νέμοιτο*, consumeretur, *was consumed*, only Β 780; mid. (1) pasci, *feed, browse, graze*, *νέμεαι*, *ονται*, *εσθαι*, Ε 777, υ 164; (2) frui, *feed one's self upon, possess*, *νέμεται*, *όμεσθ(α)*, subj. *ηαι*, opt. *οιτο*, Ζ 195, Ψ 177.—(3) incolere, *inhabit*, *νέμονται*, *ἐνέμοντο*, Υ 8, Β 496, 751.

νένιπται, see *νίζω*.

νεο-αρδέ(α), acc. (*ἄρδω*), *freshly watered*, Φ 346†.

νεο-γῑλῆς, *new-born*, *σκύλακος*, μ 86†.

νεό-δαρτον (*δείρω*), *newly flayed*, χ 363†.

νεο-θηλέα, acc. (*θάλλω*), *fresh-sprouting*, Ξ 347†.

νεοίη (*νέος*), adolescentia, *youth, youthful thoughtlessness*, Ψ 604†.

νέομαι and *νεῦμαι*, *νεῖαι*, *νεῖται*, *νέονται*, subj. *νέηαι*, *ηται*, *ώμεθ(α)*, opt. *νεοίμην*, *μεθα*, *οίατο*, imp. *νεέσθω*, *σθων*, inf. *νεόμην*, *νέοντο*, (*νεσομαι*, *νισσομαι*), often with fut. signif., (1) redire, *return*, *οἰκόνδε*, λ 176, ο 72, σ 241, ω 460, Μ 32, *κὰρ ῥόον*.—(2) ire, *go*, Υ 6, Ξ 335, δ 8, ξ 261; venire, *come*, χ 484; *ὑπὸ ζόφον*, Ψ 51.—(3) abire, *go away*, φ 374.

νέον, see *νέος*.

νεο-πενθέα (*πένθος*), *fresh-mourning*, *θυμόν*, λ 39†.

νεό-πλῡτα (*πλύνω*), *newly washed*, ζ 64†.

νεο-πρίστου (*πρίω*), *fresh-sawn*, θ 404†.

Νεο-πτόλεμος, son of Achilleus, educated in Skyros, Τ 327; conducts the Myrmidons home from Troja, weds Hermione, daughter of Menelaos, γ 189, δ 5; slays Eurypylos, λ 520.

νέος, *οιο*, *ου*, etc., no dat. pl., *νέην*, *αι*, *νέον*, *α*; comp. **νεώτερος**, *ου*, *ῳ*, *ον*, *ω*, *οι*; sup. *νεώτατος*, *η*, (novus, new), novus, recens, *new, fresh*, opp. *παλαιοί*, δ 720, θ 58; adolescens, *young* (*ἑταῖροι*), Α 463; also substantively, τ 433, Ι 36, θ 202; *νέον*, nuper, *just now, lately*, π 181, 199.

νεός, see *νηῦς*.

νεο-σμήκτων (σμάω), *freshly polished*, N 342†.

νεοσσοί, οἶσι, (νέος), pulli, *young* (birds), B 311, I 323.

νεό-στροφον (στρέφω), *newly twisted*, νευρήν, O 469†.

νεο-τεύκτου (τεύχω), *newly wrought*, κασσιτέροιο, Φ 592†.

νεο-τευχέες, pl. from -τευχής, (τεύχω), *newly made*, E 194†.

νεότητος, τηςִ, (νέος), adolescentia, *youth*, Ξ 86, Ψ 445.

νε-ουτάτου, ον, (οὐτάω), *lately wounded*, Σ 536, N 539.

νέ-ποδες (νέω), *web-footed*, lit. "swim-footed;" or better, with Curtius, *offspring*, cf. Lat. nepos, δ 404†.

νέρθε(ν), adv., (ἔνερος), *below*, H 212, Λ 535; with gen., *under*, γῆς, λ 302.

Νεστόρεος, adj. from Νέστωρ, Θ 192, 113, B 54.

Νεστορίδης, *son of Nestor*, (1) Antilochos, O 589.—(2) Peisistratos, δ 71, ο 6, 44, 202; pl. Antilochos and Thrasymedes, Π 317.

Νέστωρ, ορος, son of Neleus and Chloris, king in Pylos, Γερήνιος ἱππότα, B 336; ὁ γέρων, Λ 637; ttisecli senex, survivor of three generations of men, A 247 sqq.; λιγὺς Πυλίων ἀγορητής, A 248, Δ 293; his youthful exploits, Δ 319, Λ 669 sqq., A 262 sqq., Ψ 630 sqq.; after the Trojan war, again in Pylos, γ 17, cf. 412 sqq.

νεῦμαι = νέομαι.

νευρή, ῆς, ῆφι(ν), ῇ, ήν, fem., (σνευρή, Schnur), *bow-string*, Δ 118, Θ 300.

νεῦρον, α, ntr., (νερϝον, nervus), *sinew, tendon*, of body, Π 316; *bow-string*, Δ 122; *cord*, with which the arrow-head was bound to the shaft, Δ 151.

νευστάζων, part. prs., (νεύω), *nodding*, Υ 162; κεφαλῇ, *letting* the head *droop*; ὀφρύσι, *giving a sign by nodding* with the eyebrows, innuens, μ 194.

νεύσιεν, οντα, όντων, ipf. ἔνευε and νεῦον, aor. νεῦσ(εν), from νεύω, nuo, *nod*; capite, π 283, I 223, N 133; annuit, promisit, *assent* or *promise by a nod*, Θ 246; but κεφαλάς, demittere, *let* their heads *hang down*; often also of helmet, of plume, *nod*, Γ 337, χ 124.

νεφέλη, ῃ, ην, αι, άων, ῃσι(ν), ας, fem., (κνεφ., nebula), nubes, *cloud*; ἄχεος, grief's *dark cloud* enshrouded him, P 591.

νεφελ-ηγερέτα, nom., (ἀγείρω), Ζεύς, Zeus, *the cloud-compeller, cloud-gatherer*, A 511, α 63.

νέφος, εϊ, εα, έων, (ἑ)εσσι(ν), ntr., (κνέφας, δνοφερός, nebula), nubes, *cloud*, Δ 275; θυόεν, fragrant, O 153; ἀχλύος, dark mist; θανάτου μέλαν ν., death's gloomy cloud, Π 350, δ 180; the gods have at control red, blue, black, and golden clouds. *Thick cloud, company*, Ψ 133, P 755.

I. **νέων**, ipf. ἔννεον, (σνεϝω), nare, *swim*, Φ 11, ε 344.

II. νέω, aor. mid. **νήσαντο**, (nere), *have spun* to him with the thread, η 198†.

νη-, negative prefix, as in Lat. neuter, nemo, noenum (nenum), nullus.

νῆα, νηάδε, see νηῦς.

νη-γάτεον, ῳ, (νέον, γέγαα), *newmade*, B 43 and Ξ 185.

νήγρετος, ον, (νη, ἐγείρω), *without waking*, εὕδειν; ὕπνος, *deep*, ν 80.

νηδυίοισι, τοῖς, ntr., (νηδύς), intestinis. *bowels*, P 524†.

νή-δυμος, ον, ὕπνος, *fast, deep sleep*, B 2, ν 79; derivation doubtful, possibly from δύη, "pain," i. e. *painless, refreshing without pain*; yet see Curtius.

νηδύος, νηδὺν, fem., *belly, stomach*, N 290, ι 296; *womb*, Ω 496.

νῆες, νήεσσι, see νηῦς.

νηέω, ipf. **νήει**, νήεον, aor. νήησαν, ῆσαι, ήσας, (νέω), *heap* or *pile up*, Ψ 139; upon wagon or car, ἐπ' ἀπήνης; *fill with cargo*, I 358, and mid. νηησάσθω, σασθαι νῆα, fill one's ship with cargo.

Νηιάς, αδες, κοῦραι Διός, ν 104, 356, *Naiads*, pl. from **Νηίς**, Υ 384, Z 22.

Νήιον, spur of Mount Neriton in Ithaka, α 186†.

νήϊον (νηῦς), with and without δόρυ, *ship-timber*, Γ 62, ι 384.

νηίς, see Νηιάς.

νῆϊς, ἴδα, (νη-ἰδμεναι), ignarus, *unpracticed in*, ἀέθλων, θ 179; absol., *inexperienced*, H 198.

νη-κερδέα, δέι, (κέρδος), *useless*, P 469, ξ 509.

νηκούστησε, aor. from νηκουστέω, (νη-ἀκουστός), οὐδ' — θεᾶς, nor did he *disobey* the goddess, Υ 14.

νηλεής, sync. **νηλής**, *νηλεῖ, έα*; *εές*, (*νη-ἔλεος*), *pitiless, ruthless*, often *relentless*, fig. of *θυμός, ἦτορ, δεσμῷ, χαλκῷ, ἦμαρ*, day of death, *ὕπνῳ*, *irresistible*, μ 372.

Νηλείδης, Nestor, Ψ 652 = *Νηληϊάδης*.

νηλείτιδες, fem. from *νη-άλείτης*, *guiltless, innocent*, π 317; v. l. *νηλῖτεῖς*.

Νηλεύς, *ῆος*, son of Poseidon and of Tyro, husband of Chloris, λ 254, 281; father of Pero, ο 233, and of Nestor; driven by his brother Pelias from Iolkos in Thessaly, he wanders to Messenia and founds Pylos, γ 4; in war with Herakles, all his twelve children were slain except Nestor, Λ 692; who is called **Νηληιάδης**, Θ 100, Ο 378, Λ 618; **Νηλήιος**, *Neleian*, Ψ 514, Λ 597, Β 20.

νηλής, see word before *Νηλείδης*.

νηλιτεῖς, see *νηλείτιδες*.

νῆμα, **νήματος**, *τα*, ntr., (II. *νέω*), *that which is spun, yarn*, β 98. (Od.)

νημερτής, *έ(α), ές*, adv. *έως*, (*ἁμαρτάνω*), *unerring, infallible*, verax; *νόος*, candidus; ntr. with *εἰπεῖν*, etc., verum (a) dicere, speak the *truth*, γ 101.

Νημερτής, *ἡ*, a Nereid, Σ 46†.

νηνεμίη, *ης*, fem. from **νήνεμος**, Θ 556, (*νη-ἄνεμος*), *windless, breezeless*; also as subst., *calm*, Ε 523, ε 392.

νηός, *ῷ, όν, ούς*, masc., (*ναίω*), *dwelling of a god, temple*, Α 39, ζ 10; for an idea of the interior of the cella, cf. cut under *βωμός*, with statue of Aphrodite and altar.

νηός, gen. from *νηῦς*.

νη-πενθές (*πένθος*), *soothing sorrow*, epith. of Egyptian magic drug which lulled sorrow for a day (Opium?), δ 221†.

νηπιάας, see *νηπιέη*.

νηπιᾰχεύων (*νηπίᾰχος*), *playing childishly*, Χ 502†.

νηπίᾰχον, *οι, οις*, (*νήπιος*), *childish*, Β 338.

νηπιέη, *έῃσι(ν), άας*, (*νήπιος*), *infancy*, Ι 491; *childish follies*, α 297.

νήπιος, *ον, ε, οι*; *η*; *α*, (*νη-πυ*, im-pu-bes, puer?), *young; offspring*, Ρ 134; common phrase, *ν. τέκνα*, also of animals; *foolish, blind*, Β 873; with *αὕτως*, so young! Ζ 400; *infantile, feeble*, *βίη*.

νή-ποινοι (*ποινή*), inulti, *unavenged*, α 380, β 145; *νήποινον*, impune, *with impunity*, α 160.

νη-πῡτίον, *ι(ε), ιοι, ίοισιν*, *children*, Υ 244; *foolish*, Υ 211.

Νηρηΐδες, *Nereids*, Σ 38, 49, 52, the daughters of Nereus, the old man of the sea, who is never mentioned in Homer by name, but only as *ἅλιος γέρων*, Α 538.

Νήρικον, orig. a promontory on the coast of Akarnania; later, by cutting through an isthmus, the island of Leukas; subjugated by Laertes, ω 377†.

Νήρῐτον, mountain in northern part of Ithaka, ν 351, Β 632, ι 22.

Νήρῐτος, an Ithakan, ρ 207†.

νήριτος, see *εἰκοσι-νήριτ'*.

Νησαίη, a Nereid, Σ 40†.

νῆσος, *ου, ῳ, ον, οι, ων, οισι(ν), ους*, fem., (*νέω*, nare), *island*, α 85, Β 108.

νήστιες, *ῐας*, (*νη-ἔδω*), *not eating, fasting*, σ 370. (Od.)

νητός, adj., (*νέω, νηέω*), *piled up*, β 338†.

νηῦς, νηός, *ἰ* (dat. of accompaniment, λ 161), *α, ες, ῶν, εσσι*, and *νηυσί, ας*, and *νηάδε*; also *τὴν νέα*, pl. *νέες, ῶν, εσσιν*, and *ναῦφιν, νέας* (*νέω*, nare), navis, *ship*; its parts, as named in Homer (see cut under *ἔδᾰφος*), are as follows: of the hull, *τρόπις, πρῴρη, πρύμνη, ἐπηγκενίδεσσι, πηδάλιον, οἰήϊα, ἱστός, ἱστοπέδη, ἱστοδόκη, ζυγά, κληῖδες, κώπη, ἐρετμά, τροπός*; of the rigging, *ἱστία, πείσματα, πόδες, ἐπι-* and *πρότονος, πρυμνήσια*; see these words separately. When the word stands alone, *ship of war* is commonly implied; *ν. φορτίδος*, *ship of burden*, ε 250, ι 323; pl. *νῆες*, freq. signifies in Iliad *camp*, including *νῆες* and *κλισίαι*, Β 688. (See also plate IV., at end of volume.)

νηχέμεναι, inf. prs., ipf. *νῆχε, ον*, and **νηχόμενος**, *οι, οισι*, fut. *νήξομ(αι)*, (*σνήχω*), natare, *swim*, ε 375. (Od.)

νίζειν, imp. *νίζ(ε)*, ipf. *νίζε, ον*, and mid. *νίζετο*, fut. *νίψω, ει*, aor. *νίψ(εν)*, imp. *νίψον*, mid. aor. *νίψατο, ασθαι, άμενος, οι*, (*νίγjω, νιβ*), lavare, *wash*, *τινὰ πόδας*, the hands and feet for some one, *τὶ ἀπό τινος*, abluere, *wash off*; mid. *wash one's self*; *χεῖρας*, wash one's hands; with dat. of place (locative), Π 229; *ἁλός*, with water from the sea; χρόα ἅλμην, washed off from his body the salt sea-spray, ζ 224; pass. νένιπται αἷμα, the blood is washed off.

νικᾷς, ᾷ, etc., prs., ipf. (ἐ)νίκα, (ἐ)νίκων, iter. νικάσκομεν, fut. νικήσει, ουσι, ἔμεν, aor. ἐνίκησα, ας, ε, and νίκησα, etc., pass. aor. νικηθείς, θέντι, (νίκη), vincere, *conquer*, with dat. of manner; *surpass, excel*, with dat. of means; *vanquish, be superior to*, τινά τινί, e. g. ἀγορῇ, κάλλεϊ, μάχῃ, πόδεσσι, πύξ; phrases: Ψ 604, youth got the better of judgment; λ 545, gain a victory; σ 319, shall not outwatch me.

νίκη, only in sing., *victory*, in battle and before the tribunal, λ 544; νίκης πείρατα, H 102, cords of victory.

Νιόβη, daughter of Tantalos, wife of Amphion, king of Thebes. She exultingly compared her twelve children with the two (Apollo and Artemis) of Leto, and was punished by the death of all her children: the six sons by the arrows of Apollo; the daughters by the arrows of Artemis, while she herself, in grief at their death, was changed to stone. The legend arose from a natural rock-figure in Mount Sipylos, which resembles a woman in sitting posture, Ω 602, 606.

νίπτω, see *νίζω*.

Νιρεύς, ῆος, son of Charopos and Aglaïa of Syme, the most beautiful of the Greeks next to Achilleus, B 671 sqq.

Νῖσα, village on Mount Helikon in Boiotia, B 508†.

Νῖσος, son of Aretos, father of Amphinomos of Dulichion, π 395, σ 127, 413.

νίσομαι, νίσσεται, ὀμεθα, ὀμενον, ipf. νίσσοντο, (νέσjομαι), ire, *go*, πόλεμόνδε, into the combat; abire, M 119; redire, οἴκαδε.

Νίσυρος, small island, one of the Sporades, B 676†.

νιφάς, ἄδες, ἄδεσσι, fem., (σνιφ., nives, snow), *snow*, O 170; *flakes*, χιόνος, M 278. (Il.)

νιφετός, όν, (νιφάς), *snow-storm, snows*, nives, K 7 and δ 566.

νιφόεντος, τι, τα, (νιφάς), nivosi, *snow-clad, snow-capped*, N 754, τ 338, Kreta, Olympos, Tmolos, Thrakian mountains.

νιφέμεν, inf., (νιφάς), ningere, *snow*, M 280†. (v. l. νειφέμεν.)

νίψ', νιψάμενος, etc., see νίζω.

νοέω, εις, imp. νόει, part. νοέοντι, ούσῃ, ipf. νόει, fut. νοήσω, εις, ει, aor. ἐνόησα, σας, σ(εν), and νόησα, εν, subj. σῃ, imp. νόησον, inf. νοῆσαι, part. σας, mid. aor. νοήσατο, (γι-γνώ-σκω?), (1) sentire, *perceive, observe, become aware of*, X 136, O 453, Γ 396, π 5; freq. with part., υ 367 and B 391, Γ 21, 30, Δ 200, X 463, δ 653; ὀξὺ ν., *sharply* or *quickly see, discern*, Γ 374; (ἐν) ὀφθαλμοῖς (Ω 294), O 422; coupled with θυμῷ and οἶδα, σ 228; φρεσίν, α 322; *see with mind, discern*, A 343; ἐπεφράσατο, θ 94; ἀθρεῖν, τ 478.—(2) *think*, K 247; ἄλλα, of something else, Ψ 140, 193, β 393; πεπνυμένα πάντα, think always prudent thoughts, σ 230; ἐναίσιμον, η 299.—(3) *imagine, devise*, ρ 576; μῦθον, H 358; νόον, I 104; τεχνήσομαι ἠδὲ ν., Ψ 415.—(4) *ponder, reflect* (ἐν and μετά, γ 26, Υ 310), φρεσί, O 81; μετὰ φρ. καὶ κατὰ θυμόν, Υ 264; with ὅππως, ο 170, K 224; νοέων, π 136, ρ 193; *prudent, discreet*, A 577, Ψ 305.—(5) *be minded, intend*, φρεσί, with inf., X 235, Ω 560; τί, A 543.—(6) *think of, remember to*, with inf., E 665, cf. ι 442; οὐ ν., with inf. (mid. only K 501), I 537, λ 62, with subst. clause, Υ 264, X 445, *nor did* she think.

νόημα, ατος, τι, τα, σι, (νοέω), *that which is thought, thought*, β 363; *idea*, H 456, abstract, η 36; *plan*, P 409; *wish*, K 104, Σ 328; *schemes*, β 121; *reason*, υ 346, T 218; *disposition, character*, ζ 183, Ω 40, η 292, σ 215; *sense, heart*, υ 82.

νοήμονες (νοεῖν), *discreet*, β 282, ν 209. (Od.)

Νοήμων, ονος, (1) a Lykian, slain by Odysseus, E 678.—(2) son of Phronios in Ithaka, δ 630, β 386.—(3) a Pylian, Ψ 612.

νόθος, ον, ην, (ἄνθος, ἐνήνοθε), *illegitimate son*, or, N 173, *daughter*.

νομεύς, ῆες, ῆας, masc., (νέμω), pastor, *shepherd*, O 632; ἄνδρες, P 65.

νομεύων, part., ipf. ἐνόμευε, (νομεύς), pascere, *pasture*, ι 217, 336. (Od.)

Νομίων, father of Nastes and Amphimachos of Karia, B 871†.

νομός, οῦ, ῷ, όν, (νέμομαι), pascua, *pasture*, E 587; ἐπέων, fig. wide is the field of words, on this side, and on that, i. e. varied is their range of meaning, Υ 249; ὕλης, woodland pasture.

νόος, οιο, ου, ῳ, ον, (γιγνώσκω), (1) *consciousness*, κ 240, 494; *power of thought*, *understanding*, *prudence*, μετὰ φρεσί, Σ 419; ἐν στήθεσι, υ 366; νόῳ, *cunningly*, Α 132; *wisely*, ζ 320; Ο 643, πέπνυσαι; νόῳ, Ω 377; with βουλή, μ 211, π 374, δ 267.—(2) *thought*, *thoughts*, Ο 80, τ 479.—(3) *desire* or *aim*; here follow a variety of shades of meaning, all covered by the single English word *mind*, e. g. ὄρνυται, α 347; μενοινᾷ, β 92, Χ 382, β 124; with θυμός, *thought* and wish, Δ 309; *disposition*, σ 136, Π 35, γ 147, ζ 121, ν 229, α 3; *thought*, Ι 104; *design*, *counsel*, Διός, Ο 242, Π 103, Ρ 176, ξ 490, Ο 699, 52, δ 493, ε 23; *interior of one's soul*, *heart*, κεῦθε νόῳ, Α 363, ω 474; ἴσχανε, τ 42. Cf. Γ 63, θ 78; *thought* (intention, plan), Ψ 149, δ 256, χ 215; νόος καὶ μῆτις, *reason* and reflection, Κ 226, Ψ 590, τ 326.

νόσος, see νοῦσος.

νοστέω, only fut. **νοστήσω,** inf. σέμεν and σειν, and aor. νοστήσῃ, etc., (νόστος), redire, *return*, in various signif., but esp. φίλην ἐς πατρίδα γαῖαν, οἴκαδε, ὅνδε δόμονδε, ἐκ —, out of dangers, Τροίης, πυρός, Κ 247; πολέμοιο; κεῖσέ με νοστήσαντα, while I tarried there on my return home.

νόστἴμος (νόστος), rediturus, *destined to return*, υ 333, δ 806; νόστιμον ἦμαρ, day of one's return.

νόστος, οιο, ου, ῳ, ον, masc., (νέομαι), reditus, *return home*; Ἀχαιΐδος, to Achaia; ν 379, *his delayed return*; ε 344, νόστου, *return*, namely to the land of the Phaiakians.

νόσφ(ιν), (1) seorsum, *apart*, *away*; ἀπό, from.—(2) *aloof from*, *except*, with gen. = sine, θεῶν, Ἀχαιῶν; Β 346, form their plans *at variance with* those of the Achaians.

νοσφίζεαι, οίμεθα, prs., aor. νοσφίσατο, (σ)σαμένη, ην, aor. pass. νοσφισθείς, (νόσφι), discedere, *depart from*, τινός; τινά (Od.), derelinquere, *abandon*; neglegere, *disregard*, Ω 222.

νοτἴῃσι, ταῖς, (νότιος), imbribus, *rains*, *showers*, Θ 307†.

νότιος, ῳ, (νότος), humidus, ntr., *harbor water*, *roadstead*, δ 785.

Νότος, οιο, ου, (Ger. netzen, nass), *south wind*, bringing rain, Β 145, γ 295; ἀργεστᾶο, Λ 306, Φ 334.

νοῦς, see νόος.

νοῦσος, ῳ, ον, fem., morbus, pestilentia, *sickness*, *disease*, Α 10.

νῦ(ν), enclitic, *now*; νύ περ, *of course*, just *now*; Γ 164, *doubtless*, *methinks*; οὔ νυ, *surely* not; τί νυ, quid tandem, why *pray!*

νυκτερίς, ίδες, fem., (νύξ), vespertilio, *bat*, μ 433 and ω 6.

νύμφη, ης, ῃ, ην, ἄ, αι, άων, ῃς, ας, (nubo), *bride*, Σ 492; also of married woman still comparatively young, Γ 130.

Νύμφη, *goddess of subordinate rank*, *Nymph*, e. g. Kalypso, ε 153; Kirke, κ 543; Naiads, ν 107; mountain-nymphs, Ζ 420, ζ 123; offerings made to them, ρ 211, μ 318; Phaethusa and Lampetie, μ 132; κοῦραι Διός, ζ 105.

νυμφίου, ίον, masc., (νύμφη), *newly married*, η 65 and Ψ 223.

νῦν (nunc), *now*, of present time, more or less protracted; νῦν δή, nunc iam, nunc tandem, *now at this moment*, *just now*, Β 435; νῦν αὖ, but *now*, ν 149; ν. αὖτε, now on the contrary, now once more, Α 237, Ε 117; used with preterit tenses, where an unexpected result discloses a truth at variance with one's previous supposition, νῦν δέ, nunc autem, but now, Α 417.

νύξ, νυκτός, τί, τ(α) and νύχθ', νύκτες, ῶν, ας = nox, *night*, acc. with φυλάσσειν, ἰαύειν, watch, sleep *the live-long night*; νύκτας τε καὶ ἦμαρ, noctu diuque; διὰ νύκτα, of space and time, Β 57; ἀνὰ νύκτα, νυκτός, ἐπὶ νυκτί, noctu; *by night*, ο 34; also fig. *the night of death*, Ε 310. As goddess, *Night*, Ξ 259.

νυόν, οί, ούς, fem., (σνυσον, nurum, Schnur), nurus, *sister-in-law*, Γ 49.

Νυσήιον, τό, *region about Nysa*, where Dionysos grew up, Ζ 133†.

νύσσα, ης, ῃ, fem., meta, *turning post*, or *pillar*, round which the chariots turned, and returned to the starting-point, Ψ 332; elsewh. *starting-point* or *line*.

νύσσων, οντες, pass. ομένων, aor. νύξ(εν), ας, *prick*, *pierce*, Π 704; esp.

with weapons, M 395; *τινά τι*, Υ 487, Λ 563.

νῶ, see *νῶι*.

νωθής (*νη-* *ὄθεσθαι*?), iners, *lazy*, Λ 559†.

νῶι, nom., (*νῶι*(*ν*) gen. dat., *νῶι*, *νώ* acc. du., (nos), *we* (two); Π 99, *νῶιν*, dat.

νωΐτερον, *ην*, *of us both*, Ο 39 and *μ* 185.

νωλεμές (*νη-ορεμές*, *ἠρέμα*), *without pause*, Ξ 58; freq. with *αἰεί* at the close of verse, *χ* 228; adv. **νωλεμέως,** *unceasingly; firmly*, Δ 428.

νωμάω, **νωμᾷς,** *ᾷ*, *ῶν*, prs., ipf. *ἐνώμων*, *ας*, *α*, *νώμα*, aor. *νώμησεν*, *σαν*, *σαι*, (*νέμω*), distribuere, dispensare, *deal out*, *distribute*, food and drink, Α 471; *ply*, *πόδας καὶ γούνατα*; huc illuc versare, *handle*, *wield* (weapons); *hold*, *control*, *πόδα*, the sheet; *οἰήια*, the rudder; esp. *νόον*, *ν* 255, *revolve; κέρδεα*, shrewd plans.

νώνυμος, *ον*, *νωνύμνους*, (*νη-ὄνομα*), inglorius, *nameless*, *α* 222, Μ 70.

νώροπι, *α*, (nero, *ἀνήρ*), only of *χαλκός*, *manly*, as man's defense, Β 578, Η 206, *ω* 467.

νῶτον, *ου*, *φ*, *α*, *οισι*(*ν*), (nates) tergum, *back*, also pl., cf. terga; *back pieces*, as best portions of meat at feast, Η 321; *θαλάσσης*, Β 159.

νωχελίη, *τῇ*, (*νη-ὠκύς*), inertiae, tarditati, *sloth*, Τ 411†.

Ξ.

ξαίνειν (*ξέω*), *comb* or *card* wool, *χ* 423†.

ξανθός, *ῷ*, *όν*, *ή*, *ῆς*, *ήν*, *άς*, *ά*, (1) flavus, *blond*, *fair; κάρη*, fair countenanced, *ο* 133; *κόμης*, Α 197; *τρίχες*, *ν* 399; of mortals and of Demeter.—(2) *sorrel*, of horses, Λ 680.

Ξάνθος, (1) son of Phainops, a Trojan, Ε 152, slain by Diomedes.—(2) *Sorrel*, name of one of the horses of Achilleus, Π 149; of Hektor, Θ 185. —(3) (a) river in Lykia, flowing from Mount Tauros into the Mediterranean, Β 877; (b) another name for the Trojan Skamandros, Φ 15, Ξ 434, Ζ 4. Personified as god of this stream, Υ 40, 74, Φ 146.

ξεινήϊον, *α*, (*ξεῖνος*), *gift given by host to his guest on his departure*, Κ 269; *between host and guest*, Ζ 218; hospitium, *entertainment*, Σ 408; ironically: *hospitable return*, *ι* 370; *recompense*, *χ* 290; as adj. joined with *δῶρα*, *ω* 273.

ξεινίζειν (*ξεῖνος*), hospitio excipere, *receive as guest*, *γ* 355; fut. *ξεινίσσομεν*, aor. (*ἐ*)*ξείνισσα*, *ε*, and *ξεινίσαι*, *σας*, *entertain*.

ξείνιος, *ου*, *ον*, and **ξένιον,** hospitalis, Zeus, *protector of guests* (strangers), Ν 625, *ι* 271; *τράπεζα*, *hospitable table*, *ξ* 158; as subst. (sc. *δῶρον*, *α*), *gift bestowed upon the guest*, *ξείνιον*, *ια*, *ξενίων*, *υ* 296, *ξ* 404, *ο* 514; *παραθεῖναι*, *δοῦναι*.

ξεινο-δόκος, *ου*, *φ*, *ον*, *οι*, (*δέκομαι*), *hospitable*, *ἀνήρ*, *ο* 55; *host*, *σ* 64.

ξεῖνος, *οιο*, *ου*, *φ*, *ον*, *οι*, *ων*, *οισ*(*ιν*), *ους*, *strange*, *ἄνθρωποι*, *πάτερ*; elsewh. as subst., hospes, *stranger*, *guest*, under the protection of *Ζεὺς ξείνιος*; *guest-friend*, which relation existed from the time when *ξεινήια*, as pignora, were exchanged; hence hereditary, *πατρώϊος*, Ζ 215.

ξεινοσύνης, *τῆς*, *hospitality*, *φ* 35.

ξενίη, *τῇ*, hospitio, *entertainment*, *ω* 286; *μίξεσθαι*, hospitio mutuo usuros, enjoy each the hospitality of the other, *ω* 314.

ξένιος, see *ξείνιος*.

ξερόν, *τό*, *dry land*, *ε* 402†.

ξέσσε, aor. from *ξέω*.

ξεστοῦ, *οῖο*, *ῶν*, *οῖσι*, *όν*, (*ξέω*), *hewn*, *polished*, of cut stone, *αἴθουσαι*; *polished*, *τ* 566.

ξέω, ipf. **ἔξεον,** aor. *ξέσσε*(*ν*), *smooth*, *hew*, *polish*, *ψ* 199, *ε* 245. (Od.)

ξηραίνω, only aor. pass. **ἐξηράνθη,** *was dried up*, Φ 345.

ξίφος, *εος*, *εϊ*, *ει*, *εεσσ*(*ι*), (*ξύω*), *sword*,

Δ 530, λ 97; a *two-edged sword*, united by bands of dark metal (μελάνδετον) to the hilt (κώπῃ, ἀργυροήλῳ), worn in a sheath (κουλεός); sword and sheath were suspended by a strap (τελαμών) passing over the shoulder. (See adjacent cut.) [ῐ]

ξῦλον, *α*, Ψ 327, truncus, *trunk of a tree*; pl. ligna, *wood*.

ξυλόχοιο, *ῳ, ον*, *thicket, jungle*, Λ 415, δ 335.

ξυμ-, form used in compounds of βάλλω, πᾶς, and **ξυν-**, in composition with ἀγείρω, ἄγνυμι, ἄγω, δέω, ἐλαύνω, ἔσεσθαι, ἔχω, ἰέναι, ἱέναι,—ξύνεσις and ξυνοχή, see under συμ-, συν-.

ξυν-εείκοσι, *twenty together*, ξ 98†.

ξυν-έηκε, *έηχ', ες*, see συν-ίημι.

ξυνήϊα (ξυνός), communia, *common property*, Α 124, Ψ 809.

ξυνίει, *ιον*, see συν-ίημι.

ξυνιόντος, *ξύνισαν*, see σύν-ειμι.

ξῦνός, *ή, όν* = κοινός, communis, *common*, Ο 193; Ἐνυάλιος, *even-handed*, *changing*.

ξῦροῦ, ntr., (ξύω), ἐπὶ — ἀκμῆς, is poised upon a *razor's* edge, hangs by a hair, in ipso discrimine, Κ 173†.

ξυστόν, *ῷ, οῖσι*, (ξύω), hastile, (*polished*) *shaft* of a spear; *ναύμαχον*, ship-*pike*.

ξύω, ipf. **ξῦον**, aor. ἔξῦσε, (ξέω), *scrape*, χ 456; *make smooth*, Ξ 179.

O.

ὁ-, protheticum (= ἀ copulat.), see ὄτριχας, ὄπατρος, οἰετέας.

ὁ, ἡ, τό, (Goth. sa, sô, thata); peculiar forms: *τοῖο, τοῖιν, τοί, τοῖσι, ταί, τάων, τῇς(ι)*, I. demonstr., (**a**) simply pointing out, (1) substantively, Α 9, 12, 29, 43, 55, 57, 58, Ο 539; *τοῖσι μετέφη*, spoke among *them*; *ἐκ τοῦ*, exinde, since then, ever since; *ὁ δέ*, emphatic, accompanying not change of subj., but fresh act of same subject, nearly = αὐτός δε, Α 191; anticipatively, *it* indeed (the spear) no one thought of, to draw out = no one thought of drawing it out, Ε 665, Ο 599, Ρ 406; repeated in simile, Β 459. —(2) before an appositional subst. nearly = hic ille, indicating something as present, before one, known, etc., Α 20, these things, as ransom, ν 215, Α 33, ὁ γέρων, *he*, the old man, Λ 637, Α 11, ρ 10, Α 207, 167; Λ 69, the handfuls (as every one knows) fall; denoting opposition, Δ 399, λ 4, Κ 498, ι 375; with second of two substantives, χ 104, υ 310; with the first of several appositives, Λ 660; in arsis of first foot for emphasis, θ 388, τ 483, α 351; in classification with *μέν—δέ*, ξ 435, Ε 145, μ 73; in antithesis often only in second member, Β 217, Ν 616.—(b) referring back to what has already been mentioned, μ 201, Α 33, γ 306; ὁ δέ, after hypothetical relative sentence, λ 148; emphasizing the subject, Δ 491; with partitive division of numbers, Ε 272.—(c) calling attention to something which follows, before relative clause, Κ 322, ψ 28, φ 42; after substantive, especially in arsis of first foot, Δ 41, Ε 320, Ι 631, κ 74.—II. individualizing, fulfilling the proper function of the article, (a) rendering adj. substantive, ρ 218, Π 53, ξ 12, Α 576, Ψ 702, 325, 663, Φ 262, Θ 430, Ψ 572; here belong also, Λ 613, *τὸ πρίν, τὸ πάρος, τὰ πρῶτα*; never, in this use, before inf., which is to be construed as appositive of *τό*, e. g. harmful is *this*, to watch (cf. υ 52, α 370); (b) preceding the attribute, e. g. *ὁ καλὸς παῖς*, Κ 536, Ξ 376, Δ 42, λ 515, Ξ 503, Ο 37, Κ 408, Ξ 274; inversion of usual position of attribute, owing often to requirements of metre, e. g. *ὁ παῖς καλός*, Φ 317, Α 340, λ 492; (c) preceding the appositive (but only once expressed), λ 298, Α 288, Ξ 213; with pron., η 223, Θ 211 (rarely after demonstr., σ 114, τ 372, β 351); with gen. of poss. pron. only Ι 342; with *πᾶς*, ν 262, ω 79, etc.; *ὁ αὐτός*, rarely, η 55, 326, cf. θ 107; (d) expressing possession or propriety, *own, proper*, Λ 142, λ 492, θ 195, Α 763, ο 218, λ 339.

ὅ, ἥ, τό, esp. freq. forms beginning with τ, pr. relat., α 300, β 262; *οἵ τοί*, ζ 153; *ταί τε*, μ 63; *ὅτε*, quicunque, *whoever*, μ 40; *since he*, Α 412; *ὅ τις*, α 47, ρ 53; *τῇ περ, in which very way*, θ 510; *τὸ μέν*, Α 234.

ὀάρων, *ὀάρεσσιν*, fem., (*οσαρ-*, cf. *ὅρμος*, sermo), uxorum, ibus, *wives*, Ι 327, Ε 486.

ὀαρίζετον, *ζέμεναι*, ipf. *ὀάριζε*, (*ὄαρ*, sermo), *chat, τινί*; *converse familiarly*, Ζ 516, Χ 127 sq.

ὀαριστής, ὁ, (*ὀαρίζω*), *bosom friend*, τ 179†.

ὀαριστύς, ύν, fem., (*ὀαρίζω*), *familiar converse*, *πάρφασις*, fond discourse, beguiling the mind, etc., Ξ 216; iron. *intercourse, combat*, *πολέμου, προμάχων*.

ὀβελοῖσ(ι), *ούς*, masc., veru, *spit*, Α 465. (See cuts under *πεμπώβολα*.)

ὀβριμο-εργός, *όν*, (*ϝέργον*), immania exsequens, *worker of monstrous deeds, impious*, Ε 403 and Χ 418.

ὀβριμο-πάτρη, *ης*, *daughter of the mighty father*, Ε 747, γ 135.

ὄβριμος, *ον* (ε), incorrectly written *ὄμβρ*. Γ 357, (*βρίθω*), *mighty*, of Ares, Ο 112, Ν 444; of heroes, Θ 473, Τ 408; of things, *ponderous, heavy*, Γ 357, Δ 453, *ἄχθος*, ι 233; *θυρεόν*, ι 241.

ὀγδοάτῳ, *την*, γ 306, Τ 246, and **ὄγδοος**, *ον*, octavus, *eighth*; **ὀγδώκοντα**, octoginta, *eighty*, Β 568.

ὅγε, *ἥγε, τόγε*, (see *γε*), freq. with slight force which can not be given in translation, Α 65, 93, 68, 97.—(1) as outward sign, indicating an antithesis, Ρ 122, *αὐτάρ*, Λ 226, Μ 40, Ψ 35.—(2) in second member of antithesis, (a) referring to what has gone before, Μ 239, δ 789, Α 190; in first member of antithesis, recapitulating, β 132, γ 90, δ 821; *δ' ὅγε*, Λ 226, Ρ 130; special cases: Ν 8, 395, Ο 392, 479, 710; after *ἄρα*, Η 169, Ι 511, χ 329, 379; after recapitulating pron. or adv., Ν 88, 94, 538; *ὥς*, Λ 136, Μ 171; idem, Λ 478, Π 455; (b) pointing forward, κ 91; in simple anticipation, Α 120, ζ 182, ξ 119, in opposition to what has gone before, τ 283, π 470.

ὄγκιον, *τό*, (*ὄγκος*), *iron-basket*, basket or chest for containing iron, φ 61†.

ὄγκοι, *ους*, masc., (uncus), *barbs* of arrow, Δ 151. (Il.)

ὄγμον, *οι*, *ους*, masc., (*ἄγω*), lira, *furrow*; Σ 552, 557, *swath* made by mower or reaper.

'Ογχηστός, town on Lake Kopais in Boiotia, with grove of Poseidon, Β 506.

ὄγχνη, *η*, *ην*, *αι*, *ας*, fem., pirus, *pear-tree*; but also pirum, *pear*, η 120. (Od.)

ὀδαίων, ntr. pl. gen., (*ὁδός*), *freight, cargo*, θ 163 and ο 445.

ὀδάξ, adv., (δάκνω), *with the teeth,* λάζεσθαι, ἕλον γαῖαν, οὖδας, bite the ground, of slain in combat, X 17; ἐν χείλεσι φύντο, bit their lips in wrath.

ὅδε, ἥδε, τόδε, dat. pl. **τοῖσδε** and **τοίσδεσ(σ)ι,** pron. dem., hic, *this,* points out what lies before one, Γ 192, θ 403; yet not yet named or known, Γ 166, 226; cf. οὗτος, Γ 178, 200, 229, T 8.—(1) referring to the speaker, π 205, α 76, T 140; and to what falls within his familiar horizon, e. g. house, α 232; city, η 26; land, ο 484, people, cf. French céans, English, these here, β 317, τ 372, ο 388, 429, in widest, most general sense, χ 154, Z 326, Θ 237, A 257, Ξ 3, ρ 158, θ 197, B 324, ω 444.—(2) referring to that which is present in widest sense, υ 116, Θ 541, Φ 155, Ω 765 (usually following its subst.); yet ἥδε ὁδός, τόδε κακόν, μ 216; that in which the speaker feels a lively interest, γ 56, δ 94, β 280, A 127, 134; emphatically of that which is absent, α 185; τόδε (δεῦρο), *here,* ἱκάνω, ρ 444; explanatory, τῷδ' ἐπὶ θυμῷ.—(3) pointing out what is to follow, δ 486, K 111; esp. τόδε, referring to: inf., O 509, α 376; indirect question, H 393; substantive clause introduced by that, υ 333, χ 350, A 41; hypothetical sentence, O 208; μή, π 291; ὡς, ρ 242; relative clause, θ 564, σ 221, A 110, B 274; freq. where there is an asyndeton, β 93, ρ 274, B 301, O 36; γάρ, β 162, Π 238.—(4) special phrases: ἥδε δέ μοι κατὰ θυμὸν ἀρίστη φαίνετο βουλή, ι 318, 424, B 5, K 17; εὖ γὰρ ἐγὼ τόδε οἶδα, with asyndeton, ο 211; ἀλλ' ἄγε μοι τόδε εἰπέ, with following question, α 169, K 384, α 206, Ω 380.

ὁδεύειν, inf., (ὁδός), ire, *go,* ἐπὶ νῆας, Λ 569†.

'Οδίος, (1) leader of the Halizones, slain by Agamemnon, B 856, E 39.—(2) herald of the Greeks, I 170.

ὁδ-ίτης, αι, άων, masc., (ὁδός, εἶμι), *wayfarer,* λ 127, also ἄνθρωπος, *wending his way,* Π 263, ν 123.

ὀδμή, ήν, fem., odor, *smell, fragrance,* Ξ 415, ι 210.

ὁδοι-πόρον, masc., (περᾶν), *wayfarer,* (fellow) *traveler,* Ω 375†, hence **ὁδοιπόριον,** ntr., *reward for the journey* (*feast*), ο 506†.

ὁδός, οῖο, οῦ, ῷ, όν, ούς, fem., (1) *way, journey,* Lat. iter, A 151, as envoy; expeditio, γ 288, ξ 235; also by sea, β 273; ἦρχε δ' ὁδοῖο, she began the *way,* took the lead; πρήσσειν ὁδοῖο, accomplish the *way,* leave it behind.—(2) *path, road,* via, δ 389, cf. π 138; ἱππηλασίη, carriage-road; λαοφόρον, highway; πρὸ ὁδοῦ ἐγένοντο, progressed on their way.

ὀδούς, **ὀδόντι,** α, τες, ων, οὖσι, όντας, masc., dens, *tooth,* τ 450; λευκῷ, τ 393.

ὀδύνη, ῃ, αι, άων, ῃσι, ας, (δύη?), dolor, *pain,* Λ 398, E 417; animi= *sorrow,* α 242, β 79; O 25, 'Ηρακλῆος, *grief* for Herakles.

ὀδυνή-φατον, α, (φένω), *pain-assuaging,* E 401. (Il.)

ὀδύρομαι, εαι, εται, εο, and part., ipf. ὀδύρετο, οντο, (ὀδύνη ?), lamentari, *grieve, mourn,* X 79, α 55, θ 577, στοναχῇ τε γόῳ τε; τινός, for any one, Ψ 224, ξ 40; τινί, conqueri apud, *lament before,* δ 740; B 290, *lamenting to each other,* they desire to return home; *mourn for, deplore,* commiserari, T 345, δ 100, ν 379.

'Οδυσήιος, σ 353, adj. from **'Οδυσ(σ)εύς,** (σ)σῆος, σέος, σεῦς; σῆι, σεῖ; σσῆα, σσέα, σῆ, *Odysseus,* son of Laertes and Ktimene, king of Kephallenes, inhabiting Ithaka, Same, Zakynthos, Aigilops, Krokyleia, and a strip of opposite mainland, husband of Penelope, father of Telemachos; for Homeric explication of his name, see τ 407; the shrewd, much-tried hero of the Odyssey, πολύτροπος, πολύμητις, always able to evade danger by stratagem, and esp. conspicuous for his self-control.

ὀδύσσομαι, aor. **ὠδύσαο,** ατ(ο), aor. ὀδύσαντο, part. σσάμενος, οιο, pf. ὀδώδυσται, irasci, odisse, *be angry with, hate,* τινί; pf. pass., ε 423, mihi iratus sit.

ὀδώδει, see ὄζω; **ὀδώδυσται,** see ὀδύσσομαι; **ὄεσσι,** see ὄϊς.

ὄζος, ῳ, ον, οι, οισιν, ους, *shoot, twig,* Z 39, K 467, Π 768; Ἄρηος, *scion* of Ares, epithet of daring heroes, B 540, 745.

ὄζω, only plupf. **ὀδώδει,** *give out a smell,* transl. *was exhaled;* fragrabat, ε 60 and ι 210.

ὅθεν (ὅς), unde, *whence,* B 307, Δ 58,

η 131; also with personal antecedent, *γ* 319.

ὅθ(ι) (ὅς), ubi, *where*, B 572, 722; also further defined by follg. preposition, *λ* 191, *ξ* 533; — *τε*, introductory to a general description, *where also*, *α* 50, *μ* 3; — *περ*, *ξ* 532, even where; *καὶ* —, only *ι* 50. [ὅθῐ, Δ 516.]

ὄθομαι, *εται*, ipf. *ὄθετ(ο)*, (ὄθνος, odium), always with negation, non respicio, ***heed***, A 181; *τινός*, ***trouble one's self about***, usually with inf., with part., E 403.

ὀθονέων, *ησιν*, *ας*, fem., ***fine linen***, Γ 141, Σ 595, of women's garments; ***a web***, or ***piece of fine linen***, *η* 107.

Ὀθρῡονεύς, *ῆος*, Trojan ally from Kabesos, N 363, 370, 374, 772.

οἷ, sibi, ei, see *οὗ*.

οἷα, see *οἷος*.

οἴγνυμι, aor. **ῷξε,** and *ὤϊξε*, *αν*, *ὀΐξασα*, pass. ipf. *ὠΐγνυντο*, aperire, ***open***, *θύρας*, *πύλας*; but *γ* 392, *οἶνον*, ***broach*** the wine.

οἶδα, *ας*, *ε*, see ΕΙΔ, IV.

οἰδάνει (*οἰδέω*), ***swells***, (enrages), I 554, *νόον*; pass. *οἰδάνεται κραδίη χόλῳ*, swells with wrath, I 646.

οἰδέω, ipf. **ᾤδεε,** ***had*** all his body ***swollen***, *χρόα*, *ε* 455†.

Οἰδιπόδης, **Οἰδιπόδᾱο,** ***Oidipus***, *λ* 271, Ψ 679, son of Laios and Epikaste, father of Eteokles, Polyneikes, and Antigone.

οἴδματι, *τῷ*, ntr., (*οἰδέω*), ***swell of the sea, billow***, Φ 234 and Ψ 230.

οἰετέας, acc. pl., (*οἰέτης*, *ὁ-Fέτης*), ***of equal age***, B 765†.

ὀϊζυρός, *οῦ*, *οῖο*, *όν*, *οῖσι*, *αί*, comp. -*ώτερον*, P 446; sup. -*ώτατον*, *ε* 105; (*ὀϊζύς*), miser, ***wretched***, A 417, *γ* 95.

ὀϊζύς, *ύος*, *υῖ* *η* 270, *υν*, fem., (*οἴ*, vae), miseria, aerumna, ***woe, suffering, misery***, Z 285, Ξ 480, O 365, *δ* 35.

ὀΐζῡε, imp., ipf. *ὀϊζύομεν*, aor. part. *ὀϊζύσας*, (*ὀϊζύς*), ***endure hardship, lament, suffer***, *περί τινα*, circa; *ἀμφί τινι*, propter; *κακά*, perpeti, Ξ 89.

οἰήϊον, *α*, ntr., (*οἴσω*, *Fοιήιον*), ***tiller***, then in wider signif. ***rudder***, *ι* 483; usually pl. because the Homeric ships had two rudders, *μ* 218. (Cf. following cuts and No. 64.)

οἰήκεσσι, dat. pl., (*οἴσω*), ***rings in the***

yoke through which the reins passed, Ω 269†. (Cf. cuts Nos. 49 *h*, 10, 84 *f*.)

οἴκᾰδε (old acc. form with *δε*), domum, ***homeward, home***, hence freq. = ***to one's house, tent;*** with verbs of motion, A 19, 170, B 154, 236, Γ 72, Δ 103, H 79, I 418, *β* 176, *δ* 701, *ε* 108, *η* 326, *κ* 484, *λ* 132, *ν* 169, *ο* 431.

οἰκεύς, **οἰκῆϊ,** pl. *οἰκῆες*, *ων*, *ας*, (*οἶκος*), ***inmates of house***, Z 366; ***servants***, E 413.

οἰκέομεν (*οἶκος*), habitamus, ***inhabit, dwell***, *ζ* 204; ipf. *ᾤκει*, *ι* 200; *ᾤκεον*, Υ 218; pass. *οἰκέοιτο*, Δ 18, ***be inhabited;*** aor. *ᾠκηθεν*, ***settled***.

οἰκί(α), *τά*, (*οἶκος*), domicilium, ***abode;*** *ναίων*, habitans, dwelling, Z 15, H 221; *Ἑλλάδι*, Π 595; nidus, ***nest***, M 168, Π 261, M 221; dwelling of Aides, Υ 64.

Ὀϊκλείης, *ο* 244, son of Antiphates, father of Amphiaraos.

οἰκόθεν (*οἶκος*), ***from home***, A 632; de suo (de re familiari), H 364.

οἴκοθι (οἶκος), domi, *at home*, Θ 513, φ 398; of like signif. **οἴκοι** (locative from οἶκος), Α 113, θ 324.

οἰκόνδε (οἶκος), domum, *home; ἄγεσθαι*, the bride, ζ 159; *to women's apartment*, α 360, φ 354; *homeward*, Β 158.

οἶκος, οιο, ον, ῳ, ον, οι, ων, ους, masc., (ϝοῖκος, vicus), *house*, domus and domicilium, Ο 498; *roof, abode*, ι 478, ω 208; *tent*, Ω 471; *room*, υ 105; *hall*, τ 598; *household*, β 45, η 68, ο 375; res familiaris, *substance*, β 48, ρ 455, τ 161, β 238.

οἰκτείρων, aor. ᾤκτειρε, (οἶκτος), misereri, *pity*, Ψ 548, Ω 516.

οἴκτιστος, see *οἰκτρός*.

οἶκτος, masc., (οἶ), ἕλε (τινάς), misericordia tetigit (eos), *pity*, β 81, ω 438.

οἰκτρός, comp. -ότερ(α), sup. -οτάτην and οἰκτίστῳ, ον, (οἶκτος), miserabilis, *pitiable*, Λ 242, λ 381, 421, Χ 76, μ 258; οἰκτρ(ὰ) ὀλοφύρεσθαι, miserabiliter lamentari, κ 409; οἴκτιστα θάνοιεν, miserrime morerentur, χ 472.

οἰκ-ωφελίη (οἶκος, ὀφέλλω), *bettering one's estate, thrift*, ξ 223†.

'Οϊλεύς, ῆος, (1) king in Lokris, father of the lesser Aias and of Medon, Ν 697, Ο 333, Β 727, see Αἴας.—(2) charioteer of Bienor, slain by Agamemnon, Λ 93. Hence **'Οϊλιάδης**, Aias, Μ 365, Ν 712, Ξ 446, Π 330, Ψ 759.

οἶμα, ματ(α), ntr., (οἴσω), impetus, *spring, swoop*, Π 752, Φ 252.

οἰμάω, aor. **οἴμησε(ν)**, irruit, *dart upon*, Χ 308, ω 538; μετὰ πέλειαν, in columbam, *swoop after* a dove, Χ 140.

οἴμης, pl. ας, (εἶμι), *song, lay*, θ 481, χ 347; θ 74, cuius cantici gloria.

οἶμοι, pl. masc., (εἶμι), *stripes, bands*, Λ 24†.

οἰμωγή, ῆς, ῇ, fem., (οἰμώζω), lamentatio, *cry of grief*, Χ 409; δέδηε, resounds, υ 353.

οἰμώζω, aor. **ᾤμωξε**, opt. οἰμώξειε, part. οἰμώξας, (οἴμοι, vae mihi), lamentari, aloud, with loud voice (μέγα), *wail, lament; σμερδαλέον*, bitterly; ἐλεεινά, pitiably, Μ 162, Κ 522, Χ 33, Ψ 12, ι 506.

Οἰνείδης, *son of Oineus*, Tydeus, Ε 81?, Κ 497; **Οἰνεύς**, ῆος, son of Portheus, king of Kalydon in Aitolia, husband of Althaia, father of Tydeus and of Meleagros, guest friend of Bellerophontes; Artemis, in anger, sends upon his territory the Kalydonian boar, Β 641, Ζ 216, Ι 535, Ξ 117.

οἰνίζεσθε, imp. prs., ipf. οἰνίζοντο, (οἶνος), *supply one's self with wine*, Θ 506, Η 472, Θ 546.

οἰνο-βαρείων, part., (βαρύς), *heavy* or *drunk with wine*, ι 374, κ 555, φ 304.

οἰνο-βαρές, voc., (βαρύς), = foregoing, Α 225†.

Οἰνόμαος, (1) an Aitolian, slain by Hektor, Ε 706.—(2) a Trojan, Μ 140, Ν 506.

οἰνο-πέδοιο (πέδον), adj., *with soil fit to produce wine, wine-producing*; ἀλωῆς, wine-yielding soil, earth, α 193 subst., *vineyard*, Ι 579.

Οἰνοπίδης, *son of Oinops*, Helenos, Ε 707†.

οἰνο-πληθής (πλῆθος), *abounding in wine*, ο 406†.

οἰνο-ποτάζει, ζων, (ποτόν), *quaff wine*, ζ 309, Υ 84.

οἰνο-ποτῆρας, τούς, (ποτόν), *wine-drinkers*, θ 456†.

οἶνος, οιο, ον, ῳ, ον, (ϝοῖνος, vinum), *wine*, always mixed with water before drinking (see κρητήρ, ἀμφιφορεύς, ἀσκός, πίθος, πρόχοος, νέμειν); αἴθοπα, sparkling, Α 462; see ἐρυθρόν, μελιηδέα, μελίφρονα, ἡδύν, ἡδυπότοιο, εὐήνορα; γερούσιον, reserved in honor of the elders; places famed for quality of wine: Epidauros, Phrygia, Pedasos, Arne, Histiaia, Lemnos, Thrake, Pramne, land of the Kikones.

οἰνο-χοέω, ipf. **οἰνο-χόει** (see Α 598, ο 141), ἐῳνοχόει, part. οἰνοχοεῦντες? γ 472; aor. -χοῆσαι (-χοή), and **οἰνοχοεύει**, ειν, ων, (χοεύς), *pour out wine*, τινί (in φ 142, sc. οἰνοχόος); nectar, Δ 3.

οἰνοχόος, οιο, ον, masc., (χέω), *wine-pourer, cup-bearer*, Β 128, ι 10.

οἶνοψ, **οἴνοπος**, ι, α, ε, (οἶνος?), *glancing, gleaming*, epithet of the sea and of cattle, *dark red*, ε 132.

Οἶνοψ, an Ithakan, father of Leiodes, φ 144†.

οἰνόω, only aor. pass. part. **οἰνωθέντες**, vino ebrii, *drunken with wine*, π 292 and τ 11.

ὀίξασα, see οἴγνυμι.
οἷο = οὗ, gen. from ὅς, suus.
οἰόθεν (οἶος) οἶος, *all alone*, H 39. (Il.)
οἴομαι, see ὀίω.
οἰο-πόλῳ, οισιν, (πέλομαι), desertus, *lonely*, N 473, λ 574.
οἶος, ου, ῳ, ον, ω, οι, οισι(ν), ους, η, ης, ην, αι, ῃς, solus, *alone*; οὐκ οἴη· ἅμα τῇγε, etc., Γ 143; with εἷς, μία, δύ(ο); with νόσφι, ἄνευθέ τινος, ἐν, μετά τισι; καὶ οἶος, etiam, *even alone, unassisted*, Ω 456; unicus eximius, *alone of its kind, best*, Ω 499; with ἀπό, *isolated*, ι 192; οἶον, sc. με, met me *in single combat*, I 355.
οἷος, οἵη, οἷον, rel. pron. like ὅς, orig. demonstrative like talis, B 320, that *such a thing* had happened; apparently often = ὅτι τοῖος, *because such*, δ 611, ε 183, 303, ξ 392, π 93, Σ 166; cf. ρ 160 and ω 512; then rel. qualis, *as*; οἷον ὅτε, *as* when, ν 388; οἷος, with inf., ξ 491; οἷός τε, τ 160, *such as to, able to, capable of*; οἷον, οἷα (τε), *as* (often), ι 128; οἷον δή, causal, *since now*, σ 221. [ὄjος, N 275, Σ 105, η 312, υ 89.]
οἰός and ὄιος, see ὄϊς.
οἰο-χίτων(α), τόν, *with tunic only, lightly clad*, ξ 489†.
οἰόω, aor. pass. **οἰώθη**, *leave alone, abandon*, derelicta est (a diis), Z 1; desertus est a suis, Λ 401.
ὄϊς, ὄιος and οἰός, ὄϊν, pl. ὄιες (οἴιες ι 425, οἴεσι), ὀίων, ὀίεσσι and ὄεσσι, ὄϊς, ovis, *sheep*, masc. and fem., with ἀρνειός, ἄρσην or θήλεια.
ὀίσατο, see ὀίω. **οἴσετε**, σέμεν(αι), see φέρω. **οἶσθα**, see ΕΙΔ, IV.
ὀισθείς, see ὀίω.
ὀιστεύοντα, aor. imp. ὀίστευσον, part. σας, (ὀιστός), *shoot arrows*, τόξῳ, μ 84; τινός, at any one. The following cuts, from Assyrian reliefs, give a good idea of the way in which the arrow was held in the fingers and placed upon the bow; see also cut under πῶμα.

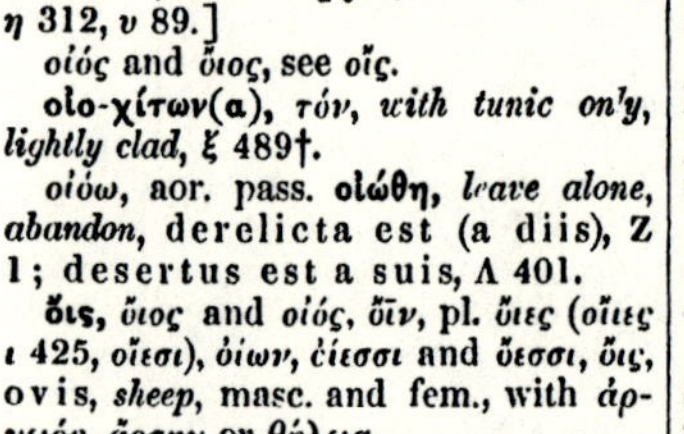

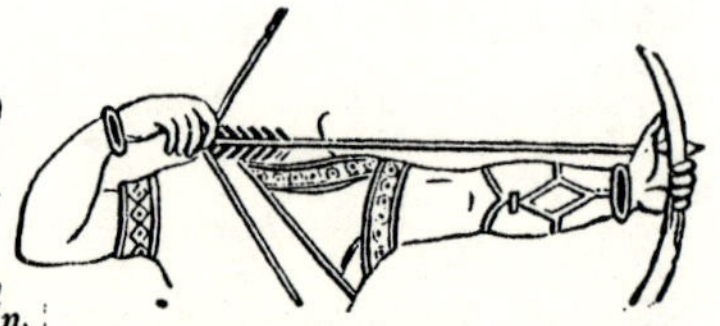

ὀιστός, οῦ, ῷ, όν, οί, ῶν, ούς, (οἰστός, φέρω, qui fertur), sagitta, *arrow*, of wood or reed, with barbed metal point, the lower end feathered and notched (γλυφίδες), or with projections, enabling the fingers to clasp firmly the arrow to draw it back; poisoned arrows are mentioned only α 261, Δ 213; πικρός, pointed, Ψ 867.
οἶστρος, ὁ, *gadfly*, χ 300†.
οἰσὕΐνῃσι (οἰσύα, vitex), ῥίπεσσι, *willow* (withes), ε 256†.
οἶτον, τόν, (οἴσω, fors ?), fortuna, *fate*, always in bad sense, I 563; usually joined with κακόν, miserâ fortunâ perire, perish by a wretched fate, Γ 417, Θ 34, α 350.
Οἴτὕλος, town on coast of Lakonike, B 585†.
Οἰχᾰλίη, town on river Peneios, home of Eurytos, B 730; **Οἰχαλίηθεν**, *from Oichalia*, B 596; **Οἰχαλιεύς**, Eurytos, B 596, θ 224.
οἰχνέω, 3 pl. **οἰχνεῦσιν**, ipf. iter. οἴχνεσκον, ε, (οἴχομαι), meare, *go, come*, E 790, γ 322.
οἴχεται, etc., prs., ᾤχετο, etc. ipf., (properly perf. with present signif. from Ϝικ-, Ger. weiche), (1) *slip away, escape*, N 672, E 472, X 213, ι 47, α 242; part. also=absens, α 281; *begone, be away*, also profectus sum, *set out for*, A 366; c. term. in quo, δ 821; c. term. in quem, ἐς, ἐπί, μετά, κατά, (πάντῃ), παρά, πρός, with acc., κεῖσε, Πύλονδε; abire, *depart*, κ 571, E 511; ferri, *fly, speed, haste, run*, A 53; κατὰ γαίης, χθονός, under the earth, μετὰ κουρὸς ἐρωήν; ὁδόν, profectus, since *thou hast set out* (on thy long and weary journey), δ 393.
ὀίω (⏑ ⏑ | – E 894), οἴω, mid. ὀίομαι, εαι, ται, etc., opt. οἴοιτο, ipf. ὠίετο, aor. ὀίσατο, pass. ὠίσθην, θη, ὀισθείς (ὀϜίω, opinor ?), suspicor, *suspect*, τί, τάδε, γόον (θυμός); often parenthetical, like Lat. opinor, π 309; *think, intend, mean*, A 170, 296. Construed with, (1)

acc. and inf., Α 59, 170, 204, 289, 427, 558, Ω 727, γ 27, χ 215, Α 78, Τ 334, α 173, χ 210; subject to be supplied from context, α 201, 323, ζ 173, ο 173, 278, π 372, Μ 66, 217, Ο 292, Υ 195, κ 193.—(2) with inf. where subj. remains unchanged, Α 296, Ζ 341, Φ 92, θ 180, τ 215, Δ 12, Ο 728, τ 581, φ 91. —(3) acc., χ 159, β 351, χ 165; with attraction, γ 255, υ 224.—(4) *ὀίσατο κατὰ θυμὸν μὴ . . . ἀμφράσσαιτο*, ne . . . agnosceret, there rose in his mind the apprehension lest, etc., τ 390.—(5) impers., τ 312, *ἀλλά μοι ὧδ' ἀνὰ θυμὸν ὀίεται ὡς ἔσεταί περ.*

οἰωνιστής, *ήν*, masc., (*οἰωνός*), *understanding the flight of birds*, Ν 70; elsewhere as subst.

οἰωνο-πόλων, gen. pl., (*πολέω*), augurum, *occupied with flight of birds, seers*, Α 69 and Ζ 76.

οἰωνός, *ῷ, όν, οί, ῶν, οἷσι(ν), ούς*, (avis), *bird of prey*, γ 271; coupled with *κύνες*, γ 259; *bird of omen, δεξιός*, seen in the east, auspicious quarter, ο 531; omen, the one best omen is, etc., Μ 243.

ὀκνείω, prs., ipf. *ὤκνεον*, (*ὄκνος*), with inf., dubitare, *shrink*, Ε 255 and Υ 155.

ὄκνος, *ῳ*, masc., (cunctari), inertia, *sluggishness*, Ε 817. (Il.)

ὀκριόωντο, ipf., (*ὀκριάω*, from *ὀκριόεις*), — *πανθυμαδόν*, exasperabantur, *were hot* with furious passion, σ 33†.

ὀκρῐόεντι, *τα* (*θ'*), (*ἄκρος*), *having sharp corners* or *points, jagged, rugged*, Θ 327, Π 735, ι 499.

ὀκρυόεντος, *οἐσσης*, (*κρύος*), horrendi, ae, *chilling, horrible*, Ι 64 and Ζ 344.

ὀκτά-κνημα, adj. ntr. pl., (*κνήμη*), *eight-spoked*, Ε 723†, of wheels, as in adjoining cut, from a painting on a

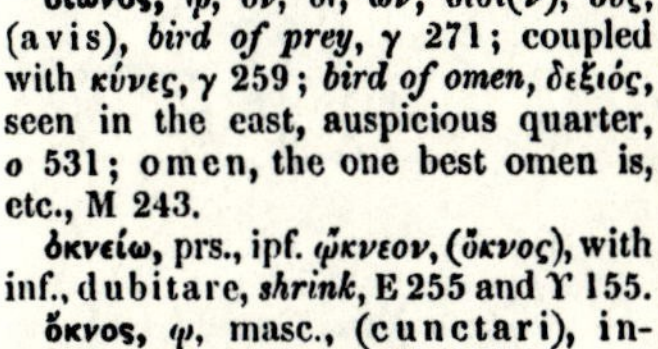

Panathenaic amphora found at Volsci.

ὀκτώ, octo, *eight*, Β 313, χ 110; *ὀκτω-καιδεκάτῃ*, duodevicesima die, ε 279, η 268, ω 65.

ὀλβιό-δαιμον, voc., (*ὄλβιος*), *blessed by the deity*, Γ 182.

ὄλβιος, *ου, ον, ε, οι*, (*ὄλβος*), beatus, *blessed*, λ 450, ρ 354; *rich*, σ 138; pl. *ὄλβια, blessings* (in their lives), η 148; *ποιήσειαν*, may they bless! ν 42.

ὄλβος, *ῳ, ον*, masc., *wealth*; γ 208, *good fortune*.

ὀλέεσθαι, *ὀλέεσκε*, see *ὄλλυμι*.

ὀλέθριον (*ὄλεθρος*) *ἦμαρ*, day of *destruction*, Τ 294 and 409.

ὄλεθρος, *ου, ῳ, ον*, (*ὄλλυμι*), pernicies; *αἰπύς*, sheer, utter *ruin*; *ψυχῆς*, vitae discrimen, most *perilous spot* to life, Χ 325; *πείρατα ὀλέθρου, destruction's* net; Ω 735, a wretched *fate*.

ὀλεῖται, see *ὄλλυμι*.

ὀλέκουσι, prs. with part., ipf. *ὄλεκον*, iter. *ὀλέκεσκεν*, pass. prs. *ὀλέκονται*, ipf. *ὀλέκοντο*, (*ὄλλυμι*), perdere, pessumdare, *destroy*, Θ 279, χ 305, Π 17, Α 10.

ὀλέσαι, *ας, σσαι, σσας, ὀλέσθαι*, see *ὄλλυμι*.

ὀλετῆρα, *τόν*, (*ὄλλυμι*), *destroyer*, Σ 114†.

ὀλιγη-πελέων, *έουσα*, *swooning*, Ο 245; infirma, τ 356.

ὀλιγη-πελίης, *τῆς*, (*πέλομαι*), *weakness, faintness*, ε 468†.

ὀλίγιστος, see *ὀλίγος*.

ὀλῐγο-δρᾰνέων, part., (*δρᾶν*), *able to do but little, feeble*, Ο 246. (Il.)

ὀλῐγος, *ου, ῳ, ον, οισι, η, ης, ῃ, ην, ον*, sup. *ὀλίγιστος*, Τ 223, paullus, brevis, exiguus, *little, small; πῖδαξ, feeble flowing; ὀπί, feeble*; ntr. *ὀλίγον*, paullum, *a little*, Ρ 538, θ 547; with comp., paullo, *by little*, Τ 217; *ὀλίγου*, paene, *almost*, ξ 37; super., Τ 223, scanty shall be the reaping.

Ὀλιζών, town in Magnesia in Thessaly, Β 717†.

ὀλισθάνω, aor. **ὄλισθε,** (for *ὀγλισθάνω*, Ger. glitschen), *slipped and fell*, Ψ 774; with *ἐκ*, Υ 470, *fell from him*.

ὄλλυμι, part. **ὀλλύς,** *ύντων, τας, ὀλλῦσαι*, fut. *ὀλέσω, σσεις, σσει*, aor. *ὤλεσα, ας, (εν), σσαν* and *ὄλεσσε(ν)*, *σσαν*, subj. *σσῃς, ῃ, σωσιν*, opt. *σειε* imp. σσον, inf. σσαι, part. σσας, σαντ(α), τες, σασα, perdere, pessum dare, delere, interimere, *destroy*, *kill*, amittere, *lose*, θυμόν, μένος, Λ 83, Θ 449; pass. mid. prs. ὀλλύμενοι, ων, ους, άων, ipf. ὄλλυντ(ο), fut. ὀλεῖται, ὀλέεσθε, σθαι, aor. ὀλόμην, ὄλεθ' = τ(ο), οντο and ὤλεο, ὤλετο, subj. ὄλωμαι, ὄληαι, ται, ωνται, opt. οισθε, inf. έσθαι, see οὐλόμενος, perire, *perish*, ὑπό τινι; with acc. of manner of death, etc., μόρον, οἶτον, ὀλέθρῳ; with dat. of means, δόλῳ; also pf. ὄλωλας, εν, ῃ, and plupf. ὀλώλει, periit, etc., Ω 729, Κ 187.

ὄλμον, τόν, (ϝολμ., volvo), *smooth round stone*, *quoit*, Λ 147†.

ὀλοιῇ, ῇσι, dat. pl., (ὀλοός), perniciosa, *destructive*, *deadly*, Χ 5, Α 342.

ὀλολῦγῇ, τῇ, (ὀλολύζω, ululare), *with a loud cry*, Ζ 301†.

ὀλολύζω, aor. **ὀλόλυξε,** αν, αι, always of female voices, ululare, *lament aloud*, δ 767; eiulare, *rejoice aloud*, χ 408, 411.

ὀλόμην, see ὄλλυμι.

ὀλοοί-τροχος, masc., (ϝολϝοι-, volvo-), *rolling stone*, *round rock*, Ν 137†.

ὀλοός, οῖο, ῷ, όν, οῖς; ή, ῆς, ήν, ῇς, άς; ά, comp. ώτερος, sup. ώτατος, τε, (ὄλλυμι), perniciosus, *destroying*, of gods, Μοῖρα, Κήρ; of men and things, Γ 133, Ω 39, Χ 5, Π 849; κῆρ, saevum; but κῆρ' = Κῆρα, saevam.

Ὀλοοσσών, όνος, town on river Eurotas in Thessaly, situated on white cliffs, Β 739†.

ὀλοό-φρων, ονος, (φρήν), *baleful*, *savage*, *stern*, saevus, Β 723, α 52.

ὀλοφυδνόν (ὀλοφύρομαι?), *pitiful*, *doleful*, miserabile, ἔπος, Ε 683, τ 362.

ὀλοφῦρομαι, εαι, etc., prs. aor. ὀλοφύραο, ατο, lamentari, miserari, *wail*, *lament*, *pity*, πολλά, much, οἰκτρ(ά), piteously, αἰνά, dreadfully, pitiably, ν 221, τ 543; freq. with προσηύδα, Λ 815, λ 472, κ 265, cf. Ο 114; with inf., χ 232 (cf. ὀκνεῖν), *bewail* that thou must be brave before the suitors; τινός (Il.), misereri, *feel pity*, Π 17, Χ 170; τινά, miserari, *show pity*, Ω 328, κ 157, τ 522.

ὀλο-φώϊα (φάος, salus?), perniciosa, *destructive*, δήνεα; subst., *wiles*, δ 410.

Ὀλυμπιάδες, Β 491†, Muses, cf. **Ὀλύμπιος,** οι, α, Α 583, 399, 18, *Olympian*, inhabiting **Οὔλυμπος** or Ὄλυμπος, *Olympus*, the mighty mountain, dwelling of gods, on left bank of river Peneios in Thessaly, penetrating with its snow-capped peaks into the upper αἰθήρ; ἀγάννιφος, αἰγλήεντος, αἰπύν, θεῶν ἕδος, μακρός, πολυπτύχου.

ὀλύρας, τάς, (ἀλέω?), a kind of grain not unlike *barley*, Ε 196 and Θ 564.

ὄλωλε, see ὄλλυμι.

ὁμάδησαν, aor. from ὁμαδέω, (ὅμαδος), *made a din*, α 365. (Od.)

ὅμᾰδος, ῳ, ον, masc., (ὁμός), *noise*, *din*, strictly of many voices, also of battle-cry, κ 556. (Il.) [σομάδῳ, Ρ 380?]

ὁμᾰλὸν ποίησαν, levigabant, made *smooth*, ι 327†.

ὁμ-αρτέων, part. prs., aor. ήσειεν, ήσαντ' = ήσαντε, τες, (ὁμοῦ, ἄρτιος), *meet*, *keep pace with*, ν 87; comitari, *attend*, Ω 438; *encounter*, Μ 400.

ὁμαρτῇ, see ἁμαρτῇ.

ὀμβριμος, -πάτρη, false reading for ὄβριμος, ὀβριμοπάτρη.

ὄμβρος, ῳ, ον, masc., (imber, μύρεσθαι?), imber, *rain*, also of heavy *snow-fall*, Μ 286.

ὀμεῖται, fut. from ὄμνυμι.

ὁμ-ηγερέες, έεσσι, (ὁμοῦ, ἀγείρω), *assembled together*, Ο 84.

ὁμ-ηγυρίσασθαι, aor. from -ηγυρίζομαι, (ἄγυρις), congregare, *convoke*, π 376†.

ὁμήγῠριν, τήν, concionem, *assembly*, Υ 142†.

ὁμ-ηλικίη, ης, ῃ, ην, (ὁμοῦ, ἧλιξ), *sameness of age*, Υ 465; aequales, (collective), *those of like age*, Γ 175, Ν 485; also aequalis, *companion*, ζ 23, χ 209.

ὁμ-ήλικα, ες, ας, (ὁμοῦ, ἧλιξ), aequalis, τινός, *of like age with*, τ 358.

ὁμ-ηρέω, aor. **ὡμήρησε,** (ἀραρεῖν), μοι, *met* me, π 468†.

ὁμῖλᾰδόν, adv., (ὅμιλος), catervatim, *in crowds*, Μ 3. (Il.)

ὁμῖλεῖν, prs., ipf. ὡμίλει, έομεν, εον, aor. ὡμίλησα, ήσωσι, ήσειεν, ήσαντες, (ὅμιλος), *introduce one's self among*, *associate with* (ἐνί, μετά, παρά), τισιν, π 271; versari inter, cum, σ 167; manus conserere, *meet in battle*, Ν 779 (μετά), τισίν; *throng about*, περί τινα, Π 641, ω 19.

ὅμῖλος, *ου, ῳ, ον,* masc., (ὁμοῦ, εἰλέω), *crowd, throng,* ἵππων τε καὶ ἀνδρῶν, etc.; *tumult of battle,* ὁμίλῳ, Φ 606; *army, host,* K 231 (in camp or otherwise), λ 514; then acervus, coetus, *mass, company,* ο 328, π 29.

ὀμίχλη, *ην,* (μιχ), nebula, *cloud,* A 359, Γ 10; κονίης, *dust-cloud.* (Il.)

ὄμμα, *τ(α), σι,* ntr., (ὦμμαι, perf. from ὁράω), oc-ulus, *eye,* A 225, Λ 614; Θ 349, better οἶμαr'.

ὄμνῦθι, from ὄμνυμι; also from ὀμνύω, ὀμνῦέτω, imp. prs., and ipf. ὤμνυε; fut. ὀμοῦμαι, εἶται, aor. ὤμοσα, ε, σαμεν, elsewh. ὀμ-, also with σσ, iurare, *swear;* alicui, τινί (πρός τινα), ὅρκον; *affirm by oath, swear,* iure iurando affirmare, τί; or with inf. as object, ἦ μέν, A 76, μή, I 132, Ψ 585, β 373; acc. with inf. μήποτ', T 127, cf. ξ 332; with inf. fut. aor. and perf. according to the sense; *swear by* a thing, τινά, O 40.

ὁμο-γάστριος, *ον,* (γαστήρ), germanus, brother *by the same mother, own brother,* Φ 95; κασίγνητος, Ω 47.

ὁμόθεν, ἐξ—, = ἐξ ὁμοῦ, *from the same* (root or spot), ε 477†.

ὁμοῖος, *ον, οι, η, ης, ῃ, ην, αι, ας,* (ἅμα, similis, Ger. samt, Eng. same), idem, *same,* π 182; with οὐ, A 278; M 270, similis, *like, similar,* τινί, in something, τί or ἐν πολέμῳ, or θέειν, also with other infs.; in abbreviated comparisons, β 121, P 51; Ψ 632, *equal,* distinguish from follg.

ὁμοιΐου and ὁμοΐον, *making like, breaking down distinctions, shared by all alike,* ω 543.

ὁμοιόω, only aor. pass. **ὁμοιωθήμεναι** ἄντην, A 187, *match himself* face to face; μῆτιν, in shrewdness, γ 120.

ὁμόκλᾱ, ipf. from ὁμοκλάω = -κλέω, ipf. **ὁμοκλέομεν,** *εον,* aor. ὁμοκλήσειε, etc., and iter. κλήσασκε, (καλεῖν, κελεύω), *call out to, exclaim,* Σ 156; Υ 448, E 439, δεινά; Ω 248, iubere, *command,* τ 155; with inf., ω 173; acc. with inf., Π 714.

ὁμο-κλῇ, *ήν, αί,* fem., (ὁμοκλᾶν), *loud call,* M 413; *commands,* ρ 189.

ὁμο-κλητῆρος, τοῦ, (ὁμοκλή), *one who calls out aloud;* ἀκούσας, hearing the *call, cry,* M 273 and Ψ 452.

ὀμόργνυμι, ipf. **ὀμόργνυ,** mid. ὠμόργνυντο, aor. ὀμορξάμενος, *ον, ην,* (mergere), *wipe off;* δάκρυα, his tears; παρειάων, de genis, from his cheeks, Σ 124.

ὁμός, *οῦ, όν, ή, ῇ, ήν,* (ἅμα, simul, similis, Ger. sam, samt, Eng. same), idem, *same,* Δ 437, κ 41; communis, *common,* N 333.

ὀμόσας, etc., see ὄμνυμι, iurare.

ὁμόσε (ὁμός), eodem, *together,* M 24 and N 337.

ὁμο-στιχάει (στείχω) βόεσσιν, una cum bobus incedit, *keeps pace with,* O 635†.

ὁμό-τῑμον, masc., (τιμή), *equally honored, entitled to equal honor,* O 186†.

ὁμοῦ (ὁμός), *together,* Δ 122, λ 573; simul, *alike, at once,* A 61, Λ 245, μ 67; una cum, νεφέεσσιν.

ὁμο-φρονέοις, *έοντε,* du. part., (φρονέω), *be of one mind,* ι 456; νοήμασι, in unity of purposes, ζ 183.

ὁμο-φροσύνην, *ῃσι,* fem., (ὁμόφρων), concordia, ζ 181; familiaritas, *intimacy,* ο 198.

ὁμό-φρονα (φρήν) θυμόν, *having like desire, harmonious,* X 263†.

ὁμωθῆναι, aor. pass. from ὁμόω — φιλότητι, *to be united in love,* Ξ 209†.

ὀμφαλόεν, Ω 269, *with a knob* or *cap* (see cut No. 5); ὀμφαλοέσσης, *αν, αι, ας,* (ὀμφαλός), *ornamented with studs,* τ 32, or *with a single great boss,* with corresponding deep concavity in interior (see cuts Nos. 17, 121). (Il.)

ὀμφαλός, *οῦ, όν, οί,* (1) umbilicus, *navel,* Δ 525, Φ 180.—(2) *boss* or *projection* on centre of shield, terminating in a button or in a point; pl., *studs* upon shield serving as ornament, Λ 34. —(3) a *knob* or *pin* on the centre of the yoke (see cut No. 49, *a*), also among the Assyrians (see cut No. 55), while the Egyptians ornamented each end of the yoke with a ball of brass (see cut on next page), Ω 273.—(4) in wider signif., *middle point, centre,* θαλάσσης, α 50. (Il.)

ὄμφᾰκες, *αί,* (ἀν-, φαγεῖν?), *unripe grapes,* η 125†.

ὀμφή, *ῆς, ῇ,* fem., (Ϝέπος, vox), *voice,* θεῶν, Υ 129; θεοῦ, γ 215; also of dream, B 41 (see πανομφαῖος); always of *divine prophetic voices.*

ὁμ-ώνῦμοι, pl., (ὄνομα), cognomines, *having the same name,* P 720†.

ὁμῶς (ὁμός), (1) *together*, *πάντες*, δ 775.—(2) *alike*, *at once*, *also*, P 644, κ 28, ν 405; with dat. = pariter ac, *equally as*, *just as*, E 535.

ὅμως (ὁμῶς), tamen, *yet*, M 393†.

ὄναρ, τό, somnium, *dream*, *vision*, K 496; opp. ὕπαρ, *reality*, τ 547, υ 90.

ὄνειᾰρ, ὀνείᾰθ' = ὀνείατα, ntr., (ὀνίνημι), *protector*, *defense*, X 433; *relief*, *refreshment*, δ 444; pl., *rich presents*, Ω 367; elsewh. *food*, *victuals*.

ὀνείδειον, οισ(ιν), (ὄνειδος), *reproachful*, μῦθον, ἐπέεσσιν, Φ 393; without ἐπ., *reproaches*, X 497.

ὀνειδίζων, aor. 2 sing. ὀνείδισας, imp. -ισον, (ὄνειδος), *reproach*, ἔπεσιν; τινί τι, I 34, or ὅτι, B 255, *censure*; exprobrare, *cast in one's teeth*, σ 380.

ὄνειδος, εα, εσι, ntr., (Goth. naiteins, neith, Ger. Neid), probrum, *reproach*, pl. κατ' χεῦαν μητέρι, χ 463, have covered (overwhelmed) my mother with reproach; II 498, *matter of reproach*, *disgrace*.

ὀνείρατα, see ὄνειρος.

ὀνειρείῃσι, fem. adj., (ὄνειρος), ἐν — πύλῃσι, at the portals *of dreams*, δ 809.

ὀνειρο-πόλοιο, ον = (ὀνειροπολούμενος), A 63, *interpreter of dreams*.

ὄνειρος, ὁ, (τὸ ὄνειρον, δ 841), φ, ον, ε, οι, ων, ους, and τὰ **ὀνείρατ(α)**, υ 87, (ὄναρ), somnium, *dream*, B 6, 8, 16; in simile, of disembodied spirits, λ 207, 222; represented as a people located on the way to Aides, ω 12; they come to mortals through two gates, τ 562 sqq., cf. δ 809.

ὀνήμενος, ὄνησα, see ὀνίνημι.

ὀνήσιος, τῆς, (ὄνησις, ὀνίνημι), ἀντιάσειεν, would that he might have such a portion of *prosperity*, i. e. none whatever, φ 402†.

Ὀνητορίδης, γ 282, Phrontis.

Ὀνήτωρ, priest of Idaean Zeus; his son Laogonos, II 604.

ὄνθος, ου, ον, masc., fimus, *dung*, Ψ 775. [Ψ]

ὀνίνησι, fut. ήσει, ειν, aor. ὤνησας, εν, αν, and ὄνησα; mid. fut. ὀνήσεαι, εται, ὀμεθ(α), 2 aor. imp. ὄνησο, part. ὀνήμενος, (cf. ὦνος), iuvare, *help*, *aid*, *cheer*, Θ 467; τινά, A 395, 503, ξ 67; by what means, τινί, A 503; μέγα, multum, Ω 45, τοῦτο, in this; mid. iuvari, ὃν θυμόν, *have profit* in his own soul, H 173; frui, *enjoy*, τινός, II 31, τ 68; part. ὀνήμενος, sc. ἔστω, may he be blessed, β 33.

ὄνομ(α) and **οὔνομα**, οὔνοματ(α), ntr., (ὄ-γνομα, nomen), *name*; καί τ' οὔνομα, vel nomen, Γ 235; = memoria, δ 710, ω 93; μοί ἐστιν, with nom., τ 183, 247, σ 5, ι 366 (η 54, τ 409, with ἐπώνυμον); τίθεσθαι, indere, give a name to —; ὅ, ττι σε κάλεον, θ 550; fama, gloria, ν 248.

ὀνομάζοι, ε, ειν, ων, ipf. ὀνόμαζες, ον, aor. ὠνόμασας, (ὄνομα), *name*, *mention*, I 515; address by name, ἐξονομακλήδην, X 415: πατρόθεν ἐκ γενεῆς, according to his descent on the father's side, K 68.

ὄνοσαι, *ονται, οιτο,* fut. *ὀνόσσεται, σθαι,* aor. *ὠνοσάμην, ὀνόσασθ(ε)* Ω 241, *ὀνόσαντ(ο), οσσάμενος,* and 2 aor. *ὤνατο* P 25, vitupero, *censure, scorn,* (exc. P 173, φ 427), always in rhetorical question or with negation, Δ 539, P 399; *κακότητος,* ε 379, fore ut te poeniteat miseriae, that thou wilt disparage, esteem lightly.

ὀνομαίνω, only aor. **ὀνόμηνας,** *εν, ω, ῃς,* (*ὄνομα*), *declare,* λ 251; *recount, name,* B 488, δ 240; *name as witnesses,* Ξ 278; *call by name,* K 522; *name as, constitute,* Ψ 90.

ὀνομακλήδην, see *ἐξονομ.*

ὀνομά-κλῦτος (*κλύω*), *of famous name, renowned,* X 51†.

ὀνομαστήν (*ὀνομάζω*), *οὐκ* —, not *to be uttered* (because ill-omened Ilios, malum omen), τ 260. (Od.)

ὄνος, masc., asinus, *ass,* Λ 558†.

ὀνόσασθε, -αιτο, ὀνοσσάμενος, see *ὄνοσαι.*

ὀνοστά, verbal adj. from *ὄνομαι, οὐκέτ'* —, non vituperanda, no *contemptible,* I 164†.

ὄνυξ, **ὀνύχεσσι,** masc., unguibus, *claws, talons* of eagle, M 202.

ὀξυ-βελής (*βέλος*), *sharp-pointed,* Δ 126†.

ὀξυόεντι, *τα,* (*ὀξύ*), *piercing, δόρυ,* Ξ 443, *ἔγχεα,* τ 33, 306. (Il.)

ὀξύς, *ύ, ύν, έες, έσι(ν); εῖ(α)* O 313, *είῃ, εῖ(αι)* Λ 272, *ῃς, ας; εῖα, έα,* sup. *ὀξύτατον,* (acer, acus), *sharp* (penetrating), *pointed,* of weapons and utensils, P 520; cliffs, ε 411; *keen, φάσγανον, ἄορ;* of light, P 372, and sound, *clear, shrill, piercing,* especially ntr. sing. and ntr. pl.; with verbs of perceiving and of calling, *sharply, keenly, quickly,* Γ 374; and of pains, Λ 268; of grief, etc., *bitter,* τ 517; *the wildly charging* Ares, Λ 836.

ὅο and **ὅου** for *οὗ,* see *ὅς, ἥ, ὅ.*

ὀπάζειν, prs., ipf. *ὄπαζεν, ὤπαζε, ζον,* fut. *ὀπάσσω, ομεν,* aor. *ὤπασα, ε, αν,* and *ὄπασσα, ε(ν),* opt. *σαιμι, σειαν,* imp. *σσον,* inf. *σσαι,* part. *σσας,* fut. mid. *ὀπάσσεται,* aor. *σσατο, σσάμενος,* (*ἕπω,* sequor), *make to follow, τινί τινα* (*ἅμα,* Σ 452, ο 310), as escort, also *μετ' ἀμφοτέροισι;* also of things, θ 430, *κῦδός τινι, ἔργοις;* of dowry of bride, X 51; *bestow, confer,* θ 498; often with inanimate subj., *γῆρας, follow hard upon, beset,* Δ 321; mid., *take to one's self as escort,* T 238; κ 59, *take with one.*

ὀπαῖα, ntr. pl., (*ὀπή*), *ἀν' ὀπαῖα,* through the *loop-holes,* i. e. between the rafters, under the eaves. These open spaces were afterward filled up, and a specific name, *μετόπαι,* given to them. This seems the simplest interpretation of α 320†, for that swallows and other birds often flew through these apertures, and into the apertures, can not be doubted. (See cut No. 90.)

ὅ-πατρος, *ον,* (*πατήρ*), eiusdem patris, *of the same father,* Λ 257 and M 371.

ὀπάων, *ονα,* masc., (*ἕπω*), comes, *armor-bearer, esquire,* K 58. (Il.)

ὅ περ, see *ὅς περ.*

ὅπ(π)η, adv., quā, (1) *where,* κ 190 sq.; *whither*(soever), M 48.—(2) *as,* θ 45.

ὀπηδεῖ, prs., ipf. *ὀπήδει,* (*ὀπηδός, ὀπάζεσθαι*), (*ἅμα,* η 165, ι 271) *τινί,* comitari, *attend, follow, ἀρετή,* etc., θ 237, P 251, *ἐκ Διός,* a Jove; *μοί,* E 216, I carry it with me in vain.

ὀπίζομαι, *εο,* prs., ipf. *ὠπίζετ(ο),* (*ὄπις*), revereri, *reverence, τί,* Σ 216, Od. always joined with *Διός, θεῶν μῆνιν; τινά,* only X 332.

ὄπιθε(ν), see *ὄπισθεν.*

ὀπῑπεύεις, and part. aor. *εύσας,* (*ὄπις*), Δ 371, circumspicere, *gaze at, τί; stare at, γυναῖκας.*

ὄπις, *ιδος, ιδα,* and *ιν,* fem., (*ὄπωπα*), *eye, θεῶν,* in sense of *avenging eye,* ultio, ξ 88; elsewh. *divine punishment,* only ξ 82 without *θεῶν,* Π 388. (Od.)

ὄπι(σ)θε(ν), adv., (*ἀπό?*), *τὰ ὄπ.,* a tergo; *στῆ,* accessit, approached *from behind,* A 197; *behind,* ρ 201; *οἱ ὄ.,* relicti; (from) *behind,* Σ 548, Φ 256; postea, *afterward,* χ 55; in posterum, *hereafter,* Δ 362; = prep. with gen., N 536.

ὀπίσ(σ)ω (*ἀπό?*), *backward,* M 272, Γ 218; *behind him,* X 137; postmodo, *hereafter,* Γ 160, 411; *πρόσω καὶ ὀπ.,* before and behind, forward and backward, describing foresight, A 343, Γ 109; *λείπειν,* leave behind.

Ὀπίτης, a Greek, slain by Hektor, Λ 301†.

ὤπλεον, ipf., (ὅπλον), *were getting ready*, ζ 73†.

ὁπλέων, gen. pl. from ὁπλή, ungularum, *hoofs*, Λ 536 and Υ 501.

ὁπλίζω, aor. **ὥπλισσε**, imp. ὅπλισσον, inf. ίσαι, pass. and mid. prs. ὁπλίζονται, ώμεθα, ipf. ὁπλίζετο, ιντο, aor. ὡπλίσαθ' = ὁπλίσσατο, άμεσθ(α), subj. όμεσθα, aor. pass. 3 pl. ὅπλισθεν, *make ready*, chariot, *prepare*, food, Ω 190; *get* ship *ready for sailing*; mid. pass., *make one's self ready*, ψ 143, Η 417; *equip, arm one's self*, Θ 55; mid. sibi parare (cenam), π 453 = **ὅπλεσθαι**, Τ 172, Ψ 159; equos suos adiungere, *harness one's horses*, Ψ 301.

ὅπλον, φ, ων, οισιν, (α), *utensil, implement*, (1) *tools*, Σ 409, γ 433.—(2) *rope, cable*, rudens, φ 390, ξ 346; pl. *cordage, rigging*, β 390.—(3) armatura, *weapons, armor*, Κ 254, Σ 614.

ὁπλότερος, οι, ων, άων, comp.; sup. -οτάτη, ην, (ὅπλον), *stronger, fresher, younger*; γενεῇ, γενεῆφιν, in age, Β 707, Ι 58; cf. Δ 325, γ 465.

Ὀπόεις, όεντος, masc., city in Lokris, home of Menoitios, Ψ 85, Σ 326, Β 531.

ὀπός, masc., (sucus), coagulum, *sap of wild fig-tree*, used, like rennet, to curdle milk, Ε 902†.

ὀπός, τῆς, see ὄψ.

ὀππόθεν (ὀκϝό-), interrogative adv., unde, *whence*, α 406, ξ 47. (Od.)

ὅπποθ(ι), rel. adv., ubi, *where*, Ι 577, γ 89.

ὁποῖος, ρ 421, τ 77, and ὁπποῖον, οίης, οἷ(α), (ὀκϝοῖος), qualis, *of what sort*, (1) interrogative, α 171; ὁπποῖ' ἄσσα, *about what sort of* garments, τ 218.—(2) rel., ρ 421, Υ 250.

ὅπου, ubi, *where*, γ 16. (Od.)

ὁππόσ, see follg.

ὁπόσσον, **ὀπ(π)ό(σ)σ(α)**, ntr., *how many*, ξ 47; ὁπόσᾱ, quantum, Ω 7; quatenus, Ψ 238; ἐπέλθω, quantum permeavero, however far I may seek, ξ 139.

ὀπ(π)ότε, adv., (ὀκϝότε), quando, *when*, with indic. after principal tenses, δ 633, υ 386; with opt. after historical tenses, Ι 191.—Conjunction = quom, I. temporal with ind., *when*, σ 409, Γ 173; fut. κέν [π 282].—II. conditional, when that is spoken of which has not yet taken place, (a) with subj., (1) *if, in case that*, where something is anticipated before the action of the principal verb follows, Α 163, Φ 112.—(2) in general propositions, Ο 210, Π 53, Ρ 98, δ 651, ρ 470; esp. in similes, Ο 382, ρ 128.—(3) designating repeated action in present, (b) with opt., (1) in cases of indefinite frequency in past, Τ 317, the verb in the principal sentence is ipf. or aor. (iter.), Γ 233, Ο 284, Σ 544, ξ 217.—(2) through assimilation with mode of principal verb, Υ 148, σ 148; (c) with subj. with κέν, in principal sentence: imp., κ 293 (ζ 303, ἄν); fut., Χ 366, Ι 703, Ξ 505, β 358, ν 394, χ 216 (ἄν, α 40, Π 62, Υ 317); prs. indic., γ 238, υ 83 (ἄν, λ 17); subj., θ 445, with ἄν.

ὀππότερος, φ, οι, οισι, η, αι, uter, *which* (of two), Γ 71, μ 57; **ὀπποτέρωθεν**, ex utra parte, Ξ 59†.

ὀπτᾰλέα, έων, (ὀπτός), assata, *roasted*, Δ 345, μ 396.

ὀπτάω, only 3 pl. ipf. **ὄπτων** = ὤπτων, aor. ὤπτησε, σαν, ὄπτησαν, ῆσαι, ήσας, σαντες, pass. aor. ὀπτηθῆναι, (ὀπτός), assare, *roast* (on the spit), γ 33, Α 466; κρεῶν, partitive gen., ο 98.

ὀπτῆρας, τούς, (ὄπωπα), speculatores, *scouts, spies*, ξ 261 and ρ 430.

ὀπτόν, ά, (ποπ-, popina, πεπ, coctum), *roasted, broiled*, π 443. (Od.)

ὀ-πυίοι, έμεν(αι), οντες, ipf. ὤπυιε, ὄπυιε, (pubes), *wed, take to wife*, uxorem ducere, Ν 429, Π 178; ὀπυίοντες, *married*; ὀπυιομένη, nupta.

ὄπωπα, see ὁράω.

ὀπωπῆς, τῆς, (ὄπωπα), visus, *sight* (vision), ι 512; adspectus, ὅπως ἤντησας, as thou hast met the view, as thine eyes have seen, γ 97.

ὀπώρη, ης, ῃ, ην, (ὀπτός, ὥρη), *time of ripening*, extending from the rising of Seirios (end of July) to the setting of the Pleiades, and corresponding nearly to our dog-days; τεθαλυῖα, luxuriant, exuberant fruit-time, λ 192.

ὀπωρῑνός, ῷ, (ὀπώρη), belonging to ὀπώρη, *midsummer*; ἀστήρ, Seirios, Ε 5.

ὅπ(π)ως, adv., (ὅκϝως), ut, I. interrogative, in indirect question, quomodo, *how*, Κ 545, Β 252; with fut. indic., often involving an intention, Ρ 635, Δ 14, α 57; with subj., ξ 329, and κέν, δ 545, Ι 681, α 296; it passes into final ut, *in order that*, γ 19, α 77, ν

365, ξ 181; joined with opt. after historical tenses, Ξ 160, ν 319, ζ 319. The transition from the use of ὅπως as indirect interrogative to that of a final conjunction can not be traced.—II. relative, *as*, corresponding to ὥς, ο 111; τοῖον, π 208, δ 109, as he is now so long away; conditional, with subj., ζ 189, with κεν, Υ 243; temporal, with preterit tense, Ε 27, Λ 459, γ 373, yet in all these passages there exists a v. l. ἐπεί.

ὁράω, **ὁρόω**, ῶ, άας, ᾶς, ᾷ, ῶμεν; **ὁρᾶτε**; ὅρα; ἆν; όων, όωντες, όωσα, ῶν, ῶντες, ῶσα; mid. ὁρῶμαι, ᾶται; ὅρηαι, ηται; ῷτο, άασθαι, ᾶσθαι, ώμενος, οι; ipf. ὁρᾶτο, ῶντο; pf. ὄπωπα, ας, plupf. ὀπώπει, aor. εἶδον and -όμην, see ΕΙΔ, V.; fut. mid. **ὄψεαι**, ει, εται, εσθ(αι), όμενος, η, αι; but ὄψεσθ(ε) (Ω 704, θ 313) is aor. imp., (*F*ορ., vereor, Ger. gewar, Eng. wary), videre, *be aware of*, *behold*, τινά, τί (ἐν, before, θ 459) ὀφθαλμοῖσιν; mid. (e. g. δ 47, Χ 166), *look on with interest*, *gaze*; φάος ἠελίοιο=ζῆν; also intelligere, *notice*, ρ 545; *look at*, *over*, *down upon*, εἰς, ἐπί, κατά τινα, τι; κατ' ὄσσε, into the eyes, Ρ 167; also with follg. ὅτι, Η 448; οἷος, Φ 108; part., Ι 360.

ὄργυι(α), αν, fem., (ὀρέγω), *fathom*, distance spanned by the outstretched arms, Ψ 327. (Od.)

ὀρεγνύς, part., parallel form to **ὀρέγων**, οντας, fut. ὀρέξω, ομεν, ειν, aor. ὤρεξε, ὀρέξῃς, ῃ, ειαν, αι, ας; mid. ὀρέγεσθαι, pf. 3 pl. ὀρωρέχαται, Π 834; plupf. ὀρωρέχατο, Λ 26; aor. ὠρέξατ(ο) and ὀρέξατ(ο), άσθω, ασθαι, άμενος, η, (por-rigo, reach), (1) *stretch out*, the hands toward heaven, or toward some person.—(2) *extend to, and give*, mid., *stretch themselves* (with the neck), Λ 26; *grasp after* any thing, with the hand; *stretch themselves*, *go at full speed*, of horses; *stride*, Ν 20; ἔγχει, *lunge out*, with the spear; τινός, at any thing; *aim at* or *hit*, δουρί; with ἔφθη. φθῇσι, and part., *hit first*, any one τινά, something τι; Ω 506, *reach out* the hands to the mouth (chin) of the murderer of my son; a general expression for the act of supplication, described in word γουνοῦσθαι, and not entirely consistent with Ω 478. Hence **ὀρεκτῇσιν**, porrectis (hastis), *by thrusting* with their spears, Β 543.

ὀρέοντο, ipf., parallel form to ὄρνυμι, coorti sunt, *rushed forth*, Β 398 and Ψ 212.

Ὀρέσ-βιος, a Boiotian from Hyle, slain by Hektor, Ε 707†.

ὀρεσί-τροφος, *mountain-bred*, Μ 299, ζ 130.

ὀρεσ-κῴοισι, ους, (κεῖμαι), *having mountain-lairs*, Α 268 and ι 155.

ὀρέστερος, ροι, (ὄρος, cf. ἀγρότερος), *of the mountains*, *mountain*-dragon, Χ 93; wolves, κ 212.

Ὀρέστης, (1) a Trojan, slain by Leonteus, Μ 139, 193.—(2) a Greek, slain by Hektor, Ε 705.—(3) son of Agamemnon, returns to Mykenai in the eighth year of the reign of Aigisthos, γ 306, whom, with his own mother, Klytaimnestra, he slays (see cut under ἕδρη, from painting on ancient Greek vase), and assumes his hereditary throne, λ 461, α 30, 40, 298, δ 546, Ι 142, 284.

ὀρεστιάδες (ὄρος) νύμφαι, *mountain-nymphs*, Ζ 420†.

ὄρεσφι, see ὄρος.

ὀρέχθεον, ipf., (ῥοχθέω), *rattled in the throat*, *bellowed in last agonies*, Ψ 30†.

ὄρθαι, see ὄρνυμι.

Ὀρθαῖος, a Trojan, Ν 791†.

Ὄρθη, town in Thessaly, Β 739†.

ὄρθι(α), ntr. pl., (ὀρθός), *with high, shrill voice*, Λ 11†.

ὀρθο-κραιράων, gen. pl. fem., (κέραα), (1) βοῶν, *with straight, upright horns*, opp. the horns of sheep and goats, μ 348, Θ 231.—(2) νεῶν, Σ 3, Τ 344, also applied to ships, with reference to pointed bow and stern, yet possibly from κεραία, *with straight* or *extended yards*, antennis porrectis instructarum.

ὀρθός, όν, (ά), ῶν, (arduus), erectus, *upright*, usually with στῇ; ἀναΐξας, starting up from his seat.

ὀρθόω (ὀρθός), aor. **ὤρθωσε**, *raise up*, Η 272; ὀρθωθείς, *raised up*, *upright*; Κ 21, *rising up*.

ὀρίνω, ει, ετον, ων, ipf. ὄρινε(ν), aor. ὤρινας, ε(ν), ὄρινα, ας, ε, ῃς, ῃ, αις, pass. pr. ὀρίνονται, ὀρινομένῳ, ον, οι, ους, η, ipf. ὠρίνετο, aor. ὠρίνθη, ὀρίνθη, είη, ἐντες, (ὄρνυμι), *stir*, *raise*; γόον, Ω 760, *aroused*; *shock*, Δ 208; *dispersed*, *affrighted*, χ 23; θυμόν, stir the heart with anger, θ 178, and other passions, Β 142, Γ 395, Δ 208, Λ 804, ρ 47, 150, 216, φ 87; fear, σ 75, χ 23; *move to pity, touch*, Λ 792, Ο 403, ξ 361, ο 486; κῆρ, ἦτορ, Π 509; pass. also grassari, *rage wildly through*, χ 360; conturbari, *troubled, confused*, Β 294, Ο 7, Π 377.

ὅρκιον, Δ 158; ὅρκι(α), pl., (ὅρκος), *pledge*, pignora foederis, (1) *oath*, Δ 158, τ 302.—(2) *victims for sacrifice*, Γ 245, 269; ταμεῖν, slaughter, hence foedus ferire, conclude a treaty, Β 124; πιστά, worthy of confidence, because under the protection esp. of Zeus, Γ 105, 107; Δ 155, as death for thee, fatal to thee; cf. also φυλάσσω, τελέω, δηλέομαι, συγχέω, ψεύδομαι, κατὰ πάτησαν.

ὅρκος, ου, ῳ, ον, ους, masc., (ἕρκος), (1) *object by which one swears*, the power called upon as witness and avenger in taking an oath, Β 755, Ο 38.—(2) *oath*, ἑλέσθαι τινός or τινί, take an oath from one, Χ 119, δ 746; καρτερόν, μέγαν, by the three realms, of the universe, of the gods, Τ 108; also in general, μέγας, mighty; θεῶν, oath by the gods, cf. Υ 313; γερούσιον, oath of the princes binding the entire people, Χ 119; ὅρκῳ πιστωθῆναι, bind yourselves by oath, ο 436.

ὁρμαθοῦ, τοῦ, (ὅρμος), *chain*, of bats hanging together, ω 8†.

ὁρμαίνων, ουσ(α), etc., part. prs., ipf. ὥρμαινε, aor. ὥρμηνε, αν, (ὁρμάω), animo volvere, *turn over in the mind*, Ξ 20; *debate, ponder*, χαλεπὰ ἀλλήλοις; (ἐνὶ) φρεσίν, κατὰ φρένα (καὶ κατὰ θυμόν), ἀνὰ θυμόν; also with ὅπως, or a double question.

ὁρμάω, only aor. **ὡρμήσαμεν,** σαν; ὁρμήσῃ, σειε, (ὁρμή), excitare, *set in motion*, τινὰ ἐς πόλεμον, πόλεμον; pass. ὁρμηθεὶς θεοῦ, a numine divi, *inspired by* the gods; surgere, with στῆναι ἐναντίβιον, ad resistendum, *make an effort* to resist; τινός, contra aliquem; mid. ipf. ὡρμᾶτ(ο), ὦντ(ο), aor. ὡρμήσατ(ο), ήσωνται, and pass. ὡρμήθη, ήτην, ησαν, and ὁρμηθήτην, ῆναι, θείς, θέντος, ι, α, ε, ες, surgere, ruere, *set out, rush on*, with inf., Κ 359; ἐκ-, currere; μετά τινα, cursu persequi, *pursue*; ἦτόρ οἱ, animus eius gestiebat, his heart *desired*; irruere, *charge upon*, τινός (ἐπί τινι) ἔγχεϊ, etc.; σὺν τεύχεσι, rise up in armor.

Ὀρμενίδης, αο, *son of Ormenos*, Amyntor, Ι 448; Ktesios, ο 414.

Ὀρμένιον, τό, town in Magnesia, Β 734†.

Ὄρμενος, (1) a Trojan, slain by Teukros, Θ 274.—(2) a Trojan, slain by Polypoites, Μ 187.—(3) and (4) see Ὀρμενίδης.

ὄρμενον, see ὄρνυμι.

ὁρμή, ῆς, ῇ, ήν, (ruo, ῥέω), impetus, ἐς ὁ. ἔγχεος ἐλθεῖν, come within the *cast* of a spear; Δ 466, curtus eius erat impetus, short was his *effort*; ε 416, irritus mihi erit, vain was my *effort*; β 403, profectionem, *departure*.

ὁρμήματα, τά, (ὁρμᾶσθαι), *longings and sorrows* of Helene, Β 356; others construe as obj. gen., *struggles and sorrows* for Helene, i. e. for her recovery.

ὁρμίζω, only aor. **ὡρμίσαμεν,** σαν, subj. ὁρμίσσομεν, (ὅρματα), *make fast, moor*, by means of stones cast from the ship, ἐπ' εὐνάων, Ξ 77, δ 785.

1. **ὅρμον,** ον, (ὁρμή ?), *landing*, the running of the flat-bottomed ship upon the shore, Α 435; μέτρον, anchorage, ν 101.

2. **ὅρμον,** ους, masc., (σειρά, series), *necklace*, ο 460, Σ 401. (See adjoining cut, also Nos. 43, 44.)

Ὀρνειαί, town in Argolis, Β 571†.

ὄρνεον, *τό*, (ὄρνις), aviculam, *bird*, N 64†.

ὄρνῑς, ῑθος, ι, ες, ων, εσσι(ν) and ὄρνῖσι, avis, ales, *bird*, in widest signif. small and large, also of birds of prey (freq. with name of the species added, λάρῳ, αἰγυπιοῖσιν), hence also *birds of omen*, K 277, ω 311, β 155; omen praesagium, evil omen, Ω 219.

ὄρνυμι, imp. **ὄρνῦθι,** *τε*, inf. ὕμεν(αι), ipf. ὤρνῠε, ον, fut. ὄρσομεν, ὄρσουσα, aor. ὦρσε, σαν, ὄρσῃ, ωμεν, (and ομεν), ητε, ὄρσας, ὄρσασ(α), aor. iter. ὄρσασκε, 2 aor. ὤρορε(ν), subj. ὀρώρῃ, (orior, ruo), *rouse*, ἐξ εὐνῆς, also, *awake*, K 518; excitare, impellere, *excite, impel*, Δ 439; τινὰ (ἐπί) τινι or ἀντία τινός, instigare; of mental states and emotions, *arouse*, Ψ 14; υ 346, *excite*. Distinguish pf. ὄρωρε, ῃ, plupf. ὀρώρει (Ψ 112, ἐπὶ, ad eos surrexerat, *arose* as their chief), ὠρώρει and mid. ὄρνῠτ(αι), ὄρνυσθ(ε), μένοιο, etc., ipf. ὤρνυθ' = ὤρνυτ(ο), ὄρνυτο, υντο, pf. ὀρώρεται, ηται, fut. ὀρεῖται, aor. ὤρετο, ὦρτ(ο), ὄροντο, ὄρηται, ὄροιτο, ὄρσ(ο) and ὄρσεο, σευ, inf. ὄρθαι, part. ὄρμενον, α, orior, *rise, arise*, of wind, dust, Λ 151; battle, tumult K 523, fire; often like ordior, with inf. η 14, *begin*; of persons, from the seat or the bed, or (for battle) against some one, χαλκῷ; ruere, πρόσω, flying onward; φίλα γούνατα, have strength; spring up, H 162, χ 364.

ὀροθύνει, prs., aor. ὀρόθῡνε, imp. νον, (ὄρνυμι), excitare, *urge on*; Φ 312, cause all the river-beds to swell.

ὄρονται, το, (Ϝορ-, ὁρᾶν, Goth. waren, Eng. be-ware), ἐπὶ δ' —, *keep ward over them*, γ 471. (Od.)

ὄρος, εος, εϊ, εα, έων, εσ(σ)ι, for gen. and dat. usually εσφι, and **οὔρεος,** εϊ, εα, εσι(ν), mons, *mountain*; Νήριτον, ι 21; Παρνησοῦ, τ 431, etc.

ὀρῷ, όν, masc., (ῥέω), serum lactis, *whey*, the watery portion of curdled milk, ι 222 and ρ 225.

ὄρουσ(εν), σαν, aor. from ὀρούω, part. σας, (ὄρνυμι), ruit, irruit, *rush forth, dart forward*, of persons and things, of missiles, Λ 359, N 505.

ὀροφῆς, τῆς, (ἐρέφω), tecti, *roof* or *ceiling*, χ 298†.

ὄροφον, τόν, (ἐρέφω), *reeds* used for thatching houses, Ω 451†.

ὀρόω, see ὁράω.

ὅρπηκας, τούς, surculos, *saplings, shoots*, Φ 38†.

ὄρσ', ὄρσεο, ὄρσευ, ὄρσας, ὄρσασκε, see ὄρνυμι.

Ὀρσίλοχος, (1) son of Alpheios, E 547 = Ὀρτίλοχος, father of Diokles, γ 489, ο 187, cf. φ 16.—(2) son of Diokles from Pherai, grandson of foregoing, E 549.—(3) a Trojan, slain by Teukros, Θ 274.—(4) fabled son of Idomeneus, ν 260.

ὀρσο-θύρη, ην, fem., (ὄρρος), *back door*, in the side wall of the men's hall (μέγαρον) of house of Odysseus, leading into the passage (λαύρη), χ 126, 132, 333. (See cut No. 90, and plate III., *b*, at end of vol.)

Ὀρτίλοχος, v. l. for Ὀρσίλοχος.

Ὀρτῠγίη (ὄρτυξ), a fabled land, ο 404, ε 123.

ὀρυκτῇ, ῇ, ήν, (ὀρύσσω), fossa, *dug*, adj. joined with τάφρος, M 72. (Il.)

ὀρῡμαγδός, only sing., (rugire), *any loud inarticulate noise, crash, roar, rattling*; esp. the *din of battle*, P 424, B 810, K 185.

ὀρύσσειν, aor. ὄρυξα, αν, subj. ομεν, inf. αι, part. ας, fodere, *dig*, κ 517; but κ 305, effodere, *dig up*.

ὀρφᾰνικόν, οί, (ὀρφᾰνός), *orphaned, fatherless*; ἦμαρ, X 490, the day that makes one an orphan, orphanhood.

ὀρφᾰναί, orbae, *orphan daughters*, υ 68†.

ὀρφναίην, acc., (ὄρφνη, ἔρεβος), tenebricosam, *murky*, νύκτα, ι 143. (Il.)

ὄρχαμος, ον, ε, (ἄρχομαι), *the first of a row, leader, chief*, ἀνδρῶν, acc.; of Eumaios (at close of verse), ξ 22, 121, ο 351, 389, π 36, ρ 184; of Peisistratos, γ 454, 482; Philoitios, υ 185, 254; Asios, B 837, M 110; Polites, κ 224; Achilleus, Z 99; Peisistratos, γ 400; voc. with λαῶν, of Menelaos (seven times); Agamemnon, Ξ 102; Patroklos, as dead, T 289; Achilleus, Φ 221; Odysseus, κ 538.

ὄρχᾰτος, ου, ον, οι, masc., (ὄρχος), *trees planted in rows, orchard*, η 112; φυτῶν, Ξ 123.

ὀρχέομαι, ipf. **ὠρχείσθην,** ὠρχεῦντ(ο), aor. inf. ὀρχήσασθαι, (ὄρχος), *dance*, properly in a ring or row, Σ 594, θ 371.

ὀρχηθμοῖο, *τοῦ, choral dance,* θ 263, N 637.

ὀρχηστήν, ὀρχησταί = **ὀρχηστῆρες,** Σ 494†, *dancers,* Π 617. (Il.)

ὀρχηστύς, *υῖ, ύν,* fem., saltatio, *dance,* α 152, 421.

Ὀρχομενός, (1) Μινυήϊῳ, λ 284; Μινύειον, B 511; very ancient city on Lake Kopais, in Boiotia, seat of the treasure-house of Minyas.—(2) city in Arkadia, B 605.

ὄρχον, *ους,* masc., *row of vines,* η 127 and ω 341.

ὄρωρε, *ει, ηται,* see ὄρνυμι.

ὀρωρέχαται, *το,* see ὀρέγω.

I. **ὅς, ἥ, ὅ,** ὅου (ὅο? B 325, α 70), ἕης, also οὗ, ἧς, etc., dat. pl. ᾗσ(ιν) E 54; orig. demonstr.; then correlative as in Z 59, μηδ' ὅν τινα—μηδ' ὅς; then apparently also interrogative.

(I.) demonstr. pr., *this, that; he, she, it,* ἥ, only ω 286, B 872, δ 367, ο 254, ρ 221, 425, υ 289, 291, Z 132, 316, 399, Π 356, Φ 198, X 201; doubled, like hi—illi, Φ 353 sq.; in first member of correlative period, τά, A 125, δ 349; ὅ, Σ 460.

(II.) relat. pron., *who, which.*—(A) position in sentence: after monosyllabic preps., but before those of more than one syllable; before, or following at an interval, a gen. part., ε 448. The relative sentence is sometimes thrown in parenthetically, χ 51; often precedes demonstrative, δ 349; specifying clauses in this case added by a dem. pron., the place of which, in apod. of conditional clauses, is sometimes supplied by δέ; two or more relative sentences succeed each other, either without connective, ψ 229, or the second relative falls away, β 54, δ 737, ξ 86; or may be replaced by a dem. or pers. pron., A 95.—(B) Construction (a) with respect to antecedent, (1) ad sensum, genere, K 278; numerus plur. after collectives, ι 96, 332; vice versâ = οἷα, μ 97, Z 228.—(2) the antecedent must sometimes be supplied, σ 286; τῶν, δ 177.—(3) antecedent assimilates to itself the case of the relative, Ψ 649, ω 30; more often the reverse, K 416. —(4) antecedent drawn into the rel. clause (attraction), B 38.—(b) as regards mode, (1) with ind. of existing circumstances, A 37; so especially in descriptions, also with κέ.—(2) with subj. of possibility (the realization of which is expected), esp. in general statements or in comparisons, δ 165. —(3) with opt., of desire, H 342; after principal verb in the preterit tense, to denote an action repeated indefinitely often, ι 94; with κέ, as in principal sentences, A 64.—(C) relative clauses may be classified, (a) simply descriptive or explanatory, H 349, I 110, K 323.—(b) hypothetical, ο 72. —(c) final, δ 389, mittit qui dicat, ὅς (κεν) ἐρεῖ, (κεν) εἴπῃ, κεν εἴποι; so also after principal verb in preterit tense, also ὅς εἶπεν.—(d) causal, B 239, 275, σ 222.—(e) apparently interrogative (in indirect question), δ 740, ρ 363, B 365, Φ 609.—(D) joined with particles, ὅς δή, *who plainly;* ὅς καί, *who also, who too;* ὅς ῥά (τε, B 522); τῷ γάρ, Z 393.

II. **ὅς, ἥ, ὅν** (properly σϝος, Lat. svos, suus, then ϝός, ϝοῖο, etc.; ϝ afterward replaced in all forms by rough breathing), also the form ἧφι, *one's own,* α 402, ι 28 [ν 320]; tuus, T 174; eius, [δ 192]; usually reflexive, suus, e. g. α 269; ὅνδε δόμονδε, *to his own* house; freq. with pron., τό, τά, etc., Φ 305, M 280, ξ 153, Σ 451, ι 250. It often precedes its noun, π 411, σ 8 (precedes the preposition, Z 500); and often follows it, E 71, Ω 36, γ 39 (follows preposition, ο 251). The noun to which it refers is often not the subject, though in the same sentence, Π 753, α 218, ι 369, λ 282, Ψ 153, ω 365; sometimes in another sentence, K 256, δ 618, 643.

ὁσίη, οὐχ —, non fas (est), it is against *divine law* to—; with inf., π 423. (Od.)

ὅσος, *οι, η, ην, αι,* ὅσον, *α,* and **ὅσσος,** *οι, οισιν, ους, η, ῃ, ας, ον, (α),* quantus, pl. quot. Quantitative adj. with varying meaning according to its antecedent, e. g. *as much as, how much, as great as, how great; as far as, how far;* its proper antecedent is τόσος, after which it is translated *as;* with τίς or τέ = quidam, fere, hence ὅσσον τε = fere; agrees in gender with the noun to which it refers, B 845; ὅσον ἔπι, *as far as,* B 616; elsewh. ὅσσον τ' ἔπι, Ψ 251, ν 114 = per quantum spatium; ἐπί θ' ὅσσον, P 368; ὅσσοι νῦν βροτοί, θ 222; ntr. **ὅσ(σ)ον,** (1) *as far as* (a certain distance), I 354.—(2) quantopere, *by as much as, by how much,* before comparatives and superlatives, A 186, 516.

ὅς περ, B 318; ὅ περ, H 114; ἥ περ, Ψ 79, etc.; τοί περ, τῶν περ = pr. rel. with πέρ (q. v.), (1) *the very one who* (*which*), B 318.—(2) *which however,* B 286.

ὄσσα, η, αν, (Ϝόκjα, vox), fama divinitus excita, *rumor,* α 282; ἐκ Διός, personified as messenger of Zeus, Fama, B 93, ω 413.

Ὄσσα, mountain in Thessaly, λ 315.

ὄσσα, see ὅσος.

ὁσσάκι, quoties, *as often as,* Φ 265; relative to τοσσάκι, λ 585.

ὁσσάτιον, masc., quantum, *how great,* E 758†.

ὄσσε, τώ, (ὄκjε, oculi), *eyes;* its adj. often pl., N 435; its verb occurs in all three nos., M 466, O 608, N 617.

ὀσσόμενος, ον, η, part. prs., ipf. ὄσσετο, οντο, (ὄσσε), *see forebode,* κ 374, Σ 224; *give to forebode, threaten,* β 152, Ξ 17; ἐνὶ φρεσί, α 115; υ 81, *see in spirit, picture to one's self.*

ὅσσος, see ὅσος.

ὅς τε, ἥ τε, τό τε, (masc. also **ὅτε,** quicunque, μ 40, ξ 221, Π 54, O 468); τάς τε, Λ 554; τά τε, B 262, E 52, ε 438 = οἷα, ν 60; differing from ὅς only in binding more closely together, and emphasizing the mutual relation between the chief and dependent clause, *that which,* Δ 361, E 332, I 117, O 130, δ 207, η 312, ξ 466; then, without general sense, like quippe qui, (ἅτε), *which in fact,* either causal, or of what is permanent or usual, ν 60: e. g. custom, Λ 779; manner, γ 73, X 127; occupation, Λ 238; ὅς ῥά τε, who, in fact.

ὀστέον, ου, ῳ, ον (α), ὀφιν, for gen. and dat. pl., (ossa), *bone,* Λ 97, M 384; λευκά, the bleached bones of the dead, λ 221, Ψ 83.

ὅστις, ἥτις, ὅτι, οὕτινος, ἧστινος, ὅντινα, οἵτινες, αἵτινες, οὕστινας, ἅστινας; also from **ὅτις,** ὅττ(ι), ὅττεο = ὅτ(τ)ευ, ὀτέῳ, pronounce ὅτjῳ, M 428; ὅτινα, ὅτεων, ὀτέοισι, ὅτινα, and ἅσσα (q. v.), quicunque, *whosoever, whichsoever,* also distributive before (ι 96) or after pl., γ 355; also indirectly interrogative, Γ 167; οὐκ οἶδ' ὅστις, mihi ignotus.

ὅτ', (1) = ὅτε.—(2) = ὅ τε, i. e. ὅτι τε.—(3) doubtful whether ε or ι is elided, the meaning is *because,* A 244.

ὅταν, better ὅτ' ἄν, see ὅτε.

ὅ τε, see ὅς τε.

ὅτε, (see ὅ), quom.—I. temporal, correlative with τότε, ἔνθα, ἔπειτα.—(A) with indic., (1) pres., *when, where, since,* B 743; -δή, β 314; ὅτε τε, *when usually,* B 471; with fut. and κέν, Υ 335.—(2) with preterit tenses, *when, how,* memini cum, A 396, Φ 396, P 627; with pf., Φ 156; plupf., E 392; ὅτε τε, with aor., E 803; ipf., η 324; ὅτε δή ῥα, Γ 221; with aor., ὡς ὅτε, *as, then, when,* Γ 33, Δ 319.—(3) iterative, ὅτε περ, E 802; introducing a simile, ὡς δ' ὅτε, with aor., Γ 33; with fut., A 518.—(B) with subj., *when,* (1) of possibility with expected realization, Φ 323, ψ 258, π 267; with ἄν, Z 448, Δ 164, Θ 373, H 459, Θ 406, (πρίν—πρίν γ' ὅτ' ἄν, δ 478); with κέν, Z 225, I 138, ν 180, ο 446, A 567, θ 243, Υ 130; εἰς ὅτε κεν, *against the time when,* β 99.—(2) iterative (a) in general, κ 486, Δ 263, η 72, π 72, φ 132, τ 567, Ω 417; after past tense, Ξ 522; with κέν, K 130, I 501; ἄν, Δ 53, ν 100, B 397, λ 17; (b) in maxims or conventional phrases, ι 6, σ 134, O 207, ξ 59; κέν, λ 218, Υ 168; (c) in similes, B 782, P 756, esp. ὡς δ' ὅτε preceding the principal sentence (with τοῖοι, Δ 141; elsewh. follg. with ὥς), B 147, X 189, ε 328, ψ 158; follg. the principal sentence, Λ 325, Δ 130; ὡς δ' ὅτ' ἄν—ὥς, κ 217, K 5, Ω 480, ε 394, ψ 233; ὡς ὅτε, without verb, tanquam, *just like,* λ 368; ἕως ὅτε, only ρ 358.—(C) with opt., *when,* (1) conditional, N 319, μ 114, Σ 465, ν 390, π 197, Ξ 248, ψ 185, N 319, ε 189.—(2) iterative, the principal sentence being iterative (a) in sense, A 610, K 78, Σ 566, P 733, θ 220, λ 510, 513, ι 208, Γ 233, ξ 220; with κέν, I 525; (b) in form, its verb being iterative, θ 87, Γ 217.—II. causal, quom, quando, *whereas, since,* A 244.

ὁτὲ μέν before ἄλλοτε or ὁτὲ δέ, Υ 49, Λ 566 = modo—modo, *now—now.*

ὀτέοισι, ὅτευ, ὀτέῳ, see ὅστις.

ὅτῐ, ὅττῐ (ntr. from ὅτις, never suffers elision), (1) as adv. = quam, with superlatives, Δ 193.—(2) as conj. = quod, *that*, ὅττι ῥα, φ 415; and *because*, B 255, ξ 52, 441.

ὅ, τι, ὅ, ττι, see ὅστις.

ὅτινα, ὅτινας, ὅτις, see ὅστις.

ὀτρᾰλέως, adv., (ὀτρηρός), *nimbly, quickly*, Γ 260, τ 100.

Ὀτρεύς, ῆος, son of Dymas, king in Phrygia, Γ 186†.

ὀτρηρός, ώ, οί, ούς, ή, (ὀτρύνω, τρέω), *nimble, busy, ready*, A 321, δ 23; adv. -ῶς, δ 735.

ὄ-τριχας, acc. pl., (θρίξ), *with like hair, like-colored*, B 765†.

Ὀτρυντεΐδης, Iphition, Υ 383, 389, son of **Ὀτρυντεύς,** king of Hyde, Υ 384.

ὀτρυντύς, ύν, fem., (ὀτρύνω), *encouragement*, T 234, 235.

ὀτρύνω, εις, ει, ἐμεν, etc., ipf. ὤτρυνον, ὄτρυνον, ε(ν), iter. ὀτρύνεσκον, fut. ὀτρῡνέω, έει, έων, etc., aor. ὤτρῡνα, (εν), ὀτρύνῃσι(ν), ῦναι, also unaugmented, impellere, *urge on*, τινὰ εἴς (ἐπί, προτί) τι, εἴσω, -δέ; also with inf., ξ 374, O 402; rarely ἵππους, κύνας, τί, *hasten*, maturare, ὁδόν τινι, *speed* one's departure; ἑταίρους, *send forth*; mid. ὀτρύνεσθε, ὤμεθ(α), ipf. ὠτρύνοντο, etc., *make haste*, κ 425.

ὅττι, see ὅτῐ. **ὅ,ττι,** see ὅστις.

οὐ, οὐκί, οὐχί, before vowels οὐκ, before rough breathing οὐχ, particle of objective or absolute negation, the thing is declared not to be so, while μή (subjective negation) declares that one thinks it is not so, *not, no;* position, usually, at end of verse, often doubled, e. g., γ 28, θ 280, κ 551, θ 32, A 86, Θ 482.—(1) in independent assertion, also subjective (opt. with κέ, A 271; fut. subj., A 262; subj. and κέ, H 197; with reference to what is past, ω 61; hypothetical, E 22).—(2) in dependent assertion after ὥς, ὅτι, οὕνεκα (not in protestation), δ 377; with inf., P 176; after verbs of thinking; in relative sentence, A 234, B 36.—(3) in causal sentence after ἐπεί, A 119; ὅτε, A 244; οὕνεκα, A 111, and conclusion. —(4) where subst. or word used substantively replaces subordinate clause, β 50.—(5) joined closely to a verb, changing its meaning into its converse, esp. with φάναι, ἐῶ, ἐθέλω, τελέω, χραίσμῃ, cf. also Δ 57, ν 143, ω 251, β 274, Γ 289; οὔτι, not a whit, by no means, δ 292; οὐ πάμπαν, οὐ πάγχυ, nequaquam, in no wise.—(6) in questions expecting affirmative answer, K 165, η 239; also in question containing a summons, η 22; cf. E 32 and ἠὲ καὶ οὐκί.—(7) οὐ μά, see μά; οὐχ ὥς, φ 427; οὐ μὰν οὐδέ, Δ 512.

οὗ, οἷ, ἕ, (orig. form σϜοῦ, etc., traces of Ϝ at hand in many forms, sui), as reflexive always retains its accent; as simple pron. of 3 pers. enclitic; gen. ἕο, εἷο, εὖ, ἕθεν, eius, and more freq. sui (εὖ, only Υ 464, sui; elsewh. eius, and enclitic); dat. οἷ, ei (ἑοῖ, without Ϝ, before αὐτῷ, sibi, N 495), and sibi; acc. ἕ, and (not enclitic, without Ϝ) ἑέ, se; not eum, eam, eos, but B 196 = eum, A 236 = id. ἓ αὐτόν, ήν, se ipsum, am, *himself, herself.*

οὔασι, ατα, see οὖς.

οὖδας, εος, εἴ, ει, (ὀδός, οὐδός), solum, *surface of the earth; ἄσπετον*, immensum; οὐδάσδε, and freq. οὖδει, *to the ground, on the earth*, κ 440; ὀδὰξ ἕλον οὖδας, they bit the dust, see ὀδάξ; also pavimentum, *pavement; κραταίπεδον*, hard-surfaced, ψ 46.

οὐδέ (οὐ δέ), neque, (1) *and not*, τὸ (τὰ) ἤδη (οἶδεν) ὅ (ὅττι), B 38; ι 408, with double meaning *nor, and not;* introduces an apodosis, E 789; causal (subordinative), B 873, δ 493, 729; οὐδὲ γὰρ οὐδέ, for *by no means*, E 22; οὐδέ τε, (a) continuative, in a negative sentence, *nor*, P 42; (b) in an affirmative sentence, *and not, nor*, β 182, A 406; — τι, *nor* at all (separated by intervening words, N 521, P 401, X 279), very freq. before οἶδα, χρή, χρεώ, with acc., δ 492; and with other verbs, A 468, Ξ 66; πολύς, λίην, πρίν, T 169; πάμπαν, by no means, ω 245.—(2) *yet not, and also not*, Γ 215, ν 243; οὐδὲ μέν, nec vero, A 154; non profecto, B 203; non enim, ο 246; — μὲν οὐδέ, *but also not*, B 703, cf. γ 27.—(3) ne—quidem, *not even*, ἠβαιόν, ne paullulum quidem, strengthens preceding negation, N 106; — περ, λ 452, elsewh. always separated; — εἰ, *not even* if, γ 115; — ὥς, ne sic quidem, *not even* thus, φ 427.—(4) — οὐδέ (not even), *nor yet*, Α 332, β 369, δ 492.—(5) *but not*, after μέν, better separated, οὐ δέ, Ε 138; *and yet not*, *nor yet*, Α 124, Γ 215; οὐδὲ —δέ, *but not*, —*but*, Γ 348.

οὐδενί, τὸ ὃν μένος, in his courage, οὐδενὶ εἴκων, yielding *to no one*; elsewh. ntr. οὐδέν, nihil, nequaquam, *nothing*, *by no means*, *in no respect*, Α 244, Χ 332, Ω 370, δ 195.

οὐδενόσ-ωρα (ὥρα), *worth no notice*, contemnenda, Θ 178†.

οὐδέ πη, neque usquam, *nor anywhere*, μ 433 = οὐδέ **ποθι**, υ 114; οὐδέ **ποτε**, neque unquam, *nor ever*, *never*, Ε 789, β 26; οὐδέ **πω**, — τί πω, nondum, *not yet*, Α 108; neque ulla ratione, *nor in any way*.

οὐδετέρωσε, in neutram partem, Ξ 18†.

οὐδός, οῖο, οὗ, όν, masc., (ὁδός), limen, δ 680, *threshold of women's apartment*; λάινος, lapideum, but υ 258, χ 127 = κρηπίδωμα, fundamentum, *stone foundation walls*.

οὐδός, ῷ, όν, fem., (ὁδός), *way*, ρ 196; γήραος, *the path* of old age; ἱκέσθαι, arrive at, tread upon the *path* of old age, commonly interpreted as *threshold* (see foregoing), which does not suit all passages.

οὖθαρ, ατα, ntr., uber, *udder*, metaphorically, *fertile*, *fat land*, Ι 141.

οὐκ, see οὐ.

Οὐκ-αλέγων, οντα, Trojan counsellor, Γ 148†.

οὐκ-ἔτι, non iam, non amplius, *no longer*, Η 357; — πάμπαν, or — πάγχυ, *no more* at all.

οὐκ-ί = οὐκ, at close of verse, δ 80.

οὐλάς, τάς, (ὅλος ?), *barley-corns*, roasted, mixed with salt, and sprinkled between the horns of victim, mola salsa, γ 441†.

οὐλᾰμόν, τόν, (2. οὖλος, εἰλέω), ἀνδρῶν, *throng*, *crowd* (of men), Δ 251. (Il.)

οὖλε (1. οὖλος), imp. pres., salve, — καὶ μάλα χαῖρε, *hail* and a hearty welcome to thee, ω 402†.

οὐλῆς, ήν, fem., (ἕλκος, vulnus ?), *scar*, cicatrix, τ 391, φ 219. (Od.)

οὔλιος (ὀλοός, οὖλος), perniciosus, *baleful*, *deadly*, Λ 62†.

οὐλο-κάρηνος (2. οὖλος), *with thick*, *curly hair*, τ 246†.

οὐλόμενον, (ε), η, ης, ῃ, ην, ων, prs. part. from οὔλομαι = ὄλλυμι, *accursed*, δ 92.

1\. **οὖλος**, ον, (σολϜος, salvus, sollus), solidus, *whole*, ρ 343 and ω 118.

2\. **οὖλος**, ων; η, ην, ας; ον, (ϜολϜειρος, vellus, Ger. wolle, Eng. wool), *woollen*, Π 224, ταπήτων and χλαῖναν, ας, τ 225, Ω 646, δ 50, ρ 89; *bushy*, *thick*, *crisp*, κόμας, ζ 231, ψ 158; ntr., *confusedly*, *incessantly*, Ρ 756.

3\. **οὖλος**, ον, ε, (ὀλϜός, ὀλοός), perniciosus, *destructive*, *murderous*, Ares, Ε 461; Achilleus, Φ 536, Ε 717; of dream, *baneful*, Β 6, 8.

οὐλο-χύτας, τάς, (οὐλάς, χέω), *sprinkled-barley*, poured or scattered from baskets, δ 761, between the horns of the victim, Α 458, as initiatory sacrificial rite; κατάρχεσθαι, = begin the solemn rites.

Οὔλυμπος, see Ὄλυμπος.

οὐμός = ὁ ἐμός, Θ 360†.

οὖν, particle, never standing alone, igitur, *then*, *therefore*, (1) resumptive, Γ 340, Ν 1; ἐπεὶ οὖν, ξ 467.—(2) continuing or further developing a thought, α 414, *hence*; μὲν οὖν, δ 780.—(3) carrying the thoughts backward, ἐπεὶ οὖν, since *once for all*; ὡς οὖν, *so* when, when *then*, Α 57 and Γ 4, Ο 363, ρ 226. —(4) used in appending an attendant circumstance in harmony with what precedes, neither *certainly* nor; neither, nor *yet*; according as it occurs in the first or second of correlative clauses: μήτ' οὖν—μήτε, ρ 401; οὔτ' οὖν—οὔτε, α 414; οὐδέ τις οὖν, ξ 254; γὰρ οὖν, for *certainly*, Β 350; εἴ γ' οὖν, if *in any case*, Ε 258.

οὕνεκα = οὗ ἕνεκα, (1) quamobrem, *therefore*, corresponding to τοὕνεκα, Γ 403.—(2) quod, quia, *because*, Α 11, δ 569.—(3) *that*, ε 216.

οὔνεσθε, see ὄνομαι.

οὔνομα, see ὄνομα.

οὔ περ, *not at all*, Ξ 416. **οὔ πη**, (1) nequaquam, *in no way*, ε 410.—(2) = οὔ **ποθ(ι)**, Α 278, Ν 309, nusquam, *nowhere*. **οὔ ποτε**, nunquam, Ζ 124. **οὔ πω**, (1) nondum, *not yet*, Α 224, β 118.—(2) = οὔ πως, *in no wise*, Γ 306. **οὔ πώ ποτ(ε)**, φ 123, μ 98, *never yet at any time*. **οὔ πως**, nulla ratione, nequaquam, *nohow*, *on no* *terms;* ἔστι, with inf., ε 103, ι 411; absolutely, χ 136.

οὖρα, see οὖρον.

οὐραῖαι, fem. pl., (οὐρά), τρίχες, hairs *of the tail,* Ψ 520†.

Οὐρᾰνίωνες, ων, (οὐρανός), caelites, *heavenly, celestial,* Ω 547; θεοί, Α 570, ι 15; also as subst., Ε 373, 898.

οὐρᾰνόθεν (οὐρανός), caelitus, *from heaven,* also with ἐξ —, Θ 19; ἀπό —, Φ 199. **οὐρᾰνόθι** πρό, *before,* i. e. not yet having passed through and beyond the vault of *the heavens, under the sky,* Γ 3†.

οὐρᾰνο-μήκης (μῆκος), *high as heaven,* ε 239†.

οὐρανός, οῦ, ῷ, όν, masc., *heaven,* (1) conceived of as fortress of brass or iron; above the αἰθήρ, Β 458; hence οὐρανὸν ἵκει, makes its way up to heaven, ι 20, ο 329.—(2) as home of gods; ἔχουσιν, inhabit; Olympus towers aloft and its summit penetrates into heaven, Α 497; invoked as witness to oath, εὐρύς, Ο 36, ε 184.

οὔρεα, see ὄρος, mons, *mountain.*

οὐρεύς, only pl. **οὐρῆες,** εῦσι, ῆας, mulus, *mule,* Α 50; but in interpolated verse, Κ 84 = οὔρους, *guard, sentry.*

οὐρή, dat. οὐρῇ, pl. -ῇσιν, cauda, *tail,* of wild beasts, Η 215; of the hound Argos, ρ 302.

οὐρίᾰχος, ον, (οὐρά), ἔγχεος, *the thicker, butt end* of spear, Ν 443, Π 612. (Il.) (See cut under ἀμφῐ-γύοισιν.)

1. **οὖρον,** α, (ὄρνυμι), ἡμιόνοιιν, ων, mules' *range,* θ 124, Κ 351, as much as a pair of mules can plough, for which the later word was πλέθρον, i. e. πέλεθρον, point at which the team, having finished the furrow, turns, *furrow's length;* δίσκου, Ψ 431, *discus-throw;* as measure of distance, θ 124.

2. **οὖρος,** ον, οι, masc., (aura), *fair wind,* ε 268; proleptically ἴκμενον, following, favoring, β 420.

3. **οὖρον,** τόν, pl. οισι, (ὅρος), *landmark, boundary,* Φ 405, Μ 421.

4. **οὖρος,** ον, masc., (Ϝόρος, ὁρᾶν), *guardian,* ο 89; Ἀχαιῶν, *bulwark* of the Achaians, γ 411.

5. οὖρος, εος, dat. pl. οὔρεσι, see ὄρος, mons.

6. οὐρός, **οὐρούς,** τούς, (ὀρύσσω), *ditches* or *channels,* serving as ways for the ships, leading from the camp down to the sea, Β 153†.

οὖς, acc. sing., ὠσίν, dat. pl., and **οὔατος,** τ(α), ασι, auris; ἀπ' οὔατος, far from the *ear,* = unheard, Σ 272; from resemblance to an ear, *handles,* Λ 633.

οὐτάζων, prs. part., ipf. οὔταζον, pass. -ζοντο, aor. οὔτασε(ν), ῃ, αι, pf. pass. οὔτασται, μένος; also from οὐτάω, aor. **οὔτησε,** iter. οὐτήσασκε, aor. pass. οὐτηθείς; from οὔτημι, imp. οὔτᾰε, aor. 3 sing. οὖτα, iter. οὔτασκε, inf. οὐτάμεν(αι), and pf. pass. οὐτᾰμένην, οι, icere, *hit, wound* by cut or thrust, αὐτοσχεδίην and αὐτοσχεδόν, τινά, also with acc. of part hit; with double acc., Δ 467, Ν 438, χ 294; with κατά, Λ 338, Ξ 446; ἕλκος, vulnus infligere.

οὔτε, neque, *neither, nor;* usually corresponding to οὔτε or οὐ; also to οὐδέ, or to τέ, καί, δέ; οὔτε τι, δ 264, Α 108.

οὐτήσασκε, see οὐτάζων.

οὔτι, see οὔτις.

οὐτῐδᾰνός, οῖο, οῖσιν, *worthless,* Α 231.

οὔτῐς, τινι, τιν(α), τινες, τι, parts often written separately, nullus, *no one,* **οὔτι,** as adv., nequaquam, *not at all, by no means,* with verbs, β 411, Β 338, β 235, Α 241; — γε, Η 142, Ι 108, Ψ 515; with adjs., Θ 81, Α 153; with advs., Α 416; οὔ μέ τι, Υ 361.

Οὖτις, τιν, fabled name, *No-man,* ι 366, 369.

οὔτοι, *certainly not,* α 203, ι 27, 211.

οὗτος, αὕτη, τοῦτο, hic, *this,* referring to what is in the mind, or to what is mentioned or known, Γ 178, 200, 229, Τ 8; in reference to second person, Κ 82; in contrast to ἐγώ, γ 359, σ 57, Θ 141; used antithetically, ν 230, Ζ 352, χ 254, 70, 78; καί μοι τοῦτ' ἀγόρευσον, α 174, δ 645, ν 232; used correlatively, Γ 177; referring back to something already mentioned, π 373, Α 126, β 256; freq. with γέ: where apparently referring to what follows, κ 431, α 267, ε 23, ν 314, η 299, φ 200, to be, however, explained as epexegetical (offering additional explanation), or οὗτος refers to what is known or has preceded; it is never used like ὅδε in wider signif., nor in reference to time.

οὕτως, before consonants οὕτω, (οὗτος), sic, *thus, so,* in reference to what is present in sight or thought, ε 377, Φ 184; with verb in 2 pers., κ 378, Δ 243, Κ 37, Ε 249; in 3 pers., Γ 42, 169, Ε 717; referring back (1) to a single thought, γ 358, φ 257, Α 131, Η 198, Τ 155 (closing a sentence, δ 485, ε 146, λ 348).—(2) to a hypothetical sentence, β 334, τ 128, Κ 129.—(3) — δή, sic igitur, *thus* then, Β 158, ε 204, θ 167, *so true* is it that; interrogative, Ξ 88, Ο 201, 553; — θην, Ν 620; referring apparently to what follows, Ν 225, Ξ 69, Ω 373, δ 148, θ 465; tantopere, Β 120; — ὡς, ξ 440, ο 341 cf. ita—ut, σ 236; *so certainly as,* Ν 825.

οὐχ, before rough breathing, see οὐ.

οὐχί, non, *no, not,* Ο 716, π 279.

ὄφειλον, ipf. indic. pl., and pass. ipf. ὀφείλετο, *owe,* with χρεῖος, a debt, Λ 688, 686, 698.

Ὀφελέστης, αο, (1) a Trojan, slain by Teukros, Θ 274.—(2) a Paionian, slain by Achilleus, Φ 210.

1. ὀφέλλω (ὀφείλω), **ὀφέλλεις,** ει, ετε, ipf. ὄφελλον, ὤφελλον, ες, ε, aor. ὄφελον, ες, (εν), and ὤφελε, ετ(ε), pass. prs. ὀφέλλεται, debere, *owe,* χρεῖος, a debt; in aor., debebam, of impossible wish, *ought to have,* etc., freq. with αἴθε, εἴθε, ὡς, also with μή, utinam, would that, Λ 380, Φ 279, Ω 764, β 184, Ι 698, Ρ 686.

2. **ὀφέλλεις,** ει, ωσι, ειεν, ειν, ουσα, ipf. ὤφελλον, ες, (ε), ὄφελλε(ν), pass. ὀφέλλετο, augere, *increase, augment,* Γ 62, Υ 242, π 174; Β 420, laborem auxit ingentem, prolepsis, *increase so as to be dreadful;* Ψ 524, *stand in stead; μῦθον, multiply* words.

ὄφελος, τό, commodum, *advantage;* with εἶναι, γενέσθαι, prodesse, *profit,* Ν 236, Χ 513.

Ὀφέλτιος, (1) a Greek, slain by Hektor, Λ 302.—(2) a Trojan, slain by Euryalos, Ζ 20.

ὀφθαλμός, οῖο, οῦ, ῷ, όν; ώ, οῖιν; οί, ῶν, οῖσ(ιν), ούς, (ὄπωπα), oculus, *eye,* Α 587; βολαί, δ 150, glances; ἐς ὀφθαλμούς, in conspectum, before one's eyes; cf. ἐν ὀφθαλμοῖσιν, θ 459; cf. also δ 47.

ὄφιν, masc., [ŏ], anguem, *snake,* Μ 208†.

ὄφρᾰ, I. temporal: (1) aliquamdiu, *sometime,* Ο 547.—(2) dum, *as long as, while,* (a) with indic. of actuality, Β 769.—(b) with subj. of probability, (*a*) *so long, as long as,* Ψ 47, Λ 477, σ 132; κεν, θ 147, Ω 553; ἄν, Χ 388; κέν and ἄν—τόφρα, β 124, ε 361, ζ 259, Λ 202; (*b*) *until,* with κέν, τ 17; with ἄν, Σ 409, Ρ 186.—II. final: *in order that* (freq. of the intention of destiny, Β 359); ὄφρα τάχιστα, Δ 269; ὄφρ' εἴπω, φ 276; εὖ εἰδῇς, Α 185, (a) with indic. fut., δ 163, ρ 6.—(b) with subj. 140 times (κέν 9, ἄν 7 times), the verb of principal sentence being (*a*) imp. or imp. inf., θ 27, χ 391, Ρ 685 (κέν, σ 182, Ω 636; ἄν, ρ 10), Ι 370, Χ 343 (κέν, κ 298); (β) subj., Ψ 83, ψ 255 (κέν, Β 440); (γ) opt., Ω 75, ο 431; (δ) indic. fut., Ζ 365, Π 423 (κέν, τ 45, γ 359); pres., π 195, 31, Μ 281 (μή, Α 579; ἄν, σ 363); pret., π 234, γ 15, Δ 486 (ἄν, κ 65, Ο 23).—(c) with opt., Η 340, 349; assimilated through influence of principal verb, υ 80.—III. special cases, referrible to I. or II. with subj., Ζ 258 (ἄν, Υ 24; κέν, Ω 431).

ὀφρυόεσσα, from ὀφρύς, cf. supercilium, on the brow or edge of a steep rock, *beetling, high-throned,* Χ 411†.

ὀφρύς, **ὀφρύος,** ύσι, ύας = ῦς, fem., *brow,* Ι 620; Υ 151, *brow of a hill.*

ὄχ(ᾰ) (cf. ἔξοχα), always before ἄριστος, α, etc., eminenter, *by far,* Α 69, ω 429, γ 129.

ὄχεσφι, see ὄχος.

ὀχετ-ηγός (ὀχετός, ἄγω), *laying out a ditch,* Φ 257†.

ὀχεύς, ῆα, ῆες, ας, masc., (ἔχω), *holder,* (1) *chin-strap of helmet,* Γ 372.—(2) *clasps* on belt, Δ 132.—(3) *bolt* (as in cut No. 32), Μ 121.

ὀχέειν, έοντας, pass. έεσθαι, ipf. 3 sing. ὀχεῖτο, ipf. iter. ὀχέεσκον, fut. mid. ὀχήσονται, aor. ὀχήσατο, vehere, *bear; play,* νηπιάας; elsewh. *endure;* pass. and mid., vehi, *be borne, drive, sail,* Ρ 77, ε 54.

Ὀχήσιος, an Aitolian, father of Periphas, Ε 843†.

ὀχθέω, **ὤχθησαν,** ὀχθήσας, (ἄχθος), aegre ferre, indignari, *bear with indignation, take ill,* Α 570; μέγ', in great wrath he spake, δ 30, ψ 182.

ὄχθης, gen., ῃ, ην, ας, ῃσιν, ας, fem., (ἔχω), ripa, litus, *bank, shore,* Φ 17, 171, 172, ι 132.

ὀχλεῦνται = έονται, from ὀχλέω, (ὀχλός), *are swept away,* Φ 261†.

ὀχλίσσειαν, 3 pl. opt. aor. from ὀχλίζω, (ὀχλός), *would heave from its place, raise,* M 448, ι 242.

1. ὄχος, **ὄχεα,** έων, έεσσι, εσφι, εα, ntr. pl., (Ϝεχ, veho), *chariots,* Λ 160, Δ 297.

2. ὄχος, **ὄχοι,** pl., (ἔχω), νηῶν, *shelters* for ships, ε 404†.

ὄψ, **ὀπός,** ί, ὄπ(α), usually with Ϝ, Ϝοπός, Ϝόπα but ὀπί, fem., (Ϝεπ-, vocis), vox, (1) *voice; ὀλίγῃ,* with faint, feeble voice; also of insects and animals, Γ 152, Δ 435.—(2) *speech, words,* H 53.

ὀψέ (ὄπισθε), postea, *afterward,* P 466, Δ 161; se ɔ, *late,* I 247, ε 272, Φ 232.

ὀψείοντες, desiderative part. from ὄψομαι, *desiring to see,* with gen., Ξ 37†.

ὀψί-γονος, ων, (ὀψέ, γόνος), *late-born, posterity,* posteri, postumus, Π 31, Γ 353.

ὄψιμον (ὀψέ), *late* (coming), B 325†.

ὄψις, **ὄψει,** fem., (ὄψομαι), *power of sight; ἰδεῖν,* see with one's eyes, Υ 205, ψ 94; conspectus, species, *appearance, exterior,* Z 468, Ω 632.

ὀψι-τέλεστον (τελέω), *late of fulfillment,* B 325†.

ὀψόμενος, etc., see ὁράω.

ὄψον, ου, ntr., (ἕψω), that which is cooked and eaten with bread; *onion,* Λ 630, ποτῷ, as relish with wine; γ 480, *flesh.*

Π.

πάγεν = πάγησαν, πάγη, see πήγνυμι.

πάγοι, masc., (πήγνυμι), scopuli, *cliffs,* ε 405 and 411.

πάγ-χαλκος, and -χάλκεος, ον, (χαλκός), *all of bronze,* θ 403; fig., a man with sinews of brass, Υ 102.

παγ-χρύσεοι (χρυσός), *all of gold,* B 448†.

πάγχυ (χέϜω, instead of παγχύδην, cf. ῥύδην, lit. "pouring out, heaping up every thing"?), prorsus, *altogether, wholly, absolutely,* ρ 217.

πάθε, έειν, ῃσθα, see πάσχω.

παιδνός (παῖς), puer, *lad, mere child,* φ 21 and ω 338.

παιδο-φόνοιο (φόνος), *murderer of one's children,* Ω 506†.

παίζουσι, part. όντων, ούσας, aor. imp. παίσατε, (παῖς), ludere, *play,* also of dance, θ 251; σφαίρῃ, game at ball, ζ 100.

Παιήων, ονος, physician of the gods, E 401, 899; from him the Egyptian physicians traced their descent, δ 232.

παιήονα, *song of triumph* or *thanksgiving* (addressed to Apollon), A 473, X 391.

Παίων, ονες, tribe in Makedonia and Thrake, on river Axios, allies of Trojans, Π 291; ἀγκυλότοξοι, K 428; δολιχεγχέας, Φ 155; ἱπποκορυστάς, Π 287.

Παιονίδης, Agastrophos, son of Παίων, Λ 339, 368.

Παιονίη, fertile territory of the Παίονες, P 350, Φ 154.

παιπαλόεντος, έσσης, ῃ, αν, (πάλλω?), *rugged, rough,* N 17, 33, P 743, κ 97. (A word of uncertain meaning.)

πάϊς, in thesis of first foot, παῖς π 337, δός, δί, (α), πάϊ; (ε); ες, ων, σί and δεσσι(ν), (πάϜ-ις, pover=puer), *child,* σ 216, δ 688; *maiden,* δ 13; *daughter,* η 313, α 278; *son,* Δ 512, I 37; *young,* Φ 282; with νέος, δ 665.

Παισός, town on the Propontis, E 612, see Ἀπαισός.

παιφάσσουσα, intensive form from stem of φά-ος, exsplendescens, *dazzling,* B 450†.

πάλαι (πάρος), olim, *long ago,* opp. νέον, I 527, νῦν, I 105; iamdiu, pridem, *long, all along,* ρ 366, υ 293, ψ 29.

πᾰλαι-γενέϊ, *ές*, dat. and voc. sing., (*γένος*), grandaevus, *full of years*, Γ 386, χ 395.

παλαιός, *οῦ, ῷ, οί, ή, αί, ῶν, ά*, (*πάλαι*), senex, *old, aged, ancient*, Ξ 108, α 395; *φωτί*, Ξ 136; vetustus, β 293, 340; comp. *παλαιοτέρους*, seniores, Ψ 788.

πᾰλαισμοσύνη, *ης*, (*παλαίω*), luctatio, *wrestling-match*, Ψ 701, θ 126.

πᾰλαισταί, masc., (*παλαίω*), luctatores, *wrestlers*, θ 246†.

πᾰλαι-φᾰτον, *α*, (*φημί*), pridem edita, *uttered long ago*; *θέσφατα*, vaticinia; *δρυός*, *famed in fable, mythical*, τ 163.

πᾰλαίω, ipf. **ἐπάλαιον,** fut. *παλαίσεις*, aor. *ἐπάλαισεν*, (*πάλη*), luctari, *wrestle*, Ψ 621, δ 343.

πᾰλάμη, *άων, ῃσ(ιν), ηφιν*, palma, *palm of the hand*, Γ 338, β 10; *hand, fist*, Γ 128, Θ 111.

1. *πᾰλάσσω*, fut. **πᾰλαξέμεν,** pass. ipf. (*ἐ*)*παλάσσετο*, pf. *πεπαλαγμένον, αι*, plupf. *πεπάλακτο*, (*πάλλω*), conspergere, inquinare, *besprinkle, stain, defile*, ν 395, Λ 169; *χεῖρας*, Λ 98.

2. *πᾰλάσσω*, mid. pf. **πεπάλασθε,** *άσθαι*, (*πάλλω*), — *κλήρῳ*, of men, *select among themselves by lot*, which was shaken in helmet, Η 171 and ι 331.

πᾰλη, *ἡ*, (*πάλλω*), luctatio, *wrestling*, Ψ 635 and θ 206.

πᾰλίλ-λογα (*πάλιν, λέγω*), rursus colligenda, recollecta, Α 126†.

πᾰλιμ-πετές, ntr., as adv., (*πέτομαι*), strictly retro volando, recidendo, = retrorsum, *back, back again*, Π 395, ε 27.

πᾰλιμ-πλάζω, only pass. aor. part. **-πλαγχθέντα,** *ας*, strictly retro repulsum, *repulsed*, ν 5; *driven back* (in disgrace), = male mulcatos, Α 59.

πᾰλιν (*πάρος*), retro, *back, back again*, Α 59; *ποίησε*, transform; also with gen., back from, *τρέπειν*, Υ 439; with *αὖτις*, back again; *ὀπίσσω*, with strengthening force; *λάζετο*, retractavit, take back, unsay; *ἐρέει*, Ι 56, contradicet, gainsay.

πᾰλιν-άγρετον (*ἄγρα*), recipiendum, *revocable*, Α 526†.

πάλιν ὁρμένω, du. part. aor. mid. from *ὄρνυμι*, retro ruentes, *rushing back*, Λ 326†.

πᾰλίν-ορσος (*ὄρνυμι*), resiliens, *springing back*, Γ 33†.

πᾰλίν-τιτα (*τίνω*), ntr., retributa, — *ἔργα* = *vengeance*, α 379 and β 144.

πᾰλίν-τονον, *α*, (*τείνω*), *bent back*, having impulse to bend backward, *elastic, quivering*, Θ 266, φ 11.

πᾰλι-ρ-ρόθιον (*ῥόθος*), *foaming back, refluent*, ε 430 and ι 485.

παλι-(ι)ωξις, *ιν*, (*ἴωξις, διώκω*), *pursuit back again, rally*, Μ 71.

παλλᾰκίς, *ίδος, ίδι*, fem., *concubine*, Ι 449, ξ 203.

Παλλάς, *άδος*, epithet of Athena, according to the explanation of the ancients, from *πάλλω*, as brandishing the Aigis and the spear, Κ 275, δ 828, Α 200, 400, Ε 1, α 125, Ε 510.

πάλλειν, *ων*, prs., ipf. *πάλλον, ε(ν), ομεν*, and mid. prs. *πάλλεται, όμενος, η, ων*; act. aor. *πῆλε, πῆλαι*, mid. 2 aor. *πάλτο*, *swing, brandish*, *χερσίν*; *shake*, *κλήρους*; mid., *cast lot for one's self* or (of several) *among each other*; iaculari, *hurl* weapons; Ο 645, *ἐν ἄντυγι*, hit himself on the shield-rim = stumbled over the shield; Χ 461, quivering at heart, with palpitating heart; Χ 452, my heart leaps up to my mouth.

Πάλμυς, *υος*, a Trojan chief, Ν 792.

πάλτο = *ἔπαλτο*, from *πάλλω*.

πᾰλύνειν, ipf. *ἐπάλυνε, πάλυνε, ον*, aor. part. *παλύνας*, (*πάλλω*, pul-vis), *strew* or *sprinkle upon*, barley meal upon meat (Σ 560, for repast), *ἀλφίτου ἀκτῇ*; inspergere, *ἄλφιτα*.

παμ-μέλαν(α), *μέλανας*, *entirely, jet black*, κ 525. (Od.)

Πάμμων, son of Priamos, Ω 250†.

πάμ-πᾰν, prorsus, *altogether*, joined with verb, Τ 334; with adj., γ 348; usually with neg. *οὐ, οὔτι, οὐκέτι, οὐδέ* = *not at all, by no means*; *μή* —, let no man whatever, σ 141.

παμ-ποικίλοι, pl., *all variegated, embroidered all over*, *πέπλοι*, Ζ 289 and ο 105.

πάμ-πρωτος, *very first*, Η 324, Ι 93; *-πρῶτον*, δ 780 (Od.), and *-πρωτα*, Δ 97, Ρ 568, *first of all*.

παμφαίνῃσι, subj., and *-ων, ονθ'* = *οντα, οντας, αῖνον*, part. prs., ipf. 3 pl. *πάμφαινον*, (redup. from *φαίνω*), *gleam, shine*, with dat., in or with, Ζ 513,

Ξ 11; *στήθεσι*, with white-shining, i. e. naked breasts.

παμφανόωντος, *α, όωσα, όωσαν*, (as if from *-φανάω, φανός*), *bright-shining, beaming, glistening*, Ε 619, δ 42, Β 458.

πάν-άγρου, gen., (*ἄγρα*), *all-catching*, of fisher's net, Ε 487†.

πάν-αίθῃσι, dat. pl., (*αἴθω*), *all glowing, burnished*, Ξ 372†.

πάν-αίολος, *ον*, (*αἰολος*), *all gleaming, glancing*, Δ 186, Κ 77.

πᾱν-ἄπάλῳ, dat., (*ἀπαλός*), *very tender, youthful*, ν 223†.

πάν-ἄποτμος (*πότμος*), *all hapless*, Ω 255 and 493.

πάν-άργυρον, *all of silver*, ι 203 and ω 275.

πάν-ἀφ-ήλῐκα (*ἧλιξ*) *τιθέναι*, *deprived of all playmates*, Χ 490†.

Πάν-αχαιοί, *ῶν*, *collective Achaians*, host of the Achaians, Β 404, α 239, etc.

πάν-ᾰ-ώριον (*ἀ-, ὥρη*), *all-immature*, having left home Ι 440, as *νήπιος*, Ω 540†.

παν-δᾰμάτωρ (*δαμᾶν*), *all-subduing*, Ω 5 and ι 373.

Πανδάρεος, *ου*, friend of Tantalos; his daughter Aëdon, τ 518; the latter carried off by the Harpies, υ 66.

Πάνδᾰρος, son of Lykaon, leader of Lykians, faithless archer, Δ 88, Ε 168, 171, 795, Β 827; slain by Diomedes, Ε 294.

πᾱν-δήμιος (*δῆμος*), *belonging to all the people, public*, σ 1†.

Πανδίων, a Greek, Μ 372†.

Πάνδοκος, *ον*, a Trojan, wounded by Aias, Λ 490†.

Πάν-έλληνες, *united Greeks*, i. e. inhabitants of Hellas or northern Greece, Β 530†.

πάν-ῆμαρ, adv., *all day long*, ν 31†.

πᾱν-ημέριος, *οι, οι, οις, ίης, ίῃ*, (*ἦμαρ*), *all day long*, i. e. (1) *from morn to eve*, δ 356, λ 11.—(2) *what remains of a day*, Α 472, cf. Α 592.

Πανθοίδης, *son of Panthoos*, (1) Euphorbos, Ρ 70.—(2) Polydamas, Ξ 454.

Πάν-θοος, *ου, ῳ*, son of Othrys, father of Euphorbos and Polydamas, priest of Apollon; at Delphi, then at Troja, a counsellor, Γ 146, Ρ 9, 23, 40, 59, Ο 522.

παν-θῡμαδόν, adv., *in full wrath*, σ 33†.

παν-νύχιος, *ον, οι, η*, and *-νυχος, ον, οι*, (*νύξ*), *the whole night long, the rest of the night*, β 434.

πάν-ομφαίῳ, dat., (*ὀμφή*), *author of all omens, all-disclosing, ὀμφαί*, Θ 250†.

Πάν-οπεύς, (1) father of Epeios, Ψ 665.—(2) city in Phokis on the Kephisos, Β 520, Ρ 307, λ 581.

Πάν-όπη, a Nereid, Σ 45†.

πάν-ορμοι, *offering moorage at all points, convenient for landing*, ν 195†.

πάν-όψιος (*ὄψις*), *in every body's eyes, openly*, palam, Φ 397†.

παν-σῠδίῃ (*σεύω*; v. l. *πασσυδίῃ*), summo impetu, *with all haste*, Λ 709.

πάντῃ, also *-ῃ*, (*πᾶς*), *on all sides, in all directions*, μ 233, Ρ 354.

πάντοθεν (*πᾶς*), *from every quarter*, Π 110.

παντοῖον, *οι, ων, οισ(ι), ους; η, ης, ην, αι, ῃς, ας*, (*πᾶς*), varius, *of every kind, manifold*, Β 397; *in various guise*, ρ 486.

πάντοσε (*πᾶς*), in first or fifth foot, *on every side*, Ε 508; in other feet, *πάντοσ'*; (*πάντοσ' ἐίσην*, round, Γ 347).

πάντως, adv., omnino, *by all means*; with *οὐ*, *by no means*, τ 91, Θ 450.

πᾰν-ὑπερτάτη, extrema, *farthest off, last*, ι 25†.

πᾰν-ύστατος, *the very last*, ι 452, Ψ 547.

παππάζουσι (*πάππας*) *τινά*, *say papa, call one father*, Ε 408†.

πάππᾰ, voc., *papa, father*, ζ 57†.

παπταίνετον, indic. 3 du., part. *-ων, οντι, ες, ε*, aor. *πάπτηνε*, part. *-ας, αντα, ασ(α)*, *look narrowly, cautiously about one, ἀμφὶ ἕ*; at, or over *ἀνά, κατά τι, κατὰ δόμον*; *look in quest of*, desiderare, *τινά*, Δ 200; *δεινόν*, torva tueri, *glare fiercely*.

πάρ, (1) = *παρά*, q. v., in anastrophe, *ὄχθας πάρ* Λ 499.—(2) = *πάρεστι*, Ι 43; = *πάρεισι*, Α 174; γ 325, praesto sunt, *are at hand*.

πᾰρά, *ᾰ* κ 242; an old case-form (cf. *πάρος*) appears as locative **πᾰραί,** Β 711: with gen., Ο 175; acc., Β 711, Γ 359; dat., Ο 280; apoc. *πάρ*, orig. as adv., *alongside, by, near*, Α 611, usually preposition.—I. with gen., *from beside, from, τινός*, from some one; *ναῦφι*, from the ships; esp. with verbs of receiving to denote the source, πὰρ Ζηνός.—II. with dat., *beside, with, by*, Α 329; ὄχεσφιν, Ε 28; ναῦφιν, Π 281; usually with verbs implying rest, but also as locative with verbs of placing, ο 488 (θεῖναι, εἷσε, etc.), πεσεῖν, κυλίνδεσθαι; penes, λ 175.—III. with acc., (1) *to* (a place), *beside, unto, along by*, esp. with verbs of motion, yet also with verbs with which, in English, no idea of motion is associated, φ 64, Ζ 34.—(2) secundum, *close to, by*, Β 522, Α 34, Μ 352.—(3) praeter, *beyond*, Λ 167; *in excess of*, δύναμιν; μοῖραν, *contrary to* right.—IV. by anastrophe, **πάρα**, Σ 400, Ω 429; παρ' (for greater clearness, πάρ', Σ 191) and πάρ, q. v.; also = **πάρεστι**, π 45, Ε 603; Τ 148, penes te est, *it rests with thee;* or = **πάρεισι**, δ 559.—V. in composition, the word appears in the significations already mentioned, but notice with βάλλω, τίθημι, the meaning *before*, Ε 369, Ι 90; and the idea of beguiling or cunningly diverting which may sometimes be expressed by *amiss, aside*, Α 555, π 287.

παρα-βαίνω, **παρ . . . βαινέτω**, let him *mount by* (thy) *side* (on the chariot), Λ 512; pf. part. παρβεβαώς, ῶτε, *standing by* one (τινί) upon the chariot, Λ 522. (Il.)

πᾰρὰ βάλλετε, imp. prs., and aor. (ἐ)βάλεν, ἔβαλον, *throw* down (fodder) *before*, Θ 504, Ε 369, δ 41; mid. βαλλόμενος, *staking*, Ι 322.

πᾰρ-έβασκε, was *standing by his side* as combatant, Λ 104†.

πᾰρα-βλήδην, adv., (βάλλω), *covertly, maliciously*, Δ 6†.

παρα-βλώσκω, pf. **παρμέμβλωκε**, *go with help to the side of*, Δ 11 and Ω 73.

πᾰρα-βλῶπες (βλέπω), *looking askance* (from shame, with acc. of respect), Ι 503†.

πᾰρ-εγίγνετο, intererat, *was present at; δαιτί*, cenae, ρ 173†.

παρα-δαρθάνω, only 2 aor. ἔδρᾰθεν, *slept beside* me (υ 88), and δρᾰθέειν φιλότητι, *share the pleasures of love with*—, Ξ 163.

παρα-δέχομαι, aor.-**εδέξατο**, perceperat, *receive at hands of*—, Ζ 178†.

παραδραθέειν, see παραδαρθάνω.

παραδραμέτην, see παρατρέχω.

πᾰρα-δράω, only **δρώωσι**, τινί, *perform in the service of*, ο 324†.

πᾰρᾰ-δύμεναι, aor. inf., (δύω), *steal past*, Ψ 416†.

πᾰρ-αείδειν, σοί, *sing before*, χ 348†.

πᾰρ-αείρω, aor. pass. **-ηέρθη**, *hung down*, Π 341†.

παραι-βᾰ́ται (βαίνω), *warriors*, who *stand beside* the charioteer, and fight, Ψ 132†.

παραιπεπίθῃσι, πιθών, see παραπείθω.

πᾰρ-αίσια (αἶσα), *adverse*, Δ 381†.

πᾰρ-ᾱίσσοντος, part. prs., aor. ῄιξεν, αν, (ἀίσσω), *charge by; τινά*, Λ 615.

παραιφάμενος, see παράφημι.

παραί-φᾰσις (φημί), *persuasion, encouragement*, Λ 793 and Ο 404.

παρακάββαλε, see follg.

πᾰρᾰ-κατα-βάλλω, aor. **κάβ-βαλεν**, ον, *lay about*, Ψ 127 and 683.

παρα-κατα-λέχω, aor. mid. **ἔλεκτο**, (λέχος), τῇ, *he had laid himself down by her*, Ι 565†.

πᾰρᾰ-κεῖται, ipf. ἔκειτο, iter. εκέσκετο, freq. in tmesis, κ 9, ν 424, Κ 75, 77; *lay near* him (οἱ), φ 416; *before* him *stood*, Ω 476; licet, χ 65.

παρὰ κιών, *passing by*, Π 263†.

πᾰρα-κλῐδόν, adv., (κλίνω), *evasively*, δ 348 and ρ 139.

πᾰρα-κλῖνας, aor. part., (κλίνω), *inclining to one side*, υ 301; *turning aside*, Ψ 424.

πᾰρα-κοίτης, ας, acc. pl., (κοίτη), *bed-fellow, husband*, maritus, Ζ 430 and Θ 156.

πᾰρά-κοιτις, ῐ, ιν, (κοίτη), *wife*, uxor, Γ 53, Φ 479.

πᾰρα-κρεμᾰ́σας, aor. part., (κρεμάννυμι), *letting hang down*, Ν 597†.

πᾰρ-ελέξᾰτο, aor., subj. λέξομαι, (λέχος), *sleep by the side of; τινὶ φιλότητι, have intercourse with*, Ξ 237, λ 242.

πᾰρ-ᾰμειψᾰ́μενος, aor. part., (ἀμείβω), *driving past*, τινά, ζ 310†.

πᾰρὰ μένῃ, subj., -μένετε, μενόντων, imp., μενέμεν, inf. prs., ipf. μένον, aor. μεῖνα, -έμεινεν, (μένω), and **μίμνων**, ipf. -έμιμνεν, *remain with*, τινί, γ 115, Λ 402, Ο 400; *tarry, hold out*, π 74, β 297.

πᾰρᾰ-μῡθησαίμην, opt., σασθαι, inf. aor., (μυθέομαι, μῦθος), *encourage, exhort*, with inf., Ι 684, Ο 45.

παρα-νηέω, see *παρ-ενήνεον*.

πἄρᾰ-νήξομαι, fut., (*νήχω*), *swim along near* (the shore), ε 417†.

πἄρ-αντᾰ (*ἄντα*), *sideways*, Ψ 116†.

παρ-απαφίσκω, aor. **ἤπᾰφε,** *cajole*, Ξ 360; with inf. in tmesis, ξ 488.

πἄραι-πείθω, aor. **ἔπεισεν,** 2 aor. red. subj. *πεπίθῃσι*, part. *πεπῖθοῦσα*, **παρ-**πεπῖθών, *όντες*, *win over*, *wheedle*, H 120; with inf., χ 213.

πἄρᾰ-πέμπω, aor. **ἔπεμψε,** *guided past*, μ 72†.

πἄρα-πλάζω, aor. **ἔπλαγξε,** *drive away from*, *τινός*, ι 81, τ 187; *confuse*, *perplex*, υ 346; part. aor. -*επλάγχθη*, *went aside*, O 464.

πἄρα-πλῆγας, acc. pl. from -*πλήξ*, (*πλάζω*), *beaten on the side* by waves, i. e. *shelving*, *sloping*, ε 418.

πἄρα-πλώω, 3 sing. aor. **-ἔπλω,** (*πλέω*), praetervecta est, *sailed by*, μ 69†.

πἄρα-πνεύσῃ, subj. aor. from *πνέω*, *blow out by the side*, *escape*, κ 24†.

πἄρα-ρρητοί, *οῖσι*, (*Ϝρητοί*, verbum), (1) *to be influenced by words*, *ἐπέεσσι*, placable, I 526.—(2) ntr., *persuasion*, N 726.

πἄρα-στᾰδόν, adv., (*παρίστημι*), *going up to*, O 22. (Od.)

πἄρα-σφάλλω, aor. **ἔσφηλεν,** *caused to glance away*, Θ 311†.

παρα-σχέμεν, aor. inf. from *παρέχω*.

παρὰ ἐτᾰ́νυσσεν, aor. from *τανύω*, (*τείνω*), *spread out before*, α 138. (Od.)

πἄρᾰ-τεκταίνομαι, aor. opt. **τεκτήναιο,** *αιτο*, (*τέκτων*), *transform*, *alter*, Ξ 54, with *ἄλλως*; *ἔπος*, fashion the matter differently than the truth, *invent a new story*, ξ 131.

παρα-τίθημι, 3 sing. **παρτιθεῖ** α 192, ipf. *παρ(ὰ) τίθει*, *ἐτίθει πάρα* ε 196, fut. *παραθήσομεν*, aor. *παρέθηχ'* = *παρέθηκε(ν)*, *πὰρ ἔθηκεν*, *θῆκεν*, *παρ' ἔθηκαν* ε 199, aor. 2 *πάρθεσαν*, *πὰρ* and *παρὰ θέσαν*, *πὰρ ἔθεσαν*, subj. -*θείω*, opt. -*θεῖεν*, imp. -*θες*, mid. aor. *πὰρ θέτο*, opt. *παραθείμην*, -*θεῖτο*, part. *παρθέμενοι*, *place* or *spread before* one, food or drink, δ 57, α 192; *bestow*, *give*, ε 91; mid., *set before one's self*, *have set before* one; *κεφαλάς*, *ψυχάς*, stake one's life, β 237.

πἄρα-τρέπω, aor. **τρέψας,** *turning sideways*; *ἔχε*, he held or guided, Ψ 398; *παραὶ δέ οἱ ἐτράπετ'*, his spear was *turned to one side*, i. e. the stroke was baffled.

πἄρα-τρέχω, aor. **ἔδρᾰμον,** *εν*, *έτην*, *run by*, K 350; *outrun*, *overtake*, Ψ 636.

πἄρ-έτρεσσαν, aor. from *τρέω*, *sprang to one side*, *shied*, E 295†.

πἄρα-τροπέων, part. pres., (*τροπή*), *misleading*, δ 465†.

πἄρα-τρωπῶσι, from -*τρωπάω*, (*τρέπω*), *change purpose*, = placant, I 500†.

πἄρ-ετύγχανε, ipf. from *τυγχάνω*, *chanced to be at hand*, Λ 74†.

πἄρ-αύδα, imp., *ῶν* part. pres., aor. *αυδήσας*, (*αὐδάω*, *αὐδή*), *address with intent to persuade*, *μύθοις*; *ταῦτα*, *persuade*; *θάνατόν τινι*, *extenuate*, *make light of*, λ 488. (Od.)

πἄρ-αυτόθι, eo ipso loco, *in that very place*, M 302†.

πἄρᾰ́-φημι, suadeo, *advise*, A 577; aor. mid. *παρφάσθαι*, *φάμενος*, *ἐπέεσσιν*, *delude*, *mislead*; *παραιφάμενος*, Ω 771, *appeasing*.

πἄρα-φθάνω, aor. opt. **φθαίῃσι,** part. *φθάς*, aor. mid. *φθᾰ́μενος*, *overtake*, *pass by*, K 346, X 197, Ψ 515.

παρ-βεβαώς, see *παραβαίνω*.

παρδᾰλέῃ, *ην*, *leopard-skin*, Γ 17 and K 29.

πάρδᾰλις, see *πόρδαλις*.

πἄρ-έζω, aor. **εἶσαν,** iuxta sistebant or collocabant, *place* or *make sit near*, γ 416; mid. pres. *παρέζεο*, imp. part. *εζόμενος*, ipf. *ἕζετο*, tmesis, ξ 448; adsidebat, iuxta considebat, *sit* or *take one's place near*, A 407, δ 738.

πἄρειαί, *άων*, *ῶν*, *άς*, (os, oris), genae, *cheeks*, Λ 393, υ 353; of eagles, β 153.

παρείθῃ, aor. pass. from *παρ-ίημι*.

1. **πἄ́ρ-**ειμι, **εστι,** *εστε*, *έασιν*, opt. *εἴη*, inf. *ἔμμεναι* and *εἶναι*, part. *ἐών*, etc., ipf. 2 *ῆσθα*, 3 *ἔην*, *παρῆεν*, *παρῆν*, 3 pl. *εσαν*, fut. *ἔσσομαι*, *ἔσσεται*, *ἔσται*, (*εἰμί*), *be present*, *at hand*, *ready*, *τινί*, versari cum, adesse; praesto esse, ρ 457; *τινί*, *belong to*, ξ 80; *δύναμις*, *be at command*, ψ 128; *παρεόντων*, of *her store*.

2. **πἄ́ρ-**ειμι, **ἰών,** praeteriens, *passing by*, δ 527; accedens, *drawing near*, ρ 233, tmesis, Λ 558; **ἴσαν,** *ἤισαν*, ω 11, 13, praeterire.

πἄρ-εῖπον, subj. *εἴπῃ*, part. *ειπών*, *οῦσ(α)*, hortari, persuadere, *persuade*, *win over*, A 555, Z 337.

παρ-έκ, before vowels **πἄρ-έξ,** I. adv., *along past*, ε 439; *close by*, Λ 486; *away from* the point, *evasively*, εἰπεῖν, ἀγορεύειν; *except this*, ξ 168. — II. prep., (1) with gen., extra, *outside of*.—(2) with acc., praetereundo, ultra, *beyond, away from*, νόον, contrary to prudence, ἄγησιν, by beguiling speeches, K 391; *along beyond*, μ 276; Ἀχιλῆα, inscio Achille, without the knowledge of Achilleus, Ω 434.

παρεκέσκετο, ipf. iter. from *παράκειμαι*.

πἄρ-εκ-προ-φῦγῃσιν, subj. aor. (φεύγω), effugiat, *elude the grasp*, Ψ 314†.

πἄρ-ελαύνω, fut. **-ελάσσεις,** aor. ἔλασσ(ε) = ἤλασε, ἤλασαν, praetervehi, *drive* or *pass by*; curru, Ψ 382; nave, μ 197; τινά, aliquem.

πἄρ-έλκετε, imp. pres., *put off*, φ 111; mid. ἕλκετο, *draw aside to one's self, get hold of*, σ 282.

παρέμμεναι, see 1. *πάρειμι*.

πἄρ-ενήνεεν, *ον*, intensive ipf., (νηέω, νέω), *heap up*, α 147 and π 51.

παρέξ, see *παρέκ*.

πἄρ-εξ-ελάαν, inf. pres., (ἐλαύνω), praetervehi, *drive* or *be borne past*; aor. tmesis, ἔλασσαν, with acc., Ω 349; subj. -ελάσῃσθα, Ψ 344.

πἄρ-εξ-ἔρχομαι, aor. **ελθεῖν,** part. ελθοῦσα, *slip by*, κ 573, K 344; elsewh. eludere, *deceive*.

παρέπλω, see *παρα-πλώω*.

παρ-έρχεται, ερχομένην, fut. ελεύσεαι, aor. ἦλθεν, subj. ἔλθῃ, opt. ἔλθοι, inf. ελθέμεν, *pass by*; τινά, *outstrip*, θ 230; *surpass*, ν 291; *evade*, A 132.

πάρεσαν, see 1. *πάρειμι*.

πἄρ-ευνάζεσθε, ipf., (εὐνάζομαι, εὐνή), *lie beside*, χ 37†.

πἄρ-έχει, *ουσιν*, subj. ἔχωσι, opt. ἔχοιμι, part. ἔχουσαι, ipf. εἶχον, 3 pl. εχον, fut. ἕξω, ει, aor. subj. σχῃ, inf. σχέμεν, σχεῖν, tmesis Ψ 50, praebere, *hold ready*, Σ 556; *supply*, food and the like, σ 133, 360; *furnish, provide*, τ 113, Ψ 835; with inf., δ 89. [πᾱρσεχῃ, in arsi, τ 113.]

παρηέρθη, see *παρ-αείρω*.

πἄρ-ήϊον, *α*, ntr., (παρειά), *cheek, jaw*, χ 404, Ψ 690; *cheek-piece* of a bridle, Δ 142.

παρήλασε, see *παρ-ελαύνω*.

πἄρ-ήμενος, *ον, ω, οι*, part. from ἧμαι, — τινί, adsidere, *sit down at* or *near*, δαιτί; also versari apud, circa, *dwell with* or *among*, ν 407; of nearness that annoys, I 311.

πἄρ-ηορίῃσι, *ας*, pl. fem., (παρήορος), *head-gear, bridle and reins* of third or running horse, Θ 87, Π 152, represented in plate I. as hanging from the ζυγόν.

πἄρ-ήορος, *ον*, masc., (ἀείρω), *floating* or *hanging beside*, (1) *flighty, foolish*, Ψ 603.—(2) a horse *harnessed by the side of the* pair, ready to take the place of either of them in case of need, tolutim iuxta currens, Π 471, 474. Plate I. represents the *παρήορος* in the background as he is led to his place. See also the adjacent cut, the first horse.—(3) *stretched out, sprawling*, H 156.

πἄρ-ήπαφε, see *παρ-απαφίσκω*.

πὰρ θείω, θέμενοι, see *παρα-τίθημι*.

παρθενικῇ, *αί*, (παρθένος), *maidenly, youthful* (νεῆνις, maiden, η 20); *maiden*, λ 39.

παρθένιος, *son of an unmarried girl*, Π 180; *παρθενίην ζώνην, virgin's* girdle.

Παρθένιος, river in Paphlagonia, B 854†.

παρθεν-οπῖπα, voc. from -οπίπης, (ὀπιπτεύω), *one who stares at maidens, seducer*, Λ 385†.

παρθένος, *οι*, fem., virgo, X 127, Σ 593, ζ 33; *young wife*, B 514.

πάρθεσαν, aor. from *παρατίθημι*.

παρ-ιαύων, part. and ipf. 3 pl. ἴαυον, iuxta cubans, *sleeping by* or *with*, I 336, 470, ξ 21.

πἄρ-ῖζεν, ipf., (ἵζω), τινί, adsidebat, *sat down by*, δ 311†.

πἄρ-είθη, aor. pass. from ἵημι, dependebat, *hung down*, Ψ 868†.

παρὰ ἰθύνετε, subj. pres., *would be able to steer by*, μ 82†.

Πάρις, Γ 437, Z 280, 503, 512, son of Priamos, seducer of Helene; see Ἀλέξανδρος.

πᾰρ-ίστημι, inf. **-ιστάμεναι,** aor. ἔστης and ἑστης, η, subj. παρστήετον, opt. παρασταίης, παρσταίη, pl. παρασταῖεν, imp. πάρ-στητε, part. παραστάς, παρστάς, ᾶσα, pf. παρέστηκεν, inf. παρεστᾰ́μεναι, plupf. 3 pl. παρέστᾰσαν, mid. pres. παρίσταμαι, σαι, ται, σο, μενος, οι, η, ipf. ἵστατο, mid. accedere, *approach*, τινί, ad aliquem, B 244, E 570; opitulari, *bring aid*, K 290, ν 301; act. aor. pf. plupf. adstare, *stand by* or *near*, σ 344, α 335; plupf. aderant, H 467; aor. accessi, *draw near*, Γ 405, E 116; hostiliter, with hostile intent, X 371, ι 52, with friendly intent, O 442; part. *drawing near*, ψ 87, Λ 261.

πᾰρ-ίσχομεν (ἴσχω), *offer*, I 638; inf. παρισχέμεν, *hold in readiness*, Δ 229.

παρ-κατ-έλεκτο, see παρα-κατα-λέχω.

παρ-μέμβλωκε, pf. from -βλώσκω.

παρμένω, see παρα-μένω.

Παρνησός, οῦ, ὄνδε, *Parnassus*, a double-peaked mountain range in Phokis; in a ravine on its southern side lay Delphi, τ 394, φ 220, ω 332.

πᾰ́ροιθ(εν), (loc. παροι, cf. παραί from πάρος), *in front*, Υ 437; antea, *heretofore*, Ψ 20, also τὸ π.; with gen., coram, pro, *in presence of*, *before*, A 360, O 154.

πᾰροίτεροι, αι, (πάρος), anteriores, (those) *in front*, Ψ 459, 480.

πᾰρ-οίχομαι, ipf. **ᾤχετο,** pf. ᾤχηκε, praeteriit, K 252, v. l. οἴχωκε, two thirds of the night *have passed by*.

πᾰ́ρος (παρά), τὸ π. 28 times, N 228, θ 31; also with πέρ, γέ (μέν), ὡς τὸ π. περ 11 times; relative with τὸ π. περ 12 times, M 346, antea, *otherwise*, *formerly*, with pres., A 553, ε 88, η 201; neg. with follg. πρίν γε, E 218; with inf. = priusquam, *before*, α 21; π. σχέμεν, hold onward, drive forward, the gen. depends upon πρότερος, Θ 254.

παρ-πεπιθών, aor. from παρα-πείθω.

Παρρᾰσίη, ης, town in Arkadia, B 608†.

παρ-σταίην, στάς, στήετον, see παρίστημι.

παρ-τιθεῖ, see παρα-τίθημι.

παρ-φάμενος, φάσθαι, see παράφημι.

πάρ-φᾰσις (φημί), *persuasion*, *allurement*, Ξ 217†.

παρ-φῠγέειν, aor. inf., (φεύγω), *slip by*, *flee past*, μ 99†.

παρ-ῴχηκα, pf. from παρ-οίχομαι.

πᾶς, πᾶσα, πᾶν, (παντ-ς, ja, orig. from παϝαντ), declined throughout as in Attic dialect, yet dat. pl. πᾶσι and πάντεσσι, gen. pl. fem. πασέων, πασᾶ́ων, sing. omnis, omnes, *all*; ἅμα π., together; π. ὁμῶς, alike; μάλα π., entirely; ἐύ π., quite; with numbers, *in all*, ε 244, θ 258, ξ 103; with superlatives, *none but*, *the very*, π 251.—(2) totus, *whole*, B 809; ἀληθείην, the *entire* truth; ρ 549, νημερτέα.—(3) pl., *all sorts* or *kinds*, A 5, 15, E 52, 60, δ 279, ε 196, δ 417; all over, πάντα, τ 475.—(4) **πάντα,** ntr. pl. adv., B 643, *in all respects*, in Iliad almost always in comparisons; in Odyssey only so in ω 446; with adj. only, θ 214, ν 209; *all over*, π 21, ρ 480.

Πᾱσῐ-θέη, one of the Graces, Ξ 276.

πᾶσι μέλουσα (μέλει), *object of interest to all*, *famous*, μ 70†.

πασσᾰλόφιν = πασσάλου, dat. φ, nom. πάσσᾰλος, (πήγνυμι), *nail* or *pin* in wall; κὰδ δ' ἐκ π. κρέμασεν, he hung it upon the *peg*, suspendit ex clavo, θ 67.

πάσσασθαι, see πατέομαι.

πάσσειν, ων, ipf. ἔπασσε(ν), πάσσε, with ἐπί, *strew* or *sprinkle upon*, E 401, 900; also with gen. part., I 214.

πάσσονα = παχίονα, from παχύς.

πασσυδίῃ, see πανσυδίῃ.

πάσχω, etc., pres., ipf. ἔπασχον, ipf. mid. πασχόμην, fut. πείσομαι, εται, εσθαι, aor. ἔπᾰθον, ες and πᾰ́θον, ες, εν, etc., inf. έειν, pf. πέπονθα, ας, 2 pl. πέποσθε (πέπᾰσθε?), Γ 99, κ 465, ψ 53; part. πεπᾰθυίῃ, plupf. ἐπεπόνθει, (πάθος), pati, *suffer ill*; τ 464, with respect to the scar, how he had *come by it*; ἔκ τινος, suffer at hands of; μή τι πάθω, ῃς, lest something should *befall* me (thee), = lest I should die, cf. δ 820; τί παθών, with finite verb, by what mischance, ω 106; κακῶς, while I am maltreated, π 275.

πᾰ́τᾰγος, φ, *dashing* of waves, *chattering* of teeth, *crash* of falling trees, *roar* of combat, N 283. (Il.)

πᾰτάσσει, ipf. ε(ν), (πάταγος), *beat*, θυμός; κραδίη, H 216. (Il.)

πατέομαι, aor. **(ἐ)πᾰσᾰ́μην,** (ἐ)πασσάμεθ(α), ἐπάσαντο, πάσσασθαι, σσάμενος, ω, plupf. πεπάσμην, (pa-sci, pabulum), comedo, *eat*, σπλάγχνα, ἀκτήν; elsewh. τινός, frui, *partake of*, *enjoy*, δ 61.

πατέω, see κατὰ πάτησαν, conculcaverunt, *tread under foot.*

πᾰτήρ, έρος, ἐρι, ἐρ(α), ερ (ε lengthened, θ 408, σ 122, υ 199), ἐρων, ἐρας, and sync. πᾰτρός, Ζ 479; ί, ῶν (πατρόθεν, on the father's side, Κ 68†), pater, *father*, ἀνδρῶν τε θεῶν τε, freq. title of Zeus; in invocation, Ζεῦ πάτερ (Diespiter); pl., maiores, *ancestors*, Δ 405.

πᾰ́τος, ου, ον, masc., *path*, *trodden way*, Υ 137; ἀνθρώπων, Ζ 202 = intercourse with men, as if it were πατῶν πάτον θηρῶν.

πάτρη, ης, ῃ, fem., (πατήρ), patria, *native country*, *fatherland*; Ν 354, *home.*

πατρίς, ἴδος, ἴδι, ἰδ(α), fem., (πατήρ), *native*, *of one's fathers*, Β 140, α 407; patria, ψ 315, ω 266.

πατρο-κᾰσιγνήτοιο, ῳ, ον, *father's brother*, patrui, Φ 469. (Od.)

Πάτροκλος, οιο, ου, ῳ, ον, (ε), and κλῆος, ῆ(α), (before ἵππευ), εις, son of Menoitios, Π 760, from Opus, elder comrade of Achilleus, fled as a youth to Peleus, on account of involuntary homicide, Λ 765 sqq. When the Trojans had burst into the camp of the Greeks, he put on Achilleus's armor, and drove them back, but was slain by the united efforts of Apollon, Euphorbos and Hektor, Π; funeral games in his honor, Ψ.

πατρο-φονῆα, τόν, (φονεύς), *parricide*, α 299. (Od.)

πατρο-φόνος, masc., (φόνος), *parricide*, Ι 461†.

πατρώϊος, ιον, ιοι, ια, (πατήρ), paternus, *from one's father*, *hereditary*; patrius, *paternal*, Υ 391, Φ 44; *hereditary*, β 286; ntr. pl. as subst., *patrimony*, π 388, χ 61.

παῦρος, οι, οισι, ους, α, and comp. παυρότερον, οι, οισι(ν), ους, parvus, exiguus, *little*, *feeble*, Β 675; pauci, *few*, Ι 545, Θ 56.

παυσωλή, fem., (παύω), *rest*, Β 386†.

παύω, prs., inf. ειν and έμεναι, ipf. iter. παύεσκον, fut. παύσομεν, aor. ἔπαυσας, ε, elsewh. unaugmented, I. *check*, *restrain*, ε 451; κ 22 *calm*, τι, Τ 67, Α 282; τινά τινος, arcere a, *keep back from*, Ο 15, Φ 137; privare re, *deprive of*, Β 595; exsolvere re, *make leave off*, δ 659, 801; also with inf., Λ 442; with part., Λ 506.—II. mid. prs. παύομαι, ipf. iter. παυέσκετο, fut. παύσεσθ(αι), aor. ἐπαύσατο, σάμεθα, elsewh. unaugmented, 1 pl. subj. ώμεσθα, pf. πέπαυμαι, ται, μένοι, *cease*, *take rest from*, *leave off*, Θ 295, υ 110, Ψ 228, μ 168; τινός, τ 268, Α 467, Σ 241; with part., Χ 502; exsolvi re, θ 540.

Παφλᾰγών, όνος, ες, inhabitant of the district of Asia Minor lying south of the Pontos Euxeinos, and bounded by the rivers Halys and Parthenios, and by Phrygia, Β 851, Ε 577, Ν 656, 661.

παφλάζοντα, part., (πομφόλυξ), *foaming*, Ν 798†.

Πάφος, fem., city in Kypros, θ 363†.

πᾰ́χετος, ον, (παχύς), *thick*, ψ 191, θ 187.

πᾰ́χιστος, sup. from παχύς.

πάχνη, fem., (πήγνυμι), pruina, *hoar frost*, ξ 476†.

παχνοῦται, pass. prs., (παχνόω), congelatur, horret, *is chilled with dread*, Ρ 112†.

πᾰ́χος, ntr., (παχύς), *thickness*, ι 324†.

πᾰχύς, έος, ύν, ύ, εῖῃ, comp. πάσσονα, sup. πᾰ́χιστος, (pinguis), *thick*, in various senses, e. g. *clotted*, *stout*, *mighty*, of blood, body, and members, μηροῦ, Π 473; neck, ι 372; hand, fist, Ε 309, ζ 128; stone, staff, Μ 446, Σ 416.

πεδάω, **πεδάᾳ,** ipf. iter. πεδάασκον, aor. ἐπέδησ(εν), πέδησε, ῆσαι, (πέδη), *fetter*, ψ 17; *bind fast*, ν 168; *delay*, Ψ 585, δ 380; ἀπὸ, arcere, ω 353; Μοῖρα, *entangle in fetters*, Δ 517; with inf., Χ 5, γ 269, constrained her to yield.

πέδας, τάς, (πούς), compedes, *fetters*, Ν 36†.

πέδῑλα, πέδῑλ' ν 225, (πούς), *sandals*, for men or women, Β 44, Ξ 186; of ox-hide, ξ 23; the gods wear golden sandals, which bear them over land and sea, Ω 340.

πεδίον, οιο, ου, ῳ, ον, ία, (πέδον), *plain*, campus; πεδίονδ(ε), *toward* *the plain, earthward,* Ψ 189, Θ 21; πεδίοιο, on or over or through the plain, διώκειν, φέβεσθαι, θέειν, ἔρχεσθαι, E 222, K 344.

πεδόθεν, *from the ground, from the beginning, from childhood,* a pueritia, ν 295†.

πέδονδε (πέδον), *to the ground, to the plain, earthward,* N 796, λ 598.

πέζῃ, τῇ, (πέζα, from πεδja, πούς), *metal ring at end of pole* (see cut No. 45), Ω 272†.

πεζός, όν, οί, ούς, masc., (πέζα), pedester, Λ 341; *on foot,* pedibus, E 204; *on land,* I 329.

πείθω, etc., ipf. ἔπειθον, (εν), elsewh. unaugmented, fut. πείσεις, σει, σειν, σέμεν, aor. πείσῃ, σειε, red. aor. πεπίθοιμεν, οιεν, εῖν, οῦσα, (fides), *persuade, win over, talk over,* τινά, A 132; τινὸς φρένας, τινὶ φρένας, θυμόν; *mollify,* A 100.—pf. **πέποιθα,** ε, ασι, ώς, ότες, ότας, subj. πεποίθω, ῃς, ομεν, plupf. πεποίθεα, 1 pl. ἐπέπιθμεν, confidere, *trust in,* τινί, with inf., Ξ 55.—mid. πείθομαι, πείθεθ' = θεται, etc., 3 pl. opt. πειθοίατο, ipf. ἐπείθετο, πείθοντο, fut. πείσομ(αι), πείσεαι, εται, ονται, εσθαι; 2 aor. ἐπίθοντο, elsewh. unaugmented πιθόμην, etc., opt. πεπίθοιθ = θοιτο, obedire, *obey,* τινί, μύθῳ; δαιτί, obey (the call to) the feast; πάντα, in all things; τί, partially; ἅ τιν' οὐ πείσεσθαι ὀίω, quae multos non secuturos opinor; credere, *confide in,* τεράεσσι, τινί, υ 45.

πείκετε, see 3. πέκω.

πεινάων, οντα, οντε, inf. ήμεναι, (πείνη), esurio, *suffer hunger, hunger after,* τινός, υ 137.

πείνη, fem., (πενία, penuria), *hunger, famine,* ο 407†.

πειράζειν, ων, prs., (πειρᾶν), tentare, *make trial of, test;* τινός, π 319.

Πειραΐδης, αο, *son of Peiraios,* Ptolemaios, Δ 228†.

Πείραιος, comrade of Telemachos, son of Klytios, ο 544, ρ 55.

1. πειραίνω, only aor. part. **πειρήναντες,** (see πεῖραρ), *bind to,* χ 175 and 192.

2. πειραίνω, only pf. pass. 3 sing. **πεπείρανται** (2. πεῖραρ), *is accomplished,* μ 37†.

1. **πεῖραρ,** ατα, *cord, rope,* μ 51, also fig. laquei, ὀλέθρου, exitii, *snares* or *cords* of destruction, cf. Psalm xviii. 6, 2 Sam. xxii. 6; οἰζύος, miseriae, *net* of woes, ε 289; πολέμοιο, νίκης, cords of war, of victory, N 358.

2. **πεῖραρ,** ατα, ασι, αθ' = ατα, (πέραν), finis, fines, *end,* of earth, Okeanos, sea, ψ 248; ἑλέσθαι, obtain a decision, Σ 501; *chief points* in each matter, Ψ 350; γ 433, that which brings to completion or end, *implement, tool.*

πειρᾶν, imp. -άτω, (πεῖρα, ex-perior), tentare, *test,* τινός; also adoriri, *attack;* conari, *attempt,* with inf., Θ 8; ὅπως, δ 545.—mid. πειρᾶται, ipf. ἐπειρᾶτο, ῶντ(ο), fut. πειρήσομ(αι), etc., aor. ἐπειρήσαντ(ο) = αντ', elsewh. unaugmented, pf. πεπείρημαι, aor. pass. πειρήθη, etc., conari, with inf., also with μή, εἰ; experiri, tentare, *make trial of, put to proof,* τινός, B 193, ν 336, K 444, B 73; τί, as to something, θ 23; with εἰ, N 806; decertare cum, *contend with* (ἀντίβιον, adversus, περί, de); of things, τινός; σθένεος, test one's strength, cf. Ψ 432; also τί, make trial of something; explorare, τινί, dat. of instr.; μύθοισιν, try one's self, find out one's skill, in words.

πειρητίζων, ipf. πειρήτιζε(ν), ον, (πειράω), tentare, *try, test,* τόξου; τινός, *make trial of, sound,* ο 304; decertare cum, *contend with;* στίχας, adoriri ordines, attack the lines, M 47.

Πειρί-θοος, son of Zeus and of Dia, wife of Ixion, king of the Lapithai in Thessaly, friend of Theseus, husband of Hippodameia; the quarrel with the Centaurs arose out of the wedding banquet, M 129, 182, φ 298, Ξ 318, A 263.

πείρινθα, τήν, (πείρατα), *wagon box* or *body,* perh. of wicker-work, ο 131.

Πείροος, εω, son of Imbrasos, chief of the Thrakians, Δ 520; slain by Thoas, Δ 525.

πείρων, οντες, ipf. ἔπειρε(ν), ον, πεῖρε(ν), aor. ἔπειραν, πεῖραν, pf. pass., part. πεπαρμένος, η, ον, (περᾶν), transfodere, *pierce through,* Υ 479; peragit, *transfix,* Π 405; *pierce with spits, spit,* γ 33, κ 124; also pass., Φ 577; *stuck full of, studded,* ἥλοισι; pierced with pains, E 399; pervehi, fig.

cleave the waves, one's way, etc., β 434, Ω 8, θ 183.

πείση, τῇ, (πείθομαι), ἐν—μένε, remained *in obedience, subjection,* υ 23†.

Πείσ-ανδρος, (1) son of Antimachos, slain by Agamemnon, Λ 122, 143.—(2) a Trojan, slain by Menelaos, N 601–619.—(3) son of Maimalos, chief of Myrmidons, Π 193.—(4) son of Polyktor, suitor of Penelope, σ 299; slain by Philoitios, χ 268.

Πεισ-ηνορίδης, *son of Peisenor,* Ops, α 429, β 347, υ 148.

Πεισ-ήνωρ, (1) father of Kleitos, O 445.—(2) father of Ops.—(3) herald in Ithaka, β 38.

Πεισί-στρᾰτος, Nestor's youngest son, Telemachos's companion to Sparta and to Pherai, γ 36, δ 155, ο 46, 48, 131, 166.

πεῖσμα, ἄτος, ατ(α), ntr., *stern-cable,* used to make the ship fast to land, ζ 269, κ 96, ν 77; *cord plaited of willow withes,* κ 167. (Od.)

πείσομαι, see πάσχω, and πείθω.

(πέκω) **πείκετε,** imp. prs., (pecto), *comb* or *card* (wool), σ 316; aor. mid. πεξαμένη χαίτας, combing her hair, Ξ 176.

πέλᾰγος, ει, εσσι(ν), ntr., (πλάζω), *wave, tide;* ε 335, *high* or *open sea.*

Πελάγων, (1) chief of the Pylians, Δ 295.—(2) attendant of Sarpedon, E 695.

πελάζειν (πέλας), aor. ἐπέλασσα, ε(ν), αν, and πέλασ(σ)ε(ν), σαν, subj. πελάσῃς, (σ)σῃ, σσομεν, imp. σσετον, inf. πελά(σ)σαι, (1) *bring near, make to approach,* adigere, τινά (τί) τινι, local dat. χθονί, οὔδει, to the earth; ἱστοδόκῃ, into the mast-crotch; ὀδύνῃσι, *bring into,* so also (Od.) εἴς τι, ἔν τινι, κ 404, οὐδάσδε; mid. only 3 pl. opt. aor. νηυσὶ πελᾰσαίᾰτο, P 341.—(2) appropinquare, *approach, draw near,* νήεσσι.—Pass. pf. πεπλημένος, aor. πελάσθη, and 3 pl. πέλασθεν, also sync. aor. mid. 3 sing. πλῆτο, pl. πλῆντο, ἔπληντο, appropinquare, Δ 449, μ 108; οὔδεϊ, χθονί, sink to earth.

πέλας, iuxta, *hard by,* κ 516; with gen. only ο 257. (Od.)

Πελασγικός, όν, epithet of Zeus in Dodona, Π 233; in Argos, q. v.

Πελασγός, οἱ, original population of Greece, first in region about Dodona; then in Thessaly, B 840, Boiotia, Attika, also in Peloponnesos, P 288; Homer mentions other Pelasgians from Kyme, on side of Trojans, K 429; and still others in Kreta, τ 177.

πέλεθρα, τά, (πέλομαι?), *plethron,* a square each of whose sides is 100 feet, i. e., as measure of surface, about ¼ acre, Φ 407, λ 577; see οὖρον.

πέλεια, αν, αι, and πελειάδες, ἄσιν, fem., (πέλειος), *wild pigeon,* Φ 493, Λ 634.

πελεκκάω, aor. **πελέκκησεν,** *hew, shape with axe,* ε 244†, from

πελέκκῳ, ntr. dat., (πέλεκυς), *axehelve,* N 612.

πέλεκυς, υν, εις, εων, εσσι, εας, *axe* or *hatchet* for felling trees, Ψ 114, P 520; double-edged, ε 234, see ἡμιπέλεκκα; serves also, in case of need, as weapon, O 711; symbol of firmness and resolution, Γ 60; *sacrificial axe,* γ 449; τ 573, *wedge-shaped blocks of iron,* resembling axes, which were placed in line, and then the attempt was made to shoot an arrow through all the helve-holes.

πελεμιζέμεν, aor. πελέμιξεν, ίξαι, (πέλω), *brandish, shake,* Π 766; φ 125, *make quiver.*—Pass. ipf. πελεμίζετ(ο), aor. πελεμίχθη, concuti, *quake,* Θ 443; repulsus est, *drive back,* Δ 535.

πελέσκετο, πέλεν, see πέλω.

Πελίης, αο, *Pelias,* son of Poseidon and Tyro, λ 254; king of Iaolkos, exiled his brother Neleus, and forced Jason, the son of his other brother Aison, into the Argonautic expedition; father of Alkestis, B 715.

πέλλας, τάς, *milk bowls* or *pails,* Π 642†.

Πελλήνη, fem., town in Achaia, B 574†.

Πέλοψ, οπος, *Pelops,* son of Tantalos, father of Atreus and of Thyestes, gained with his wife Hippodameie, the daughter of Oinomaos, the throne of Elis, B 104 sqq.

πέλει, ipf. πέλε(ν), aor. ἔπλε; mid. **πέλεται,** ονται; ηται, ώμεθ(α), ωνται; οιτο; ευ, ipf. πέλοντο, iter. πελέσκετο, aor. ἔπλευ = εο, ἔπλεθ' = ἔπλετ(ο), (πάλλω), verti, *be hurled,* Λ 392; *be in motion,* ἐπί τινι, ν 60; versari circa, *be busy about;* then, in general, versari, locum habere, δ 45, usually in mid.; *πέλε*, *project*, E 729; cf. *πέλονται*, N 632; esse, esp. with adj., e. g. *τοὶ φίλον ἔπλετο* (factum est) *θυμῷ*, H 31; *πέλει*, *rises* (to heaven), Γ 3.

πέλωρ, ntr., *monster;* the Kyklops, ι 428; Skylla, μ 87; Hephaistos, Σ 410; also **πέλωρον,** *ου*, *α*, B 321, κ 168, 219, λ 634.

πελώριος, *ον*, *α*, (*πέλωρ*), immanis, ingens, *monstrous, huge*, Γ 229, γ 290, ι 187, 190, Λ 820, Θ 424, K 439, Σ 83 = **πέλωρον,** ι 257, ο 161, M 202.

πεμπάζομαι, aor. subj. 3 sing. **πεμπάσσεται,** (*πέντε*), *he reckons up for himself* (on his five fingers), δ 412†.

πεμπταῖοι, pl., (*πέντε*), *on the fifth day*, ξ 257†.

πέμπτος, *ῳ*, *ον*, *ης*, quintus, *fifth*, ι 335, Π 197.

πέμπω, etc., prs., ipf. *ἔπεμπε*, *ον*, and *πέμπ(ε)*, *ον*, fut. *πέμψω*, *έμεναι* = *ειν*, aor. *ἔπεμψ(εν)*, *αν*, and *πέμψεν*, *αν*, etc., mitto, *send*, (*ἐπί*) *τινι*, *εἰς*, *ἐπί*, *προτί τινα*; also with *-δε*, *ζε*; with inf., Π 454, ν 206.—(2) dimitto, *dismiss, send home*, ψ 315.—(3) comitari, *escort*, τ 461, θ 556.

πεμπ-ώβολα, ntr. pl., (*ὀβολός*), *five-tined forks*, on which the flesh or inwards were spitted preparatory to roasting, A 463. (Cf. adjoining cut combined from several ancient representations.)

πενθερός, *ῷ*, masc., socer, *father-in-law*, θ 582 and Z 170.

πενθήμεναι, inf., 3 du. indic. *πενθείετον*, aor. inf. *πενθῆσαι*, (*πένθος*), desiderare, lugere, *lament, mourn for*, σ 174; esp. for the dead, Ψ 283, *γαστέρι*, by fasting, T 225.

πένθος, *εος*, ntr., (*πενία*), desiderium, luctus, *longing, grief*, Σ 73, Δ 197; *τινός*, for any one, Λ 249; *ἀέξειν*, cherish grief.

πενίῃ, *τῇ*, (*πένεσθαι*), penuriae, *poverty; εἴκων*, cedens, ξ 157†.

πενιχροῦ, *τοῦ*, egeni, *needy*, γ 348†.

πενώμεθα, subj. prs., inf. *πένεσθαι*, ipf. (*ἐ*)*πένοντο*, *be busily engaged* (about), *περί τι*, *prepare;* esp. feast, meal, ξ 251.

πεντᾰ-ετές, ntr., (*Fέτος*), *five years long*, γ 115†.

πεντᾰ-έτηρον (*Fέτος*), *five years old*, B 403, ξ 419.

πέντᾰχᾰ (*πέντε*), *in five divisions*, M 87†.

πέντε, quinque, K 317, γ 299. **πεντήκοντ(α),** quinquaginta, Z 244, B 509. **πεντηκοντό-γυιον,** *of fifty acres*, I 579†. **πεντηκόσιοι,** *five hundred*, γ 7†.

πεπαθυῖα, see *πάσχω*.

πεπείρανται, pf. pass. from *πειραίνω*.

πεπαλαγμένος, *πεπάλακτο*, see *παλάσσω*.

πεπαρμένος, see *πείρω*.

πεπάσμην, see *πατέομαι*.

πεπερημένος, see *περάω*.

πέπηγε, see *πήγνυμι*.

πεπιθεῖν, *πέπιθμεν*, *πεπιθήσω*, see *πείθω*.

πέπληγον, *πεπληγώς*, see *πλήσσω*.

πεπλημένος, see *πελάζω*.

πέπλος, *οιο*, *ου*, *οι*, *οισι*, *ους*, masc., *cover* for chariot, E 194; chairs, η 96; funeral urns, Ω 796; esp. *woman's over-garment* or *robe*, E 315, Z 90, σ 292. (Cf. cut No. 2, and the cut on next page.)

πεπνυμένος, etc., see *πνέω*.

πέποιθα, see *πείθω*.

πέπονθα, *πέποσθε*, see *πάσχω*.

πεποτήαται, see *ποτάομαι*.

πεπρωμένον, *πέπρωται*, see (*ἔ*)*πορον*.

πεπταμένας, *πέπταται*, *πέπτανται*, see *πετάννυμι*.

πεπτεότ(α), see *πί-πτω.*

πεπτηώς, *ῶτα,* see *πτήσσω.*

πεπύθοιτο, *πέπυσμαι,* see *πυνθάνομαι.*

πέπον, voc., plur. *ονες,* from nom. *πέπων,* (*πέσσω*), properly, *cooked, ripe, mellow,* then as term of endearment, *dear, pet,* Z 55, P 120, ι 447; in bad sense, *coward, weakling,* B 235, N 120.

πέρ (*περί*), post-positive and enclitic, perquam, (1) to emphasize assertion, *very,* A 416, Γ 201, H 204; very first time, Ξ 295; *by all means, at all events, at least,* A 211, B 236, ρ 13, Θ 242, υ 7, 181, I 301, A 353; *even,* γ 236.—(2) concessive after part. (cf. *καίπερ*), *although,* A 241, 588, Z 85 (also preceding part., A 131, 217, 546, 587); with *ἔμπης,* ο 361; with *καί,* A 577; *καίπερ, although,* Θ 125, I 247, ε 73.—(3) with conditional particles, if *besides,* A 81, H 117; if *that is to say,* α 188; also with *κέ,* e. g. *αἴ κέ περ,* H 387.—(4) with temporal conjunctions, *ὅτε περ,* E 802, K 7; *πρίν,* O 588.—(5) after relatives (sometimes separated from the relative) calling attention to what is known, or familiar, may often be rendered by *just,* ν 284; or by *yet, for that matter,* B 286, β 156, ν 249; coinciding in meaning with (1), Ψ 79.

περάαν, see *περάω* 1. 2.

Περαιβοί, Pelasgian tribe about Dodona and on the river Titaresios, B 749†.

περαιόω, only aor. pass. **περαιωθέντες,** (*πέραν*), transvecti, (get the start in) *crossing over,* ω 437†.

περάτη, *τῇ,* (*πέραν*), in extrema parte, *at the farthest* or *opposite border;* opp. east = *in the west,* ψ 243†.

1. *περάω,* 3 pl. **περόωσι,** inf. *περάαν,* part. *περῶντα,* ipf. 3 pl. *πέραον,* iter. *περάασκε,* fut. *περήσω, ησέμεναι = ήσειν,* aor. *ἐπέρησε, πέρησε, σαμεν,* (*πέραν*), *pass through, penetrate, traverse, τί, διά τινος,* permeare, pervehi, traicere; also *διά τινος, ἐπὶ πόντον, ἐφ' ὑγρήν,* δ 709.

2. *περάω,* inf. **περάαν,** aor. *ἐπέρασσα, ας, εν, αν,* and *πέρασαν, άσητε, άσειε,* pf. pass. part. *πεπερημένος,* (*πέραν, πράσσω, πιπράσκω*), vendere, *export for sale, sell,* (*ἐς*), *Λῆμνον,* Φ 40; *πρὸς δώματα, κατ' ἀλλοθρόους ἀνθρώπους,* ο 453.

Πέργᾰμος, fem., citadel of Ilios, Δ 508, E 446, Z 512, H 21.

Περγᾰσίδης, *son of Pergasos, Δηικόων,* E 535†.

πέρην (*πέραν*), adv., ultra, *beyond,* with gen., B 626; *opposite,* with gen., B 535.

περησέμεναι, see *περάω* 1.

πέρθω, **πέρθοντε** part. pres., fut. *πέρσειν,* aor. *ἔπερσεν, πέρσα, σε(ν), σειαν, σας, σαντες,* and 2 aor. *ἔπρᾰθον* (*ἐπράθομεν,* A 125), (perdo), delere, *sack, destroy,* Σ 342, nearly always of cities; pass. pres. *περθομένη,* ipf. *πέρθετο,* M 15; fut. *πέρσεται,* Ω 729; 2 aor. sync. *πέρθαι,* Π 708, deleri, vastari, *be laid waste.*

πέρι, properly locative of orig. comparative form para, with signif. *in higher degree* or *measure,* I. as adv., (1) *more,* magis, hence often with gen. comp., see below; then valde, *very, exceedingly,* Σ 549, Π 186; often with verbs, e. g. μ 279, θ 63, *δοῦναι;* often also like valde, when standing with the locative forms *κῆρι, φρεσί, θυμῷ,* really belonging to the verb or adjective (*ἄσπετον,* Π 157, γ 112, 95).—(2) *round about,* circa, Γ 384; esp. freq. with locatives (*αὐλῇ,* in the court, κ 10; *καπνῷ,* in the smoke, A 317; *χειῇ,* in the hole, X 95), in which cases it belongs to the verb. The transition to follg. use often can not be traced: II. as prep., **περί** (by anastrophe *πέρι*), (1) with gen., (*a*) super, *over, σπείους, over* the cave; *τρόπιος, a-straddle of* the keel; (*b*) the meaning passes from the original signif. *round about,* circa, to that of *about, for, in behalf of,* de, pro, esp. with verbs of fighting, defending, striving, Π 1; (*c*) with verbs of saying, inquiring, etc., = de, *concerning,* α 135, ρ 563; (*d*) special phrases, H 301, *πέρι* may be construed with *θυμοβόρος* as adverbial, *very* destructive, and *ἔριδος* as causal genitive, out of strife; the explanation of the genitive in phrases like (*e*) *πέρι ἔμμε-*

ναι, adjectives like *καρτερύς*, *πέρι*, *more*, *in higher measure*, *better*, is to regard them as genitive after comparative, Δ 257, *δ* 190, *α* 66, Ρ 279; also dative of respect in which, *θ* 102, Ψ 318.—(2) with dative (*a*) locative, freq. *περί* as adverb really belongs to the verb, *χροί*, *on* the body; *στήθεσσι*, *on* the breast; yet with verbs of fighting it is to be translated *for*, *in behalf of*, cf. de, pro, Ρ 133; also circa, Β 389 and λ 424, dying *around* the sword, i. e. pierced by the sword still remaining in wound; (*b*) of advantage, be anxious *about*, *for*, one, Κ 240.—(3) with acc., (*a*) *round about*, *δ* 368, Ζ 256, Ω 16, Λ 609, Λ 448; (*b*) *along*, Μ 177; *close by*, *round about*, Γ 408, Β 757, *γ* 107, *κ* 410; *πονεῖν περί τι*, of object for which one is interested, circa, *about*, *respecting*; Φ 11, *about*, *in* the eddies.

πέρι stands for *περίεστι*, Κ 244, *μ* 279.

περῐ-άγνῦται (*Ϝάγνυμι*), *breaks around*, *spreads around* (voice of Hector), Π 78†; in tmesi, Λ 559, are broken over.

περὶ ἄγωσιν, subj., (*ἄγω*), *μίν*, circa eum ducant, *draw about* him, *δ* 792†.

περὶ βαῖνε, ipf., aor. *περίβη*, *ησαν*, *ῆναι*, *βάντα*, pf. *βεβαῶτα*, *ῶσα*, plupf. *βεβήκει*, *βέβασαν*, (*περί*) *τινί*, *go about*, *surround* (to protect), defendere, *τινός*.

περῐ-βάλλει, *ετον*, ipf. *βάλλε*, *περίβαλλε*, aor. *βαλόντε(ς)*, *throw about* or *around*, a rope around, *θόλοιο*; *throw* arms *around*, *flap* wings *about*, Λ 454; superare, *excel*, Ψ 276, *ο* 17.—Mid. *βαλλομένους*, ipf. *βάλλετο*, aor. *βἄλόμην*, *βάλετ(ο)*, *throw over one's self*, *put on*, *φᾶρος*, Β 43; *ζώνην ἰξυῖ*, *κ* 544.

Περί-βοια, (1) daughter of Akessamenos, mother of Pelegon, Φ 142.—(2) daughter of Eurymedon, mother of Nausithoos by Poseidon, *η* 57.

περῐ-γίγνεται, *όμεθ(α)*, *εσθαι*, superat, *surpass*, *τινός*, *θ* 102, Ψ 318.

περι-γλᾰγέας (*γλάγος*, lac), *filled with milk*, Π 642†.

περι-γνάμπτοντα (*γνάμπτω*, *νάπος*), *Μάλειαν*, *doubling* Malea, *ι* 80†.

περῐ-δείδια, pf., aor. *περί-δεισαν*, *σασ(α)*, *σαντες*, (*δειδ-*, *δϝι*, hence vowel long by position, where others read *-δδεισαν*), timere alicui, *fear for*, *τινί*; *νέκυος*, Ρ 240; ne, *lest*, *μή*, Ρ 242. (Il.)

περῐ-δέξιος, ambidexter, *very skillful*, *expert*, Φ 163†.

περι-δίδωμι, **περῐ-δώσομαι,** *ώμεθον*, subj. aor. mid., (*δίδωμι*), *stake upon*, with gen. of thing risked, Ψ 485, *ψ* 78; *πέρι δῶκε*, *gave in high degree*, *abundantly*, *α* 66, *η* 110.

περῐ-δῑνηθήτην, 3 du. aor. pass., (*δινέω*), *ran round and round*, *πόλιν*, Χ 165†.

περὶ *γὰρ* **δ϶ίε,** aor., (*δϝι*, *δίω*), valde timuit (ei) ne, *greatly feared* lest, Ε 566, Ρ 666.

περί-δρᾰμον, see *περι-τρέχω*.

περί-δρομος, *οι*, (*δρόμος*), *running round*, *round*, *circular*, Ε 726, Β 812; *ξ* 7, *detached*, *alone*.

περι-δρύφθη (*δρύπτω*), aor. pass., *he had the skin all torn off* from his elbows, Ψ 395†.

περὶ ἔδῡνεν, Π 133; aor. *δύσετο*, *χ* 113, induit, *put on*; but aor. *περίδῡσε*, *stripped off*, Λ 100.

περι-δώσομαι, *δώμεθον*, see *περιδίδωμι*.

πέρι τ' εἰμί, *περίειμι*, *εσσι*, *εστι*, *εστε*, inf. *ἔμμεναι*, *τινός*, superior sum, *be superior*, *excel*, *τι*, in respect to, in; *τόσσον*, tanto, Θ 27; also with dat. whereby, v. l. *βουλῇ*, Α 258.

περι-έρχομαι, aor. **ἤλυθεν** and *ἤλυθε(ν)*, *come around*, *encompass*, *τινά*; of a sound, *ρ* 261; *οἶνός τινα φρένας*, *stole around* his senses, *ι* 362.

περι-έχω, aor. mid. **σχόμεθα,** imp. *σχεο*, tueri, *protect*, *ι* 199; *τινός*, Α 393.

Περι-ήρης, *εος*, father of Boros, Π 177†.

περῐ-ήχησεν, aor. from *ἠχέω*, *rang all over*, Η 267†.

περι-ίδμεναι, see *περί-οιδα*.

περῐ-ίστημι, aor. **ἔστη,** *-στησαν*, 3 pl. subj. *-στείωσι*, mid. ipf. *-ίστατο*, pass. aor. *-στάθη*, *station one's self about*, circumsistere, Β 410; cingere, Ρ 95; pass., λ 243, *rose and stood around*.

περι-καλλής, *έος*, *έϊ*, *έ(α)*, *έας*, *ές*, (*κάλλος*), pervenustus, *very beautiful*.

περῐ-καλύπτει, ipf. *κάλυπτε*, aor.

ἰκάλυψα, ε, τινί τι, *cover all over with;* κῶμα, *wrap in the cloak* of sleep, Ξ 359, K 201, σ 201.

περί-κειται, *μενον,* ipf. *-κειτο, τινί, lie around,* as a veil or covering, φ 54; amplecti, T 4; I 321, naught *remains* to me, I have won nothing.

περι-κήδετο, ipf., (*κήδομαι*), *τινός, care for; οἱ βιότου,* curabat eius rem familiarem, *take care of* his possessions.

περί-κηλα, ntr. pl., (*κῆλον*), per-arida, *well-seasoned,* ε 240 and σ 309.

Περι-κλύμενος, son of Neleus and of Pero, λ 286†.

περι-κλῦτός, *οῦ, όν, ά,* (*κλύω*), praeclarus, *famous, renowned,* of gods, A 607, θ 287; of men, *α* 325, Σ 326; of things, *δῶρα,* I 121; *ἔργα,* Z 324, *ἄστυ,* δ 9.

περι-κτεινώμεθα, pres. subj., ipf. *κτείνοντο,* circa interimi, *be killed round* about, Δ 538 and M 245.

περι-κτῖόνων, *εσσι, ας,* nom. *-κτίων,* (*κτίω*), *dwellers around, neighbors,* vicinus, P 220, T 104, β 65.

περι-κτῖται, *οἱ,* (*κτίω*), *dwellers about,* vicini, λ 288†.

περί ἑ ἔλεψε (aor. from *λέπω*), *φύλλα,* has *peeled off* from it *round about* the leaves, A 236†.

περῖ-μαιμώωσα, part. from *μαιμάω, feeling* or *groping about for,* with acc., μ 95†.

πέρι μάρναο, imp. pres., (*μάρναμαι*), *ἐμεῦ, fight for* me, Π 497†.

περί-μετρον (*μέτρον*), *beyond measure, very large,* β 95. (Od.)

Περι-μήδης, (1) companion of Odysseus, λ 23, μ 195.—(2) father of Schedios, O 515.

περι-μήκετον, acc., (*μῆκος*), *very lofty,* Ξ 287, ζ 103.

περῖ-μήκεος, *ει, εες, -μηκες, εα,* (*μῆκος*), permagnus, *very long* or *high,* ι 487, N 63.

περῖ-μηχἄνόωνται, pres., ipf. *όωντο,* (*μηχανή*), *cunningly devise; τινί,* against any one, ξ 340 and η 200.

Πέρῖμος, a Trojan, son of Meges; slain by Patroklos, Π 695†.

περῖ-ναιετάουσιν, pres., (*ναίω*), *are inhabited,* i. e. *lie round about,* δ 177; *dwell about,* β 66.

περῖ-ναιέται, *οἱ, neighbors,* Ω 488†.

περι-ξέστῃ (*ξέω*), *polished on every side,* μ 79†.

περὶ οἶδ' = *περί-οιδε,* better *πέρι οἶδε,* inf. *ἴδμεναι,* plupf. *ᾔδη,* (*οἶδα*), with inf., *know better, understand* something (*τί*) *better* than others (*ἄλλων*); τ 285, be master of.

περι-πέλομαι, aor. part. **περι-πλομένου,** *ων, ους,* aor. (*πέλομαι*), Σ 220 (ex, *ὑπό*), hostibus versantibus circa urbem, in consequence of the enemies *having surrounded* the city; elsewh. *ἐνιαυτοῦ, ῶν,* as the years *revolved, in the course of* the years.

περῖ-πευκές, ntr., (*πευκ-, πικ-,* pique), *very sharp,* Λ 845†.

περι-πλέχθη, *θείς,* aor. part. from *πλέκω,* amplexus, *embrace, τινί,* ξ 313 and ψ 33.

περι-πληθής (*πλῆθος*), *very full* (of people), *populous,* ο 405†.

περι-πλομένων, see *περι-πέλομαι.*

περι-πρό, *around and before* (him), Λ 180 and Π 699.

περι-προ-χῠθείς, part. aor. pass. from *χέω, pouring in a flood over,* Ξ 316†.

περί-ρρεε (for *σρεϝε,* ipf. from *ῥέω*), *streamed around,* with acc., ι 388†.

περι-ρρηδής (*ῥέω,* cf. Liv. 2, 20, 3, "moribundus ad terram defluxit;" or perh. better from *ϝραδινός*), *τραπέζῃ, falling down across* the table, χ 84†.

περί-ρρῠτος (for *σρυτος, ῥέω*), *seagirt,* τ 173†.

περι-σθενέων, part., (*σθένος*), *exulting in his might,* χ 368†.

περι-σκέπτῳ (*σκέπω*), *covered, shut in on all sides;* others translate, *conspicuous from every side,* α 426. (Od.)

περι-σσαίνοντες, and mid. ipf. *-σσαίνοντο,* (*σϝανjω,* schwänzeln), *wag* with the tail (*οὐρῇσι*) about one (*τινά*), *fawn upon,* κ 215. (Od.)

περι-σσείοντο, ipf. pass., (*σείω, σϝι,* schwingen), *were tossed about, floated in the air,* T 382 and X 315.

περι-στᾰδόν, adv., (*ἵσταμαι*), *drawing near from every side,* N 551†.

περι-στάθη, see *περι-ίστημι.*

περι-στείχω, 2 sing. aor. **-στειξας,** circumibas, *didst walk about,* δ 277†.

περι-στέλλω, aor. pass. **στείλασα,** *wrapping up* (in funeral clothes), ω 293†.

περι-στενᾰχίζεται, ipf. *-το, re-echoes*

on every side, αὐλῇ, (even) in the court, κ 10; ποσσίν, with the tread of feet.

περι-στένεται (στένω), is *too small*, i. e. *stuffed full*, Π 163†.

περι-στέφει, 3 sing., *surrounds on all sides*, complet, ε 303; but θ 175, his grace *is not embellished* on every side by (seemly) words.

περί-στησαν, see περι-ἵστημι.

περι-στρέφω, aor. part. **στρέψας**, *whirling around*, Τ 131, θ 189; pass. στρέφεται (better τρέφεται, *curdles*, *thickens*), *whirls around*, Ε 903.

περί-σχεο, see περι-έχω.

περι-ταμνόμενον, ους, (τέμνω) *cutting off for one's self*, *intercepting*, i. e. *driving away*, λ 402. (Od.)

περι-τελλομένου, ων, ους, (τέλλω), ἔτεος, ἐνιαυτῶν, *in the revolution of* the year, the years; *revolving*, Θ 404, Β 551.

περι-τίθημι, aor. ἔθηκαν, θῆκαν, opt. 3 pl. θεῖεν, *place round about*, splinters in the fire-pan, σ 308; δύναμίν τινι, *bestow*, γ 205; mid. aor, θήκατο χροΐ, *put on* one's body, θέτο κρατί, θέτ' ὤμῳ.

περὶ τρέπω, aor. **ἔτρᾰπον**, *went round*, κ 469†.

περι-τρέφω, ipf. **τρέφεται**, *thickens*, i. e. *curdles*, Ε 903; ipf. τρέφετο, ice *was forming* (*thickening*) on the shield, ξ 477.

περὶ τρέχω, aor. **ἔδραμε**, -δραμον, it *rolled about* in every direction, Ξ 413; *ran up* with help (from every side), Χ 369.

περι-τρέω, aor. **τρεσαν**, *fled on every side* in fear, Λ 676†.

περι-τρομέοντο, ipf. (τρομέω), *his flesh quivered with fear*, μέλεσσιν, on his limbs, σ 77†.

περι-τροπέων, έοντες, part. pres., (τρέπω), *revolving*, Β 295; *turning* (ourselves) *often about*, ι 465.

περί-τροχον, ntr., *round*, Ψ 455†.

περι-φαινομένοιο, ῳ, *visible from every side*, Ν 179; subst., *conspicuous place*, ε 476.

Περί-φᾱς, αντος, (1) son of Ochesios, an Aitolian, slain by Ares, Ε 842, 847.—(2) son of Epytos, Trojan herald, Ρ 323.

Περῑ-φήτης, (1) a Mysian, slain by Teukros, Ξ 515.—(2) son of Kopreus, from Mykenai, slain by Hektor, Ο 638.

περι-φρᾰδέως, adv., *carefully*, Α 466, ξ 431.

περι-φραζώμεθα, subj., (φράζω), νόστον, *let us consider* the return, α 76†.

περί-φρων, ονι, masc. and fem., (φρήν), *very thoughtful*, *sagacious*, Ε 412, α 329.

περι-φῦναι, φύς, φῦσ(α), amplecti, *embrace*, τ 416; τινά, π 21. (Od.)

περι-χέω, aor. **ἔχευεν**, χεῦεν, χευεν, subj. χεύῃ, part. χεύας, — τινί τι, *pour* or *shed over*, Ε 776; χρυσόν τινι, gild, γ 426; mid. χεύεται for ηται, subj. aor. ἀργύρῳ, silvers; plupf. κέχυτο, was shed over, Β 19.

περι-χώσατο (χώομαι), *was very wroth*; τινός, on account of—, Ι 449, Ξ 266.

περι-ωπῇ, ήν, (ὄπωπα), *look-out place*, Ξ 8, Ψ 451, κ 146.

περι-ώσιον, ntr. adv., (ὅσιος), *beyond measure*, Δ 359, π 203.

περκνόν, with acc., *dappled*, Ω 316†.

Περκώσιος, *inhabitant of* **Περκώτη**, a town in Troas, Λ 228, Ο 548, Β 835.

πέρνημι, part. **περνάς**, ipf. iter. πέρνασχ' = πέρνασκε, pass. prs. περνάμενα, (πέραν), vendere, *sell*, Σ 292, Χ 45. (Il.)

περονάω, aor. **περόνησε**, (περάαν), transfixit, *pierce*, Η 145; mid. ipf. περονᾶτο, aor. ήσατο, *fastened*, *made fast about her*, Κ 133.

περόνη, ῃ, ην, fem., (πείρω), *clasp*, *brooch*, *buckle*, Ε 425, σ 293; of modern form, as the cut from ancient original shows.

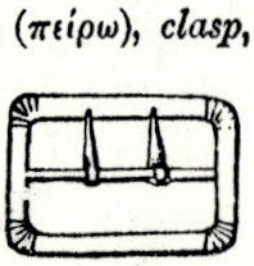

περόωσι, 3 pl. for περάουσι, from περάω.

πέρσα = ἔπερσα, aor. from πέρθω.

Περσεύς, (1) son of Danae, Ξ 320. —(2) son of Nestor, γ 414, 444.

Περσε-φόνεια, ης, ῃ, daughter of Zeus, λ 217, and of Demeter, wife of Aides, κ 494, 509, λ 213; ἐπαινή, Ι 457.

Πέρση, daughter of Okeanos, wife of Helios, mother of Aietes and of Kirke, κ 139†.

Περσηιάδης, descendant of Perseus, Sthenelos, Τ 116†.

πεσέειν, έεσθαι, see πίπτω.

πεσσοῖσιν, dat. pl. masc., *at draughts*

or *checkers*, α 107†. (Similar Egyptian game illustrated in the following cut.)

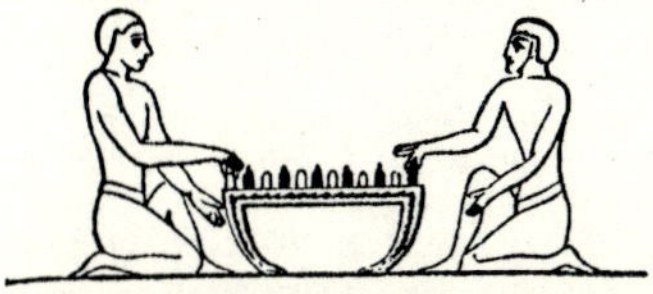

πέσσω, only prs., (coquo), *ripens*, η 119; χόλον, κήδεα, *conceal, brood over*; γέρα, *digest* = *enjoy*, B 237; Θ 513, *carry off* the missile in one, and *nurse* the wound.

πεσών, see πίπτω.

πετάλοισι, dat. pl. ntr., foliis, *leaves*, B 312, τ 520.

πετάννυμι (see πιτνάω, -ημι), aor. **πέτασ(ε),** αν, opt. άσειε, part. άσ(σ)ας, (patere), pandere, *spread out*, ζ 94, ε 269; χεῖρε, the arms, ι 417; to swim, ε 374; elsewh. as suppliant, Ξ 495; θυμόν, *open* the heart; pass. πέπταται, ανται, ατο, expanditur; πεπταμένας, patentes; aor. 3 pl. πετάσθησαν, φ 50; part. θεῖσαι.

πετεηνά, ηνῶν, οῖς, (πέτομαι), *winged*, B 459; *birds, flying things*, O 238, P 675; *fledged*, π 218.

Πετεών, ῶνος, fem., village in Boiotia, B 500†.

Πετεώς, ῶο, son of Orneus, father of Menestheus, Δ 338, M 355.

πέτομαι, **πέτεται,** ονται, εσθαι, ipf. πέτετ(ο), ἑσθην, οντο, ἐπέτοντο, aor. ἔπτἄτ(ο), subj. πτῆται, part. πτἄμένη, volare, *fly* (strictly and fig., currere, *run*, ποτὶ πτόλιος, X 198); of steeds, οὐκ ἄκοντε πετέσθην, E 366, Θ 45; with ἐκ, *fall from, escape from*, μ 203.

πετραίην, acc. fem., (πέτρη), *inhabiting a rock*, μ 231†.

πέτρη, ης, ῃ, ην, αι, άων, ῃσ(ιν), ας, saxum, *rock*, N 137, ι 243; symbol of firmness, O 618; of hard-heartedness, Π 35; *cliff, reef*, γ 293, κ 4; *rocky mountain*, ν 196, δ 501; *cave*, B 88; X 126, *stone seat*.

πετρήεσσα, ῃ, αν, (πέτρη), saxosus, *rocky*, B 496, δ 844.

πέτρῳ, ον, masc., saxum, *piece of rock, stone*, H 270.

πεύθομαι, see πυνθάνομαι.

πευκἄλίμῃσι(ν), *prudent, sagacious*; φρεσίν, Ξ 165. (Il.)

πευκεδἄνοῖο, *destructive*, K 8†.

πεύκης, ας, fem., pinus, *pine, fir*, Λ 494. (Il.)

πεύσομαι, see πυνθάνομαι.

πέφανται, see (1) φαίνω.—(2) φένω.

πεφάσθαι, see φένω.

πεφασμένος, see φαίνω.

πεφήσεται, fut. pf., (1) from φαίνω.—(2) from φένω.

πεφιδέσθαι, δήσομαι, see φείδομαι.

πέφνον, see φένω.

πέφρἄδον, δέειν, see φράζω.

πέφρικε, see φρίσσω.

πεφύασι, see φύω.

πεφυγμένον, πεφυζότες, see φεύγω.

πεφῠλαγμένον, see φυλάσσω.

πεφυυῖα, see φύω.

πεφυρμένη, ον, see φύρω.

πῆ; (v. l. πῇ), qua? (1) *whither?* E 472, Θ 94.—(2) *how?* N 307.

πή (v. l. πῄ), enclitic, aliquâ, (1) *anywhere*, χ 25; *somewhere*, Γ 400.—(2) *in any way*, Z 267, Ω 373.

πηγεσι-μάλλῳ (πήγνυμι), *thick-fleeced*, Γ 197†.

πηγαί, ἑων, ῇς, άς, fontes, *sources*, Φ 312, ζ 124.

πήγνυμι, fut. **πήξεις,** aor. ἔπηξε = πῆξε, αμεν, ῃ, αι, ας, αντ(α), (pango, pax), *fix, plant firmly* in any thing, ἐν, with local dat. χ 83, ἐπὶ τύμβῳ, λ 87; without prep., λ 129; *impale*, ἀνὰ σκολόπεσσιν, Σ 177; pass. prs. πήγνῠται, ipf. πήγνῠτο, aor. 3 pl. πῆχθεν, and 2 aor. (ἐ)πάγη, 3 pl. πάγεν, 2 pf. πέπηγε, plupf. ἐπεπήγει, haerere, *stick fast*, pf. *remain fast*, ἐν καιρίῳ, in a mortal part, Δ 185, Γ 135, N 442, Θ 298; X 453, rigescunt, *stiffen*. In ε 163, πῆξαι may be construed as imp. 1 aor. mid., or inf. 1 aor. act. used imperatively.

πηγῷ, ούς, (πήγνυμι), *firm, stout, tough*, I 124; κύματι, *mighty* wave, ε 388.

πηγῠλίς (πάγος), *frosty, ice-cold*, ξ 476†.

Πήδαιον, place in Troja, N 172†.

Πήδαιος, son of Antenor and of Theano, slain by Meges, E 69†.

πηδάλιον, ῳ, (α), (πηδόν), *rudder*, γ 281, ε 255. Strictly the word seems to denote the *handle* or *bar* connecting the two rudders (for two were used even in historical times), and serving to move them. See cuts Nos. 94, 95;

cf. Nos. 21, 40, 41, 48, 64, and adjoining cuts representing rudder of an Egyptian ship; in the first cut both rudders are portrayed, regardless of perspective, as on the same side of the vessel.

Πήδᾰσος, (1) town of the Leleges in Troas, on the Satnioeis, destroyed by Achilleus, Z 35, Υ 92, Φ 87.—(2) subject town of Agamemnon, I 152, 294.—(3) son of Abarbaree, slain by Euryalos, Z 21.—(4) steed of Achilleus, Π 152, 467.

πηδάω, ipf. **ἐπήδα,** aor. πηδῆσαι, salire, *leap*, ὑψόσε, in the air, Φ 302; *speed, escape*, Ξ 455. (Il.)

πηδῷ, τῷ, ntr., *with the oar-blade*, used collectively, η 328. (Od.)

πηκτόν, ntr., (πήγνυμι), *well joined together, firm*, K 353, ν 32.

πῆλαι, λε, see πάλλω.

Πηλεγών, son of Axios, father of Asteropaios, Φ 141, 152, 159.

Πηλεΐδης, *αο, εω*, and **Πηληιάδης,** *αο, εω* [synizesis, also in Πηλεΐδεω, A 1, O 64, θ 75], and **Πηλείων,** *ωνος, ι, α, son of Peleus*, Achilleus, A 223, O 74, X 58, Ψ 41, A 322, Ω 431, Υ 80, A 197, ω 18, Ψ 249, Υ 27, 88. **Πηλειωνάδε,** *to Peleus's son*, Ω 338†.

Πηλεύς, ῆος, (έος, when joined with υἱός, όν), *Peleus*, son of Aiakos, fugitive from Aigina to the Myrmidon Eurytion in Phthia, whose daughter Antigone he marries, but afterward the Nereid Thetis: his daughter by the former Polydora, Π 175 sqq.; his son by the latter Achilleus, I 147, 252, 289, Σ 87, Ω 61, Φ 188; hence **Πηλήιος,** adj., Σ 60.

Πηληιάδης, see Πηλεΐδης.

πήληξ, *ηκι, α*, fem., galea, *helmet*, Π 105, O 608, *α* 256. (Il.)

Πηλιάς, *ἄδα, μελίη, ην*, *Pelian* spear (from Mount Pelion), gift of Centaur Cheiron to Peleus, Υ 277, Π 143. (Il.)

Πήλιον, mountain in Thessaly, B 757, Π 144, λ 316.

πῆμ(α), ἄτος, ἄτ(α), ntr., (πά-θος), malum, *suffering, woe, harm*, Ω 547, ε 179; κακοῖο, perpessio mali, *endurance* of calamity; δύης, doloris, *depths* of wretchedness; of persons, and pestis, *bane, nuisance*, ρ 446.

πημαίνει, fut. πημανέειν, aor. 3 pl. opt. -ήνειαν, (πῆμα), *injure, distress*, O 42; ὑπὲρ ὅρκια, *work mischief* by violating the oaths; aor. pass. πημάνθῃ, ανθῆναι, laedi, τί, *to suffer* any *hurt* or *harm*, θ 563.

Πηνειός, river in Thessaly, flowing through the vale of Tempe into the Thermaic gulf, B 752, 757.

Πηνέ-λεως, εω, leader of Boiotians, B 494, Ξ 496, 487, 489, Π 340, P 597.

Πηνε-λόπεια, ης, *Penelope*, the heroine of the Odyssey, κούρη Ἰκαρίοιο, *α* 329; Ὀδυσσῆος παράκοιτις, φ 158; μήτηρ Τηλεμάχοιο, φ 311; ἐχέφρων, δ 111; περίφρων, δ 787, ε 216.

πηνίον, τό, (pannus, fano), *thread of the woof* passed from one side to the other in and out through the upright threads of the warp, before which the weaver stood, Ψ 762†.

πηός, οὖς, affinis, *brother-in-law*, Γ 163, θ 581.

Πηρείη, ἡ, region in Thessaly = Πιερίη? B 766†.

πήρης, gen., ην, fem., (pera), *knapsack, beggar's wallet*, ρ 357, 411. (Od.)

πηρόν, acc., caecum, *blind*, B 599†.

Πηρώ, οῦς, daughter of Neleus and of Chloris, wife of Bias, λ 287†.

πήχει, dat., acc. υν, du. εε, (1) *elbow, lower arm*, Φ 166; brachium, E 314, ρ 38.—(2) *the centre-piece*, which joined the arms of the ancient bow; in shooting, this piece was grasped by the left hand, and the arrow passed between the finger of the hand and the centre-piece of the bow (see cuts Nos. 112, Herakles; 133, Paris; 67, 96, 97, Assyrians), Λ 375, φ 419.

πῖαρ, ntr., (πιϜαρ), *fat*, of cattle, Λ 550; *rich, fat soil* under the surface of ground, ι 135.

πίδακος, τῆς, fontis, *spring*, Π 825†.

πιδηέσσης, *rich in springs*, Λ 183†.

Πιδύτης, ην, a Trojan from Perkote, slain by Odysseus, Z 30†.

πίε, ἐειν, aor. from πίνω.

πιέζειν, ipf. ἐπίεζε, πίεζον, pass. aor. πιεσθείς, (premo), comprimo, *squeeze, press*, μ 174, Π 510; ἐν δεσμοῖς, vinculis constringere, load with fetters.

πίειρα, irreg. fem. from πίων.

Πιερίη, region about Olympos in Makedonia, Ξ 226, ε 50; see Πηρείη.

πιθέσθαι, see πείθω.

πιθέω, apparent coll. form of πείθω, 2 fut. **πεπιθήσω**, persuadebo, *persuade*, with inf., X 223; πιθήσεις, obedies, *obey*, φ 369; aor. part. πιθήσας, with dat., fretus, confisus, *relying on*.

πίθοι, ων, *great earthen jars* for wine and oil, ψ 305, β 340, half buried in earth, as in cut No. 68.

πικρόγαμοι, nom. pl., πάντες κ' ὠκύμοροί τε γενοίατο—τε, for all would be a speedy death and a *bitter marriage*, α 266, δ 346, ρ 137.

πικρός, όν, (fem., δ 406); ήν, άς, όν, ά, *sharp-pointed*, of arrows, missiles, Δ 118; also of taste, Λ 846; and of smell, *pungent*, δ 406; *bitter*, Λ 271; *hateful*, ρ 448.

πίλνἄται, ipf. πίλνἄτο, (πέλομαι), versatur, *move about, frequent*, T 93; vertebantur, *were rolling along*, χθονί, on the ground, Ψ 368.

πῖλος, masc., pilus, *felt*, K 265.

πιμπλανεται, (πίμπλημι, plenus), impletur, *is filled with*, μένεος, I 679†.

πίμπλημι, 3 pl. **πιμπλᾶσι**, aor. 1 πλῆσε, σαν, opt. σειαν, part. σασα, impleo, *fill*, τί, Ξ 35, Φ 23; τί τινος, P 573; not with dat. (Π 373 is dat. of accompanying circumstance, amid); mid. ipf. πίμπλαντο, 1 aor. opt. 3 pl. πλησαιάτο, σάμενος, οι, like act., ξ 112; usually with reflexive reference to subject (sibi, suum), ξ 87; θυμόν, *satisfy themselves*, τ 198; pass. aor. ἐπλήσθη, 3 pl. πλῆσθεν, also 2 aor. mid. πλῆθ' = πλῆτο, pl. πλῆντο, impleri, *be filled with*, μένεος, irâ, δ 662, υ 349; δακρυόφι, δ 705; φρένας, his breast was filled, P 499. (X 402, πίτναντο.)

πινἄκι πτυκτῷ, *writing-tablet, folding tablet*, Z 169; elsewh. πίνακας κρειῶν, wooden plates or trenchers with meat, α 141; νεῶν, μ 67, ship's *timbers*.

ἐπίνυσσε, ipf. from πινύσσω, (πινυτός), *sharpen the wits*, Ξ 249†.

πῐνῠτή, ήν, *prudence, understanding*, H 289, prop. fem. from

πῐνῠτός, οῦς, ή, ῆ, (πινύσσω, πνέω), prudens, *discreet*, α 229. (Od.)

πίνων, prs., inf. ἐμεναι, ipf. iter. πίνεσκεν, fut. part. πιόμενος, aor. ἔπῐον, πίε, πίον, subj. πίω, πίῃσθα, πιῃ, opt. πίοιμι, πίοι(εν); πῐέμεν, πῐεῖν, πιών, bibere, *drink*; οἶνον, ὕδωρ, αἷμα, γάλα, ὀρόν, φάρμακα, Δ 262, portionem, each his portion; also with gen. part., λ 96 (Od.); *drain, quaff*, κρητῆρας, κύπελλα; also with dat. of place, like the French boire dans une tasse, *drink out of* a cup, ξ 112. [ῐ in aor., but in arsis also πῑέμεν.]

πίομαι, see πίνω.

πιότατον, sup. from πίων.

πίπτει, ουσι, ωσι, ων, όντων, ipf. ἔπιπτε, ον, πῖπτε(ν), ον, fut. 3 pl. πεσέονται, σέεσθαι, aor. 2 ἔπεσ(εν), ον, πέσε(ν), ἐτην, ον; ῃ(σι-ν), ητον, ωμεν, ωσι; οι, οιεν; έειν; ών, όντος, όντ(α), οῦσ(α), όντες, pf. part. πεπτεῶτα, ας [pronounced with synizesis], (ΠΕΤ), cadere, per aëra ferri, *fall, be borne through the air*, M 278; with locative, χαμαί, πεδίῳ (with ἐν, N 205; ἐπί, β 398; ὑπό, Π 378; μετά, T 110; ἔραζε, χαμάδις, ἄλλυδις); *fall over, crash*, Ψ 120, μ 410; *fall in battle*, T

227, A 243; at the hands of, ὑπό τινος (τινι), Λ 158; petere aliquid, *full upon, attack*, with ἐν, N 742; *subside*, of wind, τ 202; ἐκ, fall out of, forfeit, θυμοῦ, ex favore.

πίσεα, ntr. pl., (πίνω), *meadows*, Υ 9, ζ 124.

πίσσα, fem., (πικρός), pix, *pitch*, Δ 277.

πιστός, όν, ά, sup., πιστότατος, fidus, *trusty*, with inf., Π 147; πιστὰ γυναιξί, mulieribus confidendum; freq. ὅρκια, foedus fidum.

πιστόω, aor. mid. **ἐπιστώσαντ(ο)** = πιστώσαντο, aor. pass. 2 du. subj. ωθῆτον, inf. ωθῆναι, part. ωθείς, (πιστός), pass. confidere, *trust*, φ 218; bind one's self, fidem facere, ὅρκῳ, by oath; mid. *mutually bind each other*, Z 233.

πίσυνος, οι, (πείθω), confisus, fretus, *relying upon*, τινί, E 205, Λ 9.

πίσυρες, ας, (Aeolic for τέσσαρες), quatuor, ε 70, O 680.

Πιτθεύς, ῆος, king in Troizen, father of Aithra, Γ 144†.

πιτνάς, pres. part., ipf. πίτνα, pandere, *extending*; ipf. mid. πίτναντο, *floated, fluttered*, X 402.

Πιτύεια, town in Mysia, B 829†.

πίτυς, υσσιν, dat. pl. fem., pinus, *pine* or *fir*, N 390, ι 186.

πιφαυσκέμεν, ων, ipf. πίφαυσκε, ον, mid. πιφαύσκομαι, εαι, εται, imp. εο, part. όμενος, (πι-φαϝ-σκω, φάος), *let gleam, display*, φλόγα; M 280, *letting loose* his missiles, hence *manifest, make known*, ἔπος πάντεσσι, τί τινι. [in arsis ῑ, K 478.]

πίων, **πίονος,** ι, α, ες, fem. **πίειρα,** ῃ, αν, ας, sup. πιότατον, (opîmus?), *fat*, (1) of animals, *plump, fat*, μηρία, νῶτα, δημός, cellular tissue, paunch.—(2) of fields and soil in general, *fertile*, I 577.—(3) of localities and cities, *wealthy*, opulentus, E 512.

πλαγκταί, ἀς πέτρας, *clashing* rocks, against which every thing is dashed to pieces, myth suggested by natural phenomena in strait of Messina or the Lipari Isles, μ 61, ψ 327.

πλαγκτέ, voc., (πλάζω), either *mad*, (sc. φρένας), or, better, *vagabond*, φ 363†.

πλαγκτοσύνης, τῆς, (πλαγκτός), *roving, roaming*, ο 343†.

πλάγχθη, see πλάζω.

1. πλάζω, ipf. **πλάζ(ε),** (πέλαγος, plash), *bespattered*, Φ 269.

2. πλάζω, **πλάζουσι,** ων, ipf. πλάζε, aor. πλάγξ(ε), (πλήσσω), *drive away* (from object of one's aim), freq. with ἀπό, with inf. of result, ω 307; μέγα, greatly hinder, B 132; *confuse*, β 396; *turning its course, deflecting*, P 751; pass. mid. πλάζομαι, ετ(αι), εσθαι, όμενος, ου, οι, ipf. πλάζετ(ο), fut. πλάγξομαι, aor. πλάγχθη, θείς, θέντα, ες, oberrare, vagari, *rove, wander*, ν 204; κατά, with acc., ο 312, π 151; ἐπὶ δῆμον, ξ 43, γ 252; *be cast about*, κύματι, on the wave (collective), ε 389; *be cast away*, α 2; ἀπό, from, aberrare, ζ 278; *dash back*, Λ 351.

Πλάκος, ἡ, mountain above Thebe, in Mysia, Z 396, 425, X 479.

πλανάω, mid. **πλανόωνται,** vagantur, *rove*, Ψ 321†.

Πλάταια, town in Boiotia, B 504†.

πλατανίστῳ, fem., *plane-tree*, not unlike our maple, B 307.

πλατύς, **πλατέος,** εῖ, έ(α), *broad*, H 86, N 588; αἰπόλια αἰγῶν, *wide-roaming* herds of goats.

πλέες, ας, see **πλείων.**

πλεῖος, ου, οι; η, αι; ον, **πλέον,** πλείοις, comp. πλειοτέρῃ, plenus, *full*, K 579, Θ 162; with gen., δ 319, ο 446.

πλεῖστον, οι, ους, η, ην, αι, ον, α, (πολύς), plurimum, i, *most*, O 616; ntr. as adv., maxime, *especially*, Δ 138, T 287.

πλείων, **πλέων,** πλέονες (πλέες), όνων, όνεσσι (πλείοσι), πλέονας (πλείους, πλέας), ntr. πλέον, πλεῖον(α), comp. from πολύς, plus, plures, maior, *more, greater*, with ὁ, τό, etc., β 277, K 506, A 165. *greater part*. [σ 247, synizesis = πλεῦνες.]

πλεκτοῖς, ήν, verbal adj., (πλέκω), *braided, twisted*, χ 175, Σ 568.

πλέκω, aor. **ἔπλεξε,** *plait, twist*, Ξ 176; aor. mid. πλεξάμενος, κ 168.

πλευραί, ῶν, άς, *ribs*, Λ 437; *sides* or *flank*, latera, ρ 232, Υ 170 = **πλευρά,** acc. pl. ntr., *on the side*, Δ 468†.

Πλευρών, ῶνος, town in Aitolia, B 639, N 217, Ξ 116; inhabitant, Πλευρώνιος, Ψ 635.

πλείω, **πλεῖθ'** = πλεῖτε, πλείειν, πλέων, ουσα, σας, πλείοντες, ipf. ἔπλεον, εεν, έομεν, εον and πλέεν, ἐομεν, πλέον, fut. πλεύσεσθε, (πλέϝω), navigo, *sail; ὑγρὰ κέλευθα*, sail the watery ways, γ 71. [πλέων, synizesis, α 183.]

πλέων, έον, see πλείων.

πληγή, **πληγῆς,** ῇ, έων, ῇσι(ν), fem., (πλήσσω), *blow*, verbera, *stroke*, from stick, whip, or thong, Ο 17, δ 244; Διός, Ξ 414, stroke of lightning.

πλῆθ' = πλῆτο, see πίμπλημι.

πλῆθε, see πλήθω.

πλῆθος, dat. **πλήθεϊ,** ει [Ρ 330, Ψ 639], and **πληθύς,** ύος, ὑϊ, ύν, (πλήθω), multitudo, esp. opp. chiefs, Β 143, 278 (with pl. verb), 488, Ι 641.

πλήθω, **πλήθει,** ουσι, ωσι, ipf. πλῆθε, *be* or *become full*, with gen., of rivers, *swell*, Π 389; part. πλήθων, οντι, ουσαν, ούσας, plenus, *full*, ι 8; *swollen*, Ε 87, Λ 492; σελήνην, lunam plenam.

πληϊάδες, *Pleiades* (seven stars in the constellation Taurus), from πλέω, as the opening and close of navigation was marked by their rising and setting; the popular etymology made them doves (πελειάδες), flying before the hunter Orion, ε 272, μ 62. The Romans called the constellation Vergiliae, from vergo, to turn.

πληκτίζεσθαι (πλήσσω), depugnare, *contend with*, Φ 499.

πλήμνη, αι, fem., (πλήθω), *hub* or *nave* of a wheel, Ε 726, Ψ 339.

πλη-μῦρίς, fem., (πλήμμυρις?), *rise of the sea, flood* (tide), ι 486†.

πλήν (πλέον), with gen., *except*, θ 207†.

πλῆντο, (1) from πίμπλημι, implebantur.—(2) from πελάζω.

πλῆξα, ε, see πλήσσω.

πληξ-ίππῳ, ον, (πλήσσω), *striking* or *driving horses*, Β 104.

πλησίον, du. ίω, pl. ίοι, ίαι, (πέλας), propinquus, vicinus, *near*, ἄλλον, *neighbor*, θ 328; elsewh. adj., with gen. or dat.; ntr. as adv., prope, *hard by*, μ 102.

πλησ-ίστιον (πλήθω, ἱστίον), *filling the sail*, λ 7 and μ 149.

πλήσσω, aor. πλῆξα, ε, etc., 2 aor. (ἐ)πέπληγον, inf. πεπληγέμεν, pf. πεπληγώς, υῖα, (πλαγ-, plango), *strike*, with hand, foot, staff, whip, missile, weapon, Π 791, σ 57, υ 17, χ 20; *smite*, μ 412; pass. πληγείς, Θ 12, Ψ 694, Ο 117; κληῗδι, *thrust open by*, φ 50; θ 264, χορόν, *trod* a measure; *hit and wound*, Κ 489, Π 332; with double acc. (on), κ 161, Λ 240; mid. 2 aor. **πεπλήγετο,** οντο, reflex. se or sua, Π 125, *having smote his* thighs.

πλῆτο, (1) from πίμπλημι, implebatur.—(2) from πελάζω.

πλίσσοντο, ipf., *strode out*, ζ 318†.

πλοκάμους, masc., (πλέκω), *locks, braids*, Ξ 176†.

πλόον, masc., (πλέω), navigationem, *voyage*, γ 169†.

πλοῦτος, οιο, ῳ, ον, (πλήθω), divitiae, *wealth*, Α 171, Π 596, ξ 206.

πλοχμοί = πλόκαμοι, *locks*, Ρ 52†.

πλῠνοί, masc., *wash-troughs* or *basins* in the earth, lined with stone, ζ 40.

πλύνω, **πλυνούσῃ,** ipf. iter. 3 pl. πλύνεσκον, fut. έουσα, αι, aor. 3 pl. πλῦναν, part. ασα, (fluo), *wash, clean*, ζ 31, 59, 93.

πλωτῇ, dat. sing., (πλωτός), *floating*, κ 3†.

πλώουσι, οιεν, ειν, ipf. πλῶον, (πλόϝω from πλέω), *swim, float*, ε 240, Φ 302.

πνεύμονι, dat. masc., *lung*, Δ 528. (Il.)

πνέει, and **πνείει,** οντε, ες, ας, ουσα, αν, (πνέϝω), spirare, *breathe, live*, Ρ 447, σ 131; *smell*, δ 446; *blowing*, η 119; breathing courage, μένος, χ 203; μένεα, with souls inspired with courage; mid. pf. πέπνῦσαι, inf. ῦσθαι, plupf. πέπνῦσο, *have discretion*, κ 495; *be prudent*, Ω 377; part. pf. πεπνῦμένος, etc., prudens, *discreet*, Γ 203, α 213, δ 206, θ 388, γ 52, β 38.

πνοιῇ, ῆς, ῇ, ήν, αί, ῇσ(ιν), άς, fem., (πνέω), spiramen, *breath*, Υ 439; *panting*, Ψ 380; *hot breath, blast*, Φ 355; elsewh. of wind, ζ 20, κ 507.

Ποδᾰ-λείριος, son of Asklepios, brother of Machaon, Β 732, Λ 833.

ποδᾰ-νιπτρα, ntr., (νίπτω), *water for washing the feet*, τ 343 and 504.

Ποδ-άργη, a Harpy (storm-wind), mother of Achilleus's horses, Π 150, Τ 400.

Πόδ-αργος, horse of Hektor, Θ 185; of Menelaos, Ψ 295.

ποδ-άρκης (ἀρκέω), *swift-footed*, Α 121. (Il.)

Ποδ-άρκης, son of Iphiklos, brother

of Protesilaos, chief of the contingent from Phylake and Pyrasos, Β 704, Ν 693.

ποδ-ηνεκέ(α), ές, (ἠνεκής, stem ἐνεκ, see φέρω), *extending to the feet*, Κ 24, Ο 646.

ποδ-ήνεμος (ἄνεμος), *swift as the wind*, Β 786, of Iris. (Il.)

Ποδῆς, οῦς, ῆν, son of Eetion, slain by Menelaos, Ρ 575, 590.

ποδ-ωκείῃσι, dat. pl. fem., (ὠκύς), *swiftness of foot*, Β 792†.

ποδ-ώκης, εος, εϊ, εα, εες, εσι, εας, (ὠκύς), *fleet-footed*, Κ 316, Β 860, Ψ 249, 262, λ 471, 538,

ποθέεσκε, see ποθέω.

πόθεν, interr. adv., *whence?* unde? γ 71, ο 423; also like Lat. cujas, with gen., π. ἀνδρῶν, unde gentium, from what quarter of the world? Φ 150, α 170.

ποθέν, indefin. adv., alicunde, *from some quarter*, ω 149; freq. with εἰ.

ποθέω, έεις, ποθήμεναι, inf. prs., ipf. πόθει, εον, aor. πόθεσαν, έσαι, desidero, *desire, long for*, β 375; τινά, Α 492, λ 196.

ποθή, ῇ, ήν, (ποθέω), desiderium, *longing for*, τινός, Α 240, θ 414; σή, tui; also = inopia, *lack*, κ 505, β 126.

πόθι, interr. adv., ubi? *where?* α 170, ω 298. (Od.)

ποθί, indefin. adv., alicubi, *anywhere*, υ 114; aliqua, *somehow*, Τ 273, α 348; esp. αἴ κέ ποθι, if *in any case*, if *at all*, to see whether, α 379, β 144, μ 215, χ 252, ρ 51, 60, δ 34.

πόθος, ῳ, masc., (ποθέω), desiderium, *yearning* (after), σός, tui, Ρ 439.

Ποιάντιος υἱός, son *of Poias*, Philoktetes, γ 190†.

ποιέω, prs., ipf. ἐποίει, ποίει, ποίεον, fut. ποιησέμεν, aor. ἐποίησεν, σαν, ποίησε, σαν, σαι, etc., *make*, act., (1) *create*, εἴδωλον, φάος τινί; *build, make*, σάκος ταύρων, shield of bulls' hides; ἀθύρματα, make sport, play; with acc. and inf., ψ 258, efficere; pass. pf. πεποίηται εὐνή, η 342; σοὶ ἄριστα, optima tibi facta sunt per domum?—(2) with double acc., *cause to become, make so and so*, τινά τι (second acc. either subst. or adject.), ἄκοιτιν θνητῷ, give in marriage to a mortal; ἄιστον, cause to be forgotten; ὄλβια, bless; ἐνὶ φρεσί, put in one's thoughts. —mid. ποιεῖται, ipf. ποιεύμην, fut. ποιήσεται, aor. ποιήσατ(ο), σαντο, σασθαι, sibi facere, comparare, *make for one's self, procure*; τινὰ ἄλοχον, uxorem ducere; ἀκοίτην, nubere; υἱόν, adoptare; ῥήτρην, bind one's self by an agreement.

ποίη, ης, ῃ, ην, (ποFίη), gramen, *grass*, σ 370, Ξ 347.

ποιήεντος, gen., ποιήενθ' = ποιήεντα, ποιήεσσαν, (ποFιηFεις, ποίη), graminosus, *grassy*, Β 503, δ 337.

ποιητοῖο, οῖσι(ν), ήν, ῇσι, άς, (ποιέω), with and without εὖ, (well) *made*, Κ 262; πύκα, firmly *built*, α 333.

ποίκιλλε, ipf. from ποικίλλω, (ποικίλος), *skillfully work* or *make*, Σ 590†.

ποικίλματα, τοῖς, ntr., (ποικίλλω), *rich work, broidery*, Ζ 294 and ο 107; cf. the embroideress in cut.

ποικιλο-μήτην, voc. μῆτα, (μῆτις), prop. *with changing, versatile mind*, versatili ingenio, *rich in invention*, χ 115.

ποικίλον, ῃ, ον, (α), (pic-tus), *parti-colored, spotted, mottled*, of skin of animals; *embroidered in various colors*, Ε 735, σ 293, Χ 441; *skillfully wrought*, of objects in metal or wood, Δ 226, Κ 501.

ποιμαίνων, οντ(α), (ποιμήν), part. prs., ipf. iter. ποιμαίνεσκεν, pascere, *tend as shepherd* (ἐπ' ὄεσσι, Ζ 25), μῆλα, ι 188; pass. ipf. ποιμαίνοντο, pascebantur, *were tended*, Λ 245.

ποιμήν, ένος, ένι, ένα, ένες, έσιν, (πῶυ), pastor, *herdsman*, of sheep or oxen; λαῶν, *shepherd* (defense) of the people, epithet of chiefs, Β 243.

ποίμνησιν, dat. pl. from ἡ ποίμνη, (ποιμήν), gregibus (tenetur), (is occupied by) *flocks*, ι 122†.

ποιμνήϊον *σταθμόν*, (*ποίμνη*), *cattle-stall*, *sheep*-fold, B 470†.

ποινή, *ῆς*, *ήν*, (*ποϝινή*, poena, purus), *purification, expiation, quit-money* for bloodshed, *penalty*, *τινός*, for a person, i. e. murder of a person, I 633; for a thing, *satisfaction, price*, Γ 290, E 266, P 207; *ἄτιτοι*, unpaid; *ἀπετίνυτο*, exacted satisfaction for himself from many, Π 398.

ποῖον, *οι*, *οίη*, *ῃ*, interr. adj. pron., qualis? *of what sort? εἰτ' ἀμυνέμεν*, what sort are ye to defend? how would ye be disposed to defend? φ 195; *ποῖόν σε ἔπος φύγεν ἕρκος ὀδόντων*, in questions expressive of indignation or surprise, α 64, φ 168.

ποιπνύοντα, *ύουσαι*, ipf. (*ἐ*)*ποίπνυον*, aor. part. *ποιπνύσαντι*, (red. from *πνέω*), prop. *puff, pant, bestir one's self*, Ξ 155; *make haste*, υ 149; esp. of attendants, servants, Σ 421, A 600.

πόκον, *τόν*, (*πέκω*), *shorn wool, fleece*, vellus, M 451†.

πολέες = *πολλοί*.

πολεμήϊα, ntr., (*πόλεμος*), *ἔργα*, *toil of battle*, B 338 (*οἶδε*, understands); with *δοῦναι*, bestow *renown in battle, glory; τεύχεα, warlike* equipment.

πολεμίζω, prs. and ipf. *πολέμιζε*, *ον*, and **πτολεμίζω**, *ειν*, *ων*, fut. *ίξομεν* and *πολεμίξομεν*, (*πόλεμος*), pugnare, *fight*, *πόλεμον*, pugnam; *τινί*, contra aliquem = *ἄντα τινός*, *ἐναντίβιον*, opp. *μετά τισιν*, jointly with; impugnare, *to fight with*, Σ 258.

πολεμιστής, *ήν*, *ά*, *αί*, and **πτολεμιστῇ**, (*πολεμίζω*), bellator, *warrior*, K 549.

πόλεμος, *οιο*, *ου*, *ῳ*, *ον*, *οι*, *ων*, *ους*, and **πτόλεμος**, *οιο*, *ου*, *ῳ*, *ον*, *ους*, (*πελεμίζω*), *tumult of combat, fight*, A 492, Δ 15; esp. freq. plur., ξ 225, χ 152; also in periphrasis, *ἔρις*, *νεῖκος*, *φύλοπις πολέμοιο*, discord, fury, din of the combat. **π(τ)όλεμόνδε**, *into the combat*, Θ 400.

πολεύειν (*πέλεσθαι*), versari, *live in*, χ 223†.

πολέων = *πολλῶν*.

πόληας, *ες* = *πόλεις*.

πολίζω, aor. **πολίσσαμεν**, and plupf. pass. *πεπόλιστο*, condere, *build*, H 453 and Υ 217.

πολιήτας, *τούς* = *πολίτας*, cives, *citizens*, B 806†.

πόλινδ(ε), in urbem, *to the city*, E 224, N 820, α 189.

πολιο-κροτάφους, *τούς*, *with hoary temples* (*κρόταφος*), gray with age, Θ 518†.

πολιοῖο, *όν*, *οί*, *ῆς*, *ήν*, *άς*, (*πελλός*, pullus), canus, *hoary*, of hair (capilli, pili); of iron, sea, *ἁλός*, *with hoary foam*, A 350.

πόλῖς, *ιος* [and *ῆος*, B 811, Φ 567], *ει*, *ῖν*, *ιες*, *ίων*, *ίεσσι*, *ιας* [pronounce *ῖς*, *jας*? θ 560], *εις*; **πτόλιος**, Δ 514, etc.; *ιν*, B 130, etc.; also **πόληος**, *ηϊ*, Γ 50; *ηες*, *ηας*, urbs, civitas, *city*, with name as appos., e. g. *Τροίην*, λ 510; or as limiting gen., B 133; opp. ζ 178, *ἄστυ*, fortified dwelling-place, *πόλις*, inhabited city; P 144, community and city; *ἄκρη*, acropolis, citadel, upper town.

πολῖται, *ας*, masc., (*πόλις*), cives, *citizens*, η 131, O 558.

Πολίτης, *αο*, (1) son of Priamos, B 791, N 533, O 339, Ω 250.—(2) companion of Odysseus, κ 224.

πολλάκι(ς), adv. from *πολλός*, saepe, *many times*, Γ 232, N 666, τ 76.

πολλός, *όν*, see *πολύς*, *ύ*.

Πολῦ-αιμονίδης, *αο*, *son of Polyaimon*, Amopaon, Θ 276†.

πολῦ-αιν(ε), voc., (*αἶνος*), *much-praised*, *Ὀδυσεῦ*, I 673, Λ 430.

πολῦ-ᾶϊξ, *ᾶϊκος*, (*ἀΐσσω*), *impetuous; κάματος*, weariness *caused by impetuousness in fight*, E 811; elsewh. *πολέμοιο*, *furious* combat, A 165.

πολῦ-ανθέος (*ἄνθος*), *much-, luxuriantly blooming*, ξ 353†.

πολῦ-άρητος (*ἀράομαι*), *much-, warmly desired*, ζ 280 and τ 404.

πολῦ-αρνι, *τῷ*, (-*ϝαρνι*, lamb), *rich in lambs, possessor of many flocks*, B 106†.

πολῦ-βενθέος, gen., (*βένθος*), *very deep*, A 432; elsewh. of sea. (Od.)

Πόλῦ-βος, (1) son of Antenor, Λ 59.—(2) an Egyptian, δ 126.—(3) an Ithakan, father of Eurymachos, ο 519.—(4) a Phaiakian, θ 373.—(5) a suitor in Ithaka, χ 243, 284.

πουλῦ-βοτείρῃ, *αν*, (*βόσκω*), *much- or all-nourishing*, alma, only of the earth, *χθονί*, *α*, Z 213, Λ 619, exc. Λ 770, *Ἀχαιΐδα*.

πολῦ-βουλος (*βουλή*) *Ἀθήνη*, *deep in counsel, exceeding wise*, E 260, π 282.

πολῠ-βοῦται (*βοῦς*), *rich in cattle*, I 154 and 296.

πολῠ-γηθέες (*γηθέω*) Ὧραι, *ever gay* (conceived as never ceasing from the choral dance), Φ 450†.

πολῠ-δαίδᾰλος, *ον*, *ῳ*, *ον*, *οι*, perquam artificiosus, *highly*, *cunningly wrought*, of objects in metal and wood; of men, solertes, only Ψ 743, *skilful*.

πολύ-δακρυς, *υ*, and -*δακρῡου*, P 192, epithet of *μάχη*, *ὑσμίνη*, *ἄρηα*, *occasioning many tears*, *doleful*, *deplorable*, Γ 132.

πολῠ-δάκρῡτος, *οιο*, *much-lamented*, Ω 620; *tearful*, *γόοιο*.

Πολύ-δαμνα, wife of the Egyptian Θῶν, δ 228†.

πολῠ-δειρᾰ́δος, gen. from -*δειράς*, (*δειρή*), *many-ridged*, Οὐλύμποιο, A 499. (Il.)

πολῠ-δένδρεον, masc., (*δένδρον*), *thickly planted with trees*, δ 737, ψ 139, 359.

πολῠ-δέσμου, gen., (*δεσμός*), *firmly* (=in many places) *bound together*, epithet of Odysseus's raft, ε 33 and 338.

Πολῠ-δεύκης, acc. *εα*, *Pollux*, son of Zeus and of Leda, brother of Kastor, Γ 237, λ 300. (decus.)

πολῠ-δίψιον, ntr., (*δίψα*), *thirsty*, *dry*, of Argos in valley of Inachos, Δ 171†.

Πολῠ-δώρη, daughter of Peleus, wife of Spercheios, mother of Menestheus, Π 175†.

πολύ-δωρος (*δῶρον*), *richly dowered*, Z 394.

Πολύ-δωρος, (1) youngest son of Priamos by Laothoe, Υ 419, Φ 91, X 46; slain by Achilleus, Υ 407.—(2) a Greek, Ψ 637.

Πολύ-ειδος, v. l. for *Πολύ-ιδος*.

πολῠ-ζύγῳ (*ζυγόν*), *with many rowers' benches* = *great*, B 293†.

πολῠ-ηγερέες (*ἀγείρω*), *numerously assembled*, reading of Aristarchos in Λ 564†.

πολῠ-ηρᾰ́του, *ῳ*, *ον*, (*ἔραμαι*), *greatly loved* or *desired*, desideratus; *ἥβη*, *lovely* youthful bloom; Θήβη, λ 275.

πολῠ-ηχέι, *έα*, *many-toned*, of nightingale, τ 521; *echoing*, *resounding*, Δ 422.

πολῠ-θαρσές, *bold*, *intrepid*, audax, P 156.

Πολῠ-θερσεΐδης, *αο*, *son of Polytherses*, Ktesippos, χ 287†.

Πολύ-ῑδος (*Ϝιδος*), (1) son of Eurydamas, slain by Diomedes, E 148.—(2) seer in Korinthos, father of Euchenor, N 663, 666.

πολῠ-ιδρείησι(ν) (*ἴδρις*), consilio, *much knowledge*, *shrewdness*, β 346 and ψ 77.

πολύ-ιδρις, *ιν*, *very shrewd*, *subtle*, versutus, ο 459 and ψ 82.

πολῠ-ίππου, *rich in horses*, N 171†.

πολη-καγκέα (*κάγκανος*), *very dry*, *parching*, Λ 642†.

πολύ-καρπος, *ου*, (*καρπός*), frugifer, fructuosus, *fruitful*, η 122 and ω 221.

Πολῠ-κάστη, youngest daughter of Nestor, γ 464†.

πολῠ-κερδείῃσι (*κέρδος*), astutiâ, *great craft*, ω 167†.

πολῠ-κερδέα, acc. masc., (*κέρδος*), astutum, *cunning*, ν 255†.

πολύ-κεστος (*κεντέω*), *richly embroidered*, Γ 371†.

πολῠ-κηδέ(α), acc., (*κῆδος*), aerumnosum, *woful*, *wretched*, ι 37 and ψ 351.

πολῠ-κληῗδι, *ῖσι*, (*κληίς*), *with many thole-pins*, *many-oared*, B 74, H 88.

πολῠ-κλήρων, gen. pl., (*κλῆρος*), locupletium, *wealthy*, ξ 211†.

πολύ-κλητοι (*καλέω*), *called together in large numbers* = *from many a land*, Δ 438 and K 420.

πολῡ-κλύστῳ (*κλύζω*), *loudly surging*, δ 354. (Od.)

πολύ-κμητος, *ον*, *ον*, (*κάμνω*), *wrought with much labor*, *well-wrought*, of iron, Z 48; *θάλαμος*, δ 718, *firmly built*.

πολύ-κνημον (*κνήμη*), *with many glens* or *ravines*, B 497†.

πολῠ-κοιρᾰνίη, fem., (*κοίρανος*), *rule of many*, *mob-rule*, B 204†.

πολῠ-κτήμων (*κτῆμα*), *with much possessions*, E 613†.

Πολῠ-κτορίδης, *αο*, *son of Polyktor*, Peisandros, σ 299†.

Πολύ-κτωρ, *ορος*, (1) fabled name, Ω 397.—(2) ancient hero in Ithaka, ρ 207.—(3) father of Peisandros.

πολῠ-λήϊος (*λήϊον*), *rich in harvests*, E 613†.

πολύ-λλιστον (*λίσσομαι*), *object of many* (fervent) *prayers*, ε 445†.

Πολῦ-μήλη, daughter of Phylas, mother of Eudoros, Π 180†.

πολῦ-μήλου, gen., acc. ον, (μῆλα), *rich in sheep, rich in flocks*, B 605, 705. (Il.)

Πολῦ-μηλος, son of Argeas, a Lykian, slain by Patroklos, Π 417†.

πολῦ-μητις, ιος, (μῆτις), *rich in devices, crafty, shrewd*, freq. epithet of Odysseus, A 311; of Hephaistos, Φ 355.

πολῦ-μηχᾰνίην (μηχανή), *manifold cunning*, ψ 321†.

πολῦ-μήχᾰνος, (ε), (μηχανή), *fertile in devices, full of expedients, ever ready*, epithet of Odysseus, α 205, B 173.

πολυ-μνήστη, ην, (μνάομαι), *much-wooed, eagerly sought*, δ 770. (Od.)

πολῦ-μῦθος, ον, *of many words, fluent*, Γ 214 and β 200.

Πολῦ-νείκης, son of Oidipus, brother of Eteokles, mover of the expedition of the Epigoni (descendants) against Thebes, Δ 377†.

Πολῦ-νηος, father of Amphialos, a Phaiakian, θ 114†.

Πολύ-ξεινος, son of Agasthenes, chief of Epeioi, B 623†.

πολῦ-παίπαλοι (παιπάλη), *very artful, cunning*, ο 419†.

πολῦ-πάμονος, gen., (πέπαμαι), opulenti, *exceeding wealthy*, Δ 433†.

πολῦ-πενθέος, gen., έα, ές, (πένθος), *deeply mournful*, ψ 15, I 563.

Πολῦ-πημονίδης, fabled name (Ἀφείδας, "Spendthrift"), *son of the Great Possessor*, ω 305†.

πολῦ-πῖδακος, α, gen., also -πῖδάκου, (πίδαξ), *rich in springs*, Υ 59, Ξ 157. (Il.)

πολῦ-πικρα, as adv., (πικρός), *very bitterly*, π 255†.

πολυ-πλάγκτοιο, ῳ, οισι, ους, (πλάζω), *baffling, driving far from one's course*, Λ 308; elsewh. *far-roving, much-wandering*.

Πολῦ-ποίτης, αο, son of Peirithoos, one of the Lapithai, B 740, Z 29, M 129, 182, Ψ 836, 844.

πολῦ-πτύχου, gen., (πτύσσω), *with many folds, many-furrowed*, Θ 411. (Il.)

πολῦ-πῦρος, ου, ῳ, ον, (πῦρός), *abounding in wheat*, ο 406, Λ 756.

πολύ-ρρηνος, λ 257, and pl. -ρρηνες, (Ϝρην, Ϝάρνα), *rich in sheep*, I 154 and 296.

πολῦς, πολλή, πολῦ, besides the regular Attic forms (excluding πολλοῦ, which does not occur), are found in Homer also πολύς, N 705, πουλύς, ύν, ύ; πολέος [pronounce πολjος, υ 25], pl. πολέες, εῖς, Λ 708; πολέων [dissyll., Π 655], άων, έων, dat. πολέσι, έεσσ(ι), έσσ(ι), P 236, acc. πολέας, N 734; πουλύν, fem., K 27; also πολλός; ntr. πολλόν; comp. πλείων, ονες, οσιν, ους, ον(α), πλέων, πλέον, πλέονες, όνων, όνεσσι(ν), ονας, sup. πλεῖστον, οι, ους, η, ην, αι, α (plus, Ger. viel, voll), multus, of number, *many*; of size, strength, *much*; of time, *long*, amplus, *wide, broad*, of space; πολλοί, vulgus, plerique, *the multitude, the larger part*; also with gen., τὰ πολλά, pleraque, *the most*; τόσσον πολλόν, so *far* into the conflict, Υ 178; often coupled with other adjs., with *καί, τέ—καί, τέ—τέ*, β 188, Z 452, ο 159, B 213; ntr. πολύ, with comp., increasing comparative force = multo, *far, by far, much*, β 180, A 169, Λ 162, Ξ 467; in like manner with sup., longe, A 581, Δ 51, H 162, Ξ 442; with βούλομαι, malo, *prefer*, A 112; with φθάνω, N 815, and other words of distance where a comparative idea is involved; so likewise πολλόν, Z 479, Ψ 587, A 91, ζ 39; ἐπιδευέες, ω 171; with verbs, E 636, T 218, Ψ 742, T 113; πολλά, multa, multum, *much*, ο 401; saepe, *often*, P 430, ι 128; valde, *exceedingly*, Z 458, Θ 22; impense, *intently, earnestly*, Δ 229, E 358; *fervently, ardently*, A 35, γ 267, δ 433.

πολῦ-σκάρθμοιο (σκαίρω), *much-, far-springing, agile, fleet*, epithet of the Amazon Myrine, B 814†.

πολῦ-σπερέων, έας, (σπείρω), *wide-spread, spread over the earth*, λ 365.

πολῦ-στάφῦλον, *rich in grapes*, B 507 and 537.

πολύ-στονος, α, (στόνος), *much-sighing, mournful*, miser, τ 118; *causing many sighs, grievous*, O 451.

πολύτλας = **πολυ-τλήμων**, (τλῆναι), *much-enduring, steadfast*, esp. epithet of Odysseus, Θ 97, ε 171, H 152, σ 319.

πολύ-τλητοι (τλῆναι), aerumnosi, *having borne much, wretched*, λ 38†.

πολυ-τρήρωνα, *abounding in doves*, B 502 and 582.

πολυ-τρήτοισι (*τρητός*), *pierced with many holes, porous*, α 111. (Od.)

πολύ-τροπος, *ον*. (*τρέπω*), *versatile*, versutus, α 1 and κ 330.

πολυ-φαρμάκου, *οι*, *skilled in drugs*, Π 28, κ 276.

Πολυ-φείδης, *εος*, son of Mantios, grandson of Melampus, ο 249 and 252.

πολύ-φημος, *ον*, (*φήμη*), *abounding in songs*, χ 376; *many-voiced, buzzing*, β 150.

Πολύ-φημος, (1) son of Poseidon, Kyklops, α 70, ι 371 sqq.—(2) one of the Lapithai, A 264.

πολυ-φλοίσβοιο, gen., (*φλοῖσβος*), *θαλάσσης*, (close of verse), *loud-roaring*, A 34, ν 85.

Πολυ-φήτης, *αο*, chief of the Trojan allies from Askania, N 791†.

Πολυ-φόντης, son of Autophonos, slain before Thebes by Tydeus, Δ 395†.

πολυ-φόρβου, *ην*, (*φορβή*), *bountiful*, alma, I 568, Ξ 200. (Il.)

πολύ-φρονος, *α*, (*φρένες*), *very sagacious*, prudens, Σ 108, θ 297.

πολύ-χαλκος, *ου*, *ον*, *abounding in bronze; οὐρανός, wrought of bronze, all-brazen*, E 504, γ 2.

πολύ-χρυσος, *οιο*, *ον*, *rich in gold*, Σ 289, γ 305.

πολυ-ωπῷ (*ὀπή*) *many-meshed*, χ 386†.

πομπεύς, only pl., **πομπῆες,** *ας*, (*πομπός*), comites, *conductors, escort*, γ 325, ν 71. (Od.)

πόμπευον, ipf. from *πομπεύω*, (*πομπεύς*), comitata sum, *conduct*, ν 422†.

πομπή, *ῆς*, *ῇ*, *ήν*, (*πέμπω*), *escort*, η 193, Z 171; *sending away, dismissal*, ν 41, ε 233.

πομπός, *όν*, *οί*, *οἷσιν*, (*πέμπω*), comes, *escort*, N 416; also fem., δ 826.

πονέομαι, subj. **πονεώμεθα,** opt. *ἐοιτο*, inf. *ἐεσθαι*, part. *εύμενος*, *ον*, ipf. (*ἐ*)*πονεῖτο*, *πονέοντο*, fut. *ήσομαι*, aor. *πονήσατ(ο)*, *σάμενος*, *οι*, plupf. *πεπόνητο*, (*πόνος*), *be busy about*, *τί*, *περί τι*, Ω 444; *toil in the fight*, Δ 374; generally, *work upon*, with dat. of instrument; elaborare, *make with care*, Σ 380, ι 310.

πόνος, *οιο*, *ου*, *-ον*, *ων*, *οισ(ι)*, (*πένομαι*), labor, esp. *toil of battle*, Z 77; aerumna, *distress, grief*, B 291, that is indeed a grief, to return unsatisfied.

Ποντεύς, a Phaiakian, θ 113†.

ποντόθεν, e mari, *from the sea*, Ξ 395†. **πόντονδε,** in mare, *into the sea*, ι 495 and κ 48.

Ποντό-νοος, herald of Alkinoos, η 182, θ 65, ν 50, 53.

ποντο-πορούσης (*πορέω*), and **-πορευέμεναι,** *εύων*, *traversing the high sea*, λ 11, ε 277 sq.

ποντο-πόρος, *οιο*, *οισι(ν)*, *sailing through the sea*, H 72, μ 69.

πόντος, *οιο*, *ου*, *ῳ*, *ον*, (pons), *high sea*, ι 285, A 350, B 145; *deep*, δ 508; with adj. specifying the name, *Θρηΐκιος*, *Ἰκάριος*.

ὢ πόποι (*παπαί*), interj. of astonishment, displeasure, wrath, grief, only B 272, of pleasurable surprise; usually at beginning of verse followed by *ἦ μάλα δή* (*ῥα*), etc., ν 383, 209, A 254.

πόρδαλις, *ιος*, *ίων*, also *πάρδαλις*, *panther, leopard*, δ 457, N 103.

Πορθεύς, *εῖ*, father of Oineus, Ξ 115†.

πορθέω, ipf. (*ἐ*)*πόρθεον*, (*πέρθω*), devastare, *lay waste*, ξ 264.

πορθμῆες, pl. from *-εύς*, (*πόρος*), *ferry-men*, υ 187†.

πορθμῷ, *τῷ*, (*πόρος*), *strait, sound*, δ 671 and ο 29.

πόριες, see *πόρτιος*.

πόρκης, masc., (*πλέκω*?), *iron ring*, passing round the spear at meeting of head and shaft, Z 320 and Θ 495. (See cut No. 4.)

πόρον, acc., pl. *οι*, *οις*, *ους*, masc., (*πείρω*), vadum, *ford*, B 592, Ξ 433; pl. *paths*, μ 259.

(ἔ)πορον, (*ἔ*)*πορ(εν)*, aor. *πόρησι*, *πόρῃ*, *ωμεν*, *ωσι*, *πόροι*, *όντες*, (portio, impertio), comparare, *procure*, Ω 30; *bestow*, A 353, T 21; *provide*, υ 71; *present*, Z 218, Π 185; *commit to*, Z 168; *give*, κ 394; *grant*, σ 202; with inf., I 513; in general, *be the cause of*, τ 512; pass. perf. *πέπρωται*, *it is decreed by fate*, with acc. and inf., Σ 329; *τινί τι*, Γ 309; *πεπρωμένον*, praebitum, debitum, *destined*, *αἴσῃ*, Π 441, O 209.

πόρπας, *τάς*, nom. *ἡ πόρπη*, (*πείρω*), *buckle, brooch*, Σ 401†. (See cut No. 104.)

πορσᾰνέουσα, ipf. **πόρσῡνε,** from *πορσαίνω, σύνω,* (*πορεῖν*), prop. *make ready; λέχος καὶ εὐνήν, share* bed and couch, γ 403, Γ 411.

πόρτᾰκῐ, *τῇ,* (*πόρτις*), vitulo, *calf,* Ρ 4†.

πόρτιος, Ε 162, and **πόριες,** κ 410, fem., iuvencae, *heifer.*

πορφῦρεος, *ῳ, ον, οισ(ιν), ῃ, ην, ον,* (*α*), (purpura), *purple,* spoken of non-transparent substance with a reddish gleam, yet without distinct notion of color; of waves, *dark-gleaming,* β 428; of sea near the shore, Π 391; *θάνατος,* of death in battle, Ε 83.

πορφῦρῃ, subj. pres., ipf. *πόρφῦρε,* (*φύρω*), *boil up,* of waves, Ξ 16; elsewh. of mental disquiet, *be troubled,* δ 427.

πόσε; quo? *whither?* Π 422.

Ποσειδάων, *Poseidon,* Neptunus, son of Kronos, brother of Zeus and Aides, husband of Amphitrite, lord of the sea, Ο 190; dwells in *Αἰγαί,* also in Olympos; sends storm or favoring wind; enemy of Trojans because of faithlessness of Laomedon, Φ 443 sqq.; of Odysseus, because of Polyphemos, α 20; sets in turmoil the sea with his trident, and causes earthquakes, *ἐνοσίχθων, ἐννοσίγαιος; γαιήοχος,* earth-upholder, θ 322; *κυανοχαῖτα,* dark-haired, with hair the color of the sea; to him, as to the gods of the lower world, were sacrificed black bulls, γ 6; also boars and rams, λ 131.

Ποσῑδήιον, *place sacred to Poseidon,* ζ 266; *ἄλσος,* grove, Β 506.

1. **πόσις,** *ιος, ιν,* fem., (*ποτός*), potio, *drink,* Α 469, κ 176.

2. **πόσις,** *ιος, εϊ, ει, ιν, ιας,* masc., (*δεσπότης,* potens), *husband, spouse,* Η 411, δ 137.

ποσσ-ῆμαρ, quot dies? *how many days?* Ω 657†.

πόστον, acc., quotum, *how many a year ago?* ω 288†.

ποταμόν-δε, in flumen, *into, to the river,* Φ 13, κ 159.

ποταμός, *οῖο, οῦ, ῷ, όν, ώ, οί, ῶν, ούς,* (*δυι-πετέος*), flumen, *river,* ε 453; freq. personif. as river-god, Ε 544, Ξ 245.

ποτάομαι, **ποτῶνται,** Β 462; but **ποτέονται,** ω 7; pf. *πεπότηται, πεποτήαται,* (*πέτομαι*), volare, *fly, flutter;* of souls of departed, λ 222.

πότε, quando? *when?* Τ 227.

ποτέ, enclitic, aliquando, *once,* Ξ 45; quondam, *formerly,* Β 547, Ζ 99; olim, *hereafter,* Δ 182.

ποτέομαι, see *ποτάομαι.*

ποτέροισι, utris, *to which* (party), Ε 85†.

ποτῇ, (*πέτομαι*), *in flight,* ε 337†.

ποτής, **ποτῆτος,** *τα,* fem., (*πότος*), potionis, *drink,* δ 788, Τ 306.

ποτητά, *τά,* (*ποτάομαι*), volucres, *birds,* μ 62†.

ποτί and *ποτι-,* see *πρός, προσ-.*

ποτῐ-δέγμενος, etc., part., (*δέχομαι*), expectans, *awaiting, τινά, τί, εἰ,* ψ 91; *ὀππότ' ἄν,* Η 415.

ποτι-δόρπιον, *for* (*his*) *supper,* ι 234 and 249.

ποτι-κέκλιται, perf. from *-κλίνω.*

ποτι-νίσσεται, *go in at, enter* (through the gates, spoken of precious possessions), Ι 381†.

ποτι-πεπτηυῖαι, pf. part. (*-πτήσσω*), *λιμένος, sinking down toward* the harbor, ν 98†.

ποτι-πτυσσοίμεθα, see *προσ-πτύσσομαι.*

ποτι-τερπέτω (*τέρπω*), oblectato, *let him care for,* Ο 401†.

ποτι-φωνήεις (*φωνή*), *capable of addressing, endued with speech,* ι 456†.

πότμος, *ον,* masc., (*πίπτω*), the *lot* which *falls* from the helmet, sors; *ill fate, ἐφιέναι τινί,* (*θάνατον καὶ*) *π. ἐπισπεῖν,* meet *death,* fulfill one's *fate,* Β 359.

πότνῐ(α), *πότνᾰ,* (*πόσις*), *mistress, queen, θηρῶν; august, θεά; revered, bearing sway, μήτηρ.*

ποτόν, *οῖο, ῷ, όν,* ntr., (*πίνω*), potio, *drink,* Α 470, α 148.

ποῦ, ubi? *where?* Ε 171; quo? *whither?* Ν 219. **πού,** enclitic, aliquando, *somewhere,* λ 458; *methinks, doubtless, perhaps,* Α 178, Β 116, 136, Ι 23, θ 491, λ 449.

πουλῠ-βοτείρῃ, *αν,* Γ 89, 265, almae, *bountiful,* = *πολυβ.*

Πουλῠ-δάμας, *αντος,* son of Panthoos, a Trojan, Ξ 449, 453, Ο 339, 518, 521, Π 535; *πεπνυμένος,* Σ 249.

πουλῠ-ποδος, *τοῦ, polypus* (cuttle-fish), ε 432†.

πουλύς, θ 109 = *πολύς.*

πούς, **ποδός,** *ί, α, οῖιν* τ 444, *ες, ῶν, ποσ(σ)ί(ν), πόδεσσι(ν), ας,* pes, *foot,* of men, animals, also of birds, *talons*, ungulae; coupled with χεῖρες, χ 477; λὰξ ποδί, push with the foot, kick; ἐς πόδας ἐκ κεφαλῆς, or ἐκ κ. ἐς π., from head to foot, Σ 353; in foot race, swiftness of foot, N 325; radices montis, *foundations*, Υ 59; rope fastened to lower corners of sail to control it, *sheet* (see plate IV.), ε 260.

Πράκτιος, river in Troas, north of Abydos, B 835†.

Πραμνεῖος οἶνος, *Pramneian* wine, of dark color and fiery taste, κ 235.

πρᾰπίδων, δεσσι(ν) = φρένες, (1) praecordia, *diaphragm*, *midriff*, Λ 579.—(2) fig. *heart*, X 43; *mind*, *thoughts*, Σ 380, η 92.

πρασιή, αἱ, *garden-bed*, ω 247 and η 127.

πρέπω, *be conspicuous*, ipf. **ἔπρεπε,** διὰ πάντων, M 104†.

πρέσβᾰ, fem., (πρέσβυς), prop. *old*, then *august*, *honored*, E 721.

πρεσβήιον, (πρέσβυς), *gift of honor*, Θ 289†.

πρεσβῠ-γενής, *first-born*, Λ 249†.

πρεσβύτερος, οισιν, comp., -ύτατος, ον, η, ην, sup. from πρεσβύς, senior, *elder*, O 204; natu (γενεῇ) maximus, *oldest*, Z 24.

πρήθω, aor. (**ἔ**)**πρῆσε,** σαι, *b'ow*, *let stream forth*, Π 350 (with ἐν, A 481); *scatter*, *shower upon*, πυρί, fire, Θ 217; also πυρός, B 415, I 242.

πρηκτῆρα, τόν, (πράσσω) ἔργων, *doer*, I 443; pl. ῆρες, *traders*, θ 162.

πρηνής, έα, έες, εῖς, ές, (πρό), pronus, *forward*, *on the face* (opp. ὕπτιος, Ω 11); *head foremost*, praeceps, Z 43, Π 310.

πρῆξις, ῖν, fem., (περάω), *accomplishment*, *result*; οὔτις τινὶ γίγνεται, πέλετο, no good comes of; *enterprise*, γ 82.

πρήσσει, etc., prs., ipf. iter. πρήσσεσκον θ 259, fut. πρήξεις, ει, aor. ἔπρηξας, πρῆξαι, αντα, always after caesura in fourth foot, (πέραν), *accomplish*, *complete*, *pass over*, κέλευθον, Ψ 501; ὁδοῖο, gen. part., Ω 264, γ 476, ο 47, 219; fut. and aor., *further*, *help*, ἔργον, οὔτι.

πρῐάτο, 3 sing. aor., (περᾶν), emebat, κτεάτεσσιν, *buy* with treasure, α 430. (Od.)

Πρῐαμίδης, αο, εω, *son of Priamos*, B 817, Υ 77. (Il.)

Πρῐαμος, son of Laomedon, Υ 237, king of Troja; husband of Hekabe, who bore him 19 out of his 50 sons; already aged at the time of the Trojan war, γέρων, N 368, Ω 217, 777; descendant of Dardanos, Γ 303. His children: Hektor, Γ 314; Helenos, H 44; Echemmon, Chromios, E 160; Lykaon, Φ 35; Paris, Z 512; Polites, B 791; Gorgythion, Θ 303; Demokoon, Δ 499; Deiphobos, M 95; Isos, Antiphos, Λ 102; Kassandra, N 365, λ 421; Laodike, Γ 124.

πρίν (comp. from πρό), A. adverb: prius, *before*, B 112; τὸ πρίν γε, E 54; with indic., M 437; fut. or subj., potius, *sooner*, *first*, A 29, Σ 283, ν 427, Ω 551; with opt. and κε, γ 117; πρίν γ' ἤ, E 288, X 266; also οὐ πρίν (γε), or οὐ πάρος, or οὐ πρόσθεν with follg. πρίν γε (or ἀλλ' ὁπότ' ἂν δή, Π 62, Φ 340), E 218, E 288.—B. conjunction, *before*. I. with inf. without temporal or modal limitation, to characterize the subordinate action as unreal or impossible (if the subordinate clause has a subject, it stands in acc., Z 81); tense of inf. usually aor. after affirmative (N 172), and negative principal sentence, A 98, T 423, Φ 225, X 266, ψ 138, δ 747; also after opt. or potential sentence, Z 465, Δ 115, Ω 245, δ 668, χ 64, κ 384; cf. also E 218, 287, M 171, β 127, δ 254.—II. followed by subj. or opt., the principal sentence, as before, being negative: (1) after principal tenses, πρίν with subj. represents subordinate action at once as fut. and as the condition of principal action, Σ 135, κ 175; πρίν γ' ὁπότ' ἂν, β 374, δ 477; also after inf. used imperatively, Ω 781; even after historical tense, Σ 190.—(2) after historical tenses, πρίν with opt. represents subordinate action as future, viewed from past standpoint of principal verb, Φ 580; πρίν γ' ὅτε, I 489; transition in same sentence from II. 1 to I., β 374. [πρῖν (orig. προιν for προιον), yet not infrequently also πρῐν, δ 32, 212, B 344, 354, 413, etc.]

πριστοῦ, adj., (πρίω), ἐλέφαντος, *sawn* ivory, σ 196 and τ 564.

πρό, pro, I. adv., *before*, *forth*, οὐρανόθι, Ἰλιόθι, *in and under* (before) the sky, *around and before* Troja; also temporal, ἠῶθι, *in the morning early*, Λ 50: πρὸ φόωσδε, Π 188, *forward into the light*.—II. prep. with gen., (1) of space, pro, ante, coram, *in front of, in presence of*, τ 435, Ω 734; πρὸ ὁδοῦ, *forward* in the way, *onward*.—(2) temporal, ante, *before*, ο 524.—(3) *in behalf of, for*, μάχεσθαι, ὀλέσθαι; πρὸ ὃ τοῦ for ὁ πρὸ τοῦ, unus pro altero, one for the other, K 224; πρὸ φόβοιο, *for* (*because of*) fear.

προ-ἄλεϊ, dat. sing., (ἅλλομαι ?), *descending*, Φ 262†.

προ-βαίνω, pf. **-βέβηκας**, ε, plupf. βεβήκει, and part. pres. -βιβάς, N 18; and, as if from βιβάω, βιβῶντος, Π 609; βιβῶντι N 807, βιβῶντα Γ 22, procedere, *advance; τινός*, antecedere, *surpass; τινί*, aliqua re, Π 54.

προ-βάλλω, only aor. **-βάλόντες**, iter. βάλεσκε, projicere, *cast before*, ε 331; ἔριδα, injicere, inire, *begin*; mid. aor. -βάλοντο, *cast down before them*, A 458; Ψ 255, fundamenta iecerunt; opt. -βαλοίμην (mente te longe), antecellam, *excel*.

πρό-βἄσϊν, τήν, bona moventia, *live stock, cattle*, β 75†.

πρό-βατ(α), τά, (προβαίνω), pecora, *droves* or *flocks*, Ξ 124 and Ψ 550.

προ-βέβουλα, pf., (βούλομαι), praefero, *prefer before*, A 113†.

προ-βιβάς, -βιβῶν, see προ-βαίνω.

προ-βλής, dat. **βλῆτι**, pl. βλῆτες, ας, (προβάλλω), *projecting*, M 259.

προ-βλώσκειν, ἔμεν, aor. -μολον, imp. μολ(ε), part. μολών, οὖσα, prodire, *go* or *come forward, forth*, τ 25, ο 468, Σ 382, Φ 37.

προ-βοάω, part. **βοῶντε**, (βοή), *shouting loudly* (above the rest), M 277†.

προ-βόλῳ, τῷ, masc., (βάλλω), *jutting rock*, μ 251†.

προ-γενέστερος, οι, (γένος), senior, B 555.

προ-γίγνομαι, aor. **γένοντο**, progressi sunt, Σ 525; in tmesis, ὁδοῦ, Δ 382, *advanced* on their way.

πρό-γονοι, masc., (γόνος), *earlier born*, or *spring lambs, larger lambs*, ι 221†.

προ-δάείς, part. aor., (ἐδάην), ante sentiens, *know beforehand*, δ 396†.

προ-δοκῇσιν, dat. pl., fem., (δέχομαι), ἐν, *in ambush, lurking-place*, Δ 107†.

προ-δόμῳ, τῷ, masc., (δόμος), *vestibule, portico*, with pillars before the house (see plate III., *D D*, at end of volume), I 473, δ 302, cf. θ 57.

προ-έεργε, ipf., *hinder* (by standing before), with inf., A 569†.

προ-έηκα, ε, see προ-ίημι.

προ-εῖδον, subj. **ἴδωσι**, part. ἰδών, όντες, praevidere, *look forward, catch sight of*, ε 393, prospiciens; ἴδωνται, ν 155, prospicient.

πρό-ειμι, **πρὸ ἐόντα**, praeterita, A 70.

πρὸ εἴπομεν, praediximus, α 37†.

προ-έμεν, aor. inf. from προ-ίημι.

προ-ερέσσαμεν, σσαν, aor. from -ερέσσω (ἐρετμός), appellere, *drive forward with oars*, A 435, ι 73, ν 279, ο 497.

προ-έρυσσεν, aor., (ἐρύω), *had drawn forward*, A 308.

πρό-ες, imp. aor. from -ίημι.

προ-έχω, **προὔχουσιν**, part. οντι, α, ουσιν, οὔσῃ, σας, ipf. προέχ(ε), *jut forward*, μ 11, ω 82; *lofty*, τ 544; mid. ipf. προὔχοντο, *had before them*, γ 8; πρὸ ἔχοντο, *were holding before them*, P 355.

προ-ήκεα, ntr. pl., (ἥκης, ἀκή), praeacuta, *pointed at the end, with sharp blades*, μ 205†.

προ-θελύμνῳ, ους, α, (θέλυμνον), *along with the root*; N 130, *overlapping*, of layers of ox-hide forming a shield.

προ-θέουσι, see προ-τίθημι.

προ-θέῃσι, subj., ipf. iter. θέεσκε, praecurrere, *outstrip*, K 362, λ 515.

Προ-θο-ήνωρ, ορος, son of Areilykos, chief of Boiotians, B 495, Ξ 450, 471.

Πρό-θοος, son of Tenthredron, leader of Magnesians, B 756, 758.

προ-θορών, see προ-θρώσκω.

Προ-θόων, ωνα, a Trojan, slain by Teukros, Ξ 515†.

προ-θρώσκω, aor. **θορών**, prosiliens, *springing forward*, Ξ 363. (Il.)

προ-θῡμίῃσι, ταῖς, *zeal, courage*, B 588†.

πρό-θῠρον, ου, οιο, οισ(ιν), *pillared porch at entrance of court* (see plate III., *A*); *gateway*, α 103, γ 493; *porch before the house-door* (see plate III., *t*), *doorway*, θ 304, σ 10.

προ-ΐαλλε(ν), ipf., (ἰάλλω), *sent forth*, Θ 365.

προ-ιάπτω, fut. **ἰάψει**, *ειν*, aor. *ίαψεν*, *send* (*forth*), usually of what is untimely, premature, A 3.

προ-ίημι, **ἵησι**, 3 pl. *ιεῖσι*, imp. *ίει*, ipf. *ίειν*, *ίεις*, *ίει*, aor. *ἧκε*, = *ἧκε*, *έηκα*, *ε*(*ν*), 3 pl. *εσαν*, imp. *ες*, *έτω*, inf. *έμεν*, emittere, *send forth*, *τινά*, with inf. of purpose, κ 25; *θεῷ*, in submission to the god; also of missiles, *shoot*, *dart*, *sling*; *ὕδωρ*, *pour forth*; *ἔπος*, *let drop*; *κῦδος*, *bestow upon*; *let slip*, ε 316; τ 468, *let go*, so that it fell.

προ-ίκτης, *ῃ*, masc., (*ἱκέτης*), mendicus, *beggar*, ρ 352. (Od.)

προΐξ, **προικός**, (procus, precor), *gift*, *present*, ρ 413; but ν 15, that a single person should win for himself gratitude for a gift.

προ-ίστημι, aor. **στήσας**, in *having put* thee *forward before* the Achaians to fight, Δ 156†.

Προῖτος, king of Argives, Z 157, 177; husband of Anteia, Z 160.

προ-κăθ-ῑζόντων, gen. pl. part., (*ἵζω*), *alighting after having flown forward*, B 463†.

προ-κăλέσσατο, aor., subj. *έσσεται*, imp. *εσσαι*, (*καλέω*), evocare, *challenge*, H 39; to combat, *χάρμῃ*; *μαχέσασθαι*, H 218.

προ-κăλίζεο, imp., ipf. *καλίζετο*, (*καλέω*), evocare, *challenge*, Γ 19; *χερσί*, to boxing contest, σ 20; with inf., Δ 389, θ 228.

προ-κείμενα, part., *lying before* (them), α 149.

πρό-κλῠτα, (*κλύω*), ante audita = celebrata, *ἔπεα*, *ancient* legends, Υ 204†.

Πρόκρις, *ιδος*, daughter of Erechtheus, king of Athens, λ 321†.

προ-κρόσσας, fem. pl., (*κρόσσαι*), *in rows*, *in tiers*, Ξ 35†.

προ-κῠλίνδεται, pass., (*κυλίνδω*), provolvitur, *roll forward*, Ξ 18†.

προ-λέγω, pf. pass. part., **λελεγμένοι**, delecti, *chosen*, *élite*, N 689†.

προ-λείπω, aor. **λιπεῖν**, *ών*, *όντες*, pf. *λέλοιπεν*, deserere, *leave behind*, γ 314; deficere, *forsake*, β 279.

προ-μάχιζε, imp. pres. and ipf., (*μαχίζω*), pugnare, *τινί*, *fight in the front rank before others*, Υ 376 and Γ 16 = **προμάχεσθαί** *τινος*, Λ 217 and Ρ 358.

πρό-μᾰχος, *οιο*, *ον*, *οι*, *ων*, *οισ*(*ιν*), *ους*, (*προ-μάχομαι*), propugnator, *champion*, *foremost fighter*, σ 379, ω 526. (Il.)

Πρό-μᾰχος, son of Alegenor, Boiotian chief, Ξ 476, 482, 503.

προ-μῐγῆναι, aor. inf. pass., (*μίγνυμι*), *have intercourse with before*, *τινί*, I 452†.

προ-μνηστῖνοι, *αι*, (*πρυμνή*?), *one after another*, *successively*, φ 230 and λ 233.

προ-μολών, see *προ-βλώσκω*.

πρόμος, *ον*, (sup. from *πρό*, cf. primus), *foremost fighter*, H 75.

προ-νόησαν, *ῆσαι*, (*νοέω*), praesenserunt, *suspect*, Σ 526; ante excogitare, *devise beforehand*, ε 364.

Πρό-νοος, a Trojan, slain by Patroklos, Π 399†.

πρόξ, acc. pl. **πρόκας**, capreas, *roe*, *fawn*, ρ 295†.

προ-πάροιθε(*ν*), adv., pro, ante, porro, coram, *forward*, *formerly*, K 476, O 260; usually prep. with gen. (prepos. and postpos.), ante, *before*, O 66, Γ 22; *ἠιόνος*, *along* the shore.

προ-πᾰσας, *πᾶν*, totas, *all* (day) *long*, *all* (the ships) *together*, ι 161.

προ-πέμπω, aor. **ἔπεμψε** and *προὔπεμψα*, *ε*, *send forth*, A 442, ρ 54.

προ-πέφανται, see *-φαίνω*.

προ-πεσόντες, aor. part., (*πίπτω*), incumbentes, *bending forward*, ι 490 and μ 194.

προ-ποδίζων, (*πούς*), *striding forward*, N 158 and 806.

προ-πρηνέα, *ές*, (pronus), *leaning forward*, Γ 218; *bent*, χ 98 (v. l. *πρηνέι*).

προ-προ-κυλινδόμενος, *wandering from place to place*, ρ 525; *Διός*, ad pedes Jovis provolutus, *rolling as suppliant before*, X 221.

προ-ρέει, *ρέων*, etc., pres., profluere, M 19, ε 444.

πρό-ρριζος, *οι*, (*Fριδjα*, *ῥίζα*), radicitus, *with the roots*, Λ 157 and Ξ 415.

πρός, orig. **πρότι**, then *προτί*, to avoid the lengthening of a preceding vowel by position (exc. ω 347), **ποτί**, (*πρό*), I. adv., insuper, *moreover*, *in addition*, *δέ*, E 307, K 108.—II. prep. (a) with gen., *of point from which*, θ 29 (*toward*, K 428, X 198, ν 110, φ 347); origin, *from*, A 160, 239 *Διός*, which come from Zeus; *in the eyes of, before*, Α 339, Χ 514. Π 85, λ 302, σ 162; *in subjection to*, ἄλλης, Ζ 456; in oaths and entreaties, *by, before*, ν 324, Τ 188; (b) with dat., praeter, *besides*, κ 68; locat., *on*, ε 434, λ 423; *to, upon*, with βάλλειν, η 279; ῥαίειν, τρέπεσθαι, Ξ 403; (c) with acc. (1) local: *to, toward*, Μ 332; with verbs of going, moving, Ι 147; smiting, Δ 108, *upon*; of looking, talking, *at, with* (ξ 331, swear to), Γ 155, Α 643, 403; of changing, *with*, Ζ 235; *against*, with verbs of fighting, Ρ 98, 104.—(2) temporal: *toward*, sub vesperam, ρ 191.

προσ-άγω, aor. **ἤγαγε,** advehere, τινί, *bring upon* (us), ρ 446†.

προσ-ᾶΐξας, aor. part. from ἀίσσω, advolans, adortus, *hurry up to*, χ 337, 342, 365.

προσ-ἄλειφεν, ipf. from ἀλείφω, illinebat, *anoint*, τινί, κ 392†.

προσ-αμύνει, ομεν, pres., aor. inf. ῦναι, ward off (sc. αὐτόν), Ε 139; τινί, *help, aid*, Β 238, Π 509.

προτι-άπτω (aptus), *attach to, accord*, Ω 110†.

προσ-ἄρηρότα, ntr. pl. pf. part., (ἀραρίσκω), *closely fitted*, Ε 725†.

προσ-αυδάω, imp. **αυδάτω,** ipf. ηύδων, α, αυδήτην, ων, κ 418, ν 253, (αὐδή), alloqui, *address*, Μ 353, ψ 208, ω 320; τινά, Δ 192, Χ 7, δ 680; ἐπέεσσι, ο 440; μειλιχίοις, Ρ 431; ἔπεα πτερόεντα, Ε 871, Δ 92, β 362; with part., Φ 367, χ 435; φωνήσας, Α 201, α 122; with part. as subj., Ρ 33, ξ 79, Ο 114, Ζ 163, Ε 30, φ 192.

προσ-βαίνω, aor. **ἔβη,** ἔβαν, βάς, aor. mid. εβήσετο, adire, pervenire ad, assequi, *go to, arrive at*, τινά, τί, Β 48, Ψ 117.

προσ-βάλλω, **ἔβαλλε,** ipf., aor. βαλών, όν, in tmesi, proiicere, *dash against*, πέτρῃσι, ι 284; ἀρούρας, (sc. ἀκτῖσιν), collustrabat, *strike with rays, illumine*, Η 421; προτι-βάλλεαι, mid., increpas, *reprove*, Ε 879.

προσ-εδέρκετο, ipf. from ποτι-δέρκεται, adspicit, *look at*, υ 385, Π 10.

ποτι-δέγμενος, etc., part. pres., (δέχομαι), exspectans, *await*, τινά, τί, εἰ, ψ 91, ὁππότ' ἄν, Η 415.

πρόσ-ειμι, part. **ιόντι,** α, accedenti, em, *approach*, Ε 682. (Il.)

προσ-έειπε, ον, opt. προτι-είποι, (εἶπον), alloqui, *address*, Ω 361, ω 350; τὸν δ' αὖτε, Α 206, α 178; elsewh. τινά, Α 441, δ 542; with part., Α 105, Γ 386, ζ 56, ρ 405; μύθοισι, Γ 437, τ 252, δ 484; πρός τινα μῦθον, address a speech to, δ 803.

προσ-ερεύγεται, πέτρην, *breaks foaming against* the rock, Ο 621†.

πρόσθε(ν), adv., (πρό), *in front* (of him), ε 452; ἔχειν, hold before, Ρ 7; Υ 163, στέρνοιο; precede, ἰέναι τινί; βάλλειν, incitare, drive, urge; Ψ 639, outstripping me by their superiority in number; antea, *heretofore, formerly*, Ν 440; *before*, Ν 66, Ω 698; οἱ π., *the men of old, forefathers*. As prep. with gen. (prepos. and postpos.), ante, *before*, Ι 473, Μ 445; τινὸς ἵστασθαι, come before one for his protection, hence = ὑπέρ, Φ 587, θ 524; local and temporal, Β 359; Ν 66, τοῖιν is gen. part.

προσ-έκειτο, ipf., *were attached*, Σ 379†.

προσ-κηδέος, gen. from -κηδής, (κῆδος), diligentis, *loving, affectionate*, φ 35†.

προσ-έκλῖνε, ipf., pf. pass. ποτι-κέκλῖται, acclinare, *lean upon*, with dat., φ 138; apposita est ei, *place near*, ζ 308.

προσ-έλεκτο (λεχ-), accubuit iuxta, *reclined beside* (me), μ 34†.

προσ-πελάσας, aor. part. from πελάζω, appellere, *drive upon*, νῆα ἄκρῃ, ι 285†.

προσ-επίλνᾰτο, ipf., (πίλναμαι, πέλομαι), appropinquavit, *draw near*, ν 95†.

προσ-πλάζον, part. pres., ipf. -έπλαζε, (πέλαγος, Ger. plätschern, Eng. plash), γενείῳ, *dash against*, λ 583 and Μ 285.

προσ-πτύσσομαι, opt. **ποτι-πτυσσοίμεθα,** fut. προσ-πτύξεται, aor. -πτύξᾰτο, subj. -πτύξομαι, *fold to one's self, embrace*, τινά, amplecti, λ 451; *receive warmly*, θ 478; *welcome, greet*, γ 22; μύθῳ, adire precibus, *entreat*.

πρόσσοθεν, *before* him, Ψ 533†.

πρόσσω, see πρόσω.

προσ-στείχω, aor. **ἔστῖχε,** *strode toward*, υ 73†.

προσ-τίθημι, aor. **ἔθηκεν,** apposuerat, *place upon* (the entrance), ι 305†.

πρόσ-φασθαι, see *πρόσ-φημι.*

πρόσ-φᾰτος, Ω 757, *that may be addressed,* appearing about to speak, so unchanged = *with countenance undistorted and undisfigured,* cf. *ποτιφωνήεις.*

πρόσ-φημι, aor. **ἔφην,** *ης, η,* and pres. *φάσθαι,* alloqui, *speak to, address,* K 369, *ο* 9; *ἔπος,* ψ 106; *τινά,* H 405, N 46, *ν* 49; *ἀπαμειβόμενος,* A 560, *α* 63, A 84, 130, *ε* 214, *ω* 406; with other parts., A 148, 517, 364, Θ 38, I 196, *ι* 446, E 427.

προσ-φυέ(α), with dat., (*φύομαι*), *grown upon,* i. e. *fastened to,* *τ* 58†. (See cut No. 113.)

προσ-φύς, *φῦσα,* aor. part., (*φύομαι*), *clinging,* *μ* 433 and Ω 213.

προσ-φωνέω, ipf.**-εφώνεε,** *εον,* (*φωνή*), alloqui, *address, accost,* *ε* 159; *τινά,* Γ 389, Λ 346, 464, *χ* 355, *ο* 194; with part., Γ 413, *σ* 25, Θ 292, Γ 389; *χ* 69, *μετεφώνεε* is the better reading.

πρό(σ)σω, (porro), *forward,* Π 265; in posterum, *in the future,* A 343.

πρόσ-ωπον, *α* and *ἄτα,* dat. *ἄσι,* ntr., (*ὄπωπα*), *countenance,* Σ 24, Π 414.

προ-τᾰμών, aor. part., (*τάμνω*), *cutting up,* I 489; *cutting before one,* forward, from root toward the top, ψ 196; mid. aor. opt. *-τᾰμοίμην,* cut straight before me, draw straight before me, *σ* 375.

πρότερος, *οιο, ῳ, ον, ω, οι, ων, οισι, ους, η, ῃ, ην, ῃς,* (comp. from *πρό*), prior, *former,* Γ 140; also, instead of prius, T 183, *β* 31, Δ 67; senior, *γενεῇ, elder,* O 166; maiores, *men of former time,* Δ 308; *πόδες,* anteriores, *forefeet,* *τ* 228.

προτέρω, *forward, further,* Γ 400, K 469, *ε* 417.

προ-τεύχω, pf. pass. inf. **τετύχθαι,** facta esse, *have happened, be past,* Π 60. (Il.)

προτί, see *πρός*; **προτι-,** see *προσ-.*

Προτιάων, *ονος,* father of Astynoos, in Ilios, O 455†.

προτι-ειλεῖν (*Ϝελ-*), *press forward,* *ποτὶ νῆας,* K 347†.

προ-τίθημι, 3 pl. ipf. **-τῖθεν,** aor. *προὔθηκεν, place before,* tables, *α* 112; cast before dogs, Ω 409; *προ-θέουσι* in A 291 irregular inflection (cf. *δίδη, διδώσομεν, φορῆναι*) for *τιθέασι,* place before, give into hands of, permit.

προτι-μῡθήσασθαι, alloqui, λ 143†.

προτι-όσσομαι, imp. *εο,* ipf. *ὄσσετ(ο),* (*ὄσσε*), adspicere, *look upon,* *η* 31, ψ 365; then, with eyes of the mind, *forebode,* X 356 = recognize thee for what I had foreboded.

πρό-τμησιν, *τήν,* (*τέμνω*), *parts about the navel,* Λ 424†.

προ-τόνοισιν, *ους,* pl. masc., (*τείνω*), *fore-stay,* rope extending from the mast to the inner portion of stem, A 434, *β* 425. (See cut under the word *Σειρήν.*)

προ-τρέπω, 3 pl. ipf. mid. **τρέποντο,** 2 aor. subj. *τράπηται,* opt. *τραποίμην,* inf. *ἕσθαι,* se convertere ad, *turn in flight to, give one's self to,* *ἐπί τι, ἐπί τινος, ἄχεϊ,* Z 336.

προ-τροπάδην, adv., (*τρέπω*), *in headlong flight,* Π 304†.

προ-τύπτω, aor. **προὔτυψε,** *αν, charge forward,* *ω* 319, a prickling, smarting sensation *forced itself forward through* his nostrils (preceding the tears which he could hardly restrain).

προὔθηκε, see *προ-τίθημι.*

προὔπεμψε, see *προ-πέμπω.*

προὔχοντα, *το, προυχούσῃ,* etc., see *προέχω.*

προ-φαίνω, ipf. **προὔφαινε,** *ον, shine forth from,* *ι* 145; *revealed,* *μ* 394; mid. ipf. *προὐφαίνετο,* pf. *προπέφανται, be visible,* *ν* 169, Ξ 332; aor. pass. *προφανέντα, τε, εῖσα, appearing,* Θ 378, P 487, with *εἰς, ἐν, ἀνά* with acc.

πρό-φᾰσιν, *τήν, pretense, ostensibly,* T 262 and 302.

προ-φερέστερος, *ον, οι, αι,* and sup. *-φερέστατος,* (*προφερής*), *preferred,* *τινός,* above some one; *τινί, superior in,* *φ* 134; with inf., better in drawing, K 352.

προ-φέρω, **φέρῃσι,** *ωμεν, οις, ε, ων, ουσα, αι, bear forth, away,* *υ* 64; *proffer,* I 323, P 121; *τινὶ ἔριδα,* rivalling one another, *ζ* 92; *ὀνείδεα,* convitiari, revile; *μένος, display* courage; mid. pres. *-φέρηται ἔριδα, challenge,* *θ* 210, *begin* combat, Γ 7.

προ-φεύγω, aor. subj. **φύγῃ,** opt. *φύγοισθα,* inf. *φυγεῖν,* part. *-ών, ὄντα,* effugere, *flee away,* Λ 340; with acc., λ 107.

πρό-φρασσ(α) (. . . *φραδέος, φρήν*), propensus; *seriously,* *κ* 386; *cheerfully,* Φ 500.

πρό-φρων, *ονι, ονες*, adv. **-φρονέως,** (*φρήν*), joined with verb, cf. lubens, or lubenti animo, *gladly*, Ξ 357, E 810; *with good cheer*, ξ 54; *zealous, friendly*, π 257; *kind'y*, β 230.

προ-χέει, *ειν*, profundit, *pour forth;* pass. *-χέοντο*, ipf., effusi sunt, Φ 6. (Il.)

πρό-χνυ, adv., (*γόνυ*), *on her knees*, I 570; *ἀπολέσθαι*, be brought low and perish, perish *utterly*, Φ 460.

προ-χοῇσ(ιν), *άς*, fem., (*χέω*), *mouth, stream*, υ 65, P 263.

πρό-χοος, *ῳ, ον*, fem., vessel for drawing off wine, *pitcher, vase*, σ 397 (for the form see cuts Nos. 29, 76); used also to pour water over the hands or feet into a kettle below in washing (see cut No. 82).

πρῠλέες, *έων, έεσσ(ι)*, (proelium ?), *foot-soldiers*, Λ 49, M 77, O 517, E 744, hyperbolically, fitted to, sufficient to protect the combatants of a hundred cities.

Πρυμνεύς, *έως*, a Phaiakian, θ 112†.

πρύμνη, *ης*, puppis, *stern*, A 409, Σ 76, 447. **πρύμνηθεν,** (seize) *by the stern-post*, O 716†.

πρυμνήσι(α), *τά*, (sc. *πείσματα*), *stern*-(cables), by which the ship was made fast to the shore (*κατέδησαν, ἀνάψαι*), hence *ἔλυσαν πρυμνήσια* = naves solverunt, β 418.

πρυμνός, *οῖο, όν, οῖσι, ῆς, ῇ, ήν, όν*, extremus, *extreme end*, either *upper, lower*, or *hinder* part, Π 314, *thigh;* Π 124, 286, *stern*, cf. M 446, *below;* E 292, *root of the tongue;* M 149, *wood at the root*; E 339, ntr. *θέναρος*, *end of the palm*, just below the fingers; **-ότατον,** sup., ρ 463 = summum, where it joins the back.

πρυμν-ωρείη, *τῇ*, (*ὄρος*), *foot of a mountain*, Ξ 307†.

Πρῠτᾰνις, *ιος*, a Lykian, slain by Odysseus, E 678†.

πρῴην, adv., (*πρό*), nuper, *lately*, E 832. (Il.)

πρωθ-ῆβαι, *ας*, masc., and fem. *ην*, (*ἥβη*), pubes, *in the bloom of youth*, Θ 518, α 431.

πρῶι, adv., (*πρό*), mane, *in the morning*, Θ 530; v. l. ω 28, praemature, *untimely*.

πρωϊζ' = *πρωιζά*, (*πρῶι*), *day before yesterday*, B 303†.

πρώιον, mane, *early in the morning*, O 470†.

πρών, P 747; *πρώονες, ας*, masc., (*πρό*). *foreland, headland*, M 282. (Il.)

Πρωρεύς, a Phaiakian, θ 113†.

πρώρη, adj., (*πρό*), *νηῦς*, prora, *prow*, μ 230†.

Πρωτεσῑ-λαος, son of Iphiklos, leader of Thessalians; the first to tread on Trojan soil, and the first to fall, B 698, 706, O 705, N 681, Π 286.

Πρωτεύς, father of Eidothea, servant of Poseidon, whose seals he herds in the sea near Egypt, the wise old man of the sea, δ 365, 385.

πρώτιστος, *ῳ*, sup. from *πρῶτος*, (with *πολύ*, longe), primus, *first*, ntr. *πρώτιστον* (before vowel in third foot) (Od.) and *πρώτισθ'*, λ 168 = *πρώτιστα* (before consonants in third foot), primum, *first of all, chiefest of all*, Ξ 295, γ 57, 419, ι 224.

πρωτο-γόνων, *firstling;* *ἀρνῶν*, Δ 102. (Il.)

πρωτο-πᾰγέα, acc. sing. masc., *εῖς*, pl., (*πέπηγα*), *new-made*, E 194 and Ω 267.

πρωτο-πλόον (*πλόος*), adj., *going to sea for the first time*, θ 35†.

πρῶτος, *ῳ, ον, ω, οι, οισι(ν), ους, η, ης, ῃ, ην, αι, ας*, (sup. from *πρό*), primus, *first*, in position, *οἱ π.*, propugnatores, *θύραι* = *πρόθυρα*; in time and rank (*ἄθλα*, Ψ 275); ntr. *πρῶτον*, so also *πρῶτα* (which only occurs before consonants in first, fifth, and esp. in third foot, after *ἐπειδή, ὡς*, A 276), primum, *first of all, as soon as;* *τὸ πρῶτον* before vowels, before the feminine caesura, after *ὡς*, Δ 267; *ἐπειδή*, δ 13; *τὰ πρῶτα* in third and fourth foot only before consonants; after *ὡς*, θ 268, cf. A 6, Z 489, M 420, θ 553; after relative conjunctions, ubi primum, *as soon as.* (In ω 28, *πρῶι*, praemature, is the better reading.)

πρωτο-τόκος (*τίκτω*), *about to bear for the first time*, of heifer, P 5†.

Πρωτώ, *οῦς*, a Nereid, Σ 43†.

πρώονες, see *πρών*.

πταίρω, aor. **ἔπτᾰρεν,** *μέγ'* —, *sneezed aloud*, ρ 541†.

πτάμενος, *πτάτο*, see *πέτομαι*.

πτελέην, *αι, ας*, *elm*, Z 419. (Il.)

Πτελέος, (1) harbor-town in Thessaly, B 697.—(2) colony of Thessalian Pteleos in Elis, B 594.

πτέρνης, *τῆς*, *heel*, X 397†.

πτερόεντες, *τ(α)*, (*πτερόν*), *winged, flying*, of arrows, as feathered at the lower end, Υ 68, Δ 117.—(2) of shields, *λαισήια*, because of the fluttering apron attached to them, E 453 (see cuts Nos. 79 and 85).—(3) *ἔπεα*, A 201.

πτερόν, *ά*, ntr., (*πέτομαι*), *feather, wing* (torn, ο 527), *πυκνὰ βάλλειν*, ply rapidly; symbol of lightness, T 386, and swiftness, *η* 36; compared with oars, λ 125.

πτέρυξ, **πτέρῠγος,** *εσσι(ν)*, (*πτερόν*), *pinion, wing*, B 316.

πτήσσω, aor. **πτῆξε,** *make bend with fear, terrify*, Ξ 40, interpolated verse; pf. part. *πεπτηώς, ῶτες*, *cowering, crouching* in fear, ξ 354, χ 362.

πτοιέω, only 3 pl. aor. pass. **ἐπτοίηθεν,** pavebant, *be dismayed*, χ 298†.

Πτολεμαῖος, son of Peiraios, father of Eurymedon, Δ 228†.

πτολεμίζω, *ιστής, μος*, etc., see *πολεμίζω*, etc.

πτολίεθρον, *α*, (*πόλις*), *city*, always with follg. gen. of proper name, *Ἰλίου*; *Τρώων*, A 163, a city of the Trojans, =any whatever, not Ilios.

πτολῑ-πορθος, *ψ, ον*, and **-πόρθιον** (ι 504, 530), masc. and fem., (*πέρθω*), *destroyer, sacker of cities*, B 728, E 333, σ 356, ω 116 of Odysseus. (Il.)

πτόλις, see *πόλις*.

πτόρθον, *τόν*, surculum, *sapling*, ζ 128†.

πτύγμ(α), *τό*, *fold*, E 315†.

πτυκτῷ, dat., (*πτύσσω*), *folded*, Z 169†.

πτύξ, **πτυχί,** *ες, ας*, fem., (*πτύσσω*), (1) *layer of shield*, Σ 481; usually *the outermost, smallest layer*, e. g. in shield of Achilleus (see cut No. 135).—(2) *ravine, mountain valley*, Λ 77.

πτυόφιν=gen. sing. from *τὸ πτύον*, (*πτύω*), *winnowing shovel* or *fan*, used to throw up grain and chaff against the wind, N 588†.

πτύσσω, aor. part. **πτύξᾱσα,** *having folded together*, α 439, ζ 111; pass. ipf. *ἐπτύσσοντο*, *were bent*, N 134, doubtful reading.

πτύοντα, part. pres., (*πτύω*, spuo), *spitting forth*, Ψ 697†.

πτώξ, *ῶκα*, masc., (*πτώσσω*), timidus, *timid*, X 310; as subst. *hare*, P 676.

πτωσκαζέμεν, inf., (*πτώξ*), *crouch in fear*, Δ 372†.

πτώσσεις, *ουσι*, etc., pres., ipf. *πτώσσον* Φ 26, (*πτήσσω, πτώξ*), *cower, hide*, Δ 371; *ὑπό τινι*, before, H 129, pavere; *go cringing, begging about*, *κατὰ δῆμον*; *νέφεα*, *forsake in fear* the clouds, sky.

πτωχεύω, *ῃ, ειν*, ipf. iter. *πτωχεύεσκ(ε)*, fut. *εύσων*, (*πτωχός*), mendicari; trans. *gain by begging*, ρ 11, 17.

πτωχός, *ῷ, όν, οί, ῶν, ούς*, (*πτώσσω*), mendicus, *beggar*-(man), *ἀνήρ*, φ 327, ξ 400. (Od.)

Πυγμαῖοι, fabled race of dwarfs, *manikins, thumbkins*, lit. "fist-lings," (*πυγμή*), Γ 6†.

πυγ-μᾰχίης, *τῆς*, (*πυγμή*), *boxing*, Ψ 653 and 665; from

πυγ-μᾰ́χοι, masc., (*πυγμή*, pug-nus), pugiles, *boxers*, θ 246†. (Cf. cut.)

πυγμῇ, *τῇ*, (pugnus, Eng. fight), in the *boxing-match*, Ψ 669†.

πῡγούσιον, accus. masc., (*πυγών*), *a cubit long*; *ἔνθα καὶ ἔνθα*, in length and breadth, κ 517 and λ 25.

πύελον, *τήν*, *feeding-trough*, τ 553†.

πυθέσθαι, aor. inf. from *πυνθάνομαι*.

πυθμένι, *α, ες*, masc., (fundus, bottom), *bottom* of a vase, Λ 635; of trees, *trunk, butt-end*, ν 122, 372.

πύθω, fut. **πύσει,** Δ 174, putrefaciet, *cause to rot*; pass. *πύθεται, ομένων*, putrescere, *rot*, Λ 395, μ 46.

Πῡθώ, *οῦς, οῖ, ώ*, and **Πυθῶνα** B 519, *Pytho*, oldest name of oracle of Apollo on Parnassos, θ 80, I 405, B 519; *Πυθῶδε*, *to Pytho*, λ 581.

πῦκᾰ, *thickly, strongly*, crebro, I 588; *φρονεῖν, τρέφειν*, *wisely, carefully*, E 70.

πῠκάζοιεν, opt., *ειν*, inf. pres., aor. *πύκασε(ν), αι, ας, άσᾱσα*, pf. pass. part. *πεπῠκασμένος, α*, (*πύκα*), *cover closely*, *κάρη*; *wrap up, cover*, with dat., *ἅρματα*, chariots *overlaid with* gold; *ῥάκεσιν ὤμους*, his shoulders *wrapped in* rags; τινὰ φρένας, grief *overshadowed, encompassed* his soul; λ 320, before their chins were thickly covered with down.

πῡκῐ-μήδεος, gen., (μῆδος), prudentis, *deep-counselled*, α 438†.

πῡκῐνός, οῦ, όν, οί, οῖσι(ν), ή, ῆς, ῇ, ήν, αί, ῇς, άς, όν, (ά), and **πυκνόν**, οί, οῖσιν, ούς, ή, ήν, αί, ῇσι, ά, (πύκα), prop. spissus, frequens, *firm, close, compact*; πτερά, flap *rapidly* (in closely succeeding motions) the wings, β 151; *close-packed, crowded*, χηλός, λόχος; *firmly put together*, λέχος ψ 117, but in I 621 the adj. is rather to be understood as applying to the several bed-coverings, *closely spread; thick-foliaged*, ὄζος, δρυμός, θάμνος, ὕλη; *mighty, sore*, delusion, Ω 480; grief, Π 599; prudens, *wise, sagacious*, B 55, Σ 216, Ξ 294, Ω 282; adv. **πυκινόν**, ά, πυκνόν, ά, and **πῡκῐνῶς**, *close, fast*, then frequenter, *often, deeply*, τ 95, T 312; prudenter, *wisely*, Φ 293, α 279.

Πῡλαι-μένης, εος, king of Paphlagonians, ally of Trojans, B 851; slain by Menelaos, E 576, yet appears again N 658; his son, Harpalion, N 643.

Πῡλαῖος, son of Lethos, chief of Pelasgians, B 842†.

πῡλ-άρτᾱο, τοῦ, (-άρτης), *door-closer, gate-fastener*, epithet of Aides, Θ 367, λ 277.

Πυλ-άρτης, a Trojan, (1) wounded by Aias, Λ 491.—(2) by Patroklos, Π 696.

πῡλᾰ-ωρούς, τούς, (Fορᾶν), *gate-keepers*, Φ 530. (Il.)

πῦλαι, άων, ῃσ(ι), ας, fem., (πέλομαι?), *gate* (always pl. as in two wings), B 809; of cities, camp, heaven, dreams, τ 562; of the sun, ω 12; 'Αίδᾱο, of death, I 312.

Πυλη-γενής, see Πυλοι-γενής.

Πυλήνη, town in Aitolia, B 639†.

Πύλιοι, H 134, Ψ 633, Λ 753, ο 216, *inhabitants of* Πύλος.

Πυλοι-γενής, *born in Pylos*, Nestor, B 54; horses, Ψ 303.

Πῠλόνδε, *to Pylos*, Λ 760, β 317, γ 182, and freq.

Πῠλόθεν, π 323, *from Pylos*†.

Πύλος, *Pylos*, a city in Triphylia, south of Alpheios, Λ 671 sq. In the Odyssey a city in the Messenian Elis, opposite the south end of Sphakteria, γ 4, ἠγαθέῃ, ἱερῆς; joined with ἠμαθόεντος, τι, the word seems to designate not the city only, but the entire realm of Pylos.

πύλος, ἐν **πύλῳ**, E 397†, *in the gateway*, sc. Πυλάρταο, words from some ancient myth describing the combat of Hades and Herakles: the myth having been forgotten, later commentators wrote ἐν Πύλῳ, and thus gave to the combat an earthly arena.

Πύλων, ωνος, a Trojan, slain by Polypoites, M 187†.

πῡμάτῳ, ον, η, ης, ην, ας, ον, α, extremus, ultimus, *last*, η 138, Λ 759, Ψ 373, ι 369; N 616, *root of* the nose; ntr. used adverbially, X 203, δ 685.

πυνθάνομαι, ipf. πυνθανόμην, and **πεύθομαι**, οίαθ' = οίατο 3 pl. opt., εσθαι, έσθω, όμενος, ipf. (ἐ)πεύθετ(ο), όμεθ(α), fut. πεύσομαι, σεαι, σεται, σόμενος, ον, aor. ἐπύθοντο, and 1 sing. πυθόμην, 3 du. έσθην, ηαι, ηται, ησθε, οίμην, οιτο, οίατο, and aor. red. πεπυθοίατ(ο), pf. πέπυσμαι, σσαι, σται, ύσθαι, plupf. (ἐ)πέπυστο, 3 du. πεπύσθην, comperio, exploro, *learn by inquiry*, β 215, *from* some one, τινός, P 408; usually = audio, *ascertain at first hand*, τί, κ 147, π 412, O 379; comperio, *hear tell of*, τινός, de, ν 256, ξ 321, but Z 465, βοῆς = audire; τί τινος, P 408, from some one, also ἔκ τινος; the fact heard freq. expressed by τινά, with part. or adj., Z 50, Λ 135, cf. E 702; τινός, with part., A 257, these things from you wrangling, T 322.

πύξ, possibly for **πυξί**, adv., (pugnus, πυγμή), *at boxing*, Γ 237, θ 103.

πύξινον, ntr., (πύξος), *of box-wood*, Ω 269†.

πῦρ, πυρός, ί, ά, (Ger. Feuer), ignis, *fire*, also in fire-pans for illumination; as symbols of danger, K 246; pl. *watch-fires*; πυρὸς θερέω, warm myself *at the fire*, ρ 23.

πῡρ-άγρην, τήν, (ἀγρέω), *fire-tongs*, γ 434 and Σ 477.

Πῡρ-αίχμης, chief of the Paionians, ally of Trojans, B 848; slain by Patroklos, Π 287.

πυρακτέω, ipf. **ἐπῡράκτεον**, *I brought to a glow*, ι 328†.

Πύρᾰσος, (1) a Trojan, wounded by

Aias, Λ 491.—(2) town in Thessaly, Β 695.

πυργηδόν, adv., (*πύργος*), like a tower, *in solid masses*, Μ 43. (Il.)

πύργος, *ου, ῳ, ον, οι, ων, οις, ους*, masc., *tower, turreted wall*, ζ 262; *bulwark*, "strong tower," of Aias, λ 556; *compact body, column*, Δ 334.

πύργωσαν, 3 pl. aor., (*πυργόω*), *surround with towers. fortify*, λ 264†.

πῡρετόν, *τόν*, febrim, *fever*, Χ 31†.

πῡρή, *ῆς, ῇ, ήν, αί*, rogus, *funeral-pyre; ἀλεγεινῆς*, grievous, for the friends of the deceased, Ψ 110–177, 192–258, Ω 786–799. (Cf. cut.)

πῡρη-φόρον, see *πυρο-φόρος*.

πῡρι-ήκεα, acc., (*ἀκή, -ήκης*), *with blazing point*, ι 387†.

πῡρί-καυστος, 2, (*καίω*), praeustus, *charred*, Ν 564†.

Πῦρις, *ιν*, a Lykian, slain by Patroklos, Π 416†.

Πῡρι-φλεγέθων, river in lower world, κ 513†.

πυρ-κᾰϊή, *ῆς, ήν*, (*καίω*), *place where fire is kindled. funeral-pyre*, bustum, Ψ 158, 228, Ω 791; also Η 428, 431, *πυρκαϊῇ*, they piled the corpses on the funeral-pyre. (Il.)

πύρνον, *α*, ntr., (*πυρός*), *wheaten loaf*, ο 311. (Od.)

πῡρόν, acc. sing.; pl. *πυροί, ῶν, ούς*, *wheat* (grains) used unground, as food for animals rather than for men; yet, υ 109.

πῡρο-φόροιο, *οι*, and *πυρη-φόρον*, *wheat-bearing*, Μ 314, γ 495.

πυρ-πολέοντας, part., (colere), *tending fires*, κ 30†.

πυρσοί, masc., (*πῦρ*), *torches, signal-lights*, Σ 211†.

πώ, encl. adv., *yet, οὔ πω*, nondum, *not yet*, also nequaquam, *in no wise; οὔ πώ ποτε*, nunquam, *never*, of past.

πωλέομαι, **πωλέ**(*εαι*), *εῖται, εύμενος*, ipf. *πωλεύμην, εῖτ(ο)*, iter. *πωλέσκετο*, fut. *πωλήσεαι*, (*πέλομαι*), versari, frequentare, *frequent, consort with, εἰς, ἐπί, μετά τινας, δεῦρο*, ι 189, δ 384, β 55, Α 490, χ 352, Ε 350.

πῶλοι, *οισιν, ους*, comm., (pullus), *foal*, Λ 680, Υ 222, ψ 246.

πῶμ(α), dat. pl. *ασιν*, ntr., *cover*, of chest, Π 221; of vase, β 353; also of quiver, Δ 116. (See Herakles in cut.)

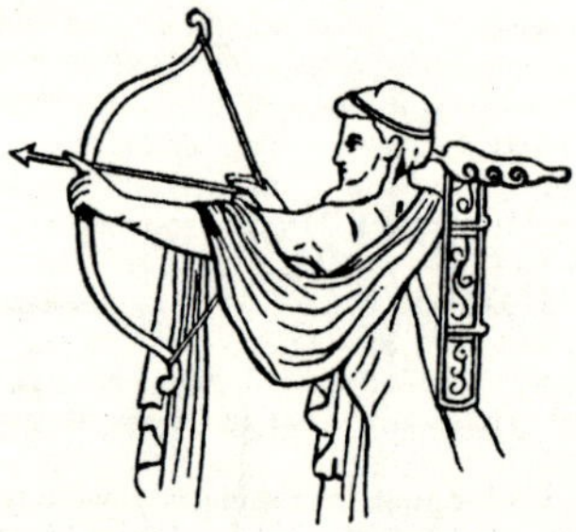

πώ-ποτε, unquam, *ever yet*, always after *οὐ*, referring to the past, μ 98.

πῶς, quomodo? *how?* in exclamatory question, κ 337; with *γάρ*, *how then?* κ 337, Α 123; with *γὰρ δή, δέ, δή*, quomodo tandem, how pray? *νῦν*, σ 223; with *τ' ἄρα*, igitur, therefore.

πώς, enclit., *somehow; αἴ κέν πως*, Α 66, si qua, if *perhaps; οὐ μέν πως*, nequaquam, by no means, Δ 158.

πωτάομαι, ipf. **πωτῶντο,** (*πέτομαι*), ferebantur, *flew*, Μ 287†.

πῶυ, *εα, εσι*, (pa-scor, Germ. Vieh), *flock, ὀίων, μήλων*, Γ 198, ω 112.

Ρ.

Ρ. Many words beginning with ρ began orig. with two consonants, esp. ϝρ and σρ; what this initial consonant orig. was can not always be determined.

ῥά, ῥ', see ἄρα.

ῥάβδον, φ, οισι, masc., (ῥέπω?), *rod, staff*, esp. *magic wand* of Hermes, Ω 343; Kirke, κ 238; Athena, ν 429; *fishing-rod*, μ 251; *pins*, Μ 297.

ῥᾰδᾰλόν, v. l. = ῥοδανόν, Σ 576.

Ῥᾰδά-μανθυς, υος, son of Zeus, brother of Minos, Ξ 322, η 323; ruler in Elysion, δ 564.

ῥαδινήν, (ϝραδ-), *slender, pliable*, Ψ 583†.

ῥᾰθάμιγγες, fem., guttae, *drops*, esp. of blood (mingled with dust), Λ 536; κονίης, *particles* of dust, Ψ 502. (Il.)

ῥαίνω (from ῥαδυjω), ipf. pass. **ῥαίνοντο**, aor. act. imp. ῥάσσατε, pass. pf. ἐρραδᾰται, plupf. ἐρράδᾰτο, conspergere, *besprinkle*, τί τινι, Λ 282, υ 150, Μ 431.

ῥαιστῆρα, acc. masc. and fem., malleum, *hammer*, Σ 477†.

ῥαίω, subj. **ῥαίησι**, ipf. ἔρραιε, fut. ῥαισέμεναι, aor. ῥαίσῃ, αι, *shatter*, νῆα; τινά, *wreck*, ζ 326, ε 221; pass. pres. ῥαίοιτο, ομένου, aor. ἐρραίσθη, *be dashed*, ι 459, πρὸς οὖδεϊ, on the ground; *shiver*, Π 339.

ϝράκος, εα, έων, εσιν, έεσσι, ntr., (λάκος, modern Greek βρακίον?), *ragged garment, tatters*, ζ 178. (Od.)

ῥαπτόν, άς, sartum, *patched*, ω 228 and 229, from

ῥάπτειν, ipf. 1 pl. ῥάπτομεν, aor. ῥάψε, ψαι, sarcio, *rivet together*, Μ 296; κακά, etc., τινί, *devise*, γ 118, π 379.

ῥάσσατε, imp. aor. from ῥαίνω, conspergite, *sprinkle*.

ῥᾰφαί, αἱ, *seams*, χ 186†.

ῥᾰχιν, fem., *chine*, piece cut lengthwise along the spine, Ι 208†.

ϜΡέα, monosyll. Ο 187, Ῥείης Ξ 203, (εὐρείης, the broad earth?), *Rhea*, daughter of Uranos, daughter and sister of Kronos, mother of Zeus, Poseidon, Aides; of Hestia, Demeter, Hera.

ῥέα, monosyll., facile, *easily*, only Il., μάλα, Υ 101. **ῥεῖα**, facile, *easily*, with verbs of moving, Ε 304; ζώοντες, *lightly* living, i. e. without care or pain, ε 122.

ῥέεθρα, τά, (ῥέω), undae, *stream, current*, also *bed*, Β 461, ζ 317.

ῥέζω, pres. and ipf., ipf. iter. ῥέζεσκον, fut. ῥέξω, ει, ομεν, ειν, aor. ἔρρεξε, ἔρεξα, etc., ῥέξ(ε) Ι 535, pass. aor. part. ῥεχθέν, έντος, (ϝρεγjω, from ϝεργjω, Ger. wirken, Eng. work), *handle, deal with*, εὖ κακῶς τινα; *attempt, avail*, Τ 90; *bring to pass*, θ 148; ἔργον, usually in bad signif., χ 315; Ι 647, *treat with contumely;* ἱερά, θαλύσια, ἑκατόμβην, *perform, offer*, sacra facere, and generally sacrificare, γ 5, Ι 535.

ῥεθέων, gen. pl. ntr., (ὄρνυμι), *limbs*, Π 856, Χ 68.

ῥεῖα, see ῥέα. **Ῥείη**, see ϜΡέα.

Ῥεῖθρον, harbor in Ithaka, α 186†.

ϝρέπω, ipf. **ϝρέπε**, *sank* (in the scale), αἴσιμον ἦμαρ, fatalis dies, destiny, Θ 72, Χ 212.

ῥερυπωμένα, see ῥυπάω.

ῥεχθέν, έντα, see ῥέζω.

ῥέων, etc., (from σρεϝω), pres., ipf. ἔρρεε, ει, εον, and ῥέε, ον, aor. ῥύη γ 455, fluere, *flow*, ὕδατι, αἵματι, *trickle;* fig., Α 249; *drop off*, κ 393.

ϝρηγμῖνος, ῖνι, ῖνα, masc., (ῥήγνυμι), *surf, breakers*, Υ 229, not on the shore alone.

ϝρήγνυμι, **ῥηγνῦσι**, ipf. iter. ῥήγνυσκε, fut. ῥήξω, ειν, aor. (ἔρ)ῥῆξ(εν), etc., (frango), *break, shatter;* πύλας, *burst through;* also of hostile ranks, φάλαγγας, στίχας; pass. pres. ipf. ῥήγνῦτο, υντο, mid. aor. ἐρρήξαντο, ῥήξασθαι, άμενος, etc., subj. ῥηξόμεθα, *break*, intrans. κῦμα, Σ 67; *unchain, let loose*, Υ 55; *burst, scatter*, Μ 440.

ϝρῆγος, εϊ, εα, εσσι, (ῥάκος, Ger. Laken), *covering, blanket*, γ 349; *woollen rug*, ζ 38, ν 73; *cushion and cover, mattress and blanket* for chair and bed,

I 661, η 336. (Cf. the Assyrian and Greek θρόνος with θρῆνυς attached.)

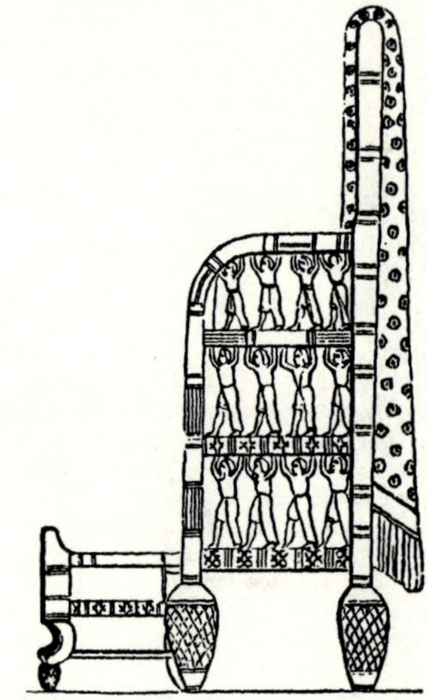

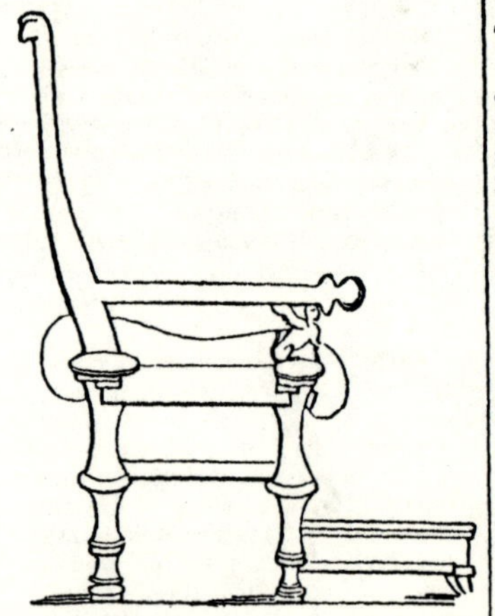

ϝρηθέντι σ 414, υ 322, part. aor. pass. from ἐρῶ, (εἰπεῖν), over a just word *clearly spoken*.

ῥηΐδίη, ιον, ι(α) Υ 265, adv. ῑδίως, Ε 808, φ 92, comp. ῥηΐτεροι, sup. ῥηΐτăτ(α), ῥηΐστη, facilis, *easy*, δ 565, φ 75; τινί, also with inf., Σ 258, Ω 243; Μ 54, facilis transitu, easy to pass.

ϝρηκτός, verbal adj. from ϝρήγνυμι, *that can be broken, vulnerable*, Ν 323†.

Ῥήνη, concubine of Oïleus, mother of Medon, Β 728†.

ῥηξ-ηνορίην, τήν, *might to break through hostile ranks, impetuosity*, ξ 217†, from

ῥηξ-ήνωρ, **ήνορος**, ι, α, *bursting hostile ranks, irresistible*, epith. of Achilleus, Η 228, δ 5.

Ῥηξ-ήνωρ, ορος, son of Nausithoos, brother of Alkinoos, η 63 and 146.

ῥῆσις, gen. **ῥήσιος**, fem., (ἐρεῖν), sermo, *speech*, φ 291†.

Ῥῆσος, son of Eïoneus, Κ 435, king of the Thrakians, slain by Odysseus and Diomedes, Κ 474, 519.

ῥήσσοντες, part. pres., (ῥήγνυμι?), *treading, stamping*, Σ 571†.

ϝρητῆρ(α), τόν, (ἐρεῖν), oratorem, *speaker*, Ι 443†.

ϝρητῷ (ἐρεῖν), conducta, *stipulated*, Φ 445†.

ϝρήτρην, τήν, (ἐρεῖν), *stipulation, bargain*, ξ 393†.

ϝρῑγεδᾰνή (ῥιγέω), *hateful, horrible*, Τ 325†.

ῥιγέω, fut. **ῥιγήσειν**, aor. ἐρρίγησε, σαν, and ῥίγησ(ε), pf. ἔρρῑγα, (ε), subj. ἐρρίγησι, plupf. ἐρρίγει, (ῥῖγος, frigus), horrere, *shudder at, start* (with fright) *from*, comm. absol. Δ 148, Ο 34, ε 116; ἰδών, Δ 279, Μ 331, 208, Π 119; pf. like pres. with inf., Γ 353; with μή, ψ 216, pertimuit, ne—.

ϝρίγιον, comp., (ῥῖγος), frigidius, *colder*, ρ 191; magis horrendum, peius, *harsher, worse*, Α 325, υ 220; sup. ῥίγιστα, pessima, Ε 873.

Ῥίγμος, son of Peiroos, from Thrake, ally of Trojans, Υ 485†.

ῥῖγος, τό, frigus, *cold*, ε 472†.

ῥιγόω, fut. **ῥῑγωσέμεν**, frigēre, *be cold*, ξ 481†.

ῥίζης, gen., ῃ, αν, αι, ῶν, ῃσι(ν), (ϝριδjα, radix, root, cf. thoroughwort), ψ 196, roots of the eye, ι 390.

ῥιζόω, aor. **ἐρρίζωσε**, *plant, fix firmly*, ν 163; pf. pass. ἐρρίζωται, *is planted out*, η 122.

ῥίμφᾰ, *swiftly*, Ζ 511, θ 193.

ῥίν, see ῥίς.

ϝρῑνόν, οῦ, ntr., corium, *hide*, Κ

155; in ι 281, *shield*, according to the ancient commentators = *cloud*, v. l. ἔρῖνον interpreted as = ἐρινεός, which suits some passages equally well, but not all.

ϝρινός, οῦ, ῷ, όν, οί, οῖς, ούς, fem., cutis, corium, *hide, skin*, of animals, K 262, Υ 276; of men, E 308; usually, with and without βοῶν, *ox-hide*, i. e. *ox-hide shield*, N 406, Δ 447; Π 636, the thud of bronze, of leather, and of ox-hide shields.

ῥῑνο-τόρος, (τορέω), *shield-piercing*, Φ 392†.

ῥίον, ntr., *peak, crag*, of Olympos, Θ 25; γ 295, *headland*.

ῥιπή, ῆς, ῇ, fem., (ῥίπτω), impetus, *impulse, weight, flight, rush*, θ 192, Θ 355, Φ 12.

Ῥίπη, town in Arkadia, B 606†.

ϝριπτάζων, part., (ῥίπτω), *hurl about*, Ξ 257†.

ϝρίπτω, ipf. iter. **ῥίπτασκον,** fut. ῥίψω, ει, aor. ἔρριψε(ν), and ῥῖψ(ε), (ϝριπ-, Ger. werfe), *hurl, throw*, τὶ μετά τινα, *toss into the hands of*, Γ 378.

ῥίπεσσι, fem., (scirpus), οἰσυΐνῃσι, *with willow withes*, viminibus, ε 256†.

ϝρίς, **ῥῑνός,** ῥῖνες, ῶν, ας, nasus, *nose*, N 616, δ 445; pl., nares, *nostrils*, Ξ 467, ε 456, T 39, per nares instillavit.

ῥοδᾰνόν, *waving, swaying*, Σ 576†.

Ῥόδιος, see Ῥόδος.

Ῥοδίος, river in Troas, rising in Mount Ida, M 20†.

ϝροδο-δάκτῠλος, *rosy-fingered*, Ἠώς, epithet originating in an appearance of the eastern sky before sunrise peculiar to southern latitudes, β 1.

ϝροδόεντι, dat., (ϝρόδον, rosa), *fragrant with roses*, Ψ 186†.

Ῥόδος, fem., *Rhodes*, famous island southwest of Asia Minor, B 654 sq., 667; the inhabitants, Ῥόδιοι, B 654.

ῥοάων, ῇσ(ι), άς, (ῥέω), fluctus, *stream*, B 869, ζ 216, ω 11.

ῥόθιον (ῥόθος), *gurgling, plashing, roaring*, ε 412†.

ῥοιαί, nom. pl., *pomegranate* (of tree and fruit), η 115 and λ 589.

ῥοιβδήσειεν, opt. aor. from ῥοιβδέω, (ῥοῖζος), *suck in*, μ 106†.

ῥοίζησεν, aor. from ῥοιζέω, *whistled*, K 502†.

ῥοίζῳ, ον, fem., *whistling, whizzing, whirr*, Π 361; of shepherd's call, ι 315.

ῥόος, όοιο, όον, masc., (σρόος, ῥέω), *stream, flow* of water, Σ 402, M 25; κὰρ ῥ., along in the current, ε 327.

ϝρόπαλον, ῳ, (α), οισι, ntr., (ῥέπω), *club, cudgel*, fustis, Λ 559, ι 319, λ 575.

ῥοχθεῖ, prs., ipf. ῥόχθει, *roar*, μ 60 and ε 402.

ῥύατο, see ῥύομαι.

ῥῠδόν, adv., (ῥέω), ἀφνειοῖο, *with floods of gold, enormously* rich, ο 426†.

ῥύη, aor. from ῥέω.

ῥῡμός, οῦ, ῷ, (ἐρύω), temo, *pole*, Z 40, K 505. (Cf. cut No. 45 for method of attachment of pole to chariot-box; cf. also Nos. 49, 99.)

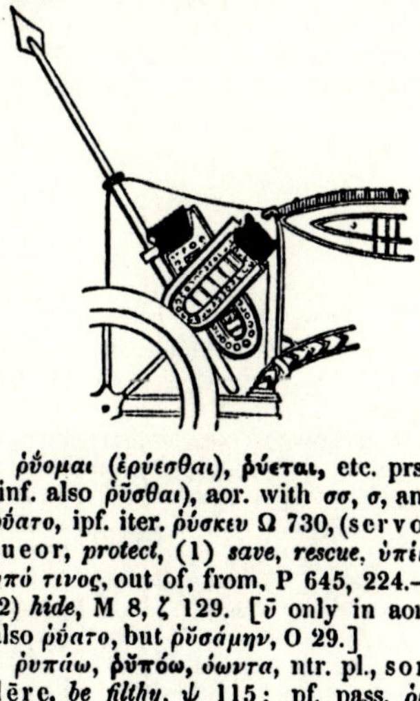

ῥῡ́ομαι (ἐρύεσθαι), **ῥύεται,** etc. prs., (inf. also ῥῦσθαι), aor. with σσ, σ, and ῥύατο, ipf. iter. ῥύσκεν Ω 730, (servo), tueor, *protect*, (1) *save, rescue*, ὑπέκ, ὑπό τινος, out of, from, P 645, 224.—(2) *hide*, M 8, ζ 129. [ῡ only in aor., also ῥύατο, but ῥῠσάμην, O 29.]

ῥυπάω, **ῥῠπόω,** όωντα, ntr. pl., sordēre, *be filthy*, ψ 115; pf. pass. ῥεῤῡπωμένα, ζ 59 (from ῥυπόω, transitive).

ῥῠ́πα, τά, sordes, *filth*, ζ 93†.

ῥῦσατ(ο) (ἐρύκω), aor., retinebat, *detain*, ψ 244†; see also ἐρῠ́ομαι and ἐρύω.

ῥῦσαι, see ῥύομαι.

ῥύσι(α), τά, (ἐρύω), ἐλαύνεσθαι, *booty dragged away*, of cattle, Λ 674†.

ῥυσί-πτολι, Z 305, v. l. for ἐρυσίπτολι.

ῥύσκεν, see ῥύομαι.

ῥῦσαί (ἐρύω, with furrows *drawn* over the face, sulcosae), rugosae, *wrinkled*, I 503†.

ῥῦσί-πτολι, *protectress of the city*, Z 305.

ῥυστάζοντας, acc. pl. part. prs., ῥυστάζεσκεν, (ἐρύω), *drag about*, Ω 755; *maltreat*, π 109.

ῥυστακτύος, τῆς, (ῥυστάζω), *misusage, ill-treatment*, σ 224†.

I. **ῥῦτῆρα,** masc., (ἐρύω), *one who draws* a bow, φ 173, σ 262.

II. **ῥῦτῆρα,** τόν, (Ϝερ-, Eng. warden), custodem, *guard*, ρ 187 and 223.

III. **ῥῦτῆρσι,** τοῖς, (ἐρύω), Π 475, they ran in between the reins, *in taut reins*, which by the fall of the παρήορος had been drawn to one side and entangled. The word is sometimes translated *traces*, but there is no mention of the use of traces in Homer. (Cf. plate I., at end of volume.)

Ῥύτιον, town in Kreta, B 648†.

ῥῦτοῖσι (ἐρύω), *dragged to the spot*, i. e., too large to carry, ζ 267 and ξ 10.

ῥωγαλέον, έην, έᾶ ξ 343, *pierced, torn, ragged*, B 417.

Ϝρῶγας (ῥήγνυμι), *clefts*, i. e. *loopholes* or *windows*, in the rear wall of the μέγαρον, to lighten the stairway behind them, χ 143. (See cut No. 90.)

ῥώομαι, ipf. **(ἐῤ)ῥώοντο,** aor. ἐρρώσαντο, (ruere), *were in rapid motion*, γούνατα, κνῆμαι; χαῖται, *fluttered*; *rushed forward*, Λ 50; *moved in armor, marched in pomp around*, ω 69; *danced*, Ω 616; Σ 417, *were running hard by* (of automatons).

ῥωπήϊα, ntr., (ῥώψ), fruticeta, *undergrowth*, Φ 559, ξ 473.

ῥωχμός, masc., (ῥώξ), *place gullied out, hollow*, Ψ 420†.

ῥώψ, acc. pl. **ῥῶπας,** fem., (ῥέπω), sarmenta, *twigs, brushwood*, κ 166, π 47.

Σ.

σ' = (1) σέ, X 351.—(2) σοί, A 170, Φ 122, cf. κ 19, δῶκε δέ μ'.—(3) σά, α 356.

Σαγγάριος, οιο, river flowing through Bithynia and Phrygia, and into Pontos Euxeinos, Γ 187, Π 719.

σαίνω (from σϜανjω, Ger. schwänzeln), **σαίνωσ(ι),** οντας, ipf. σαῖνον, *fawn upon*, with wagging of tail, π 6.

σακέσ-πᾰλος (πάλλω), *shield-swinging*, E 126†.

σάκος, εος, εϊ, εα, εσ(σ)ι(ν), ntr., *the great shield*, H 219, 222. (See cuts Nos. 9, 17, 18.)

Σᾰλᾰμίς, island near Athens, B 557, H 199, home of Aias, the son of Telamon.

Σαλμωνεύς, ῆος, son of Aiolos, father of Tyro, λ 236†.

σάλπιγξ, ἡ, *trumpet*, Σ 219†.

σαλπίζω, aor. **σάλπιγξεν,** *resounded, quaked*, Φ 388†.

Σάμη, island near Ithaka, ι 24, π 249, Kephallenia, or a part of it.

Σάμος, = (1) Σάμη, B 634. —(2) Θρηικίη, *Samothrake*, island off the coast of Thrake, N 12.

σᾰνίς, ἴδος, ίδες, ίδων, ίδεσσιν, ίδας, fem., *boards, planks*, esp. the *wings of folding doors*, fores, I 583, Σ 275; *scaffolding, stage*, φ 51.

σάος, comp. **σαώτερος,** *more safely*.

σᾰο-φροσύνης, τῆς, dat. pl. υσι, *sound sense, discretion*, ψ 30; ψ 13, bring into the *ways of reason*.

σᾰό-φρων, ονα, *discreet*, δ 158 and Φ 462.

σαόω, imp. **σάω,** v. l. σῶ ν 230 (full form σάοε), and 3 sing. ipf. σάου, σάω, σάοε, fut. **σαώσω,** aor. ἐσάωσα and σάωσε, etc., fut. mid. σαώσεαι; pass. aor. 3 pl. ἐσάωθεν, also **σώοντες,** ipf. iter. σώεσκον and (from σοάω) subj. **σόως,** σόῳ, also v. l. σόῳς, ῳ, I 681, 424, and finally **σώζων** ε 490, (σάος, salus), servare, conservare, *save, preserve*, I 78, ν 230, O 290, χ 372; ἔνθεν, inde nequaquam servaberis, thence in no way shalt thou *deliver thyself*, φ 309.

σαπήη, see σήπω.

σαρδάνιον (σαίρω ?), *grim, sarcastic*, υ 302†.

σαρκός, τῆς, sing. only τ 450; pl. σάρκες, εσσι, ας, *flesh*, Θ 380, ι 293, λ 219.

Σαρπηδών, όνος, etc., also οντος, οντι, voc. Σαρπῆδον, son of Zeus, chief of Lykians, ally of Trojans, Ψ 800, B 876, E 658, M 392, Π 464, E 633; slain by Patroklos, Π 480 sqq.; his burial, Π 667.

Σατνιόεις, εντος, forest stream in Mysia, Z 34, Ξ 445, Φ 87.

Σάτνιος, son of Enops, wounded by Aias, Ξ 443†.

σαυρωτῆρος, τοῦ, (σαῦρος), *a spike* at butt-end of spear, by which it was driven into the ground, K 153†. (See cut No. 4.)

σάφα, adv., (σάφής), *clearly, plainly*, εἶπον, ἴδμεν, ρ 106, B 192.

σάω, σαῶσαι, etc., see σαόω.

σαώτερος, see σάος.

σβέννυμι, aor. **ἔσβεσε**, σβέσαν, σβέσαι(ε), σβέσ(σ)αι, extinguere, sedare, *quench, calm*, I 678; 2 aor. ἔσβη, extinctus est, *go out*, I 471; cessavit, *cease*, γ 182.

-σε, = -δε, suffix denoting motion *toward*; κυκλό-, ὑψό-, πάντο-, ὁμό-, πό-, κεῖ-σε.

σεβάσσατο τόγε θυμῷ, aor. from σεβάζω, (σέβας), veritus hoc est in animo, *feared*, Z 167 and 417.

σέβας, τό, reverentia, *astonishment, awe*, Σ 178; μ' ἔχει, miror.

σέβεσθε, imp. prs., (σέβομαι), *are ye ashamed?* Δ 242†.

σέθεν = σοῦ, see σύ.

σεῖ(ο) or σεῦ = σοῦ, see σύ.

σειρήν, τήν, pl. άς, fem., (εἴρω, sero), *cord*, Θ 19, Ψ 115, χ 175.

Σειρήνοιιν, ῆνες, (σύριγξ, susurrus?), *Syrens*, sweetly singing enchantresses, whose allurements Odysseus found means to resist, μ 39, 42, 44, 52, 158, 167, 198, ψ 326. The cut, from an ancient gem, represents them as bird-footed, an addition of later fable; for Homer, they are beautiful maidens.

σείων (σϝειω, Ger. schwinge), οντε, ipf. σεῖον, aor. σεῖσ(ε), ασα, vibrare, *brandish*, spear, ægis, O 321; concutere (pulsare) fores, *shaking* (beat-

ing) the doors, I 583; iugum, *shake* the yoke, γ 486; pass. mid. prs. σειόμενον, (α), ipf. σείετο, (ἐ)σσείοντ(ο), aor. σείσατο, concuti, *be shaken*, Υ 59; vibrata, N 558; commovit corpus, *moved herself*, Θ 199.

Σέλαγος, ου, father of Amphios from Paisos, E 612†.

σέλας, ᾰι, τό, (σϝελ-, σείριος), *brightness, gleam* of fire, Θ 509; *fire*, P 739; *flash of lightning*, Θ 76; incendii, blaze of the burning ship, O 600; of angry look, T 17; *wondrous radiance*, T 379, Σ 214.

σελήνη, ης, ῃ, ην, fem., (σέλας), luna, *moon*, πλήθουσαν, plenam, Σ 484; symbol of splendor, δ 45.

Σεληπιάδης, αο, Euenos, *son of Selepios*, B 693†.

σέλῖνον, ου, (celery), ntr., apium, *parsley*, B 776 and ε 72.

Σελλήεις, εντος, masc., *river*, (1) in Elis near Ephyra, B 659, O 531.—(2) in Troas near Arisbe, B 839, M 97.

Σελλοί, priests of Zeus at Dodona, Π 234†.

Σεμέλη, daughter of Kadmos, mother by Zeus of Dionysos, Ξ 323 and 325.

σέο = σεῦ = σοῦ, see σύ.

ΣΕΡ (σϝερ, serere, hence σειρά, ὅρμος), pass. perf. **ἐερμένον** (αι) σ 295, plupf. ἔερτο ο 460, *was strung with* (beads of amber and gold); E 89, *firmly compacted*.

σεῦα, aor. from σεύω.

σεύω, aor. **ἔσσευα**, ε, σεῦα, ε(ν), αν, ῃ, ας, pass. pf. ἔσσυμαι, part. ἐσσύμενος, οι, etc. = citus, *quick*, with gen., cupidus, *desirous;* mid. prs. σεύονται, ipf. ἐσσεύετο, οντο, aor. σεύατ(ο), ἐσσεύαντο, σεύωνται, αιτο, ασθαι, άμενος, 2 aor. sync. ἐσσύμην, υο, υτ(ο), *set in violent motion, chase, drive,* Z 132; drive away, ζ 89, ξ 35; *hurl, throw,* Λ 147, Ξ 413; *set on,* Λ 293; E 208, *I have* really by my shot *caused* the red blood *to flow* from both; mid. freq. = act., yet also = pass., festinare, *hasten,* τ 448, Z 518; appetere, *strive for,* δ 416, N 630; *start up* (Il.), O 271; *chase,* Γ 26, Λ 415; evolare, *fly away,* Ξ 519.

σήκασθεν, 3 pl. aor. pass. from σηκάζω, (σηκός), inclusi fuissent, *pen up,* Θ 131†.

σηκο-κόρον, masc., (σηκός, κορέω), *cleaner of cattle-pens* or *sheep-folds,* ρ 224†.

σηκῷ, οί, ῶν, ούς, masc., (sepes), *pen, fold,* ι 219, 319, Σ 589.

σῆμα, ἄτι, ατ(α), also σήμᾶθ' before ἄ, ntr., *sign, mark* (by which any thing is identified), ψ 188; of recognition for us two, Ψ 326, τ 250; *mark on a lot,* H 189; on a horse, *spot, star,* Ψ 455; *a sign from heaven,* thunder, lightning, φ 413, N 244; prodigium, X 30; *funeral mound,* B 814, H 86; *mark to show the length of a throw,* θ 195; baleful *characters,* not alphabetic writing, but pictorial, Z 168.

σημαίνει, ουσιν, (ε), έτω, ειν, ων, ipf. σήμαινε, fut. σημᾰνέω, aor. σήμηνε, (σῆμα), *point out,* τέρματα, Ψ 358; *bear sway, command,* A 289; ducere, τινί, K 58, P 250; τινός, Ξ 85; ἐπί τινι, over some one, χ 427; mid. aor. ἐσημήναντο κλῆρον, suam sortem insignire, *mark,* H 175.

σημάντορος, ι, ες, ας, nom. ὁ σημάντωρ, (σημαίνω). *commander, leader,* Δ 431; *driver,* Θ 127; βοῶν, pastor.

σήμερον (τῇ ἡμέρᾳ, ho-die), hodie, *to-day,* Λ 431.

σήπεται, pf. σέσηπε, aor. pass. subj. 3 sing. σᾰπήῃ, putrescere, *rot,* B 135, T 27. (Il.)

Σήσᾰμος, town in Paphlagonia, B 853†.

Σηστός, Thrakian city on the Hellespont, opposite Abydos, B 836†.

σθεναρή (σθένος), valida, *strong,* I 505†.

Σθενέ-λᾱος, son of Ithaimenes, slain by Patroklos, Π 586†.

Σθένελος, (1) son of Kapaneus, Nestor's attendant, Θ 114; combatant before Thebes and Ilios, E 111, 108, 241, 835, B 564, Δ 367, Θ 114, I 48, Ψ 511.—(2) son of Perseus and of Andromeda, father of Eurystheus, T 116, 123.

σθένος, εος, εϊ, ει, (στα-), robur, vis, *strength,* fluminis, Oceani; *valor,* P 212, 499; in periphrasis, Ἰδομενῆος, Ὠρίωνος, Ἠετίωνος = the mighty Idomeneus, etc.; Σ 274, in concione = consultando vim assequemur, seek strength in the council, i. e. in counsel.

σῐάλοιο, ον, οισιν, ους, etc., with and without συός, *fat hog,* I 208, β 300.

σῑγᾰλόεντι, τα, nitido, a, *shining, glittering,* of garments, X 154; reins, E 226; rugs, ζ 38; ὑπερώϊα, π 449.

σίγᾱ (σϝιγ-, Ger. schweige), *hush!* imp., Ξ 90, τ 42.

σῑγῇ, dat. from ἡ σιγή, silentio, *silently,* Γ 134, H 195, ο 391.

σῐδήρεος, ῳ, ον, α, η, and **σῐδήρειος,** ον, η, ῃ, αι, (σίδηρος), ferreus, literally ὀρυμαγδός, "iron din of war," crash *of iron weapons;* fig. *hard* or *firm as iron,* inflexus, X 357; intrepidus, Ω 205; indefessus, μ 280.

σίδηρος, ου, ῳ, ον, masc., ferrum, *iron; αἴθωνι,* reddish, others glittering; πολιόν, ἰόεντα, violet blue = dark or steel blue; symbol of firmness, inexorableness, τ 494; πολύκμητος, *well-wrought, wrought with much labor,* of iron tools or weapons.

Σῑδών, ῶνος, Phoenician city, ο 425; *inhabitants of Sidon,* Σῑδόνες, Ψ 743; πολυδαίδαλοι, sollertes, skillful, and Σιδόνιοι, δ 84, 618, ο 118, Z 290; their country, Σιδονίην, ν 285; Σιδονίηθεν, Z 291†, *from Sidonia.*

σίζ(ε), ipf. from σίζω, *hissed,* ι 394.

Σῐκᾰνίη, *Sikania,* earlier form for *Sikelia,* (Sicily), ω 307; inhabitants, **Σῐκελοί,** ή, υ 383, ω 366, 389, 211.

Σῐκῠών, ῶνος, comm., *Sikyon,* a city on south shore of gulf of Corinth, subject to Agamemnon, B 572, Ψ 299.

Σῑμόεις, (1) small river rising in Mount Ida, and flowing across the Trojan plain into the Skamandros, E 774, 777, M 22, Δ 475, Z 4, Y 52.

(See plate V., at end of volume.)—(2) personified, *Simoeis*, the god of the river just described, Φ 307.

Σῑμοείσιος, son of Trojan Anthemion, slain by Aias, Δ 474, 477, 488.

σίνεται, *ηαι, οιτο,* ipf. iter. *σινέσκοντο,* rapere, *seize, despoil, τί τινι,* ζ 6 (nocet, *harms*, in ungenuine verse, Ω 45).

σίντης, *ην, αι,* (*σίνεται*), rapax, *ravenous*, Λ 481, Υ 165. (Il.)

Σίντιες (lit. "plunderers"), inhabitants of Lemnos, *ἀγριοφώνους*; θ 294, Α 594.

Σίπυλος, branch of the Tmolos mountain range, near Magnesia, on the borders of Lydia, Ω 615†.

Σίσυφος (*σοφός*), son of Aiolos, father of Glaukos, founder of Ephyra (ancient name for Acropolis of Corinth), Ζ 153 sq.; *κρατέρ' ἄλγεα πάσχων*, in the lower world, λ 593.

σιτέσκοντο, ipf. iter. from *σιτέω*, (*σῖτος*), cenabant, *used to eat*, ω 209†.

σῖτος, *οιο, ου, ῳ, ον,* masc., frumentum, *grain*, esp. *wheat; wheaten bread*, ι 9, α 139; cibus, *food*, Ω 602, Τ 306.

σῖτο-φάγῳ, *eating grain* or *bread*, ι 191†.

σιφλώσειεν, opt., (*σιφλόω*), male pessumdet, *deform, ruin*, Ξ 142†.

σῑωπᾶν, inf. pres., aor. opt. 3 pl. *ἠσειαν*, inf. *ἦσαι*, silere, *keep silence*, ρ 513 and Ψ 568.

σῑωπῇ, dat. fem., tacite, *silently*, Ι 190, ν 309; clam, *secretly*, Ξ 310; *ἀκὴν ἐγένοντο σ.*, *were* (became) hushed in silence.

σκάζων, *οντε*, and mid. *σκάζεσθαι*, claudicare, *limp*, Τ 47, Λ 811. (Il.)

Σκαιαὶ (*πύλαι*), the only one of the gates of Troy mentioned by name by Homer; it appears to have faced the Greek camp, and to have afforded a view over the Trojan plain, Γ 145, 149, 263, Ζ 237, 307, 393, Ι 354, Λ 170, Π 712, Σ 453, Χ 6, 360.

σκαιόν, *ή, ῶν,* scaevus, sinistra, *left* (hand), Α 501; *western*, γ 295.

σκαίρουσι, *οντες*, saliunt, *skip*, κ 412; tripudiantes, *beat the ground with feet in dance*, Σ 572.

(*σκαλμοί*, that *part of the gunwale* just under the thole-pin on which the oar rests as it plays. See cut No. 35, *e.*)

Σκᾰμάνδριος, (1) *πεδίον*, plain *of the Skamandros*, also *λειμών*, Β 465, 467.—(2) real name of Astyanax, Ζ 402.—(3) son of Strophios, a Trojan, slain by Menelaos, Ε 49.

Σκάμανδρος, the *Scamander* (called by gods *Ξάνθος* [yellow], now the Mendere Su, = "Scamander water"), river rising on Mount Ida, Μ 21.

Σκάνδεια, harbor of Kythera, Κ 268†.

Σκάρφη, locality in Lokris, near Thermopylai, Β 532†.

σκᾰφίδες, fem., *bowls*, ι 223†.

σκεδάννυμι, aor. (**ἐ**)**σκέδασ(εν)**, imp. *σκέδασον*, (scindo), *scatter, disperse*, Υ 341; *shed*, Η 330.

σκέδᾰσιν, *τήν*, (*σκεδάννυμι*), dispersio, *scattering; θεῖναι*, scatter, α 116 and υ 225.

σκέλλω, aor. opt. **σκήλειε**, exsiccaret, *parch*, Ψ 191†.

σκέλος, *τό, πρυμνὸν σκέλος*, upper part of *thigh*, Π 314†.

σκέπαρνον, ntr., *adze*, ε 237 and ι 391.

σκέπας, ntr., (*σκέπω*), *cover, shelter*, against the wind, *ἀνέμοιο*, ζ 210. (Od.)

σκεπάω, **σκεπόωσι,** *ward off, κῦμα* (*ἀνέμων*, raised by the winds), ν 99†.

σκέπτεο, imp. pres., ipf. *σκέπτετ(ο)*, aor. *σκεψάμενος*, (specio, Ger. spähe, Eng. spy), *look about* (after), *μετά τινα; αἴ κεν*, to see whether, with subj., Ρ 652; cavebat, Π 361.

σκηπᾰνίῳ, ntr., (*σκῆπτρον*), *staff, sceptre*, Ν 59 and Ω 247.

σκηπτ-οῦχος, *οι, ων,* (*σκῆπτρον*), *bearing a staff* or *sceptre, sceptred*, δ 64.

σκῆπτρον, *ου, ῳ, ον, α,* (scapus, Ger. Schaft, Eng. shaft), *staff*, of wanderer and beggar; *sceptre* of kings, priests, heralds, judges. (Cf. cut on next page representing Agamemnon.) He who rose to address the assembly received the sceptre on rising from the herald; symbol of royal power and dignity, Β 46; see also β 37, λ 91.

σκηπτόμενος, *ον*, innixus, *τινί*, *leaning on one's staff;* ironically, Ξ 457 = hasta transfixum.

σκηρίπτεσθ(αι), *όμενος*, inniti, *lean upon*, ρ 196; contra nitens, *push against*, λ 595.

σκιάσῃ, subj. aor., (σκιά), o b u m b r e t, *overshadow*, Φ 232†.

σκιάω, ipf. **σκιόωντο,** o b u m b r a b a n t u r, *were darkened*, β 388; Α 157, *σκιόωντα*, according to Aristarchos, *shadow-casting*, v. l. *σκιοέντα*.

σκίδνᾰται, ασθ(ε), ασθαι, ipf. σκίδναθ' = σκίδνατο, pl. ἐσκίδναντ(ο), *disperse*, ἐπί, κατά, πρός τι; with inf., Ω 2; ὑψόσε, *dash on high; diffuse its waters*, η 130.

σκῐερῷ, όν, (σκιά), o p a c u s, *shady*, Λ 480 and υ 278.

σκῐῇ, αί, u m b r a, *shadow*, λ 207; of the departed, *shade, ghost*, κ 495.

σκιόεντ-, o p a c a, *affording shade, shadowy*, Ε 525, α 365. The danger of protracted exposure to the intense rays of a southern sun gives such words as shade and shadowy much more meaning to an inhabitant of Greece or Ionia than they have to us. *σκιόωντα*, see *σκιάω*.

σκιρτάω, opt. **σκιρτῷεν,** (σκαίρω), *bound along*, Υ 226 and 228.

σκολιάς, 3, *crooked* = *perverted, unjust*, (opp. *ἰθύντατα*), Π 387†.

σκόλοπες, εσσι(ν), ας, masc., *stake for impaling*, Σ 177; *palisades*, Ο 344.

σκοπέλου, ῳ, ον, οι, οισιν, masc., s c o p u l u s, *cliff*, Β 396, μ 73.

σκοπῐαζέμεν, ων, ipf. ἐσκοπίαζον, (σκοπιή), s p e c u l a r i, *watch*, Κ 40, *search out*.

σκοπιῆς, ῇ, ήν, αί, άς, (σκοπός), s p e c u l a, *look-out place*, on a rock or mountain, Χ 145; ἔχειν, s p e c u l a r i, θ 302.

σκοπός, οῦ, όν, οί, masc., (*σκέπτομαι*), s p e c u l a t o r, *watcher, look-out*; χ 156, their (the suitors') look-out was better, = they kept a sharper watch; *overseer, person in charge*, Ψ 359, χ 396; *mark, target*, χ 6; ἀπὸ σκοποῦ, away from the mark, contrary to our idea.

σκότιον, c l a n d e s t i n u m, *in secret*, Ζ 24†.

σκοτο-μήνιος, fem., (σκότος, μήν), i l l u m i s, *darkness from absence of the moon, darkness*, ξ 457†.

σκότος, ον, masc., (σκύτος?), t e n e b r a e, *darkness, gloom*, τ 389; esp. (Il.) *the darkness of death*, μίν (ὄσσε, as to the eyes), κάλυψε, Δ 461; εἷλε, Ε 47.

σκυδμαινέμεν (σκύζομαι), *be wroth*, τινί, Ω 592†.

σκύζευ, imp., εσθαι, ομένῳ, η, ης, (σκυδρός), *be angry, wroth*, τινί, ψ 209.

σκῠλᾰκος, εσσι, ας, fem., *whelp, puppy*, ι 289. (Od.)

Σκύλλα, and η, ήν, daughter of Κραταιΐς, *Scylla*, a monster dwelling in a cave opposite Charybdis, μ 85, 235, 108, 125, 223, ψ 328.

σκύμνους, masc., (lion's) *whelps*, Σ 319†.

Σκῦρος, island northwest of Chios, λ 509, Τ 326. **Σκυρόθεν,** Τ 332, *from S.*, town of same name on the island, Ι 668.

σκῦτος, ntr., (c u t i s), c o r i u m, *hide*, ξ 34†.

σκῡτο-τόμος, *leather-worker*, Η 221†.

σκῦφον, masc., (drinking) *cup*, ξ 112†.

σκώληξ, masc., *earth-worm*, Ν 654†.

σκῶλος, masc., p a l u s, *pointed stake*, Ν 564†.

Σκῶλος, locality in Boiotia, Β 497†.

σκῶπες, masc., *horned owl*, ε 66†.

σμᾰρᾰγεῖ, aor. subj. ήσῃ, *roar, thunder*, Β 210, Φ 199; *re-echo*, Β 463.

σμερδαλέος, ῳ, ον, ω, ων, η, ην, έ(α), *fearful, terrible* (to look upon), λ 609, μ 91; ntr. as adv., έον (έα only before Ϝ and κτυπέων), of a cry or sound, χ 81; of look, Χ 95.

σμερδνή, *terrible*, Ε 742; όν as adv. with βοᾶν.

σμήχω, ipf. **ἔσμηχε,** d e t e r s i t, *wipe off, cleanse*, ζ 226†.

σμικρῇσι, p a r v i s, *small*, Ρ 757†.

Σμινθεῦ, voc., epith. of Apollo, Α 39, explained by ancient commentators as meaning the destroyer of field-mice (σμίνθοι). (The following cut, repre-

senting a mouse at work, is reproduced from the tetradrachm of Metapontion.)

σμύχοιτο, see κατὰ σμῦξαι.

σμῶδιξ, διγγες, fem., vibex, *wale*, B 267 and Ψ 716.

σόῃ, see σαόω.

σοῖο, see σός.

σόλον, τόν, rudely formed *mass of iron*, Ψ 826, 839, 844, the adj. αὐτοχόωνον (self-fused) suggests that a meteoric stone may have been meant.

Σόλῦμοι, a Lykian tribe, Z 184, 204, ε 283.

σόος, ον, οι, οις, η, salvus, integer, *safe, sound* (acc. σῶν, P 367), A 117, O 497, Ω 382; χ 28, nom. σῶς, certus, *certain*.

σορός, masc., *funeral urn*, Ψ 91†.

σός, ή, όν, etc., (σύ), tuus; joined with πόθος, ποθῇ, desiderium = tui, *for thee*; ntr. used substantively = cum patrimonio versans, *with thy possessions*, β 369.

Σούνιον, ntr., southernmost promontory of Attika, γ 278†.

σοφίης, τῆς, (σοφός, sapiens), *skill, accomplishment*, O 412†.

σόῳς, ῳ, see σαόω.

Σπάρτη, fem., capital of Lakonike, residence of Menelaos and Helena, visited by Telemachos; εὐρείῃ, λ 460; καλλιγύναικα, ν 412; B 582, Δ 52, α 93, β 214, 359. Σπάρτηθεν, *from Sparta*, β 327, δ 10. Σπάρτηνδε, *to Sparta*, α 285.

σπάρτα, τά, (σπεῖρα), *ropes*, B 135†.

σπάω, aor. **ἔσπᾰσεν,** σπάσεν, mid. aor. (ἐ)σπάσατ(ο), σπασάμην, imp. σπάσασθε, σσάμενος, pass. aor. part. σπασθέντος, *draw forth*, Λ 458; with ἐκ, E 859; mid. suum aliquid extrahere, one's hand, one's sword, etc.; κ 166, *I pulled up for myself.*

σπεῖο, imp. aor. from ἕπομαι.

σπεῖος = σπέος, specus, *cave*.

σπεῖρον, ου, α, ων, ntr., (σπείρω), *cover, garment, shroud*, β 102; *sail*, ε 318, ζ 269.

σπεῖσαι, σασκε, see σπένδω.

Σπειώ, a Nereid, Σ 40†.

σπένδησθα, subj. pres. 2 sing., ῃ, ων, οντ(α), ες, ας, ipf. iter. σπένδεσκε, ον, aor. 3 pl. σπεῖσαν, subj. σῃς, σομεν, inf. σαι, pass. σας, σαντες, aor. iter. σπείσασκε, *make a libation*, i. e. to pour out unmixed wine upon the ground, or on the altar (μ 363), in honor of the divinity, before drinking, οἶνον, τινί; yet also ὕδατι, with water, μ 363, in case of need; δέπαι, from the goblet.

σπέος, σπείους ε 68, σπῆϊ Σ 402, σπέος, σπεῖος ε 194, σπέσσι α 15, σπήεσσι, *cave, cavern, grotto*.

σπέρμα, ntr., (σπείρω), *seed, germ*; πυρός, *spark*, ε 490†.

Σπερχειός, river in Thessaly; as river-god the father of Menestheus, Π 174, 176, Ψ 144.

σπέρχωσιν, subj. pres., mid. opt. pres. σπερχοίατ(ο), and όμενος, οιο, ους, η, *move rapidly, hasten*; ἐρετμοῖς, row rapidly, ν 22; part. = adv. *hastily, rapidly*.

σπέσθαι, inf. aor. from ἕπομαι.

σπεύδουσιν, imp. ετον, ειν = ἐμεν, ων, όντεσσι, ουσ(α), etc., aor. 3 sing. σπεῦσε, subj. σομεν, imp. σατε, mid. fut. σπεύσομαι, *hasten*, Σ 373, εἴς τι, τινα, with part., = *quickly*, ι 250; περί τινος, *struggle for*, P 121; *hurry forward*, τί, γάμον, τ 137.

σπῆι, σπήεσσι, see σπέος.

σπῐδέος, *broad*, Λ 754†. (v. l. ἀσπιδέος.)

σπῖλάδες, εσσι(ν), fem., scopuli, *reefs*, ε 401, 405. (Od.)

σπινθῆρες, masc., scintillae, *sparks*, Δ 77†.

σπλάγχν(α), ων, ntr., viscera, *inward parts, entrails*, esp. *heart, liver, and lungs*; these were roasted and eaten while the other parts of the victim were burning on the altar, and served as relish to the sacrificial banquet which followed; the practice described A 464, γ 9.

σπόγγῳ, οισι, masc., (σϝόμ-γος, fungus, sponge), *sponge*, as means of cleansing the hands, Σ 414; tables and seats, α 111.

σποδιῇ, τῇ, *ash-heap*, ε 488†.

σποδοῦ, fem., *ashes*, ι 375†.

σπονδαί, αἱ, (σπένδω), libationes, *drink-offering*, *libation*, a portion of pure wine poured out before drinking in honor of the gods; *treaty* ratified by libations of unmixed wine, B 341, and Δ 159.

σπουδῆς, ῇ, fem., (studium?), *labor*, *effort*, φ 409; ἀπὸ σπ., ex animi sententia, *in earnest; σπουδῇ*, *eagerly*, *quickly*, ν 279, ο 209; *with difficulty*, *scarcely*, γ 297.

στᾰδίῃ, ἐν, (ὑσμίνῃ), *in close combat*, N 314, H 241.

στάζω, aor. **στάξ(ε)**, imp. στάξον, instillare, *drop*, *let fall*, T 39, 348.

στάθμη, ην, fem., (στῆσαι), *chalk line; ἐπὶ — ἰθύνειν*, straighten or make true to the line, ε 245; phrase used of hewing timber, setting up things in a row, digging a ditch, τάφρον, φ 121.

σταθμοῖο, ῷ, όν, οῖιν, οἱ, ῶν, οῖσι(ν), ούς, (σταθῆναι), (1) stabulum, *stall*, shelter for men and beasts, used in general for *shepherd's quarters*, T 377, ρ 20; *sheep-pen*, B 470; σταθμόνδε, *to the stall*, *homeward*.—(2) postis, *post*, Ξ 167, α 333, η 89.—(3) *weight in balance*, M 434.

στάμεν(αι), inf. aor. = στῆναι, see ἵστημι.

στᾰμίνεσσιν, ταῖς, *braces* serving to enable the ribs to resist the inward pressure of the water (see cut No. 15, *b*), ε 252†. (Yet see also plate IV., where σταμῖνες are taken as synonymous with ribs.)

στάν, 3 pl. 2 aor. from ἵστημι.

στάξ', aor. from στάζω.

στάς, part. 2 aor. from ἵστημι.

στᾰτός (ἵστημι), ἵππος, *stalled* horse, Z 506, O 263.

σταυρούς, οῖσιν, (ἱστάναι), *stake*, *pale*, Ω 453 and ξ 11.

σταφῦλή, ῇ, αἱ, ῇσι, fem., (ἀ-σταφίς), uva, *bunch of grapes*, η 121.

σταφύλῃ, τῇ, *plummet; ἐΐσαι*, matched to a hair in height, B 765†.

στᾰχύεσσιν, nom. ὁ στάχυς, aristis, *ears of grain*, Ψ 598†.

στέαρ, **στέατος** [dissyll.], ntr., (στῆναι), *hardened fat*, *tallow*, φ 178 and 183.

στείβοντες, ipf. στεῖβον, (στεμφ-, Ger. stampfen, -tapfen), *tread*, *wash* clothes *by stamping* on them, ζ 92; *trample upon*, Λ 534.

στεῖλα(ν), aor. from στέλλω.

στειλειῆς, τῆς, (στέλλω), *hole in axe*, for helve, φ 422†.

στειλειόν, ntr., (στέλλω, Ger. Stiel), *axe-helve*, ε 236†.

στεῖνος, εϊ, ει, ntr., (στεινός), angustiae, *confined space*, M 66; ὁδοῦ κοίλης, *narrow entrance*, Ψ 419.

στείνοιτο, όμενος, ipf. στείνοντο, (στεῖνος), *be crowded*, Ξ 34; ι 219, *be packed full*, with gen.; *dammed*, *weighed down*, Φ 220, ι 445; *be too narrow*, σ 386.

στεινωπός, ῷ, όν, adj., (στεῖνος), *narrow; ὁδός*, fauces, *narrow pass*, H 143; (πόντου) fretum, *strait*, μ 234.

στείομεν, subj. 2 aor. = στέωμεν, see ἵστημι.

στεῖραν, adj. fem., (στερεός), sterilem, *unfruitful*, *barren*, κ 522. (Od.)

στείρῃ, fem., (στῆναι), *fore part of keel*, *stem*, *cut-water*, A 482, β 428. (See cut No. 34, *e*.)

στείχῃσι, ειν, ων, οντα, ες, ipf. ἔστειχε, στεῖχεν, aor. ἔστιχον, (στίχος, στίχες), *go forward*, *advance*, ι 444, with θύραζε, also with acc. with ποτί, ἐς, ἀνά, *go*, *march*, B 833; also standing alone, I 86; of the sun, *climb*, λ 17.

στέλλω, **στέλλοιμι**, οντα, ας, prs., fut. στελέω, aor. στεῖλα, αν, (Ger. stellen), *put in order*, *arrange*, Δ 294; *make ready*, β 287; *send; ἱστία*, *take in* sail; mid. στέλλεσθε, *make yourselves ready*, Ψ 285; ἱστία, *take in their* sails, letting them down from the yards and getting them into the hold, A 433.

στέμμα, ματ(α), ntr., (στέφω), infula vittae, *chaplet* or *fillet of priest*, which Chryses (A 14) takes off, because he comes as suppliant; the cut on the next page shows the band in two positions—as extended at full length, and as wrapped around the head: in the second representation the ends should hang down by the sides of the head below the ears, A 28.

στενάχεσχ' = στενάχεσκε, see στενάχω.

στενᾰχίζω, ων, mid. ipf. στεναχίζετο, *wail*, *sigh*, ι 13, T 304; *groan*, B 95.

στενᾰχω, ουσι, ων, etc., ipf. iter.

στενάχεσκε Τ 132, mid. ipf. στενάχοντο, (στένω), *wail*, Π 489; *groan*, Φ 417; *puff, pant*, Π 393; *roar*, Π 391; τινά, τί, *bewail*, ι 467, Τ 301; with βαρέα, Θ 334; πυκνὰ μάλα, Σ 318; ἀδινά, Ω 123; μεγάλα, δ 516; mid. = act.

Στέντωρ, ορος, a Greek whose voice was as loud as the united cry of fifty men, Ε 785†.

στένω, **στένει** Υ 169, ipf. ἔστενε(ν), *groan, sigh*; κῆρ, in heart, Κ 16; *rage, heave*, Ψ 230.

στερεοῖς, ῇ, ῇσι, comp. -εωτέρη, (Ger. starr), *hard*, λίθος, ἐπέεσσι, κραδίη; *stiff*, βοέη; adv. **στερεῶς**, *firmly*, Κ 263, ξ 346; *obstinately* refuse, Ψ 42.

στερέω, aor. inf. **στερέσαι**, *deprive*, τινός, ν 262†.

στέρνον, οιο, ων, οισι(ν), ntr., (στόρνυμι, Ger. Stirn), *breast*, Β 479, Λ 842, Ψ 365, 508.

στεροπή, ῆς, ήν, fem., (ἀστράπτω), *thunderbolt, lightning*, Λ 66, 184; *gleam, radiance*, Τ 363, δ 72.

στεροπ-ηγερέτα (ἐγείρω) Ζεύς, *he who wakes the lightning, thunderer*, Π 298†. (Equally admissible is the derivation from ἀγείρω, *he who gathers the lightning*.)

στεῦται, ipf. στεῦτο, (στῆναι), denotes the expression of a wish by a movement or gesture, and is always followed by inf. (always fut. exc. ρ 525), *have the appearance, make as if*, with part., λ 584, *stand as if* thirsty; *pretend*, ρ 525, to have heard; also *engage, threaten, promise*.

στεφάνη, ης, ην, ας, fem., (στέφανος), that which surrounds or encompasses, (1) *head-band* or *fillet*, as woman's ornament, Σ 597. (See cuts Nos. 17, 43, 44.)—(2) *brim of helmet* projecting over the forehead, *visor*, Λ 96; *the helmet itself*, Κ 30, Η 12. (See cuts Nos. 12, 85, 87, 88, 93, 122.)—(3) *edge of a cliff*, Ν 138.

στέφανος, masc., (στέφω), *crown, ring*, Ν 736†.

στεφανόω, pass. pf. ἐστεφάνωται, plupf. -το, (στέφανος), *place all around*; πόντος, *encompasses*; Γοργώ, the Gorgon's head was placed upon it around =at the centre; νέφος, cingebat; τά τ' οὐρανός, by which the heaven is encircled; Ε 739, fig. around which panic fear was spreading itself on every side.

στέφει (στεμφ-, stipare, Ger. stopfen), *grants in abundance* grace, μορφήν, θ 170; ἀμφὶ στέφε, Σ 205, circumdedit.

στέωμεν, στῇ, στήῃ, aor. subj. from ἵσταμαι.

στῆθος, εος, εϊ, εα, εων, εσσι(ν), for gen. also **εσφι**, ntr., (στῆναι), *breast*, sing. and pl. for both sexes, of men and beasts, Β 218, Σ 51; since κῆρ, Ξ 140, κραδίη, Κ 95, ἦτορ, Α 189, are situated in the breast, it is made also the seat of θυμός, Ι 256, and in general of feelings, passions, and of reason, Α 83, Δ 208, Ε 125, Ν 732, Ξ 316, Υ 20; so also of voice, Δ 430; of breath, Ι 610.

στήλη, ην, ας, fem., (στέλλω), columna, *pillar*, Ν 437; esp. *gravestone*, Π 457 (cf. cut), Μ 259.

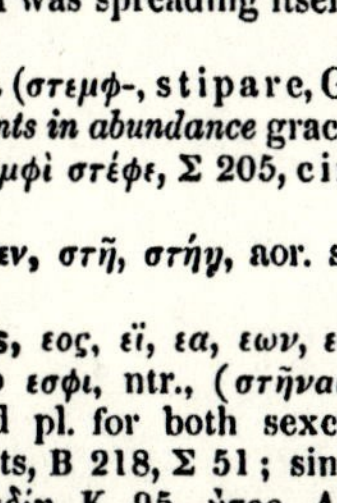

στήμεναι, inf. aor. from ἵσταμαι.

στηρίζω, aor. (ἐ)**στήριξε**, ξαι, mid. ασθαι, plupf. ἐστήρικτο, (στερεός, Ger. starr), *fix firmly*, Λ 28; *support one's self, stand upon*, μ 434, Φ 242, ποσίν, πόδεσσιν; κακὸν κακῷ, *was piled upon*, Π 111; οὐρανῷ κάρη, *rests* her head *in* the heaven, Δ 443.

στῐβᾰρόν, ῷ, οί, οῖς, ῇς, ῇσι(ν), comp. -ώτερον, adv. -ῶς, (στείβω), *close-pressed*, *trodden firm, firm, compact, strong*, of bodily members and weapons, E 400, 746, M 454.

στίβη, fem., (στείβω), *rime, hoar-frost*, ε 467 and ρ 25.

στίλβων, οντας, part., (allied to στεροπή), *glittering, gleaming*, τινί, with oil, Σ 596, also with beauty, grace.

στιλπναί (στίλβω), *sparkling* (dew-drops), Ξ 351†.

στἴχός, ες, ας, fem., (στιχ-, στοῖχος), *row, rank*, or *file* of warriors; ἐπὶ στίχας, proleptically, to the ranks (so that they formed ranks), B 687, Γ 113; κατὰ στ., by ranks, Γ 326.

στἴχάομαι, ipf. **ἐστιχόωντο,** (στίχες), *advance in rows*, in battle array, agmine incedere or vehi, B 92, 516, Γ 266.

Στἴχίος, Athenian leader, slain by Hektor, N 195, O 329, 331.

στόμ(α), ατος, ατι, ατ(α), ων, *mouth, throat*, of man and beast, B 489; διὰ στ. ἄγοντο = utter; ἀνὰ στ. ἔχων, have in one's mouth; ἐπὶ στ., praeceps; mouth of rivers, harbors, ε 441; στόμα ἠιόνος, *inlet* of the shore; O 389, at the point.

στομἄχοιο, ον, ους, masc., (στόμα), *gullet, throat*, Γ 292. (Il.)

στοναχέω, aor. inf. **στονἄχῆσαι,** *wail*, Σ 124†.

στονἄχή, ῆς, ῇ, ῆσι, άς, *sighs, groans*, B 356, ε 83.

στοναχίζω, see στεναχίζω.

στονόεντα, ες, εσσα, αν, (στόνος), plenum suspiriorum, *mournful*, ι 12; ἀοιδή, of *funeral dirge*, Ω 721; elsewh. *causing sighs and groans, grievous*, Θ 159.

στόνος, ον, masc., (στένω), *sighing, groaning*, Φ 20, ψ 40, χ 308.

στορέννυμι, aor. **ἐστόρεσεν,** σαν, στόρεσ(ε), σαν, σον, σαι, σας, pass. plupf. ἔστρωτο, (sternere), *spread out*, bed, couch, carpet, I 621, Φ 171; *scatter*, I 213; *calm*, γ 158.

Στρἄτίη, town in Arkadia, B 606†.

Στρατίος, son of Nestor, γ 413 and 439.

στρἄτός, όφιν, οῦ, ῷ, όν, οί, masc., (στρώννυμι).—(1) In Iliad *the encamped army* of the Greeks, consisting of 1186 ships; streets throughout this camp, K 66; the tents or huts stood parallel with the ships, and opposite the intervals between them, O 653 sq. At first the camp was surrounded by no wall, Achilleus's presence rendering such defense needless; but after his withdrawal, by advice of Nestor, H 436–441, a massive wall with towers and gates, M 118–123, was built. (Il.)—(2) *the host, the army* of the Greeks or Trojans, β 30.

στρατόομαι, ipf. **ἐστρἄτόωντο,** (στρατός), *be encamped*, Γ 187, Δ 378, πρὸς τείχεα, *assault*.

στρεπτοῖο, οί, οῖσι, ή, αί, (στρέφω), (1) *twisted and braided; χιτών, ringed* coat of mail (cf. cut No. 36), E 113.—(2) exorabilis, *that may be turned, placable*, φρένες, θεοί; γλῶσσα, *voluble*, Υ 248.

στρεύγεσθαι (στράγγω, Eng. struggle), *grow weary, exhausted*, O 512, μ 351.

στρεφε-δίνηθεν, aor. pass. 3 pl., (στρέφω, δινέω), vertigine rotati sunt, lit. his eyes *whirled round and round* = every thing was in a whirl before his eyes, Π 792†.

στρέφω, **στρέφει,** ipf. ἔστρεφον, ε, aor. στρέψ(ε), αν, αι, ας, αντα, ες, aor. iter. στρέψασκον, (τρέπω?), *turn*, also with chariot (ἵππους), in combat and in race, Ψ 323; or with plough, Σ 544, 546; ὄιν εἰς ἔρεβος, *turn* the sheep toward the land of shadow.—Pass. pres. στρέφεται, όμεσθα, subj. εται M 42, ipf. ἐστρέφετ(ο), fut. στρέψεσθ(αι), aor. στρεφθείς, έντος, τι, τε, εῖσ(α), *turn one's self, turn*; ἔνθα καὶ ἔνθα, huc illuc; νωλεμέως, twisting myself tightly into, i. e. twisting his wool tightly around me, ι 435.

στρέψασκον, see στρέφω.

στρόμβον, τόν, (στρέφω), *top*, Ξ 413†.

στρουθοῖο, masc., *sparrow*, B 311. (Il.)

στροφάλιγγι, τῇ, (στρέφω), vortici, *eddy, whirl*, Π 775†.

στροφἄλίζετε, imp., (στροφάλιγξ), *twirl, ply*, σ 315†.

Στρόφιος, father of Skamandros, E 49†.

στρόφος, ὁ, (στρέφω), *cord, rope*, ἀορτήρ, as support, ν 438. (Od.)

στρώννυμι, see στορέννυμι.

στρωφάω, **στρωφῶσιν,** ῶσ(α) (στρέφω), *turn constantly* (thread, yarn), ἠλάκατα; mid. ᾶσθ(αι), ipf. στρωφᾶτ(ο), *tarry, dwell*, I 463; N 557, *engage in combat against.*

στῠγερός, οῖο, οῦ, ῷ, όν, οί, ή, ῆς, ῇ, ήν, άς, adv. -ῶς, (ἔστυγον), *hated, hateful*, Ψ 79; λ 201, *wretched.*

στῠγέει, έουσι, έῃ, and έησιν, aor. ἔστῠγον, and 1 aor. opt. στύξαιμι: this last form, *make hateful*; the other forms, *hate, shudder at, be disgusted with*, Θ 370, ν 400.

Στύμφηλος, fem., town in Arkadia, B 608†.

Στύξ, Στῠγός, *Styx*, lit. "Hateful," river in the lower world, by which the gods swore their most sacred oaths; its branches, Titaresios and Kokytos, B 755, κ 514, Θ 369, Ξ 271, O 37.

Στύρα, τά, town in Euboia, B 539†.

στῠφελίζετε, ειν, aor. (ἐ)στυφέλιξε(ν), ῃ, αι, part. pres. -ομένους, (στύφω), *smite*, E 437, H 261; *scatter*, Λ 305; *thrust out* of, ἐκ(τός), A 581; *maltreat*, σ 416, π 108.

σῠ́ (for τύ, τϝέ), also τύνη, gen. τεοῖο Θ 37, σεῖ(ο), σέο encl., σεῦ Z 454, σέθεν, dat. τοι encl., τοί γε, σοί, τεΐν Λ 201, δ 619, acc. σέ, encl. and orthotone, (du. σφω(ι), and pl. ὑμεῖς, q. v.), pers. pron. of second person, tu, *thou*, often strengthened by γέ or πέρ; also orthotoned when joined with cases of αὐτός.

σῠ-βόσῖα, ntr., also written -βόσεια, (βόσις), συῶν, *herds of swine*, Λ 679, ξ 101.

σῠ-βώτης, εω, ῃ, ην, βῶτα, masc., (βόσκω), *swine-herd*, δ 640; δῖος, excellent, illustrious. (Od.)

σῠ́-γε, tu quidem.

συγ-κᾰλέσσας, aor. part., convocans, *summoning*, B 55 and K 302.

συγ-καλύπτω, see σὺν κάλυψε.

συγ-κλονέω, ipf. **συν-εκλόνεον,** perturbabant, *confound*, N 722†.

συγ-κύρσειαν, aor. opt. from κυρέω, concurrerent, *strike together*, Ψ 435†.

συγ-χέω, imp. **χει,** ipf. -χει, aor. ἔχευε, αν, inf. χεῦαι (for χεϝ-αι), part. χέας, mid. 3 sing. aor. sync. -χῠτο, confundere, *confound, confuse*, θυμόν, νόον; π 471, σύγχῠτο, *were entangled*; ὅρκια, foedus laedere, *violate*, Δ 269; κάματον, ἰούς, *make of no effect*; ἄνδρα, *break down*, θ 139.

σῡκέη (**συκῆ,** ω 246), έαι, έας, all forms pronounced with synizesis, *figtree*, η 116. (Od.)

σῦκον, σύκῳ, ntr., *fig*, η 121†.

σῡλάω (for σκυλάω, spolio), ipf. (ἐ)**σύλᾱ,** συλήτην, fut. συλήσετε, σειν, σων, aor. συλήσω, σωσι, σειε, σας, *strip off*, E 164, τεύχεα (ἀπό) τινος, Λ 110, and τινά; also τινά τι, N 201; demere, πῶμα, *take* the lid *off* the quiver, Δ 116; promere (ἐκ γωρυτοῦ), *take out* (of its case), Δ 105.

σῡλεύειν, ipf. ἐσύλευον, (σκῦλα), spoliare, *spoil*, τινά, E 48; *take away* any thing from him (Achilleus), Ω 436.

συλ-λέγω, aor. -**λέξας,** colligere, *collect, gather*; mid. fut. -λέξομαι and aor. λέξατο, sibi or sua colligere, Σ 413, β 292.

συμ (more freq. ξυμ), -βάλλω, **βάλλετον,** aor. σὺν ἔβᾰλον and σύμβᾰλον, imp. ετ(ε), aor. sync. 3 du. ξυμβλήτην, inf. -βλήμεναι, mid. fut. συμβλή(σ)εαι Υ 335, aor. σὺν ἐβάλοντο, aor. sync. ξύμβληντο, ηντο, subj. ηται η 204, part. ήμενος, miscere aquas, committere arma, pugnam, *throw, bring*, or *put together*; of rivers, *unite their waters*; of weapons, *bring in contact*; τινάς, of men, *bring against each other in battle*, Υ 55, Γ 70; τινί (with hostile intent, Π 565, Φ 578), *meet*, as also mid.; usually *meet*, also *encounter*, concurrere, μάχεσθαι, M 377.

Σύμη, fem., island off the coast of Karia, north of Rhodos; Σύμηθεν, *from Syme*, B 671†.

συμ (ξυμ) -**μάρψας,** aor., (μάρπτω), *seizing at the same time*, ι 289; but K 467, *break off.*

συμ (ξυμ) -**μητιάασθαι,** consulere, *take counsel*, K 197†.

συμ-μίσγεται, aor. 3 pl. σὺν ἔμιχθεν, *flow into*, B 753; *mingle*, Ψ 687.

συμ-μύω, pf. **σὺν μέμῡκε,** *have closed*, Ω 420†.

σύμ (ξύμ) -**παντες,** ων, ασι, ας and α, cuncti, a, *all* (*together*), B 567, η 214.

συμ-πήγνυμι, aor. **συνέπηξεν,** *curdled*, E 902†.

συμ-πίπτω, aor. **σὺν ἔπεσε,** ον, concurrit, *rush together, meet*, ε 295, H 256.

συμ-πλᾰτᾰ́γησεν (πλάταγος) χερσίν, *smote* his hands *together*, Ψ 102†.

συμ-φερτή, N 237†, where *ἀρετή* is to be repeated in the predicate, the *united* bravery even of weak men is (real) bravery.

συμ-*φέρω*, ipf. mid. **-φερόμεσθα,** fut. -*οισόμεθα*, *meet in battle*, *μάχῃ*, Λ 736; *πτόλεμόνδε*, Θ 400.

συμ-φράδμονες, pl., (*φράζω*), *joint counsellors*, B 372†.

συμ - *φράζομαι*, **φράσσομαι,** aor. *φράσσατο*, secum (*θυμῷ*) meditari, *take counsel with one's self*, *ὅπως*, ο 202; *τινί* (*βουλάς*), cum aliquo consilia inire, *concert plans with*, A 537; *have* neither word nor deed *in common with*, I 374.

σύν, from **ξύν,** which is used when it is desired to lengthen a preceding vowel by position, (*κοινός*, cum), as also freely in compounds, *with*, *along with*, *together*, K 224, κ 42; *σύν τινι*, cum aliquo; unā cum, *along with*, P 57; *by the aid of*, *σὺν Ἀθήνῃ*; of things, *with*, E 220, *ἔντεσι*, also with *νηί*; often with weapons, instrumental, *ἔντεσι*, *τεύχεσι*; with *ἀπέτῑσαν*, Δ 161, gravi poena, *with a* great price; denoting accompaniment, *along with*, *αὐτῇ σὺν πήληκι*, Ξ 498, cf. I 194. *Σὺν* freq. follows its case, ι 332, ν 303.

συν (*ξυν*) **-αγείρων,** aor. *ξυνάγειρα*, *gather together*, *assemble*, pass. -*αγειρόμενοι*, and 2 aor. mid. sync. *αγρόμενοι*, *assembled*; aor. mid.-*αγείρατ*(o), *collect for one's self*, ξ 323.

συν (*ξυν*) -*άγνυμι*, aor. **ἐ(*ϝ*)αξε,** *αν*, *αι*, tmesis, confringere, *dash to pieces*, *νῆας*, *ἅρματα*, Ψ 467; Λ 114, crush with his teeth.

σὺν (*ξυν*) -*άγω*, subj. **ξυνάγωμεν,** *ουσα*, *οντες*, *σὺν ἄγοιμι*, ipf. *ξύναγον*, *ε*, *lead together*, *νηόν*, ad templum convocare; *ὅρκια*, bring together the animals for sacrifice, Γ 269; *collect*, *φόρτον*; on the other hand, *ἄρηα*, *ἔριδα ἄρηος*, etc., *join* battle, *stir up* battle, E 861, Π 764.

συν-*αείρω*, aor. **ἤειραν,** *joined in raising* him, Ω 590; on the other hand, ipf. **ἤειρεν** K 499, aor. subj. **ἀείρεται** O 680, are from ΣϜΕΡ (*εἴρω*, *σειρά*), *couple together*.

σῦν - αίνῦτο, ipf., *gathered up*, Φ 502†.

σῦν-*αιρέω*, aor. **ελεν,** Π 740, *tore away*; - *ελών*, υ 95, *laying hold of at once*.

συν-*αντάω*, ipf. du. **αντήτην,** mid. aor. subj. *αντήσωνται*, *τινί*, *meet*, P 134 and π 333.

σῦν-αντόμενος, ipf. *ἤντετο*, 3 du. *αντέσθην*, *meet*, *τινί*; Φ 34, *encounter*.

συν-*αράσσω*, fut. **ἀράξω,** aor. *ἄραξ(εν)*, pass. *ἀράχθη*, always in tmesis, *dash to pieces*, Ψ 673, ε 426.

συν (*ξυν*) -*δέω*, ipf. 3 pl. **δέον,** aor. -*έδησα*, *ξυνέδησε*, *δῆσαι*, *bind together*, *bind fast*, A 399, χ 189; *σφενδόνῃ*, bind up with a bandage, N 599.

συν-έδραμον, see *συν-τρέχω*.

συν-*εέργω*, ipf. **-έεργον,** (for *ϝέϝεργον*), aor. *εέργαθον*, *bind together*; ξ 72, cinxit; Ξ 36, *shut in*.

(*συν* =) **ξυν-εείκοσι,** *twenty* (men) *together*, ξ 98†.

1. **σύν**-*ειμι*, fut. **ἔσεσθαι,** *be together*; *ὀιζυῖ*, *be together with*, *participate in*, η 270†.

2. *συν*-, **ξύν**-*ειμι*, **ιόντες,** *ων*, *ας*, ipf. *ξύνισαν*, du. *συνίτην*, *come* or *go together*, esp. in hostile signif. *encounter*, *περὶ ἔριδος*; *ἔριδι*, in a spirit of strife.

σῦν (*ξυν*) **-ελαύνεις,** *έμεν*, aor. *ἤλασ(ε)*, *ελάσσαμεν*, subj. *ελάσσομεν*, inf. *σσαι*, cogere, *drive together*, booty; *ὀδόντας*, *gnash* (together), σ 98; *τινὰς ἔριδι*, *bring together* in combat; only X 129, intrans. *engage in battle*.

σύν-ελον, see *συν-αιρέω*.

σῦν-εοχμῷ, masc., (vehi), *junction*, Ξ 465†.

σὺν ἐρεῖσαι, aor. from *ἐρείδω*, *close*, λ 426†.

σῦν-έρῖθος, comm., *fellow-worker*, ζ 32†.

(*συν*) **ξῦν-εσις,** fem., (*ἵημι*), *conflux*, κ 515†.

σῦν-εχές (-*σεχές*, *ἔχω*), also with *αἰεί*, perpetuo, *continuously*, ι 74.

συν (*ξυν*) -*έχω*, **ἔχουσι,** *οντες*, *ουσαν*, (tmesis), ipf. *εχον*, *hold together*, *meet*, Δ 133, Υ 415; pf. *οχωκότε*, *bent together over*, B 218.

σῦν-ημοσῦνας, *τάς*, (*συνίεμαι*), *compacts*, X 261†.

συν-ήορος (*ασϝερ*-, *σειρά*, *εἴρω*), *δαιτί*, *linked with*, *accompaniment* to the feast, θ 99†.

συν-θεσῖαι, *άων*, fem., (*συντίθημι*), conditiones, *treaty*, B 339; but E 319, *instructions*.

συν-θεύσεται, fut., (θέω), *go well,* υ 245†.

συν (ξυν) -ίημι, imp. prs. **ξυνίει,** 3 pl. ipf. ιον = ιεν, aor. ἐηκεν, 2 aor. imp. ξύνες, mid. 2 aor. ξύνετο, subj. συν-ώμεθα, *covenant, agree,* N 381; committere, ἔριδι μάχεσθαι, *bring together* in thirst for combat, to fight, A 8; *perceive, hear, attend,* ὄπα, ἔπος; also τινός, some one, B 63; something, A 273; with part., δ 76; mid. in the same sense, δ 76.

συν-ίστημι, pf.-**εσταότος,** *having arisen,* Ξ 96†.

συν-οισόμεθα, see συμ-φέρω.

σὺν ὀρίνῃς, subj., commoveas, *move,* Ω 467; ορινόμεναι, *set in motion,* Δ 332.

(συν) **ξυν-οχῇσιν,** ταῖς, (ἔχω), coniunctio, ὁδοῦ, *meeting* of out- and home-stretch, Ψ 330†.

συν-ταράσσω, aor. **ἐτάραξε,** subj. ταράξῃ, *confuse, throw into disorder,* Θ 86; *interrupt, spoil,* A 579.

σῦν-τίθημι, aor. θετο, imp. θεο, θεσθ(ε), (θυμῷ), sentire, *perceive, hear,* τί, τ 268, υ 92; *take heed to,* ο 318.

σύν-τρεις, ternos, *by threes,* ι 429†.

συν-τρέχω, aor. **ἔδρᾰμον,** concurrerunt, *rushed together,* Π 337 and 335.

συν-ώμεθα, see συν-ίημι.

σύριγξ, **σύριγγος,** ων, ξι, fem., *pipe* or *tube,* hence (1) *spear-case,* T 387.—(2) *shepherd's pipe,* K 13.

Συρίη, fem., mythical island, beyond Ortygia, far in the West, ο 403†.

συ-ρρήγνυμι (Ϝρήγνυμι), pf. pass. **συν-έρρηκται,** *is broken,* θ 137†.

σῦς, συός, ί, σῦν, σύες, ῶν, σί(ν), εσσι(ν), ας, comm., sus, *swine, hog,* boar or sow; κάπριος, *wild boar,* Λ 293, M 146, E 783, δ 457, κ 239.

σύτο = ἔσσυτο, see σεύω.

συφειοῦ κ 389, **συφεόνδε,** εοῖσιν, εούς, masc., *hog-pen, sty.* (Od.)

σῦ-φορβός, όν, έ, ῶν, masc., (φέρβω), *swine-herd;* παῖδα, Φ 282. (Od.)

σφ' = σφέ and σφί, see σφεῖς.

σφάζουσι, ειν, ipf. ἔσφαζον, aor. ἔσφαξαν, σφάξ(ε), pass. prs. σφαζόμενοι, ων, pf. ἐσφαγμένα, iugulum aperire, only of victims for sacrifice, γ 454, *cut* or *slit the throat,* so as to catch the blood (also of beast already dead, γ 449), see cut under ἀμνίον, and A 459.

σφαίρῃ, σφαῖραν, fem., *ball,* ζ 100. (Od.) **σφαιρηδόν,** adv., *like a ball,* N 204.

σφάλλω (fallo), aor. **σφῆλε,** *overthrow, make totter,* ρ 464; σφῆλαι, Ψ 719.

σφᾰρᾰγεῦντο, 3 pl. ipf. from σφαραγέομαι, (σφάραγος), *hissed,* ι 390; *were full to bursting,* ι 440.

σφάς, σφέ, see σφεῖς.

σφεδᾰνόν, adv., (σφαδάζω), *eagerly, impatiently,* Λ 165. (Il.)

σφεῖς (σϜε-, svo-), used as du. are, dat. **σφ(ίν),** acc. σφέας, σφ(έ), see also **σφωέ**; much more common are the pl. forms; gen. (ἀπὸ σφείων) σφέων orthotone and encl., σφῶν before αὐτῶν; dat. σφίσι(ν) orthotone and encl., σφ(ιν) encl.; acc. σφέας orthotone and encl., but not σφεῖας, v. l. ν 213 [pronounced as monosyll., B 96 and elsewh.]; σφᾰς encl., E 567; also σφ(έ), pron. of 3d pers., (a) reflexive, sui, sibi, se, ἀπὸ σφείων, μετὰ σφίσιν, A 368; κατὰ σφέας, B 366, and joined with αὐτῶν, ούς; (b) direct, eorum, eis, etc., esp. common dat. σφί; of things, ι 70, κ 355.

σφέλᾰς, α, ntr., *footstool,* short, thick block of wood placed before the seats of the men at banquet, σ 394 and ρ 231.

σφενδόνῃ, τῇ, (funda), *sling,* as in the cut in the hands of Assyrian; serves also as bandage for wound, N 600†.

σφετέρου, ῳ, ον, ῃσι, άων, (α), 3d

poss. pron. of 3d pers. pl., *their*, sui; cf. α 7; ad sua, α 274.

σφηκόω, plupf. pass. **ἐσφήκωντο,** (σφήξ), *were bound together*, P 52†.

Σφῆλος, οιο, son of Bukolos, father of Iasos, O 338†.

σφῆλε = ἔσφηλε, see σφάλλω.

σφήξ, **σφῆκες,** εσσιν, vespae, *wasps;* also *hornets*, M 167 and Π 259.

σφι, σφιν, see σφεῖς.

σφοδρῶς, adv., (σφεδανόν), *earnestly, eagerly*, μ 124†.

σφονδῦλίων, τῶν, masc., *vertebra of spine*, pl. *backbone*, Υ 483†.

σφός (σϝος, svos), suus, *their*, **σφοῦ,** σφούς, σφῆς, σφῇ, σφῇσι, σφάς, β 237; σφῷ, σφοῖς, Σ 231, always referring to a pl. subst.

σφῦραν, τήν, *hammer*, γ 434†.

σφῦρόν, ά, ntr., *ankle*, Δ 518, Z 117.

σφω(έ), ωίν, pron. of 3d pers. du., *they two, both of them*, A 8. (See also σφίν, σφέας, σφέ, under σφεῖς.)

σφῶι and σφω, A 257, 574; gen. σφῶιν, σφῷν, δ 62; pron. of 2d pers. du., *ye, you two*.

σφωΐτερον, poss. pron. of 2d pers. du., *of you both*, A 216†.

σχεδίης, ῃ, ην, (σχέδος, Ger. Scheit), *float, raft*, raft of Odysseus described, ε 234 sqq., the parts of which it is attempted to represent in the cut under ἁρμονίάων: *a*, the beams forming the ἔδαφος, *h*; *b*, σταμίνες; *c*, γόμφοι; *d*, ἁρμονίαι; *e*, ἐπηγκενίδες; *f*, ἴκρια; *g*, ἱστός.

σχεδίην, adv., (ἔχω), *in hand-to-hand fight*, E 830†.

Σχεδίος, (1) son of Iphitos, chief of Phokians, B 517, P 306.—(2) son of Perimedes, a Phokian, slain by Hektor, O 515.

σχεδόθεν (ἔχω), *from close at hand*, then *near at hand*, *near* (τινός, τ 447), β 267, Π 807; position in verse always the same, after caesura of third foot, ν 221.

σχεδόν, adv., (ἔχω), *near, hard by;* πηός, near kinsman, κ 441; with dat., τινί; with verbs also with gen., τινός; never with prep.; εἶναι, be at hand, N 268; M 53, the ditch, i. e. its farther bank, was not near.

σχεθέειν, see ἔχω, aor. ἔσχεθον.

σχεῖν, σχέμεν, σχέο, see ἔχω.

Σχερίη, fem., *Scheria*, the land of Phaiakes, which the ancients located in Kerkyra, whereas it really existed only in the poet's fancy, ε 34, ζ 8–263.

σχέτλιος, ε, οι, η [pronounce σχετλjη or σχἔτ-λίη, Γ 414], αι, (α), (ἔχω), strictly, *holding out, enduring*, then *merciless, unflinching, dreadful*, both in extravagant, K 164, and in seriously meant sense; always in the latter sense where reference is made to presumption or crime; ἔργα, *impious;* ὕπνος, κ 69, *wicked.*

σχέτο, aor. mid. from ἔχω.

σχίζης, ῃ, ῃσ(ιν), fem., (σκιδ-, scidi), *split wood, log*, A 462; δρυός, with the oaken billet, ξ 425.

σχοίατ(ο), opt. aor. from ἔχομαι.

σχοίνῳ, τῷ, masc. coll., *rushes*, ε 463†.

Σχοῖνος, town on river of the same name in Boiotia, B 497†.

σχόμενος, part. aor. mid. from ἔχω.

σώεσκον, σώζων, see σαόω.

σῶκος, masc., (σώζων), *saviour*, Υ 72†.

Σῶκος, son of Hippasos, a Trojan, Λ 427, 428, 440, 450, 456; slain by Odysseus, Λ 447.

σῶμα, τος, τι, τ(α), ntr., *corpse, carcass*, H 79, λ 53.

σῶς (σόος, τ 300), acc. σόον, σῶν A 117, Θ 246 (from σάος, see σαόω, sa-lus), *safe, unharmed*, X 332; *certain*, ε 305.

T.

τ', (1) = τε.—(2) = τοί, σοί, α 60, 347.—(3) = τοι after μέν, see μέν, II. 4.

τᾰγοί, pl. masc., (τάσσω), *arrangers, leaders* (v. l.), Ψ 160†.

ταθείς, τάθη, aor. pass. from τείνω.

τᾰλᾰ-εργοῦ, όν, οί, (ϝέργον), *enduring labor, patient, drudging*, mules, δ 636, Ψ 666.

Τᾰλαι-μένης, chief of Maiones, B 865†.

Τᾰλᾰϊονίδης, αο, *son of Talaos*, Mekisteus, B 566, Ψ 678.

τάλαντον, τα, ntr., (τλῆναι, tollo), (1) *scales, balance*, M 433, χρύσεια, Διός, ἱρά, in which Zeus balances the fates of men. (See cut No. 69, where Hermes occupies the place of Zeus.)—(2) a definite weight, perhaps about a *pound*, χρυσοῖο, I 122, and elsewh.

τᾰλᾰ-πείριος, ον, οι, (τλῆναι, πεῖρα), *enduring trials, much tried*, η 24, ρ 84. (Od.)

τᾰλᾰ-πενθέα, acc. (πένθος), *bearing griefs, patient in suffering*, ε 222†.

τάλᾰρον, οισι, masc., (τάλαντον), *basket*, of silver for wool, δ 125; of wicker-work for fruit, etc., Σ 568.

τάλᾰς, only voc. **τάλᾰν**, (ταλάσσῃ), *foolhardy, wretch*, σ 327 and τ 68.

τᾰλᾰσί-φρονος, α, *stout-hearted*, Δ 421, esp. of Odysseus.

ταλάσσῃς, ῃ, see τλῆναι.

τᾰλα-ύρῖνον, masc. and ntr. from -ϝρῖνον, (ϝρινός), *shield-bearing* (suspended by τελαμών, cut No. 121), in general, *brave, intrepid, valiant*, joined with Ἄρηα; —πολεμιστήν, E 289; ntr. as adv., *bravely*, H 239. (Il.)

τᾰλά-φρονα = ταλασί-φρονα, *stout-hearted*, N 300†.

Ταλθύ-βιος, herald of Agamemnon, H 276, A 320, Γ 118, Δ 192, T 196, 250, 267, Ψ 897, represented in the following cut from very ancient Greek relief.

τἆλλα, τἄλλα, see ἄλλος.

τάμε, ταμέειν, see τάμνω.

τᾰμεσί-χροα, ας, (τάμνω, χρώς), *cutting the skin, sharp-cutting*, χαλκόν, ἐγχείας, N 340. (Il.)

τᾰμίη, ης, ῃ, αι, fem., (τάμνω), *housekeeper, stewardess*, γ 392; with and without γυνή, Z 390; ἀμφίπολος, π 152.

τᾰμίης, masc., (τάμνω), *steward, dispenser*, T 44; τ. πολέμοιο, of Zeus, as controller of the combat, Δ 84; ἀνέμων, of Aiolos, κ 21.

τάμνω, **τάμνῃ**, ετε, ων, ipf. ἔταμνον, (ἔ)τάμνε, parallel form **τέμνειν** and **τέμει** (also written τεμεῖ), aor. τάμε, ον, ησιν, ωμεν, ητε, οι, έειν, ών, ταμόνθ' = όντα, όντες, secare, *cut*; of flesh, *cut up, cut in pieces*, μελεϊστί; *furrow*, with the plough, N 707; also of ships, *cut through the waves*; χρόα, *wound, maim*; ὅρκια, *conclude* a treaty *with sacrifice*, foedus icere, B 124, Γ 105; Δ 155, I *made a truce* which was death to thee; *slaughter; cut off*, τρίχας; *cut out*, the tongues of victims, an arrow from a wound; *fell* trees; *lop off* saplings from the wild fig-tree, ἐρινεὸν ὅρπηκας; *hew* beams; *mark off* an enclosure, τέμενος; mid. pass.

ταμνομένη, ους, ipf. τάμνετο, οντ(ο), mid. aor. ταμέσθαι, pf. pass. τετμημένον, ρ 195, *ready cut;* mid. contains reflexive idea, sibi, Σ 528, I 580.

τᾰνᾰ-ήκεϊ, dat., (ταναός, ἀκή), *with long edge* or *point*, of spear and sword, H 77, δ 257.

τᾰνάοιο, for ταναϜοῖο, (tenuis), *long*, Π 589†.

τᾰναύ-ποδα (ταναϜός), *long-*, i. e. *slender-legged*, ι 464†.

τᾰν-ηλεγέος (ταναός, ἄλγος), *containing long-enduring grief, deeply painful, long-lamented*, always with θανάτοιο, Θ 70, β 100, λ 171.

Τάνταλος, son of Zeus, king in Sipylos, father of Pelops, grandfather of Atreus; revealed the secrets of the gods, and was punished therefor in Hades, λ 582 sqq.

τᾰνῠ—, stem of τᾰνύς, (tenuis), *thin, stretched out*, freq. in compounds, e. g. Γ 228.

τᾰνύ-γλωσσοι (γλῶσσα), *slender-, long-tongued*, ε 66†.

τᾰνυ-γλώχῖνας (γλωχίν), *with slender, sharp point*, Θ 297†.

τᾰνῠ-ήκεας, -ηκες, -ήκεσιν, (ἀκή), *with thin, fine edge* or *point; keen*, ἄορ; *tapering*, Π 768.

τᾰνύ-πεπλος, ῳ, ε, *in finely woven garment, richly clad;* others translate, *with long flowing garment*, Γ 228, δ 305.

τᾰνυ-πτέρῠγι, γεσσι, (πτέρυξ), *with wide-extending wings*, M 237 and T 350.

τᾰνῠσί-πτεροι (τανύω, πτερόν), *broad-winged*, ε 65 and χ 468.

τᾰνυστύος, τῆς, (τανύω), *stretching* or *stringing the bow*, φ 112† (illustrated in cut No. 37).

τάνυται, see τανύω.

τᾰνύ-φλοιον, *with thin*, i. e. *smooth and tender bark*, Π 767†.

τᾰνύ-φυλλος, ον, *with long, slender leaves*, ν 102. (Od.)

τάνυμι, pass. **τᾰ́νῠται,** extenditur, *is stretched out*, P 393†.

τᾰνύω, ουσι, ειν, ων, fut. τανύουσι, φ 174, aor. (ἐ)τάνυ(σ)σε(ν), τάνυσσαν, (σ)σῃ, σειε, σσαι, σσας, pass. pf. τετάνυσται, plupf. τετάνυστο, aor. 3 pl. τάνυσθεν, σθείς, (ταν, τείνω), tendere, *stretch, strain, stretch out, put in place,* or *arrange* any thing long or broad, e. g. spears, tables, etc.; *string* a bow; *draw* the shuttle *from one side* of the warp *to the other*, κανόνα; ἵππους, *put upon their pace, drove at full speed;* of Zeus and other gods, when the comparison is with a net or noose, *extend, spread over, involve in*, yet the meaning *strain, tighten, make more intense* seems also to suit these passages, ἔριδα πολέμοιο, μάχην, πόνον, ἔριδος καὶ πολέμου πεῖραρ ἐπ' ἀμφοτέροις, N 359; pass., *be stretched out, extended;* π 175, the cheeks *became full again;* mid. ipf. τανύοντο, aor. τανυσσάμενος, and corresponding in formation and meaning, aor. pass., Π 475, *ran at full stretch; having strung his* bow, Γ 112; ι 298, *stretch one's self out.*

τᾰ́πης, ητα, ήτων, ησι, ητας, masc., *carpet, rug*, used as cover for seat and bed, κ 12, I 200. (See cuts Nos. 73, 112.)

ταπρῶτα, see πρῶτος.

τάρ from τέ and ἄρα, A 8.

τᾰράσσω (τραχύς), aor. **ἐτάραξε,** ταράξῃ, pf. τετρηχυῖα, plupf. τετρήχει, *stir up, trouble;* pf., *be in confusion,* B 95, H 346.

ταρβέω, **ταρβεῖς,** εῖ, imp. ει, ipf. τάρβει, aor. τάρβησεν, σαν, σειεν, σας, σαντε, (τάρβος), *be terrified, fear*, θυμῷ; aor. τινά and τί (Il.), *dread*, A 331, Z 469.

τάρβος, ntr., (tor-vus), terror, *dread*, Ω 152 and 181.

ταρβοσύνη, τῇ, terrore, σ 342†.

Τάρνη, Lydian city on Mount Tmolos, later Sardes, E 44†.

ταρπήμεναι, ῆναι, see τέρπω.

ταρσόν, σοί, masc., (τερσαίνω, torreo), *crate* (properly a surface for drying any thing upon), ι 219; *flat of the foot*, Λ 377, 388.

Τάρταρος, masc., *Tartaros*, dungeon, place of confinement of the lower world, situated as far below the earth as the heaven above it; here the Titans were shut up, Θ 13, 481.

ταρφέες, έεσιν, έας, ειαί, άς, ἔ(α), (τρέφω), *thick, close together, frequent;* ntr. as adv., *often, thickly*, M 47.

Τάρφη, town in Lokris, B 533†.

τάρφεσιν, nom. τὸ τάρφος, (τρέφω), *thicket*, E 555 and O 606.

ταρχύσουσι, fut., aor. subj. σωσι,

(τέρσαίνω, torreo?), orig. perh. *dry, burn*, then *solemnly bury*, στήλῃ, Π 456. (Il.)

ταυρείη, ην, (ταῦρος), *of ox-hide*, Κ 258. (Il.)

ταῦρος, οιο, ου, ον, ων, οισι, ους, taurus, *bull*, with and without βοῦς, Λ 728, Ρ 389.

τᾰφήϊον, ntr. adj., (τάφος), φᾶρος, *winding-sheet, shroud*, β 99. (Od.)

Τάφιοι, *inhabitants of the island* **Τάφος**, α 417; this Taphos has been identified with the island Meganisi between Leukas and Akarnania; the *Taphians* were notorious among the neighboring islands and on the opposite mainland for piracy, α 105, 181, 419, ξ 452, ο 427, π 426.

1. **τάφος**, τό, (τέθηπα), *astonishment*, φ 122. (Od.)

2. **τάφος**, ου, ῳ, ον, masc., (θάπτω), exsequiae, *burial*; τελέσαι, perform the rights of burial, Ω 660; *funeral banquet*, δαινύναι, γ 309.

τάφρος, οιο, ου, ῳ, ον, fem., (θάπτω), fossa, *ditch, trench*, φ 120; esp. for fortification, e. g. round the encampment of Grecian ships, Θ 179.

τᾰφών, aor. part., pf. τέθηπα, εν, ώς, ότες, ότας, plupf. ἐτεθήπεα, *be astonished, amazed*, τινά and κεῖνο, ζ 166, 168.

τάχ(ᾰ), adv. from ταχύς, *quick'y, soon*, Α 205, α 251.

τᾰχέως, *quickly*, Ψ 365†.

τάχισθ' = τάχιστ(α), etc., see ταχύς.

τάχος, ει, ntr., (ταχύς), *speed*, Ψ 406. (Il.)

τᾰχύ-πωλος, ων, (πῶλος), *with swift horses*, epithet of Δαναοί and Μυρμιδόνες, Ψ 6.

τᾰχύς, ύν, ύ, έες, έεσσι, έας, -εῖα, είης, -έ(α), comp. θάσσων, ονα, θᾶσσον, sup. τάχιστ(α) τάχισθ' θ 561, *quick, swift, fleet*; πόδας, pedibus, Σ 2; of messengers, arrows, warriors, πόδες; with inf. θείειν, Π 186; οἰωνοί, ξ 133; κύνες, Γ 26; ἐλάφοιο, αἰχμή; comp. ntr. cf. ocius, Β 440; η 152, nearly equals ὅτι τάχιστα, quam celerrime, *as quickly as possible*.

τᾰχυτῆτος, τα, fem., *swiftness, speed*, Ψ 740 and ρ 315.

τέ (τίς, τέο, quis, que), enclitic, usually postpositive, corresponding in meaning and use to que, exc. Β 136, Γ 33; I. connects things which by nature belong together, (1) -que, whether single words, Α 5, 38, Ζ 476; or sentences, Α 38, 192, 467.—(2) is often repeated, cf. et—et, Α 167, 13, 157; may connect principal and subordinate sentence, Α 81, Γ 12, Κ 225, Ψ 845; Α 218, only expressed in principal sentence; τέ—δέ, Η 418, Γ 366. —(3) τέ—καί (π 249, Α 417; in caesura, Γ 227), without marked emphasis of second clause; τέ, often repeated (γ 413, Ζ 239, Α 264), or καί (υ 365), or (Ζ 283, Α 465) first one, then the other; τε ἠδέ, Α 400; τε ἰδέ, δ 604.—II. affixed to prons. and to particles, it still serves as a connective, but can rarely be translated into English (cf. quisque, undique), (1) it may be affixed to all relatives except ὅστις, Α 86, 238, 279.—(2) to subordinate conjunctions, e. g. ὡς, ὅτε, εἴ περ, ἐπεί, Γ 33, Β 522.—(3) to co-ordinate conjunctions, e. g. καί τε, Α 521; μέν τε—δέ τε, Β 90 (ἀλλά τε, οὐδέ, δέ τ' οὐ, in second member, or δέ, δ' αὖτε, αὐτάρ), or when μέν in the first member is wanting, we find in the second member δέ τε, ἀλλά τε (after εἴπερ, Τ 164), ἀτάρ τε, Δ 484 (after ἤ ῥά τε); also οὐδέ τε, (a) *nor also*, (b) *but not*; ἤ τε, aut, *either*; doubled, *whether—or*, Λ 410, Ρ 42, and simple, quam, *than*, π 216; γάρ τε, namque.—(4) τ' ἄρα, with interrogative, Α 8, cf. Β 522. —(5) τίς τε, *any body*, δ 535. —(6) ἤ τε, Ε 201, Λ 362, Κ 450, μ 138; in οὔ νύ τ', τοι is to be understood.

Τεγέη, city in Arkadia, Β 607†.

τέγεοι, pl., (τέγος), *roofed over*, Ζ 248†.

τέγεος, τοῦ, tecti, κ 559, *roof; apartment, hall, chamber*, α 333. (Od.)

τεεῖο = σοῦ from σύ.

τεθαλυῖα, τέθηλε, see θάλλω.

τέθηπα, ότες, see ταφών.

τέθναθι, άμεν(αι), ᾶσι, εώς, ειώς, ηώς, see θνήσκω.

τεΐν = σοί, tibi.

τείνω, subj. **τείνῃ**, aor. ἔτεινε, τεῖναν, ειε, ας, pass. pf. τέτᾰται, plupf. τέτᾰτο, 3 du. τετάσθην, 3 pl. τέταντο, aor. τάθη, θείς, tendo, *stretch*, τόξον; ἡνία ἐξ ἄντυγος (see cut No. 10), *bind firmly* on the chariot rim; ὀχεύς, chin-strap *was drawn tight; ἐνὶ δεσμῷ, bind* in chains; *φάσγανον*, dependebat, *hung; λαίλαπα, spread* a tempest; *πολέμου τέλος ἴσον, strain* the even tug of war, cf. *μάχη ἐπὶ ἶσα; ἐπί τινι μάχη τέταται* (cf. *πεῖραρ*), the combat *spreads itself* around; *δρόμος ἵπποισι*, the horses *ran at full speed, at full stretch; ταθείς, stretched out, prostrate*, porrectus.

τεῖος, see *τέως*.

Τειρεσίης, *ᾱο*, Boiotian seer, dead before the Trojan war; his temple and oracle in Orchomenos, κ 537, λ 50, 89, 479, ψ 251, κ 524, λ 32, 139, 151, μ 267, ψ 323. He alone of all the shades retains his consciousness, but, like them, needs the draught of blood in order to converse with Odysseus.

τείρεα, *τά*, sidera, (*τέρας, ἀστήρ*), *constellations*, Σ 485.

τείρω, prs. ipf., (*ἔτειρε, ετο*, also unaugmented), act. and pass., terere, *wear away, fatigue*, P 745, E 153; *distress, afflict*, N 251, Z 255, δ 369; *torment*, O 61, Π 510; pass., *be hard pressed*, Z 387.

τειχεσι-πλῆτα (-pellere), voc., *stormer of walls, cities*, E 31 and 455.

τειχίζω, **ἐτειχίσσαντο**, aor. mid., *built themselves*, H 449†.

τειχῐόεσσαν (*τεῖχος*), *well-walled*, B 559, 646.

τειχίον, ntr. dimin. from *τεῖχος*, *wall of private building*, π 165 and 343.

τεῖχος, *εος, εϊ, ει, εα, εσσιν*, (Ger. Deich), *wall round a city*, Δ 308, P 558; *fortification, rampart* (draw a line of wall, *ἐλαύνειν*), M 4, *ποιήσαντο*; H 436, *ἔδειμαν*.

τείως, see *τέως*.

τέκε, τεκέειν, see *τίκτω*.

τεκμαίρομ(αι), *εται*, aor. *τεκμήρατο, αντο*, (*τέκμωρ*), *decree, appoint*, Z 349; *τινί τι*, η 317; *intend, predict, ὄλεθρον, κακά*, H 70.

τέκμωρ, *τό, goal, end; Ἰλίου, overthrow;* A 526, *pledge*.

τέκνον, voc. *φίλε τέκνον*, X 84, *α, ων*, voc. *φίλα τέκνα*, K 192, (*τίκτω*), *child*, Σ 73; in fond, conciliatory address, K 192; *young*, B 311, A 113.

τέκον, see *τίκτω*.

τέκος, *εος, εϊ, έων, τέκ(έ)εσσιν*, ntr., (*τίκτω*), *child*, Φ 229, E 71; as term of endearment, Γ 162, Θ 39, ψ 5, ζ 68; *young*, Θ 248.

τεκταίνομαι, aor. **τεκτήνατο**, *αιτο*, (*τίκτω*), *μῆτιν, devise*, K 19; *contrive, build*, E 62.

Τεκτονίδης, *ᾱο, son of Tekton* (shipbuilder), Polynaos, θ 114†.

τεκτοσῠνάων, fem. pl., (*τέκτων*), *carpenter's art*, ε 250†.

τέκτων, *ονος, ονα, ες*, masc., (*τίκτω, τεύχειν*), *maker, builder, carpenter, δούρων, νηῶν*, Z 315; *κεραοξόος, worker* in horn; *ἄνδρες*, N 390.

Τέκτων, *ονος*, father of Phereklos, E 59†.

τελᾰμών, *ῶνος, ι, α, ε, ων*, masc., (*ταλ-*, tul-), (1) *any belt* or *strap for bearing or supporting*, e. g. strap for sword (see cut No. 93), for dagger (No. 115), for shield (see cut), Ξ 404;

often cunningly wrought, λ 610.—(2) *thong* bound about or piercing the ankles, to drag dead body away, P 290; cf. cut No. 18, where the ankles of the slain Achilleus are already pierced for the thong.

Τελᾰμών, *ῶνος*, son of Aiakos, brother of Peleus, king in Salamis, father of Aias and Teukros, Θ 283, N 177, P 284, 293, λ 553.

Τελαμωνιάδης, *αο, son of Telamon*, Aias the greater, N 709.

Τελαμώνιος, son of Telamon, (1) Aias, *ὁ μέγας, υἱόν*, Λ 591.—(2) Teukros, N 170, O 462.

τελέθει, *ουσι, οντες*, (*τέλλω*), *is already here, νύξ*, H 282; generally = *to be*, η 52, I 441.

τελείων, gen. pl., (*τέλος*), *perfect, unblemished*, of victims, A 66; sup. *τελειότατον, most perfect, πετεηνῶν*, alitum, Θ 247 = aquilam (Jovis alitem).

τελείει, ipf. ἐτέλειον, and prs. pass. είεται, (τελέω), *bring to pass, fulfill,* I 456, O 593, ξ 160, τ 305, 561; *execute,* ζ 234, ψ 161.

τελεσ-φόρον εἰς ἐνιαυτόν, *bringing to perfection* or maturity, *full* (year), T 32. (Od.)

τελευτᾷ, fut. ήσω, εις, ει ο 524, ουσι, ειν, aor. τελεύτησεν, σαν, σω, σῃς, σαι, σας, aor. pass. τελευτηθῆναι, and fut. mid. ήσεσθαι in pass. signif., (τελέω), *bring to pass, fulfill,* νοήματα, Σ 328; ἐέλδωρ, φ 200; in general, λ 80, γ 62; *carry out,* β 275; ἔργα, ὅρκον, *complete,* Ξ 280; κακὸν ἦμάρ τινι, *bring* misfortune *upon.*

τελευτή, ήν, (τελέω), *end, accomplishment,* α 249; *object,* I 625, κρανέεσθαι, to be secured.

τελέω, έει, έωμεν, έοιεν, έοντες, ipf. τέλεον, fut. έω, έει, έουσι, aor. ἐτέλεσσα, ας, ε, αν, and τέλεσ(ε), σσαν, fut. (σ)σω, σσῃς, (σ)σῃ, σωσι, σαιμι, σειας, σει(εν), σαιμεν, σον, (σ)σαι; pass. prs. εἶται, ipf. ἐτελείετο, pf. τετέλεσται, σμένος, ον, α, plupf. τετέλεστο, aor. (ἐ)τελέσθη, fut. εἶται, εἶσθαι, and ἔεσθαι, (τέλος), *bring to goal,* (1) *complete,* τί, with part., *quite, altogether,* M 222, ε 409.—(2) *fulfill, accomplish,* ἔπος, μῦθον, T 107; τάδε δὴ νῦν πάντα τελεῖται, β 176; τὸ (δὲ) καὶ τετελεσμένον, *fulfilled,* ἔσται, π 440, in other phrases τετελεσμένον means *practicable.*—(3) θέμιστας, *pay* tribute, I 156.

τελήεσσας, τάς, (τέλος), *rich in fulfillment, effective,* δ 352.

τέλος, τέλοσδε, τελέεσσι(ν), ntr., (τέρμα, Ger. Ziel), *end, sum,* B 122, (1) *sum and substance,* μύθου; Π 630, πολέμοιο, *victory* in battle; ἐπέων, in words, ι 5, ρ 476.—(2) *accomplishment, reality,* γάμοιο, ἀρῇσιν; θανάτοιο, periphrasis for *death,* E 553.—(3) *completion,* Σ 378; μύθων, *conclusion* of the matter.—(4) manipulus, *division of the army, company* (Il.), Λ 730.

τέλσον, ntr., (τέλος), marks off the *limit* of the corn-field, ἀρούρης, N 707.

τέμενος, ένεα, ntr., (τέμνω), *land marked off and set apart as property of king,* λ 185; as sacred to a god, θ 363.

Τεμέση, fem., town famous for its copper mines (in Kypros ?), α 184†.

τέμνω, τέμει, τεμεῖ, see τάμνω.

Τένεδος, small island westward of Troas, A 38, Λ 625, N 33, γ 159.

Τενθρηδών, όνος, chief of Magnesians from Thessaly, father of Prothoos, B 756†.

τένοντε, du., pl. τες, τας, masc., (τείνω), *muscles; neck-muscles,* K 456; with αὐχενίους, γ 450; E 307, muscles of hip.

τέξεις, εσθαι, see τίκτω.

τέο, τεο = τοῦ, του = τίνος, τινός, see τίς 1. and 2.

τεοῖο—τεοῦ, tui, see σύ.

τεός, τεῷ, τεόν, τεώ, τεοῖσιν; τεή, τεῆς, τεῇ, τεήν, τεῇς; τεύν, τεοῖσιν, tuus, *thy,* Ω 739, γ 122, α 295, γ 94.

τέρας, τέρατα, άων, άεσσι; τέραα, (ἀστήρ, see τείρεα), prodigium, portentum, *omen* or *portent* found in some manifestation of nature, e. g. lightning, thunder, rainbow, hence Διός, since Zeus sends it, φαίνει, προφαίνει, ἵησι; but it is sent for the enlightenment or warning of men, hence with gen. ἀνθρώπων; the monster Gorgo is called, E 742, Διὸς τέρας; Λ 4, πολέμοιο τέρας, Eris holds in her hands as *dread sign of war* possibly the Gorgon's head, possibly the snakes, with which she is often represented.

τερέτρῳ, α, (τείρω), terebra, *borer, auger,* ε 246 and ψ 198.

τέρην, **τέρενα,** ntr. τέρεν, τέρεν(α), (cognate with τείρω, teres), perh. *shining, gleaming,* usually explained *tender, soft,* Δ 237, N 180; Ameis translates, π 332, *pearly* tear.

τέρμ(α), pl. τέρμαθ' = τέρματ(α), ntr., (τέλος, terminus), *goal,* pillar round which chariots had to turn at races, Ψ 309; *mark* showing how far a quoit was thrown, θ 193.

τερμιόεντα, όεσσα, (τέρμις), *encircled with a fringe* or *border,* χιτών, τ 242; ἀσπίς, furnished with tassels or tufts, Π 803. (See cut No. 93.)

Τερπιάδης, *son of Terpis,* Phemios, χ 330†.

τερπι-κέραυνος, ῳ, ον, (τέρπω), *delighting in thunder,* also sometimes referred to τρέπω, *whirling the thunderbolt,* Zeus, A 419, υ 75.

τέρπειν, prs. and ipf., (often unaugmented both in act. and mid.), mid. fut. τέρψομαι, aor. τερψάμενος, 2 aor. subj. ταρπώμεθα δ 295, aor. red. τετάρπετο, subj. τεταρπώμε(σ)θα, όμενος, οι, aor. pass. ἐτέρφθητε, ησαν, τερφθείη, 3 sing. τάρφθη, 3 pl. τάρφθεν, 2 aor. 3 du. ἐταρπήτην ψ 300, pl. τάρπημεν, ησαν, subj. **τραπείομεν** for ταρπέωμεν Γ 441, inf. ταρπήμεναι and ταρπῆναι, (τρέφω), *refresh, delight, rejoice,* τινά, θυμόν, with part., cantando, ρ 385. Mid. and pass., *satiate one's self with, satisfy,* τινός, Ω 513, I 705, γ 70; *take pleasure in, enjoy,* τινί, Θ 481; with part., α 369, E 760; θυμῷ, π 26; (ἐνὶ) φρεσίν (θ 368), T 19, or θυμόν, φρένα, Υ 23, etc.; τραπείομεν, *let us delight ourselves;* (ἐν)φιλότητι, in (the pleasures of) love; εὐνηθέντε, on the bed; κοιμηθέντες, in sleep, cf. I 337; λέκτρονδε, θ 292, to be joined with δεῦρο, which it explains.

τερπωλήν, τήν, (τέρπω), *delight, rare sport,* σ 37†.

τερσαίνω, aor. **τέρσηνε,** ῆναι, etc., (τέρσομαι), detersit, *dried up,* Π 529†.

τέρσεται, ipf. ἐτέρσετο, τέρσοντο, 2 aor. τερσήμεναι, and ῆναι, (torreo, tergo), *become* or *be dry,* of wounds, of place for drying grapes; ὄσσε δακρυόφιν, oculi lacrimis, ε 152.

τερψι-μβρότου, τοῦ, (βροτός), *delighting mortals,* Helios, μ 269 and 274.

τεσσαρᾰ́-βοιον (βοῦς), *worth four cattle,* Ψ 705†.

τεσσαρᾰ́-κοντ(α), quadraginta, *forty,* B 524, ω 340.

τέσσαρες, ας, quatuor, B 618, ξ 22.

τεταγών, aor. part., (tango), *laying hold of,* ποδός, by the foot, A 591 and O 23.

τέταται, etc., pf. part. from τείνω.

τετάρπετο, ώμε(σ)θα, όμενος, see τέρπω.

τέταρτος, ῳ, ον, ων, η, ης, and **τέτρᾰτος,** ον, (τέσσαρες), quartus, Ψ 301, 615; ntr. with and without τό, quartum, *for the fourth time,* Π 786, X 208.

τετάσθην, see τείνω.

τετεύξεται, τετεύχαται, ετον, see τεύχω.

τετευχῆσθαι, inf. pf. pass. from τευχέω, (τεύχεα), *to arm ourselves,* χ 104†.

τέτηκα, see τήκω.

τετίημαι, 2 du. **τετίησθον,** ημένος, η, αι, also pf. part. act. **τετιηότι,** ότες, (τίω), *grieve, be troubled,* Θ 447, Λ 555; ἦτορ, animo.

τέτλαθι, αίην, άμεν, άμεναι, ηώς, etc., see τλῆναι.

τετμημένον, see τέμνω.

τέτμεν, 3 pl. ον, subj. ῃς, defective aor., (τέμνω), *find,* Z 374; *reach, attain,* α 218.

τετρᾰ́-γυος (γύης), containing four γύαι η 113, τὸ -ον, as subst., *a piece of land as large as a man can plough in a day,* σ 374.

τετρᾰ-θέλυμνον (θέλυμνον), *of four layers* of ox-hide, O 479 and χ 122.

τετραίνω, aor. **τέτρηνε,** (τείρω), perforavit, *pierce with holes,* ε 247.

τετρᾰ́κις, quater, *four times,* ε 306†.

τετρᾰ́-κυκλον, οι, *four-wheeled,* ι 242.

τετρ-ᾰ́οροι (ασϝερ-, σειρά), *yoked four abreast,* ν 81†.

τετρα-πλῆ, *fourfold,* A 128†.

τέτραπτο, see τρέπω.

τέτρατος, ον, see τέταρτος.

τετρᾰ-φάληρον, *with fourfold crest,* E 743 (see cut under αὐλῶπις, where *c, e, g, f* show the four successive crests or combs of helmet).

τετρᾰ-φάλῳ, ον, *with the crest fashioned in four ridges* or *bands,* not essentially different from following, M 384 and X 315, E 743. (See cut No. 122.)

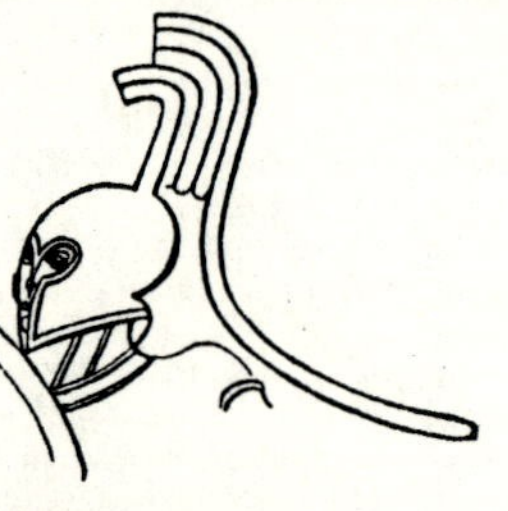

τετράφατο, see τρέπω.

τετρα-χθά, *in four parts,* Γ 363 and ι 71.

τέτρηνε, see τετραίνω.

τετρήχει, υῖα, see ταράσσω.

τετρίγει, υῖα, etc., see τρίζω.

τέτροφεν, see τρέφω.

τέττᾰ, voc., (Sanskrit, tâta), form of fond address, esp. of son to father, =*dear father,* Δ 412†.

τεττίγεσσι, τοῖς, cicada, a kind of grasshopper, probably not unlike the *katydid;* the gossiping elders at the gate of Troja are compared with τεττίγεσσιν, Γ 151†.

τετυγμένα, τετυκεῖν, έσθαι, οίμεθα, τέτυξαι, τετύχθαι, see τεύχω.

τετύχηκε, see τυγχάνω.

τεῦ, τευ = τίνος, τινός.

Τευθρανίδης, *son of Teuthras*, Axylos, Z 13†.

Τεύθρας, αντος, (1) father of Axylos.—(2) a Greek from Magnesia, slain by Hektor, E 705†.

Τεῦκρος, son of Telamon, N 170, and of Hesione of Salamis, step-brother of Aias, M 371, the best archer before Troja, M 350, 372, Z 31, Θ 322, 273, O 484.

Τευτάμίδης, αο, *son of Teutamias*, Lethos, B 843†.

τεύχε(α), έων, ε(σ)σι(ν), ntr., *implement of any kind, tackling*, π 326, 360, ο 218, elswh. arma, *equipment, arms*, Φ 301, Σ 137.

τεύχω, **τεύχοιμι,** ειν, ων, ούσῃ, ουσαι, ipf. ἔτευχε(ν), τεῦχε, 3 du. ἐτευχέτην (v. l. τετεύχετον, N 346), mid. τεύχοντ(ο), fut. act. τεύξω, etc., aor. ἔτευξα, (εν), αν, τεῦξ(ε), ῃ, ειεν, etc., also red. aor. τετυκεῖν, mid. τετύκοντο, τετυκοίμεθα, έσθαι, (τέχνη), *execute, fabricate, work*, of all kinds of handiwork, Σ 373; *build*, Z 314, Ξ 240; *prepare*, food and drink, Λ 624, ο 77; then generally, A 110, N 209, K 6; θάνατόν τινι, λ 409; γάμον, etc., κ 18, O 70; *raise*, βοήν, κ 118; *render*, (ἑλώρια, A 4), ν 397; mid. only of preparation of meals, *prepare* or *have prepared for one's self*, δόρπον, δαῖτα, etc.; pass. and fut. mid. τεύξεσθαι, pf. τετευχώς μ 423, pf. pass. τέτυξαι, τέτυκται, 3 pl. τετεύχαται, τετύχθω, τετύχθαι, τετυγμένος, ον, α, plupf. (ἐ)τετύγμην, ξο, κτο, (ἐ)τετεύχατο, aor. ἐτύχθη, also 3 fut. τετεύξεται, as pass., *be prepared*, δ 392; *be wrought of* or *in*, τινός (τινί, τ 563); *be ready*, Ξ 53, β 356; τετυγμένος, *well-wrought*, Π 225; αἰθούσῃσιν, made (furnished) with polished porticoes; well-tilled, ἀγρός; integer, well-balanced, νόος; esp. freq. in signif. *take place, happen*, fieri, θ 544; *be, become*, τέτυκται, ο, O 207, Π 622, Σ 120, Δ 84, X 30; θ 546, ἀντί τινος, takes the place of; also with πέρι, cf. περιεῖναι, surpass, P 279; δίκη, was the habit, σ 275.

τέφρη, fem., (tepere), Σ 25, Ψ 251, *ashes.*

τεχνάομαι, fut. **τεχνήσομαι,** aor. τεχνήσατο, σαιτο, σάμενος (τέχνη), *contrive, device*, Ψ 415; λ 613, where μή prepares the way for μηδ', may not he who contrived it, may he never again contrive a second like it. (Od.)

τέχνης, gen., ῃ, ην, ας, fem., (τεκεῖν, τεύχω), *art, skill*, Γ 61, λ 614; (cunning) *device*, δ 455, 529, θ 327.

τεχνήεντες, adv. -ήεντως ε 270, fem. τεχνῆσσαι, for -ήεσσαι ἱστῶν, *skillful* in weaving, η 110.

τεχνῆσαι, better τεχνῆσσαι, see τεχνήεντες.

τέῳ, τέων = τινί, τίνων.

τέως [monosyll., κ 348, ο 231, π 370], τεῖος, v. l., Y 42; v. l., T 189, αὖθι τ. (τῆος?), *so long*, Ω 658; after ἕως, Y 42; ὄφρα, T 189; *meanwhile*, ο 127, σ 190; *some time*, ο 231.

1. **τῆ** (old imper. for τῆθι or τάθι, parallel form to τείνω), *stretch out the hand here*, freq. with follg. imper. when its force may be given by *there!* Ξ 219, ε 346.

2. **τῇ** (also written τῇ, orig. old dat.), adv., (1) demonstrative, *here*, δ 847; (2) relative, also with περ, *as*, θ 510; δ 565 and τῇ ῥα M 118, *where.*

τῇδε, see ὅδε.

τήθεα, ntr., *oysters*, Π 747†.

Τηθύς, ύος, daughter of Uranos and of Gaia, wife of Okeanos, mother of river-gods, Ξ 302; of all the gods according to Ξ 201†.

τηκεδόνι, τῇ, (τήκω), *decline*, λ 201†.

τήκω, imp. **τῆκε;** θυμόν, *consume* not thy soul, τ 264; mid. τηκόμενος, ης, ipf. τήκετο, pf. act. τέτηκα, *pine away*, Γ 176; *waste one's self away* with longing disease; *melt*, of snow, τ 207.

τῆλε, *far away*, ρ 312; *far*, K 153, Σ 395, Y 482; with gen., *far from*, ρ 250, X 445; ἀπό, Ψ 880, X 468, γ 313; ἐκ, *from far away from*, B 863.

τηλεδαπός, ῷ, άων, ῶν, (τῆλε), *distant*, Φ 454; *strange, foreign*, X 45.

τηλεθάοντας, όωσα, αν, αι, ntr. άον, όωντα, (θάλλω), *luxuriant-growing, blooming*, of plants, forest, hair; παῖδες, X 423.

τηλε-κλειτοῖο, όν, οί, ῶν, ά, and **κλυτός**, α 30, (κλύω, κλεϜίω), *wide-renowned*, esp. as epithet of Trojan allies, I 233, E 491.

Τηλέ-μαχος, οιο, ον, etc., son of Odysseus and of Penelope, δ 112, α 156; visits, in search of his father, attended by Athena (in form of Nestor), Pylos, γ 1; Sparta, δ 1; returns home, ο 1; helps his father in combat with the suitors, χ 92, 267, 284, 294; ἱερὴ ἴς Τ-οιο, periphrasis, β 409; πεπνυμένος, α 213, ω 510; ἰσόθεος φώς, υ 124. (Od. and B 260, Δ 354.)

Τήλεμος, son of Eurymos, seer among the Kyklopes, ι 509.

Τηλέ-πῠλος, town of Laistrygones, κ 82, ψ 318.

τηλε-φᾰνής (φαίνομαι), *conspicuous far and wide*, ω 83†.

Τηλεφίδης, αο, *son of Telephos*, Eurypylos, λ 519.

τηλίκος, ον, *of such an age* (as), Ω 487, ρ 20.

τηλόθεν (τηλοῦ), *from far* (away), ζ 312, E 478, ι 273.

τηλόθι (τηλοῦ), *far away*, Π 233, α 22; with gen., *far from*, A 30.

τηλόσε (τηλοῦ), *to a distance, far away*, Δ 455 and X 407, ε 59.

τηλοτάτω, adv., *most distant*, η 322†.

τηλοῦ, *afar*, Λ 712; with gen., *far from*, ν 249, ψ 68.

τηλῠ-γετος, ῳ, ον, ην, (ἀταλός, τᾶλις, γέγαα?), *of tender age*, boy or girl; others explain *born long ago* (τῆλε γεν-), i. e. *full grown*; fem., Γ 175; elsewh. masc., N 470, δ 11.

τῆμος, adv., tum, *then, thereupon*, answering to ἦμος, Ψ 228; εὖτε, ν 95.

τῆπερ, see τῇ 2.

Τηρείης, ὄρος, mountain in Mysia, B 829†.

Τηῠ-γετον, mountain range in Lakonia, extending to Cape Tainaron, ζ 103†.

τηΰσίην, fem. acc., *vain, useless*, of journey, γ 316 and ο 13.

τίεσκον, see τίω.

τίη, also τί ἤ, (and τί ἤ), quidnam, *why then, why pray?* always in first or third foot follg. fem. caesura (exc. ο 326), A 407, π 421, Z 145, ρ 375; it occurs in Od. five times, in Il. twenty times; with δέ, Ξ 264; δή, M 310; after ἀλλά, P 97.

τιθαιβώσσουσι, *lay up honey*, ν 106.

τίθημι, **τίθησθα**, ησι, 3 pl. τιθεῖσι, inf. τιθήμεναι, part. τιθείς, έντες, ipf. τίθεσαν, fut. θήσω, εις, ει, etc., inf. θέμεναι, aor. ἔθηκα, ας, (εν), ἔθηχ' = ἔθηκε, καν, and θῆκα, κ(εν), καν, and θῆχ' = θῆκε; ἔθεσαν, θέσαν, subj. θείω, ῃς, ῃ, ομεν, and θήῃς, ῃ, θέωμεν, opt. θείην, ης, η, θεῖμεν, θεῖεν, imp. θές, inf. θεῖναι, θέμεν(αι), part. θέντες, θεῖσα; mid. pres. imp. τίθεσθ(ε), part. τιθήμενον, fut. θήσονται, aor. θήκατο, 2 aor. ἐθέμην, ἔθετο, θέτο, ἔθεσθε, θέσθ(ε), ἔθεντο, subj. θῆαι, opt. θεῖτο, imp. θέο, θέσθω, θέσθ(ε), inf. θέσθαι, part. θέμενος, η; also as if from τιθέω, pres. **τιθεῖ** (v. l. τίθει), ipf. (ἐ)τίθει, (condere, Ger. thun, Eng. do).—I. act., (1) ponere, collocare, *set, put, place, lay*, θεμείλια, M 29, followed by dat. without prep., or with ἐν, ἐπί, μετά, ἀμφί, ἀνά, ὑπό; by acc. with εἰς, ἀνά, ὑπό; by gen. with ἐπί; ἐν χείρεσσι, place in the hands or arms, A 45, 441; ἐπὶ γούνασι.—(2) metaphorical, put (into one's mind), *suggest, bestow*, τινὶ ἐν θυμῷ, ἐν στήθεσσι, ἐν φρεσί, in one's heart (ἔπος, μύθου τέλος, etc.), A 55.—(3) *propose* prizes in games, *deposit* gifts, statues in temple, etc.; *bury*, Ψ 83.—(4) *make, bring to pass, cause*, κακά, etc., Π 263, O 721; ἔριν μετά τισι, γ 136, cf. M 411; σῆμά τινι, give a sign, Θ 171; ἄλγεα, prepare woes for the Achaians, A 2; Π 96, bring light, i. e. rescue; σκέδασιν = σκεδαννύναι; put into a certain condition or state, *constitute, make*, αἰχμητήν, A 290; ἱέρειαν, ἄλοχον, λίθον, ν 156; with adj., *render*, Δ 363, Z 432, Φ 172; bury to half its length, X 490, λ 274, ψ 11.—II. mid. (1) *put* or *place for one's self* something of one's own, ἄορ, one's sword in its sheath; ἐν φρεσί, put into one's heart, consider by one's self; ἐλέγχεα ταῦτα, *hold* this as an insult to yourselves, φ 333; αἰδῶ ἐν στήθεσσι, N 121, O 561, 661.—(2) *make* or *prepare for one's self*, ἐπιγουνίδα; δαῖτα, δόρπον, I 88; μάχην, ἀγορήν, πόνον, Ω 402; θυμὸν ἄγριον, make one's temper savage, I 629; τινὰ γυναῖκα, take as one's wife.

τιθήνη, ης, ας, fem., (θῆσθαι), *nurse*, Z 389. (Il.)

τίθησθα, see τίθημι.

Τιθωνός, *οῖο*, son of Laomedon, carried away by Eos, Υ 237, Λ 1, ε 1.

τίκτω, **τίκτει,** ipf. *ἔτικτον, ε(ν), τίκτε,* fut. *τέξεις,* aor. *(ἔ)τέκον, τέκες, (εν), ομεν; ῃ, ωνι; οι, οιεν; έειν; ών, οῦσα,* mid. fut. *τέξεσθαι,* aor. *τέκεθ' = τέκετ(ο), έσθαι,* (*τέκτων, τεχ-, τευχ-*), gignere and parĕre, *beget* and *bring forth*, of divinity, man and beast, Τ 413, Ζ 206, Π 34, π 119.

τίλλω, ipf. **τίλλε,** *ον,* mid. *τιλλέσθην, οντο, pluck out*, hair; mid., *pluck out one's hair; τινά, tear one's hair in sorrow for*, Ω 711.

τῑμάω, **τιμᾷ,** *ῶσι, τίμα, ῶν, ῶσαι,* ipf. *ἐτίμα,* fut. *τιμήσουσι,* aor. *τιμήσῃς, ῃ, ήσομεν, τίμησον, ῆσαι, ήσας,* fut. mid. *τιμήσεσθαι,* aor. *ἐτιμήσασθ(ε), τιμήσαντο,* pf. pass. *τετίμηται, ήμεσθα, ῆσθαι,* (*τιμή*), *honor*, *τινά, τινι,* with or by any thing; pf. pass. *τιμῆς, be deemed worthy of* honor, Ψ 649; Ι 608, I deem myself *to have been* (enough) *honored* by the decree of Zeus.

τῑμή, *ῆς, ῇ, ήν,* fem., (*τίω*), *valuation*, (1) *penalty*, (*ἀπο*)*τίνειν τινί,* pay (back) a penalty to one; *ἄρνυσθαι,* exact *satisfaction* for some one, Α 159; then *punishment*, ξ 70.—(2) *honor, dignity, prerogative*, ε 335, λ 338, Δ 410.

τῑμήεις, *τιμῆς, ήεντος, α,* and *τιμῆντα, τιμήεσσα,* comp. *τιμηέστερος,* sup. *τιμηέστατον,* (*τιμή*), (1) *precious*, λ 327, δ 614. — (2) *highly honored*, σ 161.

τίμῐος (*τιμή*), *honored*, κ 38†.

τῑνάσσων, *οντας,* ipf. *τίνασσε,* aor. *ἐτίναξε(ν), τῐνάξῃ,* pass. prs. *τινάσσεται,* ipf. *τινάσσετο,* aor. 3 pl. *τίναχθεν,* mid. aor. 3 du. *τιναξάσθην, swing, shake, brandish*, weapons, etc.; Γ 385, *plucked* her garment; *θρόνον, overthrow; scatter*, ε 368; *ἐκ,* elisi sunt, *were dashed out*, Π 348; mid., β 151, *shook* their wings.

τῑνῠται, *υσθον, ύμενος,* (*τίω*), punish, *τινά, λώβην, chastise for* insolence, ω 326.

τίνειν, *ων,* fut. *τίσω,* aor. *ἔτῑσ(εν), τίσειαν, τῖσον, τῖσαι,* etc., *pay* a penalty, *τιμήν τινι; τί, atone for* something with one's life, χ 218; in good signif. *pay a debt, discharge obligation, ζωάγρια,* ransom; *reward*, ξ 166; mid. fut. *τίσομαι,* aor. *ἐτισάμην, τίσαιο,* 3 pl. *τισαίατο, indemnify one's self*, ν 15; *exact satisfaction*, (1) *τινά,* from a person, Γ 28, Β 743.—(2) *τί,* for a thing, Τ 208, ω 470.—(3) *τινά τινος,* of a person for a thing, γ 206; *τινά τι,* ο 236.

τίπτε, also *τίπτ'* (*τίφθ'* before rough breathing), from *τί ποτε,* quidnam, *why pray?* at beginning of verse or after voc.; in fifth foot only in phrase *τίπτε δὲ σὲ χρεώ*; with *αὖτε,* Α 202, λ 93; *οὕτως,* Δ 243; (*τόσσον*) *ὧδε* (ι 403), Λ 656; usually with verbs of motion, Ζ 254, Ο 90; in salutation, ε 87, λ 474.

Τίρυνς, *νθος,* fem., ancient seat of kings of Argos, of Perseus, with Cyclopean walls, Β 559†.

τίς, *τέο, τεῦ, τίνα, τίνες, τέων* [monosyll., ζ 119], ntr. *τί,* (quis), *who?* interrogative pron. *τίς δ' οὗτος,* υ 380; *οἶδεν εἰ* (*κε*), β 332; *τίς πόθεν εἷς ἀνδρῶν, who* art thou, and from where in the world dost thou come? α 170; *ἐς τί, how long? τί μοι ἀρωγῆς, what* befalls me in consequence of succor rendered? used with *ἄν* in expression of a wish, Κ 303; rarely in indirect question, ο 423. *τί*; like quid? *how? why?* Δ 371, Κ 159, α 62; *wherefore?* Λ 606, Υ 87, φ 333.

τίς, *τί,* indef. pron. enclitic, *τεῦ, τέο, τινί τεω τῳ, τινά, τί, τινέ, τινάς,* ntr. *ἄσσα,* τ 218 = *some one, something*, quidam, quoddam; *many a one, every one*, τ 265, Β 388, 355; also to indirectly designate a certain person, Α 289; often to be supplied, as suggested by an oblique case, e. g. *τινά,* suggested by *οἷ,* α 392; joined with adjs. it makes them less precise, *a certain kind of, a real*, and has often a sarcastic force, σ 382; ntr. *τί,* like aliquid, *somewhat, in a degree*, hence *οὔ τι,* nequaquam, *by no means; οὐδέ τι, and nothing whatever*, γ 184.

τῖσις, *ιν,* fem., (*τίω*), *recompense*, β 76; *punishment, vengeance*, with gen. for *τινός* (*ἔκ τινος,* proceeding from, at the hands of).

τῖτά (*τίω*) *ἔργα, vengeance*, Ω 213, better *ἄντιτα.*

τῑταίνετον, *ων,* ipf. *ἐτίταινε,* aor. *τιτήνας,* (*τανύω, τείνω*), tendo, *bend, draw*, the bow; *stretch out*, the arms; *τράπεζαν, spread* the table; *τάλαντα, poise* the balances; elsewh. *draw* chariot, plough; mid. *τιταίνοιτο,-όμε-*

νος, ἐπιταίνετο, arcum suum tendere; φ 259, *string for one's self* the bow; *stretch one's self* in running, go at full speed; πτερύγεσσιν, stretching out their wings.

Τῑτᾶνος, οιο, place (mountain or town) in Thessaly, B 735†.

Τῑτᾰρήσιος, river in Thessaly rising in Olympos, later Europos, a branch of the Peneios, B 751†.

Τιτῆνες, οἱ, *Titans*, sons of Uranos and Gaia; cast down from heaven, which they recovered by the help of Kronos, who cast them again into Tartaros, and ruled alone until his son Zeus, aided by Gaia, overpowered and shut him up in turn with the Titans, Ξ 279, ὑποταρτάριοι; οὐρανίωνες, E 898.

τιτρώσκω, see τρώω.

Τῑτυός, son of Gaia, covering in Hades nine plethra of space with his prostrate body, while vultures devour his liver, λ 576–580, η 324.

τῑτύσκεται, όμενος, οι, ων, η, αι, ipf. τιτύσκετο, (τόξον, τυχεῖν), *make ready*, πῦρ; ἵππους ὑπ' ὄχεσφι, *couple, put to;* usually *aim*, of weapons (dat.), ἄντα, straight before one; τινός, at some one; with φρεσίν, purpose, design; θ 556, *speeding* thither.

τίφθ' = τίπτε.

τίω, prs. and ipf. act. and mid. [pres. ῐ exc. I 238, ξ 84, ο 543, Θ 540; ipf. ῑ exc. N 176, O 551, α 432, τ 247, Ψ 705, so also τίεσκον, but τῑεσκεν, N 461, τῑέσκετο, Δ 46], fut. τίσω, aor. ἔτῑσε, pf. part. τετῑμένος, ον, etc., *value*, aestimare, δυωδεκάβοιον, at twelve steers' worth; ἐν καρὸς αἴσῃ, at a hair's worth; otherwise always in signif., *honor*, magni aestimare, θεὸν ὥς, etc.

τλήμων, μονα, ες, (τλῆναι), *enduring, patient*, θυμόν; *impudent*, Φ 430.

τλῆναι (ΤΑΛ, ΤΕΛ, tolero), fut. τλήσομ(αι), 1 aor. ἐτάλασσας, ταλάσσῃς, ῃ, aor. sync. ἔτλην, ης, η = τλῆ, τλῆμεν, ἔτλητε, ἔτλαν; τλαίην, ης, η, τλαῖεν, τλῆθι, τλήτω, τλῆτε; pf. τέτληκας, εν, 1 pl. τέτλαμεν, τέτλᾰθι, άτω, αίη, άμεν(αι), τετληότι, ες, τετληυῖα, *suffer, undergo*, τί; τινά, *resist;* part. pf., *steadfast, enduring*, E 873; 1 aor. animum inducere, *venture upon, presume*, O 164, N 829; *prevail upon one's self, have the heart, courage, heartlessness*, P 166.

Τληπόλεμος, ου, (1) son of Herakles and of Astyochia, fugitive on account of involuntary murder, found safety in Rhodos, where he became king, B 653, 657, 661, E 628, 631, 632, 648, 656, 660, 668.—(2) son of Damastor, slain by Patroklos, Π 416.

τλητόν (τλῆναι), *enduring*, Ω 49†.

τμήγω, aor. pass. 3 pl. **τμάγεν,** (τέμνω), discesserunt, *they dispersed*, Π 374.

τμήδην, adv., (τέμνω), *so as to cut* or *graze*, H 262†.

Τμῶλος, mountain in Lydia, near Sardes, B 866, Υ 385.

τό, *therefore*, Γ 176, M 9, θ 332; H 239, τό μοι ἔστι, therefore can I —.

τόθι, adv., ibi, *there*, ο 239†.

I. **τοί,** nom. plur. masc. from demonstrat. ὁ and from relat. ὅ.

II. **τοί** = σοί, tibi; also as unemphatic ethical dat., τ 599, see σύ.

III. **τοί** (from ethical dat. τοί, A 419, π 187), enclitic particle serving to strengthen an assertion (also in negative sentences) expressing confidence: *I assure you, verily*, A 419, 426, ο 72, π 187 (A 298); expressing emotion: *let me tell you, yet verily*, B 298, E 873, X 488, σ 230 (B 361, Γ 65); expressing conviction, *you may be sure, certainly, no doubt*, I 654, N 115, O 45 (Δ 29, Z 335, α 203); see also ἤτοι and μέν. (N 267, καί belongs to ἐμοί; is not καίτοι.)

IV. **τοιγάρ** (τοί = τῷ), *so then, accordingly*, always at beginning of a clause, with reference to an exhortation, with ἐγώ, (a) beginning a speech, A 76, K 413, α 179; (b) preceding an action, δ 612, η 28, θ 402; a second τοί is tibi, α 214.

τοῖος, ου, ον, οι, ους, τοίη, ην, αι, τοῖον, τοῖ(α), (το-), talis, *of such a kind, such*, corresponding to rel. οἷος, Σ 105, α 257, δ 345, 421, λ 499 (also to ὁποῖος, ρ 421; to ὅς, β 286; to ὅπως, π 208); τεύχεσι, *such* in his weapons; χεῖρας, in his hands; with inf., *capable, able;* with adjs., *so really, so very, just*, α 209, cf. λ 135, β 286; ntr. **τοῖον,** *so, so very*, γ 321, X 241, Ψ 246 (elsewh. only Od.).

τοιόσδε, οῦδ(ε), ῇδ(ε), όνδε, άδε, like

τοῖος, talis, *such*, with reference to something near, under one's eyes; corresponds to οἷος, followed by acc. of that in respect to which, ρ 313; ntr. τοιόνδε, *so good, so bad;* with inf., Z 463.

τοιοῦτος, ούτου, οὗτον, οὗτοι, ούτων, τοιαύτη, τοιαῦτα = τοῖος, talis, with stronger demonstrative sense, *of such a kind*, δ 650; Ἀχαιῶν, P 643; tam praestantes, *so excellent*, B 372, Π 847; tam prava, nefaria, *so heinous things*, Ψ 494, χ 315.

τοίσδεσ(σ)ι, see ὅδε.

τοῖχος, **τοίχου,** ῳ, ον, οι, ων, ους, murus, *wall of a house* or *court*, Π 212, β 342, χ 126; *sides of a ship*, μ 420, O 382.

τοκάδες, fem., (τίκτω), σύες, (swine), *having just brought forth*, ξ 16†.

τοκῆε, du., pl. τοκῆες, ήων, έων, εῦσι(ν), ῆας, (τίκτω), *parents*, α 170; ἐκ — εἶναι, Ω 387; *ancestors*, δ 596, η 54.

τόκος, οιο, ον, masc., (τεκεῖν), (1) partus, *bringing forth, delivery*, T 119, P 5.—(2) proles, *offspring*, O 141; *young*, ο 175.

τολμάω, ipf. **ἐτόλμας,** α, τόλμων, fut. τολμήσεις, aor. τόλμησεν, σειεν, σαντα, (τλῆναι, tolero), *endure*, with part., ω 162; *be bold*, K 232, E 670; *dare*, Θ 424, M 51.

τολμήεις, ήεντι, (τόλμη), *daring*, K 205; *enduring, steadfast*, ρ 284.

τολῡπεύω, ειν, aor. τολύπευσα, σε(ν), prop. *wind up as a ball* (τολύπη), hence *contrive*, δόλους; *achieve, finish*, ω 95, Ω 7.

τομήν, τήν, (τέμνω), *end left after cutting, stump*, A 235†.

τοξάζεαι, 2 sing. prs., inf. εσθαι, opt. οίμεθ(α), 3 pl. οίατο, fut. άσσεται, aor. opt. άσσαιτο, (τόξον), *shoot with bow at*, τινός, θ 218.

τοξευτῇσι, τοῖς, (τοξεύω), sagittariis, *bowmen, archers*, Ψ 850†.

τοξεύειν (τόξον), sagittas mittere, *shoot*, Ψ 855†.

τόξον, ου, ῳ, (α), ων, οισι(ν), ntr., (τιτύσκομαι, root τυκ, τευχ, τεχ-), *bow*, comm. pl. even of a single bow, either as including entire shooting apparatus, Φ 502, (O 709, sagittarum), or as in its nature pl., consisting of two pieces of horn (of the wild goat, Δ 109) fastened to a middle piece (πῆχυς). The string (νευρή) was fastened at one end of the bow, and had to have the loop at its other end slipped over the other pointed tip (κορώνη) before shooting. Cut No. 37 illustrates the method of stringing the bow ([ἐν] τανύειν); cuts Nos. 67, 96, 97, 111, 133 illustrate the method of shooting (τιταίνειν, (ἀν)έλκειν). Cuts Nos. 27, 130 represent the case for the bow. Archers were little esteemed (in comparison with πρόμαχοι), see κέραι ἀγλαέ, Λ 385, τοξότα. — τόξων, also artis sagittariae, *archery*, B 718, cf. 827.

τοξοσύνῃ, τῇ, (τόξον), *archery*, N 314†.

τοξότᾰ, voc., nom. ότης, (τόξον), *archer*, contemptuously, Λ 385†.

τοξο-φόρῳ, τῇ, (φέρω), *bow-bearing*, epithet of Artemis, Φ 483†.

τοπρίν, see πρίν.

τοπρόσθεν, see πρόσθεν.

τοπρῶτον, see πρῶτον.

τορέω? (τετραίνω), **ἔτορε,** aor., *pierce*, Λ 236†.

τορνόω, mid. aor. **τορνώσαντο,** subj. τορνώσεται, (τόρνος), *round off*, Ψ 255, ε 249.

τός, τοί, see ὁ and ὅς.

τόσ(σ)ος, σ(σ)ον, τόσσοι, ων, ους, η, ης, ην, ῃσι, τόσσας, τόσ(σ)ον, τόσ(σα), also τόσ(σ)ονδε, σσηνδε, σσαδε, and τοσ(σ)οῦτον, τοσαῦτ(α), tantus, *so great, so long, so wide*, etc., pl. tot, *so many;* cf. τρὶς τόσοι; ntr. used alone, *so much, so very*, A 64, Θ 421; with ὅσσον, Φ 370; with ἀλλά, ο 405; so also the forms with -δε, X 41; and -οῦτον, Ψ 476.

τοσσάκι, τοσσάχ' before rough breathing, (τόσος), toties, *so often*, corresponding to ὁσσάκι, quoties, as often, Φ 268.

τόσσος, τοσσοῦτον, see τόσ(σ)ος.

τότε, *at that time, then;* τῶν τότε, of those who *then* lived; freq. in apodosis in phrases, καὶ τότε δή, ῥα, ἔπειτα; esp. after protasis with ὅτε, ὁπότε, ἦμος, ἐπεί, εἰ, etc.; τότε μοι χάνοι εὐρεῖα χθών, Δ 182.

τοτέ = τότε, *at another time, anon*, A 63; usually in answering clauses, τ. μὲν—τ. δέ, modo—modo, *now—then.* (Od.)

τοῦ=gen. (1) of ὁ.—(2) of ὅς.—(3) =τίνος; **τοῦ**, encl.=τινός.

τοὔνεκα=τοῦ ἕνεκα, *on this account, therefore*, Α 291, γ 15.

τοὔνομα=τὸ ὄνομα.

τόφρα, adv., *so long*, in apodosis following ὄφρα, ἕως, ὅτε, πρίν, εὖτε, with δέ, Δ 221; *up to the time* (when), Α 509; *meanwhile*, Ν 83, μ 166.

τρᾰγους, τούς, *goats*, ι 239†.

τρᾰπεζα, ης, ῃ, αν, αι, ας, (τετρά-πεδja, four-footed), *table*, esp. *eating-table*; ξενίη, hospitable board, ξ 158; guests had, as a rule, each his own table, α 111, e. g. the suitors use their tables as shields against Odysseus's arrows; the tables were four-cornered and low, χ 84.

τρᾰπεζῆες, ῆας, pl. from -εύς, κύνες, dogs *fed from their master's table*, Ψ 173, Χ 69, ρ 309.

τραπείομεν, subj. 2 aor. pass. from τέρπω.

τρᾰπέουσι, pres., (τρέπω, torcular), *tread, press*, η 125†.

τραφέμεν, τράφεν, see τρέφω.

τραφερήν, *firm* earth, Ξ 308 and υ 98.

τρεῖς, tres, *three*, Ι 144, δ 409, see σύντρεις.

τρέμε, ipf., tremebat; ὑπὸ δ' ἔτρεμε, ον, *he trembled in* (all) his limbs, Κ 390.

τρέπω, imp. **τρέπε**, ipf. τρέπε(ν), 1 aor. (ἔ)τρέψε(ν), opt. ψειε, part. ψας, 2 aor. (ἔ)τράπε(ν), (torqueo), *turn, bend*, e. g. κεφαλὴν πρός τι, ν 29; ὄσσε ἔς τι, Ν 7; ἀπό τινος, Π 645; πάλιν, retro flectere, Υ 439, ὄσσε, *look away from, avert*; ἵππους, *turn about*, Θ 432; *guide*, νόον; θυμὸν κατὰ πληθύν, turn his fury against the mass; ὁμόσε, Μ 24; with inf., Μ 32; φύγαδε (ἵππους, Θ 157), *betake one's self* to flight, Π 657; τινὰ εἰς εὐνήν, *conduct* to bed; mid. pass. pres. **τρέπεται**, 1 aor. τρεψάμενοι, 2 aor. τράπεθ' = (ἐ)τράπετ(ο), τράποντο, ωνται, pf. part. τετραμμένος, ον, οι, αι, imp. τετράφθω, plupf. τέτραπτο, 3 pl. τετράφαθ' = φατο, aor. pass. τραφθῆναι, *turn, direct one's self*, ἰθύς, straight forward; πρὸς (ἰθύ) οἱ, right toward him, Ξ 403; ἐπὶ οἱ, toward him, Ν 542; to something, ἔς τι; πάλιν τινός, away from one, Σ 138, Φ 468; ἑκάς τινος, far from; ἀν' Ἑλλάδα, versari per Graeciam, *wander up and down* through Greece; *change*, χρώς; νόος, with inf., δ 260.

τρέφω, **τρέφει**, ipf. ἔτρεφον, ες, ε(ν), τρέφον, ε, ον, 1 aor. ἔθρεψε, θρέψ(εν), 2 aor. ἔτραφ(ε), τράφ(ε), Β 661, Φ 279, du. ἐτραφέτην, inf. τραφέμεν, transitive only in Ψ 90; pf. τέτροφε, intr. 1 aor. mid. θρέψαιο, aor. pass. τράφη (ἐτράφημεν, Ψ 84, better read τράφομέν περ), 3 pl. τράφεν, Α 251, Ψ 348, (τέρπω), *feed, nourish*, of animals, Χ 69; of plants, *let grow, tend, produce*, χαίτην, ἀλοιφήν, ἄγρια, φάρμακα; *curdle*, γάλα; of children, *educate, rear*; πῆμα γενέσθαι, with dat., rear to become a curse to some one, Χ 421; Α 414, θρέψαιο, rear for one's self; pass. with pf. and 2 aor. act., *thicken, congeal, stick firmly to*, ψ 237; *wax, grow up*, Ε 555, ξ 201.

τρέχει, aor. iter. θρέξασκον, 2 aor. ἔδραμον, (ε), *run*, of living beings; of auger, *revolve*, ι 386.

τρέω, **τρεῖ**, εἶτ(ε), εἶν, ipf. τρέε, 1 aor. ἔτρεσε, σαν, and τρέσσε, σσαν, αι, άντων, (τρήρων, Trasimenus, terror), in aor., *flee*, ζ 138; Ε 256, τρεῖν μ' οὐκ ἐᾷ Παλλὰς Ἀθήνη; elsewh. *tremble, be afraid*, Ρ 332; *dread*, with acc., Λ 554, Ρ 663. (Il.)

τρήρωνα, ες, ωσι, (τρεῖν), pavidam, *trembling*, only of doves, Χ 140.

τρητοῖο, οἶσι(ν), from (τιτράω), *perforated*, of mooring-stones, *pierced with holes for attaching the cable*; λεχέεσσι, *perforated with holes for the bed-cords*, Ω 720.

Τρηχίν, ῖνα, town in Thessaly, Β 682†.

Τρῆχος, warrior from Aitolia, slain by Hektor, Ε 706†.

τρηχύς, ύν, εἶ(α), είης, εἶαν, (τετρήχει), asper, *rough*, (1) *rugged, jagged*, λίθος, Ε 308.—(2) *stony, rocky*, ἀταρπόν, ἀκτήν, Ἑλικῶνα, Ἰθάκην, ξ 1.

τρίαιναν, τήν, *trident*, with which Poseidon stirs up the sea, and agitates the earth by earthquakes, Μ 27, δ 506.

τριβέμεναι, inf. pres., aor. τρῖψαι, pass. pres. τρίβεσθε, (τείρω, tero), properly *rub*, hence *thresh*, which was done after the Egyptian and Oriental manner represented in the following cut; *rub around in*, or perhaps *plunge* *into*, ι 333; pass., *wear one's self out*, Ψ 735.

τρί-γληνα (γλήνη), epith. of ear-rings, *with three drops* or *pearls* (lit. eyeballs), Ξ 183 and σ 297. (See cut from ancient Greek coin.)

τρι-γλώχῑνι, dat., (γλωχίν, γλῶσσα), *three-barbed*, epith. of arrow, E 393 and Λ 507.

τρί-ετες, ntr. as adv., (Ϝέτος, ἔτος), *three years long*, β 106. (Od.)

τρίζουσαι, pf. τετριγῶτας, ῦια, ῦιαι, plupf. τετρίγει, (stridere, strix), *twitter*, B 314; *squeak*, of birds and bats, ω 5, 7, 9; *gibber*, of souls of departed; of wrestlers' backs, *crack*, Ψ 714.

τριήκοντα, triginta, *thirty*, B 516. (B.)

τριηκόσιοι, κοσίοισιν, κόσι(α), trecenti, *three hundred*, ν 390 and Λ 696.

Τρίκ(κ)η, city in Thessaly, on river Peneios, B 729, Δ 202.

τρί-λλιστος (λίτομαι), *thrice-earnestly prayed for*, Θ 488†.

τρί-πλᾰκᾰ, τήν, *threefold*, Σ 480†.

τρι-πλῆ, *thrice over*, A 128†.

τρί-πολον (colere), *thrice ploughed*, Σ 542, ε 127.

τρί-πος X 164, τρί-πους, ποδος, δι, δα, δες, δων, tripus, *tripod*, a three-footed kettle for warming water, Ψ 702; also served for mixing wine in, and, being often beautifully finished, as prize in gymnastic contests. The Delphic tripod is a favorite subject of representation on ancient reliefs, from one of which the above cut is taken.

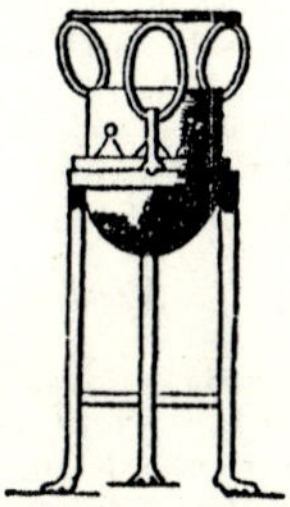

τρί-πτυχος, *triple, consisting of three layers*; meaning, as applied to τρυφάλεια, q. v., not altogether clear, Λ 353†.

τρίς, ter, *thrice*, A 213, γ 245; in Homer already a sacred number, cf. τρίλλιστος; τρὶς **μάκαρες**, *thrice-blessed*, ζ 154.

τρισ-καί-δεκᾰ, tredecim, *thirteen*, E 387; -και-δέκατον, τῃ, tertium decimum, K 495.

τρι-στοιχί, *in three rows*, K 473†.

τρί-στοιχοι, *in three rows*, μ 91†.

τρισ-χί̄λιαι, *three thousand*, Ψ 221†.

τρίτᾰτος, ῳ, ον, οισι, η, ῃ, ην, tertius, *third*, B 565, O 195, δ 97.

Τριτο-γένεια, epith. of Athena, also as proper name, Θ 39, X 183, Δ 515, γ 378; explained by old commentators as meaning *born at the lake Tritonis*, in Libya.

τρί̄τος, ῳ, ον, ων, η, ης, *third*, M 95; τὸ τρίτον, Γ 225, *for the third time*, elsewh. *in the third place*.

τρί̄-χᾰ, *threefold, in three parts*; τρ. νυκτὸς ἔην, a third of the night remained, 'twas in the third watch, μ 312. (Od.)

τρῐχ-ᾱ́ϊκες (θρίξ, ἀίσσω), *with waving, flowing plume*, τ 177†.

τρίχες, pl. from θρίξ.

τριχθά, *in three parts*, B 668, ι 71.

Τροιζήν, ῆνος, fem., town in Argolis, near the shore of Saronic gulf, B 561†.

Τροίζηνος, son of Keas, father of Euphemos, B 847†.

Τροίη, fem., (1) country of Trojans, Trojan plain, Troad, B 162.—(2) its chief town, otherwise Ἴλιος, A 129. [When the word is used to designate the *Troad*, its first syllable occurs in arsis of 1st foot five times, in thesis of 1st foot ten times, in thesis of 2d foot fifty-three times, of 3d nine times, of 4th ten times; when designating the *city*, the 1st syllable stands in thesis of 2d foot ten times, of 3d foot four times.]

Τροίηθε(ν), *from Troja*, Ω 492, γ 257.

Τροίηνδ(ε), *to Troja*, Η 390, Ω 764, γ 268.

τρομέω, **τρομέεις,** *έουσι*, ipf. *ἐτρόμεον*, mid. pres. *εοίατο, έεσθαι*, ipf. *τρομέοντο*, *tremble*, Κ 10, Ο 627, *φρένα*, animo pavere; *τινά, τί*, *dread*, π 446, υ 215; so also mid., also with *φρένες, θυμῷ*.

τρόμος, masc., (*τρέμω*), *tremor*, Γ 34; *shudder*, sickening, ω 49.

τρόπεον, 3 pl. ipf., (*τρέπω*), *were turning about*, Σ 224†.

τροπαί, pl. fem., (*τρόπος*), *ἠελίοιο*, ο 404†, *turning-places, tropics* (yet not in our sense of the word), places where the sun at evening turns about his steeds to return during the night to the east, ready to begin with morning a new day.

τρόπις, **τρόπιος,** *ιν*, fem., (*τρόπος*), *keel*, ε 130. (Od.) (See cut under *δρυόχους, a.*)

τροπός, **τροποῖς,** masc., (*τρέπω*), *thongs* or *straps*, by means of which the oars were attached to the thole-pins, *κληῖδες* (see cut No. 35, *d*), so as to play freely about them, δ 782 and θ 53. A later different arrangement is illustrated in the following cut, and in No. 41.

τροφόεντα, *swelling*, v. l. γ 290.

τροφός, *οῦ, όν*, fem., (*τρέφω*), *nurse*, ρ 31, τ 15.

τροχάω, part. pres. **τροχόωντα,** (*τρόχος*), *ἅμα*, *running about after me*, ο 451†.

τροχός, **τροχοῦ,** *όν*, (*τρέχω*), *wheel* (also *κύκλος, a*), Ζ 42; *potter's wheel*, Σ 600; *round cake of wax* or *tallow*, μ 173, φ 178.

τρυγάω, 3 pl. **τρῠγόωσιν,** opt. *τρυγόῳεν*, *gather, gather the vintage*, η 124, Σ 566.

τρύζητε, subj. pres., *gossip before me, keep dinning into my ears*, Ι 311†.

τρῦπάνῳ, *τῷ*, ntr., (*τρυπάω*), *auger, drill*, used by carpenters in boring wood, and often set in motion by a bow and string, as with us at the present day, ι 385†. (The cut is from an ancient Egyptian representation.)

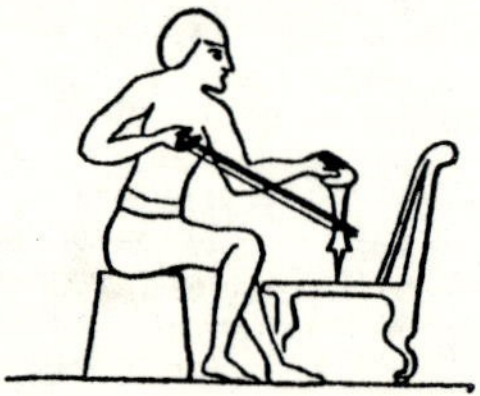

τρῡπῷ (*τρύπη, τείρω*), *bore*, ι 384†.

τρῠφάλεια, *ης, ῃ, αν, αι, ῶν*, (*τρύω, φάλος*), *helmet with crest perforated* to conveniently attach the horse-hair plumes, Γ 376. (Cf. cut on following page and No. 20.)

τροφέω, ipf. mid. **τροφέοντο,** *were swelling*, γ 290†.

τρόφι, ntr., corresponding to *τρόφις*, (*τρέφω*), *swollen, huge, κῦμα*, Λ 307†.

τρῦφος, *τό*, (*θρύπτω*), *fragment*, cf. rupes, from rumpo, δ 508†.

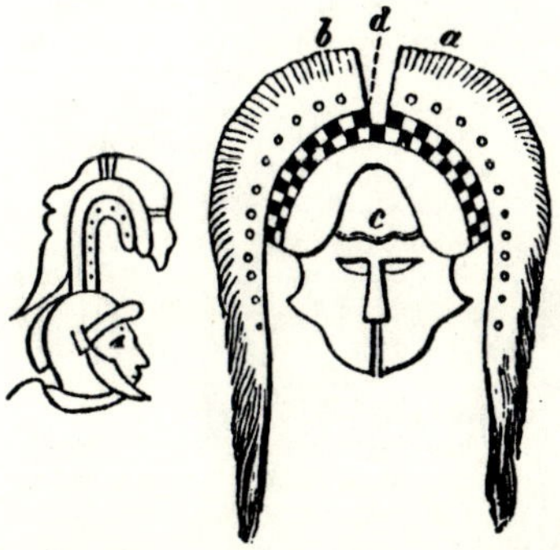

τρῦχουσι, fut. *τρύξοντα*, pass. pres. *τρυχώμεθα, όμενος*, (*τρύω*), *impoverished*, α 288, κ 177; *consume*, *οἶκον*, property.

Τρῳαί, Τρωάς, see Τρῳός.

τρώγειν, *feed upon, browse*, ζ 90†.

Τρῶες, *ώων, ωσί*, and *εσσι(ν)*, *inhabitants of Ilios and of the plain of Troas*, Τρώων πόλις = Ἴλιος; but Α 164, *πτολίεθρον*, one of the Trojan cities.

Τρωιάς, *άδος*, see Τρώιος.

Τρωικός, *κόν*, esp. *πεδίον*, the plain *of Troja*, between Ilios and the sea, Ρ 724, Κ 11.

Τρωίλος, son of Priamos and Hekabe, Ω 257†.

τρώκτης, *αι*, masc., (*τρώγω* ?), *deceiver, knave*, ξ 289 and ο 415.

Τρῳός, adj., (1) from Τρώς, *belonging to Tros*, son of Erichthonios, Π 393, Ψ 291.—(2) from Τρῶες, *belonging to the Trojans, Trojan*, fem. Τρῳαί, *ῇσιν*, Ρ 127, Ε 461; but freq. **Τρῳαί,** Γ 384, Χ 430, 57, Ζ 380, δ 259 = **Τρῳάδες,** *Trojan women*, Ζ 442, Ι 139, Ω 704; gen. also Τρωϊάδων, Σ 122; exc. ν 263, where it is adj. to ληίδος.

τρωπάω, **τρωπῶσα,** (*τρέπω*), *φωνήν*, *change* her note, τ 521; mid. *τρωπᾶσθαι* and *-ῶντο*, ipf., *turn one's self*, *πάλιν*, back, about; *φόβονδε* = *φεύγειν*.

Τρώς, *ωός*, (1) *Tros*, son of Erichthonios, father of Ilos, Assarakos, Ganymedes, Ε 265 sq., Υ 230 sq.—(2) son of Alastor, slain by Achilleus, Υ 463.

τρώσεσθαι, *τρώσῃς*, see *τρώω*.

τρωτός, verbal adjective from *τρώω*, *vulnerable*, Φ 568†.

τρωχάω, only **τρωχῶσι,** ipf. *τρώχων*, (*τρέχω*), *run*, Χ 163, ζ 318.

τρώω, **τρώει,** (*τορέω*), *sting, madden*, φ 293; aor. subj. *τρώσῃ, ητε*, *wound*, fut. mid. *τρώσεσθαι*, *to be wounded*.

τυγχάνω, ipf. **τύγχανε,** fut. *τεύξῃ, εσθαι*, aor. *ἔτυχες, τύχε, ωμι, ῃς, ησι, ῃ, οιμι, οις, ών* and 1 aor. *ἐτύχησε(ν), τύχησε, ήσας*, pf. *τετύχηκε, κώς*, (*τυκ, τύξον, τεκ, τέχνη*), (1) *τινός*, *hit*, (a) with weapon or missile; freq. *τυχών, ήσας*, with *βάλλειν, οὖτα, νύξε*, where the acc. is in each case to be construed with finite verb; *δῶκε*, φ 13; also *κατά* with acc.; (b) general sense, *happen, chance*, Θ 430; (c) *τινός*, *come upon, chance upon* some person or thing, and hence *gain, obtain*, ο 158.—(2) *happen to be, be by chance*, Λ 116, μ 106; *τετυχηκώς*, happening to be, lying, Ρ 748, κ 88; often with part. which in English becomes the principal verb, while the form of *τυγχάνω* is rendered by an adverb, *by chance, just*, etc.; *ἐτύχησε βαλών*, he had *just* hit him, Ο 581; impers., contingit, *fall to one's share*, Λ 684.

Τῡδείδης, *son of* **Τῡδεύς,** *ῆος, έος*, acc. *ῆ*, *Tydeus* is son of Oineus, Ε 813; king in Kalydon in Aitolia, father of Diomedes, Ε 163, Ζ 96; fugitive on account of his uncle's murder, he finds asylum in Argos with Adrestos, whose daughter Deipyle he marries; joins Polyneikes in the expedition against Thebes, where he is slain by Melanippos, Δ 399.

τυκτόν, *ῷ, ήν, ῇσι*, (*τεύχω*), manu factus, *well-made, well-wrought; δάπεδον, well-trodden; κακόν*, a *born* plague.

τύμβῳ, *ον*, masc., (tumulus), *funeral mound*, piled up in conical form over the urn containing the ashes of the deceased, and sometimes of enormous size, e. g. that of Aisyetes, identified with the mound now called Udschek Tepe, and 284 feet high, Δ 177, Η 336.

τυμβο-χόης, *τῆς*, (*χέω*), *the throwing up of a mound* = *funeral mound*, Φ 323† (better so read than *τυμβοχοῆσ(αι)*, for there is no analogy for the elision of *αι*).

Τυνδάρεος, Tyndareos, banished from Sparta, harbored in Aitolia by

Thestios, whose daughter Leda he weds, by Herakles he is reinstated in Sparta. —His children: Klytaimnestra, ω 199; Kastor and Polydeukes, λ 298 sq. (Helena, daughter of Zeus.)

τύνη = σύ.

τυπῇσι, ταῖς, (τύπτω), ictibus, *blow, stroke*, E 887†.

τύπτω, **τύπτετε,** ουσι, ε, ων, ipf. τύπτον, aor. τύψ(εν), ῃ, ον, ας, pass. prs. τυπτομένων, pf. τετυμμένω, aor. ἐτύπη, τυπείης, είς, *strike, cut, thrust, wound*, τινά, (on any part, τί, λαιμόν, or κατὰ γαστέρα), σχεδίην, in hand-to-hand encounter; fig. τὸν ἄχος κατὰ φρένα τύψε βαθεῖαν, sorrow *struck* deep into his soul, T 125; τύπη, with acc. ὅσσα, quot vulnera accepit. Freq. ἅλα τύπτον ἐρετμοῖς, *they were beating* (in time) the sea with their oars (see cut under ἱστίον, and No. 41); Ψ 754, *trod in* his (Ajax's) footsteps; λαίλαπι, *lashing* with the tempest.

τῡρός, **τυροῦ,** ῷ, όν, du. ώ, pl. ῶν, masc., *cheese*, δ 88; αἴγειος, cheese of goat's milk, Λ 639.

Τυρώ, *Tyro*, daughter of Salmoneus, wife of Kretheus, β 120, λ 235; mother of Pelias and Neleus by Poseidon.

τυτθός, όν, ά, *little, small, young*, X 480 and α 435, *little boy;* with διατμήξας and κεάσαιμι, hew or split up *small;* ntr. as adv., *a little*, local with ὀπίσσω, μετόπισθεν, ἐδεύησεν, it lacked *little*, ι 540; modal: ἔτισεν, φθέγγεσθαι, *low;* temporal only T 335.

τυφλόν, *blind*, Z 139†.

Τυφωεύς, έος, έι B 782, *Typhoeus*, a monster under whose form the operations of subterranean fire are symbolized.

τυχήσας, see τυγχάνω.

Τῠχίος (τεύχω), from Hylai in Boiotia, H 220†, the maker of Ajax's shield.

τῶ (τῷ), (1) *then*, α 239, γ 258, θ 467. —(2) *therefore*, θ 226, 548, ν 248, 331, ξ 67, π 445, σ 141, τ 259, Φ 190.

τώς = οὕτως, *thus*, B 330, Γ 415, τ 234.

Υ.

Ὑάδες (ὕω), *Hyades*, seven stars in the head of the Bull, whose rising marks the beginning of the rainy season, Σ 486†. The popular etymology of the word derived it from ὗς, and the Romans taking up this derivation called them Suculae, *Piglings*.

ὑᾰκινθίνῳ, *hyacinthine-colored* = *dark-colored, black*, ζ 231 and ψ 158. [ῠ]

ὑάκινθον, masc., Ξ 348†, *hyacinth*, not the same as ours, possibly the *larkspur*.

Ὑάμ-πολις, town on the river Kephisos in Phokis, B 521†.

ὑβ-βάλλειν, see ὑπο-βάλλω.

ὑβρίζεις, ων, οντες, (ὕβρις), *be insolent* or *arrogant*, α 227; trans. τινά, *insult, outrage*, υ 370, Λ 695; λώβην, *perpetrate wantonly*, υ 170.

ὕβρις, ιος, ει, ιν, fem., (ὑπέρ), superbia, *insolence, arrogance*, A 203, 214, *violence*. (Od.)

ὑβρισταί, άων, ῇσι, masc., (ὑβρίζω), *overbearing, violent, wicked persons*, N 633. (Od.)

ὑγιής (vegetus), *healthful, salutary, useful*, Θ 524†.

ὑγρόν, ήν, ά, *moist;* also of ὕδωρ, δ 458, *liquid;* ἔλαιον, *limpid*, ζ 79; κέλευθα, *watery* ways = *the sea;* ὑγρήν, subst. *the waters*, opp. τραφερήν, Ξ 308, α 97, δ 709, ε 45; ntr. ἀέντες, humide flantes, blowing *moist* or *rainy*, ε 478.

ὑδᾰτο-τρεφέων, gen. pl. from -ής, (τρέφω), *growing by the water*, ρ 208†.

Ὕδη, town on Mount Tmolos in Lydia, later Sardes? Υ 385†. [ῠ]

ὑδραίνομαι, aor. part. **ὑδρηνᾰμένη,** (ὕδωρ), *bathe, wash one's self*, δ 750. (Od.)

ὑδρεύοντο, ipf., (ὕδωρ), *were wont to draw water*, ὅθεν, η 131; act. ὑδρευούσῃ, κ 105.

ὑδρηλοί (ὕδωρ), irrigui, *moist, well-watered*, λειμῶνες, meadows, ι 133†.

ὕδρου, του, (ὕδωρ), hydrae, *water-snake*, B 723†.

ὕδωρ, ατος, ι, τ(α), ntr., (udus, unda), *water*, ἁλμυρόν, salt water; μέλαν, of water of springs, rivers, and sea, when the surface is rippled, and thus, the reflection of the sun's rays being hindered, it assumes a dark color, δ 359; ὑγρόν, flowing, liquid; αἰενάοντα, never failing; ὑ. καὶ γαῖα γένοισθε, H 99, = become dust and ashes. [ῠ, in arsi ῡ.]

ὑετόν, τόν, (ὕω), *shower*, imbrem, M 133†.

υἱός (Gothic sunus, Ger. sohn), declined from three stems, ΥΙΟ-, οῦ, ῷ, όν, έ, ῶν, οἷσι; ΥΙ-, gen. υἷος, υἷϊ, υἷα, du. υἷε; υἷες, υἱάσι, υἷας; ΥΙΕΥ-, gen. υἱέος, έϊ, έα, έες, έας, εῖς E 464, *son*, in pl. υἷες Ἀχαιῶν = Ἀχαιοί. [υἱός, όν, έ, in thesi often to be pronounced ὑός, όν, έ, Δ 473; voc. υἱέ with lengthened ε, Δ 338.]

υἱωνός, οῖο, οί, masc., (υἱός), *grandson*, B 666, ω 514.

ὑλαγμόν, τόν, (ὑλάω), *barking, howling*, Φ 575†. [ῠ]

Ὑλᾰκίδης, Κάστωρ, name invented for himself by Odysseus, ξ 204†.

ὑλᾰκόμωροι (ὑλάω), *loud-barking*, ξ 29 and π 4. [ῡ]

ὑλάκτει, εον, ipf., (ὑλακτέω, ὑλάω), *bark, bay*, Σ 586; κραδίη (growled with wrath), υ 13, 16. [ῠ]

ὑλάω, **ὑλάει, ουσι**, ipf. ὕλαον = ὑλάοντο, (ululare), *bark, bay; τινά, bark at*, π 5. (Od.) [ῠ]

ὕλη, ης, ῃ, ην, (for σύλη, solum, saltus?), (1) silva, *wood*, ι 234; *felled timber, wood for burning; clump of trees, grove*, ε 63; *forest*, freq.; *foliage*, ξ 353.—(2) *stuff* of which any thing is made, *raw material* (willow withes), ε 257. [ῡ]

Ὕλη, town in Boiotia, E 708, H 221, B 500.

ὑλήεις, εντι, τα = ὑλήενθ', ήεσσα, ης, ῃ, αν, (ὕλη), *wooded*, α 186; as comm. gender, α 246.

Ὕλλος, branch of the Hermos in Lydia, Υ 392†.

ὑλο-τόμοι, ους, (τομή), *cutting* or *felling wood*, axe, Ψ 114; *woodmen*, Ψ 123. [ῡ]

ὑμεῖς, είων, ὑμέων, with synizesis; ὑμῖν, ὕμιν, (ῡμιν), ὑμέας dissyll., parallel forms **ὕμμες**, ὑμμ(ιν), acc. ὕμμε, vos, vestri, etc. [ῡ]

ὑμέναιος, *wedding song, bridal song*, πολύς, varied, Σ 493†. [ῠ]

ὑμέτερος, ου, ον, ων, οισι(ν), ους; ης, ῃ, ῃσι, ον, (Ψ 86, ὄνδε, to *your house*), vester, *your, yours*, etc., also joined with αὐτῶν, ipsorum, *your*selves; ἑκάστου, of each one *of you*, P 226. [ῡ]

ὕμμε, ες, ι, see ὑμεῖς.

ὕμνον, τόν, (ὑφή), *strain, melody*, θ 429†.

ὑμός, only the forms, **ὑμή**, N 815; ὑμήν, E 489; ὑμά, α 375, *your*. [ῡ]

ὕπ-αγον, ε, ipf., also in tmesi, Ψ 300; as also aor., Ψ 294, ἤγαγεν, *bring* or *lead under*; ζυγόν, under the yoke, also with simple verb, *yoke, put to*; Λ 163, ἐκ—, *withdraw*.

ὑπ-αείδω, only ipf. **ὑπὸ ἄειδεν**, and aor. ἄεισεν, *accompany with voice*, Σ 570; *sang under* his hand, as he drew and let go of the bow-string, φ 411.

ὑπαί, see ὑπό.

ὕπαιθα, adv., *out from under, sidewise*, O 520; τινός, *sidewise away, at one's side*, Σ 421. [ῠ]

ὑπ-ᾱΐξει, fut., (from ἀίσσω), φρῖχ' = φρῖκα, *shall dart up under* the surface-ripple, Φ 126; aor. part. ᾱΐξας βωμοῦ, *shooting out from under* the altar, B 310.

ὑπ-ᾰκούει, aor. ὑπάκουσεν, σαι, *give ear to*, ξ 485; *reply*, κ 83, δ 283; Θ 4, ὑπὸ ἄκουον, auscultabant; π 10, ποδῶν ὕπο, (proceeding) from the feet *I hear* a noise = I hear footsteps.

ὑπ-ᾰλευάμενος, aor. part., (ἀλεύω), evitans, *avoiding, evading*, ο 275†.

ὑπ-ᾰλυξις, ιν, fem., (ἀλύσκω), *escape*, X 270 and ψ 287.

ὑπ-ᾰλύσκω, aor. **ὑπάλυξε(ν), ύξαι, ας**, (ἀλεύω), *escape, avoid*, Κῆρας; in tmesi, N 395, ψ 332; χρείως, *evade* (the payment) of his debt, θ 355.

ὑπ-αντιάσας, part. aor., (ἀντιάω), obviam factus, *having placed himself (before him)* for his defense, Z 17†.

ὕπᾰρ, ntr., *actuality, real appearance*, τ 547 and υ 90. [ῠ]

ὑπ-άρχω, aor. subj. **ὑπάρξῃ**, (so right requires), if one *have once made a beginning*, ω 286†.

ὑπ-ασπίδια (ἀσπίς), ntr. pl., used as

adv. = ὑπ ἀσπίδι, *under shelter of the shield*, προποδίζων, N 158; προβιβῶντος, Π 609.

ὕπᾰτος, ον, ε, ῳ, sup., in form from ὑπό, in meaning more nearly allied to ὑπέρ, cf. summus for sup-mus, κρειόντων, *highest*, *most exalted*, of rulers; μήστωρα, *sovereign* counsellor; θεῶν, of Zeus; πυρῇ, on the top of the pyre, Ψ 165.

ὑπ-έασι, see ὕπ-ειμι.

ὑπ-έ(δ)δεισαν, see ὑπο-δείδω.

ὑπ-έδεκτο, see ὑπο-δέχομαι.

ὑπ-εθερμάνθη, see ὑπο-θερμαίνω.

ὑπ-είκω, **ὑπο-ϝείκειν,** imp. **ὑπόεικε,** opt. εἴκοι, in tmesi, ipf. -εικον, fut. εἴξω, ομεν in Δ 62 may be aor. subj., aor. -ειξε, fut. mid. -είξομαι, εαι; everywhere with ϝ, ὑπο-ϝ., exc. ὑπείξομαι μ 117, (Ger. weichen, Eng. weak), cedere, *retire, withdraw* from—, τινός; τῷ, π 42, for, before him; χεῖρας, *escape*, elsewh. τινί, *yield*, Δ 62, Υ 266; with part. *make way for;* with dat. of advantage, Ψ 602; Ο 211, influenced by dread.

ὕπ-ειμι, 3 pl. **ὑπ-έασι,** ipf. ὑπῆσαν, in tmesi, ὑπὸ ἦεν α 131, (εἰμί), *be under*, ποσίν, a footstool *was below*, for his feet; πολλοῖσι, many *had under them* sucking foals, Λ 681.

ὑπείρ and ὑπειρ-, see ὑπέρ and ὑπερ-.

Ὑπείρ-οχος, a Trojan, slain by Odysseus, Λ 335†.

Ὑπειρ-οχίδης, *son of Hypeirochos*, Itymoneus, Λ 673†.

Ὑπείρων, ονα, a Trojan, slain by Diomedes, E 144†.

ὑπ-έκ, before vowels ὑπέξ, adv., *out from under*, freq. with gen., N 89, P 581, Σ 232.

ὑπ-εκ-προ-θέει, θέων, οντα, (θέω), praecurrere, *run on before; τυτθόν*, paullo, a little; τόσσον, as much; with acc., *outruns*, I 506.

ὑπ-εκ-προ-έλῡσαν, aor. from λύω, *loose from under* (the yoke), *put out*, ἀπήνης, ζ 88†.

ὑπ-εκ-προ-ρέει, *flows forth from* the depth below, ζ 87†.

ὑπ-εκ-προ-φύγοιμι, ών, aor., (φεύγω), fuga evadere, *escape by flight*, υ 43; Χάρυβδιν, μ 113.

ὑπεκσαόω, aor. **ὑπ-εξ-εσάωσε,** (σαόω), *save from under*, *rescue*, Ψ 292†.

ὑπέκ-φερον γ 496, and ὑπ-εξ-έφερον, ε, *raise slightly*, Θ 268; τινὰ πολέμοιο, *carry out secretly;* γ 496, *bear forward;* tmesi, Ο 628, φέρονται, pass.

ὑπ-έκ-φῠγον, ες, ε(ν), ῃ, οι, οιμεν, έειν, (φεύγω), also ὑπ-εξ-έφῠγον, εν (φεύγω), *escape secretly*, *come safely forth from*, τι, Π 687; tmesis, τινός, (Il.), N 89.

ὑπ-εμνήμυκε, see ὑπ-ημύω.

ὑπ-ένερθε(ν), opp. καθ-ύπερθεν, adv., *beneath*, Δ 186; *below*, N 30; *in the lower world*, Γ 278; with gen., *underneath*, B 150.

ὑπέξ, see ὑπ-έκ.

ὑπ-εξ-ᾰγάγοι, and in tmesi, ἀγάγωμεν, Υ 300; *bring safely forth*, *rescue*, σ 147.

ὑπ-εξ-ᾰλέασθαι, aor. inf., (ἀλεύω), *avoid*, *shun*, χεῖρας, Ο 180†.

ὑπ-εξ-ᾰνᾰ-δύς, aor. part., (-δύομαι), *emerging from under* the sea, ἁλός, N 352†.

ὑπέρ, ὑπείρ, following its word ὕπερ, super, *over*, (ὑπό), I. with gen., (1) local: *over*, *across*, Ο 382, οὐδοῦ; supra, *above; γαίης*, κεφαλῆς, *at his head*, B 20; *beyond*, τάφρου.—(2) in derived sense, *for*, *in defense of*, ῥέζειν, τι, H 449; with verbs of praying, *by*, *for the sake of*, per, Ω 466; like περί, de, *concerning*, Z 524.—II. with acc., (1) local: *over*, *beyond*, E 851; 339, *along* the surface of the hand.—(2) *beyond*, and hence *in opposition to*, *against*, αἶσαν, μοῖραν, θεόν, invito fato, deo, α 34.

ὑπερ-ᾱέϊ, dat. from -αής, (ἄημι), *loud-roaring*, Λ 297†.

ὑπερ-άλλομαι, aor. -**ᾱλτο,** ἅλμενον, (salio), *spring over*, αὐλῆς, E 138; στίχας, Υ 327.

ὑπερ-βαίνω, aor. βη, 3 pl. βᾰσαν, subj. βήῃ, aor. ἐβήσετο, tmesis, ν 63; transcendere, *step over*, ψ 88; I 501, *transgress*.

ὑπερ-βάλλω, aor. **βᾰλε,** έειν, Ψ 637; ipf. ὑπειρ-έβαλον, *cast beyond; σήματα*, all the marks; ἄκρον, over the crest of the hill; gen. only Ψ 847, τινὰ δουρί, *excel* in throwing the spear.

ὑπέρ-βασαν, 3 pl. aor. from -βαίνω.

ὑπερ-βᾰσίης, ῃ, ην, αι, ας, (βαίνω), *transgression*, *violence*, Γ 107, Π 18.

ὑπερ-βήῃ, aor. subj. from -βαίνω.

ὑπέρ-βῐος, ον, (βία), superbus,

lawless, wanton, α 368, ὕβριν; θυμός, *abrupt*, ο 212; ntr., *insolently*, π 315.

ὑπερ-δέā for δεέα, from δεής, [synizesis δjā], (δέομαι), having *very scanty* forces, Ρ 330†.

Ὑπέρεια, fem., (1) former abode of Phaiakes, near the island of the Kyklopes, ζ 4.—(2) spring in Pelasgian Argos, Ζ 457, Β 734.

ὑπ-ερείπω, aor. **ἤριπε**, *sank under* him, Ψ 691†.

ὑπ-έρεπτε, ipf., (ἐρέπτω), κονίην ποδοῖιν, *was washing away* the sand *under* his feet, Φ 271†.

ὑπερ-έσχεθον, aor. from -έχω.

ὑπερ-έχω, ipf., (**ὑπείρ-**), **εχε(ν)**, ον, aor. ἔσχε(θε), τε, σχῃ, σχοι, *hold up, above*, τί; ἡφαίστοιο, over the fire, χεῖρα(ς) τινι and τινος, *protect*, Δ 249, Ι 420; Γ 210, *overtopped* by his broad shoulders those who stood by; *rise*, of sun and stars.

ὑπέρας, τάς, (ὑπέρ), *braces* attached to the yards, by which the sails are shifted, ε 260†. (See cuts Nos. 40, 48.)

ὑπερ-ηνορέων, **ηνορέοντος**, τες, των, τας, (ἠνορέη), *tyrannical, oppressive*, esp. of the suitors of Penelope; *overbearing*, Δ 176, Ν 258. (Od.)

Ὑπερ-ήνωρ, ορος, son of Panthoos, slain by Menelaos, Ξ 516, Ρ 24. [ῠ]

Ὑπερησίη, fem., town in Achaia, Β 573, ο 254. [ῠ]

ὑπερη-φᾰνέοντες, pl. part., (φαίνω), superbi, *exulting, arrogant*, Λ 694†.

ὕπερθε(ν), adv., (ὑπέρ), *from above*, Υ 62; *above*, Β 218, Μ 55.

ὑπερ-θρώσκω, fut. **θορέονται**, aor. θορον, *spring over*, τι, Θ 179, Ι 476.

ὑπέρ-θῡμος, οιο, ον, οι, οισι, ους, (θυμός), *high-spirited, high-hearted*, of heroes, Trojans, giants, Ε 376, Ο 135, Ζ 111, η 59.

ὑπερ-θύριον, ntr., (θύρη), *lintel of a door*, opp. οὐδός, η 90†.

ὑπερ-ίημι, fut. **ήσει**, *will throw beyond* (this mark), θ 198†.

ὑπερ-ικταίνοντο, ipf., *stumbled from haste*, ψ 3†.

Ὑπεριονίδης, αο μ 176, and **Ὑπερίων**, ονος, epith. of Helios, Θ 480, Τ 398, α 8, μ 176.

ὑπερ-κᾰτᾰ-βαίνω, fut. **βήσεται**, with gen., *leap over, surmount*, Ο 382; τεῖχος, Ν 50.

ὑπερ-κύδαντας, acc. pl., (κῦδος), *of high renown*, Δ 66, 71.

ὑπερ-μενέοντες (μένος), *haughty*, τ 62†.

ὑπερ-μενής, **μενέϊ**, έα, έων, (μένος), *high-spirited* (or *courageous?*), Κρονίωνι, Διί, βασιλήων, Θ 236; ἐπικούρων, Ρ 362.

ὑπέρ-μορον has often been considered as adj., better separated, ὑπὲρ μόρον, *against fate*, more than is appointed by fate; in Β 155, really adj. used as adv. = ὑπὲρ μόρον.

ὑπερ-οπλίῃσι, ταῖς, (ὑπέροπλος), *presumption, arrogance*, Α 205†.

ὑπερ-οπλίσσαιτο, opt. aor. from -οπλίζομαι, *vanquish by force of arms*, ρ 268†.

ὑπέρ-οπλον, ntr., (ὅπλον or πέλω?), *arrogantly*, εἰπεῖν, Ο 185 and Ρ 170.

(ὑπερ-) **ὑπείρ-οχον**, (ἔχω), *eminent*, Ζ 208. (Il.)

ὑπερ-πέτομαι, aor. **πτατο**, *flew over*, Ν 408; θ 192, *flew past* (the marks of all).

ὑπ-ερράγη, aor. from ὑπο-ρρήγνυμι.

ὑπέρ-σχῃ, οι, see ὑπερ-έχω.

ὑπέρτᾰτος, sup. from ὑπέρ, *on the top, aloft*, Μ 381 and Ψ 451.

ὑπερτερίῃ, τῇ, (ὑπέρτερος), *upper part, awning, wagon-cover*, ζ 70† (others interpret as meaning *basket, crate*).

ὑπέρτερος, ον, α, comp. from ὑπέρ, *outer* (flesh), i. e. about the bone, opp. σπλάγχνα, γ 65 (Od.); *better, higher, more excellent* (Il.), Λ 786.

ὑπερ-φίᾰλος, ον, οι, ων, οισι(ν), ους, adv. ως, (ὑπερ-φυής), *overgrown*, cf. ferox, i. e. *mighty, courageous*, Ε 881; also in bad signif., *arrogant, insolent*; adv. *exceedingly, excessively*, Ν 293; insolenter, δ 663.

ὑπ-έρχομαι, aor. **ἤλυθε**, ἤλθετε, ἔλθῃ, subire, *go under, enter*, with acc., ε 476; incessit, *steal upon, seize upon*, Τρῶας (γυῖα) τρόμος, Η 215.

ὑπ-ερώησαν, *started back*, Θ 122. (Il.)

ὑπερ-ῴην, τήν, (cf. παρ-ειή), oris, *palate*, Χ 495†.

ὑπερ-ῷον, ίῳ, ῷια, and ὑπερῷ(α), ntr., *upper chamber* over the women's apartment, occupied during day and night by women and daughters of the house (not by servants), Β 514, ρ 101;

ὑπερωΐοθεν, *from the upper chamber*, α 328.

ὑπ-έστην, see ὑφ-ίστημι, mid.

ὑπ-έχω, aor. **ἔσχεθε,** *held out under* (the hand of him who offered the lot), Η 188; ὑποσχών, supponens, *putting under*, i. e. *getting with foal*, Ε 269.

ὑπ-ημύω, pf. **εμνήμῦκε,** *is* utterly (πάντα) *bowed down*, Χ 491†.

ὑπ-ήνεικαν, aor. from ὑπο-φέρω.

ὑπ-ηνήτῃ, τῷ, (ὑπήνη), *getting a beard*, κ 279 and Ω 348.

ὑπ-ηοῖοι, οίη, (ἠώς), *toward morning*, matutini, adj., = adv., Θ 530, δ 656.

ὑπ-ισχνέομαι, see ὑπ-ίσχομαι.

ὑπ-ίσχομαι, εται, όμεναι, ipf. ἔσχεο, ετο, ὑσχωμαι, ηται, ωνται, εο, ἐσθαι, όμενος, οι, (ἔχω), *take upon one's self, undertake*, μέγα ἔργον; *promise*, τινί τι; with inf., Ζ 93, 274; often also with fut. inf., Χ 114; θυγατέρα, *betroth, vow*, with acc. and inf., θ 347; Β 112, Ι 19, the part. may be read as elided dat.

ὕπνος, οιο, ου, ῳ, ον, masc., (sopor, somnus), *sleep*, relaxing the limbs, ambrosial, Β 19; νήδυμος, fast, deep sleep; ἡδέι, Δ 131; μαλακῷ, Κ 2; ὕπνον ἀωτεῖς, Κ 159; poured over the eyes of mortals; lies upon the eyelids, Κ 187. Personified, **Ὕπνος,** *Sleep*, the brother of death, Ξ 231; his sway extends over gods and men, Ξ 233.

ὑπνώοντας, part., τούς, (ὑπνόω), dormientes, *sleeping*, Ω 344, ε 48.

ὑπό, ancient locative **ὑπαί,** Κ 376 and freq., (ὕπαιθα, sub), I. adv. (1) local: *below, beneath*, Υ 37, Ε 74, Φ 270, Η 6, Φ 364, Λ 635, α 131; *down*, Α 434, Γ 217, Χ 491.—(2) causal: *there-under, there-by*, θ 380, Τ 362 sq.—II. prep. A. with acc. (1) of motion, *to* (a position) *under*, with verbs of motion, Δ 279, λ 155, 253, Χ 144, 195, Ω 274, *below*, around the end of the bolt; *under* (without idea of motion), in locating wounds, etc., Ε 67, Ν 388, 652 (the gen. in like signif., Η 12, Λ 578, Ν 412, etc.); *near by, before*, Ἴλιον, Β 216; Τροίην, δ 146.—(2) of extension *under*, χ 362, β 181, Τ 259, η 130, Γ 371, Χ 307, *down under* his thigh; also of extension in time, *during*, Π 202, Χ 102.—B. with dat., local: (1) of rest, *under*, Β 866, 307, ξ 533; sub muris, Φ 277, Ψ 81, Σ 244 (usually with gen. with λύειν, Θ 543, δ 39); of position with reference to parts of body, Ξ 236, θ 522, Ψ 265, ο 469.—(2) motion (properly locative of aim), esp. with τιθέναι, πελάζω, ἐρείδω, κλίνω, Ξ 240, Β 44.—(3) instrumental, causal: *under, by*, Β 784, Γ 13; χερσί (δαμείς, etc., Β 860, Ψ 675), ω 97, Ο 289, Ν 816; δουρί, Δ 479, Ε 653; σκήπτρῳ, Ζ 159; τινί, Ν 668, ρ 252, Π 490; flee *before*, Ε 93; with τίκτειν, *by* some one; λαίλαπι, etc., Π 384, δ 295, λ 135, δ 402, *under* the breath; χ 445, *under* the sway of the suitors; η 68, *in subjection to* their husbands.—C. with gen., (1) of situation, *under*, Θ 14, Π 375, Α 501, ὑπ' ἀνθερεῶνος, taking hold *under* the chin; also with verbs of wounding specifying the part, Δ 106, Ν 412, 671, 177.—(2) *under*, i. e. *forth from under, out from under*, Θ 543, δ 39, η 5, Ρ 224, 235; flee *before*, Φ 22, 553, Θ 149, Ν 153.—(3) causal: Β 465, Ξ 285, Φ 318, Β 268; *through*, ι 66, Ζ 134, κ 78; with verbs of moving, calling, under the hands, at the shout, Π 277, Γ 61, Ζ 73, Υ 498, Ν 27, Γ 128, Ν 334; with part., Δ 423, Μ 74, cf. Π 591; for the attendant circumstance, *under, amid*, Σ 492; *for*, ὑπὸ δείους, Κ 376, Ο 4, β 110, ω 146. [Often with accent thrown back, by anastrophe, when following its word.]

ὑπο-βάλλω, inf. **ὑβ-βάλλειν,** ipf. ὑπέβαλλε, *lay underneath*, κ 353; *interrupt*, Τ 80.

ὑπο-βλήδην, adv., (ὑποβάλλω), interpellando, *interrupting*, Α 292†.

ὑπό-βρῦχα, acc., (βρέχω), θῆκε κῦμα, the wave buried him *under water*, ε 319†.

ὑπὸ δαῖον, ipf., (δαίω, δαΐς), *kindle under*, Σ 347.

ὑπο-δάμνημι, mid. 2 sing. prs. **δάμνᾶσαι,** *thou subjectest thyself*, γ 214 and π 95.

ὑπο-δέγμενος, see ὑπο-δέχομαι.

ὑπο-δείδω (from δϝείδω), aor. **-έδεισαν,** imp. δείσατε, part. σας, ασα, αντες, pf. δείδια, plupf. ἐδείδισαν, *fear, shrink under*, κ 296; τινά, Σ 199, Χ 282; τί, Ψ 446, β 66.

ὑπο-δεξίη, fem., (δέχομαι), *hospitable welcome*, Ι 73†.

ὑπο-δέχομαι, fem. **δέξομαι,** εαι, aor. εδέξατο, aor. sync. 2 sing. -έδεξο, 3 sing. έδεκτο, inf. δέχθαι, part. δέγμενος, *receive,* I 480, so freq. with πρόφρων, gladly, οἴκῳ; κόλπῳ, in her bosom (of Thetis as personifying the sea); βίας, *receive in silence, endure; promise,* β 387.

ὑπὸ δέω, aor. **ἐδήσατο,** always in tmesi, ποσσὶ . . . πέδιλα, *bound* the sandals *under his* feet, B 44.

ὑποδήματα, τά, (ὑποδέω), that which is *bound underneath* (the foot), *sandal,* of simplest form, ο 369, σ 361.

ὑπο-δμηθεῖσα, see -δάμνημι.

ὑπο-δμώς (δάμνημι), *underling,* δ 386†.

ὑπό-δρα (δράκων), *askance, fiercely, grimly,* ἰδών, B 245, θ 165; δεινά, O 13.

ὑπο-δράω, **-δρώωσι,** ministrant, *wait upon,* ο 333†.

ὑπο-δρηστῆρες, οἱ, (ὑπο-δράω), *attendants,* ο 330†.

ὑπο-δύομαι, fut. **δύσεαι,** aor. εδύσετο and -έδῡ, δῦσα, δύντε, tmesis, ἔδυσαν, ἐδύσετο, *plunge under,* τί, Σ 145; *slip into,* θάμνους; subire, *go under to carry, take on one's shoulders;* πᾶσιν γόος, grief *penetrated* all; with gen., emergere sub, *emerge from,* θάμνων; κακῶν, *escape from* misfortune.

ὑπό-εικε, etc., see ὑπ-είκω.

ὑπο-ζεύγνυμι, fut. **ζεύξω,** *put under the yoke, harness,* ο 81†.

ὑπο-θερμαίνω, aor. pass. **εθερμάνθη,** *was warmed,* Π 333 and Υ 476.

Ὑπο-θῆβαι, town in Boiotia, B 505†.

ὑποθημοσύνῃσι, ταῖς, (τίθημι), *suggestion, counsels,* O 412 and π 233.

ὑπο-θωρήσσω, ipf. mid. **-εθωρήσσοντο,** (θώρηξ), *were arming themselves,* Σ 513†.

ὑπὸ ἔκαμψαν, aor. from κάμπτω, prep. belong. to γλώχινι, *bent under* (itself) the end of the yoke-strap, Ω 274†.

ὑπὸ κεῖται, *lies below;* ὑπό is adv., Φ 364†.

ὑπὸ κεκάδοντο, see -χάζομαι.

ὑπο κινέω, aor. **κινήσαντος,** not a compound; Ζεφύρου ὕπο, *under the impulse of* the soft-blowing Zephyros, Δ 423†.

ὑπο-κλίνω, aor. pass. **εκλίνθη** σχοίνῳ, *he lay down* in the rushes, ε 463†.

ὑπο-κλονέεσθαι (κλονέω) Ἀχιλῆι, *to crowd themselves together in flight before,* Φ 556†.

ὑπο-κλοπέοιτο (κλοπέω, κλώψ), *conceal one's self under* any thing, χ 382†.

ὑπο-κρίνονται, aor. κρίναιτο, imp. κριναι, inf. ασθαι, *answer,* τινί, H 407; *interpret,* ὄνειρον, ὧδε, M 228, cf. ο 170, τ 535, E 150.

ὑπο-κρύπτω, aor. pass. **-εκρύφθη,** *be hidden* in spray, O 626†.

ὑπό-κυκλον, *with wheels* (κύκλα) *underneath, wheeled,* δ 131†.

ὑπο-κύομαι, aor. part. **κυσαμένη,** *having conceived,* Z 26; so also of animals, mares, Υ 225.

ὑπὸ ἔλλαβε, with τρόμος, not a compound; ὑπό, adv., *underneath,* i. e. *in* his limbs, or causal, *from, at the sight.*

ὑπο-λείπω, ipf. **ἔλειπον,** *leave over,* π 50; mid. ἐλείπετο, fut. **λείψομαι,** *remain,* αὐτοῦ, ρ 276.

ὑπο-λευκαίνονται, pass., (λευκός), subalbescunt, chaff heaps *whiten,* or perh. better as two words, *grow white below,* i. e. on the ground, E 502†.

ὑπ' ὀλίζονες, not a compound; ὑπό, adv., *close by* them were the soldiers, *on a smaller scale,* Σ 519†.

ὑπο-λύω, ipf. **ἔλυεν** Ψ 513, aor. ἔλυσα, σε, (also in tmesi), aor. mid. ελύσαο, 2 aor. ἐλυντο, *loose from under, unyoke,* δ 39; *make limbs sink under* one, γυῖα, Π 805; γούνατα, O 291; *make fail,* μένος, Z 27; *paralyze by a (deadly) wound,* freq. = *slay in battle; secretly set free,* A 401.

ὑπο-μένω, aor. **ἔμεινα,** ε(ν), αν, αι, *remain,* with inf., for one to know him, α 410; ἐρωήν, *sustain;* τινά (Il.), *withstand,* E 498, P 25.

ὑπο-μιμνήσκω, fut. part. **μνήσουσα,** aor. ἐμνησεν, τινά τινος, *to remind,* ο 3; *put in mind of,* α 321†.

ὑπο-μνάομαι, ipf. **ἐμνάασθε,** γυναῖκα, *have wooed illicitly,* χ 38†.

ὑπο-νήϊον, *lying under Mount* Νήϊον, γ 81†.

ὑπο-πεπτηῶτες, see -πτήσσω.

ὑπο-περκάζουσιν (περκνός). *begin to turn, grow dark,* of grapes, η 126†.

ὑπο-πλακίῃ, situated under Mount Πλάκος, Θήβη, Z 397†.

ὑπὸ πετάννυμι, aor. part. **πετάσσας,** *spreading out underneath,* α 130†.

ὑπο-πτήσσω, pf. part. **πεπτηῶτες,** *having crouched down timidly under and hidden themselves amid* the leaves, πετάλοις, B 312†.

ὑπ-όρνυμι, 2 aor. **ὦρορε** Μοῦσα, in so moving strains *did* the muse *begin*, ω 62; but 1 aor. ὦρσε, Ψ 108, *excited;* 2 aor. mid. ὦρτο, a desire to weep *was roused*, π 215.

ὑπο-ρρήγνυμι, aor. **-ρραγη** (for ϝράγη), the limitless ether *is cleft in twain*, οὐρανόθεν αἰθήρ, Π 300 = Θ 558.

ὑπό-ρρηνον (ϝρήν), *having a lamb under her*, K 216†.

ὑπο-σσείουσι (σείω, σϝι), *whirl around*, (laying hold) *below*, ι 385†; in Ξ 285, ὕπο belongs to ποδῶν, under their feet.

ὑπο-σταίη, στάς, see ὑφ-ίστημι.

ὑπο-σταχύοιτο (στάχυς), *wax gradually like the ears of corn, increase*, υ 212†.

ὑπο-στεναχίζω, ipf. **ἐστενάχιζε**, Διί, *groaned under* Zeus, B 781†.

ὑπο-στορέννυμι, aor. **στορέσαι**, *spread out under*, υ 139; ὑπὸ ἔστρωτο, mid. he had spread out under him his shield.

ὑπο-στρέφω, ipf. **ἔστρεφε**, aor. subj. στρέψωσι, opt. ειας, part. ας, fut. mid. ψεσθαι, aor. part. στρεφθείς, *turn about*, E 581, 505; *turn in flight*, M 71, Λ 446; pass. *turn, return*, σ 23, Λ 567.

ὑπο-σχέθω, see ὑπ-έχω.

ὑπο-σχέσθαι, see ὑπ-ίσχομαι,

ὑπο-σχεσίῃσι, ταῖς, N 369, elsewh. **ὑπό-σχεσις**, ιν, B 349, 286, (ὑπίσχομαι), *promise.*

ὑπο-τάνυσσαν, aor., *placed underneath* (lengthwise, τανύω), A 486†.

ὑπο-ταρβήσαντες, aor. part. (ταρβέω, terror), τούς, *shrinking before* them, P 533†.

ὑπο-ταρταρίους, *those below in Tartaros*, Ξ 279†.

ὑπο-τίθημι, aor. θῆκε in tmesis, fut. mid. θήσομαι, εαι, εται, όμεθα, aor. θέσθαι, imp. θευ, *place under, attach*, Σ 375; mid. *suggest*, βουλήν, ἔργον, ἔπος; *counsel*, εὖ, πυκινῶς, prudently, Φ 293.

ὑπὸ (**ἔ**)**τρέμε**, his limbs *trembled beneath* (him), K 390, λ 527.

ὑπο-τρέχω, aor. **ἔδραμε**, *ran up underneath* (his weapon), *ran up to and prostrated himself before*, Φ 68 and κ 323.

ὑπο-τρέω, aor. **ἔτρεσας**, σαν, σαι, *take to flight*, P 275; τινά, *flee before* one, P 587.

ὑπο-τρομέουσι, ipf. iter. τρομέεσκον, (τρέμω), *tremble before*, X 241, Υ 28; τρομέει ὑπό (adv.), K 95.

ὑπό-τροπος, ον, (τρέπω), redux, *returning, back again*, Z 367, υ 332.

ὑπ-ουράνιον, ίων, (οὐρανός), *under the heaven*, P 675; *far and wide under the whole heaven*, ι 264.

ὑπο-φαίνω, aor. **-έφηνε**—θρῆνυν τραπέζης, *bring* a footstool *into view from under* the table, ρ 409†.

ὑπο-φέρω, aor. 3 pl. **ἤνεικαν**, *bore* me *away*, E 885†.

ὑπο-φεύγειν, subterfugere, *escape by flight*, X 200; aor. **φυγὼν ὕπο**, *escaping*, Φ 57.

ὑπο-φῆται, οἱ, (φημί), interpretes, *declarers* of the divine will, Π 235†.

ὑπο-φθάνω, aor. part. **-φθάς**, mid. φθάμενος, η, *be* or *get beforehand, anticipate*, H 144; τινά, ο 171.

ὑπο-χάζομαι, red. aor. **κεκάδοντο**, ἀνδρός, *retired before* the hero, Δ 497.

ὑπο-χείριος, *under my hands*, ο 448†.

ὑπο-χέω, aor. **ἔχευε**, *spread* (strew) *under*(neath), ξ 49, Λ 843; **χεῦεν ὕπο**, π 47.

ὑπο-χώρει, ipf., aor. χώρησαν, tmesis, Δ 505, *retire, retreat*, X 96.

ὑπ-όψιος (ὄψις), *despised* (by the rest), ἄλλων, Γ 42.

ὕπτιος, ον, οι, (ὑπό), resupinus, *back, on his back*, ι 371, Δ 108.

ὑπ-ώπια, τά, (ὤψ), vultu, *in countenance*, M 463†.

ὑπ-ωρείας, τάς, (ὄρος), *foot of a mountain, skirts of a mountain range*, Υ 218†.

ὑπ-ώρορε, see ὑπ-όρνυμι.

ὑπ-ωρόφιοι (ὀροφή), *under the* (same) *roof, table companions*, I 640†.

Ὑρίη, fem., town in Boiotia, on the Euripos, B 496†.

Ὑρμίνη, fem., harbor town in northern Elis, B 616†.

Ὑρτἄκίδης, *son of Hyrtakos*, Asios, B 837 sq., M 96, 110, 163.

Ὕρτἄκος, ου, a Trojan, husband of Arisbe, N 759 and 771.

Ὑρτῖος, son of Gyrtios, a Mysian, slain by Aias, Ξ 511†.

ὗς, **ὑός**, ὗν, ὕες, ὕεσσι(ν), ὕας, fem., (σῦς), sus, *swine;* alternating with σῦς, according to the requirements of the verse, ξ 419, ν 405, K 264.

ὑσμίνη, ης, ῃ, ην, ῖναι, ίνας, also dat. sing. ὑσμῖνι B 863, *in the conflict*, and ὑσμίνηνδ' B 477, *into the battle;* λ 417, 612, acies, *pitched combat;* δηιοτῆτος, hostile combat. (Il.)

ὑστᾰτίῃσι (ὕστατος), *last, hindmost*, O 634; ntr. ὑστάτιον, *at last.*

ὕστᾰτος, ον, οι, ον, α, sup., (ὕστερος), *last, hindmost*, B 281; ὕστατον, as adv., *last*, with πύμᾰτον, X 203, *at the very last;* also esp., in fourth foot, ὕστατα, with πύματα, δ 685.

ὕστερος, ον, α π 319, comp., (ὕστατος), posterior, *succeeding*, usually of time, *after;* γένει, natu minor, younger; σεῦ, after thee; ntr., *afterward, hereafter*, K 450, Υ 127.

ὑφαίνει, etc., prs., (subj. ῃσι, opt. οι), and ipf., iter. ὑφαίνεσκε(ν), ον, aor. ὕφηνεν, ω, ον, ας, ασα; parallel form ὑφάω, prs. **ὑφόωσι**, η 105, *weave*, ἱστόν, at the loom (which stood upright, like the Roman loom represented in the cut, or like the Egyptian loom in cut

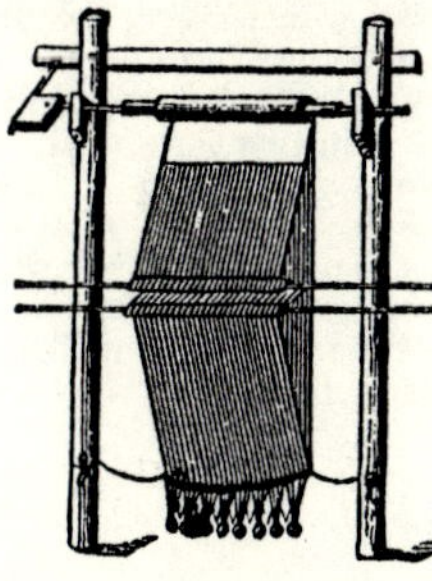

No. 63); also in general, *weave garments*, ν 108; fig. δόλον, ους, dolum, insidias struere, *spin, devise* a plot, ι 422; μῆτιν, consilium texere, *contrive* a plan, δ 678.

ὑπὸ ἤρεον, *were taking away from under*, B 154; elsewh. ὑπό is simple adv., c. g. ω 450, ὑπὸ χλωρὸν δέος ᾕρει, *seized* them *below* = in their limbs, or *by reason of what they saw.*

ὑφαντήν (ὑφαίνω), *woven*, ν 136 and π 231.

ὑφάσματα, τά, (ὑφαίνω), telas, *thing woven, web*, γ 274†.

ὑφάω, see ὑφαίνω.

ὕφ-ελκε, ipf., (ἕλκω), ποδοῖιν, *sought to drag away* by laying hold *below* at the feet, Ξ 477†.

ὑφ-ηνίοχος, masc., (ἡνίοχος), *charioteer* as subject to (ὑπό) the warrior in the chariot, Z 19†.

ὑφ-ίημι, fut. **ἥσει**, aor. ἧκεν, (part. ὑφέντες A 434, better with Aristarchos ἀφέντες), supponere, *put* or *place under*, ι 309, θρῆνυν.

ὑφ-ίσταμαι, aor. ὑπ-**έστην**, ης, η, ημεν, ἔσταν, opt. σταίη, imp. στήτω, part. στάς, *take upon one's self*, Φ 273; *promise*, τινί τι, ὑπόσχεσιν, with inf., I 445, T 195, Ψ 20, κ 483; in B 286, E 715, case ἐκπέρσαντ' (ι ? α ?) is doubtful; I 160, μοι, let him *submit* to me.

ὑ-φορβός, όν, οί, masc., (ὗς, φέρβω), *swine-herd*, with ἀνέρες, ξ 410. (Od.) [ῠ]

ὑφόωσι, see ὑφαίνω.

ὑψ-ᾰγόρην, η, masc., (ὕψι, ἀγορεύω), *big talker, boaster*, β 85, α 385. (Od.)

ὑψ-ερεφές, ntr., and **-ηρεφέος**, I 582, ές, έα, with synizesis δ 757, (ἐρέφω), *high-roofed.*

ὑψηλός, οῦ, οῖο, ῷ, όν, οί, ῶν, οῖσι(ν), ούς, ή, ῆς, ῇ, ήν, αί, άων, ῇσι, άς, όν, ά (ὕψος), *high, lofty*, of situation, *high-dwelling*, B 855.

Ὑψ-ήνωρ, ορος, (1) son of Dolopion, slain by Eurypylos, E 76.—(2) son of Hippasos, slain by Deiphobos, N 411.

ὑψ-ηρεφές, etc., see ὑψ-ερεφές.

ὑψ-ηχέες, έας, (ἠχέω), *high-neighing* (with head raised on high), E 772 and Ψ 27.

ὕψι, adv., (old locative), (1) *on high*, ἐπ' εὐνάων ὁρμίζειν, Ξ 77, make fast the ships *floating in deep water, on the high sea* (ὕψι), to the anchor-stones; βιβάς, striding along with high, i. e. long steps.—(2) *up, aloft*, Π 374, P 723, N 140.

ὑψι-βρεμέτης (βρέμω), alte tonans, *thundering aloft, high-thundering*, A 354.

ὑψί-ζῠγος (ζυγόν), lit. *on high rower's bench, high at the helm, high-ruling*, Δ 166. (Il.)

ὑψῐ-κάρηνοι (κάρη), *with lofty head* or *peak*, Μ 132†.

ὑψί-κερων, τόν, (κέρας), *with lofty antlers*, κ 158†.

ὑψῐ-κόμοιο, οισιν, ους, (κόμη), *with lofty foliage*, Ξ 398, μ 357.

ὑψῐ-πετήεις, Χ 308, and **-πέτης,** Ν 822, (πέτομαι), *high-flying.*

ὑψῐ-πέτηλον, α, (πέτηλον), *with lofty foliage*, Ν 437, λ 588.

Ὑψῐ-πύλη, wife of Iason, mother of Euneos, Η 469†.

ὑψί-πῡλον (πύλη), *high-gated*, referring to the gates in the towers, Τροίη, Π 698; and Θήβη, Ζ 416. (Il.)

ὑψόθεν, adv., (ὕψος), *from on high*, Λ 53; ἐκρέμω, thou wast hanging (swinging) *aloft*, Ο 18.

ὑψόθῐ, adv., (ὕψος), *high, on high*, Κ 16, Τ 376. (Il.)

ὑψ-ορόφοιο, ον, (ὀροφή), *with lofty covering, high-roofed*, Ω 192, 317.

ὑψόσε, adv., (ὕψος), *upward, aloft;* at beginning of verse, or in fifth foot exc. Φ 269, 302.

ὑψοῦ, adv., (ὕψος), *aloft, on high*, Α 486; ἐν νοτίῳ τήν γ' ὥρμισαν, they moored the ship, letting her ride *far out* in the roadstead, δ 785.

ὕω, ipf. **ὗε,** Ζεύς —, *sent rain;* pass. ὑόμενος, *drenched with rain*, ζ 131.

Φ.

φάανθεν, 3 pl. aor. part. from φαίνω.

φᾰάντατος, sup., (positive would be φάϝας [cf. ἄτλας, γίγας], from φαίνω), *most brilliant*, ν 93†.

φᾰγον = ἔφαγον, see ἐσθίω.

φᾰε, aor., ξ 502, for φάϝε (φάϝος, φάος), splendebat, *appeared*, fut. πεφήσεται, Ρ 155, shall have appeared.

φᾰεα, see φάος.

Φᾰέθουσα, daughter of Helios and Neaira, "new moon," μ 132†; **φᾰέθων,** masc. of foregoing (φαϝος, see φάε), splendens, *radiant*, Helios, Λ 735.

Φᾰέθων, horse of Eos, ψ 246; acc. Φαέθονθ' = οντα.

φᾰεινός, οῦ, ῷ, όν, ώ, ῶν, ούς; ή, ῆς, ῇ, ήν, αί, άς, (for φαϝεσ-ινός), comp.-εινότερον, *gleaming, shining, radiant*, Γ 419, Μ 151.

φαείνω, subj., ῃ, οιεν, φάεινε, ων, (φαεινός), *shine*, of the sun, μ 383, 385; *giving light*, σ 343.

φᾰεσί-μβροτος, ον, (φάϝος, μόρ-ος, mortalis), *bringing light to mortals*, sun, κ 138; Eos, Ω 785.

Φαίαξ, see Φαίηκες.

φαιδῐμόεντες (φαίδῐμος), *illustrious*, of Epeians, Ν 686†.

φαίδῐμος, ῳ, ον, (α), (φαϝιδ-, φάος), *shining, gleaming*, of limbs, candentes umeri, λ 128; usually of persons, *illustrious*, Aias, Hektor, υἱός, Ζ 144.

Φαίδῐμος, king of the Sidonians, δ 617, ο 117.

Φαίδρη, wife of Theseus, λ 321.†

Φαίηκες, dat. ήκεσσιν and ηξιν η 62, favored inhabitants of the fabulous Scheria, enjoying continual dolce far niente, θ 244 sqq. In earlier times their home was near the Kyklopes; they escort all those whom they receive as guests on swift ships, themselves possessing intelligence, to their desired haven, ε 34, ζ 4, θ 244 sqq.

φαινέσκετο and -ομένηφιν, see φαίνω.

Φαῖνοψ, οπος, son of Asios from Abydos, father of Xanthos and Thoon, Ρ 583, Ε 152.

φαίνω, etc., pres. inf. -έμεν, imp. φαῖν(ε), ipf. φαῖνε, aor. ἔφηνε, φήνωσι, ειε, φῆναι, (φάος), *give light, shine, make appear*, (τινί, intr. *give light*, η 102), τέρατα, σήματα, μηρούς; *show*, ὁδόν; γόνον, ἄκοιτιν, *appoint; display*, ἀρετάς; *make heard, utter*, ἀοιδήν, ἀεικείας; part. pf. μῦθον πεφασμένον (cf. θ 499), report *which has gone abroad; φαίνο-*

μαι, intr. pres., ipf., iter. φαινέσκετο, fut. φανεῖσθαι, 2 aor. (ἐ)φάνη, iter. φάνεσκε λ 587, 3 pl. φάνεν, subj. φανῇ = ῄῃ, opt. εἴη, imp. ηθι, ήτω, inf. ήμεναι = ῆναι, part., είς, έντα, εῖσα, 1 aor. pass. φαάνθη, 3 pl. φάανθεν, pf. pass. 3 sing. πέφανται, part. see above, *shine*, πυρά, ὄσσε, Ἠώς; *be visible, appear*, μάχη; *was unprotected* at the throat, X 324; *offer one's self, appear*, K 236, ω 448; σμερδαλέος, τοῖος, πῶς; Δ 278, it appears to him blacker than pitch as it advances over the sea.

Φαῖστος, son of Boros, from Tarne in Maionia, slain by Idomeneus. E 43†.

Φαιστός, city in Kreta near Gortys, B 648, γ 296.

φαλαγγηδόν, adv., (φάλαγξ), *in companies, in columns*, O 360.

φάλαγξ, **φάλαγγα,** fem., pl. ες, γξιν, ας, *line of battle, column*, Z 6, Λ 90.

φάλαρ(α), τά, (φάλος), *burnished, gleaming plates* of metal, rising above the helmet, Π 106†.

φᾰληριόωντα, part. ntr. pl. from -ιάω, (φάλαρος, α), *brightly shining, gleaming*, N 799†.

Φάλκης, a Trojan chief, N 791; Ξ 513, slain by Antilochos.

φᾰ́λον, τόν, pl. -οισι, (φάε), (1) *metal ridge* or *crest*, extending over the helmet from back to front, and furnished with a socket to receive and support the plume (see cut No. 128).—(2) in narrower signification *the rounded boss*, in which the φάλος terminated (see cut No. 20), Z 9, N 132.

φάν, see φημί.

φάνεν, εσκε, ῄῃ, ήμεναι, see φαίνω.

φᾰ́ος (from φάϝως), and φόως, dat. φάει, acc. φάος, φόως, pl. φάεα, (φάε), *light*, opp. ἀχλύς, ἠελίοιο, φόωσδε, to the *light of day*; ἐν φάει, *by daylight*; fig. lumina, *eyes*, π 15; γλυκερὸν φ., mi ocelle, light of my eyes, π 23; *deliverance, victory*, etc., Z 6.

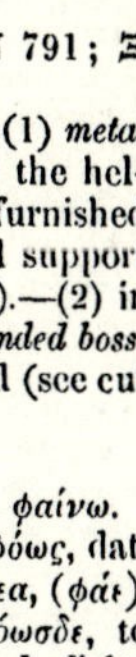

φᾰρέτρη, ης, ην, fem., (φέρω), *quiver*, Λ 45, φ 11. (Cf. cut, and Nos. 96, 97, 111.)

Φᾶρις, ιος, town in Lakonike, south of Amyklai, B 582†.

φάρμᾰκον, (α), ntr., *medicinal herbs*, δ 230; in general, *remedies*, Δ 191, Λ 741; *magic drug, potion*, κ 392; *poisonous draught, poisonous drug*, X 94, α 261, β 329, ἀνδροφόνον.

φαρμάσσων, part., *skillfully handling, tempering*, ι 393†.

φᾶρος, εϊ, ε(α), ntr., (φέρω), *large piece of cloth, a shroud*, Σ 353; *mantle, cloak*, B 43, γ 467; likewise of women, ε 230.

Φᾰ́ρος, small island at mouth of Nile, δ 355†.

φάρυγξ, **φάρῠγος,** fem., *throat*, ι 373, τ 480.

φάσγᾰνον, ου, ῳ, α, (σφάζω), *sword*, E 81, π 295.

φάσθαι, see φημί.

φάσκω, ipf. iter. **ἔφασκον,** ες, εν, εθ' = ετε, and φάσκ' = φάσκ(εν), (φημί), *declared*, λ 306; *promise*, with inf. fut., ε 135; *think*, N 100, χ 35.

φασσοφόνῳ, dat., (φάσσα, palumbes, φόνος), *dove-slayer*; ἴρηκι, pigeon-hawk, O 238†.

φάτις, ιν, fem., (φημί), fama, *report, reputation*, ἐσθλή, ζ 29; ἀνδρῶν ἠδὲ γυναικῶν, among men and women; with objective gen., ψ 362, tidings (of the slaughter) of the suitors.

φάτνῃ, ῃ̃, (πατέομαι), *crib, manger*, E 271.

Φαυσῐ̈άδης, *son of Phausios*, Apisaon, Λ 578†.

Φεαί, town in Elis, ο 297†.

φέβωμαι, ώμεθα, εσθαι, ipf. (ἐ)φέβοντο, fugari, fugere, *flee*, Λ 121, χ 299; *flee from*, E 232. (Il.)

Φειά, town on the river Jardanos, in northern Elis, H 135.

Φείδας, an Athenian chief, N 691†.

Φείδ-ιππος, son of Thessalos, B 678†.

φείδομαι, **φειδόμενος,** and φείσατ(ο), aor. red. πεφιδοίμην, οιτο, έσθαι, fut. red. πεφιδήσεται, *spare*, with gen., ι 277, Υ 464.

φειδώ, fem., *sparing, thrift*, π 315; H 409, *one must not fail* in the case of the dead *to*—.

φειδωλή, fem., (φείδομαι), *sparing, grudging use*, δούρων, X 244†.

Φείδων, king of the Thesprotians, ξ 316, τ 287.

Φεν- and φα-, roots of the follg. verbal forms, (φόνος), aor. red. **ἔπεφνον,** ες, (εν), ομεν, ετε, and πέφνε(ν), subj. ῃς, ῃ, inf. έμεν, part. πεφνόντα, pass. pf. **πέφατ(αι)**, 3 pl. *νται*, inf. *άσθαι*, 3 fut., *πεφήσεαι*, *σεται*, *slay*, θάνατος, λ 135.

Φένεος, town in Arkadia, B 605†.

Φεραί, ῶν, ῇς, important town in Thessaly, residence of Eumelos, δ 798; situated on lake Boibeis, B 711.

Φέρε-κλος, son of Harmonides, builder of the ship in which Paris carried away Helen, slain by Meriones, E 59†.

Φέρης, ητος, son of Kretheus and Tyro, father of Admetos, λ 259†.

φέριστον, ε, οι, *bravest, best*, esp. freq. in voc., Z 123, ι 269.

Φέρουσα, a Nereid, Σ 43†.

φέρτἄτος, (ε), οι, = φέριστος, sup. to **φέρτερος**, ον, οι, η, αί, praestantissimus and -ior, *pre-eminent*, both forms with πολύ, (sup. also with μέγα), χερσίν τε βίηφί τε, βίῃ; comp. with inf., *it is better*, A 169, μ 109.

φέρτε = φέρετε, imp. from φέρω.

φέρτρῳ, τῷ, ntr., (φέρω), *litter, bier* for the dead, Σ 236†.

φέρω, subj. **φέρῃσι** τ 111, imp. φέρτε, inf. φερέμεν, ipf. iter. φέρεσκον, κεν, fut. **οἴσω**, ων, mid. fut. οἴσεται, σόμενος, etc., 2 aor. imp. οἶσε, σέτω, σετε, inf. σέμεν(αι), from stem **ενεκ-**, 1 aor. **ἤνεικεν**, **καν**, and ἔνεικας, ε(ν), αμεν, ατε, αν, subj. ἐνείκω, ῃ, opt. κοι, imp. κατε, inf. ἐνεῖκαι, and opt. είκαι, part. ἐνείκας, 2 aor. (ἤνεγκεν, v. l. χ 493), inf. ἐνεικέμεν, I. act., (1) ferre, *bear, carry*, τί, with dat. instr. or with ἐν-; γαστρί, in the womb; also of the earth, *yield; bring*, (θεόν, adducere), δῶρα, τεύχεα, μῦθον, ἀγγελίην, ἔπεα, τ 565; φόως, rescue; ἦρα, χάριν, gratify; κακόν, ά; φόνον, δηιοτῆτα, ἄλγεα.—(2) vehere, *carry away, convey*, τινά, τί, subj. horses, draught animals, ἅρμα, πέδιλα, α 97; *drive*, πόντονδε, etc., freq. of winds; *scatter*, πῦρ, κονίην; *snatch away, sweep away; carry off* as plunder, esp. with ἄγειν. The part. φέρων serves often to give vividness to the narrative, A 13. The inf. (also pass.) often follows the principal verb to denote purpose, Π 671, Λ 798, or result, ε 343, μ 442.—II. pass. ferri, *be borne*, either intentionally, *charge, rush upon*, O 743; ἰθύς, straight forward, Υ 172; or, more commonly, involuntarily, *be borne, swept, hurried along*, A 592.—III. mid. sibi (au)ferre, *carry off for one's self, bear away*, esp. of victory, μέγα κράτος, N 486, and prizes, τὰ πρῶτα.

φεύγω, pres., inf. -έμεν(αι), ipf. (ἔ)φευγ(ε), and iter. φεύγεσκεν, fut. **ξομαι**, εσθ(ε), ονται, εσθαι, aor. ἔφυγες, and φύγον, ε(ν), iter. φύγεσκε, subj. ῃ(σι), opt. οιμι, etc., inf. έειν = εῖν, part.; pf. πεφεύγοι, ότες, also **πεφυζότες** Φ 6, X 1, and πεφυγμένος, ον (with ἔμμεναι, εἶναι, γενέσθαι), (fuga), fugere, *flee*, A 173, Ω 356, γ 166, ω 54; *flee from*, Λ 327, ὑπό τινος, ἐκ-; *flee one's country for crime, go into exile*, ν 259, π 424; πατρίδα, ο 228; *avoid*, τινά, μ 157, A 60; *escape*, τινά, τί, ζ 170, μ 260, κ 131; ποῖόν σε ἔπος φύγεν ἕρκος ὀδόντων, what a word *has slipped past* the fence of thy teeth! *has escaped* thee! πεφυγμένος, τί, Z 488; ἀέθλων, α 18, *escaped from* toils.

φῆ = ἔφη, from φημί.

φή, sicut, *just as, like*, B 144.

Φηγεύς, son of Dares, priest of Hephaistos in Ilios, slain by Diomedes, E 11, 15.

φήγινος, adj., (φηγός), faginus, *of oak-wood, oaken*, E 838†.

φηγῷ, όν, fem., (fāgus), *kind of oak with edible acorns;* an ancient tree of this species was one of the landmarks on the Trojan plain, H 22, I 354. (Il.)

φήμη, ην, fem., (φάναι), fama, *ominous* or *prophetic voice* or *word*, omen, υ 100, β 35.

φημί (φα, φαίνω, fari), enclitic throughout pres. exc. 2 sing. φῄς, φησί, φαμέν, φατέ, φασ(ίν), subj. φῇ-(σιν), and φήῃ, opt. φαίην, ης, η, φαῖμεν; φάς, φάντες, ipf. (ἔ)φῆν, (ἔ)φῆσθα, (ἔ)φῆς η 239, (ἔ)φῆ ω 470, (ἔ)φάμεν, 3 pl. (ἔ)φά(σα)ν, no inf., fut. φήσει; mid. = in signif. act. pres. imp. φάο, inf. φάσθαι, part. φάμενος, η, ipf. (ἐ)φάμην, (ἔ)φάτο, 3 pl. (ἔ)φάντο, *declare, make known*, opp. κεύθειν, cf. φ 194; ἔπος τ' ἔφατ', *raise the voice so as to make audible, uttered the word, spoke aloud*, Γ 398, Z 253, β 302; ἔπος, δ 370; φάτο μῦθον, as close of verse, Φ 393; *report, deliver*, τί, Σ 17; ο 377, *speak out one's mind;* ἶσον ἐμοὶ φάσθαι, *fancy himself* equal to me; mid. (exc. E 184, dico, *mean*), *think*, δ 664, χ 31, 35; *tradition says*, ζ 42; with οὐ, negare, *deny*, ο 213; ὡς φάτο, ὡς ἔφαθ', freq. as conventional phrase where it is not strictly necessary to the sense, υ 54; when the inf. follows with same subj. as the principal verb its subj. is in nom., Α 397 (exc. θ 221, where it is acc.); when the subj. changes, we find acc. with inf.; yet the subj. acc. must sometimes be supplied, Δ 351, 375, α 168, δ 638; likewise sometimes also the inf., Ι 329, Ξ 126, *εἶναι*.

Φήμιος, bard in Ithaka, α 154, 337, ρ 263, χ 331; son of Terpios.

φῆμις, *ιν*, fem., fama, *rumor, common talk* (ο 468, δήμοιο, *place of popular discussion, assembly*), Κ 207.

φῆν = ἔφην, see φημί.

φήναι, *ειε*, opt. aor. from φαίνω.

φήνη, *αι*, fem., *sea-eagle*, γ 372 and π 217.

φήρ, **φηρσίν**, τοῖς, feris, *wild beasts*, Α 268; but **φῆρας**, of Centaurs, Β 743, λαχνήεντες, hairy, shaggy.

Φηραί and Φηρῇ, Ε 543, town afterward in Messenia, but by Homer placed in domain of Lakonike, Ι 151, 293, γ 488, ο 186.

Φηρητιάδης, *αο*, *son of Pheres* = Eumelos, Β 763 and Ψ 376.

φῇς, φῆς = ἔφης, **φῆσθα** = ἔφησθα, see φημί.

φθάν, see φθάνω.

φθάνει, fut. φθήσονται, aor. ἔφθης, η, and φθῆ, 3 pl. φθάν, subj. φθῇ(σιν), φθήῃ, φθέωμεν, έωσιν [pronounce φθjῶμεν, jῶσι, π 383, ω 437], opt. φθαίη, no inf., φθάμενος, aor. mid. part. ο 171, *come before*, λ 58; *overtake, anticipate*, τινά, Φ 262; with part. may be translated *sooner, before*, π 383; so also with ἤ, e. g. λ 58, πεζὸς ἰών, thou art come sooner on foot, than—; Λ 51, with gen. of comparison, they were much (μέγα) *sooner* arranged than the horsemen; so also part. φθάμενος, *before, sooner*, Ε 119, τ 449; also with πρίν, Π 322, τοῦ ἔφθη πρὶν οὐτάσαι, hit him on the shoulder *before*—.

φθέγγομαι, subj. **φθεγγώμεθα**, imp. *εο*, part. *ομένου*, ipf. (ἐ)φθέγγοντο, aor. φθέγξατ(ο), subj. φθέγξομ(αι), part. ξάμενος, ον, η, *utter a sound, cry* or *call out*, Λ 603, κ 228; Κ 457 = χ 329, while his shout still *resounded*; ὀλίγῃ ὀπί = τυτθόν, *speaking* softly; καλεῦντες, they called *aloud*.

φθείρουσι, *destroy, ruin*, ρ 246; pass. φθείρεσθ(ε), *ruin seize ye*, Φ 128.

Φθειρῶν also **Φθερῶν**, ὄρος, mountain in Karia, Β 868.

φθέωμεν, *έωσιν*, see φθάνω.

φθῇ, φθήῃ, φθῆσιν, see φθάνω.

Φθίη, dat. Φθίηφι Τ 323, (1) *Phthia*, chief city of Myrmidons, residence of Peleus, Β 683.—(2) region about Phthia, making up with Ἑλλάς the realm of Achilleus, Ι 395, λ 496.

Φθίηνδε, *to Phthia*, Α 169, Τ 330.

φθίμενος, see φθίνω.

φθινύθει, *ουσι(ν)*, subj. *ω*; ipf. φθίνυθον and iter. φθινύθεσκε, *waste, consume*; κῆρ, one's heart = *pine away* (μευ ὀδυρόμενοι, κ 485, whose grief *breaks* my heart); intrans. *waste away*, θ 530; perire, Ζ 327.

φθίνω (parallel form φθίω, subj. **φθίῃς** β 368, ipf. ἐφθίεν Σ 446), **φθίνουσι**, *έτω, οντος, όντων*, pass. mid. fut. φθίσονται, εσθ(αι), pf. ἔφθιται, plupf. ἐφθίμην, 3 pl. ἐφθίαθ' = ατο, 2 aor. sync. ἔφθιτ(ο), subj. ωμαι, όμεσθα, opt. ἱμην, ῖτ(ο), inf. ίσθαι, part. ἱμενος, ον, οιο, οισι, aor. pass. 3 pl. ἔφθιθεν, (1) trans. only fut. φθίσει, ειν, aor. 3 pl. φθῖσαν, subj. ωμεν, inf. ῖσαι, *consume, destroy, slay*, Π 461, υ 67, π 428.—(2) intrans. (all other forms), *waste away, decay, wane, dwindle; κακὸν οἶτον, die* a wretched death; μηνός, ῶν, *wane, approach the end*, ξ 162, κ 470.

Φθῖοι, *ων*, *inhabitants of Phthia*, Ν 686, 693, 699.

φθῖσ-ήνορα, *man-consuming*, πόλεμον, Β 833. (Il.)

φθισί-μβροτος, *ον*, (βροτός), *which consumes mortals, life-destroying*, μάχη, Ν 339; αἰγίδα, χ 297.

φθογγῆς, *ήν*, fem., (φθέγγομαι), *voice*, Β 791, Π 508.

φθόγγῳ, *ον*, masc., (φθέγγομαι), *voice*; φθόγγῳ, σ 198, *aloud*, i. e. *talking*.

φθονέω, *έεις, έοιμι, έειν, έουσ(α)*, (φθίνω), *grudge, deny, refuse*, τινί τινος, ζ 68; with inf., λ 381, τ 348; acc. and inf., α 346, σ 16.

φι(ν), vestige of several old case endings, applied to the stem-vowel of the various declensions, I. ηφι and ῆφι (but ἐσχαρόφι), II. όφι, III. εσφι (but ναῦφι), of persons only in two words, (ἐκ)θεόφι and αὐτόφι: serves (1) as simple gen. only Φ 295, μ 45; with verbs, Λ 350, Π 762; with ἐπί, Τ 255, and διά.—(2) as simple dat., Β 363; with ἀτάλαντος, Γ 110; with verbs, Ν 700, ρ 4.—(3) as ablat., θ 279, ε 152, also with ἀπό, ἐκ, ὑπό, πρόσθε.—(4) as instrumental case, δακρυόφι πίμπλαντο, Ρ 696, Λ 699; ἶφι = Ϝῖφι, vi.—(5) as locative, παλάμηφιν ἀρήρει, and with ἐν, ἐπί, παρά, ἀμφί, πρός, ε 433; ὑπό, Τ 404.—(6) of doubtful classification, Μ 114, Ζ 510, Ο 267, Χ 107.

φῐάλη, ῃ, ην, fem., *large basin* or *bowl*, Ψ 270; *urn*, Ψ 243.

φῖλαι, φίλατο, see φιλέω.

φιλέω, **φιλεῖ** and έει, inf. φιλεῖν only ο 74, part. εῦντας, ipf. (ἐ)φίλει, elsewh. in pres. and ipf. always uncontracted, subj. έῃσι, opt. έοι and οίη, inf. ήμεναι, ipf. iter. φιλέεσκε, fut. inf. ησέμεν, aor. ἐφίλησα, ε, αν, and φίλησα, σ(ε); pass. 3 pl. aor. (ἐ)φίληθεν Β 668, and likewise fut. of mid. φιλήσεαι, diligere and amare, *love, hold dear, cherish*, τινὰ πέρι κῆρι, exceedingly in heart; ἐκ θυμοῦ, heartily; σχέτλια ἔργα; τινὰ παντοίην φιλότητα, bestow every mark of affection upon one; ἐφίληθεν ἐκ Διός, were loved by Zeus; also *receive as guest, welcome*, ε 135; παρ' ἄμμι φιλήσεαι, acceptus gratusque nobis eris, thou shalt be kindly welcomed by us; mid. aor. **(ἐ)φίλατο,** imp. φῖλαι περὶ πάντων, above all others, Υ 304.

φῐλ-ηρέτμοισι(ν), dat. pl., (ἐρετμόν), *fond of the oar*, Taphians and Phaiakians, α 181, ε 386. (Od.)

Φῐλ-ητορίδης, *son of Philetor*, Demuchos, Υ 457†.

Φῐλ-οίτιος, faithful herdsman of Odysseus, υ 185, 254, φ 240, 388; slays Peisandros, χ 268, and Ktesippos, χ 286.

φιλο-κέρτομε, voc., (κέρτομος), *fond of jeering* or *mocking, contemptuous*, χ 287†.

φῐλο-κτεᾰνώτατε, voc., (κτέανον), *most greedy of others' possessions*, Α 122†.

Φῐλο-κτήτης, αο, son of Poias, from Meliboia in Thessaly, γ 190, θ 219, Β 718, 725.

φῐλο-μμειδής (from σμειδής, Old Ger. smielen, Eng. smile), *laughter-loving*, Aphrodite, Γ 424, θ 362. (Il.)

Φῐλο-μηλείδης, αο, king in Lesbos, who challenged all strangers to wrestle with him, δ 343 and ρ 134.

φῐλό-ξεινοι, *loving guest-friends, hospitable*, ζ 121. (Od.)

φῐλο-παίγμονος, gen. from -μων, (παίζω), *fond of play, cheering, gay*, ψ 134†.

φῐλο-πτολέμων, οισι(ν), *fond of war, warlike*, bellicosorum, Π 65. (Il.)

φῐλος, η, ον, etc., comp. φιλίων τ 351 and ω 268, and φίλτερος, ον, οι, sup. φίλτατος, ον, ε, (φίλταθ' = ατε), οι, η, αι, suus, *one's own*, εἵματα, αἰῶνος, and esp. of parts of body, χεῖρες; pl. sui, *one's own*, servants, relatives, cf. necessarii, "one's dear ones," δ 475; then, after one's mind, *acceptable, pleasing*, τινὶ ἐστι, (εἴη, γένοιτο, ἔπλετο); with inf., Δ 372, cf. Α 107; in general, *dear*, in direct address φίλος, α 301, and φίλε τέκνον, β 363; *friendly*, μήδεα, φίλα φρονεῖν τινι, εἰδέναι, be *kindly* disposed. [φῖλε at beginning of verse, Δ 155.]

φῐλότης, ότητος, τι, τ(α), fem., (φίλος), (1) *friendship*, τιθέναι, establish; ἔταμον with ὅρκια, establish a treaty, and hallow with sacrifice the *alliance*.—(2) hospitium, *pledge of friendship, hospitable entertainment*, ο 537, 55.—(3) amores, *sexual love* or *intercourse*, esp. with ὁμωθῆναι, μίσγεσθαι, μιγάζοντο, be united in, enjoy in common *the pleasures of love*, Ν 636, θ 267.

φῐλοτήσια (φιλότης), ἔργα, *love's delights*, λ 246†.

φῐλο-φροσύνη, fem., (-φρων), *kindliness, friendly temper*, Ι 256†.

φῐλο-ψευδής (ψεῦδος), *friend of lies, false*, Μ 164†.

φίλτατος, τερος, see φίλος.

φῐλως, *gladly*, Δ 347, τ 461.

-φιν, see φι(ν).

φιτρῶν, ούς, masc., (φιτυρος, φῖτυ), *trunk, block, log*, Μ 29, μ 11. (Il.)

φλεγέθει, ουσι, οντι, pass. opt. 3 pl. φλεγεθοίατο, (φλέγω), *blaze, glow*, Φ 358, Σ 211; *consume, burn up*, Ρ 738, Ψ 197.

φλέγμᾰ, τό, (φλέγω), *flame, blaze*, Φ 337†.

Φλέγῠες or **αι,** robber tribe in Thessaly, Ν 302†.

φλέγω, **φλέγει,** (flagrare), *singe*,

consume, Φ 13; ipf. pass. φλέγετο, *blazed*.

φλέψ, **φλέβα**, τήν, (fluo), *main artery*, N 546†.

φλιῇσι, ταῖς, postibus, *door-posts*, ρ 221†.

φλόγεα, ntr. pl., (φλόξ), fulgentia, *flaming*, *gleaming*, E 745 and Θ 389.

φλοιόν, τόν, (liber), *bark*, A 237†.

φλοίσβου and οιο, gen., (φλύζω), *roar of battle*, E 322. (Il.)

φλόξ, γός, γί, γ(α), fem., (φλέγω), flamma, *flame*, *blaze*, Θ 135.

φοβέω, **φοβεῖ**, εῖτε, έουσι, aor. φόβησα, ἐφόβησας, (ἐ)φόβησε(ν), ῆσαι, fugare, *put to flight*, τινά; pass. pres. φοβεῖται, έονται, έεσθαι, εύμενος, ipf. φοβέοντο, aor. 3 pl. (ἐ)φόβηθεν, θείς, (exc. π 163 only Il.), pf. πεφοβημένος, οι, plupf. 3 pl. πεφοβήατο, *flee*, ὑπό τινος and ὑπό τινι; fut. mid. φοβήσομαί τινα, *flee from*, X 250.

φόβος, οιο, ου, ον, masc., (φέβομαι), fuga, *flight*, κρυόεντος, chilling, dreadful; μήστωρα, exciter of flight, M 39; πρὸ φόβοιο, for fear; Αἴαντι ἐν -ῶρσεν, excited in Ajax (the thought of) flight; *the horrors of flight*, E 739. **φόβονδ(ε)**, *to flight*; τρωπᾶσθαι, turn to flight; ἔχε ἵππους, ἀγορεύειν, counsel to flight, guide the horses to flight, E 252; abstained from flight, ω 57. (Il.)—**Φόβος**, attendant of Ares, O 119; son of Ares, N 299, Δ 440, Λ 37.

Φοῖβος (φοϝjος from φάϝος), *Phoebus*, the god of light; Ἀπόλλων Υ 68, preceding, elsewh. follg., freq. omitted; ἀκερσεκόμης, Υ 39; ἄνακτος, I 560; ἀφήτορος, I 405; ἑκάεργος, I 564; χρυσαόρου, E 509; ἤιε, O 365; φίλε, O 221; δεινός, Π 788.

φοινήεντα (φόνος), *blood-red*, δράκοντα, M 202 and 220.

Φοίνικες, *dwellers in* **Φοινίκη** δ 83, ξ 291, described as traders, skillful in navigation, and artful, ο 415, 419; famous alike for artistic skill and for piracy, ξ 288, Ψ 744, ν 272, ο 473; their chief city, Sidon.

φοινικόεντα, εσσαν, εσσαι [by synizesis = ουσσ], (φοῖνιξ), *purple*, *red*, K 133, Ψ 717.

φοινικο-παρῄους (παρειά), *purple* or *red cheeked*, with bows painted purple or red, λ 124 and ψ 271.

Φοῖνιξ, ικος, (1) father of Europa, Ξ 321.—(2) son of Amyntor, elder friend and adviser of Achilleus, to whose father he, under his own father's curse, had fled; Peleus constituted him lord of the Dolopes and educator of his son, whom he accompanied to Troja, I 223, 427, 432, 621, 659, 690; διίφιλος, I 168; ἀντίθεον, Ψ 360.

φοῖνιξ, (1) **φοίνῖκος**, fem., *date-palm*, ζ 163†.—(2) φοίνῖκι, purpura, *purple*, the invention of which was ascribed to the Phoenikians.—(3) adj., rufus, *gleaming with purple*; Z 219, φαεινός, *red* or *bay* (horse), *blood-bay* (?), Ψ 454†.

φοίνιον (φόνος), (*blood*) *red*, Σ 97†.

Φοίνισσα (from Φοινικjα) γυνή, *a Phoenikian woman*, ο 417.

φοινόν = φόνιον, *red*, Π 159†.

φοιτάω, **φοιτᾷ**, ῶσ(ι), ῶντε, ipf. (ἐ)φοίτων, (ἐ)φοίτα, 3 du. φοιτήτην, 3 pl. (ἐ)φοίτων, aor. φοιτήσασα, frequentare, obire, ambulare, trepidare, *go hurriedly about*, *roam*, Ω 533, E 528, O 686, ἔνθα καὶ ἔνθα κατὰ στρατόν, huc illuc per castra; παντόσε, M 266.

φολκός (falx, falcones), *bowlegged*, B 217†.

φονεύς, **φονῆος**, ῆας, masc., (φόνος), *murderer*, *homicide*, Σ 335, ω 434.

φονῇσιν, ταῖς, (φεν-), caedes, *massacre*, *murder*, K 521; *rending*, O 633.

φόνος, οιο, ου, ῳ, ον, οι, masc., (φεν-), caedes, *murder*, with κῆρα, B 352; ἀνδροκτασίαι τε; τεύχειν, prepare, E 652, δ 771; φυτεύει, β 165; μερμηρίζει, devises; φέρει, P 757; *means of death*, Π 144, T 391; = caesi, *the slain*, K 298; *blood*, *gore*, Ω 610, χ 376; αἵματος, *reeking* blood, of mangled beasts, Π 162.

φοξός (φώγειν), *sharp-pointed*, head low in front, sharp behind, a sugar-loaf head, B 219†.

Φόρβας, αντος, (1) king of Lesbos, father of Diomedes, I 665.—(2) rich Trojan, father of Ilioneus, Ξ 490.

φορβῆς, τῆς, (φέρβω, herba), *forage*, *fodder*, E 202 and Λ 562.

φορεύς, pl. **φορῆες**, οἱ, (φέρω), *carrier* of grapes in wine-harvest, *vintager* Σ 566†.

φορέω, **φορέεις**, etc., prs. always uncontracted, subj. έῃσι, inf. έειν, exc. opt.

οἰη, inf. *ἦναι*, *ήμεναι*, ipf. reg. uncontracted exc. (ἐ)*φόρει*, (ἐ)*φόρεον* [in χ 456 pronounce -*ευν*], iter. *φορέεσκε(ν)*, aor. *φόρησεν*, mid. ipf. *φορέοντο*, (*φέρω*), portare and gestare, *bear*, *carry*, β 390, O 530, T 11; ρ 245, *ἀγλαΐας ἅς φορέεις*, scatter to the wind the pomp, vanities, which *thou displayest;* vehere, B 770, K 323, Θ 528.

φορήμεναι, *φορῆναι*, see *φορέω*.

Φόρκῡνος *λιμήν*, harbor or inlet of *Phorkys* in Ithaka, ν 96†.

Φόρκυς, *υν*, (1) Phrygian chief, son of Phainops, slain by Aias, B 862, P 218, 312, 318.—(2) *Φόρκυς*, *ῡνος*, old man of the sea, father of Thoosa, α 72, ν 96, 345.

φόρμιγξ, *ιγγος*, *ι*, *α*, *ες*, fem., (fremo, Ger. brumme), a kind of *lute* or *lyre;* it had a cross-piece, *ζυγόν*; pegs, *κόλλοπες*; was held by the *ἀοιδός* (exceptionally also by heroes, Achilleus, I 186; by Apollo, Ω 63), and served to accompany the strain or recitative, A 603, θ 67, 99. In form substantially like the *κίθαρις* in cut.

φορμίζων, *touching* or *playing the lyre*, Σ 605; also said of one who plays on the *κίθαρις*. (Od.)

φορτίδος, *τῆς*, (*φόρτος*), navis oneraria, *ship of burden*, ε 250 and ι 323. (See cut.)

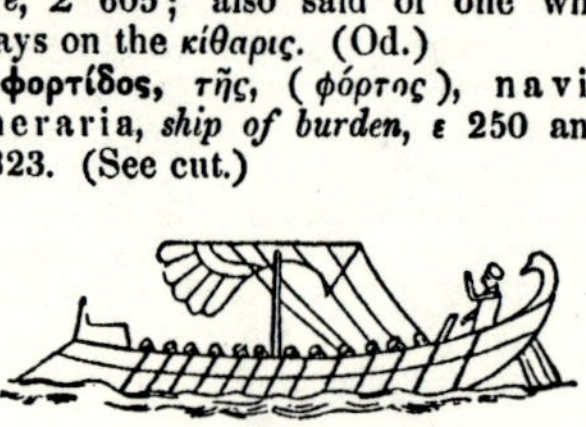

φόρτου, *ον*, masc., (*φέρω*), onus, *freight*, *cargo*, θ 163 and ξ 296.

φορύνετο, ipf. pass. *φορύνω*, (*πορ-φύρ-ω*). *was defiled*, χ 21†.

φορύξας, part. aor. from *φορύσσω*, (*πορ-φύρ-ω*), *having defiled* (thee) with much blood, σ 336†.

φόως, *φόωσδε*, see *φάος*.

φραδής, only **φραδέος** (*φράζω*), *νόου ἔργα τέτυκται*, lucida (prudenti) mente opus est, now is the need of a *clear* (*prudent*) mind, Ω 354†.

φράδμων (*φραδής*), *observing*, Π 638†.

φράζω (for *φραδjω*), aor. **φράσε,** red. *πέφρᾰδον* (ἐ)*πέφραδε(ν)*, *πεφράδοι*, *δέμεν* and *δέειν*; mid. pr. *φράζεαι*, subj. *ώμε(σ)θ(α)*, imp. *φράζεο* and *ζευ*, inf. *ζεσθαι*, ipf. iter. *φραζέσκετο*, fut. *φράσομαι*, *σσομαι*, *σσεται*, *σσόμεθ(α)*, aor. (ἐ)*φρασάμην*, *ἐφράσαθ'* = (ἐ)*φράσ(σ)ατ(ο)*, (ἐ)*φράσ(σ)αντ(ο)*, subj. *φράσεται*, imp. *φράσαι*, pass. aor. *ἐφράσθης*, (*φραδής*), *make clear*, *point out*, *show*, Ξ 500; θ 68, *showed* him how to take it with his hands, i. e. *guided* his hands to the instrument; *command*, *direct*, K 127, Ψ 138; *μῦθον*, *make known* the matter: mid. (1) *perceive*, *distinguish*, (*νοεῖν*, sentire), Ψ 450; *ἐσάντα*, *ὀφθαλμοῖσι*, *τινά*, with part.; χ 129, *look to* this approach.—(2) *make clear to one's self*, *consider*, *ponder*, A 83, ο 167, π 237, 257; with dependent clause introduced by *εἰ*, *ὅπως*, with fut. or with subj. and *κεν*, *ὥς κεν*; *μή*, videre ne, *take care* lest.—(3) *devise*, *τινί τι*, λ 624, nor was he able to devise a harder task; also, *plan for any one*, *design*, Ψ 126; of Zeus, *decree*.

φράσσω, aor. 3 sing. **φράξε,** part. *ξαντες*, mid. aor. *φράξαντο*, aor. pass. *φραχθέντες*, (farcio), ε 256, *he calked* it from end to end with willow withes (in the cracks between the planks); M 263, *having fenced around* the wall with their ox-hide shields; *δόρυ δουρί*, *joining* spear *close* to spear (so as to make a fence); O 566, *they surrounded* their ships with a brazen guard (guard of men clothed in brass).

φρέαρ, pl. **φρείατα,** ntr., *well*, Φ 197†.

φρήν K 45, *φρενός*, *ί* ζ 65, *α*, *ένες*, *ῶν*, *εσί(ν)*, *ένας*, (1) only pl., praecordia, *midriff* or *diaphragm* separating the heart and lungs from the remaining inwards, Π 481, K 10, ι 301; hence the nearly synonymous expressions: *κραδίη*, *ἦτορ*, *θυμὸς ἐνὶ φρεσίν*, *φρένες ἀμφὶ μέλαιναι*, (dark on both sides, wrapped in gloom). The meaning of the word *φρήν* in Homer stands midway between its literal and its figurative sense; it means *the heart and the parts about the heart*, and signifies (2) the *seat of thought, will, feeling; mind*, *soul*, *heart*, *consciousness*, κ 493;

even *life*, Ψ 104; θεῖναι ἐν φρεσίν, suggest, A 55; μετὰ and ἐνὶ φρεσίν, Δ 245; *discretion*, ἐσθλαί, ἀγαθῇσι, γ 266; βλάπτειν, blind, injure one's *understanding;* ἑλεῖν, ἐξέλετο, rob; *mind as will*, ἐτράπετο; often of *feelings* and *passions*, also φρένα as cognate acc., Υ 23; sing. used in reference to several persons, θ 131; κατὰ φρένα καὶ κατὰ θυμόν, in *mind* and heart.

φρήτρη, ας, ηφιν as dat. fem., (φράτηρ), gens, *clan*, B 363. (Il.)

φρίξ, φρῑκός, ἱ, φρῖχ' = φρῖκα, *ruffling, agitation;* esp. of surface of water; H 63, *a ripple* spreads over the sea.

φρίσσει, ουσι, aor. ἔφριξεν, ξας, pf. πεφρίκασι, υῖαι, horrere, *bristle*, Δ 282, H 62; *shudder at*, with acc., Λ 383, Ω 775; νῶτον, λοφιήν, are accs. of respect, bristle on the back, on the crest.

φρονέω, έεις, subj. έῃσι, ipf. φρόνεον, etc., prs. and ipf. always uncontracted, (φρήν), *have consciousness* (X 59, *live*); *think*, Z 79; *reflect*, ὧδε δέ οἱ φρονέοντι; *understand, consider*, π 136, τί, ὀπίδα; *deem*, Γ 98, I 608; ᾗ περ, just as, ἅ τε περ, the very things which; *intend*, P 286, χ 51; τὰ φρονέων ἵνα, *with this intention* that, E 564; πυκινά, *have* wise *thoughts;* ἰσόν τινι, *imagine one's self* the equal of; ἀγαθά, have noble thoughts (α 43, and Ψ 305, εἰς ἀγ., advise for one's good); φίλα, kindly; κακά, having hostile disposition, X 264; ἀταλά, gay; μέγα φρονέων, proud, bold, Π 258; ὅσσον, quantopere superbiunt, P 23; εὖ, intelligent, well-disposed, η 74; κακῶς, mean badly, σ 168; ἐφημέρια, thinking only of matters of a day, base-minded, φ 85.

Φρόνῖος, ίοιο, father of Noemon, β 386 and δ 630.

φρόνις, **φρόνιν**, τήν, (φρένες), *knowledge, counsel;* δ 258, much information.

Φρόντις, ιδος, wife of Panthoos, mother of Euphorbos and Polydamas, P 40†.

Φρόντις, ιος, son of Onetor, pilot of Menelaos, γ 282†.

Φρῠ́γες, ας, K 431, B 862, Γ 185; *Phrygians*, inhabitants of **Φρυγίη**, Γ 401, Π 719, Σ 291, a district in Asia Minor, lying partly on the Hellespontos (καθύπερθε, Ω 545), partly on the river Sangarios. Greek art is indebted to the Phrygian costume for the pointed cap, which is an attribute of skilled artisans like Hephaistos, and of shrewd wanderers like Odysseus: the cut, from a Greek relief, represents a Phrygian archer.

φῦ = ἔφυ from φύομαι.

φῠ́γἄδ(ε), *to flight*, in fugam, Θ 157. (Il.)

φῠ́γή, ῇ, fuga, *flight*, χ 306 and κ 117.

φῠγο-πτόλεμος, *cowardly*, ξ 213†.

φύζα, αν, fem., (for φυγja, fugio), flight, *consternation*, I 2; *panic*, ἐμβάλλειν.

φῠζἄκῐνῆς, ταῖς, *shy, timid*, N 102†.

φυήν, τήν, (φύομαι), naturâ, *growth*, (*in*) *bodily form, stature*, B 58, θ 134.

φῡκιόεντι, dat. from όεις, *full of seaweed. weedy*, Ψ 693†.

φῦκος, ntr., fucus, *sea-weed, sea-grass*, I 7†.

φυκτά, verbal adj. from φεύγω, only in phrase οὐκέτι—πέλονται, there is no longer *a chance of escape*, non iam effugium est, Π 128, θ 299.

φῠλἄκή, ῆς, αἱ, άς, fem., (φυλάσσω), vigilatio, excubiae, *watch, guard*, H 371; φυλακὰς ἔχον, keep guard; *outposts*, K 416.

Φῠλάκη, town in Phthiotis on northern slope of Mount Othrys, in domain of Protesilaos, λ 290, ο 236, B 695, 700, N 696, O 335.

Φῠλἄκίδης, *son of Phylakos*, Iphiklos, B 705, N 698.

φῠλάκους, τούς, (φυλάσσω), *guards*, Ω 566†.

Φύλἄκος, (1) father of Iphiklos, ο 231.—(2) Trojan, slain by Leitos, Z 35†.

φῠλακτῆρες, οἱ, nom. -κτήρ, (φυλάσσω), custodes, *guards,* I 66. (Il.)

φύλαξ, pl. **φύλᾰκες,** *ων, εσσι(ν), ας,* (φυλάσσω), custodes, vigiliae, *guards, outposts,* I 477. (Il.)

Φύλας, *αντος,* father of Polymele, king of Thesprotian Ephyra, Π 181 and 191.

φῠλάσσω, pres. (imp. φύλασσε, inf. σσέμεναι), and ipf. (ἐφύλασσεν and φύλασσε), fut. ξω, εις, ων, aor. φύλαξε, subj. ξομεν, mid. φυλάσσονται, σσομένοισι, vigilare, *keep watch,* νύκτα, per noctem; *watch over,* στρατόν; pass., K 309; δῶμα, "*keep,*" i. e. *not quit* the house; χόλον, *treasure up,* cf. β 350; *keep* faith, ὅρκια; *watch for,* νόστον τινά; mid. νύκτα, *watch for one's self; πεφυλαγμένος εἶναι, be on thy guard.*

Φῡλείδης, *εω* and *αο, son of Phyleus,* Meges, E 72, O 519, 528, Π 313.

Φῡλεύς, *έος, ῆα,* son of Augeias of Elis, banished by his father because, appointed arbiter in the dispute between him and Herakles, he decided in favor of the latter, B 628, K 110, 175, O 530, Ψ 637.

φῡλίης, *τῆς, wild olive-tree,* ε 477†.

φύλλον (φυλιον, folium), pl. **φύλλα,** *ων, οισι(ν),* ntr., *leaves,* Z 146, ε 483.

Φῡλο-μέδουσα, wife of Areithoos, H 10†.

φῦλον, *φῦλ(α), οις,* ntr., (φύομαι), *nation, people,* Πελασγῶν, Γιγάντων; *tribe, clan, family,* B 362; *class, species, host, swarm,* θεῶν, ἀνθρώπων, etc., μυίας, T 30.

φύλοπις, *ἶδος, ιδα* λ 314, and *ιν,* fem., (φῦλον), *combat, din of battle,* πολέμοιο, λ 314; also joined with πόλεμος, ἔργον, νεῖκος φυλόπιδος, angry combat, Υ 141; ἔστηκε, the combat arose, Σ 171.

Φῡλώ, *οῦς,* maid of Helene, δ 125 and 133.

φύξηλιν, acc., (φύξις), *cowardly,* P 143†.

φύξῐμον, ntr., (φύξις), *chance of escape,* ε 359†.

φύξιν, *τήν,* (φυγεῖν), *flight,* K 311, 398, 447.

φύρω, ipf. **ἔφῡρον,** fut. φύρσω, *moisten, wet,* δάκρυσιν, αἵματος; pass. pf. πεφυρμένον (η), αἵματι, δάκρυσιν, ρ 103, σ 173.

φύσας, *τάς,* (πτύω), *bellows,* Σ 412. (Σ)

φυσάω, **φῡσῶντες,** pres. part., ipf. ἐφύσων, *blow,* Σ 470 and Ψ 218.

φυσιόωντας, *τούς,* part. from -ιάω, (φῦσα), *panting,* Δ 227 and Π 506.

φῡσί-ζοος (ζωή), *producing life, life-giving,* αἶα, Γ 243.

φύσιν, *τήν,* (φύομαι), naturam, *quality, property,* κ 303†.

φῡτᾰλιῆς, *τῆς,* (φυτόν), *plantation; vineyard* or *orchard,* Z 195. (Il.)

φῡτεύει, *ουσι, ων,* ipf. φύτευεν, aor. ἐφύτευσαν, subj. φυτεύσω, inf. εῦσαι, (φυτόν), *plant,* σ 359; metaph. *devise, plan,* β 165, δ 668, O 134.

φῠτόν, *ῶν,* ntr., (φύω), *plant, tree,* coll. ω 227; ω 242, *plants.*

φύω, **φύει,** ipf. φύεν, fut. φύσει, aor. ἔφῡσε, (fui), *bring forth, produce,* φύλλα, Z 148, A 235, ποιήν, τρίχας; but pres. mid. φύονται, ipf. φύοντο, aor. ἔφῡν, ἔφυ = φῦ, φύντες, pf. **πεφύκᾰσι** = πεφύᾱσι, subj. πεφύκῃ, part. πεφυῶτας, υυῖα, plupf. πεφύκει, *grow,* of plants, Δ 484, Ξ 288, ψ 190; ἐξ ὁμόθεν, from one stem; of horns, Δ 109; see also ἐμφύομαι; only in Z 149, φύει = φύεται.

Φωκεῖς, *ήων, dwellers in* Phokis, B 517, 525, O 516, P 307.

φῶκαι, *άων, ῃσι, ας,* fem., *seals,* δ 404.

φωνέω, aor. **(ἐ)φώνησε,** *ήσας, άσης,* (φωνή), *raise the voice;* φωνήσας, *raising his voice = aloud,* with προσηύδα, προσέφη, ἀπαμείβετο; B 182, ὄπα depends upon ξυνέηκε, not so ω 535; elsewh. *speak aloud.*

φωνή, *ῇ, ήν, ῇσιν,* fem., (φάος, φάναι), *voice, cry,* P 696; of trumpet, Σ 219; *outcry,* P 111; also of beasts and birds, μ 86.

φωρῐᾰμῶν, *οῖσιν,* gen. and dat. pl. masc., (φωρέω), *chest, coffer, box,* Ω 228 and ο 104.

φῶς, φωτός, ntr., see φάος.

φώς, *φωτός, ί, (α), ε, ες, ῶν, ας,* masc., (φύω), *man,* freq. as appositive with ἰσόθεος, α 324, δ 247; differing from ἀνήρ, as having reference more to the exterior, yet alternating with it, P 98; Ἡρακλῆα, φ 26.

X.

χάδε, έειν, see χανδάνω.

χάζομαι, opt. **χαζώμε(σ)θ(α),** imp. ζεο, ipf. ἐχάζετο, χάζετ(ο), οντ(ο), fut. χάσσονται, aor. χάσσατ(ο), ασθαι, άμενος, pf. κεκάδοντο, usually with ὑπό Δ 497, cedere, *give way, withdraw before*, ἄψ, ὀπίσω, with gen., also with preps. ἐκ, ὑπό; Π 736, nor did he long retire before Hektor; elsewh. *rest from, abandon*, with gen. μάχης, δουρός. Here is also classed red. aor. **κεκαδών,** Λ 334, θυμοῦ, *depriving* of life.

χαίνω, aor. opt. **χάνοι,** part. χανών, pf. part. κεχηνότα, (hiare), *yawn*, γαῖα, χθών, may the earth *yawn for* me, i. e. *engulf* me; part. *with open mouth*, πρὸς κῦμα, μ 350, opening my mouth to the wave.

χαίρω, etc., pres., ipf. (ἔ)χαῖρε(ν), χαῖρον, iter. χαίρεσκεν, κον, fut. χαιρήσειν, aor. ἐχάρη, ημεν, ησαν, and χάρη, είη, έντες, pf. part. κεχαρηότα; mid. aor. χήρατο, also red. fut. κεχαρησέμεν, mid. fut. κεχαρήσεται, aor. κεχάροντο, οιτο, 3 pl. οίατο, (gratus), *rejoice*, ψ 32; (ἐν) θυμῷ, φρεσίν, νόῳ; φρένα, Ζ 481; χαίρων, *joyful*, δ 33, τ 461, each bidding the other a hearty farewell; also with ntr. subj., ἦτορ, κῆρ χαίρει; μέγα, greatly, exceedingly, constr. absolute, or with dat., ι 356, β 249; with part. agreeing with dat., Ε 682; with part. agreeing with subj., Γ 76; with οὕνεκα, ὅτι=quod. Χαῖρε, as salutation at meeting, *hail, welcome*, α 123, θ 408, 413, or at parting, ε 205; λ 248, because of our embrace; οὐ χαιρήσει, shall repent, Υ 363.

χαίτη, ην, αι, άων, ας, fem., *flowing hair*, Κ 15, Ξ 175, Ψ 141; juba, *mane*, Ζ 509, Ψ 282, 284.

χάλαζα, ῃ, αν, fem., grando, *hail*, Κ 6, Ο 170. (Od.)

χαλεπαίνει, οι, ε, ειν, ων, ipf. χαλέπαινε, aor. subj. χαλεπήνῃ, inf. ῆναι, (χαλεπός), *be vexed, angry*, τινί, π 114, Ξ 256, Υ 133; ἐπὶ ῥηθέντι δικαίῳ, at what has been justly said; *rage*, of wind and storm, Ξ 399; *storm*, ε 485.

χαλεπός, οῖο, ῷ, όν, οί, ῶν, οῖσι, ούς; ή, ῆς, ήν, αί, ά, comp. ώτερον, adv. ῶς, *bad, dangerous, serious*, χαλεπόν ἐστι, with (acc. and) inf., difficile est, it is *hard* or *difficult*; also pers. construction, Φ 482; Τ 80, for it is *annoying* even to one skilled (in speaking); *grievous, severe*; κεραυνός, *sharp* stroke of lightning; ὀνείδη, *harsh* insults; of persons, *angry*.

χαλέπτει, pres., (χαλεπός), irascitur, *be angry with*, δ 423†.

χᾰλῑνούς, τούς, *bit* of bridle, Τ 393†.

χᾰλι-φρονέοντα, part. from -έω, (-φρων), *thoughtless, indiscreet*, ψ 13†.

χᾰλι-φροσῦναι, αἱ, (-φρων) = levitas animi, *thoughtlessness*, π 310†.

χᾰλί-φρων (χαλάω, φρήν), *thoughtless*, δ 371 and τ 530.

χαλκεο-θωρήκων, gen. pl., *with breastplate of bronze*, Δ 448 and Θ 62.

χάλκεος, εῳ, εον, εοι, εα, and **χάλκειον,** ῳ, ων, η, ῃ, ας, (χαλκός), *of copper* or *bronze*, κύκλα, wheels; Ἄρης, clad in bronze; αὐγή, gleam of bronze; fig. brazen voice, ὄψ; ὕπνος = death, Λ 241; ἦτορ, heart of brass.

χαλκεο-φώνῳ, τῷ, (φωνή), *with voice of brass* or *bronze, loud* and *clear*, Ε 785†.

χαλκεύς, ῆες, masc., (χαλκός), faber, *coppersmith, worker in bronze*, also with ἀνήρ, ι 391, Δ 187; *worker in metals*, ι 391; *goldsmith*, γ 432.

χάλκευον, ipf., (χαλκεύς), fabricabar, *I wrought*, Σ 400†.

χαλκεῶνα, τόν, (χαλκεύς), *forge*, θ 273†.

χαλκήϊον, ια, (χαλκεύς), *smith's house, forge*, σ 328; smith's tools, γ 433.

χαλκ-ήρης, εος, εϊ, ε(α), .εσιν, εας, (ἀρηρώς), *fitted* or *furnished with bronze* = *brazen-shod*, of weapons and armor in general, Ο 544 (yet not of breastplate), Γ 316, Ο 535, Τ 53, Δ 469, Σ 534, Ν 650, Ρ 268.

χαλκίδα, τήν = κύμινδιν, Ξ 291†.

Χαλκίς, ιδος, fem., (1) town in Euboia on the strait Eurīpos, Β 537.—(2) town in Aitolia at mouth of the Euenos, ο 295.

χαλκο-βᾰρής, ές, (βάρος), *heavy with brass, of ponderous brass,* Ο 465; also fem. from βαρύς, **-βάρεια,** Λ 96, χ 259.

χαλκο-βᾰτές (βάτος), *with bronze threshold,* ν 4.

χαλκο-γλώχῖνος, gen., (γλωχίν), *with bronze point,* Χ 225†.

χαλκο-κνήμῖδες (κνημίς), *with greaves of bronze,* Η 41†.

χαλκο-κορυστῇ, ήν, (κορύσσω), *having bronze armor, brazen-clad,* Ε 699. (Il.)

χαλκο-πάρῃον, gen., (παρειά), *with side-pieces* (lit. cheeks) *of bronze,* of helmet, ω 523. (Il.)

χαλκό-ποδ(ε), du., (πούς), *with hoofs of bronze,* Θ 41 and Ν 23.

χαλκός, οῖο, and οῦ, and όφι, ῷ, όν, aes, *copper* or *bronze,* which consists of copper and tin (brass, an alloy of copper and zinc, was not known to the ancients), Ζ 48, φ 10; *utensils of bronze* of every sort, cf. ahenum, Σ 349; *knife, hook, axe, weapons* and *armor* in general, exc. shield and breastplate, φ 434 = with sword and spear; αἴθοπι, νώροπι, νηλέϊ, ταναήκεϊ, ἀτειρής; ἐπελήλατο, was riveted upon it; bronze (and gold) utensils served also as presents and ransom, Χ 50, 340.

χαλκο-τύπους (τύπτω), *inflicted with weapons of bronze,* Τ 25†.

χαλκο-χίτωνες, ων, ας, (χιτών), *with coat of bronze, brass-clad,* Α 371.

Χαλκωδοντιάδης, *son of Chalkodon,* king of the Abantes in Euboia, Elephenor, Β 541†.

Χάλκων, ωνος, a Myrmidon, the father of Bathykles, Π 595†.

χᾰμάδις, adv., (χαμαί), *to the ground,* Ζ 147, Ο 714, δ 114.

χᾰμᾶζε, adv., (χαμαί), *to the ground, down,* Γ 29; *to* or *into the earth,* Θ 134, φ 136.

χᾰμαί (old locative from χαμα, humi), *on the ground,* Ε 442; = χαμᾶζε, with πέσε, βάλλω, χύντο, Δ 482, Ε 588, Φ 181.

χᾰμαι-ευναί, pl., (εὐνή), *making their beds on the ground,* Π 235†.

χᾰμαι-ευνάδες, pl. fem., (εὐνάζω), σύες, = foreg., *lying on the ground,* κ 243 and ξ 15.

χανδάνω, ipf. **ἐχάνδᾰνον,** χάνδανε, fut. χείσεται, aor. ἔχαδε, χάδε, έειν, pf. part. κεχανδότα, plupf. κεχάνδει, (prehendo), *contain, hold,* ὅσον κεφαλὴ χάδε φωτός, he gave as loud a shout as the head of a man (*could*) *contain* (cf. Π 76), i. e. shouted as loud as he could, Λ 462.

χανδόν, adv., (χανδάνω), hiantis instar, *greedily,* φ 294†.

χάνοι, see χαίνω.

χᾰράδρης, gen., pl. αι, (χαράσσω), *gully, ravine, mountain torrent,* Δ 454 and Π 390.

χᾰρείη, χάρῃ, see χαίρω.

χαρίεις, **χᾰρίεν,** εντ(α), εσσαν, comp. ιέστερον, sup. ιέστατος, η, (χάρις), *graceful, charming, lovely,* Α 39; θ 167, winning gifts.

χᾰρίζεαι, εο, εσθαι, όμενος, η, ipf. χαρίζετο, aor. χαρίσαιτο, σασθαι, (χάρις), *show favor, gratify,* τινί; *court favor* by lies, ξ 387; ν 15, it is hard for a single person to *win for himself gratitude* for a gift, i. e. it is too much to expect that one person single-handed should make a gift and look to gratitude alone for the recompense; τί, *bestow abundantly,* Λ 134; and esp. παρεόντων, α 140, *giving freely of* her store; pass. plupf. **κεχάριστο,** *was dear* to her; pf. part. κεχαρισμένος, ε, α = χαρίεις, *pleasing, welcome;* ntr. pl., μοὶ—θείης, thou couldst gratify me.

χάρις, ῖν, ισιν, fem., (χαίρω), gratia, (1) *love, favor,* φέρειν τινί, confer upon one.—(2) *gratitude,* ἀρέσθαι, earn; Τρώεσσι, from the Trojans, ἐνεργέων, for benefits; οὔ τις ἦεν, one had no thanks; Ψ 650, may the gods grant thee in return for these things a soul-satisfying *recompense;* ἰδέω, would thank thee, χάριν Ἕκτορος, for Hektor's sake.—(3) *grace, charms,* κάλλεϊ καὶ χάρισι στίλβων, shining in beauty and grace; also of things, words, and actions, ο 320.

Χάρις, properly the same word as foreg. personified as wife of Hephaistos, Σ 382; pl. **Χάριτες,** ων, εσσι, *the Graces,* handmaids of Aphrodite, Ε 338, Ξ 267, Ρ 51, ζ 18, σ 194.

χάρμα, ατα ζ 185, ntr., (χαίρω), gaudium, *joy,* τ 471; as appositive, ζ 185; *source of malignant joy,* Ζ 82.

χάρμης, ῃ, fem., (χάρμα?), *joy in battle, desire for the fray, eagerness for combat,* χ 73, Ν 82; Δ 509, do not yield *in fury* to the Argives; also of animals, Π 823; also = *battle*, προκαλέσσατο, χάρμῃ, he had challenged to battle.

χᾰρ-οποί, *with sparkling eyes*, λ 611†.

Χάροπος, king of Syme, father of Nireus, B 672†.

Χάροψ, οπα, son of Hippasos, brother of Sokos, wounded by Odysseus, Λ 426†.

Χάρυβδις, ιος, ιν, (χάραδρα), fem., *Charybdis*, personification of the whirlpool opposite the "howling" Σκύλλα, μ 113, ψ 327; δεινήν, δῖα, μ 104, 235.

χᾰτέουσ(ιν), and part. έουσι, έουσα, (χάσκω, κῆτος), inhiare, γ 48, θεῶν, *have need of;* elsewh. *desire, demand*, ο 376, I 518.

χᾰτίζεις, ει, ων, (χατέω), with gen., (1) *have need of*, Σ 392, P 221, sc. αὐτῆς; elsewh. (2) *desire, beg*, χ 351.

χειῇ, τῇ, (χάσκω, hio), *hole*, X 93 and 95.

χεῖλος, **χείλει**, εα, εσ(σ)ι(ν) (χειῇ), *lip*, X 495, ὀδὰξ ἐν χείλεσι φύντες, biting their *lips*, α 381; *border* of the ditch, M 52, cf. δ 132, ο 116.

χεῖμα, ατος, ntr., hiems, *winter*, η 118, λ 190; *cold*, ξ 487. (Od.)

χειμά-ρροος (from σροος. ῥέω), -ρρῳ, E 88; -ρροι, ους, *swollen* (lit. flowing) *with* (water from melting) *snow*, ποταμός, N 138.

χειμερίῳ, ον, ῃ, αι, ῃσιν, (χεῖμα), *wintry*, Γ 222; ὕδωρ, *snow-water*, Ψ 420.

χειμών, ῶνος, *storm, rain*, Γ 4, P 549, δ 566.

χείρ, χειρός, (ί), (α), (ε), ες, ῶν, εσσ(ιν), ας, also χερί, χερσ(ίν) (χερ-, radical meaning "grasp," old Latin hir), manus, *hand, hand and arm*, Z 81, α 238; *fist*, στιβαρῇσιν, μ 174; ἀνέχειν, raise, in prayer, ν 355; τινί, pray to, Γ 318; pl. freq. in conventional use = sing., ν 225; 288, κατέρεξε, stroked him with the hand; ἐν χερσὶ τίθει, laid in his hands or arms, intrusted, of present or prize, A 441, γ 51; coupled with πόδες, χ 477; pl. fig. = *strength, might*, υ 237, Z 502, coupled with μένος, δύναμις, βίη; ἐπιφέρειν, ἐφιέναι, ἰάλλειν τινί, attack; (εἰς) χεῖρας ἱκέσθαι, fall into the *power*.

χειρῖδας, τάς, (χείρ), *loose* or *false sleeves*, bound over the hands instead of gloves, ω 230†.

χειρότερος, οισιν, (χέρης), = follg., Υ 436 and O 513.

χείρων, ονος, ι, α, ες, (χέρης), deterior, *inferior, worse*, O 641, λ 621, P 149, φ 325.

Χείρων, *Cheiron*, the centaur, skilled in healing and prophetic arts, intructor of Asklepios and Achilleus, δικαιότατος Κενταύρων, Λ 832, Δ 219, Π 143, T 390.

χείσεται, see χανδάνω.

χεῖσθαι, see χέω.

χελιδών, **χελῖδόνι**, hirundini, *swallow*, φ 411 and χ 240.

χέρᾰδος, τό, *gravel, pebbles*, Φ 319†.

χέρειον, see χερείων.

χερειότερος, ον, (χέρης), see follg., B 248, M 270.

χερείων, ονος, ι, α, (χέρης), deterior, *inferior, worse;* δέμας, in figure; φυήν, in size; οὔ τι χέρειον, 'tis not ill, with inf., ρ 176; τὰ χερείονα, ill counsels, A 576.

χέρης, **χέρηι**, χέρηα, χέρηες, ntr. χέρεια, (χείρ, i. e. under one's hand, subject), *humble, low, base*, A 80, Ξ 382; with gen. has force of comparative, Δ 400.

χερμάδιον, ῳ, α, οισι(ν), ntr., (χείρ), *loose stone*, of such a size as to fit the *hand* and be easily thrown, E 302, Π 774.

χερνῆτις, fem., (χείρ), *living by hand labor, woman who spins for daily hire*, M 433†.

χέρ-νῐβον (χείρ, νίπτω), *wash-basin*, Ω 304†.

χερ-νίπτομαι only aor. **-νίψαντο**, *washed their hands*, A 449†.

χέρ-νιψ, acc. **νῖβα**, *water for washing the hands*, α 136. (Od.)

Χερσι-δάμας, son of Priamos, slain by Odysseus, Λ 423†.

χέρσονδε, *on the dry land*, Φ 238†.

χέρσου, ῳ, ον, fem., *land, shore*, Δ 425, ζ 95.

χεῦαι, αν, ε, see χέω.

χεῦμα, τό, (χέω), that which is *poured out, casting*, Ψ 561†.

χέω, I. act. pres. and ipf. χέε(ν), χέον, mid. χέοντ(ο), etc., only uncontracted forms, exc. χεῖσθαι κ 518, fut. χεύω, aor. ἔχευε, εαν, (ἔ)χεῦ(εν), χεύαμεν, (ἔ)χεῦαν, subj. χεύομεν, ωσι, imp. χεῦον, άντων, inf. χεῦαι, part. χεύας, αντες, άντων, aor. mid. (ἔ)χεύατο.—II. pass. pf. κέχυνται, plupf. κέχυτ(ο), (ἐ)κέχυντο, aor. χυθείη; with pass. signif., aor. sync. (ἔ)χῦτο, (ἔ)χυντο, χυμένη, (χεϝω). I. fundo, *pour, scatter; Ζεύς ὕδωρ, it rains;* M 281, *pours down* snow; σῆμα, *raise* a monument; τύμβον, funeral mound; χθονί, *throw down, scatter* on the earth; ἔραζε, *let fall* on the ground; ἀυτμένα, *breathe forth; φωνήν, let resound;* mid. χοήν, *pour out* a libation, elsewh. with reflexive signif.; *strew upon one's* head, *throw one's arms around, they shower their missiles forth.*—II. pass. fundi, *flow, be strewn; πάλιν χύτο, flowed back, lie spread out;* with ἐκ, effundi; ἐμέ, *threw themselves* upon me, κ 415; ἀμφί τινι, *embrace.*

χηλός (χάσκω), **χηλοῖο,** οῦ, ῷ, όν, οί, οῖσιν, fem., *chest,* φ 51, Π 228.

χἠμεῖς = καὶ ἡμεῖς, B 238.

χήν, **χῆν(α),** ες, ῶν, ας, masc. and fem., (χαίνω? Ger. Gans), anser, *goose,* ο 174, B 460.

χηρᾰμόν, τόν, (χάσκω), *hole* or *crevice in a rock,* Φ 495†.

χήρατο, aor. from χαίρω.

χηρεύει (χήρη), *is deprived of, goes without,* ἀνδρῶν, hominibus, ι 124†.

χήρη, ην, αι, (χαίνω), *bereaved, widowed,* B 289; with gen. σοῦ, Z 408.

χήρωσας, ε, aor., (χήρη), *thou hast bereft,* P 36; *make desolate,* E 642.

χηρωσταί, οἱ, (χηρόω), *surviving relatives, heirs of one who dies childless,* E 158.

χήτεϊ, ει, ntr., nom. χῆτος, (χατέω), *from lack* (of), τινός, π 35. (Il.)

χθᾰμᾰλή, αί, comp. -ώτερον, sup. -ώτατον, (χαμαί), humilis, *low-lying, low,* λ 194, μ 101, N 683.

χθιζός, όν, ά, (χθές), hesternus A 424, ntr. = heri, *yesterday,* T 195; χθιζά τε καὶ πρωΐζ', it was (only) *yesterday* and day before yesterday when the ships of the Achaians were gathered in Aulis, = it was recently (verses 305–307 are parenthetical), B 303.

χθών, ονός, ί, α, humus, tellus, *ground, earth; ἐπὶ χθονί, upon the earth; ἐπὶ χθόνα, to the ground; the region,* ν 352.

χῑλῐ(α), *thousand,* H 471, Θ 562. (Il.)

χῑμαιρα (χίμαρος), *she-goat,* Z 181†.

Χῑμαιρα, fem., *Chimaera,* fire-spouting monster; its fore part a lion, its middle a goat, its hinder part a snake, sent as a plague upon Lykia, but slain by Bellerophon (the cut is from an Etruscan bronze statue of large size in the museum at Florence), Z 179 sqq., Π 328.

Χῖος, οιο, island on the Ionian coast of Asia Minor, γ 170, 172.

χιτών, **χιτῶνος,** νι, ι(α), νες, νων, ῶσι, νας, (word of Semitic origin; Heb. ketonet, Eng. cotton), *body-jacket, tunic,* Σ 595; like a shirt, but without sleeves, of woolen, white, worn by men and women next the body, and confined about the middle by a girdle, ξ 72; the cut represents Achilleus (clothed in the χιτών) taking leave of Peleus (cf. also Nos. 59, 73); there were also long tunics, see ἑλκεχίτωνες; of soldiers, *coat of mail, cuirass,* B 416, A 100 (cf. cuts Nos. 12, 17, 85, 93); λάινον, sarcastic expression for *death by stoning,* Γ 57.

χἰών, όνος, όνι, fem., *snow,* ζ 44, M 278.

χλαίνης, η, αν, αι, άων, *a piece of coarse, shaggy woollen cloth,* double or single, διπλῆ, δίπλακα, ἁπλοΐδας, freq. of purple color; *cloak, mantle,* X 493, ξ 460, 478, 480, 488, 500, 504, 516, 520, 529; it served also as covering in sleep, being in fact a sort of *blanket,* υ 4, 95, γ 349, δ 50.

χλούνην, τόν, (ἐν χλόῃ εὐνὴν ἔχοντα, etymology of ancients), *making its bed or lair in the grass,* epith. of wild boar, σῦν, I 539†.

χλωρηΐς, fem., (χλωρός), *pale green, yellow green,* epith. of nightingale as dwelling in fresh foliage, τ 518†.

Χλῶρις, ιδος, daughter of Amphion, king in Orchomenos, wife of Neleus, mother of Nestor, Chromios, Periklymenos, and of Pero, λ 281†.

χλωρός, όν, οί, άς, (χλοϜερός), flavum, *greenish yellow,* μέλι; δέος, *pale* fear, H 479, λ 43, O 4; elsewh. *fresh, verdant,* ι 379, 320.

χνόος, ὁ, (κνάω, κόνις), *foam,* ἁλός, ζ 226†.

χοάνοισιν, ntr., (χέω), *melting-pits,* Σ 470†.

χοήν, άς, (χέω), *libation, drink-offering,* esp. in sacrifices for the dead, κ 518 and λ 26.

χοῖνιξ, **χοίνῑκος,** fem., *measure for grain,* = a soldier's daily ration, about one quart; ἅπτεσθαί τινος, taste of my bread, τ 28†.

χοίρε(α), ntr., (χοῖρος), κρέα, *of swine, swine-flesh, pork,* ξ 81†.

χοῖρος, **χοίρων,** masc., porcus, *hog,* ξ 73†.

χολάδες, fem., (χορδή, haru-spex), *bowels, intestines,* Δ 526 and Φ 181.

χόλος, οιο, ου, ῳ, ον, (fel), *gall* Π 203, elsewh. *wrath,* τινός, as subj. or obj. gen. *one's wrath* or *wrath against one;* τινί, out of regard to any one, with μεθέμεν, λήσεσθαι; X 94, *rage.*

χολόω (χόλος), act. fut. **χολωσέμεν,** aor. ἐχόλωσεν, σατε, σῃς; mid. pass. pres. χολοῦμαι, οῦται, fut. ώσεαι, pf. κεχόλωται, ῶσθαι, ωμένος, etc., plupf. κεχόλωσο, ωτο, 3 pl. ώατο, 3 fut. κεχολώσομαι, σεαι, σεται, aor. (ἐ)χολώσατο, χολώσαιτο, σάμενος, etc., aor. pass. (ἐ)χολώθη, χολωθῇς, θείς, I. *provoke, enrage,* A 78, Σ 111, θ 205, σ 20.—II. mid. pass. *be angry,* θυμῷ, ἐνὶ φρεσί, κηρόθι, θυμόν, φρένα, ἦτορ, in mind, heart; τινί, at or with a person; τινός, because of (also with ἐκ, εἵνεκα, ἀμφ' ἀστραγάλοισι), I 523, N 203, P 710.

χολωτοῖσι, dat. pl., (χολόω), *angry, wrathful,* ἐπέεσσιν, Δ 241, χ 26.

χορδήν, τήν, (χολάδες), chordam, *string of gut,* φ 407†.

χοροι-τυπίῃσιν, ταῖς, (τύπτω), tripudio, *choral dance,* Ω 261†.

χοροῖο, ῳ, όν, (ὄνδε, *to the dance*), οί, masc., *choral dance,* (1) *dancing-place,* Σ 590, μ 318.—(2) *dance,* χορῷ καλή, beauteous in the dance, Π 180.

χόρτῳ, οισιν, masc., (hortus), *enclosure,* Λ 774 and Ω 640.

χραῖσμ(ε), aor., = ἔχραισμε, η(σι), ωσιν, εῖν, fut. ήσει, ησέμεν, 1 aor. χραίσμησε, ῆσαι, (χρήσιμος), always with negative, *be useful to,* τινί; with reference to—, τί; hence *help, aid,* and *ward off* any thing, A 566, 589, Λ 117, 120, Φ 193.

χράομαι (χρέος), part. **χρεώμενος,** trisyll., Ψ 834, *according to his need;* pf. κεχρημένος, ῳ, ον, with gen. *desiring,* T 262 (πρόφασιν, as a pretext); as adj. *needy,* ρ 347; plupf. φρεσὶ γὰρ κέχρητ' ἀγαθῇσιν, she had good sense, right feelings.

χραύσῃ, aor. subj. from χραύω (χράϜω, χρῶς), *scratch, graze, wound slightly,* E 138†; here belongs also aor. **ἔχραε,** άετ(ε), *fall upon, assail,* τινά; with inf. of purpose, Φ 369, φ 69; but with τοι, οἱ δαίμων, the god *has handled* (thee, him) hardly.

χράω, part. **χρείων,** *delivering an oracle,* θ 79; mid. fut. χρησόμενος, ον, ους, *to have an oracle given* to one, *for the purpose of receiving the divine response, to consult with,* θ 81, λ 165, κ 492.

χρεῖος, see χρέος.

χρείων, see χράω.

χρειώ, see χρεώ.

χρείως, see χρέος.

χρεμέτιζον, ipf., *neigh, whinny,* M 51†.

χρέος θ 353, λ 479, χρείως θ 355, also v. l. χρεῖος, τό, *want;* Τειρεσίαο κατά = *to consult with* Teiresias; elsewh. *affair, business, need,* β 45, α 409; *debt,* ὀφείλειν, owe; *payment of debt,* θ 353;

ἀποστήσωνται, recompensent, recover for themselves (pay back) *the debt* of yesterday, N 745 (v. l. ἀποτίσωνται, see themselves repaid for).

χρεώ, subst. fem., [monosyll., short, Λ 606], (χρέος, χράομαι), *want, need,* ἐστίν, γίγνεται, cf. opus est, ι 136, Φ 322, δ 634, cf. A 341, I 197; with inf., Ψ 308; τινά, α 225, K 85; with acc. and inf., Σ 406, δ 707, Φ 322; τινά τινος, I 75, 607, K 43, δ 634; parallel form **χρειώ** ἱκάνει, εται, ἵκει, *necessity* arises; τινά (τόσον, so sharply), τινός; shall he have any *need* of a tomb, Φ 322.

χρεώμενος, see χράομαι.

χρή, subst. = χρεώ, sc. ἵκει, ἐστίν, opus est, (there is) *need*, ι 50; with inf., Δ 57, Π 631, γ 209, ω 324; with pers. acc. and inf., H 331, Ψ 644, ζ 27, ω 407, cf. A 216, κ 490; οὐδέ τι (σέ) χρή, with inf. (to be supplied, Π 721, Υ 133, τ 500), or expressed, Ψ 478, α 296, τ 118; τινά τινος, H 109, α 124, χ 377.

χρηΐζεις, ζων, οντι, οντα, pres., (χρή), *need*, τινός, ρ 558, Λ 834.

χρήμᾰτ(α), ασι, ntr., (χράομαι), *what one has for need* or *use, possessions, property*, β 78, ξ 285, π 315. (Od.)

χρίμπτω, aor. pass. **χριμφθείς**, (scrimp? χρίω?), πέλας, *approaching* very near, κ 516†.

χρίω, ipf. **χρῖον**, εν, aor. ἔχρισε(ν), χρῖσεν, σαν, σον, σαι, ἐλαίῳ, *smear* with oil, *anoint*, δ 252; also bodies of dead, Ψ 186; ἀμβροσίῃ, Π 670; mid. χρίεται, εσθαι, fut. χρίσομαι, aor. σάμεναι, *anoint one's self*, ἐλαίῳ, κάλλει; ἰοὺς φαρμάκῳ, *smear* one's arrows with juice of poisonous plants, α 262.

χροιῇ, τῇ, (χρώς), prop. *surface, skin* = *body*, Ξ 164†.

χρόμᾰδος, masc., (χρεμετίζω), *grinding*, Ψ 688†.

Χρομίος, οιο, (1) son of Priamos, slain by Diomedes, E 160.—(2) son of Neleus, λ 286, Δ 295.—(3) a Lykian, slain by Odysseus, E 677.—(4) a Trojan, slain by Teukros, Θ 275.—(5) chief of Mysians, P 218, 494, 534.

Χρόμις, ιος, = Χρομίος (5), B 858.

χρόνιον, acc., (χρόνος), *after a long time*, ἐλθόντα, ρ 112†.

χρόνον, τόν, (χερ-, χραίνω?), *time*, πολύν, δηρόν, long time; τόσον, so long, Ω 670, ὀλίγον; ἕνα χ., *once for all;* ἐπί, *for a time*, μ 407.

χροός, οΐ, όα, see χρώς.

χρῡσ-άμπῡκας, acc., (ἄμπυξ), *with frontlet of gold*, of horses, E 358. (Il.)

χρῡσ-άορον, ον, (ἄορ), *with sword of gold*, Apollo, E 509 and O 256.

χρύσεος, ου, ῳ, ον, οι, οισ(ιν); ῃ, ῃ, ην, αι, ῃσιν; εον, εα, and parallel form **χρύσειον**, ῳ, οι, οις; η, ῃ, ην, αι, ῃς, ας; (α), (χρυσός), aureus, *golden, adorned with gold;* esp. of all which the gods wear or possess, Ἀφροδίτη, δ 14, *adorned with gold* (see cut No. 2); *golden* = *golden yellow*, ἔθειραι, νέφεα.

Χρύση, *Chryse*, a harbor town in Troas, with temple of Apollo, A 37, 100, 390, 431, 451.

Χρῡσηΐς, ίδος, *Chryseis*, daughter of Chryses, A 111, 143, 182, 310, 369, 439. (Her proper name was Astynome.)

χρῡσ-ηλάκᾰτος, ου, ῳ, (ἠλακάτη), *with golden arrows*, Artemis, δ 122.

χρῡσ-ήνιος (ἡνία), *gleaming with gold*, Z 205 and θ 285.

Χρύσης, αο, voc. η, *Chryses*, the priest of Apollon Smintheus at Chryse: his daughter Astynome had fallen as booty to Agamemnon; upon his refusal to release her on ransom to her father, he induces Apollo, in answer to his prayers, to send a pestilence upon the Greek camp, which compels Agamemnon to yield up the maiden, A 11, 370, 442, 450.

Χρῡσό-θεμις, daughter of Agamemnon and of Klytaimnestra, I 145 and 287.

χρῡσό-θρονος, ου, ον, (θρόνος), *on throne of gold, golden-throned* (cf. Aphrodite in cut No. 2); epithet of Eos, Hera, Artemis, A 611, ε 123.

χρῡσο-πεδίλου (πέδιλον), *golden-sandalled* [λ 604].

χρῡσό-πτερον (πτερόν), *with wings of gold*, Θ 398 and Λ 185.

χρῡσό-ρραπις, voc. ι, (ϝραπ-), *bearing a golden rod*, of Hermes with his magic staff, κ 277, 331, ε 87.

χρῡσός, οῖο, οῦ, ῳ, όν, *gold*, unwrought and wrought; τάλαντον, a pound; collective = *utensils of gold*, ο 207.

χρῡσο-χόον, *τόν*, (*χέω*), *goldsmith*, *γ* 425†.

χρώς, *ωτός*, *ῶτ(α)*, and *χροός*, gen., *οἷ*, *όα*, (*χραϝος*, *σκραυ-*), properly *surface*, esp. surface of the body, *skin*, N 191, *τ* 204, *δ* 750, *φ* 412; then, *color of the skin*, *complexion*, *τρέπεται*, changes; *body*, yet always with reference to the skin, *καλός*, *περὶ χροΐ*, *λ* 191, *χ* 113.

χυμένη, *χύτο*, see *χέω*.

χῦσις, *ιν*, fem., (*χέω*), *heap*, *ε* 483, 487, *τ* 443.

χυτλώσαιτο, aor. opt. mid. from *χυτλόω*, (*χύτλος*), *bathe and anoint one's self*, *ζ* 80†.

χῡτή, *ήν*, (*χέω*), *heaped up*, *γαῖα*, sepulchral mound, Z 464, *γ* 258.

χωλεύων (*χωλός*), *limping*, Σ 411, 417, Υ 37.

χωλός, *όν*, *αί*, claudus, *lame*, *ἕτερον πόδα*, in one foot, B 217.

χώεται, *εο*, *όμενος*, *οιο*, etc., ipf. *χώετο*, aor. (*ἐ*)*χώσατο*, subj. *σεται*, part. *σάμενος*, *η*, (*χέω*), confundi, *be in agitation*, *κῆρ*, (*κατὰ*) *θυμόν*, *φρεσίν*, in heart, in mind; *terrified*, A 380; esp. irâ suffundi, *be wroth*, at some one, *τινί*; because of something, *τινός*; also with *ὅτι*, *θ* 238.

χωρέω (*χῶρος*), fut. **χωρήσουσι**, aor. *χώρησεν*, (*ἐ*)*χώρησαν*, *σειεν*, *σαντ(α)*, *σαντες*, *give place*, *withdraw*, *τινί*, before some one, N 324; *τινός*, from something, M 406, Π 629; *ἀπό*, N 724; *τόσσον*, so far, Π 592; *πάλιν*, back.

χώρη, *ης*, *ῃ*, *ας*, (*χῶρος*), *place*, Ψ 349, *π* 352; *space*, Ψ 521, *θ* 573, *regions*, *countries*.

χωρίς, adv., (*χῆρος*), *separately*, *apart*, *by one's self*, H 470, *ι* 221 sq.

χῶρος, *ου*, *ῳ*, *ον*, (*χερ-*, Ger. fassen), *space*, *plot*, Γ 315, 344, Θ 491, where in fact *a space* (of the ground) was visible among the corpses; *spot*, *region*, N 473, Φ 262.

Ψ.

ψάμαθος, *οιο*, *ου*, *ῳ*, *ον*, *οι*, *οισι(ν)*, fem., (*ψάμμος*), *sand*, in stream, on strand, *sand hills* of the sea-shore, *δ* 426; as simile for a countless multitude, B 800.

ψάμμῳ, fem., (sabulo), *sand*, *μ* 243†.

ψᾱρῶν, gen., acc. *ψῆρας*, masc., *starlings*, *meadow-larks*, P 755 and Π 583.

ψαύουσι, ipf. *ψαῦον*, 1 aor. subj. *ψαύσῃ*, (*ψαϝω*), *touch*, *graze*, with gen. *ἐπισσώτρου*; N 132, Π 216, the helmets touched with their crests the crests of the others when they (their wearers) nodded.

ψεδνή (*ψάω*), *rubbed off*, *thin*, *sparse*, B 219†.

ψευδ-άγγελος (*ψεῦδος*), *reporting lies*, *false messenger*, O 159†.

ψευδέσσιν, *τοῖς*, nom. sing. *ψευδής*, *to liars*, Δ 235†.

ψεῦδος, *εα*, *εσσι(ν)*, ntr., *falsehood*, *lie*, *οὔτι ψ.*, in no respect as falsehood, = with perfect truth, I 115; *τ* 203, he spoke relating many *fables* resembling facts.

ψεύδονται, imp. *ε(ο)*, part. *όμενα*, fut. *σομαι*, 1 aor. *σάμενοι*, *η*, (*ψεῦδος*), mentiri, *lie*; *ὅρκια*, break the treaty; K 534, am I about (against my will) to *speak a falsehood* or the truth? *do I deceive myself* or—?

ψευστήσεις, fut. from *-έω*, (*ψεύστης*), *thou wilt* (tho' thou know'st it not) *lie*, *thou deceivest thyself*, T 107†.

ψεῦσται, *οἱ*, (*ψεύδομαι*), fraudatores, *liars*, *deceivers*, Ω 261†.

ψηλαφόων, part. from *-άω*, *feel about*, *grope*, *χερσί*, *ι* 416†.

ψῆρας, see *ψαρῶν*.

ψηφῖδες, *αἱ*, (*ψῆφος*), *pebbles*, Φ 260†.

ψῑάδας, *τάς*, guttas, *drops*, Π 459†.

ψῑλόν, *ήν*, (*ψάω*), *worn smooth and bare*, *ν* 437; *ἄροσις*, *bare* grain fields; i. e. without tree or shrub; *τήν* (*νῆα*), *μ* 421, *dismantled*, without sides.

ψολόεντι, *a.* (ψόλος, Ger. schwül), *smouldering, sulphurous,* of thunderbolt, ψ 330 and ω 539.

Ψυρίη, fem., small island between Lesbos and Chios, γ 171†.

ψυχή, ῆς, ῇ, ήν, αί, έων, άς, fem., (ψύχω), anima, properly *breath of life, life,* X 161, I 322, γ 74, regarded as escaping, like a material substance, at the moment of death from the mouth, the word is also used in the same sense of the *life* of beasts, ξ 426; then in derived sense, εἴδωλον, the *soul of the departed* in the lower world, disembodied, and so without φρένες, yet retaining the outward appearance which it had in life, described λ 207, σκιῇ εἴκελον (εἴδωλον), and yet as ψυχή, 205. ψυχή has not in Homer its later common signif. of the *soul* as the *nobler, immortal part* of man, but denotes the *spirit* only as opposed to the body.

ψῦχος, **ψύχεος,** ntr., (ψύχω), *cold, coolness,* κ 555†.

ψυχρῷ, όν, ή, ῇ, αί, (ψῦχος), frigidus, *cold,* T 358, O 171.

ψύχω, aor. part. **ψύξᾶσα,** (πτύω, spuo), *blow, breathe;* ἦκα, softly, Υ 440†.

ψωμοί, masc., (ψάω), *morsels, gobbets* of human flesh, ι 374†.

Ω.

ὦ, sign of voc., may stand between adj. and subst., δ 206; merged by synizesis with following vowel, ρ 375.

ὤ, interjection expressive of astonishment and of grief, heu, vae, *oh! alas!* ὤ μοι ἐγὼ δειλός, ε 299; ὤ πόποι, ν 209.

Ὠγυγίη, mythical island of Kalypso, α 85, ζ 172, η 244, 254, μ 448, ψ 333. The ancients identified it with Gaudes, now Gozzo, a small island near Malta.

ὧδε, adv. from ὅδε, sic, *in this wise, so, thus,* (1) referring to what is directly before the thoughts, Ω 398, β 28, ι 447, δ 141, Γ 300; *to such a degree,* γ 125, E 897; with imp. it may be translated *come; a* 182, *just, this moment,* cf. δ 159; referring to what has just happened or come to one's knowledge, β 185, Λ 656; to what in a wider sense of the term may be regarded as present, B 258, ρ 587; *so surely as,* Σ 464; φ 196, *so, right before your eyes; so,* by emphasizing one alternative, negativing all others, ζ 39, Δ 308; with following explanatory clause, ὡς, Θ 523, γ 221; adeo, K 70, M 346.—(2) referring to what follows, π 117, A 181, Ω 661, Θ 415; ὧδε δέ τις εἴπεσκεν, δ 769, B 271; ὧδε γὰρ ἐξερέω, π 440, A 212; ὧδε δέ (μοι φρονέοντι) δοάσσατο κέρδιον εἶναι, κ 153, N 458, Π 652, ε 474; ἔρξαι, ε 342; ξυνίει, ζ 289; ἐπιτέλλομαι, Λ 765.

ᾤδεε, see οἰδέω.

ὠδίνων, ουσαν, part., (αὖ, δίνη?), *writhe,* ὀδύνῃσι, with pain; *be in travail,* Λ 269.

ὠδῖνάς, τάς, (ὠδίς, ὠδίνω), *laborpains,* Λ 271†.

ὠδύσαο, ατο, see ὀδύσσομαι.

ὤθεῖ, ipf. ὤθει, iter. ὤθεσκε, aor. ἔωσε, ὦσα, ας, (εν), αν, ῃ, αιμεν, αι, iter. ὤσασκε, 1 aor. mid. ὤσατ(ο), ἀμεθ(α), αντο, αιτ(ο), αισθε, ασθαι, (Ϝοθέω), *thrust, push, shove,* ἰθὺς τάφροιο, straight toward the ditch; λ 596, *was rolling* the stone aloft; παρέξ, thrust off to one side = off from land; mid., Π 592, protruserunt, *thrust themselves = press forward;* τινά, *drive before them, force back, pursue.*

ὠίετο, ὠισθείς, see ὀίω.

ὦκ(α), adv. from ὠκύς, *quickly,* Λ 354, A 447.

Ὠκαλέη, village in Boiotia near Haliartos, B 501†.

Ὠκεανός, οῖο, (1) *mighty stream encompassing the earth and sea* (Milton's "ocean stream"); the constellations exc. the Great Bear, ε 275, sink below and emerge from its waters as they set and rise; the Pygmies dwell at its southern border; just this side of its western limit is Elysion; while with its opposite bank begins the lower world, the grove of Persephoneia, the chasm into which the waters plunge, κ 511 sqq., and here is the entrance to the dwelling of Aides.—(2) as person, the river-god *Okeanos*, husband of Tethys, father of all the streams and fountains, and indeed of all the gods, δ 568, κ 139, Ξ 311, 201. (In the adjoining cut, from a representation of the shield of Achilleus, the outer rim, No. 5, indicates the ocean stream.)

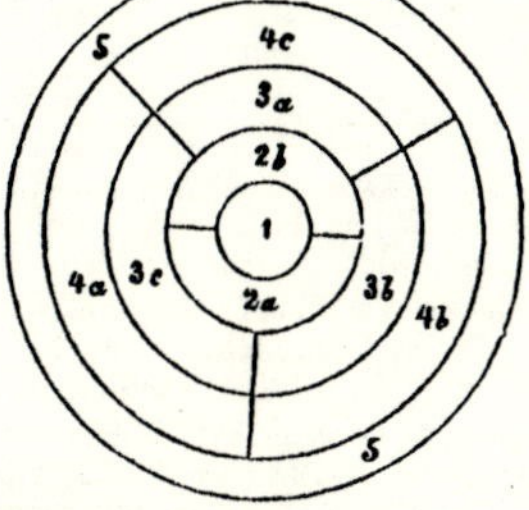

ὤκιστος, α, see ὠκύς.

ᾤκτειρε, see οἰκτείρω.

ὠκύαλος, ου, *swift-sailing* (ship), Ο 705, μ 182.

Ὠκύαλος, a Phaiakian, θ 111†.

ὠκύ-μορος, ῳ, α, ων, sup. ώτατος, Α 505, (μόρος, mors), *quickly dying, doomed to a speedy death*, Σ 95, Α 417; ἰοί, *quickly slaying*, χ 75.

ὠκυ-πέτα, du., (πέτομαι, -πέτης), *swift-flying*, Ν 24 and Θ 42.

ὠκύ-ποροι, ων, οισι(ν), (πόρος), *swift-sailing, fast-going*, ε 176, δ 708, Α 421.

ὠκύ-ποδες, ων, εσσι, (πούς), *swift-footed*, horses, Ε 296, σ 263.

ὠκύ-πτερος (πτερόν), *swift-winged*, Ν 62†.

ὠκυ-ρόῳ, for -ρρόῳ, (ῥέω), *swift-flowing*, Ε 598 and Η 133.

ὠκύς, εῖ, ύν, έες, έας, έα; εῖαι, ειάων, είῃσ(ιν), έας; ύ, έα, superl. ὠκύτατον, θ 331; ὤκιστος, ntr. α, as adv., *very quickly, at once*, χ 77, 133, (ocior), *swift, quick, fleet*, of men, animals, and things; πόδας, fleet of foot, swift-footed; adj. in predicate = adv., *quickly*, μ 374, Ψ 880.

Ὠλενίη πέτρη, *Olenian* rock, peak of Mount Skollis, on the borders of Elis, Β 617, Λ 757.

Ὤλενος, fem., town in Aitolia, on Mount Arakynthos, Β 639†.

ὠλεσί-καρποι (ὄλλυμι), *dropping their fruits*, of willows, which lose their fruit before ripening, κ 510†.

ὦλκα (for ἄϝλοκα, from ϝέλκω, ἕλκω), sulcus, *furrow*, Ν 707 and σ 375.

ὠμ-ηστής, αἱ, ῇσιν, (ὠμός, ἐσθίω), *eating raw flesh* (cf. crudelis), of animals; *savage, brutal*, ἀνήρ, Ω 207.

ὠμο-γέρων (ὠμός, cf. cruda senectus), *fresh, vigorous old man*, Ψ 791†.

ὠμο-θετεῖτο, ipf., -θέτησαν, aor., (ὠμά, θεῖναι), *place* (as offering to the gods) *raw pieces of flesh upon the* μηρία, already wrapped in the caul = *consecrate flesh*, Α 461; ξ 427, mid. *have flesh consecrated.*

ὦμος, οιο, ου, ῳ, ον, ω, οιιν, οι, ων, οισ(ιν), ους, umerus, *shoulder*, Ο 474, β 3.

ὠμόν, acc. masc., ntr. ῷ, ά, (amarus), *raw, uncooked*; opp. ὀπταλέα, μ 396; ὠμὸν βεβρώθοις, couldst eat *alive*; ὠμά, devour *raw*; γήραϊ, immaturo, in *premature* old age, ο 357.

ὠμο-φάγοι, οισ(ιν), *eating raw flesh*, epith. of wild beasts, Ε 782, Η 256. (Il.)

ᾤμωξαν, εν, see οἰμώζω.

ὤνατο, see ὄνομαι.

ὤνησας, σε, see ὀνίνημι.

ὠνητή, verbal adj., (ὠνέομαι), *bought* = *slave*-mother, ξ 202†.

ὦνον, τόν, (ϝῶνον, venum), *purchase-money*; ὀδαίων, hurry forward the delivery of the goods given in exchange for your freight, i. e. the return freight, ο 445.

ὠνοσάμην, see ὄνομαι.

ᾠνο-χόει, see οἰνο-χοέω.

ᾦξε, see οἴγνυμι.

ὥρεσσιν, see ὄαρ.

ὤρετο, see ὄρνυμι.

ὥρη, ῃ, ην, αι, ας, (Ger. Jahr, Eng. year), (1) *season, seasons*, Horae, Β 471, Ζ 148, ε 485; περὶ δ' ἔτραπον, turned about (to begin the new year); ἐπήλυθον, drew near, κ 469, both expressions representing the seasons under the figure of maidens in the choral dance, receding and approaching with measured step; εἴαρος or εἰαρινή, verna, *spring-time;* also used alone = *Spring,* B 468.—(2) generally, *the fitting time* (καιρός), ἐν, εἰς, in tempore, ad tempus; with gen. κοίτοιο, γάμου, etc., with inf., λ 373, φ 428, with acc. and inf., λ 330.—(3) personified, the *Hours,* door-keepers of Olympos and goddesses of the seasons, πολυγηθέες, Φ 450, E 749, Θ 393, 433.

Ὠρεί-θυια, a Nereid, Σ 48†.

ὥρια, τά, (ὥρη), *in their season,* ι 131†.

ὥριστος, from ὁ ἄριστος.

Ὠρίων, ωνος, (ὄαρ), *Orion,* the mighty and beautiful hunter, λ 310, Σ 486; continues the chase in the lower world, λ 572; beloved of Eos, ε 121; as constellation, Σ 488, ε 274.

ὥροpε, see ὄρνυμι.

Ὦρος, a Greek, slain by Hektor, Λ 303†.

ὦρσε, το, ὠρώρει, see ὄρνυμι.

1. **ὡς,** prep., with acc., *to,* ὡς τὸν ὁμοῖον, ρ 218†.

2. **ὡς** (old abl. of pron. ϝος, orig. ϝωτ, thence ϝως, then ὡς; in anastrophe ὥς; lengthens, by position, a preceding vowel followed by a single consonant, e. g. θεὸς ὥς, σύες ὥς, thirty-seven examples, μ 396, δ 413, Δ 482, E 78), *as,* A. **Adv.** of manner: quomodo, quam, ut, *just as, as,* before single words, where a verb may be easily supplied, e. g. ὡς τὸ πάρος πέρ, θ 31, τ 340; pleonastically with ἐοικώς, Ψ 430; especially freq. in relat. sentence, (1) modal: e. g. ἐκέλευ(σ)εν, χ 190; ἂν ἐγὼ ϝείπω πειθώμεθα, μ 213; *of what sort,* I 528; also with κέ, with opt., ψ 60 (hence the transition to B., see below).—(2) comparative: corresponding to τώς, ὥς, οὕτω, τόσσον, ξ 441; in comparisons or similes, (a) with ind. pres. and aor.; (b) with subj. pres. and aor., I 323, E 161, X 93, ε 369, θ 523, B 475; so esp. ὡς ὅτε, which always (exc. Λ 325, Δ 130, O 606, 624, Π 642) precedes the principal sentence; the principal clause follg. with ὥς thirty-one times, B 147, E 599 (τοῖοι, Δ 141); protasis begins with ὡς ὅτ' ἄν ten times, K 5, Λ 269, ε 394, χ 468; shortened to ὡς ὅτε = velut (see ὡς εἰ), *just like,* λ 368; with fut. after opt., to give assurance of the desired result; *so sure as,* ι 525 (cf. B. 3).—(3) exclamatory: *how!* π 364, ω 194.—B. **Conjunction,** (1) temporal: *as, when,* quom, always of facts, with indic., Ψ 871, when (while) he (Teukros) was (still) shooting.—(2) explanatory, after τόγε, γ 346, = ὅτι οὕτως, *that, because, for,* Δ 157, β 233, ρ 243.—(3) final: *that, in order that,* A 32, ν 402, β 316; the transition from the relative to the final use of ὡς is illustrated by follg. examples, cf. quâ ratione, (a) ὡς, with opt. and κέν, ψ 135, ω 532, β 53; and ἄν, ν 402, ο 538; more freq. (b) with subj., A 559; with imp. or inf. used as imp. in principal sentence, B 363, ρ 75 (κέν, B 385, A 32, Z 143, τ 319, τ 321, χ 117, T 151; with ἄν, π 169); with principal verb in subj., Z 259 (κέν, I 112, Ω 76, α 87; ἄν, δ 672); with principal verb to be supplied in opt., Θ 513; principal verb fut. indic. (κέν, β 316, 368, ε 144, α 205); pres., H 294 (κέν, Φ 459); pret., A 559, Ω 337 (ἄν, ω 360, π 84); expressing actual purpose with subj., Θ 182, Π 83.—(4) expressing a wish, *oh that!* with opt., Σ 107, X 286, α 47; with κέν, Z 281; μή, ο 359.

1. **ὥς** = ὡς, *as,* when it receives the accent by anastrophe, see ὡς 2.

2. **ὥς** (ὣς after οὐδ' and καί), adv., *thus,* καὶ ὥς, even so, nevertheless; οὐδ' ὥς, ne sic quidem, not even so, in no wise, (1) ὥς, at beginning of sentence, always (exc. π 28, 64) in arsi, ἔφατο, φάτο, υ 54; φαμένη, εἰπών, φωνήσας, ὥς ἔφαθ', οἱ δ' ἄρα τοῦ μ. μ., ο 220; ὥς ἔφαθ', οἱ δ' ἄρα πάντες ἀκὴν ἐγ., π 393; ὣς οἱ μὲν τοιαῦτα πρὸς ἀλλήλ. ἀγ., θ 333.—(2) correlative, ὅπως, ο 112; ὥς, talis, *such,* Δ 319, Λ 762, κ 416; *thus,* A 512; *then,* Ξ 294, T 16, Υ 424.—(3) explanatory, *so then,* Δ 157; resumptive, *thus as you think, this being the case,* τ 85, 300, ι 84; *thus for instance,* ε 121. For ὥς δ' αὔτως, ζ 166, see αὔτως.

ὡς, εἰ, ὡσεί, never separated by intervening word, *as if,* quasi, ι 314;

also with part., E 374, and without verb, *like, just as*, η 36.

ὥς περ, ὥσπερ, often separated, *just as, even as*; ὡς ἔσεταί περ, just as it shall come to pass, A 211, τ 312; ὥς περ (v. l. ὅς περ) ἂν εἴη, just as I would that it might come to pass.

ὥς τε, ὥστε (adv. from ὅς τε), *like as, just as*, Γ 23, 381, α 227, 308; also in sentences containing a comparison, with ind. or subj., B 475; explanatory, freq. followed by inf. of result, I 42, ρ 21; *as it were* (of girls), ζ 122.

ὠτειλῆς, ήν, έων, άς, fem., (οὐτᾶν), *wound*, τ 456, Σ 351.

Ὦτος, (1) son of Poseidon and of Iphimedeia, a giant, λ 308, E 385.—(2) of Kyllene, chief of the Epeians, slain by Polydamas, O 518.

ὠτώεντα, τόν, nom. -ώεις, (ὦτα), *with ears* or *handles*, Ψ 264 and 513.

ὡὐτός = ὁ αὐτός, E 396†.

ὤφελλον, ὤφελες, see ὀφείλω.

ὠχρήσαντα, part. aor. from ὠχράω, (ὦχρος), *having become pale*, λ 529†.

ὦχρος, masc., p a l l o r, *paleness*, Γ 35†.

ὦψ, only εἰς ὦπα, *in the eye, full in the face*, ἰδέσθαι; *in face, in person*, ἔοικεν, Γ 158.

Ὦψ, Ὦπος, son of Peisenor, father of Eurykleia, α 429, β 347, υ 148.

PLATE I.

PLATE II.

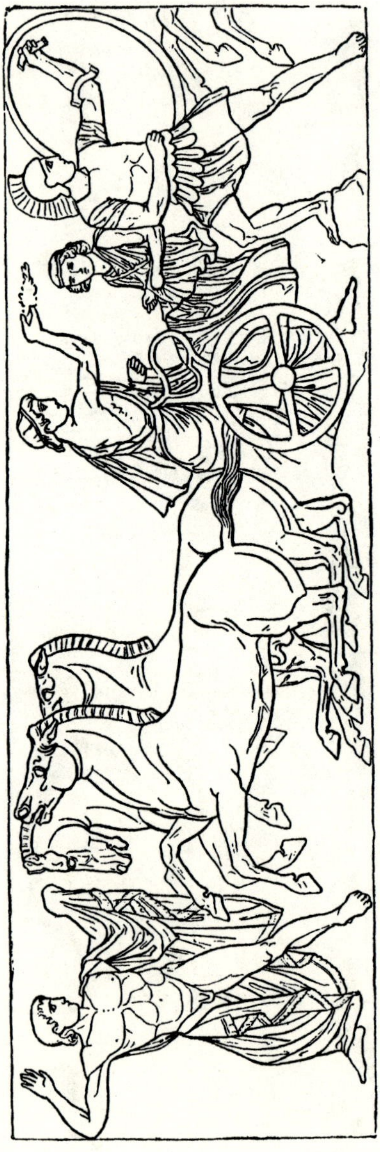

PLATE III.

House of Odysseus.

(After L. Gerlach.)

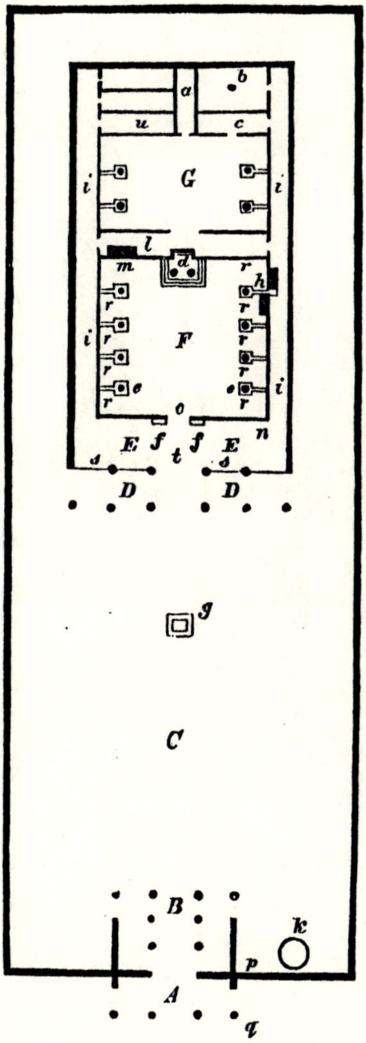

A	πρόθυρον.
B	αὐλῆς αἴθουσα, δ 678, π 342.
C	αὐλή, δ 625.
D	αἴθουσα.
E E	πρόδομος, ο 5, υ 1.
F	μέγαρον.
G	Women's apartment; overhead the ὑπερώιον.
a	Treasure-chamber.
b	Chamber of Odysseus and Penelope.
c	Chamber of Eurykleia, β 348.
d	Seats of the king and queen.
e e	Post of Odysseus as beggar.
f f	ξεστοὶ λίθοι.
g	Ζεὺς ἑρκεῖος.
h	ὀρσοθύρη.
i	λαύρη.
k	θόλος.
l	κλῖμαξ.
m	ῥῶγες.
n	στόμα λαύρης, } χ 137.
o	αὐλῆς καλὰ θύρετρα, } χ 137.
p	cf. χ 459 sq.
q	ρ 297.
r	καλαὶ μεσόδμαι, τ 37, υ 354.
s s	Wicket barriers.
t	πρόθυρον, σ 10, 33, 102.
u	Sleeping-apartment of Odysseus, ψ 190.

PLATE IV.

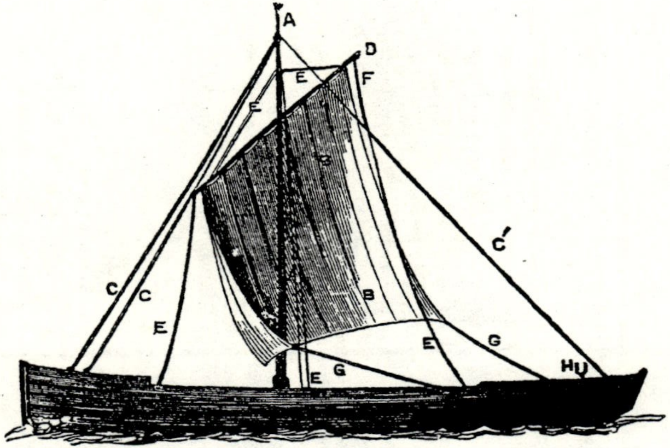

FIG. 1.—RIGGING OF HOMERIC SHIP.

A. Mast (ἱστός).
B. Sail (ἱστίον).
C C. Forestays (πρότονοι, β 425).
C'. Backstay (ἐπίτονος, μ 423).
D. Yard (ἐπίκριον, ε 254).
E E. Halliards (κάλοι, ε 260; cf. β 426).
F F. Braces (ὑπέραι, ε 260).
G G. Sheets (πόδες, ε 260).
H. Mast-crutch (ἱστοδόκη, Α 434).

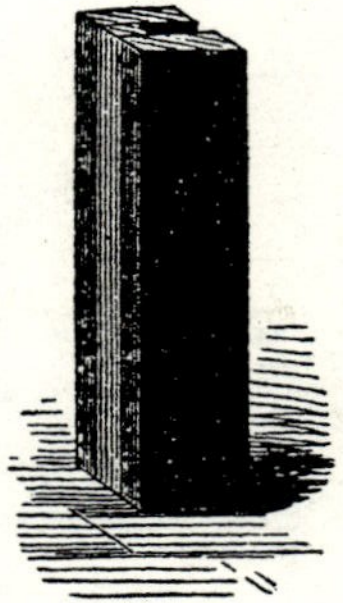

FIG. 2.—MAST-BOX.

μεσόδμη, mast-box (drawn on a larger scale), β 424, cf. τ 37.

PLATE V.

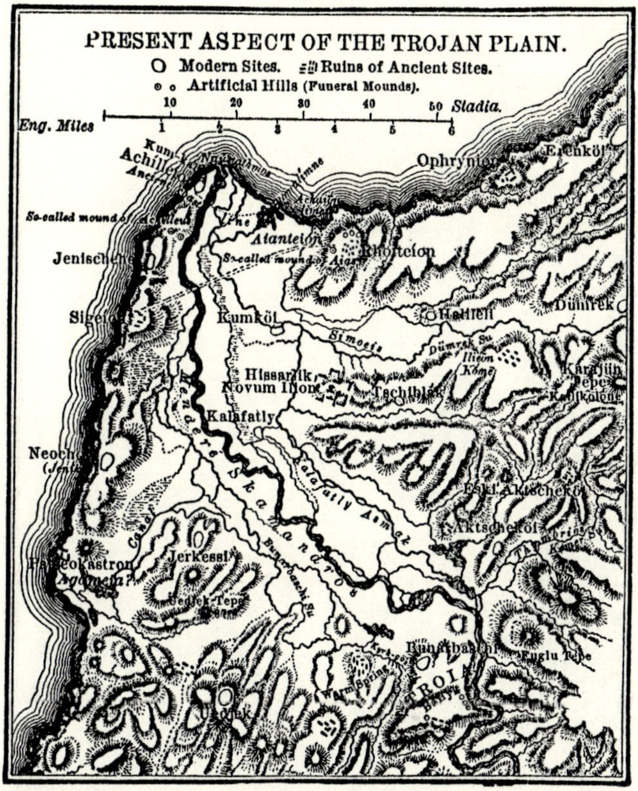

The prevalent opinion of antiquity located Homer's Troy on the hill *Hissarlik*, about three miles south of the Hellespont. The only important dissent from this view, among the ancients, was on the part of Demetrios of Skepsis, who was followed by Strabo, and who located Ilios at Ἰλιέων κώμη, some three miles east of Hissarlik, in the valley of the Simoeis.

Toward the close of the last century, the French traveller Le Chevalier visited the Troad, and boldly declared that he had identified the site of the ancient city on the height *Ballyk*, behind the village *Bunarbaschi*. Le Chevalier's view was announced with great positiveness, and has been generally received by modern scholars, e. g., Welcker, E. Curtius, Stark, Tozer, and the geographers Spratt, Kiepert, and Field-Marshal Von Moltke. In 1864 the Austrian Consul in Syra, Von Hahn, an eager partisan of Le Chevalier's theory, undertook excavations at *Ballyk*, which were prosecuted for several months, but without success.

The results of Schliemann's recent excavations at *Hissarlik* are familiar to all, and his discoveries go far to establish the fact that upon the hill *Hissarlik* the metropolis of the Trojan Plain, in prehistoric as well as in more recent times, must have stood. Among those who have advocated the claims of this site may be mentioned Gladstone, Grote, Eckenbrecker, Keller, Christ, Steitz, Büchner, and the writer of the article *Ilium* in Smith's Dictionary of Ancient Geography.

9 781585 100286